# T&T CLARK HANDBOOK OF ANTHROPOLOGY AND THE HEBREW BIBLE

# T&T CLARK HANDBOOK OF ANTHROPOLOGY AND THE HEBREW BIBLE

*Edited by Emanuel Pfoh*

LONDON • NEW YORK • OXFORD • NEW DELHI • SYDNEY

T&T CLARK

Bloomsbury Publishing Plc

50 Bedford Square, London, WC1B 3DP, UK
1385 Broadway, New York, NY 10018, USA
29 Earlsfort Terrace, Dublin 2, Ireland

BLOOMSBURY, T&T CLARK and the T&T Clark logo are trademarks of
Bloomsbury Publishing Plc

First published in Great Britain 2023
Paperback edition published 2025

Copyright © Emanuel Pfoh and contributors, 2023

Emanuel Pfoh has asserted his right under the Copyright,
Designs and Patents Act, 1988, to be identified as Editor of this work.

For legal purposes the Acknowledgements on p. x constitute an extension of this
copyright page.

Cover image: *Jacob Wrestling with the Angel* (1866) by Gustave Doré © ivan-96 / Getty Images

All rights reserved. No part of this publication may be reproduced or transmitted in any
form or by any means, electronic or mechanical, including photocopying, recording, or
any information storage or retrieval system, without prior permission in writing from the publishers.

Bloomsbury Publishing Plc does not have any control over, or responsibility for, any
third-party websites referred to or in this book. All internet addresses given in this
book were correct at the time of going to press. The author and publisher regret
any inconvenience caused if addresses have changed or sites have ceased to
exist, but can accept no responsibility for any such changes.

A catalogue record for this book is available from the British Library.

Library of Congress Number: 2022947480

ISBN: HB: 978-0-5677-0473-3
PB: 978-0-5677-0953-0
ePDF: 978-0-5677-0474-0
eBook: 978-0-5677-0476-4

Typeset by RefineCatch Limited, Bungay, Suffolk

To find out more about our authors and books visit www.bloomsbury.com
and sign up for our newsletters.

# CONTENTS

LIST OF ILLUSTRATIONS — vii
LIST OF CONTRIBUTORS — ix
ACKNOWLEDGEMENTS — x
LIST OF ABBREVIATIONS — xi

1 Introduction: Social and cultural anthropology and the Hebrew Bible in perspective — 1
*Emanuel Pfoh*

## Part One  Historiographies, theories and methods

2 Anthropologists and the Bible — 19
*Adam Kuper*

3 The Holy Land and the Bible in the nineteenth century — 39
*Eveline J. van der Steen*

4 Phantoms, factoids and frontiers: Social anthropology and the archaeology of Palestine — 69
*Dermot Nestor*

5 Ethnographic and ethnoarchaeological insights to interpret first-millennium BCE material culture — 97
*Gloria London*

6 The anthropology of the Mediterranean, the history of the southern Levant and biblical studies — 129
*Emanuel Pfoh*

## Part Two  Themes, approaches and interpretations

7 Kinship and social organization in ancient Palestine — 151
*Paula M. McNutt*

8 The many forms and foundations of power and authority in the Hebrew Bible — 189
*Victor H. Matthews*

9 Economic anthropology and the Hebrew Bible — 205
*Roger S. Nam*

| | |
|---|---|
| 10 Gender and society in ancient Israel<br>*Carol Meyers* | 223 |
| 11 Anthropologies of the Hebrew Bible<br>*Jan Dietrich* | 245 |
| 12 Honour, shame and other social values in the Hebrew Bible<br>*Philip F. Esler* | 263 |
| 13 For Moses 'Had Indeed Married a Cushite Wife': Metaphors, power and ethnicity in numbers 12<br>*Katherine E. Southwood* | 287 |
| 14 Asymmetrical reciprocal exchange in the Book of Jonah<br>*Jo-Marí Schäder* | 307 |
| 15 Neither divide nor continuum: Orality and literacy in the Hebrew Bible<br>*Robert D. Miller II* | 327 |
| 16 Telling tales: Biblical myth and narrative<br>*Karolien Vermeulen* | 351 |
| 17 A social anthropology of biblical memory<br>*Niels Peter Lemche* | 373 |
| 18 Acts that work, texts that work: Ritual in the Hebrew Bible<br>*Anne Katrine de Hemmer Gudme* | 395 |
| 19 Shaman, preacher or spirit medium? The Israelite prophet in the light of anthropological models<br>*Lester L. Grabbe* | 421 |
| 20 The anthropology of food in ancient Israel<br>*Cynthia Shafer-Elliott* | 433 |
| 21 The anthropology of death in ancient Israel<br>*Kristine Henriksen Garroway* | 455 |
| 22 Spatiality and territoriality: Power over land and power over people<br>*Stephen C. Russell* | 469 |
| 23 The anthropology of iconography in ancient Palestine<br>*Angelika Berlejung* | 491 |
| INDEX OF SOURCES | 523 |
| INDEX OF AUTHORS | 539 |

# ILLUSTRATIONS

### CHAPTER 3

| | | |
|---|---|---|
| Figure 3.1 | Jacob's well, 1879 | 46 |
| Figure 3.2 | The Pillar of Salt by Jebel Usdum, 1849 | 47 |
| Figure 3.3 | Map of Sinai, 1856 | 50 |
| Figure 3.4 | A theodolite party at work in the Holy Land, 1879 | 58 |
| Figure 3.5 | Archibald Forder in Arab dress, 1902 | 62 |
| Figure 3.6 | Jerusalem from the south-east, 1863 | 63 |

### CHAPTER 5

| | | |
|---|---|---|
| Figure 5.1a | Abandoned traditional beehive near Dhali in rural Cyprus, 1971 | 104 |
| Figure 5.1b | Beehive at Dhali, Cyprus, 1971 | 104 |
| Figure 5.2 | Traditional Cypriot breadboard, 1971 | 106 |
| Figure 5.3 | Kiln of private Kornos potter, Cyprus, 1986 | 109 |
| Figure 5.4a | Niches close to the roof in the Kornos church, Cyprus, held jugs secured by bricks and stones, 2017 | 111 |
| Figure 5.4b | Used jugs with broken rims together in a niche in Kornos church, 2017 | 111 |
| Figure 5.5a | Threshing sledge (*doukani* or *voukani*), Politiko, Cyprus, 1917 | 115 |
| Figure 5.5b | Underside of threshing board with chipped stones inserted into the wood, 1971 | 115 |
| Figure 5.6a | Wine fermentation jar at Kalokhorio, Cyprus, 1971 | 118 |
| Figure 5.6b | Impressed letters on a jar rim, 1971 | 118 |
| Figure 5.7 | Incense burner with impressed dots, Kornos, Cyprus, 1971 | 119 |

### CHAPTER 8

| | | |
|---|---|---|
| Table 8.1 | Types of power and characteristics | 192 |

### CHAPTER 9

| | | |
|---|---|---|
| Table 9.1 | *Homo economicus* versus *Homo reciprocans* | 211 |

### CHAPTER 14

| | | |
|---|---|---|
| Table 14.1 | A model of exchange in the Biblical era | 311 |

| Table 14.2 | The literary build-up of the book of Jonah as a diptych | 314 |
| Table 14.3 | A schematic representation of the sections in the book of Jonah | 315 |

## CHAPTER 17

| Figure 17.1 | Eflatun Pinar, 2015 | 383 |

# CONTRIBUTORS

**Angelika Berlejung**, University of Leipzig, Germany & University of Stellenbosch, South Africa

**Jan Dietrich**, University of Bonn, Germany

**Philip F. Esler**, University of Gloucestershire, UK

**Kristine Henriksen Garroway**, Hebrew Union College, Los Angeles, USA

**Lester L. Grabbe**, University of Hull, UK

**Anne Katrine de Hemmer Gudme**, University of Oslo, Norway

**Adam Kuper**, London School of Economics and Political Science, UK

**Niels Peter Lemche**, University of Copenhagen, Denmark

**Gloria London**, Independent Researcher, Seattle, USA

**Victor H. Matthews**, Missouri State University, USA

**Paula M. McNutt**, St. Ambrose University, USA

**Carol Meyers**, Duke University, USA

**Robert D. Miller II**, The Catholic University of America, USA

**Roger S. Nam**, Emory University, USA

**Dermot Nestor**, Australian Catholic University, Australia

**Emanuel Pfoh**, CONICET & National University of La Plata, Argentina

**Stephen C. Russell**, City University of New York, USA

**Jo-Marí Schäder**, University of Pretoria, South Africa

**Cynthia Shafer-Elliott**, Baylor University, USA

**Katherine E. Southwood**, University of Oxford, UK

**Eveline J. van der Steen**, Independent Researcher, Liverpool, UK

**Karolien Vermeulen**, University of Antwerp, Belgium

# ACKNOWLEDGEMENTS

The idea for this handbook of studies dealing with social anthropology and the Hebrew Bible started brewing at the joint meeting of the European Association of Biblical Studies and the Society of Biblical Literature in Helsinki in the summer of 2018. Dominic Mattos from Bloomsbury commented on the project to me and I was instantly imagining possibilities of themes, scopes and potential contributors. Dominic is to be thanked for this, as also is Bernhard Lang (Paderborn University), one of the pioneers in using anthropology in Old Testament studies, who thought I would be up to the task and made the contact with Bloomsbury possible. Also at Bloomsbury, I wish to thank Sarah Blake and Lucy Davies for their assistance and orientation; and Sue Littleford for her wonderful copyediting work.

This volume was produced in a good part through the *annus horribilis* that was 2020, which meant that at some point some contributors had to leave the project, others had to delay considerably the submission of their chapters, and we all essentially went through difficulties, both professional and personal, due to the Covid-19 pandemic and its aftermath. I therefore thank all the contributors for their hard work and commitment to this project.

The research group 'Anthropology and the Bible', within the European Association of Biblical Studies, and which I co-chair with Anne Katrine de Hemmer Gudme (University of Oslo), has been through the last decade or so a collective platform to think and rethink many of the themes and approaches presented and discussed in the chapters that follow. The EABS awarded me in 2015 with a small research grant and some of the results of that particular investigation are reflected in my contributions to this volume.

Four chapters in this handbook are based on previous publications and they appear here revised or updated. The following papers are reused here by kind permission of the respective publishers and editors:

Chapter 2 appeared originally as Adam Kuper, 'Anthropologists and the Bible', in R. Darnell and F.W. Gleach (eds), *Local Knowledge, Global Stage* (Histories of Anthropology Annual 10; Lincoln: University of Nebraska Press, 2016), pp. 1–30.

Chapter 7 is excerpted and revised from Paula McNutt, *Reconstructing the Society of Ancient Israel* (LAI; Louisville, KY: Westminster John Knox Press, 1999), pp. 75–96, 164–72, 197–206.

Chapter 10 appears here as an updated and revised version of the chapter 'Gender and Society: Reconstructing Relationships, Rethinking Systems', in Carol Meyers, *Rediscovering Eve: Ancient Israelite Women in Context* (New York: Oxford University Press, 2013), pp. 180–202.

Chapter 19 appeared originally as Lester L. Grabbe, 'Shaman, Preacher, or Spirit Medium? The Israelite Prophet in the Light of Anthropological Models', in J. Day (ed.), *Prophecy and Prophets in Ancient Israel: Proceedings of the Oxford Old Testament Seminar* (London: T&T Clark, 2010), pp. 117–32.

# ABBREVIATIONS

| | |
|---|---|
| 4Q184 | 4Q Wiles (*Wiles of the Wicked Woman*) |
| 4QMMT | *Halakah / Letter on Works* |
| *AABNER* | *Advances in Ancient, Biblical, and Near Eastern Research* |
| AASOR | Annual of the American School of Oriental Research |
| ÄAT | Ägypten und Altes Testament |
| ABC | The Anchor Bible Commentary |
| ABRL | The Anchor Bible Reference Library |
| ABS | Archaeology and Biblical Studies |
| *ADAJ* | *Annual of the Department of Antiquities of Jordan* |
| ADPV | Abhandlungen des deutschen Palästina-Vereins |
| AfOB | Archiv für Orientforschung Beihefte |
| *AIIN* | *Annali dell'Istituto Italiano di Numismatica* |
| AIL | Ancient Israel and Its Literature |
| *AJA* | *American Journal of Archaeology* |
| ANEM | Ancient Near Eastern Monographs |
| ANET[3] | James B. Pritchard (ed.), *Ancient Near Eastern Texts Relating to the Old Testament*: (Third Edition with Supplement; Princeton, NJ: Princeton University Press, 1969) |
| *Ant.* | Josephus, *Antiquities of the Jews* |
| AOAT | Alter Orient und Altes Testament |
| AOS | American Oriental Series |
| ASOR | American School of Oriental Research |
| ATANT | Abhandlungen zur Theologie des Alten und Neuen Testaments |
| *BA* | *Biblical Archaeologist* |
| BAR | British Archaeological Reports |
| *BASOR* | *Bulletin of the American Schools of Oriental Research* |
| *BI* | *Biblical Interpretation* |
| BI | Biblical Intersections |

| | |
|---|---|
| *Bib* | *Biblica* |
| *BibOr* | *Bibliotheca Orientalis* |
| BIS | Biblical Interpretation Series |
| *BSOAS* | *Bulletin of the School of Oriental and African Studies* |
| *BTB* | *Biblical Theology Bulletin* |
| BTS | Biblisch-Theologische Studien |
| BWANT | Beiträge zur Wissenschaft vom Alten und Neuen Testament |
| *BZ* | *Biblische Zeitschrift* |
| BZABR | Beihefte zur Zeitschrift für altorientalische und biblische Rechtsgeschichte |
| BZAW | Beihefte zur Zeitschrift für die alttestamentliche Wissenschaft |
| BZNW | Beihefte zur Zeitschrift für die neutestamentliche Wissenschaft |
| *CAJ* | *Cambridge Archaeological Journal* |
| CAT | Cuneiform Alphabetic Texts (KTU$_2$) |
| CBC | The Cambridge Biblical Commentary |
| CBET | Contributions to Biblical Exegesis and Theology |
| *CBQ* | *Catholic Biblical Quarterly* |
| CBR | Currents in Biblical Research |
| CHANE | Culture and History of the Ancient Near East |
| CIS | Copenhagen International Seminar |
| COS | W.W. Hallo and K.L. Younger, Jr (eds), *The Context of Scripture*, 3 vols (Leiden: E.J. Brill, 1997–2002) |
| CRBS | Currents in Research: Biblical Studies |
| CSAJ | J. Eggler and O. Keel, *Corpus der Siegel-Amulette aus Jordanien. Vom Neolithikum bis zur Perserzeit* (OBO.SA 25; Fribourg: Fribourg Academic Press / Göttingen: Vandenhoeck & Ruprecht, 2006) |
| CSAPI | O. Keel, *Corpus der Stempelsiegel-Amulette aus Palästina/Israel: Von den Anfängen bis zur Perserzeit. Katalog Band I: Von Tell Abu Fara' bis 'Atlit, with Three Contributions by Baruch Brandl* (OBO.SA 13; Fribourg: Fribourg Academic Press / Göttingen: Vandenhoeck & Ruprecht, 1997) |
| *CSSH* | *Comparative Studies in Society and History* |
| DANEBS | Discourses in Ancient Near Eastern and Biblical Studies |
| EA | Amarna letter |
| *ExpT* | *Expository Times* |
| FAT | Forschungen zum Alten Testament |

| | |
|---|---|
| *GGG* | O. Keel and C. Uehlinger, *Göttinnen, Götter und Gottessymbole. Neue Erkenntnisse zur Religionsgeschichte Kanaans und Israels aufgrund bislang unerschlossener ikonographischer Quellen* (QD 134; Freiburg: Herder, 5th edn, 2001 [1992]) |
| *GGIG* | O. Keel and C. Uehlinger, *Gods, Goddesses, and Images of God in Ancient Israel* (Minneapolis: Fortress Press, 1998) |
| *HAR* | *Hebrew Annual Review* |
| *HeBAI* | *Hebrew Bible and Ancient Israel* |
| HBM | Hebrew Bible Monographs |
| HBR | Handbooks of the Bible and Its Reception |
| HBS | Herders biblische Studien |
| *HBT* | *Horizons in Biblical Theology* |
| HSM | Harvard Semitic Monographs |
| *HTR* | *Harvard Theological Review* |
| *HUCA* | *Hebrew Union College Annual* |
| IAA | Israel Antiquities Authority |
| ICC | International Critical Commentary |
| *IEJ* | *Israel Exploration Journal* |
| *IJMES* | *International Journal of Middle East Studies* |
| *IPIAO* | S. Schroer and O. Keel, *Die Ikonographie Palästinas/Israels und der Alte Orient: Eine Religionsgeschichte in Bildern*, vols 1–4 (Fribourg: Fribourg Academic Press / Basel: Schwabe, 2005–18) |
| *JAA* | *Journal of Anthropological Archaeology* |
| *JAH* | *Journal of Ancient History* |
| *JANEH* | *Journal of Ancient Near Eastern History* |
| *JANES* | *Journal of the Ancient Near Eastern Society* |
| *JAOS* | *Journal of the American Oriental Society* |
| *JBL* | *Journal of Biblical Literature* |
| *JBQ* | *Jewish Bible Quarterly* |
| *JEA* | *Journal of Egyptian Archaeology* |
| *JEMAHS* | *Journal of Eastern Mediterranean Archaeology and Heritage Studies* |
| *JESHO* | *Journal of the Economic and Social History of the Orient* |
| *JFA* | *Journal of Field Archaeology* |
| *JHebS* | *Journal of Hebrew Scriptures* |

| | |
|---|---|
| JIA | *Journal of Islamic Archaeology* |
| JNES | *Journal of Near Eastern Studies* |
| JPOS | *Journal of the Palestine Oriental Society* |
| JRAI | *Journal of the Royal Anthropological Institute* |
| JSJ | *Journal for the Study of Judaism in the Persian, Hellenic and Roman Period* |
| JSNT | *Journal for the Study of the New Testament* |
| JSOT | *Journal for the Study of the Old Testament* |
| JSOTSup | Journal for the Study of the Old Testament – Supplement Series |
| JSS | *Journal of Semitic Studies* |
| JTI | *Journal of Theological Interpretation* |
| JTS | *Journal of Theological Studies* |
| KAI | H. Donner and W. Röllig, *Kanaanäische und aramäische Inschriften*, 3 vols (Wiesbaden: Harrassowitz, 1964–79) |
| LAI | Library of Ancient Israel |
| LHBOTS | Library of Hebrew Bible / Old Testament Studies |
| NEA | *Near Eastern Archaeology* |
| NRSV | New Revised Standard Version |
| NS | new series |
| OA | *Oriens Antiquus* |
| OAC | Orientis Antiqvi Collectio |
| OBO | Orbis biblicus et orientalis |
| OIP | Oriental Institute Publication |
| Or | *Orientalia* |
| ORA | Oriental Religions in Antiquity |
| OTE | Old Testament Essays |
| OTG | Old Testament Guides |
| OTL | Old Testament Library |
| PEFQS | *Palestine Exploration Fund, Quarterly Statement* |
| PEQ | *Palestine Exploration Quarterly* |
| QD | Quaestiones disputatae |
| RA | *Revue d'assyriologie et d'archéologie orientale* |
| RB | *Revue biblique* |
| RBS | Resources for Biblical Study |
| RDAC | *Report of the Department of Antiquities, Cyprus* |

| | |
|---|---|
| **RIABT** | Research on Israel and Aram in Biblical Times |
| **RSV** | Revised Standard Version |
| **SAHL** | Studies in the Archaeology and History of the Levant |
| **SBLDS** | Society of Biblical Literature – Dissertation Series |
| **SBLRBS** | Society of Biblical Literature – Resources for Biblical Study |
| **SBLSS** | Society of Biblical Literature – Symposium Series |
| **SBS** | Stuttgarter Bibelstudien |
| **SFSHJ** | South Florida Studies in the History of Judaism |
| **SHANE** | Studies in the History of the Ancient Near East |
| *SJOT* | *Scandinavian Journal of the Old Testament* |
| **SNTSMS** | Society for New Testament Studies Monograph Series |
| **SPCK** | Society for Promoting Christian Knowledge |
| **SSN** | Studia Semitica Neerlandica |
| *StTh* | *Studia Theologica* |
| **SWBAS** | Social World of Biblical Antiquity Series |
| **SWBA/SS** | Social World of Biblical Antiquity / Second Series |
| *TA* | *Tel Aviv* |
| *TDOT* | G.J. Botterweck, H. Ringgren and H.J. Fabry (eds), *Theological Dictionary of the Old Testament* (transl. J.T. Willis; Grand Rapids, MI: Eerdmans, 1977–2018) |
| *TLZ* | *Theologische Literaturzeitung* |
| **UBL** | Ugaritisch-biblische Literatur |
| *UF* | *Ugarit-Forschungen* |
| *UUÅ* | Uppsala universitetsårsskrift |
| *VT* | *Vetus Testamentum* |
| **VTSup** | Vetus Testamentum – Supplements |
| **VWGTh** | Veröffentlichungen der Wissenschaftlichen Gesellschaft für Theologie |
| **WMANT** | Wissenschaftliche Monographien zum Alten und Neuen Testament |
| **WUNT** | Wissenschaftliche Untersuchungen zum Neuen Testament |
| *ZAH* | *Zeitschrift für Althebraistik* |
| *ZAW* | *Zeitschrift für die alttestamentliche Wissenschaft* |
| *ZDPV* | *Zeitschrift des deutschen Palästina-Vereins* |
| *ZTK* | *Zeitschrift für Theologie und Kirche* |

CHAPTER ONE

# Introduction

*Social and cultural anthropology and the Hebrew Bible in perspective*

EMANUEL PFOH

When we look at the Renaissance depictions of biblical images and situations, even with little critical disposition, we rapidly realize that something is off: physical features, gestures, landscapes and, above all, the clothes of the individuals are depicted in a notably anachronistic or distorted manner, far from what we would expect nowadays to be an Oriental or Levantine or, more precisely, a 'biblical' setting, and more at home in the European country of the artist. This Western image of biblical situations in paintings and engravings, roughly between the fourteenth and seventeenth centuries, offered in itself what we now could regard an 'anti-anthropological' and equally an 'anti-historical' perspective: precisely, from modern anthropological and historical points of view, these biblical depictions were not about a biblical Other and did not have an interest in a realistic depiction of ancient cultural diacritics, but rather they were exclusively about European Christianity transposed into imagined biblical scenarios and episodes (see further Nagel and Wood 2010).

This anachronistic manner of representing episodes and social situations from the Bible would eventually change since the eighteenth century with the spirit of the Enlightenment and its focus on reason, logical reality and historicity. Building on this enlightened perspective, Western powers, along with travellers, explorers and scholars, rediscovered (or better, reinvented) the territory referred to as Near/Middle East (cf. Yilmaz 2012) through properly modern cultural perspectives: starting with the Danish Arabia Expedition of 1761–7, conceived by Johann David Michaelis (1717–91), and which had Carsten Niebuhr (1733–1815) as the only survivor (cf. Hansen 1964), and then with Constantin de Volney's (1757–1820) travels in Egypt and Syria in 1783–85 (Volney 1787). But more significantly, the decisive event is usually marked by current historiography with Napoleon Bonaparte's invasion of Egypt and Syria-Palestine during 1798–1801, when the Orient – the perceived scenario of the biblical stories – was properly opened to Western research and exploration in a historicist and rationalist manner (cf. Ben-Arieh 1979; Silberman 1982; Bar-Yosef 2005).

During the nineteenth century, in effect, we can observe the unfolding of a new epistemic worldview – actually, the irruption of a new *episteme*, as Michel Foucault would term it[1] – by which all reality had to be subjected to a certain historicity, that is, to a concrete inscription in the real world and in a chronological order following the rules of reason and nature. In this manner, the so-called biblical world evoked by painters of the pre-Enlightenment could now be recovered by a plethora of scientific disciplines, within the general framework of biblical studies. The impulse for European and then American biblical archaeology finds its rationale in this conception (cf. Ben-Arieh 1979; Silberman 1982; King 1983; Moorey 1991; Goren 2003; Davis 2004). Also, the development of geographical and cartographical studies of the Holy Land, starting with the Napoleonic investigation of Pierre Jacotin in 1799–1800 but especially with that of Edward Robinson and Eli Smith in 1838, searching for a confirmation of biblical topography (Robinson and Smith 1841), and culminating in the Palestine Exploration Fund's Survey of Western Palestine (1871–8), falls within this epistemic mode of describing and analysing what was perceived to be the land of the Bible in the nineteenth and early twentieth centuries (cf. Goren 2003; Kirchhoff 2005; Aiken 2010; Goren, Faehndrich and Schelhaas 2017).

But perhaps the most interesting expression of this rational manner of recovering the biblical world is found in the proto-ethnographic descriptions of the many Western travellers into eastern lands: they would produce for a hundred years realistic and encyclopaedic descriptions of the peoples encountered in Oriental scenarios and landscapes, most of the time related to the biblical past (cf., e.g., Lane 1836; Thomson 1859; Van-Lennep 1875; Tristram 1894; Hardy 1912; Baldensperger 1913). This proto-ethnographic genre revolved around the description of the 'manners and customs' of the local populations, which were seen as a direct window into the ancient Oriental and biblical past: since these societies were perceived from Europe as stagnant and conservative, observing and studying the Ottoman Bedouin and peasants established a cognitive bridge with the biblical past, not least for religious illumination, especially for Protestant travellers (cf. Varisco 2013; Cunningham and McGeough 2018). 'These Others, these petrified peoples, re-presented our ancient ancestors, i.e., they presented us with vivid contemporary memories of our ancient long gone past' (McGrane 1989: 94). Beyond the imperial and Orientalist epistemological mode behind these scientific productions (cf. Said 1978; further Netton 2013), it is then important to note how these Oriental others were displaced from the Ottoman present they were living into a 'biblical present' produced by pious travellers, scholars and explorers.[2] In effect, this

---

[1] Foucault (2005 [1966]: xxiii–xxiv) regards an *episteme* as an epistemological field 'in which knowledge, envisaged apart from all criteria having reference to its rational value or to its objective forms, grounds its positivity and thereby manifests a history which is not that of its growing perfection, but rather that of its conditions of possibility'. Thus, one may say that during the nineteenth century a new historicist manner of depicting the biblical past arose, particularly through the disciplines of (Semitic) philology, archaeology, geography/cartography, and ethnography.

[2] 'In the mid-nineteenth century, European scientific and military expeditions moved throughout Palestine in search of archaeological sites with biblical relevance. There was little interest in the history of Palestine or the Palestinian peoples. Indeed, the nineteenth-century European archaeologists and explorers had European and Christian interests primarily on their minds; that is the verification of Judeo-Christian roots for the recovery and preservation of their Christian, European heritage. Indirectly, such actions contributed to the increasing interest by the European nations for control of Palestine, resulting in an intensification of the religious and political struggles among the Orthodox, Protestant and Catholic churches in Palestine. The *Palestine Exploration Fund Quarterly Statement* published several articles on the need to preserve the biblical lands from the "indolent" and "ignorant" Palestinian peasantry and to place the region into the hands of the diligent and enterprising Jewish communities' (Ricks 1999: 29–30).

'denial of coevalness' – as Johannes Fabian (1983) put it – was a characteristic feature appearing not only throughout the copious pages of the writings of European travellers into the Holy Land of the period, but also in the scientific productions of Victorian evolutionary anthropology that supported this ontological projection of the Orient (cf. Stocking 1987; Kuper 2005: 1–36; Candea 2018: 20–8; see also Chapters 2 and 3 in this volume).

We find nonetheless, although later in time, the appearance of important exceptions to this drive to rediscover and resuscitate the biblical past in the present, for instance in the work of the Finnish ethnographer Hilma Granqvist (1890–1971). Regarding this sort of ahistorical parallelisms in the first volume of her *Marriage Conditions in a Palestinian Village* from 1931, she observes:

> the temptation to identify without criticism customs and habits and views of life of the present day with those of the Bible, especially of the Old Testament. Only too often one has been tempted to build a bridge from the past to the present by combining modern parallels with the Bible verses. No one can get away from the fact that much is in agreement – the land and nature determine that. But in any case one must remember the whole time that it is Muhammadan Arabs, not Jews, whose traditions are being studied, and that there is a period of 2000 years and more between them – a gap which cannot be explained away merely by citing 'the immovable East'.
>
> —Granqvist 1931: 9[3]

This critical anthropological disposition, as noted, seemed to have been an exception to the norm, rather common up to the mid-twentieth century, of perceiving both landscape and people in the southern Levant through a biblical prism. Such a disposition depended of course of the intellectual genealogy already sketched. Within Victorian anthropology, we find perhaps the most important attempts at decoding anthropologically the biblical world and its narratives in the works of William Robertson Smith (1846–94), in particular *Kinship and Marriage in Early Arabia* (1885) and *Lectures on the Religion of the Semites* (1889), and of James G. Frazer (1854–1941), notably his three-volume *Folk-Lore and the Old Testament* (1918). These works, beyond their different interests (social structures and institutions; tales and literary and mythic motifs), coincided in an evolutionary perspective deploying a comparative method and typology thought to be useful in the analysis of cultural traits that exposed levels of human development.[4] One could in fact say, with Bernhard Lang, that '[w]hile the work of Robertson Smith is still worth reading this cannot be said of Sir James Frazer's *Folk-Lore in the Old Testament* without some qualification' (1985a: 5–6; cf. Whitelam 1995). Yet, it is possible to already detect in these – still valid or failed – approaches the rise of modes of understanding the biblical past and its textual products that clearly attempt to go beyond the Bible's sole testimony for the past of Israel.

---

[3] One may trace these 'temptations to identify' – as Granqvist calls it – Bedouin with biblical characters or situations back to H.H. Milman's (1829 I: 9) depiction of Abraham as a sheik or an emir, but it may also be found continuously for two hundred years, up to, for instance, Clinton Bailey's (2018) thorough study of the Negev's Bedouin in most recent decades.

[4] Similarly, Herbert Spencer's (1820–1903) study *Hebrews and Phoenicians* (1880) offers a comparative sociology of these ancient peoples. By the way, the usual distinction between sociology as the study of industrialized societies and anthropology as the study of non-Western societies is somewhat artificial for this period in terms of epistemology since both disciplines were part of the same matrix of Victorian social science; see further in Chalcraft 2004.

Sociological enquires on Judaism are already present in Max Weber's *Das antike Judentum* (1923 [1917–19]) and also in Antonin Causse's study *Du groupe ethnique à la communauté religieuse* (1937), but these are not properly anthropological in the current sense of the term, of course.⁵ In a similar vein, building on a perspective more related to the history of religions, we have the anthology of lectures by E.O. James, nonetheless titled *The Old Testament in the Light of Anthropology* (1935). Other precursors of an analysis on ancient cultural traits through a historical perspective are, for instance, Edward Day's *The Social Life of the Hebrews* (1901), Alfred Bertholet's *Kulturgeschichte Israels* (1919), and Johannes Pedersen's *Israel: Its Life and Culture* (1991 [1926]). But it is only after half a century of developments within social and cultural anthropology, and with the replacement of Victorian evolutionism by other styles of anthropological theorizations – notably structuralism – that we encounter a properly updated interest in biblical stories by anthropologists. In effect, in 1961 Edmund Leach (1910–89) published a short paper titled 'Lévi-Strauss in the Garden of Eden', in which – and of course referring to Claude Lévi-Strauss's (1908–2009) structuralism – he analysed the narrative of the book of Genesis through a structuralist interpretation of the biblical myth (cf. also Leach 1962). Precisely, with Leach we find perhaps the first anthropological proposal of understanding the biblical text as a mythical composition – not in the vulgar understanding of the word as 'fiction', as it is misleadingly taken even nowadays in some social (and even academic) quarters, but rather as a cultural expression of a certain reality which departs from our modern and Western *episteme* (once again, as Foucault would have it). In a later study, Leach would expand his interpretative perspective, first implicitly noting the change in the epistemic disposition for reading the biblical text, notably the rationalistic understanding of an ancient religious product:

> It is only during the last 150 years that a quite different attitude has come to dominate biblical scholarship. Truth is now equated 'historical truth' and since it has become apparent that large parts of the Bible could not possibly be 'true history' in a strict sense the task of the scholar has been seen as that of sifting the true from the false. If only we could know what really happened in history then we should understand the truth, including religious truth.
>
> —Leach 1983a: 2–3

But then, and most importantly, Leach proposes an anthropological reading of the biblical text as mythic *in toto*:

> first of all I hold that anthropologists need to make a case for saying that no part of the Bible is a record of history as it actually happened. Then, on the positive side, they can show that the whole of the Bible has the characteristics of mytho-history of the sort which anthropologists regularly encounter when they engage in present-day field-research. The similarity is a matter of structure not of content. Finally they can show that if biblical texts are treated as mytho-history of this kind, then the techniques which modern anthropologists employ for the interpretation of myth can very properly be applied to biblical materials. If this is done then some parts of the text will appear

---

⁵ The more recent studies collected in Goldberg 1987 (in spite of having as a subtitle 'anthropological studies') seems to retain this particular sociological outlook after almost a century.

in a new light, or at any rate in a light which has not been generally familiar to Bible readers during the past four centuries.

—Leach 1983b: 21[6]

And finally, prefiguring a minimalist epistemology that would develop during the 1990s in Old Testament studies:

> In this regard my own position is one of extreme scepticism. If we ignore the rather small number of named biblical characters whose existence is fully vouched for by independent evidence, and by that I mean archaeology rather than Josephus, I regard all the personalities of biblical narrative, both in the Old Testament and in the New, as wholly fictional. They are there because they fill a particular role in the totality of the sacred tale and not because they actually existed in history. And even if a few of them did have some kind of real-life existence this fact is quite irrelevant.

—Leach 1983b: 10

At the time of its publication, this study – especially the epistemic statement in this last quoted paragraph – had little if any impact on European or American Hebrew Bible / Old Testament scholarship, which had had its own development in relation to the social sciences since the 1960s (see next paragraph). However, Leach's structuralist reading of the biblical myth opened up the way to other (mostly structuralist; cf. already Rogerson 1970; and Lang 1985a: 10–13) anthropological interpretations of biblical texts, of which is important to note Mary Douglas's (1921–2007) *Purity and Danger* (1966), on the Levitical laws of impurity, and her follow-ups *Leviticus as Literature* (1999) and *Jacob's Tears* (2004). In 1977, and within the tradition of British anthropology, Julian Pitt-Rivers (1919–2001) published *The Fate of Shechem*, a collection of studies focusing on Greek and Biblical stories, and expanding the potentiality of Mediterranean anthropology for interpreting ancient texts anthropologically (see Chapter 6 in this volume). Finally, Philippe Wajdenbaum's *Argonauts of the Desert* (2011) constitutes the latest comprehensive study of the Hebrew Bible from an anthropological structuralist perspective.

The 1960s were also pivotal in biblical studies. In a short article published in 1962, George E. Mendenhall would produce what is probably the first serious attempt to use modern ethnographic data to explain historically an episode of biblical relevance: the rise of early Israel in Iron Age I (*c.* 1150–1000 BCE) was explained as an indigenous process, opposing to the biblical notion of a foreign conquest of the land (Mendenhall 1962).[7] After that, other socio-anthropological studies expanded the potentialities of sociological and anthropological insights, notably Norman K. Gottwald's *The Tribes of Yahweh* (1979), which made abundant use of Karl Marx's and Émile Durkheim's theorizations and add a peasant revolt to Mendenhall's indigenous process, and Niels Peter Lemche's *Early Israel* (1985), reviewing Mendenhall's and Gottwald's models while deploying a wealth of ethnographic data from the Middle East. Further studies would appear between the 1970s and 1990s in Old Testament studies, among which it should be noted Rogerson's *Myth in Old Testament Interpretation* (1974) and *Anthropology and the Old Testament* (1978), also

---

[6] Without ever referring to Leach, we find a fine example of this interpretative disposition of the biblical narrative as myth in Thompson 1999. See also Chapter 16 in this volume.
[7] In ancient Near Eastern studies, at the same time, there was a certain move towards considering cultural anthropology as an important interpretive contribution to Cuneiform civilizations; cf. Oppenheim 1960; Kramer 1962.

*Anthropological Approaches to the Old Testament*, edited by Lang (1985b), and a two-volume selection of anthropological studies titled *Ethnologische Texte zum Alten Testament*, edited by C. Sigrist and R. Neu (1989, 1997). The anthologies by Lang and by Sigrist and Neu, in particular, collected or reproduced texts by anthropologists showing the usefulness of ethnographic cases – mostly African – for analogically interpreting biblical stories and similarly for understanding different processes (ethnogenesis, state formation) in the history of ancient Israel.[8] All these studies made an effort to grant a sociological sophistication to historical biblical interpretation in order to transcend the mere literary commentary to the text or a quick historicist correlation – even though all of them, up until the 1990s, would follow or simply accept the basic biblical scheme of progression in Israelite history (settlement – tribal formation – state formation – state fragmentation – deportation – exile) as the background for the different social processes (cf. Pfoh 2009: 69–82).

Usually conceived under the concept of 'social-science approaches', the development of these insights and interpretative methods exposed a variety of interests, mostly biblical (e.g. genealogies, prophecy, apocalypticism, sectarianism), but also illustrating more classical topics of anthropological research (e.g. politics and social organization, economics, honour and shame, family and kinship, gender, myth and narrative, religion and rituals, folklore, violence), all of which showed the potentialities of social-scientific analyses of the biblical text (see further Wilson 1977, 1984; Prewitt 1981; Culley 1982; Kirkpatrick 1988; Meyers 1988, 2013; Clements 1989; Neu 1989; Matthews and Benjamin 1993, 1994; Niditch 1993a, 1993b; Pilch and Malina 1993; Carter and Meyers 1996; Overholt 1996; McNutt 1999; Simkins and Cook 1999; Lawrence and Aguilar 2004; Esler 2006; Kessler 2006; Chalcraft 2007; Lemos 2010; Pfoh 2010b; Knight 2011; Olyan 2012, 2015; Rogerson 2013; Boer 2015; Hagedorn 2015; Goldberg 2018; Gilders 2020).

Yet, going beyond the general framework of 'social-scientific analysis of the Old Testament' (Esler and Hagedorn 2006), I think it may be useful to single out the particular relevance of a specifically anthropological perspective within this set of analytical tools (cf. Pfoh 2010a). The key issue is anthropology's emphasis on detecting cultural diversity, and with that, diverse epistemologies and ontologies. This should suffice to investigate the biblical narrative through an othering process: to regard it as an ancient source that not only needs to be linguistically translated but fundamentally culturally translated. A cultural translation of the biblical data, as a methodological principle, puts on hold the usual tendency to rapidly historicize the biblical narrative – i.e. from Joshua to Ezra and Nehemiah – or its core and its main literary characters, along with the possibility of applying social-science methods to such literary descriptions in order to achieve a realistic – if not confirmed – historical account.

Before continuing with the paramount relevance of anthropology for both biblical interpretation and historical interpretation, it is useful to clarify what is understood by

---

[8] In particular during the 1980s, anthropological discussions about lineage and segmentarism in African contexts were referred to in Old Testament studies for explaining, for instance, the rise and organization of early Israel; cf., e.g., Malamat 1973; Lemche 1985: 84–244; Rogerson 1986; further Fiensy 1987; and Sigrist and Neu 1989: 65–132. Fiensy asks the right questions: 'Does one need to accept ethnological theory to use ethnographic material? Which theory is most appropriate? How does one study a text based on observations of a society? How can one explain parallels between the Bible and contemporary primitive cultures, or is it necessary to explain them in order to utilize them exegetically?' (1987: 73).

that precise term. Already decades ago in biblical studies, Rogerson defined the connotations of the different expressions of the discipline:

> First of all, it should be noted that there are differences in the way anthropology is organized and understood, as between Britain and America. Also, European terminology seems to differ from that of Britain and America. The easiest difference to appreciate is that the German word *Anthropologie* does not entirely correspond to the British 'anthropology.' The German word is more commonly used to denote theories or speculation about the nature and being of man, and although in theological works in English it is possible to find 'anthropology' used to denote the nature and destiny of man, it would be fair to say that the modern user of English would not regard this as the *primary* sense of 'anthropology'. The German word *Ethnologie* conveys more of what is primarily meant in English by 'anthropology' and the nearest French equivalent is probably *sociologie*.
>
> —Rogerson 1978: 9

More synthetically, as Adam Kuper noted, 'American anthropology was about cultural traditions. British social anthropology was about how societies worked' (2015: 136; further Dianteill 2012).[9] In this introductory chapter, and extended to the handbook, *Social Anthropology* (British tradition), *Cultural Anthropology* (American tradition), *Ethnologie* (German tradition) and *Sociologie* (French tradition) are understood as embracing the same general and broad epistemology and methodologies, in spite of national orientations and diverging interests during the twentieth century (cf. further Augé 1982; Barth et al. 2005). Lastly, as Rogerson noted above, the German term *Anthropologie*, of common use in Old Testament studies to refer rather to human ontology (see, e.g., Wolff 1974), stands aside the proper elaborations of social and cultural anthropology since is more appropriately considered an 'internal' theological perspective in biblical texts, apart from an external analytical and/or interpretative orientation (see further Chapter 11 in this volume).

This last point introduces here the now known and accepted anthropological distinction between *emic* and *etic* perspectives of culture and social practice. An *emic* perspective aims at grasping the 'indigenous discourse' of a particular culture, group or society, namely the internal logics which produce and explain a certain reality according to the particular cultural traits of the members of that culture, group or society. An *etic* perspective, on the contrary, is constructed from outside the culture under study; it is precisely an interpretative discourse which integrates and explains the *emic* perspective through concrete analytical categories and theories (cf. the discussions in Harris 1968: 568–604; Headland, Pike and Harris 1990). In this sense, we may distinguish between the *emics* found in biblical narrative or related to them (mythic depictions, literary tropes and motifs, *Heilsgeschichten*, modern theological elaborations, etc.) and the *etics*, which explain not only the production of the biblical texts and the formation of the biblical

---

[9] 'American cultural anthropology and British social anthropology had diverged since the 1920s. They had become very different disciplines. Social anthropology was a tradition in the social sciences. It had long since abandoned historical reconstructions and taken its intellectual inspiration from the school of Durkheim. Its distinctive concept was social structure. In contrast, American anthropology stuck for a long time with the ethnological programme. The school that formed around Franz Boas at Columbia University in the early twentieth century saw its vocation as cultural history' (Kuper 2015: 136).

narrative in its ancient Near Eastern context, but also how these texts are related to the history of ancient Israel/Palestine in the Iron Age (*c.* 1150–586 BCE) and later periods, how such a history is elaborated by modern historiography, etc. (cf. already the insights in Rogerson 1989: 31–5). If we accept, with Philip R. Davies (1992), that 'ancient Israel' is a distinctive historiographical construct in modern biblical studies, blending biblical narrative with the archaeology and epigraphy of Iron Age Palestine in a rather uncritical fashion (according to historical epistemological and methodological standards), we may then consider the usual 'histories of ancient Israel' as a rather sophisticated example of an *emic* interpretation of the biblical text in modern times, which, however, fails to ultimately adopt or follow a properly *etic* approach to all the data (cf. Pfoh 2010a: 19–35).

An *etic* perspective to the biblical narrative and to the history of Israel/Palestine in antiquity is therefore one of the main analytical contributions that sociocultural anthropology makes to the investigation of the historical processes in the ancient southern Levant. In the first place, it identifies and characterizes a native or indigenous discourse about such a past (the biblical text), which has of course to be subjected to the expected criticism as a historical textual source. This native or indigenous discourse can certainly be read ethnographically – in a rather forensic manner, following a sort of ethnography of a dead culture[10] – through an integration of the logics of the mythical depictions in the biblical texts with the wider cultural traits of the Levant. In the second place, the *etic* perspective also creates the categories through which we will grant coherence and form to this past as social history, political and economic organization, religious practice, etc. This research orientation allows for having results less dependent on the biblical images of the land and its historical processes (cf. Thompson 2019), and it also allows for more sophisticated multidisciplinary approaches (cf. now Stordalen and LaBianca 2021). Lastly, we may note how ethnographic research contributes to the interpretation of the archaeological past of the southern Levant. As Albert Glock stated:

> The mental maps of ancient artisans, farmers, merchants, housekeepers and priests are fossilized in artifacts and architecture, waste debris and decayed installations. The cognitive maps of archaeologists are embedded in field procedures, laboratory analyses and excavations reports. The subtle and powerful biases inculcated by social, religious and political education have shaped the forms of both types of cultural expression. To find the past that is truly dissimilar from the present, but at the same time to be aware that the inquiry into the past serves modern needs, requires a deliberate consideration of the intellectual form and social function of the archaeological enterprise. [. . .] In sum, the use of ethnographic data in an archaeological research design enlarges the archaeologist's vision of the explanatory task and increases his capability to find probable interpretations by making visible the connections between people and place, a cultural tradition and its environment.
>
> —Glock 1983: 171, 178

To sum up, with anthropology we have analytically a 'double attack' to the past of Israel in the ancient southern Levant: on the one hand, a disposition to interpretate biblical

---

[10] Pfoh 2010a: 16–19. In fact, an anthropological perspective on a particular social situation, question or problem is more about the epistemological intervention than about 'being in the field' in the traditional Malinowskian sense; cf. Gupta and Ferguson 1997: 39: 'The idea that anthropology's distinctive trademark might be found not in its commitment to "the local" but in its attentiveness to epistemological and political issues of location surely takes us far from the classical natural history model of fieldwork as "the detailed study of a limited area."'

stories through critical conceptualizations of myth (not a mere rationalization of it), myth-making processes, and a comparison of myths with other regions and cultures of the ancient Near East, and how all this relates (or not) to the chronological and social history of the region; on the other hand, a disposition to write about the history of the region through a critical use of the archaeological and epigraphic data, and also through a critical handling of the ethnographic data for illuminating the past.

## ABOUT THIS HANDBOOK

The present handbook does not aim at being absolutely comprehensive. As with any thematic volume, there are limitations in scope and treatment and, therefore, there are indeed perspectives and themes which are wanting or missing, in particular, perspectives from Asian, African and Latino scholars dealing in particular with Asian, African and Latin contexts of biblical interpretation. Many of these insights may be found, however, in postcolonial biblical interpretation studies,[11] or in reception studies.[12] Other potential anthropological discussions that were left out the handbook may nonetheless be found in some recent thematic studies, for instance, on friendship (cf. Olyan 2017; Thiede 2022), or on dress and clothing (cf. Finitsis 2021; Quick 2021).

The chapters gathered here have as a main background what is commonly conceived of as the history of 'ancient Israel', encompassing in broad terms first-millennium BCE Palestine or, at a greater scale, the southern Levant. In Part One of the handbook, 'Historiographies, Theories and Method', Chapter 2 (Adam Kuper) surveys the relationships between British social anthropology and the Bible in the formative periods of the discipline; and Chapter 3 (Eveline J. van der Steen) expands the overview focusing on the experience of travelling to the Holy Land in the nineteenth century. Chapter 4 (Dermot Nestor) elaborates on the philosophical and epistemological ties between social anthropology and the practice of archaeology in Palestine, while Chapter 5 (Gloria London) presents a synthesis of the ethnographic approach to archaeological interpretation, namely ethnoarchaeology, including some case studies and interpretative examples. Finally in this section, Chapter 6 (Emanuel Pfoh) offers an introduction to the anthropology of the Mediterranean and how its themes and research have impacted on biblical scholarship and the history of the ancient southern Levant.

Part Two, 'Themes, Approaches and Interpretations', consists of a series of thematic case studies covering different examples of anthropological insights both on biblical aspects and on the history of Israel within its broader Levantine context. Chapter 7 (Paula M. McNutt) offers a basic yet thorough description of the social organization of Israelite society from the Iron Age I to the Persian period. This basic sociopolitical structure allows for interpretations of political authority in Chapter 8 (Victor H. Matthews), of the anthropology of economics in Chapter 9 (Roger S. Nam), and of gender issues in ancient Israelite society in Chapter 10 (Carol Meyers). An *emic* illustration of biblical anthropology is presented in Chapter 11 (Jan Dietrich), and social values like honour and shame in Israelite society are discussed in Chapter 12 (Philip F. Esler). In Chapter 13

---

[11] See, e.g., the plurality of insights gathered in Dube 2000; Sugirtharajah 2001, 2005; Moore and Segovia 2005; Brett and Havea 2014; West 2016.
[12] See, e.g., Lieb, Mason and Roberts 2011; Burnette-Bletsch 2016; Ziolkowski 2017.

(Katherine E. Southwood), an example of the relationship between power and ethnicity is studied, and Chapter 14 (Jo-Marí Schäder) investigates a case of reciprocal exchange in a biblical book. Chapter 15 (Robert D. Miller II) explores the question of orality and literacy in the Hebrew Bible, while Chapter 16 (Karolien Vermeulen) addresses issues related to narrative and myth, and Chapter 17 (Niels Peter Lemche) completes the narrative features of these chapters with a discussion on biblical memory. The ritual aspects in the Hebrew Bible are studied in Chapter 18 (Anne Katrine de Hemmer Gudme), and anthropological models for assessing biblical prophecy are illustrated in Chapter 19 (Lester L. Grabbe). The social aspects of food in the Hebrew Bible and in the archaeology of Israel appear discussed in Chapter 20 (Cynthia Shafer-Elliott). Chapter 21 (Kristine Henriksen Garroway) overviews approaches to social understandings of death in textual and archaeological sources, while the interrelationship between space, territory and power is addressed in Chapter 22 (Stephen C. Russell). Finally, Chapter 23 (Angelika Berlejung) offers a survey of approaches to and case studies on the iconography of ancient Palestine.

The studies comprising this handbook are representative of the expanding potentialities of anthropological insights in Hebrew Bible / Old Testament studies. After more than half a century, these insights have proven to be not a mere ancillary tool for biblical interpretation but an interpretative path on its own, with its own distinctive results. It is hoped that a consolidation of an anthropological study of the ancient Levant and biblical literature on its own sake is achieved in the near future, extending its competence also into the vast field of ancient Near Eastern studies.

# REFERENCES

Aiken, E.J. (2010), *Scriptural Geography: Portraying the Holy Land*, Tauris Historical Geography 3, London: I.B. Tauris.

Augé, M. (1982), *The Anthropological Circle: Symbol, Function, History*, Cambridge Studies in Social Anthropology 37, Cambridge: Cambridge University Press.

Bailey, C. (2018), *Bedouin Culture in the Bible*, New Haven, CT: Yale University Press.

Baldensperger, P.J. (1913), *The Immovable East: Studies of the People and Customs of Palestine*, London: Sir Isaac Pitman & Sons.

Bar-Yosef, E. (2005), *The Holy Land in English Culture, 1799–1917: Palestine and the Question of Orientalism*, Oxford: Clarendon Press.

Barth, F., A. Gingrich, R. Parkin and S. Silverman (2005), *One Discipline, Four Ways: British, German, French, and American Anthropology: The Halle Lectures*, Chicago: University of Chicago Press.

Ben-Arieh, Y. (1979), *The Rediscovery of the Holy Land in the Nineteenth Century*, Jerusalem: Magnes Press.

Bertholet, A. (1919), *Kulturgeschichte Israels*, Göttingen: Vandenhoeck & Ruprecht.

Boer, R. (2015), *The Sacred Economy of Ancient Israel*, LAI, Louisville, KY: Westminster John Knox Press.

Brett, M.G. and J. Havea, eds (2014), *Colonial Contexts and Postcolonial Theologies: Storyweaving in the Asia-Pacific*, New York: Palgrave Macmillan.

Burnette-Bletsch, R. (2016), *The Bible in Motion: A Handbook of the Bible and Its Reception in Film, Parts 1–2*, HBR, Berlin: De Gruyter.

Candea, M. (2018), 'Severed Roots: Evolutionism, Diffusionism and (Structural)Functionalism', in M. Candea (ed.), *Schools and Styles of Anthropological Theory*, 18–59, Abingdon: Routledge.
Carter, C.E. and C.L. Meyers, eds (1996), *Community, Identity, and Ideology: Social Science Approaches to the Hebrew Bible*, SBTS 6, Winona Lake, IN: Eisenbrauns.
Causse, A. (1937), *Du groupe ethnique à la communauté religieuse: Le problème sociologique de la religion d'Israël*, Études d'histoire et de philosophie religieuses publiées par la Faculté de Théologie Protestante de l'Université de Strasbourg 33, Paris: Alcan.
Chalcraft, D.J. (2004), 'Nineteenth-Century Comparative Sociology on Israel: The Contribution of Herbert Spencer', in L.J. Lawrence and M.I. Aguilar (eds), *Anthropology and Biblical Studies: Avenues of Approach*, 29–45, Leiden: Deo.
Chalcraft, D.J., ed. (2007), *Sectarianism in Early Judaism: Sociological Advances*, BibleWorld, London: Equinox.
Clements, R.E., ed. (1989), *The World of Ancient Israel: Sociological, Anthropological, and Political Perspectives: Essays by Members of the Society for Old Testament Study*, Cambridge: Cambridge University Press.
Culley, R.C. (1982), *Anthropological Perspectives on Old Testament Prophecy*, Semeia 21, Chico, CA: Scholars Press.
Cunningham, J.J. and K.M. McGeough (2018) 'The Perils of Ethnographic Analogy: Parallel Logics in Ethnoarchaeology and Victorian Bible Customs Books', *Archaeological Dialogues*, 25 (2): 161–89.
Davies, P.R. (1992), *In Search of 'Ancient Israel': A Study in Biblical Origins*, JSOTSup 148, Sheffield: Sheffield Academic Press.
Davis, T.W. (2004), *Shifting Sands: The Rise and Fall of Biblical Archaeology*, Oxford: Oxford University Press.
Day, E. (1901), *The Social Life of the Hebrews*, New York: Charles Scribner's Sons.
Dianteill, E. (2012), 'Anthropologie culturelle ou anthropologie sociale? Une dispute transatlantique', *L'Année sociologique*, 62: 93–122.
Douglas, M. (1966), *Purity and Danger: An Analysis of Concepts of Pollution and Taboo*, London: Routledge & Kegan Paul.
Douglas, M. (1999), *Leviticus as Literature*, Oxford: Oxford University Press.
Douglas, M. (2004), *Jacob's Tears: The Priestly Work of Reconciliation*, Oxford: Oxford University Press.
Dube, M.W. (2000), *Postcolonial Feminist Interpretation of the Bible*, St. Louis, MO: Chalice Press.
Esler, P.F., ed. (2006), *Ancient Israel: The Old Testament in Its Social Context*, Minneapolis, MN: Fortress Press.
Esler, P.F. and A. Hagedorn (2006), 'Social-Scientific Analysis of the Old Testament', in P.F. Esler (ed.), *Ancient Israel: The Old Testament in Its Social Context*, 15–32, Minneapolis, MN: Fortress Press.
Fabian, J. (1983), *Time and the Other: How Anthropology Makes Its Object*, New York: Columbia University Press.
Fiensy, D.D. (1987), 'Using the Nuer Culture of Africa in Understanding the Old Testament: An Evaluation', *JSOT*, 38: 73–83.
Finitsis, A., ed. (2021), *Dress and Clothing in the Hebrew Bible: 'For All Her Household Are Clothed in Crimson'*, LHBOTS 679, London: T&T Clark.
Foucault, M. (2002), *The Order of Things: An Archaeology of the Human Sciences*, London: Routledge [original French edn 1966].

Frazer, J.G. (1918), *Folk-Lore in the Old Testament: Studies in Comparative Religion, Legend and Law*, 3 vols, London: Macmillan.

Gilders, W.K. (2020), 'Social and Cultural Anthropology', in S.E. Balentine (ed.), *The Oxford Handbook of Ritual and Worship in the Hebrew Bible*, 125–41, Oxford: Oxford University Press.

Glock, A.E. (1983), 'The Use of Ethnography in an Archaeological Research Design', in H.B. Huffmon, F.A. Spina and A.R.W. Green (eds), *The Quest for the Kingdom of God: Studies in Honor of George E. Mendenhall*, 171–81, Winona Lake, IN: Eisenbrauns.

Goldberg, H.E., ed. (1987), *Judaism Viewed from Within and from Without: Anthropological Studies*, New York: State University of New York Press.

Goldberg, H.E. (2018), 'Anthropology and Hebrew Bible Studies: Modes of Interchange and Interpretation', *Brill Research Perspectives in Biblical Interpretation*, 3 (1): 1–81.

Goren, H. (2003), *'Zieht und erforscht das Land': Die deutsche Palästinaforschung im 19. Jahrhundert*, Göttingen: Wallstein.

Goren, H., J. Faehndrich and B. Schelhaas (2017), *Mapping the Holy Land: The Foundation of a Scientific Cartography of Palestine*, Tauris Historical Geography 11, London: I.B. Tauris.

Gottwald, N.K. (1979), *The Tribes of Yahweh: A Sociology of the Religion of Liberated Israel, 1250–1050 B.C.E.*, Maryknoll, NY: Orbis.

Granqvist, H. (1931), *Marriage Conditions in a Palestinian Village*, Vol. 1, Societas Scientiarum Fennica, Helsingfors: Akademische Buchhandlung / Leipzig: Otto Harrassowitz.

Gupta, A. and J. Ferguson (1997), 'Discipline and Practice: "The Field" as Site, Method, and Location in Anthropology', in A. Gupta and J. Ferguson (eds), *Anthropological Locations: Boundaries and Grounds of a Field Science*, 1–46, Berkeley: University of California Press.

Hagedorn, A. (2015), 'Institutions and Social Life in Ancient Israel: Sociological Aspects', in M. Sæbø (ed.), *Hebrew Bible/Old Testament: The History of Its Interpretation, Vol. III: From Modernism to Post-Modernism (The Nineteenth and Twentieth Centuries), Part 2: The Twentieth Century – From Modernism to Postmodernism*, 58–95, Göttingen: Vandenhoeck & Ruprecht.

Hansen, T. (1964), *Arabia Felix: The Danish Expedition of 1761–1767*, London: Collins [original Danish edn 1966].

Hardy, E.J. (1912), *The Unvarying East: Modern Scenes and Ancient Scriptures*, New York: Charles Scribner's Sons / London: T. Fisher Unwin.

Harris, M. (1968), *The Rise of Anthropological Theory: A History of Theories of Culture*, New York: Thomas Y. Crowell.

Headland, T.N., K.L. Pike and M. Harris, eds (1990), *Emics and Etics: The Insider/Outsider Debate*, Frontiers of Anthropology 7, London: Sage.

James, E.O. (1935), *The Old Testament in the Light of Anthropology. A Course of Public Lectures in the University of Leeds*, London: SPCK.

Kessler, R. (2006), *Sozialgeschichte des alten Israel: Eine Einführung*, Darmstadt: Wissenschaftliche Buchgesellschaft.

King, P.J. (1983), *American Archaeology in the Mideast: A History of the American Schools of Oriental Research*, Philadelphia, PA: ASOR.

Kirchhoff, M. (2005), *Text zu Land: Palästina im wissenschaftlichen Diskurs 1865–1920*, Göttingen: Vandenhoeck & Ruprecht.

Kirkpatrick, P.G. (1988), *The Old Testament and Folklore Study*, JSOTSup 62, Sheffield: JSOT Press.

Knight, D.A. (2011), *Law, Power, and Justice in Ancient Israel*, LAI, Louisville, KY: Westminster John Knox Press.

Kramer, S.N. (1962), 'Cultural Anthropology and the Cuneiform Documents', *Ethnology*, 1 (3): 299–314.

Kuper, A. (2005), *The Reinvention of Primitive Society: Transformations of a Myth*, 2nd edn, Abingdon: Routledge.

Kuper, A. (2015), *Anthropology and Anthropologists: The British School in the Twentieth Century*, 4th edn, Abingdon: Routledge.

Lane, E.W. (1836), *An Account of the Manners and Customs of the Modern Egyptians Written in Egypt During the Years 1833–1835*, London: Ward, Lock and Co.

Lang, B. (1985a), 'Introduction: Anthropology as a New Model for Biblical Studies', in B. Lang (ed.), *Anthropological Approaches to the Old Testament*, 1–20, Issues in Religion and Theology 8, Philadelphia, PA: Fortress Press / London: SPCK

Lang, B., ed. (1985b), *Anthropological Approaches to the Old Testament*, Issues in Religion and Theology 8, Philadelphia, PA: Fortress Press / London: SPCK.

Lawrence, L.J. and M.I. Aguilar, eds (2004), *Anthropology and Biblical Studies: Avenues of Approach*, Leiden: Deo.

Leach, E. (1961), 'Lévi-Strauss in the Garden of Eden: An Examination of Some Recent Developments in the Analysis of Myth', *Transactions of the New York Academy of Sciences (Series II)*, 23 (4): 386–96.

Leach, E. (1962), 'Genesis as Myth', *Discovery*, 23 (5): 30–5.

Leach, E. (1983a), 'Introduction', in E. Leach and D.A. Aycock, *Structuralist Interpretations of Biblical Myth*, 1–6, Cambridge: Cambridge University Press.

Leach, E. (1983b), 'Anthropological Approaches to the Study of the Bible During the Twentieth Century', in E. Leach and D.A. Aycock, *Structuralist Interpretations of Biblical Myth*, 7–32, Cambridge: Cambridge University Press.

Lemche, N.P. (1985), *Early Israel: Anthropological and Historical Studies on the Israelite Society Before the Monarchy*, VTSup 37, Leiden: E.J. Brill.

Lemos, T.M. (2010), *Marriage Gifts and Social Change in Ancient Palestine: 1200 BCE to 200 CE*, Cambridge: Cambridge University Press.

Lieb, M., E. Mason and J. Roberts, eds (2011), *The Oxford Handbook of the Reception History of the Bible*, Oxford: Oxford University Press.

Malamat, A. (1973), 'Tribal Societies: Biblical Genealogies and African Lineages', *Archives Européennes de Sociologie*, 14 (1): 126–36.

Matthews, V.H. and D.C. Benjamin (1993), *Social World of Ancient Israel: 1250–587 BCE*, Peabody, MA: Hendrickson.

Matthews, V.H. and D.C. Benjamin, eds (1994), *Honor and Shame in the World of the Bible*, Semeia 68, Atlanta, GA: Scholars Press.

McGrane, B. (1989), *Beyond Anthropology: Society and the Other*, New York: Columbia University Press.

McNutt, P.M. (1999), *Reconstructing the Society of Ancient Israel*, LAI, Louisville, KY: Westminster John Knox Press.

Mendenhall, G.E. (1962), 'The Hebrew Conquest of Palestine', *BA*, 25 (3): 66–87.

Meyers, C. (1988), *Discovering Eve: Ancient Israelite Woman in Context*, New York: Oxford University Press.

Meyers, C. (2013), *Rediscovering Eve: Ancient Israelite Women in Context*, New York: Oxford University Press.

Milman, H.H. (1829), *A History of the Jews*, 3 vols, 2nd edn, London: John Murray.

Moore, S.D. and F.F. Segovia, eds (2005), *Postcolonial Biblical Criticism: Interdisciplinary Intersections*, The Bible and Postcolonialism; London: T&T Clark.

Moorey, P.R.S. (1991), *A Century of Biblical Archaeology*, Cambridge: Lutterworth Press.

Nagel, A. and C.S. Wood (2010), *Anachronic Renaissance*, New York: Zone Books.

Netton, I.R., ed. (2013), *Orientalism Revisited: Art, Land, Voyage*, Culture and Civilization in the Middle East 35, London: Routledge.

Neu, R. (1989), 'Die Bedeutung der Ethnologie für die alttestamentliche Forschung', in C. Sigrist and R. Neu (eds), *Ethnologische Texte zum Altes Testament, Band 1: Vor- und Frühgeschichte Israels*, 11–26, Neukirchen: Neukirchener Verlag.

Niditch, S. (1993a), *Folklore and the Hebrew Bible*, Minneapolis, MN: Fortress Press.

Niditch, S. (1993b), *War in the Hebrew Bible: A Study in the Ethics of Violence*, New York: Oxford University Press.

Olyan, S.M., ed. (2012), *Social Theory and the Study of Israelite Religion*, SBLRBS 71, Atlanta, GA: Society of Biblical Literature.

Olyan, S.M., ed. (2015), *Ritual Violence in the Hebrew Bible: New Perspectives*, Oxford: Oxford University Press.

Olyan, S.M. (2017), *Friendship in the Hebrew Bible*, ABRL, New Haven, CT: Yale University Press.

Oppenheim, A.L. (1960), 'Assyriology – Why and How?', *Current Anthropology*, 1 (5/6): 409–23.

Overholt, T.W. (1996), *Cultural Anthropology and the Old Testament*, Guides to Biblical Scholarship, Minneapolis, MN: Fortress Press.

Pedersen, J. (1991), *Israel: Its Life and Culture*, Vol. 1, SFSHJ 28, Atlanta, GA: Scholars Press [First English translation 1926, Danish original edn 1920].

Pfoh, E. (2009), *The Emergence of Israel in Ancient Palestine: Historical and Anthropological Perspectives*, CIS, London: Equinox.

Pfoh, E. (2010a), 'Anthropology and Biblical Studies: A Critical Manifesto', in E. Pfoh (ed.), *Anthropology and the Bible: Critical Perspectives*, 15–35, BI 3, Piscataway, NJ: Gorgias Press.

Pfoh, E., ed. (2010b), *Anthropology and the Bible: Critical Perspectives*, BI 3, Piscataway, NJ: Gorgias Press.

Pilch, J.J. and B.J. Malina, eds (1993), *Biblical Social Values and Their Meaning: A Handbook*, Peabody, MA: Hendrickson.

Pitt-Rivers, J. (1977), *The Fate of Shechem, or the Politics of Sex: Essays on Mediterranean Anthropology*, Cambridge Studies and Papers in Social Anthropology 19, Cambridge: Cambridge University Press.

Prewitt, T.J. (1981), 'Kinship Structures and the Genesis Genealogies', *JNES*, 40 (2): 87–98.

Quick, L. (2021), *Dress, Adornment, and the Body in the Hebrew Bible*, Oxford: Oxford University Press.

Ricks, T. (1999), 'Memories of Palestine: Uses of Oral History and Archaeology in Recovering the Palestinian Past', in T. Kapitan (ed.), *Archaeology, History and Culture in Palestine and the Near East: Essays in Memory of Albert E. Glock*, 23–46, ASOR 3, Atlanta, GA: Scholars Press.

Robertson Smith, W. (1885), *Kinship and Marriage in Early Arabia*, Cambridge: Cambridge University Press.

Robertson Smith, W. (1889), *Lectures on the Religion of the Semites, First Series: Fundamental Institutions*, London: Adam & Charles Black.

Robinson, E. and E. Smith (1841), *Biblical Researches in Palestine, Mount Sinai and Arabia Petraea: A Journal of Travels in the Year 1838*, Vols I–II, Boston, MA: Crocker and Brewster.

Rogerson, J.W. (1970), 'Structural Anthropology and the Old Testament', *BSOAS*, 33 (3): 490–500.

Rogerson, J.W. (1974), *Myth in Old Testament Interpretation*, BZAW 134, Berlin: De Gruyter.

Rogerson, J.W. (1978), *Anthropology and the Old Testament*, Oxford: Basil Blackwell.
Rogerson, J.W. (1986), 'Was Early Israel a Segmentary Society?', *JSOT*, 36: 17–26.
Rogerson, J.W. (1989), 'Anthropology and the Old Testament', in R.E. Clements (ed.), *The World of Ancient Israel: Sociological, Anthropological, and Political Perspectives: Essays by Members of the Society for Old Testament Study*, 17–37, Cambridge: Cambridge University Press.
Rogerson, J.W. (2013), 'Expansion of the Anthropological, Sociological and Mythological Context of the Hebrew Bible/Old Testament', in M. Sæbø (ed.), *Hebrew Bible/Old Testament: The History of Its Interpretation, Vol. III: From Modernism to Post-Modernism (The Nineteenth and Twentieth Centuries), Part 1: The Nineteenth Century – A Century of Modernism and Historicism*, 119–33, Göttingen: Vandenhoeck & Ruprecht.
Said, E.W. (1978), *Orientalism: Western Conceptions of the Orient*, Harmondsworth: Penguin.
Sigrist, C. and R. Neu, eds (1989), *Ethnologische Texte zum Altes Testament, Band 1: Vor- und Frühgeschichte Israels*, Neukirchen: Neukirchener.
Sigrist, C. and R. Neu, eds (1997), *Ethnologische Texte zum Altes Testament, Band 2: Die Entstehung des Königtums*, Neukirchen: Neukirchener.
Silberman, N.A. (1982), *Digging for God and Country: Exploration, Archaeology, and the Secret Struggle for the Holy Land, 1799–1917*, New York: Doubleday.
Simkins, R.A. and S.L. Cook, eds (1999), *The Social World of the Hebrew Bible: Twenty-Five Years of the Social Sciences in the Academy*, Semeia 87, Atlanta, GA: Society of Biblical Literature.
Spencer, H. (1880), *Hebrews and Phoenicians*, compiled and abstracted by R. Scheppig, London: Williams & Northgate.
Stocking, G.W. Jr (1987), *Victorian Anthropology*, New York: Free Press.
Stordalen, T. and Ø.S. LaBianca, eds (2021), *Levantine Entanglements: Cultural Productions, Long-Term Changes and Globalizations in the Eastern Mediterranean*, Sheffield: Equinox.
Sugirtharajah, R.S. (2001), *The Bible and the Third World: Precolonial, Colonial and Postcolonial Encounters*, Cambridge: Cambridge University Press.
Sugirtharajah, R.S. (2005), *The Bible and Empire: Postcolonial Explorations*, Cambridge: Cambridge University Press.
Thiede, B. (2022), *Male Friendship, Homosociality, and Women in the Hebrew Bible: Malignant Fraternities*, Routledge Studies in the Biblical World, Abingdon: Routledge.
Thompson, T.L. (1999), *The Bible in History: How Writers Create a Past*, London: Jonathan Cape.
Thompson, T.L. (2019), 'Introduction: Creating Coherence and Continuity – Suggestions and Illustrations of Methods and Themes', in I. Hjelm, H. Taha, I. Pappe and T.L. Thompson (eds), *A New Critical Approach to the History of Palestine: Palestine History and Heritage Project 1*, 1–16, CIS, Abingdon: Routledge.
Thomson, W.M. (1859), *The Land and the Book, or Biblical Illustrations Drawn from the Manners and Customs, the Scenes and Scenery of the Holy Land*, 2 vols, New York: Harper & Brothers.
Tristram, H.B. (1894), *Eastern Customs in Bible Lands*, London: Hodder and Stoughton.
Van-Lennep, H.J. (1875), *Bible Lands: Their Modern Customs and Manners Illustrative of Scripture*, New York: Harper & Brothers.
Varisco, D.M. (2013), 'Orientalism and Bibliolatry: Framing the Holy Land in Nineteenth-Century Protestant Bible Customs Texts', in I. Netton (ed.), *Orientalism Revisited: Art, Land and Voyage*, 187–204, Culture and Civilization in the Middle East 35, London: Routledge.

Volney, C.-F. (1787), *Voyages en Syrie et en Égypte, pendant les années 1783, 1784 et 1785, avec deux cartes géographiques: Seconde édition revue et corrigée*, 2 vols, Paris: Volland et Desenne.

Wajdenbaum, P. (2011), *Argonauts of the Desert: Structural Analysis of the Hebrew Bible*, CIS, London: Equinox.

Weber, M. (1923 [1917–19]), *Gesammelte Aufsätze zur Religionssoziologie, Bd. III: Das antike Judentum*, ed. Marianne Weber, Tübingen: Mohr.

West, G.O. (2016), *The Stolen Bible: From Tool of Imperialism to African Icon*, BIS 114, Leiden: E.J. Brill.

Whitelam, K.W. (1995), 'William Robertson Smith and the So-Called New Histories of Palestine', in W. Johnstone (ed.), *William Robertson Smith: Essays in Reassessment*, 180–9, JSOTSup 189, Sheffield: Sheffield Academic Press.

Wilson, R.R. (1977), *Genealogy and History in the Biblical World*, New Haven, CT: Yale University Press.

Wilson, R.R. (1984), *Sociological Approaches to the Old Testament*, Guides to Biblical Scholarship; Philadelphia:, PA Fortress Press.

Wolff, H.W. (1974), *Anthropologie des Alten Testaments*, München: Kaiser Verlag.

Yilmaz, H. (2012), 'The Eastern Question and the Ottoman Empire: The Genesis of the Near and Middle East in the Nineteenth Century', in M.E. Bonine, A. Amanat and M.E. Gasper (eds), *Is There a Middle East? The Evolution of a Geopolitical Concept*, 11–35, Stanford, CA: Stanford University Press.

Ziolkowski, E., ed. (2017), *The Bible in Folklore Worldwide: A Handbook of Biblical Reception in Jewish, European Christian, and Islamic Folklores*, HBR 1.1, Berlin: De Gruyter.

# PART ONE

# Historiographies, theories and methods

CHAPTER TWO

# Anthropologists and the Bible

ADAM KUPER

## I

A young philosophy don, a Jerseyman at Oxford, Robert Ranulph Marett was intrigued by the subject set for the 1893 Green Prize in Moral Philosophy: 'The ethics of savage races'. He immersed himself in the literature on primitive religion, won the prize and was befriended by the only anthropologist at Oxford University, E.B. Tylor.

Tylor was the father figure of the new anthropology that had emerged in the 1860s. It was a baggy, ambitious discipline, and Tylor himself wrote about race and technology and language and marriage, but especially about religion, and this became Marett's main interest too. The first objective of the anthropology of religion was to characterize the earliest creeds and rites. The anthropologists then explained the advance of humanity from the long dark age of magic and superstition to the sunny uplands of a more spiritual religion; or they showed how metaphysical error gave way to rationality and science.

In any case, they took it for granted that religion, technology and the social order advanced in lockstep through a determined series of stages. At each stage, the beliefs and customs of societies at a similar level of development were essentially the same. So contemporary primitive societies could be treated as stand-ins for past societies at an equivalent stage of development. The notions of the American Indians, perhaps, or at a higher level, the Tahitians, provided living instances of conceptions and beliefs that had once been very widespread. To know one was to know all. Captain Cook had introduced the word *taboo* from Tahiti. Soon taboos were being discovered all over the place. Other exotic terms were soon taken up – *mana*, another Polynesian word, *totem* from the Ojibwa, *potlatch* from the Kwakiutl of British Columbia, *voodoo* from West Africa. All were elements of a universal primal religion. So Victorian anthropologists could write about Australian totems and American Indian taboos. They could even identify totem and taboo in ancient Israel.

Such beliefs and practices may once have been universal but they were surely irrational. How could so many people have believed so many impossible things for so long? Some missionaries saw the hand of the Devil here, but the anthropologists argued that there was something about the ways of thinking of primitive people that led them to make mistakes of perception and logic. After all, Darwin had shown that human evolution was paced by the development of the brain. It was widely assumed that the brains of the various races developed at different rates. The smaller-brained savages, and indeed the early Israelites, were simply not capable of thinking very clearly.

So how *did* they think? Tylor argued that primitive peoples relied on 'analogy or reasoning by resemblance' (Tylor 1881: 338). For Frazer, such 'reasoning by resemblance' accounted for the belief in magic. Robertson Smith agreed that for the savage mind there was 'no sharp line between the metaphorical and the literal', and he blamed the 'unbounded use of analogy characteristic of pre-scientific thought' for producing a 'confusion between the several orders of natural and supernatural beings' (Robertson Smith 1894: 274). Pre-scientific thinkers were particularly likely to get into a muddle when it came to causality. Robertson Smith found that primal religion was characterized by '*insouciance*, a power of casting off the past and living in the impression of the moment' which 'can exist only along with a childish unconsciousness of the inexorable laws that connect the present and the future with the past' (Robertson Smith 1894: 57).

Tylor supposed that the very earliest religion arose from a misapprehension. People everywhere have dreams and visions, but primitive people confuse dreams with real experiences. When they dream of the dead they imagine that they exist somewhere else, in another state, the state that living people experience in dreams, trances and fevers. And so, 'the ancient savage philosophers probably made their first step by the obvious inference that every man has two things belonging to him, namely, a life and a phantom' (Tylor 1871 II: 12). They then generalized this conclusion to embrace the rest of the natural world. Even trees and plants, even the planets, had souls. This was what Tylor termed 'animism'.

Rituals soon developed, notably sacrifices. In primitive animism, offerings were made to the spirits of the dead after they had appeared in dreams. In what might be called the higher animism, sacrifices were also made to 'other spiritual beings, genii, fairies, gods'. These sacrifices were gifts: 'as prayer is a request made to a deity as if he were a man, so sacrifice is a gift made to the deity as if he were a man' (Tylor 1871 II: 375). Sacrifices took the form of burnt offerings, because spirits demanded spiritual food, the souls of animals of plants (Tylor 1866: 77). Vestiges of the primitive cult – which Tylor called 'survivals' – recurred in the ceremonies of the most advanced religions.

In 1899, the young Marett achieved a certain notoriety by challenging Tylor's thesis that animism was the primeval religion. Marett identified a pre-animistic religion based on the Polynesian belief in *mana*, which he took to mean a sort of psychic energy and power. Mana was inseparable from taboo. 'Altogether, in mana we have what is *par excellence* the primitive religious idea in its positive aspect, taboo representing its negative side, since whatever has mana is taboo, and whatever is taboo has mana' (Marett 1911). His theory made some converts in Germany and in France, most notably Marcel Mauss, who made mana the dynamic force behind both the gift and sacrifice.

Tylor was already a frail old man when Marett became his friend, and Marett took responsibility for the development of anthropology at the university. He was instrumental in instituting Oxford's diploma in anthropology in 1908, and he succeeded Tylor as University Reader in Social Anthropology, a position he held for a quarter of century. When the university created a chair in anthropology in 1936 he held it for a year before the appointment of Radcliffe-Brown. From 1928 he was Rector of Exeter College. He also served for many years as Treasurer of the University Golf Club. A busy man then, but, he recalled:

> All this time [. . .] Anthropology was becoming [. . .] a passion with me [. . .] Yet I was still attending to the subject with my left hand, while the right tackled the philosophy

which after all I was paid to teach. In fact, I became a scandal to my friends, so that one of them wrote: 'A man of your talents seems rather wasted on the habits of backward races.' As it was, I divided my attention impartially between the beliefs of the savage and those of the Oxford undergraduate.

—Marett 1941: 164

## II

Tylor's theory of animism was hardly original. It was in the direct line of enlightenment accounts of the development of rationality. Indeed, it was remarkably similar to the theory that had been advanced by Charles de Brosses and Auguste Comte (de Brosses 1760; Comte 1830–42). But Tylor was also responding to the scandal provoked by two books that challenged traditional understandings of the Bible. *On the Origin of Species*, published in 1859, presented a scientific alternative to the book of Genesis. The following year *Essays and Reviews* appeared, seven essays by intellectuals in the Church of England, including Benjamin Jowett, Mark Pattison, and Frederick Temple (who was to become Archbishop of Canterbury) (Parker 1860). They downplayed miracles, questioned the story of the Creation, denied the doctrine of eternal punishment, and endorsed German critical scholarship which demonstrated that the Bible was a compilation of sometimes contradictory texts dating from different periods.

The continental champions of the new biblical criticism, Wellhausen and Kuenen, further insisted that the Jewish religion had pagan roots. The original religion of Israel was a family cult. In time the family cult became a tribal and then a national religion. Only with the emergence of great empires in Mesopotamia and Persia, which subjugated Israel, had prophets begun to formulate a universal spiritual religion, foreshadowing Christianity. But pagan elements survived (Wellhausen 1885 [1883]).

Perhaps the ordinary churchgoer could ignore these challenges. Owen Chadwick remarks that Victorian churches were full of 'worshippers who had never heard of Tylor, were indifferent to Darwin, mildly regretted what they heard of Huxley' (Chadwick 1970 II: 35). But the educated public did debate these new ideas, passionately. Samuel Wilberforce, Bishop of Oxford, son of William Wilberforce, provoked a famous public confrontation with Huxley over the descent of man ('Is Dr Huxley descended from a monkey on his father's side or on his mother's side. . .') (Hesketh 2009). The Bishop also moved to have *Essays and Reviews* condemned in the Convocation of Canterbury.

However, a new science of religion was emerging, with biblical and comparative wings, that engaged with the ideas of Darwin and Wellhausen. It brought together theologians, linguists, folklorists, archaeologists and anthropologists (Wheeler-Barclay 2010). The particular project of Tylor and the anthropologists was to discover the origins of religion, origins which could never be completely outgrown, the vestiges of ancient cults haunting even the most advanced religions.

And they had fresh evidence at their disposal, for they were able to draw on a stream of reports on primitive religions from all over the world, many of them the work of missionaries. These sources were themselves shaped by the Bible and by biblical scholarship. Protestant missionaries especially made it a priority to translate the Bible into the local language. This obliged them to identify indigenous notions that were roughly equivalent to god, spirit, sin, sacrifice and holiness. These concepts, and their ritual representations, were taken to be the essential constituents of a religion.

There is in fact no word for 'religion' in the Hebrew Bible, but it seemed obvious that ancient Judaism was the prototype of authentic religion. The Bible also gave examples of false religions, which were those of Israel's idolatrous neighbours. Similar beliefs and practices were abundantly represented in the societies to which the missionaries were called. They could now be identified as not only pagan, but primitive. The idols of false religions were totems. Their laws were barbarous taboos and had nothing to do with justice or morality. Their ceremonies, shocking exhibitions of greed and lust, featured ghastly acts of cruelty, including human sacrifice. Missionary ethnographers read the reports of their colleagues, which described surprisingly similar pagan religions in distant parts of the world, and they welcomed the guidance of Tylor and Frazer, who pointed out what they should be looking for, and explained the hold of superstition.[1]

So the anthropology of religion was from the first very largely an anthropology of the Bible, with comparative notes from all over the primitive world. Precisely because it had consequences for Christianity, it seemed to be very important. Tylor was raised as a Quaker and he believed that rituals always depended on magical thinking. Frazer argued that the comparative method 'proves that many religious doctrines and practices are based on primitive conceptions, which most civilized and educated men have long agreed on abandoning as mistakes. From this it is a natural and often a probable inference that doctrines so based are false, and that practices so based are foolish' (Frazer 1927: 282). Robertson Smith believed on the contrary that he was clearing away the debris of folklore and tribal custom so that the prophetic and historical truths in the Hebrew Bible could be properly appreciated. For their part, missionary ethnographers delighted in discovering in the most primitive communities some faint intimations of more advanced doctrines, crude versions of biblical stories, even traces in the language of the passage of one of the lost tribes of Israel. In the 1920s and 1930s this sort of thing became a speciality of the Vienna school, then a hot-house of Catholic missionary anthropology.

## III

In parallel with these studies of the development of religion, another foundational research programme of anthropology addressed the rise of marriage and the family. Was there some connection between religion, morality and social organization? In 1869, J.F. McLennan provided Tylor's animism with a social context. McLennan had himself proposed a model of the earliest societies (McLennan 1865). They were marauding nomadic bands, matrilineal and exogamous, practising marriage by capture. He now argued that these bands had an appropriate religion. Each band believed that it was descended matrilineally from a particular natural species, its totem, which was worshipped as an ancestor god and placated with rituals. Totemism was at once a religion – rather like animism, as McLennan conceded – and a social system.

Long ago, totemism had been universal. McLennan identified traces of a totemic system in Siberia, Peru, Fiji and even in classical India. The Greeks had their natural spirits. Totemism was also the point of departure of later systems of thought. It planted the seeds not only of religion but also of science. When the names of animals were given

---

[1] Some missionary scholars were also aware of the new biblical criticism. The first Anglican bishop of Zululand, John Colenso, produced sympathetic account of Zulu beliefs and practices, even endorsing polygamy, which, he noted, and as the Zulu remarked, had been practised by the biblical patriarchs. Colenso also published contributions to the new biblical criticism, and was duly tried for heresy in Cape Town (Guy 1983).

to constellations of stars, this was a legacy of totemism but also the first inklings of astronomy. Beliefs about the descent of human beings from animals gave a faint hint of what would become the theory of evolution.

McLennan suggested in passing that the serpent story in Genesis may have had a totemic significance, but his theory of totemism was first systematically applied to the Hebrew Bible by his friend, William Robertson Smith, who had been appointed to the chair of Hebrew and Old Testament at the Free Church College at Aberdeen in 1870 (see Black and Chrystal 1912). Robertson Smith accepted Wellhausen's demonstration that the Bible was a compilation of sources of various dates, and that it included mythological as well as historical elements. Following Wellhausen again, he aimed to identify the religious beliefs of the most ancient Israelites, and to trace their progressive enlightenment. He also adopted Wellhausen's view that rituals were often hangovers from more primitive times, but given fresh justifications.

How were the primitive elements to be identified? An obvious first step was to consider the practices and beliefs of Israel's pagan neighbours. Robertson Smith wrote that some ancient Jewish laws were based on principles 'still current among the Arabs of the desert' (Robertson Smith 1894: 340). He himself travelled in the Arabian interior to collect first-hand materials. However, even the Bedouin had progressed beyond the totemic stage, and they had been Muslims for many centuries. The comparative method practised by McLennan offered an alternative approach. Early Israel could be understood with reference to better-documented societies at the same level of development.

In 1880 Robertson Smith published an essay entitled 'Animal Worship and Animal Tribes Among the Arabs in the Old Testament', in which he argued that ancient Semitic societies were totemic. The evidence was admittedly patchy. Robertson Smith pointed to the Queen of Sheba as proof of early matriarchy. Some Arab marriage rituals might be interpreted as survivals of marriage by capture. Taken together with other hints scattered in the literature, Robertson Smith later pronounced, 'These facts appear sufficient to prove that Arabia did pass through a stage in which family relations and the marriage law satisfied the conditions of the totem system' (Robertson Smith 1894: 88).

Similar bits and pieces of evidence might indicate that the early Arabian religion was also totemic. Tribal groupings were often named after animals, and sometimes after the moon and sun. Sun and moon were evidently worshipped as gods, so animals presumably were also once treated as gods. And crucially it seemed that totemic beliefs survived in ancient Israel, if in an attenuated form. Robertson Smith suggested that the heathen practices against which the Hebrew prophets inveighed were totemic in origin. And the second commandment itself was apparently directed against nature worship.

This argument did not go down well with his employers. The General Assembly of the Free Church of Scotland issued a swift condemnation:

First, concerning marriage and the marriage laws in Israel, the views expressed are so gross and so fitted to pollute the moral sentiments of the community that they cannot be considered except within the closed doors of any court of this Church. Secondly, concerning animal worship in Israel, the views expressed by the Professor are not only contrary to the facts recorded and the statements made in Holy Scripture, but they are gross and sensual – fitted to pollute and debase public sentiment.

—Black and Chrystal 1912: 382

Yet Robertson Smith was not cast into outer darkness. He became co-editor of the famous ninth edition of the *Encyclopaedia Britannica* (and was reputed to have read every entry). In 1883 he was appointed Reader in Arabic at Cambridge and in 1889 he became Professor. And he elaborated his initial thesis on early Semitic religion and social organization, notably in *Kinship and Marriage in Early Arabia* (1885), and in his masterpiece, *Lectures on the Religion of the Semites* (1894 [1889]).

He remained wedded to McLennan's theory of totemism. Primitive people believed that they were physically descended from founding gods. Gods and their worshippers were originally thought of as kin who 'make up a single community, and [. . .] the place of the god in the community is interpreted on the analogy of human relationships' (Robertson Smith 1894: 53). A more sophisticated doctrine developed in ancient Israel. The divine father was conceived of in spiritual terms. But initially gods and their worshippers were thought of as blood relatives. This was also the origin of morality, for 'the indissoluble bond that united men to their god is the same bond of blood-fellowship which in early society is the one binding link between man and man, and the one sacred principle of moral obligation' (Robertson Smith 1894: 53).

The totemic gods were associated with shrines or sanctuaries. At certain times, a yet more intimate contact with the gods was required. This was achieved through sacrifice, which Robertson Smith termed 'the typical form of all complete acts of worship in the antique religions' (Robertson Smith 1894: 214). Sacrifice had been, of course, the central rite celebrated in the temple in Jerusalem, as in the temples of ancient Greece and Rome. It remained a vexing problem for Christian theology and for critical scholarship of the Bible. The priestly code represented sacrifices as acts of atonement, but Wellhausen insisted that this interpretation was anachronistic. Textual criticism revealed that the code was a post-Exilic document, which superimposed a late-priestly theology on earlier ritual practices. Originally, sacrifices were not even performed in the temple. They were associated with what Wellhausen called a natural religion, which was situated within the life of the family. Robertson Smith speculated that sacrifice was originally a sort of family meal. 'The god and his worshippers are wont to eat and drink together, and by this token their fellowship is declared and sealed'. The most primitive sacrifices were therefore not gifts, as Tylor had thought, but were 'essentially acts of communion between the god and his worshippers' (Robertson Smith 1894: 243, 271).

But what was sacrificed, what was eaten at that communion meal? Robertson Smith declared that the totemic animal itself was the original sacrificial object. Normally, a totem animal could not be killed or eaten. It was 'unclean' – taboo. Taboos were primitive anticipations of the idea of the sacred. Robertson Smith pronounced the evidence 'unambiguous': 'When an unclean animal is sacrificed it is also a sacred animal'. He concluded that among the Semites 'the fundamental idea of sacrifices is not that of a sacred tribute, but of communion between the god and his worshippers by joint participation in the living flesh and blood of a sacred victim' (Robertson Smith 1894: 345).

The argument was clearly leading up to a climax in which something would have to be said about the sacrifices of gods themselves in Semitic religions, perhaps in connection with a communion rite. Robertson Smith took the step in this passage:

> That the God-man dies for His people and that his Death is their life, is an idea which was in some degree foreshadowed by the oldest mystical sacrifices. It was foreshadowed, indeed, in a very crude and materialistic form, and without any of those ethical ideas

which the Christian doctrine of the Atonement derives from a profound sense of sin and divine justice. And yet the voluntary death of the divine victim, which we have seen to be a conception not foreign to ancient ritual, contained the germ of the deepest thought in the Christian doctrine: the thought that the Redeemer gives Himself for his people.

—Robertson Smith 1894 [1889]: 393

Frazer cited this passage in his obituary essay on Robertson Smith and remarked that it was dropped in the posthumously published second edition of the *Religion of the Semites*, which had been edited by J.S. Black (Frazer 1894).

## IV

Like Robertson Smith, James George Frazer was a Scot, and the son of a clergyman. When Robertson Smith arrived at Cambridge to take up his new professorship he commissioned Frazer to write entries on 'Taboo' and 'Totemism' for the *Encyclopaedia Britannica*. Frazer's essay on totemism turned out to be too long for the publishers, but Robertson Smith encouraged him to write a book on the subject. *Totemism* (1887) marked Frazer's debut as an anthropologist in his own right.

Frazer's most famous book, *The Golden Bough*, first published in 1890, followed up Robertson Smith's speculations about the sacrifice of a totemic god. He also drew on the theory of a German folklorist, Wilhelm Mannhardt, who had explained German peasant cults of sacred trees as survivals of ancient fertility rituals (Mannhardt 1875). Combining these elements, Frazer constructed an ethnological detective story. It began with the ritual strangling of 'the King of the Wood', the priest of the sanctuary of Nemi, near Rome. This sacred king was the embodiment of a tree-spirit. He was not simply murdered, but was sacrificed to ensure the fertility of nature. Clues drawn from a vast range of ethnographic sources showed that primitive people identified their well-being with the fate of natural spirits, whose priest-kings were sacrificed in fertility rituals. 'The result, then, of our inquiry is to make it probable that [. . .] the King of the Wood lived and died as an incarnation of the Supreme Aryan god, whose life was in the mistletoe or Golden Bough' (Frazer 1900 II: 363). Might this not imply that the Gospel accounts of Christ's crucifixion were further versions of the myth of the sacred king? Frazer wrote in a letter to a friend, in 1904, that 'the facts of comparative religion appear to me subversive of Christian theology' (Ackerman 2005: 236).

Frazer then turned his attention to the Hebrew Bible. In 1904 or 1905 the Regius Professor of Hebrew in Cambridge, Robert Hatch Kennett, was persuaded to offer a private beginner's class in Hebrew (Ackerman 1987: 183–4). It attracted a very select clientele: Jane Harrison, F.M. Cornford, A.B. Cook and Frazer. Frazer became competent enough to read the Old Testament in Hebrew and he gradually put together an anthropological commentary on the Bible, just as he had earlier issued a six-volume commentary on Pausanias' description of Greece. He published the three volumes of his *Folk-Lore in the Old Testament* in 1918.

Frazer's method was to select a myth or custom in the Bible and to identify parallels in 'primitive societies'. So in Volume 2, Chapter 4, a 300-page essay entitled 'Jacob's Marriage', he analysed Jacob's marriages to his cousins, the two daughters of his mother's brother, Laban, and posed the question whether Jacob was following established customs, and whether such customs were to be found in other primitive societies. He was, of course, able to show that these practices were indeed widespread. A chapter on Cain explained that all over the world murderers were marked in order to protect them from ghosts. Similar exercises showed that 'primitive peoples' also prayed and sacrificed to their gods, and had their myths of creation, floods, etc. As a modern biographer of Frazer comments, 'the implicit purpose of the work [was] to undermine the Bible and religion by insisting on its folkloric stratum, thereby associating it with savagery' (Ackerman 1987: 182–3).

Émile Durkheim was also inspired by Robertson Smith. In *The Elementary Forms of the Religious Life* (1971 [1912]) he adopted Robertson Smith's thesis that religion was rooted in social arrangements, and in particular that early religions developed out of family cults (a thesis that had been independently proposed for ancient Rome and Greece by Durkheim's teacher Fustel de Coulanges [1864]). Among the aboriginal peoples of Australia – apparently the most primitive surviving society – the exogamous kinship group, the clan, was associated with an emblem, the totem, which was the object of taboos and sacrifice. It was, Durkheim declared, sacred.

For Durkheim, 'the sacred was the religious' (Lukes 1973: 241), and he praised Robertson Smith for remarking the ambiguity at the core of the notion of the sacred, the biblical *qadosh*. The ambiguity lies in the fact that *qadosh* may refer to something that is holy in the Christian sense, or it may designate something that is unpropitious and taboo, like a field sown with a mixed harvest, or the *q'desha*, the temple priestess who is a cult prostitute. The key is that sacred things are set apart from profane beings. 'A whole group of rites has the object of realizing this state of separation which is essential. Since their function is to prevent undue mixings and to keep one of the two domains from encroaching upon the other, they are only able to impose abstentions or negative acts' (Durkheim 1971 [1912]: 299).

Maureen Bloom argues that Durkheim was in reality characterizing biblical Judaism, and that he was drawing upon his own education in the Hebrew Bible (Bloom 2007: Ch. 7). After all, Durkheim was the son of the rabbi of Épinal, and had been destined for the rabbinate. So once again, by another route, the Hebrew Bible shaped the anthropology of religion.

## V

The influence of the great Victorians was prolonged. The second edition of Oesterley and Robinson's influential *History of Israel*, published in 1937, still relied on Wellhausen, Robertson Smith, Tylor and Frazer. Frazer himself continued to publish on the Hebrew Bible until the 1930s. Freud – another fan of Robertson Smith – produced exercises in speculative anthropology, *Totem and Taboo* (1913), and *Moses and Monotheism* (1937), that were, at least in point of method, thoroughly Victorian.

Within anthropology a reaction set in against just-so stories of origin, but the comparative method remained in favour. Marcel Mauss (who was the grandson of a rabbi) suggested that the situation of the Hebrew patriarchs was similar to that of pastoralist elites in East Africa, who lorded it over sedentary farmers (Mauss 1926). Franz Steiner compared the patriarchal families to Nuer clans and lineages (Steiner 1954). Occasional attempts were made to rewrite chapters of *Folklore in the Old Testament* in a functionalist idiom, anthropologists citing observations from their own fieldwork to cast light on mysterious episodes in the Bible. Isaac Schapera, for example, devoted a Frazer lecture (appropriately enough) to 'the sin of Cain' (Schapera 1955).

And from the 1950s biblical scholars began to draw on more recent anthropological theories (see Rogerson 1978, 1989). Some were influenced by theories of nomadism (though not, surprisingly, by the ideas of Ibn Khaldoun). Functionalist studies of segmentary lineage systems were taken as a model of the social system of the patriarchal age. Some scholars combined the lineage model with models of state formation, or with the typology of bands, tribes and chieftaincies developed by Elman Service (1962).

Inevitably, perhaps, biblical scholars tended to place too much confidence in their chosen anthropological models. It was readily assumed, for instance, that anthropologists were quite sure what lineages are (and indeed, that any expert can distinguish minimal from maximal lineages).[2] The only issue was to identify the ancient Hebrew terms for these social units. This turned out to be very difficult. Experts could not agree whether the biblical *bêt ʾāb* or *mišpāḥāh* should be translated as a 'lineage', or whether the Hebrew words *šēbeṭ* or *maṭṭeh* referred to a 'tribe' or a 'clan'. As Niels Peter Lemche remarks, 'It is clear that the traditional literature of the OT employs a very loose terminology to describe the lower levels of the society, since [Hebrew terms usually rendered as] "house" and "father's house" are used indiscriminately of the nuclear family, the extended family, and also of the higher kinship group, the lineage'. As for the very general view that the term *mišpāḥāh* means 'clan', 'no scholar has troubled to define precisely what he meant by the word "clan"' (Lemche 1985: 260; cf. Vanderhooft 2009). Yet Lemche himself was perhaps too ready to identify 'lineages' in biblical times, and to conclude that 'clan endogamy' was widely practised (Lemche 1985: 272–4).[3]

## VI

Howard Eilberg-Schwartz (1990) has proposed a return to the comparative method, and attempts continue to generalize from exotic practices in order to illuminate puzzling biblical stories.[4] Old-fashioned ideas about primitive society still cast a long shadow in essays on the Bible. The ghosts of Robertson Smith, Frazer and Marett might find some recent exercises in the comparative method rather familiar.

But N.H. Snaith chided biblical scholars for paying more attention to primitive parallels than to textual analysis (Snaith 1944). Within anthropology there was increasing concern with the meaning of beliefs and practices for the people themselves. Marett had demanded this almost from the first. 'How then are we to be content with an explanation of taboo that does not pretend to render its sense as it has sense for those who both practice it and make it a rallying point for their thought on mystic matters? [. . .] We ask to understand it, and we are merely bidden to despise it' (Marett 1909: 97). The post-First World War generation of anthropologists, the first to spend extensive periods in the

---

[2] For a critique see Kuper 2005: Ch. 8.
[3] For some sophisticated attempts to apply the segmentary lineage model to ancient Israel, see Bendor 1996 [1986]; Frick 1985; Wilson 1977. For a review see Goldberg 1996. [Cf. also Ch. 7 in this volume].
[4] For instance, Pitt-Rivers (1977) suggested that enduring themes of Mediterranean culture explained some puzzling biblical episodes. Gilbert Lewis compared the treatment of lepers in New Guinea and ancient Israel (Lewis 1987). Meyer Fortes identified the biblical figure of Job as the prototype of some West African beliefs (Fortes 1959). Notwithstanding his clearly stated reservations, Lévi-Strauss himself published a playful comparison of origin myths of circumcision among the ancient Israelites and the penis-sheath among the Amazonian Bororo (Lévi-Strauss 1988).

field, insisted that customs had to be studied in action. Only modern ethnographic fieldwork could deliver a properly sympathetic understanding of exotic beliefs.

This was also the message of the newly fashionable linguistic philosophy. Wittgenstein read the *Golden Bough* in 1931, and reacted with furious contempt. 'Frazer is much more savage than most of his savages, for these savages will not be so far from any understanding of spiritual matters as an Englishman of the twentieth century. His explanations of the primitive observances are much cruder than the sense of the observances themselves' (Wittgenstein 1979: 8). In Wittgenstein's view, meaning was a matter of context and use.

And so they came to agree, the philosophers and the anthropologists, that concepts and practices could be understood only by appreciating their use in the business of everyday life in particular communities. Context was all. Peter Winch's *Idea of a Social Science*, published in 1958, identified the doctrines of the later Wittgenstein with the analytical practice of Oxford's new professor of social anthropology, E.E. Evans-Pritchard. As Mary Douglas put it, summing up what she took to be the position of Evans-Pritchard, 'Everyday language and everyday thought set into their social and situational context have to be the subject of inquiry' (Douglas 1980: 26).

Evans-Pritchard had read history at Exeter College as an undergraduate, and he recalled Marett as an affable fellow. When he became in his turn professor of social anthropology at Oxford and lectured on theories of primitive religion, he borrowed Marett's critical characterization of the theories of Tylor and Frazer as 'intellectualist'. He also questioned the value of psychological and sociological accounts of religion. The son of an Anglican clergyman, Evans-Pritchard was a recent convert to Catholicism, and he was inclined to believe that all religions contain a kernel of spiritual truth. This now seemed to him to be their most important feature, and he urged that spiritual beliefs should be treated seriously in their own right (Evans-Pritchard 1965).

Evans-Pritchard came to deprecate the comparative method (Evans-Pritchard 1963), but he was prepared to reverse the procedure, claiming in the introduction to his *Nuer Religion* that the religion of the Nuer and Dinka 'have features which bring to mind the Hebrews of the Old Testament'. He quoted in support an American Presbyterian working among the Nuer, who remarked that 'the missionary feels as if he were living in Old Testament times, and in a way this is true'. 'When therefore [Evans-Pritchard concluded] I sometimes draw comparisons between Nuer and Hebrew conceptions, it is no mere whim but is because I myself find it helpful, and I think others may do so too, in trying to understand Nuer ideas to note this likeness to something with which we are ourselves familiar without being too intimately involved in it' (Evans-Pritchard 1956: vii). African informants, familiar with the Bible, often made such comparisons themselves (see, e.g., Turner 1967: 135). However, Evans-Pritchard clearly intended to suggest that the Nuer had a sort of pre-knowledge of scriptural truths. In the very last sentences of the monograph he wrote that the meaning of Nuer rites 'depends finally on an awareness of God and that men are dependent on him and must be resigned to his will. At this point the theologian takes over from the anthropologist' (Evans-Pritchard 1956: 322).

## VII

According to the practitioners of the comparative method, the essential ingredients of primitive religion were totem and taboo. Its defining ritual was sacrifice. In 1950–1 Franz Steiner – an émigré Jewish mystic, a German poet, a friend of Elias Canetti, a lover of Iris Murdoch, and a lecturer in the Oxford institute of social anthropology – gave a course of lectures on taboo, which were edited and published after his death (Steiner 1999 [1956]). His central thesis was that the constructs of the comparative method had been lifted from specific ethnographic contexts. In the process they were stripped of their particularities and lost much of their meaning. When modern ethnographers apply these constructs in their own analyses, they have to be qualified if they are to be of any use at all. 'They are then redefined, and by this process they become so narrow as to lose all significance outside the individual analytical study to which they were tailored'. For example, he suggested, 'The broad significance which "Totemism" had as a comparative category has evaporated' (Steiner 1999: 105).

Steiner tagged taboo as 'a Protestant discovery', while the notion that taboos regulated social order and morality was 'a Victorian invention', one that was peculiarly interesting to prudes and snobs (Steiner 1999: 132). But taboo was actually a Polynesian concept, and Steiner proceeded to analyse the specific meaning of *tabu* in the context of Polynesian language, thought and religion. It turned out that *tabu* was not at all the same thing as the 'taboo' of the anthropologists.

Steiner then reviewed Robertson Smith's thesis that the notion of the sacred originated in ideas of taboo. Steiner had an educated knowledge of Hebrew and he argued (along the same lines as Durkheim) that the Hebrew idea of *qadosh* could not be translated simply as taboo, certainly not in the sense in which the Polynesians used the term *tabu*. He concluded that neither the Polynesian *tabu* nor the Hebrew *qadosh* were useful cross-cultural categories. The only universal was that all societies define certain acts, words and situations as pregnant with danger.

So much, then, for taboo, and perhaps even for the category of the sacred. Evans-Pritchard gave the Henry Myers lecture in 1954, which he entitled 'The Meaning of Sacrifice Among the Nuer'. He remarked that 'in Nuer sacrifice there are different shades of meaning. The pattern varies. There are shifts of emphasis'. It was difficult, if not impossible 'to present a general interpretation, to put forward a simple formula, to cover all Nuer sacrifices' (Evans-Pritchard 1954: 30). Many Nuer sacrifices regulated social relations, and might be amenable to a sociological analysis. But Evans-Pritchard noted that Father Crazzolara, a Catholic missionary among the Nuer, had distinguished a category of piacular sacrifices that were not connected to social events but, much more interesting, were concerned with a universal quest, 'the regulation of the individual's relation with God' (capitalized here, so no mere tribal deity) (Evans-Pritchard 1954).

So taboo was a Victorian invention. Sacrifice was a broad term for a range of ritual practices with unpredictable meanings, resistant to sociological analysis and to comparison. That left totemism. Lévi-Strauss's short book, *Le Totémisme aujourd'hui*, published in 1962, deconstructed the concept, concluding that totemism also was not a useful cross-cultural category. Anthropologists should rather investigate the truly universal process by which all societies classify and relate social groups and natural phenomena. In a more extended study published a few months later, *La Pensée Sauvage*, Lévi-Strauss demonstrated that arbitrary features of natural objects were given significance by their position in a series of binary oppositions. Natural species were classified with reference to these oppositions. So too were the parts of the society. They were then related to one another.

## VIII

These exemplary critiques disposed of the classical components of comparative religion, totem, taboo and sacrifice. Yet the change of paradigm was incomplete. A close reader of

Steiner and Lévi-Strauss might still be inclined to study the place of taboo and totemic marriage rules in biblical religion, even if these elements were now understood rather differently. According to Lévi-Strauss, all societies establish parallel classifications of social and natural phenomena by making a series of binary contrasts. That was totemism, properly understood. And Steiner indicated that every society marks off certain social and natural categories as dangerous. Properly understood, then, taboo was a property of a system of classification. Edmund Leach and Mary Douglas now proposed structural accounts of biblical taboos on food and marriage.

Their projects might have been similar, but Edmund Leach and Mary Douglas – like Robertson Smith and Frazer before them – began from very different points of view. Leach was a crusading atheist. His mother had hoped that he would be a missionary. Instead he became the president of the Humanist Society. Mary Douglas was a conservative Catholic. Reviewing Mary Douglas's *Natural Symbols* in *The New York Review of Books* in 1971, Leach wrote: 'All her recent work gives the impression that she is no longer much concerned with the attainment of empirical truth; the object of the exercise is to adapt her anthropological learning to the service of Roman Catholic propaganda' (Leach 1971). Reviewing Leach and Aycock's *Structuralist Interpretations of Biblical Myth* (1983) also in *The New York Review of Books*, Mary Douglas claimed that Leach imposed his own meanings on the myths, just like Frazer, and she concluded that the 'ingenious argument is extremely interesting and, to readers who are unfamiliar with Old Testament scholarship, quite plausible' (Douglas 1984).

And yet the two anthropologists had much in common, including a tendency to read back into the biblical world their own ideas about European Jews, whom they were inclined to think were too picky about food, and unreasonably prejudiced against intermarriage. To be sure, the projection of a particular understanding of the present into the past, even the very distant past, is hardly unusual. But Edmund Leach and Mary Douglas also shared more specialized ideas. Priority is difficult to establish – copies of papers circulated in draft before publication – but clearly they were already working on very similar lines in the early 1960s, drawing heavily from Lévi-Strauss.

In 1961 Leach published an essay, 'Lévi-Strauss in the Garden of Eden', which flagged his conversion to structuralism and introduced Lévi-Strauss as a better guide to the Bible than Frazer (reprinted in Leach 1969). Biblical scholars since Wellhausen and Robertson Smith had recognized mythical elements in the Hebrew Bible, the deposits of very ancient traditions, but they struggled to distinguish myths from historical texts. Leach insisted that it was all myth. And although the elements of the texts were no doubt of diverse origin, the editors of the Hebrew Bible had imposed a coherence upon this body of myth. The analyst should accordingly act 'on a presumption that the whole of the text as we now have it *regardless of the varying historical origins of its component parts* may properly be treated as a unity' (Leach and Aycock 1983: 89–112; similar pronouncements prefaced a number of Leach's biblical essays).

In his 1961 essay 'Lévi-Strauss in the Garden of Eden', Leach analysed the construction of the world and its creatures in the opening chapters of Genesis by way of a series of binary contrasts. In Leviticus 11: 'creatures which do not fit this exact ordering of the world – for instance water creatures with no fins, animals and birds which eat meat or fish, etc. – are classed as "abominations"' (Leach 1969: 13). Here and in a paper on 'Animal Categories and Verbal Abuse', published in 1964, he argued that classifications constructed by a series of binary contrasts will always throw up elements that breach boundaries. These are tabooed (Leach 1964). And taboos on anomalies reinforce boundaries.

Mary Douglas's *Purity and Danger*, published in 1966, was directly inspired by Steiner's lectures. It became famous for her first attempt at an anthropology of the Bible, a chapter on the abominations of Leviticus. Her analysis was very similar to that of Leach, the argument being that classificatory anomalies were tabooed. She did not at this stage identify the social context of these taboos, but she soon began to identify various possible functions. 'We should see taboos as the performative acts which stop the careless speaker from getting the categories confused [. . .] The performance protects boundaries around classifications [. . .] On this distinctly Durkheimian approach, impurity and taboo supply back-up for the current system of control' (Douglas 2004: 159–62).

The most important taboos concern sex and food: 'bed and board', as Mary Douglas put it (Fardon 1999: 186). Leach was more interested in the bed side of things, and he treated the biblical stories of Adam and Eve, Cain and Abel, Noah and Ham, Lot and his daughters, and Abraham and Sarah as a set of structural transformations on the theme of incest and endogamy. Arguing that all societies struggle with similar concerns he compared these stories to the myth of Oedipus, which Lévi-Strauss had selected for exemplary analysis in the first presentation of his structural method for the analysis of myth (Leach 1969; Lévi-Strauss 1963: Ch. 11).

According to Lévi-Strauss, myths grapple with existential issues, generating temporary resolutions of intractable problems. In 'The Legitimacy of Solomon', Leach set out 'to demonstrate that the biblical story of the succession of Solomon to the throne of Israel is a myth which 'mediates' a major contradiction' (Leach 1969: 31). The contradiction is between the assertion that God gave the land of Israel to the Jewish people, and that they should be endogamous, and the reality that the land accommodated a number of different populations, with whom Jews – even kings – intermarried, and for good political reasons. Leach argued that central myths in the Hebrew Bible offered resolutions of this structural contradiction.

Mary Douglas came to agree that the ancient Hebrews were obsessed by endogamy. Rereading Leach's essay, 'The Legitimacy of Solomon', 'brought home [. . .] with a resounding thud something which Old Testament scholarship had been agreed upon for a very long time [. . .] that the Pentateuch was full of concern for the evils that flowed from marriage with foreigners' (Douglas 1975: 208.) Commenting on this passage, Richard Fardon remarks that 'Tracing a general analogy between animal classification, food rules and sexual mating required, as she put it, something of a "conversion" to alliance theory in the analysis of kinship' (Fardon 1999: 186).

Dating the redaction of the Tanach is still a controversial matter, but Leach (and Mary Douglas after him) adopted the view, held by some experts, that it had been put together in its final form shortly after the return from Babylon in the sixth century BCE, and the construction of the second temple. Leach and Douglas assumed that the editors imposed a unity on the various texts incorporated into the Hebrew Bible. Their motives were political. Leach accepted the thesis that the editors were following the party line of Ezra and Nehemiah, who led the return from exile and ruled Palestine for their Persian overlords. The texts were edited to support the policies of these satraps: their land-grabbing, their xenophobic nationalism and their insistence on Jewish endogamy. Yet if there was a party line, it was not always consistent. Leach thought that myths were bound to put alternatives into play, and that myth-makers were never completely in control of their material. 'What the myth then "says" is not what the editors consciously intended to say but rather something which lies deeply embedded in Jewish traditional culture as a whole' (Leach 1969: 53).

Mary Douglas took the view that different factions had edited particular sections of the Bible. She agreed with Leach that the Persian satraps, Ezra and Nehemiah, who had led the exiles back from Babylon, were concerned with imposing endogamy, which enforced social and political boundaries.[5] But a priestly party, responsible for what biblical scholars identity as the P sources in the Bible, were prepared to tolerate exogamy. Their power base was in the temple, and their special privilege was the performance of sacrifices. In consequence, the priests were obsessed with the Levitical taboos, the rules of purity and holiness. And so distinct and conflicting political interests could be discerned behind the purity rules, on the one hand, and the rules on intermarriage on the other.

The ark, the tabernacle and the temple were the most sacred sites of Judaism. Leach sketched the outlines of structuralist geography of these sacred places (Leach 1976: 84–93). Mary Douglas argued that the rules regulating behaviour in sacred sites provided models for everyday activities. The concern for purity that regulated temple sacrifices also informed the food taboos. This was because the body was itself a temple. 'To conclude', she wrote in her final collection of essays, *Jacob's Tears*, 'the Levitical food prohibitions have plenty to do with the tabernacle. They frame the analogy between tabernacle and body: what goes for one, goes for the other' (Douglas 2004: 172). It was not enough to analyse systems of classification. One had to connect – food taboos and marriage rules; the laws of *kashrut* and the laws of sacrifice; the body and the temple; the temple and Mount Sinai and the sanctuary. In *Leviticus as Literature*, published in 1999, she introduced a further structural parallel, between the form of the book itself – a 'ring structure' – and the layout of the temple.

Some French literary structuralists also wrote essays on the Bible.[6] Yet although he had provided the inspiration, Lévi-Strauss (a grandson of the rabbi of Strasbourg) disapproved of these studies. A year after the publication of *La Pensée Sauvage*, the journal *Esprit* arranged a discussion between Lévi-Strauss and a group of philosophers led by the Christian existentialist Paul Ricoeur (Lévi-Strauss 2004). Ricoeur had just made his famous linguistic turn, and he now believed that only a hermeneutic interpretation of signs, symbols and texts could yield an understanding of the human condition. Lévi-Strauss was, of course, all in favour of a linguistic turn, but his linguistics was very different. Ricoeur charged Lévi-Strauss with privileging syntactics over semantics, structure over meaning. He conceded that this might be appropriate in analysing the ideas of simple societies, which really had very little to say for themselves. It was not helpful when it came to more complex intellectual systems. Similarly, the play of transformations in the myths of 'cold' societies were very different from the historical, logically sequential myths of 'hot' societies like ancient Greece and Israel. They had produced great narratives that were vehicles of profound reflections about human existence. Could Lévi-Strauss's method be applied to such myths?

---

[5] In her treatment of these Persian satraps, Douglas seems to have projected back from an understanding of contemporary Middle Eastern politics. Richard Fardon remarks: 'Parallels with the range of political positions occupied in contemporary Israel may be implicit in Douglas's account, but they are certainly not lost on her' (Fardon 1999: 203).

[6] French scholars from various disciplines contributed structuralist analyses of biblical texts. See, e.g., Barthes et al. 1971, and Soler 1973.

Lévi-Strauss responded that myths did not make sense in the way that Ricoeur imagined. They did not send messages. Rather they commented on one another. Symbols had only a positional significance. But Lévi-Strauss rejected the notion that there was a difference in kind between the mythologies of cold and hot societies. After all, persuasive structuralist studies of Greek myths were being published. However, the Bible was different. The problem with the Bible was, first, that while it incorporated mythical sources, these had been edited and, Lévi-Strauss said, distorted. Moreover, to understand myths one had to have some basic ethnographic information about the society in which they were current, but the ethnographic information to be gleaned from the Bible had very probably itself been mythologized (cf. Lévi-Strauss 1987).

## IX

Biblical scholars may well share Paul Ricoeur's reservations about the structuralist approach. Another reasonable complaint is that anthropologists generally lacked the scholarly preparation that their projects required. For instance, J.A. Emerton exposed Leach's dubious etymologies and other errors. He also pointed out that Leach's approach to the Bible was very selective. Leach exaggerated any biblical concern with purity of blood, and ignored that fact that intermarriage was denounced for religious rather than for racial or political reasons. The real fear was that men would follow their wives and worship foreign gods (Emerton 1976). However, Mary Douglas has been treated with more respect than Leach, perhaps in part because she was a believer and he was a crusading atheist. Distinguished scholars of the Hebrew Bible, Jacob Milgrom (2004: *passim*) and Jacob Neusner (2006: 149), have made gracious comments on her work (and see Duhaime 1998; Hendel 2008).

In any case, structuralism, broadly defined, remains the prevailing method of anthropological studies of the Bible. Leach was followed by a number of scholars, who delivered persuasive readings of biblical myths. For instance, David Pocock analysed the structural opposition of north and south in the book of Genesis (Pocock 1975), Seth Daniel Kunin (1995) covers much the same ground as Leach, but with impressive scholarship, and Édouard Conte is engaged in the structural analysis of Quranic texts on descent and incest that present further transformations of the myths of the patriarchs and the genealogy of Israel (Conte 2011a, 2011b). Other anthropologists, following on from Mary Douglas, have brought out unexpected and suggestive connections – between systems of classification, rules governing sacrifices and food prohibitions, pollution beliefs, restrictions on marriage, the politics of legitimacy, and sacred architecture and landscape. The themes of these studies are, however, rather restricted. Strangely, neither Leach nor Douglas considered the ample evidence of a preference in biblical times for cousin marriage, which had been documented long ago by Frazer (1918 II: Ch. 4). And studies of kingship have been limited to rather old-fashioned exercises in the comparative method.

The Gospels have also been relatively neglected. Leach's rather old-fashioned comparative essay on virgin birth (Leach 1966) did not attract attention from biblical scholars. His hint that the Christian Mass is a transformation of the Jewish Passover (Leach 1976: 93) was, however, developed by Gillian Feeley-Harnik, who analysed the last supper as a structural transformation of the Passover seder, where 'every critical element in the Passover is reversed' (Feeley-Harnik 1981: 19). The Talmud and the Qur'an are still little studied by anthropologists, though Maureen Bloom has produced a sophisticated anthropological analysis of mysticism and magic in the Talmud, relating Talmudic conceptions to biblical and to Babylonian sources (Bloom 2007).

Biblical scholars may be reassured that these authors do usually know Hebrew and Aramaic, even if they seldom have a mastery of the tools of Bible criticism. For their part, biblical scholars are usually uncritical in their application of anthropological examples, and rely too often on dated and discredited anthropological models. There are exceptions – R.R. Wilson's superb study of biblical genealogies comes to mind. Yet more interdisciplinary collaboration would obviously be a good idea. 'While a number of scholars make more or less overt reference to advice or counsel given by anthropology colleagues in the course of their work', James Martin remarked in 1989, 'no publication has appeared over the joint names of an anthropologist and an Old Testament scholar' (Martin 1989: 103.) I believe that the same statement could be repeated now, more than three decades later.

But perhaps the deeper problems are conceptual rather than methodological. Citing Clifford Geertz, Gillian Feeley-Harnik suggested that 'anthropologists have been studying their own religions all along, disguised as the religions of "exotic others"' (1981: 3).[7] The flip side is that anthropologists have constructed 'religions' for those 'exotic others' in the image of their own.

Although the Hebrew Bible had no word for religion, it bequeathed enduring paradigms of both genuine and false religions, setting the parameters for the classification of exotic beliefs and rituals. The 'high religions' of the East were distressingly polytheist, even inclined to idolatry, but they might be accepted as genuine because they had sacred texts, temples, hymns and prayers. Pagan cults, however, were equated with the false religion of the Philistines. They had idols instead of deities, magicians in the place of priests, orgies rather than solemn rituals. A romantic like Andrew Lang might prefer pagan sensuality, fairy tales and nature worship to the puritan church. But his was a challenge to the orthodox believer, not to the idea of religion itself. In the twentieth century, relativist anthropologists were inclined to treat all religions as equal, but the notion of religion itself was seldom put in question.

And so a distinctive realm of study was constituted, the anthropology of religion: a sacred space, occupied by myths, taboos, idols and sacrifice. Even the most secular and sceptical anthropologists accepted the parameters. They might argue about whether the distinctive feature of religion was belief or ritual, and what, if anything, distinguished religion from magic, but despite a succession of paradigm changes, the field – and its subject-matter – remained remarkably stable for 150 years. Yet surely its analytical core, the very notion of religion, is ripe for deconstruction.

# REFERENCES

Ackerman, R. (1987), *J.G. Frazer: His Life and Work*, Cambridge: Cambridge University Press.
Ackerman, R., ed. (2005), *Selected Letters of Sir James George Frazer*, Oxford: Oxford University Press.

---

[7] From one point of view, the whole history of the comparative study of religion from the time Robertson Smith undertook his investigations into the rites of the ancient Semites [...] can be looked at as but a circuitous, even devious, approach to a rational analysis of our own situation, an evaluation of our own religious traditions while seeming to evaluate only those of exotic others

—Geertz 1971: 22

Barthes, R., F. Bovon, F.-J. Leenhardt, R. Martin-Achard and J. Starobinski (1971), *Analyse structural et exégèse biblique*, Neuchâtel: Delachaux & Niestlé.
Bendor, S. (1996 [1986]), *The Social Structure of Ancient Israel: The Institution of the Family (Beit 'ab) from the Settlement to the End of the Monarchy*, Jerusalem: Simor.
Black, J. and G. Chrystal (1912), *The Life of William Robertson Smith*, London: Adam and Charles Black.
Bloom, M. (2007), *Jewish Mysticism and Magic: An Anthropological Perspective*, London: Routledge.
Brosses, Charles de (1760), *Du culte des dieux fétiches ou Parallèle de l'ancienne religion de l'Égypte avec la religion actuelle de Nigritie*, Paris: N.E.
Chadwick, O. (1970), *The Victorian Church*, 2 vols, Oxford: Oxford University Press.
Comte, Auguste de (1830–42), *Cours de philosophie positive*, 6 vols, Paris: Bachelier.
Conte, É. (2011a), 'Adam et consorts: Germanité et filiation de la Genèse au Deluge selon les traditions musulmanes', in É. Conte, E. Porqueres i Gene and J. Wilgaux (eds), *L'argument de la filiation: Aux fondements des sociétés européennes et méditerranéennes*, 39–71, Paris: Éditions de la Maison des Sciences de l'Homme.
Conte, É. (2011b), 'Elles seront des sœurs pour nous: Le mariage par permutation au Proche-Orient', *Études Rurales*, 187: 157–200.
Coulanges, F. de (1864), *La Cité Antique: Étude sur le Culte, le Droit, les Institutions de la Grèce et de Rome*, Paris: Durand.
Douglas, M. (1966), *Purity and Danger: An Analysis of Concepts of Pollution and Taboo*, London: Routledge.
Douglas, M. (1975), *Implicit Meanings*, London: Routledge.
Douglas, M. (1980), *Edward Evans-Pritchard*, London: Fontana.
Douglas, M. (1984), 'Betwixt, Bothered & Bewildered', *New York Review of Books*, 20 December.
Douglas, M. (1999), *Leviticus as Literature*, Oxford: Oxford University Press.
Douglas, M. (2004), *Jacob's Tears: The Priestly Work of Reconciliation*, Oxford: Oxford University Press.
Duhaime, J. (1998), 'Lois alimentaires et pureté corporelle dans le Lévitique. L'approche de Mary Douglas et sa réception par Jacob Milgrom', *Religiologiques*, 17: 19–35.
Durkheim, É. (1971 [1912]), *The Elementary Forms of the Religious Life*, London: Allen and Unwin.
Eilberg-Schwartz, H. (1990), *The Savage in Judaism: An Anthropology of Israelite Religion and Ancient Judaism*, Bloomington, IN: Indiana University Press.
Emerton, J.A. (1976), 'An Examination of a Recent Structuralist Interpretation of Genesis XXXVIII', *VT*, 26 (1): 79–98.
Evans-Pritchard, E.E. (1954), 'The Meaning of Sacrifice Among the Nuer', *JRAI*, 84 (1/2): 21–33.
Evans-Pritchard, E.E. (1956), *Nuer Religion*, Oxford: Oxford University Press.
Evans-Pritchard, E.E. (1963), *The Comparative Method in Social Anthropology*, London: Athlone Press.
Evans-Pritchard, E.E. (1965), *Theories of Primitive Religion*, Oxford: Oxford University Press.
Fardon, R. (1999), *Mary Douglas*, London: Routledge.
Feeley-Harnik, G. (1981), *The Lord's Table: Eucharist and Passover in Early Christianity*, Pennsylvania, PA: University of Pennsylvania Press.
Fortes, M. (1959), *Oedipus and Job in West African Religion*, Cambridge: Cambridge University Press.

Frazer, J.G. (1887), *Totemism*, London: A. & C. Black.
Frazer, J.G. (1894), 'William Robertson Smith', *Fortnightly Review*, LX: 800–7.
Frazer, J.G. (1900), *The Golden Bough*, 2nd edn, 3 vols, London: Macmillan.
Frazer, J.G. (1918), *Folk-Lore in the Old Testament*, 3 vols, London: Macmillan.
Frazer, J.G. (1927), *The Gorgon's Head*, London: Macmillan.
Freud, S. (1919 [1913]), *Totem and Taboo: Resemblances Between the Psychic Life of Savages and Neurotics*, London: Routledge.
Freud, S. (1939 [1937]), *Moses and Monotheism*, London: Hogarth Press.
Frick, F.S. (1985), *The Formation of the State in Ancient Israel: A Survey of Models and Theories*, SWBAS 4, Sheffield: Almond Press.
Geertz, C. (1971), *Islam Observed: Religious Development in Morocco and Indonesia*, Chicago: Chicago University Press.
Goldberg, H.E. (1996), 'Cambridge in the Land of Canaan: Descent, Alliance, Circumcision and Instruction in the Bible', *JANES*, 24: 9–34.
Guy, J. (1983), *The Heretic: A Study of the Life of John William Colenso, 1814–1883*, Johannesburg: Ravan Press / Pietermaritzburg: University of Natal Press.
Hendel, R.S. (2008), 'Remembering Mary Douglas: Kashrut, Culture, and Thought-Styles', *Jewish Studies*, 45: 3–15.
Hesketh, I. (2009), *Of Apes and Ancestors: Evolution, Christianity, and the Oxford Debate*, Toronto: University of Toronto Press.
Kunin, S.D. (1995), *The Logic of Incest: A Structuralist Analysis of Hebrew Mythology*, JSOTSup 185, Sheffield: Sheffield Academic Press.
Kuper, A. (2005), *The Reinvention of Primitive Society: Transformations of a Myth*, London: Routledge.
Leach, E.R. (1964), 'Anthropological Aspects of Language: Animal Categories and Verbal Abuse', in E.H. Lenneberg (ed.), *New Directions in the Study of Language*, 23–63, Cambridge, MA: MIT Press.
Leach, E.R. (1966), 'Virgin Birth', *Proceedings of the Royal Anthropological Institute for 1966*: 39–49.
Leach, E.R. (1969), *Genesis as Myth and Other Essays*, London: Jonathan Cape.
Leach, E.R. (1971), 'Mythical Inequalities', *New York Review of Books*, 28 January.
Leach, E.R. (1976), *Culture and Communication*, Cambridge: Cambridge University Press.
Leach, E.R. and J.A. Aycock (1983), *Structuralist Interpretations of Biblical Myth*, Cambridge: Cambridge University Press.
Lemche, N.P. (1985), *Early Israel: Anthropological and Historical Studies on the Israelite Society Before the Monarchy*, VTSup 37, Leiden: E.J. Brill.
Lévi-Strauss, C. (1962), *La Pensée Sauvage*, Paris: Plon.
Lévi-Strauss, C. (1963), 'The Structural Study of Myth', Ch. 9 in *Structural Anthropology*, New York: Basic Books.
Lévi-Strauss, C. (1971 [1962]), *Totemism*, Boston, MA: Beacon Press.
Lévi-Strauss, C. (1987), 'De la fidélité au texte', *L'Homme*, 27 (101): 117–40.
Lévi-Strauss, C. (1988), 'Exode sur Exode', *L'Homme*, 28 (106): 13–23.
Lévi-Strauss, C. (2004), '*Autour de la Pensée sauvage, Réponses à quelques questions:* Entretien du "groupe philosophique" d'*Esprit* avec Claude Lévi-Strauss, November, 1963', *Esprit*, 301: 169–92.
Lewis, G. (1987), 'A Lesson from Leviticus: Leprosy', *Man* New Series, 22 (4): 593–612.
Lukes, S. (1973), *Emile Durkheim, His Life and Work: A Historical and Critical Study*, Harmondsworth, UK: Penguin.

Mannhardt, W. (1875), *Der Baumkultus der Germanen und ihrer Nachbarstämme Mythologische Untersuchungen*, Berlin: Gebrüder Borntraeger.
Marett, R.R. (1909), *The Threshold of Religion*, London: Methuen.
Marett, R.R. (1911), 'Mana', in *Encyclopaedia Britannica*, 11th edition.
Marett, R.R. (1941), *A Jerseyman at Oxford*, Oxford: Oxford University Press.
Martin, J.D. (1989), 'Israel as a Tribal Society', in R.E. Clements (ed.), *The World of Ancient Israel: Sociological, Anthropological and Political Perspectives*, 95–118, Cambridge: Cambridge University Press.
Mauss, M. (1926), 'Critique interne de la "legend d'Abraham"', *Revue des études juives*, 82: 35–44.
McLennan, J.M. (1865), *Primitive Marriage: An Inquiry into the Origin of the Form of Capture in Marriage Ceremonies*, Edinburgh: Adam and Charles Black.
McLennan, J.M. (1869–70), 'The Worship of Animals and Plants', *The Fortnightly Review*, 6: 407–582; 7: 194–216.
Milgrom, J. (2004), *Leviticus*, Minneapolis, MN: Fortress Press.
Neusner, J. (2006), *Neusner on Judaism: Religion and Theology*, Aldershot: Ashgate.
Oesterley, W.O.E. and T.H. Robinson (1937), *A History of Israel*, 2 vols, 2nd edn, Oxford: Clarendon Press.
Parker, J.W., ed. (1860), *Essays and Reviews*, London: John W. Parker.
Pitt-Rivers, J. (1977), *The Fate of Shechem, or The Politics of Sex: Essays in the Anthropology of the Mediterranean*, Cambridge: Cambridge University Press.
Pocock, D.F. (1975), 'North and South in the Book of Genesis', in J.H.M. Beattie and R.G. Lienhardt (eds), *Studies in Social Anthropology*, 273–84, Oxford: Clarendon Press.
Robertson Smith, W. (1880), 'Animal Worship and the Animal Tribes Among the Arabs and in the Old Testament', *Journal of Philology*, 9: 75–100.
Robertson Smith, W. (1885), *Kinship and Marriage in Early Arabia*, Cambridge: Cambridge University Press.
Robertson Smith, W. (1894 [1889]), *Lectures on the Religion of the Semites*, 2nd edn, Edinburgh: A. and C. Black.
Robertson Smith, W. (1894), *The Old Testament in the Jewish Church*, Edinburgh: A. and C. Black.
Rogerson, J.W. (1978), *Anthropology and the Old Testament*, Oxford: Basil Blackwell.
Rogerson, J.W. (1989), 'Anthropology and the Old Testament', in R.E. Clements (ed.) *The World of Ancient Israel: Sociological, Anthropological and Political Perspectives*, 17–38, Cambridge: Cambridge University Press.
Schapera, I. (1955), 'The Sin of Cain', *Proceedings of the Royal Anthropological Institute*, 85 (1/2): 33–43.
Service, E.R. (1962), *Primitive Social Organization: An Evolutionary Perspective*, New York: Random House.
Snaith, N.H. (1944), *Distinctive Ideas of the Old Testament*, London: Epworth Press.
Soler, J. (1979), 'The Dietary Prohibitions of the Hebrews', in R. Forster and O. Ranum (eds), *Food and Drink in History*, Baltimore, MD: Johns Hopkins University Press.
Steiner, F. (1954), 'Enslavement and the Early Hebrew Lineage System: An Explanation of Genesis 47', *Man*, 54: 73–5.
Steiner, F. (1956), *Taboo*, London: Cohen and West.
Steiner, F. (1999), *Taboo, Truth, and Religion*, ed. J. Adler and R. Fardon, New York: Berghahn.
Turner, V. (1967), *The Forest of Symbols: Aspects of Ndembu Ritual*, Ithaca, NY: Cornell University Press.

Tylor, E.B. (1866), 'The Religion of Savages', *Fortnightly Review*, 6: 71–86.
Tylor, E.B. (1871), *Primitive Culture: Researches into the Development of Mythology, Philosophy, Religion, Language, Art and Custom*, 2 vols, London: John Murray.
Tylor, E.B. (1881), *Anthropology: An Introduction to the Study of Man and Civilization*, London: Macmillan.
Vanderhooft, D. (2009), 'The Israelite *mišpāḥâ*, the Priestly Writings, and Changing Valences in Israel's Kinship Terminology', in J.D. Schloen (ed.), *Exploring the Longue Durée: Essays in Honor of Lawrence E. Stager*, 485–96, Winona Lake, IN: Eisenbrauns.
Wellhausen, J. (1885 [1883]), *Prolegomena to the History of Israel*, Edinburgh: A. & C. Black.
Wheeler-Barclay, M. (2010), *The Science of Religion in Britain, 1860–1915*, Charlottesville, VA: University of Virginia Press.
Wilson, R.R. (1977), *Genealogy and History in the Biblical World*, New Haven, CT: Yale University Press.
Winch, P. (1958), *The Idea of a Social Science*, London: Routledge.
Wittgenstein, L. (1979), *Remarks on Frazer's Golden Bough*, ed. R. Rhees, Bishopstone, UK: Brynmill Press.

# CHAPTER THREE

# The Holy Land and the Bible in the nineteenth century

EVELINE J. VAN DER STEEN

We take up the Iliad and the Aeneid as works of taste and genius, and read them as much for amusement as instruction. We take up the Bible as a work which we are taught to consider infallible, and whose contents must be believed; so that we examine all that can tend to its illustration, with more than ordinary rigour. As we know that truth must always gain by investigation, and shine forth with increased brightness, when the dark clouds of error with which human weakness had obscured it are in any degree removed.

—Buckingham 1821: 491 fn

## INTRODUCTION

'The Bible is the best handbook for Palestine' is the opening sentence in one of the first guidebooks for Syria and Palestine. It was written in 1858 by Josias Porter, an Irish Presbyterian minister, for the publisher John Murray in London. Thomas Cook's company also produced a *Tourists' Handbook for Palestine and Syria*, in 1876. Its *raison d'être*, according to the introduction, was that many tourists in the area complained about how difficult it was to travel on horseback with the guidebook in one hand, and the Bible in the other. Therefore, they had included every relevant biblical reference in the book itself, 'so as to avoid the inconvenience of having to turn to the passage in the Bible' (Thomas Cook and Son 1876: iii).

Although there had always been a trickle of travellers to the Holy Land, exploration of the area really took off in the first half of the nineteenth century. Interest had been raised partly by Napoleon's expedition, and the publication of *Description de l'Égypte* (1809–29), the massive scientific publication about the history, culture and nature of the region, and partly as a direct effect of the spirit of the Enlightenment, the era of critical research that had started in the late seventeenth century and of which the *Description* itself was also a product.

Until well into the seventeenth century the Canonical Bible, 'from cover to cover', had been a yardstick against which everything, from philosophy and morality to science in all its forms, had been measured. Questioning the reliability of that yardstick was a dangerous undertaking, as people like Galileo Galilei, or Baruch Spinoza or, in Britain, Thomas Hobbes, were to find out. These seventeenth-century scholars represented the first real cracks in the authority of Scripture, and the start of the Age of Enlightenment.

When Thomas Hobbes published his *Leviathan* in 1651, he was immediately denounced as an atheist, not because of his model for the structure of society, or his views on sovereignty, but because he argued that the observable laws of nature (created by God) determined the order of everything, and took precedence over divine revelation in the Bible, throwing into doubt the existence of miracles. While this was bad enough, at least in the eyes of the religious establishment, the first man to openly reject the accepted truth that the Bible, from cover to cover, was God's word, and the Pentateuch written by Moses himself, was the Jewish-Portuguese-Dutch philosopher Baruch Spinoza (1632–77). In his main thesis, published posthumously in his *Ethica*, he drew a number of far-reaching conclusions: that the miracles in the Bible were just unexplained natural phenomena, and the Bible itself was a collection of narratives written by various authors long after the events happened, and even adapted for political or other purposes, incomplete and with bits missing. He regarded Jesus as a prophet or philosopher. It was his rejection of Cartesian dualism, the separation of mind and body, and the unity of God and Nature that branded him an atheist – if the mind and the soul were functions of the physical brain, there was no life after death, no Heaven, and more importantly, no Hell, which undermined morality.

The next step was a systematic text-critical study of the biblical narrative. This was first undertaken in Germany in the second half of the eighteenth century by the church historian and theologian Johann Semler and by the philosopher Hermann Reimarus. Both, like Spinoza, rejected the divine origins and infallibility of the Old and New Testaments, and individually developed text-critical methods to argue their case.

The Enlightenment also had its influence on the nature of politics and society. Political treatises like that of Jean-Jacques Rousseau on *The Social Contract* (published in French in 1762) or John Stuart Mill's *On Liberty* (published in 1859), questioned the place of humankind in society, which had for centuries been determined by the power of the nobility, justified by the Church's interpretation of the biblical order. The American war of Liberation, and particularly the French Revolution finally redefined that place.

Developments in science also clashed with the biblical truths. Towards the end of the eighteenth century, scholars studied the superposition of geological layers and their fossils, and concluded that the earth must be millions of years old, not 6,000 as the Archbishop Ussher had calculated from the biblical narratives. Charles Lyell's *Principles of Geology* (1830–3) saw the development of life on earth as a cyclic motion, rather than a sequence of catastrophes, while both Jean-Baptiste Lamarck and Charles Darwin overturned the story of the creation of humans.

Theologians and philosophers struggled to reconcile the new discoveries about nature, the antiquity of the earth and of life itself, with the biblical narrative. Theories like gap creationism (the idea that there is a long period between the first and the second creation stories in Genesis), as well as various theories that would later become known as 'intelligent design', became popular. On the other hand, the attacks on the authority of the Bible, be it as God's infallible word, or as a history book, which had started with Spinoza in the seventeenth century, became ever more sophisticated. Around the middle of the century a group of scholars at the University of Tübingen, Germany, developed text-critical methods to analyse the biblical narrative. One of its representatives, David Strauss, argued in his *Das Leben Jesu* (published in 1835, translated into English by George Eliot) that the miracles ascribed to Jesus were mythical later additions to the story of Jesus's life, thereby rendering every effort at finding natural explanations for those and other miracles in the Bible, a favourite pastime of scholarly explorers, obsolete.

The idea that the Bible was not the infallible word of God, but a collection of documents that had been merged into a single whole at a later date, with all its transformations, contradictions and mistakes, gave rise to a further number of text-critical theories about the origins of the biblical books and the factuality of the narrative. The most cited theory is the 'documentary hypothesis', which saw the books of the Pentateuch as a merger of four different 'documents'. This theory was most famously developed by Julius Wellhausen in his *Prolegomena zur Geschichte Israels* (1883). At the same time the other books of the Bible, as well as the narrative itself, were also studied from a text-critical as well as from a historical and archaeological point of view. The attacks on the New Testament, which was much more important for Christianity than the Old Testament, drew the ire of many travellers. David Strauss's *Das Leben Jesu*, and in 1863 Ernest Renan's *Vie de Jesus* were vilified. George Eliot's translation of Strauss's book was met with outrage. James Frazer's *The Golden Bough*, published in 1890, also drew widespread anger, because of its depiction of Christ's crucifixion as the precipitation of a primitive ritual of death and revival.

In the second half of the century politics became an increasingly important element in the exploration of the Holy Land. Ever since Napoleon's expedition into Egypt it had been clear that the Ottoman Empire was crumbling, and various Western nations had their eyes on the spoils. Its importance as the cradle of the Bible and of Christianity, as well as the protection of Christians and holy places were handy arguments, but a new element became more important: the return of the Holy Land to what was seen as its rightful owners, the Jews. Pogroms and generally bad treatment of Jewish communities in many countries was not new, but it now became more visible and less acceptable in a more enlightened society. It led to a new influx of Jewish immigrants into Palestine. The West supported these movements as a counterweight against the Turkish rule. Powerful Jewish protectors such as Moses Montefiore (1784–1885) made the case for a Jewish return to Palestine with the British government. The Dreyfus affair in France (1894), and the wave of antisemitism that followed it, inspired Theodor Herzl (1860–1904) to start his Zionist movement. By the end of the century whole Jewish communities came from eastern Europe and Russia to Palestine, and started agricultural communities.

## EARLY CRITICAL RESEARCHERS

The critical approach of the Enlightenment drew responses from several directions, when people realized that simply rejecting those criticisms on the basis of presumed biblical infallibility was no longer enough. The Bible itself needed proof, and one way of 'proving' the Bible was to go to its origins, to its ultimate homeland, Palestine.

Various seventeenth-century travellers in the region had left their eyewitness accounts, such as George Sandys and Henry Maundrell, Richard Pococke and Balthasar de Monconys, all of whom were studied and quoted extensively by later travellers. But the drive to investigate the Holy Land seriously took off towards the end of the eighteenth century. These later travellers were products of the Enlightenment, even while most were devout Christians. They were fully aware of the discrepancies between the biblical account and the natural world, and always willing to look for explanations that could reconcile both. What they did not was doubt the essential veracity of the biblical narrative.

The first truly scientific and scholarly expedition to research the origins of the biblical narrative was the ill-fated Danish expedition into Arabia Felix which set out in 1761, of which Carsten Niebuhr was the only survivor (cf. Hansen 1964). It was organized by the universities of Copenhagen and Göttingen, and funded by the King of Denmark, who as a patron of the arts took an active interest. The expedition, which consisted of a team of five experts in different fields, was provided with a list of research questions that was 325 pages long, and contained questions regarding (among many other things):

- the depth of the Red Sea, particularly where the Israelites were supposed to have crossed it
- sex with menstruating women, something that according to Moses' Law was punishable by death
- a whole series of questions about leprosy
- about the yield of corn in Asia and Africa, if it can really be a hundredfold, as mentioned in the Bible (Genesis 26)
- if there is a kind of wood that makes brackish water sweet (Exod. 15.23)
- a series of questions about the origins of Manna
- questions about frankincense
- questions about locusts
- about the benefits of circumcision for boys and girls

Most of the questions were aimed at clarifying the biblical narrative, and reconciling it with the many scientific discoveries. At the end there appeared a long appendix about the Yemen, which linked the biblical chronology with the various legends and local traditions about the Yemen, and particularly with its legendary queen of Sheba, Balkis.

There was also a sense that in order to understand the Bible, make it come to life, and comprehend its influence on Western laws and morality, one needed to go to its place of birth. As the French philosopher and orientalist Constantin de Chassebœuf, Comte de Volney (1757–1820), expressed it:

> Those are the countries in which the greater part of the opinions that govern us at this day have had their origin. In them, those religious ideas took their rise, which have operated so powerfully on our private and public manners, on our laws, and our social state. It will be interesting, therefore, to be acquainted with the countries where they had their births, the customs and manners which nourished them, and the spirit and character of the nations from whom they have been received as sacred.
> 
> —1788: v

Other scientific and scholarly expeditions followed. Napoleon, when he launched his expedition to Egypt and the lands of Palestine in 1798, brought a large team of scholars and scientists who studied every possible aspect of the lands to be conquered, which resulted in the masterpiece that is the *Description*, which also included Syria and Palestine. Ulrich Jasper Seetzen (1767–1811) travelled the region between 1805 and 1807 with a similar aim: to collect as much information as possible, particularly in the unexplored regions east of the Jordan, for his sponsor, the Duke of Gotha. He was the first westerner to explore the region east of the Jordan since the Crusaders. He was followed shortly afterwards by the Swiss Johan Ludwig Burckhardt (1784–1817), who did the same in the service of the British African Society.

These two travellers were mostly interested in discovering unexplored areas, in the manners and customs of the people, but their reference guidebook was nevertheless the Bible. There were no other guidebooks for the area east of the Jordan, and for the west there were only the accounts of earlier travellers. Both explorers identified a number of biblical place names, sometimes correctly, sometimes not. Both had a strong interest in the manners and customs of the people, villagers and Bedouin with whom they came into contact, and on occasion compared them to the Old Testament narrative (Burckhardt 1830: 216; Seetzen 1854–9 III: 32).

Seetzen, a rather sceptical Protestant traveller, likened the early history of Israel, and particularly the Exodus narratives to the *Sirat*, the great Arabic heroic epics, which were told by the campfires in Bedouin camps, and in the coffee houses in the towns and cities. Such epics and hero stories could be found in every national culture, and the Exodus stories fitted in that tradition (Seetzen 1854–9 III: 119). He also refers to Josephus' suggestion that Moses was the Egyptian renegade priest Osarseph (Seetzen 1854–9 III: 85). This kind of critical appraisal of the biblical narrative would later become unthinkable among devout Christian travellers.

For most travellers over the course of the nineteenth century, whether they considered themselves Christians or not, their reference work remained the Bible. As Porter's *Handbook* would say in 1858: 'The present work is only intended to be a companion to it [. . .] Every nook and corner of it is "holy ground"' (Porter 1858 I: v). These guidebooks also attempted to prepare the traveller for a country that was very different from Western civilized society. Nonetheless, arriving in the Middle East was often a culture shock. Charles van de Velde (1818–98), a Dutch missionary and traveller, had his first taste of it on his arrival in Beirut in 1851, when meeting and dealing with the local Arabs, and he never recovered from the shock, during all of his journey, although he reserved most of his ire for the Bedouin (cf. van de Velde 1854).

## WALKING ON HOLY GROUND

> Bible stories are grafted upon local scenes; and as is always the case in real history, these scenes have moulded and regulated, to a greater or less extent, the course of events [. . .] The parables, metaphors, and illustrations of the sacred writers were borrowed from the objects that met their eyes, and with which their first readers were familiar.
>
> — Porter 1891: ii–iii

When a traveller entered Palestine, whether from the east across the Jordan, the west through Jaffa, the north from Beirut, or the south from Cairo, the moment he set foot in Palestine, he felt himself on holy soil. In their perception the land was organized not into Turkish sanjaks, but into the tribal territories as laid out in the book of Joshua, with the familiar names of mountains, rivers, plains and towns and cities as they knew them from the Bible. Arabic geographical references were sometimes added as an afterthought, or if the traveller did not know, the biblical name. East of the Jordan it was no different; one travelled through the land of Gilead, the territories of Manasseh, Ephraim or Gad (sometimes referred to as the land of Sihon), or the Bashan of Og, and further south through Moab and Edom.

The scenery of the land inspired the traveller to quote fragments of the more poetic parts of the Bible such as the Psalms or the Song of Solomon, and biblical place names invoked extensive reminiscing of the various events and miracles that were connected with it, as if to strengthen the veracity of the story. Often travellers were moved to tears at the sight of a particular holy place. Félicien de Saulcy (1807–80), French orientalist and devout Catholic, was so moved when he entered the Cave of the Annunciation in Nazareth, that he took pieces of stone from the wall of the cave, to give to his mother and friends back home (de Saulcy 1854 I: 74–5). Dean Arthur Stanley (1815–81) looked at the ways in which the landscape had shaped what he called the Holy History, and the metaphors that were equally used in the Bible itself and by his favourite English poets (Stanley 1868: 127–32). According to him, the mountains were of particular importance for the biblical history. At the same time, he warns, the holy places themselves did not make the Holy Land. If you could remove them (as in the case of the Lady of Loreto, for example) the Land would still be Holy (Stanley 1868: 471). George Adam Smith (1856–1942), author of *The Historical Geography of the Holy Land* (1894), dedicated a chapter to the scenery of the land and the biblical poetry that celebrated it.

Most travellers saw the Bible depicted in the land. But the landscape also bore messages for the keen observer. As Edward Robinson (1794–1863) mused when he looked out over the Dead Sea:

> Lovely the scene is not; yet magnificently wild, and in the highest degree stern and impressive. Shattered mountains and the deep chasm of the rent earth are here tokens of the wrath of God, and of his vengeance upon the guilty inhabitants of the plain: when, 'turning the cities of Sodom and Gomorrah into ashes, he condemned them with an overthrow, making them an example unto them that after should live ungodly.'
>
> —Robinson and Smith 1860 I: 525

Van de Velde wrestled with his own feelings of ecstatic joy when walking on holy soil, always reminding himself that the reality of his beliefs was not to be found in those places, but in himself. To him, his own holy ecstasy was a form of superstition. It was good to see those places, because they gave him a sense of the reality of the biblical narrative, but the reality of God's presence was in the heart, not in those places (van de Velde 1854 II: 10–12). Instead, the Bible played a different, but no less important and visible role in Charles Montagu Doughty's magnum opus, *Travels in Arabia Deserta* (1888). Doughty spent two years on the Arabian Peninsula, travelling on his own and living with Bedouin tribes. He rarely refers to the Bible, but the language in which he wrote his account was moulded on the language of the King James Bible, as well as that of Chaucer and Spenser, as if designed to create an epic of biblical proportions.

# IDENTIFICATION OF HOLY PLACES

A favourite pastime of travellers and explorers of all times was the identification of biblical place names and locations. For many it was part of their mission to check or prove the truth of the biblical narrative. They were well aware of the fact that many so-called holy places in the Holy Land were fabricated, by the monks or by the local guides, for the benefit of the pilgrims and tourists, and they were determined to sift the wheat from the chaff. Edward Robinson was one of these.

Robinson was an American Biblical scholar who travelled through Palestine with his colleague Eli Smith in 1838. In their magnum opus, *Biblical Researches in Palestine* (1860 [1841]), they identified large numbers of biblical place names. The book became the standard reference for travellers in the Holy Land, and earned Robinson the honorary title of 'Father of Biblical Geography'. As they explain in the introduction, the main purpose of their expedition was to debunk the many fanciful 'identifications' of holy places and discern between what was genuine tradition and what was 'fastened upon the Holy Land by foreign ecclesiastics and monks'.

Place name identification relied heavily on linguistics: if a name sounded more or less like a biblical one, and was more or less in the right area, that was a clear argument for its identification. Claude R. Conder (1848–1910), who together with Horatio Kitchener (1850–1916) conducted the Survey of Western Palestine (1871–7) for the Palestine Exploration Fund, goes so far as to say that proper identification is impossible if the old name is lost (Conder 1879 II: 182). It helped if there were some ruins to signify ancient habitation, but as archaeological dating-methods were practically non-existent, as not much was added to the accuracy of the identification. The Presbyterian minister Josias Porter (1823–89), who wrote the first guidebook for Palestine (see above), identified the (Roman and Byzantine period) stone architecture that was typical of the Leja district in the Hauran across the Jordan, as the ancient cities of Og of Bashan (Porter 1891: 13, 25, 30).

Classical writers (particularly Josephus), early Church fathers (such as Origen, Jerome and Eusebius), and early pilgrims (Helena, who discovered the holy cross and the holy tomb, or the Pilgrim of Bordeaux, to name only a few), were also trusted on this identification, because they were chronologically closer to the original events, and therefore considered more reliable.

If a place was sacred to all three main religions, such as the Cave of Machpelah in Hebron, that was also a sure sign of its authenticity (Conder 1879 II: 80). There were some places that were not in doubt, such as Jerusalem, Bethlehem, Nazareth, Hebron or Samaria/Sichem, and others which were generally accepted as authentic by travellers, such as Rachel's tomb, or Jacob's well by Sichem (Figure 3.1), but others could be the subject of heated debates.

A favourite object of research was the Vale of Siddim, and the 'cities of the plain': Sodom, Gomorrah, Admah, Zeboim and Zoar. There were three favourite theories, apart from the suggestion that the whole story was a legend. The cities were either considered to be somewhere in the south or south-west region of the Dead Sea, close to Jebel Usdum (de Saulcy 1854; Smith 1894), or on the north-east side (Wilson 1869; Palmer 1871) or submerged in the south end of the Sea itself (van de Velde 1854; Lynch 1850). The present site of Zoara, south-east of the Dead Sea, and now generally accepted as the ancient site of Zoar, is mentioned by Seetzen and Burckhardt, although Seetzen thought that Jebel Shera was Zoar. Charles Irby and James Mangles, two English army officers who were on their way to Petra, which had just been discovered by Burckhardt, came across a site which they thought could be biblical Zoar east of Lisan, near the mouth of the Wadi Kerak (Irby and Mangles 1845: 138). While both Robinson and the American captain Lynch agreed with their identification, what they found may have been the site of Bab edh-Dhra.

The American Captain William F. Lynch (1801–65) had made a survey by boat of the River Jordan and the Dead Sea. He and his team were the first to accurately measure the level of the Jordan Valley and the Dead Sea. Lynch believed that before disaster struck

FIGURE 3.1: Jacob's well (Conder 1879: 29).

the 'cities of the plain', what is now the Dead Sea was the fertile valley that Abraham and Lot looked upon when they decided to part ways. When he got caught in a storm on the Dead Sea he exclaims 'How different was the scene before the submerging of the plain', which was 'even as the garden of the Lord!' It was a popular theory that the plain had sunk because of an earthquake, and the cities of the plain were buried under the floods as a result (Lynch 1850: 252; Figure 3.2).

Edward Robinson, on the other hand, assumed that a smaller lake already existed, but he also agreed that the 'cities of the plain' were buried in the waters of the south end of the sea.

This theory was heavily attacked by de Saulcy, who set out on a special journey to find them. He had no doubt that Jebel Usdum was Sodom, and a chain of ruins further north, up to Khirbet Qumran, formed the great city of Gomorrah. Zoar was also on the west shore of the Dead Sea, and he mocked those who 'still believe, with Irby, Mangles, and Robinson, that Zoar was on the eastern shore of the Dead Sea' (de Saulcy 1854 I: 459).

PILLAR OF SALT AT USDUM.

FIGURE 3.2: The pillar of Salt by Jebel Usdum (Lynch 1849: 308).

He even reinterpreted parts of the Bible to support his conclusions, to the disgust of van de Velde, who heard de Saulcy speak at a meeting in Brussels. Van de Velde, determined to prove de Saulcy wrong, subsequently also went to investigate the location of the 'cities of the plain', and in his opinion there could be no doubt that they were submerged in the south part of the sea. Stanley, on the other hand, thought that de Saulcy could have a point. And so did George Adam Smith, in a long argument in which he defends the historicity of the destruction against those who 'have argued that it is simply one of the many legends of overturned or buried cities, with the addition of the local phenomena of the Dead Sea, and of a very much grander moral than has ever been attached to any tale of the kind' (Smith 1894: 509). He argued that, if the cities were buried in the sea, it would have been mentioned in the biblical narrative.

In the mountains on the north-west shores of the Dead Sea, de Saulcy met a group of Arabs of the Dhullam tribe. In his zeal to find biblical names, de Saulcy immediately recognized their name as that of the biblical town of Adullam in Judah. Realizing that Adullam was in the plains, rather than the mountains, he even suggested that there could have been two Adullams. A large cave nearby could, he thought, well have been the cave of Adullam where David hid (de Saulcy 1854).

Another fiercely fought-over identification was that of Rama, the birthplace of the prophet Samuel. It was generally located north of Jerusalem, but James Silk Buckingham (1821: 163) identified Ramla, east of Jaffa, with Rama, without explaining where the extra 'l' had come from. He was roundly attacked for his identification, particularly in the conservative *Quarterly Review*. Buckingham, however, was unrepentant, using the rather cheeky argument that place names may point to a biblical identification, but not necessarily.[1] Although most explorers looked for Rama south of Jerusalem, either at Nebi Samwil or at er-Ram, Buckingham found a supporter in Constantin von Tischendorf (1815–74), who also opted for Ramla, and even explained the discrepancy in the name.

## THE STORY OF THE EXODUS

One of the biblical narratives that travellers found most baffling was the story of the Exodus. As it was fundamental not only to the history of Israel, but also to Christianity, because of the giving of the Law, this was one of the favourite expeditions for a large number of explorers. Several dedicated whole volumes to it, such as E.H. Palmer and Henry Clay Trumbull. But many others were also determined to identify the route that the Israelites followed on their journey from Egypt to the Promised Land.

Investigating the route of the Exodus was a major expedition in itself. There were no towns or villages, no hotels, even finding water was a concern. It made it easy for them to identify with the tribulations of the wandering Israelites, and bring the story to life. The journey usually started in Suez, a miserable little town according to most, but the last shred of civilization for a while. Here they were shown how drinking water for the people of Suez was brought across from the other side of the Red Sea by Bedouin. From Suez they would turn east into the desert, and debate the place where the Israelites must have

---

[1] Pococke also calls it Rama, and mentions it as the hometown of Joseph of Arimathea – but he also says that the Arabs call it Rameli (Pococke 1743: 25). Buckingham makes some other interesting mistakes: he equates Zerqa with Zara, Burza with Bosra or Bosor, and Jahaz with Jabes. It makes one wonder whether he was slightly dyslexic.

crossed the Red Sea. Seetzen put it at the small arm of the sea north-east of Suez (1854–9 III: 119) as did also Stanley (1868: 36; Palmer 1871: 36), but others looked further down the coast, to the peninsula of Ras Adabiya (e.g. Bartlett 1854: 18; Robinson and Smith 1860 I: 81; Stephens 1862 [1838]: 187). The next stop was Ayun Musa, the Wells of Moses, opposite Ras Adabiya, for many an argument in favour of that particular crossing. The bitter wells of Marah, made sweet by means of a branch of wood thrown in by Moses, were generally considered to be at Ayn Hawara, but from there the routes could differ significantly, and as Stanley (1868: 33) says: every traveller thought he had found the route the Israelites took, but only by checking every possible route could that problem be solved. In the meantime, he suggested three possible routes, a north, a middle and a south route, depending on the identification of the sacred mount, Sinai (Figure 3.3). The two main contenders were Jebel Musa, at the foot of which St Catharine's monastery stood, and Jebel Serbal, further to the south-west. The German Egyptologist Karl Richard Lepsius (1810–84) was convinced Serbal was the holy mountain (1852: 350–71), and he had his followers, but most explorers preferred Jebel Musa. Edward Henry Palmer (1840–82) explored Arab oral traditions to determine which was the mountain of the Law (cf. Palmer 1871).

Regardless of whether they favoured Jebel Musa or Serbal as the mountain of the Law, all travellers stopped at the monastery of St Catharine, although most of them showed a healthy distrust of the holy places pointed out to them by the monks: the location of the burning bush, or the various places where Moses performed his miracles. Robinson was shown the place where, according to the monks the rebels Korah, Dathan and Abiram were swallowed by the earth, 'the good fathers of the monastery, as a matter of convenience, having transferred the scene of that event from the vicinity of Kadesh to this place' (Robinson and Smith 1860 I: 113).

Another contested place was Kadesh Barnea. The American Presbyterian evangelist Henry Clay Trumbull was convinced he had finally discovered its real location, and dedicated a book to his discovery (1884). Unfortunately for him his identification with Ein Qedeis is now generally rejected, and C.L. Woolley and T.E. Lawrence's later identification with Tell Qudeirat is the generally accepted one.

One thing that baffled most travellers, was the sheer number of people that, according to the narrative, took part in the Exodus. Based on the text of Num. 1.45, which mentions 603,550 men over twenty years old (without even counting the Levites), there must have been about two million people if one included women and children. They struggled to understand how the desert could feed and particularly water two million people and their animals, during such a long period.

Very few travellers dared question the numbers. One of them was Harriet Martineau (1802–76). Martineau was a sociologist writer, who was brought up as a Unitarian, but later turned atheist. She had translated the works of Auguste Comte into English, and was a friend of Charles Darwin. She wrote extensively on social issues, and believed that the Mosaic religion represented a new phase in the progress of humanity, 'a truth so holy and so vast that even yet mankind seems scarcely able fully to apprehend it: the truth that all Ideas are the common heritage of all men, and that none are too precious to be communicated to every human mind' (Martineau 1848: 288). It made obsolete the idolatrous religions of Egypt and the surrounding countries. In the end, she claims, it failed, because Israel was not ready for it.

Martineau was not very interested in determining the route the Israelites took, or their number. According to her 'the numbers and dates of the narrative are regarded by all the

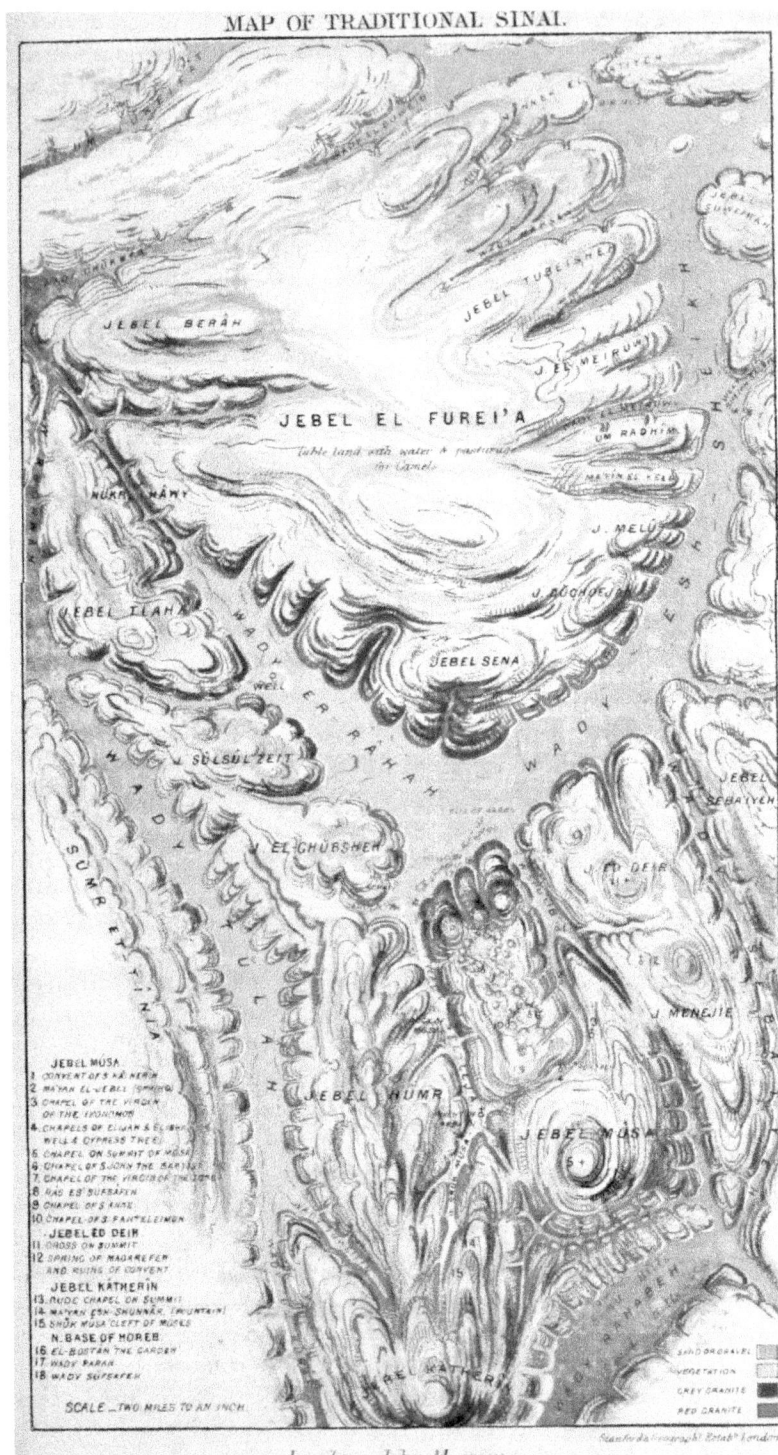

FIGURE 3.3: Map of Sinai (Stanley 1856: 42).

learned [. . .] as untenable' (1848: 307), something that was not reflected in most travel accounts.

Those that did not doubt the biblical figures had to look for other solutions. The most common suggestion was that the desert in the days of the Exodus was greener, and had more water. And, of course, there were the manna and the quails. The alternative offered by William H. Bartlett (1854: 19–21), however, rejects all such natural explanations, and urges his readers to simply accept that the Exodus was one continuous divine miracle, because it could not be anything else.

## WRITTEN HISTORY: THE BIBLE FROM COVER TO COVER

While the actual location of place names could lead to heated debates amongst scholars, another hot topic was the actual reliability of the narrative itself. For some travellers, doubting the stories of either the Old or the New Testaments was tantamount to an attack on God Himself. There were attacks from all sides. Scientific discoveries and theories, such as those of Charles Lyell about the antiquity of the earth, or later in the century Charles Darwin about the origin of species seemed to make a mockery of the creation stories. Text criticism in Germany (mostly) reduced God's word to a collection of sometimes contradictory stories. Christian travellers rushed to defend their Bible. According to Johann Nepomuk Sepp (1816–1909), a German scholar who was himself a devout Catholic, critical study of the biblical sources had become tantamount to heresy, something for which he blamed the Reformation, and he complained that the scholarship of the previous few decennia (his book was published in 1863) had created more confusion than all the monkish traditions and pilgrim superstitions together.

Various travellers sought to reconcile the scientific evidence with their beliefs. The Reverend Henry Baker Tristram (1822–1906), a clergyman and ornithologist, corresponded with Darwin about the evolution of birds, but at the same time warned against the dangers of rejecting the stories of miraculous intervention in the Scriptures (Tristram 1865: 352). George Adam Smith accepted the German methods of text criticism, which did not stand in the way of his belief that Israel's religion was unique because it was revealed to the Israelites by God Himself. Nevertheless, ethnographic and historical research of the lands of the Bible was presented as strictly independent, scholarly investigation. The prospectus of the launch of the Palestine Exploration Fund claimed: '[Our] object is strictly an inductive inquiry. We are not to be a religious society; we are not about to launch controversy; we are about to apply the rules of science, which are so well understood by us in our branches, to an investigation into the facts concerning the Holy Land'.[2]

In this investigation the biblical source was treated as a historical document. Genesis 10, the 'Table of Nations' formed the basis for a number of ethnic studies. Based on this biblical passage, the Göttingen School of History – among them we find Johann David Michaelis (1717–91) and Johann Gottfried Eichhorn (1752–1827) – coined the terms Semites, Hamites and Japhetites in the eighteenth century, after the sons of Noah. Richard Francis Burton (1821–90), one of the most colourful explorers of the Victorian era based his anthropological observations about the Arab population of the Peninsula on the Table of Nations, although he had some interesting theories of his own as well (Burton 1855: Ch. 25). Porter's handbook of Palestine (1858) also followed the Table in its historical

---

[2] https://en.wikipedia.org/wiki/Palestine_Exploration_Fund (accessed 26 July 2020).

sketch. And in a pamphlet for his home front, the evangelical missionary Archibald Forder (1863–1934) classified the population of the Arabian desert, following closely the Table of Nations, embellished with local Arab tradition. Arabs were the descendants of Ishmael, son of Abraham, and therefore close relatives of the Israelites. They inhabited Arabia Deserta. Arabia Felix was populated by the descendants of Joktan, also known as Qahtan, another descendant of Shem. The Beni Qahtan created thus the kingdoms of the Yemen and the Hedjaz. After Abraham had expelled them, Ishmael and Hagar were kindly received by these peoples. Ishmael married into the family of Jurham, one of the descendants of Joktan, and had twelve sons (Genesis 25), who went on to become great tribes, and who were the ancestors of the wandering Arabs, the 'Children of Ishmael'. And these, according to Forder, had 'preserved their language, manners and peculiar customs more perfectly than any other', so that 'one can hardly help fancying himself carried back to the days of Abraham' (Forder 1902: 84).

Conder's arguments for the historicity of the biblical narrative have undertones of typical Victorian racialism: Semitic people have no aesthetic faculty – no art, no sculpture, no poetry that we would recognize as such (Conder 1879 II: 208). They also have no love of nature for its own sake, but only as phenomena created by God. It follows that Semites cannot have a mythology, so the Old Testament cannot possibly be mythological, it must therefore be a truthful narrative of actual events (Conder 1879 II: 208). His denial of the culture of the Arab population is astonishing, as it was well known in his time that they had a rich oral tradition.

The story of Jonah was accepted as a fable by most (but not all) travellers, which did not stop them from speculating about the nature of the fish. Buckingham (1821: 149) saw a connection with the story of Perseus and Andromeda. But Jonah was an exception. Denying the existence of divine intervention in the history of Israel, as well as Jesus's miracles, where there was no natural explanation, was the greatest danger that threatened a person's beliefs.

External sources were still relatively rare in the nineteenth century. Although Egyptian hieroglyphs had been deciphered in 1822, and the various cuneiform scripts and languages around the middle of the century, translations were still fairly rare and not always accurate, and the historical documents on which travellers depended for corroboration of the biblical narrative came mainly from Greek and Latin sources. A comparison of different versions of the text itself was another way of arriving at the truth. It was the main purpose for which the German scholar von Tischendorf travelled through the Middle East, in search of ancient manuscripts of the Bible. His greatest discovery was the Codex Sinaiticus, a fourth-century manuscript of the New Testament, which he discovered in the monastery of St Catharine.

## LOCAL TRADITIONS AND THE BIBLE

References to people and events from both the Old and the New Testaments could be found everywhere in the Holy Land. Graves, mountains and wells bore the names of Old Testament heroes. Places where Jesus had dwelt, slept, eaten or performed a miracle, were invariably honoured with churches. Biblical holy places were also a handy source of income for the local population of the Holy Land. Local guides, as well as the monks who lived in the various monasteries and convents made a decent living out of identifying or assigning for the benefit of the travellers and pilgrims places connected with, as well as hand and foot prints of, the most important biblical heroes and prophets.

Some of these traditions had an obvious Christian origin, from the discovery of the True Cross by Helena and the accounts of the Church Fathers, to the location of the burning bush by St Catharine's monastery and all the places where Jesus dwelt in Jerusalem, but others were more difficult to place and some were part of the Islamic or even older local traditions. The Sinai was full of references to the Exodus: wells and mountains named after Moses or Aaron, or the last struggle of Pharaoh (Stanley 1868: 28). Stanley also thought he had found the names of Jethro and his daughters in various wadis and mountains on the peninsula (1868: 32–3).

Seetzen (1854–9 III: 15) visited a place called Madara, which, according to local tradition, had been a great city once upon a time. Its inhabitants were turned into stones by Allah, for the same crime that condemned the inhabitants of Sodom and Gomorrah. The same story was later told to other travellers (Trumbull 1884: 136–7).[3] Abraham, who, through his son Ismail, was a patriarch of both Muslims and Israelites also figured in many local stories, as did Ismail himself. David, and particularly his glamorous son Solomon were credited with various great building works, such as the temple of Baalbek, and the ruins of Palmyra (Volney 1788 II: 243). Buckingham heard a local sheikh tell of the destruction of Amman and Jerash by Solomon:

> One day [. . .] when Solomon, the son of David, paid a visit to the prince of Amman, the king of Jerash was also present; and as they ascended together the steps of the great palace (meaning the benches of the theatre at Amman), to the summer seat of the sovereign of that city, Solomon, the son of David, exclaimed, 'O! Princes! Our empires are on the decline; our cities must soon decay, and our realms be deserted and depopulated.' They expressed a hope that, under the blessing of God, that period was still far distant, when the King replied, 'Be not deceived, the sign of destruction already approaches, for, behold! Even oil hath risen to the price of three paras a skin!'
>
> —Buckingham 1825: 95

These stories were duly noted by the travellers, who, although they found them colourful and interesting, dismissed them as local folklore. The Muslim tradition, which placed Moses' grave at the site of Nebi Musa, west of the Jordan, was dismissed as a Muslim aberration of Scripture, because 'it is perfectly certain that Moses died on the further side of the Jordan, and that he was buried in a valley belonging to the land of Moab' (de Saulcy 1854 II: 195).

Many of these local traditions had been collected in the seventeenth century by the French orientalist Barthélemy d'Herbelot (1625–95), in his *Bibliotheque Orientale* (1697), a collection of Arabic and other manuscripts and traditions, and of which particularly Buckingham made extensive use in his local descriptions.

An interesting 'tradition' was noted by Henry Maundrell (1665–1701), a seventeenth-century minister to the Levant Company in Aleppo, who came to the Holy Land to celebrate Easter in Jerusalem with some of his flock. He remarked that many of the holy places he was shown seemed to be caves, even if there was no reason for it (1703: 113). He also visited the Milk Grotto, which was turned white when Mary accidentally spilt a drop of Holy Milk when feeding the Baby Jesus. Chalk from the grotto was supposed to increase a woman's milk, and was widely used 'for that purpose, and that with very good

---

[3] Trumbull suggests Madara was the site of Aaron's burial, rather than Jebel Haroun by Petra.

effect; which perhaps may be true enough, it being well known how much fancy is wont to do in things of this nature' (1703: 90).

## ETHNOGRAPHY IN THE NINETEENTH CENTURY

Lady Anne Blunt (1837–1917), who travelled to Arabia with her husband to buy horses (1881 I: xii) describes the marriage arrangement of Muhammad, a young man from Palmyra, whom they had hired as a servant for the journey. The clan to which he belonged had moved from Nejd to Palmyra about a century earlier, and they had not maintained contact with the mother tribe, but his father decided he needed a bride from the mother tribe.

> The idea and the promise were in strict accordance with Bedouin notions, and greatly delighted both him and his father Abdallah, to whom they were in due course communicated. Arab custom is very little changed on the point of marriage from what it was in the days of Abraham; and it was natural that both father and son should wish for a wife for him of their own blood, and that he should be ready to go far to fetch one.
>
> —Blunt 1881 I: xi–xii

The parallels with Isaac's quest for Rebecca are obvious, but it gets better. Once Muhammad has found his bride, her father first increases the bride price, and then tries to replace the chosen bride with her elder sister, like Laban did to Jacob, Isaac's son, and with the same argument, that he cannot marry the youngest daughter while the elder is still unmarried.

Ulrich Seetzen called Abraham 'the great Bedouin Sheikh' (Seetzen 1854–9 III: 32) and compared him and his history to the world of the Bedouin as he encountered it. The idea that the Bedouin of the desert reflected the lifestyle and philosophy of the Patriarchs in the Bible was popular, particularly by more romantically inclined travellers. Others equated the Bedouin with the traditional enemies of Israel: the Amalekites and Midianites 'and in the Tiyâha, Tawârah, or 'Alawin tribes, with their chiefs and followers, their dress, and manners, and habitations, we probably see the likeness of the Midianites, the Amalekites, and the Israelites themselves in this their earliest stage of existence' (Stanley 1868: 27).

Also, life in the villages and the fields, the labouring of the Fellahin and their skirmishes with the Bedouin were a source of inspiration. When Maundrell (1703: 188) observed farmers ploughing the field, he was particularly impressed by the goads they used to drive the oxen. He described and measured them, and suggested that Shamgar (Judges 3) used such a goad to kill the Philistines 'a weapon no less fit, perhaps fitter, than a sword for such an execution'.

Conder's (1879 II: 204–35) chapter on 'the origin of the Fellahin', is a nice Victorian-style analysis of the national character of the Semitic 'race', whether Jews or Arabs. They had a lot of good qualities, as long as they were unspoilt by the influence of 'the worst class of tourists'. But their worst vice was that of untruthfulness, a trait already found in the Old Testament, in the story of Jacob and Esau. At the same time, their conceit was also intolerable, particularly in light of the obvious superiority of the Aryan races. Again, both Jews and Arabs were guilty of it, a worthy illustration of the parable of the Publican and the Pharisee (Conder 1879 II: 212–13). However, based on the language spoken by the Fellahin, Conder concluded that they probably descended from the pre-Israelite population of Palestine, and were, as hewers of wood and drawers of water, obviously inferior to their Israelite overlords.

Laurence Oliphant (1829–88) would have concurred with that. Oliphant was a British diplomat, writer and Christian Zionist, who at had settled in Haifa. During one of his trips in the region he discovered a village in northern Galilee, Bukeia, which was inhabited by Muslims, Greek Orthodox Christians and Jews, and in which, according to his informants, the Jews had lived uninterrupted since before the destruction of the temple. The local Arabs, therefore, had to be the direct Canaanite descendants of the pre-Israelite population of the region (Oliphant 1887: 109–10). Archibald Forder also dedicated a whole chapter to verse-by-verse comparisons of biblical descriptions and Arab customs. For him those age-old customs and traditions were clear proof of the truth of the biblical narrative.

Many Bedouin customs related to hospitality, honour and warfare did indeed resemble biblical laws and customs. Robinson mentions the Bedouin custom of *thar* (blood revenge): 'this is the ancient blood-revenge of the Hebrews, which was so firmly fixed in all their habits of life, that even the inspired lawgiver did not choose to abolish it directly, but only modified and controlled its influence by establishing cities of refuge. Nothing of this kind exists among the Arabs' (Robinson and Smith 1860 I: 141).

Robinson also compared the confrontation between David's band of outlaws and Nabal to the paying of protection fees to the Bedouin by the local farmers, but he gave it a rather rose-coloured interpretation. In his version David was 'doing them good offices, probably in return for information and supplies obtained through them', rather than the protection racket that it really was (Robinson and Smith 1860 I: 498). Conder, in his *Tent Work in Palestine* (1879 II: 88) also compared the Bedouin practice of extracting *khawa* from the villages in return for protection with the story of David and Nabal.

An interesting description of Bedouin warfare is recorded by Burckhardt:

> When two hostile parties of Bedouin cavalry meet, and perceive from afar that they are equal in point of numbers, they halt opposite to each other out of the reach of musket-shot; and the battle begins by skirmishes between two men. A horseman leaves his party and gallops off towards the enemy, exclaiming, 'O horsemen, O horsemen, let such a one meet me!' If the adversary for whom he calls be present, and not afraid to meet him in combat, he gallops forwards; if absent, his friends reply that he is not amongst them. The challenged horseman in his turn exclaims, 'And you upon the grey mare, who are you?' the other answers, 'I am *** the son of ***'. Having thus become acquainted with each other, they begin to fight; none of the bystanders join in this combat, to do so would be reckoned a treacherous action; but if one of the combatants should turn back, and fly towards his friends, the latter hasten to his assistance, and drive back the pursuer, who is in turn protected by his friends. After several of these partial combats between the best men of both parties, the whole corps join in promiscuous combat.
>
> —Burckhardt 1830:174

Burckhardt leaves it to the discerning reader to draw the obvious parallels.

These comparisons between the biblical narrative and the people and customs of the land were made by most travellers but some took it further than others. William Hepworth Dixon (1821–79) in his handbook *The Holy Land* (1865) created an illustration of the Bible, using numerous sources and traditions to paint a lively impression of the life of Jesus. His chapter on the life of the Holy Family is fascinating in its detail, taken from the

Bible, the Apocrypha (gospel of James) and other traditions and sources and describes the life of Joachim and Anna, Mary and Joseph, and the whole family in fascinating detail. He calls his book 'a study of the scenery and politics of the Sacred Story' (Dixon 1865).

That the road from Jerusalem to Jericho was as dangerous as it had been in the days of Jesus, was discovered by Frederick Henniker (1793–1825) when he was robbed by Bedouin and left half dead and naked by the side of the road (Henniker 1823: 284).

Paintings of biblical scenes also changed significantly during this period, largely thanks to an increased interest in and knowledge of local dress and architecture, as well as a more critical attitude towards it (Tromans 2008). In 1821 Buckingham could still complain that paintings which he had seen in Nazareth depicted Joseph and Mary dressed up in the richest robes and finery. He could condone that in European depictions of those scenes, but in the land itself painters should have known better and depicted their characters in the more suitable local dress (1821 I: 98). But things were about to change. Painters such as William Holman Hunt (1827–1910) and David Roberts (1796–1864) travelled to the Holy Land to study and paint the landscape, the architecture and the people. In 1854 Holman Hunt settled in Jerusalem, in order to paint his *Finding Christ in the Temple*, for which he wanted portraits of Jerusalem Jews. He dressed the boy Jesus in an abaya of the kind made in Jenin. For his haunting painting of the *Scapegoat* he stayed at the south end of the Dead Sea for a fortnight, only attended by a dragoman and a guide, in order to get the right colouring of the Moab mountains by sunset at the right time of year.

## BIBLE AND POLITICS

The first premise for almost every nineteenth-century traveller to the Holy Land was that Christianity was the True Faith. George Adam Smith's proof of this is a masterpiece of circular reasoning. Evidence that the God of Israel is the real thing, is that He persevered in exile, first in Assyria and afterwards, after the destruction of the temple, in the wider world, and that He did not disappear, like all those other local religions did, but went on to conquer the world as the great religion of Christianity. Islam and even Judaism were considered false religions, but even local Christian communities, whether Arab or Monkish were poor misguided souls who did not have the True Faith (Smith 1894: 31–4).

This conviction made it easy for Christian travellers to sincerely believe that the Holy Land was destined to return into the hands of the Christian West. As William Thomson, first president of the Palestine Exploration Fund put it at the first meeting of the Fund in 1865:

> This country of Palestine belongs to you and me, it is essentially ours. It was given to the Father of Israel in the words: 'Walk through the land in the length of it, and in the breadth of it, for I will give it unto thee'. We mean to walk through Palestine in the length and in the breadth of it, because that land has been given unto us. It is the land from which comes news of our Redemption. It is the land towards which we turn as the fountain of all our hopes; it is the land to which we may look with as true a patriotism as we do in this dear old England, which we love so much.[4]

There were also the first indications of what was to become a major issue in the following half-century: the return of the land to what was seen as its rightful owners: the Jews, as

---

[4] https://en.wikipedia.org/wiki/Palestine_Exploration_Fund (accessed 26 July 2020).

opposed to those who occupied it at the time. In 1875 Lord Salisbury could describe it at a meeting of the Fund as 'a land without a people' for 'a people without a land'. The Ottoman Empire was crumbling, and Britain, which was already a world empire, considered itself eminently suited to reclaim Jerusalem, and rule Palestine for the benefit of its people and the Christian world. In the eyes of many it had every right to do so. And the Bible supported the British claim: 'With the Protestants there is a large class who base their belief in an immediately pending alteration in the political conditions under which Jerusalem now exists, upon their interpretation of prophecy. They profess to find it clearly indicated in Ezekiel, Daniel, Revelations [sic], and elsewhere in the Bible, that the protectorate of Palestine is to be vested in England' (Oliphant 1887: 313).

The English were not the only ones, however. Von Tischendorf saw a beautiful task for Germany. Standing on a height north of the town of Nazareth and looking over it he exclaimed:

> Here did the Saviour, when he looked over the ocean to the west, certainly often think of thee, thou beloved Germany! He thought of thee, because he knew that thou wouldst one day be called on as the holy avenger of the truth, to fight and bleed in opposition of falsehood; that thou wouldst found, in German hearts, a bulwark for the faith comprised within the Epistle to the Romans, when it had vanished from the palaces of the city upon the seven hills.
>
> —von Tischendorf 1847: 232

Johann Sepp (1863) also saw a noble task for Christianity: it was the duty of the Christian Western world to reconquer the Holy Land and rescue it for Christianity, just like the Crusaders had tried but failed to do 800 years earlier.

The Palestine Exploration Fund was founded in 1865 with the express aim of investigating the Holy Land, by employing 'competent persons' to examine the archaeology, manners and customs, topography, geology and natural sciences (Grove 1869; Figure 3.4). One of the first 'competent persons' to be sent out was Charles Warren (1840–1927), who excavated underneath the Haram es-Sharif in Jerusalem, in the hope of finding traces of Solomon's temple. Another aim of the scientific pursuits of the Fund was less explicitly stated, but equally important: to gain an insight into the strategically important features of the land, and particularly of Jerusalem. Charles Warren's exploration of Jerusalem therefore was as much strategic as it was archaeological.

Other scholarly societies followed: the American Palestine Exploration Society in 1870, later replaced by the American Schools of Oriental Research, the Deutsche Verein zur Erforschung Palästinas in 1877, and in 1892 the French École Biblique et Archéologique, all of which had bases in Jerusalem from which they organized and supported research into the history of the Bible.

## ZIONISM AND ANTISEMITISM

While the vast majority of the population was Arab, there always had been Jews in Palestine, particularly in the Jewish holy towns of Tiberias, Hebron and Safed, and in the Jewish quarter in Jerusalem. Most of them were desperately poor and lived on the *Halukah*, the charity from European and American Jews, and spent their time studying Torah. But during the course of the nineteenth century things began to change. During this period the number of Jews in Palestine increased steadily. Many of the newcomers

FIGURE 3.4: A theodolite party at work in the Holy Land (Conder 1879: title page).

were immigrants who worked as shopkeepers, or in agriculture or as craftsmen. Anti-Jewish sentiment, particularly in eastern Europe, enforced subscription in Russia and renewed pogroms contributed to this immigration flux. There was also encouragement from Western governments, particularly Britain, where Lord Palmerston, then foreign secretary, instructed the British consulate to support the Jewish community in Palestine

(Finn 1878 II: 56), and wealthy Jews like Moses Montefiore saw the prospect of a Jewish homeland as an increasing reality, following the probable collapse of the Turkish empire.

Protestant Christians, particularly evangelicals who believed firmly in the second coming of Christ, which was to take place in Jerusalem, felt more affinity with the Jews of the country, with whom they shared, at least partly, the same religion and the same expectations, than with the Arab population. They supported the return of Palestine to the Jews, in accordance with God's promises in the Old Testament.

James Finn (1806–72), second British consul of Jerusalem from 1845 onwards, firmly believed in the need to convert the Jewish population, and to lift them out of their misery and poverty. He was one of several people who initiated agricultural and other projects to try and make the Jewish community self-supporting. These projects often failed because of resistance by the local rabbis, who abhorred any secular interference with their community, however beneficial.

A variation on the Jewish return to Palestine was devised by Laurence Oliphant. In 1879 he suggested settling the land of Gilead, east of the Jordan, by Jewish colonies under the authority of the Porte in Istanbul. The scheme was aborted by a flat rejection by the Sultan though, and after the pogroms in eastern Europe in the early 1880s a renewed wave of Jewish refugees flocked into Palestine itself.

Charles van de Velde was another evangelical Christian traveller who expressed his conviction that the Jews would regain the country, quoting God's repeated promises in the Bible, once 'the curse had been fulfilled' (the curse in his view being the Ottoman Empire), and once they had all been converted to Christianity. He praised the activities of the London Society for Promoting Christianity Among the Jews, and lamented its lack of success (van de Velde 1854 II: 224). In effect, most travellers saw the conversion of the Jews to Christianity as a precondition for their regaining of the land. In due course these proponents would be labelled Christian Zionists.

Antisemitism in this time was largely aimed at the religion of the Jews, rather than their ethnicity. Johann Sepp compared the Old Testament with Hagar's child Ismael, and the New Testament with Sarah's child Isaac, and claimed that the Jews who stuck to the old religion were as Hagar's children who were not entitled to the inheritance (1863 I: 77). There were, however, other views. Dixon (1865), for instance, believed that the return of the Jews to Palestine could be contrived only through a miracle, not through their own efforts. He saw their attitude of keeping themselves apart from the world, and considering contact with gentiles as defiling, as the main cause for antisemitism. At the same time, it was a sense of guilt towards the Jews that led to efforts to support their return to Palestine, and paid for such projects as that James Finn tried to set up. The reason he believed these projects failed was that the Jews were too lazy, and too used to charity.

A particularly infamous book was written by Richard Burton, always a controversial man. It was called *The Jew, the Gypsy and el Islam* (1898), and it was heavily antisemitic, using quotes from the Bible, particularly from the Pentateuch and the laws of Moses to argue his case. Burton seems to have credited the stories that Jews sacrificed gentile children (1898: 34–6) explaining it as an act of revenge against the treatment they received from the world, and quoting Shakespeare's Shylock. Burton equally endorsed in his description all the other vices that had traditionally been ascribed to Jews: usury, greed, exceptionalism and a meticulous, even ridiculous, adherence to the outward religious instructions of the Talmud and the Torah. According to him Western European scholars and travellers painted a much too rosy picture of the 'Jewish race', mostly out of a sense of guilt. The book was published posthumously, in 1898, because Burton's friends, with some justification, thought it was too antisemitic and would make him a lot of enemies.

Lastly, according to Conder (1879 II: 295), 'The good qualities of the Jews are numerous: they are energetic and able, very courteous to strangers, and charitable to one another; but they are fanatical to the last degree, and Palestine under Jewish government would probably be closed against outer influence even more effectually than it is under the Turks.'

## LOCAL CHRISTIANITY

Since the beginning of Christianity there had been Christian communities in Palestine. The main local Christian communities were Greek Orthodox or Latin. Monasteries and convents were dotted all over the country, inhabited by mostly European monks, and there were Christian Arab communities, with their own Orthodox priests. Most travellers were either scathing about them, or viewed them with pity, deploring their ignorance and lack of 'true' faith (e.g. Buckingham 1821: 235–6, 1825: 47, 231). Edward Daniel Clarke (1769–1822), who travelled the region around 1800, lamented that 'The pure gospel of Christ, every where the herald of civilization and of science, is almost as little known in the Holy Land as in Caliphornia or New Holland' (1814: 246).

Since most of the local population was illiterate, oral traditions played an important role in people's religion. Buckingham, trapped by snow in es-Salt, east of the Jordan, recounts in 1821 a session of evening storytelling by the local priest, who entertained the audience with a rendering of the destruction of Sodom and Gomorrah. Conder (1879 II: 224) also mentions the garbled stories, merging local traditions with biblical narrative and heroes, and their presumed graves, and he blames the teachings of medieval monks. At the same time, he points out (1879 II: 234) that while the state of the population in the villages is generally poor and miserable, Christian villages 'thrive and grow, while Moslem ones fall into decay', seeing this as evidence of the superiority of Christianity over Islam, although he does concede that part of it may have been because of the foreign support and protection that Christian villages received.

While the travellers felt pity for the ignorance of the local Christians, they were more scathing about that of the monks, particularly those who guarded the holy places. Edward Clarke complained that 'devout but weak men' who come on their pilgrimage are either taken in by the superstitious exhibitions and embellishments, or when they see through it, end up being overwhelmed by scepticism and at risk of losing their faith altogether. While European Christians send missionaries to bring the gospel to the remotest places, 'the very land whence that gospel originated is suffered to remain as a nursery of superstition for surrounding nations'. The whole thing started with Helena, mother of Constantine, who – with the best intentions no doubt – covered every sacred spot with a church. 'Had the sea of Tiberias been capable of annihilation by her means, it would have been desiccated, paved, covered with churches and altars, or converted into monasteries and markets of indulgences, until no feature of the original remained, and this by way of rendering it more particularly holy' (Clarke 1814: 265).

Where Islamic and Old Testament traditions touched, such as in the patriarchal narratives, or some of the Exodus stories, the Jewish traditions were invariably adhered to, and the Islamic traditions dismissed, as in the traditions around Nebi Musa, the Muslim burial place of Moses west of the Jordan.

## MISSIONARIES

A special category of travellers were the missionaries. While many travellers were convinced that Islam was the curse of the region, some went with the special mission of converting the population to Christianity. An English couple, William and Jane Lethaby, with the typical predilection of many missionaries for inaccessible, dangerous and remote regions, started a mission in Kerak, which was ruled by the infamous Majali family (Durley 1910). After a few years they were joined by Archibald Forder and his wife (Figure 3.5). When the independent mission was taken over by the Church of England, Forder decided to leave, and ventured into the Arabian desert to preach the gospel to the Bedouin. He had Bibles printed to look like Qur'ans, which he distributed, risking his own life on numerous occasions for the sacred cause, and he describes his adventures with gusto. But many travellers also indulged in a bit of part-time converting, during conversations with their guides or Arab hosts.

## JERUSALEM AND THE FOOTSTEPS OF JESUS

Jerusalem was the highlight of almost every traveller's journey in the Holy Land. It was the centre of the Christian world, the place where Christianity had its roots in the footsteps of Jesus. Never mind that it was just a rather cramped and dirty little town, with narrow streets and the distinctive oriental traits of poverty, loud noises and strong smells, it was Jerusalem, it was God's own city, and it was the place where devout Jews and Christians expected the (second) coming of the Messiah.

The first reaction of travellers when seeing Jerusalem depended, at least somewhat, on the direction from which they came (Figure 3.6). The best view of the town was from the direction of Nablus. Edward Clarke and his companions, upon approaching the town from that direction, were so overwhelmed by their first sighting of the Holy City that they did not only take off their hats, but also their shoes.

> we had not been prepared for the grandeur of the spectacle which the city alone exhibited. Instead of a wretched and ruined town, by some described as the desolated remnant of Jerusalem, we beheld, as it were, a flourishing and stately metropolis; presenting a magnificent assemblage of domes, towers, palaces, churches, and monasteries; all of which, glittering in the sun's rays, shone with inconceivable splendour.
>
> —Clarke 1814: 320

Others, who came from the direction of Jaffa, were less impressed: 'the appearance of this celebrated city, independently of the feelings and recollections which the approach to it cannot fail to awaken, was greatly inferior to my expectations, and had certainly nothing of grandeur or beauty, of stateliness or magnificence, about it' (Buckingham 1821: 174–5).

The impression it made on the mind of the visitor was obviously influenced by its significance for his or her faith. De Saulcy's reaction is telling:

> The streets are narrow, filthy and loathsome, as they are in all oriental towns; the vaulted roofs which usually cover them over produce in these narrow passages a dampness and a stench exceedingly disagreeable; and lastly, the pavement is dreadfully out of order, so that people run the risk at every step of breaking their horses' legs or

FIGURE 3.5: Archibald Forder in Arab dress (Forder 1902: title page).

FIGURE 3.6: Jerusalem from the south-east (Sepp 1863: 82).

their own necks. So much for the physical impression. As to the moral effect, that is quite a different affair: we are in Jerusalem. Everything is comprised in that word.

—de Saulcy 1854 I: 118

Their awe for the holiness of the city did not extend towards its inhabitants. Volney (1788 II: 304) claimed that the inhabitants of Jerusalem had the reputation of being the vilest people in Syria, worse than those of Damascus. The Jews were the most miserable and poor, and evoked pity in most of the travellers. Muslims and the various local Christian sects were a subject of scorn. The degrading squabbles over control of the Church of the Holy Sepulchre by the various Christian groups, and the ritual of the lighting of the Holy Fire at Easter, were in for particular derision. Seetzen calls it a carnival, Maundrell a bacchanal.

Once they had overcome their culture shock at finding the city cramped and overcrowded with Muslims, Jews, monks and pilgrims, who all considered it their own Holy City, they would start looking for the Footsteps of Jesus, Bible in hand. Once again, reactions differed greatly, from being moved to tears by the awareness of being in the presence of the Saviour, to indignation at the way most of the holy places had been decorated and adorned with chapels and churches, and generally so cut up as to be unrecognizable. Nevertheless, for some the architecture of Jerusalem, its narrow, stone-paved and half-covered streets, its walls and small houses, took them back to the time when Jesus and his disciples walked the same streets – or so they imagined. There was room for heated debate: the identification of the holy places with which the town was dotted was discussed, scrutinized and rejected, and alternatives suggested.

The most important one, and the first for many to visit, was the Church of the Holy Sepulchre. Discovered by Empress Helena, the mother of Emperor Constantine, the presumed locations of Golgotha and the Tomb were covered by a church, destroyed and rebuilt several times in the following centuries, the last time in 1808, when a fire caused the dome to collapse. The authenticity of Helena's discovery was rarely doubted until the nineteenth century. The fact that Golgotha was supposed to lie outside the city was explained away by Maundrell in 1703 by stating that the sanctity of the place had 'attracted the city round about it, and stands now in the midst of Jerusalem, a great part of the hill of Sion being shut out of the walls, to make room for the admission of Calvary' (1703: 96).

Other places, however, were met with more scepticism. Maundrell expresses some doubt about the locations of the twelve stages of the cross, all conveniently laid out in the church building itself. Buckingham was shown the house of Uriah, Bathsheba's first husband, and her bath, and when he expressed scepticism, quoting a biblical passage to support it, he was told by his guide,

> that he considered the authority of the friars, who had lived here many years, to be of greater weight than any Scriptures, and that if I began to start doubt of this nature in the beginning of our visit to the holy places, there would be an end to all pleasure in the excursion. I therefore bowed assent, and remained silent.
>
> —Buckingham 1821: 186

Scepticism about the Holy Sepulchre itself also began to creep in during the nineteenth century. Early in the century both Chateaubriand and Clarke expressed their doubt, citing lack of evidence. Clarke is rather scathing about the 'evidence' that he is shown (Clarke 1814: 329–33). Edward Robinson sums up the various arguments, and while he has serious doubts about the location, he concedes that the real location of the tomb and Golgotha would probably always remain a mystery (Robinson and Smith 1860 I: 407–18); one bold suggestion was that the Holy Sepulchre itself was under the Dome of the Rock, which was built by Constantine (Fergusson 1847: 76). Oliphant, on the other hand, suggested that the Church of the Holy Sepulchre covered the tombs of the Kings of Israel (Oliphant 1887: 306).

Archaeology was also beginning to play a more important role in the identification of the holy places of Jerusalem. Already in 1817 Charles Irby (1789–1845) and James Mangles (1786–1867) were conducting secret excavations in the tombs of the Kings outside the city walls, and managed to blow a hole in one of the tombs before they were discovered. De Saulcy also conducted excavations in the tombs, and appropriated a sarcophagus for the Louvre. De Saulcy's archaeological researches relied heavily on the dating of architectural styles. Assuming erroneously that the Western Wall was part of the original temple of Solomon, he declared that this wall was so perfectly built that it could not have been Greek or Roman, it had to be original Solomonic architecture (de Saulcy 1854 II: 100). As a consequence, he 'recognized' remains of Solomonic architecture in many other places in the town.[5]

The first 'real' excavations in the town were conducted in 1867 by Charles Warren, on behalf of the Palestine Exploration Fund. The water shaft that he discovered, so-called Warren's shaft, was immediately identified as part of the tunnel system through which Joab, David's general, secretly entered the city on the eve of its conquest by David. He reported regularly in the Palestine Exploration Fund's Quarterly Statements, both on his excavations, and on a number of other subjects of archaeological or topographical interest, but always with the pen in one hand, and the Bible in the other.

---

[5] To do de Saulcy justice, though, it must be said that he was the first to suggest that Tell es-Sultan in the Jordan Valley was ancient Jericho (de Saulcy 1854 II: 41).

## CONCLUSION

The nineteenth century in Western Europe and the United States was an age of enlightenment, of great scientific discoveries and new ways of thinking about the world, life and humanity. It was an age of optimism and progress, in which the West saw itself as the guardians of civilization. This self-confidence, the sense of moral and cultural superiority, shines through in the travel books of the period. Travellers and explorers saw themselves as missionaries, representing the light of Western culture and civilization. This self-confidence emanates from the accounts of their journeys of discovery in the Holy Land, the cradle of Christianity, of their own Western morals and values. They express awe and even humility at walking on holy ground, at being in the presence of the origins of their faith, and of all the holy places mentioned in their Bible, but by doing so they claim, as it were, spiritual ownership of it. It is what Edward Said (1935–2003) condemns as nineteenth-century appropriation, a form of cultural colonialism. There was, additionally, a more politically motivated angle, which was the conviction that the Turkish empire was a disastrous influence on the region, and that only a Western government would save it for Christianity. The expected crumbling of the Ottoman Empire left a gap that should rightfully be filled by an enlightened, Western government, that could protect Christian and Jewish holy places and the Jewish population. The influx of Jewish immigrants in the second half of the century was seen as a major incentive to bring that about.

But these travel accounts display another aspect of the age of discovery. Many accepted truths from the biblical narrative, the pillars of Christianity, were thrown into doubt or simply crushed under the weight of scientific evidence. To retain their faith, explorers had to reconcile these discoveries with their beliefs. They looked for natural and scientific explanations for miracles, and evidence 'on the ground' of the biblical narrative; to claim their Bible as a proper history book. They needed to see for themselves, to find a way to accept both as truth, and live in both worlds at the same time: that of the age of discovery and that of their beliefs.

## REFERENCES

Bartlett, W.H. (1854), *Forty Days in the Desert, on the Track of the Israelites; or, A Journey from Cairo to Mount Sinai and Petra*, London: Bell and Daldy.

Blunt, A. (1881), *A Pilgrimage to Nejd, the Cradle of the Arab Race: Visit to the Court of the Arab Emir, and 'Our Persian Campaign'*, 2 vols, 2nd edn, London: John Murray.

Buckingham, J.S. (1821), *Travels in Palestine Through the Countries of Bashan and Gilead East of the River Jordan*, London: Longman, Rees, Hurst, Orme and Brown.

Buckingham, J.S. (1825), *Travels Among the Arab Tribes Inhabiting the Countries East of Syria and Palestine*, London: Longman, Rees, Hurst, Orme, Brown and Green.

Burckhardt, J.L. (1830), *Notes on the Bedouins and Wahábys, Collected During His Travels in the East*, London: Colburn and Bentley.

Burton, R.F. (1855), *Personal Narrative of a Pilgrimage to al-Medinah and Meccah*, Leipzig: Bernhard Tauchnitz.

Burton, R.F. (1898), *The Jew, the Gypsy and el Islam*, Chicago: Herbert S. Stone.

Clarke, E.D. (1814), *Travels in Various Countries of Europe, Asia and Africa: Greece, Egypt and the Holy Land, Section I*, 4th edn, New York: D. Huntington.

Conder, C.R. (1879), *Tent Work in Palestine: A Record of Discovery and Adventure, Volume 2*, London: Richard Bentley and Son.

Dixon, W.H. (1865), *The Holy Land*, Leipzig: Bernhard Tauchnitz.
Doughty, C.M. (1921 [1888]), *Travels in Arabia Deserta*, New York: Boni and Liveright.
Durley, T. (1910), *Lethaby of Moab*, London: Marshall Brothers.
Fergusson, J. (1847), *An Essay on the Ancient Topography of Jerusalem*, London: John Weale.
Finn, J. (1878), *Stirring Times, or Records from Jerusalem Consular Chronicles of 1853 to 1856*, London: C. Kegan Paul.
Forder, A. (1902), *With the Arabs in Tent and Town*, London: Marshall Brothers.
Frazer, J.G. (1890), *The Golden Bough: A Study in Comparative Religion*, 2 vols, London: Macmillan.
Grove, G. (1869), 'From the Original Prospectus', *PEFQS*, 1 (1): 1–2.
Hansen, T. (1964), *Arabia Felix: The Danish Expedition of 1761–1767*, London: Collins.
Henniker, F. (1823), *Notes During a Visit to Egypt, Nubia, the Oasis, Mount Sinai, and Jerusalem*, London: John Murray.
Irby, C.L. and J. Mangles (1845), *Travels in Egypt and Nubia, Syria, and the Holy Land, Including a Journey Round the Dead Sea, and Through the Country East of the Jordan*, London: John Murray.
Lepsius, K.R. (1852), *Discoveries in Egypt, Ethiopia, and the Peninsula of Sinai, in the Years 1842–45: During the Mission Sent Out by His Majesty Fredrick William IV. of Prussia*, London: Richard Bentley.
Lynch, W.F. (1850), *Narrative of the United States' Expedition to the River Jordan and the Dead Sea*, Philadelphia, PA: Lea and Blanchard.
Martineau, H. (1848), *Eastern Life Past and Present*, Philadelphia, PA: Lea and Blanchard.
Maundrell, H. (1703), *A Journey from Aleppo to Jerusalem at Easter A.D. 1697*, Oxford: Printed at The Theatre.
Oliphant, L. (1887), *Haifa, or Life in Modern Palestine*, Edinburgh: William Blackwood and Sons.
Palmer, E.H. (1871), *The Desert of the Exodus: Journeys on Foot in the Wilderness of the Forty Years' Wanderings*, Cambridge: Deighton, Bell.
Pococke, R. (1743), *A Description of the East, and Some Other Countries*, Vol. II, Pt 1, London: W. Bowyer.
Porter, J.L. (1858), *A Handbook for Travellers in Syria and Palestine; Including an Account of the Geography, History, Antiquities, and Inhabitants of These Countries, the Peninsula of Sinai, Edom, and the Syrian Desert; with Detailed Descriptions of Jerusalem, Petra, Damascus, and Palmyra*, 2 vols, London: John Murray.
Porter, J.L. (1891), *The Giant Cities of Bashan and Syria's Holy Places*, London: T. Nelson and Sons.
Renan, E. (1863), *Vie de Jesus*, Paris: Nelson.
Robinson, E. and E. Smith (1860), *Biblical Researches in Palestine, and in the Adjacent Regions: A Journal of Travels in the Year 1838*, Boston, MA: Crocker and Brewster.
Saulcy, F. de (1854), *Narrative of a Journey Round the Dead Sea and in the Bible Lands; in 1850 and 1851*, London: Richard Bentley and Son.
Seetzen, U.J. (1854–9), *Reisen durch Syrien, Palaestina, Phoenizien, die Trans-Jordan Länder, Arabia-Petraea und Unter Ägypten*, Berlin: G. Reimer.
Sepp, J.N. (1863), *Jerusalem und das Heilige Land. Pilgerbuch nach Palästina, Syrien und Aegypten*, Schaffhausen: Fr. Hurter.
Smith, G.A. (1894), *The Historical Geography of the Holy Land*, London: Hodder and Stoughton.
Stanley, A.P. (1868), *Sinai and Palestine in Connection with Their History*, new edn, London: John Murray.

Stephens, J.L. (1862 [1838]), *Incidents of Travel in Egypt, Arabia Petraea, and the Holy Land*, New York: Harper and Brothers.

Strauss, D.F. (1846), *The Life of Jesus, Critically Examined*, 3 vols, transl. G. Eliot, London: Chapman Bros.

Thomas Cook and Son (1876), *Cook's Tourists' Handbook for Palestine and Syria*, London: Thomas Cook and Son; Simpkin, Marshall.

Tischendorf, C. von (1847), *Travels in the East*, transl. W.E. Shuckard, London: Longman, Brown, Green and Longmans.

Tristram, H.B. (1865), *The Land of Israel: A Journal of Travels in Palestine*, London: Clay, Son and Taylor.

Tromans, N. (2008), 'The Holy City', in N. Tromans (ed.), *The Lure of the East: British Orientalist Painting*, 162–97, London: Tate Publishing.

Trumbull, H.C. (1884), *Kadesh Barnea: Its Importance and Probable Site*, New York: Scribner.

van de Velde, C.W.M. (1854), *Narrative of a Journey Through Syria and Palestine in 1851 and 1852*, 2 vols, Edinburgh: William Blackwood and Sons.

Volney, C.-F. (1788), *Travels in Syria and Egypt During the Years 1783, 1784 & 1785*, translated from the French, Perth: R. Morison.

Wellhausen, J. (1883), *Prolegomena zur Geschichte Israels*, Berlin: G. Reimer.

Wilson, C.W. (1869), 'On the Site of Ai and the Position of the Altar Which Abram Built Between Bethel and Ai', *PEFQS*, 1 (4): 123–6.

CHAPTER FOUR

# Phantoms, factoids and frontiers

*Social anthropology and the archaeology of Palestine*

DERMOT NESTOR

> Thou met'st with things dying, I with things newborn.
> —William Shakespeare, *A Winter's Tale* (3.3)

Archaeology, we are taught, is the 'study of the human past through the medium of material culture' (Thomas 2004a: 1; Boivin 2004). This statement presents as a rather unproblematic definition; one that ascribes to material culture a defining role as the primary data source of the discipline and thus the focus for the associated practices and principles of the archaeologist. It is equally clear however that the past these material items imply access to is not reconstructed in any straightforward manner. Long gone are appeals to the deceptive simplicity of von Ranke's positivist dictum and with it any understanding that the past is something that exists for the purposes of objective examination. Rather, much of the recent literature that has come to represent our field sits both comfortably and confidently within a broad hermeneutical tradition which acknowledges that the past is that which is mediated through the work of the historian (Collingwood 1946; Carr 1961).

Extending from Dilthey through Gadamer, this revelatory tradition has valorized the dynamic relationship between reader and text, between culturally conditioned preconception or disposition and literary or material artefact, as that matrix within which understanding occurs and meaning is made. While the potency of this 'fusion of horizons' has been much lauded within biblical studies and particularly since it signalled the final demise of any conception of the text as a solitary and somehow quarantined object, it is Gadamer's concept of *Wirkungsgeschichte* (Gadamer 1960) that has furnished biblical studies with the theoretical rigour its traditional practices have long assumed and, a little less intentionally, had long sought. Translated variously as the 'history of effects' or 'effective history' *Wirkungsgeschichte* seeks to articulate something of that reciprocal and mutually reinforcing relationship between what we term *tradition* and the act of *reception*. Herein, subtle forms of agency are accorded both to the interpreter who, in an engagement with a particular text, contributes to that text's tradition of hearing and heeding, and to the text itself whose tradition of interpretation exerts an influence upon the interpreter's reception and understanding. Within this relational framework, interpretation, and thus the act of historical reconstruction, presents less as an act of objectification than one of participation. Despite the obvious appeal and indeed the significant impact of this thesis, the creative tension it introduces between a text that demands to be interpreted and its interpreter whose expectations exceed the horizon of any previous audience, the approach would appear to suffer from two related and potentially debilitating limitations. First of all, the interpreting agent within the equation often seems to operate in the absence of any informed questioning or critique of the motivations, presuppositions or dispositions that inform their interpretation (Habermas 1972). Less generous commentators would suggest that there are certain interpretations that deliberately disguise the significance, even the existence, of such influences. The sceptre of unreflective and/or unchallenged modes of historical reconstruction points to the second limitation; that of *horizon*. While the etymology of this term would seemingly prescribe the limit of any individual's knowledge, experience or interest, the much-vaunted *fusion of horizons* does little to relax such constraints. On the contrary, and within the particular schemas popularized within biblical studies, participation within and/or a contribution to the interpretive tradition of any text often amounts to little more than the sterile reproduction of it. There seems to be limited scope to question or to reject the interpretive paradigms that have already established themselves and which exert their independent logic and their force. Interpretive novelty is often regulated, and any future reading seemingly already prescribed (Bourdieu 1977; Nestor 2010; Pfoh 2010).

Such observations thus acknowledge and equally affirm the important historiographic principle that the past is inevitably presented using categories and paradigms drawn from the present. In the process, they also function to problematize the quality and character of any past which the archaeologist might claim to reconstruct. As a result, one is forced to sound a cautionary note as to the status of the primary data source which that discipline has traditionally appealed to and utilized, *material culture*. For despite its seemingly fundamental role, widespread use and general acceptance, such ubiquity does not reflect a similarly universal understanding; whether of its meaning and/or significance. Rather material culture and indeed the 'archaeological record' (Patrik 1985) of whichever past it is deemed to constitute has meant different things, to different people, at different times and for different reasons. Such alterity is not an outcome of the kind of free-ranging eclecticism once derided by Marvin Harris (Harris 1979: 290) but is, at one level, a function of archaeology's distinctive and venerable relationship with the discipline of anthropology: a relationship perhaps personified by Willey and Phillip's statement that 'American archaeology is anthropology or it is nothing' (Willey and Phillips 1958; Gosden 1999; cf. Clarke 1968: 13). Where such pronounced affinity may present to some as intellectually indolent and would certainly translate as irresponsible within the context of contemporary university politics, what Willey and Phillips were signalling was not some form of capitulation or forfeit. On the contrary, they were openly acknowledging the fact that archaeology is very much part of a wider disciplinary effort that encompasses the study of all aspects of human life, past and present. That disciplinary effort is what we call social or cultural anthropology and the ideas and concepts which it has developed in an effort to understand human life have long influenced the efforts of archaeologists to recover and record past specimens of and patterns in that life.

Such mutually reinforcing effort is not in and of itself problematic. It has proven entirely possible and is indeed wholly permissible to draw insight and inspiration from one discipline in an attempt to provide clarity and intelligibility to any particular phenomenon that is relevant to another; whether it be myth, magic or religion, cult and sacrifice, totems and taboos, forms of social and political organization or, as a means of addressing questions of culture, or identity. Indeed, the divergence and disagreement that has often emerged in the appeal to or application of any particular anthropological concept or category has furnished biblical studies with an energizing and innovative dynamic that has fostered an increased sensitivity towards, appreciation for, and encouragement of difference. What reveals itself as problematic then is not in the first instance the act of application but rather the often-unacknowledged historicity and contextual evolution of the very anthropological frameworks and categories that biblical archaeologists have appealed to and *then* applied in pursuit of their own specific endeavours. These problems are certainly less obvious given they rarely impact what one might deem ordinary archaeological practice and, in many ways, are undetectable in the day-to-day efforts of archaeological field work. Such clandestine status however stands in inverse proportion to pervasiveness for as David Clarke long ago recognized, '*every* archaeologist has thoughtfully or unthinkingly chosen to use concepts of a certain kind' (Clarke 1973: 12) and these frequently constitute the paradigms within which they think and work. To that end, the focus of this chapter necessarily becomes one of conceptual affiliation long before it is one of methodological application and to address it, one is required to foreground an element of the biblical scholar's reconstructive endeavours that have been virtually invisible in their own work and liminal at best in assessments of it: epistemology.

Isolating, extricating or even identifying such conceptual entanglement and/or dependency is no easy task (Van Seters 2006; Nestor 2010). Indeed, in some respects it is a task that has been resisted, or at best frowned upon, by those for whom the unquestioned embrace of anthropological concepts and their eager conflation with archaeological data has functioned to reinforce an image of humanity derived from the biblical narratives, or to buttress a 'hermeneutic of respect' (Volf 2010) that renders historical reconstructions compatible with the 'claims of ecclesial communities, its canon, and its interpretive tradition' (Watson 2006: 120). Such challenges notwithstanding, the resurgence of this 'old morality' (Harvey 1966: 103) and its inherent if not slightly ironic scepticism as to the validity of doubt means that the principal of critical surveillance and with it the epistemological potential of reflexivity established by Troeltsch as the foundational criteria of the historical-critical method (Troeltsch 1913), remain as distant a goal as the very past that theologically or politically oriented reconstructions would seek to reveal. Indeed, the validations of biblical chronology, of biblical religion/s and of biblical peoples we frequently encounter under the guise of an archaeological or an anthropological perspective have done more to impede the project of historical reconstruction then they have to advance it.

## THINKING ABOUT THINGS

Book length treatments of the history and practice of archaeology as it relates to questions of Israelite emergence and/or presence in the land of Israel, while relatively few in number, generally display several common characteristics; principal amongst which is a celebration and veneration of the time-honoured status of archaeological activity in the region (Silberman 1982, 1989; Dever 1985; Moorey 1991; Fritz 1994; Davis 2004). Chronological in orientation and generally descriptive in character, they illustrate a shared concern with the origins of such activity that often presents as a considered, if not deliberate, effort to establish the antiquity, the singularity and, thus, the legitimacy of the endeavour. It is in this context that we read of characters such as the Empress Helena, mother of Emperor Constantine, who reportedly visited Palestine in the year 326 CE and established basilicas, most notably the Holy Sepulchre, at various sites traditionally associated with the life and passion of Christ and which allowed pilgrims to see for themselves the truth of Christianity and to worship at the holy places (Hunt 1982). Such efforts served to transform Palestine into a 'pivot' of the Christian empire and Jerusalem itself into a worldly and cosmopolitan place as opposed to the celestial refuge of the pilgrim's imagination. As sites of pilgrimage, such shrines certainly functioned to support the sojourning pilgrim's physical and spiritual needs; purposefully designed to facilitate large crowds, the sites were frequently portrayed as providing an aid to both the reading and interpretation of scripture. Yet while reactions such as those of St Jerome's disciple Paula who claimed her adoration of Jesus at the site of Golgotha paralleled a direct physical encounter with Him are certainly literalistic, they are not in any sense historical. Indeed, to assume that pilgrims deliberately sought out holy places to add to their knowledge of the scriptures or that the newly forged material evidence functioned to stimulate a belief that specific events described within those pages had actually occurred is at best an anachronism, at worst a deliberate misprision (Hunt 1982: 133). As Wilkinson's early studies have shown (Wilkinson 1977, 1981), the early European pilgrim was *not* motivated by any compelling desire to confirm the reality of biblical events by visualizing them in their hypothesized physical setting. Such authenticity was confirmed not by critical investigation, but by revelation. If that belief had not been a logical priority, the journey would not have gone beyond the proverbial first step.

For the pilgrims who travelled to the Holy Land, then, the majority of whom were from the eastern parts of the empire and aligned with various ascetic forms of Christianity, such sites functioned merely as physical settings within which specific biblical events might be proclaimed. While the prospect of worship in immediate contact with what was presented as holy constituted a powerful incentive for pilgrimage, such piety proved to be a welcome companion to, if not a catalyst for, the power of observation. Indeed, the centuries leading up to and then beyond the Crusades, while a maelstrom of religious, social and political division, proved something of a golden age in the identification of and veneration at sites associated with biblical events, the recording of biblical topography and the establishment of a scientific geography. Notwithstanding the significance of this *pilgrim's impulse*, the antiquarian interests and efforts it stimulated were neither unique nor in any way, historically prior. Aside from those accounts of earlier Jewish pilgrimage (Eliav 2005; Limor, Reiner and Frenkel 2014), general histories of archaeology (Daniel 1976; Piggott 1976; Trigger 1989; Schnapp 1997) have shown that the recovery of ancient sites was a practice already undertaken in the sixth century BCE, Nabonidus' 'excavations' at the temple of Larsa being a particular case in point. That similar accounts and myriad other examples have been documented amongst the classical Greeks, the Romans and even the Chinese might even prompt one to consider whether and to what degree such practices existed amongst preliterate societies (Turner 1973; Stott 2005; Na'aman 2011).

Collectively such accounts provide ample evidence of an awareness amongst various peoples and at various times of material things surviving into the present, an activity that would certainly qualify such activities as *antecedents* of archaeology. However, there is little if any evidence to suggest that such remains were used as material evidence in the construction of systematic knowledge of any past society or of humanity itself. They may well have been *addressing* the archaeological but there is no way in which their pursuits can be quantified or qualified as archaeological practice. Rather as Thomas reminds us, such practice 'could only come into being once a particular series of understandings of humanity, of time and of materiality had developed' (Thomas 2004a: 4).

A significant contribution to such development can be seen to come from Christianity itself and in terms of its specific anthropology, cosmology and teleology which combined to generate fundamental assumptions about the human condition and its relationship to the world in which we live. In this context, we note a fixation upon a liner conception of time, an implicit faith in perpetual progress (pending the Day of Judgement), and a creation story which, though echoing antecedent and contemporaneous ancient Near Eastern myths, posited the inexorable dominion of humans over the earthly realm (Gen. 1.28). Adam may well have been crafted from clay, but the material realm from which he was derived was something he constituted no part of. On the contrary, as someone made in God's image (Gen. 1.26) the material world was something created explicitly for his benefit, and to serve his purposes (White 1967). Successive and by no means always complimentary and/or linear developments in the history of Western philosophy served to underscore the often unacknowledged and/or overstated significance of this interpretive and inherently dualistic framework.

Thus, we encounter the experimental philosophy of Bacon, which sought to show not simply that new knowledge was a possibility but that such knowledge could be gleaned from material sources that stood outside of, and represented, a significant advance on the textual sources favoured by tradition (Shapin 1996; Gaukroger 2001; Russell 2005: 497–501). While Bacon would claim that such new knowledge would serve to magnify the greater glory of God, even if it did not deal directly with an interpretation of His divine plan, the empirical certainties he established regarding the status of objects as legitimate sources of knowledge not only imbued them with a certain objectivity but in the process set that objectivity apart from the subjective and always uncertain workings of the human mind. For where the cognitive processes of the human mind were prone to the errors of tradition and popular misconception (Gaukroger 2001: 106–26), and where sensory experience was considered of limited value pending verification through experimentation, items of material culture began to acquire the qualities of accuracy, veracity and devotion. This separation between mind and matter, or between the mental and the material that is apparent within Baconian empiricism became substantiated within the rationalism of Descartes: albeit from an entirely different perspective.

Christianity had established a cosmology in which the agency of God as first cause and creator gave way to an understanding of that creation as a resource at the disposal of human agency. Within Cartesian philosophy, the role of the divine was further marginalized, as a function of the free will and capacity for reason that God deemed fit to grant. What was for Bacon a deficiency became, for Descartes, a foundational and divinely instilled mental apparatus that consequently could not be doubted. It is in this way that the famed *cogito* established humanity and human reason at the centre of the created world and as the privileged interpreter of reality. Given the priority that is attributed to reason, other explanations for the natural order and the connections between its various elements thus had to give way; particularly that of the Renaissance, which understood the world as structured through resemblances. Over and against this hermeneutic of similarity (Foucault 1970 [1966]: 57) and the illusion it necessarily entailed, Descartes imposed a mechanical philosophy predicated on the assumption that the universe was, in essence, a machine. As a machine, its constituent parts operated not on the basis of intentionality but rather simple and invariant laws (Coley 1991). In establishing those laws, one would come to comprehend the fundamental principles and workings of nature. Because all things could thus be measured, classified and ordered, and where the measure of those things was the God-given and thus infallible project of human reason, the separation between the observing subject and observed object that was implicit in Bacon now became explicit and complete through Descartes.

Thus, while the Cartesian suggestion that mental activity takes place in a realm that is entirely separate from the material world raises a legitimate question as to the quality and nature of perception, that inconvenience is very much diminished through the prominence now attributed to epistemology. Because verifiable knowledge rested upon the subject's self-certainty and free will and because those qualities functioned to understand, translate and order the material world from which they stood apart, the question of *how* that project of understanding was to take place was established as the primary question and principal objective of philosophy. Such privileging of epistemology serves to underscore two other developments that are critical for any understanding of archaeology.

The first builds out from the broad and shared antipathy towards the contaminating and often specific effects of tradition, which prioritizes the drive towards a universal and universalizing logic. Such efforts to banish ambiguity in favour a single, authoritative and, indeed, divinely sanctioned system of knowledge naturally lead to the second; that the accumulation and production of knowledge about the material world is to be understood principally as method. As such, not only was there to be a right and a wrong way to acquire knowledge but, equally, there were criteria by which meaning, and ultimately truth, could be established.

There are certainly distinctions between the systems of thought espoused by Bacon and Descartes and, indeed, those who preceded them and whose work they openly engaged. Equally, there are sufficient and wide-ranging similarities that allow one to diagnose the emergence of something like a zeitgeist that could be seen as defining of the modern period, especially as it relates to archaeological theory and practice (Toulmin 1990; Thomas 2004a). Principal amongst these is a belief in the gradual expansion of knowledge, along with the desire to establish new foundations for that knowledge. Because that knowledge rested principally upon the application of reason, society could thus be changed by an act of will, a change that would not simply constitute alternative forms of society but more profoundly, better ones. Thus, while Foucault is certainly correct in his depiction of that tendency in European philosophical thought to aggregate around principles of order (Foucault 1970 [1966]), the equally forceful and attractive ideal was to extend those principles and measurements to a universal plane and to see them as governing all aspects of the material world. This conviction that order could be imposed upon the dizzying array of constituent elements of the natural world and through the application of human reason was extended in new ways by both Locke and Hobbes in their respective study of society and social systems. Though it was to introduce a tension between the individual and the social which was to be addressed in later developments, the political philosophy of Hobbes as articulated in *Leviathan* (Hobbes 1996 [1651]) assumes the necessary and essential status of the individual as existing *prior* to any involvement in systems of social relations. From this first principle, which radically extends the Platonic insistence on a mathematical conception of the world, Hobbes reaffirmed the Cartesian primacy of reason and, thus, the reasoned human. If the application of human reason was the critical faculty necessary to impose order upon the natural world, then a similar application by such reasoned humans should affirm that same quality in the social order. This does not mean that *Leviathan* translates as diagnostic for some particular variant of a social utopia predicated upon the actions and activities of reasoned and reasoning human agents. However, the fact that it positions just such a social order at the apex of all possibilities does mean that what currently exists can be designed for the better. Clearly an attractive concept during the period of civil war in which it was written, the possibility of future enhancement necessarily carried with it the equally plausible possibility of a more problematic alternative. It is this possibility that gives an insight into Hobbes's more profound understanding of the human condition and its development. For while reason and its application had the potential to transform social relations into civil and legitimate types, such civility and order was an outcome of reason's application; it was not and is not the natural condition. The natural condition was just that, 'the state of nature', an anarchic period in which 'natural inequalities between humans are not so great as to give anyone clear superiority; and thus all must live in constant fear of loss and violence' (Hobbes 1996 [1651]: 88). Lacking that common or central power that is the mark of a civil society which functions to impose restraint upon itself, 'everyone has a natural right to do anything one thinks necessary for preserving one's own life and life is solitary, nasty, brutish and short' (ibid.: 89). While it is certainly a leap to state that Hobbes considered human nature to be intrinsically evil (cf. Thomas 2004b: 23) since in the 'state of nature' *nothing* can be considered just or unjust, it is a perfectly valid deduction to state that for Hobbes this state of nature had a rather violent historical as well as conceptual priority.

Within the context of that appetite for and tendency towards systems of knowledge that were universal in their applicability, it would be a short step from Hobbes's treatise on ideal political forms to a historical narrative of social and technical evolution predicated on the application of reason. Indeed, it would prove to be an even shorter step to move from this hypothesis to a complementary narrative that affirmed there was a single universal condition, and a corresponding type of society to which all human beings should aspire. Inverting the more traditional trajectory of moral, social and cultural development suggested by the biblical narrative, such an arrangement would proclaim a sequential account of human liberation from the restraints of nature and the superstition of tradition – one predicted on the application of human reason and the imposition of order. While such abstract knowledge was constructed in isolation from material things, it was just such an epistemology that was to furnish material things with their meaning. In a brand of circular logic all too familiar to the biblical scholar, the meaning assigned to material things would then serve to ground and thus validate the theoretical abstraction that reason had erected. If material remains are thus to be counted as 'evidence' for anything, it is in the first place the presence and operation of such an epistemology.

This is a necessarily brief and selective review of certain tenets within the philosophical literature of the early modern period. Though such brevity certainly disguises the extent and scope of the issues at stake, its aim is simply to highlight that which is all too often overlooked. Namely, that the discipline we refer to and practise as archaeology, something surely unrecognizable to the past peoples it purports to recover, was influenced by a lofty constellation of ideological, material and social beliefs: beliefs that were decidedly oriented around notions of progress and development which functioned to forge an estrangement between the past and the present, between the mental and the material and ultimately, between God and humankind.

## THINGS AS IDEAS AND AS ADAPTIVE RESPONSES

'Give me a place to stand,' proclaimed Archimedes, 'and I will move the world' (Smith 1978: 159). Despite Smith's principled postmodern refutation of just such a stance, the conceptual foothold that Archimedes sought is one very familiar to the archaeologist – that of origin. The etymology of the term *archaeology* itself functions to establish its orientation towards the study of that which is old, which is ancient and which is hidden in the depths of the past (Bravo 2010). Indeed, it is a conventional wisdom to consider the linear process of human development to have commenced at some fixed and recognizable point in the distant past and thus for the origin of specific phenomena such as civilization, agriculture and even human groups to constitute a focus of archaeological recovery. While such concerns have been conditioned by some of the very developments noted previously, 'origin' is a fascination that has equally enthralled those who have written on the history of archaeology itself. Where these works are illustrative of a wide variety of causal factors that range from the technological (Crawford 1921, 1922), pedagogical (Schnapp 1997) and historical (Trigger 1989, 1995, 1998), they often reveal as much about the authors' personal interests and philosophical orientations as they do the subject of their study. They also reveal a near-consensus view that the origins of archaeology as a properly *scientific* discipline can be firmly located in the late nineteenth to early twentieth centuries. For while virtually all human groups can be characterized by some level of curiosity in the past, and while that curiosity has manifested itself in a startingly complex variety of forms that range from the oral circulation of mythical charters to the production of extensive narrative histories, it was only in this modern period that the necessary conditions for such a scientific archaeology existed (Thomas 2004a). This was a marked development on the earlier collection and/or veneration of specific material finds and a radical departure from the biblical view of natural, physical and moral degeneration. Rather in this period we witness an increasing realization and confidence that material remains pointed towards and provided evidence of the successive stages of humanity's technological achievements and its development.

Throughout the course of the nineteenth century an increasing amount of archaeological material was being recovered as the vastly expanding activities of the Industrial Revolution transformed Central and Western Europe into the workshop of the world (Trigger 1998: 55–9). In addition to the increasing range and volume of finds that were unearthed, this period also bears witness to the emergence of a new middle class who had the educational capital to appreciate the appeal and attraction of such finds, along with the necessary financial capital to pursue that interest. Perhaps most importantly of all, this period witnessed the emergence of a specific concept that would allow for the classification of those finds in both space and time. That concept was *culture*.

Despite its currency in the discipline of archaeology and its broad socialization within the English language, culture is a term that evidences some significant and varying conceptual difficulties (Kroeber and Kluckhohn 1952). Having an initial association with agricultural and/or horticultural activities, namely humanity's *cultivation* of nature, it soon evolved to encompass nature itself and then the specific social and historical achievements that were to define human achievement over and against that realm. In contrast to traditional religious cosmologies where all things were understood as networked together by 'connotation, sympathy, reflection and metaphor' (Foucault 1970 [1966]: 57) this emerging brand of classificatory logic not only separated reasoning humans from nature but, as a function of the very order that reason had imposed, granted them dominion over it (White 1967). While such an understanding gathered considerable momentum in the late eighteenth century and as a function of the universalizing frameworks promoted by the Enlightenment, it is the effective codification of the concept by anthropologists such as Edward Burnett Tylor and Franz Boas that was to furnish archaeology with the conceptual framework required to establish its scientific credentials.

In a formulation that has exerted vast influence since it was first put forward in his 1871 treatise *Primitive Culture*, Tylor declared that 'culture' was that 'complex whole which includes knowledge, belief, art, morals, law, custom and other capabilities and habits acquired by man as a member of a society' (Tylor 1871: 1). While such a definition could certainly be utilized in the analysis of a plurality of discrete cultural entities, it is clear that Tylor's presentation is, as was customary in his day, both singular and evolutionistic. Indeed, in his widely read textbook of anthropology, this commitment to a general evolutionary perspective is made explicit when he proclaimed:

> On the whole it appears that wherever there are found elaborate arts, abstruse knowledge, complex institutions, these are the results of gradual development from an earlier, simpler, and ruder state of life. No stage of civilization comes into existence spontaneously but grows or is developed out of the stage which came before it. This is the great principle which every scholar must lay hold of if he intends to understand either the world he lives in or the history of the past.
>
> —Tylor 1881: 20

Parsed in this way, Tylor's scheme parallels that of other socio-evolutionists such as John Lubbock who had earlier presented such development in terms of a ladder up which different people had differentially climbed (Lubbock 1870). While his was certainly devoid of the explicit racial undertones of Lubbock's work in that he did not present the relative primitiveness of specific cultures as a measure of their intellectual and hence biological inferiority, Tylor's work, and specifically on religion, did nevertheless set out a standard to which all others should aspire; that standard was, of course, the Victorian society of his own time. Though such positioning certainly functioned to reinforce an already heightened sense of Victorian self-confidence, a growing sense of political and economic insecurity along with the all too visible and wholly negative social and environmental impact of technological progress soon prompted many leading European intellectuals to jettison the thesis of unilinear cultural development along with any associated notion of progress. In its stead they appealed to a more pessimistic view of humans as naturally conservative and resistant to the type and character of change that evolutionary theories expounded. Though such notions echoed the 'transcendental anatomy' as earlier promulgated by John Knox, they did not evidence an explicit commitment to his racism, which held that variations in the external character of individuals were to be read as an expression of underlying and fixed biological types. What they did carry over, however, and in many ways extended, was Knox's emphasis on the distinctive *internal* character of these racial types; namely their morale, their temperament and their ability to construct a way of life. It was these cultural capabilities and respective idiosyncrasies that were embraced by the Romantic Movement.

Within the wider context of that tradition of Western European philosophy, the Romantic Movement constitutes something of an interruption. For while the empiricism of Bacon, the rationalism of Descartes and, indeed, the Enlightenment itself valorize the ideal that progress represented the gradual and universal unfolding of human well-being, the Romantic Movement and specifically that distillation represented by one of its earliest exponents, Johann Gottfried von Herder, marks a crucial shift towards philosophical and cultural relativism. Not gone, but certainly receiving diminished attention, were affirmations of the essential unity of the human species and in its place, the importance, both historically and politically, of *individual* cultures. Where language was understood as the vehicle through which the collective and creative energies of such peoples would come to expression, it was that collective experience, or *Geist*, that constituted his focus. In this vein, true insight into a particular culture was to be gained by reconstructing in one's own imagination the spirit that had animated it (Nestor 2010: 34). For this task Herder, obsessively attracted to questions of origin and the vitality of the primitive, turned towards folklore and poetry; traits that he believed illustrated the inherent originality, purity and thus the vitality of any nation. While the political implications of such equation between language and *Volk* was certainly not lost on his many fervent readers, the emphasis he placed upon a fundamentally idealist explanation of human cultural difference and the concomitant prominence attributed to cultural specifics as opposed to cross-cultural uniformities stimulated a development within the discipline of anthropology that was to have implications that far outstripped any initial impact.

The origins of that impact can be located in a very specific source: a paper read by Franz Boas to the American Association for the Advancement of Science in 1896. In that paper, entitled 'The Limitations of the Comparative Method in Anthropology', Boas argued, and on the basis of his own fieldwork, that the observance of apparently similar phenomena, which constituted the bulwark of the comparative method that anchored the thesis of Tylor, could be the result of such varied historical, environmental and psychological factors that the similarity of their causes could no longer be justified. In essence, Boas's argument was that the comparative method, which in its evolutionary guise sought to arrange the coexisting features of human culture into a temporal sequence of progressive development at whose peak stood Western European civilization, was based on a process of mere inference, one far too insecure to serve as a foundation for the establishment of theoretical principles. 'If anthropology wishes to establish laws governing the growth of culture', Boas claimed, 'it must not confine itself to studying the results of that growth alone, but whenever such is feasible, it must compare the process of growth' (Boas 1896: 906). While Boas never developed such general laws, his exposure of the logical and methodological flaws of evolutionary theory opened the space necessary for a redemption of that which Tylor and others had ignored; the fundamental historicity of cultural phenomena.

Though retaining a limited and somewhat liberal belief in the progress of that broader construct understood as *civilization*, Boas's thesis effectively undermined the more restrictive application of such assumptions. Over and against the single standard of evaluation that was employed by the evolutionists, Boas instead affirmed its relativity through a focus upon that traditional body of habitual behaviour that would define *each* culture. Authority, tradition and habit, the contaminating idols of Baconian empiricism, and which inhibited the acquisition of culture, were here equated with culture itself. While Boas's writings betray neither effort nor evidence of any definition of 'culture' such as is oft ascribed to Tylor, the fundamentally relativist premise that underscored his method transformed that term into a tool quite different from what it had previously been. For in changing the relation of culture from humanity's evolutionary development to the 'burden of tradition', Boas had transformed the anthropological concept itself. What had once been singular in connotation was now plural. What had once been assumed to reflect a universal process was now representative of historically conditioned and distinct cultural wholes. What once represented humanity as a general idea was now equated with the ideas of distinct peoples; peoples who, in the politically reactionary years of post-Napoleonic Germany, had quickly become the focus of archaeological enquiry.

Though he was certainly not the first person who sought to ascribe archaeological finds to specific and named past peoples, today it is the name of Gustav Kossinna who is inseparably associated with such practice. His distinctive motto, *away from Rome and away from anthropology and ethnography* certainly gives the impression that his was a singularly *archaeological* pursuit devoid of any dependency on or relation to ancillary disciplines. To accept such a claim, however, is to patently ignore the evidence. For in seeking to establish the Germanic provenance of specific material remains, for the purpose of which he developed his settlement archaeology, Kossinna's ambition was very much dependent upon a concept of culture that was derived from outside the discipline he claimed to prioritize. Though his fervent nationalism would have blinded him to this fact and would certainly have precluded him from stating it openly, a review of the core principles that define that method reveals otherwise: 'Sharply bounded archaeological provinces coincide with certain peoples or tribes throughout the ages' (Kossinna 1911: 3; author's translation).

In this definition, and its expanded version of 1926, the unacknowledged intellectual inheritance of Boas is unmistakable (cf. Kossinna 1926). Culture is a univariate and mentalistic phenomenon whose form and dynamics are reducible to a single component: ideas. Where particular constellations of such ideas, collectively held and transmitted across generations, was taken to be representative of particular and distinctive *cultures*, it was a logical inference that the archaeological record be treated as a material objectification of the unique mental template of its maker. Material remains were thus to be considered the products of internalized traditions; ways of thinking, and doing, that were passed down from generation to generation largely unchanged. What change did occur, whether in the form of artefact style or substance, would necessarily have to be explained as resulting from contact with similarly discrete, bounded entities or, as Kossinna amongst others was inclined to argue, the actual replacement of entire populations (Nestor 2010: 50–9). Within such a substantialist ontology, a direct equation between pots and people seemed wholly appropriate – more so when one considers the type of patriotic antiquarianism from which it was borne and the rising tide of nationalist sentiment it promoted. Such an equation was not, however, so inevitable. For all of its seeming rigour and its pretensions to a specifically archaeological methodology, Kossinna's settlement archaeology was dependent upon sources of evidence that stood very much outside the material domain of archaeological enquiry.

As the earlier work of Oscar Montelius illustrates, efforts to infer the nature of prehistoric societies tended to run up against a significant challenge. Material remains may well have been understood as the objectified product of the specific norms and regulative ideals constituting the unique cultural traditions of specific peoples, but this assumption was unverifiable through independent appeal to the archaeological data. Material remains were quite simply mute as to the specific question of the peoples who made them. This was a problem formalized over a century later by the first Professor in European Archaeology at Oxford University, Christopher Hawkes. Concerned with the divergences in method and modes of interpretation in what he termed 'text free archaeology' (the archaeology of periods for which no written records remain) and 'text-aided archaeology' (the archaeology of periods for which textual records do remain) Hawkes developed his now famous

'Ladder of Inference' (Hawkes 1954). Here Hawkes argued that there were several degrees of difficulty in interpreting archaeological data and which he arranged in terms of simplicity from production techniques at the bottom to religious institutions and the spiritual life at the very top. While similar limitations on archaeological inference can be read in the works of V.G. Childe (1956: 129–31) and Colin Renfrew (1985), it was one of Hawkes's singular contributions to archaeological method and theory to affirm that without some point of reference within the historical order which would reveal the specifically human and intentional mode of social life then the superstructure of past societies would forever elude archaeological enquiry (Hawkes 1954: 160). For Kossinna then, and all others who sought to infer the ideational character and quality of specific peoples with reference to specific material finds, a further standard of evidence was required: literary texts. This was the essence of the 'retrospective method' established by Montelius and which utilized the ethnic or ideational conditions of the historically documented past to infer the situation in prehistory. For Kossinna, that historically documented past was best represented by three sources that were widely considered as offering an authoritative insight into German prehistory: *The Edde, The Nibelungenlied* and Tacitus' *Germania*. Patently ignoring any source criticism of this latter work, Kossinna focused instead on the author's description of the German people as a pure-blooded people who possessed fierce blue eyes, red hair and a tall frame (Wiwjorra 1996: 169), not simply as proof of the existence of this prehistoric German type but one whose physical and hence biological conditioning was matched by a similar intellectual superiority. Here a further appeal to anthropology is evident, for in arguing that it was this slim, tall, intellectually brilliant race who gave the decisive push to the course of history by migrating from their original homeland in the north of Europe and imposing civilization upon the societies of the ancient Near East and Greece, Kossinna was drawing upon the distinction between *Kulturvölker* and *Naturvölker* which was popularized in the writings of Gustav Klemm, a scholar often credited as providing inspiration for Tylor's seminal work.

Roughly translated as proffering a description of and distinction between *culturally creative* and *culturally passive peoples* this was, for Kossinna, a distinction between Germans and all other peoples. While such an association can perhaps be read as a rather languid manipulation of the deeper intellectual inheritance of Herder, it can quite legitimately be read as a very deliberate and conscious attempt to boost nationalist sentiment. More forcefully, it translates as a concerted and intentional endorsement of Germany's innate cultural and military superiority. Kossinna of course, did not lack critics, a fact due in no small part to the provocative and polemical style of his work. Equally, he had his supporters; particularly those who viewed his advocacy of the *Kulturkreis* theory as a means of securing support for the academic study of German prehistory. Kossinna also had what can rather loosely be termed his clients; those who utilized the culture-historical paradigm he developed and who were often oblivious to its intellectual origins and sometimes ignorant of the political ends to which he had placed it in service. Though it has sometimes proven unpopular to say so, some of the most committed and often quite eager consumption of the Kossinna Method is evidenced amongst those who engaged in the project of archaeological recovery in the land of Israel. In this tradition of enquiry, one name stands out and whose work serves as something of a paragon against which the calculated errors, considered misjudgements and expedient neglect of others can be assessed: William Foxwell Albright.

Standing in a long tradition of excavation and scholarly enquiry that is often presented as stretching back to the antiquarian appetites of early pilgrims, the specifics of Albright's efforts to conjure up the feet of clay that might anchor the biblical claims of Israelite history and religion have been sufficiently well documented elsewhere to avoid repetition here (Long 1997; Nestor 2010). That the particular brand of culture-historical methodology he appealed to, whether knowingly or otherwise, has resurfaced over and over again and rather unsurprisingly, with similar results, does raise questions as to the effectiveness of the many critiques levelled against his original project. The peculiar brand of scriptural fundamentalism indulged in by Albright and his contemporaries is certainly a distant memory, even amongst those who remain devoted to the theological interpretation of the Bible as Scripture (Seitz 1998; Hays 2010; Volf 2010). The ripple effects of the Maximalist–Minimalist debate have also helped foreground questions as to the historical veracity of biblical sources and in the process stimulated a near-paranoid emphasis on evidence evaluation and methodological justification. That debate has equally sensitized scholars to the epistemological and pedagogical benefit of diversity and the inherent value of interdisciplinary agendas; whether that diversity is to be read as inherent to Israel (Stavrakopoulou and Barton 2010a) or whether it is to be applied to an analysis of the wider social, political and cultural milieu of which it was necessarily a part (Coote and Whitelam 1987). With some notable exceptions, what the debate and subsequent scholarship have not sufficiently addressed with the vigour and clarity required to register critical mass, was an appraisal of the very entity which the biblical text spoke of: Israel. Certainly, there were questions, often deemed confrontational, as to the nature and character of what it was scholars sought (Davies 1992) and analogous queries as to propriety over, and thus legitimate consumption of, the biblical text (Dever 2001). While the impulse generated by such questions has proved far-reaching, it has not stimulated an equally rigorous interrogation as to *why* an entity understood as Israel remains an object of study at all.

In part that question has been addressed in terms of biblical scholarship's seemingly *a priori* commitment to the substantialist ontology of Israel as a bounded ethnic, tribal or national entity (Nestor 2010; Crouch 2014). As a function of the degree to which that unyielding variant of psychological essentialism corroborates a heavily socialized disposition to the broader Christian tradition, biblical scholars all too frequently embrace the naturalizing categories of their informants as a frame for their own analysis. When the best books you read are those you already know (Orwell 2000: 229), it is all too easy to slip from being analysts of naturalizers to being analytic naturalizers (Brubaker 2004). Thus, whenever the object of study is set out as a specific named people, to be defined by a specific repertoire of material culture items which are collectively held to represent a specific and distinctive mental template, one most commonly expressed in terms of religion, then it will always be some version of the historical idealism promoted by Herder and Boas along with the culture-historical paradigm erected by Kossinna that will remain to the fore (Oestigaard 2007).

If the dominance of the culture-historical paradigm was to be overcome, then constructive alternatives for, as opposed to probing critiques of, it would have to sought. One such alternative was supplied by the materialist and neo-evolutionary frameworks of Julian Steward (1953) and particularly Leslie A. White (1943, 1959). As much as he was a pivotal figure in the development of American anthropological theory, Leslie A. White was a controversial one. As the proponent of an evolutionary materialism that focused attention on systems of production which harnessed ever more powerful forms of energy, White's effective affirmation of nineteenth-century cultural evolutionism placed him in direct opposition to the historical particularist orthodoxy that was the legacy of Boas. In what has been presented as one of the most courageous intellectual stands ever taken by an anthropologist, White voiced his commitment to, and the plausibility of, an eco-systemic definition of culture as the extrasomatic means of adaptation for the human organism (White 1949). Herein culture is defined as a materials-based organization of behaviour, not a univariate mental phenomenon whose form and dynamics are explicable by reduction to a single component.

The analytical consequences of this reconceptualization of culture as an adaptive mechanism were made clear in the crusading work of Lewis Binford. In a series of fighting articles that appeared through the 1960s (Binford 1962, 1965, 1968), Binford illustrated, on the basis of extensive fieldwork amongst the Nanamuit of Alaska, that there were behavioural, thus material and hence archaeological correlates of the various responses to changes in the natural environment. Where continuity and change had previously been interpreted as a consequence of the internal dynamics of cultural transmission within and between distinct cultural traditions they were now to be read as the outcome of recurring and activity-sensitive adaptive response undertaken by a single tradition. In fact, following White's formulation of the systemic model of culture Binford would argue that any similarity and/or difference in the formal traits characterizing distinct assemblages of material remains can no longer be considered a measure of the degree to which individuals or populations shared the same 'culture' or genealogical affinity. Archaeological cultures then, those collections of homogeneously shared and hence diagnostically equivalent traits are effectively removed from the equation. Gone with it was Flannery's mythical 'Indian behind the artifact' (Flannery 1967: 120). From now on, the focus of concern would be the system behind both Indian and artefact, the *only* cultural subject which, according to Binford, was archaeologically knowable.

Binford's challenge to empiricist, culture-historical assumptions about the nature of the past had obvious pragmatic appeal within biblical studies and specifically for those who saw it as providing a means of escaping the famed *tyranny of the text*. Indeed, in large part it was Binford's New Archaeology, along with the eco-systemic understanding of culture advocated by Leslie White, that provided the theoretical foundation for the many attempts that sought to emphasize the explanatory potential of large-scale and long-term cultural dynamics; those shifts and strains vital for understanding social change. As much as these provided a corrective to the unspoken and more often than not unconscious assumption that Israel was somehow impervious to the organizing principles of social evolution, efforts to establish the conditions and the circumstances within, rather than against, which Israel may have emerged were compromised by the very conceptual tools selected for the task. At one level, and within the context of that covering-law model of explanation and conformation embraced by Binford and his disciples (Hempel 1942), all explanation should be causal in nature. As such, material culture could *only* be read in a narrow and wholly functionalist manner. Every object would have its designated and specific function in terms of harmonizing systemic needs with the realities of the physical and cultural environment. What was once presented as distinctive evidence of the authentic *Geist* of a people were now simply tools for survival. In order to locate a distinctive Israelite entity within what was an otherwise largely anonymous morass of adaptive systemic responses then, biblical scholars would be forced to retreat from their proclaimed revolution and fall again upon that inferential crutch provided by the biblical narrative. Rather than signalling the departure of biblical archaeology from all previous forms of practice and orientating commitments, the application of the New Archaeology merely reflects a desire to work more efficiently and convincingly within the traditional metaphysic: one defined by the concept of culture inherited from the Romantic and ultimately nationalist context of nineteenth-century Europe.

## THINGS AS SYMBOLS

Expanding the study of the archaeological record beyond the mere subsistence levels of enquiry mandated by Hawkes's Ladder has been perhaps the single, unifying standard around which the various practitioners of what has been labelled *post-processual archaeology* can be seen to have rallied. Though such a label would appear to imply a coherent approach, even a unified body of theory or method, post-processual archaeology is better characterized as an amorphous beast, a true child of Lyotard's postmodern condition and which functions as a convenient placeholder for every reactive trend to emerge within the discipline since the 1970s (Hodder 1982, 1985, 1986). Yet while the attachment of the epithet 'post' might incline one to consign the claims of this development to a status merely relative to those that preceded them, those same reactions signal an important stage in the developing trajectory of the discipline of archaeology, one that biblical studies has eagerly sought to embrace.

Principal amongst such post-processual reactions is that which critiqued the excessive and often reductive materialism of its predecessor and which dismissed all ideas as either functionally irrelevant or tended to explain them as a form of clandestine economic rationality. In its place, post-processualism sought to restore the theoretical significance of ideas and within the context of a dialectical relationship between people and things. Material items, it argued, are not simply tools for survival, nor are they passive reflections of the unique mental templates of their makers. Rather, they are important carriers and transmitters of meaning in the living world of humans. Following the linguistic model of sign systems proposed by de Saussure, material remains are to be understood as a form of non-verbal communication that functions to project, to negotiate, to manipulate and often to subvert particular symbolic schemes. Rather than simply *active* in the adaptive strategies of particular groups then, material culture is understood to be *meaningfully constituted*: it is produced in accordance with specific symbolic schemes and structured according to the systems of meaning inherent within and determinative of particular social groupings. Over and against the objective statements about the past that processualists such as Binford felt confident could and should be made, converts to the new creed sought to articulate a view of that past as an indeterminate and open-ended network; one in which material remains necessarily have a potential multiplicity rather than a singularity of meanings.

Ascribing multivocality to material remains was an outcome of that heightened awareness within postmodernist and post-structuralist thought as to the character and status of those who could and should tell the story of the past. This certainly represented a challenge to the authority of the archaeologist and a concern to highlight those hidden prejudices that themselves are often an unacknowledged function of gender, ethnic background and religious and/or political persuasion. Surveillance of this type concomitantly stimulated what can legitimately be called a more inclusive archaeology (Hodder 1999, 2004; Meskell 2002) as the plethora of archaeological studies to emerge from and speak to the concerns of under- or misrepresented and marginalized groups would testify. Such enfranchisement has not always been greeted so enthusiastically, however, since there is a radical methodological, theoretical and ethical distinction between *having a voice* and having *control over* (Atalay 2006; Rizvi 2006). An appropriate and corrective intervention into hegemonic discourse is about much more than granting a 'voice to the voiceless'.

In enlarging that pool of voices who felt empowered or legitimized to speak about the Bible, this diffuse postmodern sensibility similarly opened up the possibility of further exploring that diversity of voices and activities that can be detected within it. For all of its feverish determination to promote the history of Israel and its religious traditions as one founded upon and representative of a covenant faith in the one God Yahweh, and centred on the one place, Jerusalem, the Hebrew Bible acknowledges that there were variations on, and deviations from, this 'national religion'. Indeed, in many ways it is the abiding legacy of Wellhausen's Documentary Hypothesis that such transformations have come to light, whatever one is to make of the manner in which he interpreted them. Aside from the various names by which the god of Israel was known (Gen. 1.1, 7.1, 49.24; Exod. 3.14), we witness such noble characters as the patriarchs worshipping, without reproach, at a variety of sanctuaries and altars (Gen. 12.7, 13.18, 14.17–20, 28.8–20, 33.8–10, 33.31); we are informed how the ark of the covenant itself rotated between a series of successive sites (Josh. 24; 1 Sam. 7.15; Judg. 18.31, 20.1–2, 21.2–3; 1 Sam. 7.1–2); and also how, during the stated period of the monarchy, religious practice was, for a long time, conducted at a variety of locations other than Jerusalem and not all of which were associated with Yahweh (1 Sam. 15.12–15, 20.6, 21.1–6; 2 Sam. 5.1–5, 21.6; Amos 8.14; Hosea 10; 1 Kings 18; 2 Kings 10; Jer. 7.12). Even the names bestowed by leading biblical figures upon their children, for example Saul (1 Sam. 14.51; 2 Sam. 2.8, 21.8) are, at the very least, to be read as indicative of an attachment to non-Yahwistic religious practices. It is largely in recognition of this internal biblical dialogue that much recent scholarship speaks of the religions rather than religion of Israel or indeed Judah (Stavrakopoulou and Barton 2010a). While in many ways such developments serve to epitomize Voltaire's critique of French history as one populated solely by 'kings, ministers and generals' (Bloch 1954: 178), they also testify to an increasingly nuanced engagement with the idea that whatever else it may be, religion is as much practice as it is the theoretical formulation of the meaning of that practice (Mayes 1997). Understood as an activity through which individuals and communities seek to relate themselves to the transcendent, then, scholarly reconstructions of 'religion' and specifically 'Israelite religion' have come to place increasing importance on the diversity of social levels and locales through which this activity may have taken place.

In addition to the national saving history or *Heilsgeschichte* of Israel, whose practice the biblical tradition seeks to firmly and unambiguously anchor in the Sinai event and within the environs of the Jerusalem Temple, a range of scholars have come to acknowledge the significance of different modes of religious expression that in many ways are uncoordinated with or unrelated to the salient features of this 'national' version. While such studies on the varied social locations of worshippers have brought into critical focus the significance and particulars of familial, even individual modes of religious practice, such diversity also functions to undermine any simplistic dichotomy such as has been hypothesized between 'Israelite' and 'Canaanite' or indeed 'official' and 'popular' religion. In illustrating how the various religions of Israel and Judah are most profitably understood as dynamic, polysemic entities, studies such as those by Mark S. Smith (1990) have embraced a 'bottom-up mode of analysis' to illustrate how this demonstrably endemic pluralism impacted upon the developing monolatrous or monotheistic Yahwism revealed within the national myth. Within the context of an uneasy process of convergence and differentiation, identification and rejection which seeks to challenge the syncretistic lens through which much Israelite religious activity has been understood, Smith continuously presses home the image of Yahwism as emerging from *within* and through rather than wholly against the polytheism that defined Israelite culture. While Yahweh may well have been the 'God of Israel' from its earliest days, as Smith's detailed studies illustrate, it was sometime before Israel was to become the people of Yahweh.

It is this essentially spectral understanding of Israelite religion as something that lends itself to a multiplicity of forms, across a variety of locations, practised by all strata of society and in respect of a multitude of deities, that furnishes the landscape upon which much recent archaeological investigation has been conducted (Mandell and Smoak 2019). With a notable absence of developed contributions by Israeli archaeologists, despite their relative proximity to the data and a near myopic focus upon the Bronze Age–Iron Age transition, this focus has resulted in several overarching syntheses (Zevit 2001; Finkelstein and Mazar 2007; Dever 2008, 2017; Albertz and Schmitt 2012; Faust 2020), that have produced pointed assessments of such issues as: distinctions between official and popular religion; the various loci of religious practice; the ornaments, amulets, animals and shrines through religious devotion came to expression; the gender and nature of religious intermediaries; and the identity and nature of the divine whose will was to be placated or enraged. Such studies have often pleaded for sufficient geographic and/or chronological breadth so that influences, continuities and/or disruptions could be observed and noted (Nakhai 2001; Zevit 2001; Hess 2007; Dever 2008; Faust 2010; Albertz and Schmitt 2012; Albertz et al. 2014). Within the context of such discussions, which are generally styled as examinations of *Israelite* religion, there are some who would read the accumulating evidence as offering a complement to rather than any immediate contradiction of that narrative tradition which emphasizes a relationship with the one God, and by a single people who understood themselves as Israel (Faust 2012). There are others who would claim the many religious practices illuminated by the archaeological data were so widespread that their existence is legitimately to be assumed, whether they are mentioned in the Bible or not. Despite the patina of authority that accompanies the proliferation of new data and the incisiveness of new critical agendas, there remains an abiding sense that, for some, such resources serve merely to reinforce a commitment to work more efficiently within the traditional metaphysic – that which is supplied by the concept of *culture*.

Nevertheless, in exposing what Zevit has referred to as the 'polydoxies and polypraxises within Yahwism' (Zevit 2001: 349) archaeological investigation of Israelite religious expression can certainly be viewed as a successful enterprise. Within the context of that wider postmodern discourse of which it is itself an expression, such work has functioned to resist any easy confidence in the notion that the historic continuity of ethnic groups can be established on the basis of similarity in material culture, an equation that has long been appealed to as a basis for claims of territorial possession and the right to dispossess. Within such narrative constructions, present-day and historic identities become so enmeshed that neither retains a meaningful existence without the other, and the resultant confluence fosters a kind of historical amnesia that ensures events of that past are recalled more vividly and more readily than any realties of the modern day (Silberman 1997; Abu el-Haj 2001; Feige 2007). That such a recruited archaeology (Ben-Yehuda 2007: 252) and the epistemic premise upon which it is constructed is deserving of critique and exposure is readily apparent, and the discipline of biblical studies has made significant strides in support of such an agenda (Whitelam 1996; Pfoh and Whitelam 2013). Despite the legitimacy and necessity of such critique, the philosophical orientation of the post-processual agenda itself functions to provide a check on optimism. For within the context of a fundamentally pagan promotion of fragmentation and discontinuity and within a world of insurmountable uncertainty, *any* effort to reify a different past in the service of the present automatically becomes ensnared in, and by, the same politics of exclusion it would seek to challenge.

The polysemic understanding of material culture generated by post-processualism can thus be seen to have stimulated as many trajectories as it has been informed by diverse stimuli. However, the overarching emphasis on social actors as thinking and plotting agents selectively and actively working their way through society in an unending series of signals and signs actually tends to draw attention *away* from the very physicality of artefacts and other material things. There remains a very real sense in reading these works that any discussion of archaeological remains relates primarily, if not entirely, to the material residues of religious activities as opposed to what the recovered materials may actually encode. Despite an increased sensitivity to the material dimension of religion, namely that religion is something that people *do* (Stavrakopoulou and Barton 2010b: 1), the material items that constitute the medium of such 'doing' are all too often framed as an entirely passive embodiment of the cultural values, thoughts and cosmological beliefs that are somehow understood to prefigure them. Things, in short, spoke messages that their human creators and/or users fully intended them to speak. While in many ways the idealism of this position is something that archaeology has long sought to exorcise, its enduring vitality reflects the degree to which the dualism of Cartesian logic continues to inform much archaeological thinking. Rather than see human action and cognition as coming to expression in and *through* material forms, archaeology – and biblical archaeology in particular – continues to separate them, to treat material remains as somehow, just there. If, as Webb Keane has recently argued, 'religions [. . .] always involve material forms' (Keane 2008: S124) then it is incumbent upon us ask what these material forms can tell us about the *lived* experience of religion.

Overcoming the Platonic dogma that subordinates principles of matter to the qualities of mind has been a defining feature of what has been widely proclaimed as the 'material turn' (Keane 2003, 2005, 2008; Boivin 2004, 2008, 2009; Miller 2005; Morgan 2010; Finch 2012; Hazard 2013; Mandell and Smoak 2019). Where the inheritance of post-processualism can be seen to lie squarely in the intellectual speculations of postmodernism and the symbolic universe described by Geertz (Appadurai 1986; Geertz 1973), the impetus for this pivot can be seen to derive from more substantive realms (Houtman and Meyer 2012). Certainly, the material turn constitutes a reaction to and critique of any reduction of the material world to a system of discourse, symbol, sign and ideology. It equally, and perhaps more powerfully, constitutes a reaction to the all too apparent impact of environmental degradation, species extinction and climate change. Where this ecological crisis calls us to reflect on whether we are integral elements of the biosphere or rulers of it (Pope Francis 2015), the equally pervasive impact of digital media and cybernetic systems calls us to question which world is in fact real. Such profound and ultimately existential questions are what constitute the principal drivers of any material turn; one whose initial and primary orientation has been a rehabilitation, if not dissolution, of conceptual dualisms, principal amongst which is that between mind and matter.

This multidisciplinary desire to collapse, if not transcend, the deeply rooted Cartesian separation of mind and body that characterizes the Western intellectual tradition finds strong empirical support in the theory of practice articulated by Pierre Bourdieu (1977, 1979, 1984, 2000, 2001). Perhaps the most influential and original French social theorist since Émile Durkheim (2001 [1912]), Bourdieu's stress on social life as simultaneously a practical logic and a logic subject to improvisation dissolves the dualism of empiricist thought that posits ideas and values as somehow prior to material forms. Rather than simply mirroring pre-existing social distinctions or ideational norms, Bourdieu's *social praxeology* (Coenen 1989) understands material forms as constituting the very medium through which these values, ideas and distinctions are produced, reproduced, legitimized and, ultimately, transformed. Material object and social subject are indelibly intertwined in a dialectical relationship where they each form part of the other. It is through things that we understand both ourselves and others – not because they are externalizations of ourselves, reflecting something more prior or basic in our consciousness or social relations but because material things are the very medium through which we make and know ourselves. It is in the creation and deployment of things that the social self is itself created. While an explicit account of this material component of human and social cultural existence is provided for in Bourdieu's well-cited examination of the Kabyle house (Bourdieu 1979), his emphasis upon the physicality of that material world, and the way in which it might stimulate rather than simply re-create thoughts and ideas (Rappaport 1999) is an insight aggressively pursued by Bruno Latour's 'actor-network theory' (Latour 1986, 2005). Although he has been critiqued for his suggestion that intentionality is a trait that applies with equal force to both the human and non-human constituents of any hypothesized network, Latour's terminological imprecision does highlight a dimension of the material world long ignored; its ability to influence and even direct behaviours and actions.

For while language may well facilitate an appreciation of religion as a particular set of beliefs to which people subscribe, the grammatical rules of this model are ill-equipped to capture an extended understanding of that phenomenon as 'an event that takes place as individuals seek to relate themselves to the transcendent' (Mayes 1997: 57). This entirely practical, and fundamentally material, attempt at engagement with what Keane has labelled the elusive and the unknown (Keane 2008: S110) cannot be forced into the distorting prism of a symbolic system any more that it can the Procrustean bed of covenant faith. Quite simply, it is the materiality of things, their tactile, visual and even olfactory qualities that evokes ideas of, and facilitates access to, the sacred and the divine.

In this context the significance of Christian faith and particularly the often-sectarian rivalry that positioned the lofty spiritualism of Protestantism against the vulgar materialism of Catholicism cannot be disregarded. For where the latter can be credited with institutionalizing the material, visual and sensual character and claims of religious experience, the former is what more often presented as stabilizing the deep-rooted conviction that *true* religion has to do with faith, or what is more generally classified as *belief*.

Where the majority of biblical scholarship has been undertaken by men of this latter persuasion, it is little surprise that the inclination to emphasize, indeed prioritize, such individual interiority as defining of religion would take hold within the discipline (Albright 1949; Wellhausen 2001 [1883]; Houtman and Meyer 2012). This is not to be read as heralding any restoration of Catholic privilege where matter sits above spirit, ritual comes before belief, and form precedes content. Some of the more celebrated anthropological engagements with biblical religion have been by Catholics who were as deeply enmeshed in the symbolic universe as the most puritanical of pastors (Kuper 2016). What it does proclaim, or at the very least suggest, is the need for a profound reorientation of our thinking around the nature and function of things in ritual or religious experience; a reorientation which, finally, may allow us to approximate an understanding of *how* religion was actually felt and experienced within specific contexts rather than simply how it was understood. At a deeper and more profound level however, an insistence upon the materiality of things, on their ability to inspire rather than simply reflect those ideas that have long been taken to define 'religion', places the demand for evidence on a different footing (Keane 2008: S110). It serves to undermine those crusading quests for the realia of the Bible, and thus supposedly 'Israelite' religious activity, by overturning the expectation that such materials provide evidence of something hidden, such as belief.

That this was a concern to the biblical writers themselves is illustrated by Stavrakopoulou's recent examination of Torah, the materiality of writing and the materiality of texts (Stavrakopoulou 2013). Avoiding any simplistic affirmation of that tendency to valorize the tradition's orientation towards lofty monotheism (Albright 1957: 281), Stavrakopoulou shows not just how the biblical texts recognize the potency of material things as mediating a relationship between the human and the divine but that they equally express a preference for specific forms of such representation: that of the divine word as represented by Torah. While such a preference points towards an implied hierarchical order of material forms, it equally points towards certain anxieties around social control and human power (Miller 2005; Ellenbogen and Tugendhaft 2011). Thus, where an appreciation of such entanglement may well confirm the initial and often ignored intuition of Marx's *Theses on Feuerbach*, it equally exposes the complexity and multiplicity of efforts to negotiate how access to the divine should be mediated, how it might be moderated and how it could be materialized; whether through ritual and place, through icon and altar, figurine or standing stone, through votive offerings and libations, or through bodily comportment and the various senses that define it. Evolutionary psychologists maintain that religious ideas are not entirely the result of cultural transition but rather are replicated by virtue of inferential processes inherent to humans' cognitive capacities. To this, however, one must add that for those inferences to circulate socially and have any sustained existence beyond that specific moment of their articulation, they must, and do, enter into material form. Failure to do so sees them remain idiosyncratic and unsupported by the rest of that person's social existence. Materiality is thus a necessary precondition for the social circulation, along with the temporal existence and persistence, of ideas (Žižek 2008).

## THINGS AS THINGS

In a letter to dated to the year 1914, the English poet Ezra Pound informed his correspondent that it took him ten years to learn his art, but a further five to unlearn it (Jenkins 2009: 149). While many have paused to enquire as to the pedagogical and hermeneutical thrust of Pound's revelation, within the context of this chapter it points to a larger series of tensions and questions that revolve around familiarity and estrangement, precision and ambiguity, singularity and multiplicity, domination and disintegration: tensions that have long defined the art of biblical scholarship and the very materials it has employed. Rather than continue to operate with such binaries and thus reinforce the ontologies they infer, the recent emphases on materiality would appear to offer an alternative; one that finds inspiration in the etymology of the term culture itself: to care, to nurture.

Representing the means by which people cultivate their world and their place within it, culture in this revised sense points towards a process of development and growth rather than any specific and historically contingent understanding of the outcome of that process. Prioritizing such *process* as the primary epistemological frame functions to shift our understanding away from the false dichotomies that position material remains as representing the embodiment of logically prior ideas or as evidencing some form of extrasomatic adaptation to the environment. It moves us away from a spectral distinction between inner and outer worlds, between mind and matter and towards a more coherent understanding of the two as necessarily and logically interdependent. It thus furnishes the possibility for new epistemological frameworks that expose the limitations inherent in traditional techniques and procedures and which remain dependent upon homogenous and fictional constructs. It represents possibilities for knowledge that invite participation and involvement yet which resist the temptation to collapse the worlds of the interpreter and the interpreted in a quest for that which is common, comfortable or convenient.

# REFERENCES

Abu el-Haj, N. (2001), *Facts on the Ground: Archaeological Practice and Territorial Self-Fashioning in Israeli Society*, Chicago: University of Chicago Press.

Albertz, R. and R. Schmitt (2012), *Family and Household Religion in Ancient Israel and the Levant*, Winona Lake, IN: Eisenbrauns.

Albertz, R., B.A. Nakhai, S.M. Olyan and R. Schmitt, eds (2014), *Family and Household Religion: Toward a Synthesis of Old Testament Studies, Archaeology, Epigraphy, and Cultural Studies*, Winona Lake, IN: Eisenbrauns.

Albright, W.F. (1949), *The Archaeology of Palestine*, Harmondsworth, UK: Penguin.

Albright, W.F. (1957), *From Stone Age to Christianity: Monotheism and the Historical Process*, 2nd edn, Baltimore, MD: Johns Hopkins University Press.

Appadurai, A., ed. (1986), *The Social Life of Things: Commodities in Cultural Perspective*, Cambridge: Cambridge University Press.

Atalay, S. (2006), 'Indigenous Archaeology as Decolonizing Practice', *American Indian Quarterly*, 30 (3/4): 280–310.

Ben-Yehuda, N. (2007), 'Excavating Masada: The Politics–Archaeology Connection at Work', in P.L. Kohl, M. Kozelsky and N. Ben-Yehuda (eds), *Selective Remembrances: Archaeology in the Construction, Commemoration and Consecration of National Pasts*, 247–76, Chicago: University of Chicago Press.

Binford, L.R. (1962), 'Archaeology as Anthropology', *American Antiquity*, 28 (2): 217–25.

Binford, L.R. (1965), 'Archaeological Systematics and the Study of Culture Process', *American Antiquity*, 31 (2, pt 1): 203–10.

Binford, L.R. (1968), 'Archaeological Perspectives', in S.R. Binford and L.R. Binford (eds), *New Perspectives in Archaeology*, 5–32, Chicago: Aldine.

Bloch, M. (1954), *The Historian's Craft*, Manchester: Manchester University Press.

Boas, F. (1896), 'The Limitations of the Comparative Method of Anthropology', *Science*, 4 (103): 901–8.

Boivin, N. (2004), 'Mind Over Matter: Collapsing the Mind–Matter Dichotomy in Material Culture Studies', in E. DeMarrais, C. Gosden and C. Renfrew (eds), *Rethinking Materiality: The Engagement of Mind with the Material World*, 63–71, Cambridge: McDonald Institute for Archaeological Research.

Boivin, N. (2008), *Material Cultures, Material Minds: The Impact of Things on Human Thought, Society, and Evolution*, Cambridge: Cambridge University Press.

Boivin, N. (2009), 'Grasping the Elusive and Unknowable: Material Culture in Ritual Practice', *Material Religion*, 5 (3): 266–87.

Bourdieu, P. (1977), *Outline of a Theory of Practice*, transl. R. Nice, Cambridge: Cambridge University Press.

Bourdieu, P. (1979), *Algeria 1960: The Disenchantment of the World, The Sense of Honour, The Kabyle House or the World Reversed*, transl. R. Nice, New York: Cambridge University Press.

Bourdieu, P. (1984), *Distinction: A Social Critique of the Judgement of Taste*, transl. R. Nice, New York: Routledge and Kegan Paul.

Bourdieu, P. (2000), *Pascalian Meditations*, transl. R. Nice, Cambridge: Polity Press.

Bourdieu, P. (2001), *Contre-feux 2: pour un mouvement social européen*, Paris: Raisons d'Agir.

Bravo, B. (2010), 'Antiquarianism and History', in J. Marincola (ed.), *A Companion to Greek and Roman Historiography*, 515–28, Oxford: Wiley-Blackwell.

Brubaker, R. (2004), *Ethnicity Without Groups*, Cambridge, MA: Harvard University Press.

Carr, E.H. (1961), *What Is History?*, Harmondsworth, UK: Penguin.

Childe, V.G. (1956), *Piecing Together the Past: The Interpretation of Archaeological Data*, London: Routledge and Kegan Paul.

Clarke, D. (1968), *Analytical Archaeology*, London: Methuen.

Clarke, D. (1973), 'Archaeology: The Loss of Innocence', *Antiquity*, 47 (185): 6–18.

Coenen, H. (1989), 'Praxeologie en strukturatietheorie preliminaire opmerkingen bij een vergelijking', *Anthropologische Verkenningen*, 8 (2): 8–17.

Coley, N. (1991), 'French Science in the Seventeenth Century', in D. Goodman and C.A Russell (eds), *The Rise of Scientific Europe, 1500–1800*, 171–96, London: Hodder and Stoughton.

Collingwood, R.G. (1946), *The Idea of History*, Oxford: Clarendon Press.

Coote, R.B. and K.W. Whitelam (1987), *The Emergence of Early Israel in Historical Perspective*, SWBAS 5, Sheffield: Almond Press.

Crawford, O.G.S. (1921), *Man and His Past*, London: Oxford University Press.

Crawford, O.G.S. (1922), 'Prehistoric Geography', *Geographical Review*, 12 (2): 257–63.

Crouch, C.L. (2014), *The Making of Israel: Cultural Diversity in the Southern Levant and the Formation of Ethnic Identity in Deuteronomy*, VTSup 162, Leiden: E.J. Brill.

Daniel, G.E. (1976), *A Hundred and Fifty Years of Archaeology*, London: Duckworth.

Davies, P.R. (1992), *In Search of 'Ancient Israel': A Study in Biblical Origins*, JSOTSup 148, Sheffield: Sheffield Academic Press.

Davis, T.W. (2004), *Shifting Sands: The Rise and Fall of Biblical Archaeology*, New York: Oxford University Press.

Dever, W.G. (1985), 'Syro-Palestinian and Biblical Archaeology', in D.A. Knight and G.M. Tucker (eds), *The Hebrew Bible and Its Modern Interpreters*, 31–74, Philadelphia, PA: Fortress Press.

Dever, W.G. (2001), *What Did the Biblical Writers Know, and When Did They Write it? What Archaeology Can Tell Us About the Reality of Ancient Israel*, Grand Rapids, MI: Eerdmans.

Dever, W.G. (2008), *Did God Have a Wife? Archaeology and Folk Religion in Ancient Israel*, Grand Rapids, MI: Eerdmans.

Dever, W.G. (2017), *Beyond the Texts: An Archaeological Portrait of Ancient Israel and Judah*, Atlanta, GA: SBL Press.

Durkheim, É. (2001 [1912]), *The Elementary Forms of Religious Life*, transl. C. Cosman, Oxford: Oxford University Press.

Eliav, Y. (2005), *God's Mountain: The Temple Mount in Time, Place, and Memory*, Baltimore, MD: Johns Hopkins University Press.

Ellenbogen, J. and A. Tugendhaft, eds (2011), *Idol Anxiety*, Stanford, CA: Stanford University Press.

Faust, A. (2010), *Israelite Society in the Period of the Monarchy*, Jerusalem: Yad Ben-Zvi [Hebrew].

Faust, A. (2012), *The Archaeology of Israelite Society in Iron Age II*, Winona Lake, IN: Eisenbrauns.

Faust, A., guest ed. (2020), 'Archaeology and Ancient Israelite Religion', *Religions* (special issue), 11 (6).

Feige, M. (2007), 'Recovering Authenticity: West Bank Settlers and the Second Stage of National Archaeology', in P.L. Kohl, M. Kozelsky and N. Ben-Yehuda (eds), *Selective Remembrances: Archaeology in the Construction, Commemoration and Consecration of National Pasts*, 277–98, Chicago: University of Chicago Press.

Finch, M.L. (2012), 'Rehabilitating Materiality: Bodies, Gods, and Religion', *Religion*, 42 (4): 625–31.

Finkelstein, I. and A. Mazar (2007), *The Quest for the Historical Israel: Debating Archaeology and the History of Early Israel*, ed. B.B. Schmidt, Atlanta, GA: Society of Biblical Literature.

Flannery, K.V. (1967), 'Cultural History v. Cultural Process: A Debate in American Archaeology', *Scientific American*, 217 (2): 119–27.

Foucault, M. (1970 [1966]), *The Order of Things: An Archaeology of the Human Sciences*, London: Tavistock.

Fritz, V. (1994), *An Introduction to Biblical Archaeology*, JSOTSup 172, Sheffield: Sheffield Academic Press.

Gadamer, H.G. (1960), *Wahrheit und Methode*, Tübingen: J.C.B. Mohr.

Gaukroger, S. (2001), *Francis Bacon and the Transformation of Early Modern Philosophy*, Cambridge: Cambridge University Press.

Geertz, C. (1973), 'Deep Play: Notes on the Balinese Cockfight', in *The Interpretation of Cultures*, 412–54, New York: Basic Books.

Gosden, C. (1999), *Archaeology and Anthropology: A Changing Relationship*, London: Routledge.

Habermas, J. (1972), *Knowledge and Human Interests*, London: Heinemann.

Harris, M. (1979), *Cultural Materialism: The Struggle for a Science of Culture*, New York: Random House.

Harvey, V.A. (1966), *The Historian and the Believer: A Confrontation Between the Modern Historian's Principles of Judgment and the Christian's Will to Believe*, New York: Macmillan.

Hawkes, C. (1954), 'Archaeological Method and Theory: Some Suggestions from the Old World', *American Antiquity*, 56: 153–68.

Hays, C.B. (2010), 'Bard Called the Tune: Whither Theological Exegesis in the Post-Childs Era?', *Journal of Theological Interpretation*, 4 (1): 139–52.

Hazard, S. (2013), 'The Material Turn in the Study of Religion', *Religion and Society: Advances in Research*, 4 (1): 58–78.

Hempel, G.C. (1942), 'The Function of General Laws in History', *Journal of Philosophy*, 39 (2): 35–48.

Hess, R.S. (2007), *Israelite Religions: An Archaeological and Biblical Survey*, Grand Rapids, MI: Baker Academic.

Hobbes, T. (1996 [1651]), *Leviathan: or The Matter, Forme and Power of a Commonwealth Ecclesiasticall and Civil*, ed. Richard Tuck, New York: Cambridge University Press.

Hodder, I. (1982), *Symbols in Action: Ethnoarchaeological Studies of Material Culture*, Cambridge: Cambridge University Press.

Hodder, I. (1985), 'Postprocessual Archaeology', *Advances in Archaeological Method and Theory*, 8: 1–26.
Hodder, I. (1986), *Reading the Past*, Cambridge: Cambridge University Press.
Hodder, I. (1999), *The Archaeological Process*, Oxford: Blackwell.
Hodder, I. (2004), *Archaeology Beyond Dialogue*, Salt Lake City: University of Utah Press.
Houtman, D. and B. Meyer (2012), 'Introduction: Material Religion – How Things Matter', in D. Houtman and B. Meyer (eds), *Things: Religion and the Question of Materiality*, 1–23, New York: Fordham University Press.
Hunt, E.D. (1982), *Holy Land Pilgrimage in the Later Roman Empire* AD *312–460*, Oxford: Clarendon Press.
Jenkins, B. (2009), *On the Camera Arts and Consecutive Matters: The Writings of Hollis Frampton*, Cambridge, MA: MIT Press.
Keane, W. (2003), 'Semiotics and the Social Analysis of Material Things', *Language and Communication*, 23 (3/4): 409–25.
Keane, W. (2005), 'Signs Are Not the Only Garb: On the Social Analysis of Material Things', in D. Miller (ed.), *Materiality*, 182–205, Durham, NC: Duke University Press.
Keane, W. (2008), 'The Evidence of the Senses and the Materiality of Religion', *JRAI NS*, 14 (1S): S110–S127.
Kossinna, G. (1911), *Die Herkunft der Germanen: Zur Methode der Siedlungsarchäologie*, Würzburg: Kabitzsch.
Kossinna, G. (1926), *Ursprung und Verbreitung der Germanen in vor- und frühgeschichtlicher Zeit*, Würzburg: Kabitzsch.
Kroeber, K.L. and C. Kluckhohn (1952), *Culture: A Critical Review of Concepts and Definitions*, Cambridge MA: Peabody Museum.
Kuper, A. (2016), 'Anthropologists and the Bible', in R. Darnell and F.W. Gleach (eds), *Local Knowledge, Global Stage*, 1–30, Histories of Anthropology Annual 10, Lincoln: University of Nebraska Press [see Chapter 2 in this volume].
Latour, B. (1986), 'The Powers of Association', in J. Law (ed.), *Power, Action and Belief: A New Sociology of Knowledge?*, 264–80, Sociological Review Monograph 32, London: Routledge and Kegan Paul.
Latour, B. (2005), *Reassembling the Social: An Introduction to Actor-Network Theory*, Oxford: Oxford University Press.
Limor, O., E. Reiner and M. Frenkel, eds (2014), *Pilgrimage: Jews, Christians, Muslims*, Raanana: Open University of Israel Press.
Long, B.O. (1997), 'Historical Imaginings, Ideological Gestures: W.F. Albright and the Reasoning Faculties of Man', in N.A. Silberman and D.B. Small (eds), *The Archaeology of Israel: Constructing the Past, Interpreting the Present*, 82–94, JSOTSup 237, Sheffield: Sheffield Academic Press.
Lubbock, J. (1870), *The Origin of Civilization and the Primitive Condition of Man*, London: Longmans Green.
Mandell, A. and J. Smoak (2019), 'The Material Turn in the Study of Israelite Religions: Spaces, Things and the Body', *JHebS*, 19: art. 5. Available online: https://doi.org/10.5508/jhs29397 (accessed 24 June 2022).
Mayes, A.D.H. (1997), 'Kuntillet Arjud and the History of Israelite Religion', in J.R. Bartlett (ed.), *Archaeology and Biblical Interpretation*, 51–66, London: Routledge.
Meskell, L. (2002), 'Negative Heritage and Past Mastering in Archaeology', *Anthropological Quarterly*, 75 (3): 557–74.

Miller, D. (2005), 'Materiality: An Introduction', in *Materiality*, 1–50, Durham, NC: Duke University Press.
Moorey, P.R.S. (1991), *A Century of Biblical Archaeology*, Louisville, KY: Westminster John Knox Press.
Morgan, D. (2010), 'Materiality, Social Analysis, and the Study of Religion' in *Religion and Material Culture: The Matter of Belief*, 55–74, Abingdon: Routledge.
Na'aman, N. (2011), 'The "Discovered Book" and the Legitimation of Josiah's Reform', *JBL*, 130 (1): 47–62.
Nakhai, B.A. (2001), *Archaeology and the Religions of Canaan and Israel*, Boston, MA: American Schools of Oriental Research.
Nestor, D.A. (2010), *Cognitive Perspective on Israelite Identity*, LHBOTS 519, London: T&T Clark International.
Oestigaard, T. (2007), *Political Archaeology and Holy Nationalism: Archaeological Battles over the Bible and Land in Israel from 1967–2000*, GOTARC Serie C 67, Göteborg: Department of Archaeology, Göteborg University.
Orwell, G. (2000), *Nineteen Eighty-Four*, intr. T. Pynchon, notes P. Davison, London: Penguin.
Patrik, L.E. (1985), 'Is There an Archaeological Record?', *Advances in Archaeological Method and Theory*, 8: 27–62.
Pfoh, E. (2010), 'Introduction: Anthropology and the Bible Revisited', in E. Pfoh (ed.), *Anthropology and the Bible: Critical Perspectives*, 3–12, BI 3, Piscataway, NJ: Gorgias Press.
Pfoh, E. and K.W. Whitelam, eds (2013), *The Politics of Israel's Past: The Bible, Archaeology and Nation-Building*, SWBA/SS 8, Sheffield: Sheffield Phoenix Press.
Piggot, S. (1976), *Ruins in a Landscape: Essays in Antiquarianism*, Edinburgh: Edinburgh University Press.
Pope Francis (2015), *Encyclical Letter Laudato Si' of the Holy Father Francis on Care for Our Common Home*. Available online: https://www.vatican.va/content/francesco/en/encyclicals/documents/papa-francesco_20150524_enciclica-laudato-si.html
Rappaport, R. (1999), *Ritual and Religion in the Making of Humanity*, Cambridge: Cambridge University Press.
Renfrew, C. (1985), *The Archaeology of Cult: The Sanctuary at Phylakopi*, British School of Archaeology at Athens Suppl. 18, London: British School of Archaeology at Athens.
Rizvi, U.Z. (2006), 'Accounting for Multiple Desires: Decolonizing Methodologies, Archaeology and the Public Interest', *India Review*, 5 (3/4): 394–416.
Russell, B. (2005), *A History of Western Philosophy*, London: Routledge Classics.
Schnapp, A. (1997), *Discovery of the Past: The Origins of Archaeology*, transl. I. Kinnes and G. Varndell, New York: Abrams.
Seitz, C.R. (1998), *Word Without End: The Old Testament as Abiding Theological Witness*, Grand Rapids, MI: Eerdmans.
Shapin, S. (1996), *The Scientific Revolution*, Chicago: University of Chicago Press.
Silberman, N.A. (1982), *Digging for God and Country: Exploration, Archaeology and the Secret Struggle for the Holy Land 1799–1917*, New York: Knopf.
Silberman, N.A. (1989), *Between Past and Present: Archaeology, Ideology and Nationalism in the Modern Middle East*, New York: Henry Holt.
Silberman, N.A. (1997), 'Structuring the Past: Israelis, Palestinians and the Symbolic Authority of Archaeological Monuments', in N.A. Silberman and D.B. Small (eds), *The Archaeology of Israel: Constructing the Past, Interpreting the Present*, 62–81, JSOTSup 237, Sheffield: Sheffield Academic Press.
Smith, J.Z. (1978), *Map Is Not Territory*, Chicago: University of Chicago Press.

Smith, M.S. (1990), *The Early History of God: Yahweh and the Other Deities in Ancient Israel*, San Francisco: Harper & Row.

Stavrakopoulou, F. (2013), 'Making Bodies: On Body Modification and Religious Materiality in the Hebrew Bible', *HeBAI*, 2 (4): 532–53.

Stavrakopoulou, F. and J. Barton, eds (2010a), *Religious Diversity in Ancient Israel and Judah*, London: T&T Clark.

Stavrakopoulou F. and J. Barton (2010b), 'Introduction: Religious Diversity in ancient Israel and Judah', in F. Stavrakopoulou and J. Barton (eds), *Religious Diversity in Ancient Israel and Judah*, 1–8, London: T&T Clark.

Steward, J. (1953), 'Evolution and Process', in A.L. Kroeber (ed.), *Anthropology Today: An Encyclopedic Inventory*, 313–26, Chicago: University of Chicago Press.

Stott, K. (2005), 'Finding the Lost Book of the Law: Re-reading the Story of "The Book of the Law" (Deuteronomy–2 Kings) in Light of Classical Literature', *JSOT*, 30 (2): 153–69.

Thomas, J. (2004a), *Archaeology and Modernity*, Abingdon: Routledge.

Thomas, J. (2004b), 'The Great Dark Book: Archaeology, Experience, and Interpretation', in J. Bintliff (ed.), *A Companion to Archaeology*, 21–36, Oxford: Blackwell.

Toulmin, S.E. (1990), *Cosmopolis: The Hidden Agenda of Modernity*, Chicago: University of Chicago Press.

Trigger, B.G. (1989), *A History of Archaeological Thought*, Cambridge: Cambridge University Press.

Trigger, B.G. (1995), 'Romanticism, Nationalism and Archaeology', in P.L. Kohl and C. Fawcett (eds), *Nationalism, Politics and the Practice of Archaeology*, 263–79, Cambridge: Cambridge University Press.

Trigger, B.G. (1998), *Sociocultural Evolution: Calculation and Contingency*, Oxford: Blackwell.

Troeltsch, E. (1913), 'Über historische und dogmatische Methode in der Theologie', *Gesammelte Schriften Band 2*, 729–53, Tübingen: Mohr.

Turner, V. (1973), 'The Center Out There: Pilgrim's Goal', *History of Religions*, 12 (3): 191–230.

Tylor, E.B. (1871), *Primitive Culture: Researches into the Development of Mythology, Philosophy, Religion, Language, Art and Custom*, 2 vols, London: John Murray.

Tylor, E.B. (1881), *Primitive Culture: Researches into the Development of Mythology, Philosophy, Religion, Language, Art and Custom*, London: Macmillan.

Van Seters, J. (2006), *The Edited Bible: The Curious History of the 'Editor' in Biblical Criticism*, Winona Lake, IN: Eisenbrauns.

Volf, M. (2010), *Captive to the Word of God: Engaging the Scriptures for Contemporary Theological Reflection*, Grand Rapids, MI: Eerdmans.

Watson, F. (2006), 'Authors, Readers, Hermeneutics', in A.K.M. Adam, S.E. Fowl, K.J. Vanhoozer and F. Watson (eds), *Reading Scripture with the Church: Toward a Hermeneutic for Theological Interpretation*, 119–24, Grand Rapids, MI: Baker Academic.

Wellhausen, J. (2001 [1883]), *Prolegomena zur Geschichte Israels*, Berlin: De Gruyter.

White, L. Jr (1967), 'The Historical Roots of Our Ecological Crisis', *Science*, 155 (3767): 1203–7.

White, L.A. (1943), 'Energy and the Evolution of Culture', *American Antiquity*, 45 (3, pt 1): 335–56.

White, L.A. (1949), *The Science of Culture*, New York: Farrar Strauss.

White, L.A. (1959), *The Evolution of Culture*, New York: McGraw-Hill.

Whitelam, K.W. (1996), *The Invention of Ancient Israel: The Silencing of the Palestinian Past*, London: Routledge.

Wilkinson, J. (1977), *Jerusalem Pilgrims: Before the Crusades*, Warminster, UK: Aris & Phillips.

Wilkinson, J. (1981), *Egeria's Travels to the Holy Land*, rev. edn, Warminster, UK: Aris & Phillips.

Willey, R.G. and P. Phillips (1958), *Method and Theory in Archaeology*, Chicago: University of Chicago Press.

Wiwjorra, L. (1996), 'German Archaeology and its Relation to Nationalism and Racism' in M. Díaz-Andreu and T.C. Champion (eds), *Nationalism and Archaeology in Europe*, 164–88, London: University College London Press.

Zevit, Z. (2001), *The Religions of Ancient Israel: A Synthesis of Parallactic Approaches*, New York: Continuum.

Žižek, Z. (2008), *Violence: Six Sideways Reflections*, New York: Picador.

# CHAPTER FIVE

# Ethnographic and ethnoarchaeological insights to interpret first-millennium BCE material culture

GLORIA LONDON

## INTRODUCTION

Beginning in the nineteenth century, men from various fields of research chronicled a diverse range of observations in order to provide an overview of local practices and lifeways in the southern Levant. By the mid-twentieth century, trained ethnographers like Anne Fuller (1970 [1961]) had embarked on more detailed descriptions of life in an individual village. More recently, ethnoarchaeological research during the second half of the twentieth century emerged with the aim of recording specific traditional artefacts and material culture used and made by an extant population. Rather than a focus on broad sociopolitical structures by interviewing people, the goal of ethnoarchaeology is to address issues and questions that arise from excavated ancient artefacts. The emphasis on artefacts requires field techniques unique to ethnoarchaeology. These studies are carried out by archaeologists with the ultimate goal of learning how ancient societies functioned day to day.

After a brief survey of early references to traditional lifestyles observed by ethnographers and others in Levant and Cyprus during the nineteenth and twentieth centuries, the subject turns to more recent ethnoarchaeological research and its relevance for creating templates to understand daily life in the first millennium BCE. Many questions that archaeologists strive to address lack simply binary solutions. As described here, ethnoarchaeological research identifies artefacts that cross from daily use to funerary use and from sacral to profane functions. Handmade pottery never disappeared despite the availability wheel-thrown wares. Men and women, young and elderly, worked as potters. Wealth is better defined in terms of covered spaces for humans and animals than in portable objects. Rather than sedentary versus mobile lifestyles, outside versus inside work, more fluid lifestyles and workplaces negate a single answer, use or understanding for excavated artefacts.

## ETHNOGRAPHIC AND ETHNOARCHAEOLOGICAL RESEARCH STRATEGIES AND TECHNIQUES

While ethnographic data often relies on visits and interviews to a specific community, ethnoarchaeology requires direct observations of people carrying out some activity. Instead of writing down what people say they do, ideally ethnoarchaeologists live in a community to witness any type of activity and collect quantitative data. When Lydia Einsler (1914) asked a potter near Ramallah, some 10 kilometres north of Jerusalem, what types and how many pots she made each year, the result is a useful list based on one woman's account of her output. We do not know how representative it is of the larger community. A single brickmaker or butcher, or the contents of one house, provides a valuable data point whose relevance is enhanced when compared and contrasted with a larger sample. Fieldwork that includes multiple households or villages offers a more comprehensive and inclusive overview than any individual, family or house. In addition to descriptive data, ethnoarchaeology involves information to quantify rates of production, frequency of animal slaughter, seasonal changes in residence or where activities take place, population density, etc.

The ability to collect quantitative data from more than a single household or individual requires time and presence. Ethnoarchaeological projects ideally entail a long-term commitment of days, weeks, months or more in order to obtain data from a valid sample of people, workshops or households. Ethnographers living full-time in a traditional community sometimes describe the artefacts that archaeologists excavate. For example, while spending the year 1937/8 in a Lebanese mountain village to learn about the economic, social, religious and political life of men, women and children Anne Fuller reported on farming tools from local or foreign sources. She mentioned women who made clay bricks for house repairs and used 'local clay ware' (Fuller 1970 [1961]: 73, 76–7, 95), without elaborating on what archaeologists want to know: where and how was it made. While living in Jerusalem in 1925–7 and in 1930 while visiting nearby Artās village, Hilma Granqvist briefly wrote about clay pots, ovens and storage bins, cave burials and other things of interest to archaeologists (Seger 1981: 9, 40, 102, 122, 125, 138, 155). Hilma Granqvist observed a resident population of 500 residents plus a 'fleeting number of the Ta'āmre tribesmen who lived in and around the village [. . .] Craftsmen stayed temporarily in the village to perform particular tasks' (Seger 1981: 32). This is a scene that likely played out repeatedly at ancient sites, for example at Tall al-'Umayri outside Amman (London 2017). Fuller and Granqvist, both remarkable pioneers in their research, were not archaeologists. Accordingly, they did not record the source of the tools and pottery or the origin of the patterns on pots. For this reason, archaeologists carry out research in communities that use or make artefacts that resemble what we excavate.

Rather than record long-lived, outdated technologies that have survived to the present as 'relics from the past' (Lyons and David 2019: 105), the goal of ethnoarchaeology is to gain information about traditional objects, processes and practices. The fieldwork often takes place in societies with a lifestyle different from that of most archaeologists and possibly comparable to ancient times. The term 'traditional' here refers to artefacts or a lifestyle that involves local or regional materials and products, an indigenous population and a lack of modern technology. For example, to answer specific questions concerning how, why, when or where people made, used or discarded artefacts, archaeologists watch people engaged in any activity that is manifested in the archaeological record. We learn how people behave and organize themselves to carry out specific tasks through direct observations, rather than interviews, and immediate note-taking during the fieldwork.

The current standards for ethnoarchaeological fieldwork do not diminish the early reports that relied on interviews and observations collected by individuals interested in male-dominated industries such as those of Gustaf Dalman (1971 [1941]). Early scholars gathered a variety of general data that is no longer available, as during the 1838 survey of Edward Robinson and Eli Smith. They observed that Gaza pottery from the Mediterranean coast reached cities located all along the *hajj* route (Salem 2009: 25; for the history of Gaza ware, see Gatt 1885a, 1885b). Jerusalem's excavator Charles Warren (1876: 513–19) noted five pottery workshops in the city. According to William Hepworth Dixon, potters offered their wares for sale at Jaffa Gate and elsewhere. Ulrich J. Seetzen mentioned pottery and pipe-bowls made at Qastel, near the road to Ramle, although pipes from Beirut workshops were superior (Ben-Arieh 1984: 41, 56). Nearly all these workshops have vanished but remain as points on the map thanks to the early observers.

When not excavating at Megiddo and Jericho, Gottlieb Schumacher (1914) travelled the countryside. He commented on the numbers of houses and tents belonging to pastoralists, thereby providing demographic information reflecting the carrying capacity of the land. Such numbers are hard to collect, even from census data. Tawfiq Canaan (1932) a physician concerned about his clientele, described occupations that usually go unnoticed, unmentioned or not considered worth recording. His description of women pounding pot sherds to provide an underlayer for Jerusalem streets is relevant for archaeologists interested in pottery reuse. The practice explains the dearth of nineteenth- and early twentieth-century sherds in Jerusalem and elsewhere.

During lulls in early twentieth-century excavations, archaeologists passed the time by visiting nearby villages where they observed people using artefacts that resembled ancient material. The abundance of workable clay and the unique benefits of pottery led to its extensive use in traditional and ancient households. Clay containers out-perform wood, stone, skins or baskets. Although pottery breaks easily, the sherds are almost indestructible. Because they survive, unlike the organic materials that burn or disintegrate over time, ancient sherds abound at first-millennium BCE sites. Based on their brief observations in the villages, archaeologists used the information to reconstruct how ancient craftspeople worked and lived. Fortuitous observations of parallels between traditional and excavated cultural material include those of Elihu Grant (1931: 34), who found the work of Ramallah potters to be 'very suggestive' with regard to ancient pottery. During excavations at Samaria, Grace Crowfoot (1932, 1940, 1957: 470–1) and E.L. Sukenik (1940) observed potters before making associations between ancient and traditional pottery in northern Israel. William Frederic Badè (1931: 5, n5) visited female potters in the central part of the country at Tell en-Nasbeh. Olga Tufnell relied on her observations of potters when publishing the Lachish volumes (Tufnell, Murray and Diringer 1958: 176, 1961; Tufnell and Ward 1966: 170). The brief contacts limit the reliability of their remarks concerning the overall industry and their applicability to the ancient artefacts but model how ancient artefacts were made and used.

Unlike the biblical scholars and more casual Victorian-era visitors who were more inclined to seek a link between past and present (Cunningham and McGeough 2018), a direct historical continuity between villagers and the ancient populations is not the goal of ethnoarchaeology. The questions that were addressed a century or more ago arose from biblical texts (Ben-Arieh 1984; see Chapter 3 in this volume). The questions that concern ethnoarchaeologists derive from the most mundane excavated artefacts and focus on recording 'variability in material culture [that is] so important to the archaeologist' (Longacre 1991: 2). Archaeologists question why pots have rounded bottoms, how pots were made, who made them, where they originated and why burnished surfaces remerged throughout the millennia. We want to know how often people consumed meat, where the animals were sheltered and if pastoralists planted fields to be harvested. By the mid-twentieth century, the re-emergence of ethnoarchaeology came when traditional technologies had largely, but not entirely, become redundant due to the availability of mass-produced goods. Pockets of traditional craftspeople persisted in remote rural areas and their work has been recorded (Seeden 1985; Kamp 1987, 1991; Köhler-Rollefson 1987; Banning and Köhler-Rollefson 1992; McQuitty 1994; Lancaster and Lancaster 1995; Mollenhauer 1997; Mulder-Hymans 1997, 2014; Palmer 1998; London 2000a, 2000b; Sutton 2000; Taxel 2006; Salem 2009; Ebeling and Rogel 2015; Whiteway 2016; Shqairat 2018). These studies offer insight into how people cope with their environment to survive from day to day.

Ethnoarchaeological research dedicated to recording the practices and behaviours to produce or distribute traditional artefacts is designed to create viable templates for how people get things done. Innumerable problems arise from short-term, fortuitous encounters, inadequate sampling strategies or lack of quantitative data, especially in communities that differ in terms of social organization from an ancient society. W.A. Longacre (1991: 5–7) regarded the selection of an appropriate society to investigate as the most essential element in designing ethnoarchaeological fieldwork. It requires taking into consideration the political, economic, physical environment and history of a region in order to investigate any question and then devise plausible interpretations of past behaviours.

My fieldwork with traditional potters in the Philippines, Jordan and in Cyprus (at Kornos and Agios Demetrios) involved traditional craftspeople, i.e. those who use local materials to make pots for local customers. In contrast are the modern potters in each country. They use modern equipment and imported clays to make objects for locals or tourists. They were not part of my research.

Had I not lived full-time for months in the villages I would have seen a simpler, less complex picture of the pottery industries. By living in the villages, I witnessed infrequent events (clay mining), as well as weekly (kiln firings) and weekday activities (shaping pottery). My findings explain why handmade unglazed jugs remained in production and at times are preferable to the glazed wheel-thrown, or metal, glass and plastic water containers. I learned that the only way to improve on the traditional techniques to ferment, process and store goat cheese is the addition of petrochemicals and other modern ingredients that can pose health risks. The choice is between chemical enhancements and preservatives or traditional technologies and clay pots.

Traditional potters in Cyprus who coil-build jugs, jars, goat-milking pots, incense burners etc. work during the six-month dry season. If a similar weather pattern of wet cold winters and hot dry summer prevailed in the first millennium BCE, pottery-making was probably a seasonal activity then, as now. Potters past and present used the same local clay sources and fired their wares in wood-burning kilns. The pots, wood fuel and kiln must dry prior to firing or will explode as the heat causes steam to form in the pots and kiln. Accordingly, April to October provides the best opportunity to achieve ideal conditions for producing pottery, now and in the past. The inference for archaeologists is that pottery in antiquity was a seasonal activity, much like sheep-shearing, cheesemaking, weaving, basketry, etc. Women would spin and knit in winter, and girls might collect grasses, herbs and colouring agents in late summer for baskets to be woven during the snowy winters when fewer other chores were feasible in the mountain regions of Lebanon (Fuller 1970 [1961]: 26).

## EXAMPLES OF ETHNOARCHAEOLOGICAL RESEARCH

Investigations of ancient pottery, food preparation and cooking, industry, agricultural and pastoral practices, architecture, population estimates, determinants of wealth, religious artefacts, gendered work and burial habits all benefit from ethnoarchaeological findings from the Levant and elsewhere. Given space limitation, most examples of ethnoarchaeological case studies discussed below derive from fieldwork carried out in western Asia and the Mediterranean. General archaeological concerns for first-millennium BCE artefacts are addressed as well as specific applications to sites or material culture.

### *Pottery for water, food, fermentation, storage and transport*

My long-term observations of traditional female potters led me to assess cookware, jugs and jars as more than mere receptacles for food or beverages. The thick-walled earthen-coloured pots were not passive containers. They interacted with foods and water. Water held in jugs became purified, filtered and cool. After young people and children carried home water from wells or springs they transferred it to a large jar that often stood near house entrances in Jordan (Mershen 1985; London and Sinclair 1991: 421; London 2016: 259). Jugs and jars, the first automatic water filterers and coolers, were in high demand for more than one reason.

The regional geology comprising calcareous rocks creates hard mineral-rich water that tastes bitter. For this reason, people across the millennia filtered water in handmade unglazed clay jugs and jars that removed the minerals. Unglazed jugs absorb water until the porous walls become saturated and leak or 'sweat'. As water migrated through the walls, the bitter-tasting minerals became trapped inside the jug. At the same time the slow evaporation cooled, cleaned and sweetened the water. After a couple of months or longer, the mineral build-up inside the jugs created a dense white deposit that clogged the pores. Eventually the dense white deposit clogging the pores rendered the jug unserviceable to cool and sweeten water. This phenomenon was observed by Gezer archaeologist R.A.S. Macalister (1912 II: 1145 n.) who reported that jug walls became choked with mineral deposits after two or three months. In his broad study of potters, Frederick R. Matson (1965: 204) found the same occurred after a couple of months or years in different Middle Eastern communities. In contrast, the non-absorbent glazed and/or wheel-thrown jugs performed less efficiently but were available. Mid-nineteenth century unglazed jugs known for cooling water were made in Beirut and found markets throughout the Middle East (Milwright 2001: 39).

Another method to compensate for the mineral-rich water involved flavouring water with a sweet syrupy *grenade* or sour *verjus*, made from pomegranate juice in medieval times (Weaver 2006: 30). Pomegranates harvested in late August into early September remain edible for a year when stored in a method still practised in Turkey (Haldane 1990: 58–9). A reliance on the fruit is attested by the third-millennium BCE seeds and hard skins excavated at Arad (Hopf 1978: 74), Tell es-Sa'idiyeh (Cartwright 2002: 106–7), Jericho and in Cyprus at Hala Sultan Tekke (Haldane 1990: 59).

Urban Cypriots fondly recall the cool, sweet water poured from red handmade jugs in their grandparents' village. Until recently, in Jordan and Egypt large wheel-thrown ceramic water jars on main roads and in towns sometimes had a cup hanging from a rope attached to a handle. Mothers dipped the cup into the water to give young children a drink. Large wheel-thrown jars, made at Zizia village in central Jordan, filled with water for use at construction sites, at least until 1989 have pointed bases either buried in the ground or inserted into a tin jerrycan (see London 2016: 126–9, Figures 10.4 and 10.5).

Ethnoarchaeological research throughout western Asia and the eastern Mediterranean reveals the usefulness of handmade unglazed versions with porous walls and why they remained in production and out-performed all other water containers. The same holds for processing, fermenting and long-term storing of dairy foods. Clay jars are surpassed only by the addition of petrochemicals and/or other modern ingredients with their potential health risks.

## Pots for fermentation and storage

Prior to refrigeration, fermented foods were a staple nutritional source. Properties inherent to unglazed clay jars allow their porous walls to absorb whatever is placed inside them. The proteins and fats found in foods are absorbed and become part of the pot. They provide the necessary 'starter' to cause fresh milk or grains to ferment. Traditional fermentation techniques process and store milk, olives, oils, birds, sugar, salt, rosewater and alcoholic beverages benefit from the memories stored in the porous walls of pottery.

Without a reliable cooling device, fresh milk might last overnight or just a few hours in the warm temperatures of the Levant. To avoid waste during the time of plentiful milk and to assure the availability of dairy products in winter, villagers regularly fermented milk into yogurt and cheese in handmade unglazed clay jars until the mid-twentieth century (London 2016: 120–3). Boiled milk transferred to a clay jar was covered and kept warm in the sun or wrapped with blankets. As the liquid separated from the dairy protein and leaked out via the porous walls it left a thickened, cultured food to be eaten or dried for long-term storage. Jar walls retained some of the soured milk which would then automatically ferment any fresh milk poured into the same jar. Wheel-thrown jars with dense walls, covered with impenetrable glazes, were less satisfactory if not undesirable for fermentation or making yogurt.

The reliance on food fermentation is demonstrated by a dried dairy food prepared throughout the Mediterranean and Asia, from the Balkans to Iran (Hill and Bryer 1995: 48–53). In Cyprus, during the late summer months, women mixed milk with ground cracked wheat which fermented in a jar embedded with bacteria. Milk replenished over the course of several days gave the mixture a desired density and flavour. Added salt, lemon, unripe grapes, or bread promoted the sour taste. Women formed the thick sticky paste into finger length rectangular strips or sour bouillon cubes, *trachanas* or *tarhana* (Albrecht 1994: 16–17). The soured pieces dried on sunny rooftops before being transferred to an airtight container that could hang from a roof rafter for months as in 2013 (London 2016: 121, Figure 10.1). In winter people would ingeniously reconstitute the dried cubes by pouring boiling water on top to make an instant warming soup without cooking or a pot. Since the nineteenth century, women in north Jordan made something similar called *kishk* (Palmer 1998: 160) comparable to *kushuk*, Syrian dried *laban* cakes (Sweet 1960: 129). These are recent versions of softened crushed grain in milk known from second millennium BCE Mesopotamian texts. In their day, the Romans ate wheat balls boiled in milk and reconstituted with water (Bottéro 1985: 43).

A second Cypriot dairy product, the *challoumi* white cheese, traditionally ripened and later was stored in a clay jar. In briny water the semi-hard cheese remains edible for a year without refrigeration. The two-handled *challoumokouza* (cheese pot), named for the cheese, never held meat (personal communication K. Demetriou, November 1986).

Small birds transported long-distance in clay jars were described by John Locke in 1553. People would: 'pickle them with vinegar and salt, and to put them in pots and send them to Venice and other places of Italy' (Cobham 1969 [1908]: 72). Pickled fowl in large jars depicted in an Eighteenth-Dynasty Theban tomb painting show plucked ducks preserved and stored in brine or oil (Wilson 2001: 40, Figure 48). Ancient porous pots throughout the first century BCE enabled the fermentation of fresh food items for shipment and trade or for storage.

Other foods fermented in clay jars embedded with bacteria and protein include grains, grape alcohol or wine and olives (London 2016: 119–34). Sourdough breads were the norm.

*First-millennium BCE cold containers for fish?*

Pickled, dried, salted or smoked fish reached inland sites in the Levant based on the bones carefully collected at excavations (Peters, Pöllath and von den Driesch 2002: 329; Gambash et al. 2019: 222). In the western Negev semi-arid zone, sixth-century CE mosaics near Kissufim depict a camel carrying jars, *gazitia*, from the pottery workshops of Gaza. Given the cooling ability of jars, might fresh fish have been transported during the first millennium BCE? The sweating, leaking porous walls of 'cooling' jars could have kept fish fresh in water cool enough to send inland. Sixth-century texts mention Mediterranean fish supplied to a resident Persian garrison and civilian population in Jerusalem. The fish arrived in ceramic 'containers' known as *maqartu*, a term that has been linked to the Aramaic word for 'cooling' (Edelman 2006: 207–9). Fresh fish could have been shipped in a 'cooling' container, i.e. a ceramic jar that kept its contents cool. Jars filled early in the morning along the coast could have been transported to some point at which the fish was transferred to fresh cooling containers filled with cool water.

*Honey*

Recent excavations at Tel Rehov in the Galilee area have unearthed Iron Age II beehives, which initiated ethnoarchaeological research on traditional beekeeping. Prior to the discovery, archaeologists did not know where to find hives, how they looked or how they were made. At Tel Rehov, unfired piles of cylindrical clay hives in the town centre belonged to an industrial apiary, which was preserved due to a huge conflagration. The accidental firing was critical to the discovery. Traditional unfired hives are similar in composition, shape, location and arrangement. At nearby Nahaf village, unfired clay, straw and dung hives stand adjacent to houses rather than in fields or outside the village (Mazar and Panitz-Cohen 2007). Cylindrical clay hives in Cyprus until the late twentieth century stood close to houses and in Agios Demetrios, Marathasa, near a schoolhouse (Figures 5.1a, 5.1b). Cypriot cylinder hives, however, were kiln-fired (London 2020b: 18–19).

Beekeeping might have more common for millennia than is currently recognized in the Levant. Sixteenth-century Ottoman-era records stipulate taxes collected from villages in Palestine, information that is supported by excavated hives (Taxel 2006). Ancient hives near houses were probably unrecognized unless the clay cylinders fired accidentally. The implication for archaeologists is that piles of clay mixed with dung and straw, within or between domestic structures, could represent ancient hives.

FIGURE 5.1a: Abandoned traditional beehive near Dhali in rural Cyprus consisting of fired ceramic cylinders arranged in six rows held in place with mud. Photographed by Knud Jensen in July 1971.

FIGURE 5.1b: Beehive at Dhali, Cyprus, piled into three rows and covered with cylindrical roof tiles. Painted crosses mark some lids. Photographed by Knud Jensen in July 1971.

## Ovens and women's networks

Women in different places traditionally relied on a variety of ovens, installations and techniques to bake bread and cook foods. The diversity helps to explain the different types of ancient hearths, cooking areas and pot shapes. Alison McQuitty (1984, 1994) recorded the advantages of closed or open heating in terms of fuel, portability and the quantity or size of breads. Ethnoarchaeological studies highlight the requirements for leavened or unleavened breads in Syria and Jordan (Mulder-Hymans 1997, 2014: 163–9; Shafer-Elliott 2013: 119–25; Ebeling and Rogel 2015).

The locations of traditional ovens and hearths, inside or outside built structures, led to traditional women's networks and cooperative work. Neighbours and extended family members shared outdoor ovens in order to conserve fuel and help each other with the heavier tasks, such as carrying wooden bread boards holding dough for six to twenty-four breads (London 2020b: Figure 10.17). Each woman could hoist her board (15 kilograms when empty) to one shoulder to carry it to the oven, but it was more easily balanced on the shoulders of two women (Figure 5.2). While the bread baked, the multitasking women shared medical, ritual and other types of knowledge. Bread would bake in the morning before the pots of food went in later. After meals, food residue burned off dirty pots placed in the ovens overnight to further maximize the heat.

## Animal bones, disposal and meat consumption

Excavated animal bones lead to questions concerning why certain bones are present, why others are habitually absent, why specific animals dominate, which animals were beasts of burden, food, milked, or raised for their skins and hair. Do bones inform on meat consumption? Archaeologists associate bones primarily with social or ritual ceremonies and feasting (Keswani 1994: 260–1) rather than the regular diet and assume that most people could not afford meat. In contrast, Justin Lev-Tov (2003) considers meat-eating as essential to maintaining a herd. He presents excavated bones and textual data from Umar, Ugarit and the Hebrew Bible as evidence of meat in the normal diet rather than a luxury food (Lev-Tov and McGeough 2007: 104–8). The availability of meat is also apparent from the animal fats identified in residue analyses of pottery, although it falls short as an indicator of the amount of meat consumed or of pot use (London 2016: 16, 110). Not all pots embedded with animal fat were used to cook meat. Instead, the fat served as a pot lining that filled the pores to limit leaking.

One example of ancient meat meals at Tall al-'Umayri included 25,000 animal bone fragments in a pit. Of the accompanying 458 LB/Iron Age I sherds, 35 per cent belonged to cookware. The deposit could represent a seasonal feast at an aggregate site where people congregated seasonally to complete work in the field, shear animals and engage in a variety of religious, social and political activities (London 2011, 2017: 356–7). Evidence of less auspicious meals with meat are harder to identify but not necessarily atypical. If the bones were shared with pets who carried them away, little remains for archaeologists to excavate. In a 1980s Syrian village, bones tossed to dogs could end up in fields or elsewhere, far from the cooking fire (Kamp 1991: 27). An ethnoarchaeological study of farmers and herders at an isolated Golan Heights Druze village found that after meals, most bones landed in the dump, while others remained in alleys and courtyards (Grantham 2000).

FIGURE 5.2: Traditional Cypriot breadboard with spaces for nine round loaves of bread seen leaning against a wall. After the dough rises on the board women carry it to the oven. The raised knob in the centre of each depression prevents the dough from sticking to the wood. Photographed by Knud Jensen in July 1971.

# FIRST-MILLENNIUM BCE POTTERY INDUSTRY: ORGANIZATION, HETEROGENEITY, DIVERSITY, AND LOCATION

## Organization

Archaeologists regularly describe the great variation of pot shapes, sizes, colours and surface treatments of paint, slip or burnish. The question remains: who made the pots? The composition of recent communities of traditional potters provides evidence of male and female professional craftspeople who produced utilitarian cookware, store jars, ovens, jugs etc. for distribution to the local populace. A similar pattern could have existed in the past if we finally expunge the ideas that male professionals dominated while women stayed close to home and were precluded from working as craft specialists in workshop or factory settings far from home. Bioarchaeological-forensic assessment of worn bones along with skeleto-muscular evidence from a first-millennium BCE female skeleton excavated in Crete at Eleutherna are consistent with protracted, heavy, repetitive movements of producing pottery with a kick-wheel and no other activity (Agelarakis 2020). Her bones prove that women worked as craft specialists, corroborating decades of ethnoarchaeological findings. Traditional female potters can and do produce thousands of pots annually in the courtyard of their homes and they formerly worked as itinerants, based on my research in Cyprus. Women figured out how to leave home to benefit their family and broader society as a whole. They produced and sold handmade wares while working in the courtyards of their homes, in a communal workspace or wherever they received a commission away from home. Some female potters temporarily relocated their entire nuclear family to produce their regular repertoire, as itinerants, in villages some 40 kilometres from home (London 2020b: 69–70). By working in Troodos Mountain foothill villages they: (1) avoided transporting the highly breakable pottery across a fragmented hilly terrain; (2) exchanged pots for foods needed to survive the winter months; (3) escaped the high humidity and temperatures of lowland Cyprus; and (4) found mates for their offspring while expanding the gene pool. Resourceful women were not limited to Cyprus. Elsewhere, Laura Swantek (2016) demonstrates the mobility of female metal- and stone-workers despite the absence of material remains indicative of their efforts. Accordingly, it is likely that first-millennium BCE male and female potters, aided by young people, shaped the ceramic containers for regional sale or exchange.

## Coexistence of handmade and wheel-thrown pottery

Despite any perceived advantages of wheel-thrown pottery, it never fully replaced handmade wares during the past 400 years in Cyprus and Jordan (London 2016: 91, 152, 2020b: 60–1; London and Dometios 2015: 210, Figure 4, which shows a mid-twentieth-century shop selling all pot types). Glazed pottery made excellent table wares but poor kitchen wares. The coexistence of both manufacturing techniques probably characterized the first-millennium BCE southern Levant. Likewise, Late Cypriot fine wares coexisted along with handmade coarse wares (Georgiou 2018: 191–2). Medieval-era handmade Geometrically Painted Ware jugs, made at multiple locations in the Levant according to petrographic analysis, defy characterization as a single industry (Gabrieli, Ben-Shlomo and Walker 2014) and contrast with the abundant contemporaneous wheel-thrown pottery. The handmade painted porous jugs made ideal containers to cool and filter water, in contrast to the wheel-thrown jugs with their dense nearly impervious walls (London 2016: 126–8).

In Jordan, medieval-era kilns at Jerash held handmade basins, bowls and roof tiles as well as wheel-turned jars (Schaefer 1986: 425). Early medieval handmade bowls, troughs, basins and lamps persisted alongside wheel-thrown containers elsewhere in the Levant (Stacy 2004: 91, 101, 104). The perpetuation of handmade wares alongside wheel-thrown pottery resulted from the different purposes each served. Both were essential, throughout history, until refrigeration and electricity became widely available.

## Seasonal and regional differences in output

Long-term fieldwork permits a more complex picture of reality. Kornos village potters produced more casseroles than deep cookware in August and September 1986. Casseroles (*ttavades*) for vegetables, with or without meat, bake in ovens, as do the deep cooking pots with meat. Casseroles lack lids, in contrast to the deep pots. Quantitative data for 1,880 pots, made from May until mid-July 1986, includes those I saw stacked, fired and unloaded from the kiln. Thousands more pots were produced in those months. Of the 1,880, 11 per cent were deep round-bottomed cookware, and casseroles accounted for 15 per cent. In August I counted 686 pots made in a Troodos Mountain village. Only 6 per cent were deep cooking pots and 3 per cent casseroles. I account for the different proportions of deep versus shallow cookware to an annual September event in Kornos. Visitors receive a regional delicacy, *ttavas* (casserole) served in a small casserole (*ttavas*). The recipe originated in Lefkara near Kornos. Potters increased casserole output in late summer for the celebration, unlike the more distant Troodos Mountain potters who had no comparable tradition. The inferences are that: (1) potters had a seasonally adjusted output; (2) different parts of Cyprus had regional foods that required particular pot types; and (3) meat cooked in deep cookware with lids while vegetables baked in casseroles.

## Dearth of ancient kilns and pottery-production locations

Ethnoarchaeology contradicts accepted explanations for the small number of excavated ancient pottery-production sites. Rather than located on the edge of town, close to the raw materials or away from residential areas to avoid potential fires and smoke (Wood 1990: 33), in Egypt (Nicholson and Patterson 1985), Cyprus (London 1989), the Philippines and Mesoamerica professional craftspeople worked and fired their wares adjacent to home (Figure 5.3). For this and other reasons, idle kilns were intentionally dismantled. They disappeared along with the material correlates of the industry. People reused the kiln bricks, stones and workspace. Pottery production and kilns located in a household courtyard occupied valuable territory and were obliterated once the craft ended or a potter retired. In addition, workshops or factories dedicated to pottery production may well have stood away from domestic space, as known during the Roman era.[1]

The 'disappearance' or invisibility of household workshops also stems from toolkits fashioned from recycled perishable organic wood, cloth, bark, string or leather. All such equipment disintegrated over time. Without durable tools, the seasonal workspaces of potters become invisible. Traditional itinerant male or female potters left no traces, especially since in Cyprus pot and jar makers fired their wares in kilns built to fire bricks. Nearly every village had a kiln to make the bricks needed to construct houses. The brick-firing kilns did double duty to fire pots when needed. Consequently, itinerant potters rarely erected their own kiln. As a result, production locations of seasonal jobs, past and present, defy detection

---

[1] For the distribution of kilns in ancient Greece, see https://atlasgreekkilns.arizona.edu/.

FIGURE 5.3: Kiln of private Kornos potter, Mrs Kyriacou Kyriacou, stands adjacent to other buildings. Stones and bricks (not seen here) were reused after it was demolished. Photograph courtesy of the author, 1986.

for two contradictory reasons: potters worked seasonally in household courtyards or they worked as itinerants far away from home (London 2020b: 174–5, 185). Multiple behaviours contribute to the difficulty archaeologists confront to identify ancient kilns and pottery-production locations. Potters who threw pots on a fast heavy wheel might have worked year-round at more permanent workshops although direct evidence is lacking.

## Repairs and residues in pottery

Another topic of ceramic ethnoarchaeology concerns the main problem with pottery: breakability. When an ancient pot cracked, people drilled holes into both sides of the break before inserting a piece of gut or metal to connect both pieces. Quantification of holes in Bronze and Iron Age sherds at Tall al-'Umayri yields a low count. Rarely are both sides of a cracked repaired pot found (London 1991a, 2017: 356–7, 2020a). Traditional communities use different ways to repair cracked pots and succeed without drilling holes. Consequently, it can be assumed that any ancient pots fixed without the holes evade detection.

The repair method employed by Cypriot men who sold new pots differs from techniques used by pot owners. At the Kornos Pottery Cooperative, I observed a man responsible for sales mend a chipped rim or fill a minor crack. He ground an old sherd before mixing the powder with water and applying it to the fired pots. Travelling salesmen would carry clay in their pocket to make repairs (personal communication, Cypriot villager 2017). Alternatively, donkey ear wax was pushed into the crack of a new pot. In contrast, pot owners plugged a larger pot hole with goat skin that was held in place with hot pitch or resin (personal communication A. Georgiades, November 2020).

## Residues in dairy pots

Residues of dairy products, extracted from Neolithic pottery excavated throughout the Levant and Turkey, are comparable to residues in recent Turkish ceramic churns for butter, cheese and yogurt. Ancient pottery preserves the fatty acids from suet or lard. Traditional ceramic churns are embedded with modern dairy, sheep, wild boar and goat fats. It is more challenging to distinguish plant residues (of olives, grains and lentils) especially when combined with animal foods (Gregg and Slater 2010: 842, 852). However, ancient food residue embedded into the wall of pots need not inform on the diet. Rather than insights about the ancient menu, or farming and herding practices, the residue analyses could inform on pre-cooking preparation techniques. In traditional societies, suet, tallow, lard, dairy or vegetal products poured into new pots coated the porous walls of cookware to minimize leakage (London 2016: 103–10). We currently lack the means to differentiate foods that were cooked in a pot from the edibles used to temper, season or prepare pot walls in order to reduce porosity. The implication for archaeologists is that the memories stored deep in pot walls reveal a full life history.

New oil jugs made in Phini and Kornos were coated with wax or a sticky product obtained at the olive oil press (personal communication, T. Pilavakis 1986). Alternatively, old water jugs with clogged pores were reused for oil, honey and other fluids. Another option for unserviceable or broken jugs was to place them on niches high on the wall of churches, or embedded into the wall, to enhance the resonance of the human voice, as was the practice in Cyprus (personal communication, M. Savvas 2017) and elsewhere in Europe (Valière et al. 2013). Cypriot jugs with chipped rims, recently removed for church renovations at Kornos, have cracked or missing handles (Figures 5.4a and 5.4b).

ETHNOGRAPHIC INSIGHTS

FIGURE 5.4a: Niches close to the roof in the Kornos church (photographed during refurbishing work) held jugs secured by bricks and stones, March 2017. Photograph courtesy of M. Savvas.

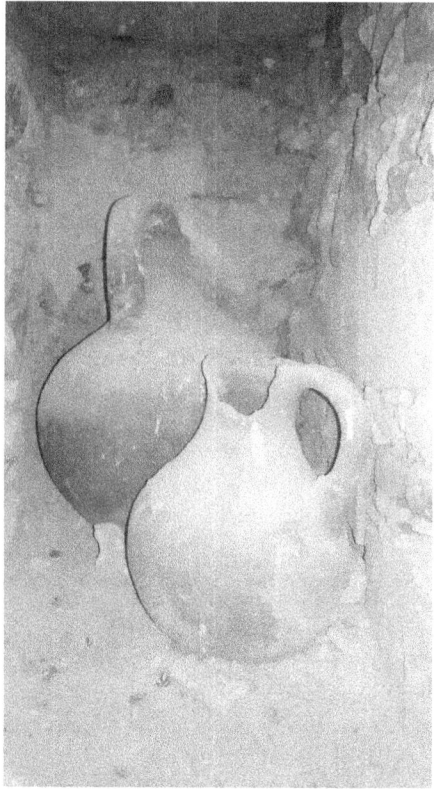

FIGURE 5.4b: Used jugs with broken rims together in a niche at the old Kornos church, March 2017. Photograph courtesy of M. Savvas.

## Architecture and spatial organization as evidence of use

To address how ancient architecture reflects its social setting, we normally attach a single purpose to a room: sleeping, cooking or storage. In an Iranian village of 150 residents, Lee Horne (1994: 9, 119, 177) found that no room in a mudbrick house was limited in purpose, regardless of the family size. Instead, the people and the types of activities carried out in any room varied and changed (Horne 1994: 159). In 1980 at the Syrian village of Darnaj, Kathryn Kamp (2000: 91) found that people worked wherever it felt best, according to season, inside or outside. Even places for sleeping and entertaining varied in the Syrian village, where people followed the shade in summer and the sun in winter (Kamp 1993: 305–7). Changes in room function need not correspond to architectural modifications but manifest in room contents (Kamp 1993: 310). Interior room usage in Cyprus, Iran and Syria followed a devolutionary trajectory as old rooms became spaces to store animals and their feed (Horne 1994: 180; London 2020b: 132). To observe the seasonal changes in the allocation of space requires the long-term presence of an ethnoarchaeologist. In the Troodos village of Agios Demetrios (Marathasa), household courtyards where women made pottery during the summer converted into a goat shelter, where in the autumn women could feed the goats a steady supply of fresh leaves and herbs before collecting milk to prepare shelf-stable foods for winter. A workspace in Kornos was converted into a storage area for vegetables and baby chicks.

In addition, rooms were in a state of transition. While demolishing part of a residence, people built, rebuilt or remodelled elsewhere in the compound. For archaeologists, the implications are that not all buildings or rooms of a structure housed people or are representative of the number of residents. To ameliorate the problem requires study of the microdeposits of floors to determine if animals had been present and an assessment of what is found in the rooms and its state of preservation. Alteration to an ancient building's interior features, walls and floors signal a change in room use. Dung mixed with soil on a floor that also has the remnants of animal feed could indicate that people no longer lived in the unit. Kamp (2000: 89) noted the quality of floor maintenance as indicative of wealth. Lack of maintenance of walls, such as annual lime whitewashing, could indicate the absence of human occupation.

During long-term field research that included the winter off-season, I witnessed potters in two Cypriot villages storing their turntables and disassembling clay mixing troughs to repurpose the space where they had made the pots in summer. The implications for archaeologists are: (1) where we find an artefact is not necessarily where it was used; and (2) courtyard activity varies seasonally. In general, women's work that involves portable pots or weaving looms can occur inside or outside, on a roof, in a building or in a courtyard, depending on the weather, lighting and other concurrent demands on their time.

## Architecture and spatial organization as evidence of population size

Most ancient population estimates tend to be exaggerated for urban and rural sites (Geva 2014). Population size based on a single attribute, such as covered interior space, is untenable in rural communities because of the seasonal need to house animals. The ethnoarchaeological study of households at Darnaj found no relationship between house size and family size given that the community of 1,500 people made extensive use of outdoor areas and the overall privacy was minimal (Kamp 2000: 86). The latter behaviour is known widely from ethnographic studies in traditional Lebanese (Fuller 1970 [1961]: 29), Palestinian (Seger 1981: 29) and Jordanian villages (Mollenhauer 1997: 422).

Kamp (1993: 305) emphasizes the impropriety of treating interior and exterior spaces as two distinct areas for specific functions. Indoor cooking or food preparation (and other work) was uncommon throughout the Middle East and Cyprus. Separately enclosed kitchens are a twentieth-century concept for traditional homes in Europe (personal communication, M. den Nijs, 1996). Late twentieth-century interior kitchens in new houses erected for Syrian villagers in the Hawran, did not eliminate dish-washing, cooking and clothes-washing outside. Kitchens became storage for food and seeds (Azar et al. 1985: 138). Women processed and prepared foods on rooftops and in courtyards (London and Sinclair 1991: 421). At the town of Salt in Jordan, the outdoor workspaces matched the size of covered interior house space (Mollenhauer 1997: 421).

Late medieval Mediterranean communities prepared foods in home kitchens that lacked running water or fire and required people to send pots of food, or breads, to be baked in shops (Levanoni 2005). An Ottoman-era prohibition on household ovens until the early nineteenth century, possibly resulted in the *klibani*, a free-standing oven used over a fire in Cyprus (Gabrieli 2006: 6.28). It is feasible that not all first-millennium BCE homes had enclosed kitchens.

People residing in traditional communities might own multiple homes for seasonal use and storage. Pastoralists who camped in tents or caves while travelling with their herds in search of grazing in southern Jordan owned permanent structures in villages where they store possessions and animal feed (Köhler-Rollefson 1987: 536–8; Lancaster and Lancaster 1995: 116; Shqairat 2018: 11). An analysis of the sixteenth-century population of Ramle found no mention of Bedouin who probably were present and were listed in regional census data for Jerusalem and Nablus (Singer 1990: 61).

Until recently, residents of upland Greek villagers slept in a nearby hamlet when tending to their terraced fields, flocks or making cheese seasonally. The reconstruction of demographic history from the official census data involves complexities emanating from changes in village names, an undercount of women or a relocation near their original siting (Sutton 2000: 84, 87). The pottery-producing village of Kornos in Cyprus relocated repeatedly in the past century. Consequently, village census lists provide incomplete data because many factors contribute to under- or over-counting. Fluidity of populations and settlement patterns probably characterized ancient communities in Greece (Sutton 2000: 105). Flexibility and seasonality of resident populations has been proposed for the late second millennium BCE at Tall al-ʿUmayri (Lev-Tov, Porter and Routledge 2011: 76–7; London 2017: 357).

The implications for archaeologists who estimate the first-millennium BCE population of ancient Israel are that building measurements, covered spaces or a reliance on texts at best provide incomplete and redacted data. Instead of a straightforward connection between houses and residents, the reality is more complicated like the complex lives of ordinary ancient people.

## *Household affluence and wealth*

To determine the status of an ancient population and its connection to the larger society, archaeologists assess evidence of long-distance trade, metals, semi-precious stones, artefact quantities and building size. In general, more and bigger is better than fewer or an absence of 'luxury' items, but are we measuring the right things and drawing meaningful conclusions? Ethnoarchaeological studies that examine the relationships between wealth/status and material possessions reveal that the numbers of pots or rooms need not correspond with wealth. Traditional Iranian villagers, regardless of affluence, owned 'costly' rugs and large copper pots to process milk or cook (Horne 1994: 157–60). Instead of portable artefacts, wealth in the Iranian village correlated with the amount of covered or roofed spaces, exactly as Kamp found in a Syrian village. The wealthiest households did not always own bigger houses filled with more material wealth. Instead, they owned more land or animals than others. Ancient architectural indices of wealth ideally include 'features that are expensive enough so that they cannot be indulged in by all households' (Kamp 2000: 89, 91). She refers to land, covered space and animals.

In the Iranian village where Horne (1994: 8, 95) spent three summers, nearly 40 per cent of the village rooms sheltered animals owned by the wealthiest people. Covered space equated not to human population, but to herd size. Furthermore, one quarter of all village roofed areas housed animals or stored straw. Ancient flock sizes remain unknown, but the need to periodically house them and store feed required interior space. It is conceivable that covered spaces in ancient villages were at a premium, not to house people but to protect the herders' highly valued flocks. Assessments of wealth and population size require consideration of the essential herds.

## Threshing floors

Archaeologists search for threshing floors in order to learn about farming practices and to determine boundaries lines. Based on recent studies in Cyprus and Jordan, there is no single place, size, shape or location for traditional threshing floors given the highly varied topography. Circular floors (12–25 metres diameter) or rectangular floors (47 × 37 and 30 × 43 metres or larger) stood within 100–200 metres from the house, near the fields or on the village/town edge (Whittaker 1996: 110, 118; 2000: 65–7; Yerkes 2000: 29). A stone enclosure wall was not mandatory but lessened grain loss and prevented animals from trespassing on the floors made of packed earth, bedrock, clay, plaster or limestone slabs.

A small threshing floor at el-Grubb in north Jordan stood in a valley below steep agricultural terraces, seen in July 1989 (London and Sinclair 1991: 421) and contrasts with earlier communal village threshing floors. Other small threshing spots stood near the fields, away from a village, on rocky outcrops or hardened earth (Palmer 1998: 152). The ethnoarchaeological research presents the range of traditional options that have changed over time. The durable material correlates of threshing areas are uniformly small chipped stones. They reveal little about their production or use date.

## Post-Stone Age chipped stone tools at threshing floors

Chipped stone flakes excavated in Bronze and Iron Age deposits are often deemed misplaced or intrusive artefacts belonging to earlier eras. Ethnoarchaeological research demonstrates that worked flint and chert were not confined to prehistoric societies. Ground stone functioned until at least the late twentieth century as observed in Cyprus. Imported basalt stones from Turkey excelled over other stones to crush sesame seeds to make *halva* in Nicosia.

Ethnoarchaeological studies of threshing boards detail their manufacture from wood and chipped stones. The 'teeth' (Isa. 41.15) made of chert or basalt that cut and crushed the grain. Cypriot threshing sleds consisted of two or more attached wooden planks (approximately 2 metres long × 60 centimetres wide), with the front end slanting upwards (Figures 5.5a, 5.5b). Each had 200–300 flakes or more wedged into parallel rows of cuts on the lower side of the boards (Whittaker 1996: 109; Given 2004: 126). The flakes

FIGURE 5.5a: Threshing sledge (*doukani* or *voukani*) pulled by two donkeys as Mr Michael Fiori stands on top at Politiko, Cyprus. Photographed by Knud Jensen in July 1971.

FIGURE 5.5b: Underside of threshing board with chipped stones inserted into the wood, photographed at Politiko, Cyprus, by Knud Jensen in July 1971.

measured 5–9 centimetres long, 2.5–4.4 centimetres wide and 1.0–1.7 centimetres thick (Whittaker 1996: 115, 118, 2000: 65; for a close-up of flints, see Yerkes 2000: 28). Itinerant craftsmen collected and roughly shaped stones at the source before returning home via the homes of farmers in the spring. Retouching or trimming work at the threshing floor, while fitting stones into the wood, left piles of slivers (Whittaker 2000: 66).

A person standing on top added weight and directed the animal(s) around the threshing floor. In 1920s Palestine, 'the sledge for threshing was of hard wood, its front turned up and cavities on the underside. In these cavities short basalt stones and pebbles were inserted. The sledge was hitched to oxen. As children our task was to sit on the sledge thus providing extra weight and pressure' (Biran 2001: 1). Basalt or flint outfitted traditional threshing boards in Lebanon (Seeden 1985: 297–8), Syria (Fuller 1970 [1961]: 76) and north Jordan. In contrast, Carol Palmer (1998: 152–4) recorded trampling bitter vetch and lentil by people and donkeys with their feet. Both foods are known from first-millennium BCE excavations. Elsewhere, in central Greece at least until 1981 (Murray and Kardulias 2000: 150), horses tethered to a central pole walked around circular threshing floors without dragging a sledge (Clarke 2000: 177). Sledges in southern Europe and south-west Asia were more efficient than flailing or trampling, even for domesticated 'free-threshing' grain varieties (Yerkes 2000: 29).

The archaeological implications are: (1) chipped stone usage spanned the millennia from the prehistoric periods to the present; (2) threshing did not always require a stone-studded board or sledge; (3) threshing floors can be close or far from structures; and (4) worked stones excavated at or near historical-era sites could belong to traditional threshing boards and were not necessarily intrusive artefacts from earlier periods. Finally, debitage (waste from shaping the flakes) together with the flattened worn stones are the material remains of threshing activity where all of the organic material no longer exists. At 'Uvda Valley in the Negev, twenty-nine threshing floors had thousands of chipped stones, leading to its designation as 'flint workshops' (Avner et al. 2003: 462–3). Perhaps they mark places to refit sledges with their 'teeth' or a temporary seasonal workspace for knappers. Similar piles of chipped stones or debitage could designate first-millennium BCE threshing sites.

## Subsistence strategies of pastoralists

Although archaeologists long assumed that non-sedentary pastoralists avoided agriculture and left minimal material remains given periodic moves searching for food for their animals. Ilse Köhler-Rollefson (1987; Banning and Köhler-Rollefson 1992) questioned the sharp dichotomy between agriculturalists and pastoralists. She demonstrated the opposite prevails in southern Jordan.

## Representations of snakes

Snake-like patterns beginning with Pre-Pottery Neolithic stone artefacts excavated near Eilat in southern Israel (Orrelle et al. 2020) represents an early use of the reptile motif that continued up to the present in the eastern Mediterranean. Painted or three-dimensional replicas on Chalcolithic-era pots and ossuaries in the southern Levant (Caselli 2020: 179–80), on Bronze Age Cypriot pottery (Herscher 1976: 16, Plates III, V), on tenth-century BCE pithoi at Tel Dan in northern Israel (Biran 1994: 166–8, Figures 126 and 128) and on Geometric Period Cycladic pots (Beaumont et al. 2014: 118, Figure 3,

Plate 31: 2; and Charalambidou 2020) demonstrate the longevity and widespread prominence of snake motifs. Three-dimensional and incised snake patterns appear on decorative traditional handmade wares and on wine fermentation pithoi (*pitharia*) in Cyprus (Dometios and London 2016: 32–3; London 2020b: 73, 107, Figures 2.10, 9.13).

People feared the strength and poisonous venom of a creature associated with the underworld and linked to the chthonic cult in Greek mythology. Simultaneous positive attributions reflect the ability of snakes to shed and rejuvenate their skin. According to Akkadian and Classical era texts, skin boiled in wine was a curative beverage (Polcaro 2019: 784).

The opposing views of snakes in part reflect the poisonous versus the non-lethal varieties. Harmless black whip snakes in Cyprus were welcome in the fields and in buildings. They guarded growing grain by eating the predators of a maturing crop. Afterwards they guarded the harvested grain stored in a clay jar. Deemed as protectors of the home, snakes controlled the rodents and preserved the family grain supply. Snake-shaped wedding breads would hang on the house wall for protection until the first born tasted it (London 2020b: 119, Figure 10.21). Snakes, as classroom pets in mid-twentieth-century schools, controlled the population mice (personal communication D. Voskaridou, 18 September 2017).

In antiquity, applied or incised wavy lines encircling jars could represent the protective snake, which was needed based on a first-millennium BCE large jar embedded into the ground at Tall al-'Umayri. It was entirely empty except for the complete skeletal remains of a mouse (personal communication, L. Geraty 2008). The ethnoarchaeological research demonstrates that the non-venomous snakes provided food security in contrast to any connection with the underworld.

## RELIGION: ARTEFACTS AND PRACTICES

### *Artefacts of religious significance*

Two traditional artefacts bearing religiously significant symbols in Cyprus had non-sacral uses. Wooden bread stamps that carry an undisputed Christian message were impressed on loaves destined for church use. The same impressions made on the shoulder or rims of traditional wine fermentation jars (London 2020b: 94–6; 183; Figures 2.3, 2.5, 9:17, 19) do not mark the wine as designated for sacral use necessarily (Figures 5.6a, 5.6b). The shallow impressions on some jars led Knud Jensen to infer that jar makers worked with older, worn stamps (London 2020b: 94). The impressions made on jars represent an explicit religious writing reused for profane purposes.

A second artefact with Christian symbols is the handmade incense burner (Figure 5.7). Some have three dots incised on the top of their handle. In 1965, 1966 and 1971, when Knud Jensen asked potters, nuns and others about the dots, some mentioned that they symbolize the Trinity, although others disputed the association. In 1986, when I asked the same question, a small survey of Greek Orthodox practitioners gave the same ambiguous responses. However, Muslims who used the same censers considered the dots as purely decorative. For archaeologists the inferences are: (1) artefacts are understood differently; (2) the same artefact has multiple meanings; and (3) a single artefact is insufficient to assign ethnic or religious identity. A censer alone does not signify a religious preference. Like the reused bread stamps, artefacts of indisputable religious purpose do not automatically imply sacral use, a single use, or unchangeable usage.

FIGURE 5.6a: Huge (1 metre tall) wine fermentation jar at Kalokhorio, Cyprus, with a raised snake-like wavy strip between two horizontal bands. An added patch of clay below the rim is impressed with a bread stamp (*typari*). It reads: IC-XC-NI-KA 'Jesus Christ conquers (or is victorious)'. Photographed by Knud Jensen in July 1971.

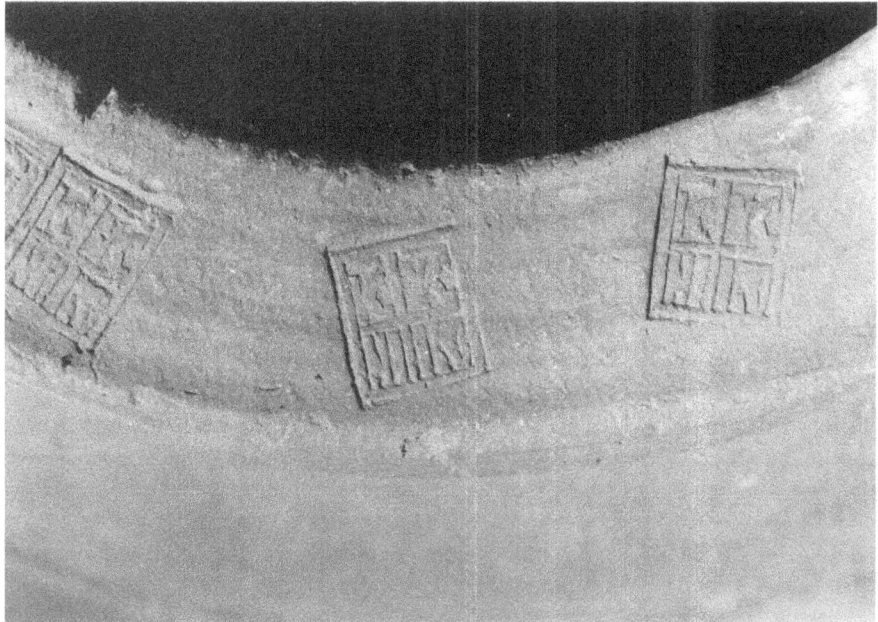

FIGURE 5.6b: The same letters are impressed on the jar rim, photographed by Knud Jensen in July 1971. (See London 2020b: 16–18.)

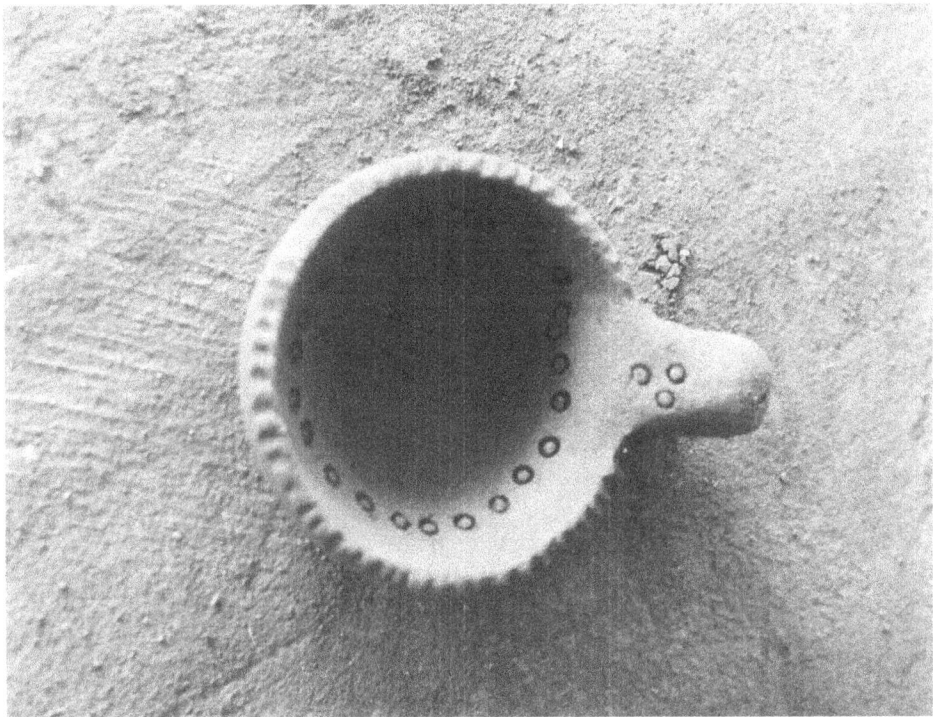

FIGURE 5.7: Incense burner with three impressed dots at the handle top plus a row encircle the interior bowl, made in Kornos, Cyprus. Photographed by Knud Jensen in June 1971.

A comparable situation involves the first-millennium BCE ceramic female figurines from the Judean Hills (Darby 2014). A single 'cultic' designation obscures changes in their use and meaning. Their initial purpose, reuse or transformation can be inferred from the different contexts in which they were excavated, their physical condition and accompanying artefacts (London 2020b: 183).

### Contemporaneous folk beliefs and formal religious practices

The coexistence of traditional Cypriot folk beliefs alongside formal religious manifestations serves as a model for first-millennium BCE religions in the Levant (London 2020b: 182). Ancient texts, names and seals record the formal religion while contemporaneous evidence of folk beliefs is plentiful. Clay figurines, symbols on pottery in ancient Israel (e.g. snakes jars at Tel Dan and region-wide), gods or goddesses wielding snakes, jewellery and cult objects at Megiddo display snakes (Loud 1948: Plates 240: 1, 4), as at Gezer (Macalister 1912 II: 339 Figure 488) or Hazor (Yadin et al. 1961: Plates 339: 5, 6).

While the parameters of a popular or folk religion are nebulous, they differ from the official religious beliefs and practices. The idea of internal 'religious pluralism' (Albertz and Schmitt 2012: 49–56), is exemplified in Cyprus where Greek Orthodoxy prevails alongside practices that take place within the home embodying long-held customs which are outside the formal religion. The coexistence of folk and formal religious traditions of the first millennium BCE is preserved in the material culture which can be ambiguous, but highly suggestive.

## Women and children

An emphasis on describing the activities often assigned exclusively to the work and efforts of men, such as large buildings and defence construction, weapons of war, trade and texts, leaves little room for the contribution of women, children and the elderly (Nakhai 2008: x). Ethnoarchaeological and ethnographic case studies reveal that considering work as a binary, either carried out by men or women, oversimplifies the reality. Men and women engaged most aspects of traditional pottery production in Cyprus. Both genders participated in every stage of the work from mining and preparing clay, shaping pots by hand, firing and selling. At times men or women might have been more prone to perform certain tasks than the other gender. By 1986 men dominated clay mining (not processing), sales and distribution (London 2016: 70–2, 75, 89–90, Figure 6.9). The involvement of a 'family team' to produce pottery in certain Mexico communities (Hirshman 2020: 15) is paralleled among traditional potters in the Philippines and in Cyprus. In all instances, the team comprises people of all ages, including the elderly and children (London 1991b: Figure 9.9, 202). Potters continue to shape pottery for sale and for personal use into their seventies and eighties.

Children had little time for play given their involvement in subsistence strategies at the Lebanese village of Buarij (Fuller 1970 [1961]: 71). The children of Mexican (Hirshman 2020: 8–11) and Cypriot potters (London, Egoumenidou and Karageorghis 1989: 69) learned the craft by performing elementary tasks while watching parents or relatives shape pots. Children carried (clay, water, fuel and pots), trampled clay (barefoot) and shaped small pots. Miniature pots made by youngsters are attempts at learning a craft and as such constitute agents of transmission rather than toys (Fassoulas, Rossie and Procopiou 2020: 51). The same can be argued for making Judean eighth-century pillar figurines, which provided a method to enculturate children on several levels. Children probably participated the household social life and subsistence strategies (Garroway 2018: 421–5).

## Burials

How are we to interpret ancient artefacts found at or in burials? It is assumed that goods deposited inside tombs furnished the dead but anything left outside the grave, as in Persian Era tombs at Shechem (Stern 2001: 472), supplied the deceased, the living or both. Ancient texts reference funerary meals and feasts intended to memorialize the deceased and the ancestors (Albertz and Schmitt 2012: 444–59). Multiple reasons account for deposits of pottery, metal, textiles, personal items etc. above grave sites that have been recorded by Autumn Whiteway in her noteworthy study of cemetery ethnoarchaeology. After interviewing more than a hundred Bedouin to learn about funerary practices she visited twenty cemeteries containing over a thousand graves in southern Jordan. Approximately 35 per cent of the material remains on the tombs involved food or drink consumption, implying that meals happened at the grave. Personal used items, rather than special funerary items, remain at the cemetery for various reasons (Whiteway 2016: 168–81). Similarly, Cypriot traditional water jugs that had been repurposed to carry wine and water for use during burial ceremonies remained on the burial deposit or were deliberately broken to stand upside-down and protect a small flame in a ceramic incense burner (London 2020b: 175–6). These two case studies reveal comparable mortuary practices for migratory and sedentary populations. Ancient tombs with old pots left on the surface probably reflect final or annual meals.

### Writings on jars, their use and regional styles

Names, initials or both incised in the wet clay designate the jar maker, owner or land manager who commissioned jars for the church in Cyprus. The names can explain the marks on first-millennium BCE transport jars (London 2020b: 163–5).

One or more wine fermentation jars embedded into storeroom floors in rural areas at high-altitude villages characterized the homes of people who harvested vineyards. The same jars found outside the grape-growing regions served other purposes, as revealed by their density, use and precise placement – whether inside or outside. Jars in towns, cities or at churches in lower elevations, where grapes for wine did not grow, usually held water or oil. The huge containers served as bathtubs for children and saunas for new mothers, for which purpose the jar was positioned slightly askew to allow easy entry (London 2020b: 44–5, Figure 6.1). For archaeologists, the implication is that one or multiple ancient jars in a store room held wine or another food stuff whereas a lone jar, in a non-rural public setting, probably contained water or served another purpose.

Regional styles for the large globular jars that span a metre or more in diameter manifest in surface treatment (London 2020b: 65–71, 91–4, 163–5). Despite their outward similarities, subtle differences in a sample of 100 jars are discernible in the types of incised or impressed patterns, decorative elements as well as the tools to render them, and the information provided by jar makers.

# SUMMARY

Ethnoarchaeological research identifies multiple explanations for why and how people use or made similar-looking artefacts. Artefacts' use changes over time. Artefacts cross from daily use to funerary use, from sacral to profane functions. An ordinary water jug became the container carried to the cemetery to sprinkle water on the deceased, the shovel and hands after the ceremony. Then it was intentionally 'killed' to protect a burning flame left at the tomb. Handmade pottery persisted alongside wheel-thrown wares, given their mutually exclusive purposes. Wealth in villages manifests in covered interior space more than in portable material possessions. Potters include males and females, young and old.

Non-binary answers to the questions that ethnoarchaeologists ask result in a more diverse and complex conceptualization of ancient societies. Instead of either sedentary or mobile lifestyles, male or female potters, ritual or secular, snakes as good or dangerous, and outside or inside work, many long-term ethnoarchaeological studies reveal a nuanced multifaceted village and urban lifestyles where there is no single answer, use or understanding. Different people can see and understand a design element differently.

Ancient domestic architecture, like pottery or animal bones, present an incomplete yet rich set of information for archaeologists to interpret based on assessing assemblages as a whole and the templates derived from long-term ethnoarchaeological studies. Most relevant is research on workshops, households or villages rather than the occasional keen observations and comments of archaeologists travelling the countryside or visiting villagers in between excavations. Instead of simple answers or binary choices for ancient people and their material remains, ethnoarchaeological research demonstrates that complexity best defines humans.

## ACKNOWLEDGEMENTS

My thanks to Emanuel Pfoh for inviting me to contribute to the current volume. I cannot express my debt of gratitude to the traditional potters of Cyprus and their families for allowing me to record their work and history. Other village members and those no longer residing in the rural communities taught me much by allowing me to share their homes, their tables and their stories. My fieldwork was made possible by grants from the Fulbright Scholar Program (1985–6), the National Endowment for the Humanities (1999–2000) and the Council for American Overseas Research Centers (2017), all administered through the Cyprus American Archaeological Research Institute (CAARI) in Nicosia and part of the American Schools of Overseas Research. For the opportunity to excavate and the study of pottery from Tall al-'Umayri since 1989, I thank the excavation directors L. Geraty, L. Herr and D. Clark. Michael Savvas, President of Kornos Village, generously took photographs of pottery in niches during the refurbishment of the village church. I thank Autumn Whiteway for permission to mention her unpublished MA thesis on cemetery archaeology. Andreas Georgiades consulted with me regarding his exceptional collection of traditional Cypriot artefacts. Discussions with Justin Lev-Tov proved highly informative. Beth Alpert Nakhai and Xenia Charalambidou kindly read and commented on an early draft of my paper. My husband, M. den Nijs, continues to provide logistical and IT support.

## REFERENCES

Agelarakis, A.P. (2020), 'Bioarchaeological Evidence Reflective of the Use of the Kick-Wheel by a Female Ceramicist in Archaic Eleutherna', in N. Stampolidis and M. Giannopoulou (eds), *Eleutherna, Crete and the Outside World*, 234–46, Athens: Rethymno.

Albertz, R. and R. Schmitt (2012), *Family and Household Religion in Ancient Israel and the Levant*, Winona Lake, IN: Eisenbrauns.

Albrecht, M. (1994), *Turkish Cypriot and Mediterranean Cookery*, London: Havellia.

Avner, U., P.C. Anderson, B.T. Mai, J. Chabot and L.S. Cummings (2003), 'Ancient Threshing Floors, Threshing Tools and Plant Remains in 'Uvda Valley, Southern Negev Desert, Israel: A Preliminary Report', in *Le Traitement des Récoltes: Un regard sur la Diversité, du Néolithique au Présent – Actes des XXIIIe Rencontres internationales d'archéologie et d'historie d'Antibes*, 455–75, Antibes: Éditions APDCA.

Azar, G., G. Chimienti, H. Haddad and H. Seeden (1985), 'Busra: Housing in Transition', *Berytus*, 33: 103–42.

Badè, W.F. (1931), 'Ceramics and History in Palestine: Presidential Address', *JBL*, 50 (2): 1–19.

Banning, E.B. and I. Köhler-Rollefson (1992), 'Ethnographic Lessons for the Pastoral Past; Camp Locations and Material Remains near Beida, Southern Jordan', in O. Bar-Yosef and A. Khazanov (eds), *Pastoralism in the Levant: Archaeological Materials in Anthropological Perspective*, 181–204, Monographs in World Archaeology 10, Madison, WI: Prehistory Press.

Beaumont, L.A., B. McLoughlin, M.C. Miller and S.A. Paspalas (2016), 'Zagora Archaeological Project: The 2013 Field Season', *Mediterranean Archaeology*, 27: 115–21.

Ben-Arieh, Y. (1984), *Jerusalem in the 19th Century: The Old City*, Jerusalem: Yad Izhak Ben Zvi Institute.

Biran, A. (1994), *Biblical Dan*, Israel Exploration Society, Jerusalem: Hebrew Union College–Jewish Institute of Religion.

Biran, A. (2001), 'More on Threshing Sledges', *NEA*, 46 (1/2): 1.

*Writings on jars, their use and regional styles*

Names, initials or both incised in the wet clay designate the jar maker, owner or land manager who commissioned jars for the church in Cyprus. The names can explain the marks on first-millennium BCE transport jars (London 2020b: 163–5).

One or more wine fermentation jars embedded into storeroom floors in rural areas at high-altitude villages characterized the homes of people who harvested vineyards. The same jars found outside the grape-growing regions served other purposes, as revealed by their density, use and precise placement – whether inside or outside. Jars in towns, cities or at churches in lower elevations, where grapes for wine did not grow, usually held water or oil. The huge containers served as bathtubs for children and saunas for new mothers, for which purpose the jar was positioned slightly askew to allow easy entry (London 2020b: 44–5, Figure 6.1). For archaeologists, the implication is that one or multiple ancient jars in a store room held wine or another food stuff whereas a lone jar, in a non-rural public setting, probably contained water or served another purpose.

Regional styles for the large globular jars that span a metre or more in diameter manifest in surface treatment (London 2020b: 65–71, 91–4, 163–5). Despite their outward similarities, subtle differences in a sample of 100 jars are discernible in the types of incised or impressed patterns, decorative elements as well as the tools to render them, and the information provided by jar makers.

# SUMMARY

Ethnoarchaeological research identifies multiple explanations for why and how people use or made similar-looking artefacts. Artefacts' use changes over time. Artefacts cross from daily use to funerary use, from sacral to profane functions. An ordinary water jug became the container carried to the cemetery to sprinkle water on the deceased, the shovel and hands after the ceremony. Then it was intentionally 'killed' to protect a burning flame left at the tomb. Handmade pottery persisted alongside wheel-thrown wares, given their mutually exclusive purposes. Wealth in villages manifests in covered interior space more than in portable material possessions. Potters include males and females, young and old.

Non-binary answers to the questions that ethnoarchaeologists ask result in a more diverse and complex conceptualization of ancient societies. Instead of either sedentary or mobile lifestyles, male or female potters, ritual or secular, snakes as good or dangerous, and outside or inside work, many long-term ethnoarchaeological studies reveal a nuanced multifaceted village and urban lifestyles where there is no single answer, use or understanding. Different people can see and understand a design element differently.

Ancient domestic architecture, like pottery or animal bones, present an incomplete yet rich set of information for archaeologists to interpret based on assessing assemblages as a whole and the templates derived from long-term ethnoarchaeological studies. Most relevant is research on workshops, households or villages rather than the occasional keen observations and comments of archaeologists travelling the countryside or visiting villagers in between excavations. Instead of simple answers or binary choices for ancient people and their material remains, ethnoarchaeological research demonstrates that complexity best defines humans.

## ACKNOWLEDGEMENTS

My thanks to Emanuel Pfoh for inviting me to contribute to the current volume. I cannot express my debt of gratitude to the traditional potters of Cyprus and their families for allowing me to record their work and history. Other village members and those no longer residing in the rural communities taught me much by allowing me to share their homes, their tables and their stories. My fieldwork was made possible by grants from the Fulbright Scholar Program (1985–6), the National Endowment for the Humanities (1999–2000) and the Council for American Overseas Research Centers (2017), all administered through the Cyprus American Archaeological Research Institute (CAARI) in Nicosia and part of the American Schools of Overseas Research. For the opportunity to excavate and the study of pottery from Tall al-'Umayri since 1989, I thank the excavation directors L. Geraty, L. Herr and D. Clark. Michael Savvas, President of Kornos Village, generously took photographs of pottery in niches during the refurbishment of the village church. I thank Autumn Whiteway for permission to mention her unpublished MA thesis on cemetery archaeology. Andreas Georgiades consulted with me regarding his exceptional collection of traditional Cypriot artefacts. Discussions with Justin Lev-Tov proved highly informative. Beth Alpert Nakhai and Xenia Charalambidou kindly read and commented on an early draft of my paper. My husband, M. den Nijs, continues to provide logistical and IT support.

## REFERENCES

Agelarakis, A.P. (2020), 'Bioarchaeological Evidence Reflective of the Use of the Kick-Wheel by a Female Ceramicist in Archaic Eleutherna', in N. Stampolidis and M. Giannopoulou (eds), *Eleutherna, Crete and the Outside World*, 234–46, Athens: Rethymno.

Albertz, R. and R. Schmitt (2012), *Family and Household Religion in Ancient Israel and the Levant*, Winona Lake, IN: Eisenbrauns.

Albrecht, M. (1994), *Turkish Cypriot and Mediterranean Cookery*, London: Havellia.

Avner, U., P.C. Anderson, B.T. Mai, J. Chabot and L.S. Cummings (2003), 'Ancient Threshing Floors, Threshing Tools and Plant Remains in 'Uvda Valley, Southern Negev Desert, Israel: A Preliminary Report', in *Le Traitement des Récoltes: Un regard sur la Diversité, du Néolithique au Présent – Actes des XXIIIe Rencontres internationales d'archéologie et d'historie d'Antibes*, 455–75, Antibes: Éditions APDCA.

Azar, G., G. Chimienti, H. Haddad and H. Seeden (1985), 'Busra: Housing in Transition', *Berytus*, 33: 103–42.

Badè, W.F. (1931), 'Ceramics and History in Palestine: Presidential Address', *JBL*, 50 (2): 1–19.

Banning, E.B. and I. Köhler-Rollefson (1992), 'Ethnographic Lessons for the Pastoral Past; Camp Locations and Material Remains near Beida, Southern Jordan', in O. Bar-Yosef and A. Khazanov (eds), *Pastoralism in the Levant: Archaeological Materials in Anthropological Perspective*, 181–204, Monographs in World Archaeology 10, Madison, WI: Prehistory Press.

Beaumont, L.A., B. McLoughlin, M.C. Miller and S.A. Paspalas (2016), 'Zagora Archaeological Project: The 2013 Field Season', *Mediterranean Archaeology*, 27: 115–21.

Ben-Arieh, Y. (1984), *Jerusalem in the 19th Century: The Old City*, Jerusalem: Yad Izhak Ben Zvi Institute.

Biran, A. (1994), *Biblical Dan*, Israel Exploration Society, Jerusalem: Hebrew Union College–Jewish Institute of Religion.

Biran, A. (2001), 'More on Threshing Sledges', *NEA*, 46 (1/2): 1.

Bottéro, J. (1985), 'The Cuisine of Ancient Mesopotamia', *BA*, 48 (1): 36–47.

Canaan, T. (1932), 'The Palestinian Arab House: Its Architecture and Folklore', *JPOS*, 12: 233–47.

Cartwright, C.R. (2002) 'Grape and Grain: Dietary Evidence from an Early Bronze Age Store at Tell es-Sa`idiyeh, Jordan', *PEQ*, 134 (2): 98–117.

Caselli, A. (2020), 'Cult and Ritual in Early Bronze Age I Southern Levant: Fragmented or Connected Landscape?', in M. Iamoni (ed.), *From the Prehistory of Upper Mesopotamia to the Bronze and Iron Age Societies of the Levant. Volume 1. Proceedings of the 5th 'Broadening Horizons' Conference (Udine 5–8 June 2017)*, 171–84, Trieste: EUT Edizioni Università di Trieste.

Charalambidou, X. (2020), 'Style and Function of Geometric Coarse Jars from Naxos: Examples from Inland and Coastal Regions of the Island', in V. Lambrinoudakis, L. Mendoni, M. Koutsoumpou, T. Panagou, A. Sfyroera and X. Charalambidou (eds), Ἔξοχος ἄλλων: Τιμητικός τόμος για την Καθηγήτρια Ε. Σημαντώνη-Μπουρνιά, 147–62, Athens: University of Athens.

Clarke, M.H. (2000), 'The Changing House and Population Size on Methana, 1880–1996', in S.B. Sutton (ed.), *Contingent Countryside: Settlement, Economy, and Land Use in the Southern Argolid Since 1700*, 169–99, Stanford, CA: Stanford University Press.

Cobham, C.D. (1969 [1908]), *Excerpta Cypria: Materials for a History of Cyprus*, transl. and transcribed by C.D. Cobham, New York: Kraus.

Crowfoot, G.M. (1932), 'Pots, Ancient and Modern', *PEQ*, 64 (4): 179–87.

Crowfoot, G.M. (1940), 'Some Censer Types from Palestine, Israelite Period', *PEQ*, 72 (4): 150–3.

Crowfoot, G.M. (1957), 'Appendix II, Burnishing Pottery', in J.W. Crowfoot, G.M. Crowfoot and K.M. Kenyon (eds), *Samaria-Sebaste III: The Objects from Samaria*, 470–1, London: Palestine Exploration Fund.

Cunningham, J.J. and K.M. McGeough (2018), 'The Perils of Ethnographic Analogy: Parallel Logics in Ethnoarchaeology and Victorian Bible Customs Books', *Archaeological Dialogues*, 25 (2): 161–89.

Dalman, G. (1971 [1941]), *Arbeit und Sitte in Palästina Band VII: Das Haus, Hühnerzucht, Taubenzucht, Bienenzucht*, New York: Georg Olms.

Darby, E. (2014), *Interpreting Judean Pillar Figurines: Gender and Empire in Judean Apotropaic Ritual*, FAT 69/2, Tübingen: Mohr Siebeck.

Dometios, P. and G. London (2016), 'Museum of Traditional Pottery in Agios Demetrios (Marathasa)', *Cyprus Today*, 53 (3): 30–4.

Ebeling, J. and M. Rogel (2015), 'The Tabun and Its Misidentification in the Archaeological Record', *Levant*, 47 (3): 328–49.

Edelman, D.V. (2006), 'Tyrian Trade in Yehud under Artaxerxes I: Real or Fictional? Independent or Crown Endorsed?', in O. Lipschits and M. Oeming (eds), *Judah and the Judeans in the Persian Period*, 207–46, Winona Lake, IN: Eisenbrauns.

Einsler, L. (1914), 'Das Töpferhandwerk bei den Bauernfrauen von Ramallah und Umgegend', *ZDPV*, 37 (3): 249–60.

Fassoulas, A., J.-P. Rossie and H. Procopiou (2020), 'Children, Play, and Learning Tasks: From North African Clay Toys to Neolithic Figurines', *Ethnoarchaeology*, 12 (1): 36–62.

Fuller, A.H. (1970 [1961]), *Buarij: Portrait of a Lebanese Muslim Village*, Harvard Middle Eastern Monograph Series VI, Cambridge, MA: Harvard University Press.

Gabrieli, R.S. (2006), 'Silent Witness: The Evidence of Domestic Wares of the 13th–19th Centuries in Paphos, Cyprus, for Local Economy and Social Organization', 2 vols, unpublished PhD diss., University of Sydney.

Gabrieli, R.S., D. Ben-Shlomo and B.J. Walker (2014), 'Production and Distribution of Geometrical-Painted (HMGP) and Plain Hand-Made Wares of the Mamluk Period: A Case Study from Northern Israel, Jerusalem and Tall Hisban', *JIA*, 1 (2): 193–229.

Gambash, G., G. Bar-Oz, E. Lev and U. Jeremias (2019), 'Bygone Fish: Rediscovering the Red-Sea Parrotfish as a Delicacy of Byzantine Negev Cuisine', *NEA*, 82 (4): 216–25.

Garroway, K.H. (2018), 'Enculturating Children in Eighth-Century Judah', in Z.I. Farber and J.L. Wright (eds), *Archaeology and History of Eighth-Century Judah*, 415–29, ANEM 23, Atlanta: SBL Press.

Gatt, G. (1885a), 'Industrielles aus Gaza', *ZDPV*, 8: 69–79.

Gatt, G. (1885b), 'Technische Ausdrücke der Töpferei und Weberei in Gaza', *ZDPV*, 8: 179–81.

Georgiou, A. (2018), 'From the Hand to the Wheel: Revisiting the Transformation of the Late Cypriot Ceramic Industry of Finewares During the 13th-to-12th c. BC Transition', in I. Caloi and C. Langohr (eds), *Technological Changes in Ceramic Production during Periods of Trouble*, 177–200, Louvain: Presses Universitaires de Louvain.

Geva, H. (2014), 'Jerusalem's Population in Antiquity: A Minimalist View', *TA*, 41 (2): 131–60.

Given, M. (2004), *The Archaeology of the Colonized*, London: Routledge.

Grant, E. (1931), *Ain Shems Excavations (Palestine) 1928–1929—1930–1931 Part I*, Biblical and Kindred Studies 3, Haverford, PA: Haverford College.

Grantham, B.J. (2000), 'Qasrin and the Druze: A Cuisine-Based Model of Bone Distributions on Archaeological Sites', *NEA*, 63 (1): 9–19.

Gregg, M.W. and G.F. Slater (2010), 'New Method for Extraction, Isolation and Transesterification of Free Fatty Acids from Archaeological Pottery', *Archaeometry*, 52 (5): 833–54.

Haldane, C.W. (1990), 'Shipwrecked Plant Remains', *BA*, 53 (1): 55–60.

Herscher, E. (1976), 'South Coast Ceramic Styles at the End of the Middle Cypriote', *RDAC*, 1976: 11–19.

Hill, S. and A. Bryer (1995), 'Byzantine Porridge: *Tracta*, *Trachanás*, and *Tarhana*', in J. Wilkins, D. Harvey and M.J. Dobson (eds), *Food in Antiquity*, 44–54, Exeter: University of Exeter Press.

Hirshman, A.J. (2020), '"They Too Can Help": Hidden Producers and Flexibility in the Organization of Collaborative Labor in Pottery-Making Households in Michoacán, México from the 1940s to 2020', *Ethnoarchaeology*, 12 (1): 1–20.

Hopf, M. (1978), 'Plant Remains, Strata V-I', in R. Amiran (ed.), *Early Arad: The Calcolithic Settlement and Early Bronze City, Vol. I*, 64–82, Jerusalem: Israel Exploration Society.

Horne, L. (1994), *Village Spaces: Settlement and Society in Northeastern Iran*, Washington, DC: Smithsonian Institution.

Kamp, K.A. (1987), 'Affluence and Image: Ethnoarchaeology in a Syrian Village', *JFA*, 14 (3): 283–96.

Kamp, K.A. (1991), 'Waste Disposal in a Syrian Village', in E. Staski and L.D. Sutro (eds), *The Ethnoarchaeology of Refuse Disposal*, 23–31, Arizona State University Research Papers 42, Temple: Arizona State University.

Kamp, K.A. (1993), 'Towards an Archaeology of Architecture: Clues from a Modern Syrian Village', *JAA*, 49 (4) 293–317.

Kamp, K.A. (2000), 'From Village to Tell: Household Ethnoarchaeology in Syria', *NEA*, 63 (1): 84–93.

Keswani, P.S. (1994), 'The Social Context of Animal Husbandry in Early Agricultural Societies: Ethnographic Insights and an Archaeological Example from Cyprus', *JAA*, 13 (3): 255–77.

Köhler-Rollefson, I. (1987), 'Ethnoarchaeological Research into the Origins of Pastoralism', *ADAJ*, 31: 535–9.

Lancaster, W. and F. Lancaster (1995), 'Land Use and Population in the Area North of Karak', *Levant*, 27 (1): 103–24.

Lev-Tov, J. (2003), '"Upon What Meat Doth This Our Caesar Feed . . .?": A Dietary Perspective on Hellenistic and Roman Influence', in S. Alkier and J. Zangenberg (eds), *Zeichen aus Text und Stein: Studien auf em Weg zu einer Archäologie des Neuen Testaments*, 420–46, Tübingen: Francke.

Lev-Tov, J. and K.M. McGeough (2007), 'Examining Feasting in Late Bronze Age Syro-Palestine Through Ancient Texts and Bones', in K.C. Twiss (ed.), *The Archaeology of Food and Identity*, 85–111, Center for Archaeological Investigations, Occasional Paper 34, Carbondale, IL: Southern Illinois University.

Lev-Tov, J., B.W. Porter and B.E. Routledge (2011), 'Measuring Local Diversity in the Early Iron Age Animal Economies: A View from Khirbat al-Mudayna al-'Aliya (Jordan)', *BASOR*, 361: 67–93.

Levanoni, A. (2005) 'Food and Cooking During the Mamluk Era: Social and Political Implications', *Mamluk Studies Review*, 9 (2): 201–22.

London, G. (1989), 'Past and Present: The Village Potters of Cyprus', *BA*, 52 (4): 219–29.

London, G. (1991a), 'Aspects of Early Bronze and Late Iron Age Ceramic Technology at Tell el-'Umeiri', in L.G. Herr, L.T. Geraty, Ø.S. LaBianca and R.W. Younker (eds), *Madaba Plains Project 2: The 1987 Season at Tell el-'Umeiri and Vicinity and Subsequent Studies*, 383–419, Berrien Springs, MI: Andrews University Press.

London, G. (1991b), 'Standardization and Variation in the Work of Craft Specialists', in W.A. Longacre (ed.), *Ceramic Ethnoarchaeology*, 182–204, Tucson: University of Arizona Press.

London, G. (2000a), 'Ethnoarchaeology and Interpretations of the Past', *NEA*, 63 (1): 2–8.

London, G. (2000b), 'Continuity and Change in Cypriot Pottery Production', *NEA*, 63 (2): 102–10.

London, G. (2011), 'Late Second Millennium BC Feasting at an Ancient Ceremonial Centre in Jordan', *Levant*, 43 (1): 15–37.

London, G. (2016), *Ancient Cookware from the Levant: An Ethnoarchaeological Perspective*, Sheffield: Equinox.

London, G. (2017), 'Marks Incised on Rims and Handles Excavated at Tall al-'Umayri, 2000', in L.G. Herr, D.R. Clark and L.T. Geraty (eds), *Madaba Plains Project 7: The 2000 Season at Tall al-'Umayri and Subsequent Studies*, 351–63, Berrien Springs, MI: Andrews University Press.

London, G. (2020a), 'Sherds with Incised Marks or Repair Holes at Tall al-'Umayri, 2004', in L.G. Herr, D.R. Douglas, and L.T. Geraty (eds), *Madaba Plains Project 9: The 2004 Season at Tall al-'Umayri and Subsequent Studies*, 293–5, University Park, PA: Eisenbrauns.

London, G. (2020b), *Wine Jars and Jar Makers of Cyprus: The Ethnoarchaeology of Pitharia*, SIMA, PB 188, Nicosia: Astrom.

London, G. and Fr Dometios (2015), 'Heritage Collection of Traditional Pottery in Ayios Demetrios, Cyprus', *JEMAHS*, 3 (3): 207–33.

London, G. and M. Sinclair (1991), 'An Ethnoarchaeological Survey of Potters in Jordan', in L.G. Herr, L.T. Geraty, Ø.S. LaBianca and R.W. Younker (eds), *Madaba Plains Project 2: The 1987 Season at Tell el-'Umeiri and Vicinity and Subsequent Studies*, 420–8, Berrien Springs, MI: Andrews University Press.

London, G., F. Egoumenidou and V. Karageorghis (1989), *Traditional Pottery in Cyprus*, Mainz: Philipp von Zabern.

Longacre, W.A. (1991), 'Ceramic Ethnoarchaeology: An Introduction', in W.A. Longacre (ed.), *Ceramic Ethnoarchaeology*, 1–10, Tucson: University of Arizona Press.

Loud, G. (1948), *Megiddo II: Seasons of 1935–39*, OIP 62, Chicago: University of Chicago Press.

Lyons, D. and N. David (2019), 'To Hell with Ethnoarchaeology . . . and Back!', *Ethnoarchaeology*, 11 (2): 99–133.

Macalister, R.A.S. (1912), *The Excavation of Gezer, 1902–1905 and 1907–1909*, 3 vols, London: John Murray.

Matson, F.R. (1965), 'Ceramic Ecology: An Approach to the Study of the Early Cultures of the Near East', in F.R. Matson (ed.), *Ceramics and Man*, 202–17, Viking Fund Publications in Anthropology 41, New York: Wenner Gren Foundation.

Mazar, A. and N. Panitz-Cohen (2007), 'It Is the Land of Honey: Beekeeping at Tel Reḥov', *NEA*, 70 (4): 202–19.

McQuitty, A. (1984), 'An Ethnographic and Archaeological Study of Clay Ovens in Jordan', *ADAJ*, 28: 259–67.

McQuitty, A. (1994), 'Ovens in Towns and Country', *Berytus*, 41: 53–76.

Mershen, B. (1985), 'Recent Hand-Made Pottery from North Jordan', *Berytus*, 33: 75–87.

Milwright, M. (2001), 'Prologues and Epilogues in Islamic Ceramics: Clays, Repairs and Secondary Use', *Medieval Ceramics*, 25: 72–83.

Mollenhauer, A. (1997), 'Historical Residential Houses in As-Salṭ: Remarks on Their Shape and Function', *ADAJ*, 41: 415–31.

Mulder-Hymans, N. (1997), 'Bread Ovens in Syria', *Journal of Primitive Technology*, 13: 48–53.

Mulder-Hymans, N. (2014), 'The Iron Age Bread Ovens in the Kitchen of Khirbet al-Mudayna, Jordan', in E. van der Steen, J. Boertien and N. Mulder-Hymans (eds), *Exploring the Narrative: Jerusalem and Jordan in the Bronze and Iron Ages*, 159–70, LHBOTS 583, London: Bloomsbury T&T Clark.

Murray, P. and P.N. Kardulias (2000), 'The Present as Past: An Ethnoarchaeological Study of Modern Sites in the Pikrodhafni Valley', in S.B. Sutton (ed.), *Contingent Countryside: Settlement, Economy, and Land Use in the Southern Argolid Since 1700*, 141–68, Stanford, CA: Stanford University Press.

Nakhai, B.A. (2008), 'Introduction', in B.A. Nakhai (ed.), *The World of Women in the Ancient and Classical Near East*, ix–xvii, Newcastle upon Tyne: Cambridge Scholars Publishing.

Nicholson, P. and H. Patterson (1985), 'Pottery-Making in Upper Egypt: An Ethnoarchaeological Study', *World Archaeology*, 17 (2): 222–39.

Orrelle, E., U. Avner, L.K. Horwitz and M. Birkenfeld (2020), 'Snakes of Stone: A Unique Stone Artefact from the LPPNB Site of Naḥal Roded 110', *Neo-Lithics*, 20: 23–31.

Palmer, C. (1998), '"Following the Plough": The Agricultural Environment of Northern Jordan', *Levant*, 30 (1): 129–65.

Peters, J., N. Pöllath and A. von den Driesch (2002), 'Early and Late Bronze Age Transitional Subsistence at Tall al-'Umayri', in L.G. Herr, D.R. Clark, L.T. Geraty, R.W. Younker and Ø.S. LaBianca (eds), *Madaba Plains Project 5: The 1994 Season at Tall al-'Umayri and Subsequent Studies*, 305–47, Berrien Springs, MI: Andrews University Press.

Polcaro, A. (2019), 'On Pots and Serpents: An Iconographic and Contextual Analysis of the Cultic Vessels with Serpent Figurines in the 4th–3rd Millennium BC Transjordan', in M. D'Andrea, M.G. Micale, D. Nadali, S. Pizzimenti and A. Vacca (eds), *Pearls of the Past: Studies on Near Eastern Art and Archaeology in Honour of Frances Pinnock*, 775–94, marru 8, Münster: Zaphon.

Salem, H.J. (2009), 'An Ethno-Archaeological Approach to Ottoman Pottery: The Case of "Gaza Grey Ware"', in B.J. Walker (ed.), *Reflections of Empire: Archaeological and Ethnographic Studies of Pottery of the Ottoman Levant*, 23–36, AASOR 64, Boston, MA: American Schools of Oriental Research.

Schaefer, J. (1986), 'An Umayyad Potters Complex in the North Theatre Jerash', in F. Zayadine (ed.), *Jerash Archaeological Project 1981–1983*, 411–59, Amman: Department of Antiquities of Jordan.

Schumacher, G. (1914), 'Unsere Arbeiten im Ostjordanlande', *ZDPV*, 37 (3): 260–6.

Seeden, H. (1985), 'Aspects of Prehistory in the Present World: Observations Gathered in Syrian Villages from 1980 to 1985', *World Archaeology*, 17 (2): 289–303.

Seger, K., ed. (1981), *Portrait of a Palestinian Village: The Photographs of Hilma Granqvist*, London: Third World Centre for Research and Publishing.

Shafer-Elliott, C. (2013), *Food in Ancient Judah: Domestic Cooking in the Time of the Hebrew Bible*, BibleWorld, Sheffield: Equinox.

Shqairat, M.A. al-Z. (2018), 'Abandoning Shammakh: Historical Archaeology Among the Villages of Southern Jordan and Its Ethno-Archaeological and Modern Economic Potential', *JAA*, 6 (1): 1–14.

Singer, A. (1990), 'The Countryside of Ramle in the Sixteenth Century: A Study of Villages with Computer Assistance', *JESHO*, 33: 51–79.

Stacy, D. (2004), *Excavations at Tiberias 1973–1974: The Early Islamic Periods*, IAA Reports 21, Jerusalem: IAA.

Stern, E. (2001), *Archaeology of the Land of the Bible: The Assyrian, Babylonian, and Persian periods, 732–332 BCE*, ABRL, New York: Doubleday.

Sukenik, E.L. (1940), 'Note on a Pottery Vessel of the Old Testament', *PEQ*, 72 (2): 59–60.

Sutton, S.B. (2000), 'Liquid Landscapes: Demographic Transitions in the Ermionidha', in S.B. Sutton (ed.), *Contingent Countryside: Settlement, Economy, and Land Use in the Southern Argolid Since 1700*, 84–106, Stanford, CA: Stanford University Press.

Swantek, L.A. (2016), 'The Mobile Woman: Using Ethnoarchaeology to Build Models of Women's Labor Contribution to Craft Production', in S.E. Kelley and T. Ardren (eds), *Gendered Labor in Specialized Economies: Archaeological Perspectives on Female and Male Work*, 237–63, Boulder, CO: University Press of Colorado.

Sweet, L.E. (1960), *Tell Toqaan: A Syrian Village*, Anthropological Papers Museum of Anthropology, University of Michigan, 14, Ann Arbor: University of Michigan Press.

Taxel, I. (2006), 'Ceramic Evidence for Beekeeping in Palestine in the Mamluk and Ottoman Periods', *Levant*, 38 (1): 203–12.

Tufnell, O. and W.A. Ward (1966), 'Relations Between Byblos, Egypt, and Mesopotamia at the End of the Third Millennium B.C.: A Study of the Montet Jar', *Syria*, 43 (3/4): 165–241.

Tufnell, O., M.A. Murray and D. Diringer (1958), *Lachish IV (Tell ed-Duweir): The Bronze Age*, London: Oxford University Press.

Valière, J.-C., B. Palazzo-Bertholon, J.-D. Polack and P. Carvalho (2013), 'Acoustic Pots in Ancient and Medieval Buildings: Literary Analysis of Ancient Texts and Comparison with Recent Observations in French Churches', *Acta Acustica United with Acustica*, 99 (1): 70–81.

Warren, C.W. (1876), *Underground Jerusalem: An Account of Some of the Principal Difficulties Encountered in the Exploration and the Results Obtained*, London: Bentley and Son.

Weaver, W.W. (2006), *The Royal Garden of Pefkou: A Study of Fruit Consumption in Medieval Nicosia*, Lefkosia: Moufflon Publications.

Whiteway, A. (2016), 'Ethnoarchaeological Perspective on the Mortuary Practices of Jordanian Bedouin', MA thesis, University of Manitoba, Winnipeg.

Whittaker, J. (1996), 'Athkiajas: A Cypriot Flintknapper and the Threshing Sledge Industry', *Lithic Technology*, 21 (2): 108–20.

Whittaker, J.C. (2000), 'Alonia and Dhoukanes: The Ethnoarchaeology of Threshing in Cyprus', *NEA*, 63 (2): 62–9.

Wilson, H. (2001), *Egyptian Food and Drink*, Princes Risborough, UK: Shire.

Wood, B.G. (1990), *The Sociology of Pottery in Ancient Palestine: The Ceramic Industry and the Diffusion of Style in the Bronze and Iron Ages*, JSOTSup 103, Sheffield: JSOT Press.

Yadin, Y., Y. Aharoni, R. Amiran, T. Dothan, M. Dothan, I. Dunayevsky and J. Perrot (1961), *Hazor III–IV: An Account of the Third and Fourth Seasons of Excavations, 1957–1958*, Jerusalem: Hebrew University of Jerusalem.

Yerkes, R.W. (2000), 'Ethnoarchaeology in Central Cyprus: Interdisciplinary Studies of Ancient Population and Agriculture by the Athienou Archaeological Project', *NEA*, 63 (1): 20–34.

# CHAPTER SIX

# The anthropology of the Mediterranean, the history of the southern Levant and biblical studies

EMANUEL PFOH

## CRITICAL EPISTEMOLOGIES AND HYBRID METHODS

Since at least the 1970s, biblical scholars have made a varied use of social anthropology – along with other social-science methods and insights – in order to better understand the cultural logics reflected in some biblical stories, as well as the historical situations in them. This interpretative disposition has not, however, been particularly present in much of ancient Near Eastern or Assyriological studies while assessing ancient texts, apart from some rather notable exceptions found, for instance, in seminal studies by Mario Liverani, Carlo Zaccagnini and Cristiano Grottanelli in the 1970s and 1980s. These Italian scholars – to note their names as probably the most relevant in retrospective – dealt in a pioneering manner with the nature of the exchange of goods, people and specialists in the ancient Near East – profiting from Marxist and substantivist economic anthropologies of the time (Liverani 1972, 1979; Zaccagnini 1973, 1983) – the logic behind ancient Near Eastern myths and evocations of the past in literature – profiting from Russian formalist approaches, semiology and linguistic anthropology (Liverani 1973, 2004) – and comparative literature and myths and the social practices reflected in such compositions (Grottanelli 1977, 1998). The anthropology of the Mediterranean has, on the other hand, focused its field of study and analysis only on recent periods of time, with an isolated yet brilliant contribution by Julian Pitt-Rivers on the nature of hospitality in Homer's *Odyssey* and the politics of honour, hospitality and sex in the biblical book of Genesis, treated among other themes in his work *The Fate of Shechem* (Pitt-Rivers 1977). In effect, this work pioneered a mode of interpreting biblical situations and performances that would thenceforth develop, especially since the 1980s, in biblical studies (cf. Matthews and Benjamin 1993; Moxnes 1993; Bolin 2004; Gudme 2019).

From this outlook, which pretends only to call the attention to some important antecedents in both fields and is far from being a nonetheless needed history of research, ancient Near Eastern scholars may therefore proceed by referencing their interpretative approach to wider anthropological studies or cases of ceremonial and goods exchange, political alliance, prestige and power, ritual and mythic evocations, etc., taken in comparison (like Liverani, Zaccagnini and Grottanelli did). Social anthropologists, instead, can certainly profit from applying ethnographic insights and analogies to dig deeper into ancient Near Eastern and biblical myths and stories.[1] These attempts, drawn from different disciplines, may, however, both agree on the principle that any text or mythic/literary tradition from the ancient past can only be unlocked in its original meaning when a cultural translation is properly performed. Such a cultural translation is met, of course, with the impossibility of ethnographic documentation and fieldwork. Notwithstanding this, an interpretative approach drawn from the methods and aims of social anthropology in order to translate the cultural remnants of ancient societies does find analytical legitimacy – not only to overcome simplistic evaluations or naïve historicist readings of written sources, but also to offer possible answers to the complexities of social practices and logics (political, economic, ritual) and ontologies expressed in textual records (like the biblical record). In this sense, we may test how 'Mediterranean' the societies behind the biblical stories were in their social practices and ontologies, in spite of the millennia that have transpired between the textual composition of these sources and ethnographic research conducted in the Mediterranean region, and also how this perspective contributes to new understandings of the ancient history of the Levant.

By 'Mediterranean' with quotation marks – it should be noted – it is meant here much more than a geographical location: it is rather intended to allude to a set of interrelated characteristics and practices present in certain historical periods, as revealed by ethnohistorical and ethnographic research, which may provide an interpretative clue to different kinds of data coming from ancient times in the East Mediterranean and the region known as the Near/Middle East – although 'South-West Asia' would be a better, less ideologically charged terminology for this territory (cf. Scheffler 2003).

## THE 'ANTHROPOLOGY OF THE MEDITERRANEAN' AS FIELDWORK AND ANTHROPOLOGICAL GENRE

Social anthropology has placed the Mediterranean basin under ethnographic scrutiny relatively recently, only since the 1950s, in spite of an already existing European intellectual tradition concerned with research on the region's societies, especially during the Classical past. As Sydel Silverman noted:

> Modern anthropological fieldwork in the Mediterranean began only in the 1950s, by which time most of the world had already been encompassed within the scope of the 'ethnographic record'. Yet, as others have pointed out – and as John Davis [1977] explicated especially well – the Mediterranean material had attracted anthropologists earlier and in greater numbers than that of perhaps any other region in the world. Maine, Fustel de Coulanges, Robertson Smith, Frazer, Durkheim, Mauss, and other luminaries drew on the Mediterranean for seminal ideas that had a profound influence

---

[1] See, for instance, Leach 1962; Leach and Aycock 1983; Kuper 2016; cf. also Grottanelli 1998: 22–38. I am very well aware that anthropology and ethnography are not monolithic fields and have of course their own intellectual history and processes (cf., e.g., Barnard 2004; Moore and Sanders 2006; Candea 2018). My intention here in this chapter is to call for a greater cross-fertilization of approaches and problem-oriented research.

on the analysis of remote societies. Their work was based primarily on literary, historical and archaeological sources, and was only occasionally connected to living peoples.

—Silverman 2001: 43[2]

Also, as observed by David Gilmore, 'Anthropology *in* the Mediterranean area [was] nothing new; some of the earliest ethnographies took place there. But an anthropology *of* the Mediterranean area which include[d] both Christian and Muslim sides [was] both new and controversial' (Gilmore 1982: 175; original emphasis).[3] Indeed, the perspective of having the European, African and Levantine shores conceived of as the scenario of shared cultural expressions marked a departure from rather old-fashioned evolutionistic views of humanity (i.e. European = culturally advanced; African and Levantine = culturally underdeveloped); but more importantly, it also started off a more sophisticated view which, however, still perceived southern Europe as the 'primitive backyard' of northern Europe (Pitt-Rivers 2000; cf. also Fabre 2007).

Pitt-Rivers's seminal and now classic ethnography *The People of the Sierra* (1954), inaugurated, in fact, the study of Mediterranean societies by British social anthropologists in the early 1950s, followed by the also relevant monographic study by J.K. Campbell, *Honour, Family and Patronage* (1964).[4] Yet, maybe 1959 is the true foundational year of the anthropology of the Mediterranean, with the celebration of a conference in Burg Wartenstein (Austria) on peasant societies in the Mediterranean basin. This academic event would trigger several successive academic meetings, which generated, too, the publication of the foundational texts of Mediterranean anthropology and their construction of themes and topics proper of such specialization, as their titles indicate: *Mediterranean Countrymen: Essays in the Social Anthropology of the Mediterranean*, edited by Pitt-Rivers (1963b); *Honour and Shame: The Values of Mediterranean Societies*, edited by John Peristiany (1965); *Contributions to Mediterranean Sociology: Mediterranean Rural Communities and Social Change*, edited by Peristiany (1968); and *Mediterranean Family Structures*, also edited by Peristiany (1976).

Eventually, constant fieldwork on northern and southern shores of the Mediterranean produced a considerable amount of ethnographic material whose cultural details and features were passible of being compared with each other (cf. Davis 1977; Leca 1977). In effect, these studies unfolded a concrete ethnographic genre, the 'anthropology of the Mediterranean', which seemed to expose a particular Mediterranean *ethos* in its different manifestations, anchored in key factors like honour and shame, amoral familism, hospitality, feuding, revenge (*vendetta*), the evil eye and related superstitions, and patron–client relations, all of them in a somehow essentialist manner and tending to manifest a

---

[2] Further on the context of these processes, cf. Flannery 1967; Silverman 2005; Schneider 2012.
[3] Cf. further Horden and Purcell 2000: 485–523.
[4] Both Pitt-Rivers and Campbell were attached to the Institute of Social Anthropology at Oxford University and were influenced by the structural-functionalism of the Oxford professor Evans-Pritchard [. . .]. Many of the early ethnographies of Southern European societies were, in fact, clearly modelled on Evans-Pritchard's *The Nuer*. In exposition they began with considerations of environment and agricultural production, and then proceeded through politics, kinship and marriage, moral values and ultimately to religion.

—Stewart 2010: 263

Further on Evans-Pritchard's anthropological circle in Goody 1995: 77–86; Kuper 2015: 42–63; and on Pitt-Rivers in Herzfeld 2017.

certain homogeneity, in spite of the regional differences of ethnographic locations like Turkey, Lebanon, Egypt, Spain, Italy, Greece, Morocco or Algeria.[5] As Christian Giordano (1990: 111) observed, 'It is interesting to note how these studies were carried out exclusively in especially marginal communities, almost as if there was an unconscious desire or a secret hope of rediscovering the "primitive", the "savage" and the "archaic" on one's back doorstep'.

This understanding was aided by the geomorphological and ecological characteristics in the Mediterranean basin, giving place to finding common elements or circumstances in different communities, several kilometres apart, as to the environment, local economy and cultural features. Such common landscape characteristics, which seemed to be (erroneously) rather constant through time, allowed for speculations on the little change social conditions would have experienced in the last millennia. Precisely, as Dionigi Albera and Anton Blok (2001: 18) affirm, regarding Louise E. Sweet's contributions to East Mediterranean ethnography:

> Sweet argues that in the past the Mediterranean basin was characterized by a 'distinctive Mediterranean culture pattern or civilization', which displays a structural, an ecological and a cultural distinctiveness [cf. Sweet and O'Leary 1969: v–xxii], including pre-industrial city-states, and urban character of peasant life (agro-towns), the predominance of large estates for the production of grains, and transhumant pastoralism of sheep and goats. Sweet emphasizes 'the recurrence of a similar climate, mountain topography, flora and fauna – natural or culturogenic (especially the vine-fig-olive, wheat-barley-beans, small-scale fishing, sheep and goat specializations) – from the Neolithic base to the present' [cf. Sweet and O'Leary 1969: i]. In passing, she mentions Mediterranean 'stereotypes', including gender segregation and the subordination of women. Whether stereotypical or not, the cultural emphasis on virginity and chastity of women together with the exclusion of women from public space (men:women/public:private/dominance:subordination) is often singled out as a most telling and diagnostic feature of the forms of life on both shores of the Mediterranean.

As it would have been expected, such a homogeneous characterization of the Mediterranean social fabric, both in spatial and temporal coordinates, configuring thus a kind of 'cultural area',[6] (even though this particular concept, as Pitt-Rivers [2000: 25] himself noted, was never used by British social anthropologists working in the Mediterranean), produced a stereotypical image soon to be criticized by Mediterranean anthropologists themselves, especially during the 1980s, accusing the promotion of exoticism, tendentious cultural homogenization and limited comparison, besides the expected ethnocentrism from the countries of northern Europe, where most Mediterranean anthropologists came from (cf. Herzfeld 1980, 1987: 5–12; Wikan 1984; Pina-Cabral 1989; Llobera 1999: 63–101). Nonetheless, the Mediterranean genre was not totally discarded in social anthropology – only its analytical 'deviations'. As Albera and Blok (2001: 18–19) have recently recognized, exposing a healthy social-anthropological reflexivity:

> It seems that a spectre is haunting those who write on the Mediterranean area: the trait-list. Two well-known dangers underlie these characterizations. First, by

---

[5] See especially Banfield 1958, where the concept of *amoral familism* was coined (in Ch. 5) to characterize these societies; but cf. the revaluations in Silverman 1968; and Stewart 2010: 265. See further now Roque 2000, 2005; Bonte 2012: 168–72; Giordano 2012: 21.

emphasizing common features you play down differences. Differences between religious beliefs and practices in the Mediterranean region are obvious, but so are the basic differences in kinship, marriage and inheritance practices, as for instance, [Jack] Goody argued in his essay 'Two Sides of the Mediterranean' [1983: 10–12]. A second and perhaps even greater danger of attempts to define the Mediterranean area is presenting an ahistoric, essentialized picture of something that is obviously in a state of flux – forms of life that have experienced a uniquely documented continuity and change over more several millennia.[7]

In this sense, criticism towards some aspects of the anthropology of the Mediterranean did not delegitimize its validity as a research field,[8] but – and once discarded the essentialist perspective, proper of a social approach based on the notion of a *Mediterranean culture area*[9] – it was rather reformulated under a more reflexive constitution: 'without necessarily essentializing or reifying the concept, it is possible to conceptualize the Mediterranean area as a field of ethnological study – as a historical formation, as a historically-constituted unit – showing enough differences and similarities for fruitful comparative research' (Albera and Blok 2001: 20).[10]

Attending too to the historical geography of the Mediterranean region and its dynamics may actually allow for a heuristic comparison of social practices and environmental adaptability through time, but without necessarily resorting to any kind of ecological (or cultural) determinism.[11] A clear aspect of Mediterranean geography, for instance, is what Peregrine Horden and Nicholas Purcell call 'the connectivity of microregions',[12] which seem to be a constant background as societies remain and change through time. Thus, a critical approach to the Mediterranean landscape would first attest particular social practices according not only to their environment but also to their historical context, in order to establish changes and continuities in a proper historical manner. In this way, it becomes in effect legitimate to propose a comparison of practices active in modern or

---

[6] On the 'culture-area', a key term in American anthropology of the early twentieth century, cf. Wissler 1927, 1928; also Hill 1941. Clark Wissler, through the study of American native societies, would conceive of defined 'culture-areas', in which ecology and material culture corresponded. To this, George Hill added the concept of 'culture type', to deepen the characterization of culture-areas. Later, Alfred Kroeber would use the concept of culture-area in opposition to the studies of Franz Boas on the indigenous peoples of California (cf. Buckley 1989). Of course, the risk of cultural essentialism and ecological determinism is very much expressed in these formulations – as it is in the foundational study of Fernand Braudel (1972 [1966]) on the Mediterranean area. The potential contribution of the *Annales* historiographical school to Levantine studies in antiquity cannot be properly dealt here within the scope of the present study. For some preliminary theoretical orientations, see Tilly 1978; Knapp 1992.
[7] See also the seminal study by Davis (1977), although from this recent reflexive outlook.
[8] The perspective has been revalidated in more recent times, with a reflexive spirit, both anthropological and historical: cf. Boissevain 1979; Gilmore 1987; Albera 1999; Horden and Purcell 2000; Roque 2000; Albera, Blok and Bromberger 2001; Harris 2005; Sant Cassia and Schäfer 2005; Albera and Tozy 2006; Giordano 2012; and most recently Ben-Yehoyada, Cabot and Silverstein 2020; Shryock 2020; Herzfeld 2020.
[9] The same criticism can be applied to characterizations of the Middle East: cf. the essentialist description by Raphael Patai (1952) on the Middle East as a 'culture area'.
[10] Also Bonte 2012: 167. Further discussion on anthropology in 'area studies' is found in Guyer 2004.
[11] Or, as has been more elegantly said by Friese (2004: 120): 'une approche susceptible de rendre compte des particularités de pratiques sociales spécifiques, de cosmologies culturelles et de leurs "imaginaires" respectifs'.
[12] Defined as 'the various ways in which microregions cohere, both internally and also one with another – in aggregates that may range in size from small clusters to something approaching the entire Mediterranean' (Horden and Purcell 2000: 123); cf. also Bresson 2005; Abulafia 2011; and for the Late Bronze Age, Knapp 1990; Hitchcock 2005; and later periods, Lichtenberger 2021.

present times and practices detected or cautiously assumed to be active in more ancient times, given a proper control of the comparison, i.e. without extracting universal laws from observing two analogous practices in similar ecological or economic settings in different periods of time. The relevant question is whether we are ultimately able to understand ancient sociopolitical practices placed in a certain environment by analysing current sociopolitical practices set in more or less similar environments. My answer is definitely positive, as long as we keep in mind the heuristic purpose of the analytical effort (cf. further Lang 1985; Matthews and Benjamin 1993: xiii–xxiii; Pfoh 2010, 2016: 63–6).

To give here a general example, the livelihood of many communities in the ancient southern Levant (in broad lines, from the third to the mid-first millennium BCE) depended on growing olives, vines and cereals, goat- and sheep-herding, and horticulture; a certain interdependence of farmers and semi-nomads was established as well.[13] Many urban settlements of relative size had a rural periphery that depended economically and politically on them, according to a common topographical fragmentation, especially in Palestine, where a cantonal landscape was evident (see Sapin 1981, 1982; Thompson 1992: 316–34; Faust 2013). As Liverani explains regarding the latter location,

> The first evident consequence of this topographic and ecologic fragmentation is political fragmentation, at least during all the period in which the dimension of political formations will be strongly conditioned by the modes of exploitation of the territory, dependent on agriculture and husbandry. [. . .] Thus, the dimension that we may qualify as 'cantonal' (a city with its hinterland destined to agriculture and husbandry) cannot be exceeded unless other factors of [territorial] unification (ethno-linguistic, religious) appear from within or proceed from external interventions. Each 'canton' remains isolated from the others due to a weakly inhabited landscape (hills, steppes, woods) quantitatively predominant.
>
> —Liverani 1990: 15[14]

This scenario is still found – or was until not so long ago – in many parts the Mediterranean, and the relationship between an urban centre and the rural space may lead us to think about the *agro-towns* of Italy's ethnographic record.[15] Now, if we extend the scope of our historical perspective, it might be possible to see a socio-economic continuum from the pastoralist semi-nomad to the peasant to the urban dweller, not only in the Eastern Mediterranean but also in the Middle East / South-West Asia, at least until around mid-twentieth century, depending on the regions or areas.[16] Said continuum is traversed by

---

[13] Cf. Thompson 1992: 316–34. For ethnographic observations from the early twentieth century, especially dealing with the productive cycle of agriculture, cf. Dalman 1932; and in relation to a Mediterranean *longue durée*, cf. Lichtenberger 2021: 130–32.

[14] The translation from the French is mine.

[15] On Mediterranean agro-towns, cf. Blok 1969; Giordano 2017. There is certainly an urban–rural continuum in the Mediterranean basin at the level of socio-economic units. As Caro Baroja (1963: 31) indicates:

> In spite of the classical authors' [Plato, Strabo] insistence on the particular quality of rural as opposed to urban life, they had very distinct ideas on the close relations of the city with the country and on their necessary connections. And it is worth noting that when they do the works of sociologists (rather than historians, geographers or moralists), they begin to see clearly something that can be defined as a linking of functions between the city and the country.

Cf., for a Middle Eastern comparison, Eickelman 2002: Chs 3–5.

[16] See the anthropological discussion in Lemche 1985: 84–244; cf. also the presentation in Lewis 1987.

relationships of economic or political dependence, which are ethnographically demonstrated to be essentially vertical – through schemes of tribal ascendancy, family networks, neighbourhood and patron–client bonds – rather than horizontal, as in a proper class order.[17] This ethnographic panorama creates, as was already observed, a spectrum of analytical possibilities through which to interpret ancient textual data describing or hinting at social and political structures and practices. The following two sections shall address further, although briefly, this insight.

## ON 'MEDITERRANEAN' FEATURES IN THE ANCIENT SOUTHERN LEVANT

In one of the aforementioned foundational works of Mediterranean anthropology, Pitt-Rivers (1963a: 9) wrote: 'The geographical form [of the Mediterranean basin] therefore favours unification by military force, settlement and, as soon as the commanding power relaxes, rebellion, but not integration into a homogeneous culture. As a result, political and religious hierarchies were able to replace one another while leaving the local community, if not unaltered, nevertheless faithful in large parts to its traditions.'

These words, read now decades after being written, may be objected to on some valid grounds, especially its blatant generalization. However, they capture well two constant realities in the history of the region of the Levant, or Syria-Palestine, in antiquity: in the first place, the rather uninterrupted occupation of the territory by successive foreign powers since the middle of the second millennium BCE until the middle of the twentieth century – almost four thousand years! – especially due to the geopolitical location of the region, as a commercial and military bridge between continents (Aharoni 1979: 3–6, 43–63; Astour 1995: 1415–16); and in the second place, what we may call the ubiquity of vertical ties of political dependence, i.e. patron–client relations, through different periods. Traditional historiography of the ancient world is confident in detecting ancient patronage only with the Roman expansion, in our case, towards the east of Europe.[18] However, patron–client relations are much older in the region and have been permanent through different periods, especially in the southern Levant (Westbrook 2005; Pfoh 2016, 2022; Pfoh and Thompson 2019).

One could ask, indeed, whether Pitt-Rivers's words do not betray a rather explicit geographical determinism as well. We should not, however, confuse geographical determinism with the concrete and documented permanence of some sociopolitical

---

[17] Cf. Eickelman 2002: Chs 6–7; Lindholm 2002. After analysing ethnographies carried out in Tell Toqaan (Syria), Al-Munsif (Lebanon) and Kufr el-Ma (Transjordan), Lemche (1985: 178) notes: 'The preceding analysis has shown that in dealing with the Middle East the relationship between city and village is not a dichotomy, but rather a continuum'. See further about this question in Lemche 1985: 164–201.

[18] The Roman period is generally the first historical example taken to illustrate patronage (and from that period comes the basic terminology of the phenomenon): see, for instance, in general Eisenstadt and Roniger 1984; Mączak 2005; Lécrivain 2007a, 2007b. For patronage in ancient Rome, Wallace-Hadrill 1989; Deniaux 2007; in ancient Greece, Finley 1983: 24–49; Pébarthe 2007; in Absolutist France, Kettering 1986. For patronage in rural settings, cf. Garnsey and Woolf 1989, for the Roman world; and Thompson 1971, for a much more modern period. On the moral economy of the peasantry and solidarity networks, cf. Fafchamps 1992. Patronage in the Middle East is well documented, cf. especially Leca and Schemeil 1983; and the studies in Gellner and Waterbury 1977, and Ruiz de Elvira, Schwartz and Weipert-Fenner 2018. For patronage in the Mediterranean basin, cf. besides the already indicated literature, Campbell 1964; Boissevain 1966; Silverman 1968; Weingrod 1968; Blok 1969, 1974; Schneider 1969. On the related phenomenon of political clientelism, cf. Briquet and Sawicki 1998.

practices through time in the same region. To focus here on one sociopolitical aspect: if patronage relations are encountered in the Levant by ethnohistory and ethnography throughout the twentieth century and even some centuries before (see, e.g., Cohen 1973; Khoury 1983; Doumani 1995; Rabinowitz 1997; Philipp 2001; Chorev-Halewa 2019), articulating internally the local community, but also linking the community and the regional power, and there is data from ancient textual sources that reflects clues that can most certainly be understood through a heuristic conceptualization of patron–client relations (cf. Lang 1982; Lemche 1985: passim; Simkins 1999; Westbrook 2005; Pfoh 2009: 113–60; Knight 2011), such an analytical operation is therefore legitimate and is far from betraying a misguided and ethnocentric essentialism of the societies of the region. Indeed, as indicated for Palestine by Robert B. Coote and Keith W. Whitelam (1987: 114), '[p]easant factionalism shaped according to patterns of elite patronage, at both village and urban levels, appears to be endemic in Palestine. Once this feature has been examined in materials dating from the seventeenth to the early twentieth centuries, it becomes quite noticeable whenever historical sources for rural life in Palestine exist in any detail'.

Contemporary examples of patronage may indeed help us explain and understand the ideological and political world view active in the ancient Levant through a careful employment of analytical analogies and being aware of the temporal and cultural distance between ancient Levantine peoples and modern ones.[19] As Horden and Purcell (2000: 464) have suggested, '[w]e can then go on to enquire what ways remain in which the ethnographic present might instruct us about the historic past'.

With patronage, of course, other elements and aspects common in traditional Mediterranean societies may be assumed to have existed, too, in the ancient Levant. Kinship structures and bonds are undoubtedly ubiquitous in any society and, in non-state societies, extended kinship offers also a main vehicle for politics and economic organization and articulation (see, e.g., Hirth 2020: 17–75). In Mediterranean societies kinship and patronage are visibly interrelated (cf. Campbell 1964), and it could well be stated that kinship and patronage constituted the main elements of social articulation in Syria-Palestine during the Late Bronze Age (c. 1550–1150 BCE) but also during the Iron Age (c. 1150–586 BCE), in the kingdoms of Israel and Judah (Pfoh and Thompson 2019; Maeir and Shai 2016). One might also conceive of the presence of situations in which personal honour and prestige, along with reciprocity and alliance, play an important role in ancient Levantine political and cultural sociability, and this may have been equally reflected in some of the textual data coming from the second- and first-millennium BCE Levant and in many biblical stories. Precisely, Johannes Pedersen (1991 [1926]) offered about a century ago a pioneering treatment of honour and shame in ancient Israelite society, although he understood the conceptual pair through biblical anthropology and Israelite psychology, rather than through social anthropology (in spite of his uses of random Middle Eastern ethnographic examples; cf. Pedersen 1991 [1926]: 213–44).[20]

---

[19] Compare, for instance, the description of Levantine politics in the mid-second millennium BCE by Liverani (1967, 1983) in the light of patron–client politics (i.e. Gellner and Waterbury 1977; Eisenstadt and Roniger 1984), as illustrated, e.g., in studies like Lemche 1996; Pfoh 2016; Pfoh and Thompson 2019.

[20] A more recent treatment of this matter, with contributions by Old and New Testaments scholars and responses by social anthropologists, is found in Victor H. Matthews and Don Benjamin's edited volume, *Honor and Shame in the World of the Bible* (1994). Olyan 1996 should be included here too, although his explicit reference to 'vassal' relationships in the Hebrew Bible (and in 'ancient Israel') must instead be understood in terms of patron–client relationships: cf. Hobbs 1997; Pfoh 2022: 17–21. A most recent discussion of premodern honour, shame and hospitality in the Ottoman Levant in connection with biblical values is found now in van der Steen 2021.

## ON 'MEDITERRANEAN' FEATURES IN BIBLICAL TEXTS

In the field of Judaism and New Testament studies, themes proper of the anthropology of the Mediterranean have been perhaps more widely discussed and treated than in Hebrew Bible / Old Testament studies, where they represent only a minority of scholars' interest. One could just mention here as different, almost opposite, examples the study by Seth Schwartz, *Were the Jews a Mediterranean Society?* (2010),[21] and works like David A. deSilva's *Honor, Patronage, Kinship and Purity* (2000) and those by the members of the Context Group in New Testament studies, like John J. Pilch and Bruce J. Malina's *Biblical Social Values and Their Meaning* (1993), Malina's *The Social World of Jesus and the Gospels* (1996), Jerome H. Neyrey and Eric C. Stewart's *The Social World of the New Testament* (2008), and Zeba A. Crook's *The Ancient Mediterranean Social World* (2020). The reason for a much more accentuated interest about Mediterranean anthropology in New Testament studies resides probably in that we have in these periods the Roman power present in the Levant and, with it, Roman culture and politics with their Mediterranean traits, which naturally affected the world in which this part of biblical literature was composed (Malina 1996).

For ancient Near Eastern and biblical studies the picture is somewhat different, although there should be little doubt that the social world of the Hebrew Bible / Old Testament was 'Mediterranean' in its social values (cf., e.g., Matthews and Benjamin 1993, 1994; Lang 2004; further Sacchi and Viazzo 2014; Huebner 2017).[22] Both of these fields, in general, have not been permeated much by social-anthropological insights and therefore archaeology and philology/linguistics have instead been the main driving forces and interpretative perspectives when attending to historical matters, at least until not so long ago.[23]

As already noted above, what the anthropology of the Mediterranean can offer us is the possibility of widening our interpretation both of ancient social logics (cultural, political, economic, religious), and of ancient myths and stories located in the ancient Levant. To attend to, once again, but one single sociopolitical factor, the notion of prestige and power, blended with expectations of honour and reciprocity, fits well within the

---

[21] Schwartz (2010: 26) argues that:

> To be sure, some biblical heroes, most prominently David (in his early life an 'outlaw' pastoralist and brigand) and the judges (who lived, the Bible repeatedly reminds, at a time when 'there was no king in Israel and each man did what was right in his eyes'), are the subjects of stories that portray them approximately as idealized Mediterranean men. Nevertheless, on the whole, the non-Pentateuchal biblical books have little good to say about Mediterranean culture [...]. [T]he Torah, for its part, has a radically anti-Mediterranean vision of Israelite society: the only fully legitimate relationship of personal dependency for Israelites is that with their God, who is their father, master, friend, and lover; hence the importance of charity, a type of redistribution intentionally set up so as to hinder the proliferation of personal ties of dependency.

One could contend, however, that personal dependency to the Israelite God was in fact modelled according to the sociopolitical arrangements of patronage, clearly an East Mediterranean practice; cf. Lemche 1996; Pfoh 2022.

[22] Compare further, on families, households and domestic spaces, the studies in Bodel and Olyan 2008 and those in Huebner and Nathan 2017.

[23] Cf. further Rogerson 2013, also Hagedorn 2015. In spite of a tradition of two hundred years of conceiving of 'the world of the Bible' by attending to ethnographic notices, Old Testament scholarship has essentially made use of social anthropology in a rather ancillary and secondary manner; see the Introduction to this volume.

ethnographic model of patron–client relations. As indicated, such relations can be found in many periods of the history of the Levant dealing, for instance, with the nature of the Hittite alliances made with the Syrian kingdoms and principalities, and with the politics of the Amarna Age (mid-fourteenth century BCE), especially between the Egyptian king and his subjects in the southern Levant – as observed above, patronage can also be found in the political dynamics of the Iron Age kingdoms, not only Israel and Judah, but also Aram in Syria and Ammon, Moab and Edom in Transjordan (see further the discussion with bibliography in Pfoh 2018).

A relatively recent monograph by Douglas A. Knight, *Law, Power, and Justice in Ancient Israel* (2011), has shown how relevant political and juridical anthropology (not only from the Mediterranean, but also from African societies) is for analytical comparison and interpretation, dealing with the understanding of law in biblical stories and their pertinence for creating knowledge about the politics in the villages and urban centres of the southern Levant in antiquity. Regarding myths and narrative compositions, the Hebrew Bible / Old Testament has already been analysed through anthropological lenses, as noted in the beginning of this chapter, especially for dealing with cultural traits and literary motifs (cf. also Rogerson 1978, 2013; Leach 1983; Lang 1985; Overholt 1996; Lawrence and Aguilar 2004). Of particular interest for the present discussion is the work of Victor H. Matthews and Don C. Benjamin, *Social World of Ancient Israel, 1250–587 BCE* (1993), where issues of prestige, honour and shame, reciprocity, and many other aspects proper to Mediterranean and Middle Eastern 'traditional' societies, as reflected in biblical stories, are articulated and treated in a very competent manner from an anthropological perspective. Perhaps a more epistemological rather than methodological criticism that may be levelled against Matthews and Benjamin's, but also against Knight's perspective (certainly, not uncommon among Old Testament scholars, even critical ones), is their overall confidence on the diachronic typologies and historical phases offered by the biblical narrative, after which we have a historical development from tribal society to a state society, namely the appearance of statehood as a major political force. For sure, the biblical texts do not necessarily reflect the sociopolitics they explicitly expose, but an implicit (later) context of composition should be instead, and more appropriately, assumed (cf. Pfoh 2009: 69–82). The relevance of the biblical texts lies instead on what they can offer when read from an ethnographic perspective, attending also to 'Mediterranean' issues (see further Chapter 12 in this volume).

But, in spite of punctual criticism, what these works mainly expose is the relevance and the legitimacy of conducting socio-anthropological research on Levantine societies and their textual products. Precisely, it is my opinion that anthropological interpretations of biblical myths and stories give us first and foremost that chance of an attempt to capture an ancient ontology at work in the text, regardless of the possibility of accounting for the precise historicity of events evoked by biblical tradition. In this sense, the biblical narrative offers the opportunity of conducting various 'textual micro-ethnographies', namely the investigation of discrete and limited episodes charged with social and symbolic cultural meaning, which the interpreter must decode by reading the text with ethnographic sensitivity. A micro-ethnographic approach does not prevent, of course, having a systematic interpretation of the whole of the Hebrew Bible / Old or New Testaments or other biblical – or further, ancient Near Eastern – literature. But it is perhaps better suited for searching within small literary compositions for symbolic clues, details and aspects regarding the hidden social meaning of events, actions and performances by biblical characters, as they can shed light – when interpreted anthropologically – on the society producing the texts and the values and world views it upholds.[24]

## A CONCLUSION

After the preceding, yet rather preliminary and programmatic, discussion and presentation, it seems to be obvious that the anthropology of the Mediterranean could indeed contribute to analysing and widening the interpretation of the social and cultural worlds of ancient Levantine peoples and biblical stories. Beyond putative criticisms towards the scope and the characteristics proper to the 'Mediterranean' perspective in anthropology, I am confident that one can overcome any kind of assumed essentialism in this perspective and recognize the historical continuities and transformations in the social practices and ontologies of the East Mediterranean region, without conceding by necessity to accepting characteristics proper of social, cultural and historical stagnation, as previous Orientalist – à la Said (1978) – understandings would imply or propose. In particular, the history, and not only the cultural features, of the ancient southern Levant roughly during the third to first millennium BCE comes also under new light after a critical 'Mediterranean' perspective, as we can attempt to understand, for instance, political practices reflected on textual data after ethnographic attestations (i.e. patron–client relationships, as I have focused on in this chapter [cf. also Chapter 14 in this volume]), which may in effect shed further light on the political ontologies at work in these periods – political ontologies that need to be properly decoded in the extant textual data.

When it comes to the biblical stories and myths, the path already trodden by Pitt-Rivers in anthropology and by Liverani and Grottanelli and others in ancient Near Eastern studies should definitely be further pursued. On this level of interpretation, degrees of 'biblical historicity' should best be left aside, for methodological reasons, in order to first and foremost grasp the ontologies behind biblical texts: what matters from a socio-anthropological perspective is the cultural voice in the texts, as translated through an ethnographic insight, and how this cultural decoding contributes to the retrieval of ancient mentalities and cultural expressions of the peoples of the Levant in antiquity. Finally, what needs to be done now – as a way to overcome both simplistic and rather complex paraphrases of the biblical text when historical interpretation is what is aimed at – is writing a proper historical anthropology of the ancient southern Levant and its different regions, treating systematically and coherently all of these aspects (see further Pfoh 2017; Thompson 2019).

## REFERENCES

Abulafia, D. (2011), *The Great Sea: A Human History of the Mediterranean*, Oxford: Oxford University Press.

Aharoni, Y. (1979), *The Land of the Bible: A Historical Geography*, rev. and enlarged edn, Philadelphia, PA: Westminster Press.

---

[24] For some results on this interpretive technique, see for instance Pfoh 2014. Furthermore, this approach should not be limited to textual readings; a properly historical reading should also be pursued after what Tilly (1978: 210) calls 'retrospective ethnography', namely 'the effort to reconstitute a round of life from the best historical equivalents of the ethnographer's observations, then to use the reconstituted round of life as a context for the explanation of collective action'.

Albera, D. (1999), 'The Mediterranean as an Anthropological Laboratory', *Anales de la Fundación Joaquín Costa*, 16: 215–32.

Albera, D. and A. Blok (2001), 'Introduction: The Mediterranean as an Ethnological Field of Study: A Retrospective', in D. Albera, A. Blok and C. Bromberger (eds), *L'anthropologie de la Méditerranée / Anthropology of the Mediterranean*, 15–37, Paris: Maisonneuve and Larose-MMSH.

Albera, D.A. Blok and C. Bromberger, eds (2001), *L'anthropologie de la Méditerranée / Anthropology of the Mediterranean*, Paris: Maisonneuve and Larose-MMSH.

Albera, D. and M. Tozy, eds (2006), *La Méditerranée des anthropologue: Fractures, filiations, contiguïtés*, Paris: Maisonneuve and Larose.

Astour, M.C. (1995), 'Overland Trade Routes in Ancient Western Asia', in J.M. Sasson (ed.), *Civilizations of the Ancient Near East, vol. 3*, 1401–20, New York: Scribner's.

Banfield, E.C. (1958), *The Moral Basis of a Backward Society*, Glencoe, IL: Free Press.

Barnard, A. (2004), *History and Theory in Anthropology*, Cambridge: Cambridge University Press.

Ben-Yehoyada, N., H. Cabot and P.A. Silverstein (2020), 'Introduction: Remapping Mediterranean Anthropology', *History and Anthropology*, 31 (1): 1–21.

Blok, A. (1969), 'South Italian Agro-Towns', *CSSH*, 11 (2): 121–35.

Blok, A. (1974), *The Mafia of a Sicilian Village, 1860–1960: A Study of Violent Peasant Entrepreneurs*, Oxford: Basil Blackwell.

Bodel, J. and S.M. Olyan, eds (2008), *Household and Family Religion in Antiquity*, Oxford: Blackwell.

Boissevain, J. (1966), 'Patronage in Sicily', *Man NS*, 1 (1): 18–33.

Boissevain, J. (1979), 'Towards a Social Anthropology of the Mediterranean [+ Comments and Reply]', *Current Anthropology*, 20 (1): 81–93.

Bolin, T.M. (2004), 'The Role of Exchange in Ancient Mediterranean Religion and Its Implications for Reading Genesis 18–19', *JSOT*, 29 (1): 37–56.

Bonte, P. (2012), 'La Méditerranée des anthropologues: Permanences historiques et diversité culturelle', in R. Abdellatif, Y. Benhima, D. König and E. Ruchaud (eds), *Construire la Méditerranée, penser les transferts culturelles: Approches historiographiques et perspectives de recherche*, 162–81, Munich: Oldenbourg.

Braudel, F. (1972), *The Mediterranean and the Mediterranean World in the Age of Philip II*, 2 vols, London: Collins [translation from the 2nd French edn 1966].

Bresson, A. (2005), 'Ecology and Beyond: The Mediterranean Paradigm', in W.V. Harris (ed.), *Rethinking the Mediterranean*, 94–114, Oxford: Oxford University Press.

Briquet, J.-L. and F. Sawicki, eds (1998), *Le clientélisme politique dans les sociétés contemporaines*, Paris: Presses Universitaires de France.

Buckley, T. (1989), 'Kroeber's Theory of Culture Areas and the Ethnology of Northwestern California', *Anthropological Quarterly*, 62 (1): 15–26.

Campbell, J.K. (1964), *Honour, Family, and Patronage: A Study of Institutions and Moral Values in a Greek Mountain Community*, Oxford: Clarendon Press.

Candea, M., ed. (2018), *Schools and Styles of Anthropological Theory*, Abingdon: Routledge.

Caro Baroja, J. (1963), 'The City and the Country: Reflections on Some Ancient Commonplaces', in J. Pitt-Rivers (ed.), *Mediterranean Countrymen: Essays in the Social Anthropology of the Mediterranean*, 27–40, The Hague: Mouton.

Chorev-Halewa, H. (2019), *Networks of Power in Palestine: Family, Society and Politics Since the Nineteenth Century*, London: I.B. Tauris.

Cohen, A. (1973), *Palestine in the 18th Century: Patterns of Government and Administration*, Jerusalem: Magnes Press.

Coote, R.B. and K.W. Whitelam (1987), *The Emergence of Early Israel in Historical Perspective*, SWBAS 5, Sheffield: Almond Press.

Crook, Z.A., ed. (2020), *The Ancient Mediterranean Social World: A Sourcebook*, Grand Rapids, MI: Eerdmans.

Dalman, G. (1932), *Arbeit und Sitte in Palästina. Band II: Der Ackerbau*, Gütersloh: C. Bertelsmann.

Davis, J. (1977), *People of the Mediterranean: An Essay in Comparative Social Anthropology*, London: Routledge and Kegan Paul.

Deniaux, É. (2007), 'Clientèle et éthique à Rome à l'époque républicaine', in V. Lécrivain (ed.), *Clientèle guerrière, clientèle foncière et clientèle électorale: Histoire et anthropologie*, 161–72, Dijon: Éditions Universitaires de Dijon.

deSilva, D.A. (2000), *Honor, Patronage, Kinship, and Purity: Unlocking New Testament Culture*, Downers Grove, IL: InterVarsity Press.

Doumani, B. (1995), *Rediscovering Palestine: Merchants and Peasants in Jabal Nablus, 1700–1900*, Berkeley: University of California Press.

Eickelman, D.F. (2002), *The Middle East and Central Asia: An Anthropological Approach*, Upper Saddle River, NJ: Prentice Hall.

Eisenstadt, S.N. and L. Roniger (1984), *Patrons, Clients and Friends. Interpersonal Relations and the Structure of Trust in Society*, Cambridge: Cambridge University Press.

Fafchamps, M. (1992), 'Solidarity Networks in Preindustrial Societies: Rational Peasants with a Moral Economy', *Economic Development and Cultural Change*, 41 (1): 147–74.

Fabre, T. (2007), 'Face to Face, Side by Side: Between Europe and the Mediterranean', *History and Anthropology*, 18 (3): 353–65.

Faust, A. (2013), 'Villages, Cities and Towns, Bronze and Iron Age', in D. Master, B.A. Nakhai, A. Faust, L.M. White and J.K. Zangenberg (eds), *Oxford Encyclopedia of Bible and Archaeology*, 203–11, New York: Oxford University Press.

Finley, M.I. (1983), *Politics in the Ancient World*, Cambridge: Cambridge University Press.

Flannery, K.V. (1967), 'Culture History v. Cultural Process: A Debate in American Archaeology', *Scientific American*, 217 (2): 119–22.

Friese, H. (2004), 'Unité et histoire croisée de l'espace méditerranéen', *Le Genre Humain*, 42: 119–37.

Garnsey, P. and G. Woolf (1989), 'Patronage of the Rural Poor in the Roman World', in A. Wallace-Hadrill (ed.), *Patronage in Ancient Society*, 153–70, London: Routledge.

Gellner, E. and J. Waterbury, eds (1977), *Patrons and Clients in Mediterranean Societies*, London: Duckworth.

Gilmore, D.D. (1982), 'Anthropology of the Mediterranean Area', *Annual Review of Anthropology*, 11: 175–205.

Gilmore, D.D., ed. (1987), *Honor and Shame and the Unity of the Mediterranean*, Washington, DC: American Anthropological Association.

Giordano, C. (1990), 'Is There a Mediterranean Anthropology? The Point of View of an Outsider', *Anthropological Journal of European Cultures*, 1 (1): 109–24.

Giordano, C. (2012), 'The Anthropology of Mediterranean Societies', in U. Kockel, M. Nic Craith and J. Frykman (eds), *A Companion to the Anthropology of Europe*, 11–31, Oxford: Blackwell.

Giordano, C. (2017), 'What Is a Mediterranean Agro-Town? On the Sense and Nonsense of Anthropological Dichotomies', *Logos*, 92: 68–83.

Goody, J. (1983), *The Development of the Family and Marriage in Europe*, Cambridge: Cambridge University Press.

Goody, J. (1995), *The Expansive Moment: The Rise of Social Anthropology in Britain and Africa 1918–1970*, Cambridge: Cambridge University Press.

Grottanelli, C. (1977), 'Notes on Mediterranean Hospitality', *Dialoghi di Archeologia*, 9/10: 186–94.

Grottanelli, C. (1998), *Sette storie bibliche*, Studi Biblici 119, Brescia: Paideia.

Gudme, A.K. de Hemmer (2019), 'Death at the Hand of a Woman: Hospitality and Gender in the Hebrew Bible', in S.L. Budin, M. Cifarelli, A. Garcia-Ventura and A. Millet Albà (eds), *Gender and Methodology in the Ancient Near East: Approaches from Assyriology and Beyond*, 327–36, Barcelona: Universitat de Barcelona.

Guyer, J.I. (2004), 'Anthropology in Area Studies', *Annual Review of Anthropology*, 33: 499–523.

Hagedorn, A.C. (2015), 'Institutions and Social Life in Ancient Israel: Sociological Aspects', in M. Sæbø (ed.), *Hebrew Bible / Old Testament: The History of Its Interpretation, Volume III: From Modernism to Post-Modernism (The Nineteenth and Twentieth Centuries), Part 2: The Twentieth Century – From Modernism to Post-Modernism*, 58–95, Göttingen: Vandenhoeck & Ruprecht.

Harris, W.V., ed. (2005), *Rethinking the Mediterranean*, Oxford: Oxford University Press.

Herzfeld, M. (1980), 'Honour and Shame: Problems in the Comparative Analysis of Moral Systems', *Man* NS, 15 (2): 339–51.

Herzfeld, M. (1987), *Anthropology Through the Looking-Glass: Critical Ethnography in the Margins of Europe*, Cambridge: Cambridge University Press.

Herzfeld, M. (2017), 'Grace and Insight: The Legacy of Julian Pitt-Rivers', in G. da Col and A. Shryock (eds), *From Hospitality to Grace: A Julian Pitt-Rivers Omnibus*, 465–72, Chicago: Hau Books.

Herzfeld, M. (2020), 'Afterword: Reclaiming the Middle Sea for Humanity', *History and Anthropology*, 31 (1): 157–64.

Hill, G.W. (1941), 'The Use of Culture-Area Concept in Social Research', *The American Journal of Sociology*, 47 (1): 39–47.

Hirth, K. (2020), *The Organization of Ancient Economies: A Global Perspective*, Cambridge: Cambridge University Press.

Hitchcock, L. (2005) '"Who Will Personally Invite a Foreigner, Unless He Is a Craftsman?": Exploring Interconnections in Aegean and Levantine Architecture', in R. Laffineur and E. Greco (eds), *Emporia: Aegeans in the Central and Eastern Mediterranean: Proceedings of the 10th International Aegean Conference / 10ᵉ Rencontre égéenne internationale, Athens, Italian School of Archaeology, 14–18 April 2004 II*, 691–9, Liège: Université de Liège.

Hobbs, T.R. (1997), 'Reflections on Honor, Shame, and Covenant Relations', *JBL*, 116 (3): 501–3.

Horden, P. and N. Purcell (2000) *The Corrupting Sea: A Study of Mediterranean History*, Oxford: Blackwell.

Huebner, S.R. (2017), 'A Mediterranean Family? A Comparative Approach to the Ancient World', in S.R. Huebner and G. Nathan (eds), *Mediterranean Families in Antiquity: Households, Extended Families, and Domestic Space*, 3–26, Chichester, UK: Wiley Blackwell.

Huebner, S.R. and G. Nathan, eds (2017), *Mediterranean Families in Antiquity: Households, Extended Families, and Domestic Space*, Chichester, UK: Wiley Blackwell.

Kettering, S. (1986), *Patrons, Brokers, and Clients in Seventeenth-Century France*, New York: Oxford University Press.

Khoury, P.S. (1983), *Urban Notables and Arab Nationalism: The Politics of Damascus 1860–1920*, Cambridge: Cambridge University Press.

Knapp, A.B. (1990), 'Ethnicity, Entrepreneurship, and Exchange: Mediterranean Inter-Island Relations in the Late Bronze Age', *The Annual of the British School at Athens*, 85: 115–53.

Knapp, A.B., ed. (1992), *Archaeology, Annales, and Ethnohistory*, Cambridge: Cambridge University Press.

Knight, D.A. (2011), *Law, Power, and Justice in Ancient Israel*, LAI, Louisville, KY: Westminster John Knox Press.

Kuper, A. (2015), *Anthropology and Anthropologists: The British School in the Twentieth Century*, 4th edn, Abingdon: Routledge.

Kuper, A. (2016), 'Anthropologists and the Bible', in R. Darnell and F.W. Gleach (eds), *Local Knowledge, Global Stage*, 1–30, Lincoln: University of Nebraska Press [see Chapter 2 in this volume].

Lang, B. (1982), 'The Social Organization of Peasant Poverty in Biblical Israel', *JSOT*, 7 (24): 47–63.

Lang, B. (2004), 'Women's Work, Household and Property in Two Mediterranean Societies: A Comparative Essay on Proverbs XXXI 10–31', *VT*, 54 (2): 188–207.

Lang, B., ed. (1985), *Anthropological Approaches to the Old Testament*, Philadelphia, PA: Fortress Press.

Lawrence, L.J. and M.I. Aguilar, eds (2004), *Anthropology & Biblical Studies: Avenues of Approach*, Leiden: Deo.

Leach, E. (1962), 'Genesis as Myth', *Discovery*, 23 (5): 30–5.

Leach, E. (1983), 'Anthropological Approaches to the Study of the Bible during the Twentieth Century', in E. Leach and D.A. Aycock, *Structuralist Interpretations of Biblical Myth*, 7–32, Cambridge: Cambridge University Press.

Leach, E. and D.A. Aycock (1983), *Structuralist Interpretations of Biblical Myth*, Cambridge: Cambridge University Press.

Leca, J. (1977), 'Pour une analyse comparative des systèmes politiques méditerranéens', *Revue française de science politique*, 27 (4/5): 557–81.

Leca, J. and Y. Schemeil (1983), 'Clientélisme et patrimonialisme dans le monde arabe', *International Political Science Review*, 4 (4): 455–94.

Lécrivain, V. (2007a), 'Le rapport de clientèle dans la perspective comparative', in V. Lécrivain (ed.), *Clientèle guerrière, clientèle foncière et clientèle électorale: Histoire et anthropologie*, 13–31, Dijon: Éditions Universitaires de Dijon.

Lécrivain, V., ed. (2007b), *Clientèle guerrière, clientèle foncière et clientèle électorale: Histoire et anthropologie*, Dijon: Éditions Universitaires de Dijon.

Lemche, N.P. (1985), *Early Israel: Anthropological and Historical Studies on the Israelite Society Before the Monarchy*, VTSup 37, Leiden: E.J. Brill.

Lemche, N.P. (1996), 'From Patronage Society to Patronage Society', in V. Fritz and P.R. Davies (eds), *The Origin of the Ancient Israelite States*, 106–20, JSOTSup 228, Sheffield: Sheffield Academic Press.

Lewis, N.N. (1987), *Nomads and Settlers in Syria and Jordan, 1800–1980*, Cambridge: Cambridge University Press.

Lichtenberger, A. (2021), 'Thoughts on Mediterranean Studies and the Study of the Graeco-Roman Holy Land', in J. Kamlah and A. Lichtenberger (eds.), *The Mediterranean Sea and the Southern Levant: Archaeological and Historical Perspectives from the Bronze Age to Medieval Times*, 121–140, ADPV 48, Wiesbaden: Harrassowitz.

Lindholm, C. (2002), *The Islamic Middle East: Tradition and Change*, rev. edn, Oxford: Blackwell.

Liverani, M. (1967), 'Contrasti e confluenze di concezioni politiche nell'età di El-Amarna', *RA*, 61 (1): 1–18.

Liverani, M. (1972), 'Elementi "irrazionali" nel commercio amarniano', *OA*, 11: 297–317.
Liverani, M. (1973), 'Memorandum on the Approach to Historiographic Texts', *Or* NS, 42: 178–94.
Liverani, M. (1979), 'Dono, tributo, commercio: ideologia dello scambio nella tarda età del bronzo', *AIIN*, 26: 9–28.
Liverani, M. (1983), 'Political Lexicon and Political Ideologies in the Amarna Letters', *Berytus*, 31: 41–56.
Liverani, M. (1990), 'De la préhistoire à l'empire perse', in A. Giardina, M. Liverani and B. Scarcia Amoretti, *La Palestine: Histoire d'une terre*, 9–79, Paris: L'Harmattan.
Liverani, M. (2004), *Myth and Politics in Ancient Near Eastern Historiography*, ed. and intro. Z. Bahrani and M. van de Mieroop, London: Routledge.
Llobera, J.R. (1999), *La identidad de la antropología*, 2nd edn, Barcelona: Anagrama.
Maeir, A.M. and I. Shai (2016), 'Reassessing the Character of the Judahite Kingdom: Archaeological Evidence for Non-Centralized, Kinship-Based Components', in S. Ganor, I. Kreimerman, K. Streit, M. Mumcuoglu (eds), *From Sha'ar Hagolan to Shaaraim: Essays in Honor of Prof. Yosef Garfinkel*, 323–40, Jerusalem: Israel Exploration Society.
Mączak, A. (2005), *Ungleiche Freundschaft: Klientelbeziehungen von der Antike bis zur Gegenwart*, Deutsche Historisches Institut Warschau: Klio in Polen 7, Osnabrück: Fibre.
Malina, B.J. (1996), *The Social World of Jesus and the Gospels*, London: Routledge.
Matthews, V.H. and D.C. Benjamin (1993), *Social World of Ancient Israel, 1250–587 BCE*, Peabody, MA: Hendrickson.
Matthews, V.H. and D.C. Benjamin, eds (1994), *Honor and Shame in the World of the Bible*, Semeia 68, Atlanta, GA: Scholars Press.
Moore, H.L. and T. Sanders, eds (2006), *Anthropology in Theory: Issues in Epistemology*, Oxford: Oxford University Press.
Moxnes, H. (1993), 'Honor and Shame', *BTB*, 23 (4): 167–76.
Neyrey, J.H. and E.C. Stewart, eds (2008), *The Social World of the New Testament: Insights and Models*, Peabody, MA: Hendrickson.
Olyan, S.M. (1996), 'Honor, Shame, and Covenant Relations in Ancient Israel and Its Environment', *JBL*, 115 (2): 201–18.
Overholt, T.W. (1996), *Cultural Anthropology and the Old Testament*, Minneapolis, MN: Fortress Press.
Patai, R. (1952), 'The Middle East as a Culture Area', *Middle East Journal*, 6 (1): 1–21.
Pébarthe, C. (2007), 'La question de la clientèle en Grèce Ancienne: Cimon versus Périclès, patronage privé contre patronage communautaire?', in V. Lécrivain (ed.), *Clientèle guerrière, clientèle foncière et clientèle électorale: Histoire et anthropologie*, 173–97, Dijon: Éditions Universitaires de Dijon.
Pedersen, J. (1991), *Israel: Its Life and Culture*, Vol. 1, SFSHJ 28, Atlanta, GA: Scholars Press [First English translation 1926, Danish original edn 1920].
Peristiany, J., ed. (1965), *Honour and Shame: The Values of Mediterranean Societies*, London: Weidenfeld and Nicolson.
Peristiany, J., ed. (1968), *Contributions to Mediterranean Sociology: Mediterranean Rural Communities and Social Change*, Paris: Mouton.
Peristiany, J., ed. (1976), *Mediterranean Family Structures*, Cambridge Studies in Social and Cultural Anthropology 13, Cambridge: Cambridge University Press.
Pfoh, E. (2009), *The Emergence of Israel in Ancient Palestine: Historical and Anthropological Perspectives*, CIS, London: Equinox.

Pfoh, E. (2010), 'Anthropology and Biblical Studies: A Critical Manifesto', in E. Pfoh (ed.), *Anthropology and the Bible: Critical Perspectives*, 15–35, BI 3, Piscataway, NJ: Gorgias Press.

Pfoh, E. (2014), 'A Hebrew *Mafioso*: Reading 1 Samuel 25 Anthropologically', *Semitica et Classica*, 7: 37–43.

Pfoh, E. (2016), *Syria-Palestine in the Late Bronze Age: An Anthropology of Politics and Power*, CIS, Abingdon: Routledge.

Pfoh, E. (2017), 'A Plea for an Historical Anthropology of Ancient Palestine', in J.G. Crossley and J. West (eds), *History, Politics and the Bible from the Iron Age to the Media Age: Essays in Honour of Keith W. Whitelam*, 41–54, LHBOTS 651, London: Bloomsbury.

Pfoh, E. (2018), 'Socio-Political Changes and Continuities in the Levant (1300–900 BCE)', in Ł. Niesiołowski-Spanò and M. Węcowski (eds), *Change, Continuity, and Connectivity: North-Eastern Mediterranean at the Turn of the Bronze Age and in the Early Iron Age*, 57–67, Philippika – Altertumswissenschaftliche Abhandlungen 118, Wiesbaden: Harrassowitz.

Pfoh, E. (2022), 'Patronage as Analytical Concept and Socio-Political Practice', in E. Pfoh (ed.), *Patronage in Ancient Palestine and in the Hebrew Bible: A Reader*, SWBA/SS 12, 1–37, Sheffield: Sheffield Phoenix Press.

Pfoh, E. and T.L. Thompson (2019), 'Patronage and the Political Anthropology of Ancient Palestine in the Bronze and Iron Ages', in I. Hjelm, I. Pappe, H. Taha and T.L. Thompson (eds), *A New Critical Approach to the History of Palestine: Palestine History and Heritage Project 1*, 200–28, CIS, Abingdon: Routledge.

Philipp, T. (2001), *Acre: The Rise and Fall of a Palestinian City, 1730–1831*, New York: Columbia University Press.

Pilch, J.J. and B.J. Malina, eds (1993), *Biblical Social Values and Their Meaning: A Handbook*, Peabody, MA: Hendrickson.

Pina-Cabral, J. de (1989), 'The Mediterranean as a Category of Regional Comparison: A Critical View', *Current Anthropology*, 30 (3): 399–406.

Pitt-Rivers, J. (1954), *The People of the Sierra*, London: Weidenfeld and Nicolson.

Pitt-Rivers, J. (1963a), 'Introduction', in J. Pitt-Rivers (ed.), *Mediterranean Countrymen: Essays in the Social Anthropology of the Mediterranean*, 9–25, The Hague: Mouton.

Pitt-Rivers, J., ed. (1963b), *Mediterranean Countrymen: Essays in the Social Anthropology of the Mediterranean*, The Hague: Mouton.

Pitt-Rivers, J. (1977), *The Fate of Shechem, or the Politics of Sex: Essays on Mediterranean Anthropology*, Cambridge Studies and Papers in Social Anthropology 19, Cambridge: Cambridge University Press.

Pitt-Rivers, J. (2000), 'Las culturas del Mediterráneo', in M.-À. Roque (ed.), *Nueva antropología de las sociedades mediterráneas: Viejas culturas, nuevas visiones*, 23–36, Barcelona: Icaria.

Rabinowitz, D. (1997), *Overlooking Nazareth: The Ethnography of Exclusion in Galilee*, Cambridge: Cambridge University Press.

Rogerson, J.W. (1978), *Anthropology and the Old Testament*, Oxford: Basil Blackwell.

Rogerson, J.W. (2013), 'Expansion of the Anthropological, Sociological and Mythological Context of the Hebrew Bible/Old Testament', in M. Sæbø (ed.), *Hebrew Bible/Old Testament: The History of Its Interpretation. Volume III: From Modernism to Post-Modernism (The Nineteenth and Twentieth Centuries)*, 119–33, Göttingen: Vandenhoeck & Ruprecht.

Roque, M.-À., ed. (2000), *Nueva antropología de las sociedades mediterráneas: Viejas culturas, nuevas visiones*, Barcelona: Icaria.

Roque, M.-À. (2005), *Antropología mediterránea: prácticas compartidas*, Barcelona: Icaria.

Ruiz de Elvira, L., C.H. Schwartz and I. Weipert-Fenner, eds (2018), *Clientelism and Patronage in the Middle East and North Africa: Networks of Dependency*, Routledge Studies in Middle Eastern Democratization and Government, Abingdon: Routledge.

Sacchi, P. and P.P. Viazzo (2014), 'Family and Household', in P. Horden and S. Kinoshita (eds), *A Companion to Mediterranean History*, 234–49, Oxford: Wiley Blackwell.

Said, E.W. (1978), *Orientalism: Western Conceptions of the Orient*, Harmondsworth, UK: Penguin.

Sant Cassia, P. and I. Schäfer (2005), '"Mediterranean Conundrums": Pluridisciplinary Perspectives for Research in the Social Sciences', *History and Anthropology*, 16 (1): 1–23.

Sapin, J. (1981), 'La géographie humaine de la Syrie-Palestine au deuxième millénaire avant J.-C. comme voie de recherche historique, I', *JESHO*, 24 (1): 1–62.

Sapin, J. (1982), 'La géographie humaine de la Syrie-Palestine au deuxième millénaire avant J.-C. comme voie de recherche historique, II–III', *JESHO*, 25 (1): 1–49; 25 (2): 113–86.

Scheffler, T. (2003), '"Fertile Crescent", "Orient", "Middle East": The Changing Mental Maps of Southwest Asia', *European Review of History*, 10 (2): 253–72.

Schneider, J. (2012), 'Anthropology and the Cold War Mediterranean', *Urban Anthropology and Studies of Cultural Systems and World Economic Development*, 41 (1): 107–29.

Schneider, P. (1969), 'Honor and Conflict in a Sicilian Town', *Anthropological Quarterly*, 42 (3): 130–54.

Schwartz, S. (2010), *Were the Jews a Mediterranean Society? Reciprocity and Solidarity in Ancient Judaism*, Princeton, NJ: Princeton University Press.

Shryock, A. (2020), 'Rites of Return: Back to the Mediterranean, Again', *History and Anthropology*, 31 (1): 147–56.

Silverman, S. (1968), 'Agricultural Organization, Social Structure, and Values in Italy: Amoral Familism Reconsidered', *American Anthropologist* NS, 70 (1): 1–20.

Silverman, S. (2001), 'Defining the Anthropological Mediterranean: Before Aix 1966', in D. Albera, A. Blok and C. Bromberger (eds), *L'anthropologie de la Méditerranée / Anthropology of the Mediterranean*, 43–57, Paris: Maisonneuve and Larose-MMSH.

Silverman, S. (2005), 'Rebellions and Reinventions', in F. Barth, A. Gingrich, R. Parkin and S. Silverman, *One Discipline, Four Ways: British, German, French, and American Anthropology*, 310–27, Chicago: Chicago University Press.

Simkins, R.A. (1999), 'Patronage and the Political Economy of Monarchic Israel', in R.A. Simkins and S.L. Cook (eds), *The Social World of the Hebrew Bible: Twenty-Five Years of the Social Sciences in the Academy*, 123–44, Semeia 87, Atlanta, GA: Scholars Press.

Stewart, C. (2010), 'Europe: Southern', in A. Barnard and J. Spencer (eds), *The Routledge Encyclopedia of Social and Cultural Anthropology*, 262–5, 2nd edn, Abingdon: Routledge.

Sweet, L.E. and T.J. O'Leary, eds (1969), *Circum-Mediterranean Peasantry: Introductory Bibliographies*, New Haven, CT: Human Relations Area Files Press.

Thompson, E.P. (1971), 'The Moral Economy of the English Crowd in the Eighteenth Century', *Past & Present*, 50: 76–136.

Thompson, T.L. (1992), *Early History of the Israelite People: From the Written and Archaeological Sources*, SHANE 4, Leiden: E.J. Brill.

Thompson, T.L. (2019), 'Introduction: Creating Coherence and Continuity – Suggestions and Illustrations of Methods and Themes', in I. Hjelm, H. Taha, I. Pappe and T.L. Thompson (eds), *A New Critical Approach to the History of Palestine: Palestine History and Heritage Project 1*, 1–16, CIS, Abingdon: Routledge.

Tilly, C. (1978), 'Anthropology, History, and the *Annales*', *Review*, 1 (3/4): 207–13.

van der Steen, E.J. (2021), 'Honor, Shame, and Hospitality: The Distribution of Power in the Premodern Levant', in T. Stordalen and Ø.S. LaBianca (eds), *Levantine Entanglements: Cultural Productions, Long-Term Changes and Globalizations in the Eastern Mediterranean*, 583–615, Sheffield: Equinox.
Wallace-Hadrill, A., ed. (1989), *Patronage in Ancient Society*, London: Routledge.
Weingrod, A. (1968), 'Patrons, Patronage, and Political Parties', *CSSH*, 10 (4): 377–400.
Westbrook, R. (2005), 'Patronage in the Ancient Near East', *JESHO*, 48 (2): 210–33.
Wikan, U. (1984), 'Shame and Honour: A Contestable Pair', *Man* NS, 19 (4): 635–52.
Wissler, C. (1927), 'The Culture-Area Concept in Social Anthropology', *American Journal of Sociology*, 32 (6): 881–91.
Wissler, C. (1928), 'The Culture-Area Concept as a Research Lead', *American Journal of Sociology*, 33 (6): 894–900.
Zaccagnini, C. (1973), *Lo scambio dei doni nel Vicino Oriente durante i secoli XV–XIII*, OAC XI, Rome: Università di Roma – La Sapienza.
Zaccagnini, C. (1983), 'On Gift Exchange in the Old Babylonian Period', in O. Carruba, M. Liverani and C. Zaccagnini (eds), *Studi orientalistici in ricordo di Franco Pintore*, 189–253, Studia Mediterranea 4, Pavia: GJES.

PART TWO

# Themes, approaches and interpretations

# CHAPTER SEVEN

# Kinship and social organization in ancient Palestine

PAULA M. MCNUTT

## SOCIOPOLITICAL ORGANIZATION AND STRUCTURE: TRIBES AND SEGMENTED SYSTEMS IN IRON AGE I

Iron Age I (c. 1150–950 BCE) is the period on which most recent social-scientific investigations of ancient Palestinian society have focused. This is due in part to its chronological association with the 'settlement', and in part to the growing lack of confidence in the biblical traditions as direct evidence for 'Israel's' early history and social life. As a consequence of the latter, more scholars have appealed to comparative studies and models developed by anthropologists and sociologists in their reconstructions of this period.

There was a clear break in type of sociopolitical organization between the Late Bronze Age and Iron Age I. The Late Bronze Age (c. 1550–1150 BCE) was characterized by complex and socially stratified urban settlements that were centres of petty kingdoms or city-states. In contrast, social organization in the new highland settlements during Iron Age I was much more limited in complexity and stratification, with very little commercial activity or craft specialization. The biblical traditions emphasize the tribal structure of this period preceding the rise of the state. Nowhere in this material, however, do we find an explanation of how the notion of tribe was conceptualized, what the composition of tribes was, how the tribes related to one another on the economic and political levels, or the structure of society in general. In some traditions there is emphasis placed on the number of tribes composing early Israel as being twelve (for example, Judges 1).[1] Judges 5, on the other hand, lists only ten. There are also tribes introduced in the narratives that are allied with 'Israel', but are never included in the lists (for example, the Calebites and the Kenites). Neither is there any evidence of precise geographical boundaries for the tribes. The city lists associated with the description of land distribution in Joshua 13–19 are now believed to reflect the situation during the monarchic period, and thus their value

---

[1] Cf. the references to twelve-tribe associations among the Ishmaelites (Genesis 17, 25), the Aramaeans (Genesis 22), and the six Arab tribes (Genesis 25).

for determining the original settlement patterns of the Iron Age I highlands is limited. They may provide information about patterns at the dawn of the monarchy, when the tribal regions were transformed into administrative districts for purposes of taxation and recruiting labour for public projects and military service. But even for this period, the lists may be idealized.[2]

In relation to social structure, only very schematic and superficial representations occur. Examples are found in Josh. 7.16–18, where society is divided into families, lineages or clans (see below) and tribes, or in census reports such as that in Num. 26.

Although we have no descriptions, there are a number of terms that occur in the biblical texts that point to conceptualizations of different levels of organization in the tribal structure. As is clear in the discussion below, there is no clear consensus on exactly what these terms mean or what level in the organization they refer to. There is also a good bit of scepticism regarding whether they in fact represent the reality of the early social organization or were later imposed by the writers of the monarchic and postexilic periods.

The difficulty in understanding the meanings of these terms can be variously explained. First, the terms we, or ancient peoples, use to identify social categories refer to *ideal* and not necessarily *empirical* categories. In this respect, members of Israelite society themselves (at whatever time) were probably not precise in their use of these terms. It is also likely that in the course of the texts' transmission the meanings of the terms changed as tribal organization became subsumed under the centralized state, and that individuals in the circles that preserved them were not familiar with their earlier usage. Another possibility is that the Israelite societies (synchronically and diachronically) did not adhere to any single system (see Lemche 1985: 202–4).

## *Kinship and genealogies*

Kinship systems and genealogies are ways of organizing and expressing relationships within a social system. In the modern Middle East, a wide variety of personal relationships are expressed in the language of family relationships (see, e.g., Eickelman 1989: 151–78). How people regard themselves in kinship terms and how they behave toward one another as 'kin' and 'family' in tribal societies, therefore, cannot be accounted for entirely in genetic terms.

Kinship is expressed through genealogies. As an organizing principle, kinship relations are significant in terms of how people understand economic and political, as well as social, relationships and their relationships with outside groups. For example, village and family property and the formation of political and economic alliances among families and among villages are kinship-based. Kinship also operates as a kind of code in which relationships of power are defined. The primary function of genealogies, then, is not to produce and transmit accurate lists of biological relationships through time, but to define social, political and economic relations, which are always open to revision, thus representing a fluid mixture of genuine and fictitious kinship connections.

---

[2] Cf. Frick 1989: 78–9. Frick assumes that while these boundary descriptions do reflect later administrative divisions under the monarchy, they derive from a source representing tribal claims during the late premonarchic period; cf. Halpern 1983. Halpern also suggests the possibility that the notion of a twelve-tribe system antedates the early monarchy (1983: 12), and that there was a full-blown tribal confederacy by the twelfth century (as indicated by Judges 5) (1983: 91–2).

Genealogies, especially those in segmented systems, also serve as memory devices for keeping track of the relationships among individuals and groups and for ranking them in terms of inheritance and succession rights. When relationships or statuses change, genealogies fluctuate in order to maintain their usefulness. When individuals or groups decline in prominence, their names are dropped. Thus, omissions are also important in understanding the dynamics of social relationships. As a result of such omissions, contrasting genealogies may exist that derive either from different times in a group's life or from different spheres of social life. Written forms are more resistant to fluidity than oral forms, but both may be adjusted as a way of keeping them functional and 'true' in relation to the existing set of relationships. Variants of written genealogies such as those in the Hebrew Bible, therefore, may not necessarily be the result of copyist error or textual corruption, but signs of the ongoing life of the genealogy.

Tribal genealogical systems have been studied extensively by anthropologists, and their conclusions have been applied to ancient Israelite society by a number of scholars (see, e.g., Johnson 1969; Malamat 1973; Wilson 1975, 1977; Flanagan 1982, 1983). In some cases, we have different versions of a genealogy, which give us some clues about how different groups in different time periods and social contexts chose to construct their understandings of a particular set of social relations according to their particular biases and agendas. The genealogies in the so-called priestly traditions, for example, are very likely stereotyped conceptions of the social structure of early 'Israel' that are meant to legitimate the writer's ideals about social relations at the time they were written down. Many of the genealogies in the Hebrew Bible are no doubt the result of such secondary and fictive systematization, constructed at the time they were written down, and later incorporated into the narrative framework. Whether any of them actually date as far back as Iron Age I is probably impossible to determine. But investigating them can nevertheless provide us with clues about the varied ways in which social, political and economic relations were understood in some periods.

In spite of problems having to do with dating the genealogies in the Hebrew Bible, anthropological models have allowed us to approach their investigation with new questions. Particularly useful in helping us to understand the nature and function of biblical genealogies are: (1) the typical distinctions in composition between oral and written genealogies; (2) the existence in tribal societies of contrasting types of genealogies with different functions – *segmented* genealogies, which have segments or 'branches' and are often preserved orally, and linear genealogies, which represent only a single line of descendants, linking the last named to those that are named before; (3) the tendency of genealogies to be fluid and flexible, with names often being moved onto, within and off lists; and (4) the multiple functions served by genealogies in the socio-economic, domestic, political and religious spheres of life (see Flanagan 1982: 24–5).

### *Early Israel as a segmented social system*

It is now widely accepted that the highland population of Iron Age I Palestine probably consisted of nomads, semi-nomads, semi-sedentary peoples, and sedentary farmers and village residents, all types of societies that would in one way or another have been engaged in symbiotic relationships with one another. Segmentation is a typical organizational principle in all these types of societies in the Middle East.

Recent descriptions of classical segmented systems include a variety of characteristics.[3] Ernest Gellner identifies the two essential characteristics of a segmented system as: (1) the primary means of maintaining order at every level of segmentation is opposition between groups; and (2) the criterion by which groups are defined is 'coextensive society itself' (Gellner 1973: 4; cited in Flanagan 1988: 278–9).

More specifically, in a segmented system society is composed of 'segments' and is characterized by considerable flexibility. Segments are units within the system that have the same structure – for example, families, clans or tribal sections (sometimes called lineages) and tribes. Individuals can have overlapping membership in more than one segment in the system at a time, as their economic, social, political and religious affiliations do not always coincide, and their regional and supra-regional identities can be based on different allegiances. Every individual is enmeshed in multiple, sometimes conflicting, affiliations and alliances, related, for example, to factions, age or gender. An individual segment is usually autonomous and tends to align itself politically so as to obtain maximum advantage for itself. This results in a continually changing organization. If the political conditions change, the subgroups may change their political and familial relationships with other subgroups within the tribe, or even with other tribes.

Individuals within this type of system conceive of relationships among themselves on the basis of shared common descent and are related *situationally* to one another. In the classic segmented system an ancestor represents political unity in a group, and symbolizes its limits. Everyone 'descended' from the ancestor is considered to be a member of the particular segment and is responsible, for example, for protecting it. Any 'segment' of society – from individuals to small, cooperative groups of close patrilineal relations, tribal sections and tribes – 'sees itself as an independent unit in relation to another segment of the same section, but sees both segments as a unity in relation to another segment' (Evans-Pritchard 1940: 147). Segments at the same 'level' are ideally equal and are defined by 'balanced opposition' toward one another.

The Rwala Bedouin, for example, have five tribal 'sections' with genealogies that are essentially fixed. Below the level of these tribal 'sections', genealogies are more flexible and reflect the situations of actual living groups. The named groups below the level of the tribal section ('minimal sections') are call *ibn 'amm* by the Rwala, and are said to be descended from a male line five generations distant. The minimal sections are essentially economic units, whose members cooperate very closely with one another.[4] The composition of descent groups below the level of tribal section changes slowly over time to accommodate shifting economic and political realities. Intermarriage is one of the ways in which individuals can claim new ties to other segments. The fact that women do not appear in the formal genealogies provides the necessary latitude for this flexibility (Eickelman 1989: 87–9; cf. Lemos 2010: 89–158).

In segmented societies, there is no permanent 'governmental' authority (according to theory). In the absence of centralized power, political order is dependent on the ways in which communities relate to one another through the segmentary principle, and efforts

---

[3] The concept of segmentation can be traced back to Émile Durkheim's *The Division of Labor in Society* (1933 [1893]: 175). E.E. Evans-Pritchard's *The Nuer* (1940) contains the most thorough application of segmentary theory to an African society. For a review of issues of segmentation in the Middle East, see, e.g., Caton 1987; Dresch 1988; Eickelman 1989: 131–8. See also Sahlins 1961; Gellner 1969, 1973; Khazanov 1984: 144–8.

[4] Reference to the minimal sections as 'lineages' is avoided, since patrilineal ties cannot be traced with precision.

are made to control conflict and maintain order at the lowest possible level. The bottom 'level' in a segmented system is composed of discrete camping clusters or rural local communities that claim common identity and may share residence in a common territory or herd together, and expect other group members to support their interests. Many households within such a community, but not necessarily all, claim common kinship ties. Conflict with other groups is understood in relation to collective honour, and members of individual groups, which are *situationally* defined, are expected to support one another. High value is placed on the autonomy and honour of individuals, as is a 'balanced opposition' of honour-bearing individuals and groups. Cultural notions of persuasion, mediation, honour and negotiation, rather than use of force, are emphasized in conflict resolution and the maintenance of social order. Thus one becomes a man of honour in such societies by learning how to be persuasive.[5] The balanced structure of segmented systems also helps to contain violence by maintaining the ideal of equality, even though in actuality egalitarianism is not absolute (Gellner 1973: 4). Even so, political leadership can exist, as long as it remains personal and is not institutionalized into an office, so that the ideal of egalitarianism can be upheld in spite of political inequality on the ground.

As an example of *flexibility* in a typical segmented group, Eickelman points to the Bni Bataw of Morocco (Eickelman 1989: 141–4). As is the case for other segmented societies, the rural local community is the most important 'level' in terms of everyday activity. Individuals in a rural local community claim patrilineal kinship to one another (among other ties), but cannot specifically identify how all members of a group are mutually related. They often point to an unspecified *ahistorical* past as a way of legitimizing present-day alignments. What counts, then, is not how individuals are in reality related by blood, but who acts together with whom in a sustained way on various ritual and political occasions.

Flexibility is also apparent in the makeup of the community's council. The council is an informal body constituted by male heads of households, who consult on such issues of mutual concern as transhumant movements, quarrels over water and pasture rights, and other types of collective obligations. When circumstances permit, individual households or groups of households who are dissatisfied with membership in a particular local community may break away to join another rural local community or to form their own in a process of fissioning and fusing.

Marriage ties, a wife's inheritance or purchasing land in another rural local community can serve as the basis for a realignment. Normally, the realignments occur only within the context of nearby local communities, and often households are not even physically relocated. What is of primary significance, then, is not a person's actual physical location, but who is aligned with whom in what circumstances.

The next 'level' in the Bni Bataw system, the *section*, is usually composed of three or four local communities and is somewhat more stable in composition over time, although composition and formal identity do tend to change gradually. The greater stability of the sections over against the lower levels in the system is connected with their recognition as administrative entities. Prior to the colonial period, for example, sections were responsible for constructing fortified compounds for collective defence against intertribal raids,

---

[5] Eickelman (1989: 132–5) emphasizes that these notions are cultural principles, not directly observable 'actual' social actions. The principle of segmentation and associated notions of person, responsibility and honour serve in a sense as 'native' models of the social order.

making collective arrangements for grazing rights to pastures controlled by neighbouring groups, and arranging 'ritual alliances' between rural local communities and sections in the same or different tribes, in which groups agreed to refrain from fighting and raiding one another and, at least in principle, to aid one another when there were threats from third parties. Such alliances were generally based on exchange of herding rights.

At the level of 'tribe', coalitions of various sections and rural local communities within the tribes often occurred, but the tribe appears to have existed more as a means of providing a range of potential identities than as a base for sustained collective action.

Interpreters of early Israel's social world continue to debate the issue of whether segmented social organizations, systems and ideologies existed and whether the segmented model is appropriate.[6] In making a determination about the utility of this model, it is important to note the distinction between segmentation and 'segmentary lineage theory'. Segmentation involves *culturally* maintained *principles* that *inform* social action in many tribal contexts, not actual observable actions and relationships. This principle should not be confused with 'segmentary *lineage* theory', which does attempt to identify real actions and relationships. Segmentary lineage theory has been criticized for its tendency to ignore cultural principles, along with its implication that political relationships of *actual groups* are formed primarily or exclusively on the basis of lineage descent, at each 'level' of society being balanced by others with roughly equal strength.[7] Objections to the model's application to the situation in early Israel, as far as I can tell, are related, then, not to the *principle* of segmentation, but to segmentary lineage theory.

In any case, this model does seem to accord well with the archaeological information from Iron Age I, and some of the texts in the Hebrew Bible seem to embody notions associated with the cultural principles of segmentation as outlined below. Even though we cannot really argue that they reflect historical reality, they nevertheless possibly tell us something about how these principles were understood by the writers and editors of the texts.

## Anthropological models of tribal organization

In his recent anthropological survey of contemporary Middle Eastern societies, Dale F. Eickelman notes that a common 'family resemblance' is identifiable among Middle Eastern notions of tribe, in spite of variations from region to region. Because of this it is possible, he argues, to make general statements about common elements or 'family resemblances' in these notions without presuming that they all must fit into a neat typology. He conceives of these common elements as 'partial similarities that can meaningfully be compared and contrasted, rather than exact, nearly botanical identities asserted by simpler but less accurate theoretical assumptions' (Eickelman 1989: 147).

Defining what a 'tribe' is, and how tribes are organized, has proven to be a notoriously complex task. Part of the problem in earlier attempts to come up with a broad, all-encompassing 'ideal type' is that tribes from different regions of the world often have little in common (see, e.g., Fried 1967, 1975). This has also been a problem in some of

---

[6] See, e.g., Crüsemann 1978: 201-15; Gottwald 1979: 322-3; Frick 1985: 51-69; Lemche 1985: 202-30; Rogerson 1986; Fiensy 1987; Flanagan 1988: 278-8.
[7] Eickelman 1989: 133-5; cf. Lemche 1985: 223-31; Rogerson 1986. Lemche and Rogerson argue that segmentary lineage theory is inadequate for understanding the situation in early 'Israel'.

the studies of tribes in ancient Palestine that have depended on models developed in studies of African tribes rather than on those relating to the geographical context of the Middle East. The concepts of tribe refer to real relations and have social and economic significance, but these are highly variable, as tribal structure and membership change constantly. Within the context of a particular tribe, as practical definitions of self-identity change, so do factional alignments over land rights, marriage strategies, access to resources, and other aspects of society. Power and leadership also shift according to current membership in changeable descent groups.

Another complicating factor is that the context and goals of the person engaged in defining 'tribe' affect the ways in which a tribe is conceptualized. *Administrative concepts* (i.e. concepts developed by administrators of states into which tribes have been incorporated), for example, frequently assume a corporate identity and fixed territorial boundaries that many 'tribes' do not possess.[8] Tribe members themselves, on the other hand, do not necessarily think of themselves primarily in relation to the state, and their social and political alignments frequently shift, even as the ways in which they conceive of boundaries tend to be blurred and flexible.[9]

It is too simplistic, then, to view tribalism as a single phenomenon, or as an undifferentiated whole, a peripheral social system, or simply a stage in the evolution of human civilization, as is often done. Rather, it is a complex system that brings people together for many different purposes, in the context of many different competing or alternative principles of alignment (LaBianca and Younker 1995: 405).

Nevertheless, as Eickelman argues, it is possible to identify some 'family resemblances' among Middle Eastern tribes. In general, a tribe is a group that is conceptualized in terms of genealogy, and may be either a *part* of a 'nation' or identical with a *whole* 'nation'. Tribes are found in a wide range of socio-economic settings, including pastoral nomads, settled farmers or even urban dwellers, and their members are often, although not necessarily, politically unified (Eickelman 1989: 73).

The composition of segments in social structure and the ways in which the structure is articulated vary from tribe to tribe and will also vary depending on whether the group is nomadic or sedentary, or a combination of both. For example, in a sedentary tribe, the village might be an identifiable segment in the system, whereas in a pastoral nomadic tribe, the 'camp' would be the corresponding segment. In terms of articulation, sedentary groups tend to develop more rigid lineages than is the case for nomadic groups. Because kin groups put a great deal of energy into working and protecting particular plots of land, their sense of ownership and investment, along with feelings of in-group loyalty and obligation, tend to be stronger.

Kin groups in nomadic societies, on the other hand, tend to have looser, more flexible lineages because of their dependence on being able to gain access to widely dispersed areas. Flexible and cooperative alignments that allow them to move beyond the social and territorial boundaries of smaller, blood-related kin groups offer advantages in this respect. By means of such processes as 'telescoping', 'fusioning', and 'grafting', pastoral nomads continually generate loose and flexible networks of cooperation and alignments, through

---

[8] This is perhaps the case in the Israelite monarchic construct of twelve tribal districts.
[9] Eickelman 1989: 128–9. For a thorough discussion of the types of relationships that exist among nomadic tribes and states, see, e.g., Khazanov 1984. The variety of ways in which tribes and states interrelate in contemporary Middle Eastern societies is also the subject of Khoury and Kostiner 1990.

which they maintain control over widespread rangeland pastures, watering places, camping sites, storage depots and burial grounds. Complicating matters further is the fact that it is not unusual for a certain amount of sedentarization and nomadization to occur among individual households, depending on their personal circumstances and shifts in economic and ecological conditions (LaBianca and Younker 1995: 404).

There are also numerous variations with respect to political organization. Some tribes are organized without strong or centralized apparatuses of power, while others are governed by a supreme tribal leader or chieftain (Lemche 1985: 111). Tribal elites tend to think of themselves as egalitarian and making decisions collectively. But in reality egalitarianism rarely exists.

Ideologies relating to tribal identity also vary, but are generally based on a concept of *political* identity formed through common patrilineal descent, as expressed through genealogies. Political actions in such tribes (the patterns in which groups of people actually come together or come in conflict with one another in a political manner) are generally explained by anthropologists in terms of *segmentary theory*, as has been indicated above, although other grounds for political action may coexist with segmentary ones. Ideologies are elaborated in varying degrees by individual members of a tribe, depending on their social positions and particular situations. Individuals who are socially and politically dominant often elaborate such ideologies in more complex ways than others, using them, for example, to solidify political alliances with members of other tribal groups and to enhance their own positions in relation to state authorities (Eickelman 1989: 128).

Another problem that arises in attempting to present a general description of tribal organization is that the terminology used to designate organizational levels varies from scholar to scholar. The use of the term 'lineage', for example, is often avoided now because of its connection to segmentary lineage theory, which implies a rigid system in which unilineal descent is associated with actual blood ties. It is also sometimes difficult to distinguish between a 'lineage' and a 'clan'. Both lineages and clans are unilineal groups that perceive themselves as being descendants of a particular individual. But they are different in that the genealogy of a lineage is more permanent, reflecting both real and postulated kinship between its members, while a clan genealogy varies according to particular clan segments, and its members, who assume common ancestry, cannot demonstrate their genealogical connections.

As is indicated in the discussion of segmented societies above, a tribe is typically segmented into at least two subdivisions (referred to variously in the literature as sections, moieties, subtribes). The form, function and significance of these subdivisions correspond in most respects to those of the tribe, but they apply to only a section of it. A section may be segmented into a number of 'clans' which, again, in terms of structure and function resemble both the subtribe and the tribe. On all three of these levels of integration it is the *concept* of blood relatedness rather than actual blood relations that motivates common activities. A clan may be segmented into a number of maximal lineages which are in turn composed of lineages and minimal lineages. In some tribes, the village or camp is also an identifiable segment in the system. Finally, the lineages themselves are subdivided into extended and nuclear families (although the extended family is not always a significant social unit).

Integration and cooperation are typically strongest at the lowest level of the nuclear or extended family, weaker in higher levels of organization, and weakest at the level of 'nation' or tribal confederacy (if one exists). The smaller units in a tribal system (for example, clans or lineages) rarely unite with each other politically. When they do, it is normally because of some threat or crisis that requires it. In between times of threat, some sense of solidarity and unity and loose bonding are maintained through economic and religious ties (for example, trade and ritual). A sense of unity is further supported by myths of common descent, fictitious kinship links by means of mythical or assumed ancestry.

Lemche's summary of the social structure of nomadic societies in the Middle East offers a good example of how individuals relate to the various levels in tribal social structure. Lemche notes that one common feature of all nomadic societies in the Middle East is that the family is the basic social and economic unit, although politically it has little significance. Extended families with up to three generations sometimes live together, but such families, he indicates, are relatively few in number. The family is exogamous, and the ideal marriage is between agnates (relatives related through male descent or on the father's side). In actuality, however, this is not necessarily the case, especially in 'princely' families, where political concerns motivate alliances outside the paternal line.

The family in nomadic tribal societies is economically autonomous, each owning its own livestock. In terms of inheritance, there is ordinarily no strict rule dictating that the oldest son must inherit a larger share than others, so ideally all sons have equal rights of inheritance.

The camp, composed of families who travel together through the annual cycle, is the next level in the structure. The camp is usually a cooperative unit in which all members share in caring for the animals and, in cases where agriculture is practised, in farming. Its organization and the principles that govern it, and the extent of its political significance in the larger structure, also vary (Lemche 1985: 112–15).

The next level in the characteristic social structure of Middle Eastern nomadic societies is the lineage, which consists of a number of related families who claim descent from a single tribal ancestor. The lineage tends to be a fairly stable social unit, in that it almost always bears a name that it retains for long periods of time. But, as has been emphasized above, it is not completely inflexible. Divisions sometimes occur that may lead to the emergence of new lineages, and the genealogies are always susceptible to adjustment when circumstances require it. The actual form of a genealogy represents the ideological basis for the composition of the lineage in question within particular situational contexts. An individual male's political and economic status within the system is also established through his position in the lineage system. Ordinarily, rights to such things as pasturage and water are connected to lineages, and the lineage is responsible for defending the rights of its members and for protecting individual members. The lineage is typically endogamous, that is, marital ties are usually formed within the lineage. Within the larger system, some lineages may have more power and status than others, and the status of the individuals within a given lineage is relatively homogeneous. Tribal leadership, if any, usually operates at the lineage level, or within the families comprising the lineage. Often, there is an officially acknowledged leader whose role is usually confined to how his lineage relates to other segments in the structure rather than governing within the lineage itself.

Maximal lineages, clans and subtribes are all above the level of the lineage, but have decreasing importance in relation to daily life. It is rare, for example, for the tribe to function collectively (Lemche 1985: 116–18).

## *Models of tribes in Iron Age I Palestine*

One of the characteristics of earlier studies that considered the nature of the tribe in Iron Age I Palestine following the 'settlement' was the assumption that a number of its features were 'survivals' of nomadic ideals (for example, Pedersen 1926–40 [1920–34]; de Vaux 1961 [1958]). As indicated above, however, recent studies of tribal societies have shown that many tribes in the recent history of the Middle East share a number of similar features, whether nomadic or sedentary. And more and more among biblical scholars there is a consensus that a significant portion of the population comprising Iron Age I highland Palestine derived from sedentary groups.

C.H.J. de Geus's work on tribes in ancient Israel was particularly important because he argued that biblical scholars should abandon the notion that the Semites, and thus the ancient 'Israelites', were originally nomads who came from the Arabian desert in successive waves of invaders (de Geus 1976).[10] He also points out the important distinction between transhumance, which is associated with agriculture, and pure nomadism. Contrary to earlier studies, he is also aware of the fact that tribal organization is not associated *only* with non-sedentary societies. For him, then, the evidence for tribal organization in sedentary societies, such as those portrayed in the biblical texts, is not evidence of survivals from an earlier nomadic stage. He also deals with the issue of the political significance of the tribe in relation to other levels of tribal organization, and concludes that the most important political group, and thus the locus of the real power in society and the basis of political organization, was not the tribe, but the *mišpāḥāh* or 'clan'. This level of Israelite social organization, he proposed, was made up of the population of a small town or, in some cases, several clans in the same town. The tribe, composed of groups of clans, was primarily a *geographic* concept that served as a means of enabling individual Israelites in a given region to define their relationships to other Israelites in other parts of the country. The tribe, therefore, had no significance in isolation from the entirety of Israel.[11]

One of the issues concerning Iron Age I sociopolitical organization that has yet to come to any kind of consensus is the question of how the various tribes in Palestine related to one another (socially, economically, politically and religiously). In his extensive study of the tribal period, Norman Gottwald agreed with de Geus on most questions of detail in relation to social structure (Gottwald 1979: 245–92). But he attributed more significance to the level of the tribes and their participation in an intertribal organization, which he perceived as being of central importance.[12] 'Israel' as a 'confederacy or league of tribes' was, in Gottwald's estimation, 'the widest societal and culture-bearing unit of associated egalitarian Yahwistic tribes' (Gottwald 1979: 338). The basic characteristics of this confederacy were a common concern for the Yahwistic cult, shared laws and ideology, a commitment to economic egalitarianism, and a readiness to organize military opposition

---

[10] Although his study was not intended so much to present a social-scientific analysis of ancient 'Israel' as it was to critique Martin Noth's amphictyonic hypothesis, and in retrospect is problematic in some respects, it was nevertheless important for providing the groundwork for further studies (for example, Gottwald's *The Tribes of Yahweh*, 1979). For critiques of de Geus's construct, see, e.g., Lemche 1985: 66–76; Martin 1989: 96.
At about the same time, George Mendenhall (1973) considered the issue of the nature of tribes and their social organization in Iron Age I Palestine. Using only Elman Service's (1962) study of the evolution of society, however, and arguing that no form can have the same function in two different societies, Mendenhall concludes that although there are some incidental similarities between the early Israelite tribes and the characteristics of tribes as identified by anthropologists, ultimately the anthropological category of 'tribe' does not fit the situation in ancient Palestine.
[11] Cf. Halpern 1983: 109–33, 145–63. Halpern makes a similar argument in his detailed discussion of the regional, historical, cultural, linguistic and economic differences among the tribes.
[12] Gottwald 1979: 345–86 and 1985: 281–84. Cf. Gottwald 1993, in which he concedes that such a tribal organization may not have existed.

against external, threatening forces such as those of the Canaanites and Philistines. For Gottwald (1979: 339), then, the tribe was 'the primary organizational segment', 'an autonomous association of segmented extended families (bēth-'āvōth) grouped in village/neighborhood protective associations (mišpāḥāh), averaging about 50 per tribe, functionally interlocking through intermarriage, practices of mutual aid, common worship, and a levy of troops'.

What shaped these tribes into such units was their common experience of oppression and rebellion, as well as their territorial grouping in areas that were determined by factors such as terrain, climate or enclaves of Canaanite city-states.[13]

In his more recent studies, Lemche (1985: 282–90, 1988: 98–109) agrees with de Geus that the Israelite tribes were primarily territorial units. On this basis he argues that the individual tribes identified themselves particularly with their respective geographical territories, and postulates that the variations in the descriptions of tribal territories in the texts correspond to the normal fissioning and fusioning processes of traditional tribal societies.

The composition of these tribes, in Lemche's estimation, essentially included the lineages and clans inhabiting the regions with which the names of particular tribes were associated. They maintained a sense of social identity on the basis of shared interest in keeping the territory in their own hands. Tribal affiliation, which would have been flexible and expressed in terms of kinship, could have been based also on any number of other factors – for example, actual or fictitious blood ties, common history, common economic interests or common external enemies.

Lemche agrees that there were probably tribal alliances, but argues that they would not necessarily have been stable and fixed. There is not, he asserts, a single concrete bit of evidence dating from the second millennium BCE that indicates that Israel was ever constituted as a permanent coalition during this period, as is implied in the 'all-Israel' construct of the Deuteronomistic traditions, or that there was any single sanctuary that might have been the centre of such a league, as such scholars as Noth and Gottwald have argued. The picture presented in the biblical texts, in his estimation, suggests that the tribes may have been united religiously in some way, but it is not certain that there was a central shrine that represented this unity. There were probably economic ties as well, expressed, for example, through trade.

## Constructs of tribal period social structure

Anthropologists have noted a tendency for tribal structure to remain intact even after a tribal territory has been incorporated into a state system, and a number of biblical scholars continue to maintain that the basic tribal structure of Iron Age I persisted, at least in rural areas, throughout Iron Age II (for example, Bendor 1996: 39). It is possible, then, that portions of the biblical construct may reflect to some extent the Iron Age I situation (cf. now the discussion in Lemos 2010: 161–79).

The three Hebrew terms that occur most frequently in the biblical texts that clearly refer to levels of social structure are *bêt 'āb*, *mišpāḥāh* and *šēbeṭ* (or *maṭṭeh*). It is far from clear, however, what each of these terms means in many of the contexts in which they occur.

---

[13] For a thorough critique of Gottwald's reconstruction, see Lemche 1985. Cf. Martin 1989.

The terms in question are normally understood to designate the nuclear or extended family (*bêt 'āb*), the clan or lineage (*mišpāḥāh*) and the tribe (*šēbeṭ* or *maṭṭeh*). Another term that is sometimes used is *'eleph* (for example, Judges 6–8), which in some contexts may refer to the same level as *mišpāḥāh* or perhaps even to another level.[14] A close examination of the writers' use of these terms, however, indicates that they very likely have a variety of different meanings, depending in part on the literary contexts in which they are used.

The term *bêt 'āb*, which occurs frequently in the ancestral narratives, seems to overlap in some instances with *mišpāḥāh*.[15] In some cases it appears to refer to the nuclear or extended family, but in others to 'lineage' or 'clan'.[16] In Gen. 7.1 and 45.1–11, for example, *bêt* clearly refers to the extended family. But in other passages it is not clear whether it refers to extended or nuclear families or to lineages (e.g. Gen. 18.19, 24.38, 24.40, 28.21). Even in passages in which *bêt 'āb* occurs together with *mišpāḥāh*, it is not easy to distinguish their relative meanings (e.g. Gen. 24.38, 40, 41; Judg. 9.1; 2 Sam. 16.5). Sometimes *mišpāḥāh* occurs but *bêt 'āb* does not, and, again, the meaning is ambiguous (e.g. Deut. 29.17; 1 Sam. 9.21, 10.21). There are also passages in Judges 6–8 in which *bêt 'āb* possibly refers to lineage rather than family or extended family, and one in Judg. 9.1 where 'mother's house' also seems to refer to a lineage. 'David's house' clearly refers to a lineage, as does 'Saul's house'.

The term *mišpāḥāh* occurs most often in census lists and genealogies, many of which are priestly, and much more rarely in narrative contexts.[17] The term *bêt 'āb*, on the other hand, is not normally used in priestly genealogies and census lists.

The census list in Numbers 26 indicates one way in which the internal organization of the tribes was conceived in the priestly traditions. Reference to the *bêt 'āb* occurs only once in this list (v. 2), where Israel's leaders are assigned to take a census of the people according to their *bêt 'ābôt*. Thereafter, the use of the term *mišpāḥāh* suggests that it represents the same basic unit as the *bêt 'āb*.

In Numbers 1, where Moses is instructed to take a census of the *mišpāḥāh* of *bêt 'āb*, the census does not penetrate below the level of tribe. The emphasis is on determining the number of grown men in the various tribes according to the various subdivisions of the tribe in question, but the nature of these subdivisions is not revealed. Numbers 1 does not really provide any information about how these two segments of society were understood. Neither of the census lists in Numbers, then, tells us much more than that at this stage in the formation of the traditions there seems to have been some uncertainty about how the terms related to social reality and to each other, and that the boundaries between them were fluid and overlapped somewhat. The stereotypical use of *mišpāḥāh* in the priestly

---

[14] In many cases *'eleph* refers to the number one thousand, but in some cases it appears to be used synonymously with *mišpāḥāh*, usually in military contexts. Gottwald (1979: 270–6) defines it as a military unit based on the *mišpāḥāh*.

[15] For a review of passages in which *bêt 'āb* and *mišpāḥāh* occur, see, e.g., Gottwald 1979: 257–70, 285–92; Lemche 1985: 245–72; Bendor 1996: passim.

[16] Lemche in particular concludes that the *bêt 'āb* is used to refer to a variety of social groupings, ranging from the nuclear family up to and including the lineage.

[17] For example, the genealogies in Genesis 10 and 36 and Exod. 6.14–25; the description of the apportionment of land in Joshua 13–21; the census/genealogy list in Numbers 26; the census list in Num. 1.1–47. Bendor (1996: 47) argues that the census lists and genealogical records, even though schematic, reflect to some extent the social pattern that existed in a number of different situations.

lists, therefore, may be a priestly systematization of kinship units that is secondary and has no relation to the social reality the term may at one time have been associated with.

Because of this confusion in the texts, anthropological models have been useful in attempts to reconstruct what the social reality might have been, even though a number of different constructs have resulted. The most thorough treatment to date of the biblical references relating to social structure is that of Bendor (1996).[18]

Bendor (1996: 31) sees the structure of Israelite society as having remained essentially the same from the time of the 'settlement' until the end of the monarchic period. He emphasizes in his study the difficulty posed by the blurring of boundaries in the biblical texts among the levels in the sequence *bêt 'āb* / *mišpāḥāh* / *šēbeṭ*, which is especially prominent as indicated above in the usage of *bêt 'āb* and *mišpāḥāh* (which he translates 'extended family' and 'sib' respectively).[19] Part of the difficulty, he suggests, may be due to varying perspectives from which the *bêt 'āb* would have been viewed: for example, the synchronic perspective of the *bêt 'āb* as constructed by its component generations would have differed from the diachronic perspective. Generational differences would also have affected the perspectives from which the *bêt 'āb* was viewed: father, son, and grandson would each have seen the *bêt 'āb* and its familial relations differently.[20] One of Bendor's aims, then, is to construct a general framework in which the dynamic balance of kinship relations can be viewed both synchronically and diachronically (that is, statically and dynamically; Bendor 1996: 40–1). He acknowledges that in attempting to do this he is presenting 'abstractions', and quotes Evans-Pritchard:

> [The anthropologist] seeks to discover the structural order of the society, the patterns of which, once established, enable him to see it as a whole, as a set of interrelated abstractions. Then the society is not only culturally intelligible [. . .] but also becomes sociologically intelligible [. . .] the social anthropologist discovers [. . .] its basic structure. This structure cannot be seen. It is a set of abstractions, each of which, though derived, it is true, from analysis of observed behaviour, is fundamentally an imaginative construct of the anthropologist himself. By relating these abstractions to one another logically so that they present a pattern he can see the society in its essentials and as a single whole.
>
> —Evans-Pritchard 1962 [1950]: 148

Most reconstructions of ancient Israelite social structure subscribe to the interpretation that the *bêt 'āb* consisted of the extended family, with as many as three generations living together as a residential group,[21] that this segment of society was the primary social and economic unit, and that it was exogamous (see, for example, Lev. 18.6–18, 20.11–12;

---

[18] Bendor's analysis is based primarily on the biblical texts, with some attention to anthropological models. For other reconstructions see, e.g., de Geus 1976; Gottwald 1979: 245–92; Lemche 1985: 244–90.

[19] A sib is a unilineal, usually exogamous, kin group based on a traditional common descent. The use of this particular term as a translation for *mišpāḥāh* is problematic, in that the ideal marriage pattern relating to this grouping in the biblical traditions appears to be endogamy rather than exogamy.

[20] Although it does not enter into Bendor's discussion, another perspective may be represented in the occasional occurrence of *bêt 'ēm* ('mother's house' – e.g. Gen. 24.28; Judg. 9.1; Ruth 1.8; Song 3.4, 8.2). With the exception of Judg. 9.1, the perspective represented is that of a woman. See Meyers 1991.

[21] Cf. Gottwald's argument that the *bêt 'āb* refers to the nuclear family and that the residential unit (which was not the *bêt 'āb* alone) contained up to five generations. Lemche notes in his review of contemporary Middle Eastern tribal societies that he did not come across any instances of a residential unit that large.

Deut. 22.30, 27.20), although there are differing nuances in their arguments. Lemche, for example, acknowledges that the emphasis in the Hebrew Bible is on extended families rather than nuclear families, but suggests that this has to do with the fact that the figures portrayed in most of the narratives are great men – that is, although the extended family was probably the ideal, in reality the nuclear family was probably more pervasive in day-to-day existence (Lemche 1985: 250–1).[22] The centrality of the nuclear family is reflected in the custom of Levirate marriage (Genesis 38; Ruth; Deut. 25.5–10), which emphasizes the survival of the nuclear family, which is threatened by extinction when the father of the house dies without having left sons.

Bendor agrees with the consensus that the *bêt 'āb* was a self-sufficient social and economic unit consisting of three or four generations, including the head of household ('father'), who had authority over it, and his wives, their sons and their wives, their unmarried daughters, the sons' offspring, and non-related dependents (Lemche 1985).[23] The *bêt 'āb* was patrilineal (descent was reckoned through the male line) and patrilocal (the wife left the *bêt 'āb* of her father to reside in the *bêt 'āb* of her husband). This segment of society, then, was composed of nuclear domestic units that consisted of the households of sons within the *bêt 'āb* (Bendor 1996: 31).[24] This household constituted a unit in its own right, although it was dependent upon the *bêt 'āb*.

The status of the individual male in a nuclear unit, according to Bendor, was dependent on his position in the *bêt 'āb* in relation to his father and brothers, especially with respect to his portion of the *naḥala*, or patrimony. This consisted of the land belonging to the kinship group as a whole, which was divided into plots inherited by the sons.[25] The plot was the basis for the nuclear unit's status in the *bêt 'āb*, just as the *naḥala* as a whole was the basis of the *bêt 'āb*'s status within the *mišpāḥāh* and of the *mišpāḥāh* in the larger society (Bendor 1996: 129–33). These nuclear units were not necessarily uniform or equal in terms of distribution of wealth and status. Although grazing pastures were shared by all member of the *bêt 'āb*, for example, flocks were the property of each nuclear unit, and the vineyards and fields belonged to the units that inherited or planted them (Bendor 1996: 202).[26]

It is very typical in Middle Eastern tribal societies, as Bendor suggests for ancient Israel, for some individuals to be accorded more prestige than others. Even though ideally they regard themselves as equals, there are nevertheless considerable differences in social status and prestige that are associated with such qualities as wealth, warlike accomplishments and eloquence (see also Lemche 1985: 120–4).

Bendor identifies the social functions of this segment of society as: protecting, cultivating and developing inherited land; clearing and preparing new land; passing knowledge from generation to generation; bearing responsibility for daily existence and survival; arranging marriages; avenging blood; maintaining internal order; redeeming

---

[22] Cf. Carney 1975: 89–92. Carney argues that in ancient societies, although the extended family was the norm among elites, the poor did not have the resources to live in extended families.

[23] The biblical material used to support this interpretation is cited on pp. 48–54 and 120–4.

[24] Passages Bendor identifies as clearly referring to the nuclear family include Gen. 42.19, 33; 45.18; Judg. 14.19. Other examples of passages in which *bêt 'āb* occurs are noted on pp. 45–7.

[25] Num. 27.1–11 and 36.1–12 refer to surviving daughters' inheriting land in the absence of sons, with the stipulation that they must marry within their own *mišpāḥāh*.

[26] Cf. Gottwald's (1979) assumption that a segmentary society is egalitarian.

land that had fallen into the hands of creditors and kinsmen who had sold themselves; safeguarding the *mišpāḥāh*'s rights of inheritance; allocating resources and dividing the obligations of the *mišpāḥāh* among its units; and performing the rituals associated with sacrifice, holidays, marriage, birth, death and burial (Bendor 1996: 118, 202–3).

In terms of the diachronic dynamics affecting social structure and status, Bendor argues that the distribution of inheritance would have determined to some extent the ways in which relations within a particular *bêt 'āb* would have shifted over time. A *naḥala* of regular size and resources, if repeatedly divided over several generations, for example, would have been reduced to a series of plots that could not support everyone in the *bêt 'āb*. Over time a point would have been reached when subdivision among heirs was no longer possible because of the limited availability of property. The *bêt 'āb* might have responded to such a situation by occasional fissioning. Or it might have responded by passing the inheritance to only some of the brothers, or only the eldest, in which case the others would be called by the name of their brothers in their *naḥala*, that is, they would no longer be units in their own right within the *bêt 'āb*.

In Bendor's construct, the *bêt 'āb* was interrelated with the *mišpāḥāh*, the next identifiable level in the social structure, in the following ways: the head of household participated in the institution of 'elders'; the *bêt 'āb* appealed to and accepted judgement from the *mišpāḥāh* in conflict situations that could not be resolved within the *bêt 'āb* itself; the *bêt 'āb* requested assistance from the *mišpāḥāh* in times of crisis and participated in periodic land distribution; it appealed to the *mišpāḥāh* for assistance in relation to blood feuds and marriages; and it participated in communal rituals (Bendor 1996: 118, 141–64).

The *mišpāḥāh* is typically understood to have been composed of a number of extended families ('father's houses') that resided together in a village or small town.[27] A territorial identity for the *mišpāḥāh* is suggested in the tribal boundary lists in Joshua 13–19, where the tribes are allotted land according to their *mišpāḥāh*. Some scholars equate it with 'clan' (e.g. de Geus 1976) a view that is generally based on Josh. 7.17, where a lot-casting procedure follows the order of *mišpāḥāh*, *bêt 'āb*, and an individual and his immediate family. Others view it as being closer in definition to lineage (a descent group composed of a number of residential groups in Lemche's definition; Lemche 1985: 244–90), and yet others as 'sib' (e.g. Bendor 1996).

Gottwald defines the *mišpāḥāh* as a 'protective association of families', consisting of: 'a cluster of extended families living in the same or nearby villages [. . .] providing socio-economic mutual aid for its constituent families, contributing troop quotas to the tribal levy, and indirectly serving alone or in concert to provide a local jural community' (Gottwald 1979: 340).[28] In addition to the *mišpāḥāh*, Gottwald suggests that there were

---

[27] For example, de Geus 1976. For this level of society, see also Gottwald 1979: 249–51, 257–70, 282–4; Lemche 1985: 260–72.

[28] Protection of the *bêt 'āb* by the *mišpāḥāh*, in Gottwald's construct, consisted of supplying a male heir if necessary, safeguarding and preventing the alienation of the *bêt 'āb*'s property, redeeming its members from enslavement, and executing blood vengeance. These actions, according to Gottwald, were taken only in emergency situations, in order to return the *bêt 'āb* to its normal state as an autonomous unit. In ordinary circumstances the *mišpāḥāh* served essentially as a reassurance for the *bêt 'āb* within it. Arguing against the view that the *mišpāḥāh* was a clan, Gottwald asserts that it provided a social fabric with some of the bonding virtues of the true clan, but without placing restrictions on the family's primacy, and that it did not have the typical characteristics of a clan that is, it was neither an exogamous unit nor a unilineal descent group.

also 'cross-cutting' associations, or sodalities, in the Iron Age I social structure. These included: protective associations that provided mutual aid and mustering a citizen army, the ritual congregation, the Levite priests, and probably the Kenites (itinerant metalworkers). In his construct, groupings of protective associations and other sodalities, tribes and an intertribal confederacy operated in various ways to provide mutual aid, external defence and a religious ideology of covenanted or treaty-linked equals (Gottwald 1979: 318–21).

Bendor disagrees in some respects with Gottwald's construct of the *mišpāḥāh*, arguing that there is no evidence that it was an 'association' rather than a genetic group (especially given the fundamentally genetic concept prevalent in the biblical texts), even though some are artificial schemes. He agrees with Gottwald, however, that the *mišpāḥāh* probably was not exogamous (that is, members of the same *mišpāḥāh* were marriageable partners), but this does not prove that it was a 'protective association' with no genetic ties (Bendor 1996: 84–6).

Lemche hypothesizes that the term *mišpāḥāh* is more likely to refer to the levels of lineage and maximal lineage than to a clan, although the formal similarities between 'clan' and 'lineage' make it difficult to determine whether the Iron Age I tribal social structure included clans. None of the biblical references to the *mišpāḥāh*, in his estimation, can clearly be identified as fitting the clan model, although neither do they, he concedes, provide enough information to argue definitively in favour of the lineage model (Lemche 1985: 96–7, 231–44).

In the biblical traditions, especially as portrayed in the Genesis narratives, the ideal Israelite marriage was endogamous within this level (e.g. Gen. 11.29, 20.12, 24.15 and ch. 29). Some traditions, particularly those in Genesis, suggest that polygyny was an acceptable practice at some points in Israel's history – probably for the purpose of acquiring more children or more prestige and power – although on the whole monogamy is the norm in the biblical construct. As in many societies, the arrangement of marriages involved an exchange of gifts to cement the relationship between the families, particularly in the form of gifts given to the bride's father (see, e.g., Gen. 34.12; Exod. 22.16–17; Deut. 22.28–29; 1 Sam. 18.25).

In his discussion of the relationship between the *bêt 'āb* and the *mišpāḥāh*, Bendor suggests that much of the dynamic of the *bêt 'āb* occurred in the blurred boundaries between the two. The demarcation between them varied according to particular situations and the points of reference of the individuals or groups concerned. This constituted a continuous process in which the *bêt 'āb* renewed itself and the *mišpāḥāh* grew, changing the points of reference for each generation (see Bendor 1996: 67–79). Sometimes this resulted in the creation of new *mišpāḥôt* as *bêt 'ābôt* naturally increased and branched out in a kind of continuous segmentation. These new *mišpāḥôt* would have continued in some cases to be associated with the traditional *mišpāḥôt*, whose territory they regarded as their patrimony. This would have been one of the factors that contributed to the continual overlap between places of settlement and *mišpāḥôt*. In other cases, the new *mišpāḥôt* would have expanded into new settlements. In such cases, as a sign of the segmentation that had occurred, a link would have been added in the genealogical record: horizontally as a 'brother', and vertically as a 'son'. In this way the collective responsibility of the *mišpāḥāh* was maintained, since the *mišpāḥāh* and *bêt 'ābôt* continued to exist as active kinship groups. The kinship group may also have been reduced in size at times. Either strategy would have contributed to the maintenance of demographic stability (Bendor 1996: 80–2).

In considering function in his reconstruction of this level in the social structure (maximal lineage or possibly clan), Lemche argues that it is unlikely that it was more important socially or politically than the *bêt 'āb* (a designation that was applicable to a variety of groups). It was the economically independent family (whether nuclear or extended) that was of decisive importance. The lineage was probably significant when irregular situations arose – for example, economic misfortune that entailed the loss of communal lands, external political pressure, or conflicts among the members of the lineage. Conflicts within lineages would have been internally resolved, and conflicts between families not affiliated by marriage would have been resolved either through negotiations or by feuds (Lemche 1985: 269–72, 1988: 95).

In the biblical text, just as the *bêt 'āb* is considered part of the *mišpāḥāh*, so the *mišpāḥāh* is considered part of the *šēbeṭ* (or *maṭṭeh*) ('tribe'), the next level in the social structure. The term appears primarily as a component in 'the twelve tribes of Israel', in the organizational schemes including the sequence *bêt 'āb / mišpāḥāh / šēbeṭ*, and in texts concerned with tribal boundaries. It is portrayed as an active social unit primarily in the literature concerning the period of settlement and the beginning of the monarchy. The names of the tribes often have geographical significance, in that they tend to appear in conjunction with geographical terms such as 'land' or 'mountain'. These references have led to the proposal that the tribe functioned primarily, although not solely, as a territorial-demographic entity, and was the least active level in terms of affecting the everyday lives of individuals.[29]

## Women

Women are an essential part of any social system. Until recently, however, there has been a tendency to ignore them in most fields of enquiry, including biblical studies, archaeology and anthropology. But in the past several decades there has been a significant increase in studies that focus on this sometimes forgotten gender. In archaeological and anthropological bibliographies, we now see such titles as *Engendering Archaeology* (Gero and Conkey 1991) and *Dislocating Masculinity* (Cornwall and Lindisfarne 1994); and in biblical studies, such titles as *Gender and Difference in Ancient Israel* (Day 1989).

The biblical traditions introduce us in an indirect way primarily to the domestic status and roles of women. Women are almost always portrayed in relation to men – who are the main characters – as wives, daughters, sisters, mothers or widows. Occasionally, other roles are represented: women as prostitutes, as having some special wisdom or skill, as foreigners, as prophetesses and as queens (although in this role the status as wife or mother of the king is what is emphasized). Very little is revealed concerning how women participated in social, political and religious institutions outside the domestic sphere.

Whether the status and roles of women changed in any significant way throughout the course of Israel's history is difficult to determine on the basis of either the biblical or archaeological information, although it is likely, at least in rural areas, that they remained consistent.

The traditions in Genesis clearly portray a patriarchal society, in which it was perfectly legitimate for men to marry more than one woman, and to have concubines as well.

---

[29] For example, de Geus 1976; Lemche 1985; Bendor 1996: 31, 36, 87–9, as noted above. Bendor does not include discussions of the nature of the tribe or of tribal society, nor does he address the problem of the tribe prior to the period of settlement or monarchy.

References to women in the Pentateuchal legal traditions treat women in a manner similar to the treatment of other kinds of property. The picture is of a society in which a woman has no power if she is not protected by a family, and even less if she is unable to participate in ensuring family continuity by providing her husband with children, especially male children to carry on the family name. According to the biblical construct, then, a woman's proper realm of influence was in relation to the family and related domestic pursuits.

One thorough construct of women's roles and status in Iron Age I Palestine is that proposed by Carol Meyers (1988, 1992). Considering biblical texts, along with archaeological information and anthropological studies of women in pre-industrial societies (for example, Whyte 1978), Meyers postulates that the absence of any sign of female dominance in the biblical texts does not necessarily mean that women were dominated. Nor, she suggests, is the apparent exclusion of women from such roles as the priesthood necessarily a sign that women were perceived as being inferior to men. And the fact that women are less visible publicly does not necessarily mean that they were submissive, or less important to the community. In support of her argument, Meyers points to anthropological studies that have drawn a distinction between 'power' and 'authority' [see also Chapter 8 in this volume]. In this distinction, authority is understood as requiring cultural legitimation, whereas power is seen as deriving from an ability to control, regardless of whether it is socially sanctioned. Women in Iron Age I Palestine, she suggests, could very well have had power, even if subordination to men with authority was what was officially sanctioned. The unauthorized power of women, then, was as important as male rights, and male authority would have been affected by female power. In further support of this argument, Meyers points to Edmund Leach's assertion that although 'myth' does express a certain kind of 'truth', it is not necessarily a 'truth' that is based on everyday reality (that is, actions do not necessarily correspond to notions). The public 'myth' of male dominance as expressed in the biblical traditions, then, according to Meyers, could well have been imposed on a situation that *functionally* was non-hierarchical (Meyers 1988: 24–46 [see also Chapter 10 in this volume]).

An important factor in Meyers's construct is her evaluation of the roles of women in relation to subsistence. She appeals to studies that have shown that the type of subsistence strategies in a given society affect the ways in which labour is distributed along gender lines, as well as how power is allocated within a community. These in turn affect the quality of relationships between men and women. Among the three factors she identifies as contributing to group survival in pre-industrial societies – reproduction, sustenance and defence – reproduction is the exclusive arena of women, sustenance requires contributions from both men and women, and defence is exclusively male. Meyers postulates that because it was necessary for men to give so much time and energy to terrace construction, it was also necessary for women to participate in the farming activities. This was in addition to attending to other responsibilities such as rearing and educating children, food preparation, sewing and weaving, and pottery production (possibly) in the domestic sphere (where women were dominant), all of which were also highly demanding in terms of energy. Because of the large amounts of energy required on the part of both men and women in order to survive in the Iron Age I 'frontier' settlements, then, gender became blurred to some extent, and thus gender hierarchy in work roles was virtually non-existent (Meyers 1988: 139–64).

Another issue that arises in relation to the role of women is the extent to which they were active in the cult. This, again, is particularly difficult to determine on the basis of the biblical traditions, which emphasize the religious roles of men. On the basis of archaeological information and comparative studies, however, it is possible to postulate that women in Iron Age I Palestine may have had a greater role than in subsequent periods. There is a growing consensus that during this period religion was practised primarily in the context of the family, and that rituals were often carried out at household shrines. Meyers suggests that the father had the role of 'priest' and 'diviner' in this context, and that the mother functioned as a kind of wise woman, as well as a 'diviner'. Again, men very likely dominated in more public expressions of religion, but women would nevertheless have had important roles at the family level (Meyers 1988: 157–64).

# SOCIOPOLITICAL ORGANIZATION AND STRUCTURE IN IRON AGE II

## Social structure

The sociopolitical and economic changes introduced by centralization during early Iron Age II (*c.* 950–586) also led to structural transformations, as well as shifts and new tensions in the relationships among various groups. The two most prominent structural changes were associated with: (1) political centralization – Israel and Judah became states with taxing and conscripting powers, and developed standing armies and hierarchical bureaucracies; and (2) social stratification. One of the important questions to consider in relation to these changes is the extent to which there was continuity in social structure, particularly at the local level (cf. now the discussion in Lemos 2010: 179–90).

Comparison of textual and archaeological material with models suggests that there was some continuity in social structure from Iron Age I to Iron Age II, at least in rural settings. It is quite possible, for example, that the notion of tribe continued to play a part in people's self-understanding and their perceptions about how they related to others. If this was the case, then the associated notions of kinship would also have retained their significance.

Studies have shown that tribal organization is not necessarily independent of states, with tribes living only on their fringes and in conflict with them. Both now and in the past, tribes have sometimes been integrated into state systems, and many states have worked through tribes rather than against them.

There are four principal, often overlapping, ways in which people construct tribal identity in the contemporary Middle East, and three of the four are possibly applicable to the Iron Age II situation. The first construct involves the elaboration and use of explicit 'native' ethnopolitical ideologies by the people themselves as a means of explaining their sociopolitical organization. The second consists of implicit *practical* notions held by people, which are not elaborated into formal ideologies. The third relates to concepts used by state authorities for administrative purposes. And the fourth relates to anthropological (analytical) concepts (Eickelman 1989: 127; cf. LaBianca and Younker 1995: 405). It is possible that each of the first three notions of tribal identity existed in Iron Age II – the first two to varying degrees among the general populace, and the third by those who participated in governing the state.[30]

---

[30] Cf. Lemche 1988: 150–1. Lemche argues that the tribe no longer had any political role, the state assumed all the former functions of the tribe. Kinship groups continued to exist, but had no significance outside local communities.

Regardless of the exact dating of the tribal boundary lists in Josh. 13.1–21.42, tribal areas probably had some kind of administrative function in the Israelite and Judean states, as is typical in the Middle East today. The numerous examples of tracing tribal descent that occur in the texts relating to the monarchic period and after testify that the *concept* of tribe, at least, had not totally disappeared.

In his reconstruction of social structure, Bendor offers the following conclusions about the tribe during the monarchic period (Bendor 1996: 92): (1) Tribe was the term by which a certain territory was identified, usually as an administrative area. (2) The tribal names served as a means by which most of the populations living in particular areas were identified. (3) The population living in a tribal territory shared some common characteristics, expressed through notions of a common past and provenience, and perhaps some other distinguishing markers of tribal identity. (4) Rituals may have been maintained in cultic sites that were associated with specific tribal territories and populations. (5) The tribe provided support and a framework for the *mišpāḥôt* that composed it, and the 'inheritance of the tribe' served as a sort of superstructure for the patrimony of the *mišpāḥôt* and *bêt 'ābôt*.

Pastoral nomadic groups probably also continued to coexist with settled populations throughout Iron Age II, although, with a few possible exceptions (for example, the Rechabites), they are not mentioned in the biblical texts relating to this period. Many Middle Eastern societies have had both nomadic and settled components, and political leadership and movements have frequently encompassed groups pursuing combinations of both forms of economic activity (cf. McNutt 1999: 69–70). Some nomadic groups have subsisted virtually as a state within a state, while others have been integrated to some extent into the wider political systems (see Lemche 1985: 111), which was most likely the case in Iron Age II Palestine.

A number of scholars have postulated in strong terms that the institution of the monarchy and urbanization resulted in the complete breakdown of the kinship structure.[31] However, some recent studies consider the possibility that the basic social structure of Iron Age I may have continued to remain essentially intact, at least in rural settings, into Iron Age II. Bendor, for example, argues that this structure 'absorbed' and adapted to the pressure imposed by the monarchy and urbanization (Bendor 1996: 32–3, 165–7, 216–28).[32] Kinship structure, in his estimation, was the 'backbone' of society, even for the institution of the monarchy itself, which was based on the king's *bêt 'āb* and *mišpāḥāh* and on the kinship units of its officials. The kinship structure, therefore, remained essentially the same, with the kinship unit maintaining its role as a self-sufficient economic unit. This would have been the case in spite of changes in the internal dynamic within and among kinship groups that resulted from the processes associated with centralization.

In contrast to arguments that the institution of the *mišpāḥāh* was replaced by communities in which kinship no longer played a role, even though their names survived, Bendor chooses to interpret the association of place names with social units as evidence that both the *mišpāḥôt* and the *bêt 'ābôt* continued to define the populations of towns

---

[31] For example, Weber 1952 [1916–19]; de Vaux 1961 [1958]; Gottwald 1985.
[32] Cf. Halpern 1981: 215–16; Lemche 1985: 261, 265, 1988: 151. Lemche argues that the local significance of the kinship group was eventually reduced, as local administrators were introduced in connection with the development of a national administration, but that the lineage system continued to function, in spite of the decline in the political significance of the tribe. Halpern suggests that tribal organization continued to exist alongside national administration, and that the kinship system did not break down.

and villages and perhaps the cities (Bendor 1996: 98–9, 219). The relationship between *mišpāḥāh* and village or town is also confirmed, Bendor believes, in the enumeration of tribal inheritances and boundaries in the book of Joshua, where the phrases 'by their *mišpāḥôt*' or 'by their *mišpāḥôt* – their cities and villages' occur. The concept behind these references for him is that both the inheritance and the localities are perceived in relation to *mišpāḥôt*.

The census lists in Numbers 1 and 26 and the genealogies in 1 Chronicles 2–8 are also cited by Bendor as verifying the continued existence and relevance of the *bêt 'āb* and *mišpāḥāh*. Regardless of whether these lists represent real or fictitious lineages, they nevertheless reflect a conception that was either recently past or contemporaneous with their composition or compilation (Bendor 1996: 102–3). According to Bendor's construct the *mišpāḥāh* would have been responsible during this period for fulfilling obligations to the monarchy in the form of taxes and conscription (both for labour and the army; Bendor 1996: 118).

Another issue that is raised in relation to social structure during this period, as in the case of Iron Age I, is the question of whether the basic socio-economic unit was the nuclear or extended family, and whether it was the same for both commoners and elites. The archaeological record (clusters of two to three houses sharing the same courtyard) indicates the probability that extended families continued at least to reside together. And the consensus seems to be that the extended family continued to be the primary socio-economic unit as well. In a study that focuses on ancient society in general, however, Carney suggests that although the extended family was the 'ideal' in most of the societies of antiquity, it was not the norm, except perhaps among elites (Carney 1975: 89–92; cf. Frick 1977: 105–6). The poor, he argues, would not have had the resources to live in extended families and thus would have had looser, less contractual types of relationships than the elites, for whom the extended family was a resource base. Whether or not Carney's construct is applicable to ancient Israel and Judah is difficult to assess, particularly given the elite perspective that permeates the biblical texts, and the fact that the traditions themselves present quite an ambivalent picture.

In any case, whether it was the nuclear or the extended family, the family was certainly very important, both socially and economically, and the interests of individuals would have been subordinate to those of the family. Marriages, for example, were probably perceived not so much in relation to the benefits and happiness of individuals, but as compacts bonding family groups and assets together under carefully regulated conditions. Within the family, gender roles were probably more sharply defined than Meyers argues was the case in Iron Age I, with the woman's being more markedly inferior and subordinate. Age divisions, again primarily within the context of the family (whether nuclear or extended), and the power and responsibility that correspond to age, were probably also strongly demarcated.

Outside and above the level of the family, socio-economic roles and statuses would have been based on division of labour and on social proximity to the ruling elites. In both cities and towns, society would have been subdivided into occupational groups, although in rural areas farming would have remained the primary occupation. The scholarly constructs of social stratification in Iron Age II Israel and Judah are based primarily on the biblical texts, comparisons of the biblical texts with other ancient Near Eastern texts and, to a lesser extent, archaeological information (see especially Mettinger 1971; de Vaux 1961 [1958]).

The lists of administrative offices in 2 Sam. 8.15–18 and 1 Kgs 4.1–6 (cf. also the lists of deportees in 2 Kings 24 and 25) refer to government, cult, defence and royal court offices. The particular offices mentioned include: priest, scribe, speaker, commander of the army, one who is in charge of the governors, friend of the king, one who is in charge of the house, and one who is in charge of forced labour. Apart from the offices mentioned in these lists, there are three others both mentioned in biblical texts and known from seals. These are: 'son of the king', 'the king's servant' and 'ruler of the city'. The latter is only mentioned in relation to Jerusalem and Samaria (1 Kings 22.26; 2 Kings 23.8; 2 Chron. 34.8). The functions of these offices are not explained, but we can assume with some certainty that those who filled them were in the upper echelon of the social hierarchy.[33]

Among these offices, the office of scribe and the question of whether scribal schools existed in ancient Israel and Judah have been the particular focus of scholarly attention.[34] Whatever form their training took, scribal activity was most likely sponsored and controlled by government authorities, and was probably confined primarily to the cities, particularly Jerusalem and Samaria but also to other administrative centres. Scribes associated with the government administrative system would have been responsible for such activities as maintaining the royal archives, writing annals, conducting correspondence within the state as well as with neighbouring states, and keeping commercial records.

Other professional classes outside the royal court possibly consisted of judges and local court officials, other administrators such as census takers, tax collectors, overseers of the corvée or forced labour that would have been used primarily for royal construction projects, district governors, and perhaps other officials who had responsibilities within the towns and villages, all of whom would have been answerable, directly or indirectly, to the king. There was probably also a class consisting of noble families associated in some way with the royal court, and a class of wealthy landowners. There may also have been a class of merchants who attained wealth and achieved elite status through contributing goods or services to the king. Individuals involved in trading activities would also have been answerable, directly or indirectly, to the government. Whether or not there were professional lenders or other similar professionals and entrepreneurs, which are typical of market economies, is open to question. Such roles are thought to have been discouraged in redistributive economic systems.

Another group of social roles would have been associated with service in the military. These would have included officers, career professionals, enlistees and conscripts, mercenaries, various specialists like runners and charioteers, and possibly sailors.

The majority of the population probably consisted of an agricultural class, including not only the owners of large estates, but also small freeholders, family farmers, agricultural workers and peasant farmers.

A number of roles were probably related to the 'official' religion of the monarchy, at least in Jerusalem. The biblical construct includes high priests, ordinary priests, temple 'doorkeepers' or supervisors, treasurers, scribes, musicians of various kinds, dancers,

---

[33] The most extensive analysis of these terms and the functions of individuals who filled these offices is Mettinger's *Solomonic State Officials* (1971). Mettinger's study is primarily a text-critical examination that considers the terms in relation to possible foreign prototypes. His analysis suggests a considerable amount of Egyptian influence. Cf. Heaton 1974. Heaton argues that these offices were a conscious imitation of Egyptian civil servants. Cf. also Redford 1972. Redford disagrees with the proposal that the system of court officials was modelled after that of Egypt, but agrees that the system of taxation was influenced by Egypt.

[34] See, e.g., Mettinger 1971: 140–57; Lemaire 1981; Crenshaw 1985; Jamieson-Drake 1991; Blenkinsopp 1995: 9–65.

keepers of vestments, those 'dedicated' to Temple service, interpreters of the law, and possibly prophets. It is particularly difficult, however, to distinguish the extent to which this construct actually reflects the situation during Iron Age II, as religious organization was a primary concern during the Persian period. The local or so-called 'popular' cults would also have required religious specialists of various kinds, possibly including priests, diviners and other types of intermediaries, although it is difficult to reconstruct from the biblical texts what these might have been.[35]

Artisans of various sorts would have played important socio-economic roles during Iron Age II, although the locus of some craft production may have remained in the household in village contexts. It is possible that some artisan groups maintained a separate and marginal status, as may have been the case during Iron Age I. But others would have been better integrated into the social structure (see McNutt 1990: 235–49, 1995), some perhaps attached to the royal court, as seems to have been typical in other ancient Near Eastern states.[36] They may also have been organized in guilds in the cities and towns (Frick 1977: 127–35). Types of artisans would have included stonemasons, builders, woodworkers, metalsmiths, jewellers, ivory and seal carvers, potters, leather workers and weavers.

In his study of ancient Israelite society, Max Weber included artisans and metalsmiths among the *gērîm* ('sojourners' or 'resident aliens'), and compared the status of the *gērîm* to the marginal social position of artisans and smiths, along with bards and musicians, among the modern Bedouin. This changed, in Weber's estimation, only during the reconstitution of the postexilic Jewish community under Ezra and Nehemiah, when artisans were divested of their tribal foreignness, were organized into guilds, and were received into the Jewish confessional community organization (Weber 1952 [1916–19]: 28–9). Whether or not his line of reasoning is valid, Weber is probably correct in his assessment that the social status of artisans and smiths changed over time, particularly as the social structure became more hierarchical. They may have continued to be socially separated to some degree (as is suggested of the Rechabites in Jer. 35.8–10),[37] perhaps as endogamous families or guilds,[38] but this social separation would not have been as radical as it was during the premonarchic period (as is suggested in the traditions about the Kenites and Midianites). If the references in 2 Kgs 24.14 and 24.16 (cf. Jer. 24.1, 29.2) to smiths and artisans as being among those of high status who were taken into exile by the Babylonians is correct, the integration may have occurred by the end of the monarchic period. Certainly by the second century BCE artisans and smiths were highly regarded, as is apparent in Sir. 38.24–34, where they are identified as individuals whose skills are necessary for the maintenance of social stability and the stability of the 'fabric of the world' (cf. Exod. 31.1–5; 1 Kings 7.13–14; 2 Chron. 2.13–14).

The lowest classes probably included resident aliens (*gērîm*), as well as indentured servants and slaves, many of them probably attached to agricultural lands. Widows, orphans, beggars and other destitute or outcast persons may have also been perceived as having similar status.[39]

---

[35] For recent social-science-oriented studies of these roles, see Blenkinsopp 1995; Grabbe 1995.
[36] On artisans in Mesopotamia, see, e.g., Gunter 1990.
[37] See Frick 1971, 1992; McNutt 1990: 243–9, 1995; Halpern 1992. The interpretation that the Rechabites may have been smiths is based on a genealogical link with the Kenites in 1 Chron. 2.55.
[38] Guild organization in the Persian period is suggested in 1 Chron. 2.55, 4.14, 21; and Neh. 3.8, 31.
[39] For a recent study of those with low status, see, e.g., Hiebert 1989.

Comparative anthropological and historical evidence suggest that slaves are distinguished from other types of dependent labourers on the basis of their 'outsider' status; that is, ideally, slaves were aliens (cf. Lev. 25.39–55). Types of slavery in the biblical construct of ancient Israel, however, range from the forced slavery of aliens to voluntary slavery of indigenous peoples.

According to the Hebrew Bible, the major factors contributing to self-enslavement, as distinct from the enslavement of aliens, were poverty and debt. In some cases, these conditions left no alternative but to sell either oneself, or minor members of one's family such as a daughter, into servitude (e.g. Exod. 21.2–11; Lev. 25.39–55; Deut. 15.16–17; 2 Kgs 4.1; Isa. 50.1; Amos 2.6, 8.6). In contrast to aliens, the laws stipulate that (ideally) 'Israelites' could not be enslaved permanently or treated as harshly (Exod. 21.2–4; Deut. 15.12–17; Lev. 25.39–55). The biblical construct also suggests that slaves were allowed to accumulate property, with which it was possible for them to purchase their freedom (2 Sam. 9.10, 16.4, 19.18, ch. 30; Lev. 25.29) (cf. Knight 2011: 209–15).

In an anthropological study of the representations of slavery in the Bible, Gillian Feeley-Harnick (1982) points out that the status of slaves seems to have been somewhat ambiguous. This is seen primarily, she suggests, in relation to kinship. On the one hand, slavery was the antithesis of kinship – that is, a slave was either an outsider who had no kin, community or nation that served as the means of self-identity, or an 'insider' who achieved this status out of necessity, a situation that, she argues, involved the destruction of kinship bonds (citing Neh. 5.5; Isa. 50.1; Amos 2.6, 8.6). On the other hand, according to her interpretation, slaves were more than kin, because by definition they did not have conflicting social ties (Feeley-Harnick 1982: 108–9).

But slaves could nevertheless be incorporated into the kinship structure, especially when there was some need relating to production or reproduction. The biblical traditions, for example, refer to fathers who sell their daughters with the condition that the masters or their sons marry them, and to masters who have children by or adopt slaves in order to acquire heirs.

There is also some ambiguity associated with the roles of slaves. In theory, slaves were perceived as property and as 'tools' to be used for carrying out the most lowly types of work (cf. Exod. 21.21; Sir. 33.24–29). But in spite of this, the legal traditions indicate that they were also perceived as fully human. In some cases, they occupied positions of trust and had the potential of social mobility. The slave–master relationship, then, was not a simple matter of exploitation and domination, but manifested contradictions and ambiguity in concepts of authority, allegiance and identity (Feeley-Harnick 1982: 125).

### Patron–client relationships

Another social institution that may have played an important role in the way in which ancient Israelite and Judean society was structured is the patron–client relationship, which was a dominant mode of relationship in the pre-industrial societies of antiquity (see Carney 1975: 171; Lemche 1995, 1996; cf. Coote 1990: 20–5). This type of relationship is typically found between individuals of differing social status at all levels of society, in both partly centralized and centralized societies.[40] In patronage societies

---

[40] Lemche (1995: 120, 1996: 110–11) suggests that patron–client relationships do not exist in bureaucratic states unless they are beginning to fall apart.

political power structures are personalized. The relationship between patron and client involves a kind of reciprocity, in which individuals with position and power use their influence to advance or protect individuals of inferior status, who thus become their clients. For example, in relation to the distribution of justice, patrons possess the ability to secure the rights of their clients. Without patrons, poor individuals have no access to official institutions that can ensure them fair treatment in, for example, conflicts with more influential members of society. Clients in turn owe their patrons loyalty, and reciprocate by providing them with resources or services. Ideally, the parties in the relationship are thus bound to ongoing mutual responsibilities. Along with the idea of loyalty, other concepts such as friendship and respect are a part of the relationship. The patron expects the client to be a friend and to show him respect as a way of expressing subordination. Potentially, the clients of powerful patrons can also become powerful and attract clients themselves.

### Women

The biblical construct of women's lives suggests that women were regarded as having no independent legal status and as being subject to the authority of men, first their fathers' and then their husbands'.

Carol Meyers's study of women suggests that the shift to an urban setting during Iron Age II almost certainly had an impact on gender relations and women's status and roles, although there may have been less change in rural settings. In particular, the shift from the family household to a centralized government with a bureaucracy composed of male officials as the place where power resided would have resulted in males' being conferred more status and privilege than women. Other factors would have included the development of an economy in which both luxury items and basic goods were more readily available, and an increase in the types of services available outside the context of the household. These would have contributed to the loss of the household's status as a self-sufficient economic unit (at least in urban contexts). As a consequence, women would have become less essential and would have had fewer potential roles to fulfil, leading ultimately to an increase in gender differentiation and a corresponding decrease in women's power and status. Meyers postulates that if city households were composed of nuclear, rather than extended, families, as some have argued, the extent to which a woman was able to exercise authority would also have decreased (Meyers 1992: 250–1; 1988: 186–96).[41]

Nevertheless, women appear occasionally in leadership roles in the biblical texts (for example as queen mother, prophets and wise women; see, e.g., Brenner 1985). Meyers suggests that these may represent a larger group of publicly active women whose identities were lost as the result of the male-controlled canonical processes.

# SOCIAL ORGANIZATION IN THE PERSIAN PERIOD

In his study of Persian-period Judah, J.P. Weinberg (1992) postulates that Judah constituted what he calls a 'citizen-temple community' (*Burger-Tempel-Gemeinde*), in which the Temple was an essential and central institution, and the social structure was based on a

---

[41] Anthropological studies cited by Meyers include Bossen 1989; Ember 1983; Silverblatt 1988. Cf. Emmerson 1989, who offers a generally positive evaluation of women's status.

unified organization of community members and the Temple priesthood.[42] Within this citizen-temple community, the primary social unit was the *bêt 'ābôt*, which consisted on average of eight hundred to one thousand men and was distinct from the preexilic *bêt 'āb* and *mišpāḥāh*. Weinberg (1992: 61) postulates that the *bêt 'ābôt*

> is an agnatic band [. . .] which unified a number of families that were related (either genuinely or fictionally). The essential characteristics of the *bêt 'ābôt* are a large quantitative composition and a complicated inner structure, an obligatory genealogy and inclusion of the name of the *bêt 'ābôt* in the full name of each of its members and a conscious solidarity based on communal ownership of lands.

This construct is based in part on Weinberg's understanding of the *gôlāh* lists in Ezra 2, Nehemiah 7, and 1 Esdras 5, which he views as sources for understanding how the social organization of the local population in the Persian period differed from that of previous periods. The citizen-temple community was grounded in the leadership of the collective of *bêt 'ābôt*, which was directly involved in the administration of property that, Weinberg suggests, belonged communally to the constituent members of the 'community'. An essential feature of the community in his construct is the inalienable property (which formally belonged to God) of the *bêt 'ābôt*, which was divided into parcels for use by the separate families comprising it (Weinberg 1992: 28). Towns were the centre of economic activity, and together the temple and the town formed a loose horizontal network of interacting and counterbalancing institutions. This combination of socio-economic interests and religious affiliation ensured land rights and citizenship within the community, and is important, Weinberg argues, for understanding the nature of the crises depicted in Ezra-Nehemiah. This structure was essentially related to agriculture, manufacturing modes of production and the appearance of money economies, and was a response to increased urbanization, the Persian taxation system and the practice by the Persian rulers of distributing estates among its elites. In the face of these Persian policies, the local community structure provided its members with an organizational unity and a means of collective self-government, as well as internal political, social and economic welfare (Weinberg 1992: 22–6). Persian-period Judah, then, according to Weinberg's construct, was a society composed of 'free and fully-enfranchised people who were socially and politically relatively similar, and who strictly distanced themselves from all those who were not community members' (Weinberg 1992: 29). Weinberg's citizen-temple community thus did not comprise the whole population of the Judean province, only those who sought separation from the royal sector and unification with the Temple (Weinberg 1992: 34–48). It is this structure and the associated concerns for boundary maintenance that account for the tensions depicted in Ezra-Nehemiah.

Although the essential place of the Temple and priesthood are generally held to have had a central role in Judean society during this period, as Weinberg argues, other aspects of his construct have been disputed. Joseph Blenkinsopp, for example, challenges Weinberg's conclusions about the relationship of the community to Persian authority, arguing that the elite were intentionally recruited from among the returnees by the Persian government, who encouraged their loyalty to the empire (Blenkinsopp 1991; cf. also, e.g., Lemche 1988: 188; Berquist 1995). The temple community, then, was semi-

---

[42] For evaluations of Weinberg's construct, see, e.g., Smith 1989; Blenkinsopp 1991; Eskenazi 1993: 67–9. See further Lemos 2010: 201–13.

autonomous and was controlled by this group of loyal elites. Blenkinsopp's construct is similar to Weinberg's in the sense that the returnees organized the community according to ancestral houses, and the community was composed of free, property-holding citizens and Temple personnel. Leadership consisted of tribal elders and an imperial representative. This cohesive social entity was jealously protective of its status and privileges. To sustain this structure, the immigrants had to regain land previously distributed to the peasants and also rebuild and secure control of the Temple.

Another study that gives attention to social structure is Daniel L. Smith's *The Religion of the Landless* (1989). Smith's study focuses on the social developments in the community of exiles as a community in crisis. The models he uses for understanding these developments, illuminating the social realities reflected in the biblical texts, and proposing hypotheses, are related to group crisis, minority behaviour and contact between ethnic groups in situations of unequal power distribution. He points in particular to structural adaptation as one of the survival mechanisms of the exiles. He argues that the exilic material from the Bible reveals both continuity and change in various aspects of the social life of the exilic community. In his construct, continuity with the past is reflected in the continuing authority of the elders, while structural adaptation is represented in the demographic changes of the *bêt 'āb* / *bêt 'ābôt*, with the *roš* as the communal leader.[43] This structural adaptation was intended to preserve identity, facilitate self-management and cope with the economic and political demands of the Babylonian conquerors.

The replacement of the *bêt 'āb* and *mišpāḥāh* with the *bêt 'ābôt* was the primary structural adaptation to social organization that was introduced among the exiles but continued to persist into the postexilic period. In terms of size and function, this new social unit resembled the pre-exilic *mišpāḥāh*, but while the *mišpāḥôt* were based on 'blood' lineage, the *bêt 'ābôt* was more artificial in the sense that there were criteria other than 'blood' lineage that were determinative for its construction, one of which was probably common residence in exile. The *bêt 'ābôt*, then, was an exilic unit that was fairly large and included the smaller *bêt 'āb*s, but also some individuals who adopted a familial fiction, most likely as an expression of social solidarity with other exiles.

Smith suggests that this structural change was a response to the social crisis brought on by the Babylonian resettlement, along with Babylonian economic policies and possibly labour needs (that is, the need for large numbers of labourers for building projects).

## Social stratification

Most studies of Persian-period Judah emphasize a sharp division between a class of elites, usually identified as deriving from the exilic population, and a poorer rural population composed of the 'people of the land' (normally identified with the population who had remained behind in Judah during the Babylonian exile). Contrary to Weinberg's arguments, many scholars now agree that during much of the period of Persian dominance the elite class was loyal to, and was supported to some extent by, the Persian authorities, whose self-interests would have been served by such a relationship. If this was in fact the case, the Jewish elites would have been in a somewhat ambiguous position in relation to

---

[43] Smith 1989: 93–126, 201–16. Cf. Bendor 1996: 228. Bendor emphasizes the fact that in the book of Nehemiah the *bêt 'āb* and the *mišpāḥāh* are still mentioned as fundamental units of the community (Neh. 4.13; 10.35 [10.34]).

the rest of the Jewish population, who on the one hand had to depend on them for support and protection, but on the other would have viewed them with hostility because of their relative wealth and privilege.

The composition of the elite class was probably similar in some respects to that of the monarchic period, with the major exceptions being that there were no royal family or officials directly connected to the king's residence. Jewish officials among the elite would have been answerable to Persian rather than local authorities. Another consequence of Persian dominance seems to have been an increase in the authority of priests and of scribes, many of whom also may have been priests.

Classes of elites clearly represented in the postexilic literature include: professional members of the cult, including Aaronic and Levitical priests (Neh. 7.1, 39, 43, 8.1–9), singers (Neh. 7.1, 23, 45), Temple servants (Neh. 3.26, 31, 7.46, 11.19), and gatekeepers (Neh. 7.1, 23, 45); a scribal class (Ezra 8.1, 9); the provincial governor, who would also have had officials serving under him (perhaps 'Solomon's servants' of Neh. 11.57–60); and 'men of the guard' (Neh. 4.23, 7.3). Artisans may also have been counted among the elite during this period (Neh. 3.8, 21–22; Ezra 3.7).

### Conflict in the postexilic community

It is clear from the biblical texts that there were internal conflicts and tensions within the province of Judah during this period. But scholarly opinion has varied with respect to its nature and extent. A number of studies focus on this issue in relation to tensions that arose between the returning exiles and the 'people of the land', especially during and after the reign of Darius, who appears to have sent exiles to Judah expressly for the purpose of organizing it more effectively for Persian benefit. The tensions may also have been associated with a related conflict between urban and rural populations (see, e.g., Berquist 1995: 78–9).

Another level of conflict portrayed in the texts is rivalry between Judah and Samaria. This rivalry is also represented in Genesis through Kings in the schism between Israel and Judah, with Israel represented as the defecting branch of the true 'Israel', whose religion is focused in Jerusalem. The nature and source of the tensions internal to Judah are constructed in a number of different ways. Paul Hanson (1979), for example, emphasizes the rise of competitive power groups within the Judean community as the basis for the development of apocalypticism. In his reconstruction, after the exile a party of ruling priests supported by a Persian mandate returned to Judah with the express purpose of building the Temple, and quickly gained the advantage in the local struggle for power. The disciples of prophets, with more egalitarian ideals, responded by challenging priestly authority. This opposition, Hanson argues, was the major source of conflict in the early postexilic period – especially as the priestly class became increasingly concerned with secular interests and their own power – and resulted in a bitter struggle for community control. The priestly class had the upper hand in this struggle, because they had the support of Persian authorities, and were able to some extent to influence Persian policy.[44]

---

[44] Cf. Berquist 1995: 8. Berquist notes that despite the persuasiveness of Hanson's reconstruction and the extent of its acceptance, more recent historians have emphasized the external influences of the Persian Empire on the Jerusalem community. Cf. also Davies 1989; Cook 1995. Davies's criticism (1989: 252) of Hanson's construct is that one cannot infer a type of society from a type of literature (apocalyptic), which is what Hanson does. In contrast to Hanson, Cook suggests that the social locus of early apocalyptic writings was possibly the priestly class that was at the centre of power in postexilic Judah, not those on the social fringes who were opposed to it.

Using Mary Douglas's (1966) work, Daniel Smith considers the issue of conflict in light of group crisis models and the role of ritual behaviour, especially purity legislation, as a means of protecting and maintaining social boundaries among colonized peoples. The exilic and postexilic elaboration of purity laws, and the emphasis on maintaining separation from the unclean, Smith argues, are related to concerns about the transfer of pollution from foreigners. This concern for boundary maintenance in relation to foreigners is represented most clearly in the dissolution of mixed marriages in Ezra-Nehemiah (Smith 1989: 203).

Smith also considers the conflict between the returning exiles and those still in the land in light of group crisis models, arguing that the 'sectarian' consciousness of the returned exiles is consistent with the social development of groups experiencing stress. His argument is that the survival of the exiles as a minority group in exile depended on their success in creating a solid community with well-defined social boundaries. The solidarity that was established in exile contributed to the later sense of separation from the population that did not share in the exile experience. The resulting conflict, then, did not reflect the 'degeneration' of religious faith on the part of those left in Palestine so much as it did different responses to the crisis, which ultimately led to different social configurations. This perceived separation is represented in the continued emphasis in the postexilic community on purity boundaries and delimiting identification markers like 'remnant', 'holy seed' and 'sons of the exile'. For Smith, then, the economic conflicts between the exiles and those who remained behind exacerbated, but did not cause, this conflict (Smith 1989: 203).

In her study of the nature of kinship and marriage in Genesis (which she analyses from the perspective that the final redaction of these traditions dates to the Persian period), Naomi Steinberg also draws conclusions about how and why boundaries were defined in the postexilic community (see Steinberg 1993: 135–47). One of the goals of the study is to investigate how the interrelationship among inheritance, descent and marriage were conceptualized in the postexilic context. She concludes that the ancestral stories in Genesis are metaphors for establishing identity and defining community boundaries, that is, the kinship structures in the texts are metaphors for social structure. More specifically, the narrative genealogy functions to establish family membership in *bêt 'ābôt*, the primary postexilic kinship group. Only those able to trace their genealogy back to the family of Jacob – that is, to those who were removed from the land and were in exile – constituted the true 'Israel', according to this biblical construct. Family, or genealogy, was thus a means of legitimating status and the power structure in postexilic community organization. Because those who had been in exile were the ones who could trace their genealogy back to the patrilineal name 'Israel', they were entitled to membership in the restored community. Ability to demonstrate inclusion within the *bêt 'ābôt* was a requirement both for membership and for defining the group's character.

The ancestral stories in Genesis, then, were intended as rationalizations for a particular social 'reality' or construct. The legitimation of community boundaries is further represented in the stories' emphasis on entering into an 'appropriate' marriage (Genesis 12–36), which excludes foreigners. That foreign wives are 'inappropriate' spouses is also an idea expressed in Ezra 9–10. Steinberg suggests that this concern is related to different standards in the exilic and in the postexilic communities – that is, while in exile people could marry whomever they wanted (since Joseph did; Genesis 36–50), but 'appropriate' wives are necessary when living in the land of inheritance.

## Women and boundary definition

As is indicated above, establishing identity, and the boundaries that define self-identity, are clearly significant issues in the Persian-period biblical literature. This is particularly apparent in the passages in Ezra 9–10 and Nehemiah 13, where intermarriage with 'foreign' women is strongly discouraged.

But there are a number of problems confronted if we try to sort out what the meaning and significance of these references are. As Tamara Eskenazi and Eleanore Judd (1994) point out, we are missing important information about these charges against mixed marriages: we are not told what constituted 'foreignness', what proportion of the community was guilty of having married these 'foreign' women, why men would have married such women, whether women also married 'foreign' men, or what, if anything, happened to these marriages. Most importantly, it is not clear who counts as a 'foreigner' or who counts as a legitimate member of 'Israel'.

Given what they do know about the demographic composition of Judah in the Persian period, Eskenazi and Judd suggest that these women could have been identified with any of the following groups: (1) They could have been Judahites or Israelites who had not been in exile or who differed ethnically and socio-economically from the returnees. If this was the case, the controversy would have concerned how Jewishness was defined, particularly on the basis of ancestry or participation in the exilic experience (perhaps also implying a conflict over land rights). (2) The women could have been members of foreign nations. (3) The women could have come from Judahite and Israelite families in the land who engaged in religious practices and beliefs different from those of the returnees. If the latter was the case, the conflict would have been related to Judaism as a religion rather than as peoplehood.

Claudia Camp (1991) makes a similar observation, noting that the terms *zār* and *nokrî* have a variety of (sometimes overlapping) meanings. They can refer to persons of foreign nationality, but they are also used to designate persons outside one's own household or family, persons who are not members of the priestly caste, or deities or practices that fall outside the covenant relationship with Yahweh.

In an earlier study, Eskenazi (1992) suggests that the opposition to mixed marriages in Ezra 9–10 was related to socio-economic issues, especially a concern about losing inherited land.[45] One of the functions of marriage was related to transferring property and social status from one group to another. Prohibition of marriage outside the group, she suggests, was a means of assuring that property and kinship-related rights remained within a closed group. If this is correct, the problem of mixed marriages would make most sense if women were able to inherit property. Because foreign wives ('foreignness' is not defined) posed a socio-economic danger to the community, opposition to intermarriage with them was also an affirmation of women who did belong to the group.

Eskenazi draws these conclusions on the basis of her examination of the sixth- to fourth-century BCE texts from the Jewish community in Elephantine. One of the aims of her study is to challenge the view that women's status declined in the postexilic period, arguing rather that conditions similar to the premonarchic period (as constructed by Carol Meyers) recurred in the postexilic period. This was partly due to a renewed emphasis on the family as the fundamental socio-economic and political unit, which

---

[45] See also Washington 1994. Washington supports Eskenazi's conclusions in his analysis of Proverbs 1–9.

resulted in a more equitable distribution of power for women. She suggests this as a background for understanding the problem of foreign wives in Ezra 9–10.

The Elephantine texts show that women in the Jewish community there were able to initiate divorce, hold property, buy and sell, and inherit property even when there was a son. Eskenazi contends that there was continuity in the practices in Jewish communities of this period, since they were all under the same Persian imperial government and would have had frequent contact and communication. References in Ezra-Nehemiah indirectly support for her the view that wives in Judah had some similar rights.

Camp (1991) argues that the marriage prohibitions related to two major issues for the returned exiles: (1) a need for family stability as a survival mechanism and to establish claims to land and political power; and (2) a need to promote the pure and proper worship of Yahweh. From her perspective, these two issues were closely linked, and crisis was reached when some men began marrying into foreign families. These marriages threatened the stability of the authority structure, particularly because intermarriage for the purpose of attaining upward mobility could bring outside challenges to the power of the leadership group (Ezra 10; Neh. 13.26–27; cf. Mal. 2.10–12). The focus on *wives* rather than husbands may, Camp proposes, represent a situation in which Judean men were marrying foreign women but not allowing their daughters to marry foreign men, possibly because the foreign brides brought as dowries actual land holdings that were claimed by members of the *gôlāh* community.

Berquist's study of Judah in the Persian period also deals with this issue (Berquist 1995: 117–18). He draws a distinction between the ways in which intermarriage is regarded in the Ezra and the Nehemiah passages, although there is a concern in both for economic and political consequences. The focus in the Ezra passage is on leadership, and there is some indication that inheritance was at least part of the problem (Ezra 9.12). Jewish men, including priests, Levites, and officials, were marrying women from neighbouring areas (Ezra 9.1–2). Nehemiah presents the problem differently. Whereas Ezra deals with *all* foreign women, Nehemiah focuses on marriages with the traditional enemies of Israel – Ashdod, Ammon, Moab (Neh. 13.23). The more specific problem identified here is that the children of such marriages speak only the languages of their mothers (Neh. 13.24). The implication, Berquist suggests, is that without a knowledge of Hebrew or Aramaic they would not be capable of assuming leadership positions within the community. Nehemiah also seems to be concerned with preventing interference in the Jewish community by foreign officials (Neh. 13.28).

Berquist also points out that the solutions to the problems differ. Nehemiah recommends discontinuing the practice, whereas Ezra recommends divorce. Berquist questions the interpretation that ethnic purity is the issue, especially in light of the fact that neither Ezra nor Nehemiah appears to be concerned with ethnic issues when dealing with the Persian court, with which both of them must have had some connection. The primary issues in Berquist's construct are matters of regional competition and economic differentiation *within* Judah. In both respects Judah was isolating itself from other geographic and political entities, while at the same time the ruling elite were distancing themselves from the economic concerns of the masses. In a situation in which economic depletion and competition from other regions were harsh realities, regulations against intermarriage would have emphasized a sense of Jewish solidarity over against other regions as a means of solidifying political control and economic security within the elite stratum of Jerusalem society. In this context, there would also have been an emphasis on marrying within one's own class, particularly as related to control over land and wealth.

In this respect, Ezra's injunction may refer not to foreign women per se but to women who were socially distant from the elites in terms of wealth and status. The *economic* consequences of intermarriage with those outside one's class, then, would have been a further depletion of already scarce resources, and the *political* effects of marrying outsiders would have included interference from other regional governments.

Eskenazi and Judd's study, referred to above, focuses on understanding the intermarriage problem in relation to ethnic groups and how ethnicity is defined. They consider both systems theory – which views society as a system of tension management between dominants and subordinates in which the dominants have responsibility as well as privilege – and power conflict theory – which also views society in terms of dominants and subordinates, but assumes groups whose interests clash over scarce resources such as economic goods, prestige and power. In both approaches, intermarriage is integral to understanding ethnic groups, and is identified as a classic example of crossing ethnic boundaries. In some cases crossing boundaries has positive value – for example, when it assists in cementing alliances. In other cases it is viewed negatively, as a violation of group integrity.

On the basis of social-scientific models, Eskenazi and Judd recommend considering three processes: (1) the structure and function of the social norms, that is, concepts associated with who benefits and how; (2) the source of deviations from those norms, that is, actual practices; and (3) the *pattern* of deviation, especially in terms of religion, race and class.

As is the case in the other studies cited above, Judah is viewed as an immigrant community in transition, adjusting to a new situation. This required a re-evaluation of norms in light of the new circumstances and, as a part of this process, establishing new boundary markers. The conflict over intermarriage in Ezra 9–10, then, needs to be evaluated in terms of the complex network of intricate variables that shape such communities in periods of transition. Eskenazi and Judd further suggest that developments in twentieth-century BCE Israel provide a useful model for understanding Ezra-Nehemiah, pointing to the potential value of comparing with Persian-period Judah the tensions between Jews from different ethnic backgrounds, between Jews and non-Jews, and between Orthodox and non-Orthodox Jews. Eskenazi and Judd focus on the third type and agree with some of the constructs introduced above that the 'foreign' women of Ezra 9–10 could very well have been Judahites or Israelites who, in the process of redefinition, came to be regarded as outsiders. Thus, although they may have been viewed as appropriate marriage partners by the early returnees, by the time of Ezra they were considered to be outside the newly defined boundaries.

In his analysis of this problem, Daniel L. Smith-Christopher (1994) agrees with other studies in viewing it in relation to land tenure and economic associations. Where he deviates from other conclusions, however, is in his argument that the returned exiles, rather than constituting a privileged elite, were a threatened minority who regarded themselves as being in a disadvantaged position, socially and economically, in relation to those who had not gone into exile. In his interpretation of Ezra, those who were considered guilty in the intermarriage problem would have been men who were attempting to 'marry up' as a means of exchanging their low status as 'exiles' for participation in aristocratic society. The consciousness of 'us' and 'them', then, is related to a threatened minority group (the returned exiles) that was intent on its internal affairs and survival over against the majority ('foreigners' – that is, those who had no connection with the returned exiles). He also deals with the question of *who* would have regarded the marriages as 'mixed' and suggests the possibility that it was only Ezra and his supporters, not necessarily the married persons themselves. The priests would have been singled out (Ezra 9.1), then, because they disagreed with Ezra about what constituted a marriage that was actually mixed. Essentially the only basis for Ezra's objection is that the foreigners were simply Jews who had not been in exile. In Nehemiah, on the other hand (as Berquist suggests), the chief danger is perceived as coming from outside Judah, not from an internal struggle. Here political considerations predominate, particularly in the form of 'power-grabbing' on the part of the leadership through strategic marriages.

The value of these studies, whether or not they agree, is that they provide some insight into the complexities associated with group and boundary definition and its interrelationship with economic and political as well as social and religious dynamics.

## REFERENCES

Bendor, S. (1996), *The Social Structure of Ancient Israel: The Institution of the Family (Beit 'ab) from the Settlement to the End of the Monarchy*, Jerusalem: Simor.

Berquist, J.L. (1995), *Judaism in Persia's Shadow: A Social and Historical Approach*, Minneapolis, MN: Fortress Press.

Blenkinsopp, J. (1991), 'Temple and Society in Achaemenid Judah', in P.R. Davies (ed.), *Second Temple Studies 1*, 22–53, JSOTSup 117, Sheffield: JSOT Press.

Blenkinsopp, J. (1995), *Sage, Priest, Prophet: Religious and Intellectual Leadership in Ancient Israel*, Louisville, KY: Westminster John Knox Press.

Bossen, L. (1989), 'Women and Economic Institutions', in S. Plattner (ed.), *Economic Anthropology*, 318–50, Stanford, CA: Stanford University Press.

Brenner, A. (1985), *The Israelite Woman: Social Role and Literary Type in the Biblical Narrative*, The Biblical Seminar 2, Sheffield: JSOT Press.

Camp, C.V. (1991), 'What's So Strange about the Strange Woman?', in D. Jobling, P.L. Day and G.T. Sheppard (eds), *The Bible and the Politics of Exegesis*, 17–38, Cleveland, OH: Pilgrim Press.

Carney, T.F. (1975), *The Shape of the Past: Models and Antiquity*, Lawrence, KS: Coronado Press.

Caton, S. (1987), 'Power, Persuasion, and Language: A Critique of the Segmentary Model in the Middle East', *IJMES*, 19 (1): 77–102.

Cook, S.L. (1995), *Prophecy and Apocalypticism: The Postexilic Social Setting*, Minneapolis, MN: Fortress Press.

Coote, R.B. (1990), *Early Israel: A New Horizon*, Minneapolis, MN: Fortress Press.

Cornwall, A. and N. Lindisfarne, eds (1994), *Dislocating Masculinity: Comparative Ethnographies*, London: Routledge & Kegan Paul.

Crenshaw, J.L. (1985), 'Education in Ancient Israel', *JBL*, 104 (4): 601–15.

Crüsemann, F. (1978), *Der Widerstand gegen das Königtum: Die antiköniglichen Texte des Alten Testamentes und der Kampf um den frühen israelitischen Staat*, Neukirchen-Vluyn: Neukirchener.

Davies, P.R. (1989), 'The Social World of Apocalyptic Writings', in R.E. Clements (ed.), *The World of Ancient Israel: Sociological, Anthropological and Political Perspectives – Essays by Members of the Society for Old Testament Study*, 251–71, Cambridge: Cambridge University Press.

Day, P.L., ed. (1989), *Gender and Difference in Ancient Israel*, Minneapolis, MN: Fortress Press.

de Geus, C.H.J. (1976), *The Tribes of Israel: An Investigation into Some of the Presuppositions of Martin Noth's Amphictyony Hypothesis*, Assen: Van Gorcum.

de Vaux, R. (1961 [1958]), *Ancient Israel*, 2 vols, New York: McGraw-Hill.
Douglas, M. (1966), *Purity and Danger: An Analysis of the Concepts of Pollution and Taboo*, London: Routledge & Kegan Paul.
Dresch, P. (1988), 'Segmentation: Its Roots in Arabia and Its Flowering Elsewhere', *Cultural Anthropology*, 3 (1): 50–67.
Durkheim, É. (1933 [1893]), *The Division of Labor in Society*, transl. George Simpson, New York: Free Press.
Eickelman, D.F. (1989), *The Middle East: An Anthropological Approach*, 2nd edn, Englewood Cliffs, NJ: Prentice-Hall.
Ember, C.R. (1983), 'The Relative Decline in Women's Contribution to Agriculture with Intensification', *American Anthropologist*, 85 (2): 285–304.
Emmerson, G.I. (1989), 'Women in Ancient Israel', in R.E. Clements (ed.), *The World of Ancient Israel: Sociological, Anthropological and Political Perspectives – Essays by Members of the Society for Old Testament Study*, 371–94, Cambridge: Cambridge University Press.
Eskenazi, T.C. (1992), 'Out from the Shadows: Biblical Women in the Postexilic Era', *JSOT*, 17 (54): 25–43.
Eskenazi, T.C. (1993), 'Current Perspectives on Ezra-Nehemiah and the Persian Period', *CRBS*, 1: 59–86.
Eskenazi, T.C. and E.P. Judd (1994), 'Marriage to a Stranger in Ezra 9–10', in T.C. Eskenazi and K.H. Richards (eds), *Second Temple Studies 2: Temple and Community in the Persian Period*, 266–85, JSOTSup 175, Sheffield: Sheffield Academic Press.
Evans-Pritchard, E.E. (1940), *The Nuer*, Oxford: Clarendon Press.
Evans-Pritchard, E.E. (1962), 'Social Anthropology: Past and Present' (1950), in *Social Anthropology and Other Essays*, 139–54. New York: Free Press.
Feeley-Harnick, G. (1982), 'Is Historical Anthropology Possible? The Case of the Runaway Slave', in G.M. Tucker and D.A. Knight (eds), *Humanizing America's Iconic Book*, 95–126, Chico, CA: Scholars Press.
Fiensy, D. (1987), 'Using the Nuer Culture of Africa in Understanding the Old Testament: An Evaluation', *JSOT*, 12 (38): 73–83.
Flanagan, J.W. (1982), 'Genealogy and Dynasty in the Early Monarchy of Israel and Judah', *Proceedings of the Eighth World Congress of Jewish Studies*, 23–8, Jerusalem: World Union of Jewish Studies.
Flanagan, J.W. (1983), 'Succession and Genealogy in the Davidic Dynasty', in H.B. Huffman, F.A. Spina and A.R.W. Green (eds), *The Quest for the Kingdom of God: Studies in Honor of George E. Mendenhall*, 35–55, Winona Lake, IN: Eisenbrauns.
Flanagan, J.W. (1988), *David's Social Drama: A Hologram of Israel's Early Iron Age*, SWBAS 7, Sheffield: Almond Press.
Frick, F.S. (1971), 'The Rechabites Reconsidered', *JBL*, 90 (3): 279–87.
Frick, F.S. (1977), *The City in Ancient Israel*, Atlanta, GA: Scholars Press.
Frick, F.S. (1985), *The Formation of the State in Ancient Israel: A Survey of Models and Theories*, SWBAS 4, Sheffield: Almond Press.
Frick, F.S. (1989), 'Ecology, Agriculture, and Patterns of Settlement', in R.E. Clements (ed.), *The World of Ancient Israel: Sociological, Anthropological and Political Perspectives – Essays by Members of the Society for Old Testament Study*, 67–93, Cambridge: Cambridge University Press.
Frick, F.S. (1992), 'Rechab', in D.N. Freedman (ed.), *Anchor Bible Dictionary*, vol. V, 630–2, New York: Doubleday.

Fried, M.H. (1967), *The Evolution of Political Society: An Essay in Political Anthropology*, New York: Random House.
Fried, M.H. (1975), *The Notion of Tribe*, New York: Random House.
Gellner, E. (1969), *Saints of the Atlas*, Chicago: University of Chicago Press.
Gellner, E. (1973), 'Introduction to Nomadism', in C. Nelson (ed.), *The Desert and the Sown*, 1–10, Berkeley: University of California Press.
Gero, J.M. and M.W. Conkey, eds (1991), *Engendering Archaeology: Women and Prehistory*, Oxford: Basil Blackwell.
Gottwald, N.K. (1979), *The Tribes of Yahweh: A Sociology of the Religion of Liberated Israel, 1250–1050 B.C.E.*, Maryknoll, NY: Orbis Books.
Gottwald, N.K. (1985), *The Hebrew Bible: A Socio-Literary Introduction*, Philadelphia, PA: Fortress Press.
Gottwald, N.K. (1993), 'Recent Studies of the Social World of Premonarchic Israel', *CRBS*, 1: 163–89.
Grabbe, L.L. (1995), *Priests, Prophets, Diviners, Sages: A Socio-Historical Study of Religious Specialists in Ancient Israel*, Valley Forge, PA: Trinity Press International.
Gunter, A.C., ed. (1990), *Investigating Artistic Environments in the Ancient Near East*, Washington, DC: Arthur M. Sadder Gallery, Smithsonian Institution.
Halpern, B. (1981), *The Constitution of the Monarchy in Israel*, Atlanta, GA: Scholars Press.
Halpern, B. (1983), *The Emergence of Israel in Canaan*, Chico, CA: Scholars Press.
Halpern, B. (1992), 'Kenites', in D.N. Freedman (ed.), *Anchor Bible Dictionary*, vol. IV, 17–22, New York: Doubleday.
Hanson, P.D. (1979), *The Dawn of Apocalyptic: The Historical and Sociological Roots of Jewish Apocalyptic Eschatology*, Philadelphia, PA: Fortress Press.
Heaton, E.W. (1974), *Solomon's New Men: The Emergence of Ancient Israel as a Nation State*, New York: Pica Press.
Hiebert, P.S. (1989), '"Whence Shall Help Come unto Me?" The Biblical Widow', in P.L. Day (ed.), *Gender and Difference in Ancient Israel*, 125–41, Minneapolis, MN: Fortress Press.
Jamieson-Drake, D.W. (1991), *Scribes and Schools in Monarchic Judah: A Socio-Archaeological Approach*, SWBAS 9, Sheffield: Almond Press.
Johnson, M.D. (1969), *The Purpose of Biblical Genealogies*, Cambridge: Cambridge University Press.
Khazanov, A. (1984), *Nomads and the Outside World*, transl. J. Crookenden, Cambridge: Cambridge University Press.
Khoury, P.S. and J. Kostiner, eds (1990), *Tribes and State Formation in the Middle East*, Berkeley: University of California Press.
Knight, D.A. (2011), *Law, Power, and Justice in Ancient Israel*, LAI, Louisville, KY: Westminster John Knox Press.
LaBianca, Ø.S. and R.W. Younker (1995), 'The Kingdoms of Ammon, Moab and Edom: The Archaeology of Society in Late Bronze I Iron Age Transjordan (*ca.* 1400–500 BCE)', in T.E. Levy (ed.), *The Archaeology of Society in the Holy Land*, 399–415, New York: Facts on File.
Lemaire, A. (1981), *Les écoles et la formation de la Bible dans l'ancien Israël*, OBO 39, Göttingen: Vandenhoeck & Ruprecht.
Lemche, N.P. (1985), *Early Israel. Anthropological and Historical Studies on the Israelite Society Before the Monarchy*, VTSup 37, Leiden: E.J. Brill.
Lemche, N.P. (1988), *Ancient Israel: A New History of Israelite Society*, The Biblical Seminar 5, Sheffield: JSOT Press.

Lemche, N.P. (1995), 'Kings and Clients: On Loyalty Between the Ruler and the Ruled in Ancient "Israel"', in D.A. Knight (ed.), *Ethics and Politics in the Hebrew Bible*, 119–32, Semeia 66, Atlanta, GA: Scholars Press.

Lemche, N.P. (1996), 'From Patronage Society to Patronage Society', in V. Fritz and P.R. Davies (eds), *The Origins of the Ancient Israelite States*, 106–20, JSOTSup 228, Sheffield: Sheffield Academic Press.

Lemos, T.M. (2010), *Marriage Gifts and Social Change in Ancient Palestine. 1200 BCE to 200 CE*, Cambridge: Cambridge University Press.

Malamat, A. (1973), 'Tribal Societies: Biblical Genealogies and African Lineage Systems', *Archives européennes de sociologie*, 14 (1): 126–36.

Martin, J.D. (1989), 'Israel as a Tribal Society', in R.E. Clements (ed.), *The World of Ancient Israel: Sociological, Anthropological and Political Perspectives – Essays by Members of the Society for Old Testament Study*, 95–118, Cambridge: Cambridge University Press.

McNutt, P.M. (1990), *The Forging of Israel: Iron Technology, Symbolism, and Tradition in Ancient Society*, SWBAS 8, Sheffield: Almond Press.

McNutt, P.M. (1995), 'The Kenites, the Midianites, and the Rechabites as Marginal Mediators in Ancient Israelite Tradition', in B.J. Malina (ed.), *Transformations, Passages, and Processes*, 109–32, Semeia 67, Atlanta, GA: Scholars Press.

McNutt, P.M. (1999), *Reconstructing the Society of Ancient Israel*, LAI, Louisville, KY: Westminster John Knox Press.

Mendenhall, G.E. (1973), *The Tenth Generation: The Origins of the Biblical Tradition*, Baltimore, MD: Johns Hopkins University Press.

Mettinger, T. (1971), *Solomonic State Officials: A Study of the Civil Government Officials of the Israelite Monarchy*, Lund: CWK Gleerup.

Meyers, C. (1988), *Discovering Eve: Ancient Israelite Women in Context*, Oxford: Oxford University Press.

Meyers, C. (1991), 'To Her "Mother's House": Considering a Counterpart to the Israelite Bêt 'āb', in D. Jobling, P.L. Day and G.T. Sheppard (eds), *The Bible and the Politics of Exegesis*, 39–51, Cleveland: Pilgrim Press.

Meyers, C. (1992), 'Everyday Life: Women in the Period of the Hebrew Bible', in C. Newsom and S.H. Ringe (eds), *The Women's Bible Commentary*, 244–51, Louisville, KY: Westminster John Knox Press.

Pedersen, J. (1926–40 [1920–34]), *Israel: Its Life and Culture*, 4 vols, London: Oxford University Press.

Redford, D.B. (1972), 'Studies in Relations Between Palestine and Egypt During the First Millennium B.C.: The Taxation System of Solomon', in J. Wevers and D.B. Redford (eds), *Studies in the Ancient Palestinian World*, 141–56, Toronto: University of Toronto Press.

Rogerson, J.W. (1986), 'Was Early Israel a Segmentary Society?', *JSOT*, 11 (36): 17–26.

Sahlins, M.D. (1961), 'The Segmentary Lineage: An Organization of Predatory Expansion', *Anthropological Quarterly*, 63 (2): 322–46.

Service, E.R. (1962), *Primitive Social Organization*, New York: Random House.

Silverblatt, I. (1988), 'Women in States', *Annual Review of Anthropology*, 17: 427–60.

Smith, D.L. (1989), *The Religion of the Landless: The Social Context of the Babylonian Exile*, Bloomington, IN: Meyer-Stone Books.

Smith-Christopher, D.L. (1994), 'The Mixed Marriage Crisis in Ezra 9–10 and Nehemiah 13: A Study of the Sociology of the Post-Exilic Judean Community', in T.C. Eskenazi and K.H. Richards (eds), *Second Temple Studies 2: Temple and Community in the Persian Period*, 243–65, JSOTSup 175, Sheffield: Sheffield Academic Press.

Steinberg, N. (1993), *Kinship and Marriage in Genesis: A Household Economics Perspective*, Minneapolis, MN: Fortress Press.

Washington, H.C. (1994), 'The Strange Woman of Proverbs 1–9 and Post-Exilic Judean Society', in T.C. Eskenazi and K.H. Richards (eds), *Second Temple Studies 2: Temple and Community in the Persian Period*, 217–42, JSOTSup 175, Sheffield: Sheffield Academic Press.

Weber, M. (1952 [1916–19]), *Ancient Judaism*, transl. H.H. Gerth and D. Martindale, New York: Free Press.

Weinberg, J.P. (1992), *The Citizen-Temple Community*, transl. D. Smith-Christopher, JSOTSup 151, Sheffield: JSOT Press.

Whyte, M.K. (1978), *The Status of Women in Preindustrial Societies*, Princeton, NJ: Princeton University Press.

Wilson, R.R. (1975), 'The Old Testament Genealogies in Recent Research', *JBL*, 94 (2): 169–89.

Wilson, R.R. (1977), *Genealogy and History in the Biblical World*, New Haven, CT: Yale University Press.

CHAPTER EIGHT

# The many forms and foundations of power and authority in the Hebrew Bible

VICTOR H. MATTHEWS

Power and authority come in many guises. The concepts of power and authority as they manifest themselves in the narratives and legal statements in the Hebrew Bible reflect that ancient society's sense of collective identity and the social, economic and political forces that influenced their lives and their history. Since kinship is the key to collective identity and behaviour in ancient Israel, the foundational measure of authority in that culture is based on the household with its hierarchy of power starting with the 'father' and that person's delegation of authority to each member of the household.[1]

By exercising his authority, the head of the household perpetuates the effort to (1) ensure that the household prospers as a social unit within their village, and (2) protect its honour as the means of demonstrating its value and right to do business with that community. Coupled with the authority invested in the head of household is a set of social protocols that govern behaviour and tie members of the household to a specific place (their portion of the land), provide a set of social expectations based on gender, age and social status, and set a tone for how they will interact with the extended range of persons identified as Israelites and those that are labelled as 'strangers' (*gerîm*).[2]

In any society, especially one that has a collective mentality and that maintains strict social protocols, it is very difficult to change patterns of behaviour once they have been established. For instance, limitations are placed on association based on membership in particular households, clans or tribes. Marriage contracts as well as other business

---

[1] The classic study on this principle is Stager 1985. A further refinement in found in Matthews and Benjamin 1993: 7–21. A recent treatment is found in Weingart 2019. Taking a broader perspective, Sanders (2012: 193) compares the eighteenth-century BCE Mari texts to the biblical book of Judges for a perspective on kinship groups 'as primary agents of history'.

[2] This label applies to two groups. First are those who are socially liminal: the female prisoner of war (Deut. 21.10–14) or the debt slave who consents to perpetual servitude by having his ear pierced at the door of his master (Deut. 15.16–17). They are transitioning by entering into a permanent covenant with a household. Second are outsiders, who are known to a household and have established economic or political covenants with the household (Deut. 16.11). See Benjamin 2017: 115–16, 134–5; and Glanville 2018: 603.

negotiations are driven by what is deemed acceptable patterns of association. Similarly, social advancement in the village context is very limited and only changes once the society becomes more urban-based and differentiation of labour, personal merit or political considerations come into play.

It is necessary to keep in mind that having the power to do something does not always grant a person authority over that power. Women have the power to reproduce, but men often retain for themselves the authority over sexual activity (marriage contracts, incest taboos, birth control).[3] In ancient Israel male authority generally superseded that of women. Thus, all forms of power and authority emerge from this foundational social model with males dominating most situations. Hence, the elders of local villages as well as the kings of Israel and Judah (once their society had evolved from the village to a more complex polity in ancient Israel) followed the same methods of delegation of authority while maintaining their own prerogatives of power over the people. Whether it involved making decisions at the local level or exercising power through a bureaucracy that attempted to combine all of the resources of the nation, all those in authority were expected to strive for the same desired goals to ensure the betterment of the people. However, like any machine that serves a particular function, there were outside or competing forces that occasionally imposed changes in the Israelite model of authority and were able instead to exercise hegemony over them for a time. And, personal ambition could also contribute to political or economic changes that had a ripple effect on society in general.

Israel's history documents many examples of local and national authority as well as the external forces that attempted to override that authority. The fact that Israel continued to exist as an identifiable people despite periods of invasion, exile, royal efforts to consolidate power, and foreign rule indicates that the original household-based authority held the people together during periods of crisis and allowed them to maintain their religious identity and their collective sense of self. It will be the task of this study to examine some aspects of the exercise of power and authority in ancient Israel at various levels. But first it is necessary to provide a theoretical underpinning for these social concepts as they apply to that ancient nation.

## THEORETICAL EVALUATION OF POWER AND AUTHORITY

Authority and power are conditions that complement each other, but it is authority that makes it possible for power to be exercised. Both can be gauged by the extent to which an individual or a group is able to influence or control other individuals or groups.[4] Of course, individuals and nations can also be influenced by outside forces beyond their control such as an epidemic or a major climatic change, but the focus here will be on human-to-human inaction (Rheinstein 1967: 323). Authority obtains its inherent abilities through association and is a function of 'all social processes' (Popitz 2017: 5). Its willingness to be employed is based on a variety of motivations and situations that call for one or more of the basic tools of power. In addition, it is manifested in direct relation to such factors as ethnic origins, kinship ties, gender, wealth, social status and personal abilities that are capable of influencing others.

Power, by its nature, is relational, acting 'on its environment and bringing about some change in it' (Wrong 1997: ix). Thus, the measure of a standard power index is based on such

---

[3] See the treatment of laws associated with male control over female sexuality in Frymer-Kensky 1998.
[4] Bannester (1969: 375) refers to this as 'sociomotive power'.

things as emotions (fear, infatuation and/or love, faith, loyalty), adherence to socialized behaviour (social protocols that determine marriage patterns, hospitality, kinship obligations), and personal desires (wealth, social advancement, opportunity). While exercised by individuals or groups, power can serve as either a positive or negative force within a community. It is most often characterized by those employing the instruments of power while being framed as being in the best interests or the defence and well-being of that community.

The basic instruments of power, both latent and extant, have been identified by Galbraith as 'condign, compensatory, and conditioned' with a combination of these three instruments often at play in every situation (Galbraith 1983: 4–6). Thus condign force (physical or psychological) combines with the fear of consequences in order to exercise control of others.[5] Compensatory power contains the potential for or promise of gain (monetary or otherwise). Conditioning power includes the effect of socialization and education as well as various forms of speech and propaganda. Implicit norms of morality and behaviour are inculcated subliminally or overtly and become the means for those in authority to increase and maintain their hold over power.

Authority and the exercise of power exist at a variety of levels depending on the social, economic, political or physical setting. For example, 'an attempt at coercion behind closed doors cannot be equated with a similar attempt when the door is open' since the potential influence of any condign act of coercion can be scaled up depending on the size of the audience, the number of participants and the frenzy associated with this exercise of power (Bannester 1969: 379). In like manner, a public display of largesse by a leader such as the 'games' in the Roman Coliseum that were sponsored by the emperors can magnify the effectiveness of such a compensatory gesture and provide a motivation or desire for more such spectacles.

There is also a basis for behaviour that involves the peculiar psychological motivation of an individual or group to act in a specific manner. It can be triggered by any of the instruments of power and can be used to an extent to predict specific future actions. Thus, a military commander can predict whether his troops will obey an order depending upon the degree to which they have been trained/socialized to obey and have previously demonstrated their expressed loyalty to the commander and to the purpose for which they serve. The individual soldier's motivation, however, may be based on fear of the consequences of disobedience, an intrinsic desire to please the officer, ambition to rise in rank or an altruistic desire to serve one's country (Hooper 1983: 499).

Developing over the past two centuries, post-Enlightenment theorists 'have portrayed modern institutions as rational forms of domination (in Weberian terms) that arose historically from confrontations with different so-called "natural" orders based on religion, kinship, castes, and personal or patrimonial domains' (Victoria 2016: 251). Because these terms tend to be 'state-centric' in their orientation, they do not fully take into account the influences of interpersonal interaction at a micro level or the macro influences of predatory imperial goals or the social and economic transformations that take place as the result of the creation of international markets and the resulting wider world view. Thus, any attempt at defining or analysing power must consider such factors and phenomena as 'informal ways of grouping and making alliances, leaderships and networking, ritual processes, and storytelling' (Victoria 2016: 254).

---

[5] Hooper points to the willingness to pay taxes to avoid a penalty, but notes that a more stable system is one 'in which individuals pay their taxes and perform other support behaviors on the basis of some kind of self-motivation' (i.e. compensatory power [1983: 497–8]).

**TABLE 8.1:** Types of power and characteristics

| Types of Power | Characteristics |
| --- | --- |
| Personal | Ability of an individual to influence others based on personal attributes (gender, hierarchical and kinship status, leadership abilities, passion, ideological conviction, ambition) |
| Hierarchical | Levels of authority clearly defined by status, wealth, gender, age, race or kinship (ethnicity, familial, clientage) |
| Political | Delegation or usurpation of authority to a hierarchy of leaders and/or groups, hegemony over contiguous territory, warfare |
| Spatial | Social and economic gridding, restrictions on use or entrance into space, defined or associated usage, sacred designation of space |
| Legal | Extent to which established principles of 'law and order' govern behaviour and are upheld by social, religious or governmental restraints |
| Social | Behavioural norms and practices inculcated through socialization determining role in society based on gender, age, health, membership in the group, or hierarchical status |
| Economic | Depending on the extent of local, regional, national or international production and commerce, systems of exchange, measures of control, and supply and demand |
| Rhetorical | The ability to influence others through speech, gesture, the use of space, recognized emblems, foundational storytelling, clothing or props, aspects of cultural norms/behaviour, intimidation and vocal propaganda |
| Visual | Monumental architecture, victory stele, clothing, socially defined and accepted symbols or props associated with authority |

Table 8.1 provides a set of categories or types of power with a list of characteristics associated with that particular form of power. The extent to which authority is or can be attached to these power categories may be based on circumstance, such as an individual's status within a particular society, political conditions at the time, and social constraints such as age or gender. Since many of these categories overlap, I will divide the discussion into five major headings that comprise the remainder of this study.

## POLITICAL POWER AND AUTHORITY

While less overtly hierarchical then in the urban setting, the village culture of ancient Israel has its own sources of power and authority. They are based on individual abilities (storyteller, craftsmen, potters, weavers, cooks), gender, age, property ownership and lineage. In addition, within the context of this social setting it is possible to refer to individuals as 'an authority', such as a master craftsman or those 'in authority' (Lincoln 1994: 3–4), which encompasses the authority exercised by the village elders (= land owners and heads of households) (Meyers 2006).

Providing a foundation for authority at a more basic level is the socialized behaviour of the community that orchestrates and obligates individuals to act and react in specific ways to each other and to strangers in order to preserve the honour of each household within the community. Particularly in the village setting these social norms are designed to maintain the physical and social viability of the community within a fragile and unforgiving physical environment. Under these conditions, the head of the household, who in most cases would also be recognized as a village elder, would be responsible for the actions of his extended family and function as an integral part of the consensus building process that ultimately serves as the means for enforcement of social protocols. For instance, Judah's summary condemnation of his daughter-in-law Tamar after she is found to be pregnant and is accused of 'playing the whore' leaves little doubt that he is fully in charge of maintaining order within his small community (Gen. 38.24). The fact that he could then overturn his own ruling when additional evidence is presented also indicates that authority is not to be exercised without reason or a sense of humility (Gen. 38.25–26).

Additional examples of how the village elders served in the capacity of community wardens can be found in Ruth 4 and in the story of the 'rebellious son' in Deut. 21.18–21. In both of these instances the elders do not serve as a police force or even as a prosecuting attorney. Instead they simply sit and listen when an issue is brought before them by another member of their village that has the potential to disrupt or endanger the entire community (Willis 2001: 277). When Boaz frames a case of levirate obligation before the village elders of Bethlehem (Ruth 4.1–12), he is not expecting them to judge the participants involved, but rather to confirm as witnesses what is already part of their legal tradition and to use their confirmation of that principle to resolve the legal disposition of Elimelech's estate and his daughter-in-law Ruth.

In the case of the disobedient and wasteful son, it becomes the obligation of his parents to present their grievance against their son before the elders at the gate. Again, it is a confirmation of an established legal principle that condemns the young man to death in order to 'purge the evil from' their midst (Deut. 21.21), not the elders' judgement of the case. And in both instances the authority of place is a significant part of the scene, since both episodes occur at the gate thereby tying the life and prosperity of the community to the physical settling of legal disputes (Matthews 2003).

It is really only within the urban-based communities such as Jerusalem that identifiable, individual political and religious leaders come into play as figures of authority who transcend or at least are able to modify normalized behaviours on a wider scale and bypass or override the traditional authority of local elders. Hierarchy in these more complex settings with its reliance on the leadership of the king still hinges on kinship relations since the early monarchs continued to practise nepotism, employing members of their own family as advisers, military leaders, or key members of the bureaucracy (see David's use of his nephew Joab as the commander of the army). However, the delegation of power became necessary beyond the kinship circle as the job of managing a wider and more complex society required expansion of kinship to encompass clientage relationships (see the mention of 550 'officers' appointed by Solomon to conduct his various building projects in 1 Kgs 9.23).[6]

Attendant with the assumption of power on the part of a high-ranking member of the priesthood, a monarch or a member of the nobility are the trappings of power that they adopt and use as recognizable symbols of their authority. Among these would be their

---

[6] The historicity of this account and the possible extent of Solomon's kingdom and activities is uncertain given a lack of extra-biblical sources and the mixed opinions on archaeological evidence at various sites including Gezer and Megiddo. See Cogan 2001: 308–9.

robes of office. Thus, the elaborate description of the priestly vestments in Exodus 28 makes them distinctive from what all other Israelites wore, setting them aside as practitioners of religious ritual and serving as reminders to them of their sacred obligation (Meyers 2005: 240–1). Rulers also would have been clothed in fine garments as a sign of their rank. Like other monarchs and gods in the ancient Near East these individuals who are clothed in robes of office separated themselves from their subjects and devotees by sitting in majesty on their throne.[7] That is graphically displayed in the placement of Ahab's and Jehoshaphat's thrones in the gate of Samaria while the two kings 'sat arrayed in their robes' of office (1 Kgs 22.10).[8]

The importance attached to royal vestments can be seen in two episodes from David's early career. As they made a pact of mutual friendship and obligation, Jonathan removes his robes, armour and weapons and gives them to David symbolizing an investiture ceremony that would eventually make David rather than Jonathan the king of Israel (1 Sam. 18.4; Cartledge 2001: 229). In a similar scene featuring the importance attached to clothing, David cuts off the corner of Saul's cloak and then regrets his action seeing it as an act that diminishes the authority of the 'Lord's anointed' and as a belligerent 'raising of the hand' against the king (1 Sam. 24.1–7).[9] In this way, David clearly equates the king's person and his authority with his robes of office.

A further aspect of how power is used to separate a political leader from those that he rules can be found in the protocol described in Est. 4.11. It is Persian policy and custom that forbids anyone to come to the king's inner court without invitation under pain of death unless the king holds out his golden sceptre to them. That gesture and the use of the sceptre as a 'prop of power' (compare Ps. 45.6; Isa. 14.5) is used to acknowledge their presence and the willingness on the part of the king to note their very existence. Esther's courage in going to the king uninvited is a gamble on her part, but also an effort to proclaim her existence and her worth to the king.

A further link to a monarch's authority is the command that he has over the space that he occupies whether it be within the palace or simply wherever he and his entourage happen to be. His presence or his association with that place (a microcosm of the state) transforms it into his exclusive domain of power for as long as he is there – that is, as long as those in attendance recognize and accept his authority. Therefore, it also is necessary that he act authoritatively so that no one else present is able to capture control over him, his speech or his actions. Thus, Jerusalem becomes David's city and seat of power when his captures it from the Jebusites (2 Sam. 5.6–10) and then brings the ark of the covenant to his capital to the acclaim of the people (2 Sam. 6.1–15). And yet, his son Absalom can stand before the gates of the city and rally strong support for himself and his political faction by pointing to David's failure to appoint judges to hear the legal cases of supplicants (2 Sam. 15.1–6). His not-so-subtle attack on his father presages an armed rebellion that temporarily drives David from Jerusalem (2 Sam. 15.13) until he and his army can once again claim that space for the king.

---

[7] For example, Yahweh claims a victory over the Elamites by proclaiming that the deity's throne will be set in Elam (Jer. 49.38).
[8] At work here also is the use of calculated 'positioning' of persons and objects in significance space as a magnified expression of power. See Matthews 2008: 119.
[9] Note that David, as an outlaw, could be seen as a covenant-breaker, not carrying out his obligations to King Saul.

The question, however, is what made Absalom a recognizable candidate for the throne. Certainly, his empathetic rhetoric was an effective tool in bringing the crowd to his side. But two other factors associated with power and authority play into this scene. First, Absalom chose daily to stage his public display in the city's gate area. That space has a long history associated with both legal and business transactions (Gen. 19.1, 34.20–24; Deut. 21.18–21, 22.13–24, 25.5–10) and, as a major part of its fortifications, is also tied to the safety and well-being of the city. Since it would have heavy traffic going in and out of the city, he can expect to be able to harangue both those who have come to bring their cases to the king but also many others who could be swayed by his promises of providing justice to the land. Second, Absalom has an entourage associated with powerful individuals: 'a chariot and horses, and fifty men to run ahead of him' (2 Sam. 15.1). A group such as this could be expected to make way for a powerful individual (compare Joseph's signs of power given him by the Pharaoh – Gen. 41.41–43) and make it known that he is to be respected and possibly feared.

An axiom that signals how those in authority make use of their power is that 'the more power becomes centralized, the easier it is for its representatives to ignore what they do not wish to see' (Herzfeld 2015: 20). Power in this sense would be political, but socially blind or at least narrowly focused. Religious leaders, the wealthy, or those of a social status that allows them a more comfortable life may not wish to take special notice of the poor or those in need since their presence is a reminder of what the affluent could be or could become if circumstances change.[10] Thus, the well-fed 'cows of Bashan' are condemned by the prophet Amos for ignoring the plight of the poor while calling on their husbands to 'bring something to drink' (Amos 4.1). This principle also applies to average citizens who may prefer to not see their 'neighbour's donkey or ox fallen in the road' (Deut. 22.4). They may wish not to get involved, but the Deuteronomic code, at least on an idealized basis, holds them to the social expectation that they will 'help to lift it up' and thereby preserve an economic asset for their neighbour. Of course, there is also a measure of reciprocity in these acts that expresses the expectation or at least the hope that the neighbour will reciprocate and thereby protect another's economy.

Other examples of prescribed proper behaviour that will not allow for the needy to become invisible include Sir. 35.17, which recounts how God 'will not ignore the supplication of the orphan, or the widow when she pours out her complaint'. In contrast, Job characterizes the 'wicked' as those who 'thrust the needy off the road' (compare Amos 5.12) and subject the poor to such scorn that they 'hide themselves' and are forced to 'lie all night naked'[11] and work 'without clothing' and are 'hungry' while 'carry[ing] the sheaves' (Job 24.4–10). The reality of desired invisibility clearly contrasts with the Deuteronomic expectations but still exists in the mind of the oppressed as in Ps. 142.4 where the lament states 'there is no one who takes notice of me'.

It is possible that yet another example of refusal of an authority figure to see something is David's arranged murder of Uriah the Hittite (2 Sam. 11.14–25)? David instructs Joab to put Uriah in the front ranks during a siege and then pull back so that he lacks necessary support and is killed. Conveniently, the king is not present, does not see the action or Uriah's death, but benefits from it. In that way the soldier becomes invisible to the

---

[10] See the arguments made by the 'Eloquent Peasant' in Egyptian wisdom literature (*ANET*³, 408–10).
[11] See the plea of the workman for justice in the Yavneh Yam ostracon in Matthews and Benjamin 2016: 395.

commander who orders him into battle – merely a piece moved across the playing board and one that can be lost or dispensed with dispassionately and with a measure of plausible deniability for those in authority.

## DIPLOMATIC POWER AND AUTHORITY

Whether it is the head of a household, a group of village elders, a king or his designated ambassador, a clear expression of authority is found in the ability of an individual or a group to negotiate a transaction, a legal settlement, or a treaty between nations. In most cases, the basic principle behind these commercial or political agreements is governed by the requirement to treat each party fairly and not renege on the terms of the agreement. For example, the inclusio in Lev. 25.14–17 that encompasses buying and selling during the Jubilee year begins and ends with the injunction 'you shall not cheat one another'. Milgrom emphasizes that in this legal pronouncement the use of 'cheat' (*tônû*) is aimed at protecting 'the underprivileged and unprotected in society' from those who otherwise had economic and political power over them (Milgrom 2001: 2176–9).

The biblical narrative contains many examples of diplomatic activity that demonstrate power relationships from a parity standpoint to a situation in which one party is clearly being coerced by the other. For instance, Solomon negotiates a mutually beneficial agreement with Hiram of Tyre to assist in constructing the Temple in Jerusalem (1 Kgs 5.1–12). While the account clearly presents Solomon in a position of higher authority (Hiram sends a diplomatic team to Jerusalem shortly after Solomon's accession to the throne, 5.1), the purchase of cedar logs for quantities of grain follows a pattern of economic exchange well documented outside the Bible.[12] The transaction in this case benefits both parties, but that is not always the case in these exchanges.

In his examination of another example of diplomatic activity in the biblical narrative, Sutherland notes that ancient Israelite society went through various phases of political development from the premonarchic council of elders in the village culture, to 'assemblies of the free adult males eligible for military service', to the monarchy when some aspects of the assemblies' authority is 'subsumed under the king's prerogatives' but still retained some measure of authority through their role as a consultative body (Sutherland 1992: 73). To illustrate his case, he points to the story in Joshua 9 of the treaty made with the Gibeonites. Even though it is based on a ruse by the Gibeonites, the negotiations include Joshua as well as the 'men of Israel' in vv. 4–7, 11–14 and 15 (*'îš-yiśā'ēl*) and the 'leaders of the congregation' (*nᵉśî ê-hā 'ēdâ*) in vv. 15b, 17–21. The use of three different power groups in the received/edited narrative is an indication that prior to the monarchy treaties and oaths could be orchestrated by local assemblies. By pairing them here with Joshua as the monarchic prototype for leadership in the divided monarchy, they retain some measure of authority as a power bloc throughout the political evolution of the Israelites (Sutherland 1992: 66–7). In the end and serving as a foundational precedent, the treaty with the Gibeonites cannot be broken because of the oath taken and the fear of divine retribution should the Israelites harm their treaty partner (Josh. 9.3–27; esp. vv. 19–20).

---

[12] See the dialogue between the Egyptian priest Wen-Amun and Tjerkerbaal, the ruler of Byblos (COS 1.41: 90–1) that describes a long history of Egypt sending representatives to obtain cedar logs from the rulers of the coastal cities of Lebanon.

That brings oath-taking into the wider realm of ancient Near Eastern treaty making and formalizes this agreement as a solemn diplomatic pact.[13]

The maintenance of international relations is not always straightforward. Thus, in the episode in which David sends emissaries to the newly crowned king of the Ammonites there are in fact underlying currents of distrust and jockeying for power (2 Sam. 10.1–5). The situation as described seems at first to be standard diplomatic procedure designed to renew and strengthen previously existing, mutually agreed upon treaty arrangements (compare Hiram's actions in 1 Kgs 5.1). However, King Hanun is warned by his assembly of 'princes' that David's intentions are not honourable and are the prelude to an attack on Ammonite territory. As a result, Hanun decides to demonstrate his disdain for what he perceives as David's predatory motives by shaming David's envoys – and by extension David himself (Esler 2006: 196–7). He symbolically emasculates them by cutting off half of their beards and half of their clothing (2 Sam. 10.3–4). David fully understands this punitive gesture and to save face for his envoys and himself orders them to remain in seclusion at Jericho until their beards grow back, and, of course, he prepares for war with Ammon (10.5–8).[14]

Sometimes the negotiation process takes the form of a plea for mercy or submission. Thus, when Jabesh-gilead is besieged by the Ammonites, the response of men of the city is a request 'to make a treaty' obligating them serve the Ammonites (1 Sam. 11.1). Such a quick surrender could be expected for a city without allies and no chance to drive off the enemy army.[15] Of course, there are instances when a city chose to hold against the besieging army. That decision, perhaps based on a hoped-for ally's assistance, could also lead to a rather undiplomatic, sarcastic speech on the part of the representative of the enemy forces (2 Kgs 18.17–25). For example, the Assyrian Rabshakeh standing before the walls of Hezekiah's besieged Jerusalem is quite articulate in laying out the situation and is quick to point out to the defenders that those who rely on aid from the Egyptians are in for a painful surprise (18.21).

## LEGAL POWER AND AUTHORITY

The exercise of legal power and authority originally is vested in the ability of the head of a household to administer the affairs of his family (see Judah's condemnation of Tamar in Gen. 38.24; Wilson 1983: 232–3). By extension and in a situation involving the honour and well-being of more than a single household, this legal authority is reflected in the power of consensus that is exhibited by a set of village elders when they are called upon to hear a case that has the power to influence their community for good or bad (see Achan's trial in Josh. 7.16–26 and the assembled elders hearing the grievance of the Levite in Judg. 20.1–11; Wilson 1983: 235–7).

On what appears to be a personal level stands the story of Jethro giving Moses advice about sharing his judicial authority with 'able men' (Exod. 18.13–23) in order to ensure timely resolution of disputes. Of course, it also spared Moses from being overwhelmed by his caseload and serves as a clear reminder to those in authority in any age that they

---

[13] See Ziegler 2007: 62–3, for the contention that oaths would have been accompanied by a significant gesture or ritual act. For discussion of ancient Near Eastern treaty language and process, see Goelet and Levine 1998.
[14] Lemos (2006: 233) also notes the relation between having half of their beard removed and the Israelites' aversion for 'asymmetry'.
[15] See the varied responses by cities in the Assyrian Annals of Shalmaneser III (COS 2.113A: 262–4), some of whom relied on the help of other rulers and some who simply paid tribute rather than face siege and destruction.

cannot expect to efficiently serve their people alone. As a parallel with a similar instance in Num. 11.16–30, what we see are efforts from two different time periods to provide an authoritative underpinning for the judiciary during the monarchy period (Cook 1999: 291–5). It is also worth noting that the actual process of sharing judicial powers probably came about as a way to deal with issues in politically or environmentally unstable times.

An interesting, if chronologically difficult, reflection of appointed authority is found in the placement of judges and officials throughout the land in every town (Deut. 16.18–20). This reference, tied as it is to Moses and thereby obtaining a form of authority through association with such a foundational figure, could also be compared to other examples of judicial reform such as the one ascribed to Jehoshaphat (2 Chron. 19.4–11). More likely, the Deuteronomic text is tied to Josiah's reform efforts to close down local shrines in Judah. The displaced 'Levites in the gates' were then given positions as judicial officers charged with implementing Josiah's reforms in the local assemblies (Benjamin 2017: 28 n.62, 54–7, 119–20). In the process, Josiah would have been able to draw on the remembered authority of both Moses and Joshua as lawgiver and national leader.

What is interesting in the Deuteronomy passage is the way that the work of these officers (*šōṭĕrîm*) is spatially tied to performing their duties locally 'in all your gates'. Furthermore, it is to be carried out without prejudice or subject to the corruption of bribes. In that way there is a continuity with the authority previously exercised by local elders in the gate (Deut. 22.15, 25.7) and is consistent with legal and prophetic injunctions that demand adherence to the principles of social justice (Exod. 23.8; Deut. 10.17; Nelson 2002: 217).

Certainly, judicial reform, especially the centralization of authority, would have been necessary over time as the society and its governing body changed its character. However, using the biblical text as our sole source is not sufficient to make a firm statement about what was actually in existence, and certainly cannot tell us whether a similar judicial system was in place in both Israel and Judah (Whitelam 1979: 167–84). What might be extrapolated from the Chronicles passage, set as it is in the social context of the Persian period, is an indication of a multi-tiered judicial system that spread authority upwards from an initial tier of royal justices hearing local cases to a second tier seated in Jerusalem that included Levites, priests and lineage heads that would 'preside over religious cases (*mišpaṭ Yhwh*) and disputes (*rîb*) (2 Chron. 19.8)' (Wilson 1983: 244, 248).

## EDUCATIONAL POWER AND AUTHORITY

What greater power is there than the power to educate and instil within the next generation the values, practices and beliefs of one's own community? As described in Galbraith's concept of 'conditioned power', education can take the form of implicit training such as teaching a skill like pottery making or weaving. But it is also something that is unconsciously absorbed without realizing it through observation and mimicry. In the process certain attitudes, such as the subordination of women, beliefs in a particular god or gods, or the acceptance of social roles and expectations are instilled (Galbraith 1983: 24–6).

In ancient Israel, the idealized social injunction to remember (*zākar*) is at the heart of the educational process for each generation.[16] Thus, an authoritative command is

---

[16] Jan Assmann (2006: 5), in referring to how the Israelites maintained their memory of Egypt and the Exodus, notes that they are based on oral tradition, anecdote and the attachment of events to a sense of social bonding.

pronounced by Moses/Deuteronomist to instruct the children to remember the events and the significance of the Exodus – Exod. 13.14; Deut. 6.20–21, 32.7 – and that includes transmission of oral tradition by the elders to the people (Judg. 6.13). To reinforce these collective memories, ritual performances were staged that also included the recitation of the nation's salvation history (Lev. 23.43 – feast of booths; Deut. 16.1–12 – Passover; Deut. 29.2–29 and Josh. 24.4–7 – covenant renewal). And, to couple these foundation events with the deity, a label or title for the power and authority of Yahweh includes the attribution, 'who brought you out of the land of Egypt and redeemed you from the house of slavery' (Exod. 20.2; Deut. 4.34–37; Josh. 24.17).

In the same way, the collections of wisdom literature compiled throughout the ancient Near East functioned as a foundation for the transmission of 'common sense' and social expectations. James Crenshaw has referred to these wisdom voices as a 'one-sided conversation' that tries to convey to students and to the young in general both what they have learned about life and what they hope their 'audience' will be able to avoid (Crenshaw 1998: 3–4). However, the existence of and reference to these wisdom sayings is an indication that their voice was intended for more that a single generation. Of course, we have little hard evidence of the educational process in ancient Israel or the degree to which the average person was literate.[17] Certainly, we can point to a few objects like the tenth century BCE Gezer Almanac that appears to be a schoolboy exercise detailing the events associated with the agricultural calendar or the abecedary from Tel Zayit that gives us a clue to the development of a Hebrew script (Tappy et al. 2006: 31–40).

For the purposes of this study, the sense of authority comes into the educational process in the form of the development of a scribal community that exercised real power in the compilation and editing of documents during the monarchy and postexilic periods. Just as the author of the Middle Kingdom Egyptian 'Satire of the Trades' notes, these individuals rise above other professionals, serving others but being their own boss and making a good living (Matthews and Benjamin 2016: 322–4). Having control over archives of information and being given the responsibility to create annals of the kings of Israel and Judah while putting a particular ideological and theological stamp on them (i.e. the Deuteronomist), makes them extremely powerful individuals. Their copying of scrolls and the editing process that they develop, which of course means shifting through the body of information known about events, makes them both the keepers of Israel's memory stream and the creators of a voice that tells their contemporaries and all later generations the story of ancient Israel. In fact, once the written tradition was formally established, it would have become the mission of written scribes to reproduce verbatim copies of the text and thus solidify the canonized version of events and stories (Evans 2017: 763).

## ECONOMIC POWER AND AUTHORITY

On the most elemental level, the ability of a household to remain viable and to maintain its economic foundation from year to year is the test of economic authority in ancient Israel. To win out over the vagaries of the weather, the pillaging of fields by wild animals and the depredations of taxes and tithes required constant vigilance and daily hard work. A picture of just how difficult this must have been is found in Isaiah's metaphorical

---

[17] Rollston (2006: 49–50) suggests that despite using an alphabetic script, proficiency in the language does require formal education to become an accomplished scribe.

depiction of the construction of a terraced field planted with a vineyard (Isa. 5.1–7). The back-breaking labour associated with constructing the stone retaining walls of the terraces and filling them with soil, removing weeds, planting the vines and cultivating them over several years until they are mature is a test of patience and endurance (Matthews 1999: 25–7).

Such willingness to scratch a living from the soil with its necessary attention to detail is coupled with the conditioned belief by each household in the ownership of a portion of the Promised Land. However idealized, the recitation of the distribution of the land to the tribal groups in Joshua 13–19 gives them a sense of ownership that at the fundamental level is found in the sacred character of the boundary stone that must not be moved (Deut. 19.14).[18] That sentiment is articulated in Naboth's simple argument when King Ahab asks to purchase his vineyard and it reflects a deep-felt tie to the land and its association with his 'ancestral inheritance' down through the generations (1 Kgs 21.2–3). Despite the abuse of royal power that eventually cost Naboth and his sons their property rights (21.8–14), the narrative also contains Elijah's prophetic judgement against the king and his family that ultimately brings a measure of posthumous justice to this case (2 Kgs 9.21–26; see Magdalene 2015).

However, it is when economic circumstances or environmental disaster drives these small landowners into debt so crushing that they could no long maintain their hold on their land that another aspect of economic power presents itself. Marvin Chaney uses Amos 2.6 to demonstrate a deliberate practice of indebtedness engaged in by large landowners who would lend the smaller farmers enough silver to cover their production costs and then recoup their loan in kind from the harvest. However, if the harvest was poor the loan could not be paid, and then foreclosure proceedings were the result (Chaney 2017: 194–7). These farmers, hopelessly in debt and further burdened by taxes imposed by the state, subsequently were forced into become landless, seasonal labourers while the urban-based elites acquired more and more of the best farmlands.[19] This practice is known as latifundialization in which a wealthy land owner is able to 'join house to house' and 'add field to field'. The fact that it continued to occur is indicated by its express condemnation in Isa. 5.8–10 and Mic. 2.2–5 (Premnath 1988: 54–7).

At the highest levels of power, there are clear signs of the growing authority of the monarchy in Judah in its efforts to manage the natural resources of the kingdom. That included the establishment of administrative centres at Lachish around the outskirts of Jerusalem (Ramat Rahel). They are indications of the government's ability to tax the people and then distribute these accumulated resources as needed. The LMLK seal impressions from the reign of Hezekiah provide graphic proof of the extent of the bureaucratic organization managing the collection and distribution of commodities of grain, wine and olive oil by the state (Lipschits, Sergi and Koch 2011). The degree to which the king saw these facilities as reflections of power can be found in Hezekiah's boastful tour that he conducted for the Babylonian envoys of his storehouses (2 Kgs 20.13–15).

---

[18] The sacred character of boundary stones and the injunction against encroaching on a neighbour's property is also found in the Egyptian 'Book of the Dead', which includes in the declarations that a soul must make to the gods of the underworld that he has 'not moved boundary markers of another's field'. See Matthews and Benjamin 2016: 235.

[19] Hopkins 1983: 201. For additional analysis of this process, see Chaney 1989: 25–7.

Although the Temple in Jerusalem also functioned as an ancillary repository for the tithes collected during the year, the authority of the priests to make use of these contributions seems to have varied over time depending on the degree to which the monarch exercised his authority over the management of the temple complex. For example, during the reign of Jehoash the funds that had been accumulated in the treasury were not being disbursed to pay workmen to make necessary repairs (2 Kgs 12.4–8). He therefore takes direct control, supplanting a portion of the priests' authority and requiring a joint accounting of the collected funds by both a priest and a king's secretary (2 Kgs 12.9–15; compare similar wording in 2 Kgs 22.3–7; Cogan and Tadmor 1988: 138, 140). It is apparent that the accounts of temple restoration during the reigns of Jehoash and Josiah parallel to some extent a similar practice by rulers in Mesopotamia, who also found it politic to take a careful look at the management of the temple community's finances (Na'aman 2013: 646–7).

During the Second Temple period when the monarchy had been supplanted by a Persian-appointed governor, a committee was created by Nehemiah to oversee the collection of both 'holy' taxes as well as the Achaemenid state taxes and both were stored in the temple treasury (Ezra 8.33; Neh. 13.12; Schaper 1997: 201–5). From these acquired commodities the Temple supplied the needs of the priesthood and their families, the daily functions of the temple rituals, and ensured that the taxes were paid to the Persian government. In that way compensatory power contributes to both the maintenance of a segment of the population and to continued peaceful relations with Persia.

## CONCLUSION

While it has not been possible in this review to touch on every aspect of power and authority in ancient Israel, the primary point being made here is that nearly everything that they experienced or did in their communities was governed and influenced by their sense of kinship. Furthermore, their understanding of the concepts of honour and shame provided a foundation for behaviour, education, legal principles, and economic interaction and exchange [see Chapter 12 in this volume]. In the course of their evolution as a nation, even as they interacted with other political entities, both on a par with themselves and with massive, predatory empires, they continued to reflect a sense of collective identity and collective memory that framed their story and reminded their leaders what was expected of them.

Ultimately, what ancient Israel's story has to say about the exercise of power and the mantle of authority acquired or inherited by heads of household, village elders, chiefs, kings and priests is the tale of a people always striving to maintain their hold on the land. Certainly, that was not always easy given the difficulties of a marginal and uncertain physical environment and their spatial placement at a crossroads between empires. However, by creating a social contract that required communities to care for the needs of all, including widows, orphans and strangers, they placed their leaders and others who were often tempted to abuse their authority on notice that they would be judged themselves by the standards of the law that governed all the people.

Power and authority are tricky concepts. They permeate societies, both ancient and modern, and at their best they provide structure for acceptable behaviour and a firm and hopefully reasonable hand in governing these societies. By examining how power and authority are expressed in terms of the exercise of, or restraints on the use of, force, on the distribution and use of natural and human resources, and on the inculcation of beliefs and social standards it is possible to grasp a sense of how communities are formed, are able to interact with other communities, and why they do or do not survive.

# REFERENCES

Assmann, J. (2006), *Religion and Cultural Memory: Ten Studies*, Stanford, CA: Stanford University Press.
Bannester, E.M. (1969), 'Sociodynamics: An Integrative Theorem of Power, Authority, Interfluence and Love', *American Sociological Review*, 34 (3): 374–93.
Benjamin, D.C. (2017), *The Social World of Deuteronomy: A New Feminist Commentary*, Cambridge: James Clarke.
Cartledge, T.W. (2001), *1 & 2 Samuel*, Macon, GA: Smyth & Helwys.
Chaney, M.L. (1989), 'Bitter Bounty: The Dynamics of Political Economy Critiqued by the Eighth-Century Prophets', in R.L. Stivers (ed.), *Reformed Faith and Economics*, 15–30, Lanham, MD: University Press of America.
Chaney, M.L. (2017), 'Producing Peasant Poverty: Debt Instruments in Amos 2.6b–8, 13–16', in *Peasants, Prophets, and Political Economy: The Hebrew Bible in Social Perspective*, 191–204, Eugene, OR: Cascade Books.
Cogan, M. (2001), *I Kings: A New Translation with Introduction and Commentary*, New York: Doubleday.
Cogan, M. and H. Tadmor (1988), *II Kings: A New Translation with Introduction and Commentary*, Garden City, NY: Doubleday.
Cook, S.L. (1999), 'The Tradition of Mosaic Judges: Past Approaches and New Directions', in S.L. Cook and S.C. Winter (eds), *On the Way to Nineveh: Studies in Honor of George M. Landes*, 286–315, Atlanta, GA: Scholars Press.
Crenshaw, J.L. (1998), *Education in Ancient Israel: Across the Deadening Silence*, New York: Doubleday.
Esler, P.F. (2006), 'David and the Ammonite War: A Narrative and Social-Scientific Interpretation of 2 Samuel 10–12', in P.F. Esler (ed.), *Ancient Israel: The Old Testament in Its Social Context*, 191–207, Minneapolis, MN: Fortress.
Evans, P.S. (2017), 'Creating a New "Great Divide": The Exoticization of Ancient Culture in Some Recent Applications of Orality Studies to the Bible', *JBL*, 136 (4): 749–64.
Frymer-Kensky, T. (1998), 'Virginity in the Bible', in V.H. Matthews, B.M. Levinson and T. Frymer-Kensky (eds), *Gender and Law in the Hebrew Bible and the Ancient Near East*, 79–96, JSOTSup 262, Sheffield: Sheffield Academic Press.
Galbraith, J.K. (1983), *The Anatomy of Power*, Boston, MA: Houghton Mifflin.
Glanville, M. (2018), 'The *Gēr* (Stranger) in Deuteronomy: Family for the Displace', *JBL*, 137 (3): 599–623.
Goelet, O., Jr and B.A. Levine (1998), 'Making Peace in Heaven and on Earth: Religious and Legal Aspects of the Treaty Between Ramesses II and Hattusili III', in M. Lubetski, C. Gottlieb and S. Keller (eds), *Boundaries of the Ancient Near Eastern World: A Tribute to Cyrus H. Gordon*, 252–99, JSOTSup 273, Sheffield: Sheffield Academic Press.
Herzfeld, M. (2015), 'Anthropology and the Inchoate Intimacies of Power', *American Ethnologist*, 42 (1): 18–32.
Hooper, M. (1983), 'The Motivational Bases of Political Behavior: A New Concept and Measurement Procedure', *Public Opinion Quarterly*, 47 (4): 497–515.
Hopkins, D.C. (1983), 'The Dynamics of Agriculture in Monarchical Israel', in K.H. Richards (ed.), *Society of Biblical Literature 1983: Seminar Papers*, 177–202, Chico, CA: Scholars Press.

Lemos, T.M. (2006), 'Shame and Mutilation of Enemies in the Hebrew Bible', *JBL*, 125 (2): 225–41.

Lincoln, B. (1994), *Authority: Construction and Corrosion*, Chicago: University of Chicago Press.

Lipschits, O., O. Sergi and I. Koch (2011), 'Judahite Stamped and Incised Jar Handles: A Tool for Studying the History of Late Monarchic Judah', *TA*, 38 (1): 5–41.

Magdalene, F.R. (2015), 'Trying the Crime of Abuse of Royal Authority in the Divine Courtroom and the Incident of Naboth's Vineyard', in A. Mermelstein and S.E. Holtz (eds), *The Divine Courtroom in Comparative Perspective*, 167–245, Leiden: E.J. Brill.

Matthews, V.H. (1999), 'Treading the Winepress: Actual and Metaphorical Viticulture in the Ancient Near East', in A. Brenner and J.W. van Heuter (eds), *Food and Drink in the Biblical Worlds*, 19–32, Semeia 86, Atlanta, GA: Scholars Press.

Matthews, V.H. (2003), 'Physical Space, Imagined Space, and "Lived Space" in Ancient Israel', *BTB*, 33 (1): 12–20.

Matthews, V.H. (2008), *More than Meets the Ear: Discovering the Hidden Contexts of Old Testament Conversations*, Grand Rapids, MI: Eerdmans.

Matthews, V.H. and D.C. Benjamin (1993), *Social World of Ancient Israel, 1250–587 BCE*, Peabody, MA: Hendrickson.

Matthews, V.H. and D.C. Benjamin (2016), *Old Testament Parallels: Laws and Stories from the Ancient Near East*, 4th edn, New York: Paulist Press.

Meyers, C. (2005), *Exodus*, New York: Cambridge University Press.

Meyers, C. (2006), 'Hierarchy or Heterarchy? Archaeology and the Theorizing of Israelite Society', in S. Gitin, J.E. Wright and J.P. Dessel (eds), *Confronting the Past: Archaeological and Historical Essays on Ancient Israel in Honor of William G. Dever*, 245–54, Winona Lake, IN: Eisenbrauns.

Milgrom, J. (2001), *Leviticus 23–27: A New Translation with Introduction and Commentary*, New York: Doubleday.

Na'aman, N. (2013), 'Notes on the Temple "Restorations" of Jehoash and Josiah', *VT*, 63 (4): 640–51.

Nelson, R.D. (2002), *Deuteronomy: A Commentary*, Louisville, KY: Westminster John Knox Press.

Popitz, H. (2017), *Phenomena of Power: Authority, Domination, and Violence*, New York: Columbia University Press.

Premnath, D.N. (1988), 'Latifundialization and Isaiah 5.8–10', *JSOT*, 13 (40): 49–60.

Rheinstein, M., ed. (1967), *Max Weber on Law in Economy and Society*, New York: Simon and Schuster.

Rollston, C.A. (2006), 'Scribal Education in Ancient Israel: The Old Hebrew Epigraphic Evidence', *BASOR*, 344: 47–74.

Sanders, S.L. (2012), 'From People to Public in the Iron Age Levant', in G. Wilhelm (ed.), *Organization, Representation, and Symbols of Power in the Ancient Near East*, 191–211, Winona Lake, IN: Eisenbrauns.

Schaper, J. (1997), 'The Temple Treasury Committee in the Times of Nehemiah and Ezra', *VT*, 47 (2): 200–6.

Stager, L.E. (1985), 'The Archaeology of the Family in Ancient Israel', *BASOR*, 260: 1–35.

Sutherland, R.K. (1992), 'Israelite Political Theories in Joshua 9', *JSOT*, 17 (53): 65–74.

Tappy, R.E., P.K. McCarter, M.J. Lundberg and B. Zuckerman (2006), 'An Abecedary of the Mid-Tenth Century B.C.E. from the Judean Shephelah', *BASOR*, 344: 5–46.

Victoria, J.L.E. (2016), 'Anthropology of Power: Beyond State-Centric Politics', *Anthropological Theory*, 16 (2/3): 249–62.

Weingart, K. (2019), '"All These Are the Twelve Tribes of Israel": The Origins of Israel's Kinship Identity', *NEA*, 82 (1): 24–31.

Whitelam, K.W. (1979), *The Just King: Monarchical Judicial Authority in Ancient Israel*, JSOTSup 12, Sheffield: JSOT Press.

Willis, T. (2001), *The Elders of the City: A Study of the Elders-Laws in Deuteronomy*, Atlanta, GA: Society of Bible Literature.

Wilson, R.R. (1983), 'Israel's Judicial System in the Preexilic Period', *Jewish Quarterly Review*, 74 (2): 229–48.

Wrong, D.H. (1997), *Power: Its Forms, Bases, and Uses*, 2nd edn, New Brunswick, NJ: Transaction.

Ziegler, Y. (2007), '"So Shall God Do . . .": Variations of an Oath Formula and its Literary Meaning', *JBL*, 126 (1): 59–81.

# CHAPTER NINE

# Economic anthropology and the Hebrew Bible

ROGER S. NAM

## INTRODUCTION

In its simplest distillation, economics is the study of systems of production, consumption and allocation of limited resources. For ancient societies, the modern academic field of economics provides limited value. Modern economic theory is highly theoretical, and tested against robust data sets. Such data is easily collectible today, but elusive in historical times. For example, consider the massive amounts of data generated by a single company such as Uber. The company is able to store and quickly sort through economic data sets against an array of factors such as time, distance and location, and to measure it against an equally dizzying array of factors for potential suppliers. Even the most generous historical sources, in terms of text and archaeological setting, cannot provide a comparable set of data. Besides the problem of lack of data for the biblical world, modern economics, particularly in the Western world, is governed by assumptions associated with capitalism, such as supply and demand. Anthropology allows us to challenge such assumptions and seek to understand an emic economic world according to whatever evidence is available. Therefore, for studies of economics in the biblical world, anthropology can serve as a much more productive avenue

Anthropology is especially valuable in that our modern economic assumptions are often subconscious. Particularly in the modern Western world, we are so accustomed to factors like prices and taxes, as well as activities such as purchasing goods and earning wages, that we do not even think about the mechanics of exchange. Consequently, there is such a strong tendency to superimpose these modern economic assumptions onto our understanding of ancient worlds. Such instincts are anachronistic and can mislead us in reconstructing social contexts and impoverish our understanding of biblical settings. To aid our interpretations, economic anthropology serves two interlocking purposes. First, anthropology can provide theoretical frames for our reconstructions. Whereas data is limited, certain stock terms of economic anthropology such as patron/client or reciprocity have been refined through studies that cross multiple cultural boundaries. These terms can then bring robust explanatory power to social systems. Second, economic anthropology can catalyse our imaginations to a wider array of possibilities. These possibilities help to hone our own reconstructions and give alternatives to our understanding of how economic systems can work. As an example, economic anthropology can interrogate seemingly axiomatic assumptions that govern our own analyses, such as the concept of unlimited wants, which has been a lasting hallmark of modern economic study.

This chapter will introduce the reader to economic anthropology as a tool to build the capacity for reconstructing more nuanced understandings of the economics of the biblical world and, in turn, better biblical readings. I will begin with a brief review of the research on economics of the biblical world and follow with the development of economic anthropology within its own intellectual history. I will then describe the nature of the sources specific to the Hebrew Bible economic world in an effort to apply different anthropological concepts, using different modes of exchange as seen in biblical and ancient Near Eastern studies. Exchange is highlighted as an activity that is traceable and necessarily interconnected, but not comprehensive. The chapter will close with suggestions on how the field of economic anthropology can continue to refine our understandings of economics in the Hebrew Bible.

## A SURVEY OF ECONOMICS AND BIBLICAL STUDIES

Explicit attention to economics in the biblical world is still in a relatively nascent stage. For so much of the modern period of biblical studies, scholars largely neglected an intentional focus on the economic systems of the Hebrew Bible. Instead of looking at broader economic systems, scholars tended to concentrate economic studies with more direct relation to theology and particular social settings behind biblical genres. Prophetic literature tended to focus on the specific historical contexts, such as the so-called eighth-century prophets. Wisdom literature, particularly the Proverbs, received much attention in economic interpretation as these texts promised wealth according to action in the line of *Tun-Ergehen-Zusammenhang* of ancient Near Eastern wisdom literature. Other approaches have examined themes with economic impact such as the role of the temple centralization or liberation approaches. None of these studies made a serious attempt at understanding the economic structures of ancient Israel. Similarly, most histories of ancient Israel did not attempt to articulate any explicit description of economic assumptions behind their reconstructions, despite the pervasive role of economics in the unfolding of political histories. This was true across the spectrum of Israelite histories, between conservative maximalist views to more sceptical historical positions. These works frequently use words like 'market', 'investment' and 'purchase' without any clarifying description of such terms. Economic anthropology can better identify our understanding of such components of an economy.

Moshe Elat's modern Hebrew language work, *Economic Relations in the Lands of the Bible (1000–539 BCE)*, published in 1977, was one of the first monographs focused primarily on economic analysis (Elat 1977). Elat utilized the Neo-Assyrian tribute lists to understand the movement of different commodities within the southern Levant. He then modelled an intricate network of exchange within the Neo-Assyrian Empire, including the Arabian Peninsula, Egypt, Phoenicia and with the biggest chapter on Israel and Judah. Overall, Elat assumed a broadly subsistence agriculture on the household level and movement within the greater empire according to modern capitalist assumptions. Elat was severely criticized, not for his economic analysis, but more for his maximalist historical reconstructions based on biblical texts. In 1983, Morris Silver published *Prophets and Markets*, the first English-language work that attempted to describe the economic structures of the Hebrew Bible.[1] Unlike Elat, who did not engage with other

---

[1] See also Silver 1986 and 1995; see critiques in Nam 2012a: 23.

viewpoints of economics, Silver explicitly argued for a pervasive capitalist economy in the Old Testament world. Silver uncritically accepted economies of the ancient world as parallel to modern economies.

Studies in Levantine archaeology provided another avenue to explore the nature of economies in the biblical world. The movements of processual archaeology and post-processual archaeology ignited research agendas that were more intellectually honest than any alleged pursuit of 'pure' historical reconstruction. These movements questioned methods and epistemologies, and thereby opened the way for more nuanced understandings of the complexities of Iron Age economies in the wake of empire. Many of these studies centred on the role of Assyria in economic exchange. Lawrence Stager suggested port-power theory as an interpretive frame, in which waterways connected local village clusters in the highlands to more established markets of the Phoenician coast.[2] Some connected the Assyrian Empire to the development of specialized industry according to a sort of economic opportunity cost, yet without full-blown capitalism (Faust and Weiss 2005). Other studies have considered the intentionality of Assyrian imperialism in the development of South Arabian incense trade.[3] Metrological studies also have investigated exchange modes, whether through studies of extant inscribed weights indicating insignificance of Judah in the wider orbit of the ancient world or the idea that the plentiful weights in even modest domestic contexts reveal a more thriving market economy (Kletter 1998; Katz 2008). More recently, a survey of the abundant sealings around Persian-period Yehud may reveal an intricate redistributive network of goods centred around Jerusalem and then a secondary administrative centre of Ramat Rahel (Lipschits 2021).

The last decade has seen the development of economic study of the biblical world accelerate. It is possible the Great Recession of 2008 and the democratization of biblical studies as an academic guild has allowed for renewed conversations on the nature of economy, particularly as related to inequalities (Nam 2020). These movements align with faith communities developing more interest in social concerns and looking for more rigorous biblical understandings to support such interests. Many studies have emerged.[4] One particularly impactful study is Roland Boer's *The Sacred Economy* (2015). This book was significant in utilizing the method of *régulation* theory, an offshoot of the Annales school that integrated economic life in the wider religious sphere. Boer argues that regulation is a procedure to navigate crisis in a way that can reinforce exploitation of the periphery. Such regulation can appear in the form of religious obligation. Thus, the very first religious centres fostered exploitation, but they reached an apex during the Neo-Assyrian times. This integration of the religious and economic spheres was long known in Assyriological studies of temple economies. Boer's work brought this conversation to biblical studies, where the guild was still sorting through the Great Recession and its impact on academic studies in arenas such as the academic job market and communities of faith wrestling with smaller endowments and reduced gifting.

---

[2] Stager introduced this concept to Late Bronze Age trade, but two of his students applied port power to Iron Age II systems, see Stager 2001; Master 2003; Aznar 2005.
[3] More recent studies have emphasized the flourishing trade in South Arabian spices due to broad contours of freedom and security through a *Pax Assyriaca* over a direct colonizing plan; see Bienkowski and van der Steen 2001.
[4] Some representative examples in Hebrew Bible studies include Adams 2014 and Altmann 2016, and in New Testament studies, Hall 2019 and Quigley 2021.

All of these studies have advanced the study of our understanding of the complex economies of the Hebrew Bible. But with the notable exception of Boer and a few others, many of these studies have not fully engaged with anthropological theories.[5] As economic anthropology continues to mature as a social science, biblical scholars may be more eager to look to these theories to frame their analyses.

## ECONOMIC ANTHROPOLOGY

It is difficult to overstate the dominant impact of Adam Smith (1723–90) in the intellectual history of economics. His publication of *An Inquiry into the Nature and Causes of the Wealth of Nations* became the foundation of our understanding of classic political economy. Smith advocated for unregulated free markets as keys to efficiency and even equity. Smith argued that such markets allow individual free will to collectively form the most effective distribution of limited resources. He summed up this idea with a well-quoted statement, 'It is not from the benevolence of the butcher, brewer, or the baker, that we expect our dinner, but from regard to their own interest' (Smith 1937 [1776] I: 82). Collectively, private interests would aggregate into collective benefit. Smith determined such free interest as so powerful that it served as an 'invisible hand,' guiding individual suppliers to decisions that would automatically be most beneficial for the common good. In advocating for a free market, Smith was protesting government intervention. He advocated for minimal government restrictions except for the protection of economic freedoms and the maintenance of true markets. Smith regarded the motivations of government officials as suspect, and less optimal than broad inputs of a collective population. In a truly free market, each person makes individual decisions that then motivates production in a way to meet the demands of the majority. Whenever possible, Smith hoped to even privatize classic public goods like bridges and highways. Interestingly, alongside *Wealth of Nations*, Smith supported a free market with certain assumptions of morality. He described this in his more philosophically oriented treatise, *The Theory of Moral Sentiments* (1976 [1759]), which emphasized the importance of altruism in humanity. Today's discourse on the morality of free markets has largely abandoned the philosophical underpinnings that informed Smith's advocacy of open capitalism.

Smith's advocacy for free markets met criticism. Perhaps most famously in the Western world, Thomas Malthus (1766–1834) stated that population growth would place a ceiling on the upper limits of production.[6] David Ricardo (1772–1823) tied such limits to arable land, as it was the most important resource directly tied to capacities for food production. These limits necessitated international trade to invoke mutual comparative benefit. John Stuart Mill (1806–73) quantified the measure of utility for individual countries in a macroeconomic world, with all of these inputs resulting in his own mechanism of price determination. Carl Menger (1840–1921) and William Stanley Jevons (1835–82) highlighted the concept of marginality as a powerful tool to determine distribution and complex systems of labour. Perhaps one of the strongest correctives to Adam Smith was John Maynard Keynes (1883–1946). The Great Depression forced economists to confront potential failure of unregulated markets with the reality of widespread poverty. Keynes

---

[5] Aside from Boer, see social scientific studies by Stansell (2006) and Matthews (2012).
[6] For a review of the reception of Adam Smith in the nineteenth century, see Nam 2012a: 30–4.

argued that certain economic cycles necessitated periods of government interventions. For Keynes, such interventions could temporarily prop up demand through arenas like public works, and this theory was implemented by Roosevelt's New Deal. Theoretically, these types of interventions would maintain stable production and wages during periods of depression. Eventually, Keynesian economics fell out of favour to a free market neoliberalism, reaching a pinnacle during the 1980s through scholars like Milton Friedman and political leaders like Ronald Reagan and Margaret Thatcher. But interestingly, the Great Recession of 2008 spurred a renewal of neo-Keynesian economics as once again, real life showed the dangers of purely unregulated markets. The Great Recession made evident the massive market inequalities that required some degree of intervention. These so-called neo-Keynesians were active before 2008, but the Recession pushed their research to more prominent spaces.

Despite all of these challenges to Adam Smith, classical political economy has continued to uphold the same Hobbesian presuppositions of economic actors. These presuppositions are largely tied to the heuristic figure of *Homo economicus*, who has the following characteristics: (1) acts selfishly; (2) exchanges for optimal utility; (3) makes decisions based on individual needs in a limited world; and (4) serves individual needs. These assumptions remain so axiomatic in Western thought that interpreters will subconsciously implant these traits onto modern treatments of ancient worlds. In fact, people only began explicitly characterizing *Homo economicus* as a response to competing economic theories.

Two of these competing theories deserve mention as we consider the field of biblical and ancient Near Eastern studies. First, Karl Marx (1818–83) had a significant impact in ancient Near Eastern histories as well as liberation theology (cf. Marx and Engels 2012 [1848]). Marx understood capitalism to occupy a central stage that could only lead to class struggle among economic actors. This struggle would eventually give way to communism. Theories of Marxism and its later trajectories were particularly attractive for ancient Near Eastern scholars for their emphasis on means of production. Marx and Engels saw the ancient (their language = 'oriental') world as highly despotic, thus preventing individuals from accumulating substantive resources. As a result, these economies were stagnant. Later interpreters developed this idea of an Asiatic Mode of Production that allowed for long-term stagnation due to exclusive controls over means of production. The pinnacle of this theory was the publication of Karl Wittfogel's *Oriental Despotism: A Comparative Study of Total Power* (1957). Wittfogel compared the Soviet Union, China and ancient Near Eastern economies as deeply dependent on centralized irrigation as a prime means of production. A group of scholars from Russia (Diakonoff, Dandamaev), as well as Western European scholars (Liverani, Zaccagnini) created hybrid versions on the Asiatic mode.[7] Several of these adaptations were centred on a two-sector model that included classes of both enslaved persons and separate free persons, who worked outside of official royal and temple sectors. These free people had limited access to their own means of production, namely their own ancestral lands. In recent years, more scholars have advocated for an offshoot of Marxism called 'world-system,' as articulated by American scholar Immanuel Wallerstein (1974). The world-system theorized that supply and demand made asymmetrical exploitation possible with a core

---

[7] Russian scholars include Diakonoff 1982; Dandamaev 1984. Prominent Western scholars include Liverani 1979; Zaccagnini 1989.

centre that continues to extract from the periphery. The extraction could transcend political borders, thus the descriptor, 'world'. Although Wallerstein developed the theory to apply to capitalist periods, it was an extremely attractive explanatory resource for the ancient world. In biblical studies, Boer's *The Sacred Economy* (2015) is one of the more influential Marxist interpretations of the wider economy with other interpretations adopting Marx's progression of clashes.

In addition, Max Weber (1864–1920) had significant influence over the interpretations of ancient economies. Unlike Marx, Weber never developed ideas of exploitation and class consciousness. Weber was actually an economics professor, firmly grounded in an era of classic political economy of Adam Smith. But Weber was unsatisfied with scientific aspects of economic study, and instead sought to identify underlying patterns to explain social behaviour in more holistic terms. Weber thought that formal economic behaviour, as described by *Homo economicus*, was a limited ideal type (*Verstehendes*) (Swedberg 1999). This type of economic behaviour was restricted to Western, capitalist systems but was by no means a universal value. Weber argued that non-economic motivations must factor into decision-making. He summarized this by protesting pure rationalist economic theories, stating, 'Economics is not a science of nature and its qualities but of people and their needs' (Weber 1976 [1897]: 32). In a sweeping statement, Weber challenged both the method of economic study as a pure science, as well as the universality of its perceived outcomes. As an illustration, Weber stated that patrimonialism was a competing ideal type in the ancient Near East. Kings and priests patterned their behaviour against patrilineal kinship structures, thereby invoking a right to govern. David Schloen (2001) cogently applied the concept of patrimonialism to the Late Bronze Age Levantine societies. He identifies a basic household model as expanding to fit a broader society with the king as a fictive patriarchal leader. This social position gives the king the right to control the resources of the family, parallel to the patriarch of an extended kinship family. Metaphors and architectural structures are designed to reify this fictive kinship structure. Schloen suggests that during the Iron Age, the arrival of 'world empires' (Assyrian, Babylonian, Persian) interrupted this kinship network. Overall, Weber's great contribution was distancing the study of economics from formal scientific inquiry. Cultural influences and social pressure can drive economic decisions that contradict profit maximization.

Both Marx and Weber influenced economic theory, but the impact was limited in the Western world. The academic discipline of economics was relatively immune to these conversations. During the early twentieth century, most college textbooks were using John Stuart Mill as a basic economics introduction with viewpoints nearly unchanged from the time of Adam Smith. The essential characteristics of *Homo economicus* were still regarded as largely universal and thus axiomatic for economic study. Ethnocentrism was particularly deleterious in preventing honest consideration of non-capitalist economic systems. Non-market economies were known, but generally regarded as unsophisticated, and thus unworthy of observation.

It was within such a context that economic anthropology as an academic discipline arose, symbolically through the work of Bronisław Malinowski (1884–1942), who pioneered approaches to anthropological study. Before Malinowski, most anthropological research was done from the comfort of a ship with short-term observations. By living among a Melanesian tribe and learning their native language, he pioneered a much more immersive approach to anthropological study, which he documented in *Argonauts of the Western Pacific* (1922). Although Malinowski was trained in the classic political economy of Adam Smith, he observed a highly efficient market civilization that did not reflect the behaviours of *Homo economicus*. In particular, Malinowski observed a ceremonial trade facilitated by long-distance canoe through a network called the *Kula* ring. This trade was highly sophisticated and technically advanced, as canoes traversed many miles of dangerous open ocean. In observing the *Kula* ring exchange network, Malinowski determined three broad categories of exchange: subsistence, prestige and *Kula*. The subsistence category involved the bringing of yams to village chiefs for use in public feasting. The prestige category was gendered with women exchanging banana leaves, which may have had some numinous protection against evil in public ceremonies such as funerals or weddings. Men traded axe heads, clay pots, tusks and other items for dowries, fees and prizes. The *Kula* category consisted of beads and necklaces in overtly ceremonial exchanges. Each of these three categories of exchange happened simultaneously in deliberate, regular patterns with a public *Kula* exchange in the foreground, and less formal exchanges on smaller household levels.

Malinowski concluded that *Kula* trade was not based on any motivations of supply and demand. Instead, Malinowski observed that the Trobriand Islanders of Melanesia were governed by a completely different set of economic assumptions, later playfully termed *Homo reciprocans*. This civilization was not primitive: rather, they were highly sophisticated and complex with a connected economic structure across many different islands separated by dangerous shark-infested waters. The Trobriand Islanders presented an economy vastly different in their understanding of classical political economy of maximizing utility. Rather, they made economic decisions based on social relationships, honour, value and kinship obligation. If the study of economics was the study of allocating limited resources among unlimited wants, the Trobriand Islander was upsetting that definition because they seemed to not have unlimited wants. The *Kula* ring trade showed a vastly contrasting system to the assumptions of *Homo economicus* (Table 9.1).

Malinowski set up *Homo reciprocans* as antithetical to *Homo economicus* in an indirect attack on the ethnocentrism of then prevailing economic theory. Many followed Malinowski to develop broader economic theories to account for non-Western systems. The assumptions of *Homo economicus* were not completely disregarded but adjusted for different cultures. Basic wants were culturally conditioned.

Malinowski's student, Raymond Firth (1901–2002), sought to expand Malinowski's theories by observing the Māori tribes of his native New Zealand (Firth 1929). There,

Table 9.1 *Homo economicus* versus *Homo reciprocans*

| Homo economicus | Homo reciprocans |
|---|---|
| 1  People act selfishly | People are socially motivated and inherently cooperative |
| 2  People exchange to maximize individual utility | People exchange for the community |
| 3  There is universal scarcity | Needs/wants are largely met |
| 4  When people are rational and have knowledge, they seek to maximize utility | People follow a complex set of traditional values, duties, obligations, beliefs, magic, social ambition and vanities |
| 5  The individual is the unit of economic analysis | The extended family or tribe is the unit of economic analysis |

Firth recognized the powerful forces of prestige and honour that motivated activity over any market motivations. Firth stated that Māori cultural norms governed their own patterns of exchange. Firth said that such motivation could fall under the general guise of supply and demand as people were willing to maximize their own utility of prestige over commodities. In his book, *The Gift: Forms and Functions of Exchange in Archaic Societies*, French scholar Marcel Mauss (1872–1950) adapted Malinowski to emphasize a kinship framework underlying exchange (Mauss 1954 [1925]). Mauss investigated the complex set of social forces behind a reciprocal gift. He stated that kinship relations were the core motivation for obligations within a group. Gifts were fundamentally different from commodities because of their social signals. And the exchange of gifts was dominant in Malinowski's *Kula* ring and Firth's Māori trade, in contrast to commodities of industrial societies. Gifts are not utilitarian in the same way as commodities, but the gifts have a crucial role in creating and maintaining kinship relations. Thus, gift exchange must take into account the social relationships between the worlds of the giver and receiver, and not merely the maximization of individual utility.

These studies were highly influential in the work of Karl Polanyi (1886–1964), who quoted generously from these anthropologists. Polanyi was a lawyer, who grew up in early twentieth-century Hungary and sought to understand the rise of fascism in relation to the economic turmoil of events like the Great Depression or post–First World War poverty. He eventually moved to the United States and became colleagues with renowned ancient Near Eastern historian, Leo Oppenheim (1904–74). This partnership helped disseminate anthropological ideas of exchange to the field of ancient Near Eastern studies. In his landmark work, *The Great Transformation* (1944), Polanyi argued that market economies did not truly exist until the Industrial Revolution. Rather, the rise of industrial production was the 'great transformation' in which economic activity was removed from social relationships. Industrial economies emphasized production efficiencies and distribution according to supply and demand, but such conditions were not universal. The mechanics of unregulated industry necessitated this degree of socially disembedded trade. Polanyi understood this transformation as disastrous for humanity, and he interpreted much of the chaos of the early twentieth century as a reaction to this great transformation. Polanyi believed that distribution according to social values over supply and demand was much more beneficial to humanity.

Polanyi described multiple modes of exchange. These descriptors remain stock terms in economic anthropology. He saw reciprocity as a form of symmetrical socially embedded trade across some real or fictive kinship relation. Redistribution was an asymmetrical form, in which a centre would extract from the periphery and redistribute back to some degree of social obligation. In his later years, Polanyi described a form of exchange as competitive feasting, in which a local power would display greatness through a feast with invited participants and thereby create allyship with the participants.[8] Polanyi described market exchange as a modern result of the Industrial Revolution, and completely absent in ancient economies. Although few people subscribe to this view today, one must understand that Polanyi was reacting to his own intellectual period, in which many people still saw *Homo economicus* as a universal figure in all history. In his later years, particularly in his posthumous book, he conceded some degree of market

---

[8] For a summary and an application to ancient Israel, see Nam 2012b.

exchange in antiquity.⁹ Polanyi was quite influential in ancient Near Eastern history, though decidedly less so in biblical studies. As most surviving ancient Near Eastern texts are economic, his work spawned rigorous conversations on the nature of markets. In order to defend his position, Polanyi and his followers outlined a set of descriptions on two types of market economies: formalist, or that describing a primarily supply-and-demand regulation, and substantivist, or an economy that was essentially socially disembedded. Much of twentieth-century economic history was a reaction to this discussion. In the twenty-first century, these debates have largely subsided as scholars recognize that economies were mixed and beyond straight binary categories.

The remainder of this chapter will explore specific social contexts of the Hebrew Bible and how economic anthropology can equip a more nuanced interpretation of biblical texts. But first, we must briefly describe the nature of sources as we seek to build some of the ways that economic anthropology can help understand the social contexts of the Hebrew Bible.

## DESCRIPTION OF SOURCES

Before we enter descriptions of exchange, I will briefly review three broad categories of sources in reconstructions of different ancient economies. First, textual evidence is primary, particularly extant extra-biblical evidence. This includes monumental inscriptions, ostraca, papyri and parchment, as well as graffiti and cave writings. Some of the valuable sources include low-level literary such as sealings, bullae and shekel weights. These examples can be drawn from the lands of Israel and Judah but also in the Transjordan, as well as from neighbouring empires of the northern Levant, Egypt or Mesopotamia. The first reconstructions of economy took evidence from Neo-Assyrian tribute lists, but the southern Levant itself has a strong amount of evidence in different formats. Such evidence need not be limited to economic texts, but literary epics and epistolary evidence can also inform economic reconstructions. The vast economic documents of the ancient Near East in cuneiform also provide excellent sources to reconstruct general contours of different ancient economies. In recent years, biblical scholars have received multiple gifts of sources. For example, the 2014 publication of the Āl Yāḫūdū archives, situated in Nippur, document a group of exiled Judeans displaced into a certain region of Nippur in order to work in labour-intensive date and barley fields (Pearce and Wunsch 2014). Thankfully for biblical studies, a group of European scholars are rapidly producing first editions of different Persian-period economic corpora to reconstruct its economic network.¹⁰

Alongside extant texts, biblical texts also have value. Of course, these are ideological texts subject to multiple revisions, and its contents are not dependable for historical reconstructions. With that said, certain portions of economic information are merely background and not ideological. Such texts may show modern readers, at the very least,

---

⁹ It is crucial to understand that Polanyi's terminology of reciprocity, redistribution and market exchange all hold to a wide semantic range in anthropology and even within Polanyi's own writings. Gareth Dale writes, 'Polanyi rarely feels the need to clarify which of these uses he has in mind, although he is aware that different definitions are in play' (Dale 2010: 73).

¹⁰ In particular, the Achaemenid Taxation Project had multiple publications in Jacobs, Henkelman and Stolper 2017.

what was plausible in ancient Israel. For example, biblical texts can be descriptive of economic activity, such as the purchase of a tract of land in Benjaminite country in Jeremiah 32. We can understand that gift-giving and gift-refusing were common place, and that people depended on land and kinship. We know that inheritances were patrilineal, but with exceptions in certain cases for the welfare of the family as with the daughters of Zelophehad. We know from biblical law that payments were both incentives and penalties as well as ways to make ransom. Women, particularly foreign women, were subject to more economic dangers. Land seemed to be a primary asset. By the eighth-century prophets, there seems to be some sort of social stratification, particularly pronounced in northern Israel. On a more macroeconomic level, long-distance trade was accepted, as was tribute between polities. Towards the later end of the Hebrew Bible chronology, coinage is mentioned. These observations are not controversial to the presented ideologies, and there is little reason to overturn these historical portrayals.

In addition to texts, archaeology plays a role in sources. With archaeology, one can trace trade, whether through the pottery typologies or even examining residues of containers. One can see evidence of storage such as silos and water systems. Surveys allow for some understanding of population data. For example, most archaeology of the Persian period does show a significant shift in population and a reduction in international trade (Carter 1999). Most archaeology is centred on elite lifestyles, but more recent turns in archaeology reveal more about particular domestic residences. For example, Avraham Faust (2012) determined that the Iron Age IIB northern kingdom showed a more economically stratified community due to different levels of luxury in the domestic spaces compared to southern counterparts. Archaeology also shows long-term processes such as movements of centralization, particularly with consistent structures of royal architecture. It can also show the introduction, assimilation and even removal of certain cultural forms such as the material culture documentation of the Sea People in the southern Levant.

But textual evidence and archaeological remains are limited, haphazard and dependent on the random controls of time. The accumulation of evidence is only a small representation of the complete economic activity. Therefore, we must turn to anthropology as a way to flesh out more complete systems of ancient economies. Anthropology can provide a broader frame by which we can integrate these limited pieces of evidence into more complete systems. Through anthropology, we can observe better documented systems, such as the *Kula* ring, that may have more commonalities with the patrilineal agrarian economies of ancient Israel. In doing so, theory provides a useful frame for making sense of this limited evidence. The following pages will exam certain anthropological terms as apt descriptors for the ancient economies of Israel. But as a note, it should be said that anthropological leanings always have the danger of orientalizing interpretations. Such interpretations are avoidable. In this sense, anthropological theories will come from their own stated contexts, and frames of interpretation should be aware of the ways that the scholar may harbour orientalist tendencies. It is hoped that some self-awareness on the part of the interpreter will help mitigate against such constructions.

## RECIPROCITY

As stated above, reciprocity is a type of economic exchange characterized by symmetry between the two parties and rooted in social relationship. When introduced to the description of reciprocity, Leo Oppenheim considered it a dominant form of exchange in ancient Mesopotamia, and he even used reciprocity to characterize long-distance trade that texts seemed to invoke competitive advantage.[11] Although Oppenheim overstated reciprocity against evidence that seemed to reveal price-setting mechanisms, it is clear that long-distance trade did rely on social motivations of *Homo reciprocans* over profit motivations of *Homo economicus*. Several scholars have identified the Amarna letters as developing a sophisticated trade network among Late Bronze Age city-states marked by reciprocal exchange. These letters comprise over three hundred cuneiform epistolary texts written in a Western Peripheral Akkadian dialect, with many of the letters documenting gift exchange between political leaders. Kevin Avruch (an anthropologist and non-Assyriologist) noted the kinship language that frames all of these letters with standard obeisance language for hospitality (Avruch 2000). One letter documents a Mitanni king sending gifts to Egypt on behalf of his family with the explicit request, 'May my brother seek friendly relations with me' (EA 17:51). Another letter turns to historical precedent as Babylonian King Burraburias II tells Pharaoh, 'Since my fathers and your fathers with one another established friendly relations, they sent to one another rich presents and they refused not one another any good request' (EA 9:7–10). One particularly significant letter records a shipment from Cyprus to Egypt of a gift of ivory and asks for ivory in return. Such an exchange has absolutely no competitive advantage! The nature of this type of trade is a hallmark of reciprocal exchange, motivated by social standing and alliances over utilitarian gain. The language for gift in the Amarna letters, *šulmānu*, implies the socially embedded nature as an attempt to maintain ties. By the Late Bronze Age, *šulmānu* signalled an 'exchange between equal rank', rather than an asymmetrical tribute or obligatory taxation, that Egypt extracted from their colonized city-states. There was some limited degree of maximizing behaviour. Cyprus sent copper from its local mines, and Babylon sent lapis lazuli, accessible from the mountains of Afghanistan. But optimizing behaviour did not define the essence of this trade. This is a nuance of reciprocity. It can take into account some degree of scarcity and competitive advantage, but at its core, it was defined and motivated by forming and maintaining social relationships between parties.

This model seems apt for much of the portrayals of biblical exchange. Two examples will suffice. In Genesis 23, Sarah dies and Abraham attempts to purchase a burial field for her. The object of purchase itself is not a subsistence item. A burial field does nothing that is strictly utilitarian. It is not necessary for life, but by definition, quite the opposite. Abraham is sojourning in a foreign land, so he attempts to buy a burial plot, knowing that it is not in his right to do so. A high price will not motivate the purchase in this social setting. Rather, Abraham gives a plea, not out of riches, but out of the social function of burial in stating that he is a foreigner. The Hittites' response shows that they are not interested in price optimization, but rather they are more interested in honour and custom. They reply in Gen. 23.6, 'Hear us, my lord; you are a mighty prince among us. Bury your dead in the choicest of our burial places; none of us will withhold from you any burial ground for burying your dead'. Presumably, they wish to establish a relationship with Abraham, and they freely use obeisance language. They do not even ask for payment, but Abraham later volunteers 'full price'. Here in this passage, there is no price negotiation, and thus no profit maximization. Rather, Genesis 23 shows the two parties arguing on a type of competition of deference, with the Hittites wanting to gift the land and Abraham

---

[11] 'The traders have become royal emissaries carrying precious gifts from one ruler to the other and are sometimes called ša mandatti, a designation which seems to refer to the source of capital' (Oppenheim 1977: 93).

insisting on payment of four hundred shekels of silver. Abraham does not use the land for any wealth generation, rather it serves as a permanent connection between Abraham and the Hittites.

Aside from individual reciprocity, the Hebrew Bible gives examples of elite reciprocity among political leaders. 1 Kings 10 is a prime example. Within this passage, the Queen of Sheba comes from afar to test Solomon against the rumours she has heard. The passage begins with emphasis on Sheba's enormous riches: vast amounts of gold, spices and precious stones that she gives to Solomon in deference to his intellectual powers. In return, Sheba gets reciprocal gifting in 'all that she desires' in the forms of lavish hospitality for her and her retinue. Again, a reciprocal arrangement does not negate certain characteristics that invoke opportunity cost. This arrangement opens up Solomon's control of Ezion Geber on the Arabian Peninsula. Also, the insertion in 1 Kgs 10.11–12 on the economic alliance with Hiram supports a level of competitive advantage exchange. With that said, the overall narrative projects Solomon as honourable, worthy of wealth from other nations. This honour is realized in that far away polities seek to make strategic alliances with Solomon. Aspects of the passage contain subtle nods to the intimacy between Solomon and the Queen of Sheba in that later Jewish, Christian and Islamic interpretations make the relationship explicitly more sexualized.

Both of these examples show far-reaching appreciation of reciprocity as a basis for exchange. It happens on elite and non-elite levels, local and distant. Certain limited aspects of optimized behaviour do not negate the nature of this exchange as essentially socially embedded. Naturally, economic decisions would understand sourcing, whether tin from Cyprus, gold from Egypt and Nubia, or horses from Anatolian ranges. But overall, economics was a means of creating and reinforcing social relationships. In the ancient world without the concept of 'money', it is natural that exchange may reflect the *Kula* ring of the Trobriand Islander much more than the New York Stock Exchange.

## REDISTRIBUTION

Whereas reciprocity is marked by symmetrical relationships, redistribution is marked by asymmetrical moves from the periphery to a real or symbolic centre, then a certain redistribution back to the periphery. Polanyi identified reciprocity and redistribution as deeply integrated mechanisms. For example, as the Amarna letters documented reciprocal exchange across long distances, it also involved the major Late Bronze Age powers, such as the Egyptians, extracting resources to their own centres. Any centralized unit, whether as small as an extended clan or as large as an empire, must involve some form of redistribution. The centre will grow in scope and power to eventually have the capacity to facilitate large-scale resources such as irrigation. Because the relationship is asymmetrical, such extractions were often coercive and unjust. A centralized power may extract in-kind goods in exchange for a religious blessing or merely the permission to live. But states had to redistribute something, otherwise the state is totalitarian and cannot exist for perpetuity. The forms of redistribution forces questions on equity in the ancient world.

Because historical evidence favours the elite and powerful, many of the archaeological sources point to redistribution. There are biases from the past as comparatively marginalized economic units (such as the simple family, the enslaved and the wanderers) did not leave much in terms of material culture. There are also biases of the present as archaeologists overwhelmingly favoured excavations of elite structures of royal and religious settings. As an example, for ancient Israel, one can consider architecture that emerges throughout Iron Age II. Regardless of one's view on precise dating of different structures, it is clear that Iron Age II began to witness a shift in developing centralized architecture, whether different layers for Megiddo, Hazor, Gezer and other major cities (regardless of whether assigning these buildings to Solomon or a later ruler like Omri). Much of the royal architecture is defensive, thereby constituting a classic public good in which every recipient benefits equally. Of particular interest to economic distribution, the appearance of storage centres – whether in the form of long tripartite structures (Hazor, Megiddo, Lachish), grain silos or even water storage centres – are all evidence of a centre collecting resources in the form of physical labour, and redistributing in the form of preserved goods. Such mechanisms are much more efficient with a centralized power coercing this allocation of resources. Alongside building architecture, epigraphic remains point to sophisticated systems of redistribution for Israel and her neighbours. In the Moabite Inscription, King Mesha boasts of various public works to benefit the peoples such as a royal palace and reservoirs, as well as highway construction and the building of a structure of Beth-Bamot, presumably for worship. In Israel and Judah, the appearance of LMLK sealings on large storage vessels is a very visible impression of a centralized power, presumably King Hezekiah, who consolidated resources to mount a collective defence against Assyrian invasion. Other corpora of Iron Age II, such as the Samaria ostraca, Arad ostraca and Lachish letters, assume a central power that controls distribution, as well as military command.

Hebrew Bible texts show redistribution on both state and temple economies. On the state level, the portrayal of Solomon's economy shows pervasive redistributive efforts. This befits the earlier covenantal promises that would culminate in a unified monarchy, at least within the biblical narrative. In 1 Kgs 4.7, twelve divisions of the united monarchy provide in-kind contributions of food to sustain the royal household. In 1 Kgs 5.27–32, the massive scale of corvée labour provides for the construction of temple materials. 1 Kgs 8.62–63 brings offerings to the centre for usage in cultic functions. The centralization is particularly strong in 1 Kgs 9.15–32 in building defence installations throughout the country. These redistributive movements contrast with the prior era of the Judges, when individual tribes cooperated or refused redistributive efforts. For Solomon, his control is complete, so much that the text then leads to complaints of abusive levels of coercion as soon as he is succeeded by Rehoboam. A closer look at the redistributive policies of Solomon indicates the massive scale of this redistribution. His labour force of 30,000 is massive collection for an agrarian society dependent on male labour. The listing of 70,000 porters and 80,000 rock cutters notably do not directly contribute to the feeding of the nation. Add to this an enormous daily ration for his private court of flour (thirty kors), meal (sixty kors), ten fattened cattle, twenty range cattle, one hundred sheep, 40,000 horse stalls for 12,000 horses, as well as gazelles, deer, roebuck and geese. In addition, Solomon traded for skilled artisans from Tyre. All of this centralized redistributive activity gives a notion of largess to the Solomonic kingdom in that 'Judah and Israel were as numerous as the sands by the sea, eating, drinking, and rejoicing in abundance' (1 Kgs 4.20) is an allusion to the Abrahamic covenant. This abundance stood for the glory of the Lord and the fulfilment of this bold covenant. But of course, redistribution is necessarily asymmetrical, and thereby subject to corruption, which soon emerges after the succession from Solomon to Rehoboam.

Redistribution also occurs through the temple economy. Religion is hardly separable for state mechanisms of exchange. But the precision on the relation of state to temple is not always clear. In the ancient Near East, temple economies were ubiquitous and sometimes dominant in the economic landscape. As Boer (2015) notes, the integration of the religious with the economic sphere has been neglected whereas in the past, life was deeply integrated. The Jerusalem temple was no exception, with temple worship serving as a means of economic centralization and perhaps even as a foundry of collection. Ezra 3 presents the temple in such a light. With the absence of a Davidic king in the postexilic period, the Persian kings take up residence and institute royal collections through the Temple. The explicit reason was for worship, but it still constituted a redistributive movement. Ezra 3.7 reads, 'So they gave money to the masons and the carpenters, and food, drink, and oil to the Sidonians and the Tyrians to bring cedar trees from Lebanon to the sea, to Joppa, according to the grant that they had from King Cyrus of Persia.' Within this single verse, redistribution comes in the form of silver/coins for natural resources, skilled labour and the provision for such labour, and all for the construction of a temple foundation through the imperial authority of King Cyrus. Although seemingly coercive, the context uses language of offering and indicates that the movement of resources to the centre was a move of religious obedience. This is merely for the foundation of the temple. Ezra-Nehemiah would continue to set in place continuous redistribution for the maintenance of proper cultic ritual. Throughout the text of Ezra-Nehemiah, there is no explicit protest against this temple centralization, though it does appear obliquely in Neh. 5.1–13, as the taxation is apparently so oppressive as to bring the people to debt slavery.

Redistribution along with reciprocity were dominant forms of exchange. Social relationships and concomitant obligations were foundational for exchange in ancient Israel. But pure substantivism is an ideological construct in economic anthropology. In reality, we must realize some existence of modernist-like motivations in the economic life of the Hebrew Bible.

## MARKET EXCHANGE

Adam Smith constructed his views of economic behaviour as universal, applying to all societies analogous to scientific theories like gravity. To his credit, he operated during the Enlightenment era where there was a strong confidence in the ability to develop theories and verify by observations. Economic anthropology has been able to refute the universality of market motivations. In more recent years, intellectual conversations are no longer confined to either end of a formalist–substantivist binary. Rather, anthropology understands that any given economic system likely had both socially embedded forms alongside market forces. Thus, the Hebrew Bible reveals traces of some market forces.

Certain Hebrew terminology seems to imply long-distance trade. For example, the word to 'trade' (Heb. *sḥr*) has its etymology in the Semitic root to travel, but its usage in the Hebrew Bible seems to refer to price-setting markets. In Gen. 37.28, the Midianite 'traders' have no desires of social relationships with the patriarchal sons. Thus they 'trade' twenty shekels of silver for the life of Joseph. Instead of forging a relationship, this exchange seems to be a pure optimizing move. The brothers have surplus (in Joseph) and they even reason that they might as well gain financially from the exchange rather than just leaving him to die. First Isaiah also labels Sidonians as 'traders,' accusing them of excessive greed. Similar terms in the Hebrew Bible seem to indicate optimizing behaviour, such as the 'men of trading' of 1 Kgs 10.15 and the Tyrians of Ezekiel 27. Another term would be markets or literally 'outside spaces' (Heb. *ḥûṣôṯ*), a later etymologically match for the Arabic word for markets, or *suq*. In 1 Kgs 20.34, an Israelite wins the trading rights to set up markets in Damascus. Considering the central location of Damascus in trade, as well as other reference to this term in a place of markets (Jer. 37.21; possibly Zeph. 3.6), it appears that the motivation was not social cohesion with this Aramean state, but rather a vehicle for greater wealth. Other have equated this term to be parallel to the Akkadian term *karum*, or a trading outpost, which was long distance and facilitated continuous exchange.

Perhaps one of the strongest verses to imply market exchange occurs at 2 Kgs 4.7. A foreign widow, with children on the verge of debt slavery, is given a miraculous supply of oil. Without any social kin, she is commanded by the prophet to go out (or to the market?) and sell the oil and pay the debt. She complies. The text does not explain anything about a mechanism of sale, nor the process by how this kinless woman can sell. Instead, the completion of the economic transaction is merely presumed. Somehow, this woman is able to exchange her commodity and use it to satisfy the terms of her debt and release her from the debtors. This clearly must be set within an economic context where non-socially embedded trade was accessible to this woman. The setting near Shunem suggests that the place was close to the rich Jezreel Valley and likely to be a place replete with traders. In such an economic setting, kinship structures would not dominate, but market exchange would exist at some level. But the degree of market exchange within this economy cannot accurately be quantified.

This is merely a brief summary of economic anthropology and a way to utilize some of its categories to help inform readings of biblical text and their social contexts. In this limited scope, this chapter is representative and not at all exhaustive. The world of economic anthropology is so much bigger, and it is hoped that this can serve as a minor introduction to how such a lens can be profitable. Economic anthropology can help characterize all movements within economic systems, including production and consumption within social settings distinct from capitalist markets. As economic anthropology continues to mature, it is also impacting modern economics. The study of modern economics is more open than ever before to non-optimizing activities. The burgeoning field of behavioural economics hit a significant milestone with its foremost adherent Richard Thaler winning the Nobel Prize in economics in 2017, and his book, *Nudge*, becoming a *New York Times* bestseller with its second edition published in 2021. It is hoped that biblical studies can continue to draw on economic anthropology as a valuable tool in recognizing the complexity of the biblical world as so different from the present.

# REFERENCES

Adams, S.L. (2014), *Social and Economic Life in Second Temple Judea*, Louisville, KY: Westminster John Knox Press.

Altmann, P. (2016), *Economics in Persian-Period Biblical Texts: Their Interactions with Economic Developments in the Persian Period and Earlier Biblical Traditions*, FAT 109, Tübingen: Mohr Siebeck.

Avruch, K. (2000), 'Reciprocity, Equality, and Status Anxiety in the Amarna Letters', in R. Cohen and R. Westbrook (eds.), *Amarna Diplomacy: The Beginnings of International Relations*, 154–64, Baltimore, MD: Johns Hopkins University Press.

Aznar, C.A. (2005), 'Exchange Networks in the Southern Levant During the Iron Age II: A Study of Pottery Origins and Distribution', PhD diss., Harvard University, Cambridge, MA.

Bienkowski, P. and E. van der Steen (2001), 'Tribes, Trade, and Towns: A New Framework for the Late Iron Age in Southern Jordan and the Negev', *BASOR*, 323: 21–47.

Boer, R. (2015), *The Sacred Economy of Ancient Israel*, LAI, Louisville, KY: Westminster John Knox Press.

Carter, C.E. (1999), *The Emergence of Yehud in the Persian Period: A Social and Demographic Study*, JSOTSup 294, Sheffield: Sheffield Academic Press.

Dale, G. (2010), *Karl Polanyi: The Limits of Markets*, Cambridge: Polity Press.

Dandamaev, M.A. (1984), *Slavery in Babylonia: From Nabopolassar to Alexander the Great, 626–331 BC*, DeKalb: Northern Illinois University Press.

Diakonoff, I.M. (1982), 'The Structure of Near Eastern Society Before the Middle of the Second Millennium B.C.', *Oikumene*, 3: 7–100.

Elat, M. (1977), *Economic Relations in the Lands of the Bible (1000–539 BCE)*, Jerusalem: Mosad Bialek.

Faust, A. (2012), *The Archaeology of Israelite Society in Iron Age II*, Winona Lake, IN: Eisenbrauns.

Faust, A. and E. Weiss (2005), 'Judah, Philistia, and the Mediterranean World: Reconstructing the Economic System of the Seventh Century B.C.E.', *BASOR*, 338: 71–92.

Firth, R. (1929), *Primitive Economics of the New Zealand Maori*, London: G. Routledge.

Hall, C. (2019), *Insights from Reading with the Poor*, Reading the Bible in the Twenty-First Century, Minneapolis, MN: Fortress Press.

Jacobs, B., W.F.M. Henkelman and M. Stolper, eds (2017), *Die Verwaltung im Achämenidenreich: Imperiale Muster und Strukturen*, Wiesbaden: Harrassowitz.

Katz, H. (2008), *A Land of Grain and Wine . . . A Land of Olive Oil and Honey: The Economy of the Kingdom of Judah*, Jerusalem: Yad Ben-Zvi Press.

Kletter, R. (1998), *Economic Keystones: The Weight System of the Kingdom of Judah*, JSOTSup 276, Sheffield: Sheffield Academic Press.

Lipschits, O. (2021), *Age of Empires: The History and Administration of Judah in the 8th–2nd Centuries BCE in Light of the Storage-Jar Stamp Impressions*, Winona Lake, IN: Eisenbrauns.

Liverani, M. (1979), 'The Ideology of the Assyrian Empire', in M.T. Larsen (ed.), *Power and Propaganda: A Symposium on Ancient Empires*, 297–317, Mesopotamia 7, Copenhagen: Akademisk.

Malinowski, B. (1922), *Argonauts of the Western Pacific: An Account of Native Enterprise and Adventure in the Archipelagos of Melanesian New Guinea*, London: George Routledge.

Marx, K. and F. Engels (2012 [1848]), *The Communist Manifesto*, New Haven, CT: Yale University Press.

Master, D.M. (2003), 'Trade and Politics: Ashkelon's Balancing Act in the Seventh Century B.C.E.', *BASOR*, 330: 47–64.

Matthews, V.H. (2012), *The Hebrew Prophets and Their Social World: An Introduction*, 2nd edn, Grand Rapids, MI: Baker Academic.

Mauss, M. (1954 [1925]), *The Gift: Forms and Functions of Exchange in Archaic Societies*, transl. I. Cunnison, Glencoe, IL: Free Press.

Nam, R.S. (2012a), *Portrayals of Economic Exchange in the Book of Kings*, Leiden: E.J. Brill.

Nam, R.S. (2012b), 'Power Relations in the Samaria Ostraca', *PEQ*, 144 (3): 155–63.

Nam, R.S. (2020), 'Biblical Studies, COVID-19, and Our Response to Growing Inequality', *JBL*, 139 (3): 600–6.

Oppenheim, A.L. (1977), *Ancient Mesopotamia: Portrait of a Dead Civilization*, rev. edn, Chicago: University of Chicago Press.

Pearce, L.E. and C. Wunsch (2014), *Documents of Judean Exiles and West Semites in Babylonia in the Collection of David Sofer*, Bethesda, MD: CDL Press.

Polanyi, K. (1944), *The Great Transformation: The Political and Economic Origins of Our Time*, New York: Farrar and Rinehart.

Quigley, J.A. (2021), *Divine Accounting: Theo-Economics in Early Christianity*, New Haven, CT: Yale University Press.

Schloen, J.D. (2001), *The House of the Father as Fact and Symbol: Patrimonialism in Ugarit and the Ancient Near East*, SAHL 2, Winona Lake, IN: Eisenbrauns.

Silver, M. (1983), *Prophets and Markets: The Political Economy of Ancient Israel*, Boston, MA: Kluwer-Nijhoff.

Silver, M. (1986), *Economic Structures of the Ancient Near East*, Totowa, NJ: Barnes and Nobles Books.

Silver, M. (1995), *Economic Structures of Antiquity*, Westport, CT: Greenwood Press.

Smith, A. (1937 [1776]), *An Inquiry into the Nature and Causes of the Wealth of Nations*, New York: Modern Library.

Smith, A. (1976 [1759]), *The Theory of Moral Sentiments*, Oxford: Clarendon Press.

Stager, L.E. (2001), 'Port Power in the Early and Middle Bronze Age: The Organization of Maritime Trade and Hinterland Production', in S.R. Wolff (ed.), *Studies in the Archaeology of Israel and Neighboring Lands in Memory of Douglas L. Esse*, 625–38, Chicago: Oriental Institute of the University of Chicago.

Stansell, G. (2006), 'Wealth: How Abraham Became Rich', in P.F. Esler (ed.), *Ancient Israel: The Old Testament in Its Social Context*, 92–110, Minneapolis, MN: Fortress Press.

Swedberg, R. (1999), 'Max Weber as an Economist and as a Sociologist: Towards a Fuller Understanding of Weber's View of Economics', *American Journal of Economics and Sociology*, 58 (4): 561–82.

Wallerstein, I. (1974), *The Modern World-System I: Capitalist Agriculture and the Origins of the European World Economy in the Sixteenth Century*, New York: Academic Press.

Weber, M. (1976 [1897]), *The Agrarian Society of Ancient Civilizations*, transl. R.I. Frank, London: NLB Press.

Wittfogel, K. (1957), *Oriental Despotism: A Comparative Study of Total Power*, New Haven, CT: Yale University Press.

Zaccagnini, C. (1989), 'Asiatic Mode of Production and Ancient Near East: Towards a Discussion', in C. Zaccagnini (ed.), *Production and Consumption in the Ancient Near East*, 1–126, Budapest: University of Budapest.

# CHAPTER TEN

# Gender and society in ancient Israel

CAROL MEYERS

## INTRODUCTION

Negative stereotypes and judgements about the relationships between women and men in ancient Israel permeate biblical scholarship. Israelite women are thought to be inferior to men, the chattel of men, even enslaved by men.

Literary critics, who tend to work directly and solely with biblical narratives, have persistently identified male dominance in biblical texts and often therefore claim to see it in ancient Israel too. One of the most pointed examples is the assertion that ancient Israel's social system was patriarchal and that it was 'a male-supremacist social and cognitive system' (Fuchs 2000: 12).[1] Supremacist is a powerful word, indicating that members of a group (in this case, men) believed themselves to be supreme and superior to others (in this case, women) and thus have the right to rule over them or otherwise control them. Patriarchy would thus be a form of supremacism – granting special rights and privileges to men and denying them to women.

This perspective echoes one made several decades ago by the prominent feminist theologian Rosemary Ruether, who chastises the biblical prophets for not objecting to the 'enslavement of persons within the Hebrew family itself: namely, women and children' (Ruether 1985: 119). And it resonates with more recent assertions that Israel was 'rigidly patriarchal' and that women were 'subordinated to men' (Marsman 2003: 26, 733, 738). These extreme views (see Lemos 2015: 227–8) are present in milder but nonetheless negative assessments that continue to label Israelite society patriarchal and to assume general male dominance (e.g. Bach 1999: xiv). The lead essay in the well-regarded *Women's Bible Commentary* refers to the 'patriarchal values embedded in all of the biblical writings' as mirroring Israelite society (Ringe 1998: 5). Even Frymer-Kensky, who heralds prominent biblical women and defends the Bible against charges of misogyny, uses the patriarchy label and asserts that women were dominated by their husbands (Frymer-Kensky 2002: xiv). The patriarchal social and cultural world of Israelites, it is assumed, was arranged to benefit men directly and to always give men power over women (O'Connor 2006: 13–14). In short, many scholars view women in biblical antiquity as powerless pawns in an all-pervasive, male-dominated hierarchical structure.

---

[1] For other examples of derogatory assumptions, see Block 2003: 61 and Lemos 2015: n.3.

Popular views are much the same. Here are some examples of what students in my course on women in the Bible and its world (see Meyers 2013: 125) say when asked in the first class to jot down their notions about women in ancient Israel:

- Women were to be seen, not heard.
- Women were shrouded and quiet.
- Are women as devalued in the Bible as they seem?
- I have very few impressions of women's roles [. . .] However, subservience is what comes to mind.
- I have always assumed that women were vastly inferior to men in biblical times.
- I think of women in the biblical period as being oppressed.

These unexamined notions stem from traditional interpretations of the Bible and its world in institutional religion, which draws on scholarly appraisals like those just mentioned. Cultural productions, including contemporary media, are also influential. For example, the website of an organization advocating religious tolerance alerts us to the status of women in biblical antiquity: women were considered 'inferior to men [. . .] Women's behavior was extremely limited [. . .] much as women are restricted in Saudi Arabia in modern-day times'.[2]

But are these views legitimate? They are typically based on biblical texts taken out of context, and they pay little or no heed to information about Israelite society from other sources. Moreover, they use the term patriarchy without attending to its origins or considering its legitimacy as a descriptor of ancient Israel. Assumptions that Israelite gender relations are marked by systemic male dominance in a patriarchal society are problematic in light of what is now known about the social reality of ancient Israel and in consideration of the deficiencies of the patriarchal paradigm. They can be contested.

In contesting the typical perspectives, this discussion first uses information about the maintenance activities (explained below) of agrarian women, arguably the majority of women throughout the period of ancient Israel (the Iron Age, c. 1200–587 BCE), to reconstruct Israelite gender relationships and thus determine whether traditional negative assessments are legitimate. It then examines the concept of patriarchy – its origins and the ways in which using it to depict ancient Israel are inappropriate – and also considers other possibilities for characterizing Israelite society. Finally, in accord with my assertion that studying ancient Israelite women necessitates an anthropological perspective that considers ordinary Israelite women apart from the admittedly biased biblical text (Meyers 2013: 14), in this chapter I engage another aspect of an anthropological perspective: the issue of evaluation. Anthropologists studying other cultures struggle with the problem of evaluation. They ask whether, as outsiders, they can or should make judgements about the group they are studying. I believe it is fitting, given the authoritative role of the Bible for so many people and the concomitant problems that its authority poses for contemporary Christian and Jewish feminists, to confront the problem of evaluation in relation to ancient Israelite women and their context.

---

[2] https://web.archive.org/web/20210317051515/http://www.religioustolerance.org/ofe_bibl.htm (accessed 13 April 2021).

# GENDER RELATIONSHIPS

The life of an Israelite agrarian was not compartmentalized, as it is for most of us, into separate domains of work and family, public and private. The domicile was the workplace, and its occupants were the workers. Although the activities of women and men overlapped at certain times and under certain circumstances, they were not the same. Texts and archaeological data along with ethnographic observations have enabled us to reconstruct women's household activities. Ethnographic examples and anthropological discussions now provide the opportunity to understand the gender dynamics embedded in women's contributions to household life and to consider the meaning of those activities for Israelite women. Recourse to several biblical passages is also illuminating, for these texts tend to corroborate what the anthropological perspective reveals – that the negative image of Israelite women in academic analyses and popular conceptions is flawed.

## *An anthropological perspective*

The negative assumptions about women in ancient Israel are hardly unique. Whether expressed implicitly or explicitly, assumptions that 'women virtually everywhere play a subordinate role' (Rogers 1975: 727) appeared repeatedly in anthropological literature until the rise of feminist anthropology.[3] Those conventional views about gender relations in premodern cultures were rooted in Victorian gender ideology,[4] which 'identified men as public, active, powerful, and dominant over women, who were considered intrinsically subordinate, domestic, passive, and powerless' (Spencer-Wood 1999: 175). That hierarchical ideology was projected onto the past to interpret 'all men's activities and roles as powerful and high status, while devaluing women's roles and activities as unimportant and low status' (ibid.). Earlier generations of anthropologists carrying out ethnographic research – mainly men who either were oblivious to the possibility of female power or who did not have access to the internal workings of a household – perpetuated these views.

More recent ethnographic studies have provided fresh data and a different perspective. In small, traditional, Mediterranean societies where, as in ancient Israel, the household is the basic economic unit of society and where women and men work very hard in mostly different sets of maintenance tasks, female power has been repeatedly documented [see further Chapter 6 in this volume]. This documentation began in the 1960s, when a report on household life in a small Greek village (population 216) – 'Appearance and Reality: Status and Roles of Women in Mediterranean Societies' (Friedl 1967) – was published in a special issue of *Anthropological Quarterly*. The author was not surprised to find that women and men contributed about equally to household labour. But because she held mid-twentieth-century views about women as powerless and subordinate in traditional societies, she was astonished to discover how influential women really were. They exerted considerable power in household decision-making about economic matters and also in choosing marital partners for their children. Despite appearances to the contrary, male dominance was not a functional reality in household life.

---

[3] Also, gender anthropology. See Meyers 2013: 10, 31–7, and the essays in Nelson 2007.
[4] As are some of the presentisms discussed in Meyers 2013: 117–23.

Other ethnographic research has similarly shown a striking absence of hierarchical male control of women. A study of rural Greek households revealed women to have as much decision-making power as their husbands, if not more (Salamone 1987: 204). Peasant women in France were observed to control 'the major portion of important resources and decisions'; and, in considering the 'actual power of peasant women and men relative to each other [. . .] women appear to be generally more powerful' (Rogers 1975: 728–9). Research on Sardinian households similarly shows facile assumptions about women's subordination to be simplistic and misleading (Assmuth 1997: 17). In Muslim Palestinian households in the early twentieth century, peasant women (unlike women in towns) were the equals of their husbands and occasionally ruled the household (Wilson 1906: 103). Similarly, Egyptian village women might seem subordinate but in fact were the managers of the household (Ammar 1954: 50). And Iranian peasant women had considerable household authority and sometimes complete control (Watson 1979: 226).

These and other studies indicate that the usual views of household power dynamics require modification when considering any traditional society (Sweely 1999: 2). Analysis of power tends to focus on institutional forms, thus highlighting visible and often coercive male power. But power can also be less visible and non-coercive, achieved (often by women) through a variety of interpersonal interactions – including affiliation, cooperation, collaboration, negotiation and inspiration. Small-scale, non-coercive power exerted by women is no less important than male power, especially in terms of the daily functioning of households and their communities. To put it another way, shared power, or 'power with' is as important, maybe more important, than 'power over' (Spencer-Wood 1999: 179). Forms of female power may look different from forms of male power, but they cannot be discounted. Conventional ideas that see women as passive and powerless in all premodern societies thus misrepresent the reality, namely that women's maintenance roles in traditional agrarian societies translate into certain kinds of power that overlap with or complement male power.

Maintenance activities are the 'basic tasks of daily life that regulate and stabilize' the life of the household and its community (González-Marcén, Montón-Subías and Picazo 2006: 3). Household maintenance is more than meeting the physical needs of the household by providing food and clothing; it also involves the care of the young and ailing, the socialization and education of children, the organization of household space, fostering links with kin and neighbours, and performing household rituals. Women's maintenance activities were time-consuming and energy-demanding; and they were interconnected and complex. Thus referring to women's household roles as maintenance activities draws attention to and valorizes women's contributions to household life. Rather than being marginalized as secondary behaviours or epiphenomena that are less important than what men do, women's activities are acknowledged for their essential role in sustaining households and communities.

Awareness of the presence and function of female power is critical for understanding gender relations in agrarian Israelite households. The maintenance roles of Israelite women,[5] which are much the same as those in the studies mentioned above, suggest a similar power dynamic. Virtually all of women's maintenance activities were indispensable to the social and economic survival of the household and contributed, in ways described

---

[5] Described in Meyers 2013: 125–70.

below, to women's household power. Carrying out household roles determined the organization and relationships of household life.

In the aggregate, women's maintenance activities probably required more technological skills than did men's. In even the simplest societies, women who transform raw products into cooked foods and produce other household commodities, as did Israelite women, are seen as having special knowledge – the ability to 'work [. . .] wonders' (Goody 1982: 70). In contrast, the food-preparation task men are most likely to perform – cooking meat at sacrificial feasts – is perhaps the least technologically complex, especially if it involves roasting over an open fire. From time immemorial, men have put the steaks on the grill and women have concocted the stews. Women's other maintenance activities similarly required specialized knowledge and skills (Meyers 2021b: 18–23). Textile work, for example, was 'one of the most complex and multi-phased processes' of any of the ancient technologies (Cassuto 2011). And making pottery, a five-stage process, each step of which requires special knowledge and skills, is considered 'a very difficult task' (Salem 1999: 70). Technological expertise certainly figured in the agrarian tasks of Israelite men, but those tasks were rarely daily ones. For example, men ploughed and planted grain seeds several times a year (Borowski 1987: 47–56) and sheared sheep annually (Borowski 1998: 70); women converted grains into edible form virtually every day, making their technological proficiency visible in daily life.

Women's control of and expertise in household technologies – transforming the raw into the cooked and producing other household foodstuffs and commodities – affords them both *personal* and *social* power. A little-recognized concomitant of women's technological skills is the valued sense of self afforded by providing items necessary for survival. Moreover, many women's tasks had direct results, providing the gratification derived from producing items that were immediately consumable or usable. The collective mindset of the Israelites (see Meyers 2013: 118–21) would not have precluded this self-awareness and self-satisfaction.

Because commodity production in subsistence households is central to their economic and social life, women's maintenance tasks positioned them to exercise certain kinds of household power. Women in traditional cultures make important household decisions by virtue of their dominance of essential household processes (Counihan 1998: 2, 4). How is this manifest? Take, for example, the production of life-sustaining foodstuffs. Women's control of their production means the control of their distribution under most circumstances (see Prov. 31.15). Those who spend considerable time and energy converting raw foodstuffs into edible form have much to say about how, when and how much food is consumed. Across cultures, people tend to control the distribution of the fruits of their labour (Whyte 1978: 68). Because their maintenance tasks generally take place in or near the domicile, women also determine the allocation and use of household space and its implements, as in traditional Palestinian villages (Hirschfeld 1995: 152, 182).

Women's power in household decision-making is not a trivial matter. Because the household is the most significant social and economic unit, household power has important consequences for the community as a whole. Ethnographic evidence indicates that when women have essential information about household or village matters, they also participate in discussions about how to solve household problems or deal with community issues (see Friedl 1967: 106). Their economic contributions to household life conferred 'a juridical position' on Sardinian women (Assmuth 1997: 92). The networks of communication with other women, established in their pattern of joint work,[6] gave Israelite women access to certain kinds of information that similarly would have figured in household, and also community, decisions about economic and political issues (see Meyers 2013: 143–6).

Highlighting their household power means rescuing Israelite women from mistaken notions of female powerlessness and subordination in household life; it also means recognizing the gender balance in Israelite households. Women in peasant households dominate in certain kinds of household activities and men in others, with significant contributions by both. As a result, female–male relationships are marked by interdependence, with a relative symmetry between the positions of women and men (Assmuth 1997: 92; Hendon 1996: 46). The marital union of women and men in rural Greece has been called an economic, social and moral partnership because of their mutual dependence on each other (Salamone 1987: 205). The designation 'partnership' resonates with the term 'partner' in the Eden tale, which portrays the first woman as the 'powerful counterpart' of the first man (Deutschmann 2022: 38–41; Meyers forthcoming).

Overall, gender interactions in peasant households are largely complementary. In some instances women may have greater decision-making powers, and in other matters (see below) men are in control. Their combined efforts are signified in ancient Israel by bread production. In most settlements bread could be obtained only by household production; and, as the fundamental nutritional commodity, bread was the *sine qua non* of food (Meyers 2021a: 385–6, 389–90). Bread production and consumption were thus the nexus of household economic, social and even religious life. Bread was a social, economic and religious substance as well as a physical one for the Israelites (see Counihan 1999: 29). It signified the processes that produced it and, as in traditional Mediterranean societies, 'confirm[ed] the complementarity of men and women' as its producers (ibid.: 37; see also Campbell 1964: 153; Hart 1992: 127, 191). Women and men in agrarian Israelite households together were 'breadwinners' responsible for the livelihood of their households. Complementary gender-linked responsibilities as parents (see Meyers 2013: 136–7) as well as providers were woven together into the overall fabric of daily life.

I have avoided looking beyond the Mediterranean basin for analogues to ancient Israelite life. But information about American frontier households, which, like Israelite ones, were largely self-sufficient, may be relevant. Diaries and other writings show that frontier women functioned in a 'partner model' with respect to household dynamics (see Kohl 1988 and Myres 1982: 164–7). They regarded their participation in decision-making to be important, for pioneer homesteads were understood to be viable only through the considerable cooperative efforts of a marital pair.

The ethnographic evidence for the complementarity of women and men in traditional agrarian households overturns the traditional views of gender hierarchy, with men controlling women in all respects. It also provides compelling evidence that the dichotomy between public and private that characterizes industrial societies (Meyers 2013: 122–3) and the associated view that low-status, female household tasks give women secondary status cannot be applied to small-scale premodern settlements.

The idea that women's maintenance activities were not valued is similarly invalid (Meyers 2013: 121–2). The significant economic, social and political value of women's

---

[6] Many household maintenance tasks were performed by women working together, often for hours at a time; this allowed them to share information. See Meyers 2013: 130, 131–2, 133, 134; Baadsgaard 2008; and Cassuto 2008.

maintenance tasks probably afforded women not only substantial household power but also the respect that accrues to any household member whose labours are essential for survival. When women are skilled managers of household production systems, they are accorded prestige and experience self-esteem. The idealized woman of Proverbs 31, after all, is praised by her husband and children for her household work. Because technical expertise was considered a form of wisdom in ancient Israel, women's technical skills and their ability to impart them to the next generation made them 'wise women'. And their tasks of socializing and educating children made women household sages (Fontaine 1990: 161; Meyers 2021b: 24–6). Finally, the religious maintenance (described in Meyers 2013: 147–79) would have not only enriched women's lives but also earned them respect for performing ritual activities considered essential for achieving biological and agricultural fertility.

This anthropological perspective of the gender dynamics implicit in women's maintenance activities suggests that a senior Israelite woman was no less powerful than her partner, and perhaps more so in some ways. Do any biblical texts, apart from the depiction of Eve as the counterpart of Adam, support the anthropological view? Biblical sources do not provide directly relevant information about the gender dynamics of ordinary Israelite women. But some of the elite women visible in the Hebrew Bible exhibit the decision-making power evident in ethnographic reports. The activities of these women resemble those of their less affluent sisters; they both supplement and confirm the ethnographic information about women's household power. (The lives of royal women were too distant socially and economically from the lives of peasant women; thus narratives about kings' wives and mothers are not examined.)

## Biblical evidence

Most of the power described in the ethnographic studies cited above was exhibited by older women with considerable experience in household maintenance tasks. Senior women, especially when extended or complex families are involved, held what today we would call managerial roles. They oversaw the assignment of tasks and use of resources, and they were responsible for organizing the work of those junior to them, including adult sons. In today's terms, the senior Israelite woman functioned as the household's COO (chief operating officer) and, if the senior male was away or incapacitated, as the acting CEO (chief executive officer; Stein 2006: 403). Household hierarchies were based on age and experience as much as on gender.

This managerial feature is visible in several biblical narratives involving women – Micah's mother, Abigail, and the great woman of Shunem – and the woman of Proverbs 31.[7] A pair of stipulations in the legal section of Exodus are also relevant. The narrative women may not be fully historical figures, and Proverbs 31 probably presents an idealized figure. Yet these images still have 'historical and sociological value' for reconstructing the lives of Israelite women (see Schroer 2000: 80, 82). Narrative details can be manipulated to produce desired effects but still reflect social conventions.

The story of *Micah's mother* (Judges 17) is about an unnamed woman who discovers that 1,100 shekels of silver have been stolen from her. Hoping to recover this considerable

---

[7] For further information about the passages discussed here, see the relevant entries and their bibliographies in Meyers, Craven and Kraemer (2000) and also the sources cited below.

amount, she utters a curse in the hope that God will punish the thief. In the biblical world curses (and blessings) were believed to be efficacious. Thus when the thief, who happens to be her son Micah, hears it, he fears divine punishment; he then confesses and returns the stolen property. But the story does not end there. Micah's mother decides that some of the silver (200 pieces) should be 'consecrated' to Yahweh. She commissions a metalsmith to make items for the household shrine.[8] Presumably she retains the other 900 pieces of silver.

This narrative, probably meant to critique the family's behaviour, in the process provides interesting details about women's decision-making powers and other behaviours. This well-to-do woman, perhaps a widow because Micah's father is not mentioned, has resources that she can use at her own discretion. She also has the right to make oaths, whether curses or blessings. She performs efficacious religious acts in uttering a curse about the theft and later offering a blessing. Forgiving her son, or perhaps rewarding him for his honesty, she says 'May my son be blessed by the Lord!' (Judg. 17.2). Like the father of the prodigal son (Lk. 15.11–32) she harbours no parental anger. Finally, she decides to commission cultic objects that contribute to the value of the household shrine.

Another fascinating narrative (1 Samuel 25) is about *Abigail*, the wife of a wealthy but 'surly and mean' man named Nabal (meaning 'fool'; v. 3). In contrast her name probably means 'her father rejoices', and she is described as 'clever and beautiful' (also v. 3). The story takes place in the days of King Saul and relates an interaction with David, who is an outlaw at the time. Boorish Nabal has insulted David. The young men working with Nabal tell Abigail about this incident, and she decides to make amends lest retributive harm come to her household. At her own initiative, and without consulting her husband, she prepares gifts for David: 'two hundred loaves, two skins of wine, five sheep ready dressed, five measures of parched grain, one hundred clusters of raisins, and two hundred cakes of figs' (1 Sam. 25.18). She loads them on donkeys and, with the young men in her household, she sets out to bring the gifts to David. When Abigail meets him, her impassioned and diplomatic plea to the future king (1 Sam. 25.24–31) averts David's ire. When she tells her husband what has happened, he suffers what seems to be a *stroke*. Appropriately, ten days later 'the Lord *struck* Nabal' (1 Sam. 25.38; my emphasis) and he dies. When David learns of this, he sends messengers to Abigail asking if she would become his wife. She agrees.

Abigail is the principal character in this story about a woman in an affluent household. The young men come to her to report the unfortunate encounter with David's men. She senses the danger to her household and takes swift action. She has access to resources – large quantities of foodstuffs – and decides how to use them. She does this on her own, without consulting Nabal; and she enlists others from the household to accompany her to meet David. Unlike the case of Micah's mother, whose words are not reported except for a brief blessing, Abigail's lengthy speech is presented. It exemplifies wisdom and diplomacy. In its use of imperatives and in the directness of its rhetoric, it displays authority and creates 'a picture of a woman used to being in charge' (Shields 2010: 53). Her intelligence – mentioned *before* her beauty at the beginning of the narrative – as well as her beauty make her a welcome member of what eventually will be the royal household. She functions as a mediator, empowered by her skill as a negotiator rather than by recourse to force. And, as is likely the case in village politics, she provides desirable food to enhance the receptivity of David to her entreaty to forego violence.

---

[8] Contra NRSV, which understands only one object although the Hebrew mentions two.

The third narrative (2 Kgs 4.8–37, 8.1–6) has been called 'one of the most remarkable in the Bible' (Camp 1998: 113). It is about an affluent woman identified as a resident of Shunem and thus called the *Shunammite woman* (2 Kgs 4.12). Unlike virtually all women in biblical narratives, she is not presented as the 'wife of' someone. This unnamed figure is described by the adjective *gĕdôlâ* (2 Kgs 4.8), a word used in the Hebrew Bible in reference to people 'of esteem and status' (Cogan and Tadmor 1988: 56). The usual translation, 'wealthy', is not incorrect yet does not do justice to the term's connotation of respect.

The prophet Elisha is visiting her town, and the Shunammite, who happens to be childless, invites him to a meal. Noting that he is frequently in the vicinity, she decides that he should have his own room in her house. Informing her husband of this, she has a room prepared for him. In gratitude, Elisha offers to commend her to the king or his general. She declines, claiming that her standing among her people needs no such intervention. The prophet then says he will see to it that her infertility problem is solved, which he does – she bears a son. Some years later, the child is in the fields with his father and becomes ill. He is brought to his mother and dies on her lap. The Shunammite immediately sets off to fetch Elisha, who comes to her domicile and revives the deceased lad.

This happy result is not the end of the Shunammite's story. Sometime later, following Elisha's advice, she moves her family to another place to get relief from a severe drought. When the drought ends, she returns to Shunem; she finds that her property has been taken by someone else. She goes directly to the king, requesting that her property be restored. The king's favourable response brings not only the restoration of the domicile and land but also what it would have produced during her absence.

Several features about the Shunammite's story are notable. First, she makes decisions autonomously: inviting the prophet to her household, reconfiguring household space, moving away to escape the consequences of drought, and appealing to the king for restitution when the household is taken over by others. Second, she is the one who tends, albeit unsuccessfully, to an ill member of the household. Third, it is her status in the community that convinces the prophet that she needs nothing special from royal or military officials. Fourth, she interacts readily with a prophet and a king. Fifth, she is the one to whom the prophet turns when warning her family to leave Shunem because of the drought. Does this autonomy and standing in the community mean that the household is her property? (suggested by Frymer-Kensky 2002: 71–3). Not necessarily. As the competent COO of the household, she manages its affairs, looking after its property. The designation 'mother's household' (cf. Meyers 2013: 112–13, 191) would surely apply to the Shunammite. When an Israelite woman entered a man's household as his wife, she identified with that household and it became hers as well as his. The household is viewed as corporate property, given the collective identity of Israelite households (Meyers 2013: 118–21).

This image of a woman running a household and making decisions about the use of resources also appears in the depiction of a *strong woman* in Prov. 31.10–31. These twenty-two verses portray the full life of a household manager. More than half refer to specifically economic processes. She provides food and engages in textile production, two of the maintenance activities discussed above. In addition, she purchases land (v. 16), takes care of her profitable business (v. 18) and sells to merchants the textiles she has produced (v. 24). Moreover, she uses some of her household's resources as charity to the poor (v. 20). Indeed, the very language of this passage 'ascribes to her physical, emotional, and intellectual strength, while the male is a bystander' (Lawrence 2010: 343). For example, the woman 'girds herself with strength, and makes her arms strong' (v. 17). The overall portrait resonates with the narrative images depicting women's autonomous resourcefulness and decision-making power.

It also resonates with a somewhat later Greek text, Xenophon's *Oeconomicus*, a treatise on household management that reveals gender relationships in elite Greek society. Xenophon does not polarize the relationship between wife and husband but rather 'views their familial and economic roles as complementary'; their powers are divided, with a woman in some instances exercising authority over her marital partner (Pomeroy 1994: 34, 36, 247).

The managerial role of Israelite women and men also appears in two verses in the Covenant Code (Exod. 20.19–23.33). Most stipulations in the Covenant Code reflect urban contexts, but a small group of cases originated in village life (Knight 2000: 177). These include Exod. 21.15, 17, which mandate the death penalty for offspring who curse or strike their mother or father. Capital punishment, which seems so harsh to us, is directed not towards children but to young adults in the household who threaten those above them 'on the authority ladder' (Westbrook and Wells 2009: 73). These cases indicate that both parents have authority over adult children. So does Prov. 20.20, part of the sections of Proverbs originating in family settings (Meyers 2013: 137–8); it proclaims that cursing either parent brings death ('your lamp [signifying life] will go out'). In the Covenant Code and Proverbs indicate the dire consequence for threatening parental authority is specified of both mother and father.

The legal rulings in Exodus and the related admonition in Proverbs make sense in the complex multigenerational families that were likely the norm in Israelite agrarian households.[9] We tend to romanticize these large family configurations, which were economically essential in biblical antiquity. But there is a downside, in that internal tensions can be more complicated than in nuclear families because more people are involved. Moreover, adult children – notably sons, for daughters marry out – at times challenge their parents. The threat of harsh punishment functions as a deterrent. At the same time, adult children have a responsibility to sustain their parents in old age. The translation 'honour' in the biblical commandment to 'honour one's father and mother' (Exod. 20.12; Deut. 5.16; cf. Lev. 19.3, where 'mother' precedes 'father') is not quite accurate in this context, for the Hebrew term for honour (root *kbd*) denotes the obligation of offspring to provide food, clothing and shelter for elderly parents (Lambert 2016: 331–2 cf. Greenfield 1982).

The Covenant Code and Proverbs texts affirming the authority of both parents arose in village or family contexts, making it likely that women's decision-making power in the narratives described above was not unique to these elite individuals but rather reflects the dynamics in agrarian households whatever their economic level. In fact, the biblical terms *baʿal* (m.) and *baʿălâ* (f.) reflect this reconstruction (Guenther 2005: 403–6). Usually translated 'master' or 'lord' and thought to indicate sexual possession, *baʿal* can better be understood as a designation for the senior male in a household, the one who 'owns' the household's property – the *naḥălâ* ('inheritance'; Meyers 2013: 108). His wife, the senior woman in a household, is thus the *baʿălâ*, the female head of a household, the manager responsible for administering the family household.

---

[9] Multigenerational families are characteristic of small-scale agrarian societies in the Mediterranean region (Huebner 2017: 12). That said, household forms are fluid and shift with the birth and death of its members, the number of children, etc.

Ethnographic data and biblical texts attest to female household power within overall gender complementarity in Israelite agrarian households. But households were the basic unit of a larger social system in which men dominated. Moreover, the term *patriarchy* is typically used to label the entire social system, household included. What does the lack of gender hierarchy within households mean for understanding Israelite society beyond the household? To answer that question, the meaning and adequacy of patriarchy as an analytical concept must be addressed.

## THE LARGER SOCIAL SYSTEM

First-wave feminist anthropologists in the 1970s and 1980s drew on the Weberian binary of informal power and legal authority in their analysis of social systems; women were associated with the former and men with the latter. My earlier work was heavily influenced by those models (Meyers 1988: 41–3 and passim). Since then a decided shift in thinking about power has occurred. Weberian (and Marxist) ideas about power focused on institutional forms and failed to take into account the way people interact with each other apart from formal structures. Power relations, it is now recognized, are not universally hierarchical or static but are rather circumstantial and continuously being negotiated (Sweely 1999). Moreover, gender is not always the most useful category of power differentials. Age and social class are frequently more relevant, especially in societies where most men as well as women are excluded from institutional positions of power. Yet societies are repeatedly deemed patriarchal, a term related to male power. The relevance of that designation is clearly problematic.

### *The patriarchy problem*

Defining patriarchy is not easy. As a theory meant to account for widespread gender stratification in human societies, it is often understood to be a general system in which power is held by adult men; and it usually implies near total male domination at the micro level of personal relationships as well as in macro institutional forms (Meagher 2011: 441). The influential feminist historian Gerda Lerner sees it as a term encompassing the 'manifestation and institutionalization of male dominance over women and children in the family and the existence of male dominance over women in society in general' (Lerner 1986: 240). This definition appears in her widely acclaimed book asserting that patriarchy as a universal condition originated with the rise of civilization in the ancient Near East. Her methodology is now considered seriously flawed (e.g. Lesko 1989: xiv; Kray 2002). Moreover, this understanding of patriarchy has been challenged by some social scientists, especially the third-wave feminists, who assert that one cannot call an entire culture patriarchal, for doing so means obscuring other, possibly more pernicious inequalities (Sered 1994; Meagher 2011: 441–2). They argue that 'the concept of patriarchy fails when the binary categories on which it depends are dismantled' (Nash 2009: 103). A glimpse at the origins and meanings of the term (not the system) is thus in order.[10]

The term *patriarchy* comes from the Greek words *pater* ('father') and *archein* ('to rule'). Its use to denote a hierarchical social system became common in the writings of nineteenth-century European social scientists. Marxist political theorists drew on newly

---

[10] For fuller discussion of patriarchy, including its origins and flaws, see Meyers 2014.

available translations of classical literature in their claim that the rise of private property in antiquity caused an original gender equality to be replaced by women's virtual servitude. The legal authority of the male head (*patria potestas*) of the ancient household (*pater familias*) was generalized to represent pervasive male control throughout society. Patriarchy was considered a system that systematically and structurally oppresses women and gives men authority over political, social and economic institutions (Gilchrist 1999: xvi). I would add religious institutions to this list.

This ideology of patriarchal dominance was aligned with nineteenth-century theories about the evolution of human societies from primitive (matriarchal or egalitarian) to a series of civilized (patriarchal) forms: tribe, chiefdom, state. It entered biblical studies in the 1880s, when two renowned biblical scholars – William Robertson Smith and Julius Wellhausen – asserted that ancient Israelite society was dominated by the universal form of the patriarchal family as it evolved from tribe to state. Fast forward to the twenty-first century, when one of the most recent studies of Israelite society adopted the notion that Israelite patrimonialism (in which all power flows from the leader down through nested units of society) originates in the 'patriarchal household government' (Schloen 2001: 52; see also King and Stager 2001: 38). Feminist biblical scholars too, as noted above, use patriarchy as a designation for both the Bible and Israelite society.

Although the term continues to be used, patriarchy is an inadequate and inappropriate designation and can no longer be seen as a cultural universal. Among the reasons for this assessment are the following:

- Classicists question the validity of the model from ancient Rome that gave rise to modern notions of patriarchy in the first place (e.g. Saller 1994: 74–132).
- Ethnographic reports from the Mediterranean world (like those cited in this chapter) and from other traditional societies indicate that much household power resides with senior women.
- When the household is the central unit of society, as in societies (like ancient Israel) in which production is at the subsistence level and supra-household structures (clan, tribe, state) impinge relatively little on household life, women have significant agency not only in the household itself but also in supra-household matters. The latter include the political-economic aspect of women's maintenance roles (described in Meyers 2013: 139–46).
- Informal organizations of female specialists in ancient Israel had their own hierarchies, independent of those in the general social system (Meyers 2013: 171–9). Women professionals would have operated outside of other hierarchical structures (Frymer-Kensky 2002: 324).
- Patriarchal models have been developed largely by analysing modern industrial societies and do not fit the interlocking social, economic and political structures of premodern groups.
- Using the patriarchy paradigm implies a fixed set of relationships, when in fact social arrangements are rarely static and power relations can shift over time.
- The focus on the subordination of women overlooks the fact that inequalities are a function of class or age as much as, if not more than, of gender. For example, insufficient regard is given to the inferior position of servants, slaves and strangers (or 'aliens', probably people of different ethnicity) in ancient Israel. And male

hereditary institutions, like the Israelite priesthood, are a little-noticed form of exclusion that excludes most men as well as women from arenas of community religious power.
- Patriarchy is a hierarchical model that cannot be uniformly applied to ancient complex societies (those with several levels of sociopolitical organization; see Stein 1998).
- Labelling traditional societies patriarchal means applying the values of capitalist societies – values that valorize male individuality – and thereby failing to recognize the importance of women's social and economic contributions in traditional societies, which are much less individualistic (Hernando 2008: 12–13).

In short, patriarchy is a value-laden and diffuse term that is probably unsuitable for characterizing any society, and there are ample reasons to discard it as a designation for Israelite society. Yet critiques of the patriarchal model have had little impact on biblical studies as biblical scholars continue to characterize Israelite society as patriarchal, although several now suggest other terms:

- Schroer would actually retain the term but define it somewhat differently and use it to designate a system in which both women and men of certain classes or groups 'exercise domination over other men, women, and children' (Schroer 1998: 90). Recognizing some female domination is important, but seeing it as limited to certain classes obscures gender complementarity and women's power in ordinary households.
- Block says that patriarchy 'places inordinate emphasis on the power a father exercised over the household' and too often connotes abusive behaviour. He then suggests that *patricentrism* would be a term that better reflects 'the normal biblical disposition' toward the senior male (Block 2003: 41). This may be suitable for describing biblical texts, but it would not be accurate in depicting household life.
- The term *patrilineal*, which I proposed in my earlier work (Meyers 1988: 37–40), certainly is important in describing the transfer of property across generations along the male line (see Meyers 2013: 108); but it is an inadequate descriptor of household gender dynamics.
- Schüssler Fiorenza (2001: 118–24) offers an intriguing proposal. She acknowledges the power inequities of monarchic rule in ancient societies and uses the term *kyriarchy*, from Greek *kyrios* ('lord') and *archein* ('to rule'), to designate 'a socio-political system in which elite educated propertied men hold power over women and other men' (ibid.: 211). She emphasizes that it is a system that subordinates men as well as women, and she focuses on the 'exploitation, dependency, and inferiority and obedience of wo/men' (ibid.: 118). Her point is well taken with respect to national and regional governance systems, but it fails to capture the gender dynamics of households and small settlements or acknowledge the agency of specialists outside hierarchical systems.

## The heterarchy alternative

Is there another, less value-laden and more suitable way to characterize social organization in ancient Israel? To answer that question, it is important first to recognize the nature of patriarchy as a hierarchical system. As anthropologists define it, *hierarchy* designates an organizational structure in which, on the basis of certain factors, some elements are subordinate to others and are usually ranked accordingly (Crumley 1979: 144). Hierarchies are often represented spatially as conical vertical structures, giving rise to phrases like 'moving up in the hierarchy' (Crumley 1995: 3). Recognizing that not all social systems are organized hierarchically, some of the social scientists who challenge the evolutionary models underlying the concept of hierarchical systems offer a more nuanced and adaptable model: *heterarchy*.

This is hardly a household term, even though it has been around since the middle of the last century.[11] A combination of Greek *heteros* ('different, other') and *archein* ('to rule'), heterarchy was introduced in the 1940s to describe neural structures, which are not always arranged hierarchically, and then was used in the 1970s to represent the diverse rankings in computer systems. It first appeared in the anthropological and archaeological literature in 1979, when Carole Crumley used it to denote an 'organizational structure [. . .] in which each element possesses the potential of being unranked (relative to other elements) or ranked in a number of different ways, depending on systemic requirements' (Crumley 1979: 144–5). More simply, the term can account for the fact that past societies had multiple sources of power that did not necessarily line up in a single set of vertical hierarchical relationships (Hays-Gilpin 2000: 98). With respect to gender, it can accommodate arenas of activity in which women have power and agency; it can also incorporate the intersection of gender with other variables like age and class.

The heterarchy model takes into account many of the flaws, noted above, in the hierarchical (patriarchal) model. For example, it does not assume that ranking is permanent or that the ranking of elements according to different criteria will always coincide. As a much more flexible concept than hierarchy, it provides a way to acknowledge the variety of patterns in organizational structures across cultures and to recognize different rankings of structures or elements of structures vis-à-vis each other (Brumfiel 1995: 125). Not surprisingly, heterarchy has been interpreted and employed in many different ways (see the examples in Ehrenreich, Crumley and Levy 1995). One of the most promising for this project is the integration of heterarchy and gender (Levy 2006).

Heterarchy provides a compelling concept for representing ancient Israelite society in the Iron Age. Perhaps its most attractive feature is that it does not eliminate hierarchies but rather recognizes that there can be a variety of hierarchies that may or may not intersect with each other. That is, heterarchies and hierarchies are not mutually exclusive concepts but rather interactive or dialectical ones (Crumley 2005: 40). A heterarchical society can be composed of various social units – including individuals, households, guilds of professionals, village communities and kinship groups – that are involved in multiple horizontal as well as vertical relationships.

In the heterarchical model, this interweaving of differently structured patterns of relationships means that an individual – an Israelite woman in an agrarian household, for example – can rank high in one modality but low in another. The maintenance activities and social structures of ancient Israel meant that daily life was rarely structured according to fixed, hierarchical gender patterns. A woman's position would vary over time, according to other factors, such as age, participation in community activities, and role in the informal network of women formed by her work patterns. And certain systems associated with

---

[11] The term's origins and development are summarized in Meyers 2006: 249–50.

women holding extra-household professional positions would have their own hierarchies and cultural authority vis-à-vis other systems. All these factors contest the existence of Israelite patriarchy, which assigns general subordination to women. Interpretative traditions that anachronistically read the gender hierarchies in biblically based Judaism and Christianity (see Meyers 2013: 203–12) back into Iron Age Israel can thus be challenged.

In other words, the perceptions cited at the beginning of this chapter about male dominance in pervasive hierarchical structures affecting all domains of human interaction and subordinating women should be replaced with the recognition that there were intersecting systems and multiple loci of power, with women as well as men shaping society. The heterarchy model allows for a more nuanced and probably more accurate view of Iron Age Israel – a view that acknowledges significant domains of female agency and power. The term patriarchy obscures the way individuals and groups were organized in complex and interlocking spheres of activity; it is not an appropriate designation for the Israelites.

The heterarchy model is important not only for understanding gender relationships. It also has great potential for understanding the diversity and complexity of Israelite society in general, as several biblical scholars have noted. Gottwald, a strong proponent of engaging social science research in the study of ancient Israel, calls heterarchy a more flexible term than the 'stark choice' of either egalitarian or hierarchical to describe Israelite social arrangements in the Iron Age I period (Gottwald 2001: 171). In his extensive study of Israelite religion as part of a dynamic and complex society, Zevit sees power throughout Iron Age Israel as heterarchical rather than hierarchical (Zevit 2001: 648, drawing on the analysis of Iron Age kingdoms east of the Jordan; see LaBianca 1999). And Nakhai (2011: 358) refers to ancient Israel's social structure as 'heterarchical'.

It is important to keep in mind that, like any model, the heterarchic one is a heuristic tool that cannot be deemed either true or false (cf. Esler 2005: 4). Rather, its value lies in helping us to understand a society that cannot be directly observed by providing new methods for interpreting existing data. Models must be modified or replaced if they are no longer helpful or if another one becomes more relevant. The hierarchy model has outlived its usefulness, especially in the way it sustains the notion of patriarchy. Perhaps the heterarchy one will endure.

Invoking heterarchy in this reconstruction of gendered life in Israelite households allows us to overcome the stereotypes of presentism and the distortions of patriarchy. The life of an ordinary Israelite women was difficult, but it did not entail all-pervasive oppression and subordination. In carrying out a wide range of maintenance activities and in managing her household, she produced life-sustaining foods and materials, performed religious acts thought essential for household survival, and was enmeshed in relationships that contributed to the vitality of her household and community.

Yet the heterarchy model does not mean that no hierarchies existed. Women's household power was significant, given the centrality of the household in the lives of most Israelites. And women held some extra-household professional positions. But these features do not mean general gender equality or the absence of male privilege. The monarchy and priesthood, and their bureaucracies, were the norm, excluding women and also most men. The male military brought men into positions of community power. Immovable property (land) was owned mainly by men. Female sexuality was controlled by men. And perhaps most important in the long run, the small group of educated elites responsible for creating or recording the Hebrew Bible was male. Whether, or how, these aspects of male position and power can be evaluated or judged must be addressed.

## EVALUATING INEQUALITIES

Should we judge the world in which ordinary Israelite women lived and the hierarchies that excluded or subordinated them? This question cannot be easily answered, given the overall anthropological approach of this chapter. That is, anthropological research generally applies the principles of *cultural relativism* (see Womack 2001: 26–7). This means not only trying to gain an emic (insider's) perspective – considering Israelite culture as a woman in an agrarian household would have experienced it. It also means trying to avoid making value judgements about her culture even though aspects would be unacceptable today. It means avoiding ethnocentrism, that is, considering the values of the researcher's culture to be superior to those of the culture being studied. Although the Hebrew Bible provides a connection of sorts between the twenty-first century academy and Iron Age settlements in the Levant, the Israelite way of life was vastly different and should be accepted as such. In short, the anthropological approach means suspending judgement.

But this is neither easy nor straightforward. Anthropologists may attempt to be neutral in understanding the customs and structures of groups they study. But inevitably some aspects seem wrong, no matter what the culture (Tilley [2000] offers a trenchant critique of relativism). Can anthropologists studying cultures that practise cannibalism or honour killings really consider them morally defensible customs? Must they refrain from criticizing blatant violations of human rights? As a philosophical stance valuing the customs and norms of all cultures equally, cultural relativism is often rejected in anthropological research. From a feminist perspective and from the perspective of an academic institution valuing diversity and equality, many aspects of the lives of Israelite women would be considered unacceptable. But the same could be said about the lives of Israelite men, for class and ethnic inequities excluded most men from positions of power and exploited many men. Like other cultures in the ancient world, Israel had a general acceptance of servitude and slavery that are now deemed intolerable (so Avalos 2011).

Having said this, a closer look at two examples of Israelite gender inequity mentioned above may be helpful. These examples – male property ownership, and male control of female sexuality – are interrelated. A household's land was its life and livelihood. This property, or 'inheritance' (*naḥălâ*), was transmitted along male lines, from father to son or sons and occasionally to daughters, if there were no sons (Num. 27.1–8). In principle, land could never be sold or transferred from one lineage or person to another. Although this principle seems to have been violated over time, with estates formed and controlled by elites, men generally did not have the option of buying or selling real property. Women were disadvantaged in this respect only slightly more than most men. It is even possible, insofar as the Israelite family household was a 'corporate household' (Meyers 2013: 119–20; cf. Stein 2006: 401–2), that household property was considered a corporate possession and not the individual domain of the senior male (as in a Greek mountain village; Campbell 1964: 187). Women took on the identity of their marital household, sharing the sense of ownership.

Because land was not only a household's life but also its identity, maintaining it within the household patrilineage was highly important, making it critical that a man's heirs were his biological children. Thus concerns about property and inheritance hover in the background of many sex regulations. If a woman engaging in extramarital sex became pregnant, the heir to household property might not be her husband's son. Without DNA tests, strong cultural incentives to refrain from extramarital sex – like the death penalty for adultery (Lev. 20.10; Deut. 22.22) – were inevitable. (But note that the death penalty for adultery applied to married men too.) Thus many biblical texts favouring men involve male control of female sexuality for reasons of inheritance. They include the divine mandate in Gen. 3.16 for men to be sexually dominant (Meyers forthcoming) and the Pentateuchal legal stipulations concerning virginity, adultery, prostitution, levirate marriage and childbirth (see Meyers 2009: 890). Property transmission was at stake for Israelites in ways that rarely exist in the developed world. Land was the chief resource, and strategies safeguarding the inheritance of household property had essential functional value. Understanding the context helps temper judgement. All told, the biblical texts in which men control women arise from socio-economic factors 'rather than from a condemnation of female sexuality per se' (Brayford 1999: 166). It must also be kept in mind that most of these legal texts, like ancient law codes in general, were not codes for ordinary conduct or adjudication of ordinary disputes and that most stipulations were meant for urban elites (see Wells 2008).

An emic perspective provides another example of context mitigating judgement. When people's lives are merged together in social units, as in a society like ancient Israel with collective group identity, women experience life not so much as individuals but as household members. The concept of either women or men striving for personal independence is antithetical to the dynamics and demands of premodern agrarians. Indeed, analysis of biblical legal materials indicates that the household and not the individual was the reigning legal entity (Kawashima 2011: 6). Moreover, gender differentials in life patterns meant complementarity and interdependence and were essential for the welfare of the household. Can we object to social arrangements that contributed to household and also community survival? To put it another way, is it really fair to criticize the past for not having the values of the present?

But offering judgement is still in order. However, I direct judgement not to Israelite society, which no longer exists, but rather to the interpretive traditions that all too often equate biblical androcentrism with social reality. I agree with some feminist theologians who insist that biblical texts themselves neither oppress nor liberate and assert that it is those who use them and the way they are used that can become oppressive or liberating (see McClintock-Fulkerson 2001: 49, 119–20, 229). And I concur with feminists who emphasize that postbiblical interpretations are sometimes more powerful and problematic than the biblical texts themselves (Fischer and Puerto 2011: 5–6, citing the Eden story as an example).

Once the Hebrew Bible became authoritative, it was interpreted according to the post-Hebrew Bible context and ideas of its interpreters (Meyers 2013: 203–12; Deutschmann 2022: 145–84). Its male perspectives and interests become the vehicle for excluding women from certain roles and otherwise restricting them. Interpreted in increasingly sexist and misogynist ways, biblical texts often became the ideological justification for the sexism and misogyny permeating many postbiblical texts. Knowledge about ancient Israel was mediated through the biblical lens and with little awareness of how the Israelite context differed from that of early Jews and Christians. Morally problematic claims about women were the result. Those patterns of interpretation grounded in biblical androcentrism are too often antithetical to current egalitarian values.

Although traditional views have occluded or distorted the social reality of ancient Israelite women, research into their world using not only the Bible but all available sources has helped us recover them. A multidisciplinary anthropological analysis, drawing on archaeology and ethnography, reveals many otherwise invisible aspects of women's everyday lives and experiences in Israelite households. This expanded knowledge in turn helps us confront the problematic stereotypes projected onto the biblical past in popular culture and biblical scholarship, both of which follow the long tradition of reading later ideas about women into Israelite contexts. Recovering the household context of women's lives also means challenging the validity of patriarchy as a designation for Israelite society. Facile use of that model not only contributes to the negative stereotypes about women in the period of the Hebrew Bible but also is less accurate than heterarchy in depicting the complexities of household life and general sociopolitical organization in the Israelite past. This alternative model allows us to see the makes the power and agency of women – especially senior women and also professionals.

# REFERENCES

Ammar, H. (1954), *Growing up in an Egyptian Village: Silwa, Province of Aswan*, London: Routledge & Kegan Paul.

Assmuth, L. (1997), *Women's Work, Women's Worth: Changing Lifecourses in Highland Sardinia*, Saarijärvi: Gummerus Kirjapaino Oy.

Avalos, H. (2011), *Slavery, Abolitionism, and the Ethics of Biblical Scholarship*, Sheffield: Sheffield Phoenix Press.

Baadsgaard, A. (2008), 'A Taste of Women's Sociality: Cooking as Cooperative Labor in Iron Age Palestine', in B.A. Nakhai (ed.), *The World of Women in the Ancient and Classical Near East*, 13–44, Newcastle upon Tyne: Cambridge Scholars.

Bach, A. (1999), 'Introduction: Man's World, Women's Place – Sexual Politics in the Hebrew Bible', in A. Bach (ed.), *Women in the Hebrew Bible: A Reader*, xiii–xxvi, New York: Routledge.

Block, D.I. (2003), 'Marriage and Family in Ancient Israel', in K.M. Campbell (ed.), *Marriage and Family in the Biblical World*, 33–102, Downers Grove, IL: InterVarsity.

Borowski, O. (1987), *Agriculture in Iron Age Israel*, Winona Lake, IN: Eisenbrauns.

Borowski, O. (1998), *Every Living Thing: Daily Use of Animals in Ancient Israel*, Walnut Creek, CA: AltaMira.

Brayford, S. (1999), 'To Shame or Not to Shame: Sexuality in the Mediterranean Diaspora', in R.A. Simkins and S.L. Cook (eds), *The Social World of the Hebrew Bible: Twenty-Five Years of Social Sciences in the Academy*, 163–76, Semeia 87, Atlanta, GA: Scholars Press.

Brumfiel, E.M. (1995), 'Heterarchy and the Analysis of Complex Societies: Comments', in R.M. Ehrenreich, C.L. Crumley and J.E. Levy (eds), *Heterarchy and the Analysis of Complex Societies*, 125–31, Arlington, VA: American Anthropological Association.

Camp, C.V. (1998), '1 and 2 Kings', in C.A. Newsom and S.H. Ringe (eds), *Women's Bible Commentary*, 102–16, rev. edn, Louisville, KY: Westminster John Knox Press.

Campbell, J.K. (1964), *Honour, Family, and Patronage: A Study of Institutions and Moral Values in a Greek Mountain Community*, Oxford: Clarendon Press.

Cassuto, D. (2008), 'Bringing Home the Artifacts: A Social Interpretation of Loom Weights in Context', in B.A. Nakhai (ed.), *The World of Women in the Ancient and Classical Near East*, 63–77, Newcastle upon Tyne: Cambridge Scholars.

Cassuto, D. (2011), 'Domestic vs. Non-Domestic: Identification and Interpretation of Weaving Workshops in the Archaeological Record', paper given at the American Schools of Oriental Research Annual Meeting, San Francisco.

Cogan, M. and H. Tadmor (1988), *II Kings: A New Translation with Introduction and Commentary*, AB 11, Garden City, NY: Doubleday.

Counihan, C.M. (1998), 'Introduction: Food and Gender – Identity and Power', in C.M. Counihan and S.L. Kaplan (eds), *Food and Gender: Identity and Power*, 1–10, Amsterdam: Harwood.

Counihan, C.M. (1999), *The Anthropology of Food and the Body: Gender, Meaning, and Power*, New York: Routledge.

Crumley, C.L. (1979), 'Three Locational Models: An Epistemological Assessment of Anthropology and Archaeology', in M.B. Schiffer (ed.), *Advances in Archaeological Method and Theory 2*, 141–73, New York: Academic Press.

Crumley, C.L. (1995), 'Heterarchy and the Analysis of Complex Societies', in R.M. Ehrenreich, C.L. Crumley and J.E. Levy (eds), *Heterarchy and the Analysis of Complex Societies*, 1–5, Arlington, VA: American Anthropological Association.

Crumley, C.L. (2005), 'Remember How to Organize: Heterarchy Across Disciplines', C.S. Beekman and W.W. Baden (eds), *Nonlinear Models for Archaeology and Anthropology: Continuing the Revolution*, 35–50. Aldershot: Ashgate.

Deutschmann, B.C. (2022), *Creating Gender in the Garden: The Inconstant Partnership of Eve and Adam*, LHBOTS 729, London: Bloomsbury T&T Clark.

Ehrenreich, R.M., C.L. Crumley and J.E. Levy, eds (1995), *Heterarchy and the Analysis of Complex Societies*, Arlington, VA: American Anthropological Association.

Esler, P.F. (2005), 'Social-Scientific Models in Biblical Interpretation', in P.F. Esler (ed.), *Ancient Israel: The Old Testament in Its Social Context*, 3–32, Minneapolis, MN: Fortress Press.

Fischer, I. and M.N. Puerto with A. Taschl-Erber (2011), 'Introduction: Women, Bible, and Reception History: An International Project in Theology and Gender Research', in I. Fischer and M.N. Puerto with A. Taschl-Erber (eds), *Torah: Hebrew Bible / Old Testament*, 1–30, The Bible and Women: An Encyclopedia of Exegesis and Cultural History 1.1, Atlanta, GA: Society of Biblical Literature.

Fontaine, C.R. (1990), 'The Sage in Family and Tribe', in J.G. Gammie and L.G. Perdue (eds), *The Sage in Israel and the Ancient Near East*, 155–64, Winona Lake, IN: Eisenbrauns.

Fuchs, E. (2000), *Sexual Politics in the Biblical Narrative: Reading the Hebrew Bible as a Woman*, Sheffield: Sheffield Academic Press.

Friedl, E. (1967), 'The Position of Women: Appearance and Reality', *Anthropological Quarterly*, 40 (3): 97–108.

Frymer-Kensky, T. (2002), *Reading the Women of the Bible*, New York: Schocken.

Gilchrist, R. (1999), *Gender and Archaeology: Contesting the Past*, London: Routledge.

González-Marcén, P., S. Montón-Subías and M. Picazo (2008), 'Toward an Archaeology of Maintenance Activities', in S. Montón-Subías and M. Sánchez-Romero (eds), *Engendering Social Dynamics: The Archaeology of Maintenance Activities*, 3–8, BAR International Series 1862, Oxford: Archaeopress.

Goody, J. (1982), *Cooking, Class, and Cuisine: A Study in Comparative Sociology*, Cambridge: Cambridge University Press.

Gottwald, N.K. (2001), *The Politics of Ancient Israel*, LAI, Louisville, KY: Westminster John Knox Press.

Greenfield, J. (1982), '*Adi balṭu* – Care for the Elderly and Its Rewards', in *Vorträge gehalten auf der 28: Rencontre Assyriologique Internationale in Wien, 6.–10. Juli 1981*, 309–16, AfOB 19, Horn: Berger.

Guenther, A. (2005), 'A Typology of Israelite Marriage: Kinship, Socio-Economic, and Religious Factors', *JSOT*, 29 (4): 387–407.

Hart, L.K. (1992), *Time, Religion, and Social Experience in Rural Greece*, Lanham, MD: Rowman & Littlefield.

Hays-Gilpin, K. (2000), 'Feminist Scholarship in Archaeology', *Annals of the American Academy of Political and Social Science*, 571: 89–106.

Hendon, J. (1996), 'Archaeological Approaches to the Organization of Domestic Labor: Household Practice and Domestic Relations', *Annual Review of Anthropology*, 25: 45–61.

Hernando, A. (2008), 'Why Did History Not Appreciate Maintenance Activities?', in S. Montón-Subías and M. Sánchez-Romero (eds), *Engendering Social Dynamics: The Archaeology of Maintenance Activities*, 9–15, BAR International Series 1862, Oxford, Archaeopress.

Hirschfeld, Y. (1995), 'The Traditional Palestinian House: Results of a Survey in the Hebron Hills', in Y. Hirschfeld (ed.), *The Palestinian Dwelling in the Roman-Byzantine Period*, 109–215, Jerusalem: Franciscan Printing Press and Israel Exploration Society.

Huebner, S.R. (2017), 'A Mediterranean Family? A Comparative Approach to the Ancient World', in S.R. Huebner and G. Nathan (eds), *Mediterranean Families in Antiquity: Households, Extended Families, and Domestic Space*, 3–26, Oxford: Wiley-Blackwell.

Kawashima, R.S. (2011), 'Could a Woman Say "No" in Biblical Israel? On the Genealogy of Legal Status in Biblical Law and Literature', *Association for Jewish Studies Review*, 35 (1): 1–22.

King, P.J. and Stager, L.E. (2001), *Life in Biblical Israel*, Louisville, KY: Westminster John Knox Press.

Knight, D.A. (2000), 'Village Law and the Book of the Covenant', in S.M. Olyan and R.C. Culley (eds), *'A Wise and Discerning Mind': Essays in Honor of Burke O. Long*, 163–79, Providence, RI: Brown Judaic Studies.

Kohl, S. (1988), 'Women's Participation in North American Family Agricultural Enterprises', in W.G. Haney and J.N. Knowles (eds), *Women and Farming: Changing Roles, Changing Structures*, 89–108, Boulder, CO: Westview.

Kray, S. (2002), '"New Mode of Feminist Historical Analysis" – Or Just Another Collusion with "Patriarchal" Bias?', *Shofar*, 20 (3): 66–90.

LaBianca, Ø.S. (1999), 'Salient Features of Iron Age Tribal Kingdoms', in B. MacDonald and R.W. Younker (eds), *Ancient Ammon*, 19–23, Leiden: E.J. Brill.

Lambert, D. (2016), 'Honor: The Hebrew Bible / Old Testament', in *Encyclopedia of the Bible and Its Reception, Vol. 12*, 330–3, Berlin: De Gruyter.

Lawrence, B. (2010), 'Gender Analysis: Gender and Method in Biblical Studies', in J.M. LeMon and K.H. Richards (eds), *Method Matters: Essays on the Interpretation of the Hebrew Bible in Honor of David L. Petersen*, 333–48, Leiden: E.J. Brill.

Lemos, T.M. (2015), 'Were Israelite Women Chattel? Shedding New Light on an Old Question', in J.J. Collins, T.M. Lemos and S.M. Olyan (eds), *Worship, Women, and War: Essays in Honor of Susan Niditch*, 227–41, Brown Judaic Studies Series 357, Providence, RI: Brown University Press.

Lerner, G. (1986), *The Creation of Patriarchy*, New York: Oxford University Press.

Lesko, B.S. (1989), 'Preface', in B.S. Lesko (ed.), *Women's Earliest Records: From Ancient Egypt and Western Asia*, xiii–xviii, Atlanta, GA: Scholars Press.

Levy, J.E. (2006), 'Gender, Heterarchy, and Hierarchy', in S.M. Nelson (ed.), *Handbook of Gender in Archaeology*, 219–46, Lanham, MD: AltaMira.

Marsman, H.J. (2003), *Women in Ugarit and Israel: Their Social and Religious Position in the Context of the Ancient Near East*, Leiden: E.J. Brill.

McClintock-Fulkerson, M. (2001), *Changing the Subject: Women's Discourses and Feminist Theology*, Eugene, OR: Wipf and Stock.

Meagher, M. (2011), 'Patriarchy', in G. Ritzier and J.M. Ryan (eds), *Concise Encyclopedia of Sociology*, 441–2, Hoboken, NJ: Wiley-Blackwell.

Meyers, C. (1988), *Discovering Eve: Ancient Israelite Women in Context*, New York: Oxford University Press.
Meyers, C. (2006), 'Heterarchy or Hierarchy? Archaeology and the Theorizing of Israelite Society', in S. Gitin, J.E. Wright and J.P. Dessel (eds), *Confronting the Past: Archaeological and Historical Essays in Honor of William G. Dever*, 245–54, Winona Lake, IN: Eisenbrauns.
Meyers, C. (2009), 'Women in the OT', in *New Interpreter's Dictionary of the Bible 5*, 888–92, Nashville, TN: Abingdon Press.
Meyers, C. (2013), *Rediscovering Eve: Ancient Israelite Women in Context*, New York: Oxford University Press.
Meyers, C. (2014), 'Was Ancient Israel a Patriarchal Society?', *JBL*, 133 (1): 8–27.
Meyers, C. (2021a), 'Food and Gender', in J. Fu, C. Shafer-Elliott and C. Meyers (eds), *T&T Clark Handbook of Food in the Hebrew Bible and Ancient Israel*, 383–98, London: Bloomsbury T&T Clark.
Meyers, C. (2021b), 'Mothers' Wisdom: Technical Training and Lessons for Life', in T.M. Lemos, J.D. Rosenblum, K.B. Stern and D.S. Ballentine (eds), *With the Loyal You Show Yourself Loyal: Essays on the Relationships in the Hebrew Bible in Honor of Saul M. Olyan*, 13–28, AIL 42, Atlanta, GA: SBL Press.
Meyers, C. (forthcoming), 'Eve in the Hebrew Bible', in C. Blyth and E. Colgan (eds), *The Routledge Companion to Eve*, Abingdon: Routledge.
Meyers, C., T. Craven and R.S. Kraemer, eds (2000), *Women in Scripture: A Dictionary of the Named and Unnamed Women in the Hebrew Bible, the Apocryphal/Deuterocanonical Books, and the New Testament*, Boston, MA: Houghton Mifflin.
Myres, S.L. (1982), *Westering Women and the Frontier Experience 1800–1915*, Albuquerque: University of New Mexico Press.
Nakhai, B.A. (2011), 'Varieties of Religious Expression in the Domestic Setting', in A. Yasur-Landau, J. Ebeling, and L. Mazow (eds), *Household Archaeology in the Ancient Israel and Beyond*, 347–60, CHANE 50, Leiden: E.J. Brill.
Nash, G.J. (2009), 'Patriarchy', in R. Kitchen and N. Thrift (eds), *International Encyclopedia of Human Geography*, 102–7, Amsterdam: Elsevier.
Nelson, S.M., ed. (2007), *Handbook of Gender in Archaeology*, Lanham, MD: AltaMira.
O'Connor, K.M. (2006), 'The Feminist Movement Meets the Old Testament: One Woman's Perspective', in L. Day and C. Pressler (eds), *Engaging the Bible in a Gendered World: An Introduction to Feminist Biblical Interpretation in Honor of Katharine Sakenfeld*, 3–24, Louisville, KY: Westminster John Knox Press.
Pomeroy, S.B. (1994), *Xenophon,* Oeconomicus: *A Social and Historical Commentary*, Oxford: Clarendon Press.
Ringe, S.H. (1998), 'When Women Interpret the Bible', in C.A. Newsom and S.H. Ringe (eds), *Women's Bible Commentary*, 1–9, rev. edn, Louisville, KY: Westminster John Knox Press.
Rogers, S.C. (1975), 'Female Forms of Power and the Myth of Male Dominance: A Model of Female/Male Interaction in Peasant Society', *American Ethnologist*, 2 (4): 727–56.
Ruether, R.R. (1985), 'Feminist Interpretation: A Method of Correlation', in L.M. Russell (ed.), *Feminist Interpretations of the Bible*, 111–24, Philadelphia, PA: Westminster.
Salamone, S.D. (1987), 'Tradition and Gender: The *Nikokyrio* – the Economics of Sex Role Complementarity in Rural Greece', *Ethos*, 15 (2): 203–25.
Salem, H.J. (1999), 'Implications of Cultural Tradition: The Case of Palestinian Traditional Pottery', in T. Kapitan (ed.), *Archaeology, History and Culture in Palestine and the Near East: Essays in Memory of Albert E. Glock*, 66–82, Atlanta, GA: Scholars Press.

Saller, R.P. (1994), *Patriarchy, Property, and Death in the Roman Family Economy*, Cambridge: Cambridge University Press.

Schloen, J.D. (2001), *The House of the Father as Fact and Symbol: Patrimonialism in Ugarit and the Ancient Near East*, SAHL 2, Winona Lake, IN: Eisenbrauns.

Schroer, S. (1998), 'Toward a Feminist Reconstruction of the History of Israel', in L. Schottroff, S. Schroer and M.-T. Wacker, *Feminist Interpretation: The Bible in Women's Perspective*, transl. M. and B. Rumscheidt, 83–176, Minneapolis, MN: Fortress Press.

Schroer, S. (2000), 'Abigail: A Wise Woman Works for Peace', in S. Schroer, *Wisdom Has Built Her House: Studies on the Figure of Sophia in the Bible*, 78–83, transl. L.M. Mahoney and W. McDonough, Collegeville, MN: Liturgical Press.

Schüssler Fiorenza, E. (2001), *Wisdom Ways: Introducing Feminist Biblical Interpretation*, Maryknoll, NY: Orbis Books.

Sered, S.S. (1994), *Priestess, Mother, Sacred Sister: Religions Dominated by Women*, New York: Oxford University Press.

Shields, M. (2010), 'A Feast Fit for a King: Food and Drink in the Abigail Story,' in T. Linafelt, C.V. Camp and T. Beal (eds), *The Fate of King David: The Past and Present of a Biblical Icon*, 38–54, LHBOTS 500, New York: T&T Clark.

Spencer-Wood, S.M. (1999), 'Gendering Power', in T. Sweely (ed.), *Manifesting Power: Gender and Interpretation of Power in Archaeology*, 175–83, London: Routledge.

Stein, D.E.S., ed. (2006), *The Contemporary Torah: A Gender-Sensitive Adaptation of the JPS Translation*, Philadelphia, PA: Jewish Publication Society.

Stein, G. (1998), 'Heterogeneity, Power, and Political Economy: Some Current Research Issues in the Archaeology of Old World Complex Societies', *Journal of Archaeological Research*, 6 (1): 1–44.

Sweely, T.L. (1999), 'Introduction', in T.L. Sweely (ed.), *Manifesting Power: Gender and Interpretation of Power in Archaeology*, 1–14, London: Routledge.

Tilley, J.T. (2000), 'Cultural Relativism', *Human Rights Quarterly*, 22 (2): 501–47.

Watson, P.J. (1979), *Archaeological Ethnography in Western Iran*, Viking Fund Publications in Anthropology 57, Tucson: University of Arizona Press.

Wells, B. (2008), 'What Is Biblical Law? A Look at Pentateuchal Rules and Near Eastern Practice', *CBQ*, 70 (2): 223–43.

Westbrook R. and B. Wells (2009), *Everyday Law in Biblical Israel: An Introduction*. Louisville, KY: Westminster John Knox.

Wilson, C.T. (1906), *Peasant Life in the Holy Land*, London: John Murray.

Whyte, M.K. (1978), *The Status of Women in Pre-industrial Societies*, Princeton, NJ: Princeton University Press.

Womack, M. (2001), *Being Human: An Introduction to Cultural Anthropology*, 2nd edn, Upper Saddle River, NJ: Prentice-Hall.

Zevit, Z. (2001), *The Religions of Ancient Israel: A Synthesis of Parallactic Approaches*, New York: Continuum.

# CHAPTER ELEVEN

# Anthropologies of the Hebrew Bible

JAN DIETRICH

The discipline of anthropology seeks insight into the human being, both emically, from an interior view, reconstructing a culture's implicit and explicit assumptions about the nature of the human being as such and of its members in particular (e.g. some practices of cultural anthropology), and etically, from an exterior view, ascertaining the essential nature of, conditions of, and data on the human being as such or of a certain culture in particular (e.g. the practices of physical anthropology), though the strict distinction between and delimitation of these perspectives have problems (cf., e.g., Lawrence 2004: 10–11). The first section reconstructs important Hebrew Bible images of the human being in general and of the Israelites in particular, especially in terms of capabilities and tasks (liminal anthropologies). The two subsequent sections portray ancient Israel's distinctive forms of social relationships (social anthropology) and its distinct modes of thinking (ancient epistemologies).

## HUMAN ABILITIES AND DUTIES – LIMINAL ANTHROPOLOGIES

In Gen. 1.26–28, the human being is created by God as the final step in Creation, receiving the highest honour. The human being is created as both male and female from the beginning and in the image (*ṣelem*) and likeness (*dᵉmût*) of God. These two terms are also found, in their ancient Aramaic form, on the statue of King Hadad-Yiši found at Tell Fekherye, describing the statue as the king's image, intended to be permanently present at the temple of the storm God in place of the king (COS 2.34; KAI 309; cf. Abou-Assaf, Bordreuil and Millard 1982). Additionally, in ancient Egypt and Mesopotamia, the king is often described as an image of the gods and/or their substitute as ruler on earth (for Egypt, cf. Ockinga 1984; for Mesopotamia, cf. Maul 1998). Therefore, in Gen. 1.26–28, the human being, as an image of God, is like an ancient Near Eastern king, taking the form of a living statue of God and as God's representative on earth, who rules over all the animals across the three dominions of the world (sea, air and land, cf. Janowski 2019: 407–15). In Gen. 1.28, the meaning of 'to rule' is presented in terms of 'to subdue' (*kābaš*) and 'to have dominion over' (*rādāh*), presenting the human being in the image of a king who rules more or less autocratically but who also has a commitment to the gods and to just principles, including defending the weak (e.g. Psalm 72; cf. Dietrich 2012). In Gen. 1.29–30, the primeval human being and the primeval animal are created vegetarian, and only after the Flood is the human being allowed to eat flesh (although without blood, Gen. 9.3–4). With God's blessing, the human being is to be fruitful, multiply and fill the earth (Gen. 1.28, 9.1), and the subsequent chapters unfold the multiplication and diversification of the human being. Gen. 5.1 and 9.6, together with the parallel text Psalm 8, present the human being such that the human image of God is not confined to the primeval state, but its royalty is conferred as it were 'democratically' on all people, elevating the status and responsibility of the human being in general (cf. Neumann-Gorsolke 2004; Schellenberg 2011).

In the second, non-priestly account of Creation (Gen. 2.4b–3.24), the human being is not said to be formed of body and soul as two parts, separate in principle, which can, as in Pythagorean and Platonic philosophy, become separated at death into an eternal soul and a decaying body (cf. Müller 2009; Alt 2013). Instead, the human being is viewed as a synthetic whole (cf. Janowski 2012). In this account, the human being (with no gender as yet)[1] is formed by God out of 'dust of the soil' ('*āfār min hā'ªdāmāh*), and God breathes the 'breath of life' (*nišmat ḥayyîm*) into his nostrils. These two sentences are synthetically concluded by a third one, which indicates that both of these constituents are needed to make man a 'living being' (*nefeš ḥayyāh* Gen. 2.7). Being made from the soil, the human being shares basic characteristics with animal life, which God forms from the soil as well (Gen. 2.19). In death, all animal life, including human life, returns to dust (Gen. 3.19; Eccl. 3.20; cf. Sir. 17.1–2).

Complementary to this idea of a return to the soil and also complementary to the culture of interment and the expression 'to be gathered to one's people' (Gen 25.8 and elsewhere; cf. Krüger 2009) is the idea of a netherworld. Here, the human being is conceived of as moving to the netherworld (*šeʾôl*) in its entirety, including both its body (Gen. 42.38; 1 Sam. 28.14; Job 17.13–16, 21.12–13) and its 'life force' or 'soul' (*nefeš*, Pss. 30.4, 86.13, 89.49; cf. *psychē* in archaic Greece, e.g. Homer, Iliad 1:3–4; *The Shield of Heracles*, l. 254). When Kohelet, the speaker of Ecclesiastes, asks whether the human breath goes up and the animal breath down to the earth at death (Eccl. 3.22), and when he later specifies that the dust turns back to the earth and the breath (of the human being) turns back to God, who gave it (Eccl. 12.7), the 'breath' (*rûªḥ*) is not described as the eternal soul of the human being but is more the single emanation or objectivation of God's life-breath (*nefeš ḥayyāh*), which returns to God from the individual human being in whom it was the power to breathe. According to some biblical and extra-biblical sources, the life force or soul (*nefeš*) seems to be a dynamic force that is separable from the dead body but in need of another corporeal container: The difficult text Num. 19.15 seems to communicate that the *nefeš* of a dead person may slip into an open vessel (cf. Michel 1994), and according to the Syrian Kutamuwa stela (line 5), the 'soul' (*nbš*) of Kutamuwa rests in his stela (cf. Pardee 2009: 53–4).

---

[1] In the second Creation account, the human being is not created at once as both male and female (as in the first account) but is initially not given any gender determination. Only after the human being is being divided into two parts are the terms 'man' (*'îš*) and 'woman' (*'išāh*) used (Gen. 2.22–24), and the generic term *'ādām* then evolves into the proper name 'Adam'. Still, this perspective appears to be a patriarchal one, as the evolution comes from the generic term *'ādām* to the male proper name 'Adam' who is the speaker in v. 23 who praises the 'woman' as being taken from his own flesh. V. 24 does not seem to imply any matriarchal lineage but that the mature man leaves his parents to become a full citizen and establish his own patriarchal family with 'his' wife (*'ištô*).

Death is not considered here as a non-existence but as a privation of life capacities (Ps. 88.5), envisaged to mean weakness (Isa. 14.10; Job 14.10) and being like a captive bird (cf. Berlejung 2001). A human being who is affected by sickness or social isolation (social death) experiences this privation of life capacities as a nearness of death, where death appears to be extending into human life. In this type of extreme situation, God may rescue a living person from the clutches of the netherworld (e.g. Psalm 18), but, once people have died, God usually is considered to have no further relationship with them (Pss. 6.6, 88.11–13), although some extra-biblical inscriptions (Khirbet el-Qom, Ketef Hinnom) seem to express a hope for a continued protective relationship in the grave (cf. Berlejung 2008). It is mostly in later Hellenistic texts that human beings appear to remain in community with God after death, in incorporeal form (Ps 49.16, 73.26). The idea of corporeal resurrection, however, is not generally present in the Old Testament. Aside from a few precursors (Isa. 26.19; Ezek. 37.12; Dan. 12.2–3; a different understanding is present in 1 Kgs 17.17–23, among other texts), it is in Hellenistic intertestamentary texts, especially in 2 Macc. 7.9–14, that we find the idea of corporeal resurrection that is later prominently expressed in the New Testament (Lk. 14.14; Acts 24.15; 1 Corinthians 15).

The second Creation account tells how the human being acquires, against God's precepts (Gen. 2.17), the capacity to understand good and evil and discern one from the other, which confers godlike status (Gen. 3.5, 3.22). This seems different from the case of Mesopotamia, where in Atra-hasis I: 237–43, from the beginning, the human being is being created with 'reason' (*ṭēmu*, cf. Oshima 2012), while in Genesis 3, reason and shame are added to the original condition.[2] To become fully godlike, however, eternal life is needed as well, and to avoid this, God ensures that the human being is prevented from accessing the tree of life (Gen. 3.22–24). With this origin story, the second Creation account explains the origin of the limited human lifespan, human understanding and the sense of shame (Gen. 3.7–10). The capacity for understanding and discerning good from evil and the ability to decide and act against God's precepts implies a presumption of autonomous decision making (cf. Deut. 30.10–14; Dietrich 2019b), the ability to decide for or against adopting the attitude of obedient listening (see section 'Modes of thinking in the Hebrew Bible – ancient epistemologies', below).

The ability to discern good from evil is located in the human heart, the organ of thinking, volition and feeling (e.g. 1 Kgs 3.9–12, 5.9) and relates to a wisdom-like orientational knowledge that helps, as in Proverbs, a person live a good and prosperous life. In many other texts, however, human insight is given in theological terms and refers to Israel's knowledge or belief in God and of his instruction (e.g. Exod. 29.45–46; Deut. 4.32–40), an insight that may be extended to the Gentiles (e.g. Ezekiel 39; Daniel 4). It builds upon God's revelation, especially his action of electing and releasing Israel, from which knowledge–belief and submission follow (e.g. Exod. 20.2–3). When this knowledge–belief is lost, prophetic and other words may bring the hope for a new Creation of the Israelite heart (Psalm 51; Jer. 31.31–34; Ezek. 11.19, 36.24–28; cf. Janowski 2019: 471–80).

---

[2] It is possible to argue for epistemological implications already being implicit in Gen. 2.15–25 (cf. Johnson 2013: 22–44), although also in this case as well, the acquisition of reasoning ability comes after the Creation narrated in Gen. 2.7.

## HUMAN RELATIONSHIPS – SOCIAL ANTHROPOLOGIES

In the Bible, the human being is highly sensitive to social, environmental and religious relationships, and its own vitality is strongly dependent upon them. To live within social relationships, or at least environmental ones, seems to be a human universal, but the sensitivity with which the Hebrew Bible perceives and depicts man's life within and dependence upon social relationships is striking, as well as the special forms of relationships to be found in ancient Israel. Here, the human being is not part of a collective personality, as scholars have long postulated (e.g. Robinson 1992; for a critique, e.g. Rogerson 1970), nor an individual in the modern sense, seeking to unfold its capabilities and expressing its inner depths (cf. Taylor 1989). Instead, the behaviour of the human being in ancient Israel and the attitudes on which this behaviour is based have the goal of maintaining honour, avoiding shame and acting in a community-promoting manner through steadfastness of character (cf. Dietrich 2017a). Customarily, maintaining one's honour and promoting one's community accompany each other, revealing how strongly 'the subject (1) is deeply embedded, or engaged, in its social identity, (2) is comparatively decentred and undefined with respect to personal boundaries, (3) is relatively transparent, socialized, and embodied (in other words, is altogether lacking in a sense of "inner depths"), and (4) is "authentic" precisely in its heteronomy, in its obedience to another and dependence upon another' (di Vito 1999: 221).

This high sensitivity to interpersonal relationships can be seen, among other places, through the interpersonal significance of the biblical body terms used where body image and social relationships overlap (cf. Berlejung 2009; Janowski 2013: esp. 63–198). The term 'life force' (*nefeš*) discussed above indicates that a person is a 'Needy Man' (Wolff 1974: 10–25), seeking to incorporate or assimilate something else, and as something seeking relationships and drawing its vital energy from the relationships in which it is involved. 'This *nephesh*-ness of the human being means that we are entirely oriented to relationship, from the very beginning' (Schroer and Staubli 2001: 58). The *nefeš* seeks physical unity to remain with a beloved person (Gen. 34.2–3); it loves (Gen. 44.30–31; Deut. 6.5; 1 Sam. 18.1; Song 1.7; among others), hates (2 Sam. 5.8; Isa. 1.14), and longs to see God (Pss. 42; 63.2, 84.3; cf. Isa. 26.9). 'The *nefesh* is that part of a human being that enables her to connect with the cultic sphere as the place of divine presence' (Schüle 2014: 152). The face (*pānîm*) that one turns toward others (*pānāh*) exhibits a similar pattern. A body term, it is used to describe relationships and designates 'real personal presence, relationship, and meeting (or refusal to meet)' (Simian-Yofre 2001: 607). A third example[3] is the heart (*leb*), the organ for thinking, volition and feeling, as noted above. Its main interpersonal significance is in its outer-directed mode of a 'listening thinking' (described in more detail below, in the section 'Modes of thinking in the Hebrew Bible – ancient epistemologies').

The family is the core actor in society and forms the character traits of the individual that are typical of most its members (cf. Fromm 1969; Dietrich forthcoming). Thus, the father figure and patriarch, as head of the household, ensures that his wife, children, maids and servants adopt appropriate cultural habits and behave according to society's expectations. The general good habits to be expected from all members of society, from the king (e.g. 1 Kings 3; Psalm 72) to the pupil and the son (e.g. Deut. 21.18–21; Proverbs

---

[3] For more examples on other body terms, cf. Schroer and Staubli 2001 and Dietrich 2017a: 25–7.

*passim*), pertain, with the help of the 'listening heart', to an outer-directed social habitus, whose main attitude is openness to ruling cultural norms and habitual forms of behaviour. For biblical texts, this means internalizing the instructions presented in traditional wisdom and law (e.g. Deut. 6.4–9; Proverbs 1–9), submitting 'to an external authority' (Newsom 2012: 12) and making listening (*šāmaʿ*), with the two aspects of hearing and obeying, a key concept for social character training, focusing on traditions that are given from outside instead on an individuals' own inner depths.

This high sensitivity to mutual social dependence is rooted in the 'family-based society' of ancient Israel (cf. Kessler 2006: 49–72), clearly present in the text of the Hebrew Bible, where the individual always appears as part of a family, kin, clan, tribe and, ultimately, a people, the people of Israel, irrespective of the fact that, from an etic point of view, the specific attribution of the relevant Hebrew terms to these institutions is subject to debate and that the term 'tribe' (*šēbeṭ*) in particular is a vague construction, seemingly a social construct (cf. Rogerson 1978: 86–101; Lemche 1985: 245–90). Individuals perceive themselves to be primarily integrated in the family and the clan, and society is considered to be and is constructed in terms of patrilineal lineages: 'Hence, family-centeredness should be understood in a directly literal sense: the family *is* the *center*, not only of the social interaction of its members, but of the system of meaning out of which such cultures arose' (McVann 1998: 75–6). In spite of the historical changes that have taken place in social structures, this part of ancient Israel's self-perception is seen to persist throughout its history, as part of its socio-anthropological *longue durée*. By contrast, other sociologically relevant, transfamilial power structures and hierarchies, from egalitarian social structures of early times to the hierarchical power and class structures found during the period of kings and to the community structures of provincial Persian society and the hierocratic structures of the Hellenistic period, all of which play an important but shifting role in the social anthropology of ancient Israel.

In Israel's family-centred society, only the *pater familias* as head of the household is a fully autonomous legal person, with his wife/wives, children and servants occupying the lower status of a legal person with fewer claims and rights (e.g. Exod. 21.2–11; Numbers 30). No sharp distinction is drawn between the human and animal worlds (cf. Riede forthcoming): the domesticated animals, like his wife/wives, children and servants, belong to the household of the patriarch, and smaller domesticated animals (sheep, goats and dogs) may stay within the house, at least at night. Legally, domesticated animals may be subject to punishment as if they were legal persons (Exod. 21.28–32; Lev. 20.15–16; cf. Exod. 11.5, 12.12–29; Deut. 13.15; Jonah 3.7–8). They may also be taken to have legal rights (Exod. 22.29, 23.4–5, 23.12, 23.19, 34.26; Lev. 22.27–28; Deut. 14.11, 25.4) and may be treated in moral contexts as if they were social persons possessing knowledge (Isa. 1.3) and needs (Lev. 18.22–24; Prov. 12.10). Some legal rules may even apply to wild animals (Exod. 23.11; Lev. 25.11; Deut. 22.6–7), and the wisdom of the wild animals may be used to teach the human being (Prov. 6.6–8, 30.24–28; cf. Job 38.36; Jer. 8.7). The hope for a world without violence includes the animal world (Isa. 11.6–10, 65.25).

Personal identity is shaped through the eyes of others, incorporating how other people see, appreciate and treat others (cf. Assmann 2011: 133–4). Honour is a social value that is awarded to each person according to their position in the community, provided that this person conducts themself 'habitually in line with the collective expectations that are "ethically" linked to their social status' (Honneth 1995: 123). In the Hebrew Bible, the pursuit of honour and the avoidance of shame are 'core values' (Plevnik 2000: 106), that is, fundamental cultural strivings that are shared by most members of society as character traits. Striving for honour here refers to typical forms of honour, especially of the body, social status, fame, the dead and the wise, and disgrace, in the form of the respective opposites of these, is avoided (cf. Dietrich 2009). Disgrace must be avoided because it expresses social relationships that are cut off (cf. Klopfenstein 1972; Grund 2013). The Psalms of lament in particular make it clear that severed relationships imply social death, and that the aim of prayer is to re-establish one's relationship with God and with the people (cf. Janowski 2013). Shame, on the other hand, can also include positive and sensible self-reflexive attitudes (cf. Dietrich 2018a) [see also Chapter 12 in this volume].

Next to honour and shame, issues of sin and guilt are among the most important questions in ancient Israel. This implies that the distinction between the so-called cultures of shame or guilt (cf. Benedict 1946) does not apply to the case of ancient Israel. Instead, we observe here a culture that distinguishes itself through its prioritization of avoiding 'guilt-based shame' (Laniak 1998: 8–9), establishing and controlling the attitudes, standards and behavioural patterns of its members (in relation to this social function of honour and shame, cf. Vogt and Zingerle 1994: 23). An honourable man keeps his word and is considered to possess both the character and the power to implement what he promises. Truthfulness and faithfulness are characteristic of an honourable man in various loyalty relationships because, with these, ethos is found in the form of solidarity (cf. Hempel 1964: 32–67). This is why terms like truthfulness ('emet/ 'emûnāh) and benevolence (ḥesed), together with justice (mišpāṭ) and fairness/righteousness (ṣedeq/ ṣedāqāh), play a decisive role in the social anthropology of the Hebrew Bible.

Steadfast people can be relied on, making 'steadfastness' ('emûnāh) another important socio-anthropological concept for the Hebrew Bible (cf. Jepsen 1974; Dietrich 2014). Whether it is a good custodian (Neh. 13.13), messenger (Prov. 25.13), friend (Prov. 27.6), servant (1 Sam. 22.14) or witness (Isa. 8.2) that is under discussion, a person in any of these roles must be reliable (neʾĕman). A reliable person ('yš 'emet Neh. 7.2; cf. Exod. 18.21) is to be characterized by a steadfast and community-oriented attitude, walking the path of 'truthfulness' (derek 'emûnāh Ps. 119.30), acting as a 'man of loyalty' ('yš 'emûnîm Prov. 20.6) and a 'friend of reliability' ('oheb 'emûnāh Sir. Ms A 6:14f; cf. Dietrich 2014; Olyan 2017). For this reason, truth and lies do not only describe knowledge but are community-supporting concepts: truth as truthfulness represents a community-promoting habitus and the lie is a community-adverse habitus (cf. Klopfenstein 1964: 353).

A similar idea is found in reciprocal behaviour, which also promotes community. Ḥesed ('benevolence') is a 'relational concept' and belongs to 'the realm of interpersonal relations' (Zobel 1986: 49, 51). Just as the 'action of Ma'at' is the basis for 'connective justice' in ancient Egypt (cf. Assmann 1990), the 'action of ḥesed' is the basis for a society rooted in mutuality, solidarity, and responsivity (cf. Dietrich 2018b) and oriented toward justice (mišpāṭ) and fairness/righteousness (ṣedāqāh) (cf. Koch 1991a). The proverb 'Whoever digs a pit will fall into it, and a stone will come back on the one who starts it rolling' (Prov. 26.27, NRSV) seems to imply, on a more theoretical level, that 'The man who does evil to another does evil to himself' (Hesiod, *Work and Days* I: 265). The responsive 'action of ḥesed' presupposes that community-enabling action is reciprocated by further community-promoting action by others (cf. Gen. 21.23; Josh. 2.12–14; 2 Sam. 2.5–6, 10.2; 1 Kgs 2.7; Zobel 1986: 47–8). That is, the way that you behave toward others will direct how the community responds to you (cf. Janowski 1999), including God, 'for those who honour me I will honour, and those who despise me shall be treated with contempt' (1 Sam. 2.30, NRSV, cf. 10.2). High sensitivity to responsive action and speech guides the behaviour of a human being in the terms in which the answer to the call of God, of fellow human beings, and animals are given (Prov. 12.10; cf. Meinhold 2002: 179). In Prov. 12.10, for example, to 'know' the needs of the animal implies a way of 'responsive knowing', i.e. attending to and caring for it.

The 'continuous *ḥesed*', meaning steadfast goodwill, is to be written on the 'tablet of the heart' (Prov. 3.3), implying that socio-ethical expectations from outside are to be internalized in the form of steadfast attitudes. Elsewhere as well, an emphasis is placed not only on outer behaviour but also on the inner attitudes that remain (for legal contexts, cf. Deut. 19.4–6; Num. 35.20). Seemingly identical outer behaviour may, therefore, be viewed differently. In Proverbs, for example, human labour is regarded positively in the contrast between the diligent and the lazy (cf. Prov. 10.4, 12.24, 13.4 and elsewhere) but negatively in the context of seeking, for its own sake, revenue, productivity and wealth in the absence of a proper ethical or religious attitude (cf. Prov. 11.28, 15.16–17).

Collective identity-building constructs Israel as a tribal or clannish people (e.g. Weingart 2014) that has been delivered by God out of Egyptian servitude (e.g. Assmann 2018).[4] This deliverance was thought of first and foremost as a legal and socio-economic as well as a 'negative' liberation, where negative is taken to mean a 'release from' (that is, a negative liberty) and not as 'freedom to' (positive liberty) (cf. Berlin 1961; Dietrich 2019b). Thus, for the ancient Israelite, the concept of liberty was an important reactive concept, as the escape from a situation of almost complete dependence. In the narrative of the Hebrew Bible, the positive implications and outcomes were the voluntary approval of, obedience to, and submission under God's law.

Cultural remembrance not only provides a connection to the past and constructs collective identity but also supports social behaviour. The idea of liberation as deliverance by God from Egyptian servitude (and from Babylonian exile, cf. Isa. 40–48) results in the use of cultural remembrance strategies in relation to the socio-economic level within the land of ancient Israel itself. The society thus envisioned is grounded on liberation, and ethical commandments are motivated by Israel's liberation. A single Israelite serving in servitude under against another Israelite is to be released every seventh year *because* the Israelites themselves, collectively, had been freed from Egyptian slavery. Highlighting collective remembrance in motivation clauses (for these, cf. Markl 2015: 329–33) uses *argumenta ex historia* for ethical and legal reasons. In Deuteronomy in particular, Israel's remembrance is evoked to support charitable attitudes. The paraenetic 'You shall remember that you were a slave in the land of Egypt' (Deut. 5.15, 15.15, 16.12, 24.18–22) serves the collective biographical actualization of the super-individual experience of past servitude to promote an attitude of support for the present *personae miserae*.

In addition, the resilient handling of disaster may have positive effects on unity and identity, promoting a collective group identity (cf. Dietrich 2015). Thus, ancient Israel responds to the disaster of exile with the identity markers of monotheism, circumcision and the Sabbath, and it sets itself apart from outsiders by prohibiting mixed marriage. Faced with the destruction of Jerusalem, Israel's concept of collective and cross-generational guilt (cf. Krašovec 1999: 110–59; Dietrich 2010) can facilitate an identity-building that can explain and cope with an experienced disaster. Here, resilience can be acquired by comprehending the origin of a disaster. This is achieved by attributing its source to two connected causes, namely, (1) the wrath of God that results from (2) human

---

[4] Collective identity-building, in its socio-constructivist dimension, grew in importance under Persian rule (cf. Berquist 2006; Knoppers and Ristau 2009).

misbehaviour pertaining to moral and religious wickedness. By adopting confessions (e.g. Ezra 9; Nehemiah 9) or atonement rituals (e.g. Leviticus 4–5, 16; 2 Samuel 21), it is possible to enter into new relationships with God as a personal cause of individual or collective disaster. For example, during the famine described in 2 Samuel 21, David asks God for the cause of the famine, and this is found to be unatoned blood-guilt incurred by Saul's slaughter of the Gibeonites. It is only with this insight that an atonement ritual can be performed to end the famine. In other cases, blood-guilt can be atoned for by a close relative, acting as an avenger and killing the perpetrator. While accepting the institution of revenge, the Hebrew Bible confines it by setting up legal (cf. Deut. 19.1–13), moral (Exod. 23.4–5; Prov. 25.21–22; Lev. 19.18) and religious boundaries (Prov. 20.22; cf. Psalm 58; Dietrich 2016).

## MODES OF THINKING IN THE HEBREW BIBLE – ANCIENT EPISTEMOLOGIES

An important aspect of ancient Hebrew anthropology bears on the question of whether there was a typical Hebrew thinking mode, in a sense that can be distinguished from ancient Greek and other thinking modes, including modern ones. Here, the term 'thinking mode' is applied in the sense of cultural–historical ways of thinking (cf. Fleck 1980; Gloy 2016), which form the basis of concrete forms of knowledge. The main aim here is to reconstruct the elementary paradigms (cf. Kuhn 1962), discourses and episteme (cf. Foucault 1966, 1969) of historical thinking that developed in ancient Israel and that formed the conditions of the possibility of developing its distinct images of the human being and its historical forms of knowledge.

Binary schemata have typically been used to oppose ancient Hebrew and Greek thinking to each other as if they constituted exclusive and exhaustive alternatives (cf. esp. Boman 1970). According to Boman, Hebrew thinking is prelogical in the way described by Lévy-Bruhl (1926), but it is logical in Greece; it is dynamic in the Hebrew Bible and static-harmonic in Greece; it is focused on hearing and listening in the Hebrew Bible, but for the Greeks, thinking is visual in the sense of Bruno Snell's definition of the Greeks as an 'ocular people' (Snell 1953: esp. 1–70).[5] After Barr's justified critique of Boman's etymological method (cf. Barr 1961: 21–45), Koch sought to uphold the quest for a typical Hebrew way of thinking, which cleared the way to placing it in a common Mediterranean cultural background (cf. Koch 1991b: 17). In this way, the quest for analysing ancient Hebrew thinking appears to have been rehabilitated as neither outdated nor anachronistic but fundamental, necessary and unavoidable (cf. Dietrich 2017b; Frevel forthcoming).

### *Synthetic thinking*

Let us begin with the way of thinking that is typical for poetic texts. In this genre, found primarily in the wisdom literature and the Psalms but also seen in the prophets and

---

[5] Hebrew thinking is described as 'analytical' by Boman, in interesting contrast to other theories in the history of comparative research in this area, and ancient Greek thought is considered 'synthetic' by him. In studies before and after Boman, however, it was typical to present ancient Hebrew thinking as holistic and synthetic, with the *parallelismus membrorum* as its typical mode of expression (cf. Pedersen 1926: 108–9, 123; Wolff 1974: 8; Avrahami 2012: 24; Müller and Wagner 2014).

elsewhere, a stereometric or synthetic way of thinking prevails, which combines the aspects of a thing or a sentence into a synthetic whole, especially through the use of the so-called *parallelismus membrorum* (cf. Wolff 1974: 8; cf. Wagner 2007). Using concrete images and metaphors, notions are often described analogically, associatively and paratactically depicting their most important facets (e.g. Prov. 25.23; Amos 3.3–8).

## *Obeying listening*

Other modes of thinking also appear. Since Boman, it has been asserted that ancient Hebrew thinking could be understood as 'listening thinking', which would include an attitude of 'obeying listening' (e.g. Kraus 1972; Wolff 1974: 74–6). In opposition to this notion, the epistemological importance of visual experience in the Hebrew Bible has been ably highlighted in recent research (e.g. Ps. 48.8–9; Job 42.5–6; cf. Carasik 2006: 32–43; Savran 2009: 320–61; Avrahami 2012: 223–76). While this makes sense as a corrective, an earlier one-sidedness should not be replaced by a novel one; instead, auditive and visual epistemologies must be differentiated and contextualized into different thinking modes and text genres (cf. Dietrich 2019a).[6] In traditional wisdom literature, such as that found in Proverbs and partly in Job, Deuteronomy and many other texts influenced by Deuteronomistic traditions (such as the wisdom Psalms, the histories and Torah), obeying listening plays a key role. Here, an outer-directed mode of listening thinking is highlighted that does not focus on unfolding the inner depths of the human being but listens to and obeys tradition, the word of God and the demands of the social world (cf. Dietrich forthcoming). In terms of a cultural attitude, obeying listening in ancient Israel is more distinct than in modern individualist cultures and was perceived as positive (e.g. Prov. 23.26). The 'listening heart' (1 Kgs 3.9) refers to the internalizing of the instructions contained in traditional wisdom and law (cf. Deut. 6.4–9; Proverbs 1–9).

## *Mnemonic thinking*

As part of obeying listening, mnemonic thinking orients itself toward the cultural memory of ancient Israel (cf. Assmann 2011). Mnemonic thinking enlivens and refreshes, in persistent oral–scribal form, the cultural knowledge present in oral communicative remembrance, and here, Israel is conceived of as a teaching and memorizing society (cf. Finsterbusch 2005). In a familial context of instruction and memorization (cf. Deut. 6.20–25), epistemic virtues such as attentiveness, mindfulness, prudence, rigor, vigilance, watchfulness and willingness to learn and to achieve insight and wisdom are made central (cf. Dietrich 2018b), presenting the concept of 'one God, one shrine, one mind' (Geller 1994: 105) to eliminate other-mindedness (cf. Deut. 21.18–21) and bring the core of Israel's cultural memory (the collective liberation from Egypt by the sole God who is worthy of worship, YHWH; e.g. Deut. 6.12) to bear as the ethical reason for socio-economic support of the needy (e.g. Deuteronomy 15) [see also Chapter 15 in this volume].

---

[6] Caution must be exercised to avoid implying that the ancient Hebrew mind sought to identify thinking and perceiving because it was unable to differentiate between them. Semantically, for example, more abstract terms like *ḥāšab* existed to express thinking in contrast with 'sensory semantics'. A simple identification of sensual experience with the acquisition of knowledge cannot be ascribed to the biblical writers (cf. Fox 2007; Johnson 2013: 65–81; Dietrich 2019a), as if thinking was, for the ancient Israelite, entirely dependent upon any sensations, whether sight or hearing.

### Taxonomic thinking

In the priestly texts (as well as in some wisdom texts, cf. Alt 1951; von Rad 1955), the ancient Israelite ability for and inclination towards abstraction, accuracy, classification, discrimination and validation occupy the centre, especially in terms of the interest in formal language (which can be recognized, e.g., by its extensive use of repetition), the use of exact terms and precise categories (e.g. the categories of clean and unclean and of the holy and the profane, as well as the different types of sacrifices and feasts) and its interest in so-called list science (*Listenwissenschaft*, cf. Dietrich 2020). The priests are tasked with distinguishing between holy and profane and between clean and unclean (Lev. 10.10, 11.47, 20.25), as well as to restrict the Israelites from mixing different kinds of animals and textiles inappropriately (Lev. 19.19; Deut. 22.9–11). Taxonomic thinking here highlights seeing as the main epistemic way of achieving insight through inspection. In Leviticus 13–14, the priest inspects (the verb used is *rā'āh*, 'to see') the surface of the human skin, textiles and houses, indicating that 'ocular thinking' is not only typical for ancient Greece but is applicable to the taxonomic thinking mode of ancient Israel as well.

### Inspired thinking

In the ancient Near East, mantic science rules supreme in its interpretation of the signs of the heavens and the earth (cf. Rochberg 2016; Maul 2018). The Hebrew Bible disapproves of the search for signs in heaven and earth (e.g. Jer. 10.2) and focuses on prophetic thinking inspired by God via auditions and/or visions of God's voice and images from him, usually while awake but sometimes also in a dream state. This kind of thinking is ecstatic, in that it does not come from the heart as the organ of thinking within the human being but from outside, inspired by an external divine source that can impart a higher form of knowledge (e.g. Isa. 55.8–9) and enable deeper insight to be achieved (cf. Vall 2007). False prophecy, by contrast, is characterized by speech from the speaker's own mind or heart (e.g. Jer. 23.16–17, 25–26; cf. Hazony 2012: 161–92). The division between true and false in religion, whose origin Assmann ascribes to the 'Mosaic distinction' (Assmann 2009)[7] seems to apply especially to the prophets and to prophetically inspired traditions which emphasize epistemic wordings of knowing and unknowing (e.g. Isa. 44.9–18, 20–25; Deuteronomy 4).

### Critical thinking

Abstract thinking, including second-order thinking, entails the ability to reflect and self-reflect, to criticize and transcend the given, and to anticipate new realms by thinking outside of what is already given. It has traditionally been argued that this type of thinking originated in ancient Greece (cf. Elkana 1986; Bellah 2011: 273–82; Schiefsky 2012). However, rational reasoning, including second-order thinking, can be found in the ancient Near East as well (cf. Machinist 1986; van de Mieroop 2016, 2018), as well as in the Hebrew Bible (cf. Tsevat 1978; Gericke 2012: 371–404, 2018; Dietrich 2017b, 2019a; Schaper 2019). The institution of law requires abstraction from single events and provides society with legal rationales in the apodictic and casuistic modes (e.g. Exod.

---

[7] In later years, Assmann developed his theory further. In his most recent book, he speaks of the distinction between friend and enemy, particularly in how it pertains to the book of Exodus (Assmann 2018).

20.22–23.33), including the application of abstract principles such as impartiality and the question of truth (Deut. 13.15, 16.19–20, 17.4, 22.20), blueprints of institutions and procedures (Deut. 17.8–20, 19.15–20) and precise criteria, definitions and differentiations (e.g. Exod. 21.28–36; Lev. 25.29–31; Deut. 19.1–13). In the priestly offering catalogue of Leviticus 1–5, an abstraction from the material value of a sacrifice emerges that can be seen to parallel the 'spiritualization' of sacrifice in the Psalms and the prophets (cf. Dietrich 2021). Ethical and religious critiques in the prophetic writings distance themselves from given attitudes, behaviours and thinking, and establish modes to think critically about all of these. The prophets use abstract social and ethical standards such as justice, righteousness, truthfulness and goodness (e.g. Isa. 1.17, 21, 27; Amos 5.14–15; Mic. 6.8; cf. Barton 2014: 227–31) as evaluative criteria beyond the usual economic or cultic realms (cf. Ernst 1994: 199). In Deutero-Isaiah, a 'monotheism of knowledge' (Assmann 2009: 37, with regard to Akhenaten's monotheism) comes to the fore with the use of epistemic terms as part of unmasking the adoration of images as a false way of thinking (Isa. 44.9–18, 20–25; cf. Berlejung 1998: 378–87) and when differentiating between godlike and human thinking (Isa. 55.8–9). In the books of Job and Ecclesiastes, the wise are shown to be thinking critically about wisdom, and an epistemological critique is sketched that shows the limits of human reason (e.g. Job 28.12–13, 20–21; Eccl. 1.16–18, 7.23–24; cf., e.g., Schellenberg 2002).

## CONCLUSIONS

This conclusion asks the question how far historical developments can be detected through the material presented here. Most of the presented modes of thinking appear to run, by and large, parallel to one another. However, some historical developments do appear at second glance. As far as can be seen in the most ancient written sources, taxonomic thinking in economic contexts may have been part of the invention of writing in early Mesopotamia (cf., e.g., Nissen, Damerow and Englund 2004). Mnemonic thinking, however, seems to have developed along a separate route, through traditional obeying listening, as a special invention of the Deuteronomistic scribes of Neo-Babylonian or early Persian times. Critical thinking, already prevalent in religious and political criticisms in the prophetic writings of pre-exilic times, finds its way, in exilic and postexilic times, into other text genres as well, such as the historical texts of the Pentateuch and the Deuteronomistic History, the later prophetic texts and the Psalms, and the critical wisdom texts of Job and Ecclesiastes. The modes and qualities of abstraction and criticism seem to have increased over time, whether in synthetic texts (cf. the 'spiritualization' of the Psalms and the critique of reason in Job and Ecclesiastes), in taxonomic texts (cf. the abstraction from the material value of things in the priestly source) or in the prophetic and Deuteronomistic texts (cf. the emergence of monotheism in Deutero-Isaiah and other late texts).

The basic structures of the social anthropologies described, with their high sensitivity for social, environmental and religious relationships, appear to be part of ancient Israel's *longue durée*, especially in regard to its family- and clan-centredness (where the *pater familias* is seen as head of the household), its core values (the steadfastness of the righteous and trustworthy character, maintaining honour and avoiding guilt-based shame) and its ideal of reciprocal behaviour. Some concepts seen here, however, seem to reflect later developments, exilic and postexilic. Collective identity-building is achieved through specific family-centred modes of cultural remembrance (found especially in Deuteronomy), together with ethical motivation clauses for lawlike behaviour ('theologization of the law') and the development of collective-identity markers, such as monotheism, circumcision, the Sabbath and the prohibition of mixed marriages. After the destruction of Jerusalem, all of these helped strengthen collective resilience, through exilic and early postexilic times. In addition, textual reflections of individual agency, although they did exist in earlier times, seem to intensify in Persian times (cf. Newsom 2012; Niditch 2015).

In regard to creation anthropologies and the human being's capabilities and duties, the idea that the human being is made from clay but provided with godlike reason is ancient indeed, found at least as far back as Atra-hasis and similar texts and traditions of ancient Mesopotamia (cf. Oshima 2012). It may well be that this idea was old in ancient Israel as well, just as was the idea of the *nefeš* as a dynamic force, death as privation of life capacities in *še'ôl*, and the heart as the thinking organ of the human being. The idea of the human being as God's image, however, seems to have a postexilic origin, at a time when there was no king in Yehud, transforming imagery from ancient royal ideology, where the king was God's image and representative, into a 'democratic' idea of the human being as God's image and representative on earth.

# REFERENCES

Abou-Assaf, A., P. Bordreuil and A.R. Millard (1982), *La statue de Tell Fekherye et son inscription bilingue assyro-araméenne* (ERC 10), Paris: Editions Recherche sur les civilisations.

Alt, A. (1951), 'Die Weisheit Salomos', *TLZ*, 76 (3): 139–44.

Alt, K. (2013), 'Unsterblichkeit', in C. Schäfer (ed.), *Platon-Lexikon: Begriffswörterbuch zu Platon und der platonischen Tradition*, 296–300, Darmstadt: Wissenschaftliche Buchgesellschaft.

Assmann, J. (1990), *Ma'at: Gerechtigkeit und Unsterblichkeit im Alten Ägypten*, München: C.H. Beck.

Assmann, J. (2009), *The Price of Monotheism*, Stanford, CA: Stanford University Press.

Assmann, J. (2011), *Cultural Memory and Early Civilization: Writing, Remembrance, and Political Imagination*, Cambridge: Cambridge University Press.

Assmann, J. (2018), *The Invention of Religion: Faith and Covenant in the Book of Exodus*, Princeton, NJ: Princeton University Press.

Avrahami, Y. (2012), *The Senses of Scripture: Sensory Perception in the Hebrew Bible*, LHBOTS 545, London: T&T Clark.

Barr, J. (1961), *The Semantics of Biblical Language*, London: Oxford University Press.

Barton, J. (2014), *Ethics in Ancient Israel*, Oxford: Oxford University Press.

Bellah, R.N. (2011), *Religion in Human Evolution: From the Paleolithic to the Axial Age*, Cambridge, MA: Belknap Press of Harvard University Press.

Benedict, R. (1946), *The Chrysanthemum and the Sword: Patterns of Japanese Culture*, Boston, MA: Houghton Mifflin.

Berlejung, A. (1998), *Die Theologie der Bilder: Herstellung und Einweihung von Kultbildern in Mesopotamien und die alttestamentliche Bilderpolemik*, OBO 162, Fribourg/Göttingen: Schweiz Universitätsverlag/Vandenhoeck & Ruprecht.

Berlejung, A. (2001), 'Tod und Leben nach den Vorstellungen der Israeliten. Ein ausgewählter Aspekt zu einer Metapher im Spannungsfeld von Leben und Tod', in B. Jankowski and B. Ego (eds), *Das biblische Weltbild und seine altorientalischen Kontexte*, 465–502, Tübingen: Mohr Siebeck.

Berlejung, A. (2008), 'Ein Programm fürs Leben: Theologisches Wort und anthropologischer Ort der Silberamulette von Ketef Hinnom', *ZAW*, 120 (2): 204–30.

Berlejung, A. (2009), 'Körperkonzepte und Geschlechterdifferenz in der physiognomischen Tradition des Alten Orients und des Alten Testaments', in B. Jankowski and K. Liess (eds), *Der Mensch im alten Israel: Neue Forschungen zur alttestamentlichen Anthropologie*, 299–37, HBS 59, Freiburg: Herder.

Berlin, I. (1961), *Two Concepts of Liberty*, Oxford: Clarendon Press.

Berquist, J.L. (2006), 'Constructions of Identity in Postcolonial Yehud', in O. Lipschits and M. Oeming (eds), *Judah and the Judeans in the Persian Period*, 53–66, Winona Lake, IN: Eisenbrauns.

Boman, T. (1970), *Hebrew Thought Compared with Greek*, New York: Norton.

Carasik, M. (2006), *Theologies of the Mind in Biblical Israel*, Studies in Biblical Literature 85, Frankfurt am Main: Peter Lang.

di Vito, R.A. (1999), 'Old Testament Anthropology and the Construction of Personal Identity', *CBQ*, 61 (2): 217–38.

Dietrich, J. (2009), 'Über Ehre und Ehrgefühl im Alten Testament', in B. Janowski and K. Liess (eds), *Der Mensch im alten Israel: Neue Forschungen zur alttestamentlichen Anthropologie*, 419–52, HBS 59, Freiburg: Herder.

Dietrich, J. (2010), *Kollektive Schuld und Haftung: Religions- und rechtsgeschichtliche Studien zum Sündenkuhritus des Deuteronomiums und zu verwandten Texten*, ORA 4, Tübingen: Mohr Siebeck.

Dietrich, J. (2012), 'Psalm 72 in Its Ancient Syrian Context', in C.L. Crouch, J. Stökl and A.E. Zernecke (eds), *Mediating Between Heaven and Earth: Communication with the Divine in the Ancient Near East*, 144–60, LHBOTS 566, London: T&T Clark.

Dietrich, J. (2014), 'Friendship with God: Old Testament and Ancient Near Eastern Perspectives', *SJOT*, 28 (2): 157–71.

Dietrich, J. (2015), 'Coping with Disasters in Antiquity and the Bible: Practical and Mental Strategies', in F. Riede (ed.), *Past Vulnerability: Volcanic Eruptions and Human Vulnerability in Traditional Societies Past and Present*, 151–67, Aarhus: Aarhus University Press.

Dietrich, J. (2016), 'Vom Umgang mit Rache im Alten Testament: Rechtliche, moralische und religiöse Grenzziehungen', in T. Moos and S. Engert (eds), *Vom Umgang mit Schuld: Eine multidisziplinäre Annäherung*, 39–50, Frankfurt am Main: Campus.

Dietrich, J. (2017a), 'Human Relationality and Sociality in Ancient Israel: Mapping the Social Anthropology of the Old Testament', in E.-M. Becker, J. Dietrich and B.K. Holm (eds), *'What Is Human?' Theological Encounters with Anthropology*, 23–44, Göttingen: Vandenhoeck & Ruprecht.

Dietrich, J. (2017b), 'Hebräisches Denken und die Frage nach den Ursprüngen des Denkens zweiter Ordnung im Alten Testament, Alten Ägypten und Alten Orient', in A. Wagner and J. van Oorschot (eds), *Individualität und Selbstreflexion in den Literaturen des Alten Testaments*, 45–65, VWGT 48, Leipzig: Evangelische Verlagsanstalt.

Dietrich, J. (2018a), 'Zur Individualität und Sozialität der Scham im Alten Testament', in A. Grund-Wittenberg and R. Poser (eds), *Die verborgene Macht der Scham: Ehre, Scham und Schuld im alten Israel, in seinem Umfeld und in gegenwärtigen Lebenswelten*, 58–83, BTS, Göttingen: Vandenhoeck & Ruprecht.

Dietrich, J. (2018b), 'Responsive Anthropologie: Zum Bild des Menschen im Alten Testament am Beispiel der Tugend-Epistemologie', in W. Bührer and R.J. Meyer zu Hörste-Bührer (eds), *Relationale Erkenntnishorizonte in Exegese und systematischer Theologie*, 145–59, Marburger Theologische Studien 129, Leipzig: Evangelische Verlagsanstalt.

Dietrich, J. (2019a), 'Empiricism or Rationalism in the Hebrew Bible? Some Thoughts About Ancient Foxes and Hedgehogs', in A. Schellenberg and T. Krüger (eds), *Sounding Sensory Profiles in the Ancient Near East*, 57–68, ANEM 25, Atlanta, GA: SBL Press.

Dietrich, J. (2019b), 'Liberty, Freedom, and Autonomy in the Ancient World: A General Introduction and Comparison', in A. Berlejung and A.M. Maeir (eds), *Research on Israel and Aram: Autonomy, Independence and Related Issues – Proceedings of the First Annual RIAB Center Conference, Leipzig, June 2016*, 3–22, RIABT 1 / ORA 34, Tübingen: Mohr Siebeck.

Dietrich, J. (2020), 'Listenweisheit im Buch Levitikus: Überlegungen zu den Taxonomien der Priesterschrift', in C. Körting and R.G. Kratz (eds), *Fromme und Frevler: Studien zu Psalmen und Weisheit – Festschrift für Hermann Spieckermann zum 70 Geburtstag*, 371–87, Tübingen: Mohr Siebeck.

Dietrich, J. (2021), 'Materialität und Spiritualität im altisraelitischen Opferkult: Religionsgeschichtliche Abstraktionsprozesse', *VT*, 71 (1): 27–47.

Dietrich, J. (forthcoming), 'Individual and Social Character in Ancient Israel', in A. Wagner, J. van Oorschot and L. Allolio-Näcke (eds), *Archaeology of Mind: Interdisciplinary Explorations in the Field of Old Testament Thinking*, Berlin: De Gruyter.

Elkana, Y. (1986), 'The Emergence of Second Order Thinking in Classical Greece', in S.N. Eisenstadt (ed.), *The Origins and Diversity of Axial Age Civilizations*, 40–64, Albany: State University of New York Press.

Ernst, A.B. (1994), *Weisheitliche Kultkritik: Zu Theologie und Ethik des Sprüchebuchs und der Prophetie des 8. Jahrhunderts*, BTS 23, Neukirchen-Vluyn: Neukirchener.

Finsterbusch, K. (2005), *Weisung für Israel: Studien zu religiösem Lehren und Lernen im Deuteronomium und in seinem Umfeld*, FAT 44, Tübingen: Mohr Siebeck.

Fleck, L. (1980), *Entstehung und Entwicklung einer wissenschaftlichen Tatsache: Einführung in die Lehre vom Denkstil und Denkkollektiv*, ed. L. Schäfer and T. Schnelle, Frankfurt am Main: Suhrkamp.

Foucault, M. (1966), *Les mots et les choses: une archéologie des sciences humaines*, Paris: Gallimard.

Foucault, M. (1969), *L'archéologie du savoir*, Paris: Gallimard.

Fox, M. (2007), 'The Epistemology of the Book of Proverbs', *JBL*, 126 (4): 669–84.

Frevel, C. (forthcoming), 'Never Mind: Some Observations on Thinking and Its Linguistic Expressions in the Hebrew Bible', in A. Wagner, J. van Oorschot and L. Allolio-Näcke (eds), *Archaeology of Mind: Interdisciplinary Explorations in the Field of Old Testament Thinking*, Berlin: De Gruyter.

Fromm, E. (1969), *Escape from Freedom*, New York: Holt, Rinehart and Winston.

Geller, S.A. (1994), 'Fiery Wisdom: Logos and Lexis in Deuteronomy 4', *Prooftexts*, 14 (2): 103–39.

Gericke, J. (2012), *The Hebrew Bible and Philosophy of Religion*, RBS 70, Atlanta, GA: Society of Biblical Literature.

Gericke, J. (2018), '"My Thoughts *Are* (Not) Your Thoughts": Transposed Second-Order Thinking in the Hebrew Bible', *Journal for Semitics*, 27 (1): 1–16.

Gloy, K. (2016), *Denkformen und ihre kulturkonstitutive Rolle*, Paderborn: Wilhelm Fink.

Grund, A. (2013), 'Scham', in M. Fieger, J. Krispenz and J. Lanckau (eds), *Wörterbuch alttestamentlicher Motive*, 347–50, Darmstadt: WBG.

Hazony, Y. (2012), *The Philosophy of Hebrew Scripture: An Introduction*, Cambridge: Cambridge University Press.

Hempel, J. (1964), *Das Ethos des Alten Testaments*, 2nd edn, Berlin: Töpelmann.

Hesiod (1991) *The Works and Days; Theogony; The Shield of Herakles*, transl. R Lattimore, Ann Arbor: University of Michigan Press.
Honneth, A. (1995), *The Struggle for Recognition: The Moral Grammar of Social Conflicts*, Studies in Contemporary German Social Thought, Cambridge, MA: MIT Press.
Janowski, B. (1999), 'Die Tat kehrt zum Täter zurück. Offene Fragen im Umkreis des "Tun-Ergehen-Zusammenhangs"', in B. Janowski (ed.), *Die rettende Gerechtigkeit*, 167–91, Beiträge zur Theologie des Alten Testaments 2, Neukirchen-Vluyn: Neukirchen-Vluyn Neukirchener.
Janowski, B. (2012), 'Konstellative Anthropologie: Zum Begriff der Person im Alten Testament', in B. Janowski (ed.), *Der ganze Mensch: Zur Anthropologie der Antike und ihrer europäischen Nachgeschichte*, 109–27, Berlin: Akademie.
Janowski, B. (2013), *Arguing with God: A Theological Anthropology of the Psalms*, Louisville, KY: Westminster John Knox Press.
Janowski, B. (2019), *Anthropologie des Alten Testaments: Grundfragen – Kontexte – Themenfelder*, Tübingen: Mohr Siebeck.
Jepsen, A. (1974), 'אמן ʾāman', *TDOT*, 1: 292–323.
Johnson, D. (2013), *Biblical Knowing: A Scriptural Epistemology of Error*, Eugene, OR: Cascade.
Kessler, R. (2006), *Sozialgeschichte des alten Israel: Eine Einführung*, Darmstadt: Wissenschaft Buchgesellschaft.
Klopfenstein, M.A. (1964), *Die Lüge nach dem Alten Testament: Ihr Begriff, ihre Bedeutung und ihre Beurteilung*, Zürich: Gotthelf.
Klopfenstein, M.A. (1972), *Scham und Schande nach dem Alten Testament: Eine begriffsgeschichtliche Untersuchung zu den hebräischen Wurzeln bôš, klm und ḥpr*, ATANT 62, Zürich: TVZ.
Knoppers, G.N. and K.A. Ristau, eds (2009), *Community Identity in Judean Historiography: Biblical and Comparative Perspectives*, Winona Lake, IN: Eisenbrauns.
Koch, K. (1991a), 'Wesen und Ursprung der "Gemeinschaftstreue" im Israel der Königszeit', in B. Janowski (ed.), *Spuren des hebräischen Denkens: Beiträge zur alttestamentlichen Theologie*, 107–27, Neukirchen-Vluyn: Neukirchener.
Koch, K. (1991b), 'Gibt es ein hebräisches Denken?', in B. Janowski (ed.), *Spuren des hebräischen Denkens: Beiträge zur alttestamentlichen Theologie*, 3–24, Neukirchen-Vluyn: Neukirchener.
Krašovec, J. (1999), *Reward, Punishment, and Forgiveness: The Thinking and Beliefs of Ancient Israel in the Light of Greek and Modern Views*, VTSup 78, Leiden: E.J. Brill.
Kraus, H.-J. (1972), 'Hören und Sehen in der althebräischen Tradition', in H.-J. Kraus, *Biblisch-theologische Aufsätze*, 84–101, Neukirchen-Vluyn: Neukirchener.
Krüger, A. (2009), 'Auf dem Weg "zu den Vätern": Zur Tradition der alttestamentlichen Sterbenotizen', in A. Berlejung and B. Janowski (eds), *Tod und Jenseits im alten Israel und in seiner Umwelt: Theologische, religionsgeschichtliche, archäologische und ikonographische Aspekte*, 137–50, FAT 64, Tübingen: Mohr Siebeck.
Kuhn, T.S. (1962), *The Structure of Scientific Revolutions*, Chicago: University of Chicago Press.
Laniak, T.S. (1998), *Shame and Honor in the Book of Esther*, Atlanta, GA: Scholars Press.
Lawrence, L.J. (2004), 'A Taste for "The Other": Interpreting Biblical Texts Anthropologically', in L.J. Lawrence and M.I. Aguilar (eds), *Anthropology and Biblical Studies: Avenues of Approach*, 9–25, Leiden: Deo.
Lemche, N.P. (1985), *Early Israel: Anthropological and Historical Studies on the Israelite Society before the Monarchy*, VTSup 37, Leiden: E.J. Brill.

Lévy-Bruhl, L. (1926), *How Natives Think*, London: George Allen & Unwin.

Machinist, P. (1986), 'On Self-Consciousness in Mesopotamia', in S.N. Eisenstadt (ed.), *The Origins and Diversity of Axial Age Civilizations*, 183–202, Albany: State University of New York Press.

Markl, D. (2015), 'Israels Moral der Befreiten: Zur Begründung der "Option für die Armen" in der geschichtlichen Identität Israels', in C. Frevel (ed.), *Mehr als Zehn Worte? Zur Bedeutung des Alten Testaments in ethischen Fragen*, 324–44, QD 273, Freiburg: Herder.

Maul, S.M. (1998), 'Der assyrische König: Hüter der Weltordnung', in J. Assmann, B. Janowski and M. Welker (eds), *Gerechtigkeit: Richten und Retten in der abendländischen Tradition und ihren altorientalischen Ursprüngen*, 65–77, München: Fink.

Maul, S.M. (2018), *The Art of Divination in the Ancient Near East: Reading the Signs of Heaven and Earth*, Waco, TX: Baylor University Press.

McVann, M. (1998), 'Family-Centeredness', in J.J. Pilch and B.J. Malina (eds), *Handbook of Biblical Social Values*, 75–9, Eugene, OR: Wipf and Stock.

Meinhold, A. (2002), 'Zur weisheitlichen Sicht des Menschen (vornehmlich nach dem Sprüchebuch, speziell Spr 20,2–30)', in T. Neumann and J. Thon (eds), *Zur weisheitlichen Sicht des Menschen: Gesammelte Aufsätze*, 177–87, Leipzig: EVA.

Michel, D. (1994), 'næpæš als Leichnam?', *ZAH*, 7: 81–4.

Müller, J. (2009), 'Seelenwanderung', in C. Horn, J. Müller and J.R. Söder (eds), *Platon Handbuch: Leben – Werk – Wirkung*, 324–8, Stuttgart: Metzler.

Müller, K. and A. Wagner, eds (2014), 'Das Konzept der synthetischen Körperauffassung in der Diskussion', in *Synthetische Körperauffassung im Hebräischen und den Sprachen der Nachbarkulturen*, 223–38, AOAT 416, Münster: Ugarit.

Neumann-Gorsolke, U. (2004), *Herrschen in den Grenzen der Schöpfung. Ein Beitrag zur alttestamentlichen Anthropologie am Beispiel von Psalm 8, Genesis 1 und verwandten Texten*, WMANT 101, Neukirchen-Vluyn: Neukirchener.

Newsom, C.A. (2012), 'Models of the Moral Self: Hebrew Bible and Second Temple Judaism', *JBL*, 131 (1): 5–25.

Niditch, S. (2015), *The Responsive Self: Personal Religion in Biblical Literature of the Neo-Babylonian and Persian Periods*, New Haven, CT: Yale University Press.

Nissen, H.J., P. Damerow and R.K. Englund, eds (2004), *5000 Jahre Informationsverarbeitung: Frühe Schrift und Techniken der Wirtschaftsverwaltung im alten Vorderen Orient*, Hildesheim: Franzbecker.

Ockinga, B. (1984), *Die Gottebenbildlichkeit im Alten Ägypten und im Alten Testament*, ÄAT 7, Wiesbaden: Harrassowitz.

Olyan, S.M. (2017), *Friendship in the Hebrew Bible*, ABRL, New Haven, CT: Yale University Press.

Oshima, T. (2012), 'When the Gods Made Us from Clay', in A. Berlejung, J. Dietrich and J.F. Quack (eds), *Menschenbilder und Körperkonzepte im Alten Israel, in Ägypten und im Alten Orient*, 407–31, ORA 9, Tübingen: Mohr Siebeck.

Pardee, D. (2009), 'A New Aramaic Inscription from Zincirli', *BASOR*, 356: 51–71.

Pedersen, J. (1926), *Israel: Its Life and Culture I–II*, London: Oxford University Press.

Plevnik, J. (2000), 'Honor/Shame', in J.J. Pilch and B.J. Malina (eds), *Handbook of Biblical Social Values*, 106–15, Peabody, MA: Hendrickson.

Riede, P. (forthcoming), 'Tiere', in J. Dietrich, B. Janowski, A. Grund-Wittenberg and U. Neumann-Gorsolke (eds), *Handbuch Alttestamentliche Anthropologie*, Tübingen: Mohr Siebeck.

Robinson, H.W. (1992), 'The Hebrew Conception of Corporate Personality' [1935], in H.W. Robinson (ed.), *Corporate Personality in Ancient Israel*, 25–44, Edinburgh: T&T Clark.

Rochberg, F. (2016), *Before Nature: Cuneiform Knowledge and the History of Science*, Chicago: Chicago University Press.

Rogerson, J.W. (1970), 'The Hebrew Conception of Corporate Personality: A Re-examination', *JTS* NS, 21 (1): 1–16.

Rogerson, J.W. (1978), *Anthropology and the Old Testament*, Oxford: Basil Blackwell.

Savran, G. (2009), 'Seeing Is Believing: On the Relative Priority of Visual and Verbal Perception of the Divine', *BI*, 17 (3): 320–61.

Schaper, J. (2019), *Media and Monotheism: Presence, Representation, and Abstraction in Ancient Judah*, Tübingen: Mohr Siebeck.

Schellenberg, A. (2002), *Erkenntnis als Problem: Qohelet und die alttestamentliche Diskussion um das menschliche Erkennen*, Fribourg/Göttingen: Universitätsverlag / Vandenhoeck & Ruprecht.

Schellenberg, A. (2011), *Der Mensch, das Bild Gottes? Zum Gedanken einer Sonderstellung des Menschen im Alten Testament und in weiteren altorientalischen Quellen*, ATANT 101. Zürich: TVZ.

Schiefsky, M. (2012), 'The Creation of Second-Order Knowledge in Ancient Greek Science as a Process in the Globalization of Knowledge', in J. Renn (ed.), *The Globalization of Knowledge in History*, Open Access, 191–202, Berlin: Epubli. Available online: https://mprl-series.mpg.de/media/studies/1/12/Studies1_chap.8.pdf (accessed 8 July 2022).

Schroer, S. and T. Staubli (2001), *Body Symbolism in the Bible*, Collegeville, MN: Liturgical Press.

Schüle, A. (2014), '"Soul" and "Spirit" in the Anthropological Discourse of the Hebrew Bible', in M. Welker (ed.), *The Depth of the Human Person: A Multidisciplinary Approach*, 147–65, Grand Rapids, MI: Eerdmans.

Simian-Yofre, H. (2001), 'pānîm', *TDOT*, 11: 589–615.

Snell, B. (1953), *The Discovery of the Mind in Greek Philosophy and Literature*, New York: Dover Publications.

Taylor, C. (1989), *Sources of the Self: The Making of the Modern Identity*, Cambridge: Cambridge University Press.

Tsevat, M. (1978), 'An Aspect of Biblical Thought: Deductive Explanation', *Shenatôn ha-miḳrâ u-le-ḥeḳer ha-mizraḥ ha-ḳadûm [. . .] An Annual for Biblical and Ancient Near Eastern Studies*, 3: 53–8.

Vall, G. (2007), 'An Epistemology of Faith: The Knowledge of God in Israel's Prophetic Literature', in M. Healy and R. Parry (eds), *The Bible and Epistemology: Biblical Soundings on the Knowledge of God*, 24–42, Milton Keynes, UK: Paternoster.

van de Mieroop, M. (2016), *Philosophy Before the Greeks: The Pursuit of Truth in Ancient Mesopotamia*, Princeton, NJ: Princeton University Press.

van de Mieroop, M. (2018), 'Theses on Babylonian Philosophy', *JANEH*, 5 (1/2): 15–39.

Vogt, L. and A. Zingerle, eds (1994), 'Einleitung: Zur Aktualität des Themas Ehre und zu seinem Stellenwert in der Theorie', in *Ehre: Archaische Momente in der Moderne*, 9–34, Berlin: Suhrkamp.

von Rad, G. (1955), 'Hiob xxxviii und die altägyptische Weisheit', in M. Noth and D.W. Thomas (eds), *Wisdom in Israel and in the Ancient Near East: Presented to Harold Henry Rowley in Celebration of His 65th Birthday, 24 March 1955*, VTSup 3, 293–301, Leiden: E.J. Brill.

Wagner, A. (2007), 'Der Parallelismus membrorum zwischen poetischer Form und Denkfigur', in *Parallelismus membrorum*, 1–26, OBO 224, Fribourg/Göttingen: Universitätsverlag / Vandenhoeck & Ruprecht.

Weingart, K. (2014), *Stämmevolk – Staatsvolk – Gottesvolk? Studien zur Verwendung des Israel-Namens im Alten Testament*, FAT 2/68, Tübingen: Mohr Siebeck.

Wolff, H.W. (1974), *Anthropology of the Old Testament*, London: SCM Press.

Zobel, H.-J. (1986), 'חסד', *TDOT*, 5: 44–64.

# CHAPTER TWELVE

# Honour, shame and other social values in the Hebrew Bible

PHILIP F. ESLER

## VALUES IN THE ISRAELITE SOCIAL SYSTEM

There is a long history of discussion on the meaning of 'values', especially within sociology, anthropology and philosophy (Jaspers 2016; Robbins and Sommerschuh 2016). For the purpose of this chapter, the following definition is adopted: 'The word "value" describes some general quality and direction of life that human beings are expected to embody in their behavior. A value is a general, normative orientation of action in a social system. It is an emotionally anchored commitment to pursue and support certain directions or types of actions' (Pilch and Malina 2016: xix).

Essential to this definition is the linkage between values and the social system in which they exist, so that different values become prominent in different social systems. From this it follows that to appreciate the values evident in the Hebrew Bible one needs to have some antecedent understanding of the ancient Israelite social system it reflects and in which it was written. The most pertinent aspects of that social system for understanding its values are: its status as an agrarian society; its group-focused rather than individualistic character (with kin the most prominent group); the centrality of patrilinearity; and the prevalence of the idea of limited good, plus the mechanisms that ameliorated its impacts, such as the practices of reciprocity and patron/client relationships. I will now consider each of these briefly.

'Agrarian society' refers to the phase in the development of human cultures originally theorized by Gerhard and Jean Lenski where, after what they called the 'horticultural' phase, the invention of the plough allowed farmers for the first time to produce a surplus of food beyond the subsistence needs of their families. Armed and bureaucratized elites then arose to seize that surplus and to establish themselves in cities. This led to a markedly vertical social stratification where a tiny and wealthy elite, served by various types of retainers, controlled the production of the rest of the population. The elite often used religious cults to legitimize the entire process (Nolan and Lenski 2014). This process comes to remarkable emic expression in 1 Sam. 8.11–17 (RSV):

> He said, 'These will be the ways of the king who will reign over you: he will take your sons and appoint them to his chariots and to be his horsemen, and to run before his

chariots; and he will appoint for himself commanders of thousands and commanders of fifties, and some to plough his ground and to reap his harvest, and to make his implements of war and the equipment of his chariots. He will take your daughters to be perfumers and cooks and bakers. He will take the best of your fields and vineyards and olive orchards and give them to his servants. He will take the tenth of your grain and of your vineyards and give it to his officers and to his servants. He will take your menservants and maidservants, and the best of your cattle and your asses, and put them to his work. He will take the tenth of your flocks, and you shall be his slaves.'

The differences between societies that are group-focused or 'collectivist' or 'allocentric', and those that are characterized by individualism (not to be equated with individuality) or 'idiocentric', have been well charted by Harry Triandis (1988). In group-oriented cultures the behaviour of most people is largely determined by the goals, attitudes and values that are shared with some group, one's family in particular. In a collectivist culture young people seek to stay embedded in their main groups, so, for example, errant teenagers in Japan are temporarily locked out of the family home. In individualistic cultures most people's behaviour is largely determined by personal goals and attitudes, with some but less influence from relevant groups to which one belongs. In these cultures, for example, young people normally seek to get away from their families, so for a teenager to be 'grounded' is a punishment. If one asks someone from a collectivist culture who they are, the first answers tend to relate to the relevant groups to which they belong, family, nation etc. The same question directed to someone from an individualist culture tends to elicit initial responses related to personal values, attributes and beliefs.

Kinship [see Chapters 7 and 10 in this volume] was by far the most important form of group belonging in ancient Israel and patrilineality was the dominant feature of Israelite kinship. Patrilinearity (sometimes 'patrilineality'), also known as 'agnatic kinship', is a system where kinship is tied to descent from the father's lineage. Male offspring inherited their father's property (land especially), a notion praised in Prov. 13.22: 'A good man will leave an inheritance to his sons' sons.' The patrilineal inheritance of property in the Hebrew Bible has been well explained by Frederick Greenspahn (1994). This was not, as is often suggested, a system of 'primogeniture', in which the first-born male inherited all the property; some was allocated to the other brothers, as may be implied in Prov. 17.2: 'A slave who deals wisely will rule over a son who acts shamefully, and will share the inheritance with one of the brothers'. The picture of brothers sharing the inheritance in Luke's Parable of the Prodigal Son (15.11–32) probably reflects older Israelite patterns. Under Israelite law patrilinearity was modified to the extent of allowing inheritance by a daughter if there were no surviving sons (Num. 27.8–9). Separate provision, moreover, was usually made for daughters during their lifetime, especially by the provision of a dowry. In a patrilineal system, having your sons marry your brothers' daughters was an attractive strategy since it kept the family property tied up in the patrilineage. Sons also took their names from their father's lineage. This feature of the social system underlies the numerous genealogies in the Hebrew Bible (Wilson 1975, 1977; Ray 2016), although they also served to emphasize the honour of the lineage (see below). Related to patrilineality was patrilocality, which refers to a social system in which a married couple resides in the house of the husband's father. High mortality rates, however, with parents dying before their children themselves marry and have children, mean that only a small minority of households, perhaps as low as 20 per cent, were likely to have fitted this pattern (Esler 2011a: 69).

Patrilinearity is not to be confused with 'patriarchy'. As Carol Meyers (2014) has shown, the latter was a term coined in the nineteenth century from observation of legal texts to denote male domination of family life in various cultures. By the early twentieth century it was adopted by sociologists (including Max Weber) to include society-wide male domination, from whom it was taken into research on ancient Israel and the Hebrew Bible. It was widely adopted by feminist scholars, with Gerda Lerner's *The Creation of Patriarchy* (1986) probably signalling the high point of that approach. Recent research, however, has led to a reappraisal, with Lerner's book being severely critiqued for its historical methodology by Susan Kray in 2002. More recently, Carol Meyers (2013, 2014) has comprehensively demonstrated that the picture it painted of largely powerless women in Israel has proven to be a false one, so that there is a strong case for the abandonment of the notion of 'patriarchy' [see further Chapter 10 in this volume].

Another aspect of the social system of ancient Israel requiring mention is the existence of a belief that all goods, material and immaterial (including honour, see below) existed in finite and non-increasing quantities and that someone could only enlarge their share thereof at the expense of someone else. This is the notion of the 'limited good' and it was first observed by George Foster during his fieldwork among peasants in Michoacán, Mexico and introduced to biblical research by Malina (1981: 75–6). While limited good is a 'cognitive orientation' (Foster 1967: 301), or part of a world view, to the extent that it motivates people to certain types of action, it also comes close to being a social value. In essence, limited good is a social construct 'which views the world as a zero-sum game' (Neyrey 2016: 103). Peasant families tend to be self-sufficient and each of them 'sees itself in perpetual, unrelenting struggle with its fellows for possession of or control over what it considers to be its share of scarce resources' (Foster 1967: 311). In this context the ideal man is someone who works to feed and clothe his family, fulfils his social obligations, minds his own business, and does not seek to be outstanding but protects his rights when necessary (ibid.: 313). Someone who betters his position threatens village stability (ibid.: 314). A sudden improvement in fortune is likely to be attributed to luck, such as by finding treasure buried in one's field (ibid.: 316–17). The striving for material gain disturbs the existing order because 'it means plunder from others' (ibid.: 320). Solid evidence exists that the idea of limited good permeated ancient Israelite society. It is directly expressed in Sir. 29.23: 'Whether you have little or much, be content with it'. Engaging in commerce was regarded as intrinsically wicked, for 'Sin will wedge itself between buying and selling' (Sir. 27.2) and 'It is difficult for a merchant to avoid doing wrong and for a small trader not to incur sin' (Sir. 26.29). The wicked increase in wealth (Ps. 73.12). The notion of buried treasure is found in Mt. 13.44 which probably reflects older tropes in Israelite society. Even God was regarded as existing in a world of limited good. In Exod. 32.19–25 the Lord describes how his people had stirred him to jealousy and how he will punish them in consequence. Yet there is a limit to his anger and he will not scatter them and wipe out remembrance of them (Exod. 32.26), 'less their adversaries should judge amiss, lest they should say, "Our hand is triumphant, the Lord has not wrought all this"' (Exod. 32.27). In other words, there is a certain amount of honour from scattering Israel's enemies and God is concerned that it might go to someone else and not him. Jerome Neyrey and Richard Rohrbaugh (2008: 242–3) note other examples. Isaac had only one blessing to give and it went to Jacob not Esau (Gen. 27.38). Similarly, God had Gideon reduce the number of men he used to defeat the Midianites to a bare minimum of 300 so that Israel could not claim the credit for a victory (Judg. 7.2), credit that in a world of limited good could only belong to God.

A negative dimension of the belief in limited good was the prevalence of envy in ancient Israelite society. Envy is a disposition to begrudge someone else the possession of a valuable asset, attribute or relationship (Malina and Seeman 2016: 51). Envy exists in every human society but in a world where all such goods are thought to exist in finite and non-increasing quantities it is likely to be particularly intense. Envy is a trigger for the activation of the evil eye, a malign force in human affairs with the power to cause great harm and which needs to be warded off by apotropaic actions, words and amulets. It has been a feature of the Mediterranean world for thousands of years (Elliott 2015). A parade example of envy and the evil eye in the Hebrew Bible, also noted by Neyrey and Rohrbaugh (2008: 242–3), is found in 1 Samuel 18. Here we are told that Saul became very angry after women of Israel had sung 'Saul has slain his thousands, and David his tens of thousands' and 'eyed David from that day on' (vv. 7–9), as powerfully depicted in a painting by Rembrandt of Saul, spear in hand, watching David as he plays his harp (Esler 1998: 254).

One process that serves various functions in numerous social systems, but that also operates to ameliorate the perceived realities of limited good, is for people to enter into various forms of non-market exchange of goods or services (labour especially), a process known as 'reciprocity'. Marshall Sahlins identified three broad types of reciprocity and this typology has been widely recognized as useful in understanding features of the ancient world, including Israel (Crook 2004; Kirk 2007; Stewart 2010 [see also Chapter 14 in this volume]). Sahlins's three types of reciprocity are:

- generalized, characterized by the altruistic supply of goods and services, without an expectation of return and typical of relationships within kin groups;
- balanced, characterized by the exchange of equal amounts of goods and services; and
- negative, characterized by the attempt to get more out of a transaction than one gives, or even to obtain nothing with impunity (Sahlins 1972: 193–6).

Phenomena comparable with reciprocity generally and with these three types are observable in the Hebrew Bible. Seth Schwartz (2010) observes the presence of notions of reciprocity in ancient Israel even though he believes they were more at home in the cultures of Greece and Rome and were often at odds with notions of Torah-based solidarity. Roger Nam finds 'symmetrical reciprocity' in the book of Kings (2012). Generalized reciprocity characterized relationships between family but also occurred in wider society: 'One man gives freely, yet grows all the richer; another withholds what he should give, and only suffers want' (Prov. 11.24 RSV) and 'A liberal man will be enriched, and one who waters will himself be watered' (Prov. 11.25 RSV). In his Gospel, Luke provides evidence of both generalized and balanced reciprocity which surely reflect patterns in Israel older than the first century CE. As to generalized reciprocity, the father in the Parable of the Prodigal Son tells the other brother, 'Son, you are always with me, and all that is mine is yours' (Lk. 15.31). As to balanced reciprocity, Jesus says to his host at a banquet, 'When you give a dinner or a banquet, do not invite your friends or your brothers lest they invite you in return, and you be repaid' (14.12), before calling for the man to practise generalized reciprocity instead: 'But when you give a feast, invite the destitute, the maimed, the lame, the blind and you will be blessed, because they cannot repay you' (14.13). Negative reciprocity can be viewed as the practices frowned upon in a limited good society, including the practice of commerce (as noted above).

Another way to mitigate the negative effects of a limited good society, which really falls within the larger category of reciprocity (Stewart 2010: 157), was to enter into a relationship with someone socially and economically superior and gain his or her assistance when necessary in return for loyalty and services as requested. This was the relationship of patron and client (sometimes mediated by a broker). It was an asymmetrical but mutually beneficial relationship sometimes presented as 'friendship' or fictive kinship. Indeed, patronage can be seen as a forum, along with kinship, for the expression of generalized reciprocity (Crook 2004: 59; Stewart 2010: 157). There is a good case to be made that in the Hebrew Bible God is often presented as acting as a patron to Israel. Thus J.-M. Schäder has argued that in Psalm 47 'God functions as Israel's patron when he subdues nations (verse 4) and chooses Israel's inheritance (verse 5) for them. Israel responds to this act of grace by proclaiming God's honour and even compelling the nations to do so as well' (2010: 256).

I will now proceed to a discussion of central values in the Hebrew Bible, beginning with by far the two most important, honour and shame. As Timothy Laniak (1998: 31) has noted in relation to Esther (but with wider application), other values (such as hospitality, generosity, obedience, anger and revenge) are 'subsidiary' to honour and shame in the sense that they are 'explicitly linked' to honour and shame. Perhaps it would be more accurate to say that in ancient Israel other values (to which one might also add purity to Laniak's list) were understood and enacted in relation to honour and shame.

## HONOUR AND SHAME: THE HISTORY OF THE DISCUSSION

Interest in honour and shame in the Hebrew Bible is not new. In 1926 Johannes Pedersen included a chapter on the subject of honour and shame in *Israel: Its Life and Culture* (Pedersen 1926: 213–44). In 1972 Martin Klopfenstein published a work on shame and disgrace (*Scham und Schande*) in the Old Testament notable for the philological thoroughness with which the relevant vocabulary was considered. A new approach, however, became possible with the arrival of the social anthropology of the Mediterranean in the 1950s and 1960s.[1] This research began with Julian Pitt-Rivers's 1954 book, *The People of the Sierra*, a study of the social structure and values of a rural community in Andalusia. In 1965 an important collection of essays appeared, inaugurating the systematic study of honour in anthropology: *Honour and Shame: The Values of Mediterranean Society* (1965), edited by John Peristiany. From the numerous detailed ethnographic studies represented in this research there emerged an understanding of honour as the dominant social value across many Mediterranean cultures, with a meaning of the worth of a person both in his or her eyes and also in the eyes of his or her relevant group (Pitt-Rivers 1965: 21). Shame was viewed in one sense as negative, the absence of honour (often, indeed, as the opposite of honour), but also in a positive sense as referring to the quality of a virtuous woman. [See also Chapter 6 in this volume.]

One of the early distinctions to be developed was between *ascribed* honour, meaning honour you possessed from whom you were (e.g. your elite family) or from what you were given, and honour that you *acquired* in social interactions with others. What has become regarded as the classic mechanism for the acquisition of honour is the social

---

[1] The use of anthropology in understanding the Hebrew Bible actually has nineteenth-century antecedents in the work of William Robertson Smith and James Frazer: see Esler and Hagedorn 2006.

dynamic of 'challenge-and-response' initially identified by Pierre Bourdieu (1965) among the Kabyle tribe of North Africa. Malina (1981: 34–9) astutely recognized and advocated the significance for biblical interpretation of this pattern of social interaction discerned by Bourdieu.

Later anthropology moved away from some of the more schematic, even reified representations of honour and shame (unsurprisingly) present in this early work and focused more deliberately on the diverse understandings and interrelationships between honour and shame in different settings. These trends are evident in *Honor and Shame and the Unity of the Mediterranean* (1987), edited by David Gilmore, and *Honor and Grace in Anthropology* (1992a), edited by Peristiany and Pitt-Rivers. In part, the latter book sought to address an issue missing in the earlier work, namely, the connection of honour with ritual and religion (Peristiany and Pitt-Rivers 1992b: 2). At one point the editors, having noted how different groups in society could have rival views of honour, rightly stated that 'It is therefore an error to regard honor as a single constant concept rather than a conceptual field within which people find the means to express their self-esteem or their esteem for others' (Peristiany and Pitt-Rivers 1992b: 4).

The anthropological research of the early period was brilliantly summarized by Bruce Malina in 1981 in his *New Testament World: Insights from Cultural Anthropology*. This book encouraged much research then and continues to do so (especially using the third edition of 2001). Many of the early adopters of Malina's advocacy of Mediterranean anthropology crystallized into the Context Group in the late 1980s and early 1990s (see Esler 2004), even though members of the Context Group all had other interests (with John H. Elliott and the present writer, for example, having a much more positive view of the role of sociology in biblical research than Malina). Gary Stansell (e.g. 1996) and Raymond Hobbs (e.g. 1997) were particularly interested in the Hebrew Bible dimensions of honour and shame. Other scholars outside the ambit of the Context Group also became interested in reading the Hebrew Bible from an honour and shame perspective. These included Victor Matthews and Don Benjamin (1993, 1996) and Renata Rabichev, who outlined important dimensions of honour and shame in relation to biblical women (1996).

In due course, however, some interpreters began to criticize Malina's approach, in part from the perspective of the more nuanced newer understanding of Mediterranean culture that was then emerging in anthropology. Some interpreters, of whom Johanna Stiebert is the most germane for present purposes, latched onto an article by Michael Herzfeld (1980) critical of the way in which honour and shame had become 'inefficient glosses' for a wide variety of phenomena.[2] They also used research by Unni Wikan (1982) conducted in Oman where some women acted contrary to expectations in relation to sexuality yet without being social ostracized and which thus appeared to contest the notion of honour and shame as opposites.

Although not mentioned by the biblical critics who enthusiastically adopted it, Herzfeld's position, however, suffered from a number of problems, principally its being an outlier in the field (of the nine anthropologists in Gilmore 1987, only Herzfeld regarded honour and shame as no longer useful in relation to the diverse phenomena of

---

[2] See Stiebert 2002: 25–86 and Lawrence 2003: 28–9 and *passim*. More recent support for Herzfeld's view comes from Lynch 2010: 509.

the Mediterranean).³ It was, and remains, questionable scholarly method by biblical scholars hostile to the notions of honour and shame to canonize the unrepresentative view of Herzfeld and to disregard the research of a majority of anthropologists who continued to use these concepts in useful ways. Herzfeld's position was also open to the charge of inconsistency in that his adoption of 'hospitality' in the place of honour was subject to much the same issues he had raised against that concept.

The significance of Wikan's article (1984) in the discussion, moreover, has been greatly overstated. Wikan did not disprove the existence of structures of honour and shame in Oman; it only showed that certain women managed to avoid some of their strictures. In her detailed ethnography, in fact, she had noted that women in Oman were generally confined to the household (being forbidden access to the market, for example), and that a powerful set of social conventions controlled women's behaviour; conventions which a few of them managed to breach without apparent consequence (1982: 64–70). In other words, this was precisely a case of the exception proving the rule. In addition, as far as I am aware, no biblical interpreter employing the framework of honour and shame has ever claimed that no one ever broke the rules! Wikan even noticed that things were very different in Cairo, since in that context women did hide their adultery from public view and that Oman represented as an exception to the general positioned outlined by Pitt-Rivers in 1965!⁴

These considerations also provide the answer to the attempt of Dianne Bergant (also, in part, reliant on Wikan) to disconnect the Song of Songs from the framework of honour and shame. According to Bergant (1996: 36): 'The general tenor of the Song of Songs throws into question most of the characteristics associated with notions of honour and shame. There is no underlying concern for male power and status and, consequently, there is no interest in controlling what might threaten it.'

On the contrary, the young woman in the Song, in a manner similar to the women of Oman (although she may be married to her beloved), simply breaches the usual conventions of her society and, in so doing, abundantly proves their existence. So she comes into conflict with her brothers and ignores their directions (Song 1.6), twice roams Jerusalem by night and on the second occasion is beaten by the city watchmen for her pains (3.1–3, 5.7), takes a lofty view of responsibility for the vineyard she has been allocated by Solomon (8.11–12) and at one point, hardly surprisingly, is concerned lest people might despise her (יְבוּזוּ־לִי; 8.1), זוב being part of the florid vocabulary of shame in the Hebrew Bible (see below). Once again, a clearer case of the exception proving the rule is difficult to imagine.

On the other hand, Wikan's view that shame was often more prominent than honour is a valuable reminder that the two are not precise opposites, while her discovery that among Omani women 'neighbourhood solidarity' was 'a primary value' is extremely

---

³ On Herzfeld's position being unrepresentative of anthropology, see Crook 2007: 252 n.4. When Timothy Laniak was working in the mid-1990s on honour and shame for his Harvard doctorate on Esther, Herzfeld encouraged him 'to disprove the reigning paradigm in Mediterranean studies'. The result is notable: 'Though fully expecting to do so, I found that the text of Esther was comprehensively ordered around these two values and that they were explicated in terms quite in keeping with the honor–shame matrix as conventionally understood' (Laniak 2002: n1).
⁴ Wikan 1984: 647: 'It [the position of adulterous women in Oman] is a far cry from Egypt, where an almost palpable fear of people's talk constrains the person in all her dealings. An Egyptian adulteress would take the utmost care to shield her misdemeanour from public view'.

valuable (1984: 643). Finally, the importance of honour in anthropology has recently been vigorously and persuasively reasserted by Charles Stewart (2015).

More recently, Tchavdar Hadjiev (2016) has very reasonably questioned the evidentiary basis for the claim often made that the pattern in some contemporary Mediterranean societies for men to be dishonoured by the (real or imagined) sexual misbehaviour of their wives, daughters or sisters is also to be found in the Hebrew Bible. His argument is strong but would be improved by a consideration of the highly pertinent evidence of Shechem's rape of Dinah and its aftermath in Genesis 34 and Absalom's killing of Amnon in response to the latter's rape of his sister, Tamar, in 2 Samuel 13. The question is what motivated the revenge of Shechem's brothers and Absalom. Perhaps it was anger at the violent affront offered to their sister or perhaps concern for the family honour or perhaps both. Dinah's brothers specifically recognize the reality of family dishonour in Gen. 34.14 and their later rejection of letting Shechem get away with treating Dinah as a prostitute (Gen. 34.31) is also compatible with such a concern. The same question of motivation arises in connection with the revenge Absalom wreaked on Amnon. In any event and as Hadjiev recognizes, this is an important discussion for the nature of social dynamics in ancient Israel that we are having because of Malina's introduction of Mediterranean anthropology into biblical interpretation.

The deployment of honour and shame as conceptual fields, rather than monovalent concepts, capable of being brought to bear on a wide variety of data, as well explained by Laniak (1998: 38–53), is really an instance of the essential role of different levels of generality in cognition, whether in relation to the natural or social world. Because the individual phenomena and stimuli we experience are so numerous there are occasions when, rather than seeking to attend to all of them individually, it is cognitively efficient to move beyond the detail and attend to the larger patterns. Thus, our sense of a landscape in a plane flying at 500 feet is very different from when we are at 30,000; both vistas are valuable but for different purposes. This is why we draw maps at small scale (e.g. 1:25,000, as in the UK Ordnance Survey Explorer maps used by hikers), medium scale (e.g. 1:600,000) or large scale (e.g. 1:50,000,000). To reject the use of conceptual fields from Mediterranean anthropology in interpretation is akin to insisting that we should restrict ourselves to small-scale maps. This consideration (together with the heuristic and non-nomistic character of social-scientific interpretation as discussed below) is the basis for doubting the persuasiveness of Gerald Downing's important argument (1999), posed with reference to a variety of ancient evidence, that the approach oversimplifies the ancient data.

It is worth noting that in 1991 Lyn Bechtel published an important article on shame as a sanction on social relations in biblical Israel that entirely overlooked Mediterranean ethnography and Malina's 1981 work but yet in many respects reached very similar conclusions. For her analysis Bechtel was, however, heavily reliant on another social anthropologist, namely, Mary Douglas, who maintained a central distinction between social systems that were oriented around the group at one end of the spectrum and individuals at the other (Bechtel 1991: 51–2; she used Douglas 1973). Bechtel cogently argued, for example, that ancient Israel was a strongly group-oriented society layered by an '"honor" hierarchy' and that since 'shame relies heavily on external pressure from the group, it works most efficiently' in such a society (Bechtel 1991: 52). Stiebert discussed Bechtel's article, but in her enthusiasm to differentiate her position from 'the claims of Neyrey, Malina or Pilch', unwisely found 'problematic' 'the view that any culture can be more fully understood by examining it through the parameters of an alleged pivotal value'

(Stiebert 2002: 59), despite the fact that Bechtel (although approaching the matter from a different starting-point) provided abundant and persuasive evidence for the benefits of doing precisely that (Bechtel 1991: 54–76).

Malina himself, it should be noted, did not propound 'honour' and 'shame' as binary opposites since most of his interest in 'shame' was in its role as speaking positively about women's virtue.[5] He also made plain that his summary was a model, but then suggested that it was to be 'tested out' against the texts; 'disprove it if you like' (1981: 48). This was unfortunate; models are not social laws to be disproved or tested; like typologies, they are tools for undertaking comparison with empirical reality. They are not true or false but useful for not (Esler 1995a: 4). More specifically, a model is: 'An abstract selective representation of the relationships among social phenomena used to conceptualize, analyze, and interpret patterns of social relations, and to compare and contrast one system of social relations with another. Models are heuristic constructs that operationalize particular theories and that range in scope and complexity according to the phenomena to be analyzed' (Elliott 1993: 132).

The comparative method can also be served not by the use of a model but by the comparison of one particular system with another; in biblical research this typically means comparing an ethnography of a particular group in the modern period with a biblical text or passage, but this still remains a heuristic process as just described. There are no social laws. The comparative process boils down to two dimensions; first, the heuristic use of models or specific ethnographic material to ask new questions of a text; and, second, the use of model or ethnography to make sense of the answers the biblical text provides to those questions, a process akin (as Elliott used to say) to 'drawing lines between the dots'. The use of modern material to fill holes in ancient data is impermissible, however, especially since it may be in the lacunas in the evidence that the ancient experience varied most greatly from the modern (Esler 1987: 11–12). Moreover, because a social pattern occurred in the Mediterranean world in the modern period does not mean it was present there in the past. On the other hand, individualism as we know it did not exist in the ancient world and was not much present in the groups studied by the Mediterranean ethnographers and both settings were also characterized by largely rural societies featuring patrilinearity. This meant the Mediterranean cultures in scope were much closer in many respects to the contexts in which the biblical texts were written than modern, individualistic, northern European and North American cultures. This factor made the comparative exercise more fruitful because interpreters from these latter contexts who delved into the settings opened up by Mediterranean ethnography suddenly had a perspective very different from their own with which to investigate biblical texts in the comparative and heuristic manner described above. This is the reason why exegesis proceeding in this way established its importance in the 1980s and has not lost it since, as evident in the research to be discussed in what follows.[6] In particular, ethnographic research into the Mediterranean world and regions a little further east that feature patrilinear social systems is continuing and provides abundant comparative material for the heuristic application to the texts of the Hebrew Bible.

---

[5] See Malina 1981: 42–4 and 48 ('Honor has a male and a female component. When considered from this perspective, the male aspect is called honor, while the female aspect is called shame').
[6] For recent explanations of the importance of biblical interpretation using Mediterranean notions of honour and shame, see Crook 2007 and 2009, and Esler 2011a.

Most of the biblical interpreters who took up Mediterranean anthropology accepted that there was a large cultural gap between people in the modern individualistic and industrialized countries of the West and the people we investigated in the Bible, while also recognizing that the very different cultures exposed by Mediterranean anthropology provided a new perspective that assisted in avoiding anachronism and ethnocentricity. That view never entailed denying that human beings are similar in many ways, even if they differ in others, as recognized by Malina (2001: 8–9). The deep structures of human cognition that developed via the evolutionary process, as well explored in the fairly recent cognitive science approach to religious phenomena, are common to all human beings. Similarly, Patterson's well-mounted argument (2019) that mechanisms of 'social dominance' feature in the mechanisms of honour and shame in both the modern world and the ancient Mediterranean fails to overturn the reality of cultural difference. The question that still remains is why social dominance takes different shapes in different cultures. The situation is analogous to the fact that our experience of being conveyed in automobiles is widely different depending on their style, size, age and condition even though most of them still have an internal combustion engine under the hood. Yet we should not despair. Even today we must often engage in intercultural communication when we travel far from home. Moreover, the cultural gap between ourselves and foreign people, including those who wrote the biblical texts, is precisely what allows them to speak to us in new and challenging ways.

## HONOUR AND SHAME LANGUAGE IN THE HEBREW BIBLE: ISAIAH AS A TEST CASE

Let us consider the extent of honour and shame in the Hebrew Bible, taking Isaiah as an example. Stiebert (2002: 87) seems to pose an initial stumbling-block: 'There are good reasons for rejecting the socio-anthropological honour/shame model when examining honour and shame in the book of Isaiah. First of all, honour (most often rendered כבד) pertaining to humans, or men in particular, as it is depicted in the anthropological literature, is not well attested in Isaiah and seldom contrasted with shame.'

Both of these observations about the text, however, are inaccurate. In fact, Isaiah is replete with words referring to the honour of both God and human beings (not always with the use of כבד, but that is inconsequential) and honour is on numerous occasions directly contrasted with shame. Here is a selection of the evidence, which also gives some idea of the very wide conceptual fields focusing on honour and shame in the Hebrew Bible, especially since nearly all of these words in Isaiah are found in other texts, often on numerous occasions. The exercise conducted below could be repeated for virtually any text from the Hebrew Bible.

First, as to the omnipresence of honour. The verb כבד appears fifteen times in Isaiah, in the meaning 'to be honoured' in the Qal (66.5) and in the Niphal (3.5, 23.8, 23.9, 43.4, 49.5, all with a human referent) and 'to get honour' (of God) in the Niphal (26.15). It appears seven times in the Piel, meaning 'to honour', on each occasion of honouring God (24.15, 25.3, 29.13, 43.20, 43.23, 58.13) or the place where he stands (60.13). It means 'honourable' in the Pual (58.13). The noun, כָּבוֹד, with the meaning of 'honour' has thirty-six occurrences, twenty of them having a divine and sixteen a human referent. But several other verbs are also employed to denote honour. In the Piel פאר, meaning 'to glorify', is applied to Israel twice (55.5, 60.9), to God (60.2) and to the place where God stands (60.13), while in the Hithpael, meaning 'to be glorified, it is used of God on four occasions

# HONOUR, SHAME AND OTHER SOCIAL VALUES

(44.23, 49.3, 60.21, 61.3). The word נִשְׂגָּב, meaning 'is exalted', is applied to the human realm (2.11, 2.17, 26.5, 30.13) and also to God (12.4, 33.5). In addition, הִגְדִּיל, the Hiphil of גָּדַל, 'to magnify', 'to exalt', is used of the honour attached to the law at 42.21. The word אדר meaning 'wide', 'great', appears in the imperfect Hiphil (יַאְדִּיר) in the same verse with the sense of 'will make glorious'. The Piel of פאר twice designates God's glorifying Israel (55.5, 60.9), while the Hithpael refers to God's being glorified on four occasions (44.23, 49.3, 60.21, 61.3). The noun cognate to פאר, namely תִּפְאָרָה, meaning 'pride' or 'glory', is used with reference to God seven times (4.2, 28.5, 60.2, 60.19, 62.3, 63.12, 63.15) and with a human referent seven times (10.12, 13.19, 20.5, 28.1, 28.4, 44.13, 52.1). A standard Hebrew word for 'pride', 'exaltation', 'glory', 'magnificence', clearly expressive of honour, is גָּאוֹן. It appears forty-two times in the Hebrew Bible and eleven times in Isaiah, more often than in any other text (2.10, 2.19, 2.21, 4.2, 13.11, 13.19, 14.11, 16.6, 23.9, 24.14, 60.15; of which four instances relate to God and the rest to human beings). The noun הָדָר has six examples in Isaiah, four with respect to God (2.10, 2.19, 2.21, 35.2) and two with respect to human beings (5.14, 53.2). Another word conveying honour is גָּבַהּ, meaning 'high' or 'exalted' and it appears in Isaiah on three occasions in relation to human or divine honour (3.16, 5.16, 52.13). The word צְבִי, meaning 'honour', 'glory', has seven instances in Isaiah (out of seventeen in the Hebrew Bible), of which three refer to God (4.2, 24.16, 28.5), while four have human referents (13.9, 23.9, 28.1, 28.4). There is also a range of words that are used when someone with honour scorns those who lack it (thus connoting arrogance), although these words can also be deployed in a positive sense, typically of God. Thus in 13.3 God refers to his honoured status with the word גַּאֲוָה, while the word is used of human haughtiness in 9.9, 13.11 and 16.6. The word רוּם, meaning 'haughtiness', 'arrogance', occurs in 2.11, 2.17 and 10.12, while רָם, meaning 'exalted', appears at 2.12, 6.1 and 26.11. In 12.5 and 26.10 גֵּאוּת is used for God's majesty and in 28.1 and 28.3 of human pride. The word זֵד, meaning 'insolent', 'presumptuous', 'arrogant', is found in 13.11. In addition, the word שֵׁם ('name') is often deployed not to identify someone – God, a person or group – but as a way of referring to their honour. This usage is apparent in relation to human beings when the Lord says in 56.5: 'I will give in my house and in within my walls a monument and a name better than sons and daughters; I will give them an everlasting name which shall not be cut off.' There is a similar usage in 66.22. There are also some twenty-one instances of the word שֵׁם applied to God in Isaiah where the connotation of honour appears.[7] Clearly, it would be a worthwhile task to explore in detail the role of honour in connection with the name of God.

To summarize this data, we thus have some 160 words in Isaiah that represent emic equivalents to our 'honour', or approximately 2.5 per chapter, and many others, for example denoting 'praise' (the appropriate response to a person of honour) that have not been included. While it is important to determine in detail the way in which honour language is functioning in any given passage, that the broad categories of honour and shame frequently provide the framework for talk of values in the text is incontrovertible. Examples of the honour and shame framework as applied in detail to particular texts in the Hebrew Bible are given below.

---

[7] 12.4 (twice), 18.7, 24.15, 25.1, 26.8, 26.13, 29.23, 30.27, 42.8, 48.1, 48.9, 50.10, 52.5, 56.6, 57.15, 59.19, 60.9, 63.12, 64.1 and 66.5.

Second, as to the opposition of honour and shame, which Stiebert alleges is 'not well attested'. The opposition between honour and shame is brought out unequivocally in Isa. 23.9 which states that the Lord of hosts has decided 'to dishonour the pride of all glory' (לְחַלֵּל גְּאוֹן כָּל־צְבִי) and 'to bring into contempt all the honourable of the earth' (לְהָקֵל כָּל־נִכְבַּדֵּי־אָרֶץ). In 2.11 'the haughty looks of humanity shall be brought low, the pride of people shall be humbled' (similarly, 2.17). In 9.1 (sometimes cited as 8.23) we learn that 'In the former time he brought into contempt (הֵקַל) the land of Zebulon and the land of Naphtali, but in the latter time he will make glorious (הִכְבִּיד) the way beyond the sea, the land beyond the Jordan, Galilee of the nations'. In a description of the coming day of the Lord God says 'I will put an end to the pride of the arrogant and I will humble (אַשְׁפִּיל) the haughtiness of the ruthless' (13.11). In 22.18 the chariots of Shebna's glory (כָּבוֹד) will be the shame (קְלוֹן) of his father's house. In 24.23 'The moon will be confounded, and the sun ashamed' (וּבוֹשָׁה) for the Lord of hosts will reign 'gloriously' (כָּבוֹד). When in 47.1 God enjoins the virgin daughter of Babylon to 'sit on the ground without a throne', the image evoked is of not just of the loss of power but of the transformation from honour to shame, as confirmed soon after in his reference to her shame (חֶרְפָּה; 47.3). The prophet announces to Israel in 61.6–7 that 'you shall eat the wealth of nations, and in their glory (וּבִכְבוֹדָם) you shall boast. Instead of your shame (בָּשְׁתְּכֶם) you shall have a double portion, and instead of dishonour (וּכְלִמָּה) you shall rejoice in your lot'. The final instance of this common pattern comes in 66.5: 'Let the Lord be glorified, that we may see your joy; but it is they who will be put to shame'. The opposition between honour and shame, especially when one is being replaced by the other in many of the social and political convulsions mentioned in the text, is thus not only 'well attested' but represents a standard feature of Isaian rhetoric.

The main emic terms in Isaiah related to the etic term 'shame' in Isaiah are: בּוֹשׁ, meaning 'to be ashamed', with twenty instances in the Qal (out of ninety-three times in the Hebrew Bible), and one in the Hiphil meaning 'to put to shame' (out of thirty-two times); the noun בֹּשֶׁת, meaning 'shame', with five instances (of twenty-eight times); the verb חָרַף, used mainly in the Piel meaning 'to reproach', with five examples (of thirty-four) and the noun חֶרְפָּה, meaning 'reproach' or 'disgrace', with six examples (of seventy-three); the verb כָּלַם in the Niphal meaning 'to be put to shame', with five instances (of twenty-six), and its cognate noun, כְּלִמָּה, meaning 'ignominy' or 'reproach', with six occurrences (of seventy-three); נָאַץ, meaning 'to despise', 'to scorn', with three examples (of twenty-three); and, finally, a word indicating 'shame' in the sense of its social lowliness, שָׁפֵל, which in the Qal means 'to become low', with nine instances (of ten) and in the Hiphil 'to abase', 'to humble', with five examples (of eighteen).[8]

The most significant of these is בּוֹשׁ. One tack taken recently by two scholars who are unsympathetic to the notion that honour and shame are such prominent values in the Hebrew Bible as others propose is to reinterpret instances of בּוֹשׁ as relating to other issues (Avrahami 2010; Lynch 2010). Both run an interesting case, with Avrahami suggesting that in the lament Psalms בּוֹשׁ means 'disappointment' rather than 'shame', while Lynch proposes that this word and its synonyms often mark physical not 'psychosocial processes'. Nevertheless, that in some places בּוֹשׁ might not mean 'shame' does not really carry much weight against the fact that in numerous locations it does. While their specific arguments are subject to critique in various ways, it is worth noting that, for

---

[8] For a discussion of shame in the Hebrew Bible, see Klopfenstein 1972; Bechtel 1991: 54; Botha 1999: 390–1.

central instances upon which they rely, the Septuagintal translators (whom they fail to mention) thought בוֹשׁ referred to 'shame'. Thus, counting against Avrahami's advocacy of 'disappointed' for אֵבוֹשָׁה in Ps. 71.1 (2010: 304) is the Septuagint's translation καταισχυνθείην ('let me not be put to shame'). His translation of יֵבֹשׁוּ יִכְלוּ in Ps. 71.13 as 'Let my accusers perish in frustration' runs up against the Septuagint's translation as Αἰσχυνθήτωσαν καὶ ἐκλιπέτωσιν' ('Let them be ashamed and utterly perish'). Finally, in relation to the use of בוֹשׁ in Ps. 71.24 Avrahami's claim that 'there is no justification for the common translation "to be shamed"' (Avrahami 2010: 306–7) comes into collision with the Septuagint's rendering of αἰσχυνθῶσι ('they are ashamed'). Similarly, Lynch's insistence that in Jeremiah 14 the verbs בוֹשׁ and כלם 'denote a process of physical weakening or diminishment', referring to 'physical processes of bodily harm occasioned by drought' (Lynch 2010: 501–2) was not something that occurred to the Septuagintal translators, who translated בֹשׁוּ in v. 4 as ἠσχύνθησαν ('they were ashamed').

## ASCRIBED AND ACQUIRED HONOUR IN ANCIENT ISRAEL

Genealogies figure prominently in the Hebrew Bible and have been attributed with a number of functions (Wilson 1975, 1977; Efthimiadis-Keith 2014: 866–9). In line with the patrilinear system operative in ancient Israel, these genealogies overwhelmingly trace descent through male ancestors. To an extent, they provide proof of the succession from an illustrious ancestor that often figures in assertions of ethnic identity, and that is clearly a large part of their function in 1 Chronicles 1–8. But they also represent a repository of ascribed honour. In ancient Israel a person was honoured by an honourable ancestor, and disgraced by a dishonourable one: 'A man's honour derives from the respect shown his father, and dishonour comes to children from their mother's disgrace' (Sir. 3.11). The living person who was the most recent addition to a genealogy enjoyed the benefit of the honour attached to his ancestors; he received this honour simply by virtue of who he was. This was ascribed honour. But honour could also be ascribed by gift from a social superior. A good example is Yahweh's appointment of Eliakim as steward over the royal household in Isa. 22.15–25 in place of Shebna. The text expressly recognizes that the honour that attaches to Eliakim by virtue of his position will spread to his family: 'And I will fasten him like a peg in a sure place, and he will become a throne of honour to his father's house' (22.23). Numerous examples can be found of the acquired honour that is won in the social dynamic of challenge-and-response. To cite one prominent case, the entirety of 2 Samuel 10–12 is explicable on this basis. The process begins with the king of Ammon challenging David by insulting his ambassadors (10.4) and, after many ups and downs, ends when David finally captures the Ammonite capital (12.29–31).[9]

## SOCIAL PRACTICES PRODUCTIVE OF SHAME

Bechtel (1991) has admirably surveyed the manifold contexts in which shaming was used as a means of judicial, political and social control in ancient Israel.[10] In all of these contexts, to shame someone entailed publicly stripping that person of honour or declaring

---

[9] See Esler 2011b. An alternative approach would be to begin with David's sending his ambassadors, which he regarded positively but was regarded negatively by the Ammonites.
[10] Also note the valuable observations on 'Shaming as a Means of Social Control' in Matthews 1997: 98–102.

that he or she lacked honour. As she notes, since 'shame relies heavily on external pressure from the group, it works most efficiently on a predominantly group-oriented society' (Bechtel 1991: 52).

Deut. 25.5–10 represents a good example of shaming in a judicial context. In a case where a man refused to marry his brother's widow, she could go to the town gate and complain about him to the elders (who were functioning judicially). When they summoned the man, and he still refused, she could pull the sandal off his foot and spit in his face (both of which were shaming acts) and then declare, 'So shall it be done to the man who does not build up his brother's house', and 'the name of his house shall be called in Israel "The house of him that had his sandal pulled off"' (Deut. 25.9–10). 'Name' (which was one facet of honour, as noted above) was, as Bechtel observes, of 'enormous importance in biblical culture' (1991: 58).

Practices of shaming also figured prominently in the conduct of warfare:

> [I]nhumane treatment and punishment of defeated warriors and leaders were not carried out for sadistic purposes alone. Such tactics were important because of their psychological impact. A captured vassal was not just vindictively tortured; he was made a *public* example for all to see [. . .] It was publicity, not necessarily pain, that was the primary motive for shameful and inhumane treatment of captives. (Bechtel 1991: 63; original emphasis)

As Lemos has noted, the Hebrew Bible never mentions pain as the reason for disfiguring a victim. Rather, mutilation of captured enemies 'functioned to shame the victim or his community'. It threatened 'what many ancient Israelites seem to have valued most, their standing in the eyes of others' (Lemos 2006: 241). Reducing captives to nakedness before leading them off into captivity was also a central feature of the shaming process. 'Humiliating captive warriors lowered them and their nation to an inferior position and raised up the victors in status' (Bechtel 1991: 64). Thus, the process involved status elevation for the victor and status degradation for the vanquished.[11] A particular feature of warfare and its aftermath in the Hebrew Bible that repays analysis from the perspective of honour and shame is the footstool (הֲדֹם רַגְלָיִם), with six occurrences in the biblical text (Isa. 61.1; Pss. 99.5, 110.1, 132.7; 1 Chron. 28.2; Lam. 2.1). The footstool is a mostly used as a metaphor for the power of king (Sutton 2016: 58). The example in Ps. 110.1 (RSV), however, directed to the king of Israel, is connected with warfare:

> The Lord says to my lord,
> 'Sit at my right hand,
> till I make your enemies
> your footstool.'

The message conveyed is that in this process the king will acquire honour and the defeated enemies will be shamed, another coupling of status elevation and status degradation in a single image (Sutton 2016). Similarly, one might add, in the Passion accounts in the Gospels there are numerous references to the dishonour that Jesus sustained, but virtually none to the pain that he undoubtedly experienced.

---

[11] One of the *Judaea Capta* coins minted after Titus had captured and sacked Jerusalem in 70 CE (an aureus from the mint in Lugdunum) perfectly captures this juxtaposition by showing Titus in his chariot and a bound Judean captive in the same image (Esler 1995b: 253, ill. 11).

The process of shaming could also have a political or diplomatic function. A good example is the way that Hanun, the new king of Ammon, treated the ambassadors David had sent to offer a continuance of good relations between the two states on the death of Hanun's father in 2 Sam. 10.1–5 (Bechtel 1991: 67–70). Taking the view that they were spies, Hanun had half their beards shaved off and half their garments cut at their hips (thus exposing their private parts). The ambassadors were greatly shamed by this (נִכְלָמִים מְאֹד), and so great in fact was the insult – an unambiguous 'challenge' requiring a robust 'response' if ever there one (see above) – that it precipitated a war with Ammon that only ended with David's capture of Rabbah, the Ammonite capital, in 2 Sam. 12.29–31 (Esler 2011b). Other examples of the use of shame for political purposes appear in Ezra/Nehemiah when the need to avoid shame is deployed by Ezra and Nehemiah for various ends, including motivating them to rebuild the Temple and the city wall and to re-establish the people as holy to the Lord (Kang 2020).

Bechtel also provides examples of the use of shame as a sanction 'publicly and informally by ordinary folk in the midst of everyday life' (1991: 70). This was clearly the most widespread arena for the production of shame. As well as specific instances from daily experience – such as scorn: mockery and being made a laughing-stock; wagging the head; gaping with an open mouth; sticking one's tongue out; spitting; hissing; striking the cheek and winking (1991: 72) – Bechtel also cites examples from the Psalms and from Job (1991: 70–4), areas of evidence considered below.

Recent research by Okyere and Effah Darko (2019) has aptly pointed to the sentiments in Prov. 10.5, 'A son who gathers in summer is prudent, but a son who sleeps in harvest brings shame', as not only revealing the extent to which shame can function as a sanction against laziness in harvest-time but as also opening up the importance of the larger task of exploring the socio-economic life of ancient Israel in the light of the dynamics of honour and shame.

# HONOUR AND SHAME IN SPECIFIC TEXTS IN THE HEBREW BIBLE

## Job

In the book of Job the lowly state into which he is transported following the discussions between God and the Satan is influenced by the social patterns of honour and shame. Thus Job observes that he has become a שְׂחֹק, a laughing-stock (12.4; twice). He remarks to Bildad the Shuhite that 'ten times you have reproached me' (תַּכְלִימוּנִי 19.3) and that his three friends have grown in honour in relation to him and have used his disgrace (חֶרְפָּה) against him (19.5). To Zophar the Naamathite he replies, 'Bear with me, and I will speak, and after I have spoken, mock on (תַּלְעִיג)' (21.3) That is to say, although he has lost his wealth and has been afflicted with sores, Job's dilemma also entails his transition from honour to disgrace (Bechtel 1991: 74). Yet, as Mbuvi has noted – in an article that is very alert to the honour/shame dimensions both of God's discussions with Satan and Job's with his interlocutors – this observation alone can only take you so far (2010: 766–7). A fuller reading of the text necessitates melding this aspect (which has hitherto not been given sufficient attention) with other textual dimensions. Mbuvi himself has focused on the way in which the discourse of honour and shame plays into the more significant theological question of 'disinterested' faith, that is, the faith that persists in spite of suffering, even though the book does not seem to answer the question of why the innocent suffer in the first place.

## The Psalms

Leonard Maré (2014: 2–4) has usefully summarized recent research on the Psalms from, he suggests, the rather neglected perspective of honour and shame. He rightly endorses the view of deSilva (2008: 288–91) that the Psalms are a rich source of evidence on this matter generally and on specific issues connected with honour and shame, such as: the use of honour and shame to signal a reversal in the fortunes of the individual and the group; the notion that honour was one of the goods that would result from a virtuous life; the fact that experience regularly contradicted the expectations of the people as they became subject to mockery and derision; the frequent wish that disgrace would instead fall on their enemies, both individuals and nations; and that God's honour often features in the Psalms. Following Tucker (2007: 469–70), he notes that sexuality is, however, not a prominent issue in the language of honour and shame in the Psalms although it is habitually present in the narrative texts of the Hebrew Bible (Maré 2014: 4). Maré's persuasive exegesis of Psalm 44 foregrounds important issues such as: Israel is honoured if the people are faithful to God's covenant; Israel's honour is intertwined with God's; God has the responsibility for shaming Israel's enemies and, at times, Israel itself; Israel's shame is reflected in a negative way on God; Israel recognizes that although God at times shames them, he is the only entity capable of restoring their honour; and Israel deploys the rhetoric of accusation against God to shame him into acting on their behalf (2014: 10–11). Sutton (2018) has posed the provocative question of whether the picture of God as a shield-bearer in Ps. 35.2, meaning that he was in a subordinate position in relation to the warrior being shielded, was intended to attach shame to Yahweh as a way of intimating Yahweh as a righteous, caring, merciful and loving God.

A notable feature of Psalms 47, 93, 96, 97, 98 and 99 is the use of the expressions 'God is king' or 'God reigns' that has led to their often being referred to as the 'enthronement Psalms'. They 'proclaim the reign of Yahweh over all nations, over the whole earth and over all creation. Yahweh's holiness, majesty, exaltedness, judgement and saving power are used to motivate the call to rejoice in his praise' (Botha 1998: 26). For present purposes, another common denominator of these Psalms is that 'Each one of them in its own right, and all of them as a group, seem to proclaim the world-wide honour of God'. An offshoot of this demand is that 'an honourable position is also claimed for Israel among the family of nations' (Botha 1998: 27). In these Psalms kingship is a metaphor for honour. For the community of believers to recognize and validate the honour of Yahweh in this way is an illocutionary act (1998: 28). In part, since Yahweh enjoys divine status his honour is ascribed, as with the references to his sitting enthroned between the cherubim (99.1) on his throne (47.9) and robed in majesty (93.1). But he also possesses acquired honour: on a cosmic level he has overcome the forces of chaos (93.3–4) and he has made the heavens (96.5). But he has also acquired honour from his treatment of Israel: he has, for example, achieved victory with his mighty arm and shown his faithfulness to Israel (98.1–3); spoken through Moses, Aaron and Samuel (99.6–8); and given his people law (93.5; Botha 1998: 29–31). In the result, 'enthronement Psalms' is a misnomer for these poems, which rather celebrate the honour of Yahweh. In a context where the honour (perhaps the existence) of Israel was at stake, their purpose seems to be to strengthen in-group identity in the face of threats from antagonistic nations and their gods, whose devotees will be put to shame (97.7; Botha 1998: 31–5).

Psalm 119 also represents another ample expression of shame in the Hebrew Bible. As Botha has observed (1999: 392–4), there are three main categories of material relating to shame: first, prayers for avoiding shame; second, prayers focusing on the removal of shame that has already been experienced; and, third, statements by the Psalmist that he will not be deterred from his doing his duty by the threat of shame. In the first category, for example, we find prayers from the Psalmist that 'I not be put to shame' (לֹא־אֵבוֹשׁ; Pss. 119.6 and 80) and in each case avoidance of shame depends upon his keeping the commandments. Second, and more frequently, are found prayers for God to remove the shame that has been incurred. The same rationale is offered, however, that the Psalmist has obeyed the law or acknowledges the worth of the divine ordinances: 'Remove scorn (חֶרְפָּה) and contempt (בּוּז) from me, for I keep your statutes' (Ps. 119.22) and 'Take away the disgrace (חֶרְפָּה) I dread, for your judgements are good' (Ps. 119.39). Examples of the third category include 'The arrogant mock me (הֱלִיצֻנִי) without restraint, but I do not turn from your law' (Ps. 119.51) and 'Though I am lowly (צָעִיר) and despised (נִבְזֶה), I do not forget your precepts' (Ps. 119.141). Although the Psalmist is more concerned with avoiding shame than gaining honour, evidence for the existence of honour occurs in the Psalm, for example when he claims to be wiser than people older than him or his teachers (vv. 99–100; Botha 1999: 395). In the Psalm the frequent references to shame and the occasional insinuations of honour are tied to the religious purpose 'professing a special relationship with Yahweh through the Torah' (Botha 1999: 397).

A gloomier picture, as Bechtel has noted, appears in the complaint Psalms,[12] where we find a constantly repeated concern with being shamed by fellow Israelites or outsiders and a wish that God would instead shame the Psalmist's opponents. Psalm 25.1–3 (RSV) is typical:

> To thee, O Lord, I lift up my soul.
> O my God, in thee I trust,
> let me not be put to shame (אֵבוֹשָׁה);
> let not my enemies exult over me.
> Yea, let none that wait for thee be put to shame (יֵבֹשׁוּ);
> Let them be ashamed (יֵבֹשׁוּ) who are wantonly treacherous.

Finally, Dennis Tucker (2007) has cogently argued for the usefulness of using the notion of patron and client relations to interpret Psalms of lament such as Psalms 44, 74 and 79. He proposes that in these psalms Yahweh fails to act 'as patron in a manner that reflects the reciprocal nature of the relationship, and further, in a manner that engenders solidarity' (ibid.: 475). The consequence is shame for the client (= the community) but also, and to a greater degree, for the patron (= Yahweh). These Psalms look to the patron to restore his honour by acting in accordance with the obligations he owes to his client. This idea emerges in verses such as 'How long, O God, will the foe taunt (חרף)? Will the enemy revile (נאץ) your name forever?' (ibid.: 477), which employ examples of the language of shame noted above. The Psalmist reminds Yahweh 'of his cosmic capacity as creator to establish order' and in doing so reasserts 'his belief in the constancy of the patron–client relation established with Yahweh' (ibid.: 477).

---

[12] She identifies (Bechtel 1991: 70–1) the following Psalms in this connection: 4, 22, 25, 31, 34, 35, 37, 39, 40, 42, 55, 57, 69, 70, 71, 74, 79, 80, 89, 102, 109, 119 and 123.

### Esther

Laniak (1998: 167–77) has shown the extent to which the conceptual fields of honour and shame find richly responsive data in the text of Esther. Several examples of the dynamic of challenge-and-response are present. The pattern evident in some of the Psalms (see above), where someone driven to despair and lamentation by the action of enemies seeks retribution in the form of disgrace that falls on those enemies, is also present in Esther. Furthermore, Laniak argues that Esther is representative of other Israelite literature, Daniel for example, in portraying Israel in the diaspora as living in a state of shame but yet at times experiencing movement from humiliation to exaltation. Moreover, the 'character of Esther provides an appropriate personification of life in Exile' (Laniak 1998: 174). This indicates the connection between the presentation of social reality and theological reflection, since in this light the text can be 'more fully appreciated as another chapter in the ongoing story of Jewish survival, another example of the *Heilsgeschichte*' (ibid.: 176–7).

## OTHER SOCIAL VALUES IN THE HEBREW BIBLE

### Hospitality

As already noted, other social values in the Hebrew Bible tend to be embedded in patterns of challenge-and-response. Hospitality, to start with, is, according to Malina (2016a: 96), 'the process of "receiving" outsiders and changing them from strangers to guests'. While this approach perhaps unnecessarily excludes food and accommodation offered to relatives and existing friends, it does cover a number of important incidents in the Hebrew Bible. In these cases 'hospitality' certainly is a value that 'serves as a means of attaining and preserving honor, the core cultural value' (ibid.). The centrality of honour in the process is apparent in the deeply disturbing account of the Levite from Ephraim and his concubine in Judges 19 who are given shelter in Gibeah one night by another Ephraimite who happens to be living there. In offering his virgin daughter and his guest's concubine to the men of the town instead of his guest whom they wish to rape, the preservation of his honour is the Ephraimite's probable motivation (especially when, in v. 24, he designates their contemplated act as נְבָלָה, often used of dishonourable conduct, for example, at 1 Sam. 25.25 and 2 Sam. 13.12). Malina has argued for a number of features that characterize the extension of hospitality to strangers and some (but not all) are comparable with the way Abraham responds to the three strangers in Gen. 18.1–15. Lee Martin has argued (2014: 1–5) that this narrative includes several elements typical of such a social interaction: travellers make themselves known but without actually seeking hospitality; the host extends an offer of modest hospitality; the hospitality is limited in time; hospitality normally includes water for washing of the guests' feet, food, drink, rest and care for animals (although there are no animals in Gen. 18.1–15); hospitality is freely given (that is, without expectation of return); the process involves entering into a social relationship as the traveller is transformed from stranger to guest; and the host accompanies the guests as they depart. A feature mentioned by Malina (on the basis of passages like Gen. 19.5) but not present here is a period of testing before hospitality is offered. Victor Matthews has published illuminating explanations of Judges 4 (1991) and Genesis 19 and Judges 19 (1992) from a similar honour and shame perspective.

## Humility

Humility is a social value that exists at the intersection of honour and limited good, since it 'directs persons to stay within their inherited social status' (Malina 2016b: 99). Humble persons refrain from threatening or challenging others in the social dynamic of challenge-and-response and do not claim more for themselves than what has been allotted to them in life. Conversely, to strive for honour that others possess is an example of proud behaviour. To humiliate oneself is 'to declare oneself powerless to defend one's status' (Malina 2016b: 99, citing 2 Chron. 33.23, 36.12; Phil. 2.8).

However, other explanations of the value reasonably designated as humility are available. Thus S.B. Dawes has, as an explanation of the ענו/ענוה semantic field in the Hebrew Bible, suggested the meaning of 'lowering oneself before a social equal', a perspective also to be found in early Christianity (1991a, 1991b). In reply to Dawes, Dickson and Rosner (2004) have argued for a rather different explanation of humility, namely, that the ענו/ענוה words in the Hebrew Bible convey other meanings, especially submission to God. The instances in 2 Chronicles cited by Malina use the different verb, כָּנַע in the Niphal, and while the sense clearly is to declare oneself powerless before another, that other is not at the same social level, being God in each case. Of the twenty-five examples of כָּנַע in the Niphal in the Hebrew Bible, there are only two reflexive (as opposed to passive) examples that refer to human beings lowering themselves before other human beings (2 Chron 30.11, 36.12, but in the second case the person is Jeremiah, God's agent). While this illustrates a social sense of this virtue, on the other fifteen occasions of 'humbling oneself' the person or people in question does so before God (1 Kgs 21.29 twice, 22.19, 2 Chron. 7.14, 12.6, 12.7 twice, 12.12, 32.26, 33.12, 33.19, 33.23 twice, 34.27 twice). Clearly, this is an area of great importance where the honour/shame dimension drawn from anthropology has made a valuable contribution but which would profit from a more extended analysis sensitive to both its social and religious dimensions.

## Purity

In 1981 Malina devoted a chapter of *The New Testament World: Insights from Cultural Anthropology* to the question of purity but his source was not Mediterranean anthropology but the work of Mary Douglas, in the form of her classic study *Purity and Danger* from 1966. The central idea in this book was that 'dirt' was matter out of place, especially because it had crossed particular boundaries that were invested with symbolic significance: 'Dirt, then, is never a unique isolated event. Where there is dirt there is a system. Dirt is the by-product of a systematic ordering and classification of matter, in so far as ordering involves rejecting inappropriate elements' (Douglas 1966: 44).

Thus, muddy boots are an accepted incident of a hike through countryside after rain; but later tramping those same boots through the front door of one's house and onto the white carpet is unacceptable. As applied to the Hebrew Bible, this insight opened up a powerful new way, aptly appropriated by Malina (1981: 122–52), to understand the numerous instances of what we call 'pollution' as exposure to substances, entities, places and times that transgress particular social boundaries. Purity is thus a state that obtains when such boundaries are not being breached or, if they have recently, appropriate rituals of cleansing have been performed. This area, recently surveyed by Wil Rogan (2018), will remain central to the understanding of numerous phenomena in the Hebrew Bible.

Other social values that can be explored using Mediterranean anthropology (perhaps starting with the various entries in Pilch and Malina 2016) include faith/faithfulness, grace/favour, gratitude, love, obedience, patience, pity, trust and zeal. In each case it will soon become clear that adopting this approach usefully enriches what is often already a rich discussion of these topics from other perspectives.

## CONCLUSION

Perspectives on social values in the Hebrew Bible using ideas drawn from anthropology, either from specialists in the Mediterranean valorizing issues of honour and shame or from other anthropologists in relation to issues like group orientation or purity, have formed part of the burgeoning social-scientific approach to biblical interpretation since the late 1970s. While this approach has inevitably attracted critiques, these have not led to its termination but have been extremely useful in encouraging its more nuanced application.[13] Looking forward, there is, in particular, ample scope for the continued deployment of specific ethnographic research in relation to particular texts and topics in the Hebrew Bible in the heuristic manner outlined above.

## REFERENCES

Avrahami, Y. (2010), 'בוש in the Psalms – Shame or Disappointment', *JSOT*, 34 (3): 295–313.

Bechtel, L. (1991), 'Shame as a Sanction of Social Control in Biblical Israel: Judicial, Political, and Social Shaming', *JSOT*, 16 (49): 47–76.

Bergant, D. (1996), '"My Beloved is Mine and I am His" (Song 2.16): The Song of Songs and Honor and Shame', in V.H. Matthews and D.C. Benjamin (eds), *Honor and Shame in the World of the Bible*, 23–40, Semeia 68, Atlanta, GA: Scholars Press.

Botha, P.J. (1998), 'The "Enthronement Psalms": A Claim to the World-Wide Honour of Yahweh', *OTE*, 11 (1): 24–39.

Botha, P.J. (1999), 'Shame and the Social Setting of Psalm 119', *OTE*, 12 (3): 389–400.

Bourdieu, P. (1965), 'The Sentiment of Honour in Kabyle Society', in J.G. Peristiany (ed.), *Honour and Shame: The Values of Mediterranean Society*, 191–241, London: Weidenfeld and Nicolson.

Crook, Z.A. (2004), *Reconceptualising Conversion: Patronage, Loyalty and Conversion in the Religions of the Ancient Mediterranean*, BZNW 130, Berlin: De Gruyter.

Crook, Z.A. (2007), 'Structure Versus Agency in Studies of the Biblical Social World: Engaging with Louise Lawrence', *JSNT*, 29 (3): 251–75.

Crook, Z.A. (2009), 'Honor, Shame, and Social Status Revisited', *JBL*, 128 (3): 591–611.

Dawes, S.B. (1991a), 'Humility: Whence This Strange Notion?', *ExpT*, 103 (3): 72–5.

Dawes, S.B. (1991b), 'Anāwa in Translation and Tradition', *VT*, 41 (1): 38–48.

deSilva, D.A. (2008), 'Honor and Shame', in T. Longman III and P. Enns (eds), *Dictionary of the Old Testament Wisdom, Poetry and Writings*, 287–300, Downers Grove, IL: IVP Academic.

Dickson, J.P. and B.S. Rosner (2004), 'Humility as a Social Virtue in the Hebrew Bible?', *VT*, 54 (4): 459–79.

---

[13] See Kelly 2015 for an essay sensitive to the complaints levelled against the use of Mediterranean anthropology in the interpretation of the Hebrew Bible yet persisting nonetheless in employing it in a sophisticated analysis of 1 Kings 22.

Douglas, M. (1966), *Purity and Danger: An Analysis of Concepts of Pollution and Taboo*, London: Routledge and Kegan Paul.
Douglas, M. (1973), *Natural Symbols*, 2nd edn, New York: Vintage Books.
Downing, G. (1999), '"Honor" Among Exegetes', *CBQ*, 61 (1): 53–73.
Efthimiadis-Keith, H. (2014), 'Genealogy, Retribution and Identity: Re-interpreting the Cause of Suffering in the Book of Judith', *OTE*, 27 (3): 860–78.
Elliott, J.H. (1993), *Social-Scientific Criticism of the New Testament: An Introduction*, Minneapolis, MN: Fortress Press.
Elliott, J.H. (2015), *Beware the Evil Eye: The Evil Eye in the Bible and the Ancient World, Volume 1 – Introduction, Mesopotamia, and Egypt*, Eugene, OR: Cascade.
Esler, P.F. (1987), *Community and Gospel in Luke–Acts: The Social and Political Motivations of Lucan Theology*, SNTSMS 57, Cambridge: Cambridge University Press.
Esler, P.F. (1995a), 'Introduction: Models, Context and Kerygma in New Testament Interpretation', in P.F. Esler (ed.), *Modelling Early Christianity: Social-Scientific Studies of the New Testament in Context*, 1–20, London: Routledge.
Esler, P.F. (1995b), 'God's Honour and Rome's Triumph: Responses to the Fall of Jerusalem in 70 CE in Three Jewish Apocalypses', in P.F. Esler (ed.), *Modelling Early Christianity: Social-Scientific Studies of the New Testament in Context*, 239–58, London: Routledge.
Esler, P.F. (1998), 'The Madness of Saul: A Cultural Reading of 1 Samuel 83–1', in J.C. Exum and S.D. Moore (eds), *Biblical Studies / Cultural Studies: The Third Sheffield Colloquium*, 220–62, JSOTSup 266, Sheffield: Sheffield Academic Press.
Esler, P.F. (2004), 'The Context Group Project: An Autobiographical Account', in M. Aguilar and L. Lawrence (eds), *Anthropology and Biblical Studies: Avenues of Research*, 46–61, Leiden: Deo.
Esler, P.F. (2011a), 'The Original Context of Old Testament Narrative', in *Sex, Wives, and Warriors: Reading Biblical Narrative with Its Ancient Audience*, 35–76, Eugene, OR: Cascade.
Esler, P.F. (2011b) 'David, Bathsheba and the Ammonite War (2 Samuel 101–2)', in *Sex, Wives, and Warriors: Reading Biblical Narrative with Its Ancient Audience*, 302–21, Eugene, OR: Cascade.
Esler, P.F. and A.C. Hagedorn (2006), 'Social-Scientific Analysis of the Old Testament: A Brief History and Overview', in P.F. Esler (ed.), *Ancient Israel: The Old Testament in Its Social Context*, 15–32, Minneapolis, MN: Fortress Press.
Foster, G.M. (1967), 'Peasant Society and the Image of the Limited Good', in J.M. Potter, M.N. Díaz and G.M. Foster (eds), *Peasant Society: A Reader*, 300–23, Boston, MA: Little, Brown [First published in the *American Anthropologist* in 1965].
Gilmore, D.D., ed. (1987), *Honor and Shame and the Unity of the Mediterranean*, American Anthropological Association 22, Washington, DC: American Anthropological Association.
Greenspahn, F.E. (1994), *When Brothers Dwell Together: The Preeminence of Younger Siblings in the Hebrew Bible*, Oxford: Oxford University Press.
Hadjiev, T.S. (2016), 'Adultery, Shame, and Sexual Pollution in Ancient Israel and in Hosea: A Response to Joshua Moon', *JSOT*, 41 (2): 221–36.
Herzfeld, M. (1980), 'Honour and Shame: Problems in the Comparative Analysis of Moral Systems', *Man* NS, 15 (2): 339–51.
Hobbs, T.R. (1997), 'Reflections on Honor, Shame, and Covenant', *JBL*, 116 (3): 501–3.
Jaspers, E. (2016), 'Values', *Oxford Bibliographies Online*. Available online: https://www.oxfordbibliographies.com/view/document/obo-9780199756384/obo-9780199756384-0182.xml (accessed 9 July 2022).

Kang, B. (2020), 'The Positive Role of Shame for Post-Exilic Returnees in Ezra/Nehemiah', *OTE*, 33 (2): 250–65.

Kelly, W.L. (2015), 'Prophets, Kings and Honour in the Narrative of 1 Kgs 22', in B. Becking and H.M. Barstad (eds), *Prophecy and Prophets in Stories: Papers Read at the Fifth Meeting of the Edinburgh Prophecy Network, Utrecht, October 2013*, 64–75, Leiden: E.J. Brill.

Kirk, A. (2007), 'Karl Polanyi, Marshall Sahlins, and the Study of Ancient Social Relations', *JBL*, 126 (1): 182–91.

Klopfenstein, M.A. (1972), *Scham und Schande nach dem Alten Testament: Eine begriffsgeschichtliche Untersuchung zu den hebräischen Wurzeln* בוש, כלם *und* חפר, ATANT 62; Zürich: TVZ.

Kray, S. (2002), '"New Mode of Feminist Historical Analysis" – Or Just Another Collusion with "Patriarchal" Bias?', *Shofar*, 20 (3): 66–90.

Laniak, T.S. (1998), *Shame and Honor in the Book of Esther*, SBLDS 165, Atlanta, GA: Scholars Press.

Laniak, T.S. (2002), 'Review of Johanna Stiebert, *The Construction of Shame in the Hebrew Bible: The Prophetic Contribution*', *Journal of Hebrew Scriptures*, 4 (4). Available online: https://doi.org/10.5508/jhs5916 (accessed 9 July 2022).

Lawrence, L. (2003), *An Ethnography of the Gospel of Matthew: A Critical Assessment of the Use of the Honour and Shame Model in New Testament Studies*, Tübingen: Mohr Siebeck.

Lemos, T.M. (2006), 'Shame and Mutilation of Enemies in the Hebrew Bible', *JBL*, 125 (2): 225–41.

Lerner, G. (1986), *The Creation of Patriarchy*, Women and History 1, New York: Oxford University Press.

Lynch, M.J. (2010), 'Neglected Physical Dimensions of "Shame" Terminology in the Hebrew Bible', *Bib*, 91 (4): 499–517.

Malina, B.J. (1981), *The New Testament World: Insights from Cultural Anthropology*, Louisville, KY: Westminster John Knox Press.

Malina, B.J. (2001), *The New Testament World: Insights from Cultural Anthropology*, 3rd edn, Louisville, KY: Westminster John Knox Press.

Malina, B.J. (2016a), 'Hospitality', in J.J. Pilch and B.J. Malina (eds), *Handbook of Biblical Social Values*, 3rd edn, 96–9, Eugene, OR: Cascade Books.

Malina, B.J. (2016b), 'Humility', in J.J. Pilch and B.J. Malina (eds), *Handbook of Biblical Social Values*, 3rd edn, 99–100, Eugene, OR: Cascade Books.

Malina, B.J. and C. Seeman (2016), 'Envy', in J.J. Pilch and B.J. Malina (eds), *Handbook of Biblical Social Values*, 3rd edn, 51–4, Eugene, OR: Cascade Books.

Maré, L.P. (2014), 'Honour and Shame in Psalm 44', *Scriptura*, 113. Available online: https://doi.org/10.7833/113-0-106 (accessed 9 July 2022).

Martin, L.R. (2014), 'Old Testament Foundations for Christian Hospitality', *Verbum et Ecclesia*, 35 (1): art 752. Available online: http://www.scielo.org.za/pdf/vee/v35n1/04.pdf (accessed 9 July 2022).

Matthews, V.H. (1991), 'Hospitality and Hostility in Judges 4', *BTB*, 21 (1): 13–21.

Matthews, V.H. (1992), 'Hospitality and Hostility in Genesis 19 and Judges 19', *BTB*, 22 (1): 3–11.

Matthews, V.H. (1997), 'Honor and Shame in Gender-Related Legal Situations in the Hebrew Bible', in V.H. Matthews, B.M. Levinson and T. Frymer-Kensky (eds), *Gender and Law in the Hebrew Bible and the Ancient Near East*, 97–112, JSOTSup 262, Sheffield: Sheffield Academic Press.

Matthews, V.H. and D.C. Benjamin (1993), *Social World of Ancient Israel 1250–587 BCE*, Peabody, MA: Hendrickson.
Matthews, V.H. and D.C. Benjamin, eds (1996), *Honor and Shame in the World of the Bible*, Semeia 68, Atlanta, GA: Scholars Press.
Mbuvi, A.M. (2010), 'The Ancient Mediterranean Values of Honour and Shame as a Hermeneutical Lens of Reading the Book of Job', *OTE*, 23 (3): 752–68.
Meyers, C. (2013), *Rediscovering Eve: Ancient Israelite Women in Context*, Oxford: Oxford University Press.
Meyers, C. (2014), 'Was Ancient Israel a Patriarchal Society?', *JBL*, 133 (1): 8–27.
Nam, R.S. (2012), 'Symmetrical Reciprocity in the Book of Kings', in *Portrayals of Economic Exchange in the Book of Kings*, 70–101, BIS 112, Leiden: E.J. Brill.
Neyrey, J.H. (2016), 'Limited Good', in J.J. Pilch and B.J. Malina (eds), *Handbook of Biblical Social Values*, 3rd edn, 103–6, Eugene, OR: Cascade Books.
Neyrey, J.H. and R. Rohrbaugh (2008), '"He Must Increase, I Must Decrease" (John 3.30): A Cultural and Social Interpretation', in J.H. Neyrey and E.C. Stewart (eds), *The Social World of the New Testament: Insights and Models*, 235–51, Peabody, MA: Hendrickson.
Nolan, P. and G. Lenski (2014), *Human Societies: Introduction to Macrosociology*, 12th edn, Oxford: Oxford University Press.
Okyere, K. and G. Effah Darko (2019), 'Honour and Shame in the Context of the Agricultural Work of Ancient Israel: The Case of Proverbs 10.5', *Theoforum*, 49 (1): 75–92.
Patterson, C. (2019), 'The World of Honour and Shame in the New Testament: Alien or Familiar', *BTB*, 49 (1): 4–14.
Pedersen, J. (1926), *Israel: Its Life and Culture, Volume 1*, London/Copenhagen: Humphrey Milford / P. Branner.
Peristiany, J.G., ed. (1965), *Honour and Shame: The Values of Mediterranean Society*, London: Weidenfeld and Nicolson.
Peristiany, J.G. and J. Pitt-Rivers, eds (1992a), *Honor and Grace in Anthropology*, Cambridge Studies in Social and Cultural Anthropology 76, Cambridge: Cambridge University Press.
Peristiany, J.G. and J. Pitt-Rivers (1992b), 'Introduction', in J.G. Peristiany and J. Pitt-Rivers, *Honor and Grace in Anthropology*, Cambridge Studies in Social and Cultural Anthropology 76, 1–17, Cambridge: Cambridge University Press.
Pilch, J.J. and B.J. Malina, eds (2016), *Handbook of Biblical Social Values*, 3rd edn, Eugene, OR: Cascade Books.
Pitt-Rivers, J. (1954), *The People of the Sierra*, New York: Criterion Books.
Pitt-Rivers, J. (1965), 'Honour and Social Status', in J.G. Peristiany (ed.), *Honour and Shame: The Values of Mediterranean Society*, 19–77, London: Weidenfeld and Nicolson.
Rabichev, R. (1996), 'The Mediterranean Concepts of Honour and Shame as Seen in the Depiction of Biblical Women', *Religion and Theology*, 3 (1): 51–63.
Ray, P. (2016), 'The Role and Function of Biblical Genealogies', *Faculty Publications*, 192, Andrews University. Available online: https://digitalcommons.andrews.edu/pubs/192 (accessed 9 July 2022).
Robbins, J. and J. Sommerschuh (2016), 'Values', *The Cambridge Encyclopedia of Anthropology*. Available online: https://www.anthroencyclopedia.com/entry/values (accessed 9 July 2022).
Rogan, W. (2018), 'Purity in Early Judaism: Current Issues and Questions', *CBR*, 16 (3): 309–39.
Sahlins, M. (1972), *Stone Age Economics*, Chicago: Aldine-Atherton.
Schäder, J.-M. (2010), 'Patronage and Client Between God, Israel and the Nations: A Social-Scientific Investigation of Psalm 47', *Journal for Semitics*, 19 (1): 235–62.

Schwartz, S. (2010), *Were the Jews a Mediterranean Society? Reciprocity and Solidarity in Ancient Judaism*, Princeton, NJ: Princeton University Press.

Stansell, G. (1996), 'Honor and Shame in the David Narratives', in V.H. Matthews and D.C. Benjamin (eds), *Honor and Shame in the World of the Bible*, 55–79, Semeia 68, Atlanta, GA: Scholars Press.

Stewart, C. (2015), 'Honour and Shame', in J.D. Wright (ed.), *International Encyclopedia of the Social and Behavioural Sciences, Volume 11*, 2nd edn, 181–4, Amsterdam: Elsevier.

Stewart, E.C. (2010), 'Social Stratification and Patronage in Ancient Mediterranean Societies', in D. Neufeld and R.E. DeMaris (eds), *Understanding the Social World of the New Testament*, 156–66, Abingdon: Routledge.

Stiebert, J. (2002), *The Construction of Shame in the Hebrew Bible: The Prophetic Contribution*, JSOTSup 346, Sheffield: Sheffield Academic Press.

Sutton, L. (2016), '"A Footstool of War, Honour and Shame?" Perspectives Induced by Psalm 110.1', *Journal for Semitics*, 25 (1): 51–71.

Sutton, L. (2018), 'A Position of Honour or Shame? YHWH as an Armour Bearer in Psalm 35.1–3', *Acta Theologica*, 38 (S26): 268–85.

Triandis, H. (1988), 'Collectivism v. Individualism: A Reconceptualisation of a Basic Concept in Cross-Cultural Social Psychology', in G.K. Verma and C. Bagley (eds), *Cross-Cultural Studies of Personality, Attitudes and Cognition*, 60–95, London: Palgrave Macmillan.

Tucker, W.D., Jr (2007), 'Is Shame a Matter of Patronage in the Communal Laments?', *JSOT*, 31 (4): 465–80.

Wikan, U. (1982), *Behind the Veil in Arabia: Women in Oman*, Chicago: University of Chicago Press.

Wikan, U. (1984), 'Shame and Honour: A Contestable Pair', *Man* NS, 19 (4): 635–52.

Wilson, R.R. (1975), 'The Old Testament Genealogies in Modern Research', *JBL*, 94 (2): 169–89.

Wilson, R.R. (1977), *Genealogy and History in the Biblical World*, New Haven, CT: Yale University Press.

CHAPTER THIRTEEN

# For Moses 'Had Indeed Married a Cushite Wife': Metaphors, power and ethnicity in numbers 12

KATHERINE E. SOUTHWOOD

Numbers 12 is an incredibly puzzling story, despite being merely sixteen verses. It contains numerous powerful themes including ethnicity, intermarriage, kinship, gender, migration, prophecy and priesthood. The episode strangely culminates with the punishment of Miriam who is struck by Yahweh with צרעת (Num. 12.10). This essay explores the specific intersection between the mention of Moses's Cushite wife in the initial verse and the striking down of Miriam with צרעת. A key contribution of this chapter is the suggestion that in this passage, ethnic boundaries are refracted through the language of the body's boundaries. In the text, Miriam represents those during the postexilic period who opposed marriage with foreign women, who are depicted as contaminating and impure. The text reverses this idea rather ironically by making Miriam (the one who criticizes Moses's intermarriage) the very source of the impurity as someone with the cultic pollution of צרעת. Rather than foreign women being unceremoniously cast out, Miriam is the one who must leave. The chapter also highlights the significance of murmuring and malicious language (such as representing foreigners as impure, or questioning the leadership of Moses) in Numbers. In Numbers 12, Miriam's murmuring polemic of Moses's intermarriage is targeted in a powerful way in order to emphasize the authority of Moses's leadership. If even the authority figure *Moses* can be depicted, and remembered, as choosing to intermarry, then later groups in postexilic Yehud who make similar choices can claim legitimacy and authenticity as in-group members (rather than being depicted as 'impure' outsiders).

 Moses's intermarriage with a woman from Cush has been a hermeneutical crux from early times, prompting reflection about the marriage from Ezekiel the Tragedian, Demetrius the Chronographer, Artapanus and Josephus (Collins 1983; Hanson 1983; Robertson 1983; Whiston 1995). Perhaps it was also a source of confusion for translators, given that the clause 'for he had married a woman of Cush' is simply omitted by the Vulgate? Some modern commentators also seem perplexed by the mention of the woman and a common way to remove the problem, it would appear, is to ignore it. For example,

Gray did not see any connection between the phrase and the rest of the story suggesting instead that Miriam and Aaron's question 'has no relation to the occasion mentioned in 1b' (Gray 1986: 122). Put more forcefully, the intermarriage is understood as 'only a pretext', 'suspicious yet scarcely fundamentally significant' or 'an irrelevant issue' (Milgrom 1991: 94; see also Noth 1968: 93; Frankel 2002: 42). If the matter is insignificant and irrelevant then the possibility has been raised that what we have in Numbers 12 is a not literary unity. Noth, for example, speculated about this but concluded that that the chapter was a 'complex which, from the literary point of view, can no longer be disentangled, two different strands have been combined' (Noth 1968: 93) but they are now 'so closely joined together that it is impossible to pursue a division into separate literary sources' (ibid.: 92). A more compelling argument is provided by Camp who offers several examples of her theory that Numbers 12 is a doubling episode. As Camp argues, 'this sort of doubling, with one episode or version of an event intercut with another, is rampant in the rebellion chapters of Numbers' (2000: 227 n.1). Furthermore, Winslow suggests that the first verse plays a key role in the chapter, functioning in a way similar to Gen. 22.1. As such, she understands the verses' repetition as emphatic, inserting the word 'indeed' into her translation (Winslow 2011a: 147). Using this as a springboard, we can translate the first verse thus: 'And Miriam and Aaron criticized[1] Moses on account of the Cushite[2] woman that he had married:[3] for he had indeed married a Cushite' (Num. 12.1). Therefore, rather than assuming the repetition of the detail about Moses's wife is redundant, or a case of sloppy editing of different units, this chapter will assume that it is a critical detail that has emphatically been pushed to the head of the episode.

If it is significant for the episode that Moses has intermarried with a woman from Cush, the next logical step is to address the woman's identity and the significance of Cush. On the former question, it is worth noticing that we are not informed about what the actual objection to the marriage is. The idea has been raised that the character is to be identified with Zipporah. However, 'no objection is made to the Non-Israelite origin' of Zipporah (Noth 1968: 94). There are scholars on each side of this debate. Some suggest that the character Zipporah can be identified with the woman mentioned here and others resist this idea (Exod. 2.21, 18.2; Num. 10.29) (Copher 1991: 156; Bellis 2007: 103; Serino 2016: 163). For example, Camp (2000: 236) suggests that Zipporah, Miriam and the Cushite can and should be read together, as three characters with overlapping identities all as strange, or Other, women. Other scholars prefer not to identify the characters as one (Noth 1968: 94; Levine 1993: 328; Adamo 1998: 70). For the purposes of this chapter, we shall not assume that the two characters are connected. Instead, we will read Numbers 12 alongside its most proximate 'murmuring motif' passage (Numbers 11), according to Coats's (1968) identification of 'murmuring motif' texts in Numbers (Numbers 11–16, 20). We ought also to note here the generally negative view of women,

---

[1] Literally, the text has the phrase ב+ דבר which can be translated as 'speak against'.
[2] The Hebrew word used is כּוּשִׁית 'Cushite woman'. Sadler (2005: 36) notes that this text 'contains the only explicit reference to a Cushite woman in the Hebrew Bible'. However, the Greek has the term Αἰθιοπίσσης 'Ethiopian'.
[3] The term לקח literally means to 'take'. However, it is regularly used in a formulaic way to suggest 'marriage'; cf. Southwood 2012: 163–81.

especially foreign women whose presence on two occasions causes a plague, that is taken in Numbers and which is in contrast to Exodus (Num. 25.6–8, 31.9–20).[4]

Regarding the significance of Cush, despite Levine's dismissal of the idea, 'race could not have been the point at issue', several scholars have made precisely this argument. Pitkänen suggests that 'some racist overtones' might be read into the text (2018: 112). For example, Olojede, though disagreeing with the thesis, certainly acknowledges the possibility that the mixed marriage 'could be interpreted [. . .] as having racial or even xenophobic undertones' (Olojede 2017: 137).[5] Williams is more emphatic, arguing that Moses's wife is a 'black African woman' and that the matter 'is a racist issue' that was 'not only the attitude of Miriam and Aaron' but also 'the attitude of the narrator also' (Williams 2002: 265). However, despite the possibility of reading this into the text (eisegesis), the evidence does not seem to suggest that racism is the problem. Indeed, in the Hebrew Bible more generally, if anything, Cush is usually a positive indicator of identity. As Sadler's systematic examination of Cush in the Hebrew Bible identifies, there are several 'types' of associations in the evidence for Cush and they are all positive. These include tropes for: military might; swiftness; dark colour; foreign gift-bearers; wealth; far-away places (Sadler 2005: 148). Adamo provides a helpful summary of Cush in the Hebrew Bible, arguing that in this material:

> Cush and Cushites [. . .] are unmistakably referring to Africa and Africans [. . .] In terms of a geographical location, it is described as the extreme part of the world (Ezk. 29.10; Isa. 45.14; Job 28.19). The inhabitants of Cush were described as tall and smooth-skinned people. Their blackness becomes proverbial (Isa. 18.2; Jer. 13.23). Moses' wife was from Cush (Nm 12.15). A Cushite man reported the death of Absalom to David (2 Sam. 18.21, 31–33). Ebed-Melech was referred to as having a Cushite ancestor (Jer. 38.6–14, 39.16–18). The Cushite power was comparable only to the power of the Assyrians. They became the hope of Judah for deliverance from the Assyrians (2 Chr. 12.3–9; Isa. 18.2; 1 Kgs. 18.19–21; 2 Chr. 32.9–15, 3.8).
>
> —Adamo 2018: 2–3

While the geographical location is not a central concern for this chapter, it is worth noting that a growing number of scholars are making connections between Cush and Africa (see Adamo 1998, 2001; Holter 2000; Lokel 2006; Olojede 2017; cf. Felder 1991; Getui, Holter and Zinkuratire 2001). What is particularly interesting, however, is the high estimation of Cush and the Cushites in the primary evidence. This attitude towards Cush and towards Moses's wife in Numbers 12 is also replicated in evidence outside of the biblical text. For example, in Josephus's retelling of the story, the woman is an Ethiopian princess (Josephus *Ant.*: 2.10.1, 239–53). In Targum Pseudo-Jonathan she is 'the queen of Cush' מלכתא דכוש. Likewise, Targum Onkelos describes the woman as 'beautiful'. The evidence seems to suggest, therefore, that through marrying the woman Moses's status is raised. This aligns well with some of the theory on intermarriage more

---

[4] Note also the contrasts between the character Miriam in Numbers and Exodus. Whereas in Exodus she is a prophetess, in Numbers she criticizes Moses, is punished for having done so, and then she dies (Exod. 15.20–21; Num. 12, 20.1). The only relatively positive story in Numbers pertaining to women is the story of the inheritance concerning the daughters of Zelophehad (Num. 27.1–11). For Exum (1996), the encoded message readers receive from the way women are portrayed is Numbers is one which perpetuates patriarchy.

[5] The suggestion that the description 'Cushite' is 'an ethnic slur based on word play' with the Arabic word '*kuss*, denoting "vulva"' is an unnecessary over-interpretation of the available evidence (cf. Hepner 2009: 234).

generally wherein hypergamy is a relatively common theme.⁶ In this case the charges that Robinson lays against Miriam, that she is 'guilty of [. . .] a small-minded jealousy of the importation of another foreign wife', although somewhat overstated perhaps, are not entirely outside the realms of possibility (Robinson 1989: 431).

Having established that Cush is a positive, then if the Cushite woman actually *elevates* Moses's status, then what accounts for Miriam and Aaron's criticism of Moses on account of her? How is this criticism connected with the emphasis on Moses's leadership in the verses that follow? Why is it that only Miriam is punished by Yahweh, when we are informed that the criticism came from both Miriam and Aaron? Some scholars answer these hermeneutical cruxes by focusing on the character Aaron. For example, Gray accounts for Aaron's lack of punishment by emphasizing the fact that the verb דבר in the first verse is third feminine singular. Therefore, he supposes that 'Miriam took the lead' in criticizing Moses's marriage (Gray 1986: 120). Similarly, Abela suggests that we should understand the *waw* in the phrase 'Miriam and Aaron' (ואהרן) as a '*waw* of accompaniment' (2008: 526). Perhaps these details are significant. However, we ought also to note that the subsequent verb reporting their speech (אמר) is plural (Num. 12.2). Likewise, in other instances where the characters appear side by side in the narrative, Aaron is mentioned first (Num. 12.4, 5). Regardless, the significance of the symbolic severing of the relationship at the beginning of the narrative between Miriam and Aaron through Yahweh's punishment of only Miriam should be noted. Perhaps, as Camp (2000: 274) argues, it is 'a point of departure for validating the Aaronite priesthood through ever-increasing narrative identification of Moses and Aaron', a move which corresponds 'to the shifting power structures, both institutional and symbolic, of the postexilic period'?⁷ Coats came to a similar conclusion, suggesting rather more tentatively in his appendix that the chapter represents a 'conflict in the priesthood' between the 'Levites and the Aaronic priesthood' (1968: 263). More recently, Erbele-Küster noted the prevalence of this sociological approach noting that the Aaronide priests 'would have used the regulations to guarantee their grip on ritual practices' thus explaining the 'social and ideological function of the Purity laws against its presumed context in the Persian period' (2017: 18). This connection is really interesting, certainly adding a new possibility for contextualizing the role of Aaron in assisting with Miriam's צרעת (Num. 12.11–12).⁸ If Aaron's intervention to Moses on Miriam's behalf is designed to emphasize his priestly role then this tightens the connections between this chapter and Leviticus 13–14. In these chapters, if צרעת occurs then the person showing signs of it 'shall be brought to Aaron the priest' (Lev. 13.2).

---

⁶ For an excellent discussion of mixed marriages in the Second Temple period, refer to the essays in Frevel 2011. Note also the connection between the setting – the desert of Paran – and the intermarriage between Abraham and his Egyptian wife, who is also this location (Gen. 21.21).

⁷ With Camp, this chapter suggests that Numbers has been edited some time during the late exilic or postexilic period. Therefore, whatever the original meaning of the story, it is not inappropriate to draw later parallels with other postexilic material. Camp provides an interesting critique of Douglas (2001: 35), who dated the redaction similarly, and who argued that the connection between Numbers (and Leviticus) was through a battle against the puritanical outlook of Ezra and Nehemiah.

⁸ We should note here that the word צרעת throughout this chapter will not be translated in order to avoid retrospective diagnosis. This word will be discussed below. We should also observe here the phrasing of Aaron's intervention on Miriam's behalf here which is ambiguous. בי אדני literally 'please, my lord' is a petition followed by a deferential address of Moses. Levine translates 'by my life, master', suggesting that this 'can mean that one offers to assume the punishment for the other's sin by asserting that the offense life in oneself' and also notes the possibility that it 'could be taken to mean "By my life, at the cost of my life"' (Levine 1993: 332).

Similarly, the quarantine period of seven days aligns with Levitical protocol, as does Miriam's dwelling outside the camp (Lev. 13.45–46, 14.8). The observation may have broader implications relating to the struggles within the priesthood in the Persian period.

However, the main focus of this chapter is intermarriage, purity and ethnicity. Therefore, although the mention of Aaron does create potential for pausing to think about a possible conflict in the priesthood informing the chapter, it does not help us here. This is because the questions about the criticism of the Cushite woman and the connections between this and the criticism of Moses's leadership still stands. What is, however, abundantly clear through the text is the special relationship between Moses and Yahweh. The criticisms of Moses, which are overheard by Yahweh, are swiftly discredited with a theophany wherein Yahweh breaks into elevated poetic parallelism on the theme of appropriate prophetic communication and attitude (Num. 12.6–7). In sharp contrast with the murmuring criticism and lust for power of Miriam and Aaron, and the congregation in the previous chapter, Moses is described as Yahweh's 'servant' who is 'humble', 'faithful' and with whom Yahweh speaks 'mouth to mouth' (Num. 12.3, 7, 8). Sturdy describes the term 'humble' (ענו) as 'a key term in the religious language of the psalms' which makes it clear that 'Moses is here given the highest valuation that Israelite piety has' (1976: 90).[9] Likewise, Sturdy notes the significance of the title 'servant' used 'especially of those who are close to God' (1976: 91). Perhaps a key image here, however, is the somatic metaphor of God speaking to Moses, not just 'face to face' as friends, but 'mouth to mouth' (Num. 12.8; cf. Exod. 33.11; Deut. 34.10). This leads Wilson to suppose that the narrative 'was originally concerned with a dispute over prophetic authority' (1980: 154). Ackerman (2002: 80) also notes that both Miriam and Aaron have indeed previously been assigned the label 'prophet' and having criticized Moses she 'appears only once more in the Exodus story, in Num. 20.1, to die' (Exod. 7.1, 15.20). The authority of Moses is certainly emphasized here through the powerful somatic metaphor which makes Moses's mouth tantamount to God's mouth. But Yahweh's speech also makes it clear that this is not only about prophetic authority and communication; clearly it is also about attitude and leadership.

If this is the case, then how does it help us to understand the leading motif in the narrative, that of Moses's Cushite wife? What, if anything, does it have to do with the challenge to Moses's authority and Miriam's punishment? In order to answer these questions, it is perhaps sensible to probe further into the social and ideological context of postexilic Yehud and the connections between the editing of this text and Persian period texts such as Haggai, Zechariah, Ezra-Nehemiah, Malachi and Proverbs 1–9. One quite direct link between the texts and Numbers 12 is the idea of the so-called 'foreign woman'.[10] This connection is widely recognized. For example, Winslow (2011b: 281) comments that,

---

[9] This aspect of Moses's characterization was demonstrated in the previous chapter, when Moses rebuked Joshua son of Nun for being 'jealous' on his behalf because of Eldad and Medad prophesying in the camp (Num. 11.24–30).

[10] The use of the term foreign has been here is encircled with inverted commas. This is a deliberate attempt to emphasize that, in this chapter, I do not approach ethnicity as a primordial entity. Nevertheless, we should recognize that the primordialist approach to ethnicity is not entirely without its uses: it certainly helps to explain the emotive, committed and passion-driven behaviour of many ethnic groups in the extremes of ethnic conflicts and violence. However, instead of thinking of ethnicity as a 'given', immutable and ineffable identity, this chapter leans instead towards understanding it from an instrumental or constructivist approach. According to the instrumentalist viewpoint, ethnicity is not intrinsically valuable but is instead a strategic basis for alliances that

The conflicts over intermarriage among previously exiled Jews, as reflected in the Persian period texts of Ezra-Nehemiah, form the context for the redaction of Numbers. The story about Moses' Cushite wife in the context of God's affirming of Moses as his most intimate prophet would have countered Ezra, Shechaniah, and Nehemiah's exclusivism [. . .] the pedagogical effect of this narrative is that protesters against those who married 'foreigners' – especially the priestly and prophetic leaders – are impertinent and should be reprimanded.

In this case, the mention of the Cushite wife in Numbers 12 is indicative of an attitude, exemplified by the character Miriam who polemically attacks exogamous unions through resistance to mixed marriages. This is a position that is similar, in some ways, to that of Douglas. Douglas (2001: 198) suggests that Miriam is a symbol for Israel and compares her with Cozbi, but her more generalized argument about the 'anti-racist leanings' of Numbers seems to compare with Winslow's point. Similarly, Burns suggests that Miriam is 'a public figure and that she is voicing a public concern' that 'stemmed from a religious objection to relations with foreign women' (1980: 109), and therefore wonders if the concern stemmed from a view of 'foreign women as occasions for apostasy' (1980: 107). Rapp also suggests that a conflict arose during the postexilic period wherein two groups wrestled for power and authority: a group who challenged the authority of Moses who produced 'mirjamfreundliche Texte' (e.g. Exod. 15.19–21; Num. 26.59; Mic. 6.4). The other group was critical of Miriam and produced 'mirjamkritische Texte' (Rapp 2002: 388). Whether, or not, we group the texts in this way, the emphasis in Rapp's discussion on conflict centred around the role of women and on attempts amongst rival groups to gain authority is helpful. This is because it strengthens the case for the postexilic period being a time wherein ethnic boundaries and 'foreign women' formed a critical focal point. As with Winslow, Rapp's theory also aligns with the suggestions that Douglas made, namely that a scenario emerged during the period between priestly groups and a dissident minority.[11] Finally, Sadler suggests that the repetition of the first verse in the Masoretic

---

enhance a group's power and wealth. Similarly, the constructivist theory suggests that ethnicity is socially constructed but fluid; it is a social category influenced by social, economic and political processes but not a 'natural' or unchanging identity. This approach is helpful on account of its tendency towards recognizing the humanity of the unknown 'Other' despite the fact that their behaviours, appearance, language, customs, myths of ancestry, religion, homeland and common past do not align with those from the in-group. Nevertheless, an acknowledged limitation of instrumental and constructivist approaches is their inability to explain why groups with similar historical, structural, socio-economic and political environments regularly behave very differently. It must be recognized that the theoretical material concerning ethnicity is, itself, not immutable or absolute. It does, however, give us some useful tools through which to reframe the way we think about ethnicity when we discern traces of the concept in primary evidence, such as (but not restricted to) the biblical texts. Cf. Hutchinson and Smith 1996.

[11] Camp has produced a thoroughly researched and convincing critique of Douglas wherein she challenges the irenic ideological coherence and inclusiveness that Douglas finds in Numbers. For Camp, Douglas too easily dismisses the conflict between priestly groups and therefore 'misses the rather important point that control of the cult always constitutes a significant social power base' (Camp 2000: 134). Camp makes this point powerfully through a set of rather provocative questions: '[H]er analysis would seem to suggest that this power struggle was resolved without residue. The "good" priests, having made a generally understood literary-theological response to a pressing socio-political problem, nonetheless lose to their opponents. Having fought the good fight, they. . . what? Ride off into the sunset?' (2000: 222). Camp's argument here suggests that the symbolic power-struggle over gender, ethnicity and deity which culminates in who can claim a 'real' Israelite identity, and with it power and authority to dictate how Yahwism is regulated ritually, would not have been simplistically resolved.

Text emphasizes that the woman is an Other, and that '[w]hat is clear is that Miriam implies the Cushite woman was Other, and that the difference mattered' (2005: 36–7). Therefore, for Sadler what we have in this story is 'an early biblical author's strategy for addressing a colour prejudice by highlighting YHWH's ironic response to Miriam's complaint' (2005: 40).[12] It seems to be the case that postexilic Yehud was, as Camp describes it, 'a society in flux' not only in terms of who gets control, but also in terms of who gets to dictate 'defining metaphors' and who has authority over 'socially accepted symbols' (2000: 275). The primary evidence does seem to point towards a generalized issue that was something to do with 'foreign' women in the postexilic period. Likewise, the scholarship around that matter makes a compelling case for deeming the story's leading issue, the matter of the Cushite union, to be the central issue that is discussed in the text, and therefore far more than a mere pretext for a discussion of Moses's leadership.

Given this context, Numbers 12 is a text that is, we suggest, largely about foreign women. But what should we interpret from the fact that the Cushite woman is silent throughout the episode and, save for her marriage to Moses and her ethnicity, anonymous? Perhaps her powerlessness in textual terms points to the greater social powerlessness that existed at the time? Or, on the contrary, perhaps being characterized in the text as a silent and largely anonymous figure would only have served to exacerbate any existing conceptions about the place in society of foreign women? We will probably never know. However, a sensible place to examine the matter further is to look again at the text and reconsider Yahweh's secondary response of punishing Miriam with צרעת. Douglas suggests here that 'the relative severity of the punishment is not merited by the offence,' but she also points out that 'Miriam's leprosy has to be taken seriously' as a 'strong pointer on how to read her story' (2001: 198, 209, 202). Given the similarities in terms of social boundaries that emerge in material concerning ethnicity and in body-metaphors in the Hebrew Bible wherein the body is a bounded system, it may be worth entertaining the possibility that Miriam's punishment and objection to Moses's intermarriage are more closely connected than may, at first, be apparent. In order to engage with this line of enquiry it is sensible to address the textual evidence in further detail.

Following Yahweh's poetic response readers are surprised by two interjections in the following verse: 'And the cloud turned away from the tent. And behold! Miriam became צרעת, as white as snow. And Aaron turned to Miriam, and Behold! She had become צרעת' (Num. 12.10).[13] The implication seems to be that Miriam's sudden condition is some form of retribution for her behaviour. This is not surprising, given the prevalence of illness (as conceived of very generally) in the Hebrew Bible as retribution for some

---

[12] The irony that Sadler refers to here is the colour-coding of the chapter, as Sadler notes, 'there is a strange irony to the story of a woman who complains against a woman identified as Cushite, implicitly dark-skinned, whose skin is then transformed as a result of YHWH's punishment, to be void of color' (2005: 39). Olojede makes a similar observation, noting 'ironically, the one who abhors another's skin color is punished with a skin disease' (2017: 138). Nevertheless, one should be cautious before jumping to conclusions about the implicit juxtaposition of skin colour in the text. As Sadler recognized, Brenner argued that 'whiteness' might be understood as skin that is flaky, like snow, thus referring to the damaged skin texture described in Leviticus 13–14 relating to צרעת rather than colour (Sadler 2005: 37, 89; Brenner 1982).

[13] Regarding צרעת, see n.8, above.

wrongdoing or other.¹⁴ However, before proceeding to analyse Aaron's, somewhat cryptic, statement in the verses that follow, a discussion of the notion of צרעת is in order.¹⁵ Hartley (1992: 187) suggests that צרעת is:

> a generic term for repulsive changes in the surface condition of human skin, clothing of wool or linen, articles of leather, and the walls of a building. [. . .] It is sometimes compared to snow (Exod. 4.6; Num. 12.10; 2 Kgs 5.27). [. . .] The term צרעת also conveyed strong feelings of dread and repulsion [. . .] for one struck by צרעת was excluded from the community with little hope of recovery.

It is sometimes a form of punishment in the Hebrew Bible (2 Chron. 24.16–23; 2 Kgs 5.26–27; 2 Sam. 3.29). It ought to be fairly obvious from the fact that the walls of a building and textiles can develop צרעת that whatever the condition indicates, it is not medical, but cultic. Therefore, little hermeneutical progress can be made by retrospectively attempting to diagnose the condition. So, what should we understand by the Miriam's punishment of צרעת? Douglas suggests that the condition is the 'ultimate defilement' (2001: 199) and that 'Miriam's punishment of leprosy [. . .] must be associated with the enemy, the false gods of death' (2001: 202). Therefore, Miriam's impurity is very obviously implied by her condition. Perhaps the reason for Douglas's argument here concerning Miriam's punishment is that she suggests 'the living God is in opposition to dead bodies' and 'total incompatibility holds between God's presence and bodily corruption' (2001: 23). There is quite a tidy logic to this argument that dichotomizes between living and dead, with 'bodily corruption' towards the latter end of the spectrum. However, the difficulty with the argument is that there is nothing in the story of

---

¹⁴ As Southwood (2021: 6 n.20) notes, examples of the link between illness and sin in the Old Testament include the diseases on Pharaoh and his household on account of Abraham's wife-sister deception (Gen 12.17); the striking blind of the men threatening Lot's house (Gen. 19.11); the closing of wombs in Abimelech's household again because of Abraham's wife-sister trickery (Gen 20.17–18); plagues and death of the Egyptian first-born on account of the genocide and forced labour of Hebrews (Exod. 7–11); Miriam's infection of תערצ on account of her and Aaron's speaking out against Moses's intermarriage with an Ethiopian woman (Num. 12.9–10); various occasions in Numbers when Yahweh threatened the Israelites with illness during their rebellions against Moses and Aaron (Num. 14.11–12, 14.36–37, 17.12–15, 25.3–9, 25.17–18, 31.16); the Philistines' rumours upon capturing in the ark (1 Sam. 5.6–6.12); the unfaithful King Jeroboam's child dies in Yahweh's manoeuvre to wipe his house out (1 Kgs 14.10–14); Yahweh refuses to heal Ahaziah because he consulted with Beelzebub (2 Kgs 1.16); greed incites תערצ in Gehazi as punishment (2 Kgs 5.26–27); the pride of King Uzziah causes him to get 2) תערצ Chron. 26.16–20); Jehoram gets an incurable illness on account of deserting Yahweh (2 Chron. 21.14–15); David's census annoys Yahweh so he is punished with a plague resulting in the death of seventy thousand people (2 Sam. 24.10–15; 1 Chron. 21.7–14). To use a poetic example, the Psalmist explicitly connects God's anger and his body's dysfunction, stating: 'There is no soundness in my flesh because of your indignation; there is no health in my bones because of my sin' and 'my wounds grow foul and fester because of my foolishness' (Ps. 38.3, 38.5). This idea continues in the New Testament material, wherein it is epitomized by the question the disciples ask in reaction to a man born blind 'Rabbi, who sinned, this man or his parents, that he was born blind?' (John 9.2).

¹⁵ The Septuagint rendered the term צרעת by λέπρα. Most Latin translators followed this rendering and therefore transliterated into Latin (lepra). Levine emphasizes the connection between Miriam and the condition in later Jewish material, stating that, 'In ancient Israel it was believed that ṣāra'at was a punishment from God, as was believed of illness generally. The present episode of the affliction of Miriam served as the primary basis for a body of postbiblical Jewish interpretation that regarded ṣāra'at as the specific punishment for malicious talk (Babylonian Talmud, Sôṭāh, 15a; Šābû'ôt, 8a)' (Levine 1993: 332). It is interesting that this material directly associates Miriam's criticisms of Moses with her condition, thus strengthening the idea of the condition as sometimes being a retribution for some wrongdoing or other. Many later texts associate צרעת with slander or gossip (4QMMT B64–72).

Numbers 12 to suggest, even implicitly, that the sudden onset of צרעת was caused by idolatry or apostasy ('false gods') on Miriam's part. Furthermore, the connection with death might be questioned slightly too. Obviously, it is there in the text; when Aaron likens Miriam to a dead person or a stillborn child 'whose skin is half consumed' (Num. 12.12). Similarly, it is mirrored in the Levitical laws, wherein one struck with צרעת not only occupied space outside the camp, but must also endure the humiliation of shouting 'unclean, unclean' and wearing mourning garments (Lev. 13.45; Olyan 2004). However, Douglas's connection between death verses the 'living God' in this chapter is slightly undermined by the fact that the text 'tacitly implies that Miriam was immediately cured of her leprosy, for the full acceptance of someone cleansed of leprosy could take place only after a seven-day period of waiting' (Num. 12.12; cf. Lev. 14.8; Noth 1968: 97).[16] Therefore, far from the צרעת being a dress-rehearsal for Miriam's imminent mortality, it is instead related to cultic pollution. The cause of the pollution is explicitly identified twice by Aaron as (חטא)[17] 'sin' on account of 'foolishness' (Num. 12.11).

But what is the significance of צרעת in the text and how does it relate to the intermarriage between Moses and the woman from Cush? Perhaps, in order to answer this question, it is sensible first to explore the implications of צרעת. Several times in Leviticus, the condition צרעת is tightly connected to the idea of being טמא: 'polluted' or 'defiled' (Lev. 13.3, 8, 11, 15, 20, 25, 27, 30, 59). Erbele-Küster (2017: 142) provides a helpful description of the issues and implications related to this term, stating:

> In Leviticus 11–15, טמא is a functional category that describes the status of an object or a person with respect to the cult and the sanctuary. [. . .] This is what the suggested renderings of טמא such as 'unsuitable for the cult', 'unclean in a ritual respect', 'compromising the cult', 'cult-abstinent', 'cult-disabled', 'ritual noncompliance', 'cultic disqualification', 'in conflict with the cult' – are intended to express. These renderings try to make visible the cultic notion of impurity in Leviticus 11–15 in contrast to the moral usage elsewhere.

Here Erbele-Küster emphasizes the distinction between different types of purity, a distinction that has become rather popular amongst scholars. For example, Klawans, who questioned Milgrom's attempt to understand the purity regulations in Leviticus as a coherent system, suggests the idea of moral impurity, in contrast with ritual impurity (Klawans 2006: 28–33, 2000; cf. Klawans 1998: 391–415). Several other scholars emphasize the need to distinguish between 'natural' impurities and those which emerge because of some specific, usually forbidden, action. For example, some impurities are 'tolerated impurities' (Anderson and Olyan 1991: 157–62). Likewise, Frymer-Kensky (1983) makes a distinction between 'ritual pollutions' and 'danger beliefs'.

More divisive, perhaps, is the way this purity-centred language is being used in the Persian period in texts such as Ezra and Nehemiah. For example, Hayes notes that during the postexilic period we have the emergence of a tendency, certainly in Ezra, 'to define

---

[16] Noth takes the rather unforgiving view that since 'Miriam had turned against Yahweh's confidant [. . .] she should really have been punished by a lifetime of suffering from leprosy' (1968: 97). This statement goes beyond the evidence within the text.

[17] Interestingly, however, 'there is no indication that Miriam herself acknowledged her guilt. In fact, Miriam is silent in the narrative after she has been described to have expressed her initial slander and challenge' (Pitkänen 2018: 113).

Jewish identity in [. . .] genealogic terms' so that 'there is a democratization of the requirement for genealogical purity' (2002: 10). Janzen also notes 'concerns about ethnic purity' and boundaries in in Ezra-Nehemiah (2002: 35). This is certainly reflected the language of Ezra, wherein the title 'holy seed' is used as a group classifier, directly linking entitlement to the land with those who returned from exile (Ezra 9–10; Neh. 13.23–27). In that set of texts, those who are constructed as 'foreign' are referred to negatively using purity language (Ezra 9–10). For those who have committed the abomination of defiling the land through intermarriage, Ezra 9–10 follows the priestly logic of Leviticus: 'Do not defile yourselves in any of these ways, for by all these practices the nations (הגוים) I am casting out before you have defiled themselves. Thus the land became defiled; and I punished it for its iniquity, and the land vomited out its inhabitants' (Lev. 18.24–25).

Assigning purity language to identity is clearly one of Ezra-Nehemiah's key tactics in its condemnation of foreigners, through the motif of foreign women. However, one thing which is particularly noteworthy in Leviticus is how purity and defilement terminology is used, not just to forge a sense of identity as with Ezra-Nehemiah, but instead it is explicitly used in connection with the human body (Leviticus 13–14). Douglas comments that 'these books [Leviticus and Numbers] never use the principle of ritual purity to separate classes or races, foreigners or natives [. . .] defilement is *not* from contact with foreigners or from lower classes' therefore 'it is not used for keeping them outside or in lower ranks' (2001: 25–6). Douglas's earlier work had emphasized the centrality of purity and order, where she had argued that purity systems are not primarily about taboo beliefs, but instead are a 'symbolic system, according to which the physical body reflects the political body' (1966: 34–7).[18] Douglas's arguments here are interesting because they illustrate the connections between the political and symbolic body. Here, the connection is emphasized between the body and purity language through the powerful metaphor of the land itself physically vomiting out the 'nations' who had defiled themselves. This potential connection between the idea of 'Israel' as a bounded ethnic group which is concretized using purity language and metaphors in Ezra-Nehemiah and purity language relating to the body as a bounded, symbolic entity is interesting.

In order to understand the significance of this connection, a brief discussion of the language concerning the body that occurs in research from medical anthropology may be helpful.[19] In a line of argument similar to Douglas, Kirmayer emphasizes the body's insistence on meaning, arguing that 'meaning resides not exclusively in the relationships between concepts [. . .] but in their connection to the body and its skills and practices. Meaning emerges from the capacity to use bodily experience (including socially embodied

---

[18] Some scholars emphasize the gendering of this purity language in a way that Douglas did not. For example, Camp, commenting on Miriam's צרעת argues 'When Miriam is given the appearance of a corpse, and shut up outside in the place of corpses, we recognize, against the ideological cover-up, that she has been *made* strange' (2000: 256). Therefore, for Camp, 'foreigners, in the form of strange women' are 'vilified in Numbers in a manner not alien to Ezra and Nehemiah' (2000: 224–5). Similarly, Erbele-Küster, focusing specifically on Leviticus 12 and 15, argues that 'The concern for order in Leviticus is effected by means of the gendered body. Hence the body serves as a boundary marker' (2017: 19).

[19] However, it is crucial to point out that in using medical anthropology as a hermeneutical tool, we are not retrospectively diagnosing or suggesting that Miriam's צרעת is an illness. As argued, the term relates to cultic pollution. Rather, we are using this research to see how it might inform our thinking when we examine the language relating to the body in Leviticus 13–14 and Numbers 12.

experience) to think with metaphorically' (1992: 334). Lupton makes a similar point, specifically with regard to bodies that visibly depart from the socially constructed 'norm', claiming that the 'appearance and deportment of the body conveys specific cultural meanings to those who observe this body' (2012: 49). Likewise, Gibbs and Franks highlight the ubiquity of metaphor in language relating to the body, arguing that people 'routinely employ a wide range of metaphorical expressions as they talk about specific diseases and their subjective experiences of illness' (2002: 140). Pilch (2000: 28–9, 45) makes a similar point about the critical role of language when constructing ideas about illness, arguing that:

> health care often overlaps with religion and other cultural systems [. . .] all realities are fundamentally semantic. Sickness becomes a human experience and an object of therapeutic attention when it becomes meaningful. Physicians make sickness meaningful by identifying the disease that fits the symptoms. Laypeople make sickness meaningful in a very subjective way, drawing upon a wide range of knowledge and ultimately constructing an illness. Thus illness realities will differ widely from individual to individual within a society, culture, or ethnic group.

What is particularly interesting about this language is the proliferation within it about beliefs.[20] Illness is explained in a personalistic way by external factors such as 'sorcery, witchcraft, and the wrath of ancestor spirits' *even* when other biomedical etiologies are available' therefore a proliferation of reinterpretation of biomedical ideas emerge 'in ways that fit local understandings of cosmology, ethnophysiology, vulnerability, and etiology' (Nichter 2008: 43–4). The research suggests that language concerning the body is important. Such language is regularly metaphoric and driven by systems of belief. Therefore, it is entirely possible that Miriam's sudden onset of צרעת is intended not only as a punishment from Yahweh on account of criticizing Moses's intermarriage. Rather, צרעת points towards a deeper symbolic and metaphoric level of meaning: Miriam is not merely punished, she is culturally unacceptable and unclean. Perhaps her body also takes on a symbolic and political role in the narrative beyond her being unclean. It is entirely possible that Miriam's culturally unacceptable body in these narrative points towards a deeper social rift between groups in the postexilic period, as Miriam becomes a symbol of those groups who did not tolerate intermarriage on the basis of the assumption that so-called 'foreigners' were impure.

If this is the case, then the connection between illness and punishment should also be probed further here for the significance of the specific punishment of צרעת to be unpacked.[21] Sontag highlights the longevity of the idea, arguing that divine wrath was the reason cited for illness in the ancient world. Judgement was meted out to people who deserved it. For example, Sontag cites 'the plague in book I of the *Iliad* that Apollo inflicts on Achaeans in punishment for Agamemnon's abduction of Chryses' daughter; the plague in *Oedipus* that strikes Thebes because of the polluting presence of the royal sinner' similarly 'the

---

[20] The connection between illness and belief systems is also made by Vindrola-Padros and Johnson who argue that 'Storytellers shape the world according to the narratives they tell. In health services research, these stories describe the complex constellations of beliefs, values, emotions, intentions, identities, attitudes, and motivations that research participants use to express themselves as individuals and embed themselves within the illness narratives they enact and tell' (2014: 1603).
[21] Refer to n.8.

stinking wound in Philoctetes' foot' (1978: 39). This is particularly divisive given the potential for language about the body and its lack of confirmation to standards of public health (or cultural purity) to make rifts between people and groups. As Lloyd (2003: 242), citing modern language concerning illness, argues: 'even in the absence of the ancient belief in objectivity in the matter of political goods, the rhetoric of disease still infects our political and moral discourse to an alarming degree. Even though we may think we are no longer in thrall to the idea of the pathology of politics, the rhetoric of politicians is still full of that imagery'.

These observations are potentially quite suggestive in light of the material relating to defilement Numbers 12. Language concerning the body, as will be demonstrated, is central in Numbers 11 and 12. The mouth and the body play a key role, as does punishment through defilement. Camp emphasizes the centrality of language and the body, arguing that Yahweh's opinions are made known in the form of language transmission that is 'often parsed with body parts' (2000: 299). In this text Miriam's punishment in the form of defilement is a direct consequence of her act of speaking out against the Cushite woman. Ethnic boundaries are questioned in a similar manner to what we have in Ezra-Nehemiah. Numbers 12 questions the restriction of ethnicity through undermining Miriam's questioning Moses's marriage to a foreign wife. But, through emphasizing the importance of language and the body in these texts, we can deduce that this undermining of strict ethnic boundaries is achieved through a mirroring system of boundaries relating to the body. Specifically, the power of the defilement and impurity metaphors when used against foreign women are being turned on their head in this instance. It is not the foreign women who are impure: it is Miriam. She receives the worst metaphoric treatment possible by the author, through being utterly defiled with צרעת.

Furthermore, as if to emphasize the level of disapproval of her, Yahweh adds a comment about her father spitting in her face. Here, the mouth of the father is contrasted with the figure Moses, who has intermarried, but who retains authority as one whose mouth is tantamount to Yahweh's. This is again contrasted with Miriam's mouth and the centrality of speech in the text. Miriam's mouth and speech criticize Moses for his intermarriage with a foreign woman. Her murmuring mouth is like the murmuring mouths of the people in ch. 11 whose constant requests for meat are met with so much of it that Yahweh says it will come out of their nostrils: another example of the centrality of the mouth and speech and how it is connected to the body in punishment. Miriam's defilement is not a 'tolerated' impurity here, it is a direct punishment from Yahweh.

As noted, in order to totally emphasize the text's condemnation of Miriam's criticism of the foreign women and intermarriage, not only is she depicted as defiled through צרעת, the author also has Yahweh strongly condemn her. This adds an extra layer of interpretation to the seven-day period of quarantine that is usually associated with צרעת (Lev. 14.8; cf. 13.45–46). Yahweh asks Moses, rhetorically, 'if her father had surely spat (ירק ירק) in her face, would she not bear her shame for seven days?' (Num. 12.14). The combination here of the infinitive absolute relating to the humiliation of a father spitting in a daughter's face and the comparison of this with the level of 'shame' (כלם) that Miriam ought to be experiencing emphasize the level of disgrace that Miriam now occupies in the eyes of Yahweh. Not only is she to live in the 'great distress' that living outside the camp in the place of the unclean would have caused, but she must also bear the added dishonour of Yahweh's fiercely worded rebuke, a rebuke communicated directly to Moses (Wenham 1979: 201). The idea of shame and a father spitting in a daughter's face is somewhat anomalous. There might be an indirect analogy to be made between the disapproval expressed by the wife of the deceased on account of the levir refusing to do his duty (Deut. 25.5–10; cf. Ruth 4.8). In other words, a 'formalized mark of contempt' (Sturdy 1976: 92). Unsurprisingly, spitting on another person is a very widespread way to express anger and contempt (Coomber, Moyle and Pavlidis 2018). Therefore, the evidence suggests that this extra level of meaning was included into the narrative in order to emphasize the shamefulness of Miriam's behaviour.

Another technique that the text uses to undermine the critique of foreign women during the postexilic period, as communicated through Miriam's speech, is to make the intermarriage not just with *any* foreign woman, but with a woman from Cush. This is hypergamy for Moses, a step up in status through marriage. Far from being threatening and impure this ethnic other is impressive. Her ethnicity is associated with wealth and strength. It should be pointed out here that Miriam's criticism is not specifically stated using the language of impurity. This is an acknowledged drawback for our theory. But it is not much of a problem considering the abundance of evidence in the Hebrew Bible that uses the impurity and defilement metaphor in order to restrict ethnic boundaries, through demonizing and emphasizing the need to separate from foreign women. The highly gendered, powerful idea of the impure and defiled 'foreign woman' becomes almost an archetype for the ethnic Other, the one who threatens the entire group, in the postexilic period. This is nowhere more clear than in Ezra-Nehemiah:

> Ezra's emphasis on cultic and moral purity is clear through the excessive use of such terminology within the intermarriage crisis: קדש (Ezr. 9.2, 8); טמא 'unclean' (Ezr. 9.11); חטא 'sin' (Neh. 9.2, 9.37, 10.33); מעל 'sacrilege' (Ezr. 9.4, 9.6, 10.2, 10.6); נדה 'defile' (*piel* Ezr. 9.11); אשם 'guilt' (Ezr. 9.6–7, 13, 10.10) אשמה 'guilt offering' (Ezr. 10.19); תעבות 'abominations' (Ezr. 9.1, 9.11, 14); בדל 'separate' (*hiphil* Ezr. 9.1, 10.8, 11, 16; Neh. 10.28; Neh. 13.3); ערב 'intermix' (*hithpael* Ezr. 9.2), as well as in other parts of the text טחור 'pure' (Ezr. 6.20; Neh. 12.30); גאל 'impure' (Ezr. 2.61–62/Neh. 7.64, 13.29). Moreover, throughout the narrative, we witness continual purification and re-purification of the community, temple and city, perhaps indicating a sense of the contagiously impure interpretation of those considered to be external to the *ethnos* (Ezr. 6.20; Neh. 12.30, 13.9, 13.22). However, this culminates in a clear indication of boundary integration through Nehemiah's self-congratulating claim of having 'purified them [the priests and the Levites] of everything foreign' וטהרתים מכל נכר (Neh. 13.30). Like Ezra, Nehemiah's conclusion represents a metamorphosis from religious divisions to ethnic boundaries.
>
> —Southwood 2012: 136[22]

However, connecting the language of purity with so-called 'foreign women' is by no means restricted to the rather extreme examples found in Ezra-Nehemiah. For example, Malachi connects the language of 'abomination' (תועבה) and the term 'profane' (חלל) with the idea of having married the 'daughter of a foreign god' (Mal. 2.11).[23] A slightly more extreme example can be found at a later period, in 4Q184, wherein the connection

---

[22] A further example, that is not included within the quotation, is the connection in Nehemiah between 'foreign women' and 'sin' (חטא) (Neh. 13.26).
[23] Though not using purity language, it is worth noting the condemnation of Solomon as 'evil' (רע) from Yahweh's perspective' on account of his marriages to Moabite, Ammonite, Edomite, Zidonian and Hittite women (1 Kgs 11.1). Similarly, Ahab's marriage to Jezebel is reported as having 'caused irritation' (כעס) to Yahweh (1 Kgs 16.33).

between the so-called 'foreign woman' and purity language are also coupled with the link to death. 4Q184 states that 'her ways are the ways of death and her path[s] are the roads to sin; her tracks lead [. . .] to iniquity and her paths are the guilt of transgression [. . .] her gates are the gates of death' (4Q184.9–10).[24] This is precisely the type of widespread language relating to foreign women in the postexilic period that is being countered in Numbers 12 with Miriam's punishment of צרעת. It is not the foreign women who 'defile' and 'pollute' the land, and potentially the Israelites. Rather, the source of the 'infection' (to continue the metaphor) is Miriam and her language with which she indirectly criticizes the foreign woman through questioning Moses's decision to intermarry with her. The way the narrative treats Miriam puts her on the other side of the type of criticism that foreign women receive in the postexilic period. Instead of the foreign women who is described as impure – sometimes to the extent that she can be linked with death and Sheol – ironically it is now Miriam, with her murmuring, who must be separated from the camp. Rather than have the wives and children cast out, as Ezra-Nehemiah does, the one being cast out and assigned the thoroughly impure label צרעת is Miriam. Effectively, what we have here is a powerful polemic against those in the postexilic period who would use purity language to disparage foreign women and intermarriage, pitched in exactly the same terms that those who resist exogamy choose to use.

Why use the same tactic of relating to defilement and pollution with ethnic differences, a tactic used to alienate so-called foreign women, against in-group members who object to intermarriage? Why counter those who choose to spread such ethnically polemical murmuring by using the exact same metaphorical tool – making Miriam one with צרעת – in a narrative against those emphasizing ethnic differences? It is impossible to know. Perhaps one answer though, is that language relating to the body and possible breaches to its boundaries, whether through cultic impurity, or to use the research from medical anthropology, through injury or illness, is a very powerful when used metaphorically to shore up ethnic boundaries. Given the ubiquitous nature of metaphor when referring to the body it is perhaps not surprising that sometimes language relating to the body and its boundaries is also used when thinking about the ethnic group and its boundaries. However, what happens when these two unrelated concepts collide using metaphor is a type of conceptual synaesthesia wherein we understand one nexus of ideas in the context of another. Through doing so a new narrative is added to the original idea. As Musolff (2007: 28) argues,

> The source cluster of body/illness/cure concepts is not an arbitrary constellation of notional elements but a complex, narrative/scenic schema or 'scenario', one that tells a mini-story, complete with apparent causal explanations and conclusions about its outcome [. . .] This narrative scenario is mapped as a whole on to the target domain, leading the hearer or reader towards the expectation that a healer will appear who will cure.

---

[24] Like the connection between negative purity language and 'foreign' women in the Hebrew Bible, death is also used to as a connection to create fear, demonize and emphasize the Otherness of so-called foreign women. Examples of the connection between death and the 'foreign' woman are plentiful in Proverbs. The foreign woman's 'house sinks down to death', her 'feet go down to death', and 'her steps grasp Sheol' (Prov. 2.16–19; 5.5; cf. Tan 2008). Moreover, her 'house' leads to 'Sheol, going down to the chambers of death', and her mouth 'is a deep pit' (Prov. 7.27; 22.14). Nevertheless, the most significant connections for our purposes between so-called foreign women and death is the example in Numbers of the incident at Baal Peor or the murder of the Midianite women who are not virgins (Num. 25.6–18, 31.5–20).

Using this mechanism, metaphor becomes a particularly powerful, and incredibly dangerous, tool that can dehumanize people by making them seem gravely unsafe, physically dirty or a source of contamination (Lakoff 1987). This can sometimes exacerbate ethnic othering through disgust which, as White and Landau (2016: 711) argue, also contributes to ethnic and racial prejudice by means of metaphor. Perhaps this is what underlies the common negative associations connected to so-called 'foreign women' in the postexilic material? At the heart of this concept is not so much the woman who happens to be perceived and constructed as being ethnically different, but the 'foreign woman'. The inverted commas indicate that the metaphor of the impure 'foreign woman' makes her into a figment or a mythical creature, an image frozen in space and time that can be projected on to any living person. The intersectionality of ethnic boundaries and gender probably, as Camp's (2000) monograph might be understood to suggest, only serve to intensify the power of this negative way of thinking about ethnic others. Therefore, in the figure of Miriam stricken by Yahweh with צרעת we see the same type of disgust against intermarriage with foreign women turned on its head. The foreign woman is not the source of disgust in this narrative. It is Miriam in the moment that Yahweh punishes her. The metaphor that 'ethnically other' equals 'impure' is repurposed and there is some sense of poetic justice, or at the very least irony, to Miriam's punishment.[25] But Miriam, unlike the foreign women as represented in other postexilic texts, is not permanently blemished. She is eventually allowed to return.

Perhaps, given this interesting reversal of the connection between impurity and ethnic others, the motif of murmuring becomes even more important. The concept of appropriate attitude and communication in the narrative – wherein murmuring criticism is contrasted with faithful prophecy and wherein the quest for authority is contrasted with humility – is emphasized through the language. For example, Abela notes that the phrase דבר+ ב is found 'no less than six times in the first eight verses, three times in the exposition and three in the Lord's climactic speech' (Abela 2008: 532; cf. Cohen 1987). Burns notes that 'in some contexts (Nm. 12.8, 21: 5, 7; Job 19.13; Ps. 50.20, 78.19) the expression certainly bears a meaning of hostile speech' however in others it 'is used of Yahweh's speaking through, with or to a person (Nm. 12.6, 8; 2 Sam. 23.2; 1 Kg. 22.28; Hos. 1.2; Hab. 2.1; cf. Zech. 1.9, 13, 2.2, 7, 4.1, 4, 5, 5: 5, 10, 6.4)' (1980: 105). It is particularly interesting to note the connections in Numbers 11 and 12 between murmuring and bodily punishment, tightening the connections between mouth and body, partly emphasized by the metaphor of eating (Num. 11.1, 4, 5, 13, 18, 19, 21, 12.12) (Jobling 1986). In ch. 12 criticism of Moses is followed by the punishment of תערֹ. In Numbers 11, the murmuring speech is, as is more common, on the mouths of the people (Num. 11.1, 4–6). Here, the request for meat is met with a curse of abundance in the form of quails with so much meat that Yahweh suggests it will be nauseating (Num. 11.20). In turn, while gathering the meat, a subsection of the people is punished by a 'very severe plague' (דאם הבר הכמ) and the

---

[25] Perhaps, given the direct relevance of this chapter to modern ethnic prejudice in present-day times a better way of repurposing metaphors that link foreignness to dirt and lack of purity is to use the metaphors themselves to attack the logic behind that connection. For example, 'racism is a deadly, highly infectious disease that is gripping politics and shutting boarders these days', or 'humanity and goodness have been consumed by a cancerous tumour of hatred that grows rapidly in present times'. These metaphors seek to attack attitudes, rather than specific people. Note the quotation earlier from Lloyd that employed this tactic, stating that 'the rhetoric of disease still infects our political and moral discourse' (2003: 242).

place they are buried designated the 'graves of lust' (קברות התאוה) (Num. 11.33–35). Likewise, a subsection of those who murmur against Moses in ch. 12 are punished. The juxtaposition between the incidents in chs 11 and 12 only serves to emphasize the often dangerous nature of speech (whether through prophesy or through criticism of Moses), the connection between the mouth and the body, and the possibility of punishment in the form of defilement. Here Moses functions as an example of good communication and attitude. His position as one spoken to 'mouth to mouth' by Yahweh is the polar opposite of Miriam's position, which in itself is a metaphor for those who oppose supposedly impure foreign women.

In conclusion, we have argued that intermarriage, ethnic boundaries and bodily boundaries are a key to understanding the dynamics in Numbers 12. We suggested that Moses's intermarriage with a Cushite woman was hypergamy and that the woman need not be identified as Zipporah. Likewise, we suggested that if an authority figure such as Moses can be depicted, or remembered, as having intermarried, then any questioning of intermarriage was severely undermined. We also argued that Miriam was symbolic of a group in the postexilic period with negative attitudes towards foreigners, who connect constructed concepts of 'foreignness' with impurity. If this is the case, we argued, then Miriam's punishment in the form of צרעת (understood as cultic pollution) repurposes metaphors connecting the breach of bodily boundaries with the breaching of ethnic boundaries. As such, purity becomes a defining metaphor in the postexilic period to divide between those who can claim in-group membership and those who are considered to be foreign. Numbers 12 turns these metaphors on their head by emphasizing the problematic nature of Miriam's murmuring criticisms of Moses's intermarriage and advocates for care to be taken, amongst audiences, in communication and speech. Here, an in-group woman is cast out as one who is severely impure, as indicated by the punishment of צרעת.

# REFERENCES

Abela, A. (2008), 'Shaming Miriam, Moses' Sister, 12,1–16: Focus on the Narrative's Exposition vv. 1-2', in T. Römer (ed.), *The Books of Leviticus and Numbers*, 521–34, Leuven: Peeters.

Ackerman, S. (2002), 'Why Is Miriam Also Among the Prophets? (And Is Zipporah Among the Priests?)', *JBL*, 121 (1): 47–80.

Adamo, D.T. (1998), *Africa and the Africans in the Old Testament*, San Francisco: Christian Universities Press.

Adamo, D.T. (2001), 'The Images of Cush in the Old Testament: Reflections on African Hermeneutics', in M. Getui, K. Holter and V. Zinkuratire (eds), *Interpreting the Old Testament in Africa: Papers from the International Symposium on Africa and the Old Testament in Nairobi, October 1999*, 65–74, New York: Peter Lang.

Adamo, D.T. (2018), 'A Silent Unheard Voice in the Old Testament: The Cushite Woman Whom Moses Married in Numbers 12.1–10', *In die Skriflig*, 52 (1). Available online: http://dx.doi.org/10.4102/ids.v52i1.2370 (accessed 10 July 2022).

Anderson, G.A. and S.M. Olyan, eds (1991), *Priesthood and Cult in Ancient Israel*, JSOTSup 125, Sheffield: JSOT Press.

Bellis, A.O. (2007), *Helpmates, Harlots, and Heroes: Women's Stories in the Hebrew Bible*, 2nd edn, Louisville, KY: Westminster John Knox Press.

Brenner, A. (1982), *Colour Terms in the Old Testament*, JSOTSup 21, Sheffield: JSOT Press.

Burns, R. (1980), '"Has the Lord Indeed Spoken Only Through Moses?" A Study of The Biblical Portrait of Miriam', PhD diss., Marquette University. Available online: https://epublications.marquette.edu/dissertations/AAI8104800/ (accessed 10 July 2022).

Camp, C.V. (2000), *Wise, Strange and Holy: The Strange Woman and the Making of the Bible*, JSOTSup 320, Sheffield: Sheffield Academic Press.

Coats, G.W. (1968), *Rebellion in the Wilderness: The Murmuring Motif in the Wilderness Traditions of the Old Testament*, Nashville, TN: Abingdon Press.

Cohen, N.G. (1987), '"כי . . . רבד": An "Enthusiastic" Prophetic Formula', *ZAW*, 99 (2): 219–32.

Collins, A.Y. (1983), 'Aristobulus (Second Century B.C.)', in J.H. Charlesworth (ed.), *The Old Testament Pseudepigrapha, Volume Two: Expansions of the 'Old Testament' and Legends, Wisdom and Philosophical Literature, Prayers, Psalms, and Odes, Fragments of Lost Judeo-Hellenistic Works*, 831–42, Peabody, MA: Hendrickson.

Coomber, R., L. Moyle and A. Pavlidis (2018), 'Public Spitting in "Developing" Nations of the Global South: Harmless Embedded Practice or Disgusting, Harmful and Deviant?', in K. Carrington, R. Hogg, J. Scott and M. Sozzo (eds), *The Palgrave Handbook of Criminology and the Global South*, 493–520, Cham: Palgrave Macmillan.

Copher, C.B. (1991), 'The Black Presence in the Old Testament', in C.H. Felder (ed.), *Stony the Road We Trod: African American Biblical Interpretation*, 146–64, Minneapolis, MN: Fortress Press.

Douglas, M. (1966), *Purity and Danger: An Analysis of Concepts of Pollution and Taboo*, London: Routledge & Kegan Paul.

Douglas, M. (2001), *In the Wilderness: The Doctrine of Defilement in the Book of Numbers*, rev. edn, Oxford: Oxford University Press.

Erbele-Küster, D. (2017), *Body, Gender and Purity in Leviticus 12 and 15*, LHBOTS 539, London: Bloomsbury T&T Clark.

Exum, J.C. (1996), *Plotted, Shot, and Painted: Cultural Representations of Biblical Women*, JSOTSup 215, Sheffield: Sheffield Academic Press.

Felder, C.H. (1991), *Stony the Road We Trod: African American Biblical Interpretation*, Minneapolis, MN: Fortress Press.

Frankel, D. (2002), *The Murmuring Stories of the Priestly School: A Retrieval of Ancient Sacerdotal Lore*, Leiden: E.J. Brill.

Frevel, C., ed. (2011), *Mixed Marriages: Intermarriage and Group Identity in the Second Temple Period*, LHBOTS 547, London: Bloomsbury T&T Clark.

Frymer-Kensky, T. (1983), 'Pollution, Purification and Purgation in Biblical Israel', in C.L. Meyers and M. O'Connor (eds), *The Word of the Lord Shall Go Forth: Essays in Honor of David Noel Freedman*, 399–414, Winona Lake, IN: Eisenbrauns.

Getui, M.N., K. Holter and V. Zinkuratire, eds (2001), *Interpreting the Old Testament in Africa: Papers from the International Symposium on Africa and the Old Testament in Nairobi, October 1999*, New York: Peter Lang.

Gibbs, R.W., Jr and H. Franks (2002), 'Embodied Metaphor in Women's Narratives About Their Experiences with Cancer', *Health Communication*, 14 (2): 139–65.

Gray, G.B. (1986), *A Critical and Exegetical Commentary on Numbers*, Edinburgh: T&T Clark.

Hanson, J. (1983), 'Demetrius the Chronographer?', in J.H. Charlesworth (ed.), *The Old Testament Pseudepigrapha, Volume Two: Expansions of the 'Old Testament' and Legends, Wisdom and Philosophical Literature, Prayers, Psalms, and Odes, Fragments of Lost Judeo-Hellenistic Works*, 803–20, Peabody, MA: Hendrickson.

Hartley, J.E. (1992), *Leviticus*, Dallas, TX: Word Books.

Hayes, C.E. (2002), *Gentile Impurities and Jewish Identities: Intermarriage and Conversion from the Bible to the Talmud*, Oxford: Oxford University Press.

Hepner, G. (2009), 'Moses' Cushite Wife echoes Hosea's Woman of Harlotries: Exposure of Unfaithfulness in the Wilderness', *SJOT*, 23 (2): 233–42.

Holter, K. (2000), 'Should Old Testament Cush Be Rendered "Africa"?', in *Yahweh in Africa: Essays on Africa and the Old Testament*, Bible and Theology in Africa, 107–14, New York: Peter Lang.

Hutchinson, J. and A.D. Smith, eds (1996), *Ethnicity*, Oxford: Oxford University Press.

Janzen, D. (2002), *Witch-Hunts, Purity and Social Boundaries: The Expulsion of the Foreign Women in Ezra 9–10*, JSOTSup 350, Sheffield: Sheffield Academic Press.

Jobling, D. (1986), *The Sense of Biblical Narrative: Structural Analyses in the Hebrew Bible*, JSOTSup 7, 2nd edn, Sheffield: JSOT Press.

Kirmayer, L. (1992), 'The Body Insistence on Meaning: Metaphor as Presentation and Representation in Illness Experience', *Medical Anthropology Quarterly* NS, 6 (4): 323–46.

Klawans, J. (1998), 'Idolatry, Incest, and Impurity: Moral Defilement in Ancient Judaism', *JSJ*, 29 (4): 391–415.

Klawans, J. (2000), *Impurity and Sin in Ancient Judaism*, New York: Oxford University Press.

Klawans, J. (2006), *Purity, Sacrifice, and the Temple: Symbolism and Supersessionism in the Study of Ancient Judaism*, Oxford: Oxford University Press.

Lakoff, G. (1987), *Women, Fire, and Dangerous Things: What Categories Reveal about the Mind*, Chicago: University of Chicago Press.

Levine, B.A. (1993), *Numbers 1–20: A New Translation with Introduction and Commentary*, New York: Doubleday.

Lloyd, G.E.R. (2003), *In the Grip of Disease: Studies in the Greek Imagination*, Oxford: Oxford University Press.

Lokel, P. (2006), 'Previously Unstoried Lives: The Case of Old Testament Cush and its Relevance to Africa', *OTE*, 19 (2): 525–37.

Lupton, D. (2012), *Fat*, Abingdon: Routledge.

Milgrom, J. (1991), *Leviticus 1–16: A New Translation with Introduction and Commentary*, New York: Doubleday.

Musolff, A. (2007), 'What Role Do Metaphors Play in Racial Prejudice? The Function of Antisemitic Imagery in Hitler's *Mein Kampf*', *Patterns of Prejudice*, 41 (1): 21–43.

Nichter, M. (2008), *Global Health: Why Cultural Perceptions, Social Representations, and Biopolitics Matter*, Tucson: University of Arizona Press.

Noth, M. (1968), *Numbers: A Commentary*, London: SCM Press.

Olojede, F. (2017), 'Miriam and Moses's Cushite Wife: Sisterhood in Jeopardy?', in L.J. Claassens and C.J. Sharp (eds), *Feminist Frameworks and The Bible: Power, Ambiguity, and Intersectionality*, 133–46, LHBOTS 630, London: Bloomsbury T&T Clark.

Olyan, S.M. (2004), *Biblical Mourning: Ritual and Social Dimensions*, Oxford: Oxford University Press.

Pilch, J.J. (2000), *Healing in the New Testament: Insights from Medical and Mediterranean Anthropology*, Minneapolis, MN: Fortress Press.

Pitkänen, P. (2018), *A Commentary on Numbers: Narrative, Ritual, and Colonialism*, Routledge Studies in the Biblical World, Abingdon: Routledge.

Rapp, U. (2002), *Mirjam: Eine feministisch-rhetorische Lektüre der Mirjamtexte in der hebräischen Bibel*, BZAW 317, Berlin: De Gruyter.

Robertson, R.G. (1983), 'Ezekiel the Tragedian', in J.H. Charlesworth (ed.), *The Old Testament Pseudepigrapha, Volume Two: Expansions of the 'Old Testament' and Legends, Wisdom and Philosophical Literature, Prayers, Psalms, and Odes, Fragments of Lost Judeo-Hellenistic Works*, 843–54, Peabody, MA: Hendrickson.

Robinson, B. (1989), 'The Jealousy of Miriam: A Note on Num. 12', *ZAW*, 101 (3): 428–32.

Sadler, R.S., Jr (2005), *Can a Cushite Change His Skin? An Examination of Race, Ethnicity, and Othering in the Hebrew Bible*, LHBOTS 425, London: T&T Clark.

Serino, R.M. (2016), 'A Sign in the Dark: Moses's Cushite Wife and Boundary Setting in the Book of Numbers', *BI*, 24 (2): 153–77.

Sontag, S. (1978), *Illness as Metaphor*, New York: Farrar, Straus and Giroux.

Southwood, K.E. (2012), *Ethnicity and the Mixed Marriage Crisis in Ezra 9–10: An Anthropological Approach*, Oxford: Oxford University Press.

Southwood, K.E. (2021), *Job's Body and the Dramatised Comedy of Moralising*, Abingdon: Routledge.

Sturdy, J. (1976), *Numbers*, CBC, Cambridge: Cambridge University Press.

Tan, N.N.H. (2008), *The 'Foreignness' of the Foreign Woman in Proverbs 1–9: A Study of the Origin and Development of a Biblical Motif*, BZAW 381, Berlin: De Gruyter.

Vindrola-Padros, C. and G.A. Johnson (2014), 'The Narrated, Nonnarrated, and the Disnarrated: Conceptual Tools for Analyzing Narratives in Health Services Research', *Qualitative Health Research*, 24 (11): 1603–11.

Wenham, G.J. (1979), *The Book of Leviticus*, Grand Rapids, MI: Eerdmans.

Whiston, W. (1995), *The Works of Josephus: Complete and Unabridged*, Peabody, MA: Hendrickson.

White, M.H., II and M.J. Landau (2016), 'Metaphor in Intergroup Relations', *Social and Personality Psychology Compass*, 10 (12): 707–21.

Williams, J. (2002), '"And She Became 'Snow White'": Numbers 12.1–16', *OTE*, 15 (2): 259–68.

Wilson, R.R. (1980), *Prophecy and Society in Ancient Israel*, Philadelphia, PA: Fortress Press.

Winslow, K.S. (2011a), 'Mixed Marriage in Torah Narratives', in C. Frevel (ed.), *Mixed Marriages, Intermarriage and Group Identity in the Second Temple Period*, 132–49, LHBOTS 547, London: Bloomsbury T&T Clark.

Winslow, K.S. (2011b), 'Moses' Cushite Marriage: Torah, Artapanus, and Josephus', in C. Frevel (ed.), *Mixed Marriages, Intermarriage and Group Identity in the Second Temple Period*, 280–302, LHBOTS 547, London: Bloomsbury T&T Clark.

CHAPTER FOURTEEN

# Asymmetrical reciprocal exchange in the Book of Jonah

JO-MARÍ SCHÄDER

## INTRODUCTION

Since the 1970s, the social sciences have demonstrated their value in reconstructing and understanding the world of the ancient Israelites. The usefulness of the social-scientific approach for biblical studies has been proven over and again (cf. Schäder 2020: 2). Social-scientific scholarship has noted similarities from the Mediterranean, through to the ancient Near East, spanning from the third millennium BCE until the legalization of Christianity (see Bolin 2004: 38–9). Within the set of social-scientific models, patronage has been useful to account for reciprocity exchanges.

The terms patron and client come to us from the study of the Graeco-Roman world, the terms being borrowed from the Roman *patronus*, a powerful aristocrat with loyal followers, known as *clientes* (Westbrook 2005: 210). However, the semantic range of such terms in the languages of the ancient Near East is very broad (Westbrook 2005: 213).[1] What studies like those of Olyan (1996) and Westbrook (2005), and also in this instance Crook (2006), aim to do is to contextualize and apply an adjusted version of these theories and values to the context of the ancient Near East and the ancient Israelites, and the Hebrew Bible specifically.

In this contribution the aim is, first, to provide an overview of the types of reciprocity as proposed by Marshall Sahlins (2017 [1972]), because even though his original work focused on primitive cultures – those without a political state – it has been found to be applicable to various cultures from different regions and times. Following upon this an overview will be provided of the adaptation of Sahlins's theory by Crook, as his focus is

---

[1] 'Kinship terms such as "father" and "son" are promiscuously employed outside of the realm of the family for all manner of social, commercial and legal relations. Terms for "gift" are frequently used in legal fictions to designate a payment that would be illegal or invalid if given its real title of price, fee or compensation. Terms of affect such as "love" are employed in servant–master / vassal–overlord relations (witness the biblical injunction that Israelites should love their god). Even terms for "friend" may designate a commercial or professional relationship' (Westbrook 2005: 213). 'A further difficulty is the nature of the sources. Most of the primary sources from the region are institutional – from the palace or the temple – and record formalized relationships of dependence' (ibid.: 214).

to contextualize Sahlins's work for application to the ancient Near East and the Hebrew Bible specifically. In his discussion on asymmetrical reciprocity – which would appear to be the most frequent manner in which reciprocal relationships manifest within the Hebrew Bible – he distinguishes between covenantal and patron–client relationships. The relationship between these two types of asymmetrical reciprocal exchange will then be dealt with, specifically focusing on their differences and similarities.

An introductory overview of the book of Jonah will be provided pertaining to its structural layout, themes and purposes of the book, its dating, and authorship and audience. This will be done in order to contextualize the application of Crook's version of asymmetrical reciprocity to the book's *emic* (insider) perspective.[2] This is because '[T]he ancient writers tell us what they wish to tell us, and they seldom explain everyday acts or behaviors' (Matthews 2007: 129). The aim of this chapter is to determine to which extent asymmetrical reciprocity is present in the book of Jonah and how applicable the model is to it.

## SAHLINS'S MODEL OF RECIPROCAL EXCHANGE

Not only has Sahlins's work been influential in economic anthropology, but also in biblical studies (see, for instance, Stansell 1999; Crook 2006; Matthews 2007). His *Stone Age Economics*, published originally in 1972,[3] has provided scholars on antiquity with a model through which we can better understand reciprocity. Sahlins's work focused on primitive cultures – those who have no political state – taking the form of hunter-gatherer societies. However, his theory has been found to be applicable to different contexts. It is an approach that can prove useful in discussing reciprocity amongst societies across geographical and temporal planes.

In his chapter 'On the Sociology of Primitive Exchange' in *Stone Age Economics*, Sahlins (2017: 113–14) pointed out:

> [F]or despite the connotation of equivalence, ordinary reciprocal exchanges are often unbalanced; that is, on the strictly material plane. Repayments are only more or less equal to the initial gifts, and they are only more or less direct in time. The variation is correlated notably with kinship distance. Balance is the material relation of distant kinship; closer to home, exchange becomes more disinterested; there is tolerance of delays or even of complete failure to reciprocate.

Crook (2006: 79) points out that Sahlins's model of reciprocity rests on two theoretical foundations, namely 'social distance' and the 'timeliness of reciprocation'. Whereas reciprocity is typically viewed as a balanced and 'unconditional one-for-one exchange', Sahlins points out that it is not the case as it consists of 'a whole class of exchanges, a continuum of forms' (Sahlins 2017: 172–3). On the one side is 'assistance freely given' (kinship, friendship and neighbourliness). It does not have 'an open stipulation of return'

---

[2] In anthropology, there is a conventional distinction between *emic* (insider) and *etic* (outsider) information and perspectives (cf. Elliott 1993: 38). Taking cognisance of the distinction between emics (insider) and etics (outsider) help us realize how the material that we study is part of a reality that is different from that of our own. We should then be sensitive not to modernize the meaning of the text to be investigated (Van Eck 1995: 163). It also aids us in overcoming 'the hermeneutical gap' that exists between 'us' and 'them' (ibid.: 163, 164). 'Implicit features in texts are thus emic data, and to make them explicit an etic interpretation is needed' (ibid.: 164).

[3] In this chapter, the latest version of this essay, published in the 2017 edition of *Stone Age Economics*, will be consulted. Even though both Crook (2006) and Matthews (2007) made use of earlier versions of Sahlins's essay, the basic tenets in the latest version remains the same.

as it would be deemed 'unthinkable and unsociable'. At the other side is 'self-interested seizure' (such as 'appropriation by chicanery or force'). It is the equivalent of the effort of *lex talionis* (namely 'negative reciprocity'; ibid.: 173). Social distance dictates the distance between the poles of reciprocity (cf. Deut. 23.20; Sahlins 2017: 173). 'It follows that close kin tend to share, to enter into generalized exchanges, and distant and nonkin to deal in equivalents or in guile' (ibid.: 178).

As has been pointed out above, Sahlins's model proposes that reciprocities occur in an abstract continuum (cf. Sahlins 2017: 174), and that 'the spirit of exchange swings from disinterested concern for the other party through mutuality to self-interest' (ibid.: 175). The reciprocities he identifies and discusses are generalized reciprocity, balanced reciprocity and negative reciprocity. What follows here is a brief overview of each of Sahlins's subtypes of reciprocity.

### *Generalized reciprocity, the solidary extreme*

These transactions are 'putatively altruistic' (Sahlins 2017: 175). The assistance returned is in line with the assistance given. Ethnographic formulas that indicate this type of reciprocity is 'pure gift' (following Bronisław Malinowski), 'sharing', 'hospitality', 'free gift', 'help' and 'generosity' (Sahlins 2017: 175). However, according to Sahlins (ibid.: 176), 'the expectation of reciprocity is indefinite'. In the case of generalized reciprocity, '[T]he requital thus may be very soon, but then again it may be never' (ibid.). This implies that in some instances there will be 'a sustained one-way flow' (ibid.). This type of reciprocity is thus selfless and open-ended and 'material concerns are subordinated to social concerns – what matters most is not the return but the support of the social system' (Crook 2006: 79).

### *Balanced reciprocity, the midpoint*

This reciprocity is a direct exchange. 'In precise balance, the reciprocation is the customary equivalent of the thing received and is without delay' (Sahlins 2017: 176). Examples of this is 'marital transactions', 'friendship compacts' and 'peace agreements' (ibid.). There is thus a narrow period that allows for the return of the equivalent of that which was given. Thus, this reciprocity is 'less 'personal' than generalized reciprocity' (ibid.: 177). Disruption of people's relationships occurs when there is a failure to reciprocate within the time allotted (cf. ibid.). This type of reciprocity may occur outside the kinship centre, but still happens within the tribe (Crook 2006: 79–80).

### *Negative reciprocity, the unsociable extreme*

This reciprocity is an attempt to get something for nothing. It consists of 'transactions opened and conducted toward net utilitarian advantage' (Sahlins 2017: 177). Some ethnographic terms Sahlins (ibid.) associates this type of reciprocity with is 'haggling' or 'barter', 'gambling', 'chicanery', 'theft' and other varieties of seizure. It is an impersonal exchange that is 'most economic' for one party. However, this exchange is still conditional and 'contingent upon mustering countervailing pressure or guile' (ibid.). This reciprocity then allows for 'the greatest social distance removed' and occurs between tribes as it is a threat to kinship stability (Crook 2006: 80).

As has already been referred to, Sahlins's model holds great potential in better understanding the types of reciprocal exchange between people from different periods and areas. So too it can be applicable to the interactions and relationships between people from the ancient

Near East, the Israelites (or Yehudites), and as reflected in the Hebrew Bible specifically. What follows is one such adaptation to make his model applicable to the biblical era.

## A MODIFICATION OF SAHLINS'S MODEL

Sahlins's model has been modified with time (cf. Stansell 1999; Matthews 2007); however, this study will focus on the modification of Crook (2006), as his typology of reciprocity – especially his explication of asymmetrical (generalized) reciprocity – will be of most aid to a practical application to the book of Jonah. Crook modifies Sahlins's model in order for it to be able to account for data from the ancient Near East, and in order to include covenantal exchange, along with patron–client relationship, as examples of asymmetrical (generalized) reciprocity.[4] What follows here is an overview of Crook's discussion of each type of modified reciprocity.

### Familial reciprocity

For Crook this reciprocity occurred in the family and broader ancient Near Eastern family (Crook 2006: 81). It is important, however, to bear in mind that not each member in the familial unit had equal status. 'Rather, the family formed a unit within which there would be equality relative to those outside the family unit' (ibid.: 91). Matthews (2007: 152) points out that the main characteristic of this type of reciprocity is that 'charity, hospitality, gifts given to kin and the circle of friends' does not require the immediate return of that which was exchanged.

### Symmetrical (balanced) reciprocity

Crook (2006: 81) motivates his choice to rename balanced reciprocity 'symmetrical reciprocity' in that the parties involved in this form of exchange are equal (symmetrical) in social status and that that which is exchanged tends to be equal (symmetrical) in value also. This type of reciprocity not only occurs between individuals, but also between families, such as in the case of marriage exchanges (the value of dowries). That which is exchanged has to be of either equal or greater value (ibid.: 81–2). Therefore another form that balanced reciprocity takes is trade and market transactions (ibid.: 82). There is also little to no delay in the repayment of this type of reciprocity. In this type of reciprocity 'the relative social status of giver and receiver can either be the same (which it must be in gift exchange) or irrelevant to the relationship (as in market exchange)' (ibid.: 63). 'The assumption here is that unbalanced exchange can create measurable tensions' (Matthews 2007: 152).

### Asymmetrical (generalized) reciprocity

The parties involved in this type of exchange are of unequal (asymmetric) social status. Goods and services shared are not of an equal value and is not repaid in kind. The

---

[4] Crook (2006) not only modifies the work of Sahlins, but also draws on that of Ekkehard and Wolfgang Stegemann (1999). The Stegemanns initially adopted Sahlins's model to reflect ancient Mediterranean forms of exchange (Crook 2006: 80). They proposed four types of reciprocal exchanges for the application to the Graeco-Roman context, namely (1) familial reciprocity (*Familiäre Reziprozität*), balanced reciprocity (*Ausgeglichene Reziprozität*), generalized reciprocity (*Generelle Reziprozität*), and negative reciprocity (*Negative Reziprozität*) (Crook 2006: 80–1). Crook modified their typology by renaming balanced reciprocity to *symmetrical reciprocity*, and by renaming generalized reciprocity to *asymmetrical reciprocity* (ibid.: 81).

recipient of asymmetrical reciprocity is then subservient to the giver, even though the language of friendship is used in such exchanges (Crook 2006: 83). The favour is repaid by 'homage and loyalty or political support or information' (ibid.: 82) or 'by giving honor, gratitude, and loyalty' (ibid.: 83). According to Crook (ibid.: 82), this then 'results in an ongoing and open-ended relationship'. Crook (ibid.: 83) argues that 'patronage and clientage has become the epitome and characteristic type of asymmetrical exchange. This presents a problem in that similar but not identical forms of asymmetrical exchange are typically collapsed into a single type'. It is then that Crook (ibid.) makes the case that there is another type of asymmetrical exchange that is not patronage and clientage, but covenantal exchange, which appears to be similar on the surface. Both are then classified as asymmetrical (generalized) reciprocity. We will return to the relationship of covenantal reciprocity and patronage and clientage in the next section of this chapter.

*Negative reciprocity*

Negative reciprocity, similar to Sahlins's explanation, is a tactic – often an aggressive one – used to obtain a greater return than that which was initially exchanged. It could also take the form of barter or theft, or getting something for nothing. These exchanges are not kin-based (Matthews 2007: 152).[5]

According to Crook (2006: 91), the main characteristics of the aforementioned exchanges is tabulated in Table 14.1.

From the preceding it ought to be clear that there are different types of reciprocal relationships reflected specifically the Hebrew Bible. However, what interests me in the next section is two types of asymmetrical reciprocal relationships, namely covenantal exchanges and patron–client relationships. The distinction and correlations between the two will now be discussed.

## TABLE 14.1: A model of exchange in the biblical era

| *Familial exchange* | *Symmetrical exchange* | *Asymmetrical exchange* | *Negative exchange* |
| --- | --- | --- | --- |
| Kinship-based | Non-kinship-based | Non-kinship-based | Non-kinship-based |
| Egalitarian (relative to non-kin); open-ended reciprocity, selfless giving | Balanced social status and balanced value of exchange | Unequal social status; unequal exchange (repayment not in kind) | Social status not relevant, treatment of enemies, opponents and strangers |
| E.g. exchanges within households, between households in clans and between clans in tribes | E.g. gift exchange, loan and loan repayment, buying/selling, trading | E.g. patronage (teacher/student, patron–client); benefaction (imperial benefactions, euergetism); covenantal exchange (treaties, oaths) | E.g. bartering, cheating, stealing |

[5] Crook (2006: 80–1) writes little on negative reciprocity apart from referring to it as one of the types of reciprocity the Stegemanns adopted and that it is a part of the model of exchange they compiled (see Table 14.1).

# ASYMMETRICAL RECIPROCITY AND THE HEBREW BIBLE

Covenantal exchanges have been primarily associated with international treaties, where the commitments of the parties involved are specified in detail. These commitments were guaranteed by oaths and were enforced by the gods, in either words or symbols, and this can be explicitly or implicitly done (Foster 2006: 40). In many contexts 'oath' and 'covenant' are synonymous with each other. Although the gods are involved in covenant relations, their involvement is limited to being witnesses and enforcers.

According to Crook (2006: 83), covenantal exchanges have three main characteristics, namely that (1) they involve a formal oath that was legally binding; (2) they had obligations that were explicitly spelled out; and (3) they were entered into by parties of unequal social status. The characteristic that distinguishes it the most from patron–client relationships is that covenantal exchange was a formal and legal agreement (Crook 2006: 84, 85, 90; cf. Matthews 2007: 155). Crook then refers to suzerain–vassal relationships and landlord–tenant relationships as examples.[6] He describes a covenantal exchange as a 'formal treaty (ratified by an oath and sworn in the name of the gods)' (Crook 2006: 84) and patronal exchange as 'loose, informal, or implied' (ibid.: 84–5).

The word בְּרִית ('covenant') does not always appear in texts where there are examples of these types of relationships in the Hebrew Bible (cf. Schäder 2010: 240). Pertaining to covenantal exchange in the Hebrew Bible, Matthews (2007: 156) points out that Israel's relationship with Yahweh is expressed in anthropomorphic terms. The condition for this covenantal relationship is that 'the people of Israel are required to limit their devotion to Yahweh alone and obey his commandments' in order for them to obtain forms of fertility, such as land and offspring (ibid.).[7] The only way the Israelites can even begin to attempt to repay the gifts of the covenant is to remain submissive and obedient to God (show their fidelity) by abstaining from the worship of other deities (see Exod. 20.3; Matthews 2007: 156, 158).[8] However, it stands to argue that there would be repercussions if the covenant was not upheld: The rains would be supressed resulting in the shrinking of harvests (cf. Jer. 3.3 and Hag. 1.6), and should divine warnings to the Israelites to return their fidelity to God fail (cf. Jer. 7.24–26), they face conquests by foreign nations (Isa. 5.24–30), or return to exile, until such a time as they are prepared to be obedient again (Isa. 40.1–2; Ezek. 36.26) (Matthews 2007: 158).

We now turn to patron–client relationships in the Hebrew Bible. It stands to argue that patron–client relationships are less formal – albeit no less binding – than covenant

---

[6] According to Pfoh (2013: 35), the native mode of political rule and subordination in Syria-Palestine was patron–client relationships. He takes issue with the term 'vassalage' as he is of the opinion that it is filled with medieval connotations and is an anachronism. He prefers the designation for these types of relationships to rather be *patron–client relationships* or *political patronage*. He is also of the opinion that the designation 'client-states' should be used instead of 'vassal states' (ibid.: 36).

[7] According to Matthews (2007: 156), a covenant can include multiple other gifts from God such as (1) protection from enemies via the aid of the Divine warrior (cf. Exod. 17.8–16), (2) nurturing to widows and orphans in his capacity as a father (Ps. 68.5–6), and (3) God's control over the forces of nature resulting in prosperity (Isa. 30.23–26; Zech. 10.1).

[8] Pilch (1998: 31) indicates that God is the most common subject of the verb 'to show compassion'. God is free to show compassion to whomever and however he wishes. Many of the occurrences of 'compassion' are linked with 'mercy' and is 'situated in the context of God's covenant promises' and 'in the Hebrew Bible compassion is most commonly ascribed to or desired from conquerors or other powerful figures' (ibid.). Obedience was not the condition for the establishment and maintenance of the covenant, but the result of it (Linington 2002: 688; cf. Cross 1998: 15).

exchanges (see Matthews 2007: 154; Crook 2006: 68, 86–7). According to Elliott (1996: 144), patronage and clientage are 'dependency relations, involving the reciprocal exchange of goods and services between socially superior "patrons" and their socially inferior "clients"'. Patron–client relationships are, therefore, relations of personal loyalty and commitment entered into voluntarily by individuals of unequal social status (Elliott 1996: 148; cf. Westbrook 2005: 211), often referred to as 'friendship' (ibid.), therefore asymmetrical in nature. Patronage is a mutually beneficial relationship between a client, whose needs have been met, and a patron, who receives grants of honour and benefaction in turn.[9] Patron–client relationships appear to be rooted in kinship obligations as members of the community (household, clan or tribe) realize that their actions will have consequences on the larger kinship group's honour and shame (Matthews 2007: 153–4).

In most cases a superior party is favoured as 'having the monopoly of coercion in the relationship', which then 'governs the whole political situation' (Pfoh 2013: 37). '[P]atronage relations are not institutionalized in society and, therefore, the presence of written treaties connoting patronage bonds would appear, *prima facie*, paradoxical' (ibid.). However, stating that patron–client relations are 'forced' would be a misnomer as it 'requires some degree of consent by the client' (ibid.: 38, n.45). Westbrook (2005: 211–12) points out that patronage is 'symbiotic' with other types of formal relationships, such as legal relations, bureaucracy, commercial exchanges and kinship obligations. Whereas it can function on an individual level, it also exists as a system.

According to Matthews (2007: 155), examples of types of patrons are the following: (1) *an individual patron:* potential clients will seek out a wealthy or influential individual who can protect and care for them, whether kin or not; (2) *village or city elders:* elders are considered to be wise men who come from influential families, and who are property owners. They sit at the gate of a city where they listen to testimony and judge cases that are brought before them in the light of the law and the community's traditions. They are thus deemed authoritative and honourable; and (3) *the king:* a king is responsible for the protection and care of the people within his realm.[10]

The most prevalent example of a patron in the Bible is when someone is referred to as 'father', but is not someone's biological father. The title refers to the role and status of the patron. The patron is like a father and the clients are like grateful and loving children. Another example of a common form of patron–client relationship is between landowners and some of their tenants (Malina 1998e: 151–3; cf. Botha 2001: 193; Crook 2006: 90).

In the case of individuals who lack the means of taking care of themselves (such as widows, orphans and strangers), and who would not readily have access to a patron, it is the responsibility of the entire community to provide them with assistance, as is expected by the prophets (cf. Zech. 7.8–10; Malina 1998f: 158; Matthews 2007: 153). Pity is then the quality that leads a person to perform acts of kindness, and to look after those in need. 'People moved by pity are prompted to act honourably toward one in need' (Malina 1998f: 157). Such a person is deemed compassionate or gracious. This is also a quality of God (Exod. 34.9; Jon. 4.2; Pss. 103.8, 13, 111.4). When his pity is withdrawn, it is a sign of judgement (e.g. Jer. 13.14; Ezek. 5.11, 7.4, 9; Malina 1998f: 157–8).

---

[9] When things ran awry, '[P]atrons and clients did not take each other to court; a dissatisfied patron simply stopped giving to a dishonoring or ungrateful client, and a dissatisfied client was more or less powerless' (Crook 2006: 89).

[10] 'The kings in Syria-Palestine, local and foreign (with exception of the pharaoh), behaved indeed like *patrons* towards their subjects and like *clients* towards their overlords' (Pfoh 2013: 40).

Gratitude can be described as 'the debt of interpersonal obligation for unrepayable favours received' (Malina 1998d: 92). The term 'faith' is also related to patron–client relationships. It refers to either 'dependability' or 'trust' (deSilva 2000: 115). Faith and faithfulness refer to the value of reliability (in interpersonal relations; Malina 1998b: 72).

As a form of asymmetrical exchange, covenantal exchanges share of course similarities with patron–client relationships: both types of exchange occur between parties of unequal social status, and that which is exchanged (either goods or services) are of unequal value ('but are based on a reciprocity of gratitude, loyalty, and honor') (Crook 2006: 86). In addition, 'loyalty/steadfast love' (חֶסֶד) was an important element in all forms of asymmetrical exchange (Crook 2006: 87; cf. Malina 1998d: 93; Esler 2006: 194).[11]

However, Crook rightly points out that 'when one approaches the texts of the ancient Near East and Israel with the current model of exchange one is forced to collapse all forms of asymmetrical exchange into patronage and clientage' (Crook 2006: 90), as these types of exchanges are 'in reality quite fluid' (ibid.: 91).

# AN INTRODUCTION TO THE BOOK OF JONAH

In this section an overview will be provided of the structural layout of the book of Jonah, its proposed themes and purposes, and this author's dating and theory of the book's authorship and audience. This is done in order to contextualize the content and argumentation that follows.

### *A structural layout of the book of Jonah*

The parallel or symmetrical structure of the book of Jonah has been identified long ago (cf. Trible 1963: 186–92, 1996: 475; cf. Potgieter 2004: 618). Spronk (2009: 3–4), indicated that the macrostructure of the book of Jonah is what he terms a diptych, consisting of parallel sections containing parallel features, and themes. Spronk's (2009: 3–4) literary build-up of the story is illustrated in Table 14.2.

**TABLE 14.2: The literary build-up of the book of Jonah as a diptych**

| Event | First appearance | Second appearance |
|---|---|---|
| Yahweh calls Jonah twice | 1.1–2 | 3.1–2 |
| Jonah stands up and goes | 1.3 | 3.3 |
| Jonah makes a short statement to the sailors/Ninevites | 1.9 | 3.4 |
| His hearers act as believers, putting their trust in Yahweh/Elohim | 1.14 | 3.5–9 |
| Yahweh calms the sea/Elohim does not destroy the city | 1.15 | 3.10 |
| Jonah prays to Yahweh | 2.2 | 4.2 |
| Jonah quotes the Psalms/Jonah quotes Exod. 34.6 | 2.2–7 | 4.2 |
| Jonah thanks Yahweh for giving him life out of the grave/Jonah prefers death over life | 2.8 | 4.8 |
| Yahweh is called a saviour/Yahweh explains why He saved Nineveh | 2.10 | 4.11 |

[11] See, for example, Deut. 7.9–12; 1 Kgs 8.23; 2 Chron. 6.14; Neh. 1.5, 9.32; see also Pss. 25.10, 89.28, 106.45, Isa. 54.10 and Dan. 9.4 (Malina 1998d: 92).

**TABLE 14.3: A schematic representation of the sections in the book of Jonah**

| Section A: Jonah 1.1–2.11 | | Section B: Jonah 3.1–4.11 | |
|---|---|---|---|
| Jonah 1.1–3 | Jonah's calling and flight | Jonah 3.1–3a | Jonah's second calling and obedience |
| Jonah 1.4–16 | Distress at sea | Jonah 3.3b-10 | Distress in Nineveh |
| Jonah 2.1–11 | Inside the fish | Jonah 4.1–11 | Outside Nineveh |

A popular manner in which to demarcate sections of the book of Jonah is to refer to the individual chapters as subsections (cf. Glaze 1972: 158; Nogalski 2011: 403, 409–10), or to consider chs 1–2 (Section A) and chs 3–4 (Section B) as the two major sections of the book (Allen 1976: 200; Potgieter 1991: 14; Simon 1999: xxv). Section A then concludes when the events in the fish comes to an end, whereas Section B begins a new series of events at a different place and at another time (Potgieter 1991: 14). According to this author, the structural layout of the book of Jonah will schematically look as set out in Table 14.3.

It is then clear that the book of Jonah consists of two major sections. At the beginning of each section the two major characters, namely Yahweh and Jonah, are introduced. All other human characters in the story are unnamed. The plot is driven by divine activity, and the response by human characters, and nature, to it. The final question in 4.11 leaves the narrative open-ended (Trible 1994: 109).

Those who adopt a fourfold division of the book of Jonah according to its four chapters are quick to point out that Jonah changes location in each of the four scenes. Each of these scenes then focuses on the interaction between Jonah and other characters, namely (1) with the (foreign) sailors in ch. 1; (2) with Yahweh in ch. 2; (3) with the inhabitants of Nineveh in ch. 3; and (4) with Yahweh again in ch. 4 (Nogalski 2011: 403).

### Themes and purpose of the book of Jonah

There are widely diverging opinions as to the purpose, themes and message of the book of Jonah. Simon (1999: vii–xiii) indicated four prominent themes that have been identified by various critics in the book of Jonah over its research history. They are:

*1. Atonement versus repentance* The Ninevites' repentance seems to be exemplary. Their repentance is accepted by the merciful God. Thus 'authentic repentance has the power to nullify the fatal decree' against them. However, if repentance was the central theme of the book of Jonah, we would expect to see it in the other episodes, beside Jonah 3, as well. The sailors are never described as transgressors, and only display great reverence for Yahweh (Simon 1999: viii).

*2. Universalism versus particularism* '[T]he book of Jonah is meant to extirpate the particularistic belief that regards the welfare of Israel as a supreme value and to assert that the prophet's love for his people must not keep him from fulfilling the mission imposed by the one universal God' (Simon 1999: viii). However, it is important to note that 'the book contains no condemnation of the sin of idolatry' (ibid.: x). To imply that Jonah symbolizes Israel and Nineveh the gentile world is based very much on an allegorical interpretation. Neither Israel, nor the kingdom of Assyria, is mentioned in the book. No mention is made of the Ninevites worshipping idols either. It would appear that the universalist view cannot be anchored in the text of the book of Jonah (ibid.).

3. *The realization versus compliance of prophecy*  This theme relates to Jonah's refusal to prophesy to the Ninevites and his anger at their deliverance. He is afraid that his credibility will be undermined if the destruction of Nineveh, which he prophesied, would not occur. However, 'there is no real sign in the book of Jonah of the prophet's anguish that his prediction did not come to pass, nor anything like this elsewhere in the Bible' (Simon 1999: xi).

4. *Compassion: justice versus mercy*  'Jonah argues on behalf of strict justice against the merciful God, who repents of His sentence.' Simon (1999: xii) then pointed out that '[O]nly when the proponent of strict justice realizes his own humanity can he understand the fundamental dependence of mortals on human and divine mercy'.

From the preceding it can be concluded that each of these themes had critique levelled against them. There is as yet then still no agreement as to the book of Jonah's purpose and message.

## Dating of the book of Jonah

Various dating has been proposed for the book of Jonah in the past,[12] however, in this contribution the book of Jonah is considered to most likely date from the late Persian Period, approximately during the fifth and early fourth centuries BCE (cf. Matthews 2012: 201). This author also considers it to have been written for the community living in Yehud (Schäder 2020: 2; cf. Ben Zvi 2003: 7–8; Handy 2007: 5, 6). Yehud (Judah) had a 'definable identity' as the area was at peace. The Persian Empire was probably compared to or regarded as the continuation of the Assyrian Empire. The book thus acquired authority during the Persian Period (Handy 2007: 6–7; Schäder 2020: 2). The legendary manner in which Nineveh is presented suggests a chronological distance. The book also appears to function as a parody on prophecy and presumes that the audience is familiar with the characteristics of biblical prophecy and the message of the biblical prophets (Bridge 2009: 116–17; Schäder 2020: 2).

## The author(s) and the audience of the book of Jonah

The book of Jonah was most likely written by a male scribe (or scribes) who was trained at Jerusalem and was responsible for writing many genres except short stories. It is likely this work was penned for the Yehudite literati who had a similar background than that of the scribe(s), and like them, had a vast biblical knowledge (see Schäder 2020: 3–4). Jonah

---

[12] There are two traditional chronological boundaries for the book of Jonah's dating. They are: (1) The eighth century BCE as the *terminus a quo* or the conservative estimate, based on the reference to a (historical?) prophet named Jonah in 2 Kings 14.23–25, who prophesied in the Northern Kingdom of Israel, during the reign of Jeroboam II (c. 750 BCE); and (2) the second century BCE as the *terminus ad quem* or the liberal estimate, based on a reference in Sir. 49.10 (c. 180 BCE) and Tob. 14.4 (c. 200 BCE) to the 'book of the Twelve' or the 'twelve prophets'. This implies that the book of Jonah might have been part of the prophetic canon by 180 BCE and could pre-date the Maccabean Period (Trible 1963: 104, 107; 1996: 466; cf. Sasson 1990: 21; Salters 1994: 23; Nogalski 2011: 1–2, 401–2).

and the Yehudite literati appear to have in common that they were both mediators or intermediaries between God and humans, or the Persian elite and commoners. They are considered to both be wealthy, to have a learned theology or education, and to have a shared knowledge of sacred texts (Schäder 2020: 5).

After this brief overview of the book of Jonah, we may now identify asymmetrical reciprocal exchanges within the book of Jonah itself and determine to what extent patron–client relationships are reflected in it.

## ASYMMETRICAL RECIPROCAL EXCHANGE IN THE BOOK OF JONAH

In this section, the relationship between Yahweh/God[13] and Jonah, and Yahweh/God with the foreigners will be discussed in the light of asymmetrical reciprocal exchange. It will be indicated how in each case there is a patron–client relationship with Yahweh/God at work. This will be followed by a short discussion on how the ungrateful Jonah serves as an unwilling broker between Yahweh and the foreigners.[14]

### *Asymmetrical exchange between Yahweh and Jonah*

It is typical to infer that the Jonah ben Amittai we read of in the book of Jonah is the same Jonah ben Amittai from Gath-hepher, active during the reign of Jeroboam son of Joash (787–747 BCE), mentioned in 2 Kgs 14.25 (Simon 1999: 4). If this is the case, we can assume an existing covenantal relationship between Jonah and Yahweh, as Jonah describes himself as a Hebrew (Jon. 1.9), representing the Israelites, namely Yahweh's chosen people.

However, the narrative commences with Jonah disobeying Yahweh's command to prophecy to the Ninevites. Instead, he flees to Tarshish (Jon. 1.3). Yahweh pursues him on the sea by causing a great storm (Jon. 1.4). Whilst the sailors pray for deliverance to their respective deities, Jonah is sleeping (1.5). Once awoken and bid to pray, it is revealed that he is the reason for the storm through divine intervention (i.e. lot casting; Jon. 1.7). Jonah answered the sailors' question as to what country and people he is from by stating what his ethnicity or tribal affiliation is, and who the deity is that he worships (Jon. 1.8-9). His answer is also the first instance that he speaks in the story, ironically with a confession of faith (Jon. 1.9):[15]

וַיֹּאמֶר אֲלֵיהֶם עִבְרִי אָנֹכִי וְאֶת־יְהוָה אֱלֹהֵי הַשָּׁמַיִם אֲנִי יָרֵא אֲשֶׁר־עָשָׂה אֶת־הַיָּם וְאֶת־הַיַּבָּשָׁה׃

And he said to them: 'I am a Hebrew, and Yahweh, the God of the heavens I fear, who made the sea and the dry land'.

---

[13] According to Bewer's (1971) famous hypothesis, the foreigners refer to God as אֱלֹהִים in the first three chapters and Jonah, the Hebrew, refers to him by his personal name יְהוָה ('Yahweh'). However, this does not appear to be consistently the case (cf. Trible 1963: 38; Salters 1994: 38).

[14] The word 'foreigners' is used to refer to the sailors and the Ninevites to place emphasis on their cultural designation in relation to that of Jonah. This is done instead of the traditional designation of 'gentiles', which places emphasis on their implied religious identity.

[15] Typical of Hebrew narrative technique, Jonah answers the last question of the sailors first. This is then an example of hysteron proteron ('last first') (Sasson 1990: 115).

The word עִבְרִי ('Hebrew') occurs thirty-five times in the Hebrew Bible. 'The word עִבְרִי is a gentilic adjective with the directive suffix יִ; this suffix is often added to names of people (i.e., Eber) and thereby converts them to tribal names' (Trible 1963: 23; cf. Snaith 1945: 18). It is postulated that עִבְרִי derives from the word עָבַר, 'to cross (over)'. It probably refers to those who lived in Eber (עֵבֶר, the land across the River (Euphrates?)). It also referred to the ethnic label associated with 'an eponymous ancestor, Eber, who was fourteen (twice seven) generations removed from Creation and who, according to Sethite genealogy, was the seventh descendant since Enoch' (Sasson 1990: 116). The Hebrews have also been associated with the *ḫabiru*; however, these peoples are not believed to have had an attachment to a specific city-state or distinct ethnicity. The term עִבְרִי was also attached to ancestors (Abraham, Joseph, Moses), in order to distinguish them from foreigners. Jonah labelling himself as a Hebrew may, then imply him distancing himself from the (foreign and other) sailors (Sasson 1990: 116–17; cf. Limburg 1993: 53; Angel 2006: 6, 11).[16] In some texts the term 'Hebrew' is even used by foreigners when referring to Israelites (by Egyptians, see Gen. 39.14, 39.17, 41.12; by Philistines, see 1 Sam. 4.6, 4.9, 13.19), or when a text marks a contrast between Israelites and other people (Gen. 43.32; Limburg 1993: 53).[17] It would appear that the terms Israelite and Hebrew are synonymous when used in the Hebrew Bible (Mendenhall 1996: 157). The Hebrew Bible also employs three distinct terms when referring to the inhabitants of Israel namely Israelite, Hebrew and Jew (from Yehudite; Sasson 1990: 115).[18] The use of 'Hebrew' may have been meant by the narrator to appeal 'to his audience's pride' (ibid.: 127). What is then clear is that the term 'Hebrew' is closely associated with Yahweh's power of salvation and his special bond with his people. Jonah defines himself narrowly in terms of a specific group occupying a specific territory, allotted to them by none other than Yahweh 'according to tradition and popular belief' (Prinsloo 2013: 20–1).

Jonah admits to fearing (revering) and being in an asymmetrical (generalized) reciprocal relationship with the creator deity Yahweh by mentioning his cultural identity. However, the irony of this confession is not lost on the reader. This deity he confesses his faith in controls all aspects of the world, namely the heavens, the seas and the dry land. Attempting to escape the presence of this deity is naturally futile. The epithet 'the God of the heavens' (אֱלֹהֵי הַשָּׁמַיִם)[19] occurs in Jon. 1.9 and is rare in older texts in the Hebrew Bible (Gen. 24.3, 7; Ps. 136.26). However, it is common in later books like Daniel, Ezra, Nehemiah, Chronicles and the apocryphal books of Judith and Tobias (Limburg 1993: 53; Simon 1999: xl).

When Jonah instructs the sailors to throw him overboard, and they eventually concede, in order for the storm and sea to stop raging, Yahweh sends a fish to save Jonah from drowning (Jon. 2.1). Jonah cannot repay Yahweh in kind (symmetrically) for saving him, but promises to sacrifice to him with a voice of thanksgiving (extolling his honour), and to pay the promises he made, i.e. vows (Jon. 2.10). However, there is no indication in the

---

[16] See, for example, Gen. 39.14, 17; 40.15; 41.12; 43.32; and Exod. 1.15, 16, 19; 2.7, 11, 13; 3.18; 5.3; 7.16; 9.1, 13; 10.3 (Angel 2006: 11).

[17] 'First Samuel 14.21 indicates that the class "Hebrews" includes more than Israelites. The expression "the LORD, the God of heaven" also occurs in Gen. 24.7 (24.3, "heaven and earth," Abraham speaks); 2 Chron. 36.23 and Ezra 1.2 (Cyrus speaks); and Neh. 1.5 (Nehemiah prays), thus always in direct address' (Limburg 1993: 53).

[18] See Sasson (1990: 115) for an elaboration on their etymological origins and brief discussion of their uses.

[19] In occurs in Hebrew in Neh. 1.4; 2.4; cf. Ps. 136.26, and in the Aramaic equivalent in Ezra 5.11, 12; 6.9, 10; 7.12, 21, 23 (twice), and Dan. 2.18, 19, 37, 44 (Limburg 1993: 53).

rest of the story that he indeed does so. He does praise Yahweh for being his source of salvation (Jon. 2.1) whilst in the fish, but not in a public domain for witnesses to hear.

In Jon. 2.9, Jonah states:

מְשַׁמְּרִים הַבְלֵי־שָׁוְא חַסְדָּם יַעֲזֹבוּ׃

Those who revere worthless idols, abandon their loyalty.

One of the expectations of the covenant between Yahweh and Israel is that they remain loyal and faithful to him alone, and not to worship idols. חֶסֶד ('loyalty/steadfast love') occurs 246 times in the Hebrew Bible and it refers to Yahweh's covenant mercy and loyalty towards his people. עָזַב ('to abandon') can be understood in a covenantal context. Israel is charged with abandoning the covenant (e.g. Deut. 29.25; Jer. 2.13, 17, 19, 22.9), and according to Hos. 4.10, the people have abandoned Yahweh. They are following other gods (cf. Hos. 1.2, 4.12). It would be impossible for the Israelites to repay God for the gifts of the covenant, therefore they have to be obedient and show their fidelity to God by abstaining from the worship of other deities (Exod. 20.3; Matthews 2007: 157–8). Like all goods, even gifts from God are limited (Malina 1998c: 90). That is probably why Jonah was angered at God's mercy to the Ninevites. Could this imply that there would be less for Israel? Nonetheless, the main character and the audience would have experienced this state of affairs as miscarried justice.

After his second calling Jonah responds with obedience and goes to Nineveh to prophesy against her (Jon. 3.3). Jonah delivers the required prophecy of doom to Nineveh (Jon. 3.4), but is angered when the Ninevites repent, and God shows them patronage in the form of mercy and pity (Jon. 3.10). Pity is in essence an act that cannot be repaid. In Jon. 4.2, Jonah states that he knows Yahweh's true nature, and that is why he fled from his commission:

וַיִּתְפַּלֵּל אֶל־יְהוָה וַיֹּאמַר אָנָּה יְהוָה הֲלוֹא־זֶה דְבָרִי עַד־הֱיוֹתִי עַל־אַדְמָתִי עַל־כֵּן קִדַּמְתִּי לִבְרֹחַ תַּרְשִׁישָׁה
כִּי יָדַעְתִּי כִּי אַתָּה אֵל־חַנּוּן וְרַחוּם אֶרֶךְ אַפַּיִם וְרַב־חֶסֶד וְנִחָם עַל־הָרָעָה׃

And he prayed to Yahweh, and he said: 'Oh, Yahweh! Was this not what I said while I was still in my own land? Therefore I was eager to flee to Tarshish, for I knew that you are a gracious and compassionate God, slow to anger and very loving, and feeling sorry over evil.'

The idiom 'gracious and compassionate' (חַנּוּן וְרַחוּם) is likely a diachronic chiasm in Jon. 4.2. Yahweh challenges Jonah whether it is reasonable for him to be angry when he displays patronage to *other* people, who in Jonah's mind, do not deserve it (Jon. 4.4). Jonah only replies to this question in Jon. 4.6. When God appointed the tiny plantlet to provide Jonah with shade, he was glad about it, but no thanks was offered for it in exchange. Jonah then comes across as an ungrateful client for the patronage that Yahweh has bestowed upon him, for saving him from death (cf. Jonah 2) and from his discomfort with the growth of the tiny plantlet (Jon. 4.6). Yahweh is then typically depicted as displaying the following attributes of a patron, namely graciousness, compassion, patience, love and mercy. Jonah in turn is disobedient and ungrateful. Incidentally it is these same attributes that Yahweh would display to the foreigners as well.

The Hebrew term for 'covenant' may not be used in the book of Jonah to describe the main character's relationship with his deity, but it is implied as there are expectations of Jonah from the outset of the narrative of what he is to do and how he should behave towards his divine superior. This relationship is implied to be anything but informal due to Jonah designating himself as a Hebrew, making the covenant stipulations applicable to him. The covenant between Israel (and Jonah) and Yahweh requires their continuous faithfulness (cf. Matthews 2007: 158). In Deut. 11.1 it is written 'You shall therefore love the Yahweh your God, and keep his charge, his statutes, his ordinances, and his commandments always'. Even though the God of Israel is authoritarian, requiring total submissiveness, he is also described as wielding 'steadfast love' and 'mercy' with those who are in a covenant with him (Malina 1998a: 13–14).

Whether a covenant is implied in the book of Jonah between Yahweh and Jonah, without the context of 2 Kgs 14.25, is questionable, but what is clear is that an asymmetrical reciprocal relationship and exchange exists between them. Yahweh then inherently functions as the divine patron to Jonah, the human client.

### *Asymmetrical exchange between Yahweh/God and foreigners*

In this section, the captain of the ship, the sailors, the king of Nineveh and the Ninevites are collectively referred to as the foreigners. Three of the five poetic prayers in the book of Jonah, were uttered by the captain of the ship (Jon. 1.6), the sailors (Jon. 1.14), and the king of Nineveh (Jon. 3.9) respectively.[20] They are as follows:

Jon. 1.6

אוּלַי יִתְעַשֵּׁת הָאֱלֹהִים לָנוּ וְלֹא נֹאבֵד׃

Perhaps this G/god will give thought to us so that we do not perish.

Jon. 1.14

אָנָּה יְהוָה אַל־נָא נֹאבְדָה בְּנֶפֶשׁ הָאִישׁ הַזֶּה וְאַל־תִּתֵּן עָלֵינוּ דָּם נָקִיא כִּי־אַתָּה יְהוָה כַּאֲשֶׁר חָפַצְתָּ עָשִׂיתָ׃

Oh, Yahweh! Please do not let us perish for this man's life. And do not give to us innocent blood, for you, Yahweh, as pleases you, you do.

Jon. 3.9

מִי־יוֹדֵעַ יָשׁוּב וְנִחַם הָאֱלֹהִים וְשָׁב מֵחֲרוֹן אַפּוֹ וְלֹא נֹאבֵד׃

Who knows?! He may turn back and God will feel sorry, and he will turn from his burning anger, so that we may not perish.

Each of these prayers occur before major changes in the narrative. The captain and the king of Nineveh's prayers share similarities in terms of theme, vocabulary and syntax. According to Trible (1994: 113), both of these prayers proclaim a theology of hope. Whereas Jon. 1.6 calls upon the help of no specific deity, this is not the case with the king's prayer where he utters it to the deity that called Jonah to prophesy against Nineveh. The collective theme of the prayers in Jon. 1.6, 1.14 and 3.9 is 'a quest for the preservation of life' (Potgieter 2004: 612).

The standard idiom of 'vowing a vow' occurs as וַיִּזְבְּחוּ־זֶבַח לַיהוָה וַיִּדְּרוּ נְדָרִים ('And they offered a sacrifice to Yahweh, and they made vows') in Jon. 1.16, pertaining to the sailors, and as וַאֲנִי בְּקוֹל תּוֹדָה אֶזְבְּחָה־לָּךְ אֲשֶׁר נָדַרְתִּי אֲשַׁלֵּמָה ('And I – I will sacrifice to you, with a voice of thanksgiving; what I have promised, I will pay') in Jon. 2.10, pertaining to Jonah.

The sailors first come to know about Yahweh when Jonah utters his confession in Jon. 1.9. They then fear Jonah's deity, as he caused the storm on the sea. Before they threw

---

[20] The other two poetic prayers are Jon. 2.3–10 and 4.2–3 and are both uttered by Jonah.

Jonah into the sea, they called to him in Jon. 1.14 as indicated above. They then pick Jonah up as he instructed and threw him overboard. Unintentionally they experience patronage when the sea ceases its raging. They then feared Yahweh greatly, and offered a sacrifice, and they made vows. There are two reasons why they are doing this. The first is in gratitude to the Yahweh who caused the storm to cease. The other is as a type of purification ritual for having thrown Jonah into the sea, to wash their hands of his death. It is unclear what becomes of the sailors after this, as they are fairly quickly faded from the scene. To argue that a covenant has been constituted between Yahweh and the sailors, because they made vows in public, is stretching the available information beyond what it probably intends to convey. Nonetheless they experience (unintended?) favour by following Jonah's advice, whereas the sailors by acting as clients experience patronage from Yahweh.

After being thrown overboard the ship, Jonah prays to Yahweh (וַיִּתְפַּלֵּל יוֹנָה) from the bowels of the fish (Jon. 2.2). After Nineveh is saved, he prays again (וַיִּתְפַּלֵּל אֶל־יְהוָה) in Jon. 4.2. Following upon the latter, we read three times that God appoints (וַיְמַן) three instruments (קִיקָיוֹן in Jon. 4.6; תּוֹלַעַת in Jon. 4.7 and רוּחַ קָדִים in Jon. 4.8) to do his bidding. This calls to mind God's appointing of the great fish (דָּג גָּדוֹל in 2.1). In this manner he is depicted as sovereign over nature as well.

Prior to Jonah 3, the only things we know of Nineveh is that it was a wicked city (Jon. 1.2), that Yahweh wanted Jonah to prophesy against her inhabitants, and that Jonah was unwilling to do so (Jon. 1.3). Nineveh is described in exaggerated terms (a great city that requires a three-day journey to cross), probably emphasizing its importance to Yahweh (cf. Jon. 1.2, 3.2, 3.3, 4.11). Jonah's prophecy of doom in Jon. 3.4 is as follows:

עוֹד אַרְבָּעִים יוֹם וְנִינְוֵה נֶהְפָּכֶת׃

Still forty days and Nineveh will be overturned!

Jonah proclaims that Nineveh will be overturned. This 'to turn, overthrow' (הָפַךְ) can be the destruction of the city, or it can mean that the city turns from her evil ways, i.e. repentance. It then appears that the inhabitants repent. To repent implies a change of heart, transformation or the broadening of boundaries. Halpern and Friedman (1980: 87) pointed out how Jonah did 'not fathom the delphic nature of his oracle'. Nineveh was indeed 'overturned' (נֶהְפָּכֶת), i.e. experienced a change of character, and not destruction, as Jonah intended to mean with his prophecy in Jon. 3.4. In essence, his prophecy was fulfilled.[21] According to Matthews (2012: 202), 'a righteous God is obliged to warn people of their failings before issuing a final judgment and imposing a sanction upon them (compare Amos 5.14–15; Joel 2.12–14)'. Whereas this warning is usually intended for the covenantal partner, this is now extended to the Ninevites. The moral change of the Ninevites is then expressed with the use of the word שׁוּב ('to return, bring back') in Jon. 3.10 (Simon 1999: 29).

The Ninevites and their animals partake in mourning rituals, by dressing in sackcloth, fasting and the king even throwing off his royal garb and sitting on ash. They do this in an attempt to avoid the destruction of the city (Jon. 3.5–8). In Jon. 3.9, they perceive this anonymous deity, who sent his prophet to deliver a prophecy of doom, as an angry one, not knowing that his attributes are mercy, compassion and patience (cf. Jon. 4.2). In

---

[21] The verb הָפַךְ denotes a change of character in 1 Sam. 10.6, 9 (cf. Exod. 14.5; Hos. 11.8; Lam. 1.20), and transformation in Deut. 23.6; Jer. 31.13; Amos 5.7; Ps. 30.12; and Neh. 13.2 (Halpern and Friedman 1980: 87).

reaction to their plight, God repents from his plan to destroy them. He acts to them as a patron showing mercy and pity to a client – the Ninevites and their animals – which they can never repay in kind. However, it is unclear how long Nineveh's repentance lasted, or how sincere it was, in the light of the book of Nahum's prophecy about its destruction.

In the cases of the foreigners, it is clear that covenants with Yahweh were not established, but that they experienced a one-off display of mercy, therefore patronage. There was no formal or legal agreement preceding their acts of sacrifice or repentance. Thus, there is no covenantal exchange present or implied. No doubt their implied reactions would be gratitude for being saved. What can be said about the salvation experienced by the Ninevites is that it would appear that Yahweh's mercy is conditional. In order to receive mercy, repentance must precede it, similar to Jonah praying to Yahweh in Jonah 2 and receiving deliverance from the fish. The withdrawal of Yahweh's pity or mercy is a sign of judgement – at least from what we know from the Israel's history. 'Any compassion God chooses to exercise with respect to that creation is a divine prerogative' (Matthews 2012: 205).

The sailors and Ninevites appear more compliant in behaving in a manner that is socially accepted of them in the circumstances that they find themselves in – being bestowed patronage by Yahweh – than the supposedly pious Jonah. They behave appropriately by bringing homage. The values pertaining to patron–client relationships dictated people how to act, and the foreigners act according to (Israelite/Hebrew) expectations.

Thus, from the above we can conclude that the foreigners, specifically collectively the sailors and the Ninevites, experiences asymmetrical reciprocity and patronage from the Hebrew God, Yahweh.

### Jonah, the unthankful client and unintentional broker

A broker is an individual who mediates between a patron and a client. 'Often a broker will function as a client to the ultimate patron and as a patron to the clients' (Esler 2006: 195). They thus 'sustains a double dyadic alliance' in this regard (Van Eck 1995: 232). An example of a broker is the mediating role of a prophet between God and his people (Esler 2006: 195). A broker then gives access to a patron (Malina 1998e: 154).

In the book of Jonah the character of Jonah functions as a non-kin to the sailors and Ninevites, and therefore does not deal with them as equals. Jonah can be considered to have inadvertently acted like a broker, mediating between Yahweh and the sailors, and God and the Ninevites. It is from him that the sailors and Ninevites first come to hear of Yahweh or God. Through a confession of faith and a prophecy of doom, he has triggered the reverence of the sailors and the mass repentance of the Ninevites. However, in both instances, it was done involuntary or unintentionally.

## SUMMARY AND CONCLUSION

In this chapter an overview of the types of reciprocity as proposed by Marshall Sahlins, followed by an overview of the adaptation of Sahlins's theory by Zeba A. Crook was provided. In turn, the distinction between covenantal exchange and patron–client relationships as examples of asymmetrical (generalized) reciprocal exchanges were discussed. This was then followed by an introductory overview of the book of Jonah.

What then proceeded was an application of asymmetrical reciprocity to the book of Jonah to determine the extent of its applicability to it.

Patron–client relationships dictated how people – and even the divine – conducted themselves in relations to each other, be it as kin or not. Based on the types of reciprocal exchanges identified by Crook, we can conclude that all reciprocal exchanges within the book of Jonah are asymmetrical, i.e. the relationship between a benefactor and a beneficiary that is open-ended and ongoing, as they are two individuals (or groups) of unequal social status, and that this patronage is not limited to Jonah alone, but also to the foreigners, namely the sailors and Ninevites. However, just like the Hebrews and Israelites, the foreigners cannot repay Yahweh in kind. They are also subservient clients to the giver, very much like Jonah is.

In this contribution it was pointed out how there is an implied covenant between Yahweh and Jonah as Jonah is taken to be a representative of Israel, Yahweh's chosen people, when the book is read in the light of the Jonah character being the same as the one mentioned in 2 Kgs 14.25. However, in his capacity as covenant partner, Yahweh also functions as patron, whereas Jonah is his client. Contrary to the foreigners that make vows and offer prayers to Yahweh or God, Jonah only makes the promise to do so (see Jonah 2) and is not described as fulfilling his word.

The type of reciprocal exchange between Yahweh and the foreigners is that of a patron–client relationship. Even though vows are made, this is not considered to be signs of a formal contract or instituting of a covenant with Yahweh, but rather is a sign of their gratefulness for the one-off act of mercy and salvation they experience.

Jonah, in turn, functions as an involuntary and unwilling broker between Yahweh and the foreigners that inadvertently made mercy towards and salvation of the foreigners possible.

What is clear from the preceding is that asymmetrical exchange appears in the Hebrew Bible, and then specifically between Jonah and the foreigners with Yahweh. Yahweh stands in a clear asymmetrical reciprocal relationship with both Jonah and Ninevites as they are his clients and are the two parties from which he has expectations that need to be fulfilled. Jonah is reluctant to do as Yahweh commands of him, but the Ninevites jump at the opportunity to change their ways and to comply with the threat of destruction.

In the light of the Persian Period dating of the book of Jonah, we can conclude that there is an element of universalism, where the foreigners are granted access to Yahweh/God. Certain circumstances and conditions were either stipulated or implied in order for them to be granted patronage, such as repentance. It would then appear that there is a doctrine of retribution at play in this book. Nonetheless, even (former) oppressors of Israel were awarded compassion when they prayed to God and turned from their wicked ways (see Jon. 3.8).

Could it then be that the book of Jonah serves as a critique on the covenantal relationship, or at least the asymmetrical reciprocal relationship, that is limited to the Israelites (or Yehudites) and Yahweh alone? Is this exclusive relationship being challenged? This would appear to be a possibility in the light of even foreigners being on the receiving end of Yahweh's patronage and their client-like behaviour.[22]

---

[22] Read in the light of a text such as Psalm 82 reinforces such a notion.

# REFERENCES

Allen, C.J., ed. (1972), *Hosea-Malachi*, Broadman Bible Commentary 7, Nashville, TN: Broadman Press.

Angel, H. (2006), '"I Am a Hebrew!" Jonah's Conflict with God's Mercy Toward Even the Most Worthy of Pagans', *JBQ*, 34 (1): 3–11.

Ben Zvi, E. (2003), *Signs of Jonah: Reading and Rereading in Ancient Yehud*, JSOTSup 367, London: Sheffield Academic Press.

Bewer, J.A. (1971), *A Critical and Exegetical Commentary on Jonah*, ICC, Edinburgh: T&T Clark.

Bolin, T.M. (2004), 'The Role of Exchange in Ancient Mediterranean Religion and Its Implications for Reading Genesis 18–19', *JSOT*, 29 (1): 37–56.

Botha, P.J. (2001), 'Social Values and the Interpretation of Psalm 123', *OTE*, 14 (2): 189–98.

Bridge, S.L. (2009), *Getting the Old Testament: What It Meant to Them, What It Means for Us*, Peabody, MA: Hendrickson.

Crook, Z.A. (2006), 'Reciprocity: Covenantal Exchange as a Test Case', in P.F. Esler (ed.), *Ancient Israel: The Old Testament in Its Social Context*, 78–91, Minneapolis, MN: Fortress Press.

Cross, F.M. (1998), *From Epic to Canon: History and Literature in Ancient Israel*, Baltimore, MD: Johns Hopkins University Press.

deSilva, D.A. (2000), *Honor, Patronage, Kinship and Purity: Unlocking New Testament Culture*, Downers Grove, IL: InterVarsity Press.

Elliott, J.H. (1993), *What Is Social-Scientific Criticism?*, Minneapolis, MN: Fortress Press.

Elliot, J.H. (1996), 'Patronage and Clientage', in R. Rohrbaugh (ed.), *The Social Sciences and New Testament Interpretation*, 144–56, Peabody, MA: Hendrickson.

Esler, P.F. (2006), '2 Samuel – David and the Ammonite War: A Narrative and Social-Scientific Interpretation of 2 Samuel 10–12', in P.F. Esler (ed.), *Ancient Israel: The Old Testament in Its Social Context*, 191–207, Minneapolis, MN: Fortress Press.

Foster, S.J. (2006), 'A Prototypical Definition of בְּרִית, "Covenant" in Biblical Hebrew', *OTE*, 19 (1): 35–46.

Glaze, A.J. (1972), 'Jonah', in C.J. Allen (ed.), *Hosea-Malachi*, 152–82, Broadman Bible Commentary 7, Nashville, TN: Broadman Press.

Halpern, B. and R.E. Friedman (1980), 'Composition and Paronomasia in the Book of Jonah', *HAR*, 4: 79–92.

Handy, L.K. (2007), *Jonah's World: Social Science and the Reading of Prophetic Story*, New York: Routledge.

Limburg, J. (1993), *Jonah: A Commentary*, OTL, London: SCM Press.

Linington, S. (2002), 'The Term בְּרִית in the Old Testament, Part I: An Enquiry into the Meaning and Use of the Word in the Contexts of the Covenants Between God and Humans in the Pentateuch', *OTE*, 15 (3): 687–714.

Malina, B.J. (1998a), 'Authoritarianism', in J.J. Pilch and B.J. Malina (eds), *Handbook of Biblical Social Values*, 12–19, Peabody, MA: Hendrickson.

Malina, B.J. (1998b), 'Faith/Faithfulness', in J.J. Pilch and B.J. Malina (eds), *Handbook of Biblical Social Values*, 72–5, Peabody, MA: Hendrickson.

Malina, B.J. (1998c), 'Grace/Favor', in J.J. Pilch and B.J. Malina (eds), *Handbook of Biblical Social Values*, 89–92, Peabody, MA: Hendrickson.

Malina, B.J. (1998d), 'Gratitude (Debt of)', in J.J. Pilch and B.J. Malina (eds), *Handbook of Biblical Social Values*, 92–4, Peabody, MA: Hendrickson.

Malina, B.J. (1998e), 'Patronage', in J.J. Pilch and B.J. Malina (eds), *Handbook of Biblical Social Values*, 151–5, Peabody, MA: Hendrickson.

Malina, B.J. (1998f), 'Pity', in J.J. Pilch and B.J. Malina (eds), *Handbook of Biblical Social Values*, 157–8, Peabody, MA: Hendrickson.

Matthews, V.H. (2007), 'Social Sciences', in V.H. Matthews, *Studying the Ancient Israelites: A Guide to Sources and Methods*, 123–58, Grand Rapids, MI: Baker Academic.

Matthews, V.H. (2012), *The Hebrew Prophets and their Social World: An Introduction*, 2nd edn, Grand Rapids, MI: Baker Academic.

Mendenhall, G.E. (1996), 'The Hebrew Conquest of Palestine' [1962], in C.E. Carter and C.L. Meyers (eds), *Community, Identity, and Ideology: Social Science Approaches to the Hebrew Bible*, 152–69, Winona Lake, IN: Eisenbrauns.

Nogalski, J.D. (1993), *Redactional Processes in the Book of the Twelve*, BZAW 218, Berlin: De Gruyter.

Nogalski, J.D. (2011), *The Book of the Twelve: Hosea-Jonah*, Smyth & Helwys Bible Commentary 18a, Macon, GA: Smyth & Helwys.

Olyan, S.M. (1996), 'Honor, Shame, and Covenant Relations in Ancient Israel and Its Environment', *JBL*, 115 (2): 201–18.

Pfoh, E. (2013), 'Loyal Servants of the King: A Political Anthropology of Subordination in Syria Palestine (ca. 1600–600 BCE)', *Palamedes: A Journal of Ancient History*, 8: 25–41.

Pilch, J.J. (1998), 'Compassion', in J.J. Pilch and B.J. Malina (eds), *Handbook of Biblical Social Values*, 30–3, Peabody, MA: Hendrickson.

Potgieter, J.H. (1991), *'n Narratologiese Ondersoek van die Boek Jona*, Hervormde Teologiese Studies Supplementum 3, Pretoria: Nederduitsch Reformed Church of Africa / Faculty of Theology (Section A), University of Pretoria.

Potgieter, J.H. (2004), 'The Nature and Function of the Poetic Sections in the Book of Jonah', *OTE*, 17 (4): 610–20.

Prinsloo, G.T.M. (2013), 'Place, Space and Identity in the Ancient Mediterranean World: Theory and Practice with Reference to the book of Jonah', in G.T.M. Prinsloo and C.M. Maier (eds), *Constructions of Space V: Place, Space and Identity in the Ancient Mediterranean World*, 3–25, LHBOTS 576, London: Bloomsbury.

Sahlins, M. (2017 [1972]), *Stone Age Economics*, London: Routledge Classics.

Salters, R.B. (1994), *Jonah and Lamentations*, OTG, Sheffield: Sheffield Academic Press.

Sasson, J.M. (1990), *Jonah: A New Translation with Introduction, Commentary, and Interpretation*, ABC, New York: Doubleday.

Schäder, J.-M. (2010), 'Patronage and Clientage Between God, Israel and the Nations: A Social-Scientific Investigation of Psalm 47', *Journal for Semitics*, 19 (1): 235–62.

Schäder, J.-M. (2020), 'A Social-Scientific Analysis of the Representation of Jonah and the Self-Perception of the Yehudite Literati During the Late Persian Period', *Journal for Semitics*, 29 (2). Available online: https://doi.org/10.25159/2663-6573/7818 (accessed 11 July 2022).

Simon, U. (1999), *Jonah* יונה, The JPS Bible Commentary, Philadelphia, PA: Jewish Publication Society.

Snaith, N.H. (1945), *Notes on the Hebrew Text of Jonah*, London: Epworth Press.

Spronk, K. (2009), 'Jonah, Nahum, and the Book of the Twelve: A Response to Jakob Wöhrle', *JHebS*, 9: art. 8. Available online: https://jhsonline.org/index.php/jhs/article/download/6237/5265 (accessed 11 July 2022).

Stansell, G. (1999), 'The Gift in Ancient Israel', in R.A. Simkins and S.L. Cook (eds), *The Social World of the Hebrew Bible: Twenty-Five Years of Social Sciences in the Academy*, 65–90, Semeia 87, Atlanta, GA: Scholars Press.

Stegemann, E.W. and W. Stegemann (1999), *The Jesus Movement: A Social History of Its First Century*, Minneapolis, MN: Fortress Press.

Trible, P.L. (1963), 'Studies in the Book of Jonah', PhD diss., Columbia University.

Trible, P.L. (1994), *Rhetorical Criticism: Context, Method, and the Book of Jonah*, Minneapolis, MN: Fortress Press.

Trible, P.L. (1996), 'The Book of Jonah: Introduction, Commentary, and Reflections', in N.M. Alexander et al. (eds), *The New Interpreter's Bible Volume VII*, 463–529, Nashville, TN: Abingdon Press.

Van Eck, E. (1995), *Galilee and Jerusalem in Mark's Story of Jesus: A Narratological and Social Scientific Reading*, Hervormde Teologiese Studies Supplementum 7, Pretoria: University of Pretoria.

Westbrook, R. (2005), 'Patronage in the Ancient Near East', *JESHO*, 48 (2): 210–33.

CHAPTER FIFTEEN

# Neither divide nor continuum

*Orality and literacy in the Hebrew Bible*

ROBERT D. MILLER II

In the twentieth century, biblical scholars wrangled and refuted over just when ancient Israel became literate. In other words, the heuristic model for discussions of 'oral tradition' was something that illiterate societies had, tales that were handed down orally until writing was discovered and then they were written. Alongside the argument of when literacy arose were claims presented for one text or another out of the Hebrew Bible being 'originally oral tradition' and later written down. Oral tradition, in that view, would be about the *forerunners* of the Bible, bits of 'pre-Bible', fragments only.

All of this picture is false. It is false first because there was no single 'discovery' of writing (Macdonald 2005: 49–50; Carr 2008: 121).[1] Writing was known in Palestine long before the twelfth century BCE, albeit not by Israelites. From almost the earliest Israelite settlement in the twelfth and eleventh centuries, there are inscriptions, including scribal exercises, although very few (Rollston 2008: 61–3). Of the multitude of seals excavated from the tenth and ninth centuries, not one is inscribed (Sanders 2008: 103–4). The ability to write one's name and draw up receipts is widespread by the eighth century (Rollston 2010: xvi; 2015: 88). By the seventh century, even common soldiers and property owners could write letters (Rollston 2010: 95, 133; 2015: 76–9). Yet there is not a single narrative piece of writing from the entire pre-exilic period. Epigraphic remains from Palestine are primarily ostraca, and most ostracon texts are ephemeral letters or economic documents.[2] Literature could not be accommodated by ostraca. Writing, even when known, does not seem to have been thought of as appropriate for literature, nor for hymnody, prophetic narrative, wisdom or law (Macdonald 2005: 53, 63; Wicomb 2018: 75–6).

That disinclination may have been due to what is a far more important reason that we should abandon the older model of oral tradition: peoples do not become reading societies upon achieving literacy (Macdonald 2005: 64–7). Historians of Israel and elsewhere have now acknowledged the anthropological work, both from fieldwork as well as from

---

[1] The acquisition of reading need not even accompany the acquisition of writing; see Macdonald 2005: 52–3.
[2] Given the ongoing debates about its contents, I am not considering the Khirbet Qeiyafa ostracon in this discussion. I do not consider it to be Hebrew in any case.

analysing texts that circulated orally, that must demolish the notion of a 'Great Divide' between two mutually exclusive media, oral and written (Carr 2005: 159–62; Egilsdóttir 2006: 215; Niditch 2008: 18; Miller 2011: 20–1; Wicomb 2018: 67). That binary opposition is a misleading, reductive approximation. Many societies produced oral and written literature simultaneously (Carr 2005: 6–7).[3] In fact, preliterate societies are *not* the most common source of oral literature. Most of the oral literature we possess and analyse was not collected from purely oral cultures. Some of this literature was collected from societies that have recently become literate but preserve much orality, but there are also many societies that have been literate from antiquity where oral literature has continued to flourish (Macdonald 2005: 74–8; Nagy 2009: 172).

Writing often supports oral tradition and vice versa. In other words, written texts circulated in oral form long after they were committed to writing; and those oral forms could be then modified into other oral forms that were not in writing, or that were put in writing some time afterwards (Harris 2016: 13; Friedrich 2019: 183). On the other hand, reading-and-writing often has a different social location than oral tradition: some genres are considered appropriate for writing, while others are not, and it is not a matter of length or textual complexity (Macdonald 2005: 63). So we cannot even speak of a 'continuum' between oral cultures and literate cultures, since there is no single spot on that continuum to place any entire society.

In ancient Egypt and Mesopotamia, audiences who knew how to read still preferred and even expected to experience their *literature* orally (Afanasjeva 1976: 123, 126–30, 135; Hodge 1989: 412, 414). Ancient Israel, even after the Exile, when a largely literate Jewish population returned to Judah, also expected to encounter their literature aurally, in performance (Gitay 2011: 37, 47). Israel and Judah were what David Carr calls an 'oral-written culture'.[4] In oral-written cultures, oral tales that circulated from bard to audience or bard to bard could be recorded in writing; they could be consulted by writers; they could be consulted by oral composers of other stories (Engnell 1969: 7, 65; Colbert 1989: 66; Wendland 2013: 95; Ready 2019: 18).

Scrolls had no spaces between words, no offset poetic lines, no chapter and verse breaks, which would have made them highly reader-unfriendly manuscripts.[5] 'An Israelite could read a book with ease only if he had previously heard it' (Levin 1995: 188, 204). In all the descriptions of texts being read in the Bible, with only one exception (2 Kings 22) it is always a text being read by a person who had already heard it (Levin 1995: 213). Even what we have written in the Bible had to be rendered orally by reciters, whether we think of them as bards or Levitical Temple priests (Wendland 2013: 84). They rendered them orally in performances, interpretive contexts mandated by tradition, to which we shall return shortly (Carr 2010: 33).

---

[3] This was recognized already by Ahlström (1966: 70); and McLuhan (1999: 139).
[4] In a fully literate society, references to all kinds of writing by all kinds of people are ubiquitous. Consider in Rome, Plautus, *Mercator*, 405–409 'My doors would be full of elegies scrawled in charcoal'; Cicero, *In Verrem* 3.2.77 'Couplets were constantly being scribbled over the dais'; and similar quips in Plutarch, *Tiberius Gracchus* 8.7; *Gaius Gracchus* 17.6; Seneca, *Suasoriae* 1.6; Cassius Dio, *Roman History* 55.27.1–2, 61.16.2a; discussed in Slater 2014.
[5] Levin 1995: 186–87, 190; Wendland 2013: 15; Cassuto 2014: 39; Edzard 2014: 52. Evans (2017: 753–4) believes such scepticism about reading vowelless, run-on scrolls is anachronistic (or ethnocentric). Levin argues the Masoretic pointing of the Hebrew Bible preserves most of ancient Israel's pronunciation. While it may well retain much from the Second Temple Period of the first century (see Khan 2018), it is impossible to say it stretches back to the biblical period.

If we have removed the notion of a Great Divide between oral tradition and literate writing, and if we also consider that the Hebrew Bible – or nearly all of it – never ceased to be performed orally in an oral-and-written society, then clearly any pursuit of 'which passages' were originally oral is misguided. Indeed, biblical scholars' continued recourse to 'oral formulaic' tests for orality based on the work of Milman Perry and Albert Lord, or even more problematically to Axel Olrik's 'epic laws' of a century ago, is lamentable (e.g. Chi 2018: 109, 112).

Our focus on this implied audience, encountering the text orally and often both orally and in writing, requires 'Performance Criticism' (Wendland 2013: 31). In order to study the biblical text within its local context of settings and participants, we will want to investigate who the implied audience is, how they are addressed and by whom: a performative schema (Ready 2019: 17). Different performative schemas would have existed for different genres, but those schemas were accepted and understood according to social and cultural conventions familiar to the original performer and audience (Hymes 1964: 16; Sherzer 1990: 119; Frog, Koski and Savolainen 2016: 24–5). Linguists and anthropologists recognize that all texts emerge in contexts in which they were actually employed, and that these contexts emerge in 'negotiations' between participants in social interactions (Sowayan 1985: 123; Shepherd 2016: 191). Governing conditions of performance like location, possible musical settings, instrumental accompaniment, gestures and much more will determine the kinds of performative schemas any society will generate (Hymes 1964: 19; King 1991; Harris 2016: 14; Shepherd 2016: 35; Patron 2018: 41). Performance Criticism focuses on the event or the dynamic complex of action of a performance. The meaning of the performance depends, then, not on some strict recitation of a text, but on a sort of social game, an interplay between a specific text, the individual performers, the setting and physical elements of the performance, and the customary performance practices that the audience expected (Busoni 1986: 208–9; King 1991: 1, 8, 19; Borges 2000: 491; Shepherd 2016: 39, 192).

The Hebrew Bible itself has almost no accounts of performances (Harris and Reichl 2012: 143). There are some depictions; these cannot be taken as necessarily historically accurate but will remain an important resource (Bergman 1979). Yet hints of performance are embedded in the text, as scribes who 'performed' the writing of the texts were usually individuals also involved in their performance (Tarkka 1993: 173; Wendland 2013: 79).

Performative schemas can also be reconstructed on the basis of evidence from other societies of the ancient Near East (Shehata 2009: 378). Yet we will also depend on ethnographic analogy: looking at societies elsewhere in history that shared the same level of literacy and the same balance of oral and written literature as ancient Israel (Zerubavel 2003: 29). As the folklorist Lauri Honko writes, 'The only way out of this dilemma seems to be more and better empirical studies on living oral epic traditions, a careful comparison of the results and their cautious application to other epics whose performance contexts will always remain poorly known but may be elucidated with the help of comparisons' (Honko 1996: 2; cf. Thomas 2005: 5). Biblical scholars have long looked to Iceland for these analogies, and with good reason, as Iceland holds many parallels to the oral-and-written world of ancient Israel (Barstad 2013: 13). As with Israel, the original contexts of composition and recitation of Icelandic literature are lost to us, only reconstructed from scenes found in the text itself, which are much later than the material's origin (Miller 2011: 31–5). As with the Hebrew Bible, Icelandic sagas and poetry drew on both oral poems and written stories, with writers deeply indebted to written material still dependent on oral tradition (Colbert 1989: 155, 158; Harris 2016: 13).

Performative schemas will differ greatly from genre to genre (Shehata 2009: 370). Nevertheless, societies of the world by and large have qualities that are common to all of their performances, regardless of genre. So some general observations are possible about the performance locations, performers, vocal elements, music and gesture of ancient Israelite performance as a whole.

Not all performance depends on a single venue; the same tales could be told in the back room of the Israelite four-roomed village house as in the court of the King of Israel in Samaria (although in some cultures certain kinds of tales are forbidden in certain seasons; Propp 2012: 306). What a performer could do in a performance is always going to be constricted by that space. Or to put it differently, the performative schema is a relationship that emerges between the space and the performer, between what the performer wants to do and what that place of performance means to the audience, its cultural resonance (McAuley 2003: 602–3, 611; Pasqualino 2008: 112). The ways in which the space imposes its reality on the performance extend far beyond physical constraints to include collective memory.

We need to consider also the performer themselves. Oral performers' behaviours are external components of the non-verbal part of the performative schema (Poyatos 2002: 338). Performers also have what Fernando Poyatos calls 'Personal sensible behavioral nonactivites', which include jewellery, body marking and clothing – and we should think here not so much of costume, as this was rare, but things like tightness of dress, appearances of self-neglect, cloaks that make distinctive sound when rustling, and so on (Poyatos 2002: 333–4; Braun 2011: 24). Poyatos's work is important, as he emphasizes that the performative schema is not a list of location, performer, techniques etc., but 'a continuum formed by verbal and nonverbal, behavioral and nonbehavioral' (Poyatos 2002: 346). Some of these will not even be consciously noticed, at least not by everyone present.

If, following Poyatos, we think of clothing as a sensible body-related personal component, then what one does with the body are sensible bodily personal components (Poyatos 2002: 328; Ready 2019: 23). Some of these are proxemics, or ways performance is constricted physically by performance space. Others are paralanguage (throat clearing, silences) and kinesics, body movements (Gerson-Kiwi 1961: 64; Hymes 1964: 25; Sherzer 1990: 31; Nord 2005: 876). The latter may be pantomime, actual expression of narration through body movements, but more often would be less explicit: slapping one's thigh, raising an arm (Pasqualino 2008: 112). These, too, will be dictated by convention.[6]

We should first of all resist drawing a sharp distinction between song and oratory (Sherzer 1990: 22). Even Greek writers like Aristotle's student Aristoxenos who discussed the difference between the two described it as a difference of degree, not kind (Winn 1981: 4). Certainly there was Hebrew musical poetry, as in the Psalms. The Prophets are also poetry. Even the narratives of Exodus and Judges, however, were probably more what musicians call Sprechstimme, midway between speech and song (Sherzer 1990: 27). Each genre probably had its own unique place on the continuum between speech and song (Gerson-Kiwi 1961: 64; Lomax 1968: 6).

Some scholars have stressed the importance of considering the rhythmic qualities of the declaimed Hebrew itself, since human beings detect rhythm as naturally as we detect changes in loudness or pitch (Lundin 1985: 113; Cohen, Douaire and Elsabbagh

---

[6] Already Wundt (1973 [1921]: 66), who greatly influenced early biblical scholars of orality.

2001: 75). Unfortunately, different societies identify different elements of speech as quantifiable – sometimes stresses, sometimes syllables – and scholars disagree widely about the rhythms of spoken ancient Hebrew (Keefer 2016: 45–58). Even at its most poetic, in the Psalms, no metre was employed, but rather free rhythmic poetry in lines of limited length variability (Dobbs-Allsopp 2015: 103, 120, 122–3, 125).

If there is little agreement among scholars about the rhythm of declaimed Hebrew, even less can be said with certainty about pitch, tone of voice and so on, although we know pitches were already classified in ancient Mesopotamia (Brown 2003: 209). Not only does every culture have its own distinct style of singing and chanting, but even the most basic categories for describing vocal sound in one culture might not be relevant for another ('Voice', in Randel 2003: 962), and include many things that we have no ordinary way of describing ('Singing Style', in Randel 2003: 783). Preferences in timbre, register, tessitura and tone quality vary vastly between societies (Flender 1992: 79).

Ancient Near Eastern texts describe harp accompaniment as part of performative schemas. In Greece, bards are depicted with lyres on vases and in the Homeric epics (Winn 1981: 14–15). The same was true in Mesopotamia (Shehata 2009: 368). In Mesopotamia, different genres and different performers employed different instruments: priests used a membranophone called a *balağ* (Shehata 2009: 368; Human 2011: 47). Numerous passages in the Hebrew Bible suggest a similar situation in ancient Israel (Human 2011: 47–8).

Lamentably, scholarship on 'music of the Bible' has been plagued with well-intentioned nonsense for centuries. From early rabbinic literature through to the twentieth century, unscientific arguments based entirely on the wording of the text ignored both archaeological evidence of actual instruments and their depiction, and the literature of the surrounding ancient Near East (Braun 2011: 24, 43, 74; Montagu 2017: 8; Dumbrill 2019: 13). Thus, although their neighbours and predecessors had them, there were no lutes or harps in ancient Israel – none until the Roman period (Manniche 2006; Braun 2011: 35, 129–31, 398, 400). The Hebrew nebel is not a harp but a lyre, as is the older, smaller *kinnôr* (Braun 2002: 18, 23, 2011: 43; Montagu 2002: 145–6).

The most commonly played instrument was the lyre, used for nearly every genre of literature and by a wide variety of performers (Gen. 4.21, 31.27; 1 Sam. 10.5, Job 30.31), but especially priests (Ps. 33.2, 92.3; 1 Chron. 13.8, 15.16, 25.1; 2 Chron. 20.28; Braun 2002: 17, 2011: 35, 45). According to the records and artistic depictions of the Assyrian King Sennacherib, who took captives from late eighth-century BCE Judah as well as receiving heavy tribute from its king, Hezekiah, lyre players were considered highly valuable (Braun 2011: 35).

The round frame drum or *tof* is attested throughout the ancient Near East (Braun 2002: 30; 2011: 96–8). Based on both the biblical text and almost a hundred terracotta figurines, it was uniquely a woman's instrument (Exod. 15.20–21; Judg. 11.34; 1 Sam. 18.6–7; Braun 2002: 118; Riley 2014: 26, 28, 30).

Each genre of the Hebrew Bible, however, needs to be treated on its own to reconstruct performative schemas more thoroughly.

## NARRATIVE

The narratives of the Hebrew Bible are dramatic. First, they use direct speech: 'Abraham said, "My son"' – indirect speech is rare (Licht 1990: 39). Second, a great many details are missing; there is no attempt at mimesis, leaving the performer to fill a lot out (Licht

1990: 64; Mathieu 2018: 150).[7] On the other hand, duplications abound, as source critics have known for centuries. But the oral-and-written nature of ancient Israel suggests another possible explanation for duplications. Antony Campbell writes, 'Texts do not always tell stories but on occasion (by including variant versions) enable stories to be told' (2004: 31). In other words, duplicate text may in some cases be presenting options that the reader or reciter was supposed to choose from in each reading (Gitay 2011: 38).

Texts are strategically selected and refigured in each oral performance, even when there are written copies already in existence.[8] In the earlier stages of the assembly of Hebrew Bible, no doubt writing down of performances took place, as in Mesopotamia (Smith 2015: 8). A given passage of the Hebrew Bible might, therefore, represent one particularly memorable ancient performance, or numerous performances as well as annotations of a later editor (Walton 2017).[9]

Nevertheless, even the latest parts of the Pentateuch, which might have been composed in writing, were performed orally (Engnell 1969: 66). Early on, this might have been quite theatrical, as we have seen (Mathieu 2018: 141, 149).[10] But even when this was no longer the primary means of performing the text, oral performance continued.

David Carr argues that what appear to be aural variants in the account of Hezekiah resisting Sennacherib in 2 Kings, 2 Chronicles, and Isaiah are evidence of ongoing oral performance, at times misheard (Carr 2015: 165). Yet, William Tooman has shown not every 'memory variant' is the result of hearing. 'Dissimilarity appears to have been a prominent and productive feature of communication-replication in ancient Hebrew literature' (Tooman 2019: 109), and dissimilarity generated by writers reading written texts 'are identical to types of dissimilarity that [. . .] Carr identif[ies] as aural- or memory-variants' (ibid.: 110). Tooman acknowledges there certainly were oral/aural variants along with writers' dissimilarities; it is just that we have no way of knowing 'the medium from which the source of a replication is drawn' (ibid.).

To reconstruct performance contexts for Israelite oral prose and narrative poetry, ancient Near Eastern evidence helps a great deal, but ethnography will be another important means to reconstruct performative schemas.[11]

In ancient Egypt, it is first necessary to remove 'audience-less' performances, the large number of attested performances that were put on only for the gods. Alongside these, there are performances of personal memoires, humorous morality tales and eulogizing of the king that involve 'reciting'. The setting is usually the royal court, minstrels are depicted in stylized 'rapt' poses, and the performer and audience together influence the composition. The fullest presentation of a performative schema is in the Middle Kingdom text 'King Cheops and the Magicians' from *Papyrus Westcar*. In the court of Pharaoh Khufu (Cheops), the story goes, 'The king's son Khafra arose [to speak, and he said: I should like to relate to your majesty] another marvel, one which happened in the time of [your] father, Nebka'

---

[7] Mathieu (2018: 145) presents a model for a staged performance of the story of Abimelech in Judges 9 that he believes belongs to the original text.
[8] Nagy 2009: 171; Wicomb 2018: 75; Smith 2015: 10, for examples from India and suggestions vis-à-vis the Homeric corpus.
[9] Harris 2016: 16, illustrates this for Icelandic literature.
[10] Also Tarkka 1993: 183, for the Nordic world; Afanasjeva 1976: 123, for Mesopotamia (Epic of Gilgamesh).
[11] Evans (2017: 755–6) suggests performance critics have imagined audiences on little basis. The contrary will be shown herein. See also Person (2018).

(1.16–20). He then tells a sort of 'marvel tale'. This is followed by, 'Bauefre arose to speak, and he said: Let me have [your] majesty hear a marvel which took place in the time of your father King Snefru' (4.18–20). There are two more such tales, each is accompanied by a favourable response from Khufu, which encourages and moulds the performance of the next one. Although we cannot assume this is an accurate record of real events, we see here a depiction of a court setting and an interplay between audience and poet.

Within various Mesopotamian narrative texts, there are numerous prologues like 'I will sing. . .' and epilogues such as 'This is a ballad in praise of . . .' or 'Whoever recites this text . . . .' The mythical *Atrahasis* epic, which contains a flood story much like Genesis, is written 'for singing'. Harps (*sammû*) and lyres are often depicted in such performative schemas. In the city of Mari, *mushtawum* minstrel poets were employed to compose and recite epic praise poetry for the king (Ziegler 2010: 127–8). We also see, however, an interplay of performance and writing. A story could be performed orally while a written form was composed from the performance on the spot (Jacobsen 1982: 131, citing the Kesh Temple Hymn).

A Canaanite Ivory plaque from Megiddo around 1200 BCE illustrates a scene reminiscent of Khufu's court, here with a lyre accompanying the rhapsode (Carter 1995: 297, 300–4). Jane Carter argues cogently that this represents the same recitation of epic poetry about heroes as found in the Homeric epics (ibid.: 307). She also argues that it is precisely the kind of performance depicted (and denounced) in Amos 6.4–7 (ibid.: 302–3).

There are accounts of performances found in some Icelandic sagas, but these must be used cautiously as they reveal only the authors' portrayal of performance. Nevertheless, those saga descriptions of performance are very similar to the ancient Near Eastern evidence. We see the audience–speaker interaction, the court setting and even the harp (Faulkes 1993: 16).

With caution we can examine the Bible's own picture of oral performance. Narrative recitation seems to have been accompanied in particular by the *kinnôr* lyre. The lyre was performed at the feasts envisioned by Isa. 5.12, and the scene looks much like that in *Papyrus Westcar* or as in Iceland.

# LAW

Most scholars understand that written law did not play a major role in the ancient Near East. We have no law codes from the Levant and the actual use of Mesopotamian 'law codes' is unproven. A good case can be made that those so-called codes were school texts, while the actual state law was customary law, oral with some written memory aids and display texts (Lemche 1995).

Textual depictions of judicial process, as Bernard Jackson writes, 'conspicuously omit any reference to the application of written rules' (Jackson 1999: 816; see Meyer 2017: 62). Even in late texts, criminal justice is based on prior decisions, not code but *stare decisis* (Falk 1964: 29).[12] David's judgement for the woman of Tekoa in 2 Sam. 14.5–7 not only does not appeal to statutory law, 'it is diametrically opposed to a known rule' in Num. 35.31–33 (Patrick 2011: 195). The same is true for Ahab and Jezebel's trial of

---

[12] Cf. Démare-Lafont 2017: 24, on *stare decisis* in Mesopotamia.

Naboth (ibid.: 196). As Jackson (2007: 373) writes, 'The use of such codes by judges in courts [. . .] remains singularly devoid of evidence'.

Further proof that the legal system must have been something other than what we have in the Pentateuch lies in the fact that the Torah lacks key areas of law (Morgenstern 1930: 32; Noth 1972: 18). It refers to divorce, modifies it, but never sets out its basics. It provides no legislation on how to marry in the first place (Pressler 2019: 290). The *Goel* is referred to but never explained (noted already by Michaelis 1814: 10, 474). Birth or war-captive grounds for slavery are never laid out in the Covenant Code, nor theft of anything other than an animal (Daube 1999: 414). All of this was known by custom (ibid.: 418–19).

Instructions for judges in Deut. 16.18 say nothing about consulting codes (Jackson 2002: 15–16). The only legal document we have from the First Temple Period, the Yavneh Yam Inscription, invokes no laws. That the Hebrew Bible regularly depicts law *recitation* from written texts (e.g. Exod. 24.3–7; Deut. 31.9–11; Josh. 8.30–35) relates not to the functioning legal system but to the performance of a display document, exactly as at the Icelandic Althing.[13]

This means the Israelite legal system was customary (Jackson 2006: 68; Schweid 2008: 108), based in a body of oral lore shared and developed by acknowledged experts who intentionally transmitted and manipulated its contents (Noth 1968: 14, 18). Law in oral-and-written Israel was much like early Iceland's: 'Law doubtless comprised an important body of oral lore which was shared and developed by acknowledged experts who deliberately passed it on to their successors' (Kjartansson 2009: 89). 'There were a number of men in [Israel], most of them probably from the social elite, with a good knowledge of the law, and these men must have taught their own sons, foster-sons and possibly sons of other members of their class' (Sigurðsson 2017: 28).

On the other hand, nothing precludes the role of writing in the customary law of ancient Israel and Judah. Iron Age legal memoranda, on ostraca, would have been memory aids for official lawmen as well as private possessions of individuals (Patrick 2011: 24; Morrow 2013: 328).

Here, then is the connection between the laws of the Hebrew Bible and the actual laws of ancient Israel. Upon a short saying, anything from an idiom of two words to a full legal maxim, a real or imaginary case is hung, or, vice versa, such a saying is added to an imaginary case (Stein 1966: 105). From that case, principles can be derived, and these are then applied to new cases 'in the gates'. The legal principle is what carries forward, however, far more than the exemplary case itself: 'When a case is done, the rule just applied returns from its brief excursion into detail, and reverts to its normal condition of generality' (Bennett 2004: 3). The Torah, then, is made of school texts (see below on the aural nature of education in ancient Israel), compendia of minute distinctions, not codes (cf. Byock 2001: 314–15; Sigurðsson 2017: 27).

The resultant 'codes' are descriptive, not proscriptive (Westbrook 1988: 5; Milstein 2018: 163). At the same time, those codes preserve signs of performance,[14] indicative – as in Iceland, and as in Greece (Sophocles, *Antigone*, 23.8.27–30; Hermippus, *Frag.* 88; Strabo, 12.2.9; Aelian, *Varia Hist.* 2.29; Plutarch, *Solon* 3; Pseudo-Aristotle, *Problemata*

---

[13] Watts (1999: 22–3) notes the parallel but entirely misses its significance, insisting it proves written law was the basis of the Israelite legal system.
[14] Démare-Lafont 2013: 73, with illustration of Hammurabi's Code.

19.28.919–20a)¹⁵ – of oral legal pedagogy and possibly of some sort of legal performance (Démare-Lafont 2013: 74). Finally, we cannot exclude the role played by the 'codes' as tokens of power, present as objects for display or whose ritual reading functioned 'magically' (Greengus 1995: 472; Schniedewind 2015: 306). As Bernard Jackson (2006: 70–1) insists, the function of the written law should not be limited to any one of these purposes.

Performative schemas for the Law will need to distinguish between pre-exilic and postexilic. Assemblies would have played an important role in the pre-exilic Israelite system (Num. 1.16, 14.10, 16.2; Josh. 24.22; Judg. 20.7–11; 1 Kgs 12.3; Prov. 5.14; Michaelis 1814: 229). The place of assembly most commonly designated is the gate (Knierim 1987: 25). The physical features of ancient Near Eastern gate complexes dispose them well for such assemblies. In fact, modifications to gate design in the Iron Age II period provided the one large open space for otherwise densely crowded towns and cities (Frese 2012: 204–5, 2020: 131). Excavated gates at Dan, Bethsaida and Tel Mevorakh have raised platforms that could have functioned for assembly leaders (Frese 2012: 228–30).

Small village moots would not have had the option of a gateworks (Matthews 1987: 29), and threshing floors had to be high ground, open to the breezes, usually circular or semi-circular, naturally suited for assembly (Aranov 1977: 168). Threshing floors sometimes serve for judicial proceedings (1 Kgs 22.10; Dietrich, Loretz and Sanmartin 1976: 1.17 ii.5–8; Aranov 1977: 158).

The lawmen active in ancient Israelite Things, if they correspond to any figures in the Hebrew Bible, are the so-called 'elders' (Alt 1968: 116; Reviv 1989: 38–9; Avalos 1995: 622; Frymer-Kenski 2003: 988; Wagner 2012: 96). City elders function as assembled representatives in Late Bronze Age Amarna Letters (EA 100) and at Alalakh (Márquez Rowe 2003: 695). A letter from Ishme-Dagan of Assyria to Yasmah-Adad refers to 'elders' gathered in 'assembly', as elders did at Emar (Westbrook 2003: 659).

The verbal contents of Israelite customary law would have been short aphorisms like Gen. 9.6, 'If anyone sheds the blood of man, by man shall his blood be shed', often with chiasms and other performative features (Jackson 2000: 215). The law in Deut. 19.16–21 seems to witness two independently circulating oral dicta for the same legal situation: 'Then you shall do to him as he meant to do to his brother' and 'Life for life, eye for eye, tooth for tooth, hand for hand, foot for foot' – the former reappearing in Judg. 1.6–7 and 15.4–11 and Prov. 24.29 (where it is contested); the latter, in 1 Kgs 20.39–43 and 2 Kgs 10.24 (Jackson 2002: 18).

---

¹⁵ Thomas 1995: 63–4; Havelock 1982: 130–1; References in Athenaeus' *Deipnosophistae*, 619b, and Strabo, *Geographica*, 12.2.9, to singing the Laws of Charondas by a *nomōidos*, 'lawsinger', and in Claudius Aelianus's *Varia Historia*, 2.39, to children of Crete learning laws with music are taken by Gagarin (2008: 34–5) to refer not to laws at all but either to *nomoi* as 'melodies' or 'general rules such as those in Hesiod's *Works and Days*', because he finds it 'nearly impossible to imagine someone putting, say, the Gortyn laws' to a melody. But no melody is mentioned, only to singing, which could easily be recitative or parlando. Gagarin also insists these are not oral laws, since they already existed in writing by this time. But, of course, that is precisely the oral-and-written phenomenon we see worldwide: oral performance of written texts, with modification happening both in the performance and in the subsequent rewriting. Gagarin retains a Great Divide between orality and literacy. It would be nice to add '8th century BC' tablets discovered in the early nineteenth century at Corinth supposedly dealing with music, which mentioned 'priests sang the nomoi' (Murhard 1825: 74). A text so at variance with the known chronology of Greek music was already deemed suspect by William C. Stafford's *History of Music* (1830: 131, footnote). It has been dismissed as 'a lengthy "text" with an even lengthier pseudo-scholarly "commentary"' (Bonds 2006: 96). I have found no indication what happened to these tablets, and the current Archaeological Mission to Corinth also has no idea.

However, we have no good way of knowing which portions of the Pentateuch's laws once served as written artefacts of, say, tenth-century Israelite law (Alt 1968: 110; Knight 2009: 111), especially since markers of performance might only be evidence of, e.g., seventh- or even fifth-century performance of written law.[16] For, as we have seen, in a legal system such as this, the resultant 'law codes' are mishmashes of various layers from different periods.[17] Editors, primarily postexilic editors, picked from the riches of the customary law of the pre-exilic community according to their own strategies, choosing to put certain laws alongside the narratives of the Pentateuch and vice versa (Greenstein 2001).

Thus, scholars have long debated whether Deut. 31.10–13, which calls for annual recitation of the Torah in which the performer has a scroll but does not read *from* it – the scroll an '*aide memoire* and physical signifier of the authority of God' (Newsom 2017: 20–1) – whether it was historically accurate for pre-exilic Israel and Judah. This debate extends to the readings of the Torah in Josh. 8.30–35 and 2 Kgs 23.1–2. This argument, however, misses seeing the value of these passages for reconstructing performative schemas *even if* those schemas turn out to be postexilic. In other words, whether or not performances like these three passages ever took place in Israel and Judah prior to the Babylonian Exile in the sixth century BCE, they reflect someone's understanding of how the text was to be performed. Moreover, they reflect a *different* kind of performance than that depicted in postexilic Nehemiah 8. There we have a much more 'liturgical' performance, with ceremonial responses ('Amen! Amen!', Neh. 8.6), gestures (bowing, face to the ground; Neh. 8.6), and quite explicitly an audience that does not understand what they are hearing (Neh. 8.7–8; Newsom 2017: 25–7).

# PROPHETS

A century ago, Mowinckel confidently spoke of three stages in the genesis of a prophetic book: the words of the prophet, a collection phase in which inauthentic additions were made, and the canonical book. Yet Theodore Robinson understood already then (building on Harris Birkeland and H.S. Nyberg) we have nothing of *ipsissima verba* of the prophet, and we have no real means to make hard and fast distinctions of what is original and what added by tradition (Nyberg 1935: 7–8, 128; Birkeland 1938: 1, 7–13; Robinson 1953: 53, 55).[18] So, 'The *biography* of Jeremiah that resulted from' early biblical scholarship 'has a strong resemblance to the lives of the nineteenth-century' liberal Protestant theologians doing the scholarship (Henderson 2016: 6).

The other problem with Mowinckel's linear progression is that writing did not *replace* oral transmission or performance (Widengren 1948: 88, 91). The books of the prophets are printed as poetry in modern Bibles because they are meant to be *heard*. Sound-play like Amos 5.5 or Isa. 24.3 is audible (Widengren 1948: 124). Rhythm, vivid imagery, and 'action-oriented language' is ubiquitous (Voth 2005: 123).

---

[16] Contra Locher 1986: 91. And why limit ourselves to Exodus? The law in Deut. 21.1–9 is also found at Ugarit, in an Akkadian letter from the King of Carchemish to Ammishtamru, Rs 20.22 (*Ugaritica* 5, 94–97); Westbrook 2008: 109.

[17] The argument to the contrary in Westbrook 1994 is based on pure analogy to Mesopotamia and logical non sequitur. See the discussion in Greengus 1994: 77; Levinson 1994: 39.

[18] The debate has been framed by Robert Carroll, Henning Graf Reventlow, and Jacques Vermeylen; for an early discussion, see Brueggemann 1987: 113–14, 120–5.

Prophets are the one genre where orality has actually been taken seriously in the past century. The supposed great achievement of the work on the prophets was isolating the oracles from each other, something now reflected in most modern published English Bibles.[19] Nevertheless, more recent scholarship concentrates the books of the Prophets as written text, rightly reacting to the early over-focus on the prophet's 'very words' (Wilson 2015: 83; Skornik 2019: 518–19 n.65).

And yet, the prophets are depicted as orators, not writers, for a reason (Wilson 2015: 84–5; Nissinen 2000: 241). Writing authors penned prophetic texts for oral delivery and performance in order to evoke the thunderous, plaintive, compassionate and grim voice of the preacher.[20] It is unlikely the books of the Prophets ever ceased being performed aloud. When Jonah is trapped in the belly of the fish, the inserted psalm, whose contents have little to do with his situation, could have been a sort of 'burden' or 'sequence' provided by a chorus. In Hab. 3.4, when the prophet describes the coming of God like a sunrise, the word 'there' in 'His brightness was like the light; rays flashed from his hand; and there he veiled his power' only makes sense if the performer of the text accompanies it with a gesture of his hand to the horizon.

## PSALMS

Oral poetry, 'insofar as it engages a body thru the voice that carries it, rejects any analysis that would dissociate it from within its social function and from its socially accorded place – more than a written text would' (Zumthor 1990: 28). One would not imagine a musicologist who only studied scores or a classicist who studied ancient Greek dramas without ever seeing them performed. Yet the standard approach to Psalms research for the past century, form criticism, focused on *literary* genres and their supposed *Sitzen im leben*, while more recent scholarship focuses on the Psalter as a book and its componental assembly. Only lately has any performance criticism examined the performance event, the dynamic complex of action that includes sound and gesture.[21]

But what is the relationship of the Psalms as we have them to the orally performed versions in ancient Israel? Bakhtin famously warned against assuming continuity between the songs of oral tradition and their written descendants (Bakhtin 1981: 14; so, too, Sigurðsson 2013: 50). Certainly, the function of the oral poems could have been quite different from functions of the poems passed on and preserved in writing (Gunnell 2016: 96). Contemporary tastes of the time of the 'recorder' may have intrusively imposed patterns and otherwise bent the Psalms to fit the conventions of the time (Zolbrod 1995: 54). Yet Eddic poetry, our best analogue to ancient Israelite oral poetry, 'was subject to a high degree of fixity' in terms of lexicology, style, structure, and narrative time and voice (Frog 2014: 148–50). As Gunnell (2016: 96, 102; also 2014: 23) writes, 'Much [. . .] can be assessed by reading the poem closely and analyzing exactly how the poems might have "worked" in performance'.

---

[19] The greatest debt is owed to Westermann (1967).
[20] Voth 2005: 119; Gitay 2011: 38; Wénin 2018: 159–60. See Nissinen 2000: 244–5, for discussion of the interplay of scribal and oral prophecy in Mari.
[21] Performance criticism arose only slightly earlier for Icelandic literature; Tarkka 1993: 168–70; cf. 'Text and Music', in Randel 2003: 876.

Pauses and periods of silence would be difficult to detect in the written remains that we have in the Psalter (Toelken 2003: 34, 36). Subordinating conjunctions repeated in regular positions at the beginning of parallel phrases, however, can serve as signs of delivery style (ibid.: 20). Eddic poems regularly indicate even more explicitly who is speaking and who is addressed (Gunnell 1995: 136–237), at times to such an obvious extent as to suggest dramatic performance (Gunnell 1995: 351, 353; Zolbrod 1995: 81). Sometimes we can name these speakers'/listeners' social identity (Hull 2014: 173). Some Psalms strongly suggest the spaces in which they could have been most effectively performed (Gunnell 2016: 102, 108). Others suggest 'blocking' or 'stage directions', including gestures.[22] Even when no actual movement occurs, the contrast between someone fairly stationary and someone in full motion can be conveyed by the dynamics of singing.

Most oral poetry is sung, not chanted or declaimed (Zumthor 1990: 142). Music is an indispensable element in its performance, while pitch and intonation are likewise essential (Cohen, Douaire and Elsabbagh 2001: 74–7, 80). Nevertheless, vocal scoring (unlike instrumentation data) would have been transmitted orally, and not encoded in written versions.

In what scholars have classically termed laments and thanksgivings, there is a sort of dialogue involved, as the rhetorical language presumes the deity is really present (Greenberg 1983: 25–8, 30–33, 36; Harkins 2012: 234; de Jong 2007: 119). In other words, the language of the Psalms especially when read aloud has a performative aspect that makes the senses understand an event between the prayer and God that is 'real in the here and now' (Harkins 2012: 235–6; also de Jong 2007: 131–2). As Angela Harkins (2012: 237) writes, the lament Psalms 'arouse vivid bodily sensations of spatiality and affect within readers'; and, even more, within hearers.

We can go further however, and postulate a soloist and a choir or congregation responding antiphonally. Sometimes this is obvious, as in Psalm 136, where the refrain 'for his mercy endures forever' is repeated stanza after stanza responsorially. There are other ways, however, of breaking up a song into fragments and distributing parts. Nissim Amzallag (2014) presents the most thorough argument for antiphonal performance of the Psalms. Psalms 121, 126 and 128 work with a complex antiphony of 'steady responsa', where the Psalm divides into two entities of equal length (Amzallag 2014: 30–1). Amzallag identifies a 'cross-responsa' or *canon cancrizans* in Psalm 87 (as well as Exodus 15; Isa. 14.4–20; and 2 Sam. 1.19–27), with a palindrome-like structure where a central verse is sung in echo by two voices in the middle of a Psalm that one voice begins and the other finished (Amzallag 2014: 32–3). And in Psalm 114, he finds a 'canonic responsa' where a second voice reiterates with a constant delay what is sung by the first voice from beginning to end (Amzallag 2014: 34). In Mesopotamia and Ugarit, too, antiphonal interplay between solo singer and choir or congregation is common.[23]

## WISDOM LITERATURE

Although there may be early elements preserved in this material, especially in Proverbs, these are among the latest books of the Hebrew Bible, the product of the highly literate postexilic period. Moreover, even the book of Proverbs is the creation of educated scribes

---

[22] Gunnell 2016: 105–6; Frog 2017: 599–600, for Iceland; Geisen 2012: 72, for Egypt.
[23] Shehata 2009: 369–70; Amzallag 2014: 31. In Greece, a conductor with a baton appears as early as a tablet from 709 BCE; cf. 'Conducting' in Randel 2003: 204.

or scribal schools. We know there were such schools, as even in the pre-exilic period; the officials in Judah who read and wrote Aramaic in the eighth and seventh centuries BCE would have required years of study, although we should envision a handful of students learning in a teacher's household, not separate institutions (Crenshaw 1998: 88; Rollston 2015: 81).

As we have seen, the uniformity of Hebrew handwriting, consistent uniform spelling and the use of the complicated Egyptian numeral system all indicate sophisticated written education for an elite few already before the Exile. In the postexilic period, the evidence for literate schools is overwhelming. After the Exile, up to the conquests of Alexander, the uses of writing expanded from economic and official uses to what we would think of as sciences and arts.[24] In fact, all the administrative inscriptions from the Persian period found in Judea were written in Aramaic (Lemaire 1992: 309). Local Jewish scholars had received formal instruction in Aramaic, while Hebrew was used mainly in the increasing amount of written codification of the books of the Hebrew Bible (Dietrich 2008: 182–3; Person 2010: 11; Van Seters 2015: 189). After the Greek conquest in the fourth century BCE, efforts were made to inculcate Greek language and culture, superseding Hebrew and Aramaic education (2 Macc. 4.12–14).[25] Proverbs 5 and Ecclesiastes 12 envision an educational setting.

And yet even this genre, seemingly the most thoroughly literary, comes from an oral literate culture.[26] We have no direct evidence of education in that 'Second Temple Period',[27] but Persian and Hellenistic provincial education both show the oral-and-written duality.

Of Persian education, scholars know very little, up to now all of it from Greek writers.[28] Strabo says Persian students 'rehearse both with and without song the deeds of gods and noble men', learning 'loud speaking', 'breathing', and 'use of their lungs' (15.3.19), all bespeaking oral education. More recently, Jonathon Riley and I have expanded our understanding of Persian education by looking at the extreme eastern end of the Persian Empire, in ancient India (this research is not yet published). That Persian education was oral-and-written. Written texts formed the basis of the curriculum, but texts were meant to be read aloud. They were memorized and then performed in pedagogical settings.

Hellenistic education, including in Ptolemaic Egyptian worked through 'imitation, drill, and monotonous repetition'[29] (Gk. Αποστοματιζω).[30] Images on Greek vases of people *reading scrolls* normally show them with musical instruments at hand; 'to read' was still 'to sing' (Loubser 2007: 20).

The Aramaic *Instructions of Ahiqar*, dated just prior to the Persian period but immensely popular during and after it, open with an account of a performance occasion and the identity of the performer. Like Ecclesiastes, a *named speaker* performs or has performed the instructions that follow, even though those instructions are really independent of this

---

[24] Cf. Loubser 2007: 17, who calls this period 'Primary Manuscript Culture'.
[25] Cf. Loubser 2007: 19, who calls this, 'Intermediate Manuscript Culture'.
[26] Vayntrub (2016: 100) seems to think it cannot be both: written *and* oral.
[27] See Crenshaw 1998: 4–5 n.6 for review of this discussion.
[28] Xenophon's *Cyropaedia* is an idealized, romanticized fiction; Herodotus (1.136) says Persians only learned riding, archery and honesty.
[29] Grubbs, Parkin and Bell 2013: 135.
[30] Cribiore 2001: 145, 181. Earlier, Classical Greek education was entirely oral, even long after the invention of the alphabet; Havelock 1982: 187.

imagined setting (Vayntrub 2016: 105). Ahiqar's nephew Nadin represents an 'ideal audience' (ibid.: 108). In other words, as Jacqueline Vayntrub has shown, *Ahiqar* mimics 'live speech performance, yet as readers we encounter these performances through written texts' (ibid.: 109).[31]

This means in ancient Israel, the performance setting for wisdom literature was 'small-scale, writing-supported, oral education of the literate elite' (Carr 2005: 208). Even in school, one learned aloud, what the Greeks called *zōsa phōnē* (Cribiore 2001: 145; Ueberschaer 2017: 33).

## CONCLUSION

Ancient Israel was an oral-and-written society – not oral, not 'literate', and not somewhere on a continuum between those two. The literature that makes up the Hebrew Bible was both written and orally performed. Performative schemas would be different for different genres, at least. Moreover, the processes of composition of the various components of the Hebrew Bible, obviously a large matter beyond the scope of this chapter, would have involved not simply composition in writing or oral composition later written down. Writers drew upon both oral tradition and written texts, and their work was then performed orally, and that performance was drawn upon by still other writers, on and on in a complex skein of transmission that is largely irrecoverable.

## REFERENCES

Afanasjeva, V. (1976), 'Mündliche überlieferte Dichtung ("Oral Poetry") und schriftliche Literatur in Mesopotamien', in J. Harmatta and G. Komoróczy (eds), *Wirtschaft und Gesellschaft im alten Vorderasien*, 121–35, Nachdruck aus den Acta Antiqua Academiae Scientarum Hungaricae 12.1–4, Budapest: Akadémiai Kiadó.
Ahlström, G.W. (1966), 'Oral and Written Transmission: Some Considerations', *HTR*, 59 (1): 69–81.
Alt, A. (1968), *Essays on Old Testament History and Religion*, Anchor Books, Garden City, NY: Doubleday.
Amzallag, N. (2014), 'The Musical Mode of Writing of the Psalms and Its Significance', *OTE*, 27 (1): 17–40.
Aranov, M.M. (1977), 'The Biblical Threshing-Floor in the Light of the Ancient Near Eastern Evidence', PhD diss., New York University, New York.
Avalos, H. (1995), 'Legal and Social Institutions in Canaan and Ancient Israel', in J.M. Sasson (ed.), *Civilizations of the Ancient Near East*, vol. I, 615–31, New York: Scribner's.
Bakhtin, M.M. (1981), *The Dialogic Imagination: Four Essays*, Austin: University of Texas Press.
Barstad, H.M. (2013), 'Eduard Nielsen's *Oral Tradition Sixty Years After*', *SJOT*, 27 (1): 8–21.
Bennett, T.W. (2004), *Customary Law in South Africa*, Cape Town: Juta.
Bergman, J. (1979), 'Commentary', in L. Honko (ed.), *Science of Religion: Studies in Methodology*, 15–21, Religion and Reason 13, The Hague: Mouton.

---

[31] Oddly, she does not think biblical wisdom literature does this, in spite of the passages cited here; cf. Vayntrub 2016: 110–11.

Birkeland, H. (1938), *Zum hebräischen Traditionswesen: die Komposition der prophetischen Bücher des Alten Testaments*, vol. I, Avhandlinger Utgitt Av Det Norse Videnskaps-Akademi, Oslo: Dybwad.

Bonds, M.E. (2006), *Music as Thought: Listening to the Symphony in the Age of Beethoven*, Princeton, NJ: Princeton University Press.

Borges, J.L. (2000), 'The Detective Story (1978)', in *Selected Non-Fictions*, ed. E. Weinberger, 491–9, New York: Penguin.

Braun, J. (2002), *Music in Ancient Israel/Palestine: Archaeological, Written, and Comparative Sources*, Grand Rapids, MI: Eerdmans.

Braun, J. (2011), *On Jewish Music: Past and Present*, rev. edn, Frankfurt: Peter Lang.

Brown, M. (2003), 'Consonance and Dissonance', in D.M. Randel (ed.), *The Harvard Dictionary of Music*, 4th edn, Cambridge, MA: Belknap.

Brueggemann, W. (1987), 'The Book of Jeremiah: Portrait of the Prophet', in J.L. Mays and P.J. Achtemeier (eds), *Interpreting the Prophets*, 113–39, Philadelphia, MN: Fortress Press.

Busoni, F. (1986), 'Sketch of a New Aesthetics of Music (1962)', in C. Dahlhaus (ed.), *Contemplating Music, Vol. 1: Substance*, 200–24, Aesthetics in Music 5, Stuyvesant: Pendragon.

Byock, J.L. (2001), *Viking Age Iceland*, London: Penguin.

Campbell, A.F. (2004), *Joshua to Chronicles: An Introduction*, Louisville, KY: Westminster John Knox Press.

Carr, D.M. (2005), *Writing on the Tablet of the Heart: Origins of Scripture and Literature*, Oxford: Oxford University Press.

Carr, D.M. (2008), 'The Tel Zayit Abecedary in (Social) Context,' in R.E. Tappy and P.K. McCarter (eds), *Literate Culture and Tenth-Century Canaan: The Tel Zayit Abecedary in Context*, 113–29, Winona Lake, IN: Eisenbrauns.

Carr, D.M. (2010), 'Torah on the Heart: Literary Jewish Textuality Within Its Ancient Near Eastern Context', *Oral Tradition*, 25 (1): 17–39.

Carr, D.M. (2015), 'Orality, Textuality, *and* Memory: The State of Biblical Studies', in B.B. Schmidt (ed.), *Contextualizing Israel's Sacred Writings: Ancient Literacy, Orality, and Literary Production*, 161–74, AIL 22, Atlanta, GA: SBL Press.

Carter, J.B. (1995), 'Ancestor Cult and the Occasion of Homeric Performance', in J.B. Carter and S.P. Morris (eds), *The Ages of Homer: A Tribute to Emily Townsend Vermeule*, 285–314, Austin: University of Texas Press.

Cassuto, P. (2014), 'La Bible: le lu, l'écrit et autres points', in P. Cassuto and P. Larcher (eds), *Oralité & écriture dans la Bible & le Coran*, 11–39, Marseille: Presses Universitaires de Provence.

Chi, A.N. (2018), 'Les traces de l'oralité en Genèse 39', in A. Gignac (ed.), *Narrativité, oralité et performance: 7e colloque international du Réseau de recherche Narratologie et Bible (RRENAB), 5 au 7 juin 2014, Université de Montréal*, 107–23, Terra Nova 4, Leuven: Peeters.

Cohen, H., J. Douaire and M. Elsabbagh (2001), 'The Role of Prosody in Discourse Processing', *Brain and Cognition*, 46 (1/2): 73–82.

Colbert, D. (1989), *The Birth of the Ballad: The Scandinavian Medieval Genre*, Skrifter Utgivna Av Svenskt Visarkiv 10, Stockholm: Svenskt Visarkov.

Crenshaw, J.L. (1998), *Education in Ancient Israel: Across the Deadening Silence*, New York: Doubleday.

Cribiore, R. (2001), *Gymnastics of the Mind: Greek Education in Hellenistic and Roman Egypt*, Princeton, NJ: Princeton University Press.

Daube, D. (1999), 'The Self-Understood in Legal History', *Green Bag*, 2: 413–19.
de Jong, A. (2007), 'Liturgical Action from a Language Perspective', in H. Schilderman (ed.), *Discourse in Ritual Studies*, 111–45, Empirical Studies in Theology 14, Leiden: E.J. Brill.
Démare-Lafont, S. (2013), 'L'écriture du droit en Mésopotamie', in O. Artus (ed.), *Loi et Justice dans la Littérature du Proche-Orient ancien*, 69–83, BZABR 20, Wiesbaden: Harrassowitz.
Démare-Lafont, S. (2017), 'Les lois dans le monde cunéiforme: codification ou mise par écrit du droit?', in D. Jaillard and C. Nihan (eds), *Writing Laws in Antiquity / L'écriture du droit dans l'Antiquité*, 21–33, BZABR 19, Wiesbaden: Harrassowitz.
Dietrich, M., O. Loretz and J. Sanmartin (1976), *Die keilalphabetischen Texte aus Ugarit: einschließlich der keilalphabetischen Texte außerhalb Ugarit*, AOAT 24, Neukirchen-Vluyn: Neukirchener.
Dietrich, W. (2008), 'Vielfalt und Einheit im deuteronomistischen Geschichtswerk', in J. Pakkala and M. Nissinen (eds), *Houses Full of All Good Things: Essays in Memory of Timo Veijola*, 169–83, Publications of the Finnish Exegetical Society 95, Helsinki: The Finnish Exegetical Society.
Dobbs-Allsopp, F.W. (2015), *On Biblical Poetry*, Oxford: Oxford University Press.
Dumbrill, R. (2019), *Semitic Music Theory (from Its Earliest Sources till the Dawn of Christianity)*, London: ICONEA.
Edzard, L. (2014), 'Oralité et écriture: les ṭəʿāmīm comme représentation prosodique de la structure morpho-syntaxique de la Bible hébraïque', in P. Cassuto and P. Larcher (eds), *Oralité & écriture dans la Bible & le Coran*, 41–52, Marseille: Presses Universitaires de Provence.
Egilsdóttir, Á. (2006), 'From Orality to Literacy: Remembering the Past and the Present in Jóns saga helga', in E. Mundal (ed.), *Reykholt som Makt- og Lærdomssenter*, 215–28, Snorrastofa 3, Reykholt: Snorrastofa.
Engnell, I. (1969), *A Rigid Scrutiny: Critical Essays on the Old Testament*, Nashville, TN: Vanderbilt University Press.
Evans, P.S. (2017), 'Creating a New "Great Divide": The Exoticization of Ancient Culture in Some Recent Applications of Orality Studies to the Bible', *JBL*, 136 (4): 749–64.
Falk, Z.W. (1964), *Hebrew Law in Biblical Times: An Introduction*, Jerusalem: Wahrmann.
Faulkes, A. (1993), *What Was Viking Poetry For? Inaugural Lecture Delivered on 27th April 1993 in the University of Birmingham*, Birmingham: University of Birmingham School of English.
Flender, R. (1992), *Hebrew Psalmody: A Structural Investigation*, Yuval Monographs 9, Jerusalem: Magnes Press.
Frese, D.A. (2012), 'The Civic Forum in Ancient Israel', PhD diss., University of California, San Diego.
Frese, D.A. (2020), *The City Gate in Ancient Israel and Her Neighbors: The Form, Function, and Symbolism of the Civic Forum in the Southern Levant*, CHANE 108, Leiden: E.J. Brill.
Friedrich, R. (2019), *Postoral Homer: Orality and Literacy in the Homeric Epic*, Hermes Einzelschrift 112, Stuttgart: Franz Steiner.
Frog, E. (2014), 'Germanic Traditions of the Theft of the Thunder-Instrument (ATU 1148b): An Approach to Þrymskviða and Þórr's Adventure with Geirrøðr in Circum-Baltic Perspective', in E. Heide and K. Bek-Pedersen (eds), *New Focus on Retrospective Methods: Resuming Methodological Discussions: Case Studies from Northern Europe*, 120–62, Folklore Fellows' Communications 307, Helsinki: Suomalainen Tiedeakatemia, Academia Scientiarum Fennica.
Frog (2017), 'Multimedial Parallelism in Ritual Performance', *Oral Tradition*, 31 (2): 583–620.

Frog, K. Koski and U. Savolainen (2016), 'At the Intersection of Text and Interpretation', in K. Koski, Frog with U. Savolainen (eds), *Genre – Text – Interpretation: Multidisciplinary Perspectives on Folklore and Beyond*, 17–43, Helsinki: Finnish Literature Society.

Frymer-Kenski, T. (2003), 'Anatolia and the Levant: Israel', in R. Westbrook (ed.), *A History of Ancient Near Eastern Law*, vol. II, 975–1046, Handbook of Oriental Studies, Section 1, The Near and Middle East 72, Leiden: E.J. Brill.

Gagarin, M. (2008), *Writing Greek Law*, Cambridge: Cambridge University Press.

Geisen, C. (2012), 'The Ramesseum Dramatic Papyrus', PhD diss., University of Toronto.

Gerson-Kiwi, E. (1961), 'Religious Chant: A Pan-Asiatic Conception of Music', *International Folk Music Journal*, 13: 64–7.

Gitay, Y. (2011), *Methodology, Speech, Society: The Hebrew Bible*, Stellenbosch: Sun Media.

Greenberg, M. (1983), *Biblical Prose Prayer: As a Window to the Popular Religion of Ancient Israel*, Berkeley: University of California Press.

Greengus, S. (1994), 'Some Issues Relating to the Comparability of Laws and the Coherence of the Legal Tradition', in B.M. Levinson (ed.), *Theory and Method in Biblical and Cuneiform Law: Revision, Interpolation and Development*, 60–87, JSOTSup 181, Sheffield: Sheffield Academic Press.

Greengus, S. (1995), 'Legal and Social Institutions of Ancient Mesopotamia', in J.M. Sasson (ed.), *Civilizations of the Ancient Near East*, vol. I, 469–84, New York: Scribner's.

Greenstein, E. (2001), 'The Relation Between Law and Narrative in the Pentateuch', paper presented at the conference Law and Literature: Mutual Negotiations, Tel Aviv, 3–5 June, 2001.

Grubbs, J.E., T.G. Parkin and R. Bell, eds (2013), *The Oxford Handbook of Childhood and Education in the Classical World*, Oxford: Oxford University Press.

Gunnell, T. (1995), *The Origins of Drama in Scandinavia*, Cambridge: D.S. Brewer.

Gunnell, T. (2014), 'Nordic Folk Legends, Folk Traditions and Grave Mounds', in E. Heide and K. Bek-Pedersen (eds), *New Focus on Retrospective Methods: Resuming Methodological Discussions: Case Studies from Northern Europe*, 17–41, Folklore Fellows' Communications 307, Helsinki: Suomalainen Tiedeakatemia, Academia Scientiarum Fennica.

Gunnell, T. (2016), 'Eddic Performance and Eddic Audiences', in C. Larrington, J. Quinn and B. Schorn (eds), *A Handbook to Eddic Poetry: Myths and Legends of Early Scandinavia*, 92–113, Cambridge: Cambridge University Press.

Harkins, A.K. (2012), 'Religious Experience Through the Lens of Critical Spatiality: A Look at Embodiment Language in Prayers and Hymns', in C. Shantz and R.A. Werline (eds), *Experientia, Vol. 2: Linking Text and Experience*, 223–42, Early Judaism and Its Literature 35, Atlanta, GA: Society of Biblical Literature.

Harris, J. (2016), 'Eddic Poetry as World Literature', *Collegium Medievale*, 29: 5–28.

Harris, J. and K. Reichl (2012), 'Performance and Performers', in K. Reichl (ed.), *Medieval Oral Literature*, 141–202, Berlin: De Gruyter.

Havelock, E.A. (1982), *The Literate Revolution in Greece and Its Cultural Consequences*, Princeton Series of Collected Essays, Princeton, NJ: Princeton University Press.

Henderson, J. (2016), 'Duhm and Skinner's Invention of Jeremiah', in E.K. Holt and C.J. Sharp (eds), *Jeremiah Invented: Constructions and Deconstructions of Jeremiah*, 1–15, LHBOTS 595, London: T&T Clark.

Hodge, C.T. (1989), 'Thoth and Oral Tradition', in M.R. Key and H.M. Hoenigswald (eds), *General and Amerindian Ethnolinguistics: In Memory of Stanley Newman*, 407–16, Contributions to the Sociology of Language 55, Berlin: Mouton de Gruyter.

Honko, L. (1996), 'Comparing the Textualization of Oral Epics', *Folklore Fellows Newsletter*, 13: 2–3, 7–8.
Hull, K.L. (2014), 'Ritual as Performance in Small-Scale Societies', *World Archaeology*, 46 (2): 164–77.
Human, D. (2011), 'Cultic Music in the Ancient Orient and in Ancient Israel/Palestine', *Verkündigung und Forschung*, 56 (2): 45–52.
Hymes, H. (1964), 'Introduction: Toward Ethnographies of Communication', *American Anthropologist*, 66 (6, pt 2): 1–34.
Jackson, B.S. (1999), 'Exodus 21:18–19 and the Origins of the Casuistic Form', *Israel Law Review*, 33 (4): 798–820.
Jackson, B.S. (2000), *Studies in the Semiotics of Biblical Law*, JSOTSup 314, Sheffield: Sheffield Academic Press.
Jackson, B.S. (2002), 'Models in Legal History: The Case of Biblical Law', *Journal of Law and Religion*, 18 (1): 1–30.
Jackson, B.S. (2006), *Wisdom-Laws: A Study of the Mishpatim of Exodus 21.1–22.16*, Oxford: Oxford University Press.
Jackson, B.S. (2007), 'Law in the Ninth Century: Jehoshaphat's "Judicial Reform"', in H.G.M. Williamson (ed.), *Understanding the History of Ancient Israel*, 369–97, Proceedings of the British Academy 143, Oxford: Oxford University Press.
Jacobsen, T. (1982), 'Oral to Written', in M.A. Dandamayev, I. Gershevitch, H. Klengel, G. Komoróczy, M.T. Larsen, and J.N. Postgate (eds), *Societies and Languages of the Ancient Near East: Studies in Honour of I.M. Diakonoff*, 129–37, Warminster: Aris & Phillips.
Keefer, A. (2016), 'Phonological Patterns in the Hebrew Bible: A Century of Studies in Sound', *CBR*, 15 (1): 45–64.
Khan, G. (2018), 'Orthoepy in the Tiberian Reading Tradition of the Hebrew Bible and Its Historical Roots in the Second Temple Period', *VT*, 68 (3): 378–401.
King, B. (1991), 'Toward and Ethnography of Listening' [rejected submission to *Language in Society*, in the Papers of Dell Hymes, American Philosophical Society].
Kjartansson, H.S. (2009), 'Law Recital According to Old Icelandic Law', *Scripta Islandica*, 60: 89–103.
Knierim, R.P. (1987), 'Customs, Judges, and Legislators in Ancient Israel', in C.A. Evans and W.F. Stinespring (eds), *Early Jewish and Christian Exegesis: Studies in Memory of William Hugh Brownlee*, 22–58, Scholars Press Homage Series 10, Atlanta, GA: Scholars Press.
Knight, D.A. (2009), 'Tradition-History-Criticism: The Development of the Covenant Code', in J.M. LeMon and K.H. Richards (eds), *Method Matters: Essays on the Interpretation of the Hebrew Bible in Honor of David L. Petersen*, 97–116, RBS 56, Atlanta, GA: Society of Biblical Literature.
Lemaire, A. (1992), 'Education: Ancient Israel', in D.N. Freedman (ed.), *The Anchor Bible Dictionary*, vol. II, 305–11, New York: Doubleday.
Lemche, N.P. (1995), 'Justice in Western Asia in Antiquity, or: Why No Laws Were Needed!', *Chicago-Kent Law Review*, 70 (4): 1695–1716.
Levin, S. (1995), 'The "Qeri" as the Primary Text of the Hebrew Bible', *General Linguistics*, 35 (1): 181–223.
Levinson, B.M. (1994), 'The Case for Revision and Interpolation Within the Biblical Legal Corpora', in B.M. Levinson (ed.), *Theory and Method in Biblical and Cuneiform Law: Revision, Interpolation and Development*, 37–59, JSOTSup 181, Sheffield: Sheffield Academic Press.
Licht, J. (1990), *Storytelling in the Bible*, Jerusalem: Magnes Press.

Locher, C. (1986), *Die Ehre einer Frau in Israel : exegetische und rechtsvergleichende Studien zu Deuteronomium 22, 13–21*, Göttingen: Vandenhoeck & Ruprecht.

Lomax, A. (1968), *Folk Song Style and Culture*, American Association for the Advancement of Science Publications 88, Washington, DC: American Association for the Advancement of Science.

Loubser, J.A. (2007), *Oral and Manuscript Culture in the Bible*, Stellenbosch: Sun Press.

Lundin, R.W. (1985), *An Objective Psychology of Music*, 2nd edn, New York: Ronald Press.

Macdonald, M.C.A. (2005), 'Literacy in an Oral Environment', in P. Bienkowski, C. Mee and E.A. Slater (eds), *Writing and Ancient Near Eastern Society: Papers in Honour of Alan R. Millard*, 45–114, LHBOTS 426, New York: T&T Clark.

Manniche, L. (2006), 'Angular Harps in the Amarna Period', *JEA*, 92 (1): 248–9.

Márquez Rowe, I. (2003), 'Alalakh', in R. Westbrook (ed.), *A History of Ancient Near Eastern Law*, vol. I, 693–718, Handbook of Oriental Studies, Section 1, The Near and Middle East 72, Leiden: E.J. Brill

Matthews, V.H. (1987), 'Entrance Ways and Threshing Floors: Legally Significant Sites in the Ancient Near East', *Fides et Historia*, 19: 25–40.

Mathieu, Y. (2018), 'Narrativité et performance dans le cycle d'Abimélek,' in A. Gignac (ed.), *Narrativité, oralité et performance: 7ᵉ colloque international du Réseau de recherche Narratologie et Bible (RRENAB), 5 au 7 juin 2014, Université de Montréal*, 125–53, Terra Nova 4, Leuven: Peeters.

McAuley, G. (2003), 'Place in the Performative Experience', *Modern Drama*, 46 (4): 598–613.

McLuhan, M. (1999), '"Achieving Relevance": Letters to Mole and Sheed' [1970], in M. McLuhan, *The Medium and the Light: Reflections on Religion*, ed. Eric McLuhan and Jacek Szklarek, 136–40, Toronto: Stoddart.

Meyer, B. (2017), *Das Apodiktische Recht*, BWANT 213, Stuttgart: Kohlhammer.

Michaelis, J.D. (1814), *Commentaries on the Laws of Moses, Vol. 1*, transl. A. Smith, London: F.C. and J. Rivington.

Miller, R.D. II (2011), *Oral Tradition in Ancient Israel*, Biblical Performance Criticism 4, Eugene, OR: Cascade.

Milstein, S.J. (2018), 'Making a Case: The Repurposing of "Israelite Legal Fictions" as Post-Deuteronomic Law', in S.M. Olyan and J.L. Wright (eds), *Supplementation and the Study of the Hebrew Bible*, 161–82, Brown Judaic Studies 361, Providence, RI: Brown Judaic Studies.

Montagu, J. (2002), *Musical Instruments of the Bible*, Lanham, MD: Scarecrow Press.

Montagu, J. (2017), 'How Music and Instruments Began: A Brief Overview of the Origin and Entire Development of Music, from Its Earliest Stages', *Frontiers in Sociology*, 2: art. 8. Available online: https://doi.org/10.3389/fsoc.2017.00008 (accessed 12 July 2022).

Morgenstern, J. (1930), 'The Book of the Covenant, Part II', *HUCA*, 7: 19–258.

Morrow, W. (2013), 'Legal Interactions: The Mišpāṭîm and the Laws of Hammurabi', *BibOr*, 70: 309–31.

Murhard, J.G. (1825), 'Discovery of Ancient Greek Tablets Relative to Music', *The Harmonicon: A Journal of Music*, 3: 55–7, 74–7.

Nagy, G. (2009), 'An Evolutionary Model for the Making of Homeric Poetry', in *Homeric Questions*, 163–79, Austin: University of Texas Press.

Newsom, C.A. (2017), 'Scenes of Reading', in J.B. Weaver and D.L. Gragg (eds), *Reading for Faith and Learning: Essays on Scripture, Community, & Libraries in Honor of M. Patrick Graham*, 19–30, Abilene, TX: Abilene Christian University Press.

Niditch, S. (2008), *Judges: A Commentary*, OTL, Louisville, KY: Westminster John Knox Press.

Nissinen, M. (2000), 'Spoken, Written, Quoted, and Invented: Orality and Writtenness in Ancient Near Eastern Prophecy,' in E. Ben Zvi and M.H. Floyd (eds), *Writings and Speech in Israelite and Ancient Near Eastern Prophecy*, 235–71, SBLSS 10, Atlanta, GA: Society of Biblical Literature.

Nord, C. (2005), 'Making Otherness Accessible: Functionality and Skopos in the Translation of New Testament Texts', *Meta: Journal des Traducteurs*, 50 (3): 868–80.

Noth, M. (1968), *The Laws in the Pentateuch and Other Studies*, Philadelphia, MN: Fortress Press.

Noth, M. (1972), *A History of Pentateuchal Traditions*, Englewood Cliffs, NJ: Prentice-Hall.

Nyberg, H.S. (1935), *Studien zum Hoseabuch*, Uppsala Universitets Arsskrift, 6, Uppsala: Lundequistska.

Pasqualino, C. (2008), 'La littérature orale comme performance', *Cahiers de la littérature orale*, 63/64: 109–16.

Patrick, D. (2011), *Old Testament Law*, Eugene, OR: Wipf & Stock.

Patron, S. (2018), 'Les catégories narratologiques et la (non-)distinction oral-écrits dans la théorie narrative (narratologie et autres théories du récit de fiction)', in A. Gignac (ed.), *Narrativité, oralité et performance: 7ᵉ colloque international du Réseau de recherche Narratologie et Bible (RRENAB), 5 au 7 juin 2014, Université de Montréal*, 19–42, Terra Nova 4, Leuven: Peeters.

Person, R.F., Jr (2010), *The Deuteronomic History and the Book of Chronicles*, AIL 6, Atlanta, GA: Society of Biblical Literature.

Person, R.F., Jr (2018), 'Texts Performed – Not Read – by Illiterate Scribes? A Response to Evans'. Available online: https://www.academia.edu/37570643/TEXTS_PERFORMED_NOT_READ_BY_ILLITERATE_SCRIBES_A_RESPONSE_TO_EVANS (accessed 12 July 2022).

Poyatos, F. (2002), *Nonverbal Communication Across Disciplines, Volume 2: Paralanguage, Kinesics, Silence, Personal and Environmental Interaction*, Philadelphia, PA: John Benjamins.

Pressler, C. (2019), 'Sexual Legislation', in B.A. Strawn (ed.), *The Oxford Encyclopedia of the Bible and Law, Vol. 2*, Oxford: Oxford University Press.

Propp, V.J. (2012), *The Russian Folktale*, transl. S. Forrester, Detroit, MI: Wayne State University Press.

Randel, D.M., ed. (2003), *The Harvard Dictionary of Music*, 4th edn, Cambridge, MA: Belknap.

Ready, J.L. (2019), *Orality, Textuality, and the Homeric Epics: An Interdisciplinary Study of Oral Texts, Dictated Texts, and Wild Texts*, Oxford: Oxford University Press.

Reviv, H. (1989), *The Elders in Ancient Israel: A Study of a Biblical Institution*, Jerusalem: Magnes Press.

Riley, S.K. (2014), 'The Hand Drum (תף) and Israelite Women's Musical Tradition', *Studia Antiqua*, 13 (1): 23–47.

Robinson, T.H. (1953), *Prophecy and the Prophets in Ancient Israel*, 2nd edn, Studies in Theology 3, London: Duckworth.

Rollston, C.A. (2008), 'The Phoenician Script of the Tel Zayit Abecedary and Putative Evidence for Israelite Literacy', in R.E. Tappy and P.K. McCarter (eds), *Literate Culture and Tenth-Century Canaan: The Tel Zayit Abecedary in Context*, 61–96, Winona Lake, IN: Eisenbrauns.

Rollston, C.A. (2010), *Writing and Literacy in the World of Ancient Israel: Epigraphic Evidence from the Iron Age*, ABS 11, Atlanta, GA: Society of Biblical Literature.

Rollston, C.A. (2015), 'Scribal Curriculum During the First Temple Period'. in B.B. Schmidt (ed.), *Contextualizing Israel's Sacred Writings: Ancient Literacy, Orality, and Literary Production*, 71–101, AIL 22, Atlanta, GA: SBL Press.

Sanders, S.L. (2008), 'Writing and Early Iron Age Israel: Before National Scripts, Beyond Nations and States', in R.E. Tappy and P.K. McCarter (eds), *Literate Culture and Tenth-Century Canaan: The Tel Zayit Abecedary in Context*, 97–112, Winona Lake, IN: Eisenbrauns.

Schniedewind, W.M. (2015), 'Scripturalization in Ancient Judah', in B.B. Schmidt (ed.), *Contextualizing Israel's Sacred Writings: Ancient Literacy, Orality, and Literary Production*, 305–22, AIL 22, Atlanta, GA: SBL Press.

Schweid, E. (2008), *The Philosophy of the Bible as Foundation of Jewish Culture: Philosophy of Biblical Law*, Reference Library of Jewish Intellectual History, Boston, MA: Academic Studies Press.

Shehata, D. (2009), *Musiker und ihr vokales Repertoire: Untersuchungen zu Inhalt und Organisation von Musikerberufen und Liedgattungen in altbabylonischer Zeit*, Göttinger Beiträge zum Alten Orient 3, Göttingen: Universitätsverlag.

Shepherd, S. (2016), *The Cambridge Introduction to Performance Theory*, Cambridge: Cambridge University Press.

Sherzer, J. (1990), *Verbal Art in San Blas: Kuna Culture Through its Discourse*, Cambridge Studies in Oral and Literate Culture 21, Cambridge: Cambridge University Press.

Sigurðsson, G. (2013), '*Vǫluspá* as the Product of an Oral Tradition: What Does that Entail?', in T. Gunnell and A. Lassen (eds), *The Nordic Apocalypse: Approaches to 'Vǫluspá' and Nordic Days of Judgement*, 45–62, Turnhout: Brepols.

Sigurðsson, J.V. (2017), 'The Education of Sturla Þórðarson (and the Icelandic Elite)', in J.V. Sigurðsson and S. Jakobsson (eds), *Sturla Þórðarson: Skald, Chieftain and Lawman*, 20–30, Northern World 78, Leiden: E.J. Brill.

Skornik, J.E. (2019), 'Between the Study of Religion and Literary Analysis: Robert Lowth on the Species of Prophetic Poetry', *Journal of Religion*, 99 (4): 492–528.

Slater, N.W. (2014), 'Speaking Verse to Power: Circulation of Oral and Written Critique in the *Lives of the Caesars*', in R. Scodel (ed.), *Between Orality and Literacy: Communication and Adaptation in Antiquity*, 289–308, Leiden: E.J. Brill.

Smith, M.S. (2015), 'The Passing of Warrior Poetry in the Era of Prosaic Heroes', in J.J. Collins, T.M. Lemos and S.M. Olyan (eds), *Worship, Women and War: Essays in Honor of Susan Niditch*, 3–15, Brown Judaic Studies 357, Atlanta, GA: Society of Biblical Literature.

Sowayan, S.A. (1985), *Nabati Poetry: The Oral Poetry of Arabia*, Berkeley: University of California Press.

Stafford, W.C. (1830), *A History of Music*, Edinburgh: Constable.

Stein, P.G. (1966), *Regulae Iuris: From Juristic Rules to Legal Maxims*, Edinburgh: Edinburgh University Press.

Tarkka, L. (1993), 'Intertextuality, Rhetorics and the Interpretation of Oral Poetry,' in P.J. Anttonen and R. Kvideland (eds), *Nordic Frontiers: Recent Issues in the Study of Modern Traditional Culture in the Nordic Countries*, 165–93, NIF Publications 27, Turku: Nordic Institute of Folklore.

Thomas, R. (1995), 'Written in Stone? Liberty, Equality, Orality and the Codification of Law', *Bulletin of the Institute of Classical Studies*, 40: 59–74.

Thomas, R. (2005), 'Performance Literature and the Written Word', *Oral Tradition*, 20 (1): 1–6.

Toelken, B. (2003), *Oral Patterns of Performance: Story and Song*, Boulder, CO: Utah State University Press.

Tooman, W.A. (2019), 'Authenticating Oral and Memory Variants in Ancient Hebrew Literature', *JSS*, 64 (1): 91–114.

Ueberschaer, F. (2017), 'Jewish Education in Ben Sira', in J.M. Zurawski and G. Boccaccini (eds), *Second Temple Jewish 'Paideia' in Context*, 29–46, BZNT 228, Berlin: De Gruyter.

Van Seters, J. (2015), *The Pentateuch: A Social-Science Commentary*, 2nd edn, London: Bloomsbury T&T Clark.

Vayntrub, J. (2016), 'The Book of Proverbs and the Idea of Ancient Israelite Education', *ZAW*, 128 (1): 96–114.

Voth, E. (2005), 'Orality and Writtenness in Ancient Near Eastern Prophecy: Its Effect on Translation as Communication in Latin America', *Bible Translator*, 56 (3): 114–28.

Wagner, V. (2012), 'Die Gerichtsverfassung Israel nach der Weisheitsliteratur des alten Testaments', *BZ*, 56 (1): 96–106.

Walton, J.H. (2017), 'Understanding Torah: Ancient Legal Text, Covenant Stipulation, and Christian Scripture', Institute for Biblical Research Plenary Address, Boston, MA.

Watts, J.W. (1999), *Reading Law: The Rhetorical Shaping of the Pentateuch*, Biblical Seminar 59, Sheffield: Sheffield Academic Press.

Wendland, E.R. (2013), *Orality and the Scriptures: Composition, Translation, and Transmission*, SIL Publications in Translation and Textlinguistics 6, Dallas, TX: SIL International.

Wénin, A. (2018), 'À vouloir être trop dissuasif . . . Rhétorique et oralité en 1 S 8, 11–18', in A. Gignac (ed.), *Narrativité, oralité et performance: 7e colloque international du Réseau de recherche Narratologie et Bible (RRENAB), 5 au 7 juin 2014, Université de Montréal*, 155–61, Terra Nova 4, Leuven: Peeters.

Westbrook, R. (1988), *Studies in Biblical and Cuneiform Law*, Cahiers de la Revue Biblique 26, Paris: Gabalda.

Westbrook, R. (1994), 'What Is the Covenant Code?', in B.M. Levinson (ed.), *Theory and Method in Biblical and Cuneiform Law: Revision, Interpolation and Development*, 15–36, JSOTSup 181, Sheffield: Sheffield Academic Press.

Westbrook, R. (2003), 'Emar and Vicinity', in R. Westbrook (ed.), *A History of Ancient Near Eastern Law*, vol. II, 657–92, Handbook of Oriental Studies, Section 1, The Near and Middle East 72, Leiden: E.J. Brill.

Westbrook, R. (2008), 'The Laws of Biblical Israel', in F.E. Greenspahn (ed.), *The Hebrew Bible: New Insights and Scholarship*, 99–119, Jewish Studies in the 21st Century, New York: New York University Press.

Westermann, C. (1967), *Basic Forms of Prophetic Speech*, London: Lutterworth.

Wicomb, Z. (2018), 'Reading, Writing, and Visual Production in the New South Africa (1995)', in *Race, Nation, Translation: South African Essays, 1990-2013*, 66–80, New Haven, CT: Yale University Press.

Widengren, G. (1948), *Literary and Psychological Aspects of the Hebrew Prophets*, UUÅ 10, Leipzig: Harrassowitz.

Wilson, R.R. (2015), 'Orality and Writing in the Creation of Exilic Prophetic Literature', in J.J. Collins, T.M. Lemos and S.M. Olyan (eds), *Worship, Women and War: Essays in Honor of Susan Niditch*, 83–96, Brown Judaic Studies 357, Atlanta, GA: Society of Biblical Literature.

Winn, J.A. (1981), *Unsuspected Eloquence: A History of the Relations Between Poetry and Music*, New Haven, CT: Yale University Press.

Wundt, W.M. (1973 [1921]), *The Language of Gestures*, The Hague: Mouton.

Zerubavel, E. (2003), *Time Maps: Collective Memory and the Social Shape of the Past*, Chicago: University of Chicago Press.

Ziegler, N. (2010), 'Teachers and Students: Conveying Musical Knowledge in the Kingdom of Mari', in R. Pruzsinszky and D. Shehata (eds), *Musiker und Tradierung: Studien zur Rolle von Musikern bei der Verschriftlichung und Tradierung von literarischen Werken*, 119–33, Wiener Offene Orientalistik 8, Vienna: LIT Verlag.

Zolbrod, P. (1995), *Reading the Voice: Native American Oral Poetry and the Written Page*, Salt Lake City: University of Utah Press.

Zumthor, P. (1990), *Oral Poetry: An Introduction*, Theory and History of Literature 70, Minneapolis: University of Minnesota Press.

CHAPTER SIXTEEN

# Telling tales

*Biblical myth and narrative*

KAROLIEN VERMEULEN

Human beings are storytellers. Whether they talk about what they did yesterday or write the next Jane Austen, they turn to stories. Therefore, some say that storytelling is a basic human capacity. It occurred and occurs all over the world (Reck 1983: 8; Dancygier 2012: 4; Gottschall 2012). Stories are conscious as well as unconscious tools that assist in both understanding and shaping the world in which we live. Precisely because of this, stories can be considered a form of social behaviour (Bruner 1991; Herman 2003). As any social behaviour, they are the product of their environment. They are produced by people in a particular time and place for specific reasons, naturally 'co-operations' with others (Fludernik 2007: 261). This is no different for the story known as the Hebrew Bible. What is more, this Bible,[1] often described as a florilegium, illustrates another important characteristic of storytelling, that is, that stories take different forms and shapes. Some tales in the Bible are short, others long. Genres go from prose and poetry to law codes and parables. Among its story themes are murder, love, war, regret, praise and power. In addition, the Hebrew Bible displays a plenitude of characters, some of whom play a role in multiple narratives whereas others appear only once. Despite this variety, which can be explained through the historical composition and growth of the text (Carr 2011), the Hebrew Bible is conceived as a coherent whole with recurring themes and concerns (Clines 1978), a divine character that features in almost all stories (Amit 2001: 82–6) and inner-biblical allusions that connect its various parts (Sommer 1998). The Bible is one big story.

This chapter will focus on two aspects of this story, or better, two concepts that are often mentioned when speaking of the story quality of the Hebrew Bible: myth and narrative. The term 'narrative' features in research early on, referring to the prose tales included in the biblical text (e.g. Linafelt 2016) as well as to the overall story of the work (e.g. Miller 2004) or a part of it (e.g. Tull 2016). Literally, narrative means that which is told, from the Latin *narrare*. It refers to both what is told and how it is told, covering the age-old division between meaning and form, or signified (*signifié*) and signifier (*signifiant*) (Saussure 1916). The term 'myth' appears as soon as scholars turn to the Bible text in terms of style and expressive modes. With a divine being as one of the protagonists and tales about the beginnings of time, some passages in the biblical text seem to fit the interpretation of myth as a story about gods and inexplicable things. Myth, from the

---

[1] In this chapter, I will use Bible as a synonym for Hebrew Bible, unless otherwise noted.

Greek *mythos*, in origin refers to a speech, thought or word, or, in a derivate sense, to a tale delivered by word of mouth. These preliminary definitions immediately reveal the connection and even (partial) overlap between the two concepts discussed here.

## MYTH AND NARRATIVE IN BIBLICAL STUDIES: KEY TERMS AND HISTORY

### *What it is about*

The introduction above offers an etymological definition of myth and narrative, as one possibly neutral way of describing the concepts. The history of research on myth and narrative in the Hebrew Bible, however, shows that both terms have been used in a variety of ways. 'We throw traditional tales, magico-religious beliefs, theology, false beliefs, superstitions, ritual formulae, literary images and symbols, and social ideas into a common pot and call the mixture mythology' (Fontenrose 1966: 53). Stephen Moore points out a similar confusion for defining narrative, and biblical narrative in particular (2016: 27). As will become clear from the overview that follows, how a term is understood changes over time and highly depends on the approach adopted. Whereas it is difficult, if not impossible or perhaps even irrelevant, to discern a clear chronological evolution, definitions can be placed on a graded continuum from more narrowly to more broadly defined. What is more, a third concept, that of metaphor, seems to explain the transfer from one end of the continuum to the other.

In its strict sense, myth is a partially if not totally fictive traditional story that explains a special event, custom or practice (e.g. Robertson Smith 1889). Think of examples such as creation narratives or stories which explain the name of a character or a festival. The explanations given are deemed unscientific or, rather, an alternative to what (modern) science would say, often involving a divine being instead. Myth says something about the relationship between this being and humans in one way or another. When defined more broadly, myth is still explanatory in nature but no longer limited to the specific closed story structure implied in the narrow definition. Whereas human–divine relations may still play a role, myth is, first and foremost, an explanatory model used by people to assess past, present and future (Pfoh 2016: 198). To summarize (and at the risk of oversimplifying matters), one could say that myth in its narrow form is a type of story with a very specific format and required elements and characters, while the broader definition of myth sees it as an interpretive frame that is present in a whole array of biblical stories, if not in the Bible as a whole.

Similarly, narrative in its strict sense is a description of events, as one finds it in novels, bedtime stories and some micro-stories within the Bible. It typically has a beginning, middle and end. Depending on the adjective used, narratives can be fictional, but also historical. Narratives have identifiable features such as time, location, characters and plot (e.g. Bar-Efrat 1979; Ryan 2007).[2] Examples from the Hebrew Bible would include the Flood account, but also the patriarchal narratives. More broadly speaking, narrative refers to a mode of communication (Fewell and Heard 2016: 114), a way in which human

---

[2] More recent studies of narrative adopt a prototypical approach, in which stories are compared to the best examples of the narrative category rather than being set against a checklist of features that determine whether they are in or out of the category (Herman 2007; Ryan 2007). This approach can also be found, although without explicitly referring to prototypicality, in studies of the apocalyptic genre in Biblical Studies (Collins 1979).

beings talk about the past, shape the present and imagine the future. This communication is often thought to reflect people's values or view on things (Dick, Segura and Dennehy 2017). Whereas the term 'narrative' may evoke the idea of prose tales,[3] one should keep in mind that its specific forms and genres are not limited to these. Narrative can be poetic, performed, open-ended, multimodal and so on (e.g. Tull 2016). When people speak of the grand narratives of a culture, they refer to narrative in its broad application. What is more, in that particular context, narrative and myth may become interchangeable, as two forms of storytelling that function as tools to understand the world outside the story.[4]

It is precisely in such a role that myth and narrative show close affinity with metaphor, an understanding of one thing through another (Lakoff and Johnson 2003 [1980]). What is more, just like myth and narrative, metaphor has a micro-level appearance in the form of specific metaphorical expressions in a text, often called literary or novel metaphors, and a macro-level appearance that consists of conceptual metaphors underlying the actual words of the text (Steen 2014: 316–17). The narrower definitions of myth and narrative respectively become the more broadly defined concepts when understood metaphorically. The small, specific story is a condensation of a world view. The broad interpretation of the concepts moves the discussion from the particular to the general, from unique expression to more universal conceptualization. There is only one priestly Creation account covering seven days (narrow definition), but there are many stories in the biblical corpus about order or about establishing a position (broad definition).[5]

The hermeneutical role of myth and narrative is intrinsically connected to the immediate communicative situation of the stories. They are told by people to other people in the real world (at least in some specific version of it). As Danna Nolan Fewell states, 'stories, even supposedly individual and private ones, are inherently social and shared' (2016a: 9). Literary research calls this setting or (social) reality in which authors and audience live the extratextual world or situation (Bal 1997: 118). Stylisticians speak of a discourse world (Gavins 2007: 9–10, 18–31). Other researchers use *Sitz im Leben* (Gunkel 1913) or the general term 'context' (Noegel 2007: 11). All these terms refer to the same concept, although emphasizing different aspects of it. Form-critical research and its *Sitz im Leben* is mostly interested in the original sociocultural setting that led up to the production of the tale, whereas in Text World Theory the discourse world refers to everything from the writer and the audience's context that impacts and interacts with how the world of the text is construed when reading it. In other words, the former focuses on what is present when the text is produced the first time, the latter on how that text actually is (re)constructed when it is read (or heard) by a specific reader, be it an ancient or a modern one.

---

[3] Consider, for example, studies such as Robert Alter's *The Art of Biblical Narrative* (1981) or Shimon Bar-Efrat's *Narrative Art in the Bible* (1989, orig. Hebrew 1979), both of which exclusively discuss prosaic stories in their respective works on biblical narrative.

[4] In her book *The Conflict Myth and the Biblical Tradition* (2015), Debra Ballentine initially seems to distinguish myth from narrative (2) but soon enough resorts to expressions such as 'mythic narrative' (3), following the work by Bruce Lincoln (1999: 147).

[5] In his study on the sea in the Hebrew Bible (Cho 2014, 2019), Paul Kang-Kul Cho brings the notions of myth, narrative and metaphor together, although using different terminology (myth, *mûthos* and metaphor) and understanding metaphor more from the rhetorical point of view than the cognitive tradition and myth in a narrower definition as stories with gods. He argues that 'once unmoored from myth, the sea *muthos* became available for later biblical writers to use as a metaphor to interpret, conceptualize and describe many historical events' (2014: 462). I suggest that the argument on a theoretical level can be expanded even more, because not only the *mûthos*, thus the narrative, but also myth, in its broader definition, can function as metaphor.

Another element fundamental to both myth and narrative is the use and role of language. Both are language products. Language is the means by which the stories and their views on a particular reality are transmitted. Scholars such as Robert Lowth (1753) and Johann von Herder (1825) acknowledged early on the importance of how things are told in the Hebrew Bible. Their concern for the expressive modes of especially biblical poetry is apparent throughout their work.[6] Whereas language is where research of the Hebrew Bible starts by definition, it forms the centre of attention in a selective set of approaches, namely literary-rhetorical approaches to myth and narrative (with a focus on literary sophistication) and (cognitive-)linguistic studies (dealing with language more generally as a [conceptual] system). For Robert Alter, for example, the literary form of the Bible is inseparable from its meaning (Alter 1981: x). As a result, he pays close attention to formal features such as repetition, wordplay and structural analogies. A scholar, such as Ellen van Wolde, draws on the Bible's language (and in particular its grammar and semantics) as a frame of reference that reflects reality, experiences and ideas about that reality, and cultural customs, including literary ones (2009).

Finally, myths and narratives come in different forms, which has led scholars to distinguish between several categories. For myth the following distinctions were made: historical myths (related to real events); philosophical-theological myths (offering explanations of the inexplicable); and artistic myths (the kind that was considered to be the product of human creativity without a historical event or a philosophical-theological need to be fulfilled) (Rogerson 1974: 3). As far as the Hebrew Bible goes, the focus was primarily on the first two categories, with the third category mainly created to avoid the issue of multiple gods inherent to some of the narrow definitions of myth (which was considered at odds with the monotheism proclaimed in the biblical text). However, some scholars would show precisely that biblical myths showcased an artistry comparable to that of their Mediterranean neighbours (e.g. Gordon and Rendsburg 1997; Smith 2008; Louden 2019). For narrative as well, scholarship created several subcategories: some topological (Creation narratives, Flood narrative, patriarchal narratives), others in terms of genre (poetic narratives, prophetic narratives, legal or historical narratives), or focalization (female narratives, animal narratives or earth narratives) (e.g. Fewell 2016b). In addition, classifications also distinguished between myth or narrative proper and mythical or narrative elements (such as motifs or characters) (Rogerson 2014: 15). Note that this separation forms an alternative to the broadening of the definition of both terms. The terms 'myth' and 'narrative' are used to refer to stories in their narrow sense, whereas the notion of mythical or narrative elements opens to understanding the respective concepts more broadly.

## How scholarship has dealt with it

Although the above draws out the similarities and connections between myth and narrative, academic scholarship has often treated one or the other. Exceptions are the work of researchers such as Lowth and Herder in the eighteenth and early nineteenth centuries, works that regularly appear in studies of both myth and (literary) narrative. Yet, as time progressed, studies on myth mostly dealt with gods and God, whereas those on

---

[6] Lowth praises the style of the Hebrew Bible, calling it 'sententious, figurative and sublime' (1815: 49). Herder focuses on its combination of image and feeling (1825: 6–7).

narrative tended to focus on the literary qualities of the biblical text with the biblical God being just one of the narrative's characters.

In his foundational work *Myth in the Old Testament*, John Rogerson (1974) offers a chronological overview of the main approaches used to study myth in relation to the Old Testament (or Hebrew Bible) from the eighteenth century onward. Key figures from this period are Robert Lowth and his study of Biblical Hebrew poetry, Christian G. Heyne's interpretation of myth as 'attempts of earliest man to understand and express his experiences by drawing analogies from the world of nature around him' (Rogerson 1974: 3), and the mythical school with Johann P. Gabler who posited that fact and perception of it are inseparable (Rogerson 1974: 7). Johann von Herder concludes the early contributions to the study of myth with a narrower definition that focuses on artistry and stories about gods (Rogerson 1974: 10–14). Already in this first wave of research, it becomes apparent that myth can be understood as both a literary form of text (narrow definition) and an explanatory model (broad definition).

In the first half of the nineteenth century, research on myths develops in two directions (or a combination thereof): philosophical-theological and historical. Wilhelm M.L. de Wette, who combines both approaches, repeats Gabler's point that the two views cannot be separated from each other. He furthermore shows that myth is not something primitive, as Heyne had suggested, by relying on contemporary philosophy for his analysis (Rogerson 1974: 16–23). Whereas de Wette's approach turned to the biblical corpus as a whole, the work by J.F.L. George and Heinrich Ewald narrows that scope significantly. George's philosophical take on myth focuses on isolated fragments in which he sees 'incorrect explanations of natural phenomena' (Rogerson 1974: 25). Ewald adopts an even narrower definition of myth as a story about gods which makes him exclude the Old Testament almost entirely, because its main story is about God (singular), not about gods (plural) (Rogerson 1974: 27–8).

The second half of the nineteenth century gives rise to comparative mythology, drawing on comparative philology. Myth evolves from the narrow definition as found in Ewald's work to a more general understanding of myth as 'the attempt to explain things' (Rogerson 1974: 54). Researchers such as Robertson Smith adopt a view of the Bible that includes both myth and history (Kuper 2016: 7). With Hermann Gunkel, it becomes clear that scholarship has at least two distinct definitions of myth: one that sees it as stories about gods (narrow definition) and one that broadens this to stories about universal questions (such as 'Where do we come from?' and 'Why do we fight?') (Rogerson 1974: 63).

Under influence of developments in other fields, the study of myth becomes intertwined with the study of ritual in the twentieth century. These practices, and thus a specific social context, are the new paradigm to explain some of the stories in the Hebrew Bible. Frazer's famous work *The Golden Bough* (1890) plays a role in this shift, not in the least because Frazer himself turns to the study of the Hebrew Bible (Kuper 2016: 11–12). The pendulum swings again to research that argues that the biblical view is radically different from mythical thought. The work by George E. Wright and the biblical theology movement is here noteworthy to mention. They argue that there is no mythology in the Hebrew Bible (Wright 1950). Leach summarizes the situation in twentieth-century scholarship as a divide between so-called symbolists, for whom myth explains the inexplicable and is even a form of word magic, and functionalists, who consider myths a justification for social action (1961: 387). The answer offered by Claude Lévi-Strauss and structuralism can be seen as a way to bridge the gap. Similarly, work by scholars such as Mary Douglas (1966) and Paul Ricoeur (1960) no longer seems to fit one or the other group but creates a new category of research on myth, combining insights from different approaches (most notably structural-linguistic, ritual and philosophical ideas, but also literary insights and socio-historical ones; Kuper 2016: 19). Whereas scholars keep on considering myth a problematic term for the biblical corpus, it does not keep them from producing insightful studies, such as Brevard Childs's *Myth and Reality in the Old Testament* (1962) and Frank Cross's *Canaanite Myth and Hebrew Epic* (1973).

The tendencies noticed by Rogerson persist in the decades that followed: a going back and forth between various understandings of myth, the adoption of new methodologies to revive old discussions, and a recurring struggle to match the mythical concept with the Hebrew Bible as a document of monotheistic faith. More recent research, however, seems to come at terms with some of these issues, under the influence of globalization as well cognitive science. As a result, the definition of myth is extended more frequently to an explanatory world view, without the restrictions of being about God, natural phenomena or events at the origin of time. This change can be attributed to the growing awareness that human behaviour shows certain universal features, regardless of the day and age one lives in. Or better, it is precisely by comparing all these different cultures and historical periods that researchers have come to realize that there is an interpretation of myth that supersedes the individual definitions. As Emanuel Pfoh has stated, myth can be considered as an 'explanatory worldview employed by "natives" to process and represent reality, past, present and future' (2016: 198). What is more, also non-natives can, with some effort, see how that explanation worked exactly. When Susan Niditch (2000 [1978]) considers underdogs and tricksters, she does this in the broader social context of the ancient Near East. The narratives, or myths if you want, are approached as illuminating the biblical world and the view of the biblical authors on matters such as gender, politics and identity.[7] Similarly, Nicolas Wyatt's study *The Mythic Mind* (2005) shows, through comparison, how the Israelite texts reflect a world view that synthesizes as well as reacts to the ideas of the surrounding cultures of Ugarit, Egypt and Mesopotamia. Likewise, Mark Smith (2010) draws on a broad definition of myth in his work on the first Creation account in Genesis. His analysis lifts myth up to the metalevel of explanation as well as framing of a certain view on reality.

The rise of cognitive science since the 1970s and 1980s is another factor that plays into a broader definition of myth. As pointed out at the beginning of this chapter, human beings are storytellers. What is more, despite fundamentally different circumstances, people's cognitive capacities to make sense of the world have remained the same, as has their physical presence in the world that frames those capacities (D'Andrade 1995).[8] Whereas one may prefer the term 'narrative' or 'story' over 'myth' nowadays, because of the last one's association with god(s), people still produce stories to understand how they were, are and will be. Since this production is inherently bound with the specific material world, stories and myths are embedded in a sociocultural reality. Note that this cognitive turn brings myth in its broad sense closer to narrative. Myth does not necessarily have to be about gods, and as will be shown below, narrative is not necessarily a literary story format detached from the real world.

---

[7] Niditch's work treats legendary narratives relying on folklore methodology. However, in her introductory chapter it becomes clear that myth is part of the larger frame in which she operates. What is more, if she would have adopted a broader definition of myth, the trickster narratives under study could have been labelled as representing a myth of the trickster as 'an essential story and [. . .] a way of seeing, understanding, and organizing reality' (2000 [1978]: 72).

[8] D'Andrade does not discuss myths in his book but outlines the rise of cognitive anthropology more broadly.

Whereas scholarship on myth has a long history, the history of narrative research starts more recently. Even though narrative is intrinsically linked to the Hebrew Bible as a text and appears as a term in almost all research of the Hebrew Bible, narrative itself is seldom the focus of study. For that, one has to wait until the 1960s and 1970s with the rise of literary criticism in biblical studies. The work by Meir Weiss (1984, orig. Hebrew 1962), Jan Fokkelman (1975), and Robert Alter (1981) firmly places narrative on the research agenda as a topic to be studied for its own sake.[9] Drawing on the assumption that the Bible is formally a narrative as any other, they analyse the text's time, space, characters, plot, motifs and other fundamental features. Opposing itself against the dominant historical-critical paradigm, the literary definition of narrative makes abstraction of the world outside the text. It looks, first and foremost, at the internal functioning of texts.[10]

According to Stephen Moore, however, 'biblical literary criticism has, by and large and relative to the often radical options on offer from the extrabiblical field of literary studies, long been a moderate, middle-of-the-road enterprise' (2016: 32). What is more, various studies look for the explanation of literary features in the world outside the text. Rather than sticking with the idea that phenomena, such as paronomasia or metaphor, draw the attention of the audience or appear merely to embellish the text, scholars investigate the social embedding of the text and consider the features' function against that background. Hence, literary features are found to be performative and far more powerful than earlier research had proposed (e.g. Noegel 2007; Vermeulen 2017a). Words were conceived as having a non-conventional link with the thing behind them, as holy (Rabinowitz 1993: 5–25), and as tools to manipulate reality (Noegel 2014: 20–6). 'What is sayable, is knowable. [. . .] Language both constructs a universe of meaning and becomes the means whereby that universe is presented to consciousness' (Fishbane 1998 [1979]: 3). In addition, the social environment in which biblical texts were produced played a role as well (Noegel 2014: 26–30). Biblical narrative is not just a neutral category of storytelling, but a means of shaping and even controlling the world outside the text.

Research on narrative also develops in another direction that is social in a different way. Rather than focusing on the way the texts fitted in the ancient world, cognitive research and especially cognitive linguistics and stylistics look at narrative as both reflecting and dealing with how people perceive the world around them. The way in which stories are told reveals something about how people understand things (e.g. Geertz 2004; van Wolde 2009). Scholars emphasize that 'our stories are never strictly our own, but are shaped by social interaction and inevitably imbued with cultural assumptions and expectations' (Fewell 2016a: 10). In other words, narratives may be particular in one way but are always inscribed in a larger discourse. It is precisely this 'balance between communicating the exceptional and the culturally recognizable and relatable', according to Fewell (2016a: 9), that is necessary for storytelling to be successful. What is more, the reading process (or the listening or viewing process) is not just a reconstruction of ancient views and what writers have tried to transmit to their audience, but it is also and always an interaction between the world of the text (and its composers) and that of an audience (Stockwell 2002: 1–11; Gavins 2007: 8–13). The imaginative process of reading is

---

[9] For a more elaborate discussion of the rise of literary criticism in Hebrew Bible studies and its current relevance, see, among others, Weitzman 2007; Vermeulen 2014; Moore 2016.
[10] Nevertheless, many of these early literary approaches of the Hebrew Bible were accused of having a hidden theological agenda (Benjamin 2007).

impacted by the world in which a reader lives and the assumptions that are out there. These assumptions interact with the views as displayed in the biblical text. This explains why modern readers respond fiercely to stories that, for example, treat women violently. These views stand in contrast with the views of the reader, personal ones but also societal ones. What is more, readers may adopt ideas embedded in the text based on the broader text's authority (e.g. O'Brien 2009).

It is precisely this idea, that narratives both are, as well as affect, social behaviour that lies at the heart of many postmodern narratological approaches. Given their interest in context, very often of the modern reader or mediated through concerns of that reader, Stephen Moore lists these ways to tend to biblical narrative together with the aforementioned cognitive approaches. 'Chameleon-like, it [i.e. narratology in general] has adapted to whatever critical environment it has found itself in' (2016: 39). Work on feminist biblical narratology, for example, has been conducted, among others by Mieke Bal (1988), Phyllis Trible (1984), Athalya Brenner (1985), Susan Ackerman (1998), and Gale Yee (2003) to name just a few. Each of these scholars unravels the narratives of biblical women as the product of their environment and invites readers to reassess the stories in light of their own environment.

As the above reveals, the current study of biblical narrative shows both an interest in the discourse world of the past (original, historical) and that of the present (feminism, ecological, queer), which is the result of an evolution that started with a focus on the text itself and its constitutive narratological parts to a broader view on narrative as a socially embedded form of communication (Fewell 2016a: 3–4).

## KEY TOPICS, QUESTIONS AND DEBATES

Whereas scholars had their specific focus or interests when studying myth and narrative in the Hebrew Bible, their research also reveals a handful of topics and questions that recur in most studies. In no particular order, these topics include the tension between myth/narrative and history, the role of situatedness, the role of God and the representative and/or interpretative nature of myth and narrative.

### *But is it true?*

One of the most debated issues is probably the relation of myth and narrative with history. The discussion seems to be especially heated when it comes to myth and history. For a long time, myth was treated as a made-up story and thus, by definition, the opposite of history, which was considered that which had really happened (Green 1990). As an example, people would point at the Creation narrative in Genesis 1 in which a divine being makes everything in a handful of days. Whereas this is a way to explain the origin of the world and human beings, this explanation differs from the Big Bang theory that science supports (e.g. Arnold 2009: 51–2). The point here is not to start a discussion about creationists versus scientists, but to illustrate that the assumption that myth and history are two different explanatory models is widely accepted. With the arrival of experimental science, the worlds of myth and facts were separated completely. Such has not always been the case. On the contrary, for a very long time and surely in biblical times, the two modes were just that, two modes that had the same goal: to offer insight into why things are the way they are (Lévi-Strauss 1963: 230). The ancient way of answering that question was to offer multiple answers. There was no need to choose one over another because all that truly mattered was offering an explanation. More recently there is a strong call to acknowledge that this distinction between fact and fiction was absent in the biblical world. It was absent in the text (Pfoh 2016: 202).[11] In other words, an analysis of the Hebrew Bible should treat both myth and history as explanatory models and consider them alongside each other and together rather than separately. In a similar way, narrative was opposed to history, and their respective methodologies in biblical studies, literary criticism and historical criticism. Here as well, 'the question is not only whether one can separate between the literary and the historical, but also whether that is necessary after all' (Vermeulen 2014: 8). In the end, a text makes its own history and history its own myths and narratives. Or as Leach has put it, 'a myth is *true* for those who believe in it; whether it is also true in a matter-of-fact, empirical, sense is irrelevant and would, in any case, usually be very difficult to demonstrate' (1983: 8, original emphasis).

## The role of situatedness

All studies of myth and narrative in the Bible emphasize the role of context, especially as in the extratextual context that gave rise to specific stories in particular forms. Social anthropologists look at who interacts with whom according to the stories, who is in power to tell stories to start with and which practices are culturally embedded (Maggio 2014: 90–3). The context is approached as a social given of which the individual is a part. Scholarship has called the ancient Israelite society 'dyadic' (Malina 1979: 128), meaning that 'individual people are not known or valued because of their uniqueness, but in terms of their dyad, that is, some other person or thing' (Neyrey 2016: 47).[12] The importance of the communal distinguishes this society, and many other ancient Mediterranean ones, from the modern Western world. This difference is also reflected in more recent approaches to context, such as Text World Theory, in which both the individual and their sociocultural background are taken into account in the analysis (Gavins 2007: 19–32).[13]

## What about God?

Biblical narrative and myth have often been defined in terms of their theological function. The Hebrew Bible is a story about God and its people. In studies about myth and the Bible, it was precisely this divine element that prompted scholars to use the term 'myth' to start with or to problematize it. Given that myth was used to describe pagan tales with multiple gods, scholarship has time and again struggled with the implied pantheon of gods when applying the term 'myth' to biblical texts. Peter Machinist speaks in that light of 'the problem of myth' (2012). As a result, the term mostly features in studies on the primordial history in Genesis 1–11, a time frame that is considered under the influence of polytheism and far enough back in time to have the biblical God mentioned alongside other gods (e.g. Smith 2010: 139–59). When myth is approached more broadly, the

---

[11] Also called a discussion on emic and etic categories (Headland, Pike and Harris 1990), for example, for literary features or other elements that we superimpose on the text without taking into account that the text and world of that text may have had different categories or a different understanding of the same categories (Noegel 2014: 19–38).
[12] Others use the term 'corporate personality' (e.g. Robinson 1964; Rogerson 1970).
[13] When Gavins introduces the concept of 'discourse world' her example touches upon what she calls a cultural difference between American and British society and their respective way of making a chicken sandwich (with or without cheese). It is precisely her belonging to one group and not the other that leads to the miscommunication she discusses.

incompatibility moves more to the background. What truly matters is the explanatory power of a myth (e.g. Fishbane 2003). For a text such as the Hebrew Bible, this often involves some influence of the divine anyway.

This self-evident inclusion of the human–divine relationship is what one finds in narrative research of the Hebrew Bible. God is treated as one of the characters in the story, regularly one of the protagonists. Debates mainly consist of the role of this divine character. Is he always the protagonist, even when hidden in the background? Or is he a major player in a tale that is, first and foremost, about human beings and their perception of the world? Much depends on the researcher's position, although in general most scholars acknowledge the divine character's role as essential to the biblical story world (Alter 1981; Sternberg 1985; Gunn and Fewell 1993; Amit 2001). Whether they extend this to the world outside the text is a different matter.

*Representation or interpretation*

The study of myth and narrative does not end with identifying the stories and their (social) background. Since these tales are a form of social behaviour, they can be approached as representing a real world or a particular view of that world, or an interpretation of these (Fishbane 2003: 81). In other words, when the Hebrew Bible portrays women's painful childbearing as a punishment for eating from the forbidden fruit of the Tree of Knowledge (Gen. 3.16), is this representing the reality of childbirth (Wurst 2000: 97) or more generally the causal relationship between transgression and punishment? Is the narrative showing a society in which labour and delivery are conceived both as negative and positive (connected to the divine realm that decides on life and death)?[14] Is the story reflecting an interpretation of a mysterious event, rendering it less of an enigma and more controllable?

Whether a story corresponds to a certain reality (childbirth, transgression and punishment) or offers an interpretation of a reality (painful labour and delivery) touches upon another issue, namely, whether the myths and narratives are conveying a general, accepted opinion or whether they form an alternative to this view. The latter includes both accepted and thus perhaps complementary views as well as more revolutionary and possibly rebellious positions. Returning to the above example, one could consider whether Genesis 3's view on labour and delivery is what most people thought or whether it presented a new view on the matter. As with the previous issues, it is clear that all these questions are entangled with concerns about the sociocultural embedding of the stories, their holistic understanding of what modern scholars would call fact and fiction, and their more inclusive take on God and gods.

# CASE STUDY 1: THE FIRST CREATION ACCOUNT AS MYTH AND NARRATIVE

One of the most studied passages of the Hebrew Bible is probably the first Creation account found in Gen. 1.1–2.4a. This tale recounts the creation of the world and all that

---

[14] Karalina Matskevich argues that the text develops several lines of thought: one on childbearing as part of the blessing of God and one of pain as part of the punishment for the humans' transgression. She notes in that respect that the word for pain used in Gen. 3.16 is the same as the one appearing in Adam's punishment in 3.17 and different from words referring to pain related to childbearing elsewhere in the Hebrew Bible (2019: 58).

is upon it in seven days. Instigator of it all is the divine being God. The text has been labelled variously as narrative (Fishbane 1998 [1979]), mythic (Fishbane 2003: 35), account (Polak 2002) and story (Sarna 1989: 3). As the list shows, both narrative and myth appear and, given the other terms in the list, are used mostly in their narrow sense, as particular story formats with a certain form and content. Myth features especially in studies that compare the story with other mythical texts that offer an account of the creation of the world. This comparison can be limited to the ancient Near East but also be widened to other cultural areas (e.g. van Wolde 1995; Gordon and Rendsburg 1997: 33–51). The term 'mythical' refers to the story's content: an account of the beginning, not as much to it including gods. As far as narrative goes, the first Creation account features as prototypical example of a biblical tale (e.g. Fishbane 1998 [1979]: 3–16). It is a closed unit in prose with a distinguishable beginning and end. It builds up to a climax and applies structural features to help its reader navigate the text. It has identifiable characters that do things and objects that undergo these things.

A very insightful study that shows how the first Creation account can be read as a myth more broadly is Mark Smith's *The Priestly Vision of Genesis 1* (2010). In this book, he places the Creation story within its societal context and shows how it not only explains a priestly world view in the tale itself but also reframes the second Creation narrative that follows it. Obviously, whereas scholars distinguish the first Creation account from the second and know the background of each of them, the average reader will read the stories as one. In other words, what is said in Genesis 1 also matters to the stories following. Text World theorists would say that is precisely where world-shifting comes in. Readers build a certain text-world with information from the text and complement it with other information readers carry already. Yet, text-worlds are dynamic. They are adapted as readers go through a text. What is more, new text-worlds are regularly created next to the text-world(s) already produced (Werth 1999: 210–58; Gavins 2007: 47–8). For the Creation narratives in particular, this means that readers cannot but incorporate Genesis 1 in their reading of Genesis 2–3 (unless they deliberately skip the first Creation account). Smith points out that that was precisely the point. By positioning this priestly account first, the explanatory model, the overarching world view as presented in the text, would extend to the second Creation narrative as well (2010: 117–38).

His discussion not only touches upon the mythical aspect of the Genesis 1 story and the world view it includes, but also addresses the role of the expressive mode and thus of the narrative techniques used. The deliberate placing of Genesis 1 before the older Creation account in Genesis 2 is a good example of that. Another example is the structure of seven days used in the story, an innovation compared to other existing creation narratives (Smith 2010: 87). Repetition is a strong mnemonic feature but also an iconic one. Evoking order is presenting order in your story. The audience can predict what is to come next, another day with a morning and an evening and something new to have been created. The text plays with schemas in our head with this repetition. A disruption of this schema creates surprise (Semino 1997: 119–25). This is the case when, on day seven God, stops creating. In addition, the description of this day differs from the other days, lacking the part that marks the end of the day (Collins 2006: 70). Note that the expressive and explanatory mode are perfectly in sync. The former tells the story with precisely that content and in such a way that fits the priestly world view best. As a result, it explains the past, but also aims to shape the future in a particular way.

The Creation account in Genesis 1 seems like the perfect example of myth as a fictive story. Its explanation is unscientific, according to the modern standards of science. The term 'historical' would only apply in the sense that it is an ancient text that has become part of our cultural history. And yet, such a conclusion would be premature. There are several elements in the Creation story that have a historical reality behind them. Take for example the distinctions between heaven and earth, day and night, animals of the sea, the land and the air, male and female. None of these are mythical or made-up entities. What is more, humans have always tried to categorize the world around them. Even today, when male and female are complemented with a third gender X, the notion of categories does not disappear. Another historical reality present in the text is the belief in the cultures surrounding ancient Israel. The biblical God may have been singular, but such was not the case in the Mesopotamian or Canaanite traditions. Scholars have gone out of their way to show that all the possible references in this first Creation narrative to polytheistic cultures are silenced by the text. Think of the echo of Tiamat in *tehom* (Cassuto 1961: 22–4), the mention of *tanninim* (Sarna 1989: 10) and the Sun and Moon (Hasel 1974: 89). Whereas they are part of (non-historical) stories of surrounding cultures, the stories themselves are real. What is more, the biblical Creation account clearly includes this reality in the tale in a way that can be considered conversational (Arnold 2009: 29–32).[15] This conversation is the result of the story's original setting or discourse world.

Scholars often point at the similarities between Genesis 1 and the Babylonian creation epic *Enuma Elish*. This story is unequivocally called a myth, as in 'a story about gods and the beginning of times'. Yet, when discussing the first story of the canonical Hebrew Bible, even with the cultural background and *Enuma Elish* in particular in mind, scholars still refrain from using the label 'myth' or 'mythical' consistently for Genesis 1. At the most, some of its themes or motifs will be called such. In other words, myth is referred to as a narrative component, not a general category, let alone an explanatory frame. The main reason for this is that Genesis 1 introduces its protagonist God as a singular god. He is the creator of everything. No other gods feature in the story. God's position as creator necessarily results in a relationship with his creatures. He controls, for example, the waters, which he separates from the dry land (Gen. 1.9–10). And he treats the human as his associate by having him rule over all that had been created previously (Gen. 1.26, 28). Scholars have described the relationship between God and humanity in Genesis 1 as rather distant and impersonal, this in contrast to Genesis 2 where God is presented in a more affectionate relationship with the human beings (Speiser 1964: 18; Kessler and Deurloo 2004: 40).

The first Creation account is an excellent example to show that myths and narratives can represent the view of a particular group in society. The priestly source is a distinct voice and Genesis 1 is a condensation of that voice's opinion in the form of a narrative and in the form of a myth. It both expresses and explains what this specific group of people thought about the world and God's role in it (Sternberg 1985: 104). Because, obviously, the story may be camouflaged as a story about the beginnings of time, but it is far more about how the biblical God, this new god on the scene, stands for a cult of order and peace and what that means for the audience, not in the past, but in the present. In that respect, the text is 'not simply descriptive of the ancient past' but also 'an ongoing prescription for Israel' (Smith 2010: 111).

---

[15] In other words, if there is a silencing of some sort, it is a conscious one, which shows that the authors were aware of the myths and narratives out there. What is more, they were placed within the orderly structure of the Creation narrative, as such being an integral part of God's Creation (Smith 2001: 38).

As far as which voice is the conventional one in the Hebrew Bible, the purposeful placing of this new account before the one that already existed shows that a new view on things was replacing or attempting to replace an older one. In that respect, the narrative is unconventional, even though it may have represented the dominant viewpoint of that particular day and age. For the biblical text, much of pinpointing this has to do with whose viewpoint we are taking. Are we reading Genesis 1 when it was just added? Or are we reading it much later when Genesis 1 and 2–3 are often read together? And does this reader know about the composition history of the text? From a modern perspective, for example, Genesis 1 may represent an old-fashioned world view, that may have been conventional at one point in time but is no longer right now. Questions about conventionality and representativeness precisely point out the importance of situatedness for understanding myths and narratives. Which extratextual situation are we considering? What did the world look like in that situation? What were the dominant ideas, in this particular case, about the creation of the world, and more generally, about the position of the Israelite God? Who communicated this view? In what way? And to whom?

To conclude this section, let us return one more time to the text. As argued in the first part of this chapter, language plays a crucial role when discussing myth and narrative. It is the means by which the stories are created and transmitted. It is also a very powerful tool that is intrinsically connected to human thought. If well formulated, stories can change the world while the world in turn may also change stories. Genesis 1 plays out this power of the word. It plays subtly with the plural Elohim at the beginning of the story, evoking the polytheistic environment in which the biblical God is trying to establish its position. It uses repetition to create predictability and reinforce the message of the story. Indeed, 'the narrative is not content with the tremendous impact of the story-stuff itself, but reinforces it by an array of original devices that are to recur with variations in future contexts' (Sternberg 1985: 105). Its language is often iconic and performative, thus representing (Vermeulen 2017a) as well as creating the reality it is imagining (Sternberg 1985: 106–8).

## CASE STUDY 2: PSALM 137 AS MYTH AND NARRATIVE

Psalm 137 is a so-called lament psalm that mourns the loss of Jerusalem during the Babylonian Exile (Savran 2000: 45; Plank 2008: 184). At the same time, the psalm is very hopeful (Bellinger 2005: 13) and even combative when it comes to the future. The singers envision the destruction of Babylon and the endurance of a heavenly Jerusalem/Zion. Research on the psalm has taken different angles, with a fair number of sociological studies on exile and its impact (e.g. Berlin 2005; Ahn 2008; Becking 2012). There are also literary analyses that discuss the use of parallelism and imagery in the psalm (Fokkelman 1998: 301–2, 2001: 61–2; Bellinger 2005).

So how can myth and narrative enlighten the discussion, for a psalm that has not been described as a myth nor as a narrative? As explained at the beginning of this chapter, both concepts can be used as communicative modes, one to explain, the other one to express. Starting with the latter, the psalm tells a story of a home, left physically but always kept close mentally. What is more, this mental home surpasses and outwits the actual place where the singers are brought to (being Babylon) by predicting its physical as well as metaphorical end (Vermeulen 2017b: 169–71). The narrative is not told chronologically but jumps back and forth as the psalmist pleases. As such, the eternity of the true home becomes even more apparent, as it is not bound to space nor time

(Couffignal 2005: 67). Even though it is a short story, it is full of suspense with a tension between Babylon and Jerusalem from the very beginning that finds its acme in the violent death of the city's future. Psalm 137 expresses a response to a situation that was life-changing if not outright traumatic (Plank 2008: 184; Lucas 2007: 38.3). It starts with what could be considered a historical reality, of exiled people mourning in Babylon to evolve into a revenge fantasy that functions as a way to deal with the situation (Vermeulen 2020: 68). Obviously, one could question whether there were really people sitting by the river and others pestering them to sing songs that used to be happy.[16] Yet, what this psalm shows is how the story supersedes history, and how it responds to that history. At least, the psalm reveals one particular response. It uses narrative techniques to voice a feeling. Features such as parallelism, the use of oppositions, personification, alliteration and chiasm allow readers to experience some of the singers' distress as well as hope. It is as if, by reading the psalm and working our way through the various storytelling strategies, we develop a coping mechanism to deal with the loss of a home (Lucas 2007: 38.5–38.7; Ahn 2011: 103; Vermeulen 2017b: 171).

Psalm 137 not only tells a story; it also explains something. That is where myth comes into play. The psalm reveals how home has been dealt with in different times and, more importantly, how these different states of home can be reconciled into a future one that is satisfying and hopeful. It explains how the Babylonian Exile was assessed, as a complex given that challenged the idea of Jerusalem as a home (Lucas 2007: 38.1; Ahn 2011: 258). The singers have to redefine home, detaching the physical aspect from mental concepts such as happiness, continuity and safety. The psalm sets up a model that explains how home is perceived in this particular exilic setting (Becking 2012: 280). At the same time, it functions as a possible model for the world of future readers as well (Hays 2005: 50). Finally, one could say that Psalm 137 is also a myth of home in a narrower sense. As a story unit, it explains where people get the idea that home is where the heart is, as one says in English. Because people were forced to leave their physical homes and their home country (Ahn 2011: 67), they could no longer identify these as fundamental to their home concept. Hence, they had to come up with another definition of home. Their focus shifted entirely to the non-tangible aspects of home, things such as prosperity, utmost happiness, familiarity, joy and endurance (Sixsmith 1986), packed in an imaginary world (Lemche 2015: 89).

In the discussion above, I have already pointed out that historical elements are interwoven with the narrative of the text (Ahn 2008). What is more, to truly understand the psalm the situatedness of the text is crucial. This is equally as true for the original setting in which, and for which, it was produced as for the later settings in which it was read. There is no reading without a discourse world outside the text. How narrative strategies are understood depends on that context. Likewise, the explanatory power of the psalm is subject to the circumstances in which it is read. A reader with a nice house in a peaceful area will consider the text less of use to explain its home concept than a person without a roof over their head living in a conflict zone. Yet, both can read Psalm 137 as an explanatory world view of the ancient situation of the Babylonian Exile.

As far as the divine–human relationship goes in this text, it clearly plays a role. It starts with the tormentors asking the singers to sing a song of Zion which is replaced by a song

---

[16] According to Hays, the abuse by the Babylonians should not be taken literally. He argues, 'it is safe to assume that nothing the Babylonians could have done would have made them look like good hosts to the psalmist' (2005: 44).

of the lord in the next verse, indicating the close connection between Zion and God (Couffignal 2005: 65; Maré 2010: 120). Perhaps for that reason the psalmist changes to use of the name Jerusalem when talking about the actual physical destruction of the city, even though in v. 6, he uses the same Jerusalem as a mental construct similar to Zion (Vermeulen 2016).[17] Whereas God is part of the absent world at the beginning of the Psalm, he takes a more present role near the end, when he is addressed. He must remember the violent destruction of Jerusalem and support an equally brutal end for Babylon. Whereas God is not an acting character in this text, the psalmist clearly has a relationship with God. This relationship is strongly rooted in the past, both in happy events (the Zion psalms) and in unhappy ones (the fall of Jerusalem). The speaker addresses God in the present, he is the one who witnessed the loss of the home and he is implicitly present in the future construction of a new home. Whereas the home concept is fundamentally human, God is part of both the story about it and the explanation given for its specific form. God does not create the home for the people, but he is there with them, siding with mental aspects such as safety and continuity. God is presented as the human's companion in their quest for home in this text (Vermeulen 2016).

When saying the psalm explains a certain view on things, the question is not only which view but also whose view. Is what we read the conventional take on things or a new, perhaps revolutionary, perspective? And does it represent a certain reality or is it an interpretation of that reality? To start with the former, the psalm is written for a changed reality the speaker experiences or has experienced (Viviers 2010). Would all people facing exile explain the situation in terms of a spatial battle between Jerusalem and Babylon? Probably not. Would they all use a turn-the-tables rhetoric? More likely, since we find this principle in various other stories in the Hebrew Bible as well as the wider ancient Near East. People strongly believed in the *lex talionis* principle in which the universe could be set right again by matching the punishment to the crime (Becking 2012: 285–6). Would all people turn to images of violated city-women and mother-cities bereft of their children? Not necessarily. There are a few passages in the biblical corpus in which the destruction of cities is imagined through such metaphors; however, there is a far greater number of passages where destroyed cities are not violated or are not even personified at all (Vermeulen 2020). However, when writers turn to this specific personification involving rape and murdered babies, the message surely hits home. Despite it being problematic and amoral, it is a powerful narrative strategy to evoke a strong response in readership (Vermeulen 2020: 67–8). 'Ps 137 might be wrong in its solutions but is not wrong in its deep-seated neurological or ideological experiences of the "other"' (Viviers 2010: 6). In addition, the imagery contributes to the complex picture of home space drawn in the psalm, a picture that tried to capture a torn home concept, one that had to go against its own principles (of safety and security) to reinvent itself. In that respect, it seems unlikely that the myth of home as told in Psalm 137 is a conventional one. It has nothing of the peaceful conversations featuring the Promised Land nor anything of the detailed descriptions of the (re)construction of Jerusalem. It is a new myth for new times.

As far as its representativeness goes, I would like to refer to my previous comments about the history-narrative/myth tension. It all depends on how one defines reality. I follow here the line of thought developed by Pfoh (2016) and others (Callender and

---

[17] If this line of thought is followed through, this would mean that the Psalmist construes Zion and Jerusalem differently. Whereas Jerusalem is presented as a physical and conceptual space, Zion's image is merely conceptual.

Green 2014) that there is no point in separating one from the other because that separation did not exist at the time of the text and, as a result, cannot feature in the views mediated through that text. The text has its own reality. What is more, it creates its own reality,[18] 'replicat[ing] for the reader the spatial dynamic that the psalmist knows on foreign shores: the loss of a center, the forceful coincidence of competing frames, and the unsettling of any "habitual order" of home' (Plank 2008: 185). Psalm 137 represents a certain view on exile, that questions such as the following can draw out further: Why does the psalmist choose an oppositional, openly violent rhetoric to talk about home space? What is the effect of personification and personal address in this psalm? What does it tell us about the relationship with God? How does this story explain exile and loss of home more generally (rather than that of a specific phase in the Babylonian Exile)?

Approaching the psalm through myth and narrative allows looking beyond the historical event of the Babylonian Exile and its traumatic experience. It is also more than noting the poetic form of the story or its use of personification for cities. It is connecting the text and its narrative with its myth, or its expression with its explanation. It is focusing on the how and why in addition to the what. It is seeing where God comes in and where he may be missing. It is understanding narrative strategies and choices within their cultural setting. It is placing the text's reality first, as an expressive and explanatory means of communication that addresses all readers, no matter where or when they live, who they are and what they believe. Human beings are storytellers, and the Hebrew Bible is a damn good story.

# REFERENCES

Ackerman, S. (1998), *Warrior, Dancer, Seductress, Queen: Women in Judges and Biblical Israel*, New York: Doubleday.

Ahn, J. (2008), 'Psalm 137: Complex Communal Laments', *JBL*, 127 (2): 267–89.

Ahn, J. (2011), *Exile as Forced Migrations: A Sociological, Literary, and Theological Approach on the Displacement and Resettlement of the Southern Kingdom of Judah*, Berlin: De Gruyter.

Alter, R. (1981), *The Art of Biblical Narrative*, New York: Basic Books.

Amit, Y. (2001), *Reading Biblical Narratives: Literary Criticism and the Hebrew Bible*, Minneapolis, MN: Fortress Press.

Arnold, B.T. (2009), *Genesis*, Cambridge: Cambridge University Press.

Bal, M. (1988), *Murder and Difference: Gender, Genre, and Scholarship on Sisera's Death*, transl. M. Gumpert, Bloomington: Indiana University Press.

Bal, M. (1997), *Narratology: Introduction to the Theory of Narrative*, 2nd edn, Toronto: University of Toronto Press.

Ballentine, D.S. (2015), *The Conflict Myth and the Biblical Tradition*, Oxford: Oxford University Press.

Bar-Efrat, S. (1979), *The Art of Narration in the Bible*, Tel Aviv: Sifriyat po'alim [Hebrew].

Bar-Efrat, S. (1989), *Narrative Art in the Bible*, JSOTSup 70, Sheffield: Almond Press.

---

[18] Understood by Ben Zvi in terms of '[a] matter[s] of identity', more broadly fitting within goal of the biblical books 'to construct a memory of the past that was central for self-identity and social reproduction within the community' (2012: 11, 1).

Becking, B. (2012), 'Memory and Forgetting in and on the Exile: Remarks on Psalm 137', in E. Ben Zvi and C. Levin (eds), *Remembering and Forgetting in Early Second Temple Judah*, 279–99, FAT 85, Tübingen: Mohr Siebeck.

Bellinger, W.H. (2005), 'Psalm 137: Memory and Poetry', *HBT*, 27: 5–20.

Benjamin, M. (2007), 'The Tacit Agenda of a Literary Approach to the Bible', *Prooftexts*, 27 (2): 254–74.

Ben Zvi, E. (2012), 'Introduction', in E. Ben Zvi and C. Levin (eds), *Remembering and Forgetting in Early Second Temple Judah*, 1–13, FAT 85, Tübingen: Mohr Siebeck.

Berlin, A. (2005), 'Psalms and the Literature of Exile: Psalms 137, 44, 69, and 78', in P.W. Flint and P.D. Miller (eds), *The Book of Psalms: Composition and Reception*, 65–86, Leiden: E.J. Brill.

Brenner, A. (1985), *The Israelite Woman: Social Role and Literary Type in Biblical Narrative*, The Biblical Seminar 2, Sheffield: JSOT Press.

Bruner, J. (1991), 'The Narrative Construction of Reality', *Critical Inquiry*, 18 (1): 1–21.

Callender, D.E. Jr and W.S. Green (2014), 'Introduction: Scholarship Between Myth and Scripture', in D.E. Callender Jr (ed.), *Myth and Scripture: Contemporary Perspectives on Religion, Language, and Imagination*, 1–11, Atlanta, GA: SBL Press.

Carr, D.M. (2011), *The Formation of the Hebrew Bible: A New Reconstruction*, Oxford: Oxford University Press.

Cassuto, U. (1961), *A Commentary on the Book of Genesis, Part One: From Adam to Noah*, Jerusalem: Magnes Press.

Childs, B.S. (1962), *Myth and Reality in the Old Testament*, 2nd edn, London: SCM Press.

Cho, P.K.-K. (2014), 'The Sea in the Hebrew Bible: Myth, Metaphor and *Muthos*', PhD diss., Harvard University, Cambridge, MA.

Cho, P.K.-K. (2019), *Myth, History, and Metaphor in the Hebrew Bible*, Cambridge: Cambridge University Press.

Clines, D.J.A. (1978), *The Theme of the Pentateuch*, JSOTSup 10, Sheffield: JSOT Press.

Collins, C.J. (2006), *Genesis 1–4: A Linguistic, Literary, and Theological Commentary*, Phillipsburg, NJ: P&R.

Collins, J.J., ed. (1979), *Apocalypse: The Morphology of a Genre*, Semeia 14, Chico, CA: Society of Biblical Literature.

Couffignal, R. (2007), 'Approches nouvelles du Psaume 137', *ZAW*, 119 (1): 59–74.

Cross, F.M. (1973), *Canaanite Myth and Hebrew Epic: Essays in the History of the Religion of Israel*, Cambridge, MA: Harvard University Press.

Dancygier, B. (2012), *The Language of Stories: A Cognitive Approach*, Cambridge: Cambridge University Press.

D'Andrade, R. (1995), *The Development of Cognitive Anthropology*, Cambridge: Cambridge University Press.

Dick, H.P., C.P. Segura, and N. Dennehy (2017), 'Narrative in Sociocultural Studies of Language', *Oxford Bibliographies*. Available online: https://www.oxfordbibliographies.com/view/document/obo-9780199766567/obo-9780199766567-0180.xml (accessed 20 October 2020).

Douglas, M. (1966), *Purity and Danger: An Analysis of Concepts of Pollution and Taboo*, London: Routledge and Kegan Paul.

Fewell, D.N. (2016a), 'The Work of Biblical Narrative', in D.N. Fewell (ed.), *The Oxford Handbook of Biblical Narrative*, 3–26, Oxford: Oxford University Press.

Fewell, D.N., ed. (2016b), *The Oxford Handbook of Biblical Narrative*, Oxford: Oxford University Press.

Fewell, D.N. and R.C. Heard (2016), 'The Genesis of Identity in the Biblical World', in D.N. Fewell (ed.), *The Oxford Handbook of Biblical Narrative*, 109–24, Oxford: Oxford University Press.

Fishbane, M. (1998 [1979]), *Biblical Text and Texture: A Literary Reading of Selected Text*, Oxford: Oneworld.

Fishbane, M. (2003), *Biblical Myth and Rabbinic Mythmaking*, Oxford: Oxford University Press.

Fludernik, M. (2007), 'Identity/Alterity', in D. Herman (ed.), *The Cambridge Companion to Narrative*, 260–73, Cambridge: Cambridge University Press.

Fokkelman, J. (1975), *Narrative Art in Genesis: Specimens of Stylistic and Structural Analysis*, SSN 17, Assen: Van Gorcum.

Fokkelman, J. (1998), *Major Poems of the Hebrew Bible at the Interface of Prosody and Structural Analysis Volume II: 85 Psalms and Job 4–14*, SSN 41, Assen: Van Gorcum.

Fokkelman, J. (2001), *Reading Biblical Poetry: An Introductory Guide*, Louisville, KY: Westminster John Knox Press.

Fontenrose, J. (1966), *The Ritual Theory of Myth*, Berkeley: University of California Press.

Frazer, J. (1890), *The Golden Bough: A Study in Magic and Religion*, 2 vols, London: Macmillan.

Gavins, J. (2007), *Text World Theory: An Introduction*, Edinburgh: Edinburgh University Press.

Geertz, A.W. (2004), 'Cognitive Approaches to the Study of Religion', in P. Antes, A.W. Geertz and R.R. Warne (eds), *New Approaches to the Study of Religion: Volume 2: Textual, Comparative, Sociological, and Cognitive Approaches*, 347–99, Berlin: De Gruyter.

Gordon, C.H. and G.A. Rendsburg (1997), *The Bible and the Ancient Near East*, 4th edn, New York: Norton.

Gottschall, J. (2012), *The Storytelling Animal: How Stories Make Us Human*, Boston, MA: Houghton Mifflin Harcourt.

Green, G. (1990), 'Myth, History, and Imagination: The Creation Narratives in Bible and Theology', *HBT*, 12: 19–38.

Gunkel, H. (1913), *Reden und Aufsätze*, Göttingen: Vandenhoeck & Ruprecht.

Gunn, D.M. and D.N. Fewell (1993), *Narrative in the Hebrew Bible*, Oxford: Oxford University Press.

Hasel, G.F. (1974), 'The Polemic Nature of the Genesis Cosmology', *Evangelical Quarterly*, 46: 81–102.

Hays, C.B. (2005), 'How Shall We Sing? Psalm 137 in Historical and Canonical Context', *HBT*, 27: 35–55.

Headland, T., K. Pike and M. Harris, eds (1990), *Emics and Etics: The Insider/Outsider Debate*, Newbury Park, CA: Sage.

Herder, J. von (1825), *Vom Geist der ebräischen Poesie: Eine Anleitung für die Liebhaber derselben und der ältesten Geschichte des menschlichen Geistes*, Leipzig: Barth.

Herman, D. (2003), 'Stories as Tool for Thinking', in D. Herman (ed.), *Narrative Theory and the Cognitive Sciences*, 163–92, Stanford, CA: CSLI.

Herman, D. (2007), 'Introduction', in D. Herman (ed.), *The Cambridge Companion to Narrative*, 3–21, Cambridge: Cambridge University Press.

Kessler, M. and K.A. Deurloo (2004), *A Commentary on Genesis: The Book of Beginnings*, New York: Paulist Press.

Kuper, A. (2016), 'Anthropologists and the Bible', in R. Darnell and F.W. Gleach (eds), *Local Knowledge, Global Stage*, 1–30, Histories of Anthropology Annual 10, Lincoln: University of Nebraska Press [see Chapter 2 in this volume].

Lakoff, G. and M. Johnson (2003 [1980]), *Metaphors We Live By*, Chicago: University of Chicago Press.

Leach, E. (1961), 'Lévi-Strauss in the Garden of Eden: An Examination of Some Recent Developments in the Analysis of Myth', *Transactions of the New York Academy of Sciences* Series II, 23 (4): 386–96.

Leach, E. (1983), 'Anthropological Studies to the Study of the Bible During the Twentieth Century', in E. Leach and D.A. Aycock (eds), *Structuralist Interpretations of Biblical Myth*, 7–32, Cambridge: Cambridge University Press.

Lemche, N.P. (2015), 'Psalm 137: Exile as Hell!', in A.K. de Hemmer Gudme and I. Hjelm (eds), *Myths of Exile: History and Metaphor in the Hebrew Bible*, 89–98, CIS, London: Routledge.

Lévi-Strauss, C. (1963), 'The Structural Study of Myth', in C. Lévi-Strauss, *Structural Anthropology*, 206–31, transl. C. Jacobson and B. Grundfest Schoepf, New York: Basic Books.

Linafelt, T. (2016), 'Poetry and Biblical Narrative', in D.N. Fewell (ed.), *The Oxford Handbook of Biblical Narrative*, 84–92, Oxford: Oxford University Press.

Lincoln, B. (1999), *Theorizing Myth: Narrative, Ideology, and Scholarship*, Chicago: University of Chicago Press.

Louden, B. (2019), *Greek Myth and the Bible*, Abingdon: Routledge.

Lowth, R. (1753), *De sacra poesi Hebraeorum: Praelectiones academicae Oxonii habitae*, Oxford: Clarendon.

Lowth, R. (1815), *Lectures on the Sacred Poetry of the Hebrews*, transl. G. Gregory, Boston: Buckingham.

Lucas, R. (2007), 'The Poet Is Always in Exile: Poetry and Mourning in Psalm 137', *The Bible & Critical Theory*, 3 (3): 38.1–38.11.

Machinist, P. (2012), 'The Problem of Myth in the Hebrew Bible', Lecture in Honor of Richard J. Clifford, Boston College School of Theology and Ministry Continuing Education, 14 March 2012. Available online: https://www.youtube.com/watch?v=9Un13LOBDFA (accessed 12 October 2020).

Maggio, R. (2014), 'The Anthropology of Storytelling and the Storytelling of Anthropology', *Journal of Comparative Research in Anthropology and Sociology*, 5 (2): 89–106.

Malina, B.J. (1979), 'Individual and the Community: Personality in the Social World of Early Christianity', *BTB*, 9 (3): 126–38.

Maré, L.P. (2010), 'Psalm 137: Exile – Not the Time for Singing the Lord's Song', *OTE*, 23 (1): 116–28.

Matskevich, K. (2019), *Construction of Gender and Identity in Genesis: The Subject and the Other*, LHBOTS 647, London: Bloomsbury T&T Clark.

Miller, J.W. (2004), *How the Bible Came to Be: Exploring the Narrative and Message*, New York: Paulist Press.

Moore, S.D. (2016), 'Biblical Narrative Analysis from the New Criticism to the New Narratology', in D.N. Fewell (ed.), *The Oxford Handbook of Biblical Narrative*, 27–50, Oxford: Oxford University Press.

Neyrey, J.H. (2016), 'Dyadism', in J.J. Pilch and B.J. Malina (eds), in *Handbook of Biblical Social Values*, 3rd edn, 46–9, Eugene: OR: Cascade.

Niditch, S. (2000 [1978]), *A Prelude to Biblical Folklore: Underdogs and Tricksters*, Chicago: University of Illinois Press.

Noegel, S.B. (2007), *Nocturnal Ciphers: The Allusive Language of Dreams in the Ancient Near East*, AOS 89, New Haven, CT: American Oriental Society.

Noegel, S.B. (2014), '"Literary" Craft and Performative Power in the Ancient Near East: The Hebrew Bible in Context', in K. Smelik and K. Vermeulen (eds), *Approaches to Literary Readings of Ancient Jewish Writings*, 19–38, SSN 62, Leiden: E.J. Brill.

O'Brien, J.M. (2009), *Nahum*, 2nd edn, Sheffield: Sheffield Phoenix Press.

Pfoh, E. (2016), 'On Finding Myth and History in the Bible: Epistemological and Methodological Observations', in Ł. Niesiołowski-Spanò, J. West and C. Peri (eds), *Finding Myth and History in the Bible: Scholarship, Scholars and Errors*, 196–208, Sheffield: Equinox.

Plank, K.A. (2008), 'By the Waters of a Death Camp: An Intertextual Reading of Psalm 137', *Literature and Theology*, 22 (2): 180–94.

Polak, F.H. (2002), 'Poetic Style and Parallelism in the Creation Account (Genesis 1.1–2.3)', in Y. Hoffman and G. Reventlow (eds), *Creation in Jewish and Christian Tradition*, 2–31, JSOTSup 319, London: Sheffield Academic Press.

Rabinowitz, I. (1993), *A Witness Forever: Ancient Israel's Perception of Literature and the Resultant Hebrew Bible*, Bethesda, MD: CDL Press.

Reck, G.G. (1983), 'Narrative Anthropology', *Anthropology and Humanism Quarterly*, 8 (1): 8–12.

Ricoeur, P. (1960), *La symbolique du mal*, Paris: Aubier.

Robertson Smith, W. (1889), *Lectures on the Religion of the Semites*, 2nd edn, London: A. and C. Black.

Robinson, W. (1964), *Corporate Personality in Ancient Israel*, Philadelphia, PA: Fortress Press.

Rogerson, J.W. (1970), 'The Hebrew Conception of Corporate Personality: A Re-examination', *JTS* NS, 21 (1): 1–16.

Rogerson, J.W. (1974), *Myth in Old Testament Interpretation*, BZAW 134, Berlin: De Gruyter.

Rogerson, J.W. (2014), '"Myth" in the Old Testament', in D.E. Callender Jr (ed.), *Myth and Scripture: Contemporary Perspectives on Religion, Language, and Imagination*, 15–26, Atlanta, GA: SBL Press.

Ryan, M.-L. (2007), 'Toward a Definition of Narrative', in D. Herman (ed.), *The Cambridge Companion to Narrative*, 22–35, Cambridge: Cambridge University Press.

Sarna, N.M. (1989), *Genesis = Be-reshit: The Traditional Hebrew Text with the New JPS Translation*, Philadelphia, PA: Jewish Publication Society.

Saussure, F. de (1916), *Cours de linguistique générale*, Paris: Payot.

Savran, G. (2000), 'How Can We Sing a Song of the Lord? The Strategy of Lament in Psalm 137', *ZAW*, 112 (1): 43–58.

Semino, E. (1997), *Language and World Creation in Poems and Other Texts*, London: Routledge.

Sixsmith, J. (1986), 'The Meaning of Home: An Exploratory Study of Environmental Experience', *Journal of Environmental Psychology*, 6 (4): 281–98.

Smith, M.S. (2001), *The Origins of Biblical Monotheism: Israel's Polytheistic Background and the Ugaritic Texts*, New York: Oxford University Press.

Smith, M.S. (2008), *God in Translation: Deities in Cross-Cultural Discourse in the Biblical World*, Tübingen: Mohr Siebeck.

Smith, M.S. (2010), *The Priestly Vision of Genesis 1*, Minneapolis, MN: Fortress Press.

Sommer, B.D. (1998), *A Prophet Reads Scripture: Allusion in Isaiah 40–66*, Stanford, CA: Stanford University Press.

Speiser, E.A. (1964), *Genesis*, Anchor Bible 1, Garden City, NY: Doubleday.

Steen, G. (2014), 'Metaphor and Style', in P. Stockwell and S. Whiteley (eds), *The Cambridge Handbook of Stylistics*, 315–28, Cambridge: Cambridge University Press.

Sternberg, M. (1985), *The Poetics of Biblical Narrative: Ideological Literature and the Drama of Reading*, Bloomington: Indiana University Press.

Stockwell, P. (2002), *Cognitive Poetics: An Introduction*, London: Routledge.

Trible, P. (1984), *Texts of Terror: Literary-Feminist Readings of Biblical Narratives*, Philadelphia, PA: Fortress Press.

Tull, P.K. (2016), 'Narrative Among the Latter Prophets', in D.N. Fewell (ed.), *The Oxford Handbook of Biblical Narrative*, 215–25, Oxford: Oxford University Press.

van Wolde, E. (1995), *Verhalen over het begin: Genesis 1–11 en andere scheppingsverhalen*, Baarn: Ten Have.

van Wolde, E. (2009), *Reframing Biblical Studies: When Language and Text Meet Culture, Cognition and Context*, Winona Lake, IN: Eisenbrauns.

Vermeulen, K. (2014), 'Introduction: Some Thoughts on Ancient Jewish Texts and the "Literary"', in K. Smelik and K. Vermeulen (eds), *Approaches to Literary Readings of Ancient Jewish Writings*, 1–16, SSN 62, Leiden: E.J. Brill.

Vermeulen, K. (2016), 'The Space in the Crack: Reading Psalm 137 with Jan Fokkelman', paper presented at the EABS Annual Meeting 2016, KULeuven, Leuven, 18 July 2016.

Vermeulen, K. (2017a), 'Verbal Creation: From Linguistic Feature to Literary Motif in Genesis 1–11', *SJOT*, 31 (2): 294–313.

Vermeulen, K. (2017b), 'Home in Biblical and Antwerp City Poems – A Journey', *Arcadia*, 52 (1): 161–82

Vermeulen, K. (2020), *Conceptualizing Biblical Cities: A Stylistic Study*, Cham: Palgrave Macmillan.

Viviers, H. (2010), 'Psalm 137: Perspectives on the (Neuro-) Psychology of Loss: Original Research', *Verbum et Ecclesia*, 31 (1): art. 397. Available online: https://verbumetecclesia.org.za/index.php/ve/article/view/397 (accessed 14 July 2022).

Weiss, M. (1984), *The Bible from Within: A Method of Total Interpretation*, Jerusalem: Magness Press [Orig. Hebrew 1962].

Weitzman, S. (2007), 'Before and After *The Art of Biblical Narrative*', *Prooftexts*, 27 (2): 191–210.

Werth, P. (1999), *Text Worlds: Representing Conceptual Space in Discourse*, London: Longman.

Wright, G.E. (1950), *The Old Testament Against Its Environment*, Studies in Biblical Theology 2, London: SCM Press.

Wurst, S. (2000), '"Beloved, Come Back to Me": Ground's Theme Song in Genesis 3?', in N.C. Habel and S. Wurst, *The Earth Story in Genesis*, 87–104, The Earth Bible 2, Sheffield: Sheffield Academic Press.

Wyatt, N. (2005), *The Mythic Mind: Essays on Cosmology and Religion in Ugaritic and Old Testament Literature*, London: Equinox.

Yee, G.A. (2003), *Poor Banished Children of Eve: Woman as Evil in the Hebrew Bible*, Minneapolis, MN: Fortress Press.

# CHAPTER SEVENTEEN

# A social anthropology of biblical memory

NIELS PETER LEMCHE

## THE TWILIGHT OF HISTORY AND THE DAWN OF MEMORY

Memory is a relative newcomer to the world of Old Testament studies, hardly attended to before the end of the twentieth or the beginning of the twenty-first century. There is a reason for the introduction of this new subject at exactly this time. History as an integral part of the traditional – since the middle of the nineteenth century – system of historical-critical scholarship was dying after it became more and more obvious that the version of Israel's history related by the historiographers of the Old Testament had little in common with actual events in ancient Palestine.[1] Gone were the days of speculating about the whereabouts of the Patriarchs; the sojourn in Egypt never happened, at least never in the form envisaged by the biblical authors; the Period of the Judges had turned out to be a collection of heroic tales from the past, and worst of all, the mighty kingdom of David and Solomon had vanished into the blue leaving (perhaps) a minor chiefdom in the central mountains of Palestine, although even the existence of this minor political entity may be questioned.

The traditional historian went out of business, so to speak. Of course, the process of deconstructing the historian's traditional discourse, aiming at reconstructing '*wie es eigentlich gewesen*' as expressed by the German historian Ludwig von Ranke in the first part of the nineteenth century, was not limited to studies of the biblical history. It was a general trend that found expression in different schools of historical research during the twentieth century leading to a general distrust in our ability to reconstruct the past. The past is a foreign country, as expressed by the North American historian David Lowenthal (2015), something we can never recover, or it is part of a 'metahistory', in the words of another North American historian, Hayden White (1973), intending at creating national histories and imagined societies, even states, in the sense of Benedict Anderson (2006 [1983]) or Hugh Trevor-Roper (2009) (cf. further Hobsbawm and Ranger 1983). The

---

[1] By using the name of Palestine about the territory today split between the modern state of Israel and the quasi-state of the Palestinians, I am referring to the classical name of this country, used by the Assyrians, and by the Greeks from Herodotus (fifth century BCE) and onwards. The Romans reinstated the name after the Jewish rebellions in the first and second centuries CE.

appearance of social history in the last part of the twentieth century was not of much help, although it created a better understanding of the circumstances that lead to history-writing. In spite of attempts by especially North American social anthropologists and archaeologists to create a system for analysing remains from the past which was intended to develop theories about the development of prehistoric societies into historical states, such attempts only led to another set of meta-histories.[2] In biblical studies such approaches were more often than not characterized by an obvious neglect of social anthropological studies in general.[3]

But in spite of all of this the biblical narratives about Israel's glorious past survived. Since the story of ancient Israel is obviously a narrative and not history-writing in any modern sense, the tools inherited from the historical-critical method of the nineteenth century were unsuited to analyse it. In many aspects the method had only led to a kind of circular argumentation that had proven fallacious.[4]

It was in this situation that memory studies came to the rescue of the history of ancient Israel. After all, memory is about the past and a meticulous application of memory approaches might perhaps be able to create a tool used for the extraction of a possible historical origin of this memory. Maybe we might after all save the lost history of ancient Israel, although only in a fragmentary state. Scholars such as Mario Liverani (2003, 2005) and Reinhard Kratz (2013, 2015) would go further and distinguish between biblical Israel whose story is told by biblical historiographers and the actual report of events of ancient Palestine as told by modern historians, but they are not inclined to give up the idea of ancient Israel as the backdrop of such a history. Other scholars made it absolutely clear what the historical purpose of memory studies aimed at, including Ronald Hendel, who states: 'The remembered past is the material with which biblical Israel constructed its identity as a people, a religion, and a culture', but also adds that 'cultural memories tend to be a mixture of historical truth and fiction, composed of "authentic" historical details, folklore motifs, ethnic self-fashioning, ideological claims, and narrative imagination' (Hendel 2005: ix, 58). We may only ask: what is not included? And we will have to realize that several issues are missing. Hendel is only referring to various forms of literary remembrance of the past, but identity is shaped by many other factors relating to food, dress, habits, the landscape and more.

It would, however, be unfair to leave Ronald Hendel alone in this place. Mark S. Smith (2004) is, if anything, even more outspoken in his way of linking history to memory. In Smith's universe, history comes first and memory is a reflection of this history. Philip R. Davies's (2008) approach is not very different. First, we have history, next comes memory. A more conscientious and multifaceted application of memory studies has recently been presented by Daniel D. Pioske (2015), who links historical events to landscapes and later memory. But still, the historical part always lurks in the background. It is obviously nearly impossible for biblical scholars to liberate themselves from this historical referent. Thus,

---

[2] So-called system theory. It became a popular tool for explaining cultural development in the 'New Archaeology' school of L.R. Binford (1972). A well-known example from historians of the early periods of Middle Eastern history is Redman (1978). For an early critique, cf. Lemche 1985: 216–19, and developed in Lemche 1990.

[3] This became abundantly clear when working on my *Early Israel* (1985). Even the most common terms from modern social anthropology were absent, such as 'lineage'. There was no proper understanding of the content of the word 'tribe', nor of 'clan', just to mention a couple of central concepts.

[4] For an overview of the historical-critical method and its shortcomings, cf. Lemche 2008.

a recent study by Matthieu Richelle (2019) clearly builds on the schema: first something happened; then it was embedded in memory, in this case in the form of cultural memory.[5] Memory is made an ancillary of history, although one might think that the relationship should go the other way, saying that history is ancillary to memory, moving from what is known to have happened in the real world to what is imagined by later remembrance. Few scholars seem to realize that there is a definite possibility that nothing happened and that the narrative about the past does not need to rely on what happened in the past but on what people imagined might have happened. Maybe the most obvious example from antiquity is the story of the Greek war against Troy narrated by Homer in the *Iliad*. Did this war ever take place – and in case it did, probably at the end of the Late Bronze Age – or is it simply a story told by a poet (tradition says a blind poet) supposed to have lived at the end of the eighth century BCE, i.e. about 500 years after the end of the Bronze Age?[6]

It is clear that biblical scholars are left in the void when it comes to a subject like cultural memory. It is a recurring story, when new subjects are included in biblical studies. Scholars do not have the proper tools for accessing new methodologies originating within other fields than their own, as they are dominated by philology and theology. This was the case towards the end of the twentieth century when social history became a dominant way of approaching historical studies, and now it is repeated again when the focus is changing to memory studies. Mario Liverani put it pointedly more than fifty years ago when he accused scholars of the Ancient Near East of focusing on philology and traditional historical method in such a way that they were intellectually unprepared to deal with changes within other fields of importance for their own subject (Liverani 1966). It was the case when social anthropology was introduced into Near Eastern studies. It seems still to be the case when social memory studies are involved. The technical part of the subject is sorely neglected.

## HISTORY, MEMORY, COLLECTIVE MEMORY, SOCIAL MEMORY, CULTURAL MEMORY: GETTING IT RIGHT

The matter of definition is alpha and omega to any academic discussion. Without proper definitions all discussions will be chaotic and purposeless. If anything, proper definitions are, in a disturbing degree, absent from modern memory studies. Or, maybe, it can also be said that there are too many and too confusing definitions blurring the discussion. Especially are the demarcations between such subjects as social memory, collective memory and cultural memory unclear.

The first issue to discuss involves the use of the word 'memory' in the 'discipline' of remembering. The second issue has as its subject the many specialized studies from Cicero to Henri Bergson of the notion of memory and its relationship to the modern idea of a collective memory. It does not stop here. We obviously see different terms used about the

---

[5] Richelle's point of departure is this quotation from Jan Assmann: 'what counts for cultural memory is not factual but remembered history. One might even say that cultural memory transforms factual into remembered history, thus turning it into myth'; cf. Assmann (2011: 37–48).
[6] Was there a Trojan War or was there not? An unending debate including almost as many sentiments as the discussion of historicity in the Old Testament. An overview is presented in Bryce 2005: 357–71.

same phenomenon: social memory, collective memory and cultural memory, but are they really identical? It would probably help if memory specialists could agree on a fixed set of terms, thereby establishing a distinction between the different forms of memory. Finally, the relationship between memory and history has never been fully explored, not least because history is in itself a not very well defined subject, relating to the origins of modern history from ancient 'histories', i.e. narratives about the past.

## Memory

'Memory' is in the Anglo-Saxon world the accepted word used in the discussion of remembrance. As such it has a long pedigree going back to Latin *memoria*. Memoria, from *memor*, has several meanings: (1) the faculty of remembering, memory, and recollection; (2) memory, remembrance; (3) a historical account, relation, narration; (4) a written account, narrative, memoir (Lewis and Short 1962 [1879]: 1130). (1) Mainly concerns memory understood to be the ability to remember; (2) is about what is stored in the mind of the person who remembers; (3) has to do with written documents the content of which is supposed to be stored in memory and (4) simply something written about the past.

When the term *loci memoriae* is invoked, a least from the time of Cicero until Giulio Camillo with his memory theatre, they *are* primarily intended to help memory; they are tools used to improve the capability of the memory. They have little to do with what is remembered, i.e. recalling the past. Thus, Cicero's *loci memoriae* did not relate to the past but made-up significant markers in the courtroom where he held his speeches, making it easier for him to remember which points should be part of his speech. The orator, so to speak, moved from one locus to the next as his speech progressed. *Loci memoriae* were rhetorical tools. They had nothing to do with the past, did not imply recollections from the past.[7]

However, when Latin *memoria* is translated into other and especially modern languages, problems arise. In French the usual translation of *memoria* is *mémoire*. Alternative translations are *souvenir* and *réminiscence*. *Mémoire* has the same connotations as *memoria*: the ability to remember, remembrance, memory, but also means something to be remembered. The gender of the word *mémoire* covering both meanings is feminine. There is also a form of *mémoir* having a masculine gender with the meaning of *memoirs*, written records of a person's life. It may also mean 'a piece of writing', more or less synonymous with the English *memorandum*, a note written as information in some concrete situation. French *souvenir* means a recollection, memory (of something), but as a verb 'to remember', 'recollect'. And finally French *réminiscence* means 'memory' both in the sense of remembering and with the meaning of the ability to remember.[8]

In German there are two basic words of importance in this connection, *Erinnerung* and *Gedächtnis*.[9] German *Erinnerung* has two basic meanings: (a) memory and remembrance, both in the sense of remembering something and of being able to remember something;

---

[7] On memory from Antiquity to the Renaissance, Yates 2014 [1966].
[8] The discussion of the French words for memory is based on the entry 'mémoire' in Blinkenberg and Høybye 1984: 1163.
[9] For an almost complete discussion of the two terms in the context of the study of memory, see Gudehus and Eichenberg 2010.

and (b) reminder. It can also be used in the sense of a memento, when something – often a physical item – is brought up as a memento about something often in the past.[10] *Gedächtnis* means memory in the sense of the ability to remember but also memorial or remembrance.[11]

So far, the different meanings of the Latin *memoria* seem to survive in modern European references to memory/*mémoire*/*Gedächtnis-Erinnerung*. This picture hardly changes when we investigate the various meanings and words relating to the phenomenon of memory in English. *Memory*, in a popular definition found on the internet, refers to the processes that are used about the mental capacity or faculty of retaining and reviving facts, events, impressions, etc., or of recalling or recognizing previous experiences.[12]

There are three major processes involved in memory: encoding, storage and retrieval. The *Oxford Learner's Dictionary* places in the first rank 'an individual person's power to remember things'. The second meaning has to do with the retrieval of the past, and therefore memory is also the period from which people may remember events. Finally, memory is also something left when you depart this world. The derived words like memorabilia, memorial etc. follows what has already been found in other languages. Thus, memory is largely concerned with the ability to store *remembrances* about something. *Recollection* also belongs in this context, but is mainly used about short-term memory.

In comparison, Webster's online dictionary has the following definition:

1. The faculty of the mind by which it retains the knowledge of previous thoughts, impressions, or events; [. . .]
2. The reach and positiveness with which a person can remember; the strength and trustworthiness of one's power to reach and represent or to recall the past; [. . .]
3. The actual and distinct retention and recognition of past ideas in the mind; [. . .]
4. The time within which past events can be or are remembered; [. . .][13]

In conclusion, the basic terminology has mainly to do with a human's ability to remember events belonging to the past *and* to the present. It can also be extended to mean the subject which is remembered, or simply recollections from the past. Still, it must be stressed that we are talking about individual memory, about an individual's talent for remembering.

## Collective memory

Until fairly modern times, the study of memory concentrated on an individual's ability to remember and about how to improve this memory through various devices such as the *loci memoriae* arranged in different ways to enhance the memory of particular points to

---

[10] Duden Online: Erinnerung: Fähigkeit, sich an etwas zu erinnern. Besitz aller bisher aufgenommenen Eindrücke; Gedächtnis Eindruck, an den jemand sich erinnert; wieder lebendig werdendes Erlebnis Andenken, Gedenken Erinnerungsstück Niederschrift von Erlebtem; Autobiografie.
[11] Duden Online: Gedächtnis: Fähigkeit, Sinneswahrnehmungen oder psychische Vorgänge (im Gehirn) zu speichern, sodass sie bei geeigneter Gelegenheit ins Bewusstsein treten können; Vermögen, Bewusstseinsinhalte aufzubewahren, zu behalten, zu speichern und sich ins Bewusstsein zurückzurufen, wieder zu beleben; Erinnerung[svermögen].
[12] https://www.dictionary.com/browse/memory.
[13] https://www.webster-dictionary.org/definition/Memory.

be included in a speech. Such *loci memoriae* might even be arranged as a kind of a computer intended to help the individual memory finding connections. The above-mentioned theatre of Camillo was constructed for exactly this purpose by allowing for the movement of thought between different stages and subjects.[14]

This changed during the following centuries, marked by an increasing interest in the individual, with contributions by thinkers such as John Locke (1632–1704), David Hume (1711–76), and Jean-Jacques Rousseau (1712–78), leading to modern psychology and sociology, in the late nineteenth century marked by Sigmund Freud (1856–1939) and Henri Bergson (1859–1941). Studying memory in an individual context was still at the centre of interest in the twentieth century (for an overview, see Rossington and Whitehead 2007).

In this context it is remarkable that the 'father' of the idea of collective memory, Maurice Halbwachs (1877–1945), started as a student of Bergson, only to be converted to sociology when he, at the beginning of the twentieth century, became acquainted with Émile Durkheim (1858–1917), exchanging Bergson's individualistic philosophy with Durkheim's collectivistic study of human sociology.[15] Halbwachs's project was to investigate the foundation of a social group (*cadre social*) in a common memory (*mémoire*), as the glue that keeps such a group together. However, group memory is not a passive recipient of past experience; it is an active player as it forms its own collective memory by adding but certainly also by forgetting recollections. A social group is thus creating its own history. We might also say that memories that are accepted as common to a certain group of people establish the identity of a social group, and thereafter the group creates its own history. It also indicates that memory, and as a consequence also history, is always in a fluid state when new members of a social group add memory to the group or even have memories removed and have history rewritten.[16] Halbwachs, furthermore, published an example of how a social group, the early Christians, formed their image of the Holy Land.[17]

Halbwachs introduced the term 'social memory'. In his later work he also called it 'collective memory'.[18] Seemingly, in the spirit of Halbwachs the two terms are used indiscriminately about the same phenomenon: group memory. The terms are interchangeable, and are used as such in the literature discussing the concept, thus in the various 'readers' and 'companions' devoted to the subject (Radstone and Schwarz 2010; Olick, Vinitzky-Seroussi and Levy 2011; Tota and Hagen 2016). Until the publications of the essentials of Halbwachs's work in English, which only followed in 1980 and 1992,[19]

---

[14] On Camillo's theatre, cf. Yates 2014 [1966]: 135–62.
[15] The introduction to *Maurice Halbwachs: On Collective Memory* (Coser 1992: 1–34), presents an overview on the career and intellectual development of as does the French specialist in Halbwachs studies, Gérard Namer (2000).
[16] Scholars of the Anglo Saxon world are mostly acquainted with the ideas of Halbwachs through the aforementioned selection of his writings in the volume published by Lewis A. Coser (1992). It mainly consists of a selection of his fundamental study, *Les Cadres sociaux de la mémoire* (1925), leaving out very important parts especially at the beginning of the work. A modern edition was prepared by Gérard Namer (Halbwachs 1994).
[17] Halbwachs 1941, of which only a few pages were included in Coser's already mentioned translation.
[18] Halbwachs's second work, *La mémoire collective* (1950), was published after his death in Buchenwald in 1945. A critical edition of the text was published by Gérard Namer (Halbwachs 1997).
[19] The English translation by Ditter and Ditter of *The Collective Memory* (Halbwachs 1980) has been out of print practically since its publication and is almost impossible to find, as noted in Olick, Vinitzky-Seroussi and Levy (2011: 139), probably because the first French edition was sub-standard. Extracts are printed in Olick, Vinitzky-Seroussi and Levy 2011: 139–49, and in Rossington and Whitehead 2007: 139–43.

little discussion of his ideas appeared, even in France as noted by Bruno Péquinot as late as 2007 in his introduction to a series of studies devoted to Halbwachs (Péquinot 2007: 5). It was probably only after Paul Connerton published his critical assessment of Halbwachs' theory in 1989 that the situation began to change.

Connerton's criticism of Halbwachs was well-founded. His point of attack was centred on the very issue of memory, about how memories survive in a social group, and how it is expressed. Because of his adherence to the Durkheim circle, Halbwachs did pay much attention to the mechanics of memory itself, and certainly to the many various forms of memory in existence. Taking up the thread Connerton distinguishes between what he calls social memory and commemorative memory referring to the *Sitz im Leben* of various forms of memory within a group, especially religious ceremonies with a fixed and repeated ritual and with a specific mythic underpinning, but he also draws special attention to bodily 'memories', physical distinctions that mark out special groups.

Connerton's studies have opened up an almost endless discussion of practically all possible aspects of memory and the relations between various forms of memory, especially as it is clear that collective memory is dependent on individual memory but not in the naïve way that it is just a combination of memories belonging to the individuals that make up a social group; it represents just as well the impression of the combined memories on the individual members, as expressed by James V. Wertsch (2009), who claims that collective memory is not only how a social group remembers but just as well how an individual remembers within a group, meaning that an individual's perception of the world is always coloured by his adherence to a social group and its collective.

This approach could be broadened by introducing another aspect of memory, individual as well as collective: what is forgotten? Since the very essence of remembering, originating in the definition of the Latin *memoria* has to do with the ability to remember, it is clear that because this ability sometimes fails and things are forgotten – either unintentionally or intentionally[20] – no memory can be complete. It will always be selective. In a modern society this is most conspicuous, and growing especially when modern demagogues make use of the human ability to forget to promote political and religious programmes that were believed to belong to the past.[21]

## *Memory and history*

Social or collective memory includes as all kinds of memory, recollections relating to the past as well as to the present (within the present generation). Without memory you have no history and no identity. However, identity is not something that stands alone as a consequence of the past; it is far more something that is operative in the present and programming both the past and the future. In spite of this, memory is often confounded

---

[20] The Romans knew this very well: things or persons might be forgotten, and it can be decided that a person should be forgotten, expressed in the *damnatio memoriae* rite, decided by the Senate, where every trace of a person was destroyed, such as was the fate of Lucius Aelius Sejanus who fell from the grace of Emperor Tiberius in 31 CE, whereupon his name was banished from all public venues (primary sources: Tacitus, *Annales*, and Suetonius, *De vitae caesarum*).

[21] On forgetting cf. Weinreich 2005 [1997]. The subject is a main subject in Radstone and Schwarz 2010, Part 3: 'Controversies' (363–464). Ricoeur (2004: 412–56) includes forgetting as an integral of his analysis of memory. Connerton published on the subject twenty years after the appearance of his *How Societies Remember* (1989): *How Modernity Forgets* (2009).

with history; we may even say that the tendency to blend history with memory is increasingly becoming a problem in modern times, when history is used as a *raison d'être* for political programmes demanding, for example, the restoration of the Russian Empire, whether the Tsarist or the Communist one, or presently with the appearance of a kind of neo-Ottomanism as a backdrop for modern Turkish political aspirations in the Middle East.[22]

Complicated as the relationship between history and memory is, it has become even more complicated in recent years, caused by the crisis of history in the modern sense of an exact investigation of what happened in the past. The problem already appears when it comes to terminology. The ancients wrote histories. We have histories in the Old Testament. As a matter of fact, all societies have, since antiquity, produced histories. In the opening of his narratives of the fate of the Greeks in the world, Herodotus wrote in his own words of *histories*:

> This is the showing forth of the Inquiry [histories] of Herodotus of Halicarnassos, to the end that neither the deeds of men may be forgotten by lapse of time, nor the works great and marvellous, which have been produced some by Hellenes and some by Barbarians, may lose their renown; and especially that the causes may be remembered for which these waged war with one another.
>
> —Herodotus 1.1

In his Ionian Greek, Herodotus writes *histories* (ἱστορίης), 'histories' (in the plural), but Greek *historia* (in the singular) does not mean 'history', but as translated here 'enquiry'. It could also be translated with 'investigations' or 'research' (Liddell and Scott 1961: 842). Not even Latin *historia* has the meaning of history, but equals *memoria* (Lewis and Short 1962 [1879]: 858). Classic authors did not write history (in the singular); they wrote histories (in the plural), the results of their investigations.

There is, in this place, no reason to discuss the origins of modern history. Nothing comparable is known from ancient times. The ancient historiographers were authors who put into writing their enquiries about what happened, in times of old and in the present – like Herodotus, and from the same period (fifth century BCE) Thucydides. The Romans adopted the Greek word *historia* with more or the less the same meaning as *memoria*. The Romans would accordingly probably have understood Herodotus to speak about remembrances, *memoriae*, from the past. Anything like modern history understood to be a methodically controlled reconstruction of past and present events was unknown.

Naturally, the relationship between history and memory being a hot spot for debate has been extensively discussed in recent years.[23] The relationship between the remembered past and modern interpretation – whether scholarly or popular – is nowhere clear. Neither has the human ability to invent histories about the past or to select stories from the past been fully explored.[24] It is evident, speaking about memory, that memory is related both to the individual person who possesses a certain memory, and to the collective communication between people where individual memories are stored and transformed.

---

[22] While the role of pan-Slavism as the ideology behind present Russian politics is well known, the case of neo-Ottomanism is not. Yavuz's *Nostalgia for the Empire: The Politics of Neo-Ottomanism* (2020) appeared too late for consideration here.

[23] Among the many works relevant to this discussion, we may mention Le Goff 1992; Hutton 1993; Climo and Cattell 2002; and Cubitt 2007. Essential discussion may also be found in other places, such as A. Assmann 2011.

[24] For discussions see especially Radstone and Schwarz 2010, Part 2: 'How Memory Works' (179–362), and here especially the second section 'Subjectivity and the Social' (235–80).

If the individual passes away, his memory is also gone, and only a vestige of it may survive. We know this especially from the memories of war veterans, because in spite of modern methods of collecting such memories from interviews with veterans, it is not possible for the outsider to understand the emotions connected with memories of this kind. As expressed by Major Richard Winters when asked about how to prepare for war, he answered: 'You cannot prepare for it. It is something you have to cope with yourself.'[25] When the veteran passes away, nobody can recall his memory; it is gone in spite of being often extensively recorded. Only a person who has similar experiences may be able to understand the basis of this memory.

Of course, memories of this kind are extreme, but the case is obvious: individual memory is short lived, basically lasting for only one generation and when lost, it can never be retrieved. No memory understood as the recollection of personal experiences survives the demise of the person who carries these recollections. Group memories are of course more robust, but the coming and going of members of the group indicates that the content of the memory is always in flux. If memories are conveyed into writing, they survive as *cultural memory*, i.e. as results of a fixation of the redaction of these memories; they belong to a different genre and are no more spontaneous recollections. Group memories include and combine, creating a forum for the memories of members of the group. They are always redacted; some memories are accepted, other are rejected, and some are retold with a different meaning. Furthermore, they are always told, meaning that they primarily exist in the communication between the members of the group. How far they spread from their group of origins depends on the character of the group in question and on the type of communication between different groups.

Individual memory cannot be controlled. They belong to the individual in question as the person's own possession. We can perhaps, to a degree, decide the manner in which the memory forms the person, creates her identity, especially if we have alternative sources to the origins of this person's memories. The same applies to collective memory. We can, on the other hand, not always check the reality of the memories, whether individual or collective. Most people have experienced exchanges of memories where disagreement arises over the precise content of the recollections told by other members of the same group. 'This never happened' or 'it did not happen as told'.

If you allow this writer to use a personal example, probably other persons may have the same experience as me, who, in 1968 was a leading member of the student's council at the University of Copenhagen and a close witness to the students' revolt that year. When the fiftieth anniversary celebrations approached, it was for me impossible to identify with the image of the rebellion described in the media in 2018. The rebellion was said to be about flower children, hippies, free drugs and more; but those things were to me never the essentials of the movement, which had a far more important purpose including a change in the way we think, programmatically claiming that nothing has any value if it cannot justify itself. The consequences could be seen during the next decade when in many sectors the academic discourse began to change in a remarkable way and many conventional theories from the past were rejected because they were unable to defend themselves, that is, were seen as obsolete.[26]

---

[25] In an interview given in combination with the miniseries *Band of Brothers* (HBO 2001).
[26] In the context of biblical studies, biblical minimalism, as expressed by the Copenhagen School of biblical studies, is one among many other examples of the changing perspective in science and especially humanities; cf. Lemche 2022.

Memories are always negotiable. They are also individualistic even if shared by many persons carrying their own interpretation of what may have happened. But are they history in the modern sense of a realistic report of events past? There is really only one way to provide an answer: a historical investigation of the content of a memory. The historical worth of a memory of the past is dependent on the person or group who entertains this memory, and as the Greeks and Romans already understood it, the worth of recollections depends on the ability of the mind to remember, or simply *memoria*. Clearly people possess different facilities for storing recollections. The same is true for groups with a collective memory. However, the problems for the use of memory in historical studies do not end here.

We have already discussed the issue of amnesia, forgetfulness. The editing of memories by individuals or groups is evident and may change the content and, even more, the meaning of the original memory. Still, one more problem exists: the human ability to invent memories of the past. Some will say: lie about the past, distort what happened, but in essence it is about redacting what is said about the past. But it goes further than that. Humans possess the ability to invent the past, to create memories that have nothing to do with real events or persons belonging to the past.

## *A case study: Eflatun Pinar*

As an example of how this may work, I will refer to the peculiar case of Eflatun Pinar, 'Plato's Well', in south-western Anatolia (Figure 17.1).[27] This monument goes back to late Hittite times (*c.* 1300 BCE) and was erected in order to provide an impression of Hittite power, marking out the territory of the Hittite kingdom vis-à-vis its neighbours. On the monument we find at the bottom a row of water gods; in the middle, Hittite mountain gods; and at the top the two major Hittite gods, the storm god and the sun goddess, and the imperial sun symbols. In the local memory nothing is left of the meaning of the monument. The modern name is, however, most interesting: *Eflatun Pınar* may mean 'the well of lilac' or 'the well of Plato', *Eflatun* meaning both 'lilac' and 'Plato' in Turkish. The problem is that the philosopher Plato never visited the region where the monument stands, but in the Middle Ages, in the time of Seljuk rule the Konya region, where Eflatun Pinar is situated, it became the centre of Sufi philosophy (as it still is) with its Neoplatonic implications. Plato therefore became a well-known name in the region, and was embraced by the inhabitants to such an extent that they named a major building complex in the outskirts of Konya the *Deyr-i Eflatun* or Eflatun Manastir, 'Plato's Monastery', sacred to the Sufis and said to be visited every year by Mevlana Rumi (1207–73), the Sufi leader.[28]

Plato's connection with the Konya region does not end here. In Seljuk tradition his grave was also found in Konya, next to the Alâeddin Mosque, as part of a church on the mound that forms the centre of the city. Sadly, this church and the grave were destroyed in 1921 or 1922, as was most of the monastery. Evidently the memory of Plato and his relations to Konya was lost at that time.

One question remains: how did the well of Plato become associated with the philosopher? It is situated about a hundred kilometres from Konya itself. Did it get its

---

[27] Sources for this case study: Mellaart 1962; Harmanşah 2015: 67–82; Yalman 2019.
[28] An article (in Turkish) by M. Sabri Doğan, 'Sille'nin efsanelere konu olan Eflatun Manastırı' (Google translation: The Legend of Sille is the Subject of Legends) includes what is known from tradition about this complex: https://www.kozanbilgi.net/sillenin-efsanelere-konu-olan-eflatun-manastiri.html (accessed 15 July 2022).

FIGURE 17.1: Eflatun Pinar, 2015 (author's photograph).

name as part of the process of domesticating the philosopher to central Anatolia? Or was it because of the healing qualities that the well was supposed to possess and which in popular memory might have been looked upon as a part of the popular image of Plato as a magician?[29] The ancient Hittite gods on the monument would probably have been seen as trolls and demons. A third option would be that the name originally meant 'the Well of the Lilac', and changed meaning because of the increasing importance of the tradition about the philosopher in the Konya region. We cannot say; it is just as possible that the well only became the well of the lilac in the twentieth century in combination with Kemal Atatürk's general settlement with religious Ottoman traditions.

This case study shows how memory – in this case a collective one – is created by elements of very different origins, including invention. The only historic reference is the philosopher Plato, but he has absolutely nothing to do with the places linked by tradition to him. Any reminiscence of the monument that was placed in connection with the philosopher is lost, as is by all means the memory of the Hittite Empire that constructed the monument.

It is true that places create memories to become, in the words of the French historian Pierre Nora, *lieux de mémoire*, places of memory.[30] It is also correct that we today live in

---

[29] The tradition of Plato as the subject of veneration from the Persian *magi* goes back to antiquity. According to Seneca such magi, living in Athens at the time of Plato's death, sacrificed at his grave (*Ad Lucilius* 58.31). This tradition is mentioned by Francesco Petrarca, in his *Seniles* XVII, 2.

[30] Nora 1989. See also the implications of this concept in the multivolume work on the history of France published by Nora (1996–8, orig. Fr. 1984–92). An up-to-date review of the discussion can be found in De Nardi et al. 2020. However, it also has to be stressed that Nora's use of the concept of memory places definitely goes back to the Roman idea of *loci memoriae*, but in essence it has little except the name in common with the Roman concept.

a world of monuments that are intended to remind us about past and present events and people, both individually and collectively. It seems that it is a special characteristic of the human race to establish memorials, and it follows our history from the Stone Age to modernity. If anything, the mania of putting up memorials has only been intensified in modern times. No modern state will be without its national monuments, no dictator will rule without having his statues put up at every square where one would fit. Buildings are plastered with inscriptions that tell us that famous persons once lived there, if only for a night or two. The question is: do we remember because we are surrounded by such memorials or are such memorials erected in order that we shall remember?

## Cultural memory

We may talk about cultural memory in this connection, and no ancient culture produced more of such memories than the one which Jan Assmann, who coined the expression 'cultural memory', has as his special field of research: ancient Egypt.[31] In his study of cultural memory, Assmann concentrates on three major ancient cultures: Egypt, Israel and Greece.[32] We will, in this place, ignore his ideas of ancient Israel as a home of cultural memory as they are based on a now obsolete idea of the history and civilization of ancient Israel that had its basis in twentieth-century German biblical scholarship and which can best today best be described as 'idealistic'.[33] Assmann's two other case studies are relevant although very different: in Egypt we may talk about a one-way communication of public memory centred on the deeds of the ruler, the Pharaoh. The memorials included both texts and images. Everyone could see and understand the images but only the literate minority would be initiated into the mysteries of the inscriptions. The impression of ancient Egypt conveyed by these monuments therefore represented the official version of Pharaoh's divine acts, recollected by members of this group and read as long as the hieroglyphs could be understood. In this way the literate elite controlled the communication of the official memory of Egypt.[34]

When the Greeks took over the control of Egypt after Alexander's conquest in 332 BCE. they adopted the Egyptian official memory and adjusted their public manifestations, although they at the same time established memories for themselves. The traditional Egyptian version lived on next to the Greek, but after the Roman annexation of Egypt in 30 BCE, it gradually went into decay with the diminishing importance of the hieroglyphs until the ability to read them finally disappeared in the course of the fourth century CE.[35]

---

[31] Jan Assmann, professor in Egyptology at the University of Heidelberg 1976–2003. His bibliography on strictly Egyptian subjects is extensive, but in this connection, it is his studies in ancient memory that draw interest. His *Cultural Memory and Early Civilization* (2011) has already been mentioned. Other studies of direct relevance include *Ägypten: Eine Sinngeschichte* (1996), *Religion und kulturelles Gedächtnis: Zehn Studien* (2007a), and *Moses der Ägypter: Entzifferung einer Gedächtnisspur* (2007b). A biography was published devoted to him and his work by Schraten (2011).

[32] Assmann 2011: part II, 147–277. This section includes four chapters, on 'Egypt', 'Israel and the Invention of Religion', 'The Birth of History from the Spirit of the Law', and 'Greece and Disciplined Thinking'.

[33] Idealistic in the way it is presenting a rationalized paraphrase of biblical historiography as essentially historical.

[34] 'Elite' is such a misleading concept in connections like this, although often used about almost everything in the media today. The *literati* as they are also sometimes called, constituted in ancient societies a minority that was of course important, but hardly belonged to the 'elite' that ruled the country. They were civil or military officers but not (normally) the ones who 'ruled'. Even today this has not changed, although in the optics of the group belonging to the 'elite' they are the persons in charge.

[35] Hieroglyphs were already interpreted as symbolic signs in the study of Horapollo, normally dated to the fifth century CE. Further on the tradition of the hieroglyphs, Iversen 1961.

Although the meaning of the hieroglyphs was forgotten, the memory of Egypt, or rather of the mystics of Egypt, lived on to this day; it even survived the decipherment of the hieroglyphs in the early part of nineteenth century CE.[36] Official and communicative memory, the message of the Egyptian state to its inhabitants was substituted gradually by a collective memory and transformed accordingly, a shift represented by the change of names of persons and places. Even the ancient name of Egypt, Kemet, was lost except in Coptic memory. The name of Egypt itself comes from Aigyptos, a Greek rendering of Hwt-ka-Ptah, one of the names of Memphis.

The Greek case is in many ways similar to the Egyptian one, but also very dissimilar. There was never a controlling force in the sense of a central government that decided what should be remembered. Neither were the memories confined to leaders of states. Memorials were put up of individuals who had done remarkable things, such as being winner at the Olympic Games, defeated the enemy, or who were great philosophers and artists, but also of mythological figures. We may talk of an ancient Egyptian state sponsored 'official memory'. In Greece memory was truly cultural and collective in a quite different sense. It was also in a way democratized as the easier access to reading and writing using a simple alphabet that was easy to learn made commemorative inscriptions accessible to a far larger community than the Egyptian hieroglyphic documents readable only by the few.

To gain an impression of the importance of the huge collections of memorials available one may go to classical geographers, especially Pausanias, the author of *Description of Greece, Hellados Periegesis* (Ἑλλάδος Περιήγησις), from the second century CE. Pausanias makes extensive use of information from monuments and statues and records such persons' deeds meticulously. For an antiquarian like Pausanias, these are living memories. Definitely the memories of ancient Greece had an important impact on posterity; not least the Romans who, like modern tourists, visited the classical localities in plenty to be part of the Greek heritage.

## CULTURAL MEMORY AND THE BIBLE

Cultural memory, as diverse as it is, has one thing in common in both Egypt and Greece: it is documented in an abundance of inscriptions and monuments put up to enforce the remembrance of the past. In comparison, nothing similar can be found in Palestine before the Hellenistic-Roman Period. There are no official inscriptions, no commemorative monuments, simply nothing. This cannot be a coincidence. Yet to a scholar like Assmann, dealing with a location with an overwhelming amount of everything commemorative, Palestine is still the place of a memory of the past which has no rivals in any other place, the Old Testament/Hebrew Bible. But ancient Palestine was not a cultural-memory culture. It was still a basically oral culture, and nothing like official inscriptions of official iconography dating from the Iron Age has ever been found here.[37]

---

[36] Contrary to the opinion of Jan Assmann, who believes that the modern direct access to the Egyptian through their writings changed Egypt from a mystic society to a historical one: 'Damit hat auch Ägypten aufgehört, ein Gegenstand der Erinnerung zu sein, und ist zu einem Gegenstand der Forschung geworden' (2010: 184).

[37] There is no reason in this place to enter the discussion of what an oral culture remembered and what it forgot, a ghost that has haunted biblical studies for at least two hundred years. This author's ideas about oral memory are very much close to those expressed by Walter Ong (2012), namely that oral societies do not remember much if anything at all. The consequence of literacy has been extensively studied, especially relating to classical culture. But cf. also Goody 2010 and, for the classical world, Havelock 1988. [Cf. also Chapter 15 in this volume].

Yet still the Old Testament is a monument of memories of the past. Nowhere in ancient Near Eastern literary remains have we found such an outspoken interest in the past. 'Remember' (*zakar*) is a dominant concept in biblical historical literature, nowhere more frequent than in Deuteronomy, in cases such as Deut. 15.15: 'You shall remember that you were a servant in the land of Egypt, and the Lord your God brought you out thence with a mighty hand and an outstretched arm; therefore the Lord your God commanded you to keep the sabbath day'; 7.18: 'You shall remember what the Lord your God did to Pharaoh and to all Egypt'; or 8.2: 'And you shall remember all the way which the Lord your God has led you these forty years in the wilderness'. Common for these and other cases is the reference to past events, but only in a few places there are connections made to specific places, as we find, for instance in the book of Genesis (28.18), where the patriarch Jacob sat up a stone in Bethel as a memorial, or in the book of Joshua (4.7): 'So these stones shall be to the people of Israel a memorial [*zikron*] for ever'. If we look for references to monumental inscriptions, the Old Testament comes to our rescue. The best-known example we find in the book of Joshua, ch. 24, where,

> Joshua wrote these words in the book of the law of God; and he took a great stone, and set it up there under the oak in the sanctuary of the Lord. And Joshua said to all the people, 'Behold, this stone shall be a witness against us; for it has heard all the words of the Lord which he spoke to us; therefore it shall be a witness against you, lest you deal falsely with your God.'
>
> —Josh. 24.26–27

Such examples show that the biblical authors had very precise ideas about the function of memory, oral and written. Memory and memorials refer to past events of the people of Israel. It is therefore astonishing that no specimens of physical memorials have been found in the archaeological remains from the territory where these Israelites were supposed to have lived. Are we only talking about a written memory, and should we see the many admonitions to remember (and in some places not to forget) what happened to Israel in the past as warnings against forgetting, or would it be possible to point at a place or an occasion where such a historical memory was kept alive? Scholars and theologians have regularly pointed at the great festivals in Jerusalem as the place where the whole people were supposed to participate, especially the Passover celebrated in remembrance of the deliverance from Egypt and the Sukkoth reminding the Israelites of the way of living in the desert when they escaped from Egypt.[38]

We are now leaving the subject of memory in the technical sense and are moving into the field of the study of biblical texts. Here there are divergences of hypotheses that are mutually exclusive. The traditional understanding as expressed by a perhaps waning majority of scholars would place the relevant text in a context towards the end of the Iron Age, i.e. before 600 BCE. Because of the preservation of both northern central Palestine/Israelite and southern/Jerusalemite traditions (memories), two periods are in focus: (1) the time after the destruction of the Kingdom of Israel in 722 BCE, when it is supposed that a large segment of the Israelite population fled to the south and settled there; their recollections merged with the Judean tradition, to form what is today known as 'ancient

---

[38] Lev. 23.14–17 establishes the rules and reason for the three great festivals in Judaism, Passover, Pentecost and Succoth.

Israel';[39] and (2) the time of King Josiah of Judah, who is said to have reformed the temple services in Jerusalem but also to have initiated a conquest of the territory of the former state of Israel, a project curtailed by the Egyptians who killed Josiah at Megiddo in 609 BCE. In connection with his expansions which included former Israelite territory, a 'national' history was established as *the* cultural memory of his state.[40]

Both options are possible but also easy to criticize.[41] They still leave us in the dark when it comes to the total lack of commemorative items such as inscriptions and iconography commemorating the incidents of this new national history. Nothing has been preserved, perhaps because there was not much; or perhaps, nothing has been preserved because there was nothing to preserve!

For more than three decades a third possibility has become increasingly widespread: the Old Testament is the product of the Hellenistic Age.[42] The basic idea is that apart from the Blessing of Aaron (Num. 6.24–26) which had been discovered in 1979 inscribed on two silver amulets in priestly graves in Jerusalem from *c.* 600 BCE (cf. Barkay et al. 2004), nothing included in the Old Testament predates the second century BCE. This means that if it is possible to explain the present Old Testament as a Hellenistic product, there is no reason to try to push its origins back into an unknown process that should have led to its formation in pre-Hellenistic times. However, being Hellenistic, it should be possible to find traces of traditions from this period in the biblical literature, and this is exactly what is happening at this moment. All kind of motifs and influences from the Greek world are being traced in biblical narrative.[43] Recently also more complex ideas such as the relationship between the Law of Moses and Plato's *Nomoi* are being discussed (Gmirkin 2017).

It is, on the other hand, impossible to overlook other influences on the biblical texts. We definitely find Mesopotamian influence, especially in the Primary History (Genesis 1–11), and in the stories about the three patriarchs (Genesis 11–37), just as Egyptian motifs are absolutely undeniable in the Joseph stories in Genesis (37–50) and in the stories in the book of Exodus about the escape of Israel from Egypt.[44] Neither are motifs and remembrances from ancient Palestine forgotten; the staging of the history of ancient Israel is definitely the scene of ancient Palestine, the land of Israel. Samarian motifs are blended with Judean ones and definitely with a 'Judean' bias, at least from the time where kings should have ruled Israel as a sacred people that had forsaken the rule of its God.

There is no reason to continue. We have three options, two in the Iron Age, and one in the Hellenistic Age. Pure literary studies will probably not help. Furthermore, it is certainly not our task in this place to present a definite solution. But all is not lost. We still possess this collection of scriptures. They represent the result of a literary process. This means that, from a sociological point of view, it should be possible to get closer to the cultural environment that produced this literature.

---

[39] This is the position of the archaeologist Israel Finkelstein, who has for many years entertained the theory that the mixing of Northern, Samarian and Judean traditions or memories happened after the Assyrian conquest of Samaria in 722 BCE.; cf. Finkelstein and Silberman 2001: 229–314 (Part Three 'Judah and the Making of Biblical History').
[40] The idea of looking at the origin of the compilation of the history of ancient Israel in the time of Kong Josiah (640–609 BCE) goes back to Alt 1953: 250–75, and has ever since been refined and edited by later scholars.
[41] This writer has provided criticism of both positions in many places, most clearly perhaps in Lemche 2010.
[42] If not for the first time, the formulation of this thesis is best remembered from Lemche 1993.
[43] Thus extensively in Wajdenbaum 2011. See also the collection of studies in Thompson and Wajdenbaum 2014.
[44] An interesting analysis of Joseph as a Hellenistic sage has been published by Jovanović 2013, placing the biblical figure of Joseph not only in Egypt but in Hellenistic Egypt.

The first requirement is the existence of a written literature. Those who wrote the stories found in the biblical books must have been able to read and write. In this connection the notion of the *literati* as a kind of 'Mandarin' class has become popular.[45] The second requirement is that there is a public who will read the products of the literati. A sociological placement of the collection of written literature like the Old Testament demands a literary culture, and here some requirements are necessary. Minor agrarian communities were not able to sustain a class of scribes writing history for the entertainment of the public, which in such places could neither write nor read. This excludes most places in ancient Palestine. We have to look for larger urban units such as residential cities with a royal administration that would have tolerated some of its members being engaged in literary productivity.

In such a case the writings originating in such an environment would most likely have a propagandistic character, sponsored by the state in question and promoting the great deeds of its sovereign. Nothing of this kind has survived. If anything, the story of ancient Israel as told by biblical historiographers is definitely anti-monarchical; the very institution of kingship is seen as blasphemous.[46] From this angle, the placement of scribal activity in Jerusalem either around 700 or around 600 BCE seems totally out of place. It simply does not make any sense.

The alternative suggested here is that the story of ancient Israel originated in a totally different environment, in the learned circles of the Museion (or even the Serapeion) in Alexandria in the Hellenistic Age.[47] Sponsored by the Ptolemaic kings of Egypt, the institution of the Museion with the famous library provided a place of study for learned people of the time, probably including members of the extensive Jewish community, or what was to become the Jewish community, in which elements from both ancient Samaria and from Jerusalem and Judah blended, merging their traditions – the collective memory – of both groups (and more). This would also be the likely place of incorporating elements of Greek literature, as this literature was present at the library, and Greek was the common language of the time in Alexandria. The Egyptian civilization was present just outside the door of the library as were its old monuments and learned priests to interpret the content of the inscriptions. Mesopotamian tradition was further away but remnants of it were present in the Greek language such as Herodotus' description of Babylonia from the fifth century BCE and most likely also Berossos' Babylonian history (see Gmirkin 2006; cf. further Haubold et al. 2013).

The product, the history of ancient Israel, was definitely a political product aiming of establishing the rights of a religious society to its alleged homeland, ancient Palestine,

---

[45] The biblical scholar who in a particular way has stressed the importance of these *literati* is Ehud Ben Zvi, who has in numerous publications emphasized the importance of such people for the formation of biblical tradition. See recently the major collections of articles on the subject in Ben Zvi 2019. It has to be added that Ben Zvi leans on a date of the historical collection that basically belongs to a pre-Hellenistic period.

[46] The anti-monarchic line of argument in biblical historiography opens with the Prophet Samuel's denunciation of kinship in 1 Samuel 8 in combination with the rise of Saul to king of Israel. And the consequence of the choice of the Israelites of a king is traced all the way through the books of Kings where every ruler is evaluated according to his good or bad relations to Yahweh, the God of Israel. Only a couple receive good marks, such as Hezekiah and Josiah; most – and all the kings from the northern part of Israel – receive bad reviews.

[47] The Museion is said to have been founded by the first Ptolemaic ruler of Egypt, Ptolemaios I Soter (r. 305–282 BCE) as a centre of learning with around a thousand alumni, all paid by the state, a huge library and other facilities. The sources for it mention how foreign – non-Greek – manuscripts were brought in from all over the known world and translated into Greek. Cf. further MacLeod 2004.

now the land of Israel, by tracing the origins of this community back to the land and creating a cultural rather than collective memory of this land and its fate at the hands of foreign conquerors. We cannot control every single element of this cultural memory of the Jewish literati, whether they relied on a genuine memory from the past or just represented invented tradition. Most likely both categories can be found in this literature, and in a few cases historical memory is definitely there, however, surprisingly almost exclusively in combination with the intrusion of foreign powers into the land of Israel, such as Sennacherib's siege of Jerusalem in 701 BCE and Nebuchadnezzar's destruction of Jerusalem in 597 or 587,[48] both commemorated in Assyrian and Babylonian official annals and iconography. Without such external evidence we are lost in tales from the past without being able to decide whether they are genuine recollections or fictive storytelling. Maybe the emergence and programme of this biblical historiography should be linked to the resurgence of the interest in Palestine as the land of Israel and its history in Hellenistic times as studied by Doron Mendels (1987, 1992).

## IN CONCLUSION

A sociological analysis of biblical memory had rather surprising consequences. Biblical historiography was not the memory of ancient Israel of its own past as imagined by Ronald Hendel and other biblical scholars. It was a learned composition put together centuries after the downfall of the petty states of Palestine at the end of the Iron Age by scholars living most likely under Greek dominion in Alexandria in Egypt, borrowing their themes and motifs from the vast literature accessible to them in the gems of the famous library in Alexandria. The Old Testament is not the collective memory of any state of the past; it is a cultural memory created by a literary circle of scholars. It was definitely composed for religious and political reasons, and it was definitely persuasive and has remained so to this day. In his *Oltre la Bibbia* (2003), Mario Liverani sees every section of the story about ancient Israel as a response to challenges belonging to the periods when these sections were put into writing. Maybe it is time to see not only the single parts as such responses; maybe it is time to consider the story in its entirety as a response to a challenge.

## REFERENCES

Alt, A. (1953), 'Die Heimat des Deuteronomiums', in A. Alt, *Kleine Schriften zur Geschichte Israels, Bd. II*, ed. M. Noth, 250–75, München: C.H. Beck.
Anderson, B. (2006 [1983]), *Imagined Communities: Reflections on the Origin and Spread of Nationalism*, rev. edn, London: Verso Books.
Assmann, A. (2011), *Cultural Memory and Western Civilization: Functions, Media, Archives*, Cambridge: Cambridge University Press.
Assmann, J. (1996), *Ägypten: Eine Sinngeschichte*, München: Carl Hanser.
Assmann, J. (2007a), *Religion und kulturelles Gedächtnis: Zehn Studien*, München: C.H. Beck.
Assmann, J. (2007b), *Moses der Ägypter: Entzifferung einer Gedächtnisspur*, Frankfurt am Main: Fischer Taschenbuch.

---

[48] For 701 BCE, compare 2 Kgs 18–20 and the Assyrian version in Luckenbill 2005 [1924]: 33–4; and for 697 BCE, Grayson 2000: 102. We have no external source for the destruction of Jerusalem in 587 BCE.

Assmann, J. (2010), *Erinnertes Ägypten: Pharaonische Motive in der europäischen Religions- und Geistesgeschichte*, Berlin: Kulturverlag Kadmos.

Assmann, J. (2011), *Cultural Memory and Early Civilization: Writing, Remembrance, and Political Imagination*, Cambridge: Cambridge University Press [German original *Das kulturelle Gedächtnis: Schrift, Erinnerung und politische Identität in frühen Hochkulturen*, München: C.H. Beck, 1999].

Barkay, G., M.J. Lundberg, A.G. Vaughn and B. Zuckerman (2004), 'The Amulets from Ketef Hinnom: A New Edition and Evaluation', *BASOR*, 334: 41–70.

Ben Zvi, E. (2019), *Social Memory Among the Literati of Yehud*, BZAW 509; Berlin: De Gruyter.

Binford, L.R. (1972), *An Archaeological Perspective*, New York: Seminar Press.

Blinkenberg, A. and P. Høybye (1984), *Fransk-Dansk Ordbog*, 2nd edn, Erhvervssproglige skrifter 8, København: Arnold Busck.

Bryce, T. (2005), *The Kingdom of the Hittites*, new edn, Oxford: Oxford University Press.

Climo, J.J. and M.G. Cattell, eds (2002), *Social Memory and History: Anthropological Perspectives*, Walnut Creek, CA: AltaMira.

Connerton, P. (1989), *How Societies Remember*, Cambridge: Cambridge University Press.

Connerton, P. (2009), *How Modernity Forgets*, Cambridge: Cambridge University Press.

Coser, L.A., ed. (1992), *Maurice Halbwachs: On Collective Memory*, Chicago: University of Chicago Press.

Cubitt, G. (2007), *History and Memory*, Manchester: Manchester University Press.

Davies, P.R. (2008), *Memories of Ancient Israel: An Introduction to Biblical History – Ancient and Modern*, Louisville, KY: Westminster John Knox Press.

De Nardi, S., H. Orange, S. High and E. Koskinen-Koivisto, eds (2020), *The Routledge Handbook of Memory and Place*, Abingdon: Routledge.

Finkelstein, I. and N.A. Silberman (2001), *The Bible Unearthed: Archaeology's New Vision of Ancient Israel and the Origin of Its Sacred Texts*, New York: Free Press.

Gmirkin, R.E. (2006), *Berossus and Genesis, Manetho and Exodus: Hellenistic Histories and the Date of the Pentateuch*, LHBOTS 433, London: T&T Clark.

Gmirkin, R.E. (2017), *Plato and the Creation of the Hebrew Bible*, CIS, Abingdon: Routledge.

Goody, J. (2010), *Myth, Ritual and the Oral*, Cambridge: Cambridge University Press.

Grayson, A.K. (2000), *Assyrian and Babylonian Chronicles*, Winona Lake, IN: Eisenbrauns.

Gudehus, C. and A. Eichenberg, eds (2010), *Gedächtnis und Erinnerung: Ein interdisziplinäres Handbuch*, Stuttgart: J.B. Metzler.

Halbwachs, M. (1925), *Les cadres sociaux de la mémoire*, Paris: Alcan.

Halbwachs, M. (1941), *La topographie légendaire des évangiles en Terre sainte: Étude de mémoire collective*, Paris: Presses Universitaires de France.

Halbwachs, M. (1950), *La mémoire collective*, Paris: Presses Universitaires de France.

Halbwachs, M. (1980), *The Collective Memory, with an Introduction by Mary Douglas*, transl. F.J. Ditter and V.Y. Ditter, New York: Harper and Row.

Halbwachs, M. (1994), *Les cadres sociaux de la mémoire: postface de Gérard Namer*, Paris: Albin Michel.

Halbwachs, M. (1997), *La mémoire collective: Éditions critique établie par Gérard Namer*, Paris: Albin Michel.

Harmanşah, Ö. (2015), *Place, Memory, and Healing: An Archaeology of Anatolian Rock Monuments*, Abingdon: Routledge.

Haubold, J., G.B. Lanfranchi, R. Rollinger and J. Steele, eds (2013), *The World of Berossos: Proceedings of the 4th International Colloquium on 'The Ancient Near East Between*

*Classical and Ancient Oriental Traditions', Hartfield College, Durham 7th–9th July 2010*, Classica et Orientalia 5, Wiesbaden: Harrassowitz.

Havelock, E.A. (1988), *The Muse Learns to Write: Reflections on Orality and Literacy from Antiquity to the Present*, New Haven, CT: Yale University Press.

Hendel, R.S. (2005), *Remembering Abraham: Culture, Memory, and History in the Hebrew Bible*, Oxford: Oxford University Press.

Herodotus (2015), *The Histories*, transl. G.C. Macaulay, Titan Read (Kindle edition).

Hobsbawm, E.J. and T. Ranger, eds (1983), *The Invention of Tradition*, Cambridge: Cambridge University Press.

Hutton, P.H. (1993), *History as an Art of Memory*, Burlington: University of Vermont Press.

Iversen, E. (1961), *The Myth of Egypt and Its Hieroglyphs*, Copenhagen: GEC Gad.

Jovanović, L. (2013), *The Joseph of Genesis as Hellenistic Scientist*, HBM 48, Sheffield: Sheffield Phoenix Press.

Kratz, R.G. (2013), *Historisches und biblisches Israel: Drei Überblicke zum Alten Testament*, Tübingen: Mohr Siebeck.

Kratz, R.G. (2015), *Historical and Biblical Israel: The History, Tradition, and Archives of Israel and Judah*, transl. P.M. Kurtz, Oxford: Oxford University Press.

Le Goff, J. (1992), *History and Memory*, New York: Columbia University Press.

Lemche, N.P. (1985), *Early Israel: Anthropological and Historical Studies on the Israelite Society Before the Monarchy*, VTSup 37, Leiden: E.J. Brill.

Lemche, N.P. (1990), 'On the Use of "System Theory", "Macro Theories" and Evolutionistic Thinking in Modern OT Research and Biblical Archaeology', *SJOT*, 4 (2): 73–88.

Lemche, N.P. (1993), 'The Old Testament – A Hellenistic Book?', *SJOT*, 7 (2): 163–93.

Lemche, N.P. (2008), *The Old Testament Between Theology and History: A Critical Survey*, LAI, Louisville, KY: Westminster John Knox Press.

Lemche, N.P. (2010), 'The Deuteronomistic History: Historical Reconsiderations', in K.L. Noll and B. Schramm (eds.), *Raising Up a Faithful Exegete: Essays in Honor of Richard D. Nelson*, 41–50, Winona Lake, IN: Eisenbrauns.

Lemche, N.P. (2022), *Back to Reason: Minimalism in Biblical Studies*, DANEBS, Sheffield: Equinox.

Lewis, C. and C. Short. (1962 [1879]), *A Latin Dictionary: Founded on Andrews' Edition of Freund's Latin Dictionary*, Oxford: Clarendon Press.

Liddell, H.G. and R. Scott (1961), *A Greek–English Lexicon: A New Edition Revised and Augmented Throughout by Henry Stuart Jones with the Assistance of Roderick McKenzie*, Oxford: Clarendon Press.

Liverani, M. (1966), 'Problemi e indirizzi degli studi storici sul Vicino Oriente antico', *Cultura e Scuola*, 20: 72–9.

Liverani, M. (2003), *Oltre la Bibbia: Storia antica di Israele*, Rome: Laterza.

Liverani, M. (2005), *Israel's History and the History of Israel*, transl. P.R. Davies and C. Peri, London: Equinox.

Lowenthal, D. (2015), *The Past Is a Foreign Country – Revisited*, Cambridge: Cambridge University Press.

Luckenbill, D.D. (2005 [1924]), *The Annals of Sennacherib*, Ancient Texts and Translations, Eugene, OR: Wipf & Stock.

MacLeod, R. (2004), *The Library of Alexandria: Centre of Learning in the Ancient World*, London: I.B. Tauris.

Mellaart, J. (1962), 'The Late Bronze Age Monuments of Eflatun Pınar and Fasıllar near Beyşehir', *Anatolian Studies*, 12: 111–17.
Mendels, D. (1987), *The Land of Israel as a Political Concept in Hasmonean Literature: Recourse to History in Second Century B.C. Claims to the Holy Land*, Texte und Studien zum Antiken Judentum 15, Tübingen: J.C.B. Mohr (Paul Siebeck).
Mendels, D. (1992), *The Rise and Fall of Jewish Nationalism*, Anchor Bible Reference Library, New York: Doubleday.
Namer, G. (2000), *Halbwachs et la mémoire sociale*, Paris: L'Harmattan.
Nora, P., ed. (1984–92), *Les Lieux de mémoire*, 3 tomes, Paris: Gallimard.
Nora, P. (1989), 'Between Memory and History: *Les Lieux de Mémoire*', *Representations*, 26: 7–24.
Nora, P., ed. (1996–8), *Realms of Memory: The Construction of the French Past*, 3 vols, New York: Columbia University Press
Olick, J.K., V. Vinitzky-Seroussi and D. Levy, eds (2011), *The Collective Memory Reader*, Oxford: Oxford University Press.
Ong, W.J. (2012), *Orality and Literacy*, 30th Anniversary Edition, with additional chapters by John Hartley, Abingdon: Routledge.
Péquinot, B., ed. (2007), *Maurice Halbwachs: le temps, la mémoire et l'émotion*, Paris: L'Harmattan.
Pioske, D.D. (2015), *David's Jerusalem: Between Memory and History*, Abingdon: Routledge.
Radstone, S. and B. Schwarz, eds (2010), *Memory: Histories, Theories, Debates*, New York: Fordham University Press.
Redman, C.L. (1978), *The Rise of Civilization: From Early Farmers to Urban Society in the Ancient Near East*, San Francisco: W.H. Freeman.
Richelle, M. (2019), 'Cultural Memory from Israel to Judah', *Semitica*, 61: 373–97.
Ricoeur, P. (2004), *Memory, History, Forgetting*, transl. K. Blamey and D. Pellauer, Chicago: Chicago University Press.
Rossington, M. and A. Whitehead. eds (2007), *Theories of Memory: A Reader*, Edinburgh: Edinburgh University Press.
Schraten, J. (2011), *Zur Aktualität von Jan Assmann: Einleitung in sein Werk*, Wiesbaden: VS Verlag.
Smith, M.S. (2004), *The Memoirs of God: History, Memory, and the Experience of the Divine in Ancient Israel*, Minneapolis, MN: Fortress Press.
Thompson, T.L. and P. Wajdenbaum, eds (2014), *The Bible and Hellenism: Greek Influence on Jewish and Early Christian Literature*, CIS, Durham, UK: Acumen.
Tota, A.L. and T. Hagen, eds (2016), *Routledge International Handbook of Memory Studies*, Abingdon: Routledge.
Trevor-Roper, H. (2009), *The Invention of Scotland: Myth and History*, New Haven, CT: Yale University Press.
Wajdenbaum, P. (2011), *Argonauts of the Desert: Structural Analysis of the Hebrew Bible*, CIS, Sheffield: Equinox.
Weinreich, H. (2005 [1997]), *Lethe: Kunst und Kritik des Vergessens*, München: C.H. Beck.
Wertsch, J.V. (2009), 'Collective Memory', in P. Boyer and J.V. Wertsch (eds), *Memory in Mind and Culture*, 117–37, Cambridge: Cambridge University Press.
White, H. (1973), *Metahistory: The Historical Imagination in Nineteenth-Century Europe*, Baltimore, MD: Johns Hopkins University Press.

Yalman, S. (2019), 'From Plato to the *Shāhnāma*: Reflections on Saintly Veneration in Seljuk Konya', in S. Yalman and A.H. Uğurlu (eds), *Sacred Spaces and Urban Networks: 11th International ANAMED Symposium*, 119–40, Istanbul: ANAMED.

Yates, F. (2014 [1966]), *The Art of Memory*, London: Bodley Head.

Yavuz, M.H. (2020), *Nostalgia for the Empire: The Politics of Neo-Ottomanism*, New York: Oxford University Press.

# CHAPTER EIGHTEEN

# Acts that work, texts that work

## *Ritual in the Hebrew Bible*

ANNE KATRINE DE HEMMER GUDME

## INTRODUCTION

The Hebrew Bible is a collection of texts teeming with ritual. This may be exemplified by the first book in that collection, Genesis. When Cain and Abel present their offering (מנחה) to Yahweh in Genesis 4, they perform a ritual, as does Noah in Genesis 8 when he offers burnt offerings (עלה) to Yahweh after the Flood. In Genesis 17, Abraham performs a ritual as he circumcises himself and his household as a sign of his covenant with God (cf. the Shechemites in Genesis 34) and again, when he buries his wife Sarah in Genesis 23 (cf. the burial of Abraham in Genesis 25, of Isaac in Genesis 35, and of Jacob in Genesis 50). In Genesis 28, Jacob performs a ritual as he makes a conditional vow (נדר) to Yahweh, promising yet more ritual activity, to set up a standing stone and create a sanctuary and to offer tithes there, if Yahweh will ensure his safety. These are all relatively clear examples of ritual practices and most readers and interpreters of the Hebrew Bible would recognize them as such.[1]

If the abovementioned examples are 'clear' cases of ritual in the Hebrew Bible, there are also less clear hints of possible ritual practices in the texts. For instance in Genesis 15, where Abraham sees a smoking oven and a burning torch pass through a row of severed animal carcasses. This text may allude to a ritual practice connected with covenant-making, the details of which are now long forgotten. Admittedly, the text may also simply be using the obscure as a narrative tool in order to relate an experience of divine revelation. A slightly less obscure reference to a seemingly ritualized gesture can be found in Genesis 24, where Abraham orders his servant to place his hand under Abraham's thigh (ירך) as he swears (שבע) an oath. This way of substantiating a speech act, a solemn promise, with a formalized gesture, placing one's hand on the recipient of the oath, can certainly be categorized as a ritual action. Similarly, the reference to bear children on the knees (ברך) of another woman in Genesis 30 may carry the echo of a ritual practice or gesture intended

---

[1] These are also texts that have been commented upon and analysed extensively and repeatedly, but focused ritual theoretical analyses of these texts remain rare.

to transfer parentage from a child's biological parents to its adopted parents. Again, it may also merely be a figure of speech in biblical Hebrew. Along the same lines, and with a similar lack of clarity, the mention of a great feast (משתה) on the day of Isaac's weaning (גמל) in Genesis 21 may allude to a customary ritual celebration of an important transition in a young child's life. However, it may also simply be a detail included by the author in this particular narrative in order to stress a father's delight in his firstborn son.

Indeed, the Hebrew Bible is so teeming with ritual, explicit and implicit, clear and obscure, that theorizing is necessary to foreground it. In the next section, I shall give an introduction to the study of ritual and outline the most prominent currents in ritual studies in recent decades. Then I shall offer a brief survey of the kinds of ritual we find in the Hebrew Bible and of the kinds of texts and literary genres that we find these rituals in. Here, I divide the Hebrew Bible into two main parts, the so-called priestly texts in the Pentateuch that have an explicit and almost programmatic interest in ritual and the non-priestly texts in the Hebrew Bible, in which ritual plays a much more subtle role. I conclude this section with a discussion of method and application, in which I offer a few reflections on the literary character of ritual in the Hebrew Bible and how best to apply ritual theory to Hebrew Bible ritual texts ('Literary Ritual and Ritual Fiction'). In the last two sections of the chapter, I present two examples to demonstrate how ritual theory may guide and inform an analysis of ritual in the Hebrew Bible.[2] The first example is ritual mourning. In the Hebrew Bible, ritual mourning is a relatively uniform set of practices, such as the absence of hygiene and personal grooming, wailing, gestures of despair and fasting, but, depending on the context of these practices, the ritual has different audiences and serves different functions. For this study, I have chosen petitionary mourning, the performance of ritual mourning behaviour in order to appeal to a deity. I have chosen this example because it illustrates three aspects of ritual particularly well: first, the relationship between one ritual form and several ritual functions, second, the connection between the 'genre' or category of a ritual action and expectations of ritual efficacy, and third, it is a good example of ritual as a category of action that mirrors social action. The specific example of King David's performance of petitionary mourning in 2 Samuel 12 is also a very good example of how a description of ritual behaviour is used as a literary tool to characterize persons in Hebrew Bible texts. The second example is the ritual behaviour prescribed for a female prisoner of war and her Israelite captor in Deut. 21.12–13. This brief legal text describes what can be called a classic rite of passage, where one of the ritual actors, the female captive, undergoes a transformation and changes her social status from captive to wife. This ritual is a good example of ritual transformation and of the tension between ritual efficacy and individual disposition. It illustrates what Roy A. Rappaport has called the *meta-performativity* of ritual – the capacity that ritual behaviour has to establish conventions of how behaviour *should* be in spite of any resistance felt by individual ritual actors (1999: 123).

---

[2] I have chosen my two examples in the sections 'Doing Things with Tears' and 'Ritual Transformation' from non-priestly Hebrew Bible texts, because so far in Hebrew Bible scholarship on ritual in general, and admittedly in my own research as well, the priestly texts have received far more attention than the non-priestly texts. With this study, I have decided to make a small contribution to correcting this bias. Readers with a particular interest in ritual theory applied to priestly texts may find Gudme 2009b on the Nazirite law in Numbers 6, Gudme 2013c on the Law of jealousy in Numbers 5 and Gudme forthcoming on the ritual use of incense in Exodus 30 and Leviticus 16 informative.

## RITUAL AND RITUAL STUDIES

Ritual studies has emerged and developed as an interdisciplinary academic field in the twentieth and twenty-first centuries.[3] The main contributions to ritual studies come from anthropology and religious studies, but theology and biblical studies also have a growing place as contributors to this field. Historically, ritual has been somewhat overlooked – or even purposefully avoided – by theologians and biblical scholars, possibly because of an anti-ritual bias influenced by Christian Protestant theology's wariness of ritual practices and 'works' in general (cf. Bell 2006: 399). Since the late twentieth century, however, ritual has increasingly come into focus in biblical studies as a steadily growing corpus of ritual-focused publications can attest.[4] Although this chapter is part of a companion to anthropology and the Hebrew Bible, I shall not limit myself to a survey of specifically anthropological contributions to ritual studies and ritual theory, but rather try to give a concise and functional summary of how ritual studies have developed in a conversation between anthropology, religious studies and their cognate academic fields. My aim is to provide a conceptual foundation and a theoretical toolbox for analysing ritual in the Hebrew Bible.

### *From defining to characterizing ritual*

The first challenge that faces anyone interested in the study of ritual is the problem of definition and delineation. What exactly *is* a ritual? Whereas most people have an almost intuitive understanding of ritual and recognize it as a category of action when they see it performed in real life or described in a text (cf. Sørensen 2007: 33–45), it has proven impossible to formulate a commonly agreed upon definition of what constitutes a ritual. In 1979, the social anthropologist Stanley J. Tambiah suggested a definition of ritual as 'a culturally constructed system of symbolic communication. It is constituted of patterned and ordered sequences of words and acts, often expressed in multiple media, whose content and arrangement are characterized in varying degree by formality (conventionality), stereotype (rigidity), condensation (fusion), and redundancy (repetition)' (1979: 119).

A shorter but somewhat similar definition was formulated by the anthropologist Roy A. Rappaport in his both metaphorically and literally big book on ritual published posthumously in 1999: 'the performance of more or less invariant sequences of formal acts and utterances not entirely encoded by the performers' (1999: 24).

In both of these oft-quoted definitions of ritual, aspects such as formality, order, repetition/invariance and cultural encoding or construction are stressed. This stress is echoed in two 'lists' of characteristic features of ritual actions: the first was compiled by

---

[3] For good introductions to the most important themes in ritual studies and to the history of research, see Bell 1997, 2006; Kreinath, Snoek and Stausberg 2006, 2007; Brosius, Michaels and Schrode 2013.
[4] It is beyond the scope of this chapter to offer an attempt at a comprehensive bibliography of literature on ritual in the Bible, but two recent publications in the influential Oxford Handbook series may serve to illustrate the place that ritual now has in biblical studies. In 2019, Oxford University Press published *The Oxford Handbook of Early Christian Ritual* (Uro et al. 2019), and in 2020 followed *The Oxford Handbook of Ritual and Worship in the Hebrew Bible* (Balentine 2020). Ritual has clearly moved from the periphery to the centre of biblical studies. It remains the case, however, that scholarship on ritual in the Bible tends to be quite undertheorized. This is regrettable, not only because theorizing can lift the quality of the analysis but also, and especially, because clear application of theory and method is the kind of scholarly 'conversation starter' that would enable a fruitful dialogue between biblical studies and cognate disciplines.

the anthropologists Caroline Humphrey and James Laidlaw in their 1994 publication on the *Archetypal Actions of Ritual*, and the second was put together by the scholar of religion and highly influential ritual theorist Catherine Bell a few years later, in 1997. Humphrey and Laidlaw's list comprises non-intentional, stipulated, elemental and archetypal and apprehensible (1997: 89). Bell's list of characteristics of ritual actions include formalism, traditionalism, invariance, rule-governance, sacral symbolism and performance (1997: 139–69). The strengths of these attempts to define ritual or to make a catalogue of ritual's most prominent features are that they do seem to capture what most people would identify as ritual. They all stress ritual as ordered, repetitive and sequential. They also stress ritual as formalized or stipulated and they all hint at the fact that ritual can somehow be apprehended or received, but that the message or communication in ritual is not necessarily invented by the ritual performers. Finally, there is a stress on performance, that ritual takes the form of acts and utterances. The weakness of these and many other attempts to define ritual is that they are not quite able to capture this phenomenon, which is seemingly formalized, rigid and invariant, but which may also sometimes be spontaneous, innovative and dynamic (Grimes 2000: 261–2).[5] There is an archaizing quality to the ritual form that gives the impression that a given ritual has been prescribed since the dawn of time, even if it is in fact performed for the very first time (cf. Bell 1997: 145–50, 2006: 397–8).

The steadily growing interest in ritual across academic disciplines has led to an increase in descriptions of ritual phenomena. This in turn has led to a dawning awareness that no one definition of ritual is going to sufficiently encompass all of ritual, just as no single 'big' theory of ritual will ever sufficiently map and explain all that ritual is and does (cf. Bell 2006: 406). Thus, generally, scholarship on ritual is gradually moving away from firm definitions of what a ritual is and towards more polythetic and fuzzy ways of categorizing rituals as phenomena that share a number of features, none of which are essential in itself for their categorization as ritual (Snoek 2006: 4–6; McClymond 2008: 25–34). In this way, it is possible to theorize actions as 'more or less' ritual, rather than as 'either or'. It follows from this way of thinking flexibly and dynamically about ritual that the working definition of ritual that one chooses, as well as the theoretical approaches that one applies, depends on the rituals that one wishes to study. In the following, I shall outline the most prominent 'trends' in ritual theory. This is not intended as a comprehensive history of research on ritual, but rather as a road map for choosing a fruitful theoretical angle when working on ritual.

## *Ritual between the social and the sacred*

Historically, the most dominant trend in ritual studies has certainly been the investigation of the interrelationship between ritual and society. This kind of investigation enquires into the social functions of ritual actions and it is therefore sometimes referred to as social functionalism, or just functionalism (Bell 1997: 23–60). An early example of this line of enquiry is the French sociologist Émile Durkheim (1858–1917), whose intellectual legacy is keenly felt in much sociological and anthropological scholarship of the twentieth

---

[5] In an attempt to capture the dynamic and diverse nature of ritual, Ronald Grimes lists the key dynamics of ritual as four paradoxical pairs: (1) rituals empower and disempower groups, (2) rituals attune and disattune bodies, (3) rituals reinforce the status quo and enact transformation, and (4) rituals make and unmake meaning (2014: 302–28).

century. In his 1912 book, *Les formes élémentaires de la vie religieuse*, Durkheim described ritual as behavioural rules intended to regulate between the domains of the profane and of the sacred, and particularly to regulate interaction with and behaviour around sacred objects (2001 [1912]: 40). Durkheim stressed that religious ritual is performed explicitly for the benefit of the sacred or the gods, but that it has a side effect, which is to recreate and reinvigorate the social (ibid.: 157–9, 283–5). When ritual participants come together to perform a ritual, they experience a feeling of 'effervescence', an experience of being part of something bigger than themselves, and this is the engine that fuels moral life and makes society possible. When a group comes together to perform a ritual, it both maintains and reaffirms itself, and thus ritual performance becomes as necessary to the moral life of society as ingestion of food is to physical life (ibid.: 284).

There is a clear line running from Durkheim's thoughts on ritual and society to the work of Rappaport and his 1999 monograph *Ritual and Religion in the Making of Humanity*, mentioned above. Rappaport also saw ritual as the foundation for human society. Rappaport divided ritual into two types of messages, canonical and self-referential. The self-referential messages say something about the current physical, mental and social state of the participants, whereas the canonical messages are the liturgical order or world view encoded in the ritual (1999: 50–2).[6] The canonical messages are what is seemingly invariable and eternal in the ritual whereas the self-referential messages take advantage of the variance in the ritual situation, namely who participates, how many participate, *if* one participates at all etc. (ibid.: 53–4). The self-referential and canonical messages relate to each other as respectively the form and substance of a ritual, and Rappaport further described their function by reference to the sign theory developed by C.S. Peirce. The canonical messages relate to their content as a *symbol* relates to that which it signifies, that is a relation, which is purely arbitrary and established by law or convention. The self-referential messages, on the other hand, relate to their content as an *index* relates to its object, i.e. a relation where the index is directly affected by or connected with its object. As she performs the ritual, the ritual participant becomes an index of the abstract content of the canonical message (ibid.: 54–8). Since the canonical messages are symbols and their relation to their content is arbitrary, theoretically this content could just as well be expressed in another form, for instance in a text, but it is the ritual form and the combination of the canonical and self-referential messages that make the ritual situation unique. The ritual form adds to the symbolically encoded ritual substance something that the ritual substance cannot express on its own, and the ritual form depends on the ritual substance in order to be interpreted and understood. Abstract concepts such as honour, faith and valour are realized when they are given a bodily sign in ritual (ibid.: 31, 58). By participating in a ritual, the ritual actor indicates to himself and to anyone present, acceptance of the canonical message, which is encoded in the ritual. Acceptance, however, is not the same as personal belief and a person may disagree with the canonical message in a given ritual and still perform the ritual (ibid.: 119–20). The implied acceptance of a ritual's canonical message does not guarantee that the ritual participant will support this world view in the future and promises or commitments given in a ritual may be broken. However, because the ritual participant has communicated acceptance of the ritual order by participating in the ritual, any actions against the ritual order will be perceived as a transgression. The ritual participant's implied acceptance does not guarantee how the

---

[6] There is a brief and helpful introduction to Rappaport's ritual theory in Jensen 2009.

ritual participant's actions *will* be, but it does create a convention of how the ritual participant's actions *should* be (ibid.: 123). To Rappaport this is the *meta-performativity* of ritual. Ritual is merely *performative* when it performs a conventional act, such as a marriage or a baptism, but ritual is *meta-performative* when at the same time it establishes and supports the conventions, which are the basis of the conventional act (ibid.: 278–80). Because of ritual's meta-performativity Rappaport names ritual *the* basic social act. By creating and maintaining social conventions and norms, ritual makes the social contract possible, which in turn makes human society possible (ibid.: 125–6, 138).

## *Practising bodies*

Rappaport stressed two aspects of ritual in particular: first that ritual is *communicative*, that it contains some kind of message and, second, that ritual is *performed*. This dual stress on communication and performance can also be found in other influential scholars' work on ritual, such as in the work of another Durkheimian, the British social anthropologist Mary Douglas (1921–2007). In her work on ritual, Douglas combined Durkheimian influence with regard to religion and the social with structuralism inspired by the work of Claude Lévi-Strauss (cf. Bell 1997: 43–6). Douglas saw ritual as a communicative system that conveyed the values of a social group, such as the group's system of categorization, its hierarchies and its social organization (2003: 53–4). The performance of ritual communicates these values to the ritual participants and in this way ritual has a regulatory effect on social behaviour. Douglas's work on ritual impurity has had a significant impact on Hebrew Bible scholarship, especially in relation to the dietary laws in Leviticus 11 (cf. Deuteronomy 14) and to the 'priestly' (see 'Ritual in the Priestly Text of the Hebrew Bible' below) world view in the Pentateuch in general.[7] Douglas' work, however, is also a good illustration of the methodological challenges posed by an approach that views ritual as communication, because it presupposes that we are able to 'read' and decipher this communication. It follows that our understanding of a ritual performance is dependent upon our ability to 'crack its code'.

Rappaport stressed that there is no intrinsic relationship between a ritual's form and a ritual's substance. For instance, there is nothing in the act of scooping handfuls of water onto an infant's head that in itself signals baptism just as there is no natural connection between the act of touching a person's shoulders with a sword and receiving the accolade (1999: 114–15). The connection between the ritual form and substance is based solely on convention, and therefore in order to decipher the message communicated in a certain ritual one will have to be socialized into or in another way informed of this ritual's symbolic system (cf. ibid.: 106, 111). In her study on Hebrew Bible dietary laws, 'The Abominations of Leviticus', which was part of her 1966 monograph *Purity and Danger* (2002: 51–71), Douglas suggested an interpretative key to the classification of clean and unclean animals in Leviticus 11. Here, the category clean corresponded with holiness, wholeness and perfection, whereas unclean was attached to the species that were perceived to be either imperfect examples of their class or whose class itself was seen to go against the scheme of the world as expressed in the creation account in Genesis 1 (ibid.: 67–71). According to Douglas, 'the dietary laws would have been like signs which at every turn

---

[7] See especially Douglas 2002, which was originally published in 1966, and her renewed interest in the books of Leviticus and Numbers in Douglas 1999 and 2004.

inspired meditation on the oneness, purity and completeness of God' (ibid.: 71). Douglas's work received much praise and a great following, but also much criticism, which she addressed and largely acceded to in her preface to the Routledge Classics edition of *Purity and Danger* published in 2002 (ibid.: xiii–xvi; see also Hendel 2008). In this preface, Douglas among other things noted 'the absence of any positive implications for the social system of the biblical Hebrews for whom the rules were made' (Douglas 2002: xiv). To place this in the context of the present discussion on ritual as a mode of communication, there was no positive information in the Hebrew Bible to support that Douglas's way of deciphering the system behind the dietary laws was correct, nor that it was a symbolic system that would have been recognized by the authors of these texts. As a twentieth-century scholar, Douglas had obviously not been socialized into an *emic* understanding of these ancient texts and the texts themselves did not give the key to the deciphering of their symbolic communication. It goes almost without saying that limited or no access to the substance of a ritual action, its symbolism or meaning, is a recurring methodological challenge to scholars studying the rituals of ancient societies. More often than not ancient ritual texts and iconography does not come with an interpretative key that may 'socialize' us into the ritual's symbolic universe. Anthropological research has shown, however, that scholars who study contemporary ritual and who have performances to watch and ritual participants and experts to interview, are in fact not much better off. In their study on the Jain *Puja* ritual, *The Archetypal Actions of Ritual*, Caroline Humphrey and James Laidlaw clearly demonstrated that both ritual experts and 'ordinary' ritual participants gave a multitude of different answers and interpretations, when asked about the 'meaning' of the ritual they performed (1994: 16–57). Based on the results of Humphrey and Laidlaw's fieldwork, the Puja ritual did not communicate one message or meaning, but rather *at least* one meaning per ritual participant. Humphrey and Laidlaw summarized this in the following way: 'Ritual acts are publicly stipulated cultural constructs, yet wide variations in how they are enacted and how they are thought about indicate that while they are in this sense not individual, they are not completely shared either' (ibid.: 133). This research indicates that the quest to decipher and 'read' a message communicated through a ritual performance may be slightly off point, because there is not necessarily a commonly agreed upon and previously encoded message built into the ritual.[8] At least if this message is there, it may be accessible neither to the ritual actors nor to an outside observer and interpreter. The ritual performance itself is all there is, and in as far as there is communication in ritual, the performance of the ritual *is* the message, or at least it is the only message that we have access to. If we frame this in Rappaport's terminology, the indexical messages is all we have, whereas the canonical messages are either non-existent or inaccessible.[9]

Humphrey and Laidlaw's work also indicates that we should see the ascription of 'meaning' to a ritual performance as a secondary product of the act rather than as a primary prerequisite for the ritual (1994: 64–81).[10] Whereas Douglas and other scholars of her

---

[8] Cf. the discussion in Jay 1992: 8–16.
[9] Interestingly, scholars of contemporary ritual have been more ready to adopt this insight than their colleagues studying ancient ritual (but see the recent treatment of this topic in Gilders 2020: 136–7). This is presumably because living ritual participants and ritual experts are able to disagree with the ways in which ritual scholars decode and 'translate' their ritual behaviour, whereas historical ritual texts and other expressions of ritual material culture are unable to 'talk back'.
[10] Cf. the critique of Mary Douglas in Kazen 2011: 23–4, and Lemos 2013.

generation imagined a symbolic system or message, which was communicated through the medium of ritual, Humphrey and Laidlaw suggested that we start with an action or a practice, which undergoes *ritualization* over time and thus becomes ritual (ibid.: 88–110, 153–5). The process of ritualization introduces a shift in the intentionality of an action and in the connection between the purpose of an action and this action's form. Whereas in everyday quotidian actions there usually is a strong and immediately perceptible link between purpose and form, this link is undermined by ritualization and appears weak in ritual actions (ibid.: 167–87). The disconnection between purpose and form in ritual actions creates a 'gap', which then calls for meaning and interpretations (ibid.: 191–208).

A focus on ritual as practice is also voiced in Catherine Bell's 1992 monograph, *Ritual Theory, Ritual Practice*, in which she proposes a 'practice approach' to ritual, inspired by the French sociologist Pierre Bourdieu (Bell 1992: 74–93). Bell sees ritual as one social practice among many, and she stresses the fact that ritual is *embodied* and that the performance of ritual requires bodily ritual mastery (ibid.: 94–108).[11] In the decades following the publication of *Ritual Theory, Ritual Practice*, it has become increasingly common in scholarship to focus on the embodied and performative aspects of ritual. This is a development which is well aligned with the general 'material turn' in the humanities in general and in religious studies in particular, where the past three decades has seen an increasing focus on practices and on the materiality of religion, rather than on beliefs and ideas (Hazard 2013; Roberts 2017).

## Acts that work

The latest trend in recent ritual theory, which I would like to highlight for the purpose of this study, is an increased focus on ritual as a category of action and on how ritual actions are efficacious. This trend has been influenced significantly by the emergence of the cognitive science of religion although it is not limited to the work of scholars, who study the relationship between human cognition and religion.[12]

In their 2002 monograph, *Bringing Ritual to Mind*, the religious studies scholar Robert N. McCauley and the philosopher Thomas E. Lawson presented their 'theory of religious ritual competence' (2002: 8), in which they described religious rituals within the framework of an Action Representation System (ibid.: 13–16). According to McCauley and Lawson, a religious ritual is an action that contains the roles of 'agent', 'act' and 'patient' and in which one of these roles includes a reference to a so-called 'culturally postulated superhuman' (CPS) agent (ibid.: 8).[13] Depending upon the role of the CPS

---

[11] For an example of an application of Bell's practice approach to ancient Near Eastern ritual, see Neumann 2019.
[12] Of the scholars mentioned in the section, Robert N. McCauley, Thomas E. Lawson and Justin Barrett all self-identify as working within the paradigm of the cognitive science of religion, whereas Jørgen Podemann Sørensen and Catherine Bell do not.
[13] In their later work, McCauley and Lawson changed their terminology from 'culturally postulated superhuman agent' (CPS agent) to 'counter intuitive agent' (CI agent), cf. McCauley and Lawson 2007. One disadvantage of McCauley and Lawson's definition of religious ritual is that it is rather exclusive:

> Our claim that all religious rituals (as opposed to religious action more broadly construed) include an agent doing something to a patient departs from popular assumptions. Priests sacrifice goats, ritual participants burn offerings, and pilgrims circle shrines, but people also pray, sing, chant, and kneel. Even though such religious activities may be parts of religious rituals, in and of themselves they do not qualify as religious rituals in our theory's technical sense.
> 
> —McCauley and Lawson 2007: 223

agent in the ritual action, McCauley and Lawson classify religious rituals as 'special agent rituals', 'special patient rituals' and 'special instrument rituals'. In special agent rituals, the CPS agent or a representative of the CPS agent fills the place of the agent in the ritual. Examples of special agent rituals are initiations, consecrations and ordinations. Special patient rituals are rituals where the CPS agent occupies the patient slot in the Action Representation System, i.e. rituals where someone does something to the gods, such as presenting them with gifts. The third and final category, special instrument rituals, includes rituals where the closest link with the CPS agent is in the act/instrument slot. A good example of special instrument rituals is rituals of divination, in which a particular object or substance is manipulated in order to divine the will of the gods. Along similar lines, in an article co-authored with Justin Barrett, Lawson describes ritual actions as mirror images of social actions in the sense that 'someone performs some kind of action in order to motivate another's action or change in disposition' (Barrett and Lawson 2001: 185).[14]

A focus on agency in ritual and on ritual as a category of action that mirrors social action can be fruitful in an analysis of ritual, because it helps to shift attention away from the social functions of ritual in order to focus on the purpose of the ritual, what the ritual participants expect their ritual to *do*.[15] This is not to say that the social function of ritual is not important to a ritual analysis, but simply to stress that ritual's impact on society and on social structures is only part of the picture. Ritual participants perform ritual for a variety of reasons, reasons that they may be more or less conscious of having, and quite often it seems that the society-facilitating aspects of ritual behaviour, which I described above, are not among the salient reasons for performing a ritual.[16] Ritual is performed rather in order to please the gods, to cure an illness, to initiate a priestess or simply to do 'good' in a vague or general sense, because there is a perception that the world *with* this ritual performance is in some way better than *without* it. This stress on the purpose or efficacy of a ritual action can be seen for instance in the work of historian of religion Jørgen Podemann Sørensen, who defines ritual as 'representative acts designed to change or maintain their object' (Podemann Sørensen 1993: 19–20). The aims of ritual actions can be as diverse as to uphold the cosmos, to cure gout or to make it rain. What ritual actions have in common is that they are designed to *work*, to have an effect: 'A ritual is designed and performed on the assumption that once it is accomplished, the world is not quite what it would have been without the ritual' (ibid.: 18). It is the context of each individual ritual that determines what the ritual is expected to achieve in a given situation. To illustrate this Podemann Sørensen mentions the singing of a hymn in different ritual circumstances. If the hymn 'A

---

[14] See also Lawson and McCauley 1990. According to Barrett and Lawson, the objective of ritual actions is to bring about 'non-natural' consequences. 'That is, rituals are actions that are performed to accomplish something that would not normally follow from this specific action. For example, a person who strikes a special pot in order to bring rain would be performing a ritual; whereas, a person who strikes a special pot in order to create pottery fragments, would not be performing a ritual' (2001: 184). This attempt to discern between ordinary quotidian actions and ritual actions is quite similar to what Humphrey and Laidlaw do in their description of ritualization, which I summarized above. Seen from an etic perspective, this division works, but seen from an emic perspective striking a special pot in order to make it rain or indeed applying blood to a curtain in order to purify it from ritual impurity (cf. Lev. 16.14) may be just as 'natural' as striking a pot in order to break it. Cf. Bell 1992: 72.
[15] Along similar lines, Ronald Grimes discerns between ritual intentions, ritual functions and ritual effects (2014: 301).
[16] With terminology borrowed from the sociologist Robert K. Merton, William K. Gilders discerns between the 'manifest' and the 'latent' functions of ritual (2004: 181–91). Manifest functions are consciously attributed by actors to their actions, whereas latent functions are generally not recognized.

Mighty Fortress Is Our God' is sung in church during a regular Sunday service its aim or purpose appears to be primarily maintaining and laudatory. However, if the same hymn is sung at sea during an awful storm the purpose of the ritual may take on a new sense of urgency and it may now be intended to rescue the ritual participants from drowning (Podemann Sørensen 2006a: 66–7; see also Podemann Sørensen 2006b).

It is the context of a ritual performance and not the ritual's form that determines the purpose of a given ritual action (cf. DeMaris 2018: 6–11). Catherine Bell has proposed six 'basic genres of ritual actions' (1997: 93–137). These are: Rites of Passage; Calendrical Rites; Rites of Exchange and Communion; Rites of Affliction; Feasting, Fasting, and Festivals; and Political Rites. Most rituals will match more than one of these basic genres, but quite often one genre does appear to be leading in relation to a given ritual more than the other genres. In this way, Bell's basic ritual genres may be a helpful tool in determining the purpose of a ritual action, what this particular ritual action is expected to have an effect on and to either change and maintain.

## RITUAL IN THE HEBREW BIBLE

Ritual in the Hebrew Bible falls into roughly two categories: ritual that appears in the so-called priestly texts in the Pentateuch and ritual in 'the rest' of the Hebrew Bible. In the following, I shall first give a brief presentation of the latter, followed by a short introduction to the former and then, finally, offer a few reflections on the literary character of ritual in the Hebrew Bible and how best to interpret these texts using anthropology and ritual theory.

### Ritual in the non-priestly texts of the Hebrew Bible

As we saw in the rough survey of the Book of Genesis in the Introduction above, the narrative texts in the Hebrew Bible have plenty of more or less explicit references to ritual practices. Just as we are told that the characters in the narrative stand up or sit down, we are also frequently informed that these characters engage in some kind of ritual performance. The challenge posed by these references to ritual practice is that they are usually incredibly terse and offer little or no detail. As an example, let us return to the text in Gen. 23.19, where it says that 'Abraham buried (קבר) Sarah his wife in the cave of the field of Machpelah facing Mamre (that is, Hebron) in the land of Canaan'.[17] This brief description leaves the reader enlightened as to the where, but completely in the dark when it comes to the how. How is a burial or just this particular burial performed?[18]

Similarly, in Josh. 5.3, we are told that 'Joshua made flint knives and circumcised the Israelites at Gibeath-haaraloth', but we are not given any details about how a circumcision is performed. For that matter, we are not told how to make flint knives either. This lack of detail on ritual in most Hebrew Bible narrative texts can probably be explained by a combination of overlapping factors. The author did not think that the details of the ritual practice were particularly important to include in the narrative, either because they were

---

[17] Here and in the following, I use the NRSV translation of the Hebrew Bible unless otherwise stated.
[18] For more on burial in the Hebrew Bible, see Bloch-Smith 1992: 114–20 and see 2 Samuel 3.31–37. For death and care for the dead in the Hebrew Bible, although not with an explicit interest in ritual theory, see Ackerman 1992: 143–51; Schmidt 1996: 1–13, 132–273; Stavrakopoulou 2010: 1–53; Suriano 2018; and Sonia 2020.

of no consequence to the story that was being told or because it was assumed that they needed no explanation, because the intended audience were as familiar with them as they needed to be. Either way, it is clear that the authors of the majority of Hebrew Bible texts have no particular interest in educating their readership on ritual. This is illustrated quite well by the Joshua passage mentioned above. Joshua 5 is completely silent to the how of the circumcision, but it does give us an answer to the why. The problem is that it is not the kind of answer we want. Josh. 5.4 begins in a very promising way by saying 'this is the reason why Joshua circumcised them'. The reason follows in v. 5: 'all the people born on the journey through the wilderness after they had come out of Egypt had not been circumcised'. Joshua circumcised the Israelites because they were uncircumcised. As Nancy Jay (1992: 9) writes: 'Why he should circumcise them in the first place is not considered to need explanation. What was problematical to the author of Joshua was not circumcision itself, but rather why all those grownup Israelites were uncircumcised. The interpretation in Jos. 5 is disappointing because it is an explanation for someone else, in some other situation, not one for us.'

If we turn to other literary genres in the Hebrew Bible, such as law texts, poetics texts, wisdom texts and prophetic texts, we also find relatively frequent and quite compact references to ritual. So, for instance in Ps. 66.13–15, where the psalmist promises to come to Yahweh's temple to pay the conditional vows (נדרי) he made to him, when he was in trouble. The psalmist intends to offer several animals as burnt offerings (עלות), fatlings, rams, bulls and goats, but that is as much detail as we get in this passage both on the ritual practice of making and paying conditional vows and on the ritual practice of making animal sacrifices.[19] Similarly, in Prov. 15.8 the sacrifice (זבח) of the wicked is compared with the prayer (תפלה) of the upright, but no additional information is offered on either practice.

As the analysis of our two Hebrew Bible examples of ritual below will show, this lack of detail in the texts does not mean that nothing whatsoever can be said about ritual practices in the Hebrew Bible. Sometimes a little actually does go a long way. It does mean, however, that one should be conscious of the limitations of the data and refrain from trying to make it yield more information than it reasonably can (cf. Gudme 2009a; Gilders 2020).

## *Ritual in the priestly texts of the Hebrew Bible*

Whereas the majority of texts in the Hebrew Bible seem to have been written by authors who took no particular interest in the details of ritual, the authors of the so-called priestly texts in the Pentateuch seem to care for little *else* than ritual. The priestly texts are concentrated especially in the books of Exodus and Leviticus, and they offer a systematic description of Yahweh's sanctuary and the rituals to be performed there.[20] These texts

---

[19] For more on conditional vows in the Hebrew Bible, see Cartledge 1992; Berlinerblau 1996; Gudme 2013a: 41–3, 2013b.
[20] The idea of a priestly textual layer or redaction in the Pentateuch originates from the early era of historical-critical biblical scholarship and the so-called documentary hypothesis; see Carr 2016: 106–14. For the priestly writings specifically, see Gorman 1997: 2–5; Hundley 2011: 1–4. For the sake of the example and simplicity, I have chosen not to include texts that seem to be ideologically related to the priestly writings, such as the holiness code in Leviticus 17–26 and the book of Ezekiel, in the discussion here, but much of what I say about the priestly texts as literary ritual in 'Literary Ritual and Ritual Fiction' below could be applied to these texts as well.

have been designated as 'priestly' in Hebrew Bible scholarship, because their focus on temple ritual and on priestly privileges makes it seem plausible that the authors were indeed priests of Yahweh by profession. Traditionally, the priestly texts have been dated to the Persian period and it is often assumed that their authors were affiliated with the Jerusalem temple in postexilic Judah/Yehud.[21]

The priestly texts are characterized by a certain literary style, by the use of a distinct terminology and by a kind of narrative logic with which it orders a body of texts that are primarily composed of ritual 'laws', divinely ordained prescriptions for the ideal Yahwist sanctuary according to the priestly authors.[22] The texts gain divine authority from the story of the revelation on Mount Sinai (Exodus 19 and 24).[23] The priestly prescriptions for the tent of meeting, Yahweh's transportable sanctuary, and the ritual practices that pertain to it, are placed in the deity's mouth as they follow immediately after the event of the revelation (Exod. 25.1–9).[24] Although the bulk of text that follows in Exodus 25–40 (minus the incident of the golden calf in chs 32–34) and Leviticus 1–16 contains very little actual narrative, the priestly ritual texts do seem to be ordered according to a narrative logic or sequence, where the various components of the sanctuary and its rituals are 'told' in the right order. First, in Exodus 25–31 Yahweh gives his instructions for the construction and furnishing of the tent of meeting. Then, in Exodus 35–40 the text meticulously and rather repetitively relates how everything is carried out in exact accordance with Yahweh's instructions, and finally, in Exod. 40.34–35, Yahweh moves in to his new sanctuary and dwells among his people exactly as he said he would in Exod. 25.8.

The careful construction of the sanctuary according to divine command is the prerequisite for installing the divine presence (cf. Exod. 40.34), in the *adyton* of the sanctuary. The indwelling of the divine presence in turn is the prerequisite for the ritual laws that follow in Leviticus 1–16, where prescriptions are given for the two most important general ritual categories in the priestly material; how to correctly present sacrifices and offerings to Yahweh (Leviticus 1–7) and how to identify, avoid and dispose of ritual impurities (Leviticus 11–15).[25] Finally, in ch. 16, the final building block is put into place as Yahweh instructs Moses on how to perform the annual ritual for purification of the sanctuary on the day of atonement or Yom Kippur. In sum, the bulk of priestly texts that stretches from Exodus 25 to Leviticus 16 can be read as a carefully constructed

---

[21] This remains the majority view on the dating of the priestly texts, but a minority sees these texts as pre-exilic or even premonarchic and possibly connected with the sanctuary in Shiloh, see Milgrom 1991: 3–35; Grabbe 2001: 92–4; Nihan 2007: 1–17.

[22] Helpful descriptions of characteristic priestly literary style and priestly theology can be found in Gorman 1990: 39–60; Jenson 1992: 15–39.

[23] The priestly 'law' is one among several Hebrew Bible law collections that draw authority from the narrative of the revelation on Mount Sinai. The same can be said about the two versions of the Decalogue (Exod. 20.1–21 and Deut. 5.1–22), the so-called 'Covenant Code' (Exod. 20.22–23.33), the 'Holiness Code' (Leviticus 17–26) and the 'Deuteronomic Law' (Deuteronomy 12–26).

[24] George 2009: 133–4. For the description of the sanctuary in Exodus 25–31 and 35–40, see Gudme 2014b: 2*–6*.

[25] These two blocks of ritual laws are linked by descriptions of the initiation of the priesthood (Leviticus 8) and the High Priest, Aaron's, first sacrifice (Leviticus 9), which is followed by the first illegitimate offering in Leviticus 10. The text instructively juxtaposes Aaron's first successful sacrifice, which is consumed on the altar by a fire that emanates from Yahweh's divine presence inside the tent of meeting (Lev. 9.24), with the unauthorized incense offering by Aaron's two sons, Nadab and Abihu. In this way, the benefits of performing rituals in accordance with Yahweh's instructions and the consequences of not doing so are very clearly illustrated in the text (Gorman 1997: 54–67).

assembly set for the ideal cult of Yahweh. First, Yahweh gives his instructions for the cult (Exodus 25–31), then Moses and Israel carry them out (Exodus 35–40), so that Yahweh can move into his new dwelling (Exod. 40.34–35). As soon as the divine presence is installed in the sanctuary, the rituals for guaranteeing divine satisfaction, sacrifices and purifications (Leviticus 1–16), are put into place (Gorman 1990: 45–8; Hundley 2011: 91–3).

Compared with the non-priestly texts in the Hebrew Bible, the priestly texts are abundant in ritual details. To mention but a few examples, they specify the dress code for the High Priest (Exodus 28), the ingredients for the sacred anointing oil (Exod. 30.22–24), what exactly a grain offering must consist of (Leviticus 2) and how to detect the ritually problematic skin disease (Leviticus 13). At the same time, in spite of their meticulous wealth of detail on the how of ritual, the priestly texts are practically silent on the why (cf. Gilders 2004: 58). Much like their non-priestly colleagues, the priestly authors do not feel a need to explain why exactly all *fat* belongs to Yahweh (Lev. 3.16), why some types of sacrifices are categorized as 'pleasing odours' for the deity and others are not, or why a discharge from the genitals is a source of ritual impurity (Leviticus 15) whereas a runny nose is not.[26]

## *Literary ritual and ritual fiction*

In terms of literary genre, the priestly ritual texts in the Pentateuch are a peculiar phenomenon. They contain a wealth of information on ritual space, ritual utensils, ritual actors and ritual practices, but they are clearly not intended to be a ritual manual or a handbook for priests. In spite of their seeming comprehensiveness and sense of detail, these texts are not functional as manuals for praxis (Smith 1987: 109; George 2009: 70–1). The exact reasons that the priestly authors wrote these texts are lost to us. It has been suggested that the priestly writings were created to legitimize a certain ritual system, a particular priestly class or family, or to support the introduction of new ritual practices.[27] Furthermore, it is unclear what relationship there is between any kind of historical or 'actual' ritual practice in Iron Age Palestine and the rituals described in the priestly texts. On the one hand, the highly idealized and programmatic nature of the priestly ritual texts point in the direction of a theological charter outlining an ideal cult or even a cultic theology (Grabbe 2003). On the other, the ritual forms mentioned in the priestly texts are generic, such as sacrifices, presentation offerings, purification rituals etc., and as such comparable with ritual practices known from ancient Mediterranean cultures in the Bronze and Iron Ages (cf. Gudme 2014a; Gane 2020). If one wishes to discover a historical 'core' in the priestly ritual texts in the Pentateuch, it requires careful 'sifting' of the information in the texts, comparison with archaeological material and cognate texts when available and a healthy dose of qualified guessing (cf. Gilders 2020: 137).

Here, I would like to move in a slightly different direction and reflect upon what it is that *literary ritual* brings to the table that ordinary performed ritual does not. By literary ritual, I mean ritual that has been turned into literature or perhaps rather ritual-as-literature: texts that prescribe and narrate ritual practices with a purpose that extends

---

[26] For a discussion on the fat, see Gudme 2019, and for a discussion of the term 'pleasing odour', see Eberhart 2002: 48–52, 186. Finally, for a discussion of the 'system' behind ritual impurity in the Hebrew Bible, see Kazen 2019.

[27] See for instance Watts 2007: 27–36; Bibb 2009: 5–69; Hundley 2012; Boorer 2016: 1–107.

beyond documenting a certain ritual performance or giving instructions for a ritual performance.[28] I take inspiration from the classicist Mary Beard, who has pointed out that 'more ritual [...] takes place in the head than on the street' (2004: 121). Beard continues: 'ritual is not solely performative. It exists as much in literary representation, in recollection, re-telling and imaginative fantasy as it does on the ground or at the altar' (ibid.: 125). I find this a helpful line of thought when analysing the priestly texts in the Pentateuch and the literary representations of ritual that we find there, but in fact also when analysing ritual in the non-priestly texts in the Hebrew Bible. These texts, these literary rituals, are part of the ritual imagination of their authors and as such they are something other and more than ritual performance.[29] Analysing literary rituals is not entirely different from analysing performed rituals. One significant difference between literary ritual and performed ritual of course is that we cannot interview the texts about the purpose of the ritual, the ritual participants' reasons for taking part etc., but as we saw in 'Practising Bodies' above, access to informants does not in itself solve the hermeneutical problem posed by ritual. In the Hebrew Bible, we only have access to the information the authors of the texts have chosen to pass on to their readers (cf. Gilders 2020: 136), and as we have also seen in 'Ritual in the Non-Priestly Text of the Hebrew Bible' and 'Ritual in the Priestly Texts of the Hebrew Bible' above providing detailed reasons for why rituals are performed or what exactly a certain ritual is expected to do is rarely on the authors' agenda.

Another difference between literary ritual and performed ritual is exactly the aspect of performance (cf. Wright 2012: 197–9). Literary rituals are not performed, they are written and (perhaps) read, and I think this is a more important aspect of literary ritual than it is sometimes given credit for. A literary ritual is not an extension of or a supplement to a performed ritual, a textual 'echo' of a practice. A literary ritual is written purposefully by an author *instead of* – or even independently of – the performance of ritual practice, and therefore we have to ask ourselves what it is that literary ritual can do that is different from or better than what a ritual performance may do.[30] The exact answers to this question certainly depend on the literary rituals that we study. If we turn to the priestly ritual texts in the Pentateuch, it is characteristic for these texts that they seem quite invested in promoting a particular ritual system as divinely ordained and therefore 'true'. Thus, in the case of the priestly texts, literary rituals may offer their authors and readers a kind of ritual virtual reality, which for one reason or another cannot be realized in real life. This may be due to a lack of influence, a lack of means, a lack of freedom, a lack of a temple, a lack of ritual competence or simply a lack of time or commitment.[31] Literary ritual has the clear advantage of offering an ideal version of reality, where no one forgets

---

[28] See the discussion on textualization of ritual in MacDonald 2016 and Frevel 2016.

[29] See McClymond 2016: 92–3 for a discussion of 'imaginal ritual' and 'discursive *representations* of ritual' (original emphasis).

[30] I find the term 'literary ritual' particularly relevant in relation to the majority of ritual texts in the Hebrew Bible. This is a collection of texts that has been compiled and heavily edited over time and this makes it very much a literary product and not a 'documentary' source. If we look to other cultures in the ancient Near East and ancient Mediterranean, we find a wider variety of different types of ritual texts, some that would fit the definition of literary ritual and others that appear to be less 'literary' and more like ritual instructions or checklists.

[31] See Podemann Sørensen 2009 for a very interesting Egyptian example of how a ritual text may store ritual competence and how the preservation of a written ritual appears to just as efficacious as the performance of this ritual. See also the interesting discussion of the priestly writings and the Holiness Code in the Pentateuch in Wright 2012: 199–209.

the words, no one spills the oil and where the fire on the altar is never obstructed by wind or rain or damp kindling.[32]

In this way, the ritual virtual reality created by literary ritual resembles the 'ritual subjunctive', a term coined by Adam B. Seligman, Robert P. Weller, Michael J. Puett and Bennett Simon to describe the conscious tension in ritual between the world as it is and the world as it should be (2008: 21–8; see also Smith 1982: 63–5). Performed ritual creates an illusion of a better world, an 'as-if' version of reality, where the world is presented as the very best version of itself. In a way, literary ritual does exactly this as well, but it is removed one step further from reality: literary ritual presents the ideal version of performed ritual, which presents an ideal version of the world. Literary ritual is subjunctive in the second degree, it lives out its authors' ritual imagination. I believe this is part of the reason for why literary ritual is such an apt medium for communicating theology. Literary ritual utilizes a category of action, ritual, that excels in constructing ideal realities to express the ideal relationship between deities and their worshippers or between members of a group. In the priestly ritual texts in the Pentateuch, the 'as-if' character of the texts is particularly noticeable in the chapters in Exodus (25–31 and 35–40) that portray the tent of meeting and its trappings. The texts are packed with sensual impressions, bright colours, luxurious textures and alluring smells. In this way, the sanctuary that is constructed in the priestly ritual texts is even more vibrant, lush, bright and fragrant than any actual physical sanctuary ever could be. There is no dust in the corners, no animal blood or dung on the floor, no stale oil or mouldy bread; there are only bright colours, glittering gold, perfumed air and the majesty of Yahweh's presence that descends on the sanctuary.[33]

If we turn to the non-priestly texts of the Hebrew Bible, we also often find ideal versions of ritual practice in these texts. For instance, in Ps. 66.13–15, which was quoted in 'Ritual in the Non-Priestly Texts of the Hebrew Bible' above, the author promises exemplary ritual behaviour and thus paints a picture of himself as a model worshipper and of Yahweh as a deity worthy of such praise. Similarly, in Job 1.5, the information that Job would get up early in the morning to sacrifice a burnt offering for each of his children in case they had sinned in their hearts, contributes to the portrayal of Job as a particularly righteous and upright man. In this way, ritual performance can be used in both poetic and narrative texts as a literary tool that constructs identity for the characters in the texts. Similarly, less-than-ideal ritual performance may be used to underline a person's moral failures, such as when the ritual offences of the ultimate 'bad king' in the Hebrew Bible, King Manasseh, are listed in 2 Kgs 21.3–6. So, although explaining the details of ritual behaviour is rarely first on the biblical authors' agenda, rituals are usually mentioned in these texts for a reason. This may be to accentuate the moral character of a person in the text, but ritual may also be used to set the scene for a story, such as when Elkanah travels to Shiloh to sacrifice with his family and this leads to his wife Hannah receiving a divine promise of a son, the prophet Samuel, in 1 Samuel 1. We can refer to this literary use of ritual as *ritual fiction*. It is ritual-as-literature, and it may be analysed as such.

---

[32] The notion of ritual failure is largely absent from the priestly texts in the Pentateuch. The exception that confirms the rule is Nadab and Abihu's failed offering in Leviticus 10 mentioned in note 25 above. This is one of the noticeable differences between the priestly texts and ritual texts from Mesopotamia, where cases of ritual gone wrong are addressed explicitly, see Ambos 2007.

[33] In a way, this is also true about the description of the construction and organization of the Jerusalem temple in 1 Chronicles 22–29 and in the much shorter account in 1 Kings 6–8. Here, we also find ideal versions of temples and cult.

# DOING THINGS WITH TEARS: PETITIONARY MOURNING IN THE HEBREW BIBLE

We can apply ritual theory developed in social anthropology and cognate fields in order to analyse the ritual in the text, just as we would analyse a ritual performed in real life. In order to see how this may be done, we shall turn to our first example, ritual mourning in the Hebrew Bible.[34] Let us begin with an extract from 2 Samuel 12. In this part of the David story, the child born to David by Bathsheba has been struck with an illness by Yahweh as a punishment for David's sin in stealing another man's wife and causing her husband's death (2 Sam. 12.14–15). The child is gravely ill for seven days and during this time David lies on the floor and will accept no food. The child dies and when he is told of the death, David's reaction surprises his servants:

> Then David rose from the ground, washed, anointed himself, and changed his clothes. He went into the house of Yahweh, and worshipped; he then went to his own house; and when he asked, they set food before him and he ate. Then his servants said to him, 'What is this thing that you have done? You fasted (צום) and wept (בכה) for the child while it was alive; but when the child died, you rose and ate food.' He said, 'While the child was still alive, I fasted and wept; for I said, "Who knows? Yahweh may be gracious to me, and the child may live." But now he is dead; why should I fast? Can I bring him back again? I shall go to him, but he will not return to me.'
>
> —2 Sam. 12.20–23

What David does in this narrative is to engage in a distinct type of behaviour that signals a ritualized expression of mourning.[35] This behaviour is characterized by an inversion of everyday life. Instead of eating and drinking, the ritual actor will fast, instead of attending to personal hygiene and grooming, the ritual actor will have a shabby an unkempt appearance and the ritual actor may sit or lie directly on the floor or ground instead of using furniture. Finally, gestures and expressions of grief and distress may accompany this behaviour (Olyan 2004: 29–34).

In a number of Hebrew Bible texts, this ritual behaviour is associated with mourning the dead. For instance, in 2 Sam. 1.11–12, where David and his men mourn (ספד) the deaths of Saul and Jonathan by tearing their clothes, weeping (בכה) and fasting (צום).[36] However, in 2 Samuel 12, David is clearly not mourning the dead, for as soon as the child dies, he ceases to mourn and returns to normal life. In the narrative, David himself provides the explanation: 'While the child was still alive, I fasted and wept; for I said, "Who knows? Yahweh may be gracious to me, and the child may live"'. David performed ritual mourning, because he hoped that this behaviour would persuade Yahweh to spare the child. Thus, we see two distinct types of ritual mourning, mourning the dead

---

[34] In this section, I have shamelessly stolen the first part of the title from Paul Delnero's brilliantly titled recent book, *How to Do Things with Tears: Ritual Lamenting in Ancient Mesopotamia* (2020). I hope Delnero will take this in the spirit it is intended: imitation is the highest praise.

[35] Ritual mourning is well-described in Hebrew Bible scholarship. A clear and systematic treatment of the topic can be found in Olyan 2004, but see also Hvidberg 1962; Anderson 1991; Pham 1999; Kozlova 2017.

[36] See also the informative instruction on how to fake mourning behaviour in 2 Sam. 14.2: 'Joab sent to Tekoa and brought from there a wise woman. He said to her, "Pretend to be in mourning [אבל in Hithpael]; put on mourning garments, do not anoint yourself with oil, but behave like a woman who has been mourning many days for the dead"'. For more examples, see Olyan 2004: 28–40.

like David and his men do in 2 Sam. 1.11–12 and petitionary mourning in 2 Samuel 12 (Olyan 2004: 62–96).[37]

Here, I would like to pick up on two points from the sections 'Practising Bodies' and 'Acts that Work', above. The first is related to the relationship between ritual's form and substance and to the context-dependence of determining a ritual's function or purpose. Rappaport stressed that there is no intrinsic relationship between a ritual's form and a ritual's substance (1999: 114–15). This connection is based on convention in a culture, and there is no 'natural' or 'obvious' connection between the distinct set of behaviours summarized as ritual mourning above and the purpose of either mourning the dead or petitioning the gods.[38] This is also a good example of how the same ritual form, in this case mourning behaviour, may be performed to achieve various purposes. This illustrates Podemann Sørensen's point that it is the context of each individual ritual that determines what the ritual is expected to achieve in a given situation (2006a: 66–7). The reaction of David's servants in 2 Samuel 12.21 reveals that they seemingly interpreted David's ritual mourning as mourning associated with death and therefore it baffles them that he ceases to mourn exactly when death has occurred. David's explanation clarifies that his behaviour was intended as petitionary mourning, and he hints that he, at least in this case, finds mourning the dead a complete waste of time: 'Why should I fast? Can I bring him back again?' (2 Sam. 12.23).[39] This is also a good illustration of Humphrey and Laidlaw's observation that 'ritual acts are publicly stipulated cultural constructs, yet wide variations in how they are enacted and how they are thought about indicate that while they are in this sense not individual, they are not completely shared either' (1994: 133). In the story, David's servants recognize David's behaviour as ritual mourning and thus display a shared knowledge of a ritual form, but they mistake David's individual purpose in performing this ritual: they assume that he is mourning the (almost) dead child, but he is in fact attempting to petition Yahweh.

My second point has to do with how ritual actions mirror social actions and with Barrett and Lawson's point that ritual actions are intended to 'motivate another's action or change in disposition' (2001: 185). In 2 Samuel 12, David performs a ritual in order to bring about a change in Yahweh's disposition and to motivate him to spare the child. According to McCauley and Lawson's theory of religious ritual competence (2002: 8), the ritual performed by David is a special patient ritual, a ritual in which the culturally postulated superhuman (CPS) agent, Yahweh, occupies the patient slot in the Action Representation System. In short, David does something to Yahweh. If we turn to Catherine Bell's six basic genres of ritual actions (1997: 93–137), we can classify David's petitionary mourning as a Ritual of Affliction.[40] This category of ritual 'attempt[s] to rectify a state of

---

[37] Compare with Delnero's distinction between lamenting the dead and proactive lamenting intended to prevent a catastrophe (2020: 31–8).

[38] Olyan identifies four distinct sets of mourning behaviour in the Hebrew Bible: mourning the dead, petitionary mourning, non-petitionary mourning in times of calamity, and the mourning of the individual afflicted with skin disease. This distinction is helpful for analytical purposes, but in practice these may not always be distinct and exclusive ritual actions. For instance, one could, in the act of mourning, be petitioning the god(s) to make sure the dead successfully make the transition to the world of the dead. I am grateful to Richard E. DeMaris for pointing this out.

[39] In other situations, David seems to put mourning the dead to good use for political purposes. See for instance 2 Sam. 3.36–37, where David's enthusiasm in mourning Abner persuades the people that David had no part to play in Abner's death, see Olyan 2004: 51–6.

[40] This classification sets petitionary mourning apart from mourning the dead, which is usually categorized as a rite of passage, see Bell 1997: 94–102; Davies 2017: 25–7.

affairs that has been disturbed or disordered; they heal, exorcise, protect and purify' (Bell 1997: 115).[41] In 2 Samuel 12, the state of affairs that requires rectifying is a dying child and the means to do so is to sway Yahweh with petitionary mourning. Sadly, David's petitionary mourning does not have the outcome he hopes for and the child dies. This is not always the case with petitionary mourning in the Hebrew Bible, however. In a humorous story, in the book of Jonah, the King of Nineveh and his subjects (including the animals!) manage to change Yahweh's mind by performing petitionary mourning. The King removes his robe and covers himself in sackcloth (שׂק) and ashes (אפר). Then he commands all of Nineveh to follow his example and to fast and to 'cry mightily to God' (Jon. 3.6–8). When Yahweh sees this, he 'changed his mind about the calamity that he had said he would bring upon them; and he did not do it' (Jon. 3.10). As the reader knows, Yahweh's change of heart and Nineveh's survival causes considerable grief for the prophet Jonah (cf. Jonah 4).

In 2 Samuel 12, the description of David's petitionary mourning portrays him in a particular light. I would say that his ritual behaviour characterizes him as a man of action rather than a man of tradition. He engages in ritual as long as it serves a clear and well-defined purpose such as averting Yahweh's anger, but once the tragedy has occurred and the child is dead, David moves on and returns to his duties. David's refusal to mourn the dead child portrays him as an unsentimental and somewhat cynical person, one who is not ruled by cultural norms or the expectations of others. David mourns if and when it suits him. It is interesting to compare David's violent public expression of grief over the deaths of his two adult sons, Amnon (2 Sam. 13.31–36) and Absalom (2 Sam. 18.33–19.4), with his reaction to the death of a baby in 2 Samuel 12.[42] David is clearly not portrayed as a man who holds no affection for his children in general, but he reacts much more strongly to the deaths of grownup sons and potential heirs to the throne than to the death of an infant.[43]

# RITUAL TRANSFORMATION: THE FEMALE PRISONER OF WAR IN DEUT. 21.12–13

My second example is a passage from the law code in the book of Deuteronomy (Bultmann 2001: 144–51).[44] It follows not immediately but quite soon after the Deuteronomic description of ideal warfare in Deuteronomy 20, and it is placed in a section of the text

---

[41] One could make a case for interpreting David's petitionary mourning as a ritual of 'Exchange and Communion' (Bell 1997: 108–14), where David's abstention from food, hygiene and comfort can be seen as a 'negative gift' (cf. the discussion in Berlinerblau 1996: 175–6) offered to Yahweh in return for his clemency.

[42] 2 Sam. 19.1–8 is another example of how David's behaviour goes against common expectations even to the point where it causes embarrassment. The usurper, Absalom, has been killed by David's soldiers and therefore David-the-king should be glad, but David-the-father displays such violent grief in public that the victory feast in the city is turned to shame (see Olyan 2004: 54–5).

[43] There may also be an element of gendered ideal behaviour in this narrative. Whereas Bathsheba is in need of comfort over the death of her child (2 Sam. 12.24), David does not dwell on their loss. I cannot help but hearing a faint echo of the ideal of a composed response to the death of their two-year-old daughter for which Plutarch commends his wife in *Consolatio ad Uxorem* 4.

[44] Unlike the priestly texts in the Pentateuch (see 'Ritual in the Priestly Texts of the Hebrew Bible' above), ritual in the book of Deuteronomy has not been paid much attention in Hebrew Bible scholarship, but see Melissa D. Ramos's (2021) recent monograph on rituals of covenant re-enactment in Deuteronomy 27–30. See also Brett E. Maiden's reading of Deuteronomic theology as 'cognitively costly religion', a reading inspired by corporate social responsibility and signalling theory (2020: 64–132).

that deals with various cases of family law (Deut. 21.10–21; Bultmann 2001: 149; Beukenhorst 2021). It reads:

> When you go out to war against your enemies, and Yahweh your God hands them over to you and you take them captive, suppose you see among the captives a beautiful woman whom you desire and want to marry, and so you bring her home to your house: she shall shave her head, pare her nails, discard her captive's garb, and shall remain in your house for a full month, mourning (בכה) for her father and mother; after that you may go in to her and be her husband, and she shall be your wife. But if you are not satisfied with her, you shall let her go free and not sell her for money. You must not treat her as a slave, since you have dishonoured her.
>
> —Deut. 21.10–14

The ritual prescribed here seems intended to transform a female ritual actor from a prisoner of war to the wife of an Israelite man. In a Deuteronomistic context, the content of this law is somewhat surprising because of its relaxed attitude to exogamy (Beukenhorst 2021: 276), a practice that is generally forbidden in the strongest terms both in the book of Deuteronomy (e.g. Deuteronomy 7) and in the Deuteronomistic History (e.g. 1 Kings 11). The ritual consists of three stages. First, the woman is selected and brought to the man's house. Second, once inside the house, the woman must undergo some physical changes. She has to shave off her hair, clip her nails and discard the clothes that she was wearing as a prisoner. Then she must spend a month in the house mourning or weeping over (בכה) her parents. Lastly, the Israelite man can have sex with her and take her as his wife. This ritual can be categorized as a Rite of Passage according to Catherine Bell's six basic genres of ritual actions (1997: 93–137). This type of ritual 'culturally mark[s] a person's transition from one stage of social life to another' (Bell 1997: 94). Arnold van Gennep first described rites of passage as consisting of three distinct phases. A phase of separation, where the ritual actor is set apart from society, a liminal phase in which a symbolic threshold (*limen*) of some sort is crossed and a transformation takes place, and a phase of incorporation, where the ritual actor is re-integrated into society in a new social role (1960: 10–11, 116–45). If we apply this scheme to the ritual in Deut. 21.12–13 it fits relatively well. The first phase, the separation, takes place when the woman is brought to the man's house. She is separated from her fellow prisoners of war from which she was singled out and taken, and she is separated from the people of Israel, because she is to be kept inside her captor's house. The second phase, the phase of transformation, takes place in the house, which becomes a liminal space for the woman.[45] Here, she must shed her hair, her nails and her clothes and shed tears for her parents, who are now presumably lost to her.[46] The text offers no explanation for why these particular actions are required, but the repeated shedding of body tissue, of garments and of tears does seem to call forth a mental image of leaving the past behind. The month-long weeping and the reference to cutting hair and removing clothes overlap to a certain extent with ritual

---

[45] One could argue that the physical transformation is part of the phase of separation and not of the phase of transformation, because especially the shaved head will set the woman apart from others.

[46] There is an echo of Ps. 45.10–11 here: 'Hear, O daughter, consider and incline your ear; *forget your people and your father's house*, and the king will desire your beauty. Since he is your lord, bow to him' (emphasis added). For a much-needed critical look at so-called marriage by rape, see Bowen 2003 on Psalm 45, Niditch 2014: 197–200 on Deuteronomy 21, and Parker 2020 on 'trafficking' of women in the Hebrew Bible in general.

mourning (see 'Doing Things with Tears' above), but the focus in this ritual text seems to be on the woman's transformation rather than on her mourning her parents (Olyan 1998: 617–19, 2000: 97–8; Niditch 2008: 130; Quick 2021: 58–9). The final phase of the ritual, the phase of incorporation, is when the woman becomes the man's wife. She is now no longer a captive, but the wife of an Israelite and as such a member of the people of Israel.

Here, I bring in Rappaport's work on ritual and how he described the relationship between what he called the canonical and self-referential messages in ritual (cf. 'Ritual Between the Social and the Sacred', above). The self-referential messages say something about the current physical, mental and social state of the ritual participant, whereas the canonical messages are the liturgical order or worldview encoded in the ritual (1999: 50–4). By participating in a ritual, the ritual actor indicates to herself, and to anyone present, acceptance of the canonical message, which is encoded in the ritual. Acceptance, however, is not the same as personal belief or personal desire, and a person may disagree with the canonical message in a given ritual and still perform the ritual (ibid.: 119–20). Let us try to apply this to a ritual such as the one described in Deut. 21.12–13. This ritual's canonical message is something along the lines of what we find in the book of Deuteronomy and it contains ideas about the mighty deity Yahweh and about his chosen people, Israel, and their special privileged relationship that makes Yahweh deliver other peoples into the hands of Israel to do with as they please. The difference between Israel and other people is so significant that it is necessary to bring about a transformation in order to make someone a member of Israel. Part of this canonical message is certainly also a patriarchal view of sex and society, where male desire (Deut. 21.11) is relevant, whereas female consent and a woman's right over her own body is irrelevant (cf. Deut. 22.13–30). Finally, the canonical message seems to consider the female prisoner of war as something other than a 'sex slave', since she cannot be sold on as a slave once she has been used as a wife (cf. Exod. 21.8–11). If a woman were to perform the ritual stipulated in Deut. 21.12–13, her performance would make her an indexical sign of this ritual's canonical message and she would appear to indicate acceptance of this message. This is so, even if her participation was forced by her captor and his family and she was secretly plotting her escape as she went through the motions of cutting her hair and nails etc. Because of what Rappaport called the *meta-performativity* of ritual, the woman's implied acceptance creates a convention of how her actions *should* be (1999: 123). This means that if she were to try to make a run for it either during her one-month detention in her captor's house or at any point after this, she would most likely be viewed by her captor and his family and by their community as a transgressor. She would be seen as a wayward wife, who tried to abandon her husband—master (בעל), and not as a courageous woman, who managed to regain her freedom and control over her own body.

The ritual procedure in Deut. 21.12–13 is part of a host of laws in the book of Deuteronomy, and just as it is the case in the priestly ritual laws in the Pentateuch, these rules are framed in Deuteronomy as uttered by Yahweh during the revelation on Mount Sinai and thus given the highest possible authority (Bultmann 2001: 135–6). It is uncertain if a law and a ritual such as this one has ever been practised, but as it sits in the text it becomes part of Deuteronomy's description of the ideal existence in the promised land, which Yahweh will give to his people – an existence in which, according to Deut. 21.10–14, Israel will be victorious thanks to Yahweh and Israelite men will be able to take their pick from beautiful and desirable captive women. It is a ritual fiction that describes an ideal life in an ideal land in accordance with divine law.

## IN CONCLUSION: TEXTS THAT WORK

The Hebrew Bible is a collection of texts teeming with ritual, and although these texts are indeed *texts*, cases of literary ritual and ritual fiction, it is still possible to utilize terminology and theory from anthropology and cognate fields when analysing them. We can use ritual theory to identify ritual in the text and to categorize these rituals in order to speculate about their would-be functions – with regard to both ritual and literary efficacy – that the authors may have envisioned as they wrote their texts.

## ACKNOWLEDGEMENTS

I dedicate this study to my two mentors in ritual studies, Bent Flemming Nielsen and Jørgen Podemann Sørensen, in deep appreciation and gratitude of their inspiring teaching and generous supervision. I am also grateful to the editor of this volume, Emanuel Pfoh, for his patience, advice and kind encouragement, and to Richard E. DeMaris for offering thoughtful and constructive feedback along the way.

## REFERENCES

Ackerman, S. (1992), *Under Every Green Tree: Popular Religion in Sixth-Century Judah*, Atlanta, GA: Scholars Press.

Ambos, C. (2007), 'Types of Ritual Failure and Mistakes in Ritual in Cuneiform Sources', in U. Hüsken (ed.), *When Rituals Go Wrong: Mistakes, Failure and the Dynamics of Ritual*, 25–47, Leiden: E.J. Brill.

Anderson, G.A. (1991), *A Time to Mourn, A Time to Dance: The Expression of Grief and Joy in Israelite Religion*, University Park: Pennsylvania State University Press.

Balentine, S.E., ed. (2020), *The Oxford Handbook of Ritual and Worship in the Hebrew Bible*, Oxford: Oxford University Press.

Barrett, J.L. and E.T. Lawson (2001), 'Ritual Intuitions: Cognitive Contributions to Judgments of Ritual Efficacy', *Journal of Cognition and Culture*, 1 (2): 183–201.

Beard, M. (2004), 'Writing Ritual: The Triumph of Ovid', in A. Barchiesi, J. Rüpke and S. Stephens (eds), *Rituals in Ink: A Conference on Religion and Literary Production in Ancient Rome*, 115–26, Stuttgart: Franz Steiner.

Bell, C. (1992), *Ritual Theory, Ritual Practice*, New York: Oxford University Press.

Bell, C. (1997), *Ritual: Perspectives and Dimensions*, New York: Oxford University Press.

Bell, C. (2006), 'Ritual', in R.A. Segal (ed.), *The Blackwell Companion to the Study of Religion*, 397–411, Malden, MA: Blackwell.

Berlinerblau, J. (1996), *The Vow and the 'Popular Religious Groups' of Ancient Israel: A Philological and Sociological Inquiry*, JSOTSup 210, Sheffield: Sheffield Academic Press.

Beukenhorst, M. (2021), 'The War Laws in Deuteronomy', in D. Edelman, B. Rossi, K. Berge and P. Guillaume (eds), *Deuteronomy in the Making: Studies in the Production of Debarim*, 271–88, BZAW 533, Berlin: De Gruyter.

Bibb, B.D. (2009), *Ritual Words and Narrative Worlds in the Book of Leviticus*, New York: T&T Clark.

Bloch-Smith, E. (1992), *Judahite Burial Practices and Beliefs About the Dead*, JSOTSup 123, Sheffield: Sheffield Academic Press.

Boorer, S. (2016), *The Vision of the Priestly Narrative: Its Genre and Hermeneutics of Time*, AIL 27, Atlanta, GA: Society of Biblical Literature.

Bowen, N.R. (2003), 'A Fairy Tale Wedding? A Feminist Intertextual Reading of Psalm 45', in B.A. Strawn and N.R. Bowen (eds), *A God So Near: Essays on Old Testament Theology in Honor of Patrick D. Miller*, 53–71, Winona Lake, IN: Eisenbrauns.

Brosius, C., A. Michaels and P. Schrode, eds (2013), *Ritual und Ritualdynamik: Schlüsselbegriffe, Theorien, Diskussionen*, Göttingen: Vandenhoeck & Ruprecht.

Bultmann, C. (2001), 'Deuteronomy', in J. Barton and J. Muddiman (eds), *The Oxford Bible Commentary*, 135–58, Oxford: Oxford University Press.

Carr, D.M. (2016), 'The Formation of the Hebrew Bible: Sources, Compositional Layers, and Other Revisions', in S. Niditch (ed.), *The Wiley Blackwell Companion to Ancient Israel*, 103–17, Malden, MA: Wiley Blackwell.

Cartledge, T.W. (1992), *Vows in the Hebrew Bible and the Ancient Near East*, JSOTSup 147, Sheffield: Sheffield Academic Press.

Davies, D. (2017), *Death, Ritual and Belief: The Rhetoric of Funerary Rites*, 3rd edn, London: Bloomsbury Academic.

Delnero, P. (2020), *How To Do Things With Tears: Ritual Lamenting in Ancient Mesopotamia*, Berlin: De Gruyter.

DeMaris, R.E. (2018), 'Introduction: With Respect to Ritual', in R.E. DeMaris, J.T. Lamoreaux and S.C. Muir (eds), *Early Christian Ritual Life*, 1–15, Abingdon: Routledge.

Douglas, M. (1999), *Leviticus as Literature*, Oxford: Oxford University Press.

Douglas, M. (2002), *Purity and Danger: An Analysis of Concept of Pollution and Taboo, with a New Preface by the Author*, Abingdon: Routledge.

Douglas, M. (2003), *Natural Symbols: Explorations in Cosmology*, Abingdon: Routledge.

Douglas, M. (2004), *Jacob's Tears: The Priestly Work of Reconciliation*, Oxford: Oxford University Press.

Durkheim, É. (2001 [1912]), *The Elementary Forms of Religious Life, A New Translation by Carol Cosman*, Oxford: Oxford University Press.

Eberhart, C. (2002), *Studien zur Bedeutung der Opfer im Alten Testament: Die Signifikanz von Blut- und Verbrennungsriten im kultischen Rahmen*, WMANT 94, Neukirchen-Vluyn: Neukirchener.

Frevel, C. (2016), 'Practicing Rituals in a Textual World: Ritual *and* Innovation in the Book of Numbers', in N. MacDonald (ed.), *Ritual Innovation in the Hebrew Bible and Early Judaism*, 129–50, BZAW 468, Berlin: De Gruyter.

Gane, R.E. (2020), 'Ritual and Religious Practices', in S.E. Balentine (ed.), *The Oxford Handbook of Ritual and Worship in the Hebrew Bible*, 223–39, Oxford: Oxford University Press.

George, M.K. (2009), *Israel's Tabernacle as Social Space*, Atlanta, GA: Society of Biblical Literature.

Gilders, W.K. (2004), *Blood Ritual in the Hebrew Bible: Meaning and Power*, Baltimore, MD: Johns Hopkins University Press.

Gilders, W.K. (2020), 'Social and Cultural Anthropology', in S.E. Balentine (ed.), *The Oxford Handbook of Ritual and Worship in the Hebrew Bible*, 125–41, Oxford: Oxford University Press.

Gorman, F.H., Jr (1990), *Ideology of Ritual: Space, Time and Status in the Priestly Theology*, JSOTSup 91, Sheffield: Sheffield Academic Press.

Gorman, F.H., Jr (1997), *Divine Presence and Community: A Commentary on the Book of Leviticus*, International Theological Commentary 3, Grand Rapids, MI: Eerdmans.

Grabbe, L.L. (2001), 'Leviticus', in J. Barton and J. Muddiman (eds), *The Oxford Bible Commentary*, 91–110, Oxford: Oxford University Press.

Grabbe, L.L. (2003), 'The Priests in Leviticus – Is the Medium the Message?', in R. Rendtorff and R.A. Kugler (eds), *The Book of Leviticus: Composition and Reception*, 207–24, VTSup 93, Leiden: E.J. Brill.

Grimes, R.L. (2000), 'Ritual', in W. Braun and R.T. McCutcheon (eds), *Guide to the Study of Religion*, 259–70, London: Cassell.

Grimes, R.L. (2014), *The Craft of Ritual Studies*, Oxford: Oxford University Press.

Gudme, A.K. de Hemmer (2009a), 'Practice Behind the Text? The Conditional Vow in Hebrew Bible Narrative Texts', in A.K. Gudme (ed.), *Text and Ritual: Papers Presented at the Symposium Text and Ritual in Copenhagen in November 2008*, 71–81, Copenhagen: Faculty of Theology, University of Copenhagen.

Gudme, A.K. de Hemmer (2009b), 'How Should We Read Hebrew Bible Ritual Texts? A Ritualistic Reading of the Law of the Nazirite (Num 6,1–21)', *SJOT*, 23 (1): 64–84.

Gudme, A.K. de Hemmer (2013a), *Before the God in this Place for Good Remembrance: A Comparative Analysis of the Aramaic Votive Inscriptions from Mount Gerizim*, BZAW 441, Berlin: De Gruyter.

Gudme, A.K. de Hemmer (2013b), 'Barter-Deal or Friend-Making Gift? A Reconsideration of the Conditional Vow in the Hebrew Bible', in M.L. Satlow (ed.), *The Gift in Antiquity*, 189–201, Malden, MA: Wiley-Blackwell.

Gudme, A.K. de Hemmer (2013c), 'A Kind of Magic? An Analysis of the "Law of Jealousy" in Numbers 5.11–31 as Magical Ritual and as Ritual Text', in H. Jacobus, P. Guillaume and A.K. Gudme (eds), *Magic and Divination in the Biblical World*, 149–67, BI 11, Piscataway, NJ: Gorgias Press.

Gudme, A.K. de Hemmer (2014a), 'Dyed Yarns and Dolphin Skins: Temple Texts as Cultural Memory in the Hebrew Bible', *Jewish Studies*, 50: 1*–14*.

Gudme, A.K. de Hemmer (2014b), '"If I Were Hungry, I Would Not Tell You" (Ps 50,12): Perspectives on the Care and Feeding of the Gods in the Hebrew Bible', *SJOT* 28 (2): 172–84.

Gudme, A.K. de Hemmer (2019), 'Liquid Life: Blood, Life, and Conceptual Metaphors in the Hebrew Bible and the Ancient Near East', in R. Nikolsky, I. Czachesz, F. Tappenden and T. Biró (eds), *Language, Cognition, and Biblical Exegesis: Interpreting Minds*, 63–70, London: Bloomsbury Academic.

Gudme, A.K. de Hemmer (forthcoming), 'Sensing a Sanctuary: The Ritual Use of Incense in Exodus 30 and Leviticus 16', in M. Bradley, A. Grand-Clément, A.-C. Rendu Loisel and A. Vincent (eds), *Sensing Divinity: Incense, Religion and the Ancient Sensorium*, Cambridge University Press.

Hazard, S. (2013), 'The Material Turn in the Study of Religion', *Religion and Society: Advances in Research*, 4: 58–78.

Hendel, R.S. (2008), 'Mary Douglas and Anthropological Modernism', *Journal of Hebrew Scriptures* 8: art. 8. Available online: https://doi.org/10.5508/jhs.2008.v8.a8.

Humphrey, C. and J. Laidlaw (1994), *The Archetypal Actions of Ritual*, Oxford: Clarendon Press.

Hundley, M.B. (2011), *Keeping Heaven on Earth: Safeguarding the Divine Presence in the Priestly Tabernacle*, FAT 2, Reihe 50, Tübingen: Mohr Siebeck.

Hundley, M.B. (2012), 'The Way Forward is Back to the Beginning: Reflections on the Priestly Texts', in E. Ben Zvi and C. Levin (eds), *Remembering and Forgetting in Early Second Temple Judah*, 209–24, FAT 85, Tübingen: Mohr Siebeck.

Hvidberg, F.F. (1962), *Weeping and Laughter in the Old Testament: A Study of Canaanite–Israelite Religion*, Leiden/Copenhagen: E.J. Brill / Arnold Busck.

Jay, N.B. (1992), *Throughout Your Generations Forever: Sacrifice, Religion, and Paternity*, Chicago: University of Chicago Press.

Jensen, H.J.L. (2009), 'Ritual and Text in the Hebrew Bible: Theoretical Reflections', in A.K. Gudme (ed.), *Text and Ritual: Papers Presented at the Symposium Text and Ritual in Copenhagen in November 2008*, 5–13, Copenhagen: Faculty of Theology, University of Copenhagen.

Jenson, P.P. (1992), *Graded Holiness: A Key to the Priestly Conception of the World*, JSOTSup 106, Sheffield: Sheffield Academic Press.

Kazen, T. (2011), *Emotions in Biblical Law: A Cognitive Science Approach*, HBM 36, Sheffield: Sheffield Phoenix Press.

Kazen, T. (2019), 'Purification', in R. Uro, J.J. Day, R.E. DeMaris and R. Roitto (eds), *The Oxford Handbook of Early Christian Ritual*, 220–44, Oxford: Oxford University Press.

Kozlova, E. (2017), *Maternal Grief in the Hebrew Bible*, Oxford: Oxford University Press.

Kreinath, J., J.A.M Snoek and M. Stausberg, eds (2006), *Theorizing Rituals, Volume 1: Issues, Topics, Approaches, Concepts*, Leiden: E.J. Brill.

Kreinath, J.A.M., J. Snoek and M. Stausberg, eds (2007), *Theorizing Rituals, Volume 2: Annotated Bibliography of Ritual Theory, 1966–2005*, Leiden: E.J. Brill.

Lawson, E.T. and R.N. McCauley (1990), *Rethinking Religion: Connecting Cognition and Culture*, Cambridge: Cambridge University Press.

Lemos, T.M. (2013), 'Where There Is Dirt, Is There System? Revisiting Biblical Purity Constructions', *JSOT*, 37 (3): 265–94.

MacDonald, N. (2016), 'Strange Fire Before the Lord: Thinking About Ritual Innovation in the Hebrew Bible and Early Judaism', in N. MacDonald (ed.), *Ritual Innovation in the Hebrew Bible and Early Judaism*, 1–10, BZAW 468, Berlin: De Gruyter.

Maiden, B.E. (2020), *Cognitive Science and Ancient Israelite Religion: New Perspectives on Texts, Artifacts, and Culture*, Cambridge: Cambridge University Press.

McCauley, R.N. and E.T. Lawson (2002), *Bringing Ritual to Mind: Psychological Foundations of Cultural Forms*, Cambridge: Cambridge University Press.

McCauley, R.N. and E.T. Lawson (2007), 'Cognition, Religious Ritual, and Archaeology', in E. Kyriakidis (ed.), *The Archaeology of Ritual*, 209–54, Los Angeles: Cotsen Institute of Archaeology Press.

McClymond, K. (2008), *Beyond Sacred Violence: A Comparative Study of Sacrifice*, Baltimore, MD: Johns Hopkins University Press.

McClymond, K. (2016), *Ritual Gone Wrong: What We Learn from Ritual Disruption*, Oxford: Oxford University Press.

Milgrom, J. (1991), *Leviticus 1–16: A New Translation with Introduction and Commentary*, New York: Doubleday.

Neumann, K. (2019), 'Sensing the Sacred in the Neo-Assyrian Temple: The Presentation of Offerings to the Gods', in A. Hawthorn and A.C. Rendu Loisel (eds), *Distant Impressions: The Senses in the Ancient Near East*, 23–62, University Park, PA: Eisenbrauns.

Niditch, S. (2008), *'My Brother Esau Is a Hairy Man': Hair and Identity in Ancient Israel*, Oxford: Oxford University Press.

Niditch, S. (2014), 'A Messy Business: Ritual Violence After the War', in B.E. Kelle, F.R. Ames and J.L. Wright (eds), *Warfare, Ritual, and Symbol in Biblical and Modern Contexts*, 187–204, AIL 18, Atlanta, GA: SBL Press.

Nihan, C. (2007), *From Priestly Torah to Pentateuch: A Study in the Composition of the Book of Leviticus*, FAT 25, Tübingen: Mohr Siebeck.

Olyan, S.M. (1998), 'What Do Shaving Rites Accomplish and What Do they Signal in Biblical Ritual Contexts?', *JBL*, 117 (4): 611–22.

Olyan, S.M. (2000), *Rites and Rank: Hierarchy in Biblical Representations of Cult*, Princeton, NJ: Princeton University Press.

Olyan, S.M. (2004), *Biblical Mourning: Ritual and Social Dimensions*, Oxford: Oxford University Press.

Parker, J.F. (2020), 'Hardly Happily Ever After: Trafficking of Girls in the Hebrew Bible', *BI*, 28 (5): 540–56.

Pham, X.H.T. (1999), *Mourning in the Ancient Near East and in the Hebrew Bible*, JSOTSup 302, Sheffield: Sheffield Academic Press.

Podemann Sørensen, J. (1993), 'Ritualistics: A New Discipline in the History of Religions', in T. Ahlbäck (ed.), *The Problem of Ritual: Based on Papers Read at the Symposium on Religious Rites Held at Åbo, Finland, on the 13th–16th of August 1991*, 9–25, Stockholm: Almqvist & Wiksell.

Podemann Sørensen, J. (2006a), *Komparativ religionshistorie*, Janua Religionum 2, Copenhagen: Books on Demand.

Podemann Sørensen, J. (2006b), 'Efficacy', in J. Kreinath, J.A.M. Snoek and M. Stausberg (eds), *Theorizing Rituals, Volume 1: Issues, Topics, Approaches, Concepts*, 523–31, Leiden: Brill.

Podemann Sørensen, J. (2009), 'Ritual Text as Knowledge and as Performance', in A.K. Gudme (ed.), *Text and Ritual: Papers Presented at the Symposium Text and Ritual in Copenhagen in November 2008*, 39–50, Copenhagen: Faculty of Theology, University of Copenhagen.

Quick, L. (2021), *Dress, Adornment, and the Body in the Hebrew Bible*, Oxford: Oxford University Press.

Ramos, M.D. (2021), *Ritual in Deuteronomy: The Performance of Doom*, Abingdon: Routledge.

Rappaport, R.A. (1999), *Ritual and Religion in the Making of Humanity*, Cambridge: Cambridge University Press.

Roberts, J.L. (2017), 'Things: Material Turn, Transnational Turn', *American Art*, 31 (2): 64–9.

Schmidt, B.B. (1996), *Israel's Beneficent Dead: Ancestor Cult and Necromancy in Ancient Israelite Religion and Tradition*, Winona Lake, IN: Eisenbrauns.

Seligman, A.B., R.P. Weller, M.J. Puett and B. Simon (2008), *Ritual and Its Consequences: An Essay on the Limitations of Sincerity*, Oxford: Oxford University Press.

Smith, J.Z. (1982), *Imagining Religion: From Babylon to Jonestown*, Chicago: University of Chicago Press.

Smith, J.Z. (1987), *To Take Place: Toward Theory in Ritual*, Chicago: University of Chicago Press.

Snoek, J.A.M. (2006), 'Defining "Rituals"', in J. Kreinath, J. Snoek and M. Stausberg (eds), *Theorizing Rituals, Volume 1: Issues, Topics, Approaches, Concepts*, 1–14, Leiden: E.J. Brill.

Sonia, K.M. (2020), *Caring for the Dead in Ancient Israel*, ABS 27, Atlanta, GA: SBL Press.

Stavrakopoulou, F. (2010), *Land of Our Fathers: The Roles of Ancestor Veneration in Biblical Land Claims*, LHBOTS 473, London: T&T Clark.

Suriano, M.J. (2018), *A History of Death in the Hebrew Bible*, Oxford: Oxford University Press.

Sørensen, J. (2007), *A Cognitive Theory of Magic*, Lanham, MD: AltaMira Press.

Tambiah, S.J. (1979), 'A Performative Approach to Ritual', *Proceedings of the British Academy*, 65: 113–69.

Uro, R., J.J. Day, R.E. DeMaris and R. Roitto, eds (2019), *The Oxford Handbook of Early Christian Ritual*, Oxford: Oxford University Press.

van Gennep, A. (1960), *The Rites of Passage*, Chicago: University of Chicago Press.

Watts, J.W. (2007), *Ritual and Rhetoric in Leviticus: From Sacrifice to Scripture*, Cambridge: Cambridge University Press.
Wright, D.P. (2012), 'Ritual Theory, Ritual Texts, and the Priestly-Holiness Writings of the Pentateuch', in S.M. Olyan (ed.), *Social Theory and the Study of Israelite Religion: Essays in Retrospect and Prospect*, 195–216, RBS 71, Atlanta, GA: Society of Biblical Literature.

# CHAPTER NINETEEN

# Shaman, preacher or spirit medium?

## The Israelite prophet in the light of anthropological models

LESTER L. GRABBE

It is fair to say that most biblical scholars who study prophetic literature are primarily interested in prophecy as literature and theology. There are occasional discussions of the prophetic persona, but this tends to be a secondary interest. The uniqueness of Israelite prophecy is assumed: it is not often discussed explicitly but just taken for granted. The question of uniqueness of theological message is a subjective one and beside the point here. Yet even though prophecy has been looked at from an anthropological point of view for many years, one notices a knee-jerk negative reaction when it is suggested that Israelite prophets might have acted in similar fashion to shamans or spirit mediums or those in a trance.

All we know about Israelite prophets comes from the biblical text. There are no other sources of information so far. Anthropology does not give us additional data. Its importance is that examples of prophetic or related figures in other cultures can be studied *in situ*. How prophetic figures actually live, perform and act can be observed and recorded. By comparing the scientific description of a living figure with the literary description in the text, we might learn something new. We might see new possibilities for understanding the biblical picture. Most of all, we might break through the constraints of our prejudices, assumptions and teachers. My intent in this chapter is to discuss possible models for Israelite prophets and prophetic activity and to discuss what they might suggest about Israelite religion (cf. Grabbe forthcoming).

## ANTHROPOLOGICAL EXAMPLES

### *Wana shamanship*[1]

The Wana are a rice-growing forest people in the interior of Sulawesi, Indonesia. During the head-hunting days of the nineteenth century the Wana tended to be the victims. They were often oppressed by a succession of coastal regimes and developed the capacity to move quickly and disappear when danger threatened. The Dutch and later the independent

---

[1] The main study is Atkinson 1989.

Indonesian government attempted to get the Wana to settle on the coast, but most of them managed to avoid this and escape back into the interior.

This and other experiences have created centrifugal tendencies in Wana settlements. The Wana concept of selfhood is that the person consists of a series of vital elements. This picture applies only in the context of illness, but the cohesion of these elements is dependent on powers external to the person. Since these elements are unstable, they can become dislocated or dispersed and can be managed only by the specialist. Sometimes the person's soul can fly away into the spiritual realm. The shamans play a central role among the people not only as healers and exorcists but also in integrating the polity of the community and countering the centrifugal tendencies noted above.

There are mainly two shamanic rituals. The lesser is the *potudu* where the shaman only sings. The other, the *mabolong*, is a communal event, a public forum in which the shaman has the chance to demonstrate his power – and also a chance for the people to see his ability tested and demonstrated (or not). In a shamanistic ritual he calls for his spirit allies, and his ability to summon and control them is the measure of his power and reputation. In some cases, the shaman must ascend to the sky to Pue, which translates as the 'Lord' or 'Owner', who seems to be some sort of supreme being. Such a drastic action is taken only when other treatments are considered insufficient.

The view of the ill person as having vital elements dispersed seems to be a major metaphor of Wana society. Just as the body has vital elements that can become disassociated, so Wana society is subject to forces that press toward its fragmentation. When knowledge, power and wealth were present in the community, it would thrive, like a healthy person, but when these were dispersed, the Wana people were like the individual who suffered soul loss. The *mabolong* had an integrative function for the community as a whole. Atkinson's (1989: 298) analysis shows that the 'Wana have relied on "men of prowess" with special access to exogenous knowledge to promote social cohesion and to cope with the hegemonic advances of a succession of coastal regimes – a trend that has only gained in strength in recent Wana history'.

In the nineteenth century, chiefdoms existed in the Wana region, and the 'men of prowess' were chiefs who sponsored priestly functionaries to conduct liturgy-centred rituals that stabilized communities. But the chiefdoms collapsed with the coming of the Dutch shortly after 1900. The result has been for present-day communities to depend on charismatic ritual leaders to give cohesion and direction (Atkinson 1989: 299).

### *Tenskwatawa*[2]

Shortly after 1800, a crisis developed among the Shawnee Indians of Ohio, at a time when the various native American tribes were being pushed back west of the Ohio river. The Shawnee chief Tecumseh had a ne'er-do-well brother with a reputation for being lazy, dissolute and frequently drunk. But he had guardian spirits and worked as a healer and exorcist. He had a vision, as a result of which he changed immediately, to everyone's astonishment, and began to preach a message of repentance to all of his people who would listen. We have a contemporary account of his message from a Shaker who was sent as part of a mission to meet Tenskwatawa, known as 'The Prophet', in 1807 and

---

[2] The basic information on Tecumseh and the Prophet is taken from Sugden 1997 and Mooney 1896. Some other literature is cited below.

listened to him sympathetically, as well as other contemporary records.[3] He began to preach a message of morality and nativism: whisky was for Whites and should not be drunk by Indians; murder and warfare were wrong; monogamy should be practised and fornication avoided. Men should dress as was traditional in an earlier age; only wild animals were to be eaten, not cattle and pigs (though horses were allowed to be ridden); bows and arrows were to be used rather than firearms; and fire should be started with sticks instead of flint and steel. One of his biggest innovations was in regard to medicine bundles. These were traditional to Indian culture, symbols of guardian spirits acquired at puberty. Part of Tenskwatawa's message was about the evils of witchcraft and sorcery, and so he called on all to give up their medicine bundles. He also instituted a witch-hunt that ended with the executions of some prominent leaders of the community.

### The Dodo possession spirits of southern Niger[4]

The dominant possession cult in parts of Western Africa is the *bori* cult, which includes a couple of hundred divinities. Those possessed by *bori* spirits do the traditional things expected of spirit mediums: they heal, they promote fertility on behalf of women, they exorcize and they divine the future. In recent years, however, the *bori* institutions have often been taken over by an increasing number of ambitious young men who see possession as a road to fame and riches. They compete openly but lack knowledge of traditional medicine, are not concerned about their clientele, charge exorbitant prices and generally behave corruptly. It is against this background that Dodo spirit possession arose. The Dodo spirits have particular ethical requirements that militate against exploitation, money grubbing, immorality or greed. They require their mediums to be committed to serving their clientele; as a result, they have a reputation for being much superior to *bori* mediums with regard to healing and divining. But Dodo spirits are very strict and will leave a medium who does not toe the line. The result is that most Dodo mediums retain their spirits only for a limited period of time.

Among the 'moral' precepts of the Dodo spirits is a rejection of Western commodities. They hearken back to an idealized past – a past that never in fact existed. The purpose of this is 'to regain control over a moral order whose viability hinges on the strength of spiritual bonds rather than on the power of market relations' (Masquelier 1999: 37). Most Dodo mediums will refuse to ride in a car. They might reject the wearing of rubber sandals instead of the traditional leather ones. They criticize schools and education, and sometimes even literacy. Capitalist society and modernity as a whole are repudiated, though there are some – often inconsistent – exceptions, such as using coloured enamel cookware and kerosene lamps, drinking Nescafé, and even wearing a watch.

### Civil war in northern Uganda[5]

In the period after the fall of Idi Amin a civil war developed between the army that liberated Uganda from his grip and another group called the National Resistance Army. The National

---

[3] The handwritten Shaker account is not signed but was written by one of the three men who formed the party sent to find and talk to Tenskwatawa. This account is published in Andrews 1972. For other contemporary accounts, see Sugden 1997: 116–26.
[4] This section is based on the data in Masquelier 1999.
[5] The information in this section is derived from Behrend 1999a and 1999b.

Resistance Army won out but sent soldiers to occupy the region of Acholi. A young spirit medium woman named Alice Lakwena, who had previously worked as a healer, began to organize resistance to this new government in the shape of the 'Holy Spirit Mobile Forces'. She was able to do this because she was possessed by a variety of spirits who formed a hierarchy that lent itself to military command. The spirits would take possession of her before a military action, and a clerk of the spirit would translate and record Alice's words. She freed the soldiers from the threat of witchcraft and evil spirits and promised protection again enemy bullets. After some remarkable successes, she marched on Kampala, at which point her army was defeated, and she fled to Kenya. Her spirits abandoned her, and she was succeeded by her rival Joseph Kony. She eventually died in January 2007.

### *Tromba spirits of north-west Madagascar*[6]

In northern Madagascar the Sakalava people were organized into a kingdom before the coming of the French. The site of the royal tombs was an island called Nosy Faly. The spirits of the dead royal ancestors were called *tromba*. The greatest and oldest of the spirits would occasionally possess a woman (it always seems to have been a woman) who would then journey in a trance to the island of Nosy Faly. She would be subjected to stringent tests, but if she passed them, she would be allowed to join the *saha*, the group of mediums possessed by these spirits, and would usually remain in the royal village for the rest of her life.

The value of the *tromba saha* mediums became apparent in an outbreak of possession of young people by evil spirits. The traditional healers could not deal with them, and the more powerful *tromba* mediums had to be called in. Their aid was further enlisted in a dispute over profitable fishing rights around the island of Nosy Faly. In another example, they were consulted on and approved the opening of a new school that might have been opposed by the Sakalava. Here we see a possession cult – incidentally, made up of women – that has considerable power and is able to pronounce on national matters and to be heeded by the powers that be.

### *Hopi prophecy*[7]

Among the Hopi Indians of the American Southwest a tradition of prophecy has developed in at least the last 150 years. We cannot speak about the pre-Columbian period, since no records are available, nor about the long period of Spanish rule, since the Spanish written records say nothing about it. But beginning about the middle of the nineteenth century, when the Hopi came under American domination, we have the record of a continuing prophetic tradition to the present day. It appears to be a native development, not the result of Christian influence, for these prophecies arise from and are interpretations of a central Hopi creation myth. Although there are a number of versions, the essence of the myth does not change. It describes how the Hopi people migrated through four worlds, one above the other until they emerged into the present world. It was empty except for Maasaw (the Hope tutelary deity), who allowed them to settle in it. They created the sun and moon to give light (since the world was previously dark). They asked the Maasaw for land and were told that they could settle; however, he would not give up title to the land

---

[6] This section depends on Sharp 1999 for the data cited.
[7] The main source for information in this section are the writings of Armin Geertz, mainly Geertz 1994.

but would see how they lived in the future. A good deal of space is given to the migrations of the various clans, and the myths vary in detail from clan to clan in this part of the narrative. An essential part of the myth concerns two brothers, an elder and a younger, who journeyed in the land. The elder moved faster and went towards the east and the rising sun. He gave rise to the White people, who would eventually return to help his younger brother. The Hopi sprang from the younger brother and settled about the centre of the earth. This myth underlies and supports Hopi society (Geertz 1994: 77):

> [T]his core narrative is enhanced, mobilized, and reiterated in hundreds of ways in social praxis. One can even postulate that every ceremonial and social drama either refers explicitly to the narrative or assumes it. The narrative and its prophetic framework follow the Hopi individual from the cradle to the grave. It defines his or her world view and provides the individual with powerful instruments in the creation of meaning and significance.

It is also the source of the series of prophecies that have been recorded over the last century and a half. The interesting thing is that as time has gone on, the prophecies have been embellished to incorporate new technologies and events. Thus, around the turn of the century leaders of two opposing factions in the community both agreed that the split had been prophesied. Later on, the prophecies were said to envisage a highway in the sky, 'cobwebs' by which people would communicate, and a 'jar of ashes' that would rain destruction on the earth (interpreted as the atomic bomb). During the 1960s and 1970s the prophecies took on an ecological character that would appeal to the counterculture and the many hippies who came to live in the Hopi community.

The prophecies were mainly utterances of elders and community leaders. A number of them were the product of the 'Traditionalist Movement' that was seeking to present an image compatible with left-wing White expectations, such as movie and rock stars, ecologists, and members of the counterculture. Their success was evident in the claims that the Hopis lived a pure life in harmony with nature and had prophesied the evils of modernity long before. In fact, no prophecy can be shown to precede the event prophesied. A catalogue of the recorded prophecies shows that none is earlier than a decade after the event; for example, the first recorded reference to the 'gourd full of ashes' appears in 1956 (Geertz 1994: 430), though it is supposed to have been mentioned in a meeting in 1948 (ibid.: 141), but the report of this utterance was not made until 1984.

## Shamanism in the Mongol state[8]

Shamans were central to Mongol society in the pre-state period, as one of several religious specialists and healers. Some also seem to have been war leaders.

The one thing linking China and the hinterland was the concept of heaven as the all-encompassing principle of cosmic order and human destiny (Humphrey 1994: 196). There were two kinds of religious specialist, one focusing on lineal clans, the other being responsible for biological reproduction. Shamans were involved in both but not exclusively or dominantly. Shamans tended to belong to one of two sorts. The first, the 'patriarchal', focused on the sky spirits, mainly calling down spirits through divination and sacrifice. They performed a liturgy-centred ritual, though shamans were often replaced by clan

---

[8] The main source for this section is the study of Humphrey 1994, with some data from Humphrey 1996.

elders or Buddhist lamas in the ritual area. The other, 'the transformational', used trance and performance-centred ritual. The aim of the ritual was to restore balance to the world. This type of shaman competed with midwives and those who used magic because they performed some of the same functions. After the consolidation of the state, shamans specializing in such practices tended to be in the backwaters.

Caroline Humphrey argues that different manifestations of shamanic practice may support or undermine political authority. Using examples from twelfth or thirteenth century, she argues that inspirational practices were deeply implicated in the formation of Inner Asian states. During the formation of the Mongol state, shamans gave characteristic discourses on prophecy and interpreted omens (e.g. natural phenomena). When the state was consolidated, prophecy became less significant and discourse related more to interpersonal power and identity, with different registers, depending on whether it was central or peripheral. Under the Manchus, concern for genealogies led to associating spirits with the ancestors, which gave an emphasis to the patriarchal form of shamanism. The shamans had much in common with priests and became 'a largely hereditary social class, responsible for maintaining the regular sacrifices for the well-being of the government and empire' (Humphrey 1994: 211). The Manchus had essentially a shamanic state religion until the end of the dynasty.

Nevertheless, the other sort of shamanism survived. Judging from interviews with modern Mongol peoples, such as the Daurs, shamanism on the periphery was different. It was less interested in the 'patriarchal' form of shamanism and more in the *yadgan* or 'transformational shamans', who were masters of spirits and able to travel to the other world to rescue souls. The emperor Hongli issued an edict to renew the court shamanic ritual by drawing on this peripheral shamanism in the mid-eighteenth century.

### *Swahili possession cults*[9]

In the 1980s Linda Giles studied possession cults in a number of coastal sites in Kenya and Tanzania in which Islam was the dominant religious culture. In spite of Quranic teachings, spirit possession is not uncommon even among 'good Muslims'. The spirit may be Muslim or pagan. When spirit possession is suspected (because of illness, misfortune, or perhaps more direct manifestations), one can go to a diviner who is able to provide a diagnosis as to whether the person is possessed. If so, the diviner will refer the person to a *mganga* who is able to treat such problems. Sometimes the spirit is exorcized, but more often the spirit is appeased and the person comes to terms with living with it. Because many people are usually possessed by the same spirit or spirits, the possessed individual will usually be initiated into a possession cult.

What Giles discovered is that such cults do not occupy the peripheral position often assumed. Possession cults are much more widespread than might be at first realized, even among Muslims. Giles, 'found all societal categories in the cult, including those from highly respected, well-educated or economically well-off families. I also found representatives from various racial and ethnic backgrounds, running the full continuum from "Arab" to "African", as well as from various age groups' (1987: 242).

Rather than being an opportunity for the marginal or powerless to protest, the cults provided a much more tangible set of benefits (1987: 247).

---

[9] The information here is taken from Giles 1987.

## PROPHETIC THEMES

An analysis of the anthropological examples catalogued above, and also the many biblical passages on prophets, yields several themes that cut across both the anthropological and the biblical material:

### *Importance of cosmology/theology as the basis for prophecy*

Shamans practise their art in a context which is founded on a particular cosmology. Among the Hopis, their emergence myth structures a great deal in their society, and it is the source and basis of their prophecy. Israelite prophets subscribed to a world view in which Yahweh decided matters in a divine council (to which the true prophet had access: 1 Kgs 22.15–23; Jer. 23.18, 23.22) and Israel was punished by conquest from foreign powers for its sins (Isaiah 8–10; Jeremiah 20–21, 27–29), from which Israel might occasionally (and only temporarily) be delivered through intervention by a righteous king and/or prophet (2 Kings 18–19//Isaiah 36–37). God had enormous heavenly armies at his disposal, if he should choose to use them (2 Kgs 6.15–17). The prophet could be a dangerous figure who could call on God to strike his enemies or those threatening him (2 Kgs 1.9–15; Jer. 28.15–17).

### *Social and ethical criticism*

One of the insights arising out of the nineteenth-century discussion of prophecy was that prophets were 'forthtellers' – they criticized society and the unethical actions of the people and, especially, their rulers. Criticism of those actions and institutions that violate cultural norms were documented throughout the examples examined in this study. Alice Lakwena, Tenskwatawa, the Wana shamans and the Dodo spirits all uphold cultural norms or condemn violations of actions viewed as evil in their respective societies. It is not just Israelite prophets who are 'forthtellers'; most prophetic figures in some way speak out about morality and ethics in their own society. The view that only Israel's prophets ('true prophets') spoke of ethics/morality is thoroughly mistaken.

### *Religious criticism*

Biblical scholars have often emphasized how prophets were commentators on the evils of the society around them. What is often overlooked is how little of the contents of prophetic writings have to do with social criticism. For example, in the book of Isaiah what we would call social or moral critique is found primarily in ch. 5, which talks about drunkenness and taking bribes to pervert the course of justice. Most of the content of the book actually has to do with *religious* criticism – incorrect worship, abandoning Yahweh, following others gods, and the like. Prophets, of whatever favour, do not usually make the modern differentiation between ethical and religious criticism: they regard their ethical, social and religious critique as all part of one whole. In the prophetic literature of the Hebrew Bible, the 'religious' critique (false worship) is much more prominent than the 'ethical'.

### *Multiple roles*

The idea types discussed below associate a single role with each religious specialist, yet in actual societies the prophet may practise a number of roles. For example, Samuel was simultaneously a prophet (1 Sam. 3.20, 9.9, 19.20), a civil leader (1 Sam. 7.6, cf. 8.1) and a priest (although perhaps not called a priest as such, he definitely acts as a priest: cf. 1 Sam. 2.35, 7.7–10, 9.6–14). We know a number of prophets who were priests – Jeremiah (Jer. 1.1), Ezekiel (Ezek. 1.3), probably Malachi (cf. Mal. 1.6–2.9) – though it is not clear that any of them practised that office while engaged in prophetic activity. There is also the question of whether some of the prophets were cult prophets – a subject that unfortunately could not be explored here because of space constraints (but see Grabbe 1995: 112–13). Shamans generally have multiple roles in their society, usually acting as priest, healer, prophet and even sometimes civic leader (e.g. among the Wana). Elijah and Elisha healed, raised the dead and fed people miraculously (1 Kings 17; 2 Kings 4).

### Relationship with the establishment

It is often assumed that prophets opposed the powers that be. One thinks of the frequent prophetic criticism of the reigning king and his officers. Yet anthropological examples illustrate the extent to which spirits support more than one grouping within society; indeed, they may even change sides as the social dynamics change. In some cases the spirits supported movements that resisted the central administration (Alice Lakwena, some Mongol shamans), but in other cases they supported the established government (the *tromba* mediums, some Mongol shamans). The same was true with Israelite prophets, a number of whom supported the reigning king in certain cases (e.g. Isaiah's support of Hezekiah and Huldah's support of Josiah).

### Prophet as war leader

It was the duty of priests in ancient Israel to bless and encourage the Israelite army before it went out (Deut. 20.2–4). This precise description is not given with regard to prophets, though it seems that for a religious specialist to be associated with a military campaign is not unusual – even to the point of leading them into battle. Samuel rallied the troops with prayer, fasting and sacrifice before fighting the Philistines (1 Sam. 7.5–10). Ahab consulted prophets of Yahweh before battle (1 Kgs 22.5–28). Elisha is credited with delivering Israel from the Aramaean army on more than one occasion (2 Kgs 6.8–23, 7). We might think some of these stories incredible, but they are on the same level as other miraculous stories told about prophets; what is more, they are on the same level as stories told to anthropologists about the exploits of prophetic figures. Tenskwatawa promised to make his warriors invulnerable to the Whites' bullets. After the death of Tecumseh, he was declared war leader (Tecumseh's son being the civil leader). Alice Lakwena apparently made a similar promise to her troops against the weapons of the government forces. Her spirit masters were also military leaders in their own right and ostensibly directed the military activities of the 'Holy Spirit Army'.

### Prophetic cults

The existence of prophetic groups or bands seems to be often overlooked or ignored in discussions, but they are mentioned in several contexts (1 Sam. 10.5–13, 19.18–24; 1 Kgs 2.3, 2.5, 2.15, 4.1, 4.38–41, 6.1–7, 9.1–10, 20.35–43). We are left with many more questions than answers. What was their function? What did they do? Were they permanent groups or did people drift in and out? But one cannot help wondering whether there is some resemblance between the 'sons of the prophets' and the possession cults known widely in various parts of the world (e.g. the Swahili possession cults, the *tromba* mediums).

## *Prophetic conflict*

In living societies with several prophet figures that have been studied, prophet rivalry is ubiquitous: prophetic figures naturally compete with each other, and prophetic conflict is normal. The Bible puts it in terms of true and false prophecy, but this is precisely what we would expect. Thus, Jeremiah contrasts himself with other prophets whom he says have not stood in the council of Yahweh and who have prophesied good things (Jer. 23.18, 23.22, 28.8–9); of course, a number of prophecies in the Bible predict good, including some in Jeremiah. Among the anthropological examples looked at here, there are a number of examples: the shamans of Wana, the Mongol shamans, Alice Lakwena.

## *Literary development of the prophetic tradition*

A century and a half or more of biblical scholarship has thoroughly analysed the prophetic corpus. There is practically universal acceptance that a great deal of literary growth, development and evolution have gone on. Whatever original prophetic oracles there were have been added to and edited, perhaps enormously. Therefore, when we talk about prophets, must we not include scribes and editors who have also contributed to the prophetic corpus? Unfortunately, it is difficult to know how these scribal editors saw their work. Did they feel under inspiration? Did the spirit come upon them? Or was it just a mundane scribal duty to 'update' the literature that they copied? Hopi prophecy seems to offer a remarkable parallel. The central core myth is known, even if there are various versions of it. But the prophecies recorded in the twentieth century show additions to the core myth to bring in developing technology (motor cars, aeroplanes, the atomic bomb, space trips to the Moon), even though there is no evidence that such information was found in the original myth(s) – the prophecies have been 'updated' to take account of the developing knowledge of the information age. Thus, scribes, editors and tradents have all made their contribution: 'My Lord Yahweh has spoken: who will not prophesy?' (Amos 3.8).

# IDEAL TYPES AND PROPHET MODELS

We should consider several ideal types (in the Weberian sense) of prophets and related figures that may help us to understand prophets in Israelite society. Certain figures that have a place in some societies will not be considered here because they do not seem relevant for Israelite society: witch-finders were not part of this society; some prophets were priests but there seems to be no connection between this and their prophetic call.

## *The diviner*

I begin with divination for a particular reason. Divination seeks to ascertain God's will and other esoteric knowledge, usually by some sort of manipulation. It often uses mechanical techniques or physical objects, but divination can use such a wide range of techniques that it becomes hard to characterize it. It might involve the interpretation of written texts or extensive questioning of the person consulting the diviner, but can be by means of the spirit of a medium or shaman. Since prophets gain esoteric knowledge by means of the divine spirit, prophecy can usually be considered a type of divination. This is why I put this idea type first, since I argue that most prophecy – including Israelite prophecy – is a form of divination (Grabbe 1995: 139–41).

### The shaman

The main distinguishing characteristic of a shaman is being a master of spirits: to call them up when needed and also to journey to the spirit world on occasion.[10] The Israelite prophets most resembling the traditional shaman are Elijah and Elisha, who control the weather (1 Kgs 17.1, 18.1, 18.41–45), make miraculous journeys (1 Kgs 18.46), conjure food from nowhere and heal and raise the dead (1 Kings 17; 2 Kings 4), and even recover lost objects (2 Kgs 6.1–7). Most of the time we are not told the context for a revelation from Yahweh: did it come out of thin air or did the prophet evoke the message? At times we know that the prophet instigated a revelation ('enquired of Yahweh'), which resembles the shamanic call up of spirits (2 Kgs 3.11–20; Ezekiel 14, 20). It seems to have been common to 'stand in the council of Yahweh' (or at least have a vision of it: 1 Kgs 22.15–28; Jer. 23.18, 23.22).

### The spirit medium

These figures are instruments in the hands of the spirit master. The spirit speaks through them and may even replace their personality. They often remember nothing about what they said or did, and it is accepted by onlookers that it is not the person but the spirit who is acting. Yet an experienced medium may be able to go into a trance and call down the spirit almost at will, which means that the traditional distinction between shaman and spirit medium becomes rather blurred in such cases. They are regularly sought out for specialist help and information about disease, personal troubles and important decisions. Spirit mediums often exist in societies that have other religious specialists, such as priests, diviners or witch-finders. Most of the Israelite prophets fit well this model. In most cases, the prophet seems to be a medium for Yahweh's revelations or communications.

### The scribe

The basic job of the scribe is to write, but his duties usually go beyond this. He not only may put dictated text into words, but might well compose writings himself – we have what seem to be a variety of scribal works from antiquity. In some cases, scribes interpret the prophetic utterances in the process of recording them (e.g. with Alice Lakwena). Thus, the scribe not only keeps records but might edit existing literature and even extend this literature by composing additions to it. It looks as if a considerable portion of prophetic literature in the Bible was written by scribes.

There are two points to keep in mind about ideal types: first, they do not necessarily occur in real life; second, they do not serve to describe reality but to interrogate it. That is, ideal types are simply a way to ask questions about the real world. The descriptions

---

[10] This differs somewhat from the definition of Eliade (1964), who puts his emphasis on the heavenly journey of the shaman, but my impression is that those who distinguish the shaman from the spirit medium and other individuals engaged in spirit possession usually have the same emphasis as that here: the shaman is able in some sense to control the spirits, though this can include his ability to journey to the spirit world to consult them.

given above are abstractions, whereas real religious specialists live in a specific cultural environment that develops, adapts and evolves over time.

One can ask whether there is an 'Israelite prophet' or only a variety of different but related types; the latter seems more likely. None of these ideal types precisely fits any of the prophets known from the biblical text, but the Israelite prophets have similarities to a number of these ideal types: shaman and spirit medium in particular, with the scribe making his contribution more in the process of transmission. The purpose of anthropological models is not to impose a structure found in one cultural situation onto another. It is only a means of trying to probe more deeply into the tradition – the biblical tradition in our case – and ask whether there is more to be discovered and learned.

## CONCLUSIONS

My aim here has been to seek clarity and illumination. Various models have been looked at to see whether they help us to understand the data of the Hebrew Bible. This might lead to the criticism that the exercise is illegitimate because – after all – Israelite prophets were not spirit mediums or shamans or witch-finders. I would make two responses to such criticisms. First, these models are just that – models. No model is actually like the real thing, and some of the models were clearly unlike Israelite prophets in some particulars. Some have even rejected the term 'prophet' for anyone but the prophets of the Bible. I would dispute that, but this aspect of the question is not essential for what I am doing here. I have emphasized resemblances in my discussion because this is where the models are likely to provide help, but I take for granted that many differences will also be noticeable without the need to draw attention to them.

Second, the point is not that these models provide something exactly like what we find in Israel. Rather, they suggest how prophets might have functioned, forcing us back to the biblical texts to read more carefully, to notice forgotten details, and to put aside our prejudices. For how do we know – *a priori* – whether the Israelite prophets were or were not shamans or spirit mediums? Is it only because such an idea goes contrary to your own subjective – prejudiced – image of what a prophet would have been? My opinion is that we should not answer these questions prematurely or close off possibilities until we have carefully investigated the matter. I think I have demonstrated how at least some biblical prophets have characteristics in common with shamans and spirit mediums. We might decide that 'shaman' and 'spirit medium' is not the way we want to characterize them, but this should be decided in the context of discussing scholarly definition, not simply from religious bias.

## REFERENCES

Andrews, E.D. (1972), 'The Shaker Mission to the Shawnee Indians', *Winterthur Portfolio*, 7: 113–28.

Atkinson, J.M. (1989), *The Art and Politics of Wana Shamanship*, Berkeley: University of California Press.

Behrend, H. (1999a), *Alice Lakwena and the Holy Spirits: War in Northern Uganda 1986–97*, Eastern African Studies, Oxford: James Currey.

Behrend, H. (1999b), 'Power to Heal, Power to Kill: Spirit Possession and War in Northern Uganda (1986–1994)', in H. Behrend and U. Luig (eds), *Spirit Possession: Modernity and Power in Africa*, 20–33, Oxford: James Currey.

Eliade, M. (1964), *Shamanism: Archaic Techniques of Ecstasy*, Bollingen Series 76, Princeton, NJ: Princeton University.

Geertz, A.W. (1994), *The Invention of Prophecy: Continuity and Meaning in Hopi Indian Religion*, Berkeley: University of California Press.

Giles, L.L. (1987), 'Possession Cults on the Swahili Coast: A Re-examination of Theories of Marginality', *Africa*, 57 (2): 234–58.

Grabbe, L.L. (1995), *Priests, Prophets, Diviners, Sages: A Socio-historical Study of Religious Specialists in Ancient Israel*, Valley Forge, PA: Trinity Press International.

Grabbe, L.L. (forthcoming), *Prophets and Prophecy in Ancient Israel: A Cross-Cultural Perspective*, London/New York: Bloomsbury T & T Clark.

Humphrey, C. (1994), 'Shamanic Practices and the State in Northern Asia: Views from the Center and Periphery', in N. Thomas and C. Humphrey (eds), *Shamanism, History, and the State*, 191–228, Ann Arbor: University of Michigan Press.

Humphrey, C. with U. Onon (1996), *Shamans and Elders: Experience, Knowledge, and Power Among the Daur Mongols*, Oxford Studies in Social and Cultural Anthropology, Oxford: Clarendon Press.

Masquelier, A. (1999), 'The Invention of Anti-Tradition: Dodo Spirits in Southern Niger', in H. Behrend and U. Luig (eds), *Spirit Possession: Modernity and Power in Africa*, 34–49, Oxford: James Currey.

Mooney, J. (1896), *The Ghost-Dance Religion and the Sioux Outbreak of 1890: Fourteenth Annual Report of the Bureau of Ethnology, 1892–93, Part 2*, Washington, DC: Government Printing Office [reprinted Lincoln: University of Nebraska, 1991].

Sharp, L.A. (1999), 'The Power of Possession in Northwest Madagascar: Contesting Colonial and National Hegemonies', in H. Behrend and U. Luig (eds), *Spirit Possession: Modernity and Power in Africa*, 3–21, Oxford: James Currey.

Sugden, J. (1997), *Tecumseh: A Life of America's Greatest Indian Leader*, New York: Henry Holt.

CHAPTER TWENTY

# The anthropology of food in ancient Israel

CYNTHIA SHAFER-ELLIOTT

You are what you eat. While this proverb may induce the obligatory eye-roll or waves of guilt, the essence of it, like most proverbs, rings true. Archaeologist Kathryn Twiss expands upon this proverb with, 'We are also where we eat, how we eat, and with whom we eat' (Twiss 2007: 1). Albeit the essential nature of food to human survival is obvious; food as a matter of enquiry within many of the social sciences, however, was overlooked or considered too mundane to matter until somewhat recently (Meyers, Shafer-Elliott and Fu 2022: 2–3). Today the study of food has become a hot topic, so to speak, with the field of anthropology taking the lead.[1] Moreover, 'Food Studies' has evolved since the 1980s into a distinctive discipline that can be described as 'an academic field that critically examines the ways in which food shapes and is shaped by the human experience' (Zhen 2018). Food studies is interdisciplinary in nature and engages with diverse topics, disciplines, theoretical approaches and methodologies. Two of the more recent disciplines to engage in food studies is Hebrew Bible Studies and Archaeology of the Southern Levant.

Historically, much of the study of ancient Israel has focused on its monumental contexts, meaning the monumental or significant people, places and performances; such as priests and kings, temples and palaces, battles and cultic ritual (Meyers 2002: 15). The Hebrew Bible itself is more interested in providing accounts of monumental people, places and events through the lens of Israel's theologies, such as military conquests, the anointing of a new king, the development of law codes and (again) cultic ritual. Likewise, the archaeology of ancient Israel has been accused of being 'Tell-minded' or the preference to excavate large, urban settlements, even though most Israelites lived in rural villages, hamlets and farmsteads (Meyers 2013: 42; Faust 2015: 248).

In regard to the study of food within Hebrew Bible studies, it must be noted that the subject of food was not fully ignored; rather, it chiefly focused on a very narrow, monumental aspect of food – that is, the food-related cultic rituals (i.e. sacrificial animals and foods as found in Leviticus 1–7 and Deut. 12.15–19) and the priestly concerns regarding food prohibitions in the Torah (Lev. 11.2–23; Deut. 14.3–20) (Shafer-Elliott

---

[1] For a collection of so-called classics in the anthropology of food see the anthology in Counihan, Van Esterik and Julier (2019).

2013: 1; Meyers, Shafer-Elliott and Fu 2022: 4).² Within the archaeologies of the Southern Levant and of the ancient Near East, zooarchaeology (i.e. the study of animal bones) and feasting as displayed in iconography (i.e. representational art) were early foci of food studies (Altmann and Fu 2014: 7; for instance, Wapnish and Hesse 1991; Collon 1992; Wapnish 1993; Ziffer 2002a, 2002b). More specifically, within the archaeology of ancient Israel and Judah the focal point of the study of food was primarily relegated to food as an identity marker (e.g. the presence or absence of pig remains). Of course, there are some exceptions to these norms including Oded Borowski's work on agriculture and animal husbandry, Carol Meyer's contribution to women and food preparation, and Nathan MacDonald's study of the Israelite diet and the symbolism of food in the Hebrew Bible (Borowski 1987, 1998; Meyers 2002; MacDonald 2008a, 2008b). Fortunately, the progress made in anthropology and food studies has made its way to the study of the Hebrew Bible and ancient Israel with MacDonald's books in 2008, as can be seen in the rise in publications on matters related to food.³

Be that as it may, in order for us to focus on the role of food in ancient Israelite society, we must shift our focus from the monumental to the mundane or the ordinary people, places and performances of the everyday. Unfortunately, the mundane or ordinary is typically overlooked or ignored in the Hebrew Bible unless, of course, it takes part in setting the scene for the narrative or the like. Furthermore, Meyers (2014: 19) notes that the Hebrew Bible is an elite, androcentric text that systematically ignores the lives of the average ancient Israelite men, women and children. Consequently, for the purpose of this study, we will make use of social-scientific approaches that will help us understand the social role of food in the lives of ordinary ancient Israelites during the Iron Age (c. 1200–586 BCE). Approaches such as food studies (previously mentioned) and household archaeology will be most helpful in appreciating the social complexity of food in ancient Israel. The purpose of this chapter is to provide a general presentation on the basic, social and cultural meanings of food in ancient Israel within domestic contexts. In other words, our aim is to better understand how everyday ancient Israelite society related to food and how it contributed to making their lives more meaningful. Unfortunately, we cannot cover all aspects of the social and cultural dynamics of food in this chapter; consequently, we will limit our focus to the sociability of food in every day and special occasions, and the politics of food and gender made visible within the Israelite household.

## TOOLS FOR THE TASK

As mentioned earlier, food studies is interdisciplinary, making use of a variety of methodologies. One of the tools that will best help us in our task of understanding the potential uses and meanings of food in the daily lives of the average ancient Israelites is household archaeology, which can be loosely defined as 'a branch of settlement archaeology specializing in the study of the activities and facilities associated with ancient households or houses' (Archaeology Wordsmith n.d.). Household archaeology is also interdisciplinary and can be broken down into two simple steps: the first being the employment of spatial

---

² For a fuller history of food-related scholarship within Hebrew Bible studies and the archaeology of the Southern Levant, see MacDonald 2008a; Altmann 2011; Greer 2013; Altmann and Fu 2014.
³ This list is by no means exhaustive: MacDonald 2008a, 2008b; Altmann 2011; Greer 2013; Altmann and Fu 2014; Peters 2016; Welton 2020; Fu, Shafer-Elliott and Meyers 2022.

analysis when excavating a house or houses; and the second is the use of secondary sources to help infer activities from the activity areas. These secondary sources include, but are not limited to: texts, comparative archaeological data, ethnography, ethnoarchaeology, iconography, gender archaeology and experimental archaeology (Hardin 2004: 74, 2010: 22, 27, 33). In order to fully appreciate how household archaeology can be utilized in food studies, it is important to flesh out the concept more fully.

In their landmark paper essentially introducing household archaeology, Richard Wilk and William Rathje characterize the household as 'the most common social component of subsistence, the smallest and most abundant activity group' (1982: 618), and argue that the study of the household can be categorized into three main groups: the material, social and behavioural aspects. The material aspect includes the physical reality of the household, which is primarily made up of the dwelling, its activity areas and possessions. The second is the social aspect including the household members and their relationships to each other. Finally, the third consists of the behavioural aspect or the activities the household members perform (ibid.).

Of course, archaeologists can only excavate the physical remains (i.e. the material aspect) of a household, with the social and behavioural aspects inferred from the excavated dwelling and its material culture.[4] Utilizing the methodology of spatial analysis on an excavation allows the archaeologist to recognize and understand patterns and regularities that would have been otherwise missed, by mapping in detail the vertical and horizontal relationships of the dwelling and the remains found within it (Hardin 2010: 26–7). Recognizing the spatial relationships of and patterns in the material culture can then be linked to specific activities, where these activities occurred, and who possibly carried them out (ibid.: 10). For example, we employed spatial analysis in our excavation of an Iron IIB (eighth century BCE) house at Tell Halif, Israel. In one room, a number of broken storage jars were found next to a grinding installation that, coupled with the micro artefacts sampled, suggest that the activity of food preparation, more specifically the grinding of grain into flour, was conducted in this space (Shafer-Elliott 2022b: 241).

Inferring behaviour from activities can be aided by the concept of 'habitus'. Habitus is defined as 'the practical logic and sense of order that is learned unconsciously through the enactment of everyday life' (Gilchrist 1999: 14). Repeated activities, or habits, communicate what societies value and devalue. The repetitive domestic activities uncovered by household archaeology and spatial analysis provide clues about what a household valued and its attitudes, including those related to identity, class and gender. Food-related repetitive activities that occurred daily or on special occasions can tell us not just what the household grew and raised, or what food was prepared and how, but they can also provide insight into what customs and norms ancient Israelite society deemed acceptable or not.

Wilk and Rathje note that there are four basic functions that households perform on a daily basis, which further clarify the household's social and economic roles. These functions include: production, distribution, transmission and reproduction. Here production is defined as 'human activity that procures resources or increases their value'. Distribution, or 'the process of moving resources from producers to consumers and could include the consumption of resources', differs from transmission, which is 'a special form of distribution that involves transferring rights, roles, land, and property between

---

[4] I.e. the physical evidence of a culture in the objects and architecture they have made.

generations'. Finally, reproduction, which is 'the rearing and socializing of children' (Wilk and Rathje 1982: 622, 624, 627, 630). Of course, the implementation of these functions is going to vary depending on the society and its environment, social strata and phase of cultural evolution; not to mention what other social groups (such as lineages, villages, monarchies etc.) are complementing, replacing or competing with the household (ibid.: 621). The basic functions of a household are similar, but we must make allowances for how households differ across time and space.

## THE ISRAELITE HOUSEHOLD

In order to better perceive the average household in ancient Israel, we shall break it down into the three main aspects of a household as suggested by Wilk and Rathje: the material, social and behavioural aspects.

The material aspect of the ancient Israelite household would include the dwelling, any other secondary buildings or caves, and its fields, orchards and vineyards. The dwelling was the centre of the household's activity, which served as a workplace as much as it did a place to live. The basic form of the so-called 'Israelite house' during the Iron Age consisted of a two-storey rectangle-shaped building typically made of stone foundations and mudbrick walls and had a flat roof. The bottom floor was made up of a room in the back running the width of the house (often called 'the broad room'), and one to three rooms separated by pillars running perpendicular to the broad room. A forecourt (or courtyard) is often found at the front of the house. The bottom floor and forecourt is where many of the domestic activities took place. The top floor of the house would primarily be used for sleeping and light household chores, while the flat roof of the house could also be used for certain tasks (e.g. the drying of flax, see Josh. 2.6) and for sleeping in the hot summer months.[5]

The social aspect includes those who are members of the household and what their relationship is to each other. Before all else, a distinction needs to be made between the term 'family' and 'household'. Sociologists define a family by kinship, descent and marriage, whereas a household is defined by co-residence and co-working (Wilk and Rathje 1982: 620). A household is a broader term that takes into consideration the fact that not all who live and or work together are related. A household would normally consist of a family, but would also include those who live with or work for the family.

In ancient Israel, a family unit would be multigenerational and would typically consist of the patriarch and matriarch (i.e. the male and female heads of the family), their married sons and their families, any unmarried children, and possibly unmarried or widowed patrilineal female members; if there was a secondary wife and children, these too would be included. The ancient Israelite *household*, on the other hand, would include the family unit as well as any non-related members who lived and/or worked for the household, such as hired seasonal workers, slaves and guests. For instance, a hired worker could live with the family while they are helping with the harvest but return to their own household once

---

[5] Unlike the topic of food, much has been written on the preferred style of house in Israel during the Iron Age, too many to list here. A selection of sources include: Shiloh 1970; Stager 1985; Kempinski and Reich 1992; Schloen 2001; Faust and Bunimovitz 2003; Hardin 2010; Yasur-Landau, Ebeling and Mazow 2011; Battini, Brody and Steadman (forthcoming).

the task is finished. A guest would stay with the family but rules of hospitality would forbid them from working. A slave would both live and work with the household. Anyone who lived and or worked with the household would be considered as part of that household for the duration of their connection. [See also Chapter 10 in this volume.]

Ancient Israelite society was kinship-based with the household, often referred to as the *bêt 'āb* or 'or house of the father' (Gen. 46.31) and occasionally *bêt 'em* or 'house of the mother' (Gen. 24.28), as its nucleus. The next concentric circle outside the nucleus would be the clan, or *mišpāḥāh* (Exod. 6.14, 25; Num. 1.2), followed by the circle made up of the tribe, *šēbeṭ* or *maṭṭeh*. Several clans, *mišpāḥôt*, that claimed a common ancestor made up a tribe and lived within the boundaries of their tribe's geographical territory (Gen. 49.28; Num. 1.16). Once a monarchy, or *mamlakah*, was established, this would be the final and largest circle in the kinship structure (1 Sam. 24.20; Backfish and Shafer-Elliott, forthcoming.) In its most basic form, a rural village consisted of a *mišpāḥôt* or clan made up of several households, or *bâttîm 'ab*. Judges 17–21 can serve as an example of an Israelite household. The household of Micah the Ephraimite includes Micah (the patriarch), his widowed mother, his sons and, more than likely, their families (Mic. 17.2, 18.22) living in several dwellings surrounded by a boundary wall (Mic. 18.14–16, 22). The household grows when Micah hires a young Levite to serve as the household priest (Mic. 17.10–12). [See also Chapter 7 in this volume].

The behavioural aspect included the daily and special occasion activities of the Israelite household. The average ancient Israelites were 'agro-pastoralists' meaning they lived on a mixture of agriculture and livestock herding, often on a mere-subsistence level. Iron Age houses excavated in Israel clearly suggest that households were engaged in the customary domestic activities of production, distribution, transmission, reproduction and – I would add – religious ritual. Undoubtedly, daily activities related to food were imperative to the survival of the household.

## FOODWAYS IN ANCIENT ISRAEL

Food studies as a discipline examines the intersection of food, culture and history. One concept that helps in this endeavour is 'foodways', which is particularly interested in the cultural, social and economic practices, attitudes and beliefs relating to the production and consumption of food. *Basic* questions related to ancient Israelite foodways include: what foodstuffs did the Israelites consume? And how did they acquire it? *Socially* relevant questions focus on who is part of the preparation group? The consumption group? What is their relationship to each other? Who is included and who is excluded? And finally, there are *cultural* questions pertaining to Israel's attitudes, practices and rituals around food and what do they inform us about Israel's most basic beliefs about the world and themselves (Harris, Lyon and McLaughlin 2005: viii–ix)? In addition, how does food relate to power, gender and politics found in Israelite society? These three categories (basic, social and cultural) will guide us as we look at ancient Israelite foodways more deeply.

### Basic foodways

Social anthropologist Jack Goody created a detailed classification system of food production that can be used to answer basic questions related to food in ancient Israel. Goody argues that there are four primary categories of food, each with aspects and phases to consider.⁶ The first category is production, which concerns agriculture and animal husbandry. Some aspects of production related to agriculture include planting, cultivating, labour, resources and technology; while those of animal husbandry involve breeding, slaughtering, labour and techniques. Distribution, the second category, includes the various types of transactions (e.g. allocation, gifts and reciprocal exchange) and aspects of the act of distribution itself (e.g. storage and transport). Preparation, or the art of cooking and cuisine, is the third category with phases concerned with preliminary work (such as the butchering of meat and the grinding of cereals), cooking or the application of heat or other transforming agents (cold, vinegar, salt etc.), and the dishing up. Other aspects of the preparation phase to consider include: the cooking group (i.e. who cooks with whom), the consumption group (i.e. for whom is the food being cooked); and technology of cooking (hearths, containers, instruments, ovens, spits and fuels). The final category is consumption, which is associated with the serving, eating and cleaning away of cooked food including its distribution in time, structure, manners, technology of eating, the eating group and the differentiation of cuisine (Goody 1982: 44–9; see also Shafer-Elliott 2013: 23).

Ancient Israel's basic foodways can best be found in the household, whose own rhythm moved according to the agricultural calendar. The household economy throughout the Iron Age was based on subsistence-level agro-pastoralism (or farming and animal husbandry), meaning that the household was responsible for the production of food, its consumption and its limited distribution. According to Walton, a subsistence household economy was concerned with reducing risk, producing diverse goods locally, and limiting trade or surplus production beyond storage against potentially bad years (Walton 2022: 59). As such, the Israelite diet mainly consisted of (or came from) products that they grew or raised including cereals, legumes, olive oil, wine, dairy products (such as cheese, curds and butter), nuts (almond, pistachio and walnut), and seasonal fruits (grape, fig, pomegranate, olive, date, sycamore) and vegetables (cucumber, watermelon, onion, leek, garlic). Unlike our meals today, the average Israelite most likely did not eat meat on a daily basis; rather, depending on the economic conditions, meat (mainly domesticated bovids such as sheep, goats, and cattle) was usually reserved for special occasions (like a wedding or agricultural/religious festival) or if the herd needed to be culled. More importantly, domesticated bovids supplied secondary products in the form of fibre, milk and traction (Lev-Tov 2022: 86); consequently, the household was dependent upon their herds for these products and would not endanger their survival just because they had a hankering for lamb chops.

Products were stored in ceramic containers of various sizes, pits, skins, sacks, baskets, wooden chests, and silos, depending on the volume of the commodities to be conserved and how long they needed to be preserved (short, medium or long term) (Ilan 2022: 261; see also Frank 2018). Out of all the products cultivated in ancient Israel, cereals were by far the most important, providing an estimated 50 per cent of daily caloric intake (Meyers 2002: 14, 21; Borowski 2003: 66). In order for grain to transform from an inedible to edible form, it must go through a multistep process of parching or soaking, milling or grinding, heating and/or leavening. Meyers estimates that two hours every day were spent processing grain, most likely by the women of the household (Meyers 1997: 25–7).

---

⁶ Goody (1982: 48) also notes that some may choose to add a fifth category of disposal for the disposal of leftovers from both sacred and profane meals.

Ground grain could be made into porridge or gruel and, of course, bread. The Israelite diet relied on bread so heavily that the Hebrew word for it, *lechem*, is metonymic with food (Gen. 28.20; Exod. 2.20; Lev. 3.16; Num. 15.19; Ruth 1.6; 2 Sam. 9.10; Job 42.11; Ps. 132.15).

Olives (for oil) and grapes (for wine) were also high on the list of important commodities produced by ancient Israel; however, there is one product whose importance in the daily fare is often overlooked – that of the legume and its pulses.[7] Legumes are economical and excellent sources of protein, carbohydrates and fibre (Zohary, Hopf and Weiss 2012: 75). Both the Hebrew Bible and archaeological samples from the southern Levant indicate that several types of legumes were widely used: broad bean, lentil, chickpea, bitter vetch, peas and fenugreek. Pulses were roasted, cooked and eaten whole, ground into flour and used for cakes, and most commonly used in soups and stews (Zohary 1982: 82–4). Interestingly, the word pulse comes from the Latin word *puls*, which can be interpreted as 'porridge', referring to the legume seeds that can be made into porridge, stew or a thick soup (Shafer-Elliott 2022a: 150).

It is difficult to say with certainty what types of meals were consumed and at what intervals. Borowski suggests that breakfast would have been a quick and easy meal of porridge or gruel since daily chores would start early most of the year. Lunch would be light and picnic-style since household members could be conducting various chores often at a distance from the dwelling. This type of meal would need to be efficient, raw and light, and could include bread, cheese, yogurt, dried fruit, parched grain, water, and seasonal vegetables and fruit (Ruth 2.14). The main hot meal seems to have been the evening meal, which more than likely was prepared by those whose activities were centred at the dwelling (Borowski 2003: 74). This evening meal probably consisted of bread and a stew. Mesopotamian sources emphasize the preference for stews in the ancient Near East. At least a hundred different soups or stews are mentioned in one Assyrian 'encyclopedia'. The recipes found in the Yale Babylonian Culinary Tablets include many recipes for stews made from vegetables, lentils and various meats (Bottéro 1995: 48; Shafer-Elliott 2013: 132). Furthermore, *nazid* is the Hebrew word for stew and is used to describe stews of vegetables or legumes (Gen. 25.29, 34; 2 Kgs 4.38–40; Hag. 2.12). In times of crisis, such as famine, war, drought or economic difficulties, normal food items could be scarce. In these circumstances, it is likely that porridge was served again as the main meal.

A variety of tools and technologies within the dwelling were used to prepare food, the most important of which was the oven. On excavations in Israel, ovens are often found in domestic contexts; however, they are usually incomplete so it is challenging to say what ovens in ancient Israel looked like exactly. Ethnographic and ethnoarchaeological studies in the Middle East can be helpful here, since some of the oven types observed may be the modern descendants of ancient ovens. The first type of oven is not technically an oven at all; rather, an open fire or hot rocks within the fire would constitute as the most simple of cooking technologies. The *saj*, or a rounded metal disc, is placed over the fire or the rocks and was used to quickly bake thin bread. Of course, the ancient Israelites would not have used their precious metal in such a way, but this method of baking could illustrate how bread was baked on hot rocks (1 Kgs 19.6), on the coals of a fire (Isa. 44.19), or on a clay

---

[7] A pulse is the edible seed within the pod of legume plants.

griddle or baking tray (Lev. 2.5, 6.21, 7.9; Ezek. 4.3; Borowski 2003: 66; Shafer-Elliott 2013: 119).

A second type of oven observed by ethnographers in the Middle East is a *tabun* (Arabic plural: *tawabin*), which is a low truncated, dome-shaped oven made of clay between 25 and 50 centimetres tall. *Tawabin* have a domed top with one opening on the side, others have a second opening located in the domed top. The *tabun* could be heated from either the outside or the inside with the dough placed usually on the floor to bake. Cooking pots could also be placed on the floor or over the top opening, if there was one (McQuitty 1984: 261, 1994: 55–7; van der Steen 1991: 135; Bottéro 2004: 49–50). Even though the term *tabun* is used to describe ovens found in archaeological excavations in Israel, it is an anachronistic term because the *tabun* style of oven is not found in archaeological contexts any earlier than the seventh century CE nor is the term *tabun* found in the Hebrew Bible or the Talmud (van der Steen 1991: 135; Ebeling and Rogel 2015: 328–30).

Ovens found in archaeological excavations resemble the *tannur* style of oven (Arabic plural: *tannaneer*) used in the Middle East. A modern *tannur* is a conical or beehive-shaped oven about a metre high, which is lit from the inside with dough baked on interior walls (Shafer-Elliott 2013: 120; Ebeling and Rogel 2015: 329). Unlike the term *tabun*, the term *tannur* is found in the Hebrew Bible fifteen times, seven of which refer to an oven used to bake bread (Exod. 7.28; Lev. 2.4, 7.9, 11.35, 26.26; Hos. 7.4, 6–7). A lid could be placed over the top opening of both *tawabin* and *tannaneer*, which would allow the oven to retain its heat and thus permitted cooking pots to be placed on top or even inside to cook (McQuitty 1984: 261, 1994: 56; van der Steen 1991: 135; Shafer-Elliott 2013: 120–1; Ebeling and Rogel 2015: 330). One complete clay oven (*tannur*) was found in a dwelling dated to the tenth-century BCE Stratum VI at the Tel Rehov archaeological excavations in Israel. The oven is 56 centimetres high from base to top with walls 4 centimetres thick; its base is 56 centimetres in diameter with its top opening 30 centimetres in diameter with flattened edges. Unlike other ovens found in archaeological excavations, the Rehov oven has two preserved openings. The oven's exterior was lined with large, closely packed potsherds set in clay, which helped insulate the oven (Mazar 2016: 118).

*Tannur*-type ovens are found both in indoor and outdoor central, living room–type spaces in Iron Age dwellings. Some have argued that the presence of ovens indicate they are in a courtyard space (Fritz and Kempinski 1983: 27–34; Herzog 1984: 76–7; Hardin 2012: 544; Oksuz, Hardin and Wilson 2019: 238); however, ethnographic and ethnoarchaeological studies in the Middle East indicate that ovens were located in indoor spaces as well as outdoors. Indoor ovens are usually located in a central space inside the dwelling proper or in their own baking hut in the open forecourt of the house (Parker 2011). Ovens inside the dwelling are a fundamental indicator of a living room–type space that was a focal point for the household, especially during the cold winter months (Watson 1979: 122; Amiry and Tamari 1989: 20; Horne 1994: 145; Holladay 1997: 339; Klein 2010: 20). Outside ovens were typically communal, reducing the use and cost of fuel, and facilitating group cohesion (Lev. 26.26; Parker 2011).

Meals were prepared mostly in cooking pots. In the Hebrew Bible, words for cooking pots include *parur* (Num. 11.8, Judg. 6.19, 1 Sam. 2.14), *siyr* (Exod. 16.3; 2 Kgs 4.38–41; Jer. 1.13; Ezek. 11.3, 7, 11; Mic. 3.3; Zech. 14.20–21), *qallachat* (1 Sam. 2.14; Mic. 3.3), and *dud* (1 Sam. 2.14; Shafer-Elliott 2013: 220).[8] Archaeologically speaking,

---

[8] For more on Hebrew terminology related to food and foodways, see Peters 2022; also Peters 2016; Pleins 2017.

cooking pots can be categorized into three basic forms that evolved throughout the Bronze and Iron Ages and were greatly influenced by Philistines. These basic forms include the Bronze Age pot or bowl, the (Philistine) jug and the hybrid pot.[9]

The typical pot of the Bronze Age looked like a shallow bowl; they were often larger, handless, open-mouthed with an everted rim, round base and carinated body. As the Bronze Age progressed, the cooking pots kept the traditional bowl-shape but with some size variations and more carinated in shape, adding a folded-over, everted rim with a triangular flange during the Late Bronze Age II. The open mouth, shallow bowl and type of cooking ware of this style of cooking pot[10] supported several cooking techniques, including steaming, frying, simmering and boiling; and its ample size allowed for the cooking of larger food items (like meat) and for serving more people. The popularity of this style of cooking pot continued to the end of the Iron Age (Killebrew 1999: 84, 92–5, 106–9).

Cooking jugs were another style of cooking pot in ancient Israel. However, it seems that the increase in cooking jugs is related to the appearance of the Philistines in the Late Bronze and Early Iron I Ages. A particular style of cooking pot is labelled the 'Philistine jug' for two notable reasons: one, because it nearly replaced the traditional cooking pot/bowl style at sites characterized as Philistine on the southern coastal plain; and two, because this type of jug is less frequently found at sites outside of Philistia. The so-called Philistine cooking jug resembled Cypriot and Aegean cooking jugs of the Late Cypriot IIC and IIIA and Late Helladic IIIC periods. The jug shape included a globular to ovoid shape, a closed mouth and one or two loop handles from the everted rim to its shoulder with modifications evolving throughout the Iron Age. The small size and shape of the Philistine jug is not conducive to multiple types of cooking.[11] Rather, its thin walls were best used for slow, low-heat cooking of liquid dishes, while its small size limited both the size and amount of ingredients, as well as the size of the portions and the consumption group (Killebrew 1999: 93–5, 107; Ben-Shlomo et al. 2008; Gur-Arieh, Maeir and Shahack-Gross 2011).

The third category of cooking pot used in ancient Israel was a blending of the Bronze Age bowl style with the cooking jug, which came to be called by some as the 'hybrid cooking pot'. The hybrid pot combined the rounded body and open mouth of the Bronze Age pot and the handles and shape of the Philistine jug, with slightly varying forms. Depending on the type of ware used, the hybrid pot could be used for slow, low-heat cooking as well as for rapid, high-temperature cooking. Furthermore, size and quantities of ingredients and people served was subject to the size and capacity of the cooking pot. All three categories of cooking pots could be suspended over a fire if they had handles, placed in a fire pit, next to or on top of a hearth, inside a *tannur*, and, according to some reconstructions, covering the *tannur*'s upper opening (Killebrew 1999: 93–5, 107; Ben-Shlomo et al. 2008).

## Social foodways

The main concern for any subsistence-level household economy in ancient societies would have been survival. The continuity of the household in the here and now, and into the

---

[9] For more on cooking pots in Iron Age Israel, see Panitz-Cohen 2022.
[10] The diameter of the mouth averaged 9.8–15.7 inches (25–40 centimetres) and the height 5.9–7.8 inches (15–20 centimetres).
[11] Philistine jugs were typically uniform in size, with a volume of about 0.4–0.6 imperial gallons (2–3 litres), a maximum height of *c.* 7.8 inches (20 centimetres), a maximum body diameter of *c.* 7 in (18 centimetres), and a diameter at the mouth of 3.5–4.7 inches (9–12 centimetres).

future, was imperative in ancient Israel. As a concept, survival was so essential that all members of the household were expected (and depended upon) to participate in the household economy, regardless of their sex, age or any other differential. However, Meyers argues that three overlapping factors of protection, procreation and production played a significant role in the social life of domestic Israel (Meyers 1983: 574–6). These factors do imply that, regardless of the unifying task of survival, some sort of gender-based roles did occur – probably due to biological or reproductive considerations. As we shall see, these factors will affect the social questions related to food.

The protection factor is considered to be managed by the household males (Meyers 1983: 577). Matthews and Benjamin suggest that protection of the household and its members was one of the primary responsibilities of the patriarch (Matthews and Benjamin 1993: 8, 12). Furthermore, it was common in ancient Israel (especially before a professional army became customary) for war-age males to be called to war (ibid.: 97). The narratives of Jacob and Dinah (Gen. 34.1–31) and Jephthah and his unnamed daughter (Judg. 11.1–40) illustrate the protection role of the patriarch (whether they are successful in their protection or not is up to the interpreter); while Judg. 19.29–30 and 20.1–7 depicts the call to arms albeit in a gruesome manner.

A vital element into the continuity of the household is fertility: fertility of the household land, animals and members. In ancient Israel, the procreation factor of the household members fell under the female domain primarily because it was the females of the household who were involved with their own reproductive role and concerns, mainly those pertaining to menstruation, conception, birth, lactation and weaning. Therefore, it seems likely that household activities performed by the females of the household were conducted within or near the dwelling itself (Meyers 1983: 574, 1997: 25). This point is illustrated by Amiry and Tamari's ethnographic study of Palestinian village peasants in the central highlands. They observed that the men would gather at the village square instead of at each other's houses. When asked about this, the men stated they met at the village square because the house was considered 'female territory', as was the spring and the bread oven (Amiry and Tamari 1989: 15). In ancient Israel, the reproduction role of the household females is thought to be under the purview of the household matriarch. Bird (1997: 35) notes that motherhood was the leading position of honour generally available to women and the highest status most women could achieve, which could be one reason why the authors/compilers/redactors of the book of Genesis address the issue of barrenness and the Hebrew matriarchs. For example, in Genesis 16, Sarah (Sarai), the matriarch of the household, is barren; thereupon, Sarah provides her husband and household patriarch, Abraham (Abram) with a surrogate (Hagar) who would bear children in her stead. Not only was designating a surrogate a legal action that helped the household survive, but it also helped to preserve the honour of the barren woman (Matthews and Benjamin 1993: 25, 33).

The factor that joined the Israelite household together was the production factor. As was mentioned earlier, all members of the household were expected to engage in domestic activities that generated production, whether they were related to agriculture, the rearing of animals, or the manufacturing of assorted goods, such as pottery and fabric. Ethnographic studies of traditional Palestinian villages in 1970s and 1980s demonstrate that household men, women and children worked together to bring in the barley and wheat harvest. 'In the fields, men reaped the crops using sickles, while women and older children gathered the sheaves of wheat and tied them into manageable bundles. [. . .] Women and young girls also carried bundles on their heads as the whole family headed towards the village threshing floor' (Amiry and Tamari 1989: 35).

While all physically able household members were required to assist at times of planting and harvest (Meyers 1997: 24), it was the household women who were required to bear the full burden of production when the household men were called to war (Meyers 1983: 574).

## Women and food preparation

The production factor was a concern for the entire household, although one aspect of production – food preparation – seems to have been the responsibility of the women of the household, and under the supervision of its matriarch. The reason for this may be directly related to the procreation factor of the women of the household. If most women of childbearing age were trying to conceive, were pregnant, had just given birth, were breastfeeding or weaning, it is unlikely that they would regularly perform household activities far from the dwelling. Of course, there were probably scenarios where 'all hands on deck' were required; however, in all likelihood, the daily activities women performed were conducted at or near the dwelling largely due to their reproductive role. Activities conducted at the dwelling chiefly consisted of those related to food preparation; thus, the connection of women to household foodways is significant.

In her study on the social life of food, archaeologist Christine Hastorf incorporates numerous ethnographic and archaeological case studies. These studies indicate that women have been or are responsible for the majority of food preparation. Hastorf records that, 'In cross-cultural studies of 185 societies, women completed most food preparation and cooking tasks, performing *more than* 80 percent of these tasks in any one group' (Hastorf 2017: 183; emphasis added). Furthermore, she notes that 'the only [food-related] tasks that men tended to dominate in were hunting, butchering, generating fire, and farming (plowing)' (ibid.). Of course, the value and importance of food preparation will vary with each society; however, food is a necessity and those who dominate the preparation of it often have more technological skill, power and prestige than meets the eye. Hastorf writes that it is 'through these acts [of food preparation] women acquire their own place and enablement, with their productive contributions being linked especially to familial prestige and position as well as training the next generations in these useful skills' (ibid.).

In ancient Israel, Meyers notes that the daily activities conducted by women were time-consuming and energy-demanding, and required more technological skill than did those daily activities conducted by the men of the household (Meyers 2013: 184). Women transformed raw products into edible food, which demanded skills that were indispensable to the household. The matriarch, as the senior woman, served as the household 'manager' of sorts who oversaw the storage and preparation of ingredients into foodstuffs and meals, which would have included having oversight of who ate, when they ate and how much they ate. Several examples from the Hebrew Bible illustrate this point. In 1 Samuel 25, the foolish Nabal insults David (through his messengers) at the sheep-shearing feast. Abigail, the wife of Nabal, neutralizes the potentially dangerous situation with food by sending David enough household food for a feast: two hundred loaves, two skins of wine, five sheep ready dressed, five measures of parched grain, a hundred clusters of raisins and two hundred cakes of figs. Abigail does not ask for permission to send a massive amount of the household provisions, she just does it. Another example can be found in the nameless woman of Shuman in 2 Kings 4.8–10, who chooses to prepare a meal for the prophet Elijah when he was in the region. Additionally, she has a small room built and furnished on the roof of her house for Elijah (v. 10). Once more, the woman of Shuman does not ask, she does. Our best description of the matriarch as the manager of the household foodways comes from Prov. 31.10–31 where in vv. 14–15 it states, 'she is like the ships of a merchant, she brings her food from far away. She rises while it is still night and provides food for her household and tasks for her servant girl'. And later in v. 27, 'She looks well to the ways of her household, and does not eat the bread of idleness'. These examples depict women having control over the household provisions and they alone decide what to do with it. The matriarch's influence over and impact on the household foodways and thus its economy is tremendous, requiring exceptional skill, expertise and diplomacy, resulting in the maintenance and endurance of the household (Shafer-Elliott 2021: 9).

## Cultural foodways

Cultural norms are the unwritten rules of a specific culture that can take the form of a practice, belief, diet, ritual or set of expectations; furthermore, cultural norms are often unquestioningly followed and come to govern all aspects of life (Wright and Novotny 2018). Food and the meals created from them are significant carriers of cultural norms in any society. Meals are about much more than the food served; they are social events rich with meaning. Mary Douglas writes, '[T]he meaning of a meal is found in a system of repeated analogies. Each meal carries something of the meaning of other meals; each meal is a structured social event which structures others in its own image' (Douglas 1972: 69–70). The repetition (or habitus) of meals reinforces its value among its participants. However, the repetition of the meal itself is not just about the recurring event of the meal; rather, it is also about the repeated construction and maintenance of the household's foodways. As Simoons argues, foodways, or 'the modes of feeling, thinking, and behaving about food that are common to a cultural group [. . .] serve to bind individuals in larger social groups through shared understandings of cultural conventions' (Simoons 1967: 3; Wood 1995: 40). Twiss elaborates on this point when she writes that food '[is used to express] not only who we are but also who we wish to be, asserting our membership in certain groups and distancing ourselves from others' (Twiss 2007: 1). In other words, to quote the familiar proverb, the family (or in ancient Israel's case, the household) who eats together stays together.

The power of food is often overlooked even though, as archaeologist Yannis Hamilakis notes, that food 'is constantly used in the generation, maintenance, legitimation and deconstruction of authority and power' (1999: 40). The habitus of the preparation, serving and consumption of both everyday and special occasion meals provides the setting for the construction and reinforcement of accepted cultural norms within a social group. Food is inherently political. 'Gastro-politics' (Appadurai 1981), or the politics of food, is characterized as 'the political discourse that encircles all things linked to eating and invokes the charged meanings underlying all culinary events' (Hastorf 2017: 182). As a political tool, meals have a capacity to both break down barriers and build boundaries. For instance, an illustration of how meals can be used to break down barriers can be seen in ancient Near Eastern and Mediterranean hospitality norms. Hospitality norms dictate the serving of a meal (more like a feast), which is used to decipher if a stranger poses a potential threat or if they could be a potential ally (Gudme 2019: 91). The hospitality meal Abraham serves the divine messengers in Genesis 18 demonstrates the diplomacy used to determine if a guest is friend or foe. At the same time, meals build boundary walls by reinforcing group identity. Most societies have food-related practices that demonstrate group membership, including using meals to model behaviour to children, what foods are acceptable or unacceptable to eat, and what foods are traditionally eaten at everyday meals versus those foods that are reserved for special occasion festive meals. The description of prohibited and permitted foods in Leviticus 11 embody how group identity is moulded through its gastro-politics.

Meals reflect how the group views itself in both identity and values. Households, therefore, are the most important of social relationships because of their influence on the household's gastro-politics. Special occasion meals, or feasts, occupied a central place in the manifestation of a household's gastro-politics. Jonathan Greer defines feasts as 'the specialized consumption of food, often meat, and drink, in a communal setting set apart precisely because of the "highly condensed" symbolic importance of the event' (Greer 2013: 3). Meyers elaborates further on the definition of a feast by noting several features of a typical festive meal. A feast is arranged for a special purpose, such as weddings or as part of religious ritual, and typically lasts longer than the average meal – it may even consist of several meals over several days. Feasts typically have more participants; for example, a household feast would include neighbours and other kinship-related households. In addition, the amount and quality of food and drink at a feast is superior to an average meal (Meyers 2013: 157).

It is important to note, however, that there are potential differences between feasting in elite contexts versus average, domestic contexts. All of the features commonly associated with a feast would be greatly exaggerated in an elite feast, especially the type and amount of special foodstuffs consumed, with meat serving as the most prestigious of food items. For example, at David's anointing as king over all of Israel in 1 Chron. 12.38–40, enough provisions of meal, cakes of figs, clusters of raisins, wine, oil, oxen and sheep were brought in to hold a three-day feast of eating and drinking. A second example comes from 1 Kgs 1.9 when Adonijah celebrates his assumed kingship with a sacrificial feast where only the finest sheep, oxen and fatted cattle (or fatlings) are served to his guests. However, as the feast is in progress, Solomon is anointed king instead of Adonijah leaving the guests fearful of their host (vv. 41, 49). Feasts are celebratory events that include abundant food and drink. Elite feasts and household feasts may have had differing amounts and types of food but, more importantly, what they had in common was what special occasions were recognized and celebrated with a feast.

## Household feasts

Household feasts in ancient Israel can be categorized into two main groups: regular or occasional feasts. Regular feasts were connected to events that occurred annually, monthly and weekly, while occasional feasts were often related to life-cycle events (Meyers 2013: 157).

Regular yearly feasts observed the annual agricultural festivals, primarily those of Passover/Unleavened Bread, Weeks and Booths (Deut. 16.1–17; Exod. 23.14–17; and Lev. 23.4–25). Even though they originated as agricultural harvest festivals, within the Hebrew Bible we see that these festivals soon adopted further significance for religious and group identity and came to be considered as high holy days. The major festivals included an animal sacrifice, which became the main dish of the feast. The Hebrew Bible gives the impression that sacrifices were conducted only at official locations, like a local shrine, or later in the Jerusalem Temple. However, Meyers argues that the sacrifices for feasts, including those for Passover, Weeks and Booths, that were held at official locations were modelled after the religious feasts held within the household – that the 'festivals and feasts were elaborated versions of ordinary household foodways' (Meyers 2013: 165).

In fact, the Hebrew Bible supports the notion that religious feasting occurred within the household. For instance, in Job 1.4, Job's children took turns hosting the feast-day in their homes (Job 1.4). While Deut. 14.22–27 lays out the acceptable products that the household could offer as their tithe at the feast, including grain, wine, oil and the firstlings of the herd and flock. These tithes were a sacrifice to be offered at the location God chooses (presumably Jerusalem); however, the passage goes on to state that if the distance was too great, the tithe could be sold and the money earned could be spent 'for whatever you wish – oxen, sheep, wine, strong drink, or whatever you desire. And you shall eat there in the presence of the Lord your God, you and your household rejoicing together' (Deut. 14.26). The trading in and eating of the tithe by the household reinstates the role of the household in religious ritual and its function as an event that solidified group identity (Altmann 2011: 211–40). What is more, the Passover regulations in Exodus 12.3–4a, 7–9 state that the feast was primarily a household celebration:

> [T]ake a lamb for each family, a lamb for each household. If a household is too small for a whole lamb, it shall join its closest neighbour in obtaining one. [. . .] They shall take some of the blood and put it on the two doorposts and the lintel of the houses in which they eat it. They shall eat the lamb that same night; they shall eat it roasted over the fire with unleavened bread and bitter herbs. Do not eat any of it raw or boiled in water, but roasted over the fire with its head, legs and inner organs.

The Passover feast was a household activity that was used to both celebrate and strengthen the kinship social structure and national identity of ancient Israel (Barton and Muddiman 2007: 75); a point to which there are ethnographic parallels. Among the Bedouin and pre-Islamic Arabs, Johnstone notes that a household would hold a feast when they were on the cusp of a new beginning, such as a new well, year, house or marriage. This particular ritual of the communal feast not only celebrated the new beginning, but also functioned as a way to secure the household during this precarious time by discouraging the household god(s) from committing any harmful behaviour against the household (Childs 1974: 197–8; Johnstone 1990: 40–3).

The primordial beginnings of the yearly festivals was as a household celebration of the harvest and to thank the household deity(ies) for their provision. The Hebrew Bible instructs that sacrifices are to be offered at the yearly festivals with the superior portion offered to the Lord and the rest of the meat prepared as a festive meal for the household (Exod. 12.3–4a, 7–9; Lev. 7.15). The sacrifice and the subsequent feast were probably viewed as a meal being shared between the household and their deity. The British anthropologist Mary Douglas suggested a connection between the altar and the 'table'. She theorizes that the altar was in essence a table and the sacrifice offered on the altar/table was a feast between the giver of the sacrifice (i.e. the household) and the receiver of the sacrifice (i.e. the deity; Douglas 1972: 71). If there is merit to this idea, then one could say that sacrifices within domestic contexts should be viewed as an indicator of household feasting.

Regular monthly feasts celebrated within the household include the new moon celebration held on the first day of the lunar month (Num. 10.10; Ps. 81.3; 2 Chron.

8.12–13; Hos. 2.11; Amos 8.5).[12] The requirements for the new moon sacrifices are found in Num. 28.11–15 and include the following: a burnt offering of two young bulls with three-tenths of an ephah of choice flour for a grain offering, mixed with oil, for each bull; one ram with two-tenths of choice flour for a grain offering, mixed with oil for the one ram; seven male lambs a year old without blemish with one-tenth of choice flour mixed with oil as a grain offering for every lamb. These burnt offerings were also to include drink offerings: a half a hin of wine for a bull, one-third of a hin for a ram, and one-quarter of a hin for a lamb. In addition, one male goat was to be offered as a sin offering to the Lord in addition to the regular burnt offering and its corresponding drink offering. As specific as these instructions are, the observance of the new moon feast was condemned by the prophets Isaiah and Amos. The inhabitants of Judah and Jerusalem were criticized by Isaiah for what he saw as their empty religious rituals on the new moon, Sabbath and appointed festivals (Isa. 1.13–14). Amos was a little more specific when he rebuked the merchants for their deceit and impatience for the new moon and Sabbath observances to pass (Amos 8.5–6). We also see the kinship nature of the new moon festival in 1 Samuel 20, when David and Jonathan use it as part of their plan to uncover King Saul's true intentions towards David. In vv. 5–6, David said to Jonathan, 'Tomorrow is the new moon, and I should not fail to sit with the king at the meal, but let me go, so that I may hide in the field until the third evening. If your father misses me at all, then say, "David earnestly asked leave of me to run to Bethlehem, his city, for there is a yearly sacrifice there for all the family"'. It seems that David's presence is expected at King Saul's new moon feast since he is in the service of the king. Seeing that the new moon feast is one traditionally observed and celebrated with one's household, David uses it as his pretence to be absent from Saul's feast. David's absence would allow Jonathan to observe Saul's current state of mind about David.

The Sabbath was probably the prevailing weekly special occasion for the household. The Hebrew Bible commands that the Israelites and their households were to cease from working including the household slaves, animals and eventually the land itself (Exod. 20.8–11, 23.10–12; Lev. 23.2–3, ch. 25; Deut. 5.12–15, 15.1–18). Furthermore, the Israelite household was to present a drink offering and a burnt offering, which included two male lambs and choice flour mixed with oil (Num. 28.9–10). Other passages in the Hebrew Bible clearly indicate that the Sabbath rules were not always strictly observed (Lev. 26.34–35; Num. 15.32–36; Ezek. 20.24). Jer. 17.21–23 specifically points out the failure of the Israelite household to observe the Sabbath, 'And do not carry a burden out of your houses on the Sabbath or do any work, but keep the Sabbath day holy, as I commanded your ancestors. Yet they did not listen or incline their ear; they stiffened their necks and would not hear or receive instruction.'

Seeing that the Sabbath was a cessation of work for the household, it was also the household that celebrated it with a special meal taken from the sacrifice (Meyers 2011: 124–6; 2013: 157–62). As we can see, the ancient Israelite household had a regular schedule of yearly, monthly and weekly special occasions that consisted of domestic religious ritual and feasting.

Included in the social and cultural calendar would be occasional feasts celebrating various life-cycle events, primarily those related to birth, circumcision, puberty, marriage and death. As was discussed earlier, the survival of the household was dependent upon the

---

[12] The new moon festival on 17 Tishri became especially important. See King and Stager 2001: 353.

fertility of the household members, the infertility of which could install fear of the decline and/or possible extinction of the family. Consequently, the household had a continuous focus on the fertility of the household females with some religious rituals motivated by the safe conception, pregnancy, delivery and survival of mother and child (Gen. 16, 25.19–23, 29.15–30.24; Judges 13; 1 Samuel 1; 2 Kgs 4.8–37). Petitions related to fertility through religious ritual to both Yahweh and other deities are visible in the Hebrew Bible. For instance, in the book of Jeremiah, Jeremiah calls out the Judahite households for offering domestic sacrifices to the Queen of Heaven: 'The children gather wood, the fathers kindle fire, and the women knead dough, to make cakes for the queen of heaven; and they pour out drink offerings to other gods' (Jer. 7.18). The Queen of Heaven is thought to be the synthesis of two ancient Near Eastern fertility goddesses, Astarte and Ishtar (Ackerman 1989: 116, 2012: 145), which, if true, suggests that the activities Jeremiah mentions in v. 18 were activities related to the domestic religious ritual itself – a special occasion feast related to household fertility.

Other life-cycle events related to fertility include birth rituals, name-giving ceremonies, perhaps a circumcision ceremony for males, and possibly weaning (Gen. 17.12, 21.4; Meyers 2013: 157–60). Like the regular feasts, occasional feasts celebrating life-cycle events included food and drink offerings to the household god(s), which then supplied the main course for the household feast. For example, after the birth of a child the mother is to offer sacrifices as part of her purification, with the consecrated food becoming a festive meal (Lev. 7, 12.6). What is more, while the marriage narratives in the Hebrew Bible provide few details, they do illustrate that weddings included a festive meal, often over several days (Gen. 29.22; Judg. 14.10; and see Tob. 7.13–14).

As we have seen, the Hebrew Bible documents that religious feasting occurred within the ancient Israelite household. A spatial analysis of an Iron Age II (Stratum VIB, c. 800–700 BCE) house at Tell Halif supports this image. The back broad room of the house (called the F7 house) was divided into two rooms (labelled Rooms 1 and 2). Numerous artefacts related to both religious ritual and feasting were uncovered in Room 2, indicating that religious feasting occurred in this space. Items related to the storage and preparation of food include: three storage jars, one pithos, and a variety of other items (for example, grinding stone), while the cooking pots, krater and bowls found in Room 2 are evidence of the serving and consumption of meals. The micro-artefactual samples (grape pips, cereals, legumes, and fish bones and scales) and zooarchaeological remains (cow and sheep) further support the notion that both the preparation and consumption of food occurred in this room. Cooking pots and kraters were often used for the serving and sharing of food, a point supported by ethnographic observations that document various traditional African societies sharing meals together and eating out of large krater-like bowls (Hendrickson and McDonald 1983). Artefacts associated with religious rituals uncovered in Room 2 include a polished triangular-shaped stone, two standing stones (*maṣṣebot*) squared with bevelled edges, a broken pillar figurine and a fenestrated stand (Hardin 2010: 133–43; Shafer-Elliott 2014: 205, 207).[13] The two bevelled and dressed standing stones (*maṣṣebot*) could have several functions: as presentation tables, altars or incense stands. The triangular-shaped stone could have been used as a table or platform for cultic activities and food preparation (Jacobs 2001), or quite possibly as another

---

[13] For more on items and categories of possible cultic paraphernalia, see Albertz and Schmitt 2012: 59–75 and Appendix A.

biblical *maṣṣebâ* (Gen. 28.18, 22; Deut. 7.5; 1 Kgs 14.23), which are often found in groups and used to secure the presence of the household deities (Hardin 2010: 138–43; Shafer-Elliott 2014: 210).

The Hebrew Bible designates many occasions that justify the need for a household feast, including regular events, such as Passover and the new moon celebrations, and occasional events, such as the safe birth of a healthy baby. Feasts are by nature religious rituals that were seen as a bonding meal between the household and their deities. The use of household archaeology and spatial analysis at Tell Halif provides us with a possible physical manifestation of domestic religious feasting, including the performance of purification rites, food and libation offerings, the burning of incense, and the serving and consumption of communal meals by the household members and their guests.

## SUMMARY

The basic, social and cultural roles of food in the lives of ordinary ancient Israelites provide us with a glimpse into the power of food. The use of food studies, household archaeology, textual sources (including the Hebrew Bible), ethnography and ethnoarchaeology have broadened our understanding of the social complexity of food in ancient Israel. The preparation and consumption of every day meals and celebration feasts (both regular yearly, monthly and weekly feasts and those special occasion feasts related to life-cycle events) illustrate how ancient Israelite society related to food and how food made their lives more meaningful. We also observed how the gastro-politics of the household made gender and authority more visible, indicating that the women and matriarch of the household possessed more power and authority than typically thought. Food is, in essence, political. Food binds people together, creates memories, enforces accepted cultural norms, and serves in the negotiation of power and boundaries. How can such a simple topic as food provide us with so much information? It is simple really and was best put by the American chef, James Beard, who wrote: 'Food is our common ground, a universal experience' (2007 [1974]: xi). Food is the common denominator across time and space, which makes learning about people through their food *nonpareil*.

## REFERENCES

Ackerman, A. (1989), '"And the Women Knead Dough": The Worship of the Queen of Heaven in Sixth-Century Judah', in P.L. Day (ed.), *Gender and Difference in Ancient Israel*, 109–24, Minneapolis, MN: Fortress Press.

Ackerman, A. (2012), 'Household Religion, Family Religion, and Women's Religion in Ancient Israel', in J. Bodel and S.M. Olyan (eds), *Household and Family Religion in Antiquity*, 127–58, Chichester: Wiley-Blackwell.

Albertz, R. and Schmitt, R. (2012), *Family and Household Religion in Ancient Israel and the Levant*, Winona Lake, IN: Eisenbrauns.

Altmann, P. (2011), *Festive Meals in Ancient Israel: Deuteronomy's Identity Politics in Their Ancient Near Eastern Context*, BZAW 422, Berlin: De Gruyter.

Altmann, P. and J. Fu, eds (2014), *Feasting in the Archaeology and Texts of the Bible and the Ancient Near East*, Winona Lake, IN; Eisenbrauns.

Amiry, S. and V. Tamari (1989), *The Palestinian Village Home*, London: British Museum.

Appadurai, A. (1981), 'Gastro-Politics in Hindu South Asia', *American Ethnologist*, 8 (3): 494–511.

Archaeology Wordsmith (n.d.), 'Household Archaeology'. Formerly available at: https://archaeologywordsmith.com/search.php?q=household (accessed 21 December 2020).

Backfish, E.H.P. and C. Shafer-Elliott (forthcoming), *Old Testament Theology in Its Cultural Context: Theology from the Ground Up*, Grand Rapids, MI: Baker Academic.

Barton, J. and J. Muddiman, eds (2007), *The Oxford Bible Commentary*, Oxford: Oxford University Press.

Battini, L., A. Brody and S.R. Steadman, eds (forthcoming), *No Place Like Home: Ancient Near Eastern Houses and Households*, Ancient Near Eastern Archaeology, Oxford: Archaeopress.

Beard, J. (2007 [1974]), *Beard on Food: The Best Recipes and Kitchen Wisdom from the Dean of American Cooking*, New York: Bloomsbury.

Ben-Shlomo, D., I. Shai, A. Zuckerman and A.M. Maier (2008), 'Cooking Identities: Aegean-Style Cooking Jugs and Cultural Interaction in Iron Age Philistia and Neighboring Regions', *AJA*, 112 (2): 225–46.

Bird, P.A. (1997), *Missing Persons and Mistaken Identities: Women and Gender in Ancient Israel*, Minneapolis, MN: Augsburg Fortress.

Borowski, O. (1987), *Agriculture in Iron Age Israel*, Winona Lake, IN: Eisenbrauns.

Borowski, O. (1998), *Every Living Thing: Daily Use of Animals in Ancient Israel*, Walnut Creek, CA: AltaMira.

Borowski, O. (2003), *Daily Life in Biblical Times*, ABS 5, Atlanta, GA: Society of Biblical Literature.

Bottéro, J. (1995), *Textes culinaires mésopotamiens*, Winona Lake, IN: Eisenbrauns.

Bottéro, J. (2004), *The Oldest Cuisine in the World: Cooking in Mesopotamia*, transl. T.L. Fagan, Chicago: University of Chicago Press.

Childs, B.S. (1974), *Exodus: A Critical, Theological Commentary*, OTL, Louisville, KY: Westminster John Knox Press.

Collon, D. (1992), 'Banquets in the Art of the Ancient Near East', in R. Gyselen (ed.), *Banquets d'Orient*, 23–30, Leuven: Peeters.

Counihan, C., P. Van Esterik and A. Julier, eds (2019), *Food and Culture: A Reader*, 4th edn, New York: Routledge.

Douglas, M. (1972), 'Deciphering a Meal', *Daedalus*, 101 (1): 61–81.

Ebeling, J. and M. Rogel (2015), 'The Tabun and its Misidentification in the Archaeological Record', *Levant*, 47 (3): 328–49.

Faust, A. (2015), 'Chronological and Spatial Changes in the Rural Settlement Sector of Ancient Israel During the Iron Age: An Overview', *RB*, 122 (2): 247–67.

Faust, A. and S. Bunimovitz (2003), 'The Four Room House: Embodying Iron Age Israelite Society', *NEA*, 66 (1/2): 22–31.

Frank, T. (2018), *Household Food Storage in Ancient Israel and Judah*, Oxford: Archaeopress.

Fritz, V. and A. Kempinski (1983), *Ergebnisse der Ausgrabungen auf der Ḫirbet el-Mšāš (Tēl Māśōś) 1972–1975*, Wiesbaden: Harrassowitz.

Fu, J., C. Shafer-Elliott and C. Meyers, eds (2022), *The T&T Clark Handbook of Food in the Hebrew Bible and Ancient Israel*, London: Bloomsbury T&T Clark.

Gilchrist, R. (1999), *Gender and Archaeology: Contesting the Past*, London: Routledge.

Goody, J. (1982), *Cooking, Cuisine and Class: A Study in Comparative Sociology*, Cambridge: Cambridge University Press.

Greer, J. (2013), *Dinner at Dan: Biblical and Archaeological Evidence for Sacred Feasts at Iron Age II Tel Dan and Their Significance*, CHANE 66, Leiden: E.J. Brill.

Gudme, A.K. de Hemmer (2019), 'Invitation to Murder: Hospitality and Violence in the Hebrew Bible', *StTh*, 73 (1): 89–108.

Gur-Arieh, S., A.M. Maeir and R. Shahack-Gross (2011), 'Soot Patterns on Cooking Vessels: A Short Note', in V. Karageorghis and O. Kouka (eds), *On Cooking Pots, Drinking Cups, Loom Weights and Ethnicity in Bronze Age Cyprus and Neighbouring Regions: An International Archaeological Symposium Held in Nicosia, November 6th–7th 2010*, 349–55, Nicosia: A.G. Leventis Foundation.

Hamilakis, Y. (1999), 'Food Technologies/Technologies of the Body: The Social Context of Wine and Oil Production and Consumption in Bronze Age Crete', *World Archaeology*, 31 (1): 38–54.

Hardin, J.W. (2004), 'Understanding Domestic Space: An Example from Iron Age Tel Halif', *NEA*, 67 (2): 71–83.

Hardin, J.W. (2010), *Lahav II: Households and the Use of Domestic Space at Iron II Tell Halif: An Archaeology of Destruction*, Winona Lake, IN: Eisenbrauns.

Hardin, J.W. (2012), 'Household Archaeology in the Southern Levant: An Example from Iron Age Tell Halif', in B.J. Parker and C.P. Foster (eds), *New Perspectives on Household Archaeology*, 519–58, Winona Lake, IN: Eisenbrauns.

Harris, P., D. Lyon and S. McLaughlin (2005), *The Meaning of Food*, Guilford, CT: Globe Pequot Press.

Hastorf, C.A. (2017), *The Social Archaeology of Food: Thinking About Eating from Prehistory to the Present*, New York: Cambridge University Press.

Hendrickson, E.F. and M.M.A. McDonald (1983), 'Ceramic Form and Function: An Ethnographic Search and an Archaeological Application', *American Anthropologist* NS, 85 (3): 630–43.

Herzog, Z. (1984), *Beer-Sheba II: The Early Iron Age Settlements*, Institute of Archaeology Publications 7, Tel Aviv: Tel Aviv University, Institute of Archaeology.

Holladay, J.S. Jr (1997), 'Four-Room House', in E. Meyers (ed.), *The Oxford Encyclopedia of Archaeology in the Near East*, vol. 2, 337–42, Oxford: Oxford University Press.

Horne, L. (1994), *Village Spaces: Settlement and Society in Northeastern Iran*, Smithsonian Series in Archaeological Inquiry, Washington DC: Smithsonian Institution Press.

Ilan, D. (2022), 'Storage', in J. Fu, C. Shafer-Elliott and C. Meyers (eds), *The T&T Clark Handbook of Food in the Hebrew Bible and Ancient Israel*, 251–65, London: Bloomsbury T&T Clark.

Jacobs, P. (2001), 'Reading Religious Artifacts: The Shrine Room at Judahite Tell Halif', *Journal of Biblical Studies*, 1 (2). Available online: https://web.archive.org/web/20101118023529/http://journalofbiblicalstudies.org/Issue2/Articles/Tell_Halif/multi.html (accessed 17 July 2022).

Johnstone, W. (1990), *Exodus*, OTG, Sheffield: JSOT Press.

Kempinski, A. and R. Reich, eds (1992), *The Architecture of Ancient Israel: From the Prehistoric to the Persian Periods*, Jerusalem: Israel Exploration Society.

Killebrew, A.E. (1999), 'Late Bronze and Iron I Cooking Pots in Canaan: A Typological, Technological, and Functional Study', in T. Kapitan (ed.), *Archaeology, History and Culture in Palestine and the Near East: Essays in Memory of Albert E. Glock*, 83–126. American Schools of Oriental Research 3, Atlanta, GA: Scholars Press.

King, P.J. and L.E. Stager (2001), *Life in Biblical Israel*, LAI, Louisville, KY: Westminster John Knox Press.

Klein, F. (2010), 'Reports About the Life, Customs and Practices of the Fellahin in Palestine, Part 1', in *Palestinian Life, Customs and Practices: German Articles from the Late 19th and Early 20th Centuries*, 11–23, transl. R. Schick, Amman, Jordan: History of Bilad al-Sham Committee.

Lev-Tov, J. (2022), 'Animal Husbandry: Meat, Milk, and More', in J. Fu, C. Shafer-Elliott and C. Meyers (eds), *T&T Clark Handbook of Food in the Hebrew Bible and Ancient Israel*, 77–98, London: Bloomsbury T&T Clark.

MacDonald, N. (2008a), *Not Bread Alone: The Uses of Food in the Old Testament*, Oxford: Oxford University Press.

MacDonald, N. (2008b), *What Did the Ancient Israelites Eat? Diet in Biblical Times*, Grand Rapids, MI: Eerdmans.

Matthews, V.H. and D.C. Benjamin (1993), *Social World of Ancient Israel: 1250–587 BCE*, Grand Rapids, MI: Baker Academic.

Mazar, A. (2016), 'Discoveries from Tel Rehov, the Early Days of the Israelite Monarchy', in I. Ziffer (ed.), *It Is the Land of Honey: Discoveries from Tel Rehov, the Early Days of the Israelite Monarchy* (exhibition catalogue), 12–154, Tel Aviv: Eretz Israel Museum.

McQuitty, A. (1984), 'An Ethnographic and Archaeological Study of Clay Ovens in Jordan', *ADAJ*, 28: 259–67.

McQuitty, A. (1994), 'Ovens in Town and Country', *Berytus*, 39: 53–76.

Meyers, C. (1983), 'Procreation, Production, and Protection: Male–Female Balance in Early Israel', *Journal of the American Academy of Religion*, 51 (4): 569–93.

Meyers, C. (1997), 'The Family in Early Israel', in L. Perdue, J. Blenkinsopp, J.J. Collins and C. Meyers (eds), *Families in Ancient Israel*, 1–47, Louisville, KY: Westminster John Knox Press.

Meyers, C. (2002), 'Having Their Space and Eating There Too: Bread Production and Female Power in Ancient Israelite Households', *Nashim: A Journal of Jewish Women's Studies & Gender Issues*, 5: 14–44.

Meyers, C. (2011), 'Household Religion', in F. Stavrakopoulou and J. Barton (eds), *Religious Diversity in Ancient Israel and Judah*, 118–34, London: T&T Clark.

Meyers, C. (2013), *Rediscovering Eve: Ancient Israelite Women in Context*, Oxford: Oxford University Press.

Meyers, C. (2014), 'Was Ancient Israel a Patriarchal Society?', *Journal of Biblical Literature*, 133 (1): 8–27.

Meyers, C., C. Shafer-Elliott and J. Fu (2022), 'Introduction: Food, the Hebrew Bible, and the Ancient Israelites', in J. Fu, C. Shafer-Elliott and C. Meyers (eds), *The T&T Clark Handbook of Food in the Hebrew Bible and Ancient Israel*, 1–14, London: Bloomsbury T&T Clark.

Oksuz, L., J. Hardin and J. Wilson (2019), 'The K8 House: A New Domestic Space from the Iron Age II at Tell Halif, Israel', *PEQ*, 151 (3/4): 218–44.

Panitz-Cohen, N. (2022), 'Ceramics in the Iron Age', in J. Fu, C. Shafer-Elliott and C. Meyers (eds), *The T&T Clark Handbook of Food in the Hebrew Bible and Ancient Israel*, 197–214, London: Bloomsbury T&T Clark.

Parker, B. (2011), 'Bread Ovens, Social Networks and Gendered Space: An Ethnoarchaeological Study of *Tandir* Ovens in Southeastern Anatolia', *American Antiquity*, 76 (4): 603–27.

Peters, K. (2016), *Hebrew Lexical Semantics and Daily Life in Ancient Israel: What's Cooking in Biblical Hebrew?*, Leiden: E.J. Brill.

Peters, K. (2022), 'Language of Food and Cooking in the Hebrew Bible', in J. Fu, C. Shafer-Elliott and C. Meyers (eds), *T&T Clark Handbook of Food in the Hebrew Bible and Ancient Israel*, 481–93, London: Bloomsbury T&T Clark.

Pleins, J.D. with J. Homrighausen (2017), *Biblical Hebrew Vocabulary by Conceptual Categories: A Student's Guide to Nouns in the Old Testament*, Grand Rapids, MI: Zondervan.

Schloen, J.D. (2001), *The House of the Father as Fact and Symbol: Patrimonialism in Ugarit and the Ancient Near East*, SAHL 2, Winona Lake, IN: Eisenbrauns.

Shafer-Elliott, C. (2013), *Food in Ancient Judah: Domestic Cooking in the Time of the Hebrew Bible*, Sheffield: Equinox.

Shafer-Elliott, C. (2014), 'The Role of the Household in the Religious Feasting of Ancient Israel and Judah', in P. Altmann and J. Fu (eds), *Feasting in the Archaeology and Texts of the Hebrew Bible and Ancient Near East*, 199–221 Winona Lake, IN: Eisenbrauns.

Shafer-Elliott, C. (2021), 'The Heroines of Every Day Life: Ancient Israelite Women in Context', in L.J. Greenspoon (ed.), *Jews and Gender*, Studies in Jewish Civilization, 1–13, West Lafayette, IN: Purdue University Press.

Shafer-Elliott, C. (2022a), 'Fruits, Nuts, Vegetables, and Legumes', in J. Fu, C. Shafer-Elliott and C. Meyers (eds), *T&T Clark Handbook of Food in the Hebrew Bible and Ancient Israel*, 139–55, London: Bloomsbury T&T Clark.

Shafer-Elliott, C. (2022b), 'Putting One's House in Order: Household Archaeology at Tell Halif, Israel', in C. Shafer-Elliott, K. Joachimsen, E. Ben Zvi and P. Viviano (eds), *The Hunt for Ancient Israel: Essays in Honour of Diana V. Edelman*, 233–57, Sheffield: Equinox.

Shiloh, Y. (1970), 'The Four-Room House: Its Situation and Function in the Israelite City', *IEJ*, 20 (3/4): 180–90.

Simoons, F. (1967), *Eat Not This Flesh: Food Avoidances in the Old World*, Madison: University of Wisconsin Press.

Stager, L.E. (1985), 'The Archaeology of the Family in Ancient Israel', *BASOR*, 260: 1–35.

Twiss, K.C. (2007), 'We Are What We Eat', in K.C. Twiss (ed.), *The Archaeology of Food and Identity*, Occasional Paper 34, 1–15, Carbondale, IL: Center for Archaeological Investigations.

van der Steen, E. (1991), 'The Iron Age Bread Ovens from Tell Deir 'Alla', *ADAJ*, 35: 135–53.

Walton, J. (2022), 'Economy and Trade', in J. Fu, C. Shafer-Elliott and C. Meyers (eds), *T&T Clark Handbook of Food in the Hebrew Bible and Ancient Israel*, 57–74, London: Bloomsbury T&T Clark.

Wapnish, P. (1993), 'Archaeozoology: The Integration of Faunal Data with Biblical Archaeology', in A. Biran and J. Aviram (eds), *Biblical Archaeology Today, 1990: Proceedings of the Second International Congress on Biblical Archaeology, Jerusalem, June–July 1990*, 426–42, Jerusalem: Israel Exploration Society.

Wapnish, P. and B. Hesse (1991), 'Faunal Remains from Tel Dan: Perspectives on Animal Production at a Village, Urban, and Ritual Center', *ArchaeoZoologia*, 4 (2): 9–86.

Watson, P.J. (1979), *Archaeological Ethnography in Western Iran*, Viking Fund Publications in Anthropology 57, Tucson: University of Arizona Press.

Welton, R. (2020), *'He Is a Glutton and a Drunkard': Deviant Consumption in the Hebrew Bible*, Leiden: E.J. Brill.

Wilk, R. and W.L. Rathje (1982), 'Household Archaeology', *American Behavioral Scientist*, 25 (6): 617–39.

Wood, R.C. (1995), *The Sociology of a Meal*, Edinburgh: Edinburgh University Press.

Wright, K. and K. Novotny (2018), *Bodies: A Digital Companion*, Champlain College Center for Publishing. Available online: https://scalar.usc.edu/works/bodies/index (accessed 18 July 2022).

Yasur-Landau, A., J.R. Ebeling and L.B. Mazow, eds (2011), *Household Archaeology in Ancient Israel and Beyond*, CHANE 50, Leiden: E.J. Brill.

Zhen, W. (2018), 'An Introduction to Food Studies', in *Bloomsbury Food Library Bibliographic Guides*, London: Bloomsbury. Available online: http://dx.doi.org/10.5040/9781474209427.ch-003 (accessed 16 December 2020).

Ziffer, I. (2002a), 'Symbols of Royalty in Canaanite Art in the Third and Second Millennia B.C.E.', *Bulletin of the Israeli Academic Center in Cairo*, 25: 11–20.

Ziffer, I. (2002b), 'From Acemhöyük to Megiddo: The Banquet Scene in the Art of the Levant in the Second Millennium BCE', *TA*, 32 (2): 133–67.

Zohary, D., M. Hopf and E. Weiss (2012), *Domestication of Plants in the Old World: The Origin and Spread of Domesticated Plants in Southwest Asia, Europe, and the Mediterranean Basin*, 4th edn, Oxford: Oxford University Press.

Zohary, M. (1982), *Plants of the Bible: A Complete Handbook to All the Plants with 200 Full-Color Plates Taken in the Natural Habitat*, Cambridge: Cambridge University Press.

# CHAPTER TWENTY-ONE

# The anthropology of death in ancient Israel

KRISTINE HENRIKSEN GARROWAY

Death is an experience that tears at the social fabric of a society. Simply put, death is disruptive. Feeling the need to restore balance within society, different groups have processed death in various ways. The anthropology of death addresses a complex matrix, examining how societies understand and define death, the dying body, funerary rites, burial and post-mortem care for the dead.

## THE DYING BODY

Dying is a process during which the body transitions from what it was in life, to what it will be in death. In this respect dying is a rite of passage, or transitional ritual. Rites of passage have been described as a tripartite journey (van Gennep 1960: 146–65; Turner 1967: 69). The individual first begins as a part of society, then leaves society in order to transform, and is ultimately reincorporated into society in their new, transformed state. During the middle portion of this journey the individual enters a liminal space; they are betwixt and between. The liminal space is paradoxical as it both separates and joins. On the one hand, individuals are separated from their original society. At the same time, they are joined together in *communitas* with those who have gone through the same transformation (Turner 1967: 96–7). With death, the transition is multifaceted. Because the body is embodied, it is a social construct (Hertz 1960: 89–113; Saxe 1970; Mauss 1979 [1934]; Durkheim 2001 [1912]). Therefore, the dying body transforms socially (Meskell 1999) in that during the dying process, the dying body goes through a period wherein the living become reacquainted with the dead in their new state, usually through a cult of the dead. The dying body also transforms physiologically. First the heart stops. For bodies that are interred, body either decomposes or is defleshed by animals or the elements, until only the bones remain. Various phases can also be understood for bodies that are cremated or cannibalized.

Once the dying body has completed its transition, it is then reincorporated into the household of the afterlife. In this way, dying is relational (Bloch and Parry 1982; Metcalf and Huntington 1991; Parker Pearson 1993; Suriano 2018). The ways in which this reincorporation occurs is socially and culturally constructed. For example, Christians believe that their spirit will be reunited with other Christians in a heavenly afterlife. Hindus and Buddhists, on the other hand, understand the spirit to be eternal and hold to the possibility of the spirit being reincarnated into a new earthly body. Accordingly, the dead are brought back to the households of the living in a new form. Reincorporation can also be quite literal. Cultures practising human sacrifice might first imbue the sacrificial victim with the divine presence. Eating the individual or a part of the individual then becomes a way of spiritually enhancing the living (Obeyesekere 2005: 261–3). Other cultures, such as that of ancient Mesopotamia, believed that deceased ancestors stayed close to the family home, protecting the household of the living (van der Toorn 1996; Steinberg 2009). Throughout the entire dying process, the living are in constant relationship with the dead (Suriano 2018: 2). In some cases, there is no belief in an afterlife. In these cases, the final transition is a transition from life to nothingness. Beliefs in an afterlife are also age-dependent. For example, children and infants might not enjoy the same afterlife as an adult in the same society (Lemos 2017: 7–15). In the same way, a living being's social status and attributed personhood can affect the type of afterlife an individual might expect.

# FUNERARY RITES, MORTUARY RITES, AND CULTS OF THE DEAD

Funerary rites help the living members of a society process the dying body, moving it from what it was known as in the household of the living, to the place it will have in the household of the dead. Funerary rites include mourning rituals and the treatment of the dead. Such events occur surrounding the biological death and transformation of an individual. They are by nature temporary and do not necessarily presume the continuation of a being into an afterlife (Goody 1962: 18). Here one thinks of physical preparations the body undergoes pre-burial. The elite of ancient Egypt had a very elaborate system of mummification which had to take place before the body could be interred. When the body was prepared, it was placed into a coffin accompanied by spells to protect the deceased along its journey to the afterlife (Meskell 1999: 107–35; Müller 2001). Grave goods also function as a means of helping the dying body transition. While funerary rites are done by the living for the dead to help facilitate their dying process, they can also function as a means of helping the living to process the death of a loved one.

A very basic example of a funerary rite would be a funeral service. The Jewish practice of sitting shiva for seven days after the death of a family member is another example (Washofsky 2001: 184–204). Embedded within the funerary rites are ways in which the living members of a society process their emotion through ritual (Kan 2016: 17). For example, in the contemporary Western world, the decaying body presents the living with an emotional issue (Walter 1993). Rather than accepting the dying process, those in the United States prefer to temporarily halt the decaying process by embalming the body, while many in the UK prefer to forgo any interaction with the deceased's body and opt for cremation. Thus, in modern times, deposition of the dead has become a way to process an emotional need. This differs from concerns of purity and impurity that may have arisen surrounding the dying body in ancient Israel. While these are examples of a single event, funerary rites might include a variety of rituals that take place over the course of many days. All funerary rites are part of the process meant to mend the tear in the social fabric caused by death.

Like funerary rites, mortuary rites vary in how long they last, how many phases are involved, and the emotions that surround them (Nilsson Stutz and Tarlow 2013: 5). While mortuary rites can function like funerary rites, there are some marked differences. Mortuary rites are those rituals that occur regularly after the individual is buried, such as a 'cult of the dead' (Schmidt 1996: 1–13). For many Westerners, steeped in the cultural milieu of Christianity, the term 'cult of the dead' or 'death cult' has negative connotations, because the word cult is associated with paganism, and the 'other'. Here, definition becomes necessary as a way to move beyond a polarizing term. Émile Durkheim's definition of a death cult has been foundational for how anthropologists have come to think about death. He stated a death cult included 'repeated standardized practices oriented toward the dead'. Furthermore, these practices were generally done at specific 'ritual locations associated with the dead' (Durkheim 2001 [1912]: 64). Practices that are repeated and standardized imply that a group of people has agreed upon certain actions. Most importantly, these practices are done in ritualized locations. For example, Jews recite Yizkor each year during Yom Kippur in order to remember their deceased relatives. Recitation of the deceased's name is a way for subsequent generations to keep their memory alive. The Chinese Qingming, or 'tomb-sweeping' day, done on the anniversary of the loved one's death, involves cleaning the grave, burning incense and presenting offerings of food and drink that the deceased might use in the afterlife. Ritual need not only be done at a tomb or in a public place of religious worship, such as a shrine, synagogue, church or mosque. Ritual can take place in the domicile as well. Here one might consider the *ofrenda* (offering) with its various traditional elements that is set up in houses for the Día de los Muertos (day of the dead). The *ofrenda* transforms a quotidian space on a yearly basis into a ritual space using a standardized set of ritual elements.

Discussions regarding cults of the dead bring up the question of how the dead are understood to operate after they are no longer living. In some cases, the dead have no power. Once the dying body has transitioned to its final form, the deceased's ability to interact with the living realm has been severed. Other cultures understand the dead to be active, retaining the ability to affect things that occur in the world of the living. In such cases, the dead might be venerated or worshipped (Schmidt 1996: 9–10). Venerating the dead implies a belief that the dead can intercede with the divine on behalf of the living. Whether or not the dead themselves are considered divine differs based on the society in question. The Roman Catholic view of saints provides a helpful distinction between venerating and worship. Under the doctrine of the Communion of Saints, Roman Catholics venerate (pray to) saints so that they might intercede before the throne of God on their behalf (Abbott 1966; Schmidt 1996: 9). On the other hand, dead who are worshipped are believed to have achieved a deified place in the afterlife. Many ancient cultures believed their rulers were the embodiment or representative of a god on earth. For example, Egyptian pharaohs enjoyed a royal cult both in life and death (Müller 2001), and the kings of Ugarit, an ancient kingdom in northern Syria, were divinized and worshipped after death (Hays 2011: 108–15). Ancestors can also be worshipped, especially if they are thought to have the power to provide beneficiary outcomes for the living. The Mesopotamian *kispu*, or cult of the dead kin, could be offered to both royal and non-royal individuals, by individuals who may or may not have been direct descendants of the dead (Sonia 2020: 8–11). The living honoured their dead through the rites of *kispu* (Tsukimoto 1985) with meals and worship so as not to anger the dead or incur their wrath (van der Toorn 1996: 48–52; Hays 2011: 43).

# BURIAL AND POST-MORTEM CARE

Not all cultures practise inhumation, but all cultures have a concept of what qualifies as a 'good' or proper deposition of the dying body and post-mortem care for the dead. For example, while laying the dead out to be eaten by vultures might seem less than ideal to a Westerner, a sky burial (celestial funeral) is considered a proper way for Tibetan Buddhists to be buried (Wylie 1964: 232). In cultures where inhumation is practised, there are beliefs that the body should be protected as it moves through decomposition. Cultures that believe in a future resurrection of the dead emphasize the importance of keeping the elements of the body in one place. Here one might consider Muslims, who do not endorse cremation except in cases of disease, for the Muslim belief in bodily resurrection states that Allah will resurrect the body from the tailbone. Inhumations in coffins, tombs, cist graves, bone boxes or other containers are a way of enclosing the dying body in a safe space. The degree of protection afforded a person might also be related to their personhood, especially if personhood is marked by 'protection from physical harm – and/or by public rituals that convey or reaffirm that individual's value' (Lemos 2017: 11). For those of a lower social class, or those who might not be considered full participants in a society, burials might look different. Young children might be buried away from the other members of society, have smaller memorials atop their graves, or be buried with different grave goods (Watson 1979: 42; Green 2017 Garroway 2018: 255–61).

Care for the dead is generally carried out by members of the deceased individual's family. In some cases, non-kin individuals might create fictional kinship bonds with the deceased by caring for them with the intent to 'assert continuity through kinship and, thus, mitigate perceived social and political ruptures' (Sonia 2020: 10). This is particularly apt on the level of the royal cult as seen in Roman imperial families, where sons who were adopted during an emperor's lifetime continued to honour the deceased emperor via the imperial cult. The relationship between Octavian and his adoptive father Julius Caesar is exemplary in this regard. Care for the dead includes, inter alia, keeping the grave site clean and beautified, making sure the grave site is not desecrated, erecting a monument for the dead, and providing food and libations for the dead – whether in veneration or in worship (ibid.: 21). In some cases, it might also mean the repatriation of the deceased's body or bones to bury in a family burial plot. Such might be the case for those who die in war or while on a journey.

## DEATH IN THE HEBREW BIBLE

Each of the different elements discussed above as general components of an anthropology of death are culturally specific. Uncovering the different cultural nuances regarding death is a task much more easily accomplished for living societies. To provide the fullest picture of death in ancient Israel, a combination of both textual evidence and archaeological realia is necessary. Regarding the Hebrew Bible, it is important to note that it is an ideologically driven text. It is difficult to know how normative the rules and regulations within the text actually were, or how accurately they reflected the society about which they are written (Meyers 2013: 24). The text was not written in a vacuum, however, and it is possible to identify practices that reflect general aspects of Israelite beliefs. Archaeology can be a valuable source for illuminating some of the practices described within the texts of the Hebrew Bible and can provide a picture of how life 'on the ground' may have lined up with life described 'on the page'.

Ancient Israel, as described in the biblical text, was a kinship-based society (see Chapter 7 in this volume). The *bêt ʾāb* was the smallest unit of society, comprising the nuclear family. The biblical text also describes extended family arrangements where multiple generations or different relatives lived together (Meyers 2013: 110–11). It was the responsibility of the living members of the family to bury their dead, transitioning them from the household of the living to the household of the dead. The rituals surrounding death helped maintain ties between the living and the dead and strengthen the bonds between kin. Hints of how this happened appear in verses suggesting the dead were fed and tended at burial markers, on hilltops, in tombs and at shrines (Bloch-Smith 1992: 220; inter alia Deut. 26.14; Gen. 31.54; Isa. 57.8; 1 Sam. 1.21). The texts hint at venerating ancestors (1 Sam. 1.6) and even consulting the dead (1 Samuel 28; Isa. 8.19).

## THE DYING BODY IN THE HEBREW BIBLE

A belief in an afterlife or household of the dead meant something very specific in ancient Israel. Unlike Christian concepts of a soul going to reside in heaven or hell, the Hebrew Bible describes what is called functional immortality. Many societies today understand the physical body to be a shell that holds a separate entity designated as the spirit or soul. In this framework, the death of the physical body releases the spirit or soul, but it does not necessitate that the spirit or soul ceases to exist. This understanding stems from Cartesian dualism, which finds its roots in the Greek philosophers, namely Plato and Socrates (Martin 1995: 3–37). The same concept of 'soul' is not present in the texts of the Hebrew Bible or ancient Israel. The term *npš* found in the biblical texts and Northwest Semitic inscriptions refers to either the dead body or the persona of the dead (Suriano 2018: 133–53). When referring to the persona of the dead, the *npš* 'should be viewed as an element of selfhood that is ritually embodied' (ibid.: 148). These definitions of *npš* and its embodiment represent a Foucauldian notion of the soul as 'the prison of the body' (Foucault 1995: 30). It is the *npš* or personhood which lives on. Functional immortality is the 'preservation and endurance of one's legacy' (Suriano 2018: 6). Legacy refers to the things related to an individual's personhood such as their inheritance, reputation or name. In order for functional immortality to operate, the living must preserve the personhood of the dead for future generations. This can happen by continually passing down physical items, such as land, money or belongings, but it also happens by ritually caring for the dead throughout the entire dying process and then keeping their name alive.

### *Descriptions of the dying process*

As the individual went through the dying process, the living began to prepare the dying for their transition to the household of the dead. Most narrative reports of death in the Hebrew Bible are of men, particularly important men. Therefore, our picture of death and rituals surrounding it skews towards the elite male realm. In addition, much like with marriage, divorce, adoption or other mundane social institutions, the biblical text does not expound much on the exact process of dying. What is presented in detail are the unusual occurrences of death or the exceptions to what was likely considered a normal practice. For example, prior to the deaths of Jacob and Joseph, the matriarchs, patriarchs and their sons are described as breathing their last and then being buried and gathered to their ancestors (Gen. 25.7–10, 25.17). There is no description of the care that is given to the body. Similarly, what happens in the mourning rituals is absent. Sarah dies, Abraham mourns, and then seeks out a burial plot (Gen. 23.1–20). The rituals are implied for those dying in the land, whereas in the deaths of Jacob and Joseph, which take place outside the

Promised Land, the rituals are presented in detail. The dying bodies of Jacob and Joseph were cared for with Egyptian rituals. Here, Jacob's narrative serves as the primary example. Once Jacob breathed his last breath, the dying body was protected during the intervening liminal phrase before burial by the embalmers. For forty days he was embalmed, and for seventy days the Egyptians mourned him (Gen. 50.1–3). The body then needed burial. Joseph takes leave of the Egyptian court to transport the body back to the family burial cave. The solemn parade of individuals and the continual mourning is constantly highlighted as 'other', as Egyptian, by the text (Gen. 50.1–11).

*Sheol*

Where information is lacking regarding preparation of the body, there are texts that give some hint as to the transitional process from the perspective of the dead. Biblical texts portray the netherworld as a destination. Sheol, for example, appears as a mythologized realm of the dead. It is deep, dark and dusty (Deut. 32.22; Job 17.13; Ps. 22.16). It is a liminal space from which one can be delivered and, like the process of dying, a transitory place that slowly strips an individual of their identity (Suriano 2018: 215–48, esp. 247). As a mythical realm, Sheol's boundaries are not clearly defined. In Isa. 38.10, Hezekiah states that one must cross through gates to reach it. Ps. 16.10 refers to it as a place where God is absent. Arrival in this place is not desired and remaining there is not a good death. Sheol is often paired with 'the pit'. These terms can mean a physical place, such as a tomb where one enters a forgetful state and is forgotten (Eccl. 9.10; Ps. 88.5). The association of 'the pit' with a place that is dug into the ground, reflects a culture where in the dead are interred. Scholars have wondered if 'the pit' refers to a bone repository (see below) found in most Judean bench tombs (Hays 2011: 177).

# FUNERARY RITES, MORTUARY RITES AND CULTS OF THE DEAD

An anthropology of death is related to religion, in as much as religion functions as a way for the living to process the death of their loved ones. Since the Hebrew Bible is intent on pushing a Yahweh-centric religious ideology, it presents the Israelites as following a unique and proscribed set of rituals regarding the dead, one that upholds only Yahweh (see here Stavrakopoulou 2010). This impression comes from negative descriptions of practices echoing those of Egypt (Lewis 1999; Hays 2011: 57–92), Mesopotamia (van der Toorn 1991, 1996; Scurlock 1997, 2002), the Neo-Hittite state (Collins 2002: 224–38), and Ugarit (Smith and Bloch-Smith 1988; van der Toorn 1991; Hays 2011: 98–130). A careful reading, however, finds that beliefs about the afterlife in the biblical text are heterodox. There is no one set of funerary or mortuary rites that appear consistently with every reference to the dead. Because of this, discussions regarding death and a cult of the dead have proved divisive in biblical scholarship.

The history of scholarship on the cult of the dead in the Hebrew Bible is long and storied. Like a pendulum, support for the concept has swung back and forth. Those arguing for some form of a cult of the dead in ancient Israel include, inter alia, Albright (1968), Brichto (1973), Spronk (1986), Lewis (1989), Pope (1977, 1981), Smith and Bloch-Smith (1988), von Rad (2001 [1957]), Hays (2011), Suriano (2018) and Sonia (2020). What exactly this cult looked like, how it was carried out, and the place of the dead within the cult has been a matter of some debate. Around the turn of the twentieth century, scholars working in comparative religion were influenced by the anthropological approaches of those scholars who thought that a common feature of natural religion was the worship of the dead, evidenced by plural term in Hebrew 'Elohim' (gods), which represented dead spirits (Spronk 1986: 28; Hays 2011: 135 n.8). Worship of the dead has become a sticking point within biblical studies. Texts that suggested the dead could be consulted (1 Samuel 28; Isa. 8.19; Deut. 18.11) were thought to show ancient Israel was not unique in their understanding of death, but that they followed a belief system similar to that of surrounding cultures (von Rad 2001: 276–7). Questions surrounding whether the dead were beneficent or harmful, powerful or weak, reflections of a Canaanite background or Mesopotamian retrojections have made for lively scholarly debate (see too, Schmidt 1996; Lewis 1999; Hays 2011: 143–7; Sonia 2020: 26–64).

## *The* Rephaim *and* rpum

The *Rephaim* have come to play an important role in the discussion of ancestor cults and how the dead were perceived in ancient Israel. Interpretations of the *Rephaim* include beings who are semi-divine, a class of warriors, a mythic tribe or deified royal ancestors (Spronk 1986: 195; Schmidt 1996: 33). These meanings are derived from context and have been suggested based on proposed Semitic roots (Lewis 1999: 118). One possible root is *rph*, meaning 'to sink down, be weak', while the favoured possibility is *rp'*, meaning 'to heal'. Depending on the root, the powers afforded to the dead are quite different – they are either weak and powerless, or powerful healers. A similar term, *rpum*, is found in the Ugaritic literature. With Ugarit just to the north of Israel, it is likely that the Ugaritic and Hebrew terms refer to beings who were understood in a similar manner. Accordingly, comparisons have been made with the Ugaritic literature in order to illuminate what the Hebrew term might have meant. Ugaritic texts describe the *rpum* as the recipients of a cult in which food, libations and offerings were given to the dead on a regular basis (The Epic of Aqhat *CAT* 1.17 and the 'Rapiuma texts' *CAT* 1.20–2). These regular interactions meant the living remained in relationship with the dead because the dead were understood to have some power to affect the living in a beneficial manner.

The degree to which the Ugaritic *rpum* might apply in cases of the biblical *Rephaim* is uncertain. Did the dead, like the *rpum*, also have power to affect the living? Perhaps, as Hays argues, the biblical texts reflect a background in which the dead were understood as powerful beings, but where 'the fear of the wrath of the dead that was prevalent in Mesopotamia seems to have been as muted in Israel and Judah as it was in Ugarit' (Hays 2011: 168). For example, Deut. 3.11 recalls a time when the *Rephaim* were a tribe of giants. 'Now only King Og of Bashan was left of the remnant of the Rephaim. In fact, his bed, an iron bed, can still be seen in Rabbah of the Ammonites. By the common cubit it is nine cubits long and four cubits wide'.[1] Consider too, Isa. 14.9, which presents the *Rephaim* as dead (deified?) royalty. 'Sheol beneath is stirred up to meet you when you come; it rouses the shades (*Rephaim*) to greet you, all who were leaders of the earth; it raises from their thrones all who were kings of the nations'. What is clear is that the term was known and demythologized by the biblical authors. This fact, however, does not undermine the possibility of a cult of the dead.

---

[1] All biblical translations are from the NRSV unless otherwise noted.

### Dining with the dead

Feeding or feasting with the dead seems to have been a regular part of ancient West Asian cults of the dead. The Ugaritic texts refer to a *marziḥu* as feast and sacrifice linked with the cult of the ancestors (*CAT* 1.21). A similar situation appears, albeit described in a negative fashion, along with the term *marzēaḥ* in Jer. 16.5–7 (Hays 2011: 163–5). The Mesopotamian *kispu* (cult of dead kin) also included a ritual meal shared with dead ancestors (Bayliss 1973; Tsukimoto 1985; van der Toorn 1996: 48–52; Sonia 2020: 27). Monumental inscriptions from Sam'al also discuss feeding the dead on a regular basis (Bonatz 2014; Sonia 2020: 44–50). Within the archaeological remains of Iron Age Israel, tombs commonly include ceramic items related to eating and drinking. Interpreting the meaning behind such ceramics is difficult. As Suriano (2018: 156) states: 'Was the placement of food symbolic or real? Do these remains indicate a type of propitiation, based on the belief that the dead were powerful and dangerous? Or do the remains suggest a type of commensality that involved the sustenance for the dead inside the tomb?' An examination of Iron Age family tombs and their contents (ibid.: 157, 2021) finds grave goods were mostly near the head and feet of individuals. When making room for a subsequent interment, both the grave goods and the skeletal remains they were associated with were moved to a repository niche, thus indicating an association between the person and their grave goods. The sheer quantity and variety of vessels related to both cooking and eating implies that the dead had the same needs as the living.

Whether the living feasted along with their deceased relatives is unknown and is further complicated by passages from the Hebrew Bible that appear to indicate that food within tombs is impure. Deut. 26.14 is commonly cited as prohibiting feeding the dead and, in turn, a denial of the cult of ancestors. The rationale is that Israelite ancestors did not need feeding because if they did, then they would be dependent upon the living and not Yahweh in the afterlife. Lest the Israelites become too much like their neighbours and follow their pagan practices, the dead should not be fed, or so the argument goes. However, this verse does not prohibit feeding the dead, rather it prohibits tithing food to Yahweh that had become impure by being in contact with either the dead or a person in mourning. Nowhere in the Hebrew Bible does it prohibit caring for the ancestors or feeding the dead (most recently, Suriano 2018: 154–72; Sonia 2020 174–5; Suriano 2021).

## BURIAL AND POST-MORTEM CARE: GATHERED TO THE ANCESTORS

'Therefore, I will gather you to your ancestors, and you shall be gathered to your grave in peace; your eyes shall not see all the disaster that I will bring on this place.' They took the message back to the king.

—2 Kings 22.20

### A good death

The phrase 'to be gathered to one's ancestors' has a double meaning. Here, in 2 Kings 22.20, God assures King Josiah that he will die a good death. A good death is generally afforded to those individuals who led a righteous life. In this way, it became biblical shorthand for 'this person was considered morally good'. The association of a good death with a good life is in some ways similar to the Egyptian belief that when one dies, the heart is weighed against Ma'at to determine whether the individual proceeds on to the afterlife. Egyptians determine one's fate during the 'Weighing of the Heart', which is described in detail in Spell 125 of the Egyptian Book of the Dead. If a person is not worthy, their heart is eaten by the god Ammit and they do not continue on their journey to the underworld. While there are differences between the two cultures, it is important to remember that the Hebrew Bible was not unique in its judgement of individuals when they died; it came from a world that believed there were good deaths and bad deaths.

Logistically, being afforded a good death meant one was also physically 'gathered to their ancestors'. Association with family in death underlines the position that individuals were a part of a house, both in life and in death, further emphasizing the importance of family in ancient Israel and the ties between family and land (Stavrakopoulou 2010). The early references to burials in the Promised Land note that Abraham, Isaac and Jacob were all buried with their ancestors in the cave of Machpelah (Gen. 25.9, 35.27–9, 50.13). Here, archaeology can be helpful in providing an image of what this practice looked like. Once a location was established as a burial ground, an individual would be prepared for burial and then buried. Grave goods generally accompanied the burial. When a subsequent family member died, the family cave would be reopened. Earlier burials would be swept to the side making space for the new burials. Bones might be intermingled overtime as bones swept aside were literally gathered together with the bones of their ancestors (Bloch-Smith 1992: 36–7). In reopening the tomb and intermingling with deceased relatives, the living actively participated in upholding the social memory of the family (Cradic 2018). Cave tombs were popular in the highlands of Canaan during the Late Bronze Age and into the early Iron I period (Gonen 1979; Bloch-Smith 1992: 39).

## *Judahite family tombs*

By beginning of the Iron II period, rock-cut bench tombs became synonymous with 'Judahite burial'. Like cave tombs, they functioned as a burial ground in which families could be kept together. The rock-cut bench tombs, however, appear to belong to the upper class (Bloch-Smith 2002: 128–9; Ilan 2017: 56). The architectural plan of the rock-cut tombs is distinct. An entrance shaft, sometimes with descending stairs, led to the burial chamber(s). Bench tombs, as opposed to the similarly constructed arcosolia tombs, had more than one chamber or room (Gonen 1979: 108; Bloch-Smith 1992: 41). Benches were carved along the walls of the rooms and somewhere in the tomb there was a repository pit. Bodies would be laid in primary burials on the benches, where they would transform into a skeleton. Once the body was decomposed, it would be removed to the repository pit to make room for a new burial (Ilan 2017: 54–5). The placement of the body within the tomb is a pivotal moment in the dying process. Suriano (2018: 207–8) argues that in the narrative describing the matriarch Sarah's death, Sarah is described as marginalized between the time she dies and the time she is laid to rest (Gen. 23.3–15). Suriano notes the Hebrew calls her *met*, 'dead', using the Hebrew masculine participle, indicating that she exists in a liminal state, robbed of all identity, including her gender. Only once she is interred in the cave of Machpelah does she regain her identity as Abraham's wife and her place within the family. 'And then Abraham buried his wife Sarah in the cave of the field of Machpelah' (Gen. 23.19). Notably, the 'structural plan of a conventional bench tomb is similar to intramural tombs, or tombs built beneath homes, such as those at Megiddo during the MB [Middle Bronze Age]. Intramural tombs emulated the house and thus created a means of unifying generations both living and dead' (Suriano 2018: 58; also Cradic 2018).

The layout of the bench tomb has also been associated with the so-called Israelite four-room house, the latter of which is thought to be the locus of the *bêt 'āb*. It has been suggested that that the 'rock-cut tomb was an attempt to immortalize the *bet 'av* in stone' (Faust and Bunimovitz 2008: 151, 162). Whether the tombs are evidence of the elite class developing alongside state formation (Fantalkin 2008) or were used as resistance between established lineages in the area and the new monarchy (Faust and Bunimovitz 2008), they served to strengthen lineage links between the living and dead and claims to the land where the deceased were buried (Brichto 1973; Stavrakopoulou 2010: 9–18).

## MEMORIALIZING THE DEAD IN ANCIENT ISRAEL

The Hebrew Bible references a number of ways in which the living remembered the dead. Memorializing and remembering the deceased served as yet another way to keep the dead alive in the social memory and create ties between the living household and the dead household, which again attests to the position held by the Hebrew Bible that death has a relational component to it. The most visible means of memorializing an individual was through the tomb itself. The family tomb served as a place of remembrance to which later generations would return to bury their dead (Cradic 2018). It also served as a visible marker on the landscape indicating that a family had a claim to the land. Land and landholdings became linked to the ancestral burial plots. The inalienable rights attached to the land via ancestral plots with or without graves hovers in the background of many texts, most notably the narrative concerning Naboth's vineyard in 1 Kings 21 (Lewis 1991). Francesca Stavrakopoulou (2010) has demonstrated the important role that burials play in delineating territorial boundaries within the Hebrew Bible. She points to Joshua's burial at the boundary of his ancestral estate (Josh. 24.30; Judg. 2.8–9) and Rachel's burial (Stavrakopoulou 2010: 81) on the boundary of the territory of Benjamin (Gen. 25.19; 1 Sam. 10.2). Stavrakopoulou notes, 'These traditions are suggestive of a territoriality of burial familiar from social-scientific studies of communities in which the dead (usually imaged as ancestors) play an acknowledged social role' (2010: 12).

At times, additional monuments were attached to grave sites. Similar to how we might understand a headstone, these monuments were meant to carry on the deceased's name into an unknown point in the future. For example, Rachel's burial was marked with a pillar (Gen. 48.7). Isa. 56.3–5 offers another example of a stele or pillar being used as a memorial. The concern in Isaiah is for the eunuch who has no children to carry on his name. God asserts that all who follow God's ways will be remembered. God will set up a *yād wā-šēm*. A literal translation of this phrase is a 'hand and a name', which is a hendiadys for a commemorative monument (Sonia 2020: 53). The term *yād* is also found in other texts meaning monument (1 Sam. 15.12 and Isa. 57.8). In the case of Isaiah 57.8 *yād* is paired with *zikkaron*, which carries the sense of remembrance, like 'name' (Ackerman 1990). Both these texts in Isaiah are concerned with fertility and death. However, the need to make sure one's name lives on in perpetuity is best exemplified in the narrative of Absalom. Lacking a son to carry on his name, he sets up a pillar by which to be remembered. 'Now Absalom in his lifetime had taken and set up for himself a pillar that is in the King's Valley, for he said, "I have no son to keep my name in remembrance"; he called the pillar by his own name. It is called Absalom's Monument to this day' (2 Sam. 18.18). Absalom is concerned with functional immortality. Without a son to carry on his lineage and remember him, his memory would soon cease to exist. The pillar takes the place of the son as all who walk by would (hypothetically) say, 'That is Absalom's Pillar'. Commemoration, therefore, also means the recitation of the deceased's name (Brichto 1973: 20–1; Sonia 2020: 53). Many ancient West Asian funerary monuments were inscribed with messages including the deceased's name and imprecations to keep the tomb intact. The desire that the tomb be undisturbed, and the memory of the dead kept alive, further argue in favour of a belief in post-mortem existence (Suriano 2018: 98–127).

At some point, an individual might cease to be remembered and functional immortality is lost. This could happen in two ways. First, it happens when the social role of the *npš* is lost. If personhood is tied to both memory and things, loss of personhood might occur when there are either no more family members left who remember the dead, or if the dead had no one to remember them in the first place. The belongings of the deceased, whether they be land or other valuables, would cease to be passed on. In other cases, a person may be forgotten with intention, via an effort to erase their memory. This might be the case with bodies exposed to the elements and not afforded a proper burial. Consider Jezebel, who was thrown out of a window. Before they could bury her with proper burial rites, she was eaten by dogs (2 Kgs 9.34–7). These burial rites are described in Hebrew as *piqdû* which is often compared to care provided in the Mesopotamian cult of the dead kin, called *pāqidu* (Lewis 1989: 120–2; Sonia 2020: 10). Only Jezebel's skull, feet and hands remained (2 Kgs 9.35). 2 Kgs 9.37 states that without an entire corpse to bury, Jezebel would not receive any type of burial. 'The carcass of Jezebel shall be like dung on the ground, in the field of Jezreel, so that none will be able to say: "This was Jezebel"'. The texts suggest Jezebel's memory would be forgotten and her *npš* lost. For Jezebel there would be no functional immortality.

# CONCLUSION

When regarding the archaeological record alongside the textual record, one sees that caring for the dead was not discouraged, but rather encouraged. This set of data provides a preponderance of evidence against which to read those biblical texts that have been used to argue against a cult of the dead, or at the very least, the reduction of such a cult in in the face of YHWH-centred monotheism. Moreover, the matrix of death-related activities can even be applied to YHWH. For example, both Ezek. 37.11–14 and Isa. 56.3–5 show how YHWH fulfils the role of caregiver post-mortem to those who die outside of their ancestral land and to those who have no one to remember them (Sonia 2020: 165–201; contra Stavrakopoulou 2010: 125). 'Instead of condemning the cult, the biblical writers depict YHWH [in the postexilic period] as the cultic caregiver par excellence. This depiction does not undermine the cult of dead kin but instead draws on a broader motif in ancient West Asia of a benevolent god or king acting as caregiver for the marginalized, including the untended dead' (Sonia 2020: 183). Based on the importance placed on commemoration and functional immortality, the attribution of YHWH, a being who transcends ancestral location and whose memory lasts forever (Ps. 45.17), as a caregiver would be a very compelling tenet for the ancient Israelites who were displaced in the diaspora. This idea is equally powerful for those who were of the lower classes and could not afford elaborate family sepulchres. Without the money to spend on long-lasting monuments that would be revisited in generations to come, those without means would be buried in simple pits, and therefore subject to a shorter functional immortality in the afterlife.

As this brief exploration has shown, concepts within the Hebrew Bible of death, the dying body, funerary rites, burial and post-mortem care for the dead are not uniform; nor are they too disparate to prevent a description – albeit a broad description – of an anthropology of death in ancient Israel. Hays's observation regarding beliefs and practices concerning death is most apt. He states that the Hebrew Bible 'contains some proscription, much description, but an almost total lack of prescription' (Hays 2011: 153). In short, much like one finds in contemporary societies, descriptions of death and the afterlife in ancient Israel are heterodox, representing a rich and complex understanding of 'what happens next'.

# REFERENCES

Abbott, W.M., ed. (1966), *The Documents of Vatican II*, New York: Guild Press.
Ackerman, S. (1990), 'Sex, Sacrifice and Death: Understanding a Prophetic Poem', *Bible Review*, 6 (1): 38–44.
Albright, W.F. (1968), *Yahweh and the Gods of Canaan: A Historical Analysis of Two Contrasting Faiths*, Winona Lake, IN: Eisenbrauns.
Bayliss, M. (1973), 'The Cult of the Dead Kin in Assyria and Babylonia', *Iraq*, 35 (2): 115–25.
Bloch, M. and J. Parry, eds (1982), *Death and the Regeneration of Life*, Cambridge: Cambridge University Press.
Bloch-Smith, E. (1992), *Judahite Burial Practices and Beliefs About the Dead*, JSOTSup 123, Sheffield: JSOT Press.
Bloch-Smith, E. (2002), 'Life in Judah from the Perspective of the Dead', *NEA*, 65 (2): 120–30.
Bonatz, D. (2014), 'Katumuwa's Banquet Scene', in V.R. Herrmann and J.D. Schloen (eds), *In Remembrance of Me: Feasting with the Dead in the Ancient Middle East*, 39–44, Chicago: Oriental Institute of Chicago.
Brichto, H. (1973), 'Kin, Cult, Land and Afterlife – A Biblical Complex', *HUCA*, 44: 1–54.
Collins, B.J. (2002), 'Necromancy, Fertility and the Dark Earth: The Use of Ritual Pits in Hittite Cult', in P. Mirecki and M. Meyer (eds), *Magic and Ritual in the Ancient World*, 224–41, Leiden: E.J. Brill.
Cradic, M.S. (2018), 'Residential Burial and Social Memory in the Bronze Age Levant', *NEA*, 81 (3): 191–201.
Durkheim, É. (2001 [1912]), *The Elementary Forms of Religious Life*, transl. C. Cosman, Oxford: Oxford University Press.
Fantalkin, A. (2008), 'The Appearance of Rock-cut Bench Tombs in Iron Age Judah as a Reflection of State Formation', in A. Fantalkin and A. Yasur-Landau (eds), *Bene Yisrael: Studies in the Archaeology of Israel and Levant during the Bronze and Iron Ages in Honour of Israel Finkelstein*, 17–54, CHANE 31, Leiden: E.J. Brill.
Faust, A. and S. Bunimovitz (2008), 'The Judahite Rock-Cut Tomb: Family Response at a Time of Change', *IEJ*, 58 (2): 150–70.
Foucault, M. (1995), *Discipline and Punish: The Birth of the Prison*, New York: Vintage Books.
Garroway, K.H. (2018), *Growing Up in Ancient Israel: Children in Material Culture and Biblical Texts*, ABS 23, Atlanta, GA: Society of Biblical Literature.
Gonen, R. (1979), 'Burial in Canaan of the Late Bronze Age as a Basis for the Study of Population and Settlements', PhD diss. [Hebrew], Hebrew University, Jerusalem.
Goody, J. (1962), *Death, Property and the Ancestors: A Study of the Mortuary Customs of the Lo Dagaa of West Africa*, Stanford, CA: Stanford University Press.

Green, J.D.M. (2007), 'Anklets and the Social Construction of Gender and Age in the Late Bronze and Early Iron Age Southern Levant', in S. Hamilton, R.D. Whitehouse and K.I. Wright (eds), *Archaeology and Women: Ancient and Modern Issues*, 283–311, Walnut Creek, CA: Left Coast Press.

Hays, C.B. (2011), *A Covenant with Death: Death in the Iron Age II and Its Rhetorical Uses in Proto-Isaiah*, Grand Rapids, MI: Eerdmans.

Hertz, R. (1960), *Death and the Right Hand*, transl. R. Needham and C. Needham, Glencoe, IL: Free Press.

Ilan, D. (2017), 'Iron Age Mortuary Practices and Beliefs in the Southern Levant', in J. Bradbury and C. Scarre (eds), *Engaging with the Dead: Exploring Changing Human Beliefs About Death, Mortality, and the Human Body*, 51–66, Studies in Funerary Archaeology 13, Philadelphia, PA: Oxbow.

Kan, S. (2016), *Symbolic Immortality: The Tlingit Potlatch of the Nineteenth Century*, 2nd edn, Seattle: University of Washington Press.

Lemos, T.M. (2017), *Violence and Personhood in Ancient Israel and Comparative Contexts*, Oxford: Oxford University Press.

Lewis, T. (1989), *Cults of the Dead in Ancient Israel and Ugarit*, HSM 39, Atlanta, GA: Scholars Press.

Lewis, T. (1991), 'The Ancestral Estate (naḥlat elohîm) in 2 Samuel 14.16', *JBL*, 110 (4): 597–612.

Lewis, T. (1999), '*Israel's Beneficent Dead: Ancestor Cult and Necromancy in Ancient Israelite Religion and Tradition*, by Brian B. Schmidt: A Review Article', *JAOS*, 119 (3): 512–14.

Martin, D.B. (1995), *The Corinthian Body*, New Haven, CT: Yale University Press.

Mauss, M. (1979 [1934]), 'Techniques of the Body', in *Sociology and Psychology: Essays*, 95–123, transl. B. Brewster, London: Routledge & Kegan Paul.

Meskell, L. (1999), *Archaeologies of Social Life: Age, Sex, Class et cetera in Ancient Egypt*, Oxford: Blackwell.

Metcalf, P. and R. Huntington (1991), *Celebrations of Death: The Anthropology of Mortuary Ritual*, 2nd edn, Cambridge: Cambridge University Press.

Meyers, C. (2013), *Rediscovering Eve: Ancient Israelite Women in Context*, Oxford: Oxford University Press.

Müller, M. (2001), 'Afterlife', in D. Redford (ed), *The Oxford Encyclopedia of Ancient Egypt*, transl. R. Shillenn and J. McGary, Oxford: Oxford University Press. Available online: https://www.oxfordreference.com/view/10.1093/acref/9780195102345.001.0001/acref-9780195102345-e-0013 (accessed 18 July 2022).

Nilsson Stutz, L. and S. Tarlow (2013), 'Beautiful Things and Bones of Desire: Emerging Issues in the Archaeology of Death and Burial', in S. Tarlow and L. Nilsson Stutz (eds), *The Oxford Handbook of the Archaeology of Death and Burial*, 1–14, Oxford: Oxford University Press.

Obeyesekere, G. (2005), *Cannibal Talk: The Man-Eating Myth and Human Sacrifice in the South Seas*, Berkeley: University of California Press.

Parker Pearson, M. (1993), 'The Powerful Dead: Archaeological Relationships Between the Living and the Dead', *CAJ*, 3 (2): 203–29.

Pope, M.H. (1977), 'Notes on the Rephaim Texts from Ugarit', in M. de Jong Ellis (ed.), *Essays on the Ancient Near East in Memory of Jacob Joel Finkelstein*, 163–82, Memoirs of the Connecticut Academy of Arts and Sciences 19, Hamden, CT: Archon Books.

Pope, M.H. (1981), 'The Cult of the Dead at Ugarit', in G.D. Young (ed.), *Ugarit in Retrospect: Fifty Years of Ugarit and Ugaritic*, 159–79, Winona Lake, IN: Eisenbrauns.

Saxe, A. (1970), 'Social Dimensions of Mortuary Practices', PhD diss., University of Michigan, Ann Arbor.

Schmidt, B.B. (1996), *Israel's Beneficent Dead: Ancestor Cult and Necromancy in Ancient Israelite Religion and Tradition*, Winona Lake, IN: Eisenbrauns.

Scurlock, J. (1997), 'Ghosts in the Ancient Near East: Weak or Powerful?', *HUCA*, 68: 77–96.

Scurlock, J. (2002), *Magico-Medical Means of Treating Ghost-Induced Illnesses in Ancient Mesopotamia*, Ancient Magic and Divination 3, Leiden: E.J. Brill.

Smith, M. and E. Bloch-Smith (1988), 'Death and Afterlife in Ugarit and Israel', *JAOS*, 108 (2): 277–84.

Sonia, K. (2020), *Caring for the Dead in Ancient Israel*, ABS 27, Atlanta, GA: SBL Press.

Spronk, K. (1986), *Beatific Afterlife in Ancient Israel and in the Ancient Near East*, AOAT 219, Neukirchen-Vluyn: Neukirchener.

Stavrakopoulou, F. (2010), *Land of Our Fathers: The Roles of Ancestor Veneration in Biblical Land Claims*, LHBOTS 473, London: T&T Clark.

Steinberg, N. (2009), 'Exodus 12 in Light of Ancestral Cult Practices', in P. Dutcher-Walls (ed.), *The Family in Life and in Death: The Family in Ancient Israel – Sociological and Archaeological Perspectives*, 89–105, LHBOTS 504, New York: T&T Clark.

Suriano, M. (2018), *A History of Death in the Hebrew Bible*, Oxford: Oxford University Press.

Suriano, M. (2021), 'What Did Feeding the Dead Mean? Two Case Studies from Iron Age Tombs at Beth Shemesh', *AABNER*, 1 (3): 119–42.

Tsukimoto, A. (1985), *Untersuchungen zur Totenpflege (kispum) im alten Mesopotamien*, AOAT 216, Neukirchen-Vluyn: Neukirchener.

Turner, V. (1967), *The Forest of Symbols: Aspects of Ndembu Ritual*, Ithaca, NY: Cornell University Press.

van der Toorn, K. (1991), 'Funerary Rituals and Beatific Afterlife in Ugaritic Texts and the Bible', *BibOr*, 48: 40–66.

van der Toorn, K. (1996), *Family Religion in Babylonia, Ugarit, and Israel: Continuity and Changes in the Forms of Religious Life*, Leiden: E.J. Brill.

van Gennep, A. (1960), *The Rites of Passage*, Chicago: University of Chicago Press.

von Rad, G. (2001 [1957]), *Old Testament Theology, Vol. 1: The Theology of Israel's Historical Traditions*, OTL, Louisville, KY: Westminster John Knox Press.

Walter, T. (1993), 'Dust Not Ashes: The American Preference for Burials', *Landscape*, 32 (1): 42–8.

Washofsky, M. (2001), *Jewish Living: A Guide to Contemporary Reform Practice*, New York: UAHC Press.

Watson, P.J. (1979), *Archaeological Ethnography in Western Iran*, Tucson: University of Arizona.

Wylie, T. (1964), 'Mortuary Customs at Sa-skya, Tibet', *Harvard Journal of Asiatic Studies*, 25: 229–42.

# CHAPTER TWENTY-TWO

# Spatiality and territoriality

*Power over land and power over people*

STEPHEN C. RUSSELL

## INTRODUCTION

Since the turn of the millennium, the study of space, land, place and territory has received renewed attention within biblical studies and its allied fields. To be sure, historically grounded approaches to the Bible and ancient Israel have long paid attention to land, which is one of the Bible's major themes. But a number of recent studies have approached the topic in conversation with the work of geographers, sociologists and philosophers (for example, George 2009; Wazana 2013; Pioske 2015; Waters 2015; Russell 2016; James 2017). Biblical studies has been involved in what Warf and Arias (2009) have called the spatial turn across academic disciplines.[1] In this regard, Henri Lefebvre's work on space (1991) has been especially influential in shaping the analysis of space within biblical studies.[2] Lefebvre's central insight, that space is a social product, has opened up new avenues of enquiry for biblical studies. In my estimation, Lefebvre's work will continue to be central to any analysis of spatiality and territoriality in the Bible and ancient Israel (Russell 2017).

In the context of this handbook on social anthropology and the Bible, I wish to highlight the work of four anthropologists who have received comparatively little attention among biblical scholars treating the theme of land in the Bible. I focus here on Max Gluckman (1965), Edmund Leach (1961), Caroline Humphrey (1983) and Katherine Verdery (2003). The first three of these completed their doctoral training in the UK, where the distinction between social anthropology and cultural anthropology was more clearly maintained. The last, Verdery, completed her doctoral training in the United States, where social anthropology has not generally been treated as a separate field from

---

[1] The renewed focus on space and territory has been nurtured especially by the Constructions of Space Ancient Seminar of the American Academy of Religion and the Society of Biblical Literature, from 2000 to 2005, and the Space, Place, and Lived Experience in Antiquity Program Unit of the Society of Biblical Literature, from 2005 to the present. Several volumes of essays have come out of the work of these fora (Berquist and Camp 2007; Camp and Berquist 2008; George 2013; Prinsloo and Maier 2013; Økland, de Vos and Wenell 2016).

[2] Among biblical scholars, Soja's (1996) interpretation of Lefebvre has been especially influential, though I (2017) have situated myself within an interpretive tradition of Lefebvre that includes Elden (2004, 2007) and Merrifield (1993, 2006)

cultural anthropology. They have all worked in the tradition of the great social anthropologist Bronisław Malinowski. In the final volume of his trilogy treating the Trobriand Islanders, Malinowski wrote, 'To understand how land is owned, it is above all necessary to know how it is used and why it is valued' (1935: 323). The anthropologists I discuss here have clarified in a variety of contexts how land is owned, used and valued.

As we will see, Gluckman advanced Malinowski's legacy by continuing to dispel the notion of primitive communal land ownership, which had been one intellectual handmaid to the colonial enterprise.[3] Gluckman provided a general legal framework for understanding land rights in many societies, especially those structured around an ideology of kinship. Leach worked within the empirical tradition of Malinowski and asserted that social structure is best understood as a statistical order that emerges from myriad data.[4] For Leach, land and relationships to it shape social structure rather than the other way around. A major contribution of Humphrey[5] and Verdery[6] has been to advance Malinowski's legacy by relating legal rules of land tenure to an extralegal framework – Humphrey exploring unwritten rules and Verdery charting the concept of value. Together, these anthropologists suggest a range of possible approaches to understanding land rights and territoriality that I think biblical scholars will find helpful as they approach the theme of land in the Bible.

Scholars working on space and territory across academic disciplines have come to use a set of terms that carry certain nuances. Before I take up the work of Gluckman, Leach, Humphrey and Verdery, let me make explicit some of what scholars imply with this specialized language. Spatial terminology is somewhat fluid and I do not present here universally accepted technical definitions of space, territory, land and related concepts. But I hope to orient the reader unfamiliar with spatial studies to how these terms carry special connotations within scholarly literature on the topic.

---

[3] In seeking to give a more precise definition of ownership, Gluckman cites Malinowski:

> We can appreciate therefore why Malinowski in 1926 insisted that that the 'ownership and use of the canoe [in the Trobriand Islands] consist of a series of obligations and duties uniting a group of people into a working team', and concluded that 'ownership, therefore, can be defined neither by such words as "communism" nor "individualism," nor by reference to "joint-stock company" system or "personal enterprise" but by the concrete facts and conditions of use. It is the sum of duties, privileges and mutualities which bind the joint owners to the object and to each other.'
>
> —Gluckman 1965: 165–6 citing Malinowski 1926: 18, 20–1

[4] Contrasting Malinowski's work to that of Radcliffe-Brown, Leach writes,

> It follows that custom, in Malinowski's conception, is like Durkheim's 'suicide rate', a symptom; it is not something imposed by rule, nor is it itself coercive, it simply corresponds to the state of affairs. Custom "makes sense" not in terms of some external, logically ordered, moral system, but in terms of the private self-interest of the average man in that particular cultural situation.
>
> —1961: 298

[5] Humphrey writes, 'I shall be using the anthropological approach to property rights initiated by Malinowski and developed by Firth and Goodman' (1983: 118).

[6] Verdery presents as an epigraph to her second chapter Malinowski's statement, 'To understand how land is owned, it is above all necessary to know how it is used and why it is valued'. She writes, 'I follow Bronislaw Malinowski's dictum and ask how socialism's resources were used (Malinowski 1935: 323). This strategy enables me to examine socialist property in something like its own terms, instead of as a failed form of western property' (2003: 47).

As used by scholars studying spatiality and territoriality, the term 'space' does not usually refer to the celestial realm of stars, black holes and galaxies. Rather, it primarily refers to the terrestrial realm within which humans make their home, at scales ranging from the body to the planet. Spatial studies does not treat space as an abstract, idealized geometric grid, but as the real product of human beings. Space results from human economic activity, it is conceptualized by human imagination and it derives meaning from human culture. The active role humans play in perceiving, conceiving and living in space is sometimes emphasized by the term 'spatiality'.

'Territory' commonly refers to space at a societal scale but within spatial studies territory can refer to space at other scales. The term territory emphasizes human power over space. But this power is not understood as being an end in itself. Rather, human power over space is understood as a means of establishing power over people. Territory thus connotes a distinction between those with a legitimate right to use space and those who are not considered to have such a right. Territory implies boundaries that demarcate the space over which power is exercised. At times, a single legitimate centre is imagined as being separated from an illegitimate, chaotic periphery by an extended frontier zone (see especially Wazana 2013). At other times multiple legitimate centres are imagined as being separated by relatively thin borders. And even within a single territory, territoriality connotes a hierarchy of power. As Robert D. Sack writes, 'Territoriality for humans is a powerful geographic strategy to control people and things by controlling area' (1986: 5).

Compared to other academic disciplines within which space has been explored, social anthropology has focused especially on land tenure. Within spatial studies, the term 'land' often connotes space's economic function. It refers to space as used for farming, grazing, mining and so forth. Land is space as one factor of economic production. Like territory, the term land can imply legitimate and illegitimate users and uses of space. Social anthropologists have considered both formal systems of jural rules governing human use of land and the social, technological, ecological, economic and ideological contexts of these rules. In examining land tenure, social anthropologists have worked at the intersections of various subfields, each of which has become increasingly specialized since the 1950s.

One focus of twentieth-century social anthropology was the relationship between jural rules governing land tenure and patterns of kinship. Kinship refers to the network of social relationships formed through descent and marriage. But anthropologists recognize kinship as ideological in so far as it presents inequitable relations of power as natural. Societies and individuals often frame social relationships in ways that do not entirely match historical and biological reality. Indeed, co-residence can give rise to social relationships that come to be formulated in the language of kinship. Kinship is treated in greater detail in Chapter 7 of this handbook (see also Chapter 10). With this basic orientation to terminology in mind, let us turn to the work of Gluckman, Leach, Humphrey and Verdery.

# MAX GLUCKMAN

The social anthropologist who has most influenced my work on land rights and territoriality in the biblical world is Max Gluckman (Russell 2013, 2014b, 2016, 2017, 2018a, 2018b). Gluckman's analysis of land tenure (1943, 1965) grew both out of his fieldwork among the Lozi (Barotse), conducted from 1939 onwards, and his familiarity with the scholarly tradition in which anthropologists worked to come to terms with concepts of property in many societies.⁷ As such, he offered both an interpretation of Lozi land tenure in its particulars and a framework for analysing property in a wide variety of societies.⁸ Because Gluckman aims at a general framework, I will not discuss in great detail the Lozi and will instead emphasize the general principles Gluckman develops as part of his treatment of Lozi jurisprudence.

Gluckman presents a legal framework for understanding land tenure. *The Ideas in Barotse Jurisprudence* grew out of the Storrs Lectures that Gluckman delivered at Yale Law School in 1963 and reflects deeper engagement with twentieth-century jurisprudential thought than much anthropological writing. His chapter on land tenure sits comfortably within a network of chapters covering other legal topics recognizable to jurists – constitutional law, legal administration, contract, injury, liability and debt, among others. The reader senses behind Gluckman's focus on the legal legitimacy of Lozi land tenure an anti-colonial impulse. Born and raised in South Africa, Gluckman trained at Oxford and spent much of his career at the University of Manchester. He was a political activist and openly criticized colonialism (see Gordon 2018: 388–91). In presenting a legal framework for Lozi land tenure, Gluckman emphasizes its validity.

To my mind, Gluckman's analysis of Barotse landholding involves three major insights that are of special interest to biblical scholars. First, Gluckman situates his analysis of land tenure within a jurisprudential discourse that eschews the multi-referential concept 'ownership' and that instead analyses property relations in terms of rights. Drawing on Wesley N. Hohfeld, American legal scholar Arthur L. Corbin had argued that legal relations do not exist between people and objects but between individuals and other individuals (Corbin 1919: 165; Hohfeld 1919). Although a person may have a physical relation to an object such as a house, from a legal standpoint that person has several legal relations with other individuals with respect to the house (Corbin 1919: 165). An individual may have the right to use a house in a certain way. This right constitutes a legal relation in so far as it permits or prohibits another person from using the house in a similar or different way. Gluckman works within this jurisprudential tradition that emphasizes rights. At the same time, he speaks generally of rights without classifying them further according to Hohfeld's taxonomy of demand-right, privilege-right, power, and immunity (Gluckman 1965: 79).

Gluckman's second major insight is that different individuals can hold different kinds of rights in the same piece of land. He distinguishes between productive rights and administrative rights, which among the Lozi are nested in a hierarchy. By productive rights, he refers to the right to use land for primary economic activity. Among the Lozi, this especially involves rights, 'to cultivate, to pasture stock, to fish, or to collect wild products' (1965: 90). Gluckman emphasizes that, 'a parcel of land is not a specific area, but an area used for a certain purpose at a certain time' (ibid.).

By administrative rights, Gluckman refers to wardenship or management rather than direct use. The nature of administrative rights is best illustrated by the ultimate administrator of all land among the Lozi, the king. The king is understood to be the

---

⁷ Among others, Gluckman draws on Lowie 1920; Malinowski 1926; Firth 1936; Wilson 1938; Richards 1939; Schapera 1943; Meek 1949; Elias 1951; Goodenough 1951; Sheddick 1954; Colson 1960; Lloyd 1962.
⁸ For example, Gluckman writes, 'The main principles of Barotse landholding, which I am now going to describe and analyse, are to be found in most tribal societies' (1965: 78).

owner of all land. In fact, the king's title, Litunga, means 'the land' (1965: 79). But not all land is available to the king for private use. Nor can the king simply seize at will land in use by a household (ibid.: 83). Gluckman's focus on rights allows him to explain the king's ownership as akin to wardenship. The king's ownership has limits. Gluckman delineates the king's administrative rights in land in a section worth quoting in full:

> (1) he can claim allegiance from any one settling on or using his land; (2) he is held to be the immediate owner of all land in his territory not yet taken up by his subjects; (3) this gives rise to a power to request that land allocated to subjects but not yet used by them be returned to him; (4) he inherits any land for which no heir of the dead holder can be found, and takes over land abandoned by a family or left by a banished family; (5) his ownership is held to be the basis of his right to demand a portion of the produce as tribute; (6) he can control the settlement of the people on the surface of the land; and (7) he has the power to legislate about holding and use of the land.
>
> —1965: 79

Between the king with ultimate administrative rights in land and households with productive rights in land, Lozi administrative rights in land are held in a hierarchy.[9] 'As the Lozi see the allocation of land, it is in a chain of distribution from the king to the village headman, to household head, to subordinates in the household; and therefore landholding is formulated in a straightforward series of allocations' (Gluckman 1965: 85). In speaking in this way, Gluckman does not refer to the complicated historical processes through which Lozi land was actually acquired but to the schematization of land distribution. The number of levels within the hierarchy could multiply as individuals with productive rights in land allocated land to others thereby acquiring an administrative right in the land. Or the number of levels could be reduced in various situations of default.

Gluckman emphasizes the security of the rights of those lower down the hierarchy against those higher up the hierarchy. For example, he writes, 'Once the king has given land to a subject the latter has in it rights which are protected against all comers including the king himself' (1965: 83). And he writes,

> In saying that the primary holder retains his holding in the secondary estates granted in his estate, I again emphasize that this is a revisionary or residual right; i.e. he can exercise it only if the secondary holder abandons the estate or is expelled from the group. Any estate, once granted, is held securely against all comers, including the grantor – and I repeat, even if he be the king.
>
> —ibid.: 92

Administrative rights are also held securely. Among the Lozi, individuals with rights in land had power to redistribute land but they could not ignore the administrative rights held by those higher up the hierarchy. An individual could not simply take their land rights with them to another village, for example. 'If a man leaves a village, he loses his rights in all land he worked as a member of that village [. . .] He works the land by grace of the headman to whom it is attached' (1965: 83). In sum, then, Gluckman showed how several individuals could hold different kinds of rights in the same land.

Gluckman's third major insight on land tenure is that property rights inhere in status within society. Among the Lozi, 'rights to land are an incident of political and social

---

[9] Biebuyck (1960) notes that a rigid hierarchy is not characteristic of all African agrarian systems.

status' (1965: 78). To emphasize this connection between rights and status, Gluckman refers throughout to 'estates of administration', 'estates of production' and a 'hierarchy of estates'. The primary implication of this is that rights to land also entail and are contingent upon responsibilities. 'In practice in these systems persons can maintain rights of tenure only if they fulfil their obligations both to superiors and to subordinates. Tenure of land therefore arises from, and is maintained by, fulfilment of obligations to other persons and not from title to the land itself' (ibid.: 79). Failure to fulfil responsibilities places rights in jeopardy. Thus, a banished family gave up its rights to land, which then defaulted up the administrative hierarchy to the king. Even the king's rights in land involved obligations. For example, the king had the responsibility to provide all members of society with access to land and the obligation to defend the property rights of his subjects (ibid.: 80). Of the three broad insights I have discussed in Gluckman's analysis, his emphasis on status is perhaps the one that is least universally translatable. Even so, biblical and other ancient Near Eastern legal systems embrace a connection between legal rights and legal responsibilities.

In a series of studies, I have tried to show the relevance of Gluckman's main insights for thinking about property rights as portrayed in the Bible and in other documents from the ancient Near East (Russell 2013, 2014b, 2016, 2017, 2018a, 2018b). His framework brings analytical clarity to an assessment of the legal concepts underpinning many land tenure systems. At the same time, it has its limits. As a general framework it cannot account for all the details of a specific case. The next anthropologist we will examine emphasized the particularities of land tenure as evidenced in a particular place at a particular time.

## EDMUND LEACH

Compared to Gluckman's broad claim that he examines, 'Barotse landholding – and African landholding in general' (1965: 71), Leach is adamant in asserting that his focus is 'extremely narrow' (1961: 1). In *Pul Eliya*, he offers a detailed case study of the relationship between land tenure and kinship systems in a single year, 1954, in a single village in northern Ceylon, now Sri Lanka, that consisted of 146 individuals and had about 135 acres under cultivation (1961: 1). He writes, 'I do not suggest that it is in any special way "typical" of all such villages or that it is in any sense a statistically "average" village. [. . .] [M]y first concern is not with general characteristics, but with the workings of a particular social system in all the details of its singular particularity' (1961: 1, 3–4). And yet, for precisely this reason, I think it worthwhile to examine his work here. Let me begin by summarizing some of the specific data Leach treats before discussing the broader implications of his work.

Leach sets his examination of property rights in ecological, geographical and historical context. The village of Pul Eliya lies in a dry zone so that scarcity of water rather than scarcity of land is of primary importance (Leach 1961: 15, 17). The village was once part of the Sinhalese kingdom, which largely conformed to Wittfogel's (1957) thesis of a hydraulic society (Leach 1961: 16). Endogamy and the caste system produced close bonds of kinship among villagers, with strict rules governing their relationships with members of neighbouring villages (ibid.: 23–8). Leach observes a distinction between political rights exercised by men in a variety of contexts and property rights connected to inheritance exercised by both women and men (ibid.: 36–7).

Leach presents a map of the village territory with accompanying analysis and explanation (1961: 43–66). In 1954, land was held under three categories of tenure, which were rooted in land categories established half a century earlier. In 1900 the central government undertook a survey of villages in the area that recognized lands under cultivation as *paravēni*, ancestral private property. All other land was treated as belonging directly to the crown (ibid.: 46). This *paravēni* constituted the old field of Pul Eliya. A major point made by Leach is that this land was not held communally. Rather, individual men and women held rights in land, including the right to pass their land on to heirs.[10] In 1954, in addition to the old field and crown lands, there were lands which had been bought outright from the government in the intervening years, so-called *sinakkara*, 'freehold acre land' (1961: 49–50). From 1935, no crown land could be sold. But two-acre plots of crown land could be leased, so-called *badu adam*. Such land was inheritable, but could only be passed on to a single heir. The rights of tenants were less secure than the rights of those in other categories of tenure.

There were three main types of ground in Pul Eliya: irrigated rice fields, tank ground and building ground. The majority of village cultivation was limited to the irrigated fields dedicated to this purpose. But climatic and economic factors sometimes drove villagers to utilize surrounding scrub jungle for cash crops, a practice discouraged by the government.

The village was served by two main water tanks, the larger held by the crown and the smaller by the temple. There were also a few small tanks long held by feudal lords and temple officials and a few small privately held tanks whose rights of ownership were acquired by virtue of the labour exerted in refurbishing long-abandoned ancient tanks. In exchange for use of the crown tank, villagers owed *rājakāriya*, corvée labour for the maintenance of the tank (1961: 43, 46). Tanks were open-air, so that they served as collection areas during the rainy seasons and could serve as pasturage during dry seasons (ibid.: 53). A prohibition on cultivation of the government-owned main tank was intended to prevent damage to the tank bund.

Other ground in Pul Eliya was devoted to buildings, especially to private dwellings and their accompanying small gardens. Some private dwellings were considered to be ancestral property, while a few, all held by individuals with outside status, were more recently constructed on land bought or leased from the crown. In addition to private dwellings, there were a few public buildings. The temple compound included an ancient temple, a recently built one, and a residence for the village priest. There was a separate site with a small shrine to the god Pulleyar (Ganesha). The school was owned by the government and included a residence for the schoolmaster's family. There was also a derelict medical building used by a travelling government medical officer.

Leach gives details of the thirty-nine household heads dwelling in Pul Eliya in 1954 and their distribution into thirteen compound groups (1961: 67–144). He shows how property rights were enjoyed both by individuals, male and female, and by the compound groups of kinship relations he maps. Property rights would pass from mother and father to children according to rules Leach defines. As such, land tenure at any point in time was shaped by marriages in immediately preceding generations. Particular kinship relations, for example elder brother and younger brother, were accompanied by rights and responsibilities, which Leach outlines. The local court played a major role in settling land

---

[10] The principle of private rights in land is illustrated by the case of plots of land that were undivided, i.e. owned by 'the heirs of X the previous owner' (1961: 48). These heirs, Leach asserts, were not coparceners. Rather, they were partners, 'each of whom has a separate title to a particular mathematical proportion of the total' (ibid.: 49). Each heir had clearly defined individual rights.

disputes between relations and it could evict individuals from their land and from the village with just cause. In precise detail, Leach traces the jural rules governing land tenure and the economic and legal facts he encountered – including the allocation of water, corvée duties, the history of ownership of each plot from 1889 to 1954 and the organization of labour (ibid.: 145–295).

At least two broadly relevant principles can be discerned within Leach's detailed, particular analysis of land tenure at Pul Eliya in 1954. First, Leach recognizes the discrepancies between the theory of land tenure, formulated according to legal rules, and the facts on the ground. Second, Leach asserts the primacy of ground in shaping social relations.[11] Leach writes:

> At no point in time is there ever a perfect functional fit between the facts of the kinship system and the facts of the land tenure system; both are always in a process of modification. Land tenure and kinship structure are both 'patterns of jural relationships,' but they are relative ideas which cannot be viewed separately and both are aspects of something else. The continuity of the society does not depend upon any continuing pattern of jural relationships; within certain limits the pattern can vary rapidly and quite drastically. The limits in question are not jural but topographical, the size of the tank and the shape of the field [. . .] Pul Eliya society is an ordered society, but the order is of a statistical and not a legal kind.
>
> —1961: 145

Statistical analyses of economic relations are fundamental to Leach's analysis, while jural rules governing kinship relations are considered secondary (1961: 9). He shows that unilineal descent, as treated by Sir Edward Evans-Pritchard (1940, 1951) and Alfred R. Radcliffe-Brown (1950, 1952), was not a factor at Pul Eliya. He does not propose an alternative categorization for Pul Eliya, such as a bilateral kinship structure. Rather, he emphasizes that here, 'it is locality rather than descent which forms the basis of corporate grouping' (Leach 1961: 7).

Leach's claims about statistical order in society are a response to an alternative approach that explains anthropological phenomena in what Leach regards as mystical terms (1961: 298).[12] The approach he rejects invokes social equilibrium or social solidarity as real forces, as though society itself was a real entity separate from the parts of which it is composed. For Leach, social structure, 'is a byproduct of the sum of many individual human actions, of which the participants are neither wholly conscious nor wholly unaware. It is normal rather normative' (ibid.: 300). Thus, the ground itself – including how topography, climate and geology shape its use – imposes a statistical order that anthropologists read as social structure. The land shapes kinship.

What are the implications of Leach's approach to land tenure for biblical scholars? Principally, his work serves as a caution against overly optimistic extrapolations from the relatively sparse biblical data to the social world that produced the text. While a few jural rules might be inferred from the biblical text, these are hardly sufficient to allow a reconstruction of land tenure as practised in any particular locale at any particular time in the southern Levant. Leach's work also serves as a caution against applying anthropological

---

[11] On this point, see Cohn's (1962) review of Leach.
[12] On this point, see Straus's (1961) review of Leach.

models of kinship from one setting or another onto the biblical text. While Malinowski's work on unilineal descent groups might prove generative in some contexts, it need not match the facts on the ground in ancient Israel and Judah. Only the ancient data, much of which is no longer available to the historian, could definitively establish the relationships between land tenure and kinship in the region. And yet, Leach's work also provides another kind of anthropological analogue to which biblical scholars might turn. In recent decades historians and archaeologists have emphasized the continuity in material culture between Late Bronze Age Canaan and Iron Age Israel. This data suggests that ancient Israel was indigenous. If so, how can biblical scholars explain the prevalence of kinship ideology in the Bible? Leach provides one historical example showing how residence, how locality, can be prior to and can shape kinship.

## CAROLINE HUMPHREY

Edmund Leach's student Caroline Humphrey (1983) showed how informal, unwritten rules shape human territoriality. In the 1960s and 1970s she conducted several months of fieldwork among Buryat communities on two collective farms in Siberia that coincidentally shared a name, Karl Marx kolkhoz in Selenga and Karl Marx kolkhoz in Barguzin. Humphrey's *Karl Marx Collective* is based on this fieldwork and on extensive documentary research in Russian, Mongolian and Buryat materials that had been almost entirely inaccessible to Western scholars. The Buryat had traditionally been nomadic herders. Humphrey picks up the story of land tenure among them a half a century after the formation of the Buryat-Mongol Autonomous Soviet Socialist Republic, which drastically shifted the nature of their relationship to their land.

Humphrey sets the local communities she examines within the larger political (esp. 1983: 300–72), economic (esp. 140–299) and ideological (esp. 73–117) structure of the Soviet state. Collective farms, which typically had some three to five thousand members, were set up to mirror the hierarchy of the Soviet state. In this structure, lower organizational levels report information to higher levels who act on it by providing directives to lower levels (ibid.: 2, 73–117). The collective farm is conceptualized according to four hierarchical levels, 'the enterprise management, the brigade or sector, the production team, and the household', with information and commands transmitted between these via, 'the functional organization of the kolkhoz, the Soviets, and the Party' (ibid.: 3). But reality does not match this simple model. Humphrey shows how conflict and informal social relationships play an important part in Soviet collective farms (ibid.). She places emphasis on 'unplanned for, or hidden, or heterodox, but even non-cognised, economic and social phenomena' (ibid.).

Drawing on Gluckman, Humphrey traces the hierarchy of property rights on Buryat collective farms (1983: 118–39). Humphrey identifies within Soviet collective farms, 'several levels of estates of production (households, work-teams, and brigades or sectors)' (ibid.: 6). She delineates the property rights of the chairman of the kolkhoz, the committee of the kolkhoz, the party secretary, the chairman of the rural soviet, the brigades, production units within the brigades – variously devoted to milk, sheep, horses, hay and agricultural fields – households, and individual workers. She emphasizes that individuals could hold different types of rights by virtue of occupying multiple positions within the hierarchy. 'For example, the head of a sheep-production brigade might hold rights as a Soviet citizen, as a household head, as a kolkhoznik, as a brigadier, and as a member of the Communist Party' (ibid.).

Humphrey shows that the property rights of members of the collective farm inhere in their status as kolkhoznik, 'originally derived from becoming a shareholder in the collective, but subsequently passed on to succeeding generations by virtue of birth in the family of a kolkhoznik' (1983: 5).[13] Rights, Humphrey asserts, also relate to another kind of status, membership in the Communist Party (ibid.). It is precisely because of the relationship of rights to status that property cannot adequately by summarized purely in terms of legal statutes (ibid.: 118).

One theme to which Humphrey returns in various ways is the relationship between land and other forms of property. The Soviet system within which the collective farms operate prohibits certain kinds of private transactions. As a result, 'individually owned goods tend to be used as leverage for attaining status in the public sphere, or at least for negating differences inherent in that sphere' (1983: 11). Humphrey shows that chattel rights are not subject to the same kind of hierarchy of rights that define immovable property. Shaping patterns of rights in immovable property is the fact that the kolkhoz has the right to seize private livestock that exceeded a household's legal limit (ibid.: 394).[14] This has the effect of discouraging individuals from accumulating wealth in livestock. Instead, individuals use their movable property for 'personal social influence by means of gift-debt relations' (ibid.: 11). Humphrey outlines these rituals of exchange, especially those surrounding marriage (ibid.: 378–401).

Movable property is also important at higher levels of kolkhoz administration. What Humphrey terms 'manipulable resources', especially movable goods, prove crucial to administrator's ability to negotiate with those below and above them (1983: 195–227). A central dynamic is the discrepancy between production targets set by the central government for farm administrators and the resources available to them. Administrators require cooperative labour, providing a situation in which individuals and teams can use their labour to bargain for preferential treatment and access (ibid.: 228–66). Within the internal dynamics of the collective farm, then, actors engage in legal and illegal operations to serve ends that sometimes are quite legitimate (ibid.: 227). Immovable property, and not just land, are crucial to the functioning of the farm's administrative hierarchy.

In the background to Humphrey's analysis was a perception of a crisis in Soviet agriculture caused by the apparent low productivity of collective farming and the comparatively high productivity of private farming. Humphrey shows that there is no simple opposition between the two, 'since the "rights" over the means of production and the produce are in fact distributed in a complex way over the entire range of "private" and public spheres. In other words, the "private" is not as private as it may seem, nor is the "public" as public' (1983: 1).

What are the implications of Humphrey's work for historians interested in land rights and territoriality in the ancient world? Although there are vast differences between land tenure as managed by national and international royal administrations in the ancient world and land tenure as managed within the Soviet state in the 1960s and 1970s, both involved complex interactions between local actors and larger institutional structures that cannot be fully described by recourse to the official legal system of property rights. Humphrey points the historian towards 'unplanned for, or hidden, or heterodox, but

---

[13] Humphrey notes, 'After 1969 the status of kolkhoznik was no longer inherited and became a matter of choice at the age of sixteen' (1983: 6).
[14] On this aspect of Humphrey's work, see Hill 1985.

even non-cognised, economic and social phenomena' (1983: 3) at work within systems of land tenure. Her work encourages the historian to look beyond land tenure as defined according to jurisprudential regulations and to consider a wide range of territorial strategies employed by actors at all levels of society.

## KATHERINE VERDERY

In her review of Caroline Humphrey's *Karl Marx Collective*, Katherine Verdery (1984) praises Humphrey for linking, at several categories of analysis, 'local-level forms and behavior to the overall organization and official ideology of the Soviet system'. Verdery's *The Vanishing Hectare: Property and Value in Postsocialist Transylvania* is characterized by the same effortless movement between local, regional and international actors around the question of property. Verdery takes up the story of land tenure in another part of what had been the Soviet Union some two decades after Humphrey's analysis of Soviet land tenure. She examines former state farms undergoing decollectivization in the village of Aurel Vlaicu in Romania. She traces how land in Vlaicu came once more to be held privately by families who had owned it generations earlier and she shows how land held different kinds of value for different social actors – international organizations, Romanian politicians, former members of the collective farm, local authorities, banks, courts and many others.

For Verdery, property is, 'a historical and political process' (2003: 4). A major assertion of the book is that the Western concept of property, which has 'long presumed an object-relations view of the world', is not 'universal, natural, and neutral' (ibid.: 16, 17). In fact, Verdery asserts the existence of a Soviet property regime, in which the state, socialist cooperatives and organizations, and individuals or households held various kinds of legally recognized property (ibid.: 40–76). And she usefully applies Gluckman's notion of a hierarchy of rights to the Soviet property regime (ibid.: 55–9).

While affirming the anti-colonial impulse behind Gluckman's assertion of a clearly defined system of land rights among the Lozi (2003: 15), Verdery adopts a broader definition of property than Gluckman's. She writes, 'Property is not just about bundles [of rights] but about the entire process of bringing a good into use' (ibid.: 355). Something of this broader approach is inherent in Gluckman's analysis of the relationship between property rights and social and political status, but Verdery makes the full process of bringing a good into use a much more explicit part of her analysis. Like Humphrey, then, Verdery is concerned with the relationship between formal, legally recognized rights in land and extralegal strategies, practices and ideologies related to land.

Compared to the other anthropologists we have examined here, Verdery focuses especially on the value of land.[15] At times her analysis of value relates directly to economic outcomes. In the wake of the collapse of the Soviet Bloc in 1989, Romanian households came to own land in a different way from that they had under the Soviet property regime. They held rights in land. But, Verdery asserts, 'obtaining rights often failed to generate ownership that was effective, in which owners could actually do something with their land' (2003: 4). Although land was relatively available in post-Soviet Romania, shortages in labour and capital made it difficult for landholders to realize value from their land

---

[15] On the concept of value, see Anderson's (2005) review of Verdery.

(ibid.: 212–23, 244–56). Furthermore, specific agrarian laws and policies, which Verdery discusses, often hindered the ability of households to realize value from their land (e.g. ibid.: 100–13, 132–40). The value of land also related to the social location of the owner, which could facilitate access to markets, licensing systems and equipment.[16] Without additional resources and access, 'land could become a negative rather than a positive asset' (ibid.: 114).

In Verdery's analysis, land also has value unrelated to economic outcomes. She writes, 'Throughout the decollectivization process, rights to land held multiple and conflicting significances for different actors' (2003: 9).[17] For example, collective farms under the Soviet property regime in Romania had defined value differently from how the international agencies and private firms implementing privatization in Romania defined value. What had been considered valuable was often accounted as a liability in the process of privatization (ibid.: 23). Families cared about the connection plots of land provided to their ancestors, while firm managers placed little stock in this attachment value (ibid.: 22).[18]

Verdery recognizes that value is not static. She attends to processes of valuation and devaluation, which were frequently quite rapid in the shifting political and economic context of post-Soviet Romania. And she sets these shifts in value in national and international context (e.g. 2003: 282–3). In the fluid economic and legal environment, 'One person's write-off became another's source of income' (ibid.: 23).

What are the implications of Verdery's work for biblical scholars examining land in the ancient world? Her work provides categories of analysis that allow us to interrogate ancient evidence in fresh ways. I find her focus on value especially compelling. How do actors extract value from land by utilizing social networks, accumulated capital and the like? Is there evidence that might challenge the notion of completely independent ancient households engaged in agriculture and herding on their ancestral lands? How is land valued differently by social actors? Indeed, a difference in how land is valued is central to the dramatic tension in a biblical narrative we now examine.

## READING THE STORY OF NABOTH'S VINEYARD

As an example of how these four anthropological treatments of land tenure provide categories of analysis that can help biblical scholars examining the ancient data for spatiality and territoriality let us consider the biblical story of Naboth's vineyard. 1 Kings 21 dramatizes a conflict over land (Zakovitch 1984: 382–3). The story's victim is Naboth, a Jezreelite, about whom almost nothing is known. Its villains and the targets of its literary critique are the Israelite royal family: Ahab, son of Omri, and his Phoenician wife Jezebel. Ahab, according to the story, wishes to purchase Naboth's vineyard adjoining the royal estate in order to use it as a vegetable garden. But Naboth refuses to sell. Jezebel arranges for Naboth to be executed on trumped up charges, paving the way for Ahab to take possession of the vineyard.

The story is not objective in its reporting, nor even likely to be based on a historical encounter in which Ahab met with Naboth to negotiate a land acquisition. Rather, the scribes who produced the account developed a known tradition about the murder of

---

[16] On social relations and actualizing value, see Cartwright's (2004) review of Verdery.
[17] On the different meanings attributed to land, see Hayden's (2004) review of Verdery.
[18] On attachment to ancestral lands, see especially Shipton 2009.

Naboth and his sons – a tradition reflected in 2 Kgs 9.25–26 – into the story as we have it in 1 Kings 21 with clear political intent (cf. Rofé 1988: 95–7; McKenzie 1991: 73–4; White 1994; Na'aman 2008: 202–3; Russell 2014b). The narrative aims to justify Jehu's overthrow of Ahab's royal house – described in 2 Kings 9–10 – by pointing to the royal house's abuse of territorial power.[19] The scribes who produced the account relied on the issue of land rights to convince the story's ancient audience that Ahab and his sons fully deserved their brutal murder at the hands of Jehu. Nor did scribes leave it to the audience's imagination to draw the connection.[20] Rather, the narrative presents Yahweh himself as instructing the prophet Elijah to intercept Ahab en route to the vineyard and to pronounce a death sentence against him because of this abuse of territorial power.[21]

Many wonderful historical, philological and literary studies have clarified aspects of the narrative and its function in the book of Kings.[22] Elsewhere, I have summarized some of the most compelling of these (Russell 2014a, 2014b). In the context of this handbook on social anthropology and the Bible, I wish to present another kind of analysis: how would Gluckman, Leach, Humphrey and Verdery read 1 Kings 21? How would their insights on the nature of land tenure, gained from anthropological fieldwork conducted in the twentieth century, shape their interpretation of this biblical story in its ancient literary and historical context?

Gluckman's work clarifies the legal logic of 1 Kings 21. To be sure, the narrative has a political aim. But the legal logic of land tenure provides the threads out of which the narrative weaves its political tapestry. Let us take a few of these points of law in turn. In a terse, even sparse, narrative, why does the text mention the purpose for which Ahab intends to use land? The narrative places in Ahab's mouth's the words, 'Sell me your vineyard that I may have it as a vegetable garden because it is directly beside my house' (v. 2a). Gluckman's framework for land rights provides a partial, narrowly legal answer to this question. He explicates ownership in terms of the right to use land in a particular way. Here, Ahab specifies the new use to which he will put the land. Abraham too, in the story of his purchase of Ephron's cave, notes the new use to which he hopes to put the land he buys (Gen. 23.4; Russell 2013: 162–3). And David likewise notes the new use he intends for Araunah's threshing floor (2 Sam. 24.21; Russell 2016: 16–39). As part of standard legal negotiations of sale, then, Ahab discloses the new use to which he will put the land. The narrative utilizes this disclosure in order to contrast Naboth's and Ahab's perspective on the land, as I note further below.

Why does Ahab sulk after Naboth refuses to sell him the vineyard in Jezreel? According to the narrative, following Naboth's refusal to sell Ahab returns home sullen and downcast. The narrator draws attention to Ahab's mood by depicting him as prostrate in bed, with his face turned, or perhaps twisted. The king has even lost his appetite. Scholars who read

---

[19] On the biblical presentation of Jehu's reign, see Lamb 2008; Robker 2012.
[20] The redactional history of the chapter is more complicated than can be addressed here. For different approaches to the editorial history of the narrative describing Elijah's confrontation of Ahab, see Rofé 1988; McKenzie 1991: 67, 73–4, 85–6, 94; Blum 2000; Cronauer 2005: 167–85.
[21] In our narrative, the distinctive language of the Deuteronomistic School is found in the prophetic speech in vv. 20–26. See Zakovitch 1984: 399–401; Weinfeld 1992: 18–20; Cronauer 2005: 102–9.
[22] Baltzer 1965; Andersen 1966; Seebass 1974; Würthwein 1978; Zakovitch 1984; Oeming 1986; Rofé 1988; Martin-Achard 1991; McKenzie 1991: 67–74; Westbrook 1991: 32–4; Walsh 1992; White 1994; Sarna 1997; Thiel 1999; Blum 2000; Cronauer 2005; Na'aman 2008; Halpern and Lemaire 2010: 145; Seidel 2012; Amit 2015; Fleishman 2015; Franklin, Ebeling and Guillaume 2015; Kitz 2015; Shemesh 2015; Sutskover 2015.

the narrative against the background of the purported right of ancient Near Eastern kings to confiscate land struggle to make sense of this feature of the account. But royal power over land in the ancient Near East was limited (Oden 2012; Russell 2014b). Ancient Near Eastern kings could only confiscate land in certain situations of default. For example, in an Akkadian tablet from Alalakh, AT 17 (see Wiseman 1953), King Niqmepa justifies the confiscation of property from Apra by noting that he had become a criminal (Russell 2016: 28–9). And in a tablet from ancient Ugarit written in Akkadian (Ras Shamra tablet, field no. 16.145), King Yaqauru justifies the confiscation of property from 'Ili-ba'lu by pointing to his status as a criminal (Russell 2016: 29). Gluckman's approach to land rights, which acknowledges a connection between rights and responsibilities and which recognizes the security of the rights of those lower down the hierarchy against those higher up the hierarchy, provides a fruitful framework within which to interpret 1 Kings 21. Within the narrative, Ahab sulks because he cannot violate Naboth's rights to land. This legal principle allows the narrative to set the stage for the abuse of power that will lead to the downfall of the royal family.

Why is Naboth's murder so complicated? Elsewhere in biblical narrative, the crown uses loyal military officials to dispatch its enemies with great efficiency. For example, Benaiah executes Joab at Solomon's command in 1 Kgs 2.29–34. But in 1 Kings 21, Jezebel writes and seals letters in Naboth's name to the elders of his town. They arrange for false witnesses to accuse Naboth. An assembly is held. Naboth is executed publicly. Why, within the narrative logic of the episode, is this murder so complicated? Gluckman's insights on land tenure offer a partial answer to this question. Jezebel arranges Naboth's murder precisely to produce a situation of default like the historical examples noted above in AT 17 and RS 16.145. If she had simply asked one of Ahab's military officers to dispatch Ahab, the vineyard would have passed to Naboth's heirs. But the situation of default arranged by Jezebel paves the way for Ahab to take possession of the vineyard. Of course, the default is manufactured through a false denunciation and the narrative seizes on this to justify the overthrow of Ahab's house.

Edmund Leach's work on land tenure serves as a caution to historians about extrapolating too much from the story of Naboth's vineyard in their attempts to reconstruct the system of land tenure in ninth-century BCE Samaria. To be sure, for the narrative to have accomplished its literary aim of justifying Ahab's overthrow the system of land rights it assumes it must have seemed plausible to its ancient audience. But this need only be true in a general way. One certainly cannot read the narrative as an example of the inalienability of land in ancient Israel as advocated by the jubilee laws in Leviticus 25, as some scholars have done.

In her treatment of Soviet collective farms, Humphrey emphasized the extralegal strategies, practices and ideologies that shape legal title to land. In our story too, extralegal strategies are key to the characters' attempts to maintain or obtain legal rights in land. Let us begin with the language of Naboth's refusal, 'Defilement for me from Yahweh if I should sell you my ancestral inheritance!' Why does Naboth invoke Yahweh? On the face of things, Ahab's offer to purchase the vineyard is perfectly reasonable (Seebass 1974: 477). The opening pattern of his words resembles quite closely the language of the biblical heroes Abraham (Gen. 2.4) and David (2 Sam. 24.21) in narratives about their purchase of land. And the price he offers seems fair, perhaps even generous. Naboth does not simply decline. He invokes Yahweh. This invocation is best understood against the background of ancient Near Eastern conditional self-curses, which have been carefully mapped by Anne Marie Kitz (2014: 96–133). In effect, Naboth calls down Yahweh's divine punishment on himself if he should ever sell his land to Ahab (Russell 2016: 135–6). Some commentators read Naboth's refusal as piety, as though he were following a divine sanction against alienating land also reflected in the jubilee legislation in Leviticus 25 (cf. Fohrer 1957: 72–3; Malamat 1962: 149; Baltzer 1965: 78–9; Andersen 1966: 49; Pixley 1992: 58; Fleishman 2015). But Yahweh's name is invoked here as one who will enforce the curse in the future rather than as one who has given instructions in the past. By invoking Yahweh, Naboth precludes the possibility of further negotiations with Ahab. This is the strongest form of 'No' he can utter. Ahab understands this and returns to his house forlorn. Naboth's invocation of Yahweh, then, can be read as part of an extralegal strategy for maintaining his legal title to land, a strategy that will ultimately fail.

The narrative devotes considerable attention to Jezebel's political manoeuvring. To be sure, her actions are meant to evoke a negative response from the audience (cf. Shemesh 2015). But Jezebel's actions as they are portrayed in the story also reflect broader patterns of extralegal territorial strategy in the biblical world. She employs technologies and networks of royal correspondence that are well attested in the ancient world and that have been traced in Radner (2014). She writes letters, seals with Ahab's seal, and presumably delivers the letters through messenger networks that are elided in the narrative. Jezebel also exploits the system of legal administration. Kitz (2015) sets the portrayal of Jezebel's actions within the context of historical examples of denunciation in the ancient Near East. She points out that since the directive comes from the crown itself, Jezebel knows there will be no higher authority to whom Naboth can successfully appeal once the elders of his town pass judgement on him.[23] By working with local authorities to carry out Naboth's execution, she makes them complicit in Naboth's murder and so removes the possibility of local opposition to Ahab's future use of the vineyard.

The elders and nobles of Naboth's town also engage in extralegal territorial strategy. Humphrey emphasizes the dynamics of power between centralized authority, local authorities and individual households. I suspect that the curiously repetitive references to the relationship between Naboth and the local authorities who betray him (vv. 8, 11) is designed to elicit disappointment or even shock from the audience, even as the narrative's primary critique is reserved for Ahab's house. The audience probably would have expected locals to side with one of their own against an outsider unless their fellow had wronged them in some way – compare the loyalty shown by Benjamites to one of their own in Judg. 20.12–13. But the behaviour of the elders and nobles of Naboth's town is comprehensible in the context of known patterns of territorial strategy in the ancient Near East. Town leaders negotiated between insiders and outsiders and had to reckon with the relative strength of outsiders. Towns are known to have sided with outsiders against one of their own. For example, the collective leadership of Philistine Ekron handed over their King Padi to Hezekiah of Judah, as recounted by Sennacherib in his annals.[24] The circumstances of this historical encounter differ substantially from the fictive account in 1 Kings 21. But both situations reflect the negotiated, intermediary power of local collective leadership, which engaged in a variety of extralegal strategies in

---

[23] The narrative of Absalom's quest for power in 2 Sam. 15.1–6 rests on the assumption that legal parties could appeal their cases to the crown. See Russell 2015.

[24] For a translation of the relevant section of Sennacherib's annals, see Grayson and Novotny 2012: 64–5.

order to maintain their position with respect both to those lower down and those higher up the administrative hierarchy.

Verdery attends to differences in how land is valued. Her concept of value helps the reader understand one aspect of Naboth's response to Ahab. In refusing to sell, he calls the land 'my ancestral inheritance' (v. 3). But in reporting the incident to Jezebel, Ahab places in Naboth's mouth the words 'my vineyard' (v. 6) just as his initial request was for the purchase of 'your vineyard' (v. 2). This difference in terminology points to a difference in how the actors Ahab and Naboth value the land.[25] For Ahab, the land's value consists in its ability to produce vegetables and its convenient location adjacent to the royal estate. Naboth values the land because of the connection it provides to his ancestors. He would not sell it at any price. I do not think it necessary to assume here that Naboth's ancestors were buried on this land, as some have suggested.[26] Indeed, archaeological evidence from the period suggests that burial on family land would have been quite unusual and we would therefore expect the narrative to make any such basis to Naboth's refusal more explicit.[27] All we can say from the narrative is that the vineyard provides Naboth with a connection to his ancestors. Perhaps they tended its vines, which could take decades to come to maturity (cf. Davis 2008: 112).[28] Perhaps it was simply the bequest itself that was meaningful to him. When a wide range of biblical texts emphasizing the connection between land and ancestors is considered, it is possible to contextualize Naboth's perspective on the land's value within a broader ideology of attachment to ancestral land, which is well attested in several streams of biblical tradition (Russell 2014a).[29] But 1 Kings 21 does not make the logic of Naboth's attachment explicit. Regardless, a difference in how the characters value land is at the centre of the story's dramatic tension.

In sum, I have traced in this chapter land tenure and related concepts in the work of anthropologists Max Gluckman, Edmund Leach, Caroline Humphrey and Katherine Verdery. Gluckman provides a general legal framework for understanding land rights. Leach emphasizes the statistical order of land tenure and kinship in a particular time and place. Humphrey attends to extralegal strategies, practices and ideologies that shape legal rights in land. Verdery traces how and why social actors value land. Together, these anthropologists provide useful axes of analysis for considering how land tenure functioned in the Iron Age Levant and how it is depicted in the Hebrew Bible, as I briefly illustrated with reference to the biblical story of Naboth's vineyard.

---

[25] On the difference in terminology, compare Zakovitch 1984: 388; Rofé 1988: 91; Garsiel 2015. In my view, the narrative is not meant as an allegory in which Naboth stands in for traditional, tribal, covenantal values while Ahab stands in for royal values (cf. Burnside 2011: 188–9). The narrative's critique is of the house of Ahab in particular and not of monarchy in general. Indeed, the story of Naboth is part of a larger narrative sequence that will present King Jehu quite positively.

[26] On connections between families, their dead ancestors, and family lands see Brichto 1973; Stavrakopoulou 2010.

[27] Bloch-Smith 1992 summarizes the three locations in which Iron Age burials have been discovered: on the slopes of archaeological tells, on cliffs or hills facing tells, and in a single necropolis framed by Dhahr Mirzbaneh in the south and 'Ein es-Samiya in the north. On the biblical texts reflecting an ideology of attachment to ancestral lands, see Russell 2014a.

[28] On the remains of a winery discovered at Jezreel, see Franklin, Ebeling and Guillaume 2015.

[29] Compare the description of ancestors and land in Firth 1936: 374.

# REFERENCES

Amit, Y. (2015), 'Shaping and Meaning in the Story of Naboth's Vineyard (1 Kgs 21)', *Beit Mikra: Journal for the Study of the Bible and Its World*, 60 (1): 19–36 [Hebrew].

Andersen, F.I. (1966), 'The Socio-Juridical Background of the Naboth Incident', *JBL*, 85 (1): 46–57.

Anderson, D.G. (2005), 'Review of *The Vanishing Hectare: Property and Value in Postsocialist Transylvania* by Katherine Verdery', *JRAI*, 11 (1): 184–5.

Baltzer, K. (1965), 'Naboth's Weinberg (1 Kön. 21): Der Konflikt zwischen israelitischem und kanaanäischem Bodenrecht', *Wort und Dienst* NS, 8: 73–88.

Berquist, J.L. and C.V. Camp, eds (2007), *Constructions of Space I: Theory, Geography, and Narrative*, LHBOTS 481, New York: T&T Clark.

Biebuyck, D. (1963), 'Introduction', in D. Biebuyck (ed.), *African Agrarian Systems: Studies Presented and Discussed at the Second International African Seminar, Lovanium University, Leopoldville, January 1960*, 15–16, London: Oxford University Press.

Bloch-Smith, E. (1992), *Judahite Burial Practices and Beliefs About the Dead*, JSOTSup 123, Sheffield: JSOT Press.

Blum, E. (2000), 'Die Nabotüberlieferungen und die Kompositionsgeschichte der Vorderen Propheten', in R.G. Kratz, T. Krüger and K. Schmid (eds), *Schriftauslegung in der Schrift: Festschrift für Odil Hannes Steck zu seinem 65 Geburtstag*, 111–28, Berlin: De Gruyter.

Brichto, H.C. (1973), 'Kin, Cult, Land and Afterlife – A Biblical Complex', *HUCA*, 44: 1–54.

Burnside, J.P. (2011), *God, Justice, and Society: Aspects of Law and Legality in the Bible*, Oxford: Oxford University Press.

Camp, C.V. and J.L. Berquist, eds (2008), *Constructions of Space II: The Biblical City and Other Imagined Spaces*, LHBOTS 490, New York: T&T Clark.

Cartwright, A. (2004), 'Review of *The Vanishing Hectare: Property and Value in Postsocialist Transylvania* by Katherine Verdery', *Anthropological Quarterly*, 77 (4): 871–5.

Cohn, B.S. (1962), 'Review of *Pul Eliya: A Village in Ceylon* by Edmund Leach', *JAOS*, 82 (1): 104–6.

Colson, E. (1960), *Social Organization of the Gwembe Tonga*, Manchester: Manchester University Press.

Corbin, A.L. (1919), 'Legal Analysis and Terminology', *Yale Law Journal*, 29 (2): 163–73.

Cronauer, P.T. (2005), *The Stories About Naboth the Jezreelite: A Source, Composition, and Redaction Investigation of 1 Kings 21 and Passages in 2 Kings 9*, LHBOTS 424, London: T&T Clark.

Davis, E.A. (2008), *Scripture, Culture, and Agriculture: An Agrarian Reading of the Bible*, Cambridge: Cambridge University Press.

Elias, T.O. (1951), *Nigerian Land Law and Custom*, London: Routledge and Kegan Paul.

Elden, S. (2004), *Understanding Henri Lefebvre: Theory and the Possible*, London: Continuum.

Elden, S. (2007), 'There is a Politics of Space Because Space is Political: Henri Lefebvre and the Production of Space', *Radical Philosophy Review*, 10 (2): 10–16.

Evans-Pritchard, E.E. (1940), *The Nuer*, Oxford: Oxford University Press.

Evans-Pritchard, E.E. (1951), *Kinship and Marriage among the Nuer*, Oxford: Clarendon Press.

Firth, R. (1936), *We the Tikopia: A Sociological Study of Kinship in Primitive Polynesia*, London: Allen and Unwin.

Fleishman, J. (2015), 'The Significance of Ahab's Request of Naboth, and Naboth's Response', *Beit Mikra: Journal for the Study of the Bible and Its World*, 60 (1): 92–116 [Hebrew].

Fohrer, G. (1957), *Elia*, Zurich: Zwingli.
Franklin, N., J. Ebeling and P. Guillaume (2015), 'An Ancient Winery in Jezreel', *Beit Mikra: Journal for the Study of the Bible and Its World*, 60 (1): 9–18 [Hebrew].
Garsiel, M. (2015), 'The Significance of Repetitions and Comparisons for Understanding Characters, Points of View and Messages in the Story of Naboth's Vineyard', *Beit Mikra: Journal for the Study of the Bible and Its World*, 60 (1): 37–64 [Hebrew].
George, M.K. (2009), *Israel's Tabernacle as Social Space*, AIL 2, Atlanta, GA: Society of Biblical Literature.
George, M.K. (2013), *Constructions of Space IV: Further Developments in Examining Ancient Israel*, LHBOTS 569, New York: T&T Clark.
Gluckman, M. (1943), *Essays on Lozi Land and Royal Property*, Livingstone, Northern Rhodesia: Rhodes-Livingstone Institute.
Gluckman, M. (1965), *The Ideas in Barotse Jurisprudence*, New Haven, CT: Yale University Press.
Goodenough, W.H. (1951), *Property, Kin, and Community of Truk*, New Haven, CT: Yale University Press.
Gordon, R.J. (2018), *The Enigma of Max Gluckman: The Ethnographic Life of a 'Luckyman' in Africa*, Lincoln: University of Nebraska Press.
Grayson, A.K. and J.R. Novotny (2012), *The Royal Inscriptions of Sennacherib, King of Assyria*, Winona Lake, IN: Eisenbrauns.
Halpern, B. and A. Lemaire (2010), 'The Composition of Kings', in B. Halpern and A. Lemaire (eds), *The Books of Kings: Sources, Composition, Historiography and Reception*, 123–54, Leiden: E.J. Brill.
Hayden, R.M. (2004), 'Review of *The Vanishing Hectare: Property and Value in Postsocialist Transylvania* by Katherine Verdery', *East European Politics and Societies: and Cultures*, 18 (4): 710–14.
Hill, P. (1985), 'Review of *Karl Marx Collective: Economy, Society, and Religion in a Siberian Collective Farm* by Caroline Humphrey', *Man NS*, 20 (1): 177–9.
Hohfeld, W.N. (1919), *Fundamental Legal Conceptions as Applied in Judicial Reasoning and Other Legal Essays*, ed. Walter Cook, New Haven, CT: Yale University.
Humphrey, C. (1983), *Karl Marx Collective: Economy, Society and Religion in a Siberian Collective Farm*, Cambridge: Cambridge University Press.
James, E.T. (2017), *Landscapes of the Song of Songs: Poetry and Place*, New York: Oxford University Press.
Kitz, A.M. (2014), *Cursed Are You! The Phenomenology of Cursing in Cuneiform and Hebrew Texts*, Winona Lake, IN: Eisenbrauns.
Kitz, A.M. (2015), 'Naboth's Vineyard After Mari and Amarna', *JBL*, 134 (3): 529–45.
Lamb, D.T. (2008), *Righteous Jehu and His Evil Heirs: The Deuteronomist's Negative Perspective on Dynastic Succession*, Oxford: Oxford University Press.
Leach, E.R. (1961), *Pul Eliya, a Village in Ceylon: A Study of Land Tenure and Kinship*, Cambridge: Cambridge University Press.
Lefebvre, H. (1991), *The Production of Space*, transl. D. Nicholson-Smith, Oxford: Blackwell.
Lloyd, P.C. (1962), *Yoruba Land Law*, London: Oxford University Press.
Lowie, R.H. (1920), *Primitive Society*, New York: Bonnie and Liveright.
Malamat, A. (1962), 'Mari and the Bible: Some Patterns of Tribal Organization and Institutions', *JAOS*, 82 (2): 143–50.
Malinowski, B. (1926), *Crime and Custom in Savage Society*, New York: Harcourt, Brace.
Malinowski, B. (1935), *Coral Gardens and Their Magic: A Study of the Methods of Tilling the Soil and of Agricultural Rites in the Trobriand Islands*, London: Allen and Unwin.

Martin-Achard, R. (1991), 'La vigne de Naboth (1 Rois 21) d'après des études récentes', *Études théologiques et religieuses*, 66 (1): 1–16.

McKenzie, S.L. (1991), *The Trouble with Kings: The Composition of the Book of Kings in the Deuteronomistic History*, VTSup 42, Leiden: E.J. Brill.

Meek, C.K. (1949), *Land Law and Custom in the Colonies*, London: Oxford University Press.

Merrifield, A. (1993), 'Place and Space: A Lefebvrian Reconciliation', *Transactions of the Institute of British Geographers*, 18 (4): 516–31.

Merrifield, A. (2006), *Henri Lefebvre: A Critical Introduction*, New York: Routledge.

Na'aman, N. (2008), 'Naboth's Vineyard and the Foundation of Jezreel', *JSOT*, 33 (2): 199–204.

Oden, D. (2012), 'Grapes from a Distant Vineyard: Power over Land in Ancient Syrian Legal Documents and Its Characterization in 1 Kings 21:1–16', PhD diss., New York University.

Oeming, M. (1986), 'Naboth, der Jesreeliter Untersuchungen zu den theologischen Motiven der Überlieferungsgeschichte von 1 Reg 21', *ZAW*, 98 (3): 363–82.

Økland, J., J.C. de Vos and K.J. Wenell, eds (2016), *Constructions of Space III: Biblical Spatiality and the Sacred*, LHBOTS 540, New York: T&T Clark.

Pioske, D.D. (2015), *David's Jerusalem: Between Memory and History*, New York: Routledge.

Pixley, J.V. (1992), *Biblical Israel: A People's History*, Minneapolis, MN: Fortress Press.

Prinsloo, G.T.M. and C.M. Maier, eds (2013), *Constructions of Space V: Place, Space and Identity in the Ancient Mediterranean World*, LHBOTS 576, New York: T&T Clark.

Radcliffe-Brown, A.R. (1950), 'Introduction', in A.R. Radcliffe-Brown and D. Forde (eds), *African Systems of Kinship and Marriage*, 1–85, London: Oxford University Press.

Radcliffe-Brown, A.R. (1952), *Structure and Function in Primitive Society: Essays and Addresses*, Glencoe, IL: Free Press.

Radner, K., ed. (2014), *State Correspondence in the Ancient World: From New Kingdom Egypt to the Roman Empire*, New York: Oxford University Press.

Richards, A.I. (1939), *Land, Labour and Diet in Northern Rhodesia: An Economic Study of the Bemba Tribe*, London: Oxford University Press.

Robker, J.M. (2012), *The Jehu Revolution: A Royal Tradition of the Northern Kingdom and Its Ramifications*, BZAW 435, Berlin: De Gruyter.

Rofé, A. (1988), 'The Vineyard of Naboth: The Origin and Message of the Story', *VT*, 38 (1): 89–104.

Russell, S.C. (2013), 'Abraham's Purchase of Ephron's Land in Anthropological Perspective', *BI*, 21 (2): 153–70.

Russell, S.C. (2014a), 'Ideologies of Attachment in the Story of Naboth's Vineyard', *BTB*, 44 (1): 29–39.

Russell, S.C. (2014b), 'The Hierarchy of Estates in Land and Naboth's Vineyard', *JSOT*, 38 (4): 453–69.

Russell, S.C. (2015), 'Gate and Town in 2 Sam 15:1–6: Collective Politics and Absalom's Strategy', *JAH*, 3 (1): 2–21.

Russell, S.C. (2016), *The King and the Land: A Geography of Royal Power in the Biblical World*, New York: Oxford University Press.

Russell, S.C. (2017), *Space, Land, Territory, and the Study of the Bible*, Leiden: E.J. Brill.

Russell, S.C. (2018a), 'Biblical Jubilee Laws in Light of Neo-Babylonian and Achaemenid Period Contracts', *ZAW*, 130 (2): 189–203.

Russell, S.C. (2018b), 'The Legal Background of the Theme of Land in the Book of Joshua', *Hebrew Studies*, 59: 111–28.

Sack, R.D. (1986), *Human Territoriality: Its Theory and History*, Cambridge: Cambridge University Press.

Sarna, N.M. (1997), 'Naboth's Vineyard Revisited (1 Kings 21)', in M. Cogan, B.L. Eichler, and J.H. Tigay (eds), *Tehillah le-Moshe: Biblical and Judaic Studies in Honor of Moshe Greenberg*, 119–26, Winona Lake, IN: Eisenbrauns.

Schapera, I. (1943), *Native Land Tenure in the Bechuanaland Protectorate*, Lovedale, South Africa: Lovedale Press.

Seebass, H. (1974), 'Der Fall Naboth in 1 Reg. XXI', *VT*, 24 (4): 474–88.

Seidel, H.-J. (2012), *Nabots Weinberg, Ahabs Haus, Israels Thron: textpragmatisch fundierte Untersuchung von 1 Kön 21 und seinen Bezugstexten*, Berlin: LIT.

Sheddick, V. (1954), *Land Tenure in Basutoland*, London: Statistical Office.

Shemesh, Y. (2015), '"She Sealed Them with His Seal": A Gendered Reading of the Story of Naboth's Vineyard', *Beit Mikra: Journal for the Study of the Bible and Its World*, 60 (1): 117–49 [Hebrew].

Shipton, P. (2009), *Mortgaging the Ancestors: Ideologies of Attachment in Africa*, New Haven, CT: Yale University Press.

Soja, E. (1996), *Thirdspace: Journeys to Los Angeles and Other Real-and-Imagined Places*, Cambridge, MA: Blackwell.

Stavrakopoulou, F. (2010), *Land of Our Fathers: The Roles of Ancestor Veneration in Biblical Land Claims*, LHBOTS 473, London: T&T Clark.

Straus, M.A. (1961), 'Review of *Pul Eliya: A Village in Ceylon – A Study of Land Tenure and Kinship* by E.R. Leach', *Journal of Asian Studies*, 21 (1): 121–2.

Sutskover, T. (2015), 'Space and Its Meaning in the Narrative of Naboth's Vineyard', *Beit Mikra: Journal for the Study of the Bible and Its World*, 60 (1): 65–91 [Hebrew].

Thiel, W. (1999), 'Der Todesrechtsprozeß Nabots in 1 Kön 21', in S. Beyerle, G. Mayer and H. Strauß (eds), *Recht und Ethos im Alten Testament: Gestalt und Wirkung: Festschrift für Horst Seebass zum 65. Geburtstag*, 72–6, Neukirchen-Vluyn: Neukirchener.

Verdery, K. (1984), 'Review of *Karl Marx Collective: Economy, Society, and Religion in a Siberian Collective Farm* by Caroline Humphrey', *Contemporary Sociology*, 13 (6): 745–6.

Verdery, K. (2003), *The Vanishing Hectare: Property and Value in Postsocialist Transylvania*, Ithaca, NY: Cornell University Press.

Walsh, J.T. (1992), 'Methods and Meanings: Multiple Studies of 1 Kings 21', *JBL*, 111 (2): 193–211.

Warf, B. and S. Arias, eds (2009), *The Spatial Turn: Interdisciplinary Perspectives*, Abingdon: Routledge.

Waters, J.L. (2015), *Threshing Floors in Ancient Israel: Their Ritual and Symbolic Significance*, Minneapolis, MN: Augsburg Fortress.

Wazana, N. (2013), *All the Boundaries of the Land: The Promised Land in Biblical Thought in Light of the Ancient Near East*, transl. L. Qeren, Winona Lake, IN: Eisenbrauns.

Weinfeld, M. (1992), *Deuteronomy and the Deuteronomic School*, Winona Lake, IN: Eisenbrauns.

Westbrook, R. (1991), *Property and the Family in Biblical Law*, JSOTSup 113, Sheffield: JSOT Press.

White, M.C. (1994), 'Naboth's Vineyard and Jehu's Coup: The Legitimation of a Dynastic Extermination', *VT*, 44 (1): 66–76.

Wilson, G. (1938), *The Land Rights of Individuals Among the Nyakyusa*, Livingstone, Northern Rhodesia: Rhodes-Livingstone Institute.

Wiseman, D.J. (1953), *The Alalakh Texts*, Occasional Publications of the British Institute of Archaeology at Ankara 2, London: British Institute of Archaeology.
Wittfogel, K.A. (1957), *Oriental Despotism: A Comparative Study of Total Power*, New Haven, CT: Yale University Press.
Würthwein, E. (1978), 'Naboth-Novelle und Elia-Wort', *ZTK*, 75 (4): 375–97.
Zakovitch, Y. (1984), 'The Tale of Naboth's Vineyard: 1 Kings 21', in M. Weiss (ed.), *The Bible from Within: The Method of Total Interpretation*, 379–405, Jerusalem: Magnes Press.

# CHAPTER TWENTY-THREE

# The anthropology of iconography in ancient Palestine

ANGELIKA BERLEJUNG

## INTRODUCTION

Contrary to the opinion that, because of the Old Testament's ban against images, there were no pictorial representations in ancient 'Israel' – a once common view still held in some circles – there is an abundance of iconographic source material in the region going back to the earliest periods and extending without a break up into the Islamic period, and this abundance of iconographic material is growing steadily thanks to ongoing excavations. For quite some time now, the material from Palestine (the coastland and West and East Jordan) and its neighbouring regions (Egypt, Syria, Cyprus, Anatolia, Mesopotamia, Iran etc.) has been collected and studied within the framework of individual scientific disciplines like prehistorical studies, Classical or ancient Near Eastern archaeology, Egyptology, Art History etc. It was Othmar Keel and his school in Fribourg, Switzerland who established biblical iconography in the 1970s as a distinctive discipline which lead to a series of publications collecting and studying the pictorial material from or about (e.g. the Assyrian reliefs of Lachish) Palestine/Israel (Keel 1977, 1992, 1997; Winter 1983; Schroer 1987; Herrmann 1994, 2002, 2006; Uehlinger 1997, 2001; *CSAPI*; *GGG*; *GGIG*; Keel and Staubli 2001; Keel and Schroer 2004; *IPIAO*). Keel did not really develop a method of art interpretation by himself, but accepted and used the methods as they had been coined and introduced by the art historian Erwin Panofsky (1932, 1939, 1994a, 1994b) in the first half of the twentieth century. Panofsky's method gives rise to a three-step method, beginning with phenomenological description of the pictorial elements (style, motifs etc.), followed by iconographic-analytical allocation of pictorial representations to specific themes, and ending in iconological interpretation of the actual meaning of a representation in its intellectual-historical context. The basic assumption is that pictorial repertoires and their associated meanings are not arbitrary, but have been standardized by models, tradition and technical competence. Because there is a high degree of system conformity of the artefacts, the pictures can be interpreted (in the third step) as an indicator of their period, culture and society.

For a special *biblical* iconography the point is made that it has to be understood as part of the methodological study of the religion of ancient Israel and Judah in connection with historical and religious-historical work on and with the Old Testament. Biblical iconography, or rather the iconography of Palestine or the iconography of the biblical world, has the task of researching the visual sign system of the ancient Israelite/Judean religion and its historical development. To the same degree that biblical iconography deals with images as part of the world of the Old (and New) Testament, it also enters into a constructive dialogue with text-oriented biblical studies. It can contribute substantially to the understanding of biblical texts and needs to be viewed as an additional and corrective tool to traditional text-oriented historical-critical biblical studies (on the relation between images and the Bible see Bonfiglio 2016: 37–63, more generally on images and texts and 'iconographic exegesis' see Bonfiglio 2016: 64–116; see also de Hulster, Strawn and Bonfiglio 2015).

In a combination of Panofsky and standard archaeological methods, the archaeological methods for dating and contextualizing the material image-bearing objects are used (as e.g. stratigraphy, the use of datable parallels, less often C14), the researcher describes the pictorial material in terms of their image-bearing objects, techniques, peculiarities in style, individual motifs and 'constellations' of meaning (complexes of ideas and stories reduced to the icon[1]), pictorial themes, pictorial organization etc., and analyses them in terms of picture composition and themes. Based on the assumption that images are artefacts, which follow a system of norms, conventions and rules specific to religion, culture or social group that can be (re)constructed empirically on the basis of surviving pictorial documents, the researcher usually begins with the reconstruction of the rules according to which a culture produces its images, distributes them and assigns meaning to them. He tries to interpret the individual pictorial programmes by using parallels, captions or by relating them to other sources (e.g. texts). The researcher seeks to contextualize the iconographic sources, for example by grouping motifs into a typology, arranging them regionally or diachronically, and by studying them in terms of the history of styles and motifs as well as in terms of general cultural, social and religious history. For the assessment of the significance of pictures for religious communication, the genre of the image carriers, their material, the context of their use or dissemination are to be taken into account, including aspects of media and communication theory.

In spite of the term biblical iconography, the analysis is not at all limited in scope to the short span of time related in the Hebrew Bible (mid-second millennium until second century BCE) but extends deep into the other periods as well (see *IPIAO*). This is particularly promising because it allows structures and themes of a *longue durée* to be traced back even to pre-scriptural periods. The material provides valuable information about the life and ideas of a specific region, epoch and culture, as well as about prominent intercultural contacts and sometimes even fashion trends in a given period. The depiction and representation of human beings or anthropological issues (e.g. the iconography of birth, death, honour, gender etc.) are usually embedded in these studies without giving them a special attention.

Although biblical iconography is concerned with the analytical study and synthetic historical interpretation of ancient Near Eastern pictorial sources, the terms 'image' and 'picture' and the processes of their cognition are mostly underdetermined (see now Bonfiglio 2016: 171–94, referring to Thomas W.J. Mitchell, David Freedberg and Alfred

---

[1] For the term 'constellation' as used here, see *GGIG*: §6.

Gell) or adopted from neighbouring sciences. Thus, semiotic methods of image theory and interpretation are sometimes used when images were considered as signs and carriers of meaning (Sonesson 1993; Schelske 1997; Scholz 2004; Lobinger 2012) and the 'reading' of pictures with the levels of visual syntax, semantics and pragmatics is included. Less established is the approach based on phenomenology or perception theory (Wiesing 2000, 2005, 2016), which considers pictures as 'artificial presences', whose necessary key characteristic is the 'mere visibility' for visual perception, which (in contrast to the anthropological theory of images) can also arise without any human intervention.

Communication-theoretical orientations are also applied, which (partly in combination with semiotic approaches) can easily be assigned to overarching cultural-anthropological studies, so that aspects of communication, performance and relevance to action are included (Uehlinger 2000; Bonatz 2002a, 2002b; Frevel 2005). In addition, there are first approaches that want to make the constructivist approach fruitful (for an overview see Weibel 2001; Weissenrieder and Wendt 2005) for the analysis of ancient Near East pictorial material, also in connection with sociological (Bourdieu 1996 [1992]) aspects (Berlejung 2017b, 2021a, 2021b).

Even if the sign status as a conceptual criterion of a pictorial theory is controversial (and even more Charles Sanders Peirce's [1983, 1991] three categories of signs: icon, index and symbol) and is rejected by representatives of phenomenology, perception theory (Wiesing 2016) and anthropological image theory (see below), there is fundamental agreement that images are media that can be divided into three parts:

- what the picture refers to (the depicted object or denotation; in semiotics: extension);
- the picture-bearing object (material expression; in semiotics: carrier of signs); and
- the pictorial object's characteristics (content, meaning, significance, connotation, iconic type or depiction; in semiotics: attributes referenced by the sign/intension).

A picture is the unity of this three-part difference and is involved in various processes of perception, memory, communication and distribution.

It is clear that the study of the cognitive construction processes of the individual must be complemented by a theory of social systems, so that the embedding of cognitive construction processes in social and cultural processes that influence and condition them has to be included. Pictures are produced by people for people, perceived by people and, in the case of a successful cognition and communication process, recognized and understood, disseminated and passed on (or destroyed) by people. Pictures motivate people to positioning or actions. This brings us to the starting point of an anthropological theory of images.

## *HOMO PICTOR* AND ANTHROPOLOGICAL PICTORIAL THEORIES

With the search for an essentialist definition, an anthropology can aim at the production or identification of an unambiguous distinction – a *differentia specifica* – which is to guarantee the identity of being human. Hans Jonas gave a clear answer to this with his essay 'Homo pictor und die Differentia des Menschen', first published in 1961. With 'man as image creator' Jonas (2010a) describes the *differentia specifica* of humans compared to animals, because only *Homo sapiens* has the ability to create a picture which represents the presence of absence. The pictorial competence of man – who is therefore described as *Homo pictor* – is decisive for him and justifies speaking of a picture-anthropology. This anthropology wants to formulate an anthropological constant and to examine the making and recognizing of pictures as an exclusive ability of humankind. While in the course of the heterogeneous research in image science or picture theory (German: *Bildwissenschaft*) of the last thirty years (keyword: 'visual/pictorial turn') a consensus on what is to be understood by an image and picture could hardly be found anymore, Jonas was still sure that one could quickly agree on a definition of picture/image. He himself got by with the minimal condition that similarity is a constitutive characteristic of pictoriality, and that a picture (and the similarity) must have been produced intentionally. What makes *Homo pictor* human is, therefore, the ability of intentional image production, and above all the condition underlying this ability: freedom. Each making of a picture presupposes a decision process, which concerns material, scale, style, colour, motif choice and much more.

Because for Jonas this making of a picture always implies the making of a reference to reality, degrees of freedom already lie in the choice of the way of this reference. For Jonas, the degrees of freedom increase from the image-immanent compulsion of incomplete similarity, to the possibility of an own artistic style, up to the creation of never seen, thus freely invented, forms. Thus, the freedom of *Homo pictor* consists above all in the possibility of appropriating the world and reality (which serve as a template for the pictorial realization) in a picture. This freedom of forming corresponds to the freedom of seeing (Jonas 2010b).

Since Hans Jonas's essentialist definition of being human (in contrast to being animal) as *Homo pictor* ('man as creator of pictures') in 1961 and his understanding of pictures as a form of appropriation of reality (with incomplete similarity), the anthropological picture theory has developed further (understood as anthropology in the sense of historical and cultural anthropology); it rightly refers to the fact that pictures are produced as a cultural process, as a specific cultural strategy by people for people. Alfred Gell (1998) is worth mentioning. He sketched an anthropological theory of visual arts that focused (less on art production as the *differentia specifica* of humankind as Jonas did but) on the social context of art production, circulation and reception. As a theory of the nexus of social relations involving works of art, Gell suggests that art objects should not be seen as signs, bearers of meaning or aesthetic values, but as forms mediating social action. Thus in certain contexts, 'art objects are the equivalent of persons, or more precisely, social agents' (Gell 1998: 7), whose immediate interactive fields of action in social processes are central. Consequently they 'have to be treated [. . .] as person-like; that is, sources of, and targets for, social agency' (ibid.: 96). Since images are treated as living persons in the context of worship and cult, he offers a general theory of (mainly Greek) idolatry and artefacts as interaction partners. This fits into his definition of 'art as a system of action, intended to change the world rather than encode symbolic propositions about it' (ibid.). With his action-centred approach and his focus on social agency he is not that far from the prospective aspects of images that have been observed in constructivist theories, or from media- and communication-theoretical approaches that match with cultural-anthropological issues as e.g. the role of images in non-verbal communication, as archives and transfer modes of collective memory and as active agents within social interaction processes.

Hans Belting has devoted himself to the origins of pictorial art and claimed a 'close and fundamental interrelation (and interaction) of image, body and medium as components in every attempt at picture-making' (Belting 2011: 3). In terms of image anthropology, he considers the living human body as the locus of images, since it is the body that perceives, identifies/recognizes and generates images – materially and mentally. Images, especially mental ones, i.e. imagination and fantasy, cannot be separated from the body (ibid.: 37–61). His body-centred anthropological image theory emphasizes the coordinates of body, time and space, the performativity of images, involves memory (individual as well as collective), possible memory transformations and imagination, and interprets image seeing as action (Schuhmacher-Chilla 2018).

## PICTORIAL ANTHROPOLOGICAL CONCEPTS

While the previous section was about human-based image/picture theories, this section will be devoted to picture-based concepts of humankind. Thus, it is no longer a question of how the concept and term 'image' and 'picture' is defined from the human being, but how the human being is defined in visible material images. This approach deals with the history, practice and a critical discourse about how one communicates anthropological concepts pictorially.

In the specialist literature, one of the terms used here is visual anthropology. Visual anthropology is a subfield of sociocultural anthropology (understood as the study of patterns of behaviour in human societies and cultural variations) and encompasses the anthropological study of all visual representations. Visual anthropology wants to complete textual research and claims to have a holistic view: human artefacts of the present or past are not merely an object of art or merely a product of culture but active sites of cultural practice. They are a window into the customs, techniques, practices, social organization, ideas, processes, concepts or constructs of reality, access to and transfer of resources, and capitals of the respective time of its production.

With the study of iconographic sources, visual anthropology therefore contributes to the (re-)construction of history of humankind in terms of anthropological constants as well as in cultural changes and processes in very different aspects. There are several possible approaches to the field: e.g. visual anthropology as the sociocultural and historical study of pictorial media, or visual culture or as an inclusive sociocultural anthropology of visual communication. The key questions for the anthropologist are how the pictures operate to mediate human communication, and how such mediation is embedded in broader social and historical processes. The historically oriented visual anthropologist is a scholar of the visible and pictorial world of antiquity but he is also an image-maker himself even if he is not creating pictures but synthetic images of the past.

Based on the assumption that pictures are embedded in materiality and in a variety of social, cultural, religious, anthropological processes, concepts, agencies and strategies, the following paragraphs try to sketch some insights about the human being, *emically* by an inside-view, reconstructing a culture's own implicit and explicit assumptions about the human being as such and its group members in particular [cf. Chapter 11 in this volume]. For the interpretation of concrete iconographical material from ancient cultures, in our actual context of ancient 'Israel', more precisely the Southern Levant, the aforementioned meta-reflexive systematic considerations on iconography, anthropological pictorial theories, pictorial anthropological concepts and empirical and historical issues have to be tied together. The remainder of the chapter will focus upon the study of pictorial material from the Southern Levant in the Iron Ages as representing the 'inside perspective' and on the Assyrian reliefs depicting the siege of Lachish (post–701 BCE) and the Black Obelisk of Shalmaneser III (858–824 BCE) representing an 'outside perspective' on the local population. These depictions are taken as sources for (re)constructing the images of the human being in general and of the Israelites/Judeans in particular regarding the following topics:

1. gendered corporeality, status of honour,
2. roles and functions of human beings and their social relationships and
3. the relationship of human beings to nature and their environment.

Cultural-anthropological and social science interpretation and modelling have identified various cultural guidelines and core values that were part of the collective thinking style in ancient Israel and Judah as supra-individual predetermined mindsets. They were passed on from generation to generation through texts and images. According to this the following parameters were valid through the ages:

1. the collectivist/dyadic/constellational/social (role) conformist model of personality = life as being embedded in social associations (clan, family, etc.), connectivity and identity formation through recognition of others;
2. agonism = social life as permanent competition for honour, as well as honour/shame as the centre of the social code of values;
3. binary gender-constructs with the attribution of given gender roles; and
4. the hierarchization of each social unit.

These four points will be included in the following, as they provide starting points such as categories for the interpretation and understanding of the pictorial sources. Before we start with the first subsection, some special characteristics of the ancient pictorial material of the Southern Levant (and of the ancient Near East) have to be mentioned briefly:

- Palestine, Israel and Judah were part of the ancient Near East, thus the ancient Near East is the horizon of understanding of the textual and of the pictorial sources (Berlejung 2017a). This is evidenced in the Masoretic Text among other things, by numerous loan words from languages related to Hebrew (e.g. Aramaic, Akkadian, Arabic), and in the iconography inter alia by the integration and reception of pictorial motifs from the neighbouring cultures.

- What is true for images in general, is true for the ancient Near East (including the Southern Levantine) images: they present complex contents to the viewer simultaneously (more correctly in terms of perception psychology: in a very short time; Scholz 2004: 109): the relationship of several single elements to each other and to the whole is fixed in the picture and recognizable at a glance. Therefore, proportions of the human body, complex social connections, hierarchies or spatial relationships are easier and faster to comprehend through a pictorial representation than through a textual description.

- The pictorial representation can have a 'natural' similarity to the thing to be depicted, which seems to allow recognition on the basis of assigning similarities between image and depicted object without the need for prior training or instruction. Nevertheless, the competence to recognize and understand images and to produce comprehensible images had to be acquired by ancient people as well.

- Much of the art was commissioned by the elite upper class. Especially, depictions that were made for displaying prestige, or the rulership of the depicted king or deity needed to go conform with the political or theological programmes (Berlejung 2017b).

- Nature, landscapes, plants, animals, realia and objects of daily use (such as bowls, altars or weapons) or even non-elitist people in practical activities (such as hunting, praying or singing) are usually depicted (even if sometimes schematic) in naturalistic proportions (*IPIAO* 4: Figure 1684, Kuntillet ʿAjrud, Iron Age IIB). However, these pictures are not to be understood as verisimilar depictions or copies of a reality (Bahrani 2003: 87–93), but rather as its interpretation. They are not intended to mimic but to change the world and the view of the onlooker. This means that depictions of beasts, nature, landscapes or persons are idealized/stylized and do not correspond to their natural setting, actual geographical features or their actual age or physical condition. Any indications of deviations of the ideal, destruction or decay are also stylized but always attributed to the 'other', enemy or foreign country.

- Representations of humans, especially members of the elites and kings, and deities were idealized/stylized. They were not conceived as portraits; instead, persons and gods are shown as representatives of a certain role or function. Thus, for example, the Israelite king Jehu of Israel on the Black Obelisk of the Assyrian king Shalmaneser III is depicted in the same manner and attitude of humility as the subdued king Sua of Gilzanu (an area in modern Azerbaijan) on the same side of the stele. Little or no attention was paid to individual features, either of human beings or of deities. Hierarchic scaling can play a role for indicating hierarchies and high rank; however, more significant seems to be the clothing, decoration, headdresses, gesture, the objects held in the hands and the arrangement of accompanying pictorial elements. Perhaps the colouring has to be added which is lost in most cases.

- Particularly typical is the form of depiction of anthropomorphically designed figures (humans and gods) in flat reliefs or in paintings. Here (as in Egypt) the head is depicted in profile from the side, an eye, shoulders and chest from the front, the hips and legs from the side (*IPIAO* 4: Figure 1440, Beth Zur, Iron Age IIB). This striking stylistic element is called 'aspective' (cf. Emma Brunner-Traut (e.g. 1992); e.g. *IPIAO* 4: Figure 1669; Kuntillet ʿAjrud painting Iron Age IIB). Frontality is possible ('woman in the window', e.g. *IPIAO* 4: Figure 1556, Samaria Iron Age IIB), for some pictorial groups even characteristic, e.g. plaques, cult stands or masks (cf. Berlejung, Kohlhaas and Stein 2018) but especially for paintings, bas-reliefs, ivories (with the aforementioned exception) and seals uncommon.

- The depth of the space is usually not depicted. Homogeneous groups (e.g. breads, animals, people) are geometrically precise ordered upwards or backwards so that the number can be counted from the top view (*IPIAO* 4: Figure 1671, cylinder seal, Tell es-Saʿidiye, Iron Age IIB [breads]).

- Events that followed one after the other in time, are displayed right beside each other (cf. relief of Lachish, SW Palace in Nineveh, reign of Sennacherib).

- *Horror vacui*. Empty spaces are usually filled in. It is not always clear how the filling relates to the main motif.

- No distinction was made between craftsman and artist, signatures by name are uncommon.
- The aforementioned characteristics are partly also valid for Egyptian, Syrian and Mesopotamian art. Artefacts found or made in the Southern Levant are characterized by a certain mixed or hybrid style that mirrors the internationalization of society and the setting of Palestine within the multicultural sphere influenced by Egypt (see the iconography of the ruler in Kuntillet ʿAjrud *IPIAO* 4: Figure 1669, Iron Age IIB), Syria, Phoenicia, Mesopotamia (see the iconography of the ruler on the sherd from Ramat Rahel, cf. *IPIAO* 4: Figure 1943, Iron Age IIC), Minor Asia, Persia, Cyprus and (with increasing influence in the Achaemenid period) Greece.

## *The gendered corporeality and status of honour*

Since humans are mostly depicted as living or dying/dead bodies in iconography, a body-oriented visual anthropology (Schroer and Staubli 2017 [1998]) makes sense, which is closely connected to the construct of the body in ancient Israel/Judah. That body perception and evaluation (and its depiction) is a cultural construct has now been extensively studied (Asher-Greve 1998; Berlejung 2009, 2012, 2021c [ideal male and female bodies in the Song of Songs]). The concepts and pictures of human bodies are culturally generated and mediated; they are inherently subject to cultural interpretations and culturally determined attributions of meaning and conventions of representation.

The social construction concerns the corporeality of the living body and that of the corpse. It is noticeable that pictures of human bodies are clearly binarily gendered, so that men and women can be easily distinguished. In larger representations, the primary and secondary sexual characteristics are clearly recognizable, in smaller ones often less, which is due to the quality of the image. However, despite schematic representation, one can assume that men are depicted when one sees schematic figures in a short kilt with bare legs in walking position (*IPIAO* 4: Figure 1351 scaraboid from Tell Halif, Iron Age IIA). Women usually wear floor-length robes and are less expansive in posture. The hair length or a veil or a visible beard are also often decisive. In general, there are quantitatively far fewer depictions of women than of men, which is probably due to the fact that women (and children) were socially located in the inner, domestic sphere, which is less frequently thematized in pictorial media than public space or courtly, economic or martial life, in which men played the central role.

In the context of a biblical, text-oriented anthropology, it is common to start from the human body and to trace the meaning of individual body parts (Wolff 1994 [1973]: §2–9; Schroer and Staubli 2017 [1998]). This approach seems to be of limited suitability for pictorial material, as the picture interpreter must counter the danger of reading textual implications into the depiction of a human body. Human bodies are mostly depicted quite naturalistically, but e.g. the biblical focus on the human face with the forehead, eyes, nose, ears and mouth, and the meanings associated with these body parts in the texts (forehead as the seat of pride and stubbornness; ears as the seat of wisdom, understanding, hearing; eyes as the seat of desire, envy, demand; nose as the seat of anger and patience; mouth as the place of speech, prayer, singing and eating) can hardly be transferred linearly to the pictures. The heads and faces on pictorial sources are mostly depicted schematically with the anatomical parts, but without individualizing features, emotions or qualitative character differentiations (e.g. pride, envy, desire, anger). If individual features can be identified on faces, their emotionally controlled composure is striking (e.g. *IPIAO* 4: Figure 1669, Kuntillet ʿAjrud painting Iron Age IIB), with which the depicted person turns towards his viewer or the neighbouring pictorial elements in the respective pictorial context.

In the iconography, the representation of the physical integrity of the living human being is of essential importance. At the same time, it becomes clear that the human body is very vulnerable, so that clothing has a protective function, but is also charged with sociocultural meaning (see below). Ideally, the human body is complete, intact, well proportioned and without deformities from the head down to the feet. In the ruler's self-portrayal as preserved, for example, in the statue of Yarih-ʿezer from Amman (Berlejung 2017b: 170–4 and Figure 3), in addition to this emotionally controlled composure, the face and body ideals are: symmetry, the controlled tension and closed arrangement of the body limbs, a body hierarchy that grants more detail to the head/top and the front than to the feet/bottom and the back. It is possible that traits of an 'archaic smile' (actually an element of Greek art from *c.* seventh century BCE), can be identified in this statue or other representations of rulers (e.g. painting from Ramat Rahel, cf. *IPIAO* 4: Figure 1943, Iron Age IIC; faience head from Tel Abel Beth Maacah, cf. Yahalom-Mack, Panitz-Cohen and Mullins 2018, Iron Age IIA). This is a mimic convention evoked by indicating the slight raising of the corners of the mouth or even just the tightening of the sulcus nasolabialis or the protrusion of the cheekbones. Bared teeth are not shown to express laughter or anger, because this would probably contradict the social ideal of emotional countenance that characterizes the ruler.

The hairstyle of men and women is depicted according to the prevailing convention, although in Palestine conventions overlap: while Egypt and Egyptian-influenced depictions of men show shaved, beardless heads or heads with wigs (*IPIAO* 4: Figure 1401, faience head from Yoqneam, Iron Age IIB), Asian-styled men are characterized by half-length hair and beard (*IPIAO* 4: Figure 1943, painted sherd from Ramat Rahel [Cornelius 2015], Iron Age IIC; faience head of a figurine from Tel Abel Beth Maacah Iron Age IIA, cf. Yahalom-Mack, Panitz-Cohen and Mullins 2018). Thick, dark hair and beard growth signal health, vitality and youth in the living man and belong to the body ideal as it is sedimented in pictures and in biblical texts. Socially and in texts, thick hair on the heads of men and women is also connoted with eroticism and the dynamism of the living human body, which in fact constitutes its beauty. The dynamism of the human being can also be translated into colour when the skin of the idealized human being is figuratively marked with the colour red (Yarih-ʿezer, see Berlejung 2017b: Figure 3; painting from Kuntillet ʿAjrud, cf. *IPIAO* 4: Figure 1669, Iron Age IIB; limestone statue of a naked male from Khirbet al-Mudayna, Iron Age IIB cf. Daviau forthcoming) which also stands for vitality in texts. In contrast, the faience head of an elite man from Tel Abel Beth Maacah (Yahalom-Mack, Panitz-Cohen and Mullins 2018, Iron Age IIA) stands out with its white face, from which the brown hair, brown beard and naturalistic brown eyes are clearly distinguished.

The physiognomic ideal of bright eyes that radiate dynamism is quite tangible in texts, but not in the pictorial material of the Southern Levant. This is at least partly due to the state of preservation. The eyes of the statue of Yarih-ʿezer were perhaps designed with shining inlays, but these are no longer preserved. What they might have looked like can be deduced from a find from Ashdod-yam, where naturalistically shaped bronze eye outlines were found together with the inlays of white shells that represented the eyeballs; a rounded shape was given for the iris and pupil, but the ancient inlays were lost (Iron Age IIB/C; Berlejung and Fantalkin 2017).

The bodily integrity of the living person is further usually depicted in such a way that the human body can be seen in its completeness in orderly movements, standing upright, walking or sitting (rarely lying on the bed, cf. lovers). The living person is in control of his body. The living body, when embedded in more complex pictorial contexts, as in seals, paintings or reliefs, stands in relation to other persons, deities, living beings or objects, which can be expressed by the turning of the face, arms, hands or the position of the feet. Gestures are interaction and are depicted according to social conventions: an arm raised to strike represents aggression, two arms raised to the sky are gestures of prayer, two arms placed on the head are gestures of mourning, the right hand raised in greeting/blessing indicates positive attention, and the forehead on the ground indicates submission. There also seems to be a certain higher esteem of the right as opposed to the left half of the body, for it is often the right hand that is iconographically raised in greeting by gods and humans in encounter, which probably corresponds to the convention of real social greeting gestures. Thus, the depiction of a body signals not only the physical presence of a person, but also a relationship and encounter. For pictorial art, people are primarily bodies that relate to each other or to their world in a way that is towards or away from them – but always in some way. This basic definition of being human as being a relational being in the picture can be correlated with the Hebrew concepts and terms of the body. They are relationally connoted with communicative meaning (Dietrich 2015). It also fits together with central texts of biblical anthropology that emphasize the human being's turn towards communication and interaction partners.

When living (i.e. under tension) human bodies are visually related to each other, this relationship can be further qualified by the positioning of the bodies (one above, one below) and by the representation of posture and gesture, i.e. with the posture of arm, hand and foot. In the pictorial representation of the body, head and limbs thus not only have a general relational and communicative aspect, but are also used to hierarchize the relationship of the interaction partners. If a human body is under the foot or under the raised arm of another being (human, divine or zoomorphic), or is forced by the latter's hand into a body position (e.g. kneeling) that it would not assume without this force, it is quite clearly classified as deprived of its integrity, mobility and thus inferior. The arm, hand and foot in dynamics also appear in textual sources in the field of interpersonal encounters with communicative, interactive and juridical significance. Their position expresses existing hierarchies in interactions. Physical integrity also stands for the status of a person's bodily honour. In pictorial media, this status can be expressed not only through the depiction of an intact, upright body that is not exposed to attack, but also through hierarchic scaling. This means that superior persons in the standing area stand higher or are depicted larger than subordinates. The challenge to the honour status of the opponent is expressed iconographically through corresponding postures or gestures that attempt to physically immobilize or dominate the opponent. Violence is always physical violence; a verbal attack cannot be depicted.

The social status of people is differentiated iconographically by their clothing, headgear, jewellery, insignia or furniture. This corresponds to the social experience that simple people have simple clothes, whereas luxurious clothes and jewellery as well as throne furniture correspond to a higher social status. Economic capital is closely related to social and symbolic capital. The exclusive status of a king's bodily honour and access to capital is visually translated in depictions of kings in such a way that thrones or pedestals, clothes, crowns, jewellery and insignia clearly distinguish him from other mortals. Rulers are sometimes approximated to anthropomorphic gods in the depiction, from whom they often differ only in details that are difficult to recognize (such as the divine crown of horns, insignia). Rulers standing in a pictorial context together with a deity and on the same stand line appear in physical proximity to deities and entitled to access the sacred space (Baluʿa stele, Iron Age I; see Berlejung 2017b: 158–69, Figure 1). Sharing the luxury setting and the gestures of dominance, iconographically only kings can claim to be the representative image of god. It is well known that biblical anthropology (Genesis 2–3) democratized this exclusive view of kingship. For the Old Testament, every male-female human being is a representative image of god, obliged to take over royal responsibilities toward Yahweh, his neighbour and creation.

From the previous section it is clear that the notion of 'nakedness' stood in opposition to clothing and was imbued with sociocultural meaning. Clothing was considered 'normative', while nakedness was situational, and nudity restricted to specific contexts and spheres (Asher-Greve and Sweeney 2006: 125–31): mythic/religious (the naked goddess through the ages, the naked Horus-child, Bes, the nude male hero from the late Persian period onward as evidenced by bullae from Wadi Daliyeh, and Persian period seals, bullae and coins featuring Heracles and other Greek gods, see Pyschny 2019), cultic/ritual, war (prisoners of war), lovemaking, sports (swimming) and death (naked dead bodies of slain enemies). The clothed body stood in contrast to the unclothed body in order to signify rank and status (elite versus non-elite, prestige versus humiliation), honour versus shame, binary gender differences and sexuality or age (children versus adults). Childhood nudity, nakedness during erotic encounters and sports or the loss of clothing in captivity may reflect situations in real life. But they also express the fact that the naked bodies of children, captives, sportsmen and lovers are also highly vulnerable and exposed to the support, goodwill or respect of their human interaction partners.

The depiction of nudity is a provocation to the viewer. This is true for all kinds of depictions of unclothed adult human bodies, erotic or not. Erotic nudity depicts an unclothed adult living human body in intact corporal integrity and in self-control of its movements; it evokes desire or is an object of desire, enhances pleasure, and/or is a sexual object, attracting the viewer of the picture personally and positively. Naked adult bodies whose corporal integrity is disturbed and who lost self-control or even are under control of a dominating god, person or beast provoke social distancing. Pictorial media of this type surely teach the viewer to avoid to get into a similar situation.

The maximum loss of honour and social status iconographically coincides with the loss of life. Several

> visual forms of dying and dead human bodies can be differentiated relatively clearly. Here, it is noticeable that in each case the depiction of the dead/dying person in the context of the picture is always in relation to (at least) one living body (optically marked as such by height, upright position), be it a human being, animal, hybrid creature or god.
>
> —Berlejung 2021b: 373

Iconographically, the human body that lies disarticulated, unnaturally twisted and lifeless on the ground, whose drooping limbs indicate that there is no longer any purposeful ability to move, is limp, mutilated or naked, has lost body control and limbs and can no longer fend off attacks by animals or enemies, is clearly assigned to the sphere of death (for examples see Berlejung 2021b). Dying bodies are distinguished from dead bodies by the fact that they lie on the ground or are about to go down, whereby a movement and tension posture of the body is still recognizable (extremities or head). A body that is still capable of movement is often depicted falling, kneeling or supine (with the mostly unarmed hands/arms raised towards the aggressor or used backwards for support). Any loss of control, dynamics and tension distinguishes the living from the dead human body. It is striking that most of the images depicting the dying and the dead belong to the discourse of rulership and motifs of triumph. The people shown die as a result of external violence, whereas the 'everyday' causes of death (such as dying at home from illness, childbirth or hunger) are not included in pictures. The motif of triumph, which in Palestinian and Phoenician art adopts especially Egyptian ruler poses or depictions of inferiority,[2] and which shows victorious, living and inferior, dying and dead bodies, aims to communicate royal ideology or theology: it performs the superior ruler/Pharaoh/god as lord over life and death, honour and dishonour. The loss of bodily integrity is marked as dishonour in these contexts where the ruler/deity does violence to someone and takes away his life, limb and bodily honour. It is the inferior to whom the shame is assigned, whereas all honour belongs to the ruler/god.

### *Roles and functions of human beings and their social relationships*

Anthropomorphic depictions of people (not deities) can be divided into kings, courtiers or officials, warriors (here probably also the horsemen from the eighth century BCE onwards), hunters, captives, worshippers, sacrificers, priests or musicians, rarely scribes. Women are rarely found (musicians, lamentation women[3]), children mostly only in the company of their mother. The king is depicted in various functions, whereby his enthroned or fighting positioning represents an intersection with enthroned and fighting deities, from which he can only be clearly distinguished if the crowns and paraphernalia typical of the gods are visible. Quantitatively, representations of rulers predominate, which can be classified into the following types, which can also be combined (Berlejung 2017b: 155–6): the enthroned king; the king with insignia; the king before a deity; the king with dignitary(s); the fighting king in a chariot; with enemy(s), animal(s), mixed creatures; or hunting (mostly with a bow). These scenes of dominance, war, hunting and submission perform the king as a guarantor of order, whereas the scenes in which he is depicted with deities communicate the ruler's physical closeness to gods and his divine legitimacy.

From these roles attributed to people or the king in pictorial material, we can conclude that images express that being human as well as being king means being embedded in relationships and taking on certain roles: One exercises dominion over someone, one pays loyalty and reverence to someone, one wages war and hunts against someone, one is captured by someone, one makes music for someone and one mourns the loss of someone. There are three possibilities of social partners: deities (or hybrid beings), fellow human beings and living beings from nature (flora or fauna). All relationships among them are hierarchical. It goes without saying that the encounters between humans and deities are clearly asymmetrically hierarchized and that only images of deities that are consensual in the plausibility system of a culture are transmitted in this culture. The fact that every

---

[2] See e.g. *CSAJ*: Irbid, no. 7 (cylinder seal; Late Bronze Age); war victim under a chariot: *CSAPI*/1: Tell el-'Aǧul, no. 302 (scarab; Late Bronze Age); *IPIAO* 4: Figure 1023, Tell el Qasile, Iron Age IB; lion over enemy: *IPIAO* 4: Figure 1377, Lachish, Iron Age IIB; Pharaoh smiting the enemy: *IPIAO* 4: Figure 1381–2, Samaria and Megiddo Iron Age IIB.

[3] The pictorial evidence of wailing women from Palestine/Israel or the Levant is sparse and all dates from the Late Bronze Age or Early Iron Age. They bear witness to Egyptian and Aegean influences, see Schroer 2014.

social unit of people is also hierarchized is part of the implicit basic convictions as they are sedimented in pictures and texts of the entire ancient Near East and therefore also in Palestine/Israel. Hierarchical structures also determine the interactions of humans with nature and creatures from nature, as humans often either worship, dominate, kill them or are killed by them in the pictorial repertoire. At the top of the social pyramid and of the created world order is the king (in unity with his gods), who also largely dominates the pictorial sources.

The quantity of motifs with kings and people in scenes of dominance, war, hunting and submission reflects social life as a permanent competition for status and honour. Since only men could actively participate in this competition for honour, and women were embedded in the honour of the man responsible for them – father or husband (Berlejung 2004: 45, 2009: 319) – women do not appear in this pictorial repertoire.

The pictures were part of the social identity formation processes that were supposed to help the members of the collective to create an image of themselves as a community, which strengthened the group identity, and also gave the individual guidelines for his or her behaviour. Thus, the material images are not only about the retrospective cultural memory of shared memories or beliefs, but also about the transmission of memory processes and prospectively about the stabilization and expansion of current social relations and social networks. The pictures with scenes of dominance, war, hunting and submission in particular are part of the socially constructed social networks and patriarchal hierarchies, which they perform as intact, stable and successful as well as protected by gods and rulers. Thus, in very many images, the validity of the religious symbol system, loyalty, solidarity as well as the acceptance of existing social hierarchies and assignments of honour status are propagated. This can be seen particularly well in the aforementioned triumph motifs, which visualize rulers and gods as lords over life and death and communicate the message to the viewer that a ruler and a deity are to be met with unequivocal loyalty and submission. The eternal validity of these principles can be underlined by the material: royal self-representations (Berlejung 2017b) are mainly preserved as stone statuary or stone reliefs. The material in itself ensures a detemporalization of the representation and its message of legitimacy of rulership, as it stands for permanence, indestructibility and solidity.

*Pictures as social agents in service for the rulers* Pictures of rulers are good sources of what values and traditions determined the respective society or its construct of power and leadership (Berlejung 2017b: 152–3). In the cognition and communication process, a construction of shared perspectives of meaning is carried out between the picture and the viewer that generates support in the viewer. This support, which manifests itself on the systemic level of rule as well as on the level of the subjects, feeds back in both directions. The royal self-representation in the picture simultaneously performs the claim, assertion and – if publicly displayed and exhibited without damage or copied or purchased by subjects – acceptance of a king's legitimacy. Royal self-depictions, i.e. royal images commissioned and authorized by the king himself, are only known from Jordan and without clear contextualization (statue of Yarih-ʿezer, stele of Baluʿa; cf. Berlejung 2017b; colossal basalt statue of a king from the Amman theatre, *c*. ninth-seventh century BCE, Burnett and Gharib 2019). They clearly indicate that representations of the ruler that were to have a convincing legitimizing function had to feature the ruler in traditional roles and pictorial constellations. The ruler (dynastic or a usurper) had to be visualized as a rule-abiding guardian of laws, orders and socially accepted rules, if his picture was to support and advance his legitimacy. In this respect, depictions of rulers were bound to conventions and conformity to rules, since breaking conventions and traditions was considered illegitimacy.

The few attested representations of rulers from first-century BCE Israel/Judah were probably not commissioned as self-representations, yet they are local products and provide insights into existing ruler constructs. To mention are a painted sherd in Assyrian style from Ramat Rahel (*IPIAO* 4: Figure 1943, Iron Age IIC) and an earlier mural painting in Egyptian style on the pilaster at the entrance of Building A from Kuntillet 'Ajrud (*IPIAO* 4: Figure 1669, Iron Age IIB).[4] The mixed style of the painting constructs in Kuntillet 'Ajrud for the king of Judah or Israel (according to Ornan [2016b: 7] the painting shares features with the Northern Kingdom) in Iron Age IIB an identity, which – according to the iconography – is characterized as an interface identity, with the ruler being a 'citizen of the world' between local and Egyptian traditions (Beck 2012: 189–92; Ornan 2016b: 6–8). Since in this case the context is preserved and the enthroned ruler was depicted on the entrance pilaster of Building A, painting and building are to be related: 'Thus, the figure of the enthroned king in the entrance to Building A, the largest among the surviving wall paintings, conveyed to all entering into it that this was a royal domain' (Ornan 2016b: 8). The Egyptianization of local ruler symbolism in the painting from Kuntillet 'Ajrud goes back to the Late Bronze Age and is very traditionalistic. Among other things the use of the lotus as a sceptre refers to these conventions. The lotus visually translates that authority, vitality and fertility accompany the ruler. Behind the king, a standing courtier or musician is discernible, so that the painting is possibly a banquet or audience scene. The seated ruler surrounded by his courtiers shows that he is guarding domestic peace and is surrounded by loyal members of the elite. The message is communicated that the person who is entering has to join the queue of those who also recognize the king's rule as legitimate in the picture.

The painting on the sherd from Ramat Rahel Iron Age IIC also constructs the identity of the ruler as an interface identity, but he is a citizen of the world between Judah and contemporary Assyria (Cornelius 2015). Both paintings justify the right to rule not transcendentally through the gods, but within society through the incorporation of the known and handed-down traditions of the Late Bronze Age and Egypt (Kuntillet 'Ajrud) or Assyria (Ramat Rahel). Both paintings are examples of how the local elite of Judah and Israel respectively assimilated into the international elite culture. The reference to Egyptian and Neo-Assyrian as well as local traditions was important in order to present the (nameless) rulers as conforming to the socially accepted rules and thus legitimate. The respective chosen leading culture, Egypt in Kuntillet 'Ajrud in the Iron Age IIB, and Assyria in Ramat Rahel in the Iron Age IIC corresponds to the socio-historical conditions. In fact, the recognizable affinity to Assyria and Egypt is something that is recognizable in the Old Testament as a permanent conflict in the Israelite and Judean elites, and which led to a political seesaw between Egypt and Assyria in the local royal houses in the Iron Age.

Both rulers wear elaborate clothing or symbols of power, so that their high social rank and economic as well as symbolic capital are visible. Both paintings show (like the statue

---

[4] The throne details share some similarities with a statuette made from hippopotamus tusk from Tel Rehov (Iron Age IIA). According to Mazar (2007) the seated male is a king of Israel; less probable is the proposal in *IPIAO* 4: Figure 1092 to identify the enthroned person with the Egyptian god Ptah. For another ivory depicting an enthroned ruler see *IPIAO* 4: Figure 1670 (Samaria, Iron Age IIB).

of Yarih-ʿezer) that a legitimate ruler had to conform to the basic rule of being a 'man in his prime', physically intact, in full possession of health and strength (hair and beard intact in Ramat Rahel; sidelock in Kuntillet ʿAjrud, but shaved smooth according to Egyptian convention), well dressed and coiffed, at peace with himself and traditionalist in his overall design as a man on the throne. He is internationally networked (Egyptian motifs, Assyrian motifs), and is himself an aesthetically pleasing being whose emotional superiority can be inferred from his resting facial features. Even if the contexts of both pictures are destroyed, the gestures of both rulers show their quality of rulership, as both sit sovereignly opposite the viewer and the partners in the picture (destroyed); one signals greetings to his opposite partner (Ramat Rahel) while the other enjoys a lotus (Kuntillet ʿAjrud) and is surrounded by courtiers. Both fulfil their duties as keeper of peace and order. Pictorial themes of this kind perform the practical level of public and exemplary acceptance of rulership through significant subjects and thus demonstrate the legitimacy of the king. Images of this type function as social agents for the king and invite the viewer to join his group.

*Pictures as social agents stabilizing social hierarchies and role conformism* Successful social relationships are visualized in pictures as relationships of loyalty that run according to the rules and stabilize community. The pictures say something about which rules had to be complied with, what had to be done and what had to be avoided. Gods and kings beneficially turn to people who approach them according to the socially applicable rules, laws, traditions or customs. In contrast, kings and gods fight everything and everyone who threatens what they protect. In doing so, kings act in unity with the gods, whose partners and representatives they are. In this respect, pictures of rulers and gods implement the socially recognized and demanded qualifications of rulers and the collectively defined goals of rulership. Images of these motifs are part of the active and interactive construction of the social actors, so that they have very active roles: they constitute, reproduce and perform the valid social hierarchies and systems of plausibility. The pictorial repertoire, which included conformity to rules and roles and the acceptance of authority structures, contributed to the negotiation of social norms and orders. It had a reinforcing and refigurative effect at the same time. Pictures have a clear task in this context, which is not only to visualize the 'faith' in one's own religious and social system, but to dynamically advance the interactive constructions of social relations and their basis of justification (the gods as a socially recognized form of the source of authority of the human ruler and the applicable social rules).

In the world of pictures, the main subjects of interaction among men are loyalty, hierarchy and authority acceptance, as well as competitions for honour. Their setting is outside the home. The social role of women, as already mentioned, was fixed to their tasks within the home and the family. This domicile within the home is reflected and propagated as a role-conforming ideal in the depictions that show women looking out or down from windows or buildings. They remain static, neither reaching out through arms nor legs, and appear like an audience watching what is happening before their eyes. One could mention the well-known ivory motif of the courtly 'woman in the window' (*IPIAO* 4: Figure 1556, Samaria Iron Age IIB) or the many house or temple models showing women on thresholds (Schroer 2017; *IPIAO* 4: 68.79). Whether they are goddesses can be doubted for the 'women in the window', the clothed females and the musicians; they are rather mortals. As an implicit cultural axiom, these representations of women tied to buildings reflect and transmit the following ideal: the ideal woman keeps to herself in the house and leaves social life and its struggles outside the house to the man. She does not take part in competitions outside the home, but waits. She reacts to successes of men and gods with music (women with drums *IPIAO* 4: Figures 1186–8; 1548–52), to failures, death and catastrophes with lamentation (*IPIAO* 4: Figure 1226).

Men have to manage the honour and business of their family outside the house. Reliability and mutual loyalty as an ideal among men is shown in depictions of members of the upper classes among themselves or with the king. The pictorial arrangement that visually translates the acceptance of social hierarchy also communicates the message that everyone knows his place and honour status and does not dispute it with his counterpart. The level of exemplary agreement of valid hierarchies was implemented in iconography when the ruler was acknowledged by significant social partners (subordinates, officials, deities) in court, banquet, audience and submission scenes (see above).

A loyalty picture is a stamp seal impression, depicting the armed ruler/king who is handing over a bow and three arrows to a non-armed courtier, perhaps the *sr h'r* 'city governor' (stamp seal impression, unprovenanced, *IPIAO* 4: Figure 1941, Iron Age IIC?) and owner of the seal. The pictorial theme is a mutual proving of legitimacy for both men: the city governor was appointed by his king, and acknowledged the king as a legitimate source of authority. This kind of representation visualizes the symbolic (prestige, reputation, potential for trust) and social capital of the ruler and of his courtier; both are shown in their social network as reliable partners in interaction. This also seems to be evident in the foot posture, when the communication partners each have both feet on the ground. Social-anthropologically and in the Old Testament, steadfastness is a term with positive connotations and is associated with reliability. A lunge with one leg forward expresses a spatial encroachment and thus a challenge (of honour) and aggression. It therefore belongs in the iconography of the attacking ruler (or god), not at all in that of his officials.

The embedding of the human being in his family context occurs rather rarely in the pictorial material (for an example, which is, however, Neo-Assyrian, see *IPIAO* 4: Figure 1876). Even kings do not seem to have perpetuated themselves with their family in the pictorial material (apparently only Pharaohs of the Amarna period), but appear in the dominance motifs in splendid isolation. Although according to social history and in textual sources the family unit must be considered the most effective form of social organization, a regular family structure can rarely be discerned in the pictures. Kinship-based relationships that shaped the life and thinking of the individual are rather rare in the material images.

An example that does not come from Palestine, but represents an outside-view on Palestine through attributing life conditions and social structures to the people of Judah, is the Assyrian relief depicting the conquest of Lachish.[5] There, women, men and children of various ages are displayed together with their mobile goods and domestic animals as fellow sufferers in a wagon train. One could interpret a single wagon unit together with the people on and in front of the wagon as a closed family unit. Women and small children are sitting on the wagon, while mostly the men, together with the older children, actively walk themselves, drive and lead the wagon with the draught animals. They all go into

---

[5] For an image of Judean prisoners in the relief of the siege of Lachish at the British Museum, see: https://commons.wikimedia.org/wiki/File:The_fall_of_Lachish,_King_Sennacherib_reviews_Judaean_prisoners..JPG#/media/File:The_fall_of_Lachish,_King_Sennacherib_reviews_Judaean_prisoners..JPG (accessed 28 July 2022).

exile under the control of Assyrian soldiers, who in turn execute treacherous upper-class people in front of their (?) children. In all this, they are acting on behalf of the Assyrian king, so that the relief plays in several levels of social hierarchies at once. This relief also makes its contribution in the claiming and assertion of hierarchies, or more generally in the interaction of the actors, for it drives forward the interactive constructions of the interrelationships. The relief can be identified as an agent, but also as a 'mirror' of legitimizing mechanisms and social consensus formation in matters of domination and social roles. Of Lachish it sketches (from the external perspective) a complete social pyramid with corresponding loyalty requirements, ranging from the Assyrian king, through his courtiers, the male Assyrian elite and soldiers, to the male Judean elite (divided into executed traitors and submissive loyalists) and their children, to soldiers, and to the Judean nuclear families, comprising wives, sons and daughters of various ages. From the Assyrian perspective, no one falls out of this system of complex loyalty owed to the Assyrian king and life-promoting rule conformity, no matter how rich or poor, big or small, male or female, adult or child.

### *The relationship of human beings to nature and their environment*

In pictorial media, animals and plants can accompany deities, be their attribute and even represent them fully. It is therefore not always clear when watching an animal or tree on pictorial media what one is dealing with. If a pictorial motif shows people together with flora or fauna, then the motif can refer to the relationship of people to nature, but it can also refer to the religious symbolic universe. In contrast to the Old Testament, where God and nature are clearly distinguished, in iconography the forces and creatures of nature and the world of the gods are closely related. An animal, its horn, a tree or even just a twig (see e.g. the twig-goddess of the Middle Bronze Age IIB) can stand for a deity whom humankind has to encounter according to culturally accepted religious conventions.

*Animals* The interpretations of depictions of a bull (from the Middle Bronze Age on the pedestal and theomorphic presence marker of the Syro-Levantine storm-god), of a horse (in the Late Bronze Age the pedestal of Qudshu/Qedeshet, attribute animal of martial Astarte) or of a dove (since the Middle Bronze Age connected as attribute to female deities; *IPIAO* 4: 68–9) vary, especially when they are the sole motif on seals or in coroplastic art. Scholarship usually discusses a 'profane-secular' and a 'religious-sacred' meaning. After all, there is no denying that cattle- and horse-breeding[6] and dovecotes existed in Palestine and that these animals were kept in the first millennium BCE as domestic, farm or riding animals and for consumption, so that representations of bulls, pigeons and horses do not always have to be transparent to deities.

For wild game, which was not domesticated at any time but was hunted, the same is true, although the names of the deities it represents are not always clear: serpents (attribute of Qudshu/Qedeshet in the Late Bronze Age cf. *IPIAO* 3: Figures 859, 864–6, of several deities in the Iron Age – often in the shape of the Egyptian uraeus, see Ornan 2012),

---

[6] The donkey was the oldest means of transport for people and goods in Palestine. In the local pictorial material, it is ridden only by high-ranking men (cf. Sinai stelae of the second millennium, see Schroer 2006: 114–15). From the Late Bronze Age onwards, the horse comes to the fore for riding, and after their domestication dromedary camels enter the stage as beasts of burden (less as riding animals). Owning work animals not only contributed to mobility and the improved access to resources, but undoubtedly to an elevated status of honour.

caprids (ibex, doe, antelope, gazelle, oryx, deer; since the Pottery Neolithic Age in association with goddesses, but since the Bronze Age also linked with Baal and Reshef, cf. Ornan 2011: 264–7), ostriches or lions can be associated with deities. Being their zoomorphic shape and embodying divine presence, they can be adorated (adoration of a caprid, see *IPIAO* 4: Figure 1250 Beth Shemesh, Iron Age IIAB; adoration of an ostrich, see *IPIAO* 4: Figure 1533 Arad, Iron Age IIB; adoration of a lion, cf. Rowe 1936: no. 317). Wild game can also be considered as embodiment of the wilderness which has to be fought and controlled by a king/pharaoh, hero, a specific deity or the nameless 'master (or mistress) of the animals'. The latter motif occurs with various wild animals (bovine, ostriches, lions, caprids, crocodiles, scorpions, serpents). Lions in particular are an important part of the ancient Near Eastern and Egyptian iconography. They appear in the Late Bronze Age and Iron Ages as guardians (Weippert 2017) or representatives of royal power (since the Early Bronze Age the lion represents the pharaoh). They also serve as a divine pedestal for male and female divinities (Baal-Seth, Qudshu/Qedeshet, Ishtar [medallion from Ekron]) and as attribute animals flanking deities (Reshef) communicating the triumph of the deity over his/her archetypal enemy (Strawn 2005: 77–128).

Pictorial themes with bulls, horses, doves, serpents, caprids, ostriches, lions and other living beings do not always mirror, transmit and push forward the social construct about the relationship of human beings to nature and wildlife but refer to social constructs of the divine or royal spheres. However, the imagery attests to the human and divine interwovenness with nature and to the perception of these living beings that are brought into culturally accepted relations to deities or kingship. Animals that are depicted as zoomorphic representation or attribute of a deity indicate some of its key characteristics and bring them to the point. A double preselection and reduction of complexity has to be done: the most typical characteristic of the complex theological profile of a deity and the most typical characteristic of a specific animal have to be selected and co-related. This can differ culturally and diachronically, depend on the context of the pictorial medium and its intention. The typical characteristic that is attributed to an animal can be backed by special observations, as, for example, by observing that serpents shed their skin and lions battle and kill nearly all other animals; however, their interpretation and inclusion into iconography are a pure cultural construct.

Apart from the intertwining between the animal and the divine worlds, the existing visual sources of the Southern Levant show that the interest in depicting animals can be prioritized: *domestic food animals* (sheep, goat, cattle, pig) are not often attested in the local iconographic material. From the *domestic non-food animals* (dogs, cats), cat images can only rarely be found in the local imagery; as amulets they are backed by Egyptian religion. In contrast, there are some more attestations of dogs which can be shown side by side with chariots or in hunting contexts – referring to their function in everyday life.

Much more depictions exist of *work animals* (equids, bovines, camels) with a clear priority of bulls and horses (on bulls and horses see Daviau 2020), while dromedary camels remain scarce. Bovines are depicted on different media and in various materials (clay, bronze, ivory carvings, on seals, reliefs and stela), while the majority of horses are made of clay. The latter are terracottas with (e.g. Tel Mozah, Iron Age IIA, and very often in the Persian period) and without a rider, referring to a possible religious or martial context. Bovines can be depicted in splendid isolation, in adoration scenes (see above), grazing and lactating, with persons horizontally above the animal's back (leaping?) (*CSAPI*/1: Akko, no. 124, Iron Age IIA), or in front of it (*CSAPI*/1: Akko, no. 131, Iron Age IIA) or in hunting scenes (*IPIAO* 4: Figure 1629, Tell Abu Haraz, Iron Age IIB). It can usually not be decided whether the animal is depicted in its wild or domesticated form. The latter is surely the case in the Neo-Assyrian reliefs from Sennacherib's siege of Lachish mentioned above. They show the deportees taking their cattle as draught animals and dromedary camels as pack animals with them. The work animals are seen as part of the mobile goods of the Judean families. A double Neo-Assyrian message to the viewer can be suggested: the human beings are the animal's owners; however, animals and humans face the same fate – labour in Assyria; on the other hand it is well known that work animals were always scarce in Mesopotamia and part of the conquered booty.

*Non-food wild animals* that were hunted because of their teeth, horns, feathers or eggs (e.g. elephants, hippos, rhinos, ostriches[?]) occur quite sparsely in the iconographic sources, while *food wild game* (caprids, gazelles and deer) are a frequent motif. Caprids appear alone on seals and ivory carvings. Terracotta figurines are few. The caprid is mainly depicted as a suckling, sometimes with a scorpion or vulture (*GGIG*: Figure 318a) in the scene. Caprids are often shown as victims of violence and attacked by lions, dogs, the nameless 'master of the animals' (see above) or archers (*CSAPI*/1: Akko, no. 123; Iron Age IIA). On seals, cult stands and paintings, caprids are often associated with plant elements, flanking a tree (striding or standing upright; *GGIG*: Figures 182, 184, 219 [Kuntillet ʿAjrud], 362). The pictorial motif of wild caprids on a tree, documented since the earliest times, is transparent to the numinous forces that were assumed to be behind the regeneration of nature. Even if goats and other caprids are able to climb on trees for food, the setting of the caprids at the naturalistic trees or symbolic trees of life in no way mimics their natural surrounding and thus emphasizes the symbolism of the scene. Perhaps the antithetical layout of the animals flanking the tree from both sides marks a visual merism, indicating the totality of faunal life depending on the flora. Pictorial themes with (grazing, browsing, suckling, climbing) caprids communicate less aggressivity than lions, serpents and other wild beasts. They are fleeing and prey animals, not predators. Their survival does not depend on hunting, competing or killing; they are vegetarians being fed by the power of nature and deities. In this respect, these species do not give the impression of danger, neither in the context of the picture nor in the viewer (until today). Competition or conflict is limited to the mating behaviour and rivalry between males and usually does not end up with the death of one of the participants but with its flight. The coherence of the motif of grazing, browsing, suckling, climbing caprids, and caprids flanking trees sets flora and fauna in harmonious interaction. Humans play no role in the pictorial theme and watch as onlookers from the outside that nature is in balance with its ongoing life cycle and forces. The motif communicates an atmosphere of peace that does not fear any intervention by predators or human beings. From an anthropocentric perspective grazing or browsing caprids are usually considered to be mediating agents that granted supernatural protection and blessing (Ornan 2016a: 291).

In Iron Age I and II, caprids with offspring are newly added to the Palestinian pictorial repertoire. The lactating caprids are also often combined with scorpions (*IPIAO* 4: 66, 69–70) which is associated with concepts of nutrition, motherly care, fertility and female goddesses (Ornan 2016a: 294). The interest in these herd animals and their offspring in the Early Iron Age might be due to a change of perspective: the pictorial themes include the lifeworld of the pastoralist in the countryside and less the wilderness-construct of the urbanite. Herd animals guarantee the survival of people even when harvests are poor, as they can find food almost everywhere. The combination of the lactating mother animal with the scorpion, which has been one of the attribute animals of the goddesses since the Middle Bronze Age, is often interpreted in such a way that the mother animal with her reproduction and maternity was placed under the constellation of the scorpion, which is important for agriculture (Staubli 2010). In my opinion, it is rather a female scorpion that is depicted carrying its young on its back until the first moult, thus also documenting motherly care. Nevertheless, the scorpion (especially the female variant that is carrying offspring) is a dangerous animal that provokes viewers to keep their distance from the picture.

Last but not least, the depictions of *non-food wild animals without possible economic exploitation but with high symbolic meaning* have to be mentioned (lions and other felids, serpents, crocodiles, scorpions, scarab beetles). The most frequent motif is the scarab whose symbolism of life, regeneration and survival is very well known. Also, the scorpion seems to be related to life-giving powers (see above). On seals, the crocodile is often combined with the lion but it can also occur with caprids. Its association with the falcon-headed god (*GGIG*: Figures 34a, 34b) or 'the master of the crocodiles' point to its Egyptian background. Serpents are also a very common motif on seals, ivories, decorations of vessels, cult stands and altars, or as votives made of metal. The majority are uraei in Egyptian tradition, reflecting the protective force of the animal. As already mentioned above, the lion plays a major role in royal and divine iconography, in postures of dominance and triumph. The animal can also be depicted alone on seals, or to decorate weapons, furniture, vessels, royal and cultic equipment and other items. Terracotta lions are few (cf. Darby and de Hulster 2022). In violent scenes with the lion not being the victim (of human, heroic, divine hunters) but the aggressor he most frequently leaps on a caprid, sometimes on bovines, rarely a boar (Pithos A from Kuntillet 'Ajrud, *GGIG*: Figure 219). The lion as a sole motif stamped on handles in the glyptics of Judah (already an earlier local motif but mainly attested in the sixth century BCE and later) is usually interpreted as expressing kingship and uncontested authority – of a mortal (*IPIAO* 4: 62–3) or divine king (Yahweh; cf. Ornan and Lipschits 2020).

It can be observed that domestic animals that were primarily consumed because of their meat (cf. Sapir-Hen 2019) or exploited because of their secondary products (milk, wool), to differ from work animals (exploited because of their labour, cf. Sapir-Hen 2020), non-food domestic animals with special skills, food wild game, non-food wild game that was hunted because of the teeth or horn and non-food wild game without economic but only symbolic exploitation options (e.g. lions, serpents) were perceived by humans in different ways. Iconographical sources mainly included *work animals*, *food wild game* and *non-food wild animals* without possible economic exploitation but with high symbolic meaning into the repertoire. 'Cattle stands out as it bears a symbolic status both in its wild and domestic form' (Sapir-Hen 2020: 88). Regarding iconography the following main motifs with wild animals can be observed: (1) as pedestals, (2) as attributes of deities, (3) being worshipped, (4) as sole motif, (5) being hunted, (6) being grabbed by the tail/neck, (7) predators hunt themselves, (8) grazing peacefully, (9) at a tree and (10) lactating their offspring. In spite of their very important economic role for human life and development, the motifs including domestic food animals, domestic non-food animals and work animals do not have the same spectrum. Also, the ritual practice with all the aforementioned animals differed based on the symbolic perception of these animals by humans. The reasons are a matter of debate: in some cases, the economic contribution of an animal to society and its symbolic role and high esteem can be co-related (e.g. the donkey until the early IA, partly replaced by the horse and dromedary camel). But as the high status of some non-food and non-work animals (e.g. lion, serpent, scarabs) which cannot be exploited economically indicates, this is not always decisive (contra Sapir-Hen

2020: 89–90). In particular, the hunting of lions had a ceremonial and highly symbolic and prestigious aspect, making them the most appropriate animal to be used in motifs of domination and triumph.

Thus, the human view on nature is quite complex: wild and domesticated animals were seen from an economic perspective as work or food animals, they were used in ceremonies and rituals, and they were regarded as status symbols, as identity markers of groups or as representatives of numinous powers, gods, forces of vitality or wilderness and destructive power. In any case, humans exploited the creatures of nature to take them into their service, whether by taming them, using them for humankind's own purposes, eating them, sacrificing them, or attributing characteristics and interpretations to them that, zoologically speaking, are completely alien to them. Animals were assigned to an anthropocentric world view. Implicit axioms and cultural expectations are tied to the attributions associated with certain animals, especially wild animals, which can actually be dangerous to humans and stand for strength, speed, aggression, high honour status, invincibility and danger to life. Used as guardian animals (mainly uraeus and lions), they protect what is behind them. Their control is a key issue in royal ideology and theology. Whether human or divine – whoever stands on a wild animal in a pictorial motif or grabs them by the neck or tail restricts their bodily integrity and dynamism and must have the enduring strength to assume this position of dominance. In this respect, the strength and aggression of the human, heroic or divine serpent or lion conqueror always exceeds that of the serpent or lion.

It is precisely these cultural expectations and attributions that the iconography of gods and rulers ties in with. Numerous depictions of seals show the ruler in battle or hunting against lions or other wild animals, which is one of the subjugation motifs already mentioned. The wild animals, whose status (dangerousness for humans and competitiveness with humans) is set as high as possible in this fight, stand for the threat to the order, which the king successfully fends off. The king's honour, status and prestige grow with the status of the opponent he kills or dominates, which is why kings fight lions, which are considered the strongest wild animals, or even potent mixed creatures, not rabbits. The fact that wild animals – including lions – essentially want to be left alone by humans, only attacking for their food supply and when threatened, plays no role in anthropocentric iconography. Even if the animals are rendered naturalistically, their depictions are not about to mimic or copy nature but to propose an interpretation of these animals within the given traditional and transmitted worldview. The iconography reflects and transmits the cultural axiom that domestic and work animals are fully under human control and can be exploited, while wild animals are dangerous to humans and must be controlled or eradicated so that humans can move about without danger. The relationship between humans and wild animals is thus fundamentally competitive and conflictual. Wild animals as representatives of the wilderness and their dominance, control or killing by humans or gods are an expression of a basic disposition that assumes that wild nature is humankind's enemy, not its ally. Wild animals and wild nature are allied with humans or gods only (for example as guardian and postament animals) when they are mastered or tamed, thus when they give up their wilderness.

Overall, it can be stated that dangerous wild animals and predators signal a danger, challenge, conflict potential, competition, enmity or even a fear factor to the viewer of the picture. Danger recognition, distance and the need to fight back and triumph are the attitudes expected towards these creatures. Even if it is in reality the human being who lays claim to the wild animal's life, offspring or habitat (no animal has ever set fire to a forest and cleared it!), the animal is always considered to be the aggressor. Domesticated animals and non-predators as pictorial motifs show the orderly and controlled world whose existence is secured by the fact that humans can rely on the reproductive power of these non-predatory creatures to survive, depending only on plants, air and water.

*Plants* Just as animals, plants can mark divine presence or be a divine attribute. Especially in the Bronze Ages, the naked goddess and the Middle Bronze Age twig-goddess are clearly associated with plants. The connection of the anthropomorphic naked goddess and plants is less significant in the Iron Ages. However, even if they are not combined any more, naked females persist (mainly as terracottas) as well as depictions of plants and trees. Also, the connection between trees, twigs and goddesses is still present, though the goddesses are dressed now (*GGIG*: Figure 323, Lachish, Iron Age IIC). Male and female gods can hold various types of plant attributes or sceptres, mainly consisting of a tree, twig, papyrus stalk, lotus/waterlily (held by the Late Bronze Age Qudshu, *IPIAO* 3: Figure 860, 862–4), or unidentified blossom referring to the power to grant earth's fertility and reproduction (*IPIAO* 3: Figure 933). In the Iron Age IIB regeneration of life is represented in Egyptian style by the sun-god as sun-child, sitting or kneeling on a lotus blossom (*GGIG*: Figures 240–1a–c). Especially the lotus/waterlily – a plant without economic exploitation function (even if there is some evidence for eating lotus) but high symbolic status expressing the regenerative powers of nature – also played an important role in royal iconography. Kings often hold a lotus flower or another blossom as a sceptre (Kuntillet ʿAjrud = *GGIG*: Figure 238a), while the much later coinage of Yehud and Samaria attest the lily (Wyssmann 2014: 249–50), or lily-shaped sceptres (ibid.: 230).

Plants were also among the resources that humans exploited, and which they depicted and perceived differently: *food plants* cultivated in agriculture and gardens (wine, olives, fruit and nut trees), *food plants growing without agriculture* (berries, mushrooms etc.), *non-food plants whose products can be exploited* (papyrus, flax, plants, trees and bushes for their wood, incense, medical use, spices, shade), *non-food plants that cannot be used economically* and have a *positive* (lotus or lily) or a *negative symbolic meaning* (weeds, thorns, thistles, see Gen. 3.18; Isa. 7.23–25; Jer. 12.13). Food plants and plants that could be exploited or which had a positive symbolic meaning were included in cult ceremonies and iconography – thorns, thistles and weeds apparently not. Also, in Palestine it was a common experience that, where cultivated land was not constantly worked, thorns and thistles spread again unhindered (Isa. 7.23–24) and destroyed what human labour had created with much effort and time (Isa. 14.13). Thorns and thistles, plants of the desert, were seen as the representatives of the wilderness and non-ordered world. As such, and for pragmatic reasons, they had to be pulled out or burnt. In contrast to the battle against the faunal representatives of wilderness (see above), the fight against thorns, thistles and weeds is no pictorial theme in the Southern Levant. A possible explanation is that this was not an activity that was considered to be of high social prestige – no trophy could be displayed – even if it clearly had a high economic meaning.

Usually, it is not that easy to identify plants in pictorial media. Once more, the Neo-Assyrian reliefs on the siege of Lachish are instructive: they depict Palestine as an area of food plants: vines and fig, pine, olive and pomegranate trees. Palestine is shown as a well-cultivated land with a developed agriculture. It was not the intention of Neo-Assyrian art to create a survey of the different plant species from Palestine or the floral landscape of the Shephelah. Rather, they were interested in displaying lifelike representations of foreign plants to demonstrate their victorious power over the conquered country and its products.

In local Southern Levantine iconography, plants could be used as the main motif or as ornamental element (see e.g. the name seals of the Iron Age IIC decorated with a variety of plants in *GGIG*: Figures 349–53, 355). The choice of the plants (palmettes, twigs, pomegranates, lotus, pine cones and papyrus) indicates that they are not simply decoration but also symbolize growth, blessing and prosperity. Trees can be depicted naturalistically or stylized, serve as a mere graphical separator, a side decoration or as the centre of the scene. Plants can fill the background in depictions of wildlife behaviour (e.g. grazing caprids), or be the setting of human beings hunting wild animals (e.g. duck-hunting in the marshes with papyrus in the background, *GGIG*: Figure 68b), cutting down trees during a military campaign (a Neo-Assyrian practice, see Wright 2012), or – in this case perhaps representing a garden – having erotic encounters (*GGIG*: Figure 41; see also the Neo-Assyrian relief with Ashurbanipal in the arbour).

The most important representation of plants with the highest status and symbolic meaning is the sacred tree, symbolizing the ongoing life cycle, divine blessing, fertility, life and order. In Syria-Palestine, the sacred tree can be depicted as a stylized date-palm ('palmette'), some more or less elaborated bough or twig or as a complex composite tree combining the stylized palm as the basic upright stem with papyrus umbels, lilies or lotus blossoms (*GGIG*: Figures 14a–15c; 219 [Kuntillet ʿAjrud]; 223). The sacred tree can also be linked with the cosmic tree, which represents the centre and axis of the world. Grounding in the depths, it bears the firmament and thus connects and stabilizes underworld, heaven and earth. This tree is a key element of the Levantine symbolic universe (Winter 2002) and can be included into pictorial scenes with hybrid beings (*GGIG*: Figures 231ab, 232b) or human beings touching, adoring or dancing around it (*GGIG*: Figures 14a–c, 179–81, 233). Also, animals can be centred around the 'tree of life', such as birds (*GGIG*: Figure 16), and, more often, caprids (see above). The motif of caprids eating from the tree does not show food plants suitable for humans but only for animals. Therefore, the motif is about nature as a closed functioning system which is watched by human beings from the outside. Plants that are depicted side by side with permanently grazing and feeding animals communicate the message that the vegetation constantly regrows, providing food. This refers to the human observation and generalized expectation that plants can be distinguished from animals (and humans) because they have the regenerative power to sprout again even after they have been eaten away, cut down, burnt and even seem to die yearly (Job 14.7–10). The flourishing of nature as seen in the growth of plants and reproduction of the animals has been interpreted as the manifest expression of the blessing of the gods (Pss. 67.7, 85.13). According to the iconography and textual sources, the appropriate human reaction to this well-ordered life cycle is the adoration of the gods. Unlike the Old Testament (e.g. Deut. 20.19, 22.6–7, 25.4; Prov. 12.10; Riede 2016) environmental protection is no topic in the pictorial material.

# CONCLUSION

Based on the assumption that culture and society are unfolding rather than fixed realities, pictures are in all stages, during their production, circulation and reception, part of these unfolding cultural processes and social dynamics including sociocultural phenomena of continuity (referring to historical precedents of given images and conventions) and change.[7]

The pictorial material of the Southern Levant testifies to how deeply the region was rooted in the ancient Near East, as various motifs show a *longue durée*, some of which go back to the Neolithic Age or can be traced back to Egyptian or Syro-Mesopotamian influences. To the question: 'How do people of the Southern Levantine culture of the Iron Age "see" their world and themselves?' one could therefore answer that the people understood their culture as tradition-bound in space and in time and were prepared to integrate motifs and styles from the past and from neighbouring cultures into their pictorial repertoire. Especially in the iconography of rulership, in dominance and triumphal themes, the connection to Bronze Age traditions and Egypt plays a prominent role, while Assyrian influences are also reflected in the Iron Age IIC. Upper-class identity was constructed in the pictures as an interface identity between local and Egyptian or local and Assyrian traditions, so that they communicate the message that internationality in combination with tradition-boundness are to be seen as a value, rather than isolation being the ideal.

Pictures are social agents, sources of, and targets for, social agency. This is also true for the material images from Palestine/Israel. They mirror and transmit different implicit axioms and social cues and stimulate communication and action. The pictures are involved in processes of non-verbal communication, they are archives and transfer modes of collective memory and very active agents within social interaction processes. The pictorial material of ancient Palestine/Israel is less intended to change the world but to stabilize it, its socially accepted hierarchies, role conformities, symbolic universes and plausibilities.

As social agents, pictures are also part of the social transfer of capitals. Their materiality mirrors the economic capital that had been invested to produce or buy them and transfers economic into cultural, social and symbolic capital. As part of this process, material images convey prestige and honour, their destruction, loss and shame. Pictures are therefore deeply embedded in social processes of identity formation, negotiation of social roles, status assignments and the legitimation of social hierarchies and constructs of plausibilities [further on honour, see Chapter 12 in this volume].

Regarding the depictions of human beings and (anthropomorphically depicted) deities we can observe a clear body-centrism, the corporeality of the living and dead body, several body ideals, the acceptance of gender as category and the social construct of several binarities as given realities. To be mentioned is the ideal of bodily integrity of the living body with the self-control of movements and emotions, while the disarticulation of the human body, its dominance by external violence corresponds to the loss of bodily integrity, dishonour and death. Bodies of males/females, gods/goddesses, animals or other beings organize and qualify space when beings are shown that belong to the ordered world or to the wilderness. Through the arrangement of the bodies and their limbs, pictures visualize relationships which are deeply rooted in social constructs, e.g. the conflict of the beings of the ordered world with the beings of the wilderness, rulers or deities clashing with enemies or lions.

---

[7] On the transformation of collective structures of meaning over time, see, e.g., Sahlins 1987. He examines processes and symbolisms of social practice equally, thus overcoming the seeming contradiction of stability and change, static and dynamic. The terms cultural concept, symbolic system and structure can be used synonymously, in his opinion, because interconnected processes take place. The fact is: the transformation of interpretive patterns is an everlasting process of change; its triggers are debatable.

Pictures reflect, communicate and transmit and also shape different anthropological concepts that can be identified according to the motifs which show human beings in their social roles and functions, interactions and interrelations with their possible interactive partners: humans, deities and nature. The material images mirror and transmit the basic assumption, that being human means to take over roles and functions, to be part of interactions and interrelations that are clearly defined by gender, social roles, social status and hierarchical structures.

Pictures depicting males, often kings and members of the elite, frequently qualify the represented relationships as competitive, manifesting that royal and male life is embedded in competitions about resources, status, honour, prestige – generally speaking about all kinds of capitals (in Bourdieu's sense) – including the defence of the order against enemies of all kind. Women are usually depicted in reaction to activities of others (usually males), observing from a safe position in the interior house, feasting/music-making, mourning or accompanying the head of the family (Lachish reliefs). Activities outside the house, in economy, war, hunt or competition neither belong to the pictorial repertoire of females nor to their social field. Women are excluded from making any prestigious triumph and its display. Instead, they are shown expressing emotions or fulfilling their social role as mothers taking care of a child. Thus, the pictures communicate the acceptance of social role conformity, hierarchies and loyalty to them (females to males, males to the king, the king to the gods) as ideal social behaviour. Kinship-based relationships are rather rare in the pictorial repertoire (except the motif 'mother with child'), while patron–client relationships with higher social strata (e.g. ruler with loyal officials in banquet scenes, or scenes of audience) or with protective deities (e.g. kings closed to deities, human beings in adoration scenes) are displayed in different pictorial motifs communicating that relationships of this type are a win–win situation for both sides: role conformity and loyalty to rulers and deities is rewarded with protection and blessing. In contrast, any attempt to transgress the borders and orders given and protected by them is combated by them – and they always win (e.g. scenes of triumphs and dominance) against the aggressor. The pictures were social agents in service for the rulers and disseminated royal ideology; but they also were part of the social identity formation processes that were supposed to help the members of the collective to create an image of themselves as a community, which strengthened the group identity, and also gave the viewer guidelines (e.g. role conformism) for his or her behaviour. Thus, ideal social interactions are *mise-en-scène* and depict very often the ruler, males and rarely females in fulfilling their social roles in paradigmatic interactions. The viewer has to understand that humans have to be persons who are always related to others and who derive their identity from the relational connections that they actually have and from their past traditions. The successful human being accepts, keeps and supports (with loyalty, solidarity, steadfastness) the given social relations, institutions and roles, the inherited status of honour, and the given hierarchies that are legitimated by the culturally accepted supernatural powers and traditions. The material images visualize an approach to life that supports the community.

Also, broader social and historical processes are tangible in the images when the visual construct of rulership and its legitimacy not only adopts traditional and local motifs, but includes an international flair that is inspired by the actual political hegemonies – such as a royal figure showing typical Egyptian features in Kuntillet ʿAjrud in the Iron Age IIB, while in the Iron Age IIC Assyrian dress codes and body concepts (see the 'muscle man' from Ramat Rahel) were preferred.

Regarding the relation of human beings to nature the pictorial themes communicate several aspects: in general, nature and its creatures are perceived, prioritized and structured in a very anthropocentric way. Wild and domesticated animals were seen from an economic perspective as work or food animals, they were used in ceremonies and rituals, and they were regarded as status symbols, as identity markers of groups or as representatives of numinous powers, gods, constructive forces of vitality or wilderness and destructive power. Human hierarchies, behaviour and constructs were transposed and projected into wildlife, when beasts were used in imagery to represent social behaviour as rulership, triumph, guardianship or subordination (e.g. the lion as representative of the pharaoh), motherly care or mating (e.g. suckling caprids and cows). In the social view promoted in the pictorial themes, kings and men clearly share some characteristics with predators (aggressivity, killing) and replace in combat their human physical deficits and bodily vulnerability with weapons (knives instead of teeth and claws, chariots to increase the speed and protective distance). In addition, the pictorial themes construct nature as a danger to human beings (see the images of predators, and wildlife), but flora and fauna in an ongoing continuity and equilibrium of life. Animals are not depicted as interaction partners for human beings on eye level but as objects that have to be hunted, killed, consumed, domesticated, controlled, exploited, tamed and ridden or watched with some distance from the outside (e.g. grazing, at trees or suckling). The presence of non-predators with or without plants on pictorial media indicates a balance of flora and fauna under divine preservation, only rarely aggression, but never danger. Considering that images also evoke emotions in the reception process, images with non-predators are more likely to create a feel-good zone than images with predators. In this respect, it is not surprising that utopian scenarios that envision a general world of peace proclaim general animal peace between predators and non-predators (Isa. 11.6–8, 65.25) and thus correspond to the creation's longing for an end to general killing.

# REFERENCES

Asher-Greve, J.M. (1998), 'The Essential Body: Mesopotamian Conceptions of the Gendered Body', in M. Wyke (ed.), *Gender and the Body in the Ancient Mediterranean*, 8–37, Oxford: Wiley-Blackwell.

Asher-Greve, J.M. and D. Sweeney (2006), 'On Nakedness, Nudity, and Gender in Egyptian and Mesopotamian Art', in S. Schroer (ed.), *Images and Gender: Contributions to the Hermeneutics of Reading Ancient Art*, 125–76, OBO 220, Fribourg: Fribourg Academic Press / Göttingen: Vandenhoeck & Ruprecht.

Bahrani, Z. (2003), *The Graven Image: Representation in Babylonia and Assyria*, Philadelphia: University of Pennsylvania Press.

Beck, P. (2012), 'The Drawings and Decorative Designs', in Z. Meshel, *Kuntillet 'Ajrud (Ḥorvat Teman): An Iron Age II Religious Site on the Judah-Sinai Border*, 143–203, Jerusalem: Israel Exploration Society.

Belting, H. (2011), *An Anthropology of Images: Picture, Medium, Body*, transl. T. Dunlap, Princeton, NJ: Princeton University Press.

Berlejung, A. (2004), 'Frau nach Maß: Physiognomische Omina für die Frau als Quellen für Überlegungen zur Mentalität und Kultur der altorientalischen Gesellschaft im 1. Jt. v. Chr.', in R. Kampling (ed.), *Sara lacht . . . Eine Erzmutter und ihre Geschichte: Zur Interpretation und Rezeption der Sara-Erzählung*, 27–63, Paderborn: Schöningh.

Berlejung, A. (2009), 'Körperkonzepte und Geschlechterdifferenz in der physiognomischen Tradition des Alten Orients und des Alten Testaments', in B. Janowski and K. Liess (eds), *Der Mensch im alten Israel: Neue Forschungen zur alttestamentlichen Anthropologie*, 299–337, HBS 59, Freiburg: Herder.

Berlejung, A. (2012), 'Menschenbilder und Körperkonzepte in altorientalischen Gesellschaften im 2. und 1. Jt. v. Chr.: Ein Beitrag zur antiken Körpergeschichte', in A. Berlejung, J. Dietrich and J.-F. Quack (eds), *Menschenbilder und Körperkonzepte im Alten Israel, in Ägypten und im Alten Orient*, 367–97, ORA 9, Tübingen: Mohr Siebeck.

Berlejung, A. (2017a), 'Bibel und Orient', in W. Dietrich (ed.), *Die Welt der hebräischen Bibel: Umfeld – Inhalte – Grundthemen*, 17–30, Stuttgart: Kohlhammer.

Berlejung, A. (2017b), 'Dimensionen der Herrschaftslegitimität: Ikonographische Aspekte königlicher Selbstdarstellung in den Kulturen der südlichen Levante der Eisenzeit anhand der Bildwerke von Baluʿa, Yarih-ʿezer und Askalon', in C. Levin and R. Müller (eds), *Herrschaftslegitimation in vorderorientalischen Reichen der Eisenzeit*, 147–88, ORA 21, Tübingen: Mohr Siebeck.

Berlejung, A. (2021a), 'The Reduction of Complexity: The Theological Profile of a Deity and its Iconographic Expression – The God Aššur in First-Millennium B.C.E. Assyria as a Case Study', in *Divine Secrets and Human Imaginations: Studies on the History of Religion and Anthropology of the Ancient Near East and the Old Testament*, 247–89, ORA 42, Tübingen: Mohr Siebeck.

Berlejung, A. (2021b), 'Images of the Dead – Images for the Living: Life and Death in the Iconography of Ancient Mesopotamia, Egypt and Palestine', in *Divine Secrets and Human Imaginations: Studies on the History of Religion and Anthropology of the Ancient Near East and the Old Testament*, 369–413, ORA 42, Tübingen: Mohr Siebeck.

Berlejung, A. (2021c), '"Man and Woman, and Woman and Man Reach Up to the Godhead's Span": Eroticism and the Utopia of Transformations in the Song of Songs', in *Divine Secrets and Human Imaginations: Studies on the History of Religion and Anthropology of the Ancient Near East and the Old Testament*, 617–44, ORA 42, Tübingen: Mohr Siebeck.

Berlejung, A. and A. Fantalkin (2017), 'Ausgrabungen in Aschdod-yam 2017: Hafenzentrum und Klosterstadt', *Welt und Umwelt der Bibel*, 2017 (4): 66–8.

Berlejung, A., S. Kohlhaas and J. Stein (2018), 'Katalog der anthropomorphen Masken der südlichen Levante vom präkeramischen Neolithikum B bis zum Beginn der hellenistischen Zeit (9. Jt. – 4. Jh. v. Chr.)', in A. Berlejung and J. Filitz (eds), *The Physicality of the Other: Masks as a Means of Encounter / Die Leibhaftigkeit des Anderen: Masken als Medium der Begegnung*, 397–550, ORA 27, Tübingen: Mohr Siebeck.

Bonatz, D. (2002a), 'Sprache ohne Worte. Aspekte der nonverbalen Kommunikation durch Bilder im Alten Orient', in D. Bonatz and M. Heinz (eds), *Bild – Macht – Geschichte. Visuelle Kommunikation im Alten Orient*, 137–62, Berlin: Reimer.

Bonatz, D. (2002b), 'Agens Bild: Handlungszusammenhänge altorientalischer Bildwerke', in D. Bonatz and M. Heinz (eds), *Bild – Macht – Geschichte: Visuelle Kommunikation im Alten Orient*, 53–70, Berlin: Reimer.

Bonfiglio, R.P. (2016), *Reading Images, Seeing Texts: Towards a Visual Hermeneutics for Biblical Studies*, OBO 280, Fribourg: Fribourg Academic Press / Göttingen: Vandenhoeck & Ruprecht.

Bourdieu, P. (1996 [1992]), *The Rules of Art: Genesis and Structure of the Literary Field*, transl. S. Emanuel, Stanford, CA: Stanford University Press.

Brunner-Traut, E. (1992), *Frühformen des Erkennens: am Beispiel Altägyptens*, 2nd edn, Darmstadt: Wissenschaftliche Buchgesellschaft.

Burnett, J.S. and R. Gharib (2019), 'The Amman Theatre Statue and the Ammonite Royal Ancestor Cult', *The Ancient Near East Today*, 7 (12). Available online: https://www.asor.org/anetoday/2019/12/Amman-Theatre-Statue-and-Ammonite-Royal-Ancestor-Cult (accessed 21 July 2022).

Cornelius, I. (2015), 'Revisiting the Seated Figure from Ḥirbet Ṣāliḥ / Rāmat Rāḥẹ l', *ZDPV*, 131 (1): 29–43.

Darby, E.D. and I.J. de Hulster, eds (2022), *Iron Age Terracotta Figurines from the Southern Levant*, CHANE 125, Leiden: E.J. Brill.

Daviau, P.M.M. (2020), 'Bulls and Horses, Gods and Goddesses: The Religious Iconography of Israel's Neighbors', in C. Cornell (ed.), *Divine Doppelgängers: YHWH's Ancient Look-Alikes*, 219–37, University Park, PA: Eisenbrauns.

Daviau, P.M.M. (forthcoming), 'Cultural Multiplicity in Northern Moab: Figurines and Statues from Khirbat al-Mudayna Thamad', in Y. Alian (ed.), *Studies in the History and Archaeology of Jordan 14*, Amman: Department of Antiquities of Jordan.

de Hulster, I.J., B.A. Strawn and R.P. Bonfiglio (2015), 'Introduction: Iconographic Exegesis: Method and Practice', in I.J. de Hulster, B.A. Strawn and R.P. Bonfiglio (eds), *Iconographic Exegesis of the Hebrew Bible / Old Testament: An Introduction to Its Method and Practice*, 19–42, Göttingen: Vandenhoeck & Ruprecht.

Dietrich, J. (2015), 'Sozialanthropologie des Alten Testaments: Grundfragen zur Relationalität und Sozialität des Menschen im alten Israel', *ZAW*, 127 (2): 224–43.

Frevel, C., ed. (2005), *Medien im antiken Palästina: materielle Kommunikation und Medialität als Thema der Palästinaarchäologie*, FAT II/10, Tübingen: Mohr Siebeck.

Gell, A. (1998), *Art and Agency: An Anthropological Theory*, Oxford: Clarendon Press.

Herrmann, C. (1994), *Ägyptische Amulette aus Palästina / Israel*, OBO 138, Fribourg: Fribourg Academic Press / Göttingen: Vandenhoeck & Ruprecht.

Herrmann, C. (2002), *Ägyptische Amulette aus Palästina / Israel II*, OBO 184, Fribourg: Fribourg Academic Press / Göttingen: Vandenhoeck & Ruprecht.

Herrmann, C. (2006), *Ägyptische Amulette aus Palästina / Israel III*, OBO.SA 24, Fribourg: Fribourg Academic Press / Göttingen: Vandenhoeck & Ruprecht.

Jonas, H. (2010a), 'Homo pictor: Von der Freiheit des Bildens / Die Freiheit des Bildens: Homo pictor und die Differentia des Menschen' (1961), in D. Böhler et al. (eds), *Kritische Gesamtausgabe der Werke von Hans Jonas, I.1: Organismus und Freiheit – Philosophie des Lebens und Ethik der Lebenswissenschaften*, 277–303, Freiburg: Rombach.

Jonas, H. (2010b), 'Der Adel des Sehens: Eine Untersuchung zur Phänomenologie der Sinne' (1953), in D. Böhler et al. (eds), *Kritische Gesamtausgabe der Werke von Hans Jonas, I.1: Organismus und Freiheit – Philosophie des Lebens und Ethik der Lebenswissenschaften*, 243–67, Freiburg: Rombach.

Keel, O. (1977), *Jahwe-Visionen und Siegelkunst: Eine neue Deutung der Majestätsschilderungen in Jes 6, Ez 1 und 10 und Sach 4*, SBS 84/85, Stuttgart: Katholisches Bibelwerk.

Keel, O. (1992), *Das Recht der Bilder, gesehen zu werden: Drei Fallstudien zur Methode der Interpretation altorientalischer Bilder*, OBO 122, Fribourg: Fribourg Academic Press / Göttingen: Vandenhoeck & Ruprecht.

Keel, O. (1997), *The Symbolism of the Biblical World: Ancient Near Eastern Iconography and the Book of Psalms*, Winona Lake, IN: Eisenbrauns.

Keel, O. and S. Schroer (2004), *Eva – Mutter alles Lebendigen: Frauen- und Göttinnenidole aus dem Alten Orient*, Fribourg: Fribourg Academic Press.

Keel, O. and T. Staubli (2001), *'Im Schatten Deiner Flügel': Tiere in der Bibel und im Alten Orient*, Fribourg: Fribourg Academic Press.

Lobinger, K. (2012), *Visuelle Kommunikationsforschung: Medienbilder als Herausforderung für die Kommunikations- und Medienwissenschaft*, Wiesbaden: Springer.

Mazar, A. (2007), 'An Ivory Statuette Depicting an Enthroned Figure from Tel Rehov', in S. Bickel, S. Schroer, R. Schurte and C. Uehlinger (eds), *Images as Sources: Studies on Ancient Near Eastern Artefacts and the Bible Inspired by the Work of Othmar Keel*, 101–10, OBO Sonderband, Fribourg: Fribourg Academic Press / Göttingen: Vandenhoeck & Ruprecht.

Ornan, T. (2011), '"Let Ba'al Be Enthroned": The Date, Identification and Function of a Bronze Statue from Hazor, *JNES*, 70 (2): 253–80.

Ornan, T. (2012), 'Member in the Entourage of Yahweh: A Uraeus Seal from the Western Wall Plaza Excavations, Jerusalem', '*Atiqot*, 72: 15*–20*.

Ornan, T. (2016a), 'The Beloved, Ne'ehevet, and Other Does: Reflections on the Motif of the Grazing or Browsing Wild Horned Animals', in I. Finkelstein, C. Robin and T. Römer (eds), *Alphabets, Texts and Artifacts in the Ancient Near East: Studies Presented to Benjamin Sass*, 279–302, Paris: Van Dieren.

Ornan, T. (2016b), 'Sketches and Final Works of Art: The Drawings and Wall Paintings of Kuntillet 'Ajrud Revisited', *TA*, 43 (1): 3–26.

Ornan, T. and O. Lipschits (2020), 'The Lion Stamp Impressions from Judah: Typology, Distribution, Iconography, and Historical Implications – A Preliminary Report', *Semitica*, 62: 69–91.

Panofsky, E. (1932), 'Aufsätze zu Grundfragen der bildenden Kunst', *Logos*, 21: 103–19 [republished as *Aufsätze zu Grundfragen der Kunstwissenschaft*, ed. by H. Oberer and E. Verheyen, 85–97, Berlin: Hessling, 1964].

Panofsky, E. (1939), *Studies in Iconology: Humanistic Themes in the Art of the Renaissance*, New York: Oxford University Press.

Panofsky, E. (1994a), 'Zum Problem der Beschreibung und Inhaltsdeutung von Werken der bildenden Kunst', in E. Kaemmerling (ed.), *Ikonographie und Ikonologie: Theorien – Entwicklung – Probleme: Bildende Kunst als Zeichensystem 1*, 6th edn, 185–206, Köln: DuMont.

Panofsky, E. (1994b), 'Ikonographie und Ikonologie', in E. Kaemmerling (ed.), *Ikonographie und Ikonologie: Theorien – Entwicklung – Probleme: Bildende Kunst als Zeichensystem 1*, 6th edn, 207–25, Köln: DuMont.

Peirce, C.S. (1983), *Phänomen und Logik der Zeichen*, ed. and transl. H. Pape, Frankfurt am Main: Suhrkamp.

Peirce, C.S. (1991), *Naturordnung und Zeichenprozeß: Schriften über Semiotik und Naturphilosophie*, ed. H. Pape, Frankfurt am Main: Suhrkamp.

Pyschny, K. (2019), 'Concepts and Contexts of Female and Male Nudity in the Iconography of the Southern Levant', in C. Berner, M. Schäfer, M. Schott, S. Schulz and M. Weingärtner (eds), *Clothing and Nudity in the Hebrew Bible*, 127–62, London: T&T Clark.

Riede, P. (2016), 'Geschaffen – anvertraut – bewundert: Die biblische Tierwelt als Spiegel des Menschen', *BiKi*, 71: 202–6.

Rowe, A. (1936), *A Catalogue of Egyptian Scarabs, Scaraboids, Seals and Amulets in the Palestine Archaeological Museum*, Le Caire: L'Institut Français d'Archéologie Orientale.

Sahlins, M.D. (1987), *Islands of History*, Chicago: University of Chicago Press.

Sapir-Hen, L. (2019), 'Late Bronze and Iron Age Livestock of the Southern Levant: Their Economic and Symbolic Roles', *TA*, 46 (2): 227–36.

Sapir-Hen, L. (2020), 'Human–Animal Relationship with Work Animals. Symbolic and Economic Roles of Donkeys and Camels During the Bronze and Iron Ages in the Southern Levant', *ZDPV*, 136 (1): 83–94.

Schelske, A. (1997), *Die kulturelle Bedeutung von Bildern: Soziologische und semiotische Überlegungen zur visuellen Kommunikation*, Wiesbaden: DUV.

Scholz, O.E. (2004), 'Was heißt es, ein Bild zu verstehen?', in K. Sachs-Hombach and K. Rehkämper (eds), *Bild – Bildwahrnehmung – Bildverarbeitung. Interdisziplinäre Beiträge zur Bildwissenschaft*, 2nd edn, 105–17, Bildwissenschaft 15, Wiesbaden: DUV.

Schroer, S. (1987), *In Israel gab es Bilder: Nachrichten von darstellender Kunst im Alten Testament*, OBO 74, Fribourg: Fribourg Academic Press / Göttingen: Vandenhoeck & Ruprecht.

Schroer, S. (2006), 'Gender und Ikonographie – aus der Sicht einer feministischen Bibelwissenschaftlerin', in S. Schroer (ed.), *Images and Gender: Contributions to the Hermeneutics of Reading Ancient Art*, 107–24, OBO 220, Fribourg: Fribourg Academic Press / Göttingen: Vandenhoeck & Ruprecht.

Schroer, S. (2014), 'Tod und Gender im alten Israel und seinen Nachbarkulturen', in S. Schroer (ed.), *Sensenfrau und Klagemann: Sterben und Tod mit Gendervorzeichen*, 43–52, Zürich: TVZ.

Schroer, S. (2017), 'The Iconography of Shrine Models of Khirbet Qeiyafa', in S. Schroer and S. Münger (eds), *Khirbet Qeiyafa in the Shephelah: Papers Presented at a Colloquium of the Swiss Society for Ancient Near Eastern Studies Held at the University of Bern, September 6, 2014*, 137–58, OBO 282, Fribourg: Fribourg Academic Press / Göttingen: Vandenhoeck & Ruprecht.

Schroer, S. and T. Staubli (2017 [1998]), *Body Symbolism in the Bible*, Collegeville, MN: Liturgical Press [first pub. in German as *Die Körpersymbolik der Bibel*].

Schuhmacher-Chilla, D. (2018), *Anthropologische Kunsttheorie*, Kunstpädagogische Positionen 42, Hamburg: Universität Hamburg.

Sonesson, G. (1993), 'Die Semiotik des Bildes: Zum Forschungsstand am Anfang der 90er Jahre', *Zeitschrift für Semiotik*, 15 (1/2): 127–60.

Staubli, T. (2010), 'Bull Leaping and Other Images and Rites of the Southern Levant in the Sign of Scorpius', *UF*, 41: 611–30.

Strawn, B.A. (2005), *What is Stronger than a Lion? Leonine Image and Metaphor in the Hebrew Bible and the Ancient Near East*, OBO 212, Fribourg: Fribourg Academic Press / Göttingen: Vandenhoeck & Ruprecht.

Uehlinger, C. (1997), 'Anthropomorphic Cult Statuary in Iron Age Palestine and the Search for Yahweh's Cult Images', in K. van der Toorn (ed.), *The Image and the Book: Iconic Cults, Aniconism, and the Rise of Book Religion in Israel and the Ancient Near East*, 97–155, CBET 21, Leuven: Peeters.

Uehlinger, C., ed. (2000), *Images as Media – Sources for the Cultural History of the Ancient Near East and the Eastern Mediterranean (1st Millennium BCE): Proceedings of an International Symposium Held in Fribourg on November 25–29, 1997*, OBO 175, Fribourg: Fribourg Academic Press / Göttingen: Vandenhoeck & Ruprecht.

Uehlinger, C. (2001), 'Bildquellen und "Geschichte Israels": grundsätzliche Überlegungen und Fallbeispiele', in C. Hardmeier (ed.), *Steine – Bilder – Texte: Historische Evidenz außerbiblischer und biblischer Quellen*, 25–77, Arbeiten zur Bibel und ihrer Geschichte 5, Leipzig: Evangelische Verlagsanstalt.

Weibel, P. (2001), 'Kunst als soziale Konstruktion', in A. Müller, K.H. Müller and F. Stadler (eds), *Konstruktivismus und Kognitionswissenschaft: Kulturelle Wurzeln und Ergebnisse*, 2nd edn, 193–208, New York: Springer.

Weippert, H. (2017), 'Die von Löwen und anderen Wesen getragene und beschützte Welt: Ein Erbe der bronzezeitlichen Stadtkultur Palästinas an ihre eisenzeitliche Nachfolgerin – Mit einem Exkurs von Henrike Michelau', in J. Kamlah, R. Schafer and M. Witte (eds), *Zauber und Magie im antiken Palästina und in seiner Umwelt: Kolloquium des Deutschen Vereins zur Erforschung Palästinas vom 14. bis 16. November 2014 in Mainz*, 199–251, ADPV 46, Wiesbaden: Harrassowitz.

Weissenrieder, A. and F. Wendt (2005), 'Images as Communication: The Methods of Iconography', in A. Weissenrieder, F. Wendt and P. von Gemünden (eds), *Picturing the New Testament: Studies in Ancient Visual Images*, 3–49, WUNT II/193, Tübingen: Mohr Siebeck.

Wiesing, L. (2000), *Phänomene im Bild*, München: Fink.

Wiesing, L. (2005), *Artifizielle Präsenz: Studien zur Philosophie des Bildes*, Frankfurt am Main: Suhrkamp.

Wiesing, L. (2016), *The Visibility of the Image: History and Perspectives of Formal Aesthetics*, transl. N.A. Roth, New York: Bloomsbury [orig. pub. 2008, as *Die Sichtbarkeit des Bildes. Geschichte und Perspektiven der formalen Ästhetik*, Frankfurt am Main: Campus].

Winter, U. (1983), *Frau und Göttin: Exegetische und ikonographische Studien zum weiblichen Gottesbild im Alten Israel und in dessen Umwelt*, OBO 53, Fribourg: Fribourg Academic Press / Göttingen: Vandenhoeck & Ruprecht.

Winter, U. (2002), 'Der Lebensbaum im Alten Testament und die Ikonographie des stilisierten Baumes in Kanaan/Israel', in U. Neumann-Gorsolke and P. Riede (eds), *Das Kleid der Erde: Pflanzen in der Lebenswelt des alten Israel*, 138–62, Stuttgart: Calwer.

Wolff, H.W. (1994 [1973]), *Anthropologie des Alten Testaments*, 6th edn, Kaiser Taschenbücher 91, Gütersloh: Gütersloher Verlagshaus.

Wright, J.L. (2012), 'Die Zerstörung des Ökosystems als Element der Kriegsführung im Alten Israel', in A. Berlejung (ed.), *Disaster and Relief Management / Katastrophen und ihre Bewältigung*, 179–203, FAT 81, Tübingen: Mohr Siebeck.

Wyssmann, P. (2014), 'The Coinage Imagery of Samaria and Judah in the Late Persian Period', in C. Frevel, K. Pyschny and I. Cornelius (eds), *A 'Religious Revolution' in Yehûd? The Material Culture of the Persian Period as a Test Case*, 221–66, OBO 267, Fribourg Academic Press / Göttingen: Vandenhoeck & Ruprecht.

Yahalom-Mack, N., N. Panitz-Cohen and R. Mullins (2018), 'From a Fortified Canaanite City-State to "a City and a Mother" in Israel: Five Seasons of Excavation at Tel Abel Beth Maacah', *NEA*, 81 (2): 145–56.

# INDEX OF SOURCES

**Ancient Near Eastern Sources**

Alalakh Tablet
17     482

*ANET³*
408–10     195 n.10

Atra-hasis
I 237–43     247

CAT
1.17     461
1.20–2     461
1.21     462

COS
1.41: 90–1     196 n.12
2.113A: 262–4     197 n.15
2.34     245

EA
9:7–10     215
17:51     215
100     335

KAI
309     245

*Papyrus Westcar*
1.16–20     332-3
4.18–20     333

Ras Shamra Texts
16.145     482
20.22     336 n.16

**Biblical Sources**

Hebrew Bible/Old Testament
*Genesis*
1–11     359, 387
1     358, 361–3, 400
1.1     84
1.1–2.4a     360
1.9–10     362
1.26     73, 362
1.26–28     245
1.28     73, 245, 246, 362
1.29–30     245
2–3     361, 363, 501
2     361–3
2.4     482
2.4b–3.24     246
2.7     246, 247 n.2
2.15–25     247 n.2
2.17     247
2.19     246
2.22–24     246 n.1
2.23     246 n.1
3     247
3.5     247
3.7–10     247
3.16     239, 360, 360 n.14
3.17     360 n.14
3.18     512
3.19     246
3.22     247
3.22–24     247
4     395
4.21     331
5.1     246
7.1     84, 162
8     395
9.1     246
9.3–4     246
9.6     246, 335
10     162 n.17
11–37     387
11.29     166
12.7     84
12.17     294 n.14
12–36     179
13.18     84
14.17–20     84
15     395
16     442, 448

| | | | |
|---|---|---|---|
| 17 | 395 | 33.31 | 84 |
| 17.12 | 448 | 34 | 395 |
| 18 | 444 | 34.1–31 | 442 |
| 18.1–15 | 280 | 34.2–3 | 248 |
| 18.19 | 162 | 34.12 | 166 |
| 19 | 280 | 34.14 | 270 |
| 19.1 | 195 | 34.20–24 | 195 |
| 19.5 | 280 | 34.31 | 270 |
| 19.11 | 294 n.14 | 35 | 395 |
| 20.12 | 166 | 35.27–9 | 463 |
| 20.17–18 | 294 n.14 | 38.24 | 197 |
| 21 | 396 | 36 | 162 n.17 |
| 21.4 | 448 | 36–50 | 179 |
| 21.21 | 290 n.6 | 37–50 | 387 |
| 21.23 | 250 | 37.28 | 218 |
| 22.1 | 288 | 38 | 164 |
| 23 | 215, 395 | 38.24 | 193 |
| 23.1–20 | 459 | 38.25–26 | 193 |
| 23.3–15 | 463 | 39.14 | 318 n.16, 318 |
| 23.4 | 246 n.1, 481 | 39.17 | 318 n.16, 318 |
| 23.6 | 215 | 40 | 162 |
| 23.19 | 404, 463 | 40.15 | 318 n.16 |
| 24 | 395 | 41 | 162 |
| 24.3 | 318 | 41.12 | 318, 318 n.16 |
| 24.7 | 318 n.17 | 41.41–43 | 195 |
| 24.15 | 166 | 42.19 | 164 n.24 |
| 24.28 | 163 n.20, 437 | 42.33 | 164 n.24 |
| 24.38 | 162 | 42.38 | 246 |
| 24.40 | 162 | 43.32 | 318, 318 n.16 |
| 25 | 52, 395 | 44.30–31 | 248 |
| 25.7–10 | 459 | 45.1–11 | 162 |
| 25.8 | 246 | 45.18 | 164 n.24 |
| 25.9 | 463 | 46.31 | 437 |
| 25.17 | 459 | 48.7 | 464 |
| 25.19–23 | 448 | 49.24 | 84 |
| 25.19 | 464 | 49.28 | 437 |
| 25.29 | 439 | 50 | 395 |
| 25.34 | 439 | 50.1–3 | 460 |
| 27.38 | 265 | 50.1–11 | 460 |
| 28 | 395 | 50.13 | 463 |
| 28.8–20 | 84 | | |
| 28.18 | 386, 449 | *Exodus* | |
| 28.21 | 162 | 1.15 | 318 n.16 |
| 28.22 | 449 | 1.16 | 318 n.16 |
| 28.20 | 439 | 1.19 | 318 n.16 |
| 29 | 166 | 2.7 | 318 n.16 |
| 29.15–30.24 | 448 | 2.11 | 318 n.16 |
| 29.22 | 448 | 2.13 | 318 n.16 |
| 30 | 395 | 2.20 | 439 |
| 31.27 | 331 | 2.21 | 288 |
| 31.54 | 459 | 3.14 | 84 |
| 33.8–10 | 84 | 3.18 | 318 n.16 |

# INDEX OF SOURCES

| | | | |
|---|---|---|---|
| 4.6 | 294 | 24 | 406 |
| 5.3 | 318 n.16 | 24.3–7 | 334 |
| 6.14 | 437 | 25–31 | 406, 406 n.24, 407, 409 |
| 6.25 | 437 | 25–40 | 406 |
| 7–9 | 446 | 25 | 406 |
| 7–11 | 294 n.14 | 25.1–9 | 406 |
| 7.1 | 291 | 25.8 | 406 |
| 7.16 | 318 n.16 | 28 | 407 |
| 7.28 | 440 | 29.45–46 | 247 |
| 13.14 | 199 | 30 | 396 n.2 |
| 6.14–25 | 162 n.17 | 30.22–24 | 407 |
| 9.1 | 318 n.16 | 31.1–5 | 173 |
| 9.13 | 318 n.16 | 32–34 | 406 |
| 10.3 | 318 n.16 | 32.19–25 | 265 |
| 11.5 | 249 | 32.26 | 265 |
| 12.3–4a | 446 | 32.27 | 265 |
| 14.5 | 321 n.21 | 33.11 | 291 |
| 15 | 338 | 34.6 | 314 |
| 15.19–21 | 292 | 34.9 | 313 |
| 15.20–21 | 289 n.4, 331 | 34.26 | 249 |
| 15.20 | 291 | 35–40 | 406, 406 n.24, 407, 409 |
| 16.3 | 440 | 40.34–35 | 406, 407 |
| 17.8–16 | 312 n.7 | 40.34 | 406 |
| 18.2 | 288 | | |
| 18.13–23 | 197 | *Leviticus* | |
| 18.21 | 250 | 1–5 | 255 |
| 19 | 406 | 1–7 | 406, 433 |
| 20.1–21 | 406 n.23 | 1–16 | 406–7 |
| 20.2–3 | 247 | 2 | 407 |
| 20.2 | 199 | 2.4 | 440 |
| 20.3 | 312, 319 | 2.5 | 440 |
| 20.8–11 | 447 | 3.16 | 407, 439 |
| 20.12 | 232 | 4–5 | 252 |
| 20.19–23.33 | 232 | 6.21 | 440 |
| 20.22–23.33 | 255, 406 n.23 | 7 | 448 |
| 21.8–11 | 414 | 7.9 | 440 |
| 21.2–11 | 174, 249 | 7.15 | 446 |
| 21.2–4 | 174 | 8 | 406 n.25 |
| 21.15 | 232 | 9 | 406 n.25 |
| 21.17 | 232 | 9.24 | 406 n.25 |
| 21.21 | 174 | 10 | 406 n.25, 409 n.32 |
| 21.28–32 | 249 | 10.10 | 254 |
| 21.28–36 | 255 | 11–15 | 295, 406 |
| 22.16–17 | 166 | 11 | 400, 445 |
| 22.29 | 249 | 11.2–23 | 433 |
| 23.4–5 | 249, 252 | 11.35 | 440 |
| 23.8 | 198 | 11.47 | 254 |
| 23.10–12 | 447 | 12.6 | 448 |
| 23.11 | 249 | 12.12–29 | 249 |
| 23.12 | 249 | 13–14 | 254, 290, 293 n.12, 296 |
| 23.14–17 | 445 | 13 | 407 |
| 23.19 | 249 | 13.2 | 290 |

| | | | |
|---|---|---|---|
| 13.3 | 295 | 11.20 | 301 |
| 13.45–46 | 291, 295, 298 | 11.21 | 301 |
| 14.8 | 291, 295, 298 | 11.24–30 | 291 n.9 |
| 15 | 407 | 11.33–35 | 302 |
| 16 | 252, 396 n.2, 406 | 12 | 287–9, 289 n.4, 291–3, 295, 296 n.19, 298, 300–2 |
| 16.14 | 403 n.14 | | |
| 17–26 | 406 n.23 | 12.1 | 288 |
| 18.6–18 | 163 | 12.2 | 290 |
| 18.22–24 | 249 | 12.3 | 291 |
| 18.24–25 | 296 | 12.4 | 290 |
| 19.3 | 232 | 12.5 | 290 |
| 19.18 | 252 | 12.6–7 | 291 |
| 19.19 | 254 | 12.6 | 301 |
| 20.10 | 239 | 12.7 | 291 |
| 20.11–12 | 163 | 12.8 | 291, 301 |
| 20.15–16 | 249 | 12.9–10 | 294 n.14 |
| 20.25 | 254 | 12.10 | 287, 293–4 |
| 22.27–28 | 249 | 12.11–12 | 290, 295 |
| 23.2–3 | 447 | 12.12 | 295, 301 |
| 23.4–25 | 445 | 12.14 | 298 |
| 23.14–17 | 386 n.38 | 12.15 | 289 |
| 23.43 | 199 | 13.8 | 295 |
| 25 | 447, 482–3 | 13.11 | 295 |
| 25.11 | 249 | 13.15 | 295 |
| 25.14–17 | 196 | 13.20 | 295 |
| 25.29 | 174 | 13.25 | 295 |
| 25.29–31 | 255 | 13.27 | 295 |
| 25.39–55 | 174 | 13.30 | 295 |
| 26.26 | 440 | 13.59 | 295 |
| 26.34–35 | 447 | 14.10 | 335 |
| | | 14.11–12 | 294 n.14 |
| *Numbers* | | 14.36–37 | 294 n.14 |
| 1 | 162, 171 | 15.19 | 439 |
| 1.1–47 | 162 n.17 | 15.32–36 | 447 |
| 1.2 | 437 | 16.2 | 335 |
| 1.16 | 335, 437 | 17.12–15 | 294 n.14 |
| 5 | 396 n.2 | 19.15 | 246 |
| 6 | 396 n.2 | 20.1 | 289 n.4, 291 |
| 6.24–26 | 387 | 21.5 | 301 |
| 10.2 | 288 | 21.7 | 301 |
| 10.10 | 446 | 25.3–9 | 294 n.14 |
| 11–16 | 288 | 25.6–8 | 289 |
| 11 | 288, 298, 301–2 | 25.6–18 | 300 n.24 |
| 11.1 | 301 | 25.17–18 | 294 n.14 |
| 11.4 | 301 | 26 | 152, 162, 162 n.17, 171 |
| 11.4–6 | 301 | 26.2 | 162 |
| 11.5 | 301 | 26.59 | 292 |
| 11.8 | 440 | 27.1–8 | 238 |
| 11.13 | 301 | 27.1–11 | 164 n.25, 289 n.4 |
| 11.16–30 | 198 | 28.9–10 | 447 |
| 11.18 | 301 | 28.11–15 | 447 |
| 11.19 | 301 | 30 | 249 |

INDEX OF SOURCES

| | | | |
|---|---|---|---|
| 31.5–20 | 300 n.24 | 19.4–6 | 251 |
| 31.9–20 | 289 | 19.14 | 200 |
| 31.16 | 294 n.14 | 19.15–20 | 255 |
| 35.20 | 251 | 19.16–21 | 335 |
| 35.31–33 | 333 | 20 | 412 |
| 36.1–12 | 164 n.25 | 20.2–4 | 428 |
| | | 20.19 | 513 |
| *Deuteronomy* | | 21 | 413 n.46 |
| 3.11 | 461 | 21.1–9 | 336 n.16 |
| 4 | 254 | 21.10–14 | 189 n.2, 414 |
| 4.32–40 | 247 | 21.10–21 | 413 |
| 4.34–37 | 199 | 21.11 | 414 |
| 5.1–22 | 406 n.23 | 21.12–13 | 396, 412–4 |
| 5.12–15 | 447 | 21.18–21 | 193, 195, 249, 253 |
| 5.15 | 251 | 21.21 | 193 |
| 5.16 | 232 | 22.4 | 195 |
| 6.4–9 | 249, 253 | 22.6–7 | 249, 513 |
| 6.5 | 248 | 22.9–11 | 254 |
| 6.12 | 253 | 22.13–24 | 195 |
| 6.20–21 | 199 | 22.13–30 | 414 |
| 6.20–25 | 253 | 22.15 | 198 |
| 7 | 413 | 22.20 | 255 |
| 7.5 | 449 | 22.22 | 239 |
| 7.9–12 | 314 n.11 | 22.28–29 | 166 |
| 7.18 | 386 | 22.30 | 164 |
| 8.2 | 386 | 23.6 | 321 n.21 |
| 10.17 | 198 | 23.20 | 309 |
| 11.1 | 320 | 24.18–22 | 251 |
| 12–26 | 406 n.23 | 25.4 | 249, 513 |
| 12.15–19 | 433 | 25.9–10 | 276 |
| 13.15 | 249, 255 | 25.5–10 | 164, 195, 276, 299 |
| 14 | 400 | 25.7 | 198 |
| 14.3–20 | 433 | 26.14 | 459, 462 |
| 14.11 | 249 | 27–30 | 412 n.44 |
| 14.22–27 | 446 | 27.20 | 164 |
| 14.26 | 446 | 29.2–29 | 199 |
| 15 | 253 | 29.17 | 162 |
| 15.1–18 | 447 | 29.25 | 319 |
| 15.12–17 | 174 | 30.10–14 | 247 |
| 15.15 | 251, 386 | 31.9–11 | 334 |
| 15.16–17 | 174, 189 n.2 | 31.10–13 | 336 |
| 16.1–12 | 199 | 32.7 | 199 |
| 16.1–17 | 445 | 32.22 | 460 |
| 16.11 | 189 n.2 | 34.10 | 291 |
| 16.12 | 251 | | |
| 16.18 | 334 | *Joshua* | |
| 16.18–20 | 198 | 2.6 | 436 |
| 16.19–20 | 255 | 2.12–14 | 250 |
| 17.4 | 255 | 4–7 | 196, 386 |
| 17.8–20 | 255 | 5 | 405 |
| 18.11 | 461 | 5.3 | 404 |
| 19.1–13 | 252, 255 | 5.4 | 405 |

| | | | |
|---|---|---|---|
| 5.5 | 405 | *Ruth* | |
| 7.16–18 | 152 | 1.6 | 439 |
| 7.16–26 | 197 | 1.8 | 163 n.20 |
| 8.30–35 | 334, 336 | 2.14 | 439 |
| 9 | 196 | 4.1–12 | 193 |
| 9.3–27 | 196 | 4.8 | 299 |
| 9.19–20 | 196 | | |
| 11–14 | 196 | *1 Samuel* | |
| 13–19 | 151, 200 | 1 | 409, 448 |
| 13–21 | 162 n.17 | 1.6 | 459 |
| 13.1–21.42 | 170 | 1.21 | 459 |
| 15.15b | 196 | 2.14 | 440 |
| 15.17–21 | 196 | 2.30 | 250 |
| 24 | 84, 386 | 2.35 | 428 |
| 24.4–7 | 199 | 3.20 | 428 |
| 24.17 | 199 | 4.6 | 318 |
| 24.22 | 335 | 5.6–6.12 | 294 n.14 |
| 24.26–27 | 386 | 7–9 | 266 |
| 24.30 | 464 | 7.1–2 | 84 |
| | | 7.5–10 | 428 |
| *Judges* | | 7.6 | 428 |
| 1 | 151 | 7.7–10 | 428 |
| 1.6–7 | 335 | 7.15 | 84 |
| 2.8–9 | 464 | 8 | 388 n.46 |
| 4 | 280 | 8.1 | 428 |
| 5 | 152 n.2 | 8.11–17 | 263 |
| 6–8 | 162 | 9.6–14 | 428 |
| 6.13 | 199 | 9.21 | 162 |
| 6.19 | 440 | 10.2 | 464 |
| 7.2 | 265 | 10.5 | 331 |
| 9 | 322 n.7 | 10.5–13 | 428 |
| 9.1 | 162, 163 n.20 | 10.6 | 321 n.21 |
| 11.1–40 | 442 | 10.9 | 321 n.21 |
| 11.34 | 331 | 10.21 | 162 |
| 13 | 448 | 11.1 | 197 |
| 14.10 | 448 | 14.51 | 84 |
| 14.19 | 164 n.24 | 15.12 | 464 |
| 15.4–11 | 335 | 15.12–15 | 84 |
| 17–21 | 437 | 18 | 266 |
| 17 | 229 | 18.1 | 248 |
| 17.2 | 230 | 18.4 | 194 |
| 18.31 | 84 | 18.6–7 | 331 |
| 19 | 280 | 18.25 | 166 |
| 19.24 | 280 | 19.18–24 | 428 |
| 19.29–30 | 442 | 20 | 447 |
| 20.1–2 | 84 | 20.5–6 | 447 |
| 20.1–7 | 442 | 20.6 | 84 |
| 20.1–11 | 197 | 21.1–6 | 84 |
| 20.7–11 | 335 | 22.14 | 250 |
| 20.12–13 | 483 | 24.1–7 | 194 |
| 21.2–3 | 84 | 24.20 | 437 |
| | | 25 | 230, 443 |

# INDEX OF SOURCES

| | | | |
|---|---|---|---|
| 25.3 | 230 | 21.8 | 84 |
| 25.18 | 230 | 23.2 | 301 |
| 25.24–31 | 230 | 24.10–15 | 294 n.14 |
| 25.25 | 280 | 24.21 | 481–2 |
| 25.38 | 230 | 30 | 174 |
| 28 | 459, 461 | | |
| 28.14 | 246 | *1 Kings* | |
| | | 1.9 | 445 |
| *2 Samuel* | | 1.41 | 445 |
| 1.11–12 | 410–1 | 1.49 | 445 |
| 1.19–27 | 338 | 2.3 | 428 |
| 2.5–6 | 250 | 2.7 | 250 |
| 2.8 | 84 | 2.29–34 | 482 |
| 3.29 | 294 | 3 | 248 |
| 3.31–37 | 404 n.18 | 3.9 | 253 |
| 3.36–37 | 411 n.39 | 3.9–12 | 247 |
| 5.1–5 | 84 | 4.1–6 | 171 |
| 5.6–10 | 194 | 4.7 | 217 |
| 5.8 | 248 | 4.20 | 217 |
| 6.1–15 | 194 | 5.1 | 196–7 |
| 8.15–18 | 171 | 5.1–12 | 196 |
| 9.10 | 174, 439 | 5.9 | 247 |
| 10–12 | 275 | 5.27–32 | 217 |
| 10.1–5 | 197, 277 | 6–8 | 409 n.33 |
| 10.3–4 | 197 | 7.13–14 | 173 |
| 10.4 | 275 | 8 | 84 |
| 10.5–8 | 197 | 8.23 | 314 n.11 |
| 11.14–25 | 195 | 8.62–63 | 217 |
| 12 | 396, 410–12 | 9.15–32 | 217 |
| 12.14–15 | 410 | 9.23 | 193 |
| 12.20–23 | 410 | 10 | 216 |
| 12.21 | 411 | 10.11–12 | 216 |
| 12.23 | 411 | 11 | 413 |
| 12.24 | 412 n.43 | 11.1 | 299 n.23 |
| 12.29–31 | 275, 277 | 12.3 | 335 |
| 12.42 | 412 | 14.10–14 | 294 n.14 |
| 13.12 | 280 | 10.15 | 218 |
| 13.31–36 | 412 | 14.23 | 449 |
| 14.2 | 410 n.36 | 16.33 | 299 n.23 |
| 14.5–7 | 333 | 17 | 428, 430 |
| 15.1 | 195 | 17.1 | 430 |
| 15.1–6 | 194, 483 n.23 | 17.17–23 | 247 |
| 15.13 | 194 | 18.19–21 | 289 |
| 16.4 | 174 | 18.46 | 430 |
| 16.5 | 162 | 19.6 | 439 |
| 18.18 | 464 | 20.34 | 219 |
| 18.21 | 289 | 20.39–43 | 335 |
| 18.33–19.4 | 412 | 21 | 464, 480–82 |
| 19.1–8 | 412 n.42 | 21.2 | 484 |
| 19.18 | 174 | 21.2a | 481 |
| 21 | 252 | 21.2–3 | 200 |
| 21.6 | 84 | 21.8 | 483 |

| | | | |
|---|---|---|---|
| 21.8–14 | 200 | 22 | 328 |
| 21.11 | 483 | 22.3–7 | 201 |
| 21.29 | 281 | 22.20 | 462 |
| 22.5–28 | 428 | 23.1–2 | 336 |
| 22.10 | 194 | 23.8 | 172 |
| 22.15–28 | 430 | 24 | 171 |
| 22.15–23 | 427 | 24.14 | 173 |
| 22.19 | 281 | 24.16 | 173 |
| 22.26 | 172 | 25 | 171 |
| 22.28 | 301 | | |

*1 Chronicles*

| | | | |
|---|---|---|---|
| *2 Kings* | | 1–8 | 275 |
| 1.9–15 | 427 | 2–8 | 171 |
| 1.16 | 294 n.14 | 2.55 | 173 nn.37-8 |
| 2.5 | 428 | 4.14 | 173 n.38 |
| 2.15 | 428 | 12.38–40 | 445 |
| 3.11–20 | 430 | 13.8 | 331 |
| 4 | 428, 430 | 21 | 173 n.38 |
| 4.1 | 174, 428 | 21.7–14 | 294 n.14 |
| 4.38–40 | 439 | 22–29 | 409 n.33 |
| 4.38–41 | 428, 440 | 28.2 | 276 |
| 4.7 | 219 | | |
| 4.8 | 231 | *2 Chronicles* | |
| 4.8–10 | 443 | 2.13–14 | 173 |
| 4.8–37 | 231, 448 | 6.14 | 314 n.11 |
| 4.12 | 231 | 7.14 | 281 |
| 5.26–27 | 294, 294 n.14 | 8.12–13 | 447 |
| 5.27 | 294 | 12.3–9 | 289 |
| 6.1–7 | 428, 430 | 19.4–11 | 198 |
| 6.8–23 | 428 | 19.8 | 198 |
| 6.15–17 | 427 | 21.14–15 | 294 n.14 |
| 7 | 428 | 24.16–23 | 294 |
| 8.1–6 | 231 | 26.16–20 | 294 n.14 |
| 9–10 | 481 | 20.28 | 331 |
| 9.1–10 | 428 | 30.11 | 281 |
| 9.21–26 | 200 | 32.9–15 | 289 |
| 9.25–26 | 481 | 34.8 | 172 |
| 9.34–7 | 465 | 36.23 | 318 n.17 |
| 9.35 | 465 | | |
| 9.37 | 465 | *Ezra* | |
| 10 | 84 | 1.2 | 318 n.17 |
| 10.24 | 335 | 2 | 176 |
| 12.4–8 | 201 | 2.61–62 | 299 |
| 12.9–15 | 201 | 3 | 218 |
| 14.23–25 | 316 n.12 | 3.7 | 178, 218 |
| 14.25 | 317, 320, 323 | 5.11 | 318 n.18 |
| 18–19 | 427 | 5.12 | 318 n.18 |
| 18.17–25 | 197 | 6.9 | 318 n.18 |
| 18.21 | 197 | 6.10 | 318 n.18 |
| 20.13–15 | 200 | 6.20 | 299 |
| 20.35–43 | 428 | 7.12 | 318 n.18 |
| 21.3–6 | 409 | 7.21 | 318 n.18 |

| | | | |
|---|---|---|---|
| 7.23 | 318 n.18 | 9.2 | 299 |
| 8.1 | 178 | 9.32 | 314 n.11 |
| 8.9 | 178 | 9.37 | 299 |
| 8.33 | 201 | 10.28 | 299 |
| 9–10 | 179–82, 296 | 10.33 | 299 |
| 9 | 252 | 10.35 | 177 n.43 |
| 9.1 | 183, 299 | 11.19 | 178 |
| 9.1–2 | 181 | 11.57–60 | 178 |
| 9.2 | 299 | 12.30 | 299 |
| 9.4 | 299 | 13 | 180 |
| 9.6 | 299 | 13.2 | 321 n.21 |
| 9.6–7 | 299 | 13.3 | 299 |
| 9.8 | 299 | 13.9 | 299 |
| 9.11 | 299 | 13.12 | 201 |
| 9.12 | 181 | 13.13 | 250 |
| 9.13 | 299 | 13.22 | 299 |
| 9.14 | 299 | 13.23 | 181 |
| 10 | 181 | 13.23–27 | 296 |
| 10.2 | 299 | 13.24 | 181 |
| 10.6 | 299 | 13.26–27 | 181 |
| 10.8 | 299 | 13.26 | 299 n.23 |
| 10.10 | 299 | 13.28 | 181 |
| 10.11 | 299 | 13.29 | 299 |
| 10.16 | 299 | 13.30 | 299 |
| 10.19 | 299 | 21–22 | 178 |

*Nehemiah*

*Esther*

| | | | |
|---|---|---|---|
| 1.4 | 318 n.18 | 4.11 | 194 |
| 1.5 | 314 n.11, 318 n.17 | | |
| 2.4 | 318 n.18 | *Job* | |
| 3.8 | 173 n.38, 178 | 1.4 | 446 |
| 3.26 | 178 | 1.5 | 409 |
| 3.31 | 173 n.38, 178 | 12.4 | 277 |
| 4.13 | 177 n.43 | 14.7–10 | 513 |
| 4.23 | 178 | 14.10 | 247 |
| 5.1–13 | 218 | 17.13 | 460 |
| 5.5 | 174 | 17.13–16 | 246 |
| 7 | 176 | 19.3 | 277 |
| 7.1 | 178 | 19.5 | 277 |
| 7.2 | 250 | 19.13 | 301 |
| 7.3 | 178 | 21.3 | 277 |
| 7.23 | 178 | 21.12–13 | 246 |
| 7.39 | 178 | 24.4–10 | 195 |
| 7.43 | 178 | 28.12–13 | 255 |
| 7.45 | 178 | 28.19 | 289 |
| 7.46 | 178 | 28.20–21 | 255 |
| 7.64 | 299 | 30.31 | 331 |
| 8.1–9 | 178 | 38.36 | 249 |
| 8.6 | 336 | 42.5–6 | 253 |
| 8.7–8 | 336 | 42.11 | 439 |
| 9 | 252 | | |

*Psalms*

| | |
|---|---|
| 4 | 279 |
| 6.6 | 247 |
| 8 | 246 |
| 12.6 | 281 |
| 12.7 | 281 |
| 12.12 | 281 |
| 15.16 | 331 |
| 16.10 | 460 |
| 18 | 247 |
| 22 | 279 |
| 22.16 | 460 |
| 25 | 279 |
| 25.1 | 331 |
| 25.1–3 | 279 |
| 25.10 | 314 n.11 |
| 30.4 | 246 |
| 30.12 | 321 n.21 |
| 31 | 279 |
| 32.26 | 281 |
| 33.2 | 331 |
| 33.12 | 281 |
| 33.19 | 281 |
| 33.23 | 281 |
| 34 | 279 |
| 34.27 | 281 |
| 35 | 279 |
| 35.2 | 278 |
| 36.12 | 281 |
| 37 | 279 |
| 38.3 | 294 n.14 |
| 38.5 | 294 n.14 |
| 39 | 279 |
| 40 | 279 |
| 42 | 248, 279 |
| 44 | 278–9 |
| 45 | 413 n.46 |
| 45.6 | 194 |
| 45.10–11 | 413 n.46 |
| 45.17 | 465 |
| 47 | 267, 278 |
| 47.4 | 267 |
| 47.5 | 267 |
| 47.9 | 278 |
| 48.8–9 | 253 |
| 49.16 | 247 |
| 50.20 | 301 |
| 51 | 247 |
| 55 | 279 |
| 57 | 279 |
| 58 | 252 |
| 63.2 | 248 |
| 66.13–15 | 405, 409 |
| 67.7 | 513 |
| 68.5–6 | 312 n.7 |
| 69 | 279 |
| 70 | 279 |
| 71 | 279 |
| 71.1 | 275 |
| 71.13 | 275 |
| 71.24 | 275 |
| 72 | 245, 248 |
| 73.12 | 265 |
| 73.26 | 247 |
| 74 | 279 |
| 78.19 | 301 |
| 79 | 279 |
| 80 | 279 |
| 81.3 | 446 |
| 82 | 323 n.22 |
| 84.3 | 248 |
| 85.13 | 513 |
| 86.13 | 246 |
| 88.5 | 247, 460 |
| 88.11–13 | 247 |
| 89 | 279 |
| 89.28 | 314 n.11 |
| 89.49 | 246 |
| 92.3 | 331 |
| 93 | 278 |
| 93.1 | 278 |
| 93.3–4 | 278 |
| 93.5 | 278 |
| 96 | 278 |
| 96.5 | 278 |
| 97 | 278 |
| 97.7 | 278 |
| 98 | 278 |
| 98.1–3 | 278 |
| 99 | 278 |
| 99.1 | 278 |
| 99.5 | 276 |
| 99.6–8 | 278 |
| 102 | 279 |
| 103.8 | 313 |
| 103.13 | 313 |
| 106.45 | 314 n.11 |
| 109 | 279 |
| 110.1 | 276 |
| 111.4 | 313 |
| 114 | 338 |
| 119 | 278–9 |
| 119.6 | 279 |
| 119.22 | 279 |

INDEX OF SOURCES 533

| | | | |
|---|---|---|---|
| 119.30 | 250 | 31.15 | 227 |
| 119.39 | 279 | 31.27 | 444 |
| 119.51 | 279 | | |
| 119.141 | 279 | *Ecclesiastes* | |
| 121 | 338 | 1.16–18 | 255 |
| 123 | 279 | 3.20 | 246 |
| 126 | 338 | 3.22 | 246 |
| 128 | 338 | 7.23–24 | 255 |
| 132.7 | 276 | 9.10 | 460 |
| 132.15 | 439 | 12 | 339 |
| 136.26 | 318, 318 n.18 | 12.7 | 246 |
| 137 | 363-6 | | |
| 137.6 | 365 | *Song of Songs* | |
| 142.4 | 195 | 1.6 | 269 |
| 199.99–100 | 279 | 1.7 | 248 |
| | | 3.1–3 | 269 |
| *Proverbs* | | 3.4 | 163 n.20 |
| 1–9 | 180 n.45, 249, 253, 291 | 5.7 | 269 |
| 2.16–19 | 300 n.24 | 8.1 | 269 |
| 3.3 | 251 | 8.2 | 163 n.20 |
| 5 | 339 | 8.11–12 | 269 |
| 5.5 | 300 n.24 | | |
| 5.14 | 335 | *Isaiah* | |
| 6.6–8 | 249 | 1.3 | 249 |
| 7.27 | 300 n.24 | 1.13–14 | 447 |
| 10.4 | 251 | 1.14 | 248 |
| 10.5 | 277 | 1.17 | 255 |
| 11.24 | 266 | 1.21 | 255 |
| 11.25 | 266 | 1.27 | 255 |
| 11.28 | 251 | 2.10 | 273 |
| 12.10 | 249, 251, 513 | 2.11 | 273–4 |
| 12.24 | 251 | 2.12 | 273 |
| 13.4 | 251 | 2.17 | 273–4 |
| 13.22 | 264 | 2.19 | 273 |
| 15.8 | 405 | 2.21 | 273 |
| 15.16–17 | 251 | 3.5 | 272 |
| 17.2 | 264 | 3.16 | 273 |
| 20.6 | 250 | 4.2 | 273 |
| 20.20 | 232 | 5.1–7 | 200 |
| 20.22 | 252 | 5.8–10 | 200 |
| 22.14 | 300 n.24 | 5.12 | 333 |
| 23.26 | 253 | 5.14 | 273 |
| 24.29 | 335 | 5.16 | 273 |
| 25.13 | 250 | 5.24–30 | 312 |
| 25.21–22 | 252 | 6.1 | 273 |
| 25.23 | 253 | 7.23–25 | 512 |
| 26.27 | 250 | 8.2 | 250 |
| 27.6 | 250 | 8–10 | 427 |
| 30.24–28 | 249 | 8.19 | 459, 461 |
| 31 | 229 | 8.23 | 274 |
| 31.10–31 | 231, 444 | 9.1 | 274 |
| 31.14–15 | 444 | 9.9 | 273 |

| | | | |
|---|---|---|---|
| 10.12 | 273 | 40–48 | 251 |
| 11.6–8 | 516 | 40.1–2 | 312 |
| 11.6–10 | 249 | 42.8 | 273 n.7 |
| 12.4 | 273, 273 n.7 | 42.21 | 273 |
| 12.5 | 273 | 43.4 | 272 |
| 13.3 | 273 | 43.20 | 272 |
| 13.9 | 273 | 43.23 | 272 |
| 13.11 | 273–4 | 44.9–18 | 254–5 |
| 13.19 | 273 | 44.13 | 273 |
| 14.4–20 | 338 | 44.19 | 439 |
| 14.5 | 194 | 44.20–25 | 254–5 |
| 14.9 | 461 | 44.23 | 273 |
| 14.10 | 247 | 45.14 | 289 |
| 14.11 | 273 | 47.1 | 274 |
| 14.13 | 512 | 47.3 | 274 |
| 16.6 | 273 | 48.1 | 273 n.7 |
| 18.2 | 289 | 48.9 | 273 n.7 |
| 18.7 | 273 n.7 | 49.3 | 273 |
| 20.5 | 273 | 49.5 | 272 |
| 22.15–25 | 275 | 50.1 | 174 |
| 22.18 | 274 | 50.10 | 273 n.7 |
| 22.23 | 275 | 52.1 | 273 |
| 23.8 | 272 | 52.5 | 273 n.7 |
| 23.9 | 272, 274 | 52.13 | 273 |
| 24.3 | 336 | 53.2 | 273 |
| 24.14 | 273 | 54.10 | 314 n.11 |
| 24.15 | 272, 273 n.7 | 55.5 | 272 |
| 24.16 | 273 | 55.8–9 | 254–5 |
| 24.23 | 274 | 56.3–5 | 464–5 |
| 25.1 | 273 n.7 | 56.5 | 273 |
| 25.3 | 272 | 56.6 | 273 n.7 |
| 26.5 | 273 | 57.8 | 459, 464 |
| 26.8 | 273 n.7 | 57.15 | 273 n.7 |
| 26.9 | 248 | 58.13 | 272 |
| 26.10 | 273 | 59.19 | 273 n.7 |
| 26.11 | 273 | 60.2 | 272 |
| 26.13 | 273 n.7 | 60.9 | 272, 273 n.7 |
| 26.15 | 272 | 60.13 | 272 |
| 26.19 | 247 | 60.15 | 273 |
| 28.1 | 273 | 60.19 | 273 |
| 28.3 | 273 | 60.21 | 273 |
| 28.4 | 273 | 61.1 | 276 |
| 28.5 | 273 | 61.3 | 273 |
| 29.13 | 272 | 61.6–7 | 274 |
| 29.23 | 273 n.7 | 62.3 | 273 |
| 30.13 | 273 | 63.12 | 273, 273 n.7 |
| 30.23–26 | 312 n.7 | 63.15 | 273 |
| 30.27 | 273 n.7 | 64.1 | 273 n.7 |
| 33.5 | 273 | 65.25 | 249, 516 |
| 35.2 | 273 | 66.5 | 272, 273 n.7, 274 |
| 36–37 | 427 | 66.22 | 273 |
| 38.10 | 460 | | |

# INDEX OF SOURCES

*Jeremiah*
| | |
|---|---|
| 1.1 | 428 |
| 1.13 | 440 |
| 2.13 | 319 |
| 2.17 | 319 |
| 2.19 | 319 |
| 3.3 | 312 |
| 7.18 | 448 |
| 7.12 | 84 |
| 7.24–26 | 312 |
| 8.7 | 249 |
| 9.9 | 428 |
| 10.2 | 254 |
| 12.13 | 512 |
| 13.14 | 313 |
| 13.23 | 289 |
| 14 | 275 |
| 14.4 | 275 |
| 16.5–7 | 462 |
| 17.21–23 | 447 |
| 18.1 | 430 |
| 18.41–45 | 430 |
| 19.20 | 428 |
| 20–21 | 427 |
| 22.9 | 319 |
| 23.16–17 | 254 |
| 23.18 | 427, 429–30 |
| 23.22 | 427, 429–30 |
| 23.25–26 | 254 |
| 24.1 | 173 |
| 27–29 | 427 |
| 28.8–9 | 429 |
| 28.15–17 | 427 |
| 29.2 | 173 |
| 31.13 | 321 n.21 |
| 31.31–34 | 247 |
| 31–33 | 289 |
| 32 | 214 |
| 35.8–10 | 173 |
| 37.21 | 219 |
| 38.6–14 | 289 |
| 39.16–18 | 289 |
| 49.38 | 194 n.7 |

*Lamentations*
| | |
|---|---|
| 1.20 | 321 n.21 |
| 2.1 | 276 |

*Ezekiel*
| | |
|---|---|
| 1.3 | 428 |
| 4.3 | 440 |
| 5.11 | 313 |
| 7.4 | 313 |
| 9 | 313 |
| 11.3 | 440 |
| 11.7 | 440 |
| 11.11 | 440 |
| 11.19 | 247 |
| 14 | 430 |
| 20.24 | 447 |
| 27 | 218 |
| 29.10 | 289 |
| 36.24–28 | 247 |
| 36.26 | 312 |
| 37.11–14 | 465 |
| 37.12 | 247 |
| 39 | 247 |

*Daniel*
| | |
|---|---|
| 2.18 | 318 n.18 |
| 2.19 | 318 n.18 |
| 2.37 | 318 n.18 |
| 2.44 | 318 n.18 |
| 4 | 247 |
| 9.4 | 314 n.11 |
| 12.2–3 | 247 |

*Hosea*
| | |
|---|---|
| 1.2 | 301, 319 |
| 2.11 | 447 |
| 4.10 | 319 |
| 4.12 | 319 |
| 6–7 | 440 |
| 7.4 | 440 |
| 10 | 84 |
| 11.8 | 321 n.21 |

*Joel*
| | |
|---|---|
| 2.12–14 | 321 |

*Amos*
| | |
|---|---|
| 2.6 | 174, 200 |
| 3.3–8 | 253 |
| 4.1 | 195 |
| 5.5 | 336 |
| 5.7 | 321 n.21 |
| 5.12 | 195 |
| 5.14–15 | 255, 321 |
| 6.4–7 | 333 |
| 8.5 | 447 |
| 8.5–6 | 447 |
| 8.6 | 174 |
| 8.14 | 84 |

## Jonah

| | |
|---|---|
| 1.1–2 | 314 |
| 1.1–3 | 315 |
| 1.2 | 321 |
| 1.3 | 314, 317, 321 |
| 1.4 | 317 |
| 1.4–16 | 315 |
| 1.5 | 317 |
| 1.6 | 320 |
| 1.7 | 317 |
| 1.8–9 | 317 |
| 1.9 | 314, 317–8, 320 |
| 1.14 | 314, 320–1 |
| 1.15 | 314 |
| 1.16 | 320 |
| 2 | 319, 322–3 |
| 2.1 | 318–9, 321 |
| 2.1–11 | 315 |
| 2.2 | 314, 321 |
| 2.2–7 | 314 |
| 2.3–10 | 320 n.20 |
| 2.8 | 314 |
| 2.9 | 319 |
| 2.10 | 314, 318, 320 |
| 3 | 321 |
| 3.1–2 | 314 |
| 3.1–3a | 315 |
| 3.2 | 321 |
| 3.3 | 314, 319, 321 |
| 3.3b-10 | 315 |
| 3.4 | 314, 319, 321 |
| 3.5–8 | 321 |
| 3.5–9 | 314 |
| 3.6–8 | 412 |
| 3.7–8 | 249 |
| 3.8 | 323 |
| 3.9 | 320–1 |
| 3.10 | 314, 319, 321, 412 |
| 4 | 412 |
| 4.1–11 | 315 |
| 4.2 | 313–4, 319, 321 |
| 4.2–3 | 320 n.20 |
| 4.4 | 319 |
| 4.6 | 319, 321 |
| 4.7 | 321 |
| 4.8 | 314, 321 |
| 4.9 | 318 |
| 4.11 | 314, 321 |
| 13.19 | 318 |
| 24.7 | 318 |

## Micah

| | |
|---|---|
| 2.2–5 | 200 |
| 3.3 | 440 |
| 6.4 | 292 |
| 6.8 | 255 |
| 17.2 | 437 |
| 17.10–12 | 437 |
| 18.14–16 | 437 |
| 18.22 | 437 |

## Habakkuk

| | |
|---|---|
| 2.1 | 301 |
| 3.4 | 337 |

## Zephaniah

| | |
|---|---|
| 3.6 | 219 |

## Haggai

| | |
|---|---|
| 1.6 | 312 |
| 2.12 | 439 |

## Zechariah

| | |
|---|---|
| 1.9 | 301 |
| 1.13 | 301 |
| 2.2 | 301 |
| 2.7 | 301 |
| 4.1 | 301 |
| 4.4 | 301 |
| 4.5 | 301 |
| 5.5 | 301 |
| 5.10 | 301 |
| 6.4 | 301 |
| 7.8–10 | 313 |
| 10.1 | 312 n.7 |
| 14.20–21 | 440 |

## Malachi

| | |
|---|---|
| 1.6–2.9 | 428 |
| 2.10–12 | 181 |
| 2.11 | 299 |

## New Testament
## Matthew

| | |
|---|---|
| 13.44 | 265 |

## Luke

| | |
|---|---|
| 14.12 | 266 |
| 14.13 | 266 |
| 14.14 | 247 |
| 15.11–32 | 230, 264 |
| 15.31 | 266 |

# INDEX OF SOURCES

| | |
|---|---|
| 31.16 | 231 |
| 31.17 | 231 |
| 31.18 | 231 |
| 31.20 | 231 |

*John*
| | |
|---|---|
| 9.2 | 294 n.14 |

*Acts*
| | |
|---|---|
| 24.15 | 247 |

*1 Corinthians*
| | |
|---|---|
| 15 | 247 |

Apocrypha/Deuterocanonical Books
*Tobit*
| | |
|---|---|
| 7.13–14 | 448 |
| 14.4 | 316 n.12 |

*Ecclesiasticus/Sirach*
| | |
|---|---|
| 3.11 | 275 |
| 17.1–2 | 246 |
| 26.29 | 265 |
| 27.2 | 265 |
| 29.23 | 265 |
| 33.24–29 | 174 |
| 35.17 | 195 |
| 38.24–34 | 173 |
| 49.10 | 316 n.12 |
| Ms A 6:14f. | 250 |

*2 Maccabees*
| | |
|---|---|
| 4.12–14 | 339 |
| 7.9–14 | 247 |

*1 Esdras*
| | |
|---|---|
| 5 | 176 |

Qumran Texts
| | |
|---|---|
| 4Q184 | 299, 300 |
| 4Q184.9–10 | 300 |
| 4QMMT B64–72 | 294 n.15 |

Rabbinic Literature
Babylonian Talmud
| | |
|---|---|
| Sôṭāh 15[a] | 294 n.15 |
| Šābû'ôt 8[a] | 294 n.15 |

**Other Ancient Sources**

Aelian
*Varia Hist.*
| | |
|---|---|
| 2.29 | 334 |

Athenaeus
*Deipnosophistae*
| | |
|---|---|
| 619b | 335 n.15 |

Cassius Dio
*Roman History*
| | |
|---|---|
| 55.27.1–2 | 328 n.4 |
| 61.16.2[a] | 328 n.4 |

Cicero
*In Verrem*
| | |
|---|---|
| 3.2.77 | 328 n.4 |

Claudius Aelianus
*Varia Historia*
| | |
|---|---|
| 2.39 | 335 n.15 |

Flavius Josephus
*Jewish Antiquities*
| | |
|---|---|
| 2.10.1, 239–53 | 289 |

Hermippus
*Frag. 88* | 334 |

Herodotus
*Histories*
| | |
|---|---|
| 1.1 | 380 |
| 1.136 | 339 n.28 |

Hesiod
*Work and Days*
| | |
|---|---|
| I: 265 | 250 |

Homer
*Iliad*
| | |
|---|---|
| 1:3–4 | 246 |

Plautus
*Mercator*
| | |
|---|---|
| 405–409 | 328 n.4 |

Plutarch

*Solon*
3 334

*Tiberius Gracchus*
8.7 328 n.4

*Gaius Gracchus*
17.6 328 n.4

Pseudo-Aristotle
*Problemata*
19.28.919–20ª 334-5

Seneca
*Ad Lucilius*
58.31 383 n.29

*Suasoriae*
1.6 328 n.4

Sophocles
*Antigone*
23.8.27–30 334

Strabo
*Geographica*
12.2.9 334, 335 n.15
15.3.19 339

Xenophon
*Oeconomicus* 232

**Renaissance Sources**

Petrarca
*Seniles* XVII, 2 383 n.29

# INDEX OF AUTHORS

Abbott, W.M. 457
Abela, A. 290, 301
Abou-Assaf, A. 245
Abu el-Haj, N. 85
Abulafia, D. 133 n.12
Ackerman, A. 448
Ackerman, R. 25–6
Ackerman, S. 291, 358, 404 n.18, 464
Adamo, D.T. 288–9
Adams, S.L. 207 n.4
Afanasjeva, V. 328, 332 n.10
Agelarakis, A.P. 107
Aguilar, M.I. 6, 138
Aharoni, Y. 135
Ahlström, G.W. 328 n.3
Ahn, J. 363–4
Aiken, E.J. 2
Albera, D. 132–3, 133 n.8
Albertz, R. 85, 119–20, 448 n.13
Albrecht, M. 102
Albright, W.F. 80–1, 87–8, 460
Allen, C.J. 315
Alt, A. 254, 335–6, 387 n.40
Alt, K. 246
Alter, R. 354, 357, 360
Altmann, P. 207 n.4, 434, 434 nn.2–3, 446
Ambos, C. 409 n.32
Amiry, S. 440, 442
Amit, Y. 351, 360, 481 n.22
Ammar, H. 226
Amzallag, N. 338, 338 n.23
Andersen, F.I. 481 n.22, 483
Anderson, B. 373
Anderson, D.G. 479 n.15
Anderson, G.A. 295, 410 n.35
Anderson, P.C. 116
Andrews, E.D. 423 n.3
Angel, H. 318, 318 n.16
Appadurai, A. 86, 444
Aranov, M.M. 335
Arias, S. 469
Arnold, B.T. 358, 362
Asher-Greve, J.M. 498, 501
Assmann, A. 380 n.23

Assmann, J. 198 n.16, 249–51, 253–5, 254 n.7, 375 n.5, 384–5, 384 n.31, 385 n.36
Assmuth, L. 226–8
Astour, M.C. 135
Atalay, S. 83
Atkinson, J.M. 421 n.1, 422
Augé, M. 7
Avalos, H. 238, 335
Avner, U. 116
Avrahami, Y. 252 n.5, 253, 274–5
Avruch, K. 215
Azar, G. 113
Aznar, C.A. 207 n.2

Baadsgaard, A. 228 n.6
Bach, A. 223
Backfish, E.H.P. 437
Badè, W.F. 99
Bahrani, Z. 497
Bailey, C. 3 n.3
Bakhtin, M.M. 337
Bal, M. 353, 358
Baldensperger, P.J. 2
Ballentine, D.S. 353 n.4
Baltzer, K. 483
Banfield, E.C. 132 n.5
Bannester, E.M. 190 n.3, 191
Banning, E.B. 100, 116
Bar-Efrat, S. 352, 353 n.3
Bar-Yosef, E. 1
Barkay, G. 387
Barnard, A. 130 n.1
Barr, J. 252
Barrett, J.L. 402 n.12, 403, 403 n.14, 411
Barstad, H.M. 329
Barth, F. 7
Barthes, R. 32 n.6
Bartlett, W.H. 49, 51
Barton, J. 81, 84, 86, 255, 446
Battini, L. 436
Bayliss, M. 462
Beard, J. 449
Beard, M. 408

Beaumont, L.A. 116
Bechtel, L. 270–1, 274 n.8, 275–7, 279, 279 n.12
Beck, P. 504
Becking, B. 363–5
Behrend, H. 423 n.5
Bell, C. 397–8, 397 n.3, 400, 402, 402 n.12, 403 n.14, 404, 411 n.40, 412–3, 412 n.41
Bell, R. 339 n.29
Bellah, R.N. 254
Bellinger, W.H. 363
Bellis, A.O. 288
Belting, H. 494–5
Ben Zvi, E. 316, 366 n.18, 388 n.45
Ben-Arieh, Y. 1–2, 99
Ben-Shlomo, D. 107, 441
Ben-Yehoyada, N. 133 n.8
Ben-Yehuda, N. 85
Bendor, S. 27 n.3, 161, 162 n.15, n.17, 163–6, 164 n.24, 167 n.29, 170–1, 177 n.43
Benedict, R. 250
Benjamin, D.C. 6, 129, 134, 136 n.20, 137–8, 189 nn.1–2, 195 n.11, 198–9, 200 n.18, 268, 442
Benjamin, M. 357 n.10
Bennett, T.W. 334
Bergant, D. 269
Bergman, J. 329
Berlejung, A. 10, 247–8, 255, 493, 496–9, 501–3
Berlin, A. 363
Berlin, I. 251
Berlinerblau, J. 405 n.19, 412 n.41
Bertholet, A. 4
Berquist, J.L. 176, 178, 178 n.44, 181, 183, 251 n.4, 469 n.1
Beukenhorst, M. 413
Bewer, J.A. 317 n.13
Bibb, B.D. 407 n.27
Biebuyck, D. 473 n.9
Bienkowski, P. 207 n.3
Binford, L.R. 82–3, 374 n.2
Biran, A. 116
Bird, P.A. 442
Birkeland, H. 336
Black, J. 23, 25
Blenkinsopp, J. 172 n.34, 173 n.35, 176, 176 n.42
Blinkenberg, A. 376 n.8
Bloch, Marc 84
Bloch, Maurice 455

Bloch-Smith, E. 404 n.18, 459–60, 463, 484 n.27
Block, D.I. 223 n.1, 235
Blok, A. 132–3, 133 n.8, 134 n.15, 135 n.18
Bloom, M. 26, 33–4
Blum, E. 481 n.20, n.22
Blunt, A. 54
Boas, F. 7 n.9, 77–9, 81, 133 n.6
Bodel, J. 137 n.22
Boer, R. 22, 207–8, 208 n.5, 210, 218
Boissevain, J. 133 n.8, 135 n.18
Boivin, N. 69, 86
Bolin, T.M. 129, 307
Boman, T. 252–3, 252 n.5
Bonatz, D. 462, 493
Bonds, M.E. 335 n.15
Bonfiglio, R.P. 492
Bonte, P. 132 n.5, 133 n.10
Boorer, S. 407 n.27
Bordreuil, P. 245
Borges, J.L. 329
Borowski, O. 227, 434, 438–40
Bossen, L. 175 n.41
Botha, P.J. 274 n.8, 278–9, 313
Bottéro, J. 102, 439–40
Bourdieu, P. 70, 86–7, 268, 402, 493, 515
Bowen, N.R. 413 n.46
Braudel, F. 133 n.6
Braun, J. 330–1
Bravo, B. 76
Brayford, S. 239
Brenner, A. 175, 293 n.12, 358
Bresson, A. 133 n.12
Brett, M.G. 9 n.11
Brichto, H. 460, 464–5, 484 n.26
Bridge, S.L. 316
Briquet, J.-L. 135 n.18
Brody, A. 436 n.5
Bromberger, C. 133 n.8
Brosius, C. 397 n.3
Brosses, Ch. de. 21
Brown, M. 331
Brubaker, R. 81
Brueggemann, W. 336 n.18
Brumfiel, E.M. 236
Bruner, J. 351
Brunner-Traut, E. 497
Bryce, T. 375 n.6
Bryer, A. 102
Buckingham, J.S. 39, 48, 48 n.1, 52–3, 56, 60–1, 64
Buckley, T. 133 n.6

INDEX OF AUTHORS

Bultmann, C. 412–14
Bunimovitz, S. 436, 464
Burckhardt, J.L. 43, 45, 55
Burnett, J.S. 503
Burnette-Bletsch, R. 9 n.12
Burns, R. 292, 301
Burnside, J.P. 484 n.25
Burton, R.F. 51, 59–60
Busoni, F. 329
Byock, J.L. 334

Cabot, H. 133 n.8
Camp, C.V. 180–1, 231, 288, 290, 290 n.7, 292 n.11, 293, 296 n.18, 298, 469 n.1
Campbell, A.F. 332
Campbell, J.K. 131, 131 n.4, 135 n.18, 136, 228, 238
Canaan, T. 99
Candea, M. 3, 130 n.1
Carasik, M. 253
Carney, T.F. 164 n.22, 171, 174
Caro Baroja, J. 134 n.15
Carr, E.H. 69
Carr, D.M. 327–8, 332, 340, 351, 405 n.20
Carter, C.E. 214
Carter, J.B. 333
Cartledge, T.W. 194, 405 n.19
Cartwright, A. 480 n.16
Cartwright, C.R. 101
Caselli, A. 116
Cassuto, D. 227, 228 n.6
Cassuto, P. 328 n.5
Caton, S. 154 n.3
Cattell, M.G. 380 n.23
Causse, A. 4
Chadwick, O. 21
Chalcraft, D.J. 3 n.4, 6
Chaney, M.L. 200, 200 n.19
Charalambidou, X. 117
Chi, A.N. 329
Childe, V.G. 80
Childs, B.S. 446
Cho, P.K.-K. 353 n.5
Chorev-Halewa, H. 136
Chrystal, G. 23
Clarke, D. 70–1
Clarke, E.D. 60–1, 64
Clarke, M.H. 116
Clements, R.E. 6
Climo, J.J. 380 n.23
Clines, D.J.A. 351

Coats, G.W. 288, 290
Cobham, C.D. 103
Coenen, H. 87
Cogan, M. 193 n.6, 201, 231
Cohen, A. 136
Cohen, H. 330
Cohen, N.G. 301
Cohn, B.S. 476 n.11
Colbert, D. 328–9
Coley, N. 74
Collingwood, R.G. 69
Collins, A.Y. 287
Collins, B.J. 460
Collins, C.J. 361
Collins, J.J. 352 n.2
Collon, D. 434
Colson, E. 472 n.7
Comte, A. de. 21, 49
Conder, C.R. 45–6, 52, 54–5, 58, 60
Conkey, M.W. 167
Connerton, P. 379, 379 n.21
Conte, É. 33
Cook, S.L. 6, 178 n.44, 198
Cook, T. 39
Coomber, R. 299
Coote, R.B. 81, 136, 174
Copher, C.B. 288
Corbin, A.L. 472
Cornelius, I. 499, 504
Cornwall, A. 167
Coser, L.A. 378 nn.15–17
Couffignal, R. 364–5
Coulanges, F. de. 26
Counihan, C.M. 227–8, 433 n.1
Cradic, M.S. 463–4
Craven, T. 229 n.7
Crawford, O.G.S. 76
Crenshaw, J.L. 172 n.34, 199, 339, 339 n.27
Cribiore, R. 339 n.30, 340
Cronauer, P.T. 481 nn.20–2
Crook, Z.A. 137, 266–7, 269 n.3, 271 n.6, 307–14, 308 n.2, 310 n.4, 311 n.5, 313 n.9, 322–3
Cross, F.M. 312 n.8
Crouch, C.L. 81
Crowfoot, G.M. 99
Crumley, C.L. 236
Crüsemann, F. 156 n.6
Cubitt, G. 380 n.23
Culley, R.C. 6
Cunningham, J.J. 2, 99

Dale, G. 213 n.9
Dalman, G. 99, 134 n.13
Damerow, P. 255
Dancygier, B. 351
D'Andrade, R. 356, 356 n.8
Daniel, G.E. 72
Darby, E.D. 119, 510
Daube, D. 334
Daviau, P.M.M. 499, 508
Davies, D. 411 n.40
Davies, P.R. 8, 81, 178 n.44
Davis, E.A. 484
Davis, J. 130–1, 133 n.7
Davis, T.W. 2, 71
Dawes, S.B. 281
Day, E. 4
Day, P.L. 167
de Geus, C.H.J. 160–1, 163 n.18, 165, 165 n.27, 167 n.29
de Hulster, I.J. 492, 510
de Jong, A. 338
De Nardi, S. 383 n.30
de Vaux, R. 160, 170 n.31, 171
Delnero, P. 410 n.34, 411 n.37
Démare-Lafont, S. 333 n.12, 334 n.14, 335
DeMaris, R.E. 404, 411 n.38
Dennehy, N. 353
Deniaux, É. 135 n.18
deSilva, D.A. 137, 278, 314
Deurloo, K.A. 362
Deutschmann, B.C. 228, 239
Dever, W.G. 71, 81, 85
di Vito, R.A. 248
Diakonoff, I.M. 209, 209 n.7
Dianteill, E. 7
Dick, H.P. 353
Dickson, J.P. 281
Dietrich, J. 9, 245, 247–8, 248 n.3, 250–5, 253 n.6, 500
Dietrich, M. 335
Dietrich, W. 339
Diringer, D. 99
Dixon, W.H. 55–6, 59, 99
Dobbs-Allsopp, F.W. 331
Dometios, P. 107, 117
Douglas, M. 5, 28, 30–3, 32 n.5, 179, 270, 281, 290 n.7, 292–6, 292 n.11, 296 n.18, 355, 400–1, 400 n.7, 401 n.10, 444, 446
Doughty, C.M. 44
Doumani, B. 136
Downing, G. 270

Dresch, P. 154 n.3
Driesch, A. von den. 103
Douaire, J. 330, 338
Dube, M.W. 9
Duhaime, J. 33
Dumbrill, R. 331
Durkheim, É. 5, 7 n.9, 26, 29, 87, 130, 154 n.3, 378–9, 398–9, 455, 457, 470 n.4
Durley, T. 61

Ebeling, J. 100, 105, 436 n.5, 440, 481 n.22, 484 n.28
Eberhart, C. 407 n.26
Edelman, D.V. 103
Edzard, L. 328 n.5
Effah Darko, G. 277
Egilsdóttir, Á. 328
Egoumenidou, F. 120
Ehrenreich, R.M. 236
Eichenberg, A. 376 n.9
Eickelman, D.F. 134 n.15, 135 n.17, 152, 154, 154 n.3, 155–8, 169
Eilberg-Schwartz, H. 27
Einsler, L. 98
Eisenstadt, S.N. 135 n.18, 136 n.19
Elat, M. 206
Elden, S. 469 n.2
Eliade, M. 430 n.10
Elias, T.O. 472 n.7
Eliav, Y. 72
Elkana, Y. 254
Ellenbogen, J. 88
Elliott, J.H. 266, 268, 271, 308 n.2, 313
Elsabbagh, M. 330, 338
Ember, C.R. 175 n.41
Emerton, J.A. 33
Emmerson, G.I. 175 n.41
Engels, F. 209
Englund, R.K. 255
Engnell, I. 328, 332
Erbele-Küster, D. 290, 295, 296 n.18
Ernst, A.B. 255
Eskenazi, T.C. 176 n.42, 180, 180 n.45, 181–2
Esler, P.F. 6, 9, 197, 237, 264, 266, 267 n.1, 268, 271, 271 n.6, 275 n.9, 276 n.11, 277, 314, 322
Evans, P.S. 328 n.5
Evans-Pritchard, E.E. 28–9, 131 n.4, 154, 154 n.3, 163, 476
Exum, J.C. 289 n.4

# INDEX OF AUTHORS

Fabian, J. 3
Fabre, T. 131
Faehndrich, J. 2
Fafchamps, M. 135 n.18
Falk, Z.W. 333
Fantalkin, A. 464, 499
Fardon, R. 31, 32 n.5
Fassoulas, A. 120
Faulkes, A. 333
Faust, A. 85, 134, 207, 214, 433, 436 n.5, 464
Feeley-Harnik, G. 33–4
Feige, M. 85
Felder, C.H. 289
Ferguson, J. 8 n.10
Fergusson, J. 64
Fewell, D.N. 352–4, 357–8, 360
Fiensy, D.D. 156 n.6, 6 n.8
Finch, M.L. 86
Finitsis, A. 9
Finkelstein, I. 85, 387 n.39
Finley, M.I. 135 n.18
Finn, J. 59
Finsterbusch, K. 253
Firth, R. 211–12, 470 n.5, 472 n.7, 484 n.29
Fischer, I. 239
Fishbane, M. 357, 360–1
Flanagan, J.W. 153–4, 156 n.6
Flannery, K.V. 82, 131 n.2
Fleck, L. 252
Fleishman, J. 481 n.22, 483
Fludernik, M. 351
Fokkelman, J. 357, 363
Fohrer, G. 483
Fontaine, C.R. 229
Fontenrose, J. 352
Forder, A. 52, 55, 61–2
Fortes, M. 27 n.4
Foster, G.M. 281
Foster, S.J. 312
Foucault, M. 1, 2 n.1, 4, 73–4, 76, 252, 459
Fox, M. 253 n.6
Frank, T. 438
Frankel, D. 288
Franklin, N. 481 n.22, 484 n.28
Franks, H. 297
Frazer, J.G. 3, 20, 22, 25–30, 33, 41, 130, 267 n.1, 355
Frenkel, M. 72
Frese, D.A. 335
Freud, S. 26, 378
Frevel, C. 252, 290 n.6, 408 n.28, 493

Frick, F.S. 27 n.3, 152 n.2, 156 n.6, 171, 173, 173 n.37
Fried, M.H. 156
Friedl, E. 225, 227
Friedman, R.E. 209, 321, 321 n.21
Friese, H. 133 n.11
Fritz, V. 71, 440
Frog, E. 329, 338 n.22
Frog 337
Fromm, E. 248
Frymer-Kensky, T. 190 n.3, 223, 231, 234, 295
Fu, J. 433–4, 434 nn.2–3
Fuchs, E. 223
Fuller, A.H. 97–8, 101, 112, 116, 120

Gabrieli, R.S. 107, 113
Gadamer, H.G. 69
Gagarin, M. 335 n.15
Galbraith, J.K. 191, 198
Gambash, G. 103
Gane, R.E. 407
Garnsey, P. 135 n.18
Garroway, K.H. 10, 120, 458
Garsiel, M. 484 n.25
Gatt, G. 99
Gaukroger, S. 73
Gavins, J. 353, 357, 359, 359 n.13, 361
Geertz, A.W. 357, 424 n.7, 425
Geertz, C. 34, 34 n.7, 86
Geisen, C. 338 n.22
Gell, A. 493–4
Geller, S.A. 253
Gellner, E. 135 n.18, 136, 154, 154 n.3, 155
George, M.K. 407, 469, 469 n.1
Georgiou, A. 107
Gericke, J. 254
Gero, J.M. 167
Gerson-Kiwi, E. 330
Getui, M.N. 289
Geva, H. 112
Gharib, R. 503
Gibbs, R.W., Jr 297
Gilchrist, R. 234, 435
Gilders, W.K. 6, 401 n.9, 403 n.16, 405, 407–8
Giles, L.L. 426, 426 n.9
Gilmore, D.D. 131, 133 n.8, 268
Giordano, C. 132, 132 n.5, 133 n.8, 134 n.15
Gitay, Y. 328, 332, 337 n.20
Given, M. 114
Glanville, M. 189 n.2

Glaze, A.J. 315
Gloy, K. 252
Gluckman, M. 469–74, 470 n.3, 472 nn.7–8, 477, 479, 481–2, 484
Gmirkin, R.E. 387–8
Goelet, O., Jr 197 n.13
Glock, A.E. 8
Goldberg, H.E. 4 n.5, 6, 27 n.3
Gonen, R. 463
González-Marcén, P. 226
Goodenough, W.H. 472 n.7
Goody, J. 131 n.4, 133, 227, 385 n.37, 437–8, 438 n.6, 456
Gordon, C.H. 354, 361
Gordon, R.J. 472
Goren, H. 2
Gorman, F.H., Jr 405 n.20, 406 n.22, n.25, 407
Gosden, C. 70
Gottschall, J. 351
Gottwald, N.K. 5, 156 n.6, 160–1, 160 n.10, n.12, 161 n.13, 162 nn.14–15, 163 n.18, n.21, 164 n.26, 165–6, 165 nn.27–8, 170 n.31, 237
Grabbe, L.L. 10, 173 n.35, 406 n.21, 407, 421, 428, 430
Granqvist, H. 3, 3 n.3, 98
Grant, E. 99
Grantham, B.J. 105
Gray, G.B. 288, 290
Grayson, A.K. 389 n.48, 483 n.24
Green, G. 358, 366
Green, J.D.M. 458
Greenberg, M. 338
Greenfield, J. 232
Greengus, S. 335, 336 n.17
Greer, J. 434 nn.2–3, 445
Gregg, M.W. 110
Grimes, R.L. 398, 398 n.5, 403 n.15
Grottanelli, C. 129–30, 130 n.1, 139
Grove, G. 57
Grubbs, J.E. 339 n.29
Grund, A. 250
Gudehus, C. 376 n.9
Gudme, A.K. de Hemmer 10, 129, 396 n.2, 405, 405 n.19, 406 n.24, 407, 407 n.26, 444
Guenther, A. 232
Guillaume, P. 481 n.22, 484 n.28
Gunkel, H. 353, 355
Gunn, D.M. 360
Gunnell, T. 337–8

Gunter, A.C. 173 n.36
Gupta, A. 8 n.10
Gur-Arieh, S. 441
Guy, J. 22 n.1
Guyer, J.I. 133 n.10

Habermas, J. 70
Hadjiev, T.S. 270
Hagedorn, A. 6, 137 n.23, 267
Hagen, T. 378
Halbwachs, M. 378–9, 378 nn.15–19
Haldane, C.W. 101
Hall, C. 207 n.4
Halpern, B. 152 n.2, 160 n.11, 170 n.32, 173 n.37, 321, 321 n.21, 481 n.22
Hamilakis, Y. 444
Handy, L.K. 316
Hansen, T. 1, 42
Hanson, J. 287
Hanson, P.D. 178, 178 n.44
Hardin, J.W. 435, 436 n.5, 440, 448–9
Hardy, E.J. 2
Harkins, A.K. 338
Harmanşah, Ö. 382 n.27
Harris, J. 328–9
Harris, M. 7, 70, 359 n.11
Harris, P. 437
Harris, W.V. 133 n.8
Hart, L.K. 228
Hartley, J.E. 294
Harvey, V.A. 71
Hasel, G.F. 362
Hastorf, C.A. 443–4
Haubold, J. 388
Havea, J. 9 n.11
Havelock, E.A. 335 n.15, 339 n.30, 385 n.37
Hawkes, C. 79–80, 83
Hayes, C.E. 295
Hays, C.B. 81, 364, 364 n.16, 457, 460–2, 466
Hays-Gilpin, K. 236
Hazard, S. 86, 402
Hayden, R.M. 480 n.17
Hazony, Y. 254
Headland, T.N. 7, 359 n.11
Heard, R.C. 352
Heaton, E.W. 172 n.33
Hempel, G.C. 82
Hempel, J. 250
Hendel, R.S. 33, 374, 389, 401
Henderson, J. 336
Hendon, J. 228

Hendrickson, E.F. 448
Henkelman, W.F.M. 213 n.10
Henniker, F. 56
Hepner, G. 289 n.5
Herder, J. von 78, 354–5, 354 n.6
Herman, D. 351, 352 n.2
Hernando, A. 235
Herrmann, C. 491
Herscher, E. 116
Hertz, R. 455
Herzfeld, M. 131 n.3, 132, 133 n.8, 195, 268–9, 268 n.2, 269 n.3
Herzog, Z. 440
Hesketh, I. 21
Hess, R.S. 85
Hesse, B. 434
Hiebert, P.S. 173 n.39
Hill, G.W. 133 n.6
Hill, P. 478 n.14
Hill, S. 102
Hirschfeld, Y. 227
Hirshman, A.J. 120
Hirth, K. 136
Hitchcock, L. 133 n.12
Hobbes, T. 40, 74–5
Hobbs, T.R. 136 n.20, 268
Hobsbawm, E.J. 373
Hodder, I. 83
Hodge, C.T. 328
Hohfeld, W.N. 472
Holladay, J.S. Jr 440
Holter, K. 289
Honko, L. 329
Honneth, A. 249
Hooper, M. 191, 191 n.5
Hopf, M. 101, 439
Hopkins, D.C. 200 n.19
Horden, P. 131 n.3, 133, 133 n.8, n.12, 136
Horne, L. 112, 114, 440
Houtman, D. 86–7
Huebner, S.R. 137, 137 n.22, 232 n.9
Hull, K.L. 338
Human, D. 331
Humphrey, C. 398, 401–2, 403 n.14, 411, 425–6, 425 n.8, 469–71, 470 n.5, 477–9, 478 n.13, 481–4
Hundley, M.B. 405 n.20, 407, 407 n.27
Hunt, F.D. 72
Huntington, R. 455
Hutchinson, J. 292 n.10
Hutton, P.H. 380 n.23
Hvidberg, F.F. 410 n.35

Hymes, H. 329–30
Høybye, P. 376 n.8

Ilan, D. 438, 463
Irby, C.L. 45–6, 64
Iversen, E. 384 n.35

Jackson, B.S. 333–5
Jacobs, B. 213 n.10
Jacobs, P. 448
Jacobsen, T. 333
James, E.O. 4
James, E.T. 469
Jamieson-Drake, D.W. 172 n.34
Janowski, B. 245–8, 250
Janzen, D. 296
Jaspers, E. 263
Jay, N.B. 401 n.8
Jenkins, B. 88
Jensen, H.J.L. 399 n.6
Jenson, P.P. 406 n.22
Jepsen, A. 250
Jobling, D. 301
Johnson, D. 247 n.2, 253 n.6
Johnson, G.A. 297 n.20
Johnson, M. 353
Johnson, M.D. 153
Johnstone, W. 446
Jonas, H. 493–4
Jovanović, L. 387 n.44
Judd, E.P. 180, 182
Julier, A. 433 n.1

Kamp, K.A. 100, 105, 112–14
Kan, S. 456
Kang, B. 277
Kardulias, P.N. 116
Katz, H. 207
Kawashima, R.S. 239
Kazen, T. 401 n.10, 407 n.26
Keane, W. 86–8
Keefer, A. 331
Keel, O. 491
Kelly, W.L. 282 n.13
Kempinski, A. 436 n.5, 440
Kessler, M. 362
Kessler, R. 6, 249
Keswani, P.S. 105
Kettering, S. 135 n.18
Khan, G. 328 n.5
Khazanov, A. 154 n.3, 157 n.9
Khoury, P.S. 136, 157 n.9

Killebrew, A.E. 441
King, B. 329
King, P.J. 2, 234, 447 n.12
Kirchhoff, M. 2
Kirk, A. 266
Kirkpatrick, P.G. 6
Kirmayer, L. 296
Kitz, A.M. 481 n.22, 482–3
Kjartansson, H.S. 334
Klawans, J. 295
Klein, F. 440
Kletter, R. 207
Klopfenstein, M.A. 250, 267, 274 n.8
Kluckhohn, C. 76
Knapp, A.B. 133 n.6, n.12
Knierim, R.P. 335
Knight, D.A. 6, 136, 138, 174, 232, 336
Knoppers, G.N. 251 n.4
Koch, I. 200
Koch, K. 250, 252
Kohl, S. 228
Kohlhaas, S. 497
Koski, K. 329
Kossinna, G. 79–81
Kostiner, J. 157 n.9
Kozlova, E. 410 n.35
Köhler-Rollefson, I. 100, 113, 116
Kraemer, R.S. 229 n.7
Kramer, S.N. 5 n.7
Krašovec, J. 251
Kratz, R.G. 374
Kraus, H.-J. 253
Kray, S. 233, 265
Kreinath, J.A.M. 397 n.3
Kroeber, K.L. 76, 133 n.6
Krüger, A. 246
Kuhn, T.S. 252
Kunin, S.D. 33
Kuper, A. 3, 7, 9, 27 n.2, 87, 130 n.1, 131 n.3, 355–6

LaBianca, Ø. 8, 157–8, 169, 237
Laidlaw, J. 398, 401–2, 403 n.14, 411
Lakoff, G. 301, 353
Lamb, D.T. 481 n.19
Lambert, D. 232
Lancaster, F. 100, 113
Lancaster, W. 100, 113
Landau, M.J. 301
Lane, E.W. 2
Lang, B. 3, 5–6, 134, 136–8
Laniak, T.S. 250, 267, 269 n.3, 270, 280

Latour, B. 87
Lawrence, B. 231
Lawrence, L. 268 n.2
Lawrence, L.J. 6, 138, 245
Lawson, E.T. 402, 402 nn.12–13, 403, 403 n.14, 411
Le Goff, J. 380 n.23
Leach, E. 4–5, 5 n.6, 30–3, 130 n.1, 138, 168, 355, 359, 469–71, 474–7, 476 nn.11–12, 481–2, 484
Leca, J. 131, 135 n.18
Lécrivain, V. 135 n.18
Lefebvre, H. 469, 469 n.2
Lemaire, A. 172 n.34, 339, 481 n.22
Lemche, N.P. 5, 6 n.8, 10, 27, 134 n.16, 135 n.17, 136, 136 n.19, 137 n.21, 152, 156 nn.6–7, 158–9, 160 n.10, 161, 161 n.13, 162 nn.15–6, 163 n.18, n.21, 164–5, 165 n.27, 166–7, 167 n.29, 169 n.30, 170, 170 n.32, 174, 174 n.40, 176, 249, 333, 364, 374 n.2, n.4, 381 n.26, 387 nn.41–2
Lemos, T.M. 6, 154, 161, 169, 176 n.42, 197 n.14, 223, 223 n.1, 276, 401 n.10, 456, 458
Lenski, G. 263
Lepsius, K.R. 49
Lerner, G. 233, 265
Lesko, B.S. 233
Lev-Tov, J. 105, 113, 438
Levanoni, A. 113
Lévi-Strauss, C. 4, 27 n.4, 29–33, 355, 358, 400
Levine, B.A. 197 n.13, 288–9, 290 n.8, 294 n.15
Levinson, B.M. 336 n.17
Levy, D. 378, 378 n.19
Levy, J.E. 236
Lévy-Bruhl, L. 252
Lewis, C. 376, 380
Lewis, G. 27 n.4
Lewis, N.N. 134 n.16
Lewis, T. 460–1, 464–5
Licht, J. 331
Lichtenberger, A. 133 n.12
Liddell, H.G. 380
Lieb, M. 9 n.12
Limburg, J. 318, 318 n.17, n.19
Limor, O. 72
Linafelt, T. 351
Lincoln, B. 192, 353 n.4
Lindholm, C. 135 n.17

Lindisfarne, N. 167
Linington, S. 312 n.8
Lipschits, O. 200, 207, 510
Liverani, M. 129–30, 134, 136 n.19, 139, 209, 209 n.7, 374–5, 389
Llobera, J.R. 132
Lloyd, G.E.R. 298, 301 n.25
Lloyd, P.C. 472 n.7
Lobinger, K. 493
Locher, C. 336 n.16
Lokel, P. 289
Lomax, A. 330
London, G. 9, 98, 100–3, 105, 107–8, 110, 112–14, 117–21
Long, B.O. 81
Longacre, W.A. 100
Loretz, O. 335
Loubser, J.A. 339, 339 nn.24–5
Loud, G. 119
Louden, B. 354
Lowenthal, D. 373
Lowie, R.H. 472 n.7
Lowth, R. 354–5, 354 n.6
Lubbock, J. 77
Lucas, R. 364
Luckenbill, D.D. 389 n.48
Lukes, S. 26
Lundin, R.W. 330
Lupton, D. 297
Lynch, M.J. 274–5
Lynch, W.F. 45–7
Lyon, D. 437
Lyons, D. 98

Macalister, R.A.S. 101, 119
McAuley, G. 330
McCauley, R.N. 402–3, 402 nn.12–13, 403 n.14, 411
McClintock-Fulkerson, M. 239
McClymond, K. 398, 408 n.29
Macdonald, M.C.A. 327, 327 n.1, 328
McDonald, M.M.A. 448
MacDonald, N. 408 n.28, 434, 434 nn.2–3
McGeough, K.M. 2, 99, 105
McGrane, B. 2
Machinist, P. 254, 359
McKenzie, S.L. 481 n.20, n.22
McLaughlin, S. 437
McLennan, J.M. 22–4
MacLeod, R. 388 n.47
McLuhan, M. 328 n.3
McNutt, P.M. 6, 9, 170, 173, 173 n.37

McQuitty, A. 100, 105, 440
McVann, M. 249
Maeir, A.M. 136, 441
Magdalene, F.R. 200
Maggio, R. 259
Maiden, B.E. 412 n.44
Maier, C.M. 469 n.1
Malamat, A. 153, 483, 6 n.8
Malina, B.J. 6, 137, 263, 265–6, 268, 270–2, 271 n.5, 280–2, 313–14, 314 n.11, 319–20, 322, 359
Malinowski, B. 210–12, 309, 470, 470 nn.3–6, 472 n.7, 477
Mandell, A. 85
Mangles, J. 45–6, 64
Mannhardt, W. 25
Manniche, L. 331
Maré, L.P. 278, 365
Marett, R.R. 19–21, 27–8
Márquez Rowe, I. 335
Markl, D. 251
Marsman, H.J. 223
Martin, D.B. 459
Martin, J.D. 34, 160 n.10, n.13
Martin, L.R. 280
Martin-Achard, R. 481 n.22
Martineau, H. 49
Marx, K. 5, 88, 209–10
Mason, E. 9 n.12
Masquelier, A. 423, 423 n.4
Master, D.M. 207 n.2
Mathieu, Y. 332, 332 n.7
Matskevich, K. 360
Matson, F.R. 101
Matthews, V.H. 6, 9, 129, 134, 136 n.20, 137–8, 189 n.1, 193, 194 n.8, 195 n.11, 199–200, 200 n.18, 208 n.5, 268, 275 n.10, 280, 308, 308 n.3, 310–13, 312 n.7, 316, 319–22, 335, 442
Maul, S.M. 245, 254
Mauss, M. 20, 26, 212, 455
Mayes, A.D.H. 84, 87
Mazar, A. 85, 103, 440, 504 n.4
Mazow, L.B. 436 n.5
Mączak, A. 135 n.18
Mbuvi, A.M. 277
Meagher, M. 233
Meek, C.K. 472 n.7
Meinhold, A. 251
Mellaart, J. 382 n.27
Mendels, D. 389
Mendenhall, G.E. 5, 160 n.10, 318

Merrifield, A. 469 n.2
Mershen, B. 101
Meskell, L. 83, 455–6
Metcalf, P. 455
Mettinger, T. 171, 172 nn.33–4
Meyer, B. 86–7, 333
Meyers, C.L. 6, 9, 163 n.20, 168–9, 171, 175, 175 n.41, 180, 192, 194, 224, 225 nn.3–4, 226 n.5, 227–9, 228 n.6, 229 n.7, 231–5, 233 n.10, 236 n.11, 237–9, 265, 433–4, 434 n.3, 438, 442–3, 445–8, 458–9
Michaelis, J.D. 1, 51, 334–5
Michaels, A. 397 n.3
Michel, D. 246
Milgrom, J. 33, 196, 288, 295, 406 n.21
Millard, A.R. 245
Miller, D. 86, 88
Miller, J.W. 351
Miller, R.D. II 10, 328–9
Milman, H.H. 3 n.3
Milstein, S.J. 334
Milwright, M. 101
Mollenhauer, A. 100, 112–13
Montagu, J. 331
Montón-Subías, S. 226
Mooney, J. 422 n.2
Moore, H.L. 130 n.1
Moore, S.D. 352, 357, 357 n.9, 358
Moorey, P.R.S. 2, 71
Morgan, D. 86
Morgenstern, J. 334
Morrow, W. 334
Moxnes, H. 129
Moyle, L. 299
Mulder-Hymans, N. 100, 105
Mullins, R. 499
Murhard, J.G. 335 n.15
Murray, M.A. 99
Murray, P. 116
Musolff, A. 300
Müller, J. 246
Müller, K. 252 n.5
Müller, M. 456–7
Myres, S.L. 228

Na'aman, N. 72, 201, 481, 481 n.22
Nagel, A. 1
Nagy, G. 328, 332 n.8
Nakhai, B.A. 85, 120, 237
Nam, R.S. 9, 206 n.1, 207, 208 n.6, 212 n.8, 266
Namer, G. 378 nn.15–16, n.18

Nash, G.J. 233
Nathan, G. 137 n.22
Nelson, R.D. 198
Nelson, S.M. 225 n.3
Nestor, D.A. 9, 70–1, 78–9, 81
Netton, I.R. 2
Neu, R. 6, 6 n.8
Neumann, K. 402 n.11
Neumann-Gorsolke, U. 246
Neusner, J. 33
Newsom, C.A. 249, 256, 336
Neyrey, J.H. 137, 265–6, 270, 359
Nicholson, P. 108
Nichter, M. 297
Niditch, S. 6, 256, 328, 356, 356 n.7, 413 n.46, 414
Nihan, C. 406 n.21
Nilsson Stutz, L. 456
Nissen, H.J. 255
Nissinen, M. 337, 337 n.20
Noegel, S.B. 353, 357, 359 n.11
Nogalski, J.D. 315, 316 n.12
Nolan, P. 263
Nora, P. 383, 383 n.30
Nord, C. 330
Noth, M. 161, 288, 295, 334
Novotny, K. 444, 483 n.24
Nyberg, H.S. 336

O'Brien, J.M. 358
O'Connor, K.M. 223
O'Leary, T.J. 132
Obeyesekere, G. 456
Ockinga, B. 245
Oden, D. 482
Oeming, M. 481 n.22
Oesterley, T. 26
Oestigaard, T. 81
Oksuz, L. 440
Okyere, K. 277
Olick, J.K. 378, 378 n.19
Oliphant, L. 55, 57, 59, 64
Olojede, F. 289, 293 n.12
Olyan, S.M. 6, 9, 136 n.20, 137 n.22, 250, 295, 307, 410, 410 nn.35–6, 411, 411 nn.38–9, 412 n.42, 414
Ong, W.J. 385 n.37
Oppenheim, A.L. 5 n.7, 212, 214–15, 215 n.11
Ornan, T. 504, 507–10
Orrelle, E. 116
Orwell, G. 81

Oshima, T. 247, 256
Overholt, T.W. 6, 138
Økland, J. 469 n.1

Palmer, C. 100, 102, 114, 116
Palmer, E.H. 45, 48-9
Panitz-Cohen, N. 103, 441 n.9, 499
Panofsky, E. 491-2
Pardee, D. 246
Parker, B. 440
Parker, J.F. 413 n.46
Parker, J.W. 21
Parker Pearson, M. 455
Parkin, T.G. 339 n.29
Parry, J. 455
Pasqualino, C. 330
Patai, R. 133 n.9
Patrick, D. 333-4
Patrik, L.E. 70
Patron, S. 329
Patterson, C. 272
Patterson, H. 108
Pavlidis, A. 299
Pearce, L.E. 213
Pébarthe, C. 135 n.18
Pedersen, J. 4, 136, 160, 252 n.5, 267
Peirce, C.S. 399, 493
Péquinot, B. 379
Peristiany, J. 131, 267-8
Person, R.F., Jr 332 n.11, 339
Peters, J. 103
Peters, K. 434 n.3, 440 n.8
Pfoh, E. 6, 8-9, 70, 85, 134-6, 136 nn.19-20, 137 n.21, 138-9, 139 n.24, 312 n.6, 313, 313 n.10, 352, 356, 359, 365
Pham, X.H.T. 410 n.35
Philipp, T. 136
Phillips, P. 70
Picazo, M. 226
Piggot, S. 72
Pike, K.L. 7, 359 n.11
Pilch, J.J. 6, 137, 263, 270, 282, 297, 312 n.8
Pina-Cabral, J. de 132
Pioske, D.D. 374, 469
Pitkänen, P. 289, 295 n.17
Pitt-Rivers, J. 5, 27 n.4, 129, 131-2, 131 n.4, 135, 139, 267-9
Pixley, J.V. 483
Plank, K.A. 363-4, 366
Pleins, J.D. 440 n.8
Plevnik, J. 249
Pocock, D.F. 33

Pococke, R. 41, 48 n.1
Podemann Sørensen, J.P. 397, 402 n.12, 403-4, 408 n.31, 411
Polak, F.H. 361
Polanyi, K. 212-13, 213 n.9, 216
Polcaro, A. 117
Pöllath, N. 103
Pomeroy, S.B. 232
Pope Francis 86
Pope, M.H. 460
Popitz, H. 190
Porter, B.W. 113
Porter, J.L. 39, 43, 45, 51
Potgieter, J.H. 314-15, 320
Poyatos, F. 330
Premnath, D.N. 200
Pressler, C. 334
Prewitt, T.J. 6
Prinsloo, G.T.M. 318, 469 n.1
Procopiou, H. 120
Propp, V.J. 330
Puerto, M.N. 329
Puett, M.J. 409
Purcell, N. 131 n.3, 133, 133 n.8, n.12, 136
Pyschny, K. 501

Quick, L. 9, 414
Quigley, J.A. 207 n.4

Rabichev, R. 268
Rabinowitz, D. 136
Rabinowitz, I. 357
Radcliffe-Brown, A.R. 20, 470 n.4
Radner, K. 483
Radstone, S. 378, 379 n.21, 380 n.24
Ramos, M.D. 412 n.44
Randel, D.M. 331, 337 n.21, 338 n.23
Ranger, T. 373
Rapp, U. 292
Rappaport, R.A. 87, 396-7, 399-400, 411, 414
Rathje, W.L. 435-6
Ray, P. 264
Ready, J.L. 328-30
Reck, G.G. 351
Redford, D.B. 172 n.33
Redman, C.L. 374 n.2
Reich, R. 436 n.5
Reichl, K. 329
Reiner, E. 72
Renan, E. 41
Rendsburg, G.A. 354, 361

Renfrew, C. 80
Reviv, H. 335
Rheinstein, M. 190
Richards, A.I. 472 n.7
Richelle, M. 375, 375 n.5
Ricks, T. 2 n.2
Ricoeur, P. 32–3, 355, 379 n.21
Riede, P. 249, 513
Riley, S.K. 331
Ringe, S.H. 223
Ristau, K.A. 251 n.4
Rizvi, U.Z. 83
Robbins, J. 263
Roberts, J. 9 n.12
Roberts, J.L. 402
Robertson, R.G. 287
Robertson Smith, W. 3, 20, 22–7, 29–30, 34 n.7, 130, 234, 267 n.1, 352, 355
Robinson, B. 290
Robinson, E. 2, 44–6, 49, 55, 64, 99
Robinson, H.W. 248
Robinson, T.H. 336
Robinson, W. 359 n.12
Robker, J.M. 481 n.19
Rochberg, F. 254
Rofé, A. 481, 481 n.20, n.22, 484 n.25
Rogan, W. 281
Rogel, M. 100, 105, 440
Rogers, S.C. 226
Rogerson, J.W. 5–8, 6 n.8, 27, 137 n.23, 138, 156 nn.6–7, 248–9, 354–6, 359 n.12
Rohrbaugh, R. 265–6
Rollston, C.A. 199 n.17, 327, 339
Roniger, L. 135 n.18, 136 n.19
Roque, M.-À. 132 n.5, 133 n.8
Rosner, B.S. 281
Rossie, J.-P. 120
Rossington, M. 378 n.19
Routledge, B.E. 113
Rowe, A. 508
Ruether, R.R. 223
Ruiz de Elvira, L. 135 n.18
Russell, B. 73
Russell, S.C. 10, 469, 471, 474, 481–4, 483 n.23, 484 n.27
Ryan, M.-L. 352, 352 n.2

Sacchi, P. 137
Sack, R.D. 471
Sadler, R.S., Jr 288 n.2, 289, 292–3, 293 n.12
Sahlins, M.D. 154 n.3, 266, 307–11, 308 n.3, 310 n.4, 322, 514 n.7

Said, E.W. 2, 65, 139
Salamone, S.D. 226, 228
Salem, H.J. 99–100, 227
Saller, R.P. 234
Salters, R.B. 316 n.12, 317 n.13
Sanders, S.L. 189 n.1, 327
Sanders, T. 130 n.1
Sanmartin, J. 335
Sant Cassia, P. 133 n.8
Sapin, J. 134
Sapir-Hen, L. 510
Sarna, N.M. 361–2, 481 n.22
Sasson, J.M. 316 n.12, 317 n.15, 318, 318 n.18
Saulcy, F. de 44–6, 48, 53, 61, 63–4, 64 n.5
Saussure, F. de 83, 351
Savolainen, U. 329
Savran, G. 253, 363
Sawicki, F. 135 n.18
Saxe, A. 455
Schaefer, J. 108
Schäfer, I. 133 n.8
Schaper, J. 201, 254
Schapera, I. 26, 472 n.7
Schäder, J.-M. 10, 267, 307, 312, 316–17
Scheffler, T. 130
Schelhaas, B. 2
Schellenberg, A. 246, 255
Schelske, A. 493
Schemeil, Y. 135 n.18
Schiefsky, M. 254
Schloen, J.D. 210, 234, 436 n.5
Schmidt, B.B. 404 n.18, 457, 461
Schmitt, R. 85, 119–20, 448 n.13
Schnapp, A. 72, 76
Schneider, J. 131 n.2
Schneider, P. 135 n.18
Schniedewind, W.M. 335
Scholz, O.E. 493, 496
Schraten, J. 384 n.31
Schrode, P. 397 n.3
Schroer, S. 229, 235, 248, 248 n.3, 491, 498, 502 n.3, 505, 507 n.6
Schuhmacher-Chilla, D. 495
Schumacher, G. 99
Schüle, A. 248
Schüssler Fiorenza, E. 235
Schwartz, C.H. 135 n.18
Schwartz, S. 137, 137 n.21, 266
Schwarz, B. 378, 379 n.21, 380 n.24
Schweid, E. 334
Scott, R. 380

## INDEX OF AUTHORS

Scurlock, J. 460
Seebass, H. 481 n.22, 482
Seeden, H. 100
Seetzen, U.J. 42–3, 45, 49, 53–4, 63, 99
Seger, K. 98, 112
Segovia, F.F. 9 n.11
Segura, C.P. 353
Seidel, H.-J. 481 n.22
Seitz, C.R. 81
Seligman, A.B. 409
Semino, E. 361
Sepp, J.N. 51, 57, 59, 63
Sered, S.S. 233
Sergi, O. 200
Serino, R.M. 288
Service, E.R. 27
Shafer-Elliott, C. 10, 105, 433–4, 434 n.3, 435, 437–40, 444, 448–9
Shahack-Gross, R. 441
Shai, I. 136
Shapin, S. 73
Sharp, L.A. 424 n.6
Sheddick, V. 472 n.7
Shehata, D. 329–31, 338 n.23
Shemesh, Y. 481 n.22, 483
Shepherd, S. 329
Sherzer, J. 329–30
Shields, M. 230
Shiloh, Y. 436 n.5
Shipton, P. 480 n.18
Short, C. 376, 380
Shqairat, M.A. al-Z. 100, 113
Shryock, A. 133 n.8
Sigrist, C. 6, 6 n.8
Sigurðsson, G. 337
Sigurðsson, J.V. 334
Silberman, N.A. 1–2, 71, 85, 387 n.39
Silver, M. 206, 206 n.1, 208
Silverblatt, I. 175 n.41
Silverman, S. 130–1, 131 n.2, 132 n.5, 135 n.18
Silverstein, P.A. 133 n.8
Simian-Yofre, H. 248
Simkins, R.A. 6, 136
Simon, B. 409
Simon, U. 315–18, 321
Simoons, F. 444
Sinclair, M. 101, 113–14
Singer, A. 113
Sixsmith, J. 364
Skornik, J.E. 337
Slater, G.F. 110

Slater, N.W. 328 n.4
Smith, A. 208–10, 208 n.6, 218
Smith, A.D. 292 n.10
Smith, D.L. 176 n.42, 177, 179
Smith, E. 2, 44–5, 49, 55, 64, 99
Smith, G.A. 44–5, 48, 51, 56
Smith, J.Z. 76, 407, 409
Smith, M.S. 84–5, 332, 332 n.8, 354, 356, 359, 361–2, 362 n.15, 374, 460
Smith-Christopher, D.L. 182
Smoak, J. 85–6
Snaith, N.H. 27, 318
Snell, B. 252
Snoek, J.A.M. 397 n.3, 398
Soja, E. 469 n.2
Soler, J. 32 n.6
Sommer, B.D. 351
Sommerschuh, J. 263
Sonesson, G. 493
Sonia, K.M. 404 n.18, 457–8, 460–2, 464–5
Sontag, S. 297
Southwood, K.E. 10, 288 n.3, 294 n.14, 299
Speiser, E.A. 362
Spencer, H. 3 n.4
Spencer-Wood, S.M. 225–6
Spronk, K. 314, 460–1
Stacy, D. 108
Stafford, W.C. 335 n.15
Stager, L.E. 189 n.1, 207, 207 n.2, 234, 436 n.5, 447 n.12
Stanley, A.P. 44, 48–50, 53–4
Stansell, G. 208 n.5, 268, 308, 310
Staubli, T. 248, 248 n.3, 491, 498, 510
Stausberg, M. 397 n.3
Stavrakopoulou, F. 81, 84, 86, 88, 404 n.18, 460, 463–5, 484 n.26
Steadman, S.R. 436 n.5
Steen, G. 353
Stegemann, E.W. 310 n.4
Stegemann, W. 310 n.4
Steinberg, N. 179, 456
Stephens, J.L. 49
Stein, D.E.S. 229, 238
Stein, G. 235
Stein, J. 497
Stein, P.G. 334
Steiner, F. 26, 28–30
Stern, E. 120
Sternberg, M. 360, 362–3
Steward, J. 81
Stewart, C. 131 n.4, 132 n.5, 270
Stewart, E.C. 266–7

Stiebert, J. 268, 268 n.2, 270–2, 274
Stocking, G.W. Jr 3
Stockwell, P. 357
Stolper, M. 210 n.13
Stordalen, T. 8
Stott, K. 72
Strauss, D.F. 41
Strawn, B.A. 492, 508
Sturdy, J. 291, 299
Sugden, J. 422 n.2, 423 n.3
Sugirtharajah, R.S. 9 n.11
Sukenik, E.L. 99
Suriano, M.J. 404 n.18, 455–6, 459–60, 462–5
Sutherland, R.K. 196
Sutskover, T. 481 n.22
Sutton, L. 276, 278
Sutton, S.B. 100, 113
Swantek, L.A. 107
Swedberg, R. 210
Sweely, T.L. 226, 233
Sweeney, D. 501
Sweet, L.E. 102, 132
Sørensen, J. 397

Tadmor, H. 201, 231
Tamari, V. 440, 442
Tambiah, S.J. 397
Tan, N.N.H. 300 n.24
Tappy, R.E. 199
Tarkka, L. 329, 332 n.10, 337 n.21
Tarlow, S. 456
Taxel, I. 100, 103
Taylor, C. 248
Thiede, B. 9
Thiel, W. 481 n.22
Thomas, J. 73–6
Thomas, R. 329, 335 n.15
Thompson, E.P. 135 n.18
Thompson, T.L. 5 n.6, 8, 134, 134 n.13, 135–6, 136 n.19, 139, 387 n.43
Thomson, W.M. 2, 56
Tilley, J.T. 238
Tilly, C. 133 n.6, 139 n.24
Tischendorf, C. von 48, 52, 57
Toelken, B. 338
Tooman, W.A. 332
Tota, A.L. 378
Toulmin, S.E. 74
Tozy, M. 133 n.8
Trevor-Roper, H. 373
Triandis, H. 264

Trible, P.L. 314–15, 316 n.12, 317 n.13, 318, 320, 358
Trigger, B.G. 72, 76
Tristram, H.B. 2, 51
Troeltsch, E. 71
Tromans, N. 56
Trumbull, H.C. 48–9, 53
Tsevat, M. 254
Tsukimoto, A. 457, 462
Tucker, W.D., Jr 278–9
Tufnell, O. 99
Tugendhaft, A. 88
Tull, P.K. 351, 353
Turner, V. 28, 72, 455
Twiss, K.C. 433, 444
Tylor, E.B. 19–22, 24, 26, 28, 77–8

Ueberschaer, F. 340
Uehlinger, C. 491, 493
Uro, R. 397 n.4

Valière, J.-C. 110
Vall, G. 254
Van-Lennep, H.J. 2
van de Mieroop, M. 254
van der Steen, E.J. 9, 136 n.20, 207 n.3, 440
van der Toorn, K. 456–7, 460, 462
van de Velde, C.W.M. 43–5, 48, 59
Van Eck, E. 308 n.2, 322
Van Esterik, P. 433 n.1
van Gennep, A. 413, 455
Van Seters, J. 71, 339
van Wolde, E. 354, 357, 361
Vanderhooft, D. 27
Varisco, D.M. 2
Vayntrub, J. 340, 340 n.31
Verdery, K. 469–71, 479–81, 479 n.15, 484
Vermeulen, K. 10, 357, 357 n.9, 359, 363–5
Viazzo, P.P. 137
Victoria, J.L.E. 191
Vindrola-Padros, C. 297 n.20
Vinitzky-Seroussi, V. 378, 378 n.19
Viviers, H. 365
Vogt, L. 250
Volf, M. 71, 81
Volney, C.-F. 1, 42, 53, 63
von Rad, G. 254, 460–1
Voth, E. 336

Wagner, A. 252 n.5, 253
Wagner, V. 335

Wajdenbaum, P. 5, 387 n.43
Walker, B.J. 107
Wallace-Hadrill, A. 135 n.18
Wallerstein, I. 209–10
Walsh, J.T. 481 n.22
Walter, T. 456
Walton, J.H. 332, 438
Wapnish, P. 434
Ward, W.A. 99
Warf, B. 469
Warren, C.W. 57, 64, 99
Washington, H.C. 180 n.45
Washofsky, M. 456
Waterbury, J. 135 n.18, 136 n.19
Waters, J.L. 469
Watson, F. 71
Watson, P.J. 226, 440, 458
Watts, J.W. 407 n.27
Wazana, N. 469, 471
Weaver, W.W. 101
Weber, M. 4, 170 n.31, 173, 210, 233, 265, 429
Weibel, P. 493
Weinfeld, M. 481 n.21
Weinberg, J.P. 175–6, 176 n.42, 177
Weingart, K. 189 n.1, 251
Weingrod, A. 135 n.18
Weinreich, H. 379 n.21
Weipert-Fenner, I. 135 n.18
Weippert, H. 508
Weiss, E. 207
Weiss, M. 357
Weissenrieder, A. 493
Weitzman, S. 357 n.9
Weller, R.P. 409
Wellhausen, J. 21, 23–4, 26, 30, 41, 84, 87, 234
Wells, B. 232, 239
Welton, R. 434 n.3
Wendland, E.R. 328–9, 328 n.5
Wendt, F. 493
Wenell, K.J. 469 n.1
Wenham, G.J. 298
Wénin, A. 337 n.20
Werth, P. 361
Wertsch, J.V. 379
West, G.O. 9 n.11
Westbrook, R. 135–6, 232, 307, 307 n.1, 313, 334–5, 336 nn.16–17, 481 n.22
Westermann, C. 337 n.19
Wheeler-Barclay, M. 21
Whiston, W. 287
White, H. 373
White, L. Jr 73, 77

White, L.A. 81–2
White, M.C. 481, 481 n.22
White, M.H., II 301
Whitehead, A. 378, 378 n.19
Whitelam, K.W. 3, 81, 85, 136, 198
Whiteway, A. 100, 120
Whittaker, J. 114, 116
Whittaker, J.C. 116
Whyte, M.K. 168, 227
Wicomb, Z. 327–8, 332 n.8
Widengren, G. 336
Wiesing, L. 493
Wikan, U. 132, 268–9
Wilk, R. 435–6
Wilkinson, J. 72
Willey, R.G. 70
Williams, J. 289
Willis, T. 193
Wilson, C.T. 226
Wilson, C.W. 45
Wilson, G. 472 n.7
Wilson, H. 103
Wilson, J. 440
Wilson, R.R. 6, 27 n.3, 153, 197–8, 264, 275, 291, 337
Winch, P. 28
Winn, J.A. 330–1
Winslow, K.S. 228, 291–2
Winter, U. 491, 513
Wiseman, D.J. 482
Wissler, C. 133 n.6
Wittfogel, K. 209
Wittgenstein, L. 228
Wiwjorra, L. 80
Wolff, H.H. 7, 248, 252 n.5, 253, 498
Womack, M. 238
Wood, B.G. 108
Wood, C.S. 1
Wood, R.C. 444
Woolf, G. 135 n.18
Wright, D.P. 408, 408 n.31
Wright, G.E. 355
Wright, J.L. 513
Wright, K. 444
Wrong, D.H. 190
Wundt, W.M. 330 n.6
Wunsch, C. 213
Wurst, S. 360
Würthwein, E. 481 n.22
Wyatt, N. 356
Wylie, T. 458
Wyssmann, P. 512

Yadin, Y. 119
Yahalom-Mack, N. 499
Yalman, S. 382 n.27
Yasur-Landau, A. 436 n.5
Yates, F. 376 n.7
Yavuz, M.H. 380 n.22
Yee, G.A. 358
Yerkes, R.W. 114, 116
Yilmaz, H. 1
Younker, R.W. 157–8, 169

Zaccagnini, C. 129–30, 209, 209 n.7
Zakovitch, Y. 480, 481 nn.21–2, 484 n.25
Zerubavel, E. 329
Zevit, Z. 85, 237
Zhen, W. 433
Ziegler, N. 333
Ziegler, Y. 197 n.13
Ziolkowski, E. 9 n.12
Ziffer, I. 434
Zingerle, A. 250
Zinkuratire, V. 289
Žižek, Z. 88
Zobel, H.-J. 250
Zohary, D. 439
Zohary, M. 439
Zolbrod, P. 337–8
Zumthor, P. 337–8

www.ingramcontent.com/pod-product-compliance
Lightning Source LLC
Chambersburg PA
CBHW080529300426
44111CB00017B/2659